GUN TRADER'S GUIDE

Thirty-Fourth Edition

A Comprehensive, Fully-Illustrated Guide to Modern Firearms with Current Market Values

Edited by Stephen D. Carpenteri

Skyhorse Publishing

Contents

Copyright © 2012 by Stephen D. Carpenteri

All Rights Reserved. No part of this book may be reproduced in any manner without the express written consent of the publisher, except in the case of brief excerpts in critical reviews or articles. All inquiries should be addressed to Skyhorse Publishing, 307 West 36th Street, 11th Floor, New York, NY 10018.

Skyhorse Publishing books may be purchased in bulk at special discounts for sales promotion, corporate gifts, fund-raising, or educational purposes. Special editions can also be created to specifications. For details, contact the Special Sales Department, Skyhorse Publishing, 307 West 36th Street, 11th Floor, New York, NY 10018 or info@skyhorsepublishing.com.

Skyhorse® and Skyhorse Publishing® are registered trademarks of Skyhorse Publishing, Inc.®, a Delaware corporation.

Visit our website at www.skyhorsepublishing.com.

10 9 8 7 6 5 4 3 2 1

Library of Congress Cataloging-in-Publication Data is available on file.
ISBN: 978-1-61608-843-9

Printed in Canada

Introduction

This thirty-fourth edition of Skyhorse Publishing's *Gun Trader's Guide* is designed to provide the professional and amateur firearms enthusiast with more specifications and photographs of collectible firearms than ever before. In the past fifty years, the *Gun Trader's Guide* has grown to over six hundred pages and now lists more than six thousand standard firearms and their variations.

The first edition of the *Gun Trader's Guide* contained some 1,360 listings accompanied by 100 illustrations. Now, after more than thirty editions later, the book has evolved into one of the most comprehensive catalogs targeting the most common smokeless-powder rifles, shotguns, and handguns of the late-nineteenth and twentieth centuries. Over two million gun buffs have made the *Gun Trader's Guide* their primary reference for identification and comparison of sporting, military, and law enforcement firearms, including rare and unusual collectibles and commemoratives. The current edition of the *Gun Trader's Guide* has been expanded to include more list-

ings than ever before, with nearly 2,750 photographs. Not every gun ever made can be listed in any catalog of this type, but we have made every effort to include the makers and models that are most popular with American owners and collectors today.

The format of the *Gun Trader's Guide* is simple and straightforward, listing thousands of firearms manufactured since the late 1800s in the United States and abroad. Most entries include complete specifications, including: model number and name; caliber or gauge; barrel length; overall length; weight; distinguishing features; variations; the dates of manufacture (when they can be accurately determined); and dates of discontinuation. Many illustrative photos accompany the text to help the reader with identifications and comparisons. Also, first and last entries are listed at the top of the page for additional ease in finding a particular manufacturer.

The *Gun Trader's Guide* is revised annually to ensure that its wealth of information is both current and detailed. The princi-

pal features that contribute to the unique nature of this firearms reference guide include the extensive pictorial format and accompanying comprehensive specifications. It provides a convenient procedure for identifying vintage firearms while simultaneously determining and verifying their current value.

SIMPLIFIED STRUCTURE

Production data for each gun includes:

- Specifications
- Variations of different models
- Dates of manufacture and/or discontinuation
- Current values

The catalog is also set up to provide ease of use, including:

- Tabbed sections for user friendly reference
- Complete index of all firearms

Values shown are based on national averages obtained by conferring with knowledgeable gun dealers, traders, collectors, and auctioneers around the country, and not by applying an arbitrary mathematical formula that could produce unrealistic figures. The values listed herein accurately reflect the nationwide average at the time of publication and are updated annually.

In some rare cases, such as the Winchester Model 1873 "One of One Thousand" rifle or the Parker AA1 Special shotgun in 28 gauge, where very little trading takes place, active gun collectors were consulted to obtain current market values.

ORGANIZATION OF LISTINGS

In the early editions of *Gun Trader's Guide*, firearms were frequently organized chronologically by date of production within manufacturers' listings because many gun-making companies used the date that a particular model was introduced as the model number. For example, the Colt U. S. Model 1911 semiautomatic pistol was introduced in 1911, the French Model 1936 military rifle was introduced in 1936, and the Remington Model 32 shotgun debuted in 1932. However, during the first quarter of the twentieth century, gun makers began assigning names and numbers that did not relate to the year the gun was introduced. As these recent models and their variations multiplied through the years, it became increasingly difficult to track them by date, especially for the less-experienced collector.

Additionally, some Winchester and Remington firearms have been grouped differently in this edition. For example, The Winchester Model 1894, in its many variations, was produced beginning in 1894 and later manufactured as the "Model 94" by U. S. Repeating Arms Co. (Collector's note: this Model 1894 lever-action rifle, the famed Model 70 Winchester, and the Model 1300 pump shotgun, all Winchester standards, were discontinued in 2006.) In general, Winchester used the year of introduction to name its firearms; that is, Model 1890, 1892, 1894, 1895, and so forth. Shortly after World War I, Winchester dropped the first two digits and listed the models as 90, 92, 94, 95, and so on. Later, guns were given model numbers that had no relation to the date of manufacture. Marlin and several other manufacturers used a similar approach in handling model designations.

As a result, Winchester rifles are grouped alphanumerically in two different groups: early Winchesters manufactured before 1920 under the four-digit model-date designations and guns manufactured after 1920 with their revised model format designations. If any difficulty is encountered in locating a particular model, the models and

their variations are cross-referenced in the index.

In past years, some readers reported difficulty in finding certain Remington rifles. In this edition, Remington rifles have been grouped according to action type (i.e., single-shot rifles, slide actions, autoloaders, etc.). Our surveys revealed this to be the easiest way to locate a specific firearm. The index may also be used if difficulty is encountered in finding a particular model.

In researching data for this edition, some manufacturers' records were unavailable and some information was unobtainable. For example, many early firearms production records were destroyed in a fire that ravaged the Winchester plant. Likewise, some manufacturers' records have been lost or were simply not maintained accurately. These circumstances resulted in some minor deviations in the presentation format of certain model listings. For example, production dates may not be listed when manufacturing records are unclear or unavailable. As an alternative, approximate dates of manufacture may be listed to reflect the availability of guns from a manufacturer or distributor. These figures may represent disposition dates indicating when that particular model was shipped to a distributor or importer. Frequently, and especially with foreign manufacturers, production records are unavailable. Therefore, information on availability is often based on importation records that reflect domestic distribution only.

All of this is meant to explain the procedure and policy used regarding these published dates and to establish the distinction between "production dates," which are based on manufacturers' records, and "availability dates," which are based on distribution records in the absence of recorded production data.

To ensure that we have the most accurate information available, we encourage and solicit the users of *Gun Trader's Guide* to communicate with our research staff at the Skyhorse Publishing, Inc., offices (address below) and forward any verifiable information they may have, especially in relation to older, out-of-production models.

CAUTION TO READERS

An amendment to the Gun Control Act of 1968 prohibited the manufacture, transfer, or possession of firearms intended for disposition to the general public designed to accept large capacity ammunition feeding devices. Manufacturers who produced such arms were required to redesign those models to limit their capacities to 10

rounds or less, or discontinue production or importation. The law applied to all such devices manufactured after October 13, 1994. Post-ban feeding devices must meet the capacity limit requirements. However, the grandfather clause of this amendment exempts all such devices lawfully possessed at the time the legislation became law. Pre-ban arms (manufactured before October 13, 1994) may therefore be bought, sold, or traded with no additional restrictions imposed by this law, which was ultimately rescinded in 2004 under the sunset provision and is no longer in effect. Any student of firearms should study the provisions of the Gun Control Act of 1968 for more information on firearms ownership, sales, and transfers in the United States. For updates and current firearms regulations, contact the Bureau of Alcohol, Tobacco, Firearms and Explosives at www.atf.gov.

For the purposes of this book, models previously designed to accept high capacity feeding devices will be listed at their original specifications and capacities if only the feeding device was modified to reduce that capacity.

Regarding shotguns, the reader should be aware that shotgun barrels must be 18 inches or longer except when used by

military or law enforcement personnel. A special permit from the Bureau of Alcohol, Tobacco, Firearms and Explosives is required to possess shotguns with barrel lengths that are shorter than 18 inches.

Because state and federal laws vary and may change annually, it is in the collector's best interest to inquire about the legality of ownership, concealment, or display of specific firearms in his or her state, town, or county. Firearms restrictions are not universal and ignorance of the law is not a legal defense. Protect yourself by knowing which guns you may own, purchase, and transport under the laws of your state.

ACKNOWLEDGMENTS
The publisher wishes to express special thanks to the many collectors, dealers, manufacturers, shooting editors, firearms' firms, distributors' personnel, and other industry professionals who provided product information and willingly shared their knowledge in making this the best *Gun Trader's Guide* yet.

Readers may send comments or suggestions to:
Stephen D. Carpenteri, Editor
Gun Trader's Guide
Skyhorse Publishing, Inc.
307 West 36th Street, 11th Floor
New York, NY 10018

How to Use This Guide

Are you planning on buying or selling a used rifle, shotgun, or handgun? Perhaps you just want to establish the value of a favorite rifle, shotgun, or handgun in your collection. No matter what your interest in collectible smokless-powder firearms, today's enthusiast inevitably turns to *Gun Trader's Guide* to determine specifications, date of manufacture, and the average value (in the United States) of a specific modern firearm.

Opening this book, the collector asks himself the first obvious question: "How much is my used gun worth?"

Gun prices contained within should be considered "retail"; that is, the average price a collector anywhere in the United States may expect to pay for a firearm in similar condition. Don't leap to the conclusion that your firearm will bring top dollar! There is no right or wrong price for any collectible firearm. The listings shown here are based on national averages and may be higher or lower depending on where you live and the strength of the market in your area. There is a market for everything from folk art to xylophones to used firearms, but the range of values can be extreme and only items in perfect condition will bring top dollar.

Many variables must be considered when buying or selling a used gun. Scarcity, demand, geographic location, the buyer's position, and the gun's condition ultimately govern the selling price of a particular firearm. Sentiment often shades the value of a particular gun in the seller's mind, but the market value of Grandpa's old .30–30 cannot be logically cataloged nor effectively marketed (except possibly to someone else in the family!).

TEST SALE

To illustrate how the price of a particular gun may fluctuate, let us consider the popular Winchester Model 94 (discontinued in 2006 after 110 years of continuous production) and see what its value might be.

The Model 1894 (or Model 94) is a lever-action, solid-frame repeater. Round or octagon barrels of 26 inches were standard when the rifle was first introduced in 1894. However, half-octagon barrels were offered for a slight increase in price. Various magazine lengths were also available.

Fancy-grade versions in all Model 94 calibers were available with 26-inch round, nickel steel barrels. This grade featured a checkered fancy walnut pistol grip stock and forearm and was available with either shotgun or rifle-type butt plates.

In addition, Winchester produced this model in carbine-style with a saddle ring on the left side of the receiver. The carbine had a 20-inch round barrel and full or half magazine. Some carbines were supplied with standard-grade barrels while others were made of nickel steel. Trapper models were also available with shorter 14-, 16-, or 18-inch barrels.

In later years, the Rifle and Trapper models were discontinued and only the carbine remained. Eventually, the saddle ring was eliminated from this model and the carbine butt stock was replaced with a shotgun-type butt stock and shortened forend.

After World War II, the finish on Winchester Model 94 carbines changed to strictly hot caustic bluing; thus, pre-war models usually demand a premium over post-war models.

In 1964 (a turning point for many American firearms manufacturers), beginning with serial number 2,700,000, the action on the Winchester Model 94 was redesigned for easier manufacture. Many collectors and firearms enthusiasts considered this (and other) design changes to be inferior to former models. Therefore, the term "pre-64" has become the watchword for collectors when it comes to setting values on Winchester-made firearms. This will likely be the case in the future as the now-discontinued models 70, 94, and 1300 Winchesters reach the collectible market.

Whether this evaluation is correct or not is unimportant. The justification for an immediate increase in the value of pre-64 models was that they were no longer available. This diminished availability placed them in the "scarce" class, making them more desirable to collectors.

Shortly after the 1964 transition, Winchester began producing Model 94 commemorative models in great numbers, adding confusion to the concept of "limited production." Increased availability adversely affected the annual appreciation and price stability of these commemorative models. The negative response generated by this marketing practice was increased when Winchester was sold in the 1980s. The name of this long-established American firearms manufacturer was changed to U. S. Repeating Arms Company, which manufactured the Model 94 in both standard carbine and big bore models until 2006. Later, the Angle-Eject model was introduced, a design change that allowed for the mounting of scope sights directly above the action.

With the above facts in mind, let's explore *Gun Trader's Guide* to establish the approximate value of your particular Model 94. We will assume that you recently inherited the rifle, which has Winchester Model 94 inscribed on the barrel. Turn to the Rifle Section of the book and look under the W listings until you find Winchester. The Index (at the back of the book) is another possible means of locating your rifle.

The listings in *Gun Trader's Guide* are arranged within each manufacturer's entry, first by model numbers in consecutive numerical order followed by model names in alphabetical order. At first glance, you see that there are two model designations that may apply: the original designation (Model 1894) or the revised, shorter designation (Model 94). Which of these designations applies to your recently acquired Winchester?

The next step in the process is to try to match the appearance of your model with a photo in the book. The photos may all look alike at first glance, but close evaluation and careful attention to detail will enable you to eliminate models that are not applicable. Further examination of your gun might reveal a curved or crescent-shaped butt plate. By careful observation of your gun's characteristics and close visual comparison of the photographic examples, you may logically conclude that your gun is the Winchester Model 94 Lever Action Rifle. (Please note that the guns shown in *Gun Trader's Guide* are not always shown in proportion to one another; that is, a carbine barrel might not appear to be shorter than a rifle barrel.)

You have now tentatively determined your model, but, to be sure, you should read through the specifications for that model and establish that the barrel on the pictured rifle is 26 inches long; you should also determine if it is round, octagonal, or half-octagonal.

Upon measuring, you find that the barrel on your rifle is approximately 26 inches, perhaps a trifle under, and it is round. Additionally, your rifle is marked .38-55 (the caliber designation). The caliber offerings listed in the specifications include .38-55, so you are further convinced that this is your gun. You may read on to determine that this rifle was manufactured from 1894 to 1937. After that date, only the shorter-barreled carbine was offered by Winchester, and then only in .25-35, .30-30, and .32 Special.

At this point, you know you have a Winchester Model 94 rifle manufactured before World War II. You read the value and take the rifle to your dealer to initiate a sale.

Here is a look at some of the scenarios you may encounter:

SCENARIO I
If the rifle is truly in excellent condition—hat is, if it retains at least 95 percent of its original finish on both the metal and wood and has a perfect bore—then the gun does in fact have a collectible value as noted. However, keep in mind that the dealer is in business to make a profit. If he pays you the full value of the gun, he will have to charge more than this when he sells it in order to make a reasonable profit. If more than the fair market value is charged, the gun will not sell or someone will pay more for the gun than it is actually worth

Therefore, expect a reputable dealer to offer you less than the published, maximum value for the gun in its present condition. The exact amount will vary for a variety of reasons. For example, if the dealer already has a dozen or so of the same model on his shelf and they do not sell well his offer will be considerably lower. On the other hand, if the dealer does not have any of this model in stock and knows several collectors who want it, chances are his offer will be considerably higher.

SCENARIO II
Perhaps you overestimated the true state of the rifle's condition. Suppose the gun's finish is flawed and not much of the original bluing remains. There are several shiny, bare-metal spots mixed with a brown patina over the remaining metal. Also, much of the original varnish on the wood has been worn off from extended use. Consequently, the rifle is not considered to be in "excellent" condition and is worth proportionately less than the value shown in this book.

SCENARIO III
Your Winchester Model 94 rifle looks nearly new, as if it were just out of the box, and the rifle works perfectly. Therefore, you are convinced that the dealer

should pay you the full value of the gun (less a reasonable profit of 25 to 35 percent). When the dealer offers you about half what you expect, you are shocked!

Although the rifle looks new to you, the experienced dealer has detected that the gun (or parts of it) has been refinished. Perhaps you did not notice the rounding of the formerly sharp edges on the receiver or the slight funneling of some screw holes—all dead giveaways that the rifle has been refinished. If so, your rifle is not in "excellent" condition as you originally assumed and is therefore worth less than "high book" value.

A knowledgeable gun dealer will check each firearm to determine that it functions properly, and the condition of interior parts may also be a factor in determining the value of any firearm. Even when a collectible firearm has been expertly refinished to "excellent" condition it is no longer "original," and a rule of thumb is to deduct 50 percent from the value listed in this book. If the job is poorly done, deduct 80 percent or more.

Now, if you are somewhat of an expert and know for certain that your rifle has never been refinished or otherwise repaired or damaged, has at least 95 percent of its original finish left, and you believe you have a firearm that is truly worth full book value, understand that a dealer will still only offer you from 25 percent to 50 percent less for it due to profit margins, overstocked goods, and so forth.

TOP-DOLLAR OPTIONS

One alternative for getting top dollar for your gun is to advertise your item in a local newspaper and sell the firearm directly to a private collector. Many collectors have a special interest in certain models, manufacturers, or product lines and will happily pay full price (and sometimes more) for a hard-to-find piece. However, this approach may prove time-consuming, frustrating, and expensive. In addition, there may be federal and local restrictions on the sale of firearms in your area, so check with the local police chief or sheriff before you proceed with a private sale.

If you experience such complications, chances are the next time you have a firearm to sell you will be more than happy to take it to a dealer and let him make his fair share of profit!

STANDARDS OF CONDITION

The condition of a firearm is an important factor in determining its value. In some rare and unusual models, a variation in condition from "Excellent" to "Very Good" can mean a value difference of 50 percent or more. Therefore, you must be able to determine the gun's condition before you can accurately evaluate the value of the firearm.

Several sets of value standards have been used in gun trading, but the National Rifle Association Standards of Condition of Modern Firearms are probably the most popular. In recent years, condition has been established by the percentage of original finish remaining on the wood and metal of the firearm.

Here's a look at how these standards are applied:

Excellent

For the purpose of assigning comparative values as a basis for trading, firearms listed in this book are assumed to be in Excellent condition if they have 95 percent or more remaining original finish, no noticeable marring of wood or metal, and the bore has no pits or rust.

To the novice, this translates to meaning a practically new gun, almost as though it had just been removed from its shipping box. The trained eye, however, will see the difference between "new" or "mint" condition and merely "excellent."

Very Good

Any other defects, no matter how minor, diminish the value of a firearm below those listed in this book. For example, if more than 5 percent of the original finish is gone and there are minor surface dents or scratches, regardless of how small, the gun is no longer in Excellent condition. Instead, it is considered to be in Very Good condition provided the gun is in perfect working order. Despite the minor defects, the gun will still look relatively new to the untrained buyer.

Good

If the gun is in perfect working condition and functions properly but has minor wear on working surfaces (perhaps some deep scratches on the wood or metal), the gun is considered to be in Good condition, one grade below Very Good, according to NRA standards. Again, the price shown in this book for that particular firearm must be reduced to reflect its true value.

The two remaining NRA conditions fall under the headings of Fair and Poor. These guns normally have little value unless they are of historical importance or an aficionado simply must have them to complete his collection. The value of such guns is then determined by the price the buyer is willing to pay.

In any case, do not sell any gun until you have researched its history and value. Many plain-looking guns have sold for thousands of dollars for a variety of reasons. Many an innocent widow has literally given away her deceased husband's guns, not knowing they were of extremely high value. Avoid buyers who are in a hurry to make a purchase or who quickly offer what seems to be more money than the gun is worth. Not every gun is priceless, but many of them are!

Previous editions of *Gun Trader's Guide* offered multiplication factors to use for firearms in other than Excellent condition. These factors are listed below. Be aware that the figures given are not etched in stone. Instead, they are simply another rough means of establishing the value of a particular firearm.

For guns in other than Excellent condition, multiply the price shown in this book for the model in question by the following factors:

Multiplication Factors for Guns Not in Excellent Condition:

CONDITION	X	FACTOR
Mint or New (NiB)		1.25
Excellent (Ex)		1.00
Very Good (VG)		.85
Good (Gd)		.68
Fair		.45
Poor		.15

PARTING THOUGHTS

Remember, the word "guide" in *Gun Trader's Guide* should be taken literally. This book is meant to be a reference only and is not the gospel of the collectible trade. We sincerely hope, however, that you find this publication useful when you decide to buy or sell a used, collectible modern firearm. Study all available references, manufacturers' histories, and visit state and regional auction houses and dealers to develop an accurate assessment of your firearm's true value before you let it go.

Also, keep in mind that gun values vary from region to region. For this reason, we recommend that you attend local gun shows and auctions to develop a better understanding of gun values and pricing. And, whenever you travel, check the prices of guns you're familiar with to compare their values in other parts of the country. The difference can be surprising!

Finally, beware of guns that have been refinished or refurbished, either by amateurs or even expert gunsmiths. A century-old gun that looks brand new has probably been refinished and will actually be worth far less than a time-worn original. Every new screw, pin, or spring added to an original firearm diminishes its value—the worn, pitted original parts of a firearm enhance its value far more than modern replacements. Refinishing a gun may improve its looks and satisfy the final owner, but it will lose collectible value that will never be recovered.

GUN SHOWS AROUND THE COUNTRY

The majority of private, non-commercial gun deals in the United States take place in living rooms and garages, spur-of-the-moment transactions that involve a seller who needs cash and a buyer who wants to buy that particular firearm. The seller simply wants as much money as he can get for the piece and the buyer just wants a good deal for a firearm he hopes to resell at a profit. In most one-time purchases, both parties go away happy with the outcome. But before one enters the world of serious firearms collecting, start attending organized gun shows. This is where gun lovers converge on hundreds of booths containing thousands of guns ranging in value from less than $10 to $100,000 or more.

GO TO THE SHOW!
To learn the most about the value and condition of used guns, nothing beats a weekend gun show. Dealers from throughout the region, and often from across the country, will be on hand to show, sell, buy, and trade new and used guns of every type. Some dealers specialize in guns made by a specific manufacturer (Beretta, Benelli, Winchester, Remington, Savage, Ruger, Stevens, etc.) while some deal in just one model of firearm (i.e., pre-64 Winchester Model 70s). Others may offer custom guns or firearms made by European or Asian manufacturers, while others offer a variety of collectibles including swords, knives, and ancient weaponry.

Gun buyers, collectors, and dealers benefit from attending gun shows because it's a chance to see a wide variety of firearms, their condition and value, on the local level. This is the place to really learn about guns and how their value is determined. Most dealers will gladly explain the nuances of gun condition, why perfectly refurbished guns are worth so much less than a rusted, beat-up original, and what makes one gun worth so much while another, seemingly similar model, is worth so much less.

GUN SHOW ETIQUETTE
Unless otherwise noted, all gun shows in the United States are open to the public. Ticket prices are reasonable and food and beverages are usually available. Of course, there are security requirements that must be met and procedures that must be followed, but in general anyone attending a gun show may bring guns for appraisal, sale, or trade. Laws vary from state to state, so be sure to check with show promoters or local law enforcement personnel before bringing a gun to any show!

Most gun shows are well-attended, often crowded, and sales can be brisk. Be patient while moving between booths. If a particular dealer or booth is overrun with customers, come back later to talk. There are always slow periods at gun shows (early in the day, around lunch time, and just before closing) so schedule your visits to dealers and make the most of the time you have available.

In general, don't bring a gun to a commercial show and expect to get top dollar for it.

Show dealers often work in volume sales and may have a dozen or more of your model on the table. This is especially true of the cheaper imports, WWII Japanese and Italian rifles, and other "by the barrel" items.

Specialty guns, of course, will draw any dealer's attention, and once in a while you will get far more than you expected from a particular firearm. However, it's best to bring your gun in for appraisal only. See what the dealer is willing to give you for it and compare that to the prices listed in this book. If he's offering you a much higher price, tell him you'll think about it and then go do a little more research; you may have a unique model that commands a much higher price!

In most cases there will be too much confusion, conversation, and diversion at gun show booths to allow you to make a serious sale or trade. If you're feeling rushed or pressured, move on to another dealer or ask for his card and plan to make a personal, one-on-one visit later in the week or month. Most gun dealers follow the gun show circuit and may be found again in a week or two at another location or at their shop or home, so don't feel rushed to sell. Work the shows, study the guns and prices, and make your best deal when you are ready to commit to a final transaction.

WORK THE CROWD
While huge crowds at gun shows can be a hindrance when you're trying to buy or sell a gun, you can use the crowd to your advantage by carrying your locked and tagged "for sale" gun with you as you move around the arena. There will be a wide variety of gun buyers, dealers, and fans in the crowd who may stop you and want to discuss your firearm. A buyer who needs a particular piece to com-

plete his collection could easily offer you more than the gun is listed for, more than the dealer offered, and more than you ever expected to get for it.

Remember: Everyone attending a gun show is in the market to trade, buy, or sell. Even if you don't make a sale while you are there, you can make valuable contacts that may come in handy for future transactions. For example, you may encounter a dealer who trades only in vintage Savage rifles, and on your next trip to the family farm you may find that your grandfather left his trusty Model 99 in .300 Savage in an upstairs closet. Or you may find a pre-64 Winchester Model 70 Super Grade in your uncle's attic. Having met the right people at the local gun show, you can buy, sell, or trade your new collectibles quickly and profitably because you took the time to find the right people.

Commercial gun shows are on-going events that occur weekly, monthly, or annually in various towns and cities around the country. Some shows are sponsored by the same organizations in the same location each time, so it is easy to keep track of them.

It is possible to attend a different gun show every weekend somewhere in the United States. For a complete, updated list of gun shows near you, log onto www.gunshows-usa.com. This useful site includes a listing of all the gun shows presently scheduled in every state and the list is updated weekly.

Be sure to call ahead to verify show times, dates, ticket fees, and regulations, including tips on how to bring firearms into the show for trade, sale, or appraisal.

Colt Model 1911 Semi-Automatic Pistol

Adopted by the U.S. Ordnance Department in 1911, the Colt semi-automatic pistol was originally manufactured by Colt and the government's Springfield Armory. In 1917, with the US entry into World War I, the government contracted with Colt for one million pistols and contracts were signed for the production of a total of two million more pistols with Remington-UMC, North American Arms, Savage, Winchester, National Cash Register Co., Burroughs Adding Machine, Lamston Monotype, and Caron Bros. A total of 629,000 pistols were completed by the war's end in1918. Production was resumed in 1924 with a series of design modifications introduced during the inter-war period resulting in the Model 1911 A1. From the onset of World War II until its end in 1945 Colt, Remington UMC, Remington-Rand, Ithaca, Singer, and Union Switch and Signal Company manufactured nearly 2 million M1911A1s.

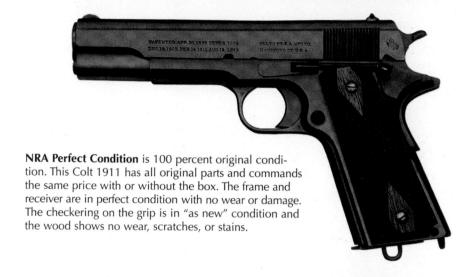

NRA Perfect Condition is 100 percent original condition. This Colt 1911 has all original parts and commands the same price with or without the box. The frame and receiver are in perfect condition with no wear or damage. The checkering on the grip is in "as new" condition and the wood shows no wear, scratches, or stains.

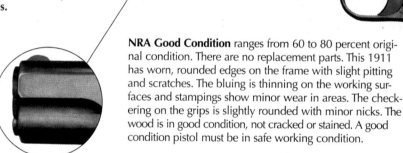

NRA Good Condition ranges from 60 to 80 percent original condition. There are no replacement parts. This 1911 has worn, rounded edges on the frame with slight pitting and scratches. The bluing is thinning on the working surfaces and stampings show minor wear in areas. The checkering on the grips is slightly rounded with minor nicks. The wood is in good condition, not cracked or stained. A good condition pistol must be in safe working condition.

NRA Fair Condition ranges from 20 to 60 percent original condition. This Model 1911 is in well-worn condition with the frame retaining only 40 percent of its original finish. Some major and minor parts have been replaced and scratches and pitting from rust and corrosion are evident on the frame and slide. Serial numbers and other markings are shallow and difficult to identify. While the grips on this pistol are not badly scratched or soiled, they show worn checkering and several large and small dents. The gun must function and shoot properly.

Winchester Model 94

Winchester produced approximately 2,550,000 Model 94 lever action rifles between 1894 and 1962. The Model 94 was manufactured in both rifle and carbine versions with several configurations that included pistol- and straight-grip stocks, various grades of wood, and several different barrel lengths and magazine capacities. Crescent and shotgun style buttstocks and take-down barrels were also offered. The Model 94 was produced in 25-35, 30, 30-30, 32-40 and 38-55 calibers.

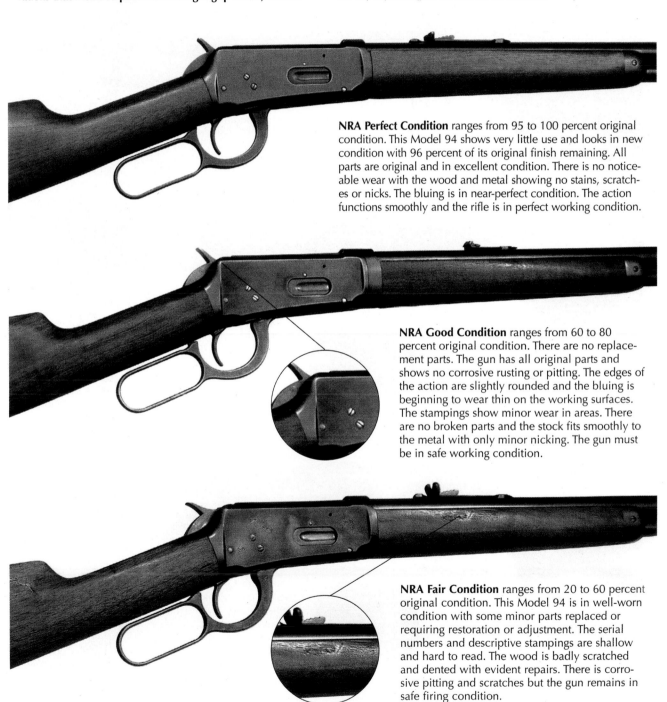

NRA Perfect Condition ranges from 95 to 100 percent original condition. This Model 94 shows very little use and looks in new condition with 96 percent of its original finish remaining. All parts are original and in excellent condition. There is no noticeable wear with the wood and metal showing no stains, scratches or nicks. The bluing is in near-perfect condition. The action functions smoothly and the rifle is in perfect working condition.

NRA Good Condition ranges from 60 to 80 percent original condition. There are no replacement parts. The gun has all original parts and shows no corrosive rusting or pitting. The edges of the action are slightly rounded and the bluing is beginning to wear thin on the working surfaces. The stampings show minor wear in areas. There are no broken parts and the stock fits smoothly to the metal with only minor nicking. The gun must be in safe working condition.

NRA Fair Condition ranges from 20 to 60 percent original condition. This Model 94 is in well-worn condition with some minor parts replaced or requiring restoration or adjustment. The serial numbers and descriptive stampings are shallow and hard to read. The wood is badly scratched and dented with evident repairs. There is corrosive pitting and scratches but the gun remains in safe firing condition.

Winchester Model 12

When introduced in 1912, the hammerless Model 12 slide-action shotgun was offered only in 20-guage with a 2½-inch chamber. In 1914 12- and 16-guage versions were introduced followed by a 28-guage in 1937. The Model 12 was available with various chokes and with walnut, straight or pistol grip stock and forearm. Winchester sold more than 1,900,000 Model 1912s during the shotgun's 51-year history.

NRA Perfect Condition is 100 percent original condition. This Model12 is in NIB condition and has not been previously sold at retail. The shotgun shows no signs of use and retains 100 percent of its original finish. All parts are original and in new condition.

NRA Good Condition ranges from 60 to 80 percent original condition. This gun has all original parts in good condition. There is no corrosive pitting or rusting and the action displays only slightly rounded edges. The gun retains 70 percent of its original finish with bluing beginning to wear on the working surfaces. The stock fits smoothly to the metal and has only minor nicking. The shotgun must be in good working order.

NRA Fair Condition ranges from 20 to 60 percent original condition. Showing a well-worn condition, this gun may require minor parts to be replaced or adjusted. The serial numbers and descriptive stamping are shallow and difficult to read. The wood is badly scratched and dented with evident repairs. Corrosive pitting and scratches in the metal, while considerable, do not render the gun unsafe.

MODERN ARs:
THE NEW COLLECTIBLES?

For over 130 years the term "collectible firearms" invariably referred to rifles, shotguns, and handguns made in the smokeless powder era using steel and wood. Prior to 1964, when modern manufacturing processes changed to machine-made, stamped, and plastic parts in order to keep retail prices low, most American- and foreign-made firearms were still hand fitted, carved, checkered, and finished. The best examples of those labor-intensive products now bring premium prices among dealers and collectors as well as at auction. Interest in these and other "pre-64" models are likely to continue to increase in popularity and value among those who prefer the classic lines of a well-designed, wood-stocked firearm.

During the Vietnam War, however, the look and feel of firearms began to change. Colt's M-16 and the many variations that followed were considered cheap, inferior, and of little collectible value. Mostly of poor quality and made with cheap powdered metal or stamped

parts with plastic stocks and grips, those early "black rifles" were unpopular with the troops who used them. These first ARs were neither accurate nor dependable. Troops despised them and complaints about their poor performance filled the shooting press for decades.

As might be expected, ARs (which is simply named for Armalite, the company that first designed them) were not popular with collectors either, and their value was low even for "new in the box" specimens. Used, abused, and constantly repaired ARs were tossed into the military bins where Japanese, Russian, Italian, and other low-end firearms were often sold at gun shows for less than the price of admission.

It's been nearly forty years since the M-16 ("Matty Mattel" as it was wryly referred to by disenchanted troops) was first introduced, and it is long forgotten except among those who carried them. Few would offer the price of a cup of specialty coffee to own one.

Much has changed since

1975. For those who enjoy and prefer today's AR offerings, the choices are many and, in most cases, far superior to the original M-16. Built to tight tolerances, solid and accurate, one can reasonably expect to pay (new) $1,000 and up for a base-model AR, not including sling, scope, bipod, night sights, and other accessories that could easily bump the start-up cost to $5,000.

Today's assault rifles are a far cry from the AK-47 and other Kalashnikov knock-offs that, by design and necessity, were easy to assemble from cheap, mass-produced parts. Famously dependable and accurate enough for close-quarter combat, most in the gun collecting world know the AK-47 for what it is and few collect them other than for the quick "wow" factor they provide.

Dozens of manufacturers now produce some version of an AR for range, law enforcement, military, self-defense, or sporting use. The majority has morphed into long-range, sniper-type rifles and invariably include the term "tactical" in their nomenclature, primarily to appeal to former military, police officers, and fans of the SWAT genre. The best of these rifles are capable of minute-of-angle accuracy at 100 yards and, properly equipped with high-powered scopes and a steady rest, most will "ring the gong" at 1,000 yards or more on silhouette targets specifically designed for ultra long-range shooting.

In most cases ARs are like new cars: they lose value the instant you walk out of the gun store. What makes any gun valuable is its condition, history, rarity, and its quality of construction. Other than the M-16, AR-15, and the AK-47, few of these rifle models are well known or familiar to collectors. ARs chambered for the .338 Lapua, .300 Winchester Magnum, and .308 Winchester have the highest "face" and collectible value, but few are presently worth more than their original MSRP. This will likely change in the future, particularly with models that were produced in small production runs, have unusual or unique features, or were chambered for custom or uncommon calibers. Only "the market" knows the answers to these questions and will reveal its findings in its own good time.

The best advice would be to hold on to any ARs and black guns you have in your possession, keep them clean, operable, and in "as new" condition, and wait patiently for the market to develop (which could be twenty years or more).

A key point in collecting any firearm is maintaining its "as new" condition, which includes the original shipping box, supplied accessories and parts, the owner's manual, and other inserts. If your AR was shipped with a scope, extra magazines, and bipod as standard accessories, having them on hand will increase the value of the piece when it is time to sell or trade. It's likely that the base rifle will be the base selling point. Accessories and add-ons will increase its value by a percentage depending on condition, quality of workmanship, and original selling price. Most gun shops, dealers, and auctioneers will likely begin hoarding ARs for future sale and trade as the present demand for these guns increases and more of them enter the market over time.

Few gun catalogs and collectible listings contain ARs as of 2012 because these products are too new and relatively unknown to those who dabble in collectibles. Even seasoned firearms dealers and auctioneers aren't sure how to price a modern AR other than to offer it at some percentage less than

MSRP based on condition or manufacturer. Too soon for "classic" status and too new to be considered "antique," today's selection of ARs may be a good investment for collectors looking for a higher return some time down the road. Only popular demand can establish a greater value.

When considering the purchase of a modern AR, the buyer is advised to carefully examine the condition of the firearm. Unfortunately, many ARs have a variety of plastic or powdered-metal parts that are subject to scratches, dents, and breakage, all of which can drive the value down. Do not be tempted to replace damaged parts with (relatively cheap) new pieces and never attempt to repair or replace ARs or parts at home. Any sign of replacement or repair will reduce the value of these firearms, which are likely to be relatively low to begin with unless they are unique, short-run, or otherwise unusual pieces.

Keep in mind that even with the most valuable standard firearm, the top value is rarely offered and is used primarily for insurance purposes. The range of value for any firearm, including antiques, can be 50 percent to 200 percent above or below its "as new" value.

34th Edition
GUN TRADER'S GUIDE

Handguns

NOTE: *Abbreviations used throughout the Handgun section: DA = Double Action; SA = Single Action; LR = LR; WMR = Winchester Magnum Rimfire; Adj. = Adjustable; Avail. = Available; Bbl., = Barrel; Disc. = Discontinued; TT = Target Trigger; TH = Target Hammer.*

Accu-Tek Model AT .380

Accu-Tek Model BL-9

Accu-Tek HC-380SS

A.A. ARMS — Monroe, North Carolina

AP-9 SERIES
Semiautomatic recoil-operated pistol w/polymer integral grip/frame design. Fires from a closed bolt. Caliber: 9mm Parabellum. 10- or 20-round magazine, 3- , 5- or 11-inch bbl., 11.8 inches overall w/5-inch bbl., Weight: 3.5 lbs. Fixed blade, protected post front sight adjustable for elevation, winged square notched rear. Matte phosphate/blue or nickel finish. Checkered polymer grip/frame. Made from 1988-99.

AP9 model
(pre-94 w/ventilated bbl., shroud . . NiB $426 Ex $353 Gd $253
AP9 Mini model
(post-94 w/o bbl., shroud). . . . . NiB $240 Ex $235 Gd $175
AP9 Target model
(pre-94 w/11-inch bbl.). . . . . NiB $630 Ex $398 Gd $285
Nickel finish, add. $20

ACCU-TEK — Chino, California

MODEL AT-9 AUTO PISTOL
Caliber: 9mm Para. 8-round magazine, Double action only. 3.2-inch bbl., 6.25 inches overall. Weight: 28 oz. Fixed blade front sight, adj. rear w/3-dot system. Firing pin block with no external safety. Stainless or black over stainless finish. Checkered black nylon grips. Announced 1992, but made from 1995-99.
Satin stainless model . . . . NiB $310 Ex $249 Gd $172
Matte black stainless . . . . NiB $281 Ex $233 Gd $183

MODEL AT-25 AUTO PISTOL
Similar to Model AT380 except chambered .25 ACP w/7-round magazine, Made from 1992-96.
Lightweight w/aluminum frame. . . . . . NiB $152 Ex $125 Gd $99
Bright stainless (disc. 1991). . . . . NiB $152 Ex $125 Gd $99
Satin stainless model . . . . NiB $152 Ex $125 Gd $99
Matte black stainless . . . . NiB $152 Ex $125 Gd $99

MODEL AT-32 AUTO PISTOL
Similar to Model AT-.380 except chambered .32 ACP. Made from 1990-2003.
Lightweight w/aluminum
Frame (disc. 1991). . . . . NiB $190 Ex $133 Gd $99
Satin stainless model . . . . NiB $190 Ex $133 Gd $99
Matte black stainless . . . . NiB $195 Ex $138 Gd $104

MODEL AT-40 DA AUTO PISTOL
Caliber: .40 S&W. Seven-round magazine, 3.2-inch bbl., 6.25 inches over-all. Weight: 28 oz. Fixed blade front sight, adj. rear w/3-dot system. Firing pin block with no external safety. Stainless or black over stainless finish. Checkered black nylon grips. Announced 1992, but made from 1995-96.
Satin stainless model . . . . NiB $260 Ex $147 Gd $105
Matte black stainless . . . . NiB $265 Ex $152 Gd $1105

MODEL AT-380 AUTO PISTOL
Caliber: .380 ACP. Five-round magazine, 2.75-inch bbl., 5.6 inches overall. Weight: 20 oz. External hammer w/slide safety. Grooved black composition grips. Alloy or stainless frame w/steel slide. Black, satin aluminum or stainless finish. Made from 1992-2003.
Standard alloy frame (disc. 1992) . . . NiB $262 Ex $152 Gd $99
Satin stainless model . . . . NiB $262 Ex $152 Gd $99
Matte black stainless . . . . NiB $267 Ex $157 Gd $104

MODELS BL-9, BL 380 . . . . NiB $188 Ex $147 Gd $118
Ultra compact DAO semiautomatic pistols. Calibers: .380 ACP, 9mm Para. 5-round magazine, 3-inch bbl., 5.6 inches overall. Weight: 24 oz. Fixed sights. Carbon steel frame and slide w/black finish. Polymer grips. Made 1997 to 1999.

MODELS CP-9, CP-40, CP-45
Compact, double action only, semiautomatic pistols. Calibers: 9mm Parabellum, .40 S&W, .45 ACP, 8-, 7- or 6-round magazine, 3.2-inch bbl., 6.25 inches overall. Weight: 28 oz. Fixed blade front sight, adj. rear w/3-dot system. Firing-pin block with no external safety. Stainless or black over stainless finish. Checkered black nylon grips. Made1997-2002 (CP-9), 1999 (CP-40), 1996 (CP-45).
Black stainless model . . . . NiB $228 Ex $167 Gd $125
Satin stainless model . . . . NiB $228 Ex $167 Gd $125

MODEL HC-380SS AUTO PISTOL . . . . NiB $246 Ex $218 Gd $185
Caliber: .380 ACP. 13-round magazine, 2.75-inch bbl., 6 inches overall. Weight: 28 oz. External hammer w/slide safety. Checkered black composition grips. Stainless finish. Made 1993 to 2003.

ACTION ARMS — Philadelphia, Pennsylvania

See also listings under CZ pistols. Action Arms stopped importing firearms in 1994.

AT-84S DA AUTOMATIC PISTOL. . . NiB $475 Ex $338 Gd $281
Caliber: 9mm Para. 15-round magazine, 4.75-inch bbl., 8 inches overall. Weight: 35 oz. Fixed front sight, drift-adj. rear. Checkered walnut grips. Blued finish. Made in Switzerland from 1988 to 1989.

AT-84P DA AUTO PISTOL . . . . NiB $480 Ex $332 Gd $281
Compact version of the Model AT-84. Only a few prototypes were manufactured in 1985.

AT-88P DA AUTO PISTOL . . . . NiB $500 Ex $456 Gd $347
Compact version of the AT-88S w/3.7-inch bbl. Only a few prototypes of this model were manufactured in 1985. Note: The AT-88 pistol series was later manufactured by Sphinx-Muller as the AT-2000 series.

AT-88S DA AUTOMATIC PISTOL. . . NiB $500 Ex $456 Gd $347
Calibers: 9mm Para. or .41 Action Express, 10-round magazine, 4.6-inch bbl., 8.1 inches overall. Weight: 35.3 oz. Fixed blade front sight, adj. rear. Checkered walnut grips. Imported 1989 to 1991.

ADVANTAGE ARMS — St. Paul, Minnesota

MODEL 422 DERRINGER . . . . NiB $155 Ex $110 Gd $90
Hammerless, top-break, 4-bbl., derringer w/rotating firing pin. Calibers: .22 LR and .22 Mag., 4-round capacity, 2.5 inch bbl., 4.5 inches overall. Weight: 15 oz. Fixed sights. Walnut grips. Blued, nickel or PDQ matte black finish. Made from 1985 to 1987.

S. A. ALKARTASUNA FABRICA DE ARMAS — Guernica, Spain

"RUBY" AUTOMATIC PISTOL. . . . . NiB $329 Ex $258 Gd $191
Caliber: .32 Automatic (7.65mm). Nine-round magazine, 3.63-inch bbl., 6.38 inches overall. Weight: About 34 oz. Fixed sights. Blued finish. Checkered wood or hard rubber grips. Made from 1917-22. Note: Mfd. by a number of Spanish firms, the Ruby was a secondary standard service pistol of the French Army in World Wars I and II. Specimens made by Alkartasuna bear the "Alkar" trademark.

Action Arms AT-84 with
Prototype of Model AT-84P
in background

AMERICAN ARMS — Kansas City, Missouri

Importer of Spanish and Italian shotguns, pistols, and rifles. Acquired by Trisatan Arms, Ltd., in 2000.

BISLEY SA REVOLVER . . . . NiB $445 Ex $399 Gd $300
Uberti reproduction of Colt's Bisley. Caliber: .45 LC. Six-round cylinder, 4.75-, 5.5- or 7.7-inch bbl., Case-hardened steel frame. Fixed blade front sight, grooved top strap rear. Hammer block safety. Imported from 1997 to 1998

CX-22 DA AUTOMATIC PISTOL
Similar to Model PX-.22 except w/8-round magazine, 3.33-inch bbl., 6.5 inches overall. Weight: 22 oz. Made from 1990 to 1995.
Standard w/chrome
Slide (disc. 1990) . . . . NiB $175 Ex $129 Gd $117
Classic model . . . . NiB $185 Ex $135 Gd $115

EP-380 DA AUTOMATIC PISTOL . . . . NiB $385 Ex $279 Gd $145
Caliber: .380 Automatic. Seven-round magazine, 3.5-inch bbl., 6.5 inches overall. Weight: 25 oz. Fixed front sight, square notch adj. rear. Stainless finish. Checkered wood grips. Made 1989 to 1991.

ESCORT DA AUTO PISTOL . . . . NiB $290 Ex $209 Gd $136
Caliber: .380 ACP. 7-round magazine, 3.38-inch bbl., 6.13 inches overall. Weight: 19 ounces. Fixed, low-profile sights. Stainless steel frame, slide, and trigger. Nickel-steel bbl., Soft polymer grips. Loaded chamber indicator. Made from 1995 to 1997.

MATEBA AUTO REVOLVER
Unique combination action design allows both slide and cylinder to recoil together causing cylinder to rotate. Single or double action. Caliber: .357 Mag. Six-round cylinder, 4- or 6-inch bbl., 8.77 inches overall w/4-inch bbl., Weight: 2.75 lbs. Steel/alloy frame. Ramped blade front sight, adjustable rear. Blue finish. Smooth walnut grips. Imported from 1997-99.
Mateba model (w/4-inch bbl.) . . . . NiB $1180 Ex $949 Gd $678
Mateba model (w/6-inch bbl.) . . . NiB $1245 Ex $1001 Gd $723

P-98 DA AUTOMATIC PISTOL . . . . . NiB $190 Ex $115 Gd $95
Caliber: .22 LR. Eight-round magazine, 5-inch bbl., 8.25 inches overall. Weight: 25 oz. Fixed front sight, square notch adj. rear. Blued finish. Serrated black polymer grips. Made 1989 to 1996.

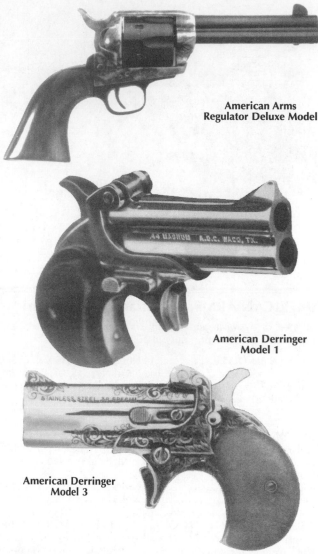

American Arms
Regulator Deluxe Model

American Derringer
Model 1

American Derringer
Model 3

PK-22 DA
AUTOMATIC PISTOL . . . . **NiB $175 Ex $124 Gd $135**
Caliber: .22 LR. Eight-round magazine, 3.33-inch bbl., 6.33 inches overall. Weight: 22 oz. Fixed front sight, V-notch rear. Blued finish. Checkered black polymer grips. Made from 1989 t5o 1996.

PX-22 DA AUTOMATIC PISTOL . . . **NiB $215 Ex $168 Gd $149**
Caliber: .22 LR. Seven-round magazine, 2.75-inch bbl., 5.33 inches overall. Weight: 15 oz. Fixed front sight, V-notch rear. Blued finish. Checkered black polymer grips. Made from 1989-96.

PX-25 DA AUTOMATIC PISTOL . . . **NiB $225 Ex $179 Gd $159**
Same general specifications as the Model PX-22 except chambered for .25 ACP. Made from 1991-92.

REGULATOR SA REVOLVER
Similar in appearance to the Colt Single-Action Army. Calibers: .357 Mag., .44-.40, .45 Long Colt. Six-round cylinder, 4.75- or 7.5-inch bbl., blade front sight, fixed rear. Brass trigger guard/backstrap on Standard model. Casehardened steel on Deluxe model. Made from 1992 to 2000.
Standard model . . . . **NiB $279 Ex $195 Gd $114**

Standard combo set
(45 LC/.45 ACP & .44-.40/.44 Spec.) . . . . **NiB $419 Ex $335 Gd $251**
Deluxe model . . . .**NiB $356 Ex $291 Gd $209**
Deluxe combo set (.45 LC/.45
ACP & .44-40/.44 Spec.) . . . . **NiB $429 Ex $369 Gd $235**
Stainless steel . . . . **NiB $395 Ex $328 Gd $228**

BUCKHORN SA REVOLVER
Similar to Regulator model except chambered .44 Mag. w/4.75-, 6- or 7.7-inch bbl., Fixed or adjustable sights. Hammer block safety. Imported 1993 to 1996.
Buckhorn model (standard sights) . . **NiB $385 Ex $318 Gd $235**
W/adjustable sights, add **$25**

SPECTRE DA AUTO PISTOL
Blowback action, fires closed bolt. Calibers: 9mm Para., .40 S&W, .45 ACP. 30-round magazine, 6-inch bbl., 13.75 inches overall. Weight: 4 lbs. 8 oz. Adj. post front sight, fixed U-notch rear. Black nylon grips. Matte black finish. Imported 1990 to 1994.
9mm Para. . . . . **NiB $510 Ex $417 Gd $246**
.40 S&W (disc. 1991) . . . . **NiB $479 Ex $385 Gd $275**
.45 ACP . . . . **NiB $525 Ex $428 Gd $271**

WOODMASTER SA AUTO PISTOL . . . . . . **NiB $260 Ex $210 Gd $162**
Caliber: .22 LR. 10-round magazine, 5.88-inch bbl., 10.5 inches overall. Weight: 31 oz. Fixed front sight, square-notch adj. rear. Blued finish. Checkered wood grips. Disc. 1989.

454 SSA REVOLVER. . . . . **NiB $750 Ex $645 Gd $500**
Umberti SSA chambered 454. Six-round cylinder, 6-inch solid raised rib or 7.7-inch top-ported bbl., satin nickel finish. Hammer block safety. Imported from 1996 to 1997.

AMERICAN DERRINGER CORPORATION —
Waco, Texas

MODEL 1 STAINLESS
Single-action pocket pistol similar to the Remington O/U derringer. Two-shot capacity. More than 60 calibers from .22 LR to .45-70. Three-inch bbl., 4.82 inches overall, weight: 15 oz. Automatic bbl., selection. Satin or high-polished stainless steel. Rosewood grips. Made from 1980 to date.
**.45 Colt, .44-40 Win., .44
Special, .410** . . . . **NiB $560 Ex $376 Gd $315**
**.45-70, .44 Mag., 41 Mag.,
.30-30 Win., .223 Rem.** . . . . **NiB $625 Ex $539 Gd $433**
**.357 Max., .357 Mag., .45 Win.
Mag., 9mm Para.** . . . . **NiB $625 Ex $539 Gd $433**
**.38 Special, .38 Super, .32 Mag.,
.22 LR, .22 WRM.** . . . . **NiB $625 Ex $539 Gd $433**

MODEL 2 STEEL "PEN" PISTOL
Calibers: .22 LR, .25 Auto, .32 Auto (7.65mm). single-shot. Two-inch bbl., 5.6 inches overall (4.2 inches in pistol format). Weight: 5 oz. Stainless finish. Made from 1993 to 1994.
.22 LR . . . . **NiB $379 Ex $298 Gd $167**
.25 Auto. . . . . **NiB $375 Ex $288 Gd $153**
.32 Auto. . . . . **NiB $415 Ex $318 Gd $168**

DA 38 DOUBLE ACTION
Calibers: .22LR, .357 Mag., .38 Special, 9mm Para., .40 S&W. 3-inch bbls., satin stainless with aluminum grip frame. DA trigger, hammerblock thumb safety. Weight: 14.5 oz. New 1990.
Standard . . . . **NiB $590 Ex $298 Gd $137**
.357 or .40 cal. . . . . **NiB $645 Ex $338 Gd $187**
Lady Derringer. . . . . **Add $15**

MODEL 3 STAINLESS STEEL . . . . NiB $95   Ex $68   Gd $41
Single-shot. Calibers: .32 Mag. or .38 Special. 2.5-inch bbl., 4.9 inches overall. Weight: 8.5 oz. Rosewood grips. Made from 1984 to 1995.

MODEL 4 DOUBLE DERRINGER
Calibers: .357 Mag., .357 Max., .44 Mag., .45 LC, .45 ACP (upper bbl., and 3-inch .410 shotshell (lower bbl.). 4.1-inch bbl, 6 inches overall. Weight: 16.5 oz. Stainless steel. Staghorn grips. Made from 1984 to date. .44 and .45-70 disc. 2003.

.357 Mag., .357 Max . . . . NiB $760   Ex $427   Gd $316
.44 Mag., .45 LC, .45 ACP . . . . NiB $865   Ex $532   Gd $421
Engraved, add $125

MODEL 6
Caliber: .22 Mag., .357 Mag., .45 LC, .45 ACP or .45 LC/.410 or .45 Colt. Bbl.: 6 inches, 8.2 inches overall. Weight: .22 oz. Satin or high-polished stainless steel w/rosewood grips. Made 1986 to date.

.22 Magnum . . . . NiB $745   Ex $389   Gd $325
.357, .45 ACP, .45 LC. . . . . NiB $495   Ex $389   Gd $330
.45/LC/.410 O/U . . . . NiB $495   Ex $389   Gd $330
Engraved, add $125

MODEL 7
Same general specifications as the Model 1 except high-strength aircraft aluminum used to reduce its weight to 7.5 oz. Made from 1986 to date. (.44 Special disc. then reintroduced in 2008.)
.22 LR, .22 WMR. . . . . NiB $550   Ex $295   Gd $149
.44 Calibers . . . . NiB $500   Ex $256   Gd $155

MODEL 10
Same general specifications as the Model 7 except chambered for .38 Special, .45 ACP or .45 Long Colt.
.38 Special or .45 ACP . . . . NiB $525   Ex $322   Gd $271
.45 Long Colt. . . . . NiB $470   Ex $367   Gd $315
Model 11 (Disc. 2003). . . . . NiB $525   Ex $322   Gd $271
Same general specifications as Model 7 except with a matte gray finish only, weight: 11 oz. Made from 1980 to date.

25 AUTOMATIC PISTOL
Calibers: .25 ACP or .250 Mag. Bbl.: 2.1 inches, 4.4 inches overall. Weight: 15.5 oz. Smooth rosewood grips. Limited production.
.25 ACP blued
(est. production 50) . . . . NiB $595   Ex $452   Gd $350
.25 ACP stainless
(est. production 400) . . . . NiB $452   Ex $370   Gd $299
.250 Mag. stainless
(est. production 100) . . . . NiB $619   Ex $558   Gd $431

MODEL 38 DA DERRINGER
Hammerless, double action, double bbl (o/u). Calibers: .22 LR, .38 Special, 9mm Para., .357 Mag., .40 S&W. Three-inch bbl., weight: 14.5 oz. Made from 1990 to date.
.22 LR or .38 Special . . . . NiB $496   Ex $449   Gd $400
9mm Para. NiB $285   Ex $228   Gd $165
.357 Mag. NiB $528   Ex $498   Gd $452
.40 S&W . . . . NiB $326   Ex $269   Gd $195

ALASKAN SURVIVAL MODEL . . . . . NiB $548   Ex $487   Gd $350
Same general specifications as the Model 4 except upper bbl., chambered for .45-70 or 3-inch .410 and .45 Colt lower bbl. Also available in .45 Auto, .45 Colt, .44 Special, .357 Mag. and .357 Max. Made from 1985 to date.

COP DA DERRINGER . . . . NiB $293   Ex $320   Gd $220
Hammerless, double-action, four-bbl., derringer. Caliber: .357 Mag. 3.15-inch bbl., 5.5 inches overall. Weight: 16 oz. Blade front sight,

American Derringer
Model .38 DA

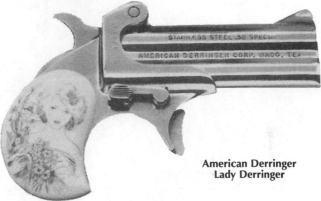

American Derringer
Lady Derringer

open notched rear. Rosewood grips. Intro. 1990, disc. 1994.

LADY DERRINGER
Same general specifications as Model 1 except w/custom-tuned action fitted w/scrimshawed synthetic ivory grips. Calibers: .32 H&R Mag., .32 Special, .38 Special (additional calibers on request). Deluxe Grade engraved and highly polished w/French fitted jewelry box. Made from 1991 to date. Deluxe and Engraved models disc. 1994.
Lady Derringer . . . . NiB $715   Ex $490   Gd $357
Deluxe. . . . . NiB $670   Ex $440   Gd $285
Gold Engraved . . . . Rare

MINI-COP DA DERRINGER . . . . . . NiB $263   Ex $182   Gd $111
Same general specifications as the American Derringer Cop except chambered for .22 Magnum. Made from 1990 to 1995.

SEMMERLING LM-4
Manually operated repeater. Calibers: .45 ACP or 9mm. Five-round (.45 ACP) or 7-round magazine (9mm)., 3.6-inch bbl., 5.2 inches overall. Weight: 24 oz. Made from 1997 to date. Limited availability.
Blued finish . . . . NiB $3499   Ex $2342   Gd $1591
Stainless steel . . . . NiB $3499   Ex $2342   Gd $1591

TEXAS COMMEMORATIVE
Same general specifications as Model 1 except w/solid brass frame, stainless bbls. and rosewood grips. Calibers: .22 LR, .32 Mag., .38 Special, .44-40 Win. or .45 Colt. Made from 1991 to date.
.38 Special . . . . NiB $385   Ex $284   Gd $199
.44-40 or .45 Colt . . . . NiB $595   Ex $466   Gd $320

AMT
.45 ACP Backup

AMT
.45 ACP Hardballer

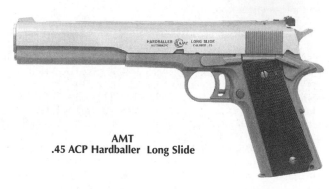

AMT
.45 ACP Hardballer Long Slide

AMERICAN FIREARMS MFG. CO., INC. — San Antonio, Texas

25 AUTO PISTOL
Caliber: .25 Auto. 8-round magazine, 2.1-inch bbl., 4.4 inches over-all. Weight: 14.5 oz. Fixed sights. Stainless or blued ordnance steel. Smooth walnut grips. Made from 1966 to 1974.
Stainless steel model . . . . NiB $195 Ex $150 Gd $103
Blued steel model . . . . NiB $165 Ex $130 Gd $102

380 AUTO PISTOL. . . . . NiB $706 Ex $528 Gd $361
Caliber: .380 Auto. 8-round magazine, 3.5-inch bbl., 5.5 inches overall. Weight: 20 oz. Stainless steel. Smooth walnut grips. Made from 1972 to 1974.

AMT (ARCADIA MACHINE & TOOL) — Irwindale, California (Previously Irwindale Arms, Inc.)

NOTE: *The AMT Backup II automatic pistol was introduced in 1993 as a continuation of the original .380 backup with the traditional double action function and a redesigned double safety.*

45 ACP HARDBALLER
Caliber: .45 ACP. Seven-round magazine, 5-inch bbl., 8.5 inches overall. Weight: 39 oz. Adj. or fixed sights. Serrated matte slide rib w/loaded chamber indicator. Extended combat safety, adj. trigger and long grip safety. Wraparound Neoprene grips. Stainless steel. Made 1978-2001.
.45 ACP Hardballer . . . . NiB $513 Ex $359 Gd $235
Long slide conversion kit
(disc. 1997), add $300

45 ACP HARDBALLER LONG SLIDE
Similar to the standard AMT Hardballer except w/2-inch-longer bbl. and slide. Also chambered for .400 Cor-Bon. Made from 1980-2001
.45 ACP long slide . . . . NiB $487 Ex $409 Gd $291
.400 Cor-Bon long slide
(Intro.1998) . . . . NiB $477 Ex $394 Gd $287
5-inch conversion kit
(disc. 1997), add $300

1911 GOVERNMENT MODEL
AUTO PISTOL . . . . NiB $387 Ex $335 Gd $255
Caliber: .45 ACP. Seven-round magazine, 5-inch bbl., 8.5 inches overall. Weight: 38 ounces. Fixed sights. Wraparound Neoprene grip. Made from 1979 to date.

AUTOMAG II
AUTOMATIC PISTOL . . . . NiB $465 Ex $340 Gd $227
Caliber: .22 Mag. Seven- or 9-round magazine, bbl., lengths: 3.38-4.5-, 6-inch. Weight: 32 oz. Fully adj. Millett sights. Stainless finish. Smooth black composition grips. Made from 1986 to 2001.

AUTOMAG III
AUTOMATIC PISTOL . . . . NiB $549 Ex $461 Gd $408
Calibers: .30 M1 and 9mm Win. Mag. Eight-round magazine., 6.38-inch bbl., 10.5 inches overall. Weight: 43 ounces. Millet adj. sights. Stainless finish. Carbon fiber grips. Made from 1992 to 2001.

AUTOMAG IV
AUTOMATIC PISTOL . . . . NiB $565 Ex $499 Gd $408
Calibers: 10mm Mag., .45 Win. Mag. 8- or 7-round magazine, 6.5- or 8.63-inch bbl., 10.5 inches overall. Weight: 46 oz. Millet adj. sights. Stainless finish. Carbon fiber grips. Made from 1992-2001.

AUTOMAG V
AUTOMATIC PISTOL . . . . NiB $972 Ex $853 Gd $765
Caliber: .50 A.E. Five-round magazine, 7-inch bbl., 10.5 inches overall. Weight: 46 oz. Custom adj. sights. Stainless finish. Carbon fiber grips. Made from 1994 to 1995.

BACKUP AUTOMATIC PISTOL
Caliber: .22LR, .380 ACP. Eight-round (.22LR) or 5-round (.380 ACP) magazine, 2.5-inch bbl., 5 inches overall. Weight: 18 oz. Open sights. Carbon fiber or walnut grips. Stainless steel finish. Made from 1990 to 1998.
.22 LR (disc. 1987) . . . . NiB $200 Ex $153 Gd $111

BACKUP II

AUTOMATIC PISTOL . . . . **NiB $322 Ex $240 Gd $188**
Caliber: .380 ACP, 5-round magazine, 2.5-inch bbl., 5 inches overall. Weight: 18 oz. Open sights. Stainless steel finish. Carbon-fiber grips. Made from 1993 to 1998.

BACKUP DAO AUTO PISTOL

Calibers: .380 ACP, .38 Super, 9mm Para., .40 Cor-Bon, .40 S&W, .45 ACP. Six-round (.380, .38 Super 9mm) or 5-round (.40 Cor-Bon, .40 S&W, .45 ACP) magazine, 2.5-inch bbl., 5.75-inches overall. Weight: 18 oz. (.380 ACP) or 23 oz. Open fixed sights. Stainless steel finish. Carbon fiber grips. Made from 1992 to date.
.380 ACP . . . . **NiB $270 Ex $219 Gd $170**
.38 Super, 9mm . . . . **NiB $288 Ex $227 Gd $155**
.40 Cor-Bon, .40 S&W,
.45 ACP . . . . **NiB $298 Ex $251 Gd $178**

BULL'S EYE

TARGET MODEL . . . . **NiB $460 Ex $392 Gd $364**
Caliber: .40 S&W. Eight-round magazine, 5-inch bbl., 8.5 inches overall. Weight: 38 oz. Millet adjustable sights. Wide adj. trigger. Wraparound Neoprene grips. Made from 1990 to 1992.

JAVELINA . . . . **NiB $662 Ex $529 Gd $415**
Caliber: 10mm. Eight-round magazine, 7-inch bbl., 10.5 inches overall. Weight: 48 oz. Long grip safety, beveled magazine well, wide adj. trigger. Millet adj. sights. Wraparound Neoprene grips. Stainless finish. Made from 1991 to 1993.

LIGHTNING AUTO PISTOL

Caliber: .22 LR. 10-round magazine, 5-, 6.5-, 8.5-, 10-inch bbl., 10.75 inches overall (6.5-inch bbl.). Weight: 45 oz. (6.5-inch bbl.). Millett adj. sights. Checkered rubber grips. Stainless finish. Made from 1984 to 1987.
Standard model . . . . **NiB $420 Ex $295 Gd $198**
Bull's-Eye model . . . . **NiB $490 Ex $410 Gd $334**

ON DUTY DA PISTOL

Calibers: .40 S&W, 9mm Para., .45 ACP. 15-round (9mm), 13-shot (.40 S&W) or 9-round (.45 ACP) magazine, 4.5-inch bbl., 7.75 inches overall. Weight: 32 oz. Hard anodized aluminum frame. Stainless steel slide and bbl., Carbon fiber grips. Made from 1991-94.
9mm or .40 S&W . . . . **NiB $435 Ex $354 Gd $297**
.45 ACP . . . . **NiB $480 Ex $393 Gd $250**

SKIPPER AUTO PISTOL . . . . **NiB $435 Ex $328 Gd $290**
Calibers: .40 S&W and .45 ACP. Seven-round magazine, 4.25-inch bbl., 7.5 inches overall. Weight: 33 oz. Millet adj. sights. Walnut grips. Matte finish stainless steel. Made from 1990 to 1992.

ANSCHUTZ PISTOLS — Ulm, Germany Mfd. by J.G. Anschutz GmbH Jagd und Sportwaffenfabrik

Currently imported by Accuracy International, Boseman, MT and AcuSport Corporation, Bellefontaine, OH

MODEL 64P

Calibers: .22 LR or .22 Magnum. Five- or 4-round magazine, 10-inch bbl., 64MS action w/two-stage trigger. Target sights optional. Rynite black synthetic stock. Imported from 1998 to 2003.
.22 LR . . . . **NiB $445 Ex $230 Gd $170**
.22 Mag. . . . . **NiB $490 Ex $259 Gd $190**
W/tangent sights, add **$75**

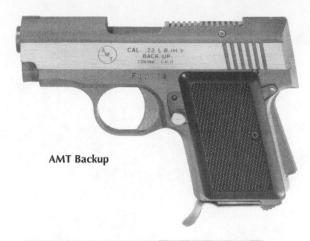

AMT Backup

AMT Backup DAO

AMT Bull's Eye Target

AMT Skipper

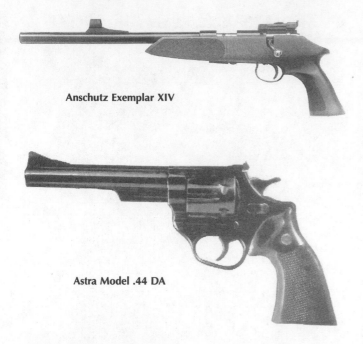

Anschutz Exemplar XIV

Astra Model .44 DA

EXEMPLAR (1416P/1451P) BOLT-ACTION PISTOL
Caliber: .22 LR, single-shot or 5-round clip. Seven- or 10-inch bbl., 19 inches overall (10-inch bbl.). Weight: 3.33 lbs. Match 64 action. Slide safety. Hooded ramp post front sight, adjustable open notched rear. European walnut contoured grip. Exemplar made from 1987-95 and 1400 series made from 1997. Disc. Note: The .22 WMR chambering was advertised but never manufactured.

Exemplar w/7- or 10-inch bbl.	NiB $399	Ex $305	Gd $244
Left-hand model (disc. 1997)	NiB $518	Ex $420	Gd $355
Model 1451P (single-shot)	NiB $434	Ex $322	Gd $261
Model 1416P (5-round repeater)	NiB $1100	Ex $870	Gd $566

EXEMPLAR HORNET . . . . NiB $950 Ex $753 Gd $644
Based on the Anschutz Match 54 action, tapped and grooved for scope mounting with no open sights. Caliber: .22 Hornet, 5-round magazine, 10-inch bbl., 20 inches overall. Weight: 4.35 lbs. Checkered European walnut grip. Winged safety. Made from 1990 to 1995.

EXEMPLAR XIV . . . . NiB $836 Ex $524 Gd $441
Same general specifications as the standard Exemplar bolt-action pistol except with 14-inch bbl., weight: 4.15 lbs. Made from 1989 to 1995.

ARMSCOR (Arms Corp.) — Manila, Philippines
Currently imported by K.B.I., Harrisburg, PA. (Imported 1991-95 by Ruko Products, Inc., Buffalo NY. Previously by Armscor Precision, San Mateo, CA.)

MODEL M1911-A-1
AUTOMATIC PISTOL . . . . NiB $357 Ex $296 Gd $173
Caliber: .45 ACP. Eight-round magazine, 5-inch bbl., 8.75 inches overall. Weight: 38 oz. Blade front sight, drift adjustable rear w/3-dot system. Skeletonized tactical hammer and trigger. Extended slide release and beavertail grip safety. Parker-ized finish. Checkered composition or wood stocks. Imported from 1996 to 1997. Disc. 1991.

MODEL M1911-A-1
COMMANDER . . . . NiB $365 Ex $265 Gd $175
Caliber: .45 ACP. Similar to M1911-A-1 except with Commander configuration and 4-inch bbl. Rear slide serrations only. Disc. 1991.
Two-tone finish . . . . add $40
Stainless . . . . add $75

MODEL M1911-A-1 COMBAT . . . . . NiB $355 Ex $280 Gd $210
Caliber: .45 ACP. Similar to M1911-A-1 except with Combat configuration. Bbl.:3.5 inches. Checkered hardwood grips. Weight: 2.16 pounds. Disc. 1991.
Two-tone finish . . . . add $40
Stainless . . . . add $75

MODEL M1911-A-1
MEDALLION SERIES . . . . $449 Ex $329 Gd $248
Caliber: 9mm Para., .40 S&W, .45ACP. Standard or Tactical, blue finish standard. Bbl.: 5 inches. Custom model with match barrel, checkered wood Pachmayr grips. Disc. 1991.
Two-tone finish (Tactical) . . . . add $200
Chrome (Tactical) . . . . add $2050

MODEL200DC/TC
DA REVOLVER . . . . NiB $199 Ex $179 Gd $150
Caliber: .38 Special. Six-round cylinder, 2.5-, 4-, or 6-inch bbl.; 7.3, 8.8, or 11.3 inches overall. Weight: 22, 28, or 34 oz. Ramp front and fixed rear sights. Checkered mahogany or rubber grips. Disc. 1991.

MODEL 202A REVOLVER . . . . NiB $141 Ex $106 Gd $81
Caliber: .38 Special. Similar to Model 200 (DC) revolver except does not have barrel shroud. Disc. 1991.

MODEL 206 REVOLVER . . . . NiB $216 Ex $162 Gd $137
Caliber: .38 Special. Similar to Model 200 (DC) revolver except has a 2-7/8-inch bbl. Weight: 24 ounces. Disc. 1991.

MODEL 210 REVOLVER . . . . NiB $185 Ex $149 Gd $101
Caliber: .38 Special. Similar to Model 200 (DC) except has a 4-inch ventilated rib bbl., adjustable rear sight. Weight: 28 ounces. Disc. 1991.

ASAI AG — Advanced Small Arms Industries Solothurn, Switzerland
Currently imported by Magnum Research Inc., Minneapolis, MN.

See listings under Magnum Research Pistols

ASTRA PISTOLS — Guernica, Spain
Manufactured by Unceta y Compania
Currently imported by E.A.A. Corporation, Sharpes, FL.

MODEL 357 DA REVOLVER . . . . . . NiB $345 Ex $270 Gd $221
Caliber: .357 Magnum. Six-round cylinder. 3-, 4-, 6-, 8.5-inch bbl., 11.25 inches overall (with 6-inch bbl.). Weight: 42 oz. (with 6-inch bbl.). Ramp front sight, adj. rear sight. Blued finish. Checkered wood grips. Imported from 1972 to 1988.

MODEL 44 DA REVOLVER
Similar to Astra ..357 except chambered for .44 Magnum. Six- or 8.5-inch bbl., 11.5 inches overall (6-inch bbl.). Weight: 44 oz. (6-inch bbl.). Imported from 1980 to 1993.
Blued finish (disc. 1987) . . . . NiB $360 Ex $287 Gd $250
Stainless finish (disc. 1993) . . . . NiB $360 Ex $287 Gd $250

MODEL 41 DA REVOLVER ....NiB $350 Ex $282 Gd $195
Same general specifications as Model 44 except in .41 Mag. Imported from 1980-85.

MODEL 45 DA REVOLVER .... NiB $346 Ex $287 Gd $261
Similar to Astra .357 except chambered for .45 Colt or .45 ACP. Six- or 8.5-inch bbl., 11.5 inches overall (with 6-inch bbl.). Weight: 44 oz. (6-inch bbl.). Imported from 1980-87.

MODEL 200 FIRECAT
VEST POCKET AUTO PISTOL .....NiB $294 Ex $244 Gd $227
Caliber: .25 Automatic (6.35mm). Six-round magazine, 2.25-inch bbl., 4.38 inches overall. Weight: 11.75 oz. Fixed sights. Blued finish. Plastic grips. Made 1920 to date. U.S. importation disc. in 1968.

MODEL 202 FIRECAT
VEST POCKET AUTO PISTOL ..... NiB $550 Ex $460 Gd $410
Same general specifications as the Model 200 except chromed and engraved w/pearl grips. U.S. importation disc. 1968.

MODEL 400 AUTO PISTOL....... NiB $700 Ex $435 Gd $220
Caliber: 9mm Bayard Long (.38 ACP, 9mm Browning Long, 9mm Glisenti, 9mm Para. and 9mm Steyr cartridges may be used interchangeably in this pistol because of its chamber design). Nine-round magazine., 6-inch bbl., 10 inches overall. Weight: 35 oz. Fixed sights. Blued finish. Plastic grips. Made 1922-45. Note: This pistol, as well as Astra Models 600 and 3000, is a modification of the Browning Model 1912.

MODEL 600 MIL./POLICE-TYPE
AUTO PISTOL .... NiB $515 Ex $399 Gd $265
Calibers: .32 Automatic (7.65mm), 9mm Para. Magazine: 10-round (.32 cal.) or 8-round (9mm)., 5.25-inch bbl., 8 inches overall. Weight: About 33 oz. Fixed sights. Blued finish. Checkered wood or plastic grips. Made from 1944 to 1945.

MODEL 800 CONDOR
MILITARY AUTO PISTOL...... NiB $1862 Ex $1540 Gd $1270
Similar to Models 400 and 600 except has an external hammer. Caliber: 9mm Para. Eight-round magazine, 5.25-inch bbl., 8.25 inches overall. Weight: 32.5 oz. Fixed sights. Blued finish. Plastic grips. Imported from 1958 to 1965.

MODEL 2000 CAMPER
AUTOMATIC PISTOL .... NiB $350 Ex $248 Gd $200
Same as Model 2000 Cub except chambered for .22 Short only, has 4-inch bbl., overall length, 6.25 inches, weight: 11.5 oz. Imported from 1955 to 1960.

MODEL 2000 CUB
POCKET AUTO PISTOL.......... NiB $300 Ex $245 Gd $163
Calibers: .22 Short, .25 Auto. Six-round magazine, 2.25-inch bbl., 4.5 inches overall. Weight: About 11 oz. Fixed sights. Blued or chromed finish. Plastic grips. Made 1954 to date. U.S. importation disc. in 1968.

MODEL 3000
POCKET AUTO PISTOL.......... NiB $850 Ex $535 Gd $380
Calibers: .22 LR, .32 Automatic (7.65mm), .380 Auto (9mm Short). Ten-round magazine (.22 cal.), 7-round (.32 cal.), 6-round (.380 cal.). Four-inch bbl., 6.38 inches overall. Weight: About 22 oz. Fixed sights. Blued finish. Plastic grips. Made from 1947 to 1956.

MODEL 3003
POCKET AUTO PISTOL........ NiB $2165 Ex $1110 Gd $634
Same general specifications as the Model 3000 except chromed and engraved w/pearl grips. Disc. 1956.

Astra Model
3003 Pocket

Astra Model
4000 Falcon

MODEL 4000
FALCON AUTO PISTOL .... NiB $610 Ex $450 Gd $287
Similar to Model 3000 except has an external hammer. Calibers: .22 LR, .32 Automatic (7.65mm), .380 Auto (9mm Short). Ten-round magazine (.22 LR), 8-round (.32 Auto), 7-round (.380 Auto), 3.66-inch bbl., 6.5-inches overall. Weight: 20 oz. (.22 cal.) or 24.75 oz. (.32 and .380). Fixed sights. Blued finish. Plastic grips. Made from 1956 to 1971.

CONSTABLE DA AUTO PISTOL
Calibers: .22 LR, .32 Automatic (7.65mm), .380 Auto (9mm Short). Magazine capacity: 10-round (.22 LR), 8-round (.32), 7-round (.380). 3.5-inch bbl., 6.5 inches overall. Weight: about 24 oz. Blade front sight, windage adj. rear. Blued or chromed finish. Imported from 1965 to 1992.
Stainless finish................. NiB $330 Ex $261 Gd $205
Blued engraved finish .... NiB $550 Ex $381 Gd $270
Chrome finish (disc. 1990) .... NiB $500 Ex $335 Gd $234

MODEL A-60 DA
AUTOMATIC PISTOL .... NiB $395 Ex $263 Gd $180
Similar to the Constable except in .380 only, w/13-round magazine and slide-mounted ambidextrous safety. Blued finish only. Imported from 1980 to 1991.

MODEL A-70 COMPACT AUTO PISTOL
Calibers: 9mm Para., .40 S&W. Eight-round (9mm) or 7-round (.40 S&W) magazine., 3.5-inch bbl., 6.5 inches overall. Blued, nickel or stainless finish. Weight: 29.3 oz. Imported from 1992 to 1996.
Blued finish.................... NiB $359 Ex $288 Gd $196
Nickel finish .... NiB $380 Ex $309 Gd $227
Stainless finish................. NiB $510 Ex $375 Gd $313

MODEL A-75 ULTRALIGHT ...... NiB $370 Ex $291 Gd $224
Similar to the standard Model 75 except 9mm only w/24-oz. aluminum alloy frame. Imported from 1994 to 1997.

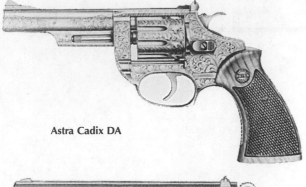

Astra Cadix DA

Astra Constable DA

**Auto-Ordnance 1927
A-5 w/drum magazine**

MODEL A-80 AUTO PISTOL . . . . . . NiB $415 Ex $370 Gd $250
Calibers: 9mm Para., .38 Super, .45 ACP. 15-round magazine or 9-round (.45 ACP). Bbl.: 3.75 inches., 7 inches overall. Weight: 36 oz. Imported from 1982 to 1989.

**MODEL A-90 DA
AUTOMATIC PISTOL . . . . .NiB $455 Ex $370 Gd $260**
Calibers: 9mm Para., .45 ACP. 15-round (9mm) or 9-round (.45 ACP) magazine, 3.75-inch bbl., 7 inches overall. Weight: about 40 oz. Fixed sights. Blued finish. Checkered plastic grips. Imported 1985 to 1990.

MODEL A-100 DA AUTO PISTOL
Same general specifications as the Model A-90 except selective double action chambered for 9mm Para., .40 S&W or .45 ACP. Imported from 1991 to 1997.
Blued finish . . . . NiB $425 Ex $376 Gd $270
Nickel finish . . . . NiB $450 Ex $385 Gd $260
For night sights, add $90

CADIX DA REVOLVER
Calibers: .22 LR, .38 Special. Nine-round (.22 LR) or 5-round (.38 cal.) cylinder. Four- or 6-inch bbl., Weight: About 27 oz. (6-inch bbl.). Ramp front sight, adj. rear sight. Blued finish. Plastic grips. Imported from 1960-68.
Standard model . . . . NiB $247 Ex $206 Gd $135
Lightly engraved model . . . . NiB $367 Ex $293 Gd $215
Heavily engraved model (shown) . . . . . NiB $678 Ex $550 Gd $390

MODEL A-75 DECOCKER AUTO PISTOL
Similar to the Model 70 except in 9mm, .40 S&W and .45 ACP w/decocking system and contoured pebble-textured grips. Imported from 1993-97.
Blued finish, 9mm or .40 S&W . . . . NiB $349 Ex $280 Gd $215
Nickel finish, 9mm or .40 S&W. . . . NiB $366 Ex $280 Gd $210
Stainless, 9mm or .40 S&W. . . . . . . NiB $374 Ex $288 Gd $217
Blued finish, .45 ACP. . . . . NiB $355 Ex $285 Gd $195
Nickel finish, .45 ACP . . . . NiB $372 Ex $305 Gd $190
Stainless, .45 ACP . . . . NiB $375 Ex $335 Gd $265

AUTAUGA ARMS — Prattville, Alabama

**MODEL 32 (MK II)
DAO AUTOMATIC PISTOL . . . . NiB $325 Ex $270 Gd $220**
Caliber: .32 ACP. Six-round magazine, 2-inch bbl., weight: 11.36 oz.. Double action only. Stainless steel. Black polymer grips. Made from 1996 to 2000.

AUTO-ORDNANCE CORPORATION —
West Hurley, New York

1911 A1 GOVERNMENT AUTO PISTOL
Copy of Colt 1911 A1 semiautomatic pistol. Calibers: 9mm Para., .38 Super, 10mm, .45 ACP. 9-round (9mm, .38 Super) or 7-round 10mm, .45 ACP) magazine. Five-inch bbl., 8.5 inches overall. Weight: 39 oz. Fixed blade front sight, rear adj. Blued, satin nickel or Duo-Tone finish. Checkered plastic grips. Made 1983 to 1999.
.45 ACP caliber . . . . NiB $445 Ex $350 Gd $275
9mm, 10mm, .38 Super. . . . . NiB $445 Ex $350 Gd $275

1911A1 .40 S&W PISTOL . . . . NiB $450 Ex $340 Gd $260
Similar to the Model 1911 A1 except has 4.5-inch bbl., w/7.75-inch overall length. Eight-round magazine, weight: 37 oz. Blade front and adj. rear sights w/3-dot system. Checkered black rubber wraparound grips. Made from 1991 to 1999.

1911 "THE GENERAL". . . . . NiB $385 Ex $295 Gd $205
Caliber: .45 ACP. Seven-round magazine, 4.5-inch bbl., 7.75 inches overall. Weight: 37 oz. Blued nonglare finish. Made 1992 to 1999.

1927 A-5 SEMIAUTOMATIC PISTOL
Similar to Thompson Model 1928A submachine gun except has no provision for automatic firing and does not have detachable buttstock. Caliber: .45 ACP, 5-, 15-, 20- and 30-round detachable box magazines. 30-round drum also available. 13-inch finned bbl., 26 inches overall. Weight: About 6.75 lbs. Adj. rear sight, blade front. Blued finish. Walnut grips. Made from 1977 to 1994.
W/box magazine . . . . NiB $1055 Ex $765 Gd $535
W/drum magazine (illustrated) . . . . Add $300

**ZG-51 PIT BULL
AUTOMATIC PISTOL . . . . NiB $385 Ex $300 Gd $250**
Caliber: .45 ACP. Seven-round magazine, 3.5-inch bbl., 7 inches overall. Weight: 32 oz. Fixed front sight, square-notch rear. Blued finish. Checkered plastic grips. Made from 1991 to 1999.

LES BAER —Hillsdale, Illinois

1911 CONCEPT SERIES AUTOMATIC PISTOL
Similar to Government 1911 built on steel or alloy full-size or compact frame. Caliber: .45 ACP. Seven-round magazine, 4.25- or 5-inch bbl. Weight: 34 to 37 oz. Adjustable low mount combat or BoMar target sights. Blued, matte black, Two-Tone or stainless finish. Checkered wood grips. Made from 1996 to date.

Concept models I & II . . . . .NiB $1235 Ex $985 Gd $690
Concept models III, IV & VII . . . . NiB $1350 Ex $1090 Gd $775
Concept models V, VI & VIII . . . . NiB $1399 Ex $1245 Gd $785
Concept models IX & X . . . . NiB $1390 Ex $1125 Gd $795

1911 PREMIER SERIES AUTOMATIC PISTOL
Similar to the Concept series except also chambered for .38 Super, 9x23 Win., .400 Cor-Bon and .45 ACP. 5- or 6-inch bbl. Weight: 37 to .40 oz. Made from 1996 to date.

Premier II
(9x23 w/5-inch bbl.) . . . . NiB $1487 Ex $1199 Gd $855
Premier II (.400
Cor-Bon w/5-inch bbl.) . . . . NiB $1354 Ex $1100 Gd $770
Premier II (.45 ACP
w/5-inch bbl.) . . . . NiB $1264 Ex $1028 Gd $727
Premier II (.45 ACP
S/S w/5-inch bbl.) . . . . NiB $1392 Ex $1150 Gd $795
Premier II (.45/.400
combo w/5-inch bbl.) . . . . NiB $1550 Ex $1260 Gd $890
Premier II (.38
Super w/6-inch bbl.) . . . . NiB $1783 Ex $1433 Gd $990
Premier II (.400
Cor-Bon w/6-inch bbl.) . . . . NiB $1580 Ex $1295 Gd $913
Premier II (.45 ACP
w/6-inch bbl.) . . . . NiB $1490 Ex $1241 Gd $865

S.R.P. AUTOMATIC PISTOL
Similar to F.B.I. Contract "Swift Response Pistol" built on a (customer-supplied) Para-Ordance over-sized frame or a 1911 full-size or compact frame. Caliber: .45 ACP. Seven-round magazine, 5-inch bbl., weight: 37 oz. Ramp front and fixed rear sights, w/Tritium Sight insert.

SRP 1911 Government
or Commanche model . . . . NiB $2159 Ex $1732 Gd $1222
SRP P-12 model . . . . NiB $2442 Ex $1966 Gd $1371
SRP P-13 model . . . . NiB $2210 Ex $1808 Gd $1259
SRP P-14 model . . . . NiB $2102 Ex $1696 Gd $1190

1911 ULTIMATE MASTER COMBAT SERIES AUTOMATIC PISTOL
Model 1911 in Combat Competition configuration. Calibers: .38 Super, 9x23 Win., .400 Cor-Bon and .45 ACP. Five- or 6-inch NM bbl., weight: 37 to 40 oz. Made from 1996 to date.

Ultimate MC (.38 or 9x23
w/5-inch bbl.) . . . . NiB $2235 Ex $1808 Gd $1259
Ultimate MC (.400 Cor-Bon
w/5-inch bbl.) . . . . NiB $2049 Ex $1665 Gd $1164
Ultimate MC (.45 ACP
w/5-inch bbl.) . . . . NiB $1964 Ex $1589 Gd $1117
Ultimate MC (.38 or 9x23
w/6-inch bbl.) . . . . NiB $2286 Ex $1854 Gd $1299
Ultimate MC (.400 Cor-Bon
w/6-inch bbl.) . . . . NiB $2137 Ex $1721 Gd $1207
Ultimate MC (.45 ACP
w/6-inch bbl.) . . . . NiB $2001 Ex $1620 Gd $1132
Ultimate "Steel Special"
(.38 Super Bianchi SPS) . . . . NiB $2521 Ex $2038 Gd $1420
Ultimate "PARA" (.38, 9x23
or .45 IPSC comp) . . . . NiB $2559 Ex $2078 Gd $1440
W/Triple-Port Compensator, add $95

Auto-Ordnance ZG-51 Pit Bull

1911 CUSTOM CARRY SERIES AUTOMATIC PISTOL
Model 1911 in Combat Carry configuration built on steel or alloy full-size or compact frame. 4.5- or 5-inch NM bbl., chambered for .45 ACP. Weight: 34 to 37 oz.

Custom carry (steel frame
w/4.24- or 5-inch bbl.) . . . . NiB $1445 Ex $1169 Gd $825
Custom carry (alloy frame
w/4.24-inch bbl.) . . . . NiB $1651 Ex $1335 Gd $935

BAUER FIREARMS CORPORATION — Fraser, MI

.25 AUTOMATIC PISTOL . . . . NiB $158 Ex $110 Gd $80
Stainless steel. Caliber: .25 Automatic. Six-round magazine, 2.13-inch bbl., 4 inches overall. Weight: 10 oz. Fixed sights. Checkered walnut or simulated pearl grips. Made from 1972 to 1984.

BAYARD PISTOLS — Herstal, Belgium
Mfd. by Anciens Etablissements Pieper

MODEL 1908
POCKET AUTOMATIC PISTOL . . . . NiB $349 Ex $294 Gd $175
Calibers: .25 Automatic (6.35mm). .32 Automatic (7.65mm), .380 Automatic (9mm Short). Six-round magazine, 2.25-inch bbl., 4.88 inches overall. Weight: About 16 oz. Fixed sights. Blued finish. Hard rubber grips. Intro. 1908. Disc. 1923.

MODEL 1923 POCKET
.25 AUTOMATIC PISTOL . . . . NiB $366 Ex $285 Gd $142
Caliber: .25 Automatic (6.35mm). 2.13-inch bbl., 4.31 inches overall. Weight: 12 oz. Fixed sights. Blued finish. Checkered hard-rubber grips. Intro. 1923. Disc. 1930.

MODEL 1923 POCKET
AUTOMATIC PISTOL . . . . NiB $379 Ex $300 Gd $192
Calibers: .32 Automatic (7.65mm), .380 Automatic (9mm Short). Six-round magazine, 3.31-inch bbl., 5.5 inches overall. Weight: About 19 oz. Fixed sights. Blued finish. Checkered hard-rubber grips. Intro. 1923. Disc. 1940.

MODEL 1930 POCKET
.25 AUTOMATIC PISTOL . . . . NiB $360 Ex $234 Gd $171
This is a modification of the Model 1923, which it closely resembles.

BEEMAN PRECISION ARMS, INC. — Santa Rosa, CA

P08 AUTOMATIC PISTOL . . . . NiB $399 Ex $327 Gd $223
Caliber: .22 LR. 10-round magazine, 3.8-inch bbl., 7.8 inches overall. Weight: 25 oz. Fixed sights. Blued finish. Checkered hardwood grips. Imported from 1969 to 1991.

Benelli MP90S

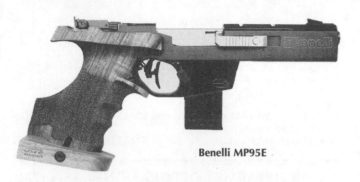

Benelli MP95E

Beretta Model 21

MINI P08 AUTOMATIC PISTOL . . . NiB $439 Ex $353 Gd $267
Caliber: Same general specifications as P08 except shorter 3.5-inch bbl., 7.4 inches overall. Weight: 20 oz. Imported 1986 to 1991.

SP METALLIC SILHOUETTE PISTOLS
Caliber: .22 LR. Single-shot. Bbl. lengths: 6-, 8-, 10- or 15-inches. Adj. rear sight. Receiver contoured for scope mount. Walnut target grips w/adj. palm rest. Models SP made 1985 to 1986 and SPX 1993-94.

SP Standard W/8-or 10-inch bbl....	NiB $285	Ex $235	Gd $172
SP Standard W/12-inch bbl.	NiB $330	Ex $266	Gd $191
SP Standard W/15-inch bbl.	NiB $344	Ex $286	Gd $200
SP Deluxe W/8-or 10-inch bbl.....	NiB $346	Ex $276	Gd $199
SP Deluxe W/12-inch bbl.........	NiB $355	Ex $291	Gd $209
SP Deluxe W/15-inch bbl.........	NiB $374	Ex $306	Gd $215
SPX Standard W/10-inch bbl.	NiB $679	Ex $548	Gd $387
SPX Deluxe W/10-inch bbl........	NiB $925	Ex $744	Gd $524

BEHOLLA PISTOL — Suhl, Germany
Mfd. by both Becker and Holländer and Stenda-Werke GmbH

POCKET AUTOMATIC PISTOL .... NiB $250 Ex $200 Gd $140
Caliber: .32 Automatic (7.65mm). Seven-round magazine, 2.9-inch bbl., 5.5 inches overall. Weight: 22 oz. Fixed sights. Blued finish. Serrated wood or hard rubber grips. Made by Becker and Hollander 1915 to 1920, by Stenda-Werke circa 1920 to 1925. Note: Essentially the same pistol was manufactured w/the Stenda version as the "Leonhardt" by H. M. Gering and as the "Menta" by August Menz.

BENELLI PISTOLS — Urbino, Italy
Imported by Benelli USA

MP90S WORLD CUP TARGET PISTOL
Semiautomatic blowback action. Calibers: .22 Short, .22LR, .32 W.C. Five-round magazine, 4.33-inch fixed bbl. 6.75 inches overall. Weight: 36 oz. Post front sight, adjustable rear. Blue finish. Anatomic shelf-style grip. Imported from 1992 to 2001.

MP90S (.22 LR)	NiB $1264	Ex $1075	Gd $950
MP90S (.22 Short, disc. 1995)....	NiB $1146	Ex $944	Gd $662
MP90S (.32 WC)	NiB $1390	Ex $1200	Gd $1080
W/conversion kit, add............................... $550			

MP95E SPORT TARGET PISTOL
Similar to the MP90S except with 5- or 9-round magazine, 4.25- inch bbl., Blue or chrome finish. Checkered target grip. Imported from1994 to date.

Blue MP95 (.22 LR)	NiB $776	Ex $642	Gd $410
Blue MP95 (.32 WC)	NiB $900	Ex $776	Gd $545
Chrome, add $60			

BERETTA USA CORP. — Accokeek, Maryland

Beretta firearms are manufactured by Fabbrica D'Armi Pietro Beretta S. p. A. in the Gardone Val Trompia (Brescia), Italy. This prestigious firm has been in business since 1526. In 1977, Beretta U.S.A. Corp., a manufacturing and importing facility, opened in Accokeek, MD. (Previously imported by Garcia Corp., J.L. Galef & Son, Inc. and Berben Corporation.) Note: Beretta also owns additional firearms manufacturing companies including: Benelli, Franchi, Sako, Stoeger, Tikka and Uberti.

MODEL 20 DA AUTO PISTOL..... NiB $245 Ex $194 Gd $130
Caliber: .25 ACP. Eight-round magazine, 2.5-inch bbl., 4.9 inches overall. Weight: 10.9 oz. Plastic or walnut grips. Fixed sights. Made 1984 to 1985.

MODEL 21 DA AUTO PISTOL
Calibers: .22 LR and .25 ACP. Seven-round (.22 LR) or 8-round (..25 ACP) magazine, 2.5-inch bbl., 4.9 inches overall. Weight: About 12 oz. Blade front sight, V-notch rear. Walnut grips. Made from 1985 to date. Model 21EL disc. 2000.

Blued finish	NiB $245	Ex $190	Gd $158
Nickel finish (.22 LR only)........	NiB $255	Ex $201	Gd $177
Model 21EL engraved model	NiB $315	Ex $265	Gd $225

MODEL 70
AUTOMATIC PISTOL .... NiB $215 Ex $168 Gd $109
Improved version of Model 1935. Steel or lightweight alloy. Calibers: .32 Auto (7.65mm), .380 Auto (9mm Short). Eight-round (.32) or 7-round (.380) magazine, 3.5-inch bbl., 6.5 inches overall. Weight: Steel, 22.25 oz.; alloy, 16 oz. Fixed sights. Blued finish. Checkered plastic grips. Made 1959 to 1985. Note: Formerly marketed in U.S. as

"Puma" (alloy model in .32) and "Cougar" (steel model in .380). Disc.

MODEL 70S. . . . . **NiB $377 Ex $247 Gd $165**
Similar to Model 70T except chambered for .22 Auto and .380 Auto. Longer bbl. guide and safety lever blocking hammer. Front blade and rear sight fixed on breechblock. Weight: 1 lb., 7 oz. Made 1977 to 1985.

MODEL 70T
AUTOMATIC PISTOL . . . . **NiB $275 Ex $208 Gd $184**
Similar to Model 70. Caliber: .32 Automatic (7.65mm). Nine-round magazine, 6-inch bbl., 9.5 inches overall. Weight: 19 oz. adj. rear sight, blade front sight. Blued finish. Checkered plastic grips. Intro. in 1959. Disc.

MODEL 71
AUTOMATIC PISTOL . . . . **NiB $220 Ex $162 Gd $106**
Same general specifications as alloy Model 70. Caliber: .22 LR. Six-inch bbl., 8-round magazine, Adj. rear sight frame. Single action. Made 1959 to 1989. Note: Formerly marketed in U.S. as the "Jaguar Plinker."

Beretta Model 71

MODEL 72 . . . . **NiB $275 Ex $230 Gd $175**
Same as Model 71 except has 6-inch bbl., weight: 18 oz. Intro. in 1959. Disc. Note: Formerly marketed in U.S as "Jaguar Plinker."

MODEL 76
AUTO TARGET PISTOL
Caliber: .22 LR. 10-round magazine, 6-inch bbl., 8.8 inches overall. Weight: 33 oz. adj. rear sight, front sight w/interchangeable blades. Blued finish. Checkered plastic or wood grips. Made from 1966 to 1985. Note: Formerly marketed in the U.S. as the "Sable."
Model 76 w/plastic grips . . . . **NiB $345 Ex $301 Gd $250**
Model 76W w/wood grips . . . . **NiB $385 Ex $342 Gd $290**

Beretta Model 72

MODEL 81 DA AUTO PISTOL . . . . . **NiB $300 Ex $204 Gd $169**
Caliber: .32 Automatic (7.65mm). 12-round magazine, 3.8-inch bbl., 6.8 inches overall. Weight: 23.5 oz. Fixed sights. Blued finish. Plastic grips. Made principally for the European market 1975 to 1984, w/similar variations as implemented on the Model 84.

MODEL 82W DA AUTO PISTOL . . . **NiB $290 Ex $209 Gd $115**
Caliber: .32 ACP. Similar to the Model 81 except with a slimmer-profile frame designed to accept a single column 9-round magazine. Matte black finish. Importation disc. 1984.

Beretta Model 84

MODEL 84B DA AUTO PISTOL . . . **NiB $288 Ex $209 Gd $156**
Same as Model 81 except made in caliber .380 Automatic w/13-round magazine, 3.82-inch bbl., 6.8 inches overall. Weight: 23 oz. Fixed front and rear sights. Made from 1975 to 1982.

MODEL 84B DA AUTO PISTOL . . . **NiB $296 Ex $204 Gd $122**
Improved version of Model 84 w/strengthened frame and slide, and firing-pin block safety added. Ambidextrous reversible magazine release. Blued or nickel finish. Checkered black plastic or wood grips. Other specifications same. Made circa 1982 to 1984.

MODEL 84(BB) DA AUTO PISTOL
Improved version of Model 84B w/further-strengthened slide, frame and recoil spring. Caliber: .380 ACP. 13-round magazine, 3.82-inch bbl., 6.8 inches overall. Weight: 23 oz. Checkered black plastic or wood grips. Blued or nickel finish. Notched rear and blade front sight. Made circa 1984-94.
Blued w/plastic grips . . . . **NiB $350 Ex $275 Gd $180**
Blued w/wood grips . . . . **NiB $405 Ex $428 Gd $230**
Nickel finish w/wood grips . . . . **NiB $565 Ex $464 Gd $335**

Beretta Model 84
Cheetah (Nickel finish)

MODEL 84
CHEETAH SEMI-AUTO PISTOL
Similar to the Model 84 BB except with required design changes as mandated by regulation, including reduced magazine capacity (10-round magazine) and marked as 9mm short (.380) as a marketing strategy to counter increased availability of 9mm chamberings from other manufacturers. Made from 1994 to 2002, reintro. 2004.
Blued w/plastic grips . . . . **NiB $580 Ex $397 Gd $280**
Blued w/wood grips . . . . **NiB $595 Ex $428 Gd $305**
Nickel finish w/wood grips . . . . **NiB $647 Ex $449 Gd $325**

Beretta Model 85

Beretta Model 85BB

Beretta Model 86 Cheetah

MODEL 85
DA AUTO PISTOL . . . . NiB $585 Ex $394 Gd $245
Similar to the Model 84 except designed with a slimmer-profile frame to accept a single column 8-round magazine, no ambidextrous magazine release. Matte black finish. Weight: 21.8 oz. Introduced in 1977 following the Model 84.

MODEL 85B DA AUTO PISTOL . . . NiB $375 Ex $290 Gd $179
Improved version of the Model 85. Imported from 1982-85.

MODEL 85BB DA PISTOL
Improved version of the Model 85B w/strengthened frame and slide. Caliber: .380 ACP. Eight-round magazine, 3.82 inch bbl., 6.8 inches overall. Weight: 21.8 oz. Blued or nickel finish. Checkered black plastic or wood grips. Imported from 1985 to 1994.

Blued finish
w/plastic grips . . . . NiB $444 Ex $357 Gd $248
Blued finish
w/wood grips . . . . NiB $480 Ex $395 Gd $283
Nickel finish
w/wood grips . . . . NiB $535 Ex $450 Gd $315

MODEL 85 CHEETAH
SEMI-AUTO PISTOL
Similar to the Model 85 BB except with required design changes as mandated by regulation and marked as 9mm short (.380) as a marketing strategy to counter increased availability of 9mm chamberings from other manufacturers. Made from 1994 to date.
Blued finish
w/plastic grips . . . . NiB $585 Ex $357 Gd $260
Blued finish
w/wood grips . . . . NiB $615 Ex $411 Gd $296
Nickel finish
w/wood grips . . . . NiB $645 Ex $445 Gd $326

MODEL 85F
DA PISTOL
Similar to the Model 85BB except has re-contoured trigger guard and manual ambidextrous safety w/decocking device. Bruniton finish. Imported in 1990 only.
Matte black Bruniton
finish w/plastic grips . . . . NiB $375 Ex $301 Gd $244
Matte black Bruniton
finish w/wood grips . . . . NiB $400 Ex $328 Gd $270

MODEL 86 CHEETAH
DA AUTO PISTOL . . . . NiB $560 Ex $455 Gd $255
Caliber: .380 auto. Eight-round magazine, 4.4- inch bbl., 7.3 inches overall. Weight: 23.3 oz. Bruniton finish w/wood grips. Made from 1986-89. (Reintroduced 1990 in the Cheetah series.)

MODEL 87 CHEETAH
AUTOMATIC PISTOL
Similar to the Model 85 except in .22 LR w/8- or 10- round magazine (Target) and optional extended 6-inch bbl. (Target in single action). Overall length: 6.8 to 8.8 inches. Weight: 20.1 oz. to 29.4 oz (Target). Checkered wood grips. Made from 1987 to date.
Blued finish
(double-action) . . . . NiB $660 Ex $435 Gd $240
Target model
(single action) . . . . NiB $692 Ex $468 Gd $265

MODEL 89
GOLD STANDARD TARGET
AUTOMATIC PISTOL . . . . NiB $630 Ex $503 Gd $390
Caliber: .22 LR. Eight-round magazine, 6-inch bbl., 9.5 inches overall. Weight: 41 oz. Adj. target sights. Blued finish. Target-style walnut grips. Made from 1988 to 2000.

MODEL 90
DA AUTO PISTOL . . . . NiB $275 Ex $206 Gd $156
Caliber: .32 Auto (7.65mm). Eight-round magazine, 3.63-inch bbl., 6.63 inches overall. Weight: 19.5 oz. Fixed sights. Blued finish. Checkered plastic grips. Made from 1969 to 1983.

MODEL 92 DA AUTO
PISTOL (1ST SERIES) . . . . NiB $755 Ex $622 Gd $330
Caliber: 9mm Para. 15-round magazine, 4.9-inch bbl., 8.5 inches overall. Weight: 33.5 oz. Fixed sights. Blued finish. Plastic grips. Initial production of 5,000 made in 1976.

MODEL 92D DA AUTO PISTOL

Same general specifications as Model 92F except DA only w/bobbed hammer and 3-dot sight. Made from 1992 to 1998.
Model 92D . . . . NiB $608 Ex $425 Gd $327
With Tritium
sight system add $90

MODEL 92F COMPACT

DA AUTOMATIC PISTOL . . . . NiB $600 Ex $534 Gd $266
Caliber: 9mm Para. 12-round magazine, 4.3-inch bbl., 7.8 inches overall. Weight: 31.5 oz. Wood grips. Square-notched rear sight, blade front integral w/slide. Made from 1990-93.

MODEL 92F COMPACT L TYPE M DA AUTOMATIC PISTOL

Same general specifications as the original 92F Compact except 8-round magazine, Weight: 30.9 oz. Bruniton matte finish. Made from 1998 to 2003.
Model 92F
Compact L Type M . . . . NiB $600 Ex $536 Gd $260
Model 92F
Compact L Type M Inox . . . . NiB $600 Ex $536 Gd $260
W/Tritium
sight system, add $90

MODEL 92F DA AUTOMATIC PISTOL

Same general specifications as Model 92 except w/slide-mounted safety and repositioned magazine release. Replaced Model 92SB. Blued or stainless finish. Made from 1992 to 1998.
Blued finish . . . . NiB $560 Ex $433 Gd $268
Stainless finish . . . . NiB $560 Ex $433 Gd $268
Model 92F-EL gold . . . . Add $175

MODEL 92FS DA AUTOMATIC PISTOL

Calibers: 9mm, 9mmx19 and .40 S&W. 15- round magazine, 4.9-inch bbl., 8.5 inches overall. Weight: 34.4 to 35.3 oz. Ambidextrous safety/decock lever. Chrome-lined bore w/combat trigger guard. Bruniton finish w/plastic grips or Inox finish w/rubber grips. Made from 1999 to 2003.
Model 92FS . . . . NiB $560 Ex $457 Gd $345
Model 92FS, B-lok . . . . NiB $585 Ex $484 Gd $350
Model 92FS — Brigadier
(Made 1999 to date) . . . . NiB $690 Ex $511 Gd $360
Model 92FS —
Brigadier Inox . . . . NiB $690 Ex $600 Gd $450
Model 92FS — Centurion
(Made 1992 to date) . . . . NiB $460 Ex $325 Gd $245
Model 92FS — 470th Anniver.
(Made 1999) . . . . NiB $1955 Ex $1740 Gd $1548

MODEL 92S DA AUTO

PISTOL (2ND SERIES) . . . . NiB $575 Ex $430 Gd $325
Revised version of Model 92 w/ambidextrous slide-mounted safety modification intended for both commercial and military production. Evolved to Model 92S-1 for U.S. Military trials. Made from 1980 to 1985.

MODEL 92SB DA

AUTO PISTOL (3RD SERIES) . . . . . . NiB $525 Ex $405 Gd $310
Same general specifications as standard Model 92 except has slide-mounted safety and repositioned magazine release. Made 1981 to 1985.

MODEL 92 SB-F

DA AUTO PISTOL . . . . NiB $655 Ex $530 Gd $321
Caliber: 9mm Para. 15-round magazine, bbl.: 4.9 inches, 8.5 inches overall. Weight: 34 oz. Plastic or Beretta Model 92 SB-F DA Auto Pistol wood grips. Square-notched rear sight, blade front sight integral w/slide. This model, also called Model 92S-1, was the standard-issue sidearm for the U.S. Armed Forces. Disc. 1985.

Beretta Model 92F

Beretta Model 92 Compact L Type M

Beretta Model 92FS Brigadier Inox

Beretta Model 96

Beretta Model 949
Olimpionico

Beretta Model 950BS
Jetfire

MODEL 96 DA AUTO PISTOL
Same general specifications as Model 92F except in .40 S&W. 10-round magazine (9-round in Compact model). Made from 1992 to 1998.
Model 96 D (DA only) . . . . NiB $460 Ex $385 Gd $275
Model 96 Centurion (compact) . . . . NiB $525 Ex $420 Gd $275
W/Tritium sights, add $90
W/Tritium sights system, add $95

MODEL 101 . . . . NiB $255 Ex $200 Gd $172
Same as Model 70T except caliber .22 LR, has 10-round magazine, Intro. in 1959. Disc.

MODEL 318 (1934) AUTO PISTOL . NiB $255 Ex $180 Gd $150
Caliber: .25 Automatic (6.35mm). Eight-round magazine, 2.5-inch bbl., 4.5 inches overall. Weight: 14 oz. Fixed sights. Blued finish. Plastic grips. Made from 1934 to c. 1939.

MODEL 949
OLYMPIC TARGET AUTO PISTOL . . NiB $655 Ex $600 Gd $401
Calibers: .22 Short, .22 LR. Five-round magazine, 8.75-inch bbl., 12.5 inches overall. Weight: 38 oz. Target sights. Adj. bbl., weight. Muzzle brake. Checkered walnut grips w/thumbrest. Made from 1959 to 1964.

MODEL 950B AUTO PISTOL . . . . . . NiB $195 Ex $154 Gd $99
Same general specifications as Model 950CC except caliber .25 Auto, has 7-round magazine, Made from 1959 to date. Note: Formerly marketed in the U.S. as "Jetfire."

MODEL 950B JETFIRE SA PISTOL
Calibers: .25 ACP or .22 Short (disc.1992). Seven- or 8-round magazine, 2.4- or 4- inch bbl., 4.5 to 4.7 inches overall. Weight: 9.9 oz. Fixed blade front and V-notch rear sights. Matte Blue or Inox (Stainless) finish. Checkered black plastic grips. Made from 1987 to date.
Blued finish . . . . NiB $151 Ex $100 Gd $74
Nickel finish . . . . NiB $200 Ex $155 Gd $120
Inox finish . . . . NiB $215 Ex $175 Gd $131
W/4-inch bbl.,
(.22 Short) . . . . NiB $224 Ex $184 Gd $135

MODEL 950CC
AUTO PISTOL . . . . NiB $139 Ex $108 Gd $92
Caliber: .22 Short. Six-round magazine, hinged 2.38-inch bbl., 4.75 inches overall. Weight: 11 oz. Fixed sights. Blued finish. Plastic grips. Made from 1959 to date. Note: Formerly marketed in the U.S. as "Minx M2."

MODEL 950CC
SPECIAL AUTO PISTOL . . . . NiB $135 Ex $108 Gd $95
Same general specifications as Model 950CC Auto except has 4-inch bbl. Made from 1959 to date. Note: Formerly marketed in the U.S. as "Minx M4."

MODEL 951 (1951)
MILITARY AUTO PISTOL . . . . NiB $285 Ex $225 Gd $190
Caliber: 9mm Para. Eight-round magazine, 4.5-inch bbl., 8 inches overall. Weight: 31 oz. Fixed sights. Blued finish. Plastic grips. Made from 1952 to date. Note: This is the standard pistol of the Italian Armed Forces, also used by Egyptian and Israeli armies and by the police in Nigeria. Egyptian and Israeli models usually command a premium. Formerly marketed in the U.S. as the "Brigadier."

MODEL 1915
AUTO PISTOL . . . . NiB $1490 Ex $1290 Gd $1006
Calibers: 9mm Glisenti and .32 ACP (7.65mm). Eight-round magazine, 4-inch bbl., 6.7 inches overall (9mm), 5.7 inches (.32 ACP). Weight: 30 oz. (9mm), 20 oz. (.32 ACP). Fixed sights. Blued finish. Wood grips. Made 1915-1922. An improved postwar 1915/1919 version in caliber .32 ACP was later offered for sale in 1922 as the Model 1922.

MODEL 1923 AUTO PISTOL . . . NiB $2005 Ex $1950 Gd $1564
Caliber: 9mm Glisenti (Luger). Eight-round magazine, 4-inch bbl., 6.5 inches overall. Weight: 30 oz. Fixed sights. Blued finish. Plastic grips. Made circa 1923 to 1936.

MODEL 1934 AUTO PISTOL
Caliber: .380 Automatic (9mm Short). Seven-round magazine, 3.38-inch bbl., 5.88 inches overall. Weight: 24 oz. Fixed sights. Blued finish. Plastic grips. Official pistol of the Italian Armed Forces. Wartime pieces not as well made and finished as commercial models. Made from 1934 to 1959.
Commercial model . . . . NiB $2200 Ex $1975 Gd $1240
War model . . . . NiB $550 Ex $351 Gd $276

MODEL 1935 AUTO PISTOL
Caliber: .32 ACP (7.65mm). Eight-round magazine, 3.5-inch bbl., 5.75 inches overall. Weight: 24 oz. Fixed sights. Blued finish. Plastic grips. A roughly-finished version of this pistol was produced during WW II. Made from 1935 to 1959.
Commercial model . . . . NiB $1699 Ex $1357 Gd $1013
War model. . . . . NiB $550 Ex $399 Gd $297

MODEL 3032 DA SEMIAUTOMATIC TOMCAT
Caliber: .32 ACP. Seven-round magazine, 2.45-inch bbl., 5 inches overall. Weight: 14.5 oz. Fixed sights. Blued or stainless finish. Made from 1996 to date.
Matte blue. . . . . NiB $309 Ex $242 Gd $160
Polished blue. . . . . NiB $366 Ex $301 Gd $230
Stainless. . . . . NiB $377 Ex $325 Gd $230

Beretta Model 3032 Tomcat

MODEL 8000/8040/8045 COUGAR DA PISTOL
Calibers: 9mm, .40 S&W and .45 Auto. Eight- or 10- shot magazine, 3.6 to 3.7- inch bbl., 7- to 7.2 inches overall. Weight: 32 to 32.6 oz. Short recoil action w/rotating barrel. Fixed sights w/3-dot Tritium system. Textured black composition grips. Matte black Bruniton finish w/alloy frame. Made from 1995 to 2005.
8000 Cougar D
(9mm DAO). . . . . NiB $670 Ex $614 Gd $372
8000 Cougar F
(9mm DA) . . . . NiB $715 Ex $600 Gd $362
8040 Cougar D
(.40 S&W DAO). . . . . NiB $665 Ex $600 Gd $362
8040 Cougar F
(.40 S&W DA) . . . . NiB $665 Ex $600 Gd $362
8045 Cougar D
(.45 Auto DAO) . . . . NiB $715 Ex $619 Gd $389
8045 Cougar F
(.357 Sig SA/DA). . . . . NiB $665 Ex $520 Gd $375

Beretta Model 8000 Cougar D

MODEL 8000/8040/8045 MINI COUGAR DA PISTOL
Calibers: 9mm, .40 S&W and .45 Auto. Six- 8- or 10-round magazine, 3.6- to 3.7- inch bbl., 7 inches overall. Weight: 27.4 to 30.4 oz. Fixed sights w/3-dot Tritium system. Ambidextrous safety/decocker lever. Matte black Bruniton finish w/anodized aluminum alloy frame. Made from 1995 to 2008.
8000 Mini
Cougar D (9mm DAO) . . . . NiB $635 Ex $560 Gd $317
8000 Mini
Cougar F (9mm DA) . . . . NiB $635 Ex $560 Gd $317
8040 Mini
Cougar D (.40 S&W DAO) . . . . . . NiB $635 Ex $560 Gd $317
8040 Mini
Cougar F (.40 S&W DA) . . . . NiB $635 Ex $560 Gd $317
8045 Mini
Cougar D (.45 Auto DAO) . . . . NiB $635 Ex $560 Gd $317
8045 Mini
Cougar F (.45 Auto DA). . . . . NiB $635 Ex $560 Gd $317

Beretta Model 8000 Cougar F

MODEL 9000S SUBCOMPACT PISTOL SERIES
Calibers: 9mm, .40 S&W. 10-round magazine, 3.5- inch bbl., 6.6 inches overall. Weight: 25.7 to 27.5 oz. Single/double and double-action only. Front and rear dovetail sights w/3- dot system. Chrome-plated barrel w/Techno-polymer frame. Geometric locking system w/tilt barrel. Made from 2000 to 2005.
Type D (9mm) . . . . NiB $400 Ex $325 Gd $275
Type D (.40 S&W) . . . . NiB $400 Ex $325 Gd $275
Type F (9mm). . . . . NiB $400 Ex $325 Gd $275
Type F (.40 S&W). . . . . NiB $400 Ex $325 Gd $275

Beretta Model 8040 Mini Cougar D

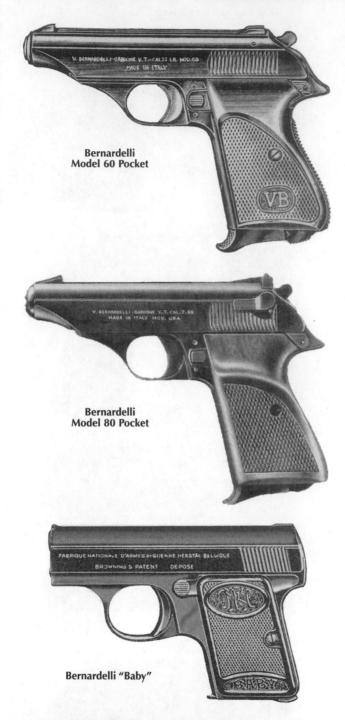

Bernardelli
Model 60 Pocket

Bernardelli
Model 80 Pocket

Bernardelli "Baby"

BERNARDELLI, VINCENZO S.P.A.
Gardone V. T. (Brescia), Italy

MODEL 60 POCKET
AUTOMATIC PISTOL . . . . **NiB $223 Ex $200 Gd $177**
Calibers: .22 LR, .32 Auto (7.65mm), .380 Auto (9mm Short). Eight-round magazine (.22 and .32), 7-round (.380). 3.5-inch bbl., 6.5 inches overall. Weight: About 25 oz. Fixed sights. Blued finish. Bakelite grips. Made from 1959 to 1990.

MODEL 68 AUTOMATIC PISTOL . . . **NiB $145 Ex $104 Gd $72**
Caliber: 6.35. Five- and 8-round magazine, 2.13-inch bbl., 4.13 inches overall. Weight: 10 oz. Fixed sights. Blued or chrome finish. Bakelite or pearl grips. This model, like its .22-caliber counterpart, was known as the "Baby" Bernardelli. Disc. 1970.

MODEL 69 AUTOMATIC
TARGET PISTOL . . . . **NiB $650 Ex $533 Gd $361**
Caliber: .22 LR. 10-round magazine, 5.9-inch bbl., 9 inches overall. Weight: 2.2 lbs. Fully adj. target sights. Blued finish. Stippled right- or left-hand wraparound walnut grips. Made from 1987 to date. This was previously Model 100; not imported to the U.S.

MODEL 80
AUTOMATIC PISTOL . . . . **NiB $185 Ex $100 Gd $63**
Calibers: .22 LR, .32 ACP (7.65mm), .380 Auto (9mm Short). Magazine capacity: 10-round (.22), 8-round (.32), 7-round (.380). 3.5-inch bbl., 6.5 inches overall. Weight: 25.6 oz. adj. rear sight, white dot front sight. Blued finish. Plastic thumbrest grips. Note: Model 80 is a modification of Model 60 designed to conform w/U.S. import regulations. Made from 1968 to 1988.

MODEL 90
SPORT TARGET . . . . **NiB $215 Ex $180 Gd $130**
Same as Model 80 except has 6-inch bbl., 9 inches overall, weight: 26.8 oz. Made from 1968 1990.

MODEL 100 TARGET
AUTOMATIC PISTOL . . . . **NiB $395 Ex $340 Gd $266**
Caliber: .22 LR. 10-round magazine, 5.9-inch bbl., 9 inches overall. Weight: 37.75 oz. Adj. rear sight, interchangeable front sights. Blued finish. Checkered walnut thumbrest grips. Made from 1969-86. Note: Formerly Model 69.

MODEL AMR AUTO PISTOL . . . . . . **NiB $390 Ex $300 Gd $242**
Simlar to Model USA except with 6-inch bbl. and target sights. Imported from 1992 to 1994.

"BABY" AUTOMATIC PISTOL . . . . . **NiB $288 Ex $211 Gd $155**
Calibers: .22 Short, .22 Long. Five-round magazine, 2.13-inch bbl., 4.13 inches overall. Weight: 9 oz. Fixed sights. Blued finish. Bakelite grips. Made from 1949 to 1968.

MODEL P010
AUTOMATIC PISTOL . . . . **NiB $675 Ex $495 Gd $322**
Caliber: .22 LR. Five- and 10-round magazine, 5.9-inch bbl. w/7.5-inch sight radius. Weight: 40 oz. Interchangeable front sight, adj. rear. Blued finish. Textured walnut grips. Made from 1988 to 1992 and 1995 to 1997.

P018 COMPACT MODEL . . . . **NiB $545 Ex $434 Gd $336**
Slightly smaller version of the Model P018 standard DA automatic except has 14-round magazine and 4-inch bbl., 7.68 inches overall. Weight: 33 oz. Walnut grips only. Imported from 1987 to 1996.

P018 DOUBLE-ACTION
AUTOMATIC PISTOL
Caliber: 9mm Para. 16-round magazine, 4.75-inch bbl., 8.5 inches overall. Weight: 36 oz. Fixed combat sights. Blued finish. Checkered plastic or walnut grips. Imported from 1987 to 1996.
W/plastic grips . . . . **NiB $488 Ex $370 Gd $281**
W/walnut grips . . . . **NiB $528 Ex $410 Gd $322**

P-ONE DA AUTO PISTOL
Caliber: 9mm Parabellum or .40 S&W. 10- or 16-round magazine, 4.8-inch bbl., 8.35 inches overall. Weight: 34 oz. Blade front sight, adjustable rear w/3-dot system. Matte black or chrome finish. Checkered walnut or black plastic grips. Imported from 1993 to 1997.

Model P-One blue finish . . . . NiB $585 Ex $495 Gd $335
Model P-One chrome finish . . . . . . NiB $662 Ex $525 Gd $360
W/walnut grips, add $40

P-ONE PRACTICAL VB AUTO PISTOL
Similar to Model P One except chambered for 9x21mm w/2-, 4- or 6-port compensating system for IPSC competition. Imported 1993 to 1997.
Model P One
Practical (2 port) . . . . NiB $1125 Ex $1047 Gd $770
Model P One
Practical (4 port) . . . . NiB $1234 Ex $1033 Gd $767
Model P One
Practical (6 port) . . . . NiB $1645 Ex $1366 Gd $975
W/chrome finish, add $75

SPORTER AUTOMATIC PISTOL . . . . . NiB $305 Ex $220 Gd $114
Caliber .22 LR. Eight-round magazine, bbl., lengths: 6-, 8- and 10-inch, 13 inches overall (10-inch bbl.). weight: About 30 oz. (10-inch bbl.) Target sights. Blued finish. Walnut grips. Made 1949 to 1968.

MODEL USA AUTO PISTOL
Single-action, blowback. Calibers: .22 LR, .32 ACP, .380 ACP. Seven-round magazine or 10-round magazine (.22 LR). 3.5-inch bbl., 6.5 inches overall. Weight: 26.5 oz. Ramped front sight, adjustable rear. Blue or chrome finish. Checkered black bakelite grips w/thumbrest. Imported from 1991 to 1997.
Model USA blue finish . . . . NiB $385 Ex $304 Gd $241
Model USA chrome finish. . . . . NiB $440 Ex $364 Gd $195

VEST POCKET
AUTOMATIC PISTOL . . . . NiB $250 Ex $175 Gd $110
Caliber: .25 Auto (6.35mm). Five- or 8-round magazine, 2.13-inch bbl., 4.13 inches overall. Weight: 9 oz. Fixed sights. Blued finish. Bakelite grips. Made from 1945 to 1968.

BERSA PISTOLS — Argentina

Currently imported by Eagle Imports, Wanamassa, NJ (Previously by Interarms & Outdoor Sports)

MODEL 83 DA AUTO PISTOL
Similar to the Model 23 except for the following specifications: Caliber: .380 ACP. Seven-round magazine, 3.5-inch bbl., Front blade sight integral on slide, square-notch rear adj. for windage. Blued or satin nickel finish. Custom wood grips. Imported from 1988 to 1994.
Blued finish . . . . NiB $255 Ex $188 Gd $107
Satin nickel . . . . NiB $292 Ex $245 Gd $59

MODEL 85 DA AUTO PISTOL
Same general specifications as Model 83 except 13-round magazine, Imported from 1988 to 1994.
Blued finish . . . . NiB $295 Ex $210 Gd $147
Satin nickel . . . . NiB $545 Ex $368 Gd $194

MODEL 86 DA AUTO PISTOL
Same general specifications as Model 85 except available in matte blued finish and w/Neoprene grips. Imported from 1992 to 1994.
Matte blued finish . . . . NiB $315 Ex $259 Gd $195
Nickel finish . . . . NiB $335 Ex $289 Gd $220

Bernardelli P010

Bernardelli P018

Bersa Model 85

Bersa Model 383

Bersa Thunder .380

Bersa Thunder .380 Deluxe

MODEL 95 DA AUTOMATIC PISTOL

Caliber: .380 ACP. Seven-round magazine, 3.5-inch bbl., weight: 23 oz. Wraparound rubber grips. Blade front and rear notch sights. Imported from 1995 to date.

Blued finish . . . . NiB $300 Ex $193 Gd $137
Nickel finish . . . . NiB $282 Ex $216 Gd $160

MODEL 97 AUTO PISTOL . . . . NiB $357 Ex $312 Gd $199

Caliber: .380 ACP. Seven-round magazine, 3.3-inch bbl., 6.5 inches overall. Weight: 28 oz. Intro. 1982. Disc.

MODEL 223

Same general specifications as Model 383 except in .22 LR w/10-round magazine capacity. Disc. 1987.

Double-action . . . . NiB $228 Ex $196 Gd $136
Single-action . . . . NiB $218 Ex $186 Gd $132

MODEL 224

Caliber: .22 LR. 10-round magazine, 4-inch bbl., weight: 26 oz. Front blade sight, square-notched rear adj. for windage. Blued finish. Checkered nylon or custom wood grips. Made 1984. SA. disc. 1986.

Double-action . . . . NiB $228 Ex $197 Gd $136
Single-action . . . . NiB $132 Ex $195 Gd $129

MODEL 226

Same general specifications as Model 224 but w/6-inch bbl. Disc. 1987.

Double-action . . . . NiB $238 Ex $196 Gd $136
Single-action . . . . NiB $328 Ex $186 Gd $133

MODEL 383 AUTO PISTOL

Caliber: .380 Auto. Seven-round magazine, 3.5-inch bbl. Front blade sight integral on slide, square-notched rear sight adj. for windage. Custom wood grips on double-action, nylon grips on single action. Blued or satin nickel finish. Made 1984. SA. disc. 1989.

Double-action . . . . NiB $215 Ex $135 Gd $90
Single-action . . . . NiB $200 Ex $120 Gd $75

MODEL 622 AUTO PISTOL . . . . NiB $182 Ex $150 Gd $110

Caliber: .22 LR. Seven-round magazine, 4- or 6-inch bbl., 7 or 9 inches overall. Weight: 2.25 lbs. Blade front sight, square-notch rear adj. for windage. Blued finish. Nylon grips. Made from 1982 to 1987.

MODEL 644 AUTO PISTOL . . . . NiB $269 Ex $224 Gd $150

Caliber: .22 LR. 10-round magazine, 3.5-inch bbl., weight: 26.5 oz. 6.5 inches overall. Adj. rear sight, blade front. Contoured black nylon grips. Made from 1980 to 1988.

THUNDER 9 AUTO PISTOL . . . . . . NiB $375 Ex $237 Gd $152

Caliber: 9mm Para. 15-round magazine, 4-inch bbl., 7.38 inches overall. Weight: 30 oz. Blade front sight, adj. rear w/3-dot system. Ambidextrous safety and decocking device. Matte blued finish. Checkered black polymer grips. Made from 1993 to 1996.

THUNDER .22 AUTO PISTOL (MODEL 23)

Caliber: .22 LR, 10-round magazine, 3.5-inch bbl., 6.63 inches overall. Weight: 24.5 oz. Notched-bar dovetailed rear, blade integral w/slide front. Black polymer grips. Made from 1988 to 1998.

Blued finish . . . . NiB $239 Ex $200 Gd $157
Nickel finish . . . . NiB $246 Ex $214 Gd $174

THUNDER .380 AUTO PISTOL
Caliber: .380 ACP. Seven-round magazine, 3.5-inch bbl., 6.63 inches overall. Weight: 25.75 oz. Notched-bar dovetailed rear, blade integral w/slide front. Blued, satin nickel, or Duo-Tone finish. Made from 1995 to 1998.

Blued finish	NiB $275	Ex $201	Gd $143
Satin nickel finish	NiB $306	Ex $232	Gd $174
Duo-Tone finish	NiB $276	Ex $202	Gd $144

THUNDER .380 PLUS AUTO PISTOL
Same general specifications as standard Thunder .380 except has 10-round magazine and weight: 26 oz. Made from 1995 to 1997.

Matte finish	NiB $265	Ex $215	Gd $155
Satin nickel finish	NiB $297	Ex $247	Gd $187
Duo-Tone finish			Add $20

BROLIN ARMS — La Verne, California

"LEGEND SERIES" SA AUTOMATIC PISTOL
Caliber: .45 ACP. Seven-round magazine, 4- or 5-inch bbl., weight: 32-36 oz. Walnut grips. Single action, full size, compact, or full size frame compact slide. Matte blued finish. Lowered and flared ejection port. Made from 1995 to 1998.

Model L45	NiB $434	Ex $363	Gd $280
Model L45C	NiB $440	Ex $339	Gd $276
Model L45T	NiB $440	Ex $339	Gd $276

"PATRIOT SERIES" SA AUTOMATIC PISTOL
Caliber: .45 ACP. Seven-round magazine, 3.25- and 4-inch bbl., weight: 33-37 oz. Wood grips. Fixed rear sights. Made 1996 to 1997.

Model P45	NiB $595	Ex $443	Gd $265
Model P45C (disc. 1997)	NiB $610	Ex $561	Gd $430
Model P45T (disc. 1997)	NiB $621	Ex $529	Gd $345

"PRO-STOCK AND PRO-COMP" SA PISTOL
Caliber: .45 ACP. Eight-round magazine, 4- or 5-inch bbl., weight: 37 oz. Single action, blued or two-tone finish. Wood grips. Bomar adjustable sights. Made from 1996 to 1997.

Model Pro comp	NiB $820	Ex $628	Gd $548
Model Pro stock	NiB $685	Ex $528	Gd $448

TAC SERIES
Caliber: .45 ACP. Eight-round magazine, 5-inch bbl., 8.5 inches overall. Weight: 37 oz. Low profile combat or Tritium sights. Beavertail grip safety. Matte blue, chrome or two-tone finish. Checkered wood or contoured black rubber grips. Made from 1997 to 1998.

Model TAC 11 service	NiB $609	Ex $482	Gd $373
Model TAC 11 compact	NiB $610	Ex $498	Gd $385
W/Tritium sights, add			$90

BANTAM MODEL .... NiB $370 Ex $263 Gd $188
Caliber: 9mmPara., .40 S&W. Single or double-action, super compact size, concealed hammer, all steel construction; 3-dot sights; royal blue or matte finish. Manufactured 1999 only.

BRONCO PISTOL — Eibar, Spain
Manufactured by Echave y Arizmendi

MODEL 1918 POCKET
AUTOMATIC PISTOL .... NiB $184 Ex $110 Gd $77
Caliber: .32 ACP (7.65mm). Six-round magazine 2.5-inch bbl., 5 inches overall. Weight: 20 oz. Fixed sights. Blued finish. Hard rubber grips. Made circa 1918- to 1925.

Browning Model 25 Automatic

VEST POCKET AUTO PISTOL ...... NiB $159 Ex $103 Gd $46
Caliber: .25 ACP, 6-round magazine, 2.13-inch bbl., 4.13 inches overall. Weight: 11 oz. Fixed sights. Blued finish. Hard rubber grips. Made from 1919 to 1935.

BROWNING PISTOLS — Morgan, Utah

The following Browning pistols have been manufactured by Fabrique Nationale d'Armes de Guerre (now Fabrique Nationale Herstal) of Herstal, Belgium, by Arms Technology Inc. of Salt Lake City and by J. P. Sauer & Sohn of Eckernforde, W. Germany. (See also FN Browning and J.P. Sauer & Sohn listings.)

.25 AUTOMATIC PISTOL
Same general specifications as FN Browning Baby (see separate listing). Standard Model, blued finish, hard rubber grips. Light Model, nickel-plated, Nacrolac pearl grips. Renaissance Engraved Model, nickel-plated, Nacrolac pearl grips. Made by FN from 1955 to 1969.

Standard model	NiB $554	Ex $502	Gd $255
Lightweight model	NiB $564	Ex $502	Gd $255
Renaissance model	NiB $1070	Ex $838	Gd $478

.32 AND .380 AUTOMATIC PISTOL, 1955 TYPE
Same general specifications as FN Browning .32 (7.65mm) and .380 Pocket Auto. Standard Model, Renaissance Engraved Model as furnished in .25 Automatic. Made by FN from 1955 to 1969.

Standard model (.32 ACP)	NiB $455	Ex $409	Gd $286
Standard model (.380 ACP)	NiB $425	Ex $358	Gd $255
Renaissance model	NiB $1135	Ex $891	Gd $659

.380 AUTOMATIC PISTOL, 1971 TYPE
Same as .380 Automatic, 1955 Type except has longer slide, 4.44-inch bbl., is 7.06 inches overall, weight: 23 oz. Rear sight adj. for windage and elevation, plastic thumbrest grips. Made 1971 to 1975.

Standard model	NiB $464	Ex $366	Gd $263
Renaissance model	NiB $1071	Ex $865	Gd $582

BDA DA AUTOMATIC PISTOL
Similar to SIG-Sauer P220. Calibers: 9mm Para., .38 Super Auto, .45 Auto. Nine-round magazine (9mm and .38), 7-round (.45 cal), 4.4-inch bbl., 7.8 inches overall. Weight: 29.3 oz. Fixed sights. Blued finish. Plastic grips. Made from 1977 to 1980 by J. P. Sauer.

BDA model, 9mm, .45 ACP	NiB $575	Ex $437	Gd $297
BDA model, .38 Super	NiB $695	Ex $431	Gd $339

**Browning
BDA .380 Nickel Finish**

**Browning
BDM 9mm DA**

**Browning
Buck Mark 22 Field (5.5)**

**Browning
Buck Mark 22 Bullseye**

**Browning
Buck Mark 22 Plus**

BDA .380 DA AUTOMATIC PISTOL

Caliber: .380 Auto. 10- or 13-round magazine, bbl. length: 3.81 inches., 6.75 inches overall. Weight: 23 oz. Fixed blade front sight, square-notch drift-adj. rear sight. Blued or nickel finish. Smooth walnut grips. Made from 1982 to 1997 by Beretta.

Blued finish .NiB $555 Ex $410 Gd $264
Nickel finish . . . . NiB $625 Ex $494 Gd $356

BDM SERIES AUTOMATIC PISTOLS

Calibers: 9mm Para., 10-round magazine, 4.73-inch bbl., 7.85 inches overall. Weight: 31 oz., windage adjustable sights w/3-dot system. Low profile removable blade front sights. Matte blued, Bi-Tone or silver chrome finish. Selectable shooting mode and decocking safety lever. Made from 1991 to 1997.

BDM Standard . . . . NiB $575 Ex $395 Gd $343
BDM Practical . . . . NiB $550 Ex $465 Gd $346
BDM-D Silver Chrome . . . . NiB $650 Ex $475 Gd $354

BUCK MARK .22 AUTOMATIC PISTOL

Caliber: .22 LR. 10-round magazine, 5.5- inch bbl., 9.5 inches overall. Weight: 32 oz. Black molded grips. Adj. rear sight. Blued or nickel finish. Made from 1985 to date.

Blued finish . . . . NiB $335 Ex $217 Gd $140
Nickel finish . . . . NiB $395 Ex $279 Gd $199

BUCK MARK .22 BULLSEYE PISTOL

Same general specifications as the standard Buck Mark 22 except w/7.25-inch fluted barrel, 11.83 inches overall. Weight: 36 oz. Adjustable target trigger. Undercut post front sight, click-adjustable Pro-Target rear. Laminated, Rosewood, black rubber or composite grips. Made from 1996 to 2006.

Standard model (composite grips) . . NiB $440 Ex $317 Gd $224
Target model . . . . NiB $426 Ex $343 Gd $219

BUCK MARK .22

BULLSEYE TARGET . . . . NiB $440 Ex $363 Gd $235
Caliber: .22 LR. 10-round magazine, 7.25- inch fluted bbl., 11.83 inches overall. Weight: 31 oz. Rosewood wrap-around finger groove grips w/matte blued finish. Made from 1996 to 2005.

BUCK MARK .22 FIELD

(5.5) AUTO PISTOL . . . . NiB $455 Ex $299 Gd $213
Calibers: .22 LR. 10-round magazine, 5.5- inch bbl., 9.58 inches overall. Weight: 35.5 oz. Standard sights. Matte Blue finish. Made from 1991 to date.

BUCK MARK .22 MICRO AUTOMATIC PISTOL

Same general specifications as standard Buck Mark .22 except w/4-inch bbl., 8 inches overall. Weight: 32 oz. Molded composite grips. Ramp front sight, Pro Target rear sight. Made from 1992 to date.

Blued finish . . . . NiB $335 Ex $247 Gd $155
Nickel finish . . . . NiB $390 Ex $300 Gd $225

**Browning
Buck Mark .22 Silhouette**

**Browning
Buck Mark .22 Target (5.5)**

BUCK MARK .22 MICRO PLUS AUTO PISTOL

Same specifications as the Buck Mark .22 Micro except ambidextrous, laminated wood grips. Made from 1996 to 2001.

Blued finish . . . . NiB $265 Ex $275 Gd $177
Nickel finish . . . . NiB $365 Ex $290 Gd $225

BUCK MARK .22 PLUS AUTO PISTOL

Same general specifications as standard Buck Mark .22 except for black molded, impregnated hardwood grips. Made from 1987 to 2001.

Blued finish . . . . NiB $365 Ex $265 Gd $160
Nickel finish . . . . NiB $396 Ex $2905 Gd $175

BUCK MARK .22 TARGET (5.5) AUTO PISTOL

Caliber: .22 LR. 10-round magazine, 5.5- inch bbl., 9.6 inches overall. Weight: 35.5 oz. Pro target sights. Wrap-around walnut or contoured finger groove grips. Made from 1990 to 2009.

Matte blue finish . . . . NiB $420 Ex $335 Gd $199
Nickel finish (1994 to date). . . . . . . NiB $475 Ex $385 Gd $345
Gold finish (1991-99) . . . . NiB $355 Ex $249 Gd $155

BUCK MARK .22 SILHOUETTE . . . . NiB $425 Ex $345 Gd $199

Same general specifications as standard Buck Mark .22 except for 9.88-inch bbl. Weight: 53 oz. Target sights mounted on full-length scope base, and laminated hardwood grips and forend. Made from 1987 to 1999.

**Browning
Buck Mark .22 Micro Plus**

BUCK MARK .22
UNLIMITED SILHOUETTE . . . . NiB $519 Ex $399 Gd $265

Same general specifications as standard Buck Mark .22 Silhouette except w/14-inch bbl., 18.69 inches overall. Weight: 64 oz. Interchangeable post front sight and Pro Target rear. Nickel finish. Made from 1991 to 1999.

BUCK MARK .22
VARMINT AUTO PISTOL. . . . . NiB $315 Ex $255 Gd $205

Same general specifications as standard Buck Mark .22 except for 9.88-inch bbl. Weight: 48 oz. No sights, full-length scope base, and laminated hardwood grips. Made from 1987 to 1999.

CHALLENGER AUTOMATIC PISTOL

Caliber: .22 LR. 10-round magazine, bbl. lengths: 4.5 and 6.75-inches. 11.44 inches overall (with 6.75-inch bbl.). Weight: 38 oz. (6.75-inch bbl.). Removable blade front sight, screw adj. rear. Standard finish, blued, also furnished gold inlaid (Gold model) and engraved and chrome-plated (Renaissance model). Checkered walnut grips. Finely figured and carved grips on Gold and Renaissance models. Standard made by FN 1962-75, higher grades. Intro. 1971. Disc.

Standard model . . . . NiB $550 Ex $395 Gd $265
Gold model . . . . NiB $2950 Ex $2370 Gd $1675
Renaissance model . . . . NiB $2950 Ex $2370 Gd $1675

**Browning Challenger
Standard Model**

CHALLENGER II
AUTOMATIC PISTOL . . . . NiB $325 Ex $244 Gd $140

Same general specifications as Challenger Standard model w/6.75-inch bbl. except changed grip angle and impregnated hardwood grips. Original Challenger design modified for lower production costs. Made by ATI from 1976 to 1983.

**Browning Challenger
Renaissance Model**

Browning
Challenger III Sporter .22

Browning
Hi-Power Mark III

Browning
9mm Hi-Power w/Molded Grips

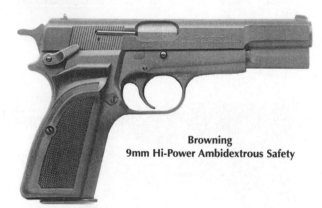

Browning
9mm Hi-Power Ambidextrous Safety

Browning
Hi-Power Captain

CHALLENGER III

AUTOMATIC PISTOL . . . . NiB $240 Ex $217 Gd $134
Same general description as Challenger II except has 5.5 inch bull bbl., alloy frame and new sight system. Weight: 35 oz. Made from 1982-84. Sporter Model w/6.75-inch bbl.. Made from 1982-85.

HI-POWER AUTOMATIC PISTOL

Same general specifications as FN Browning Model 1935 except chambered for 9mm Para., .30 Luger and .40 S&W. 10- or 13-round magazine, 4.63-inch bbl., 7.75 inches overall. Weight: 32 oz. (9mm) or 35 oz. (.40 S&W). Fixed sights, also available w/rear sight adj. for windage and elevation, and ramp front sight. Ambidextrous safety added after 1989. Standard model blued, chrome-plated or Bi-Tone finish. Checkered walnut, contour-molded Polyamide or wraparound rubber grips. Renaissance Engraved model chrome-plated, w/Nacrolac pearl grips. Made by FN from 1954 to 2002.
Standard model,
fixed sights, 9mm . . . . NiB $825 Ex $654 Gd $489
Standard model, fixed sights,
.40 S&W (intro. 1986) . . . . NiB $748 Ex $652 Gd $555
Standard model, .30
Luger (1986-89). . . . . NiB $900 Ex $667 Gd $463
Renaissance model,
fixed sights. . . . . NiB $3797 Ex $3526 Gd $2612
W/adjustable
rear sight, add $50
W/ambidextrous
safety, add $95
W/moulded grips,
deduct $40
W/tangent rear sight
(1965-78), add* $295
W/T-Slot grip &
tangent sight
(1965-78), add* $595
*Check FN agent to certify value

HI-POWER

CAPITAN AUTOMATIC . . . . NiB $755 Ex $580 Gd $400
Similar to the standard Hi-Power except fitted w/adj. 500-meter tangent rear sight and rounded serrated hammer. Made from 1993 to 2000.

HI-POWER MARK

III AUTOMATIC PISTOL . . . . NiB $750 Ex $467 Gd $369
Calibers: 9mm and .40 S&W. 10-round magazine, 4.75-inch bbl., 7.75 inches overall. Weight: 32 oz. Fixed sights with molded grips. Durable non-glare matte blue finish. Made from 1985 to 2000.

**Browning
Hi-Power Practical**

**Browning
Hi-Power Silver Chrome**

HI-POWER PRACTICAL AUTOMATIC PISTOL
Similar to the standard Hi-Power except has silver-chromed frame and blued slide w/Commander-style hammer. Made from 1991 to 2006.

W/fixed sights . . . . NiB $695 Ex $508 Gd $369
W/adj. sights . . . . Add $60

HI-POWER SILVER CHROME
AUTOMATIC PISTOL . . . . NiB $750 Ex $626 Gd $384
Calibers: 9mm and .40 S&W. 10-round magazine, 4.75-inch bbl., 7.75 inches overall. Weight: 36 oz. Adjustable sights with Pachmayer grips. Silver-chromed finish. Made from 1991 to 2000.

HI-POWER 9MM CLASSIC
Limited Edition 9mm Hi-Power, w/silver-gray finish, high-grade engraving and finely-checkered walnut grips w/double border. Proposed production of the Classic was 5000 w/less than half that number produced. Gold Classic limited to 500 w/two-thirds proposed production in circulation. Made from 1985 to 1986.

Gold classic . . . . NiB $5225 Ex $4866 Gd $3409
Standard classic . . . . NiB $825 Ex $630 Gd $502

INTERNATIONAL
MEDALIST EARLY MODEL
TARGET PISTOL . . . . NiB 1150 Ex $960 Gd $773
Modification of Medalist to conform w/International Shooting Union rules. 5.9-inch bbl., Smaller grip with no forearm. Weight: 42 oz. Made from 1970-73. Subtract 30% for post 1974 models

MEDALIST AUTOMATIC TARGET PISTOL
Caliber: .22 LR. 10-round magazine, 6.75-inch bbl. w/vent rib, 11.94 inches overall. Weight: 46 oz. Removable blade front sight, click-adj. micrometer rear. Standard finish, blued also furnished gold-inlaid (Gold Model) and engraved and chrome-plated (Renaissance Model). Checkered walnut grips w/thumbrest (for right- or left-handed shooter). Finely figured and carved grips on Gold and Renaissance Models. Made by FN from 1962 to 1975. Higher grades. Intro. 1971.

Standard model . . . . NiB $1500 Ex $1292 Gd $1034
Gold model . . . . NiB $2098 Ex $1789 Gd $997
Renaissance model . . . . NiB $2557 Ex $2115 Gd $1365

NOMAD
AUTOMATIC PISTOL . . . . NiB $457 Ex $305 Gd $203
Caliber: .22 LR. 10-round magazine, bbl. lengths: 4.5 and 6.75-inches, 8.94 inches overall (4.5-inch bbl.). Weight: 34 oz. (with 4.5-inch bbl.). Removable blade front sight, screw adj. rear. Blued finish. Plastic grips. Made by FN from 1962 to 1974.

**Browning
Hi-Power 9mm Classic**

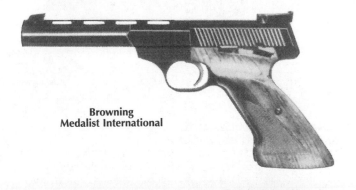

**Browning
Medalist International**

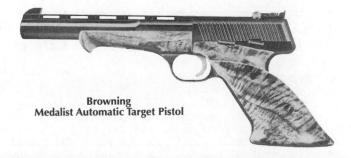

**Browning
Medalist Automatic Target Pistol**

Browning Renaissance

Charter Arms Bonnie

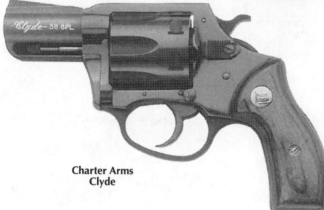

Charter Arms Clyde

RENAISSANCE 9MM, .25 AUTO AND .380 AUTO (1955) ENGRAVED

MODELS, CASED SET . . . . NiB $3746 Ex $3320 Gd $3035
One pistol of each of the three models in a special walnut carrying case, all chrome-plated w/Nacrolac pearl grips. Made by FN from 1964 to 1975. Options and engraving varies.

BRYCO ARMS INC. — Irvine, California Distributed by Jennings Firearms. Inc. Carson City, NV

MODELS J22, J25 AUTO PISTOL
Calibers: .22 LR, .25 ACP. Six-round magazine, 2.5-inch bbl., about 5 inches overall. Weight: 13 oz. Fixed sights. Chrome, satin nickel or black Teflon finish. Walnut, grooved black Cycolac or resin-impregnated wood grips. Made from 1981 to 1985.
Model J-22 (disc. 1985) . . . . NiB $65 Ex $46 Gd $30
Model J-25 (disc. 1995) . . . . NiB $108 Ex $76 Gd $61

MODELS M25, M32, M38 AUTO PISTOL
Calibers: .25 ACP, .32 ACP, .380 ACP. Six-round magazine, 2.81-inch bbl., 5.31 inches overall. Weight: 11oz. to 15 oz. Fixed sights. Chrome, satin nickel or black Teflon finish. Walnut, grooved, black Cycolac or resin-impregnated wood grips. Made from 1988 to 2000.
Model M25 (disc.) . . . . NiB $107 Ex $82 Gd $66
Model M32 . . . . NiB $127 Ex $97 Gd $73
Model M38 . . . . NiB $135 Ex $108 Gd $77

MODEL M48
AUTO PISTOL . . . . NiB $117 Ex $96 Gd $71
Calibers: .22 LR, .32 ACP, .380 ACP. Seven-round magazine, 4-inch bbl., 6.69 inches overall. Weight: 20 oz. Fixed sights. Chrome, satin nickel or black Teflon finish. Smooth wood or black Teflon grips. Made from 1989 to 1995.

MODEL M58
AUTO PISTOL . . . . NiB $117 Ex $96 Gd $71
Caliber: .380 ACP. 10-round magazine, 3.75-inch bbl., 5.5 inches overall. Weight: 30 oz. Fixed sights. Chrome, satin nickel, blued or black Teflon finish. Smooth wood or black Teflon grips. Made 1993 to 1995.

MODEL M59
AUTO PISTOL . . . . NiB $117 Ex $107 Gd $71
Caliber: 9mm Para. 10-round magazine, 4-inch bbl., 6.5 inches overall. Weight: 33 oz. Fixed sights. Chrome, satin nickel, blued or black Teflon finish. Smooth wood or black Teflon grips. Made 1994 to 1996.

MODEL NINE SA
AUTO PISTOL . . . . NiB $152 Ex $122 Gd $91
Similar to Bryco/Jennings Model M59 except w/redesigned slide w/loaded chamber indicator and frame mounted ejector. Weight: 30 oz. Made from 1997 to 2003.

MODEL 5 . . . . NiB $90 Ex $60 Gd $40
Caliber: .380 ACP, 9mm Para.; 10- or 12-shot magazine. Bbl: 3.25 inches. Blue or nickel finish, black synthetic grips. Weight: 36 oz. Disc. 1995.

BUDISCHOWSKY PISTOL — Mt. Clemens, Michigan, Mfd. by Norton Armament Corporation

TP-70 DA AUTOMATIC PISTOL
Calibers: .22 LR, .25 Auto. Six-round magazine, 2.6-inch bbl., 4.65 inches overall. Weight: 12.3 oz. Fixed sights. Stainless steel. Plastic grips. Made from 1973 to 1977.
.22 LR . . . . NiB $445 Ex $320 Gd $245
.25 ACP . . . . NiB $330 Ex $226 Gd $154

CALICO LIGHT WEAPONS SYSTEM, Hillsboro OR

MODEL 110 AUTO PISTOL . . NiB $610 Ex $544 Gd $446

Caliber: .22 LR. 100-round magazine, 6-inch bbl., 17.9 inches overall. Weight: 3.75 lbs. Adj. post front sight, fixed U-notch rear. Black finish aluminum frame. Molded composition grip. Made from 1986 to 1994.

MODEL M-950 AUTO PISTOL . . . . NiB $795 Ex $456 Gd $347
Caliber 9mm Para. 50- or 100-round magazine, 7.5-inch bbl., 14 inches overall. Weight: 2.25 lbs. Adj. post front sight, fixed U-notch rear. Glass-filled polymer grip. Made from 1989 to 1994.

CHARTER ARMS CORPORATION — Shelton, Connecticut

MODEL 40 AUTOMATIC PISTOL..... NiB $265 Ex $205 Gd $157
Caliber: .22 RF. Eight-round magazine, 3.3-inch bbl., 6.3 inches overall. Weight: 21.5 oz. Fixed sights. Checkered walnut grips. Stainless steel finish. Made from 1985 to 1986.

**MODEL 79K
DA AUTOMATIC PISTOL** .... NiB $326 Ex $268 Gd $216
Calibers: .380 or .32 Auto. Seven-round magazine, 3.6-inch bbl., 6.5 inches overall. Weight: 24.5 oz. Fixed sights. Checkered walnut grips. Stainless steel finish. Made from 1985 to 1986.

BONNIE AND CLYDE SET........ NiB $420 Ex $329 Gd $277
Matching pair of shrouded 2.5-inch bbl., revolvers chambered for .32 Magnum and .38 Special. Blued finish w/scrolled name on bbls.. Made 1989 to 1990.

BULLDOG .44 DA REVOLVER
Caliber: .44 Special. Five-round cylinder, 2.5- or 3-inch bbl., 7 or 7.5 inches overall. Weight: 19 or 19.5 oz. Fixed sights. Blued, nickel-plated or stainless finish. Checkered walnut Bulldog or square buttgrips. Made from 1973 to 1996.
**Blued finish/
Pocket Hammer (2.5-inch)** .... NiB $225 Ex $179 Gd $112
**Blued finish/
Bulldog grips (3-inch disc. 1988)** .... NiB $229 Ex $184 Gd $132
Electroless nickel .... NiB $256 Ex $209 Gd $149
**Stainless steel/
Bulldog grips (disc. 1992)** .... NiB $199 Ex $178 Gd $122
**Neoprene grips/
Pocket Hammer** .... NiB $224 Ex $183 Gd $131

BULLDOG .357 DA REVOLVER... NiB $185 Ex $14 3 Gd $112
Caliber: .357 Magnum. Five-round cylinder, 6-inch bbl., 11 inches overall. Weight: 25 oz. Fixed sights. Blued finish. Square, checkered walnut grips. Made from 1977 to 1996.

BULLDOG NEW POLICE DA REVOLVER
Same general specifications as Bulldog Police except chambered for .44 Special. Five-round cylinder, 2.5- or 3.5-inch bbl. Made from 1990 to 1992.
Blued finish .... NiB $258 Ex $197 Gd $145
Stainless finish (2.5-inch bbl. only) ..... NiB $198 Ex $163 Gd $112

BULLDOG POLICE DA REVOLVER
Caliber: .38 Special or .32 H&R Magnum. Six-round cylinder, 4-inch bbl., 8.5 inches overall. Weight: 20.5 oz. Adj. rear sight, ramp front. Blued or stainless finish. Square checkered walnut grips. Made from 1976-93. No shroud on new models.
Blued finish .... NiB $232 Ex $188 Gd $135
Stainless finish .... NiB $222 Ex $183 Gd $124
.32 H&R Magnum (disc.1992) ..... NiB $237 Ex $191 Gd $135

BULLDOG PUG DA REVOLVER
Caliber: .44 Special. Five-round cylinder, 2.5 inch bbl., 7.25 inches overall. Weight: 20 oz. Blued or stainless finish. Fixed ramp front sight, fixed square-notch rear. Checkered Neoprene or walnut grips. Made from 1988 to 1993.
Blued finish .... NiB $242 Ex $202 Gd $151
Stainless finish .... NiB $195 Ex $142 Gd $101

BULLDOG TARGET DA REVOLVER
Calibers: .357 Magnum, .44 Special (latter intro. in 1977). Four-inch bbl., 8.5 inches overall. Weight: 20.5 oz. in .357. Adj. rear sight, ramp front. Blued finish. Square checkered walnut grips. Made 1976 to 1992.
Blued finish (disc.1989) .... NiB $235 Ex $175 Gd $126

**Charter Arms
Bulldog Police**

**Charter Arms
Bulldog Police**

**Charter Arms
Bulldog Target**

Charter Arms
Explorer II

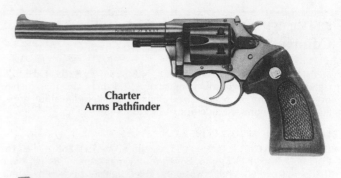

Charter
Arms Pathfinder

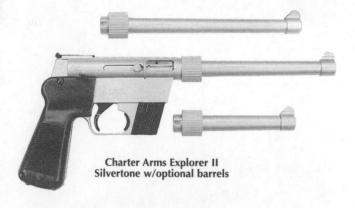

Charter Arms Explorer II
Silvertone w/optional barrels

Charter Arms Police Undercover
.32 H&R Magnum

Charter Arms Undercover
.32 S&W Long

Charter Arms
Undercover Stainless

BULLDOG TRACKER
DA REVOLVER. . . . . **NiB $180 Ex $127 Gd $95**
Caliber: .357 Mag. Five-round cylinder, 2.5-, 4- or 6-inch bbl., 11 inches overall (6-inch bbl.). Weight: 21 oz. (2.5-inch bbl.). Adj. rear sight, ramp front. Checkered walnut grips. Blued finish. 4- or 6-inch bbl., Disc.1986. Reintroduced 1989 to 1992.

EXPLORER II SEMIAUTO SURVIVAL PISTOL
Caliber: .22 RF. Eight-round magazine, 6-, 8- or 10-inch bbl., 13.5 inches overall (6-inch bbl.). Weight: 28 oz. finishes: Black, heat cured, semigloss textured enamel or silvertone anticorrosion. Disc. 1987.
Standard model . . . . **NiB $130 Ex $102 Gd $71**
Silvertone (w/optional
6- or 10-inch bbl.) . . . . **NiB $140 Ex $121 Gd $81**

OFF-DUTY DA REVOLVER
Calibers: .22 LR or .38 Special. Six-round (.22 LR) or 5-round (.38 Spec.) cylinder. Two-inch bbl., 6.25 inches overall. Weight: 16 oz. Fixed rear sight, Partridge-type front sight. Plain walnut grips. Matte black, nickel or stainless steel finish. Made from 1992 to 1996.
Matte black finish . . . . **NiB $172 Ex $148 Gd $107**
Nickel finish . . . . **NiB $214 Ex $184 Gd $132**
Stainless steel . . . . **NiB $235 Ex $176 Gd $122**

PATHFINDER DA REVOLVER
Calibers: .22 LR, .22 WMR. Six-round cylinder, bbl. lengths: 2-, 3-, 6-inches, 7.13 inches overall (in 3-inch bbl.), and regular grips. Weight: 18.5 oz. (3-inch bbl.). Adj. rear sight, ramp front. Blued or stainless finish. Plain walnut regular, checkered Bulldog or square buttgrips. Made 1970 to date. Note: Originally designated "Pocket Target," name was changed in 1971 to "Pathfinder." Grips changed in 1984. Disc. 1990.
Blued finish . . . . **NiB $188 Ex $153 Gd $112**
Stainless finish . . . . **NiB $228 Ex $173 Gd $112**

CHARTER ARMS PIT BULL DA REVOLVER

Calibers: 9mm, .357 Magnum, .38 Special. Five-round cylinder, 2.5-, 3.5- or 4-inch bbl., 7 inches overall (2.5-inch bbl.). Weight: 21.5 to 25 oz. All stainless steel frame. Fixed ramp front sight, fixed square-notch rear. Checkered Neoprene grips. Blued or stainless finish. Made from 1989 to 1991.

Blued finish . . . . NiB $237 Ex $205 Gd $124
Stainless finish . . . . NiB $240 Ex $206 Gd $124

CHARTER ARMS UNDERCOVER DA REVOLVER

Caliber: .38 Special. Five-round cylinder,. bbl., lengths: 2-, 3-, 4-inches, 6.25 inches overall (2-inch bbl.), and regular grips. Weight: 16 oz. (2-inch bbl.). Fixed sights. Plain walnut, checkered Bulldog or square buttgrips. Made from 1965 to 1996.

Blued or nickel-plated finish . . . . NiB $190 Ex $108 Gd $87
Stainless finish . . . . NiB $260 Ex $209 Gd $132

CHARTER ARMS UNDERCOVER

Same general specifications as standard Undercover except chambered for .32 H&R Magnum or .32 S&W Long, has 6-round cylinder and 2.5-inch bbl.

.32 H&R Magnum (blued) . . . . NiB $310 Ex $248 Gd $167
.32 H&R Magnum nickel . . . . NiB $208 Ex $168 Gd $107
.32 H&R Magnum (stainless) . . . . . . NiB $325 Ex $263 Gd $182
.32 S&W Long (blued) disc. 1989 . . . . . NiB $297 Ex $221 Gd $175

CHARTER ARMS UNDERCOVER POCKET POLICE DA REVOLVER

Same general specifications as standard Undercover except has 6-round cylinder and pocket-type hammer. Blued or stainless steel finish. Made from 1969 to 1981.

Blued finish . . . . NiB $317 Ex $265 Gd $194
Stainless steel . . . . NiB $335 Ex $280 Gd $219

CHARTER ARMS UNDERCOVER POLICE DA REVOLVER

Same general specifications as standard Undercover except has 6-round cylinder. Made from 1984 to 1989. Reintroduced 1993.

Blued, .38 Special . . . . NiB $205 Ex $163 Gd $127
Stainless, .38 Special . . . . NiB $244 Ex $193 Gd $142
.32 H&R Magnum . . . . NiB $225 Ex $180 Gd $132

CHARTER ARMS UNDER-
COVERETTE DA REVOLVER . . . . . . NiB $155 Ex $106 Gd $75
Same as Undercover model w/2-inch bbl. except caliber .32 S&W Long, 6-round cylinder, blued finish only. Weight: 16.5 oz. Made 1972 to 1983.

CIMARRON F.A. CO. — Fredricksburg, Texas

CIMARRON EL PISTOLERO
SINGLE-ACTION REVOLVER . . . . . NiB $416 Ex $310 Gd $232
Calibers: .357 Mag., .45 Colt. Six-round cylinder, 4.75- 5.5- or 7.5-inch bbl., polished brass backstrap and triggerguard. Otherwise, same as Colt Single-Action Army revolver w/parts being interchangeable. Made from 1997 to 1998.

COLT'S MANUFACTURING CO., INC. — Hartford, Connecticut

Previously Colt Industries, Firearms Division. Production of some Colt handguns spans the period before World War II to the postwar years. Values shown for these models are for earlier production. Those manufactured c. 1946 and later generally are less desirable to collectors and values are approximately 30 percent lower.

NOTE: *For ease in finding a particular firearm, Colt handguns are grouped*

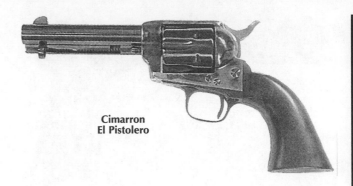

**Cimarron
El Pistolero**

into three sections: Automatic Pistols, Single-Shot Pistols, Derringers and Revolvers. For a complete listing, please refer to the Index.

AUTOMATIC PISTOLS

COLT MODEL 1900 .38 AUTOMATIC PISTOL

Caliber: .38 ACP (modern high-velocity cartridges should not be used in this pistol). Seven-round magazine, 6-inch bbl., 9 inches overall. Weight: 35 oz. Fixed sights. Blued finish. Hard rubber and plain or checkered walnut grips. Sharp-spur hammer. Combination rear sight and safety unique to the Model 1900 (early production). In mid-1901 a solid rear sight was dovetailed into the slide. (SN range 1-4274) Made 190003. Note: 250 models were sold to the military (50 Navy and 200 Army).

Early commercial model
(w/sight/safety) . . . . NiB $15,000 Ex $13,000 Gd $10,000
Late commercial model
(W/dovetailed sight) . . . . NiB $15,000 Ex $13.008 Gd $10,000
Army Model w/U.S. inspector
marks (1st Series - SN 90-150
w/inspector mark J.T.T) . . . . NiB $30,000 Ex $26,000 Gd $20,000
(2nd Series - SN 1600-1750
w/inspector mark R.A.C.) . . . . NiB $10,337 Ex $8290 Gd $5669
Navy model (Also marked
w/USN-I.D. number) . . . . NiB $18,228 Ex $12,263 Gd $9292

COLT MODEL 1902 MILITARY .38 AUTOMATIC PISTOL

Caliber: .38 ACP (modern high-velocity cartridges should not be used in this pistol). Eight-round magazine, 6-inch bbl., 9 inches overall. Weight: 37 oz. Fixed sights w/blade front and V-notch rear. Blued finish. Checkered hard rubber grips. Round back hammer, changed to spur type in 1908. No safety but fitted w/standard military swivel. About 18,000 produced with split SN ranges. The government contract series (15,001-15,200) and the commercial sales series (15,000 receding to 11,000) and (30,200-47,266). Made from 1902 to 1929.

Early military model (w/front
slide serrations) . . . . NiB $5790 Ex $3548 Gd $3325
Late military model (w/rear
slide serrations) . . . . NiB $5750 Ex $3490 Gd $2270
Marked "U.S. Army" (SN 15,001-
15,200) . . . . NiB $18,199 Ex $16,055 Gd $14,710

COLT MODEL 1902 SPORTING
.38 AUTOMATIC PISTOL . . . . NiB $4855 Ex $2955
Gd $2131
Caliber: .38 ACP (modern high-velocity cartridges should not be used in this pistol). Seven-round magazine, 6-inch bbl., 9 inches overall. Weight: 35 oz. Fixed sights w/blade front and V-notch rear. Blued finish. Checkered hard rubber grips. Round back hammer was standard but some spur hammers were installed during late production. No safety and w/o swivel as found on military model. Total production about 7,500 w/split SN ranges (4275-10,999) and (30,000-30,190) Made from 1902 to 1908.

Colt
Model 1902 Military

Colt
1903 Early Hammer

Colt
Model 1903 Pocket Hammerless

MODEL 1903 POCKET .32 AUTOMATIC PISTOL
FIRST ISSUE - COMMERCIAL SERIES
Caliber: .32 Auto. Eight-round magazine, 4-inch bbl., 7 inches over-all. Weight: 23 oz. Fixed sights. Blued or nickel finish. Checkered hard rubber grips. Hammerless (concealed hammer). Slide lock and grip safeties. Fitted w/barrel bushing but early models have no magazine safety. Total production of the Model 1903 reached 572,215. The First Issue maded from 1903 to 1908 (SN range 1-72,000).
Blued finish . . . . NiB $1040 Ex $713 Gd $547
Nickel finish . . . . NiB $1150 Ex $734 Gd $562

MODEL 1903 POCKET .32 AUTOMATIC PISTOL
SECOND ISSUE - COMMERCIAL SERIES
Same as First Issue but with 3.75-inch bbl. and small extractor. Made from 1908 to 1910 (SN range 72,001 -105,050).
Blued finish . . . . NiB $765 Ex $572 Gd $432
Nickel finish . . . . NiB $799 Ex $650 Gd $463

MODEL 1903 POCKET .32 AUTOMATIC PISTOL,
THIRD ISSUE - COMMERCIAL SERIES
Caliber: .32 Auto. Similar to Second Issue w/3.75-inch bbl. except with integral barrel bushing and locking lug at muzzle end of bbl. Production occurred 1910 to 1926 (SN range 105,051-468,096).
Blued finish . . . . NiB $1250 Ex $987 Gd $737
Nickel finish . . . . NiB $1400 Ex $1190 Gd $877

MODEL 1903 POCKET .32 AUTOMATIC PISTOL
FOURTH ISSUE - COMMERCIAL SERIES
Caliber: .32 Auto. Similar to Third Issue except a slide lock safety change was made when a Tansley-style disconnector was added on all pistols above SN 468,097, which prevents firing of cartridge in chamber when the magazine is removed. Blued or nickel finish. Checkered walnut grips. These design changes were initiated 1926 to 1945 (SN range 105,051-554,446).
Blued finish . . . . NiB $1248 Ex $958 Gd $740
Nickel finish . . . . NiB $1450 Ex $1077 Gd $890

MODEL 1903 POCKET (HAMMER) .38 AUTOMATIC PISTOL
Caliber: .38 ACP (modern high-velocity cartridges should not be used in this pistol). Similar to Model 1902 Sporting .38 but w/shorter frame, slide and 4.5-inch bbl. Overall dimension reduced to 7.5 inches. Weight: 31 oz. Fixed sights w/blade front and V-notch rear. Blued finish. Checkered hard rubber grips. Round back hammer, changed to spur type in 1908. No safety. (SN range 16,001-47,226 with some numbers above 30,200 assigned to 1902 Military). Made from 1903 to 1929.
Early model
(round hammer) . . . . NiB $1910 Ex $1629 Gd $1321
Late model
(spur hammer). . . . . NiB $2173 Ex $1873 Gd $1583

MODEL 1903 POCKET HAMMERLESS (CONCEALED HAMMER) .32 AUTOMATIC PISTOL - MILITARY
Caliber: .32 ACP. Eight-round magazine, Similar to Model 1903 Pocket .32 except concealed hammer and equipped w/magazine safety. Parkerized or blued finish. (SN range with "M" prefix M1-M200,000) Made from 1941 to 1945.
Blued service model (marked
"U.S. Property") . . . . NiB $1250 Ex $1100 Gd $800
Parkerized service model (marked
"U.S. Property") . . . . NiB $2075 Ex $1700 Gd $1450
Blued documented
Officer's model . . . . NiB $3000 Ex $2771 Gd $1671
Parkerized documented
Officer's model . . . . NiB $3000 Ex $2771 Gd $1671

MODEL 1905 .45 AUTOMATIC PISTOL
Caliber: .45 (Rimless) Automatic. Seven-round magazine, 5-inch bbl., 8 inches overall. Weight: 32.5 oz. Fixed sights w/blade front and V-notch rear. Blued finish. Checkered walnut, hard rubber or pearl grips. Predecessor to Model 1911 Auto Pistol and contributory to the development of the .45 ACP cartridge. (SN range 1-6100) Made from 1905 to 1911.
Commercial model . . . . NiB $7209 Ex $5399 Gd $3649
W/slotted backstrap
(500 produced). . . . . NiB $10,430 Ex $8680 Gd $7180
W/shoulder stock/holster . . . . Add $7500 to $10,000

MODEL 1905 .45 (1907)
CONTRACT PISTOL . . . . . . NiB $21,150 Ex $16,610 Gd $9360
Variation of the Model 1905 produced to U.S. Military specifications, including loaded chamber indicator, grip safety and lanyard loop. Only 201 were produced, but 200 were delivered and may be identified by the chief inspector's initials "K.M." (SN range 1-201) Made from 1907 to 1908.

MODEL 1908 POCKET .25 HAMMERLESS AUTO PISTOL

Caliber: .25 Auto. Six-round magazine, 2-inch bbl., 4.5 inches over-all. Weight: 13 oz. Flat-top front, square-notch rear sight in groove. Blued, nickel or Parkerized finish. Checkered hard rubber grips on early models, checkered walnut on later type, special pearl grips illustrated. Both a grip safety and slide lock safety are included on all models. The Tansley-style safety disconnector was added in 1916 at pistol No. 141000. (SN range 1-409,061) Made 1908 to 1941.

Blued finish . . . . NiB $1649 Ex $1331 Gd $1075
Nickel finish . . . . Add $100
Marked "U.S. Property"
(w/blued finish) . . . . NiB $3000 Ex $2744 Gd $2458

MODEL 1908 POCKET .380 AUTOMATIC PISTOL

Similar to Pocket .32 Auto w/3.75-inch bbl. except chambered for .380 Auto w/seven-round magazine. Weight: 23 oz. Blue, nickel or Parkerized finish. (SN range 1-138,009) Made from 1908 to 1945.

First Issue (made 1908-11, w/bbl.,
lock and bushing, w/SN 1-6,250) . . NiB $1654 Ex $1466 Gd $1202
Second Issue (made 1911-28,
w/o bbl., lock and bushing,
w/SN 6,251-92,893) . . . . NiB $1920 Ex $1608 Gd $1448
Third Issue (made 1928-45,
w/safety disconnector,
w/SN 92,894-138,009) . . . . NiB $1654 Ex $1466 Gd $1202
Parkerized service model
(Marked "U.S. Property" made
1942-45, w/SN "M" prefix.) . . . . . NiB $2515 Ex $1891 Gd $1631
Documented officer's model
(service model w/military
assignment papers) . . . . NiB $3010 Ex $2450 Gd $1734

NOTE: *During both World Wars, Colt licensed other firms to make these pistols under government contract, including Ithaca Gun Co., North American Arms Co., Ltd. (Canada), Remington-Rand Co., Remington-UMC, Singer Sewing Machine Co., and Union Switch & Signal Co. M1911 also produced at Springfield Armory.*

MODEL 1911 AUTOMATIC PISTOL

Caliber: .45 Auto. Seven-round magazine, 5-inch bbl., 8.5 inches overall. Weight: 39 oz. Fixed sights. Blued finish on Commercial model. Parkerized or similar finish on most military pistols. Checkered walnut grips (early production), plastic grips (later production). Checkered, arched mainspring housing and longer grip safety spur adopted in 1923 (on M1911A1).

Model 1911
commercial (C-series) . . . . NiB $14,895 Ex $12,543 Gd $10,794
Model 1911A1 commercial
(Pre-WWII) . . . . NiB $3750 Ex $3064 Gd $2134

U.S. GOVERNMENT MODEL 1911

Colt manufacture . . . . NiB $10,000 Ex $8720 Gd $6692
North American Arms Co.
manufacture . . . . NiB $35,868 Ex $28,693 Gd $24,071
Remington-UMC manufacture . . . . NiB $5949 Ex $3951 Gd $2377
Springfield manufacture . . . . . . NiB $5950 Ex $3951 Gd $2377
Navy Model M1911 type . . . . . . NiB $8500 Ex $6499 Gd $4750

U.S. GOVERNMENT MODEL 1911A1

Singer manufacture . . . . . NiB $44,936 Ex $37,748 Gd $24,109
Colt, Ithaca, Remington-
Rand manufacture . . . . NiB $2500 Ex $2145 Gd $1804
Union Switch &
Signal manufacture . . . . NiB $6500 Ex $6252 Gd $5896

**Colt
Model 1905 Military**

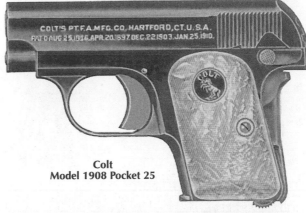

**Colt
Model 1908 Pocket 25**

**Colt
Model 1911**

**Colt
1991 A1**

Colt Cadet .22

Colt All American
Model 2000

MODEL M1991 A1 SEMIAUTO PISTOL
Reissue of Model 1911A1 (see above) w/a continuation of the original serial number range 1945. Caliber: .45 ACP. Seven-round magazine, 5-inch bbl., 8.5 inches overall. Weight: 39 oz. Fixed blade front sight, square notch rear. Parkerized finish. Black composition grips. Made from 1991 to date. (Commander and Compact variations intro. 1993).
Standard model.................... NiB $1860 Ex $1512 Gd $1309
Commander w/4.5-inch bbl., ... NiB $1145 Ex $943 Gd $803
Compact w/3.5-inch bbl., (six-round) ..... NiB $842 Ex $707 Gd $551

.22 CADET AUTOMATIC PISTOL .... NiB $450 Ex $316 Gd $255
Caliber: 22 LR. 10-round magazine, 4.5-inch vent rib bbl., 8.63 inches overall. Weight: 33.5 oz. Blade front sight, dovetailed rear. Stainless finish. Textured black polymer grips w/Colt medallion. Made 1993 to 1995. Note: The Cadet Model name was disc. under litigation but the manufacturer continued to produce this pistol configuration as the Model "Colt 22". For this reason the "Cadet" model will command slight premiums.

.22 SPORT AUTOMATIC PISTOL. .... NiB $428 Ex $340 Gd $189
Same specifications as Cadet Model except renamed Colt .22 w/composition monogrip or wraparound black rubber grip. Made 1994 to 1998.

.22 TARGET PISTOL............. NiB $435 Ex $289 Gd $159
Similar to Colt 22 Sport Model except w/6-inch vent rib bbl., 10.12 inches overall. Weight: 40.5 oz. Partridge style front sight, adjustable white outline rear on full length grooved rib. Made from 1995 to 1999.

ACE AUTOMATIC PISTOL
Caliber: .22 LR (regular or high speed). 10-round magazine. Built on the same frame as the Government Model .45 Auto w/same safety features, etc. Hand-honed action, target bbl., adj. rear sight. 4.75-inch bbl., 8.25. inches overall. Weight: 38 oz. Made 1930 to 1940.
Commercial model .... NiB $4500 Ex $3660 Gd $3147
Service model (1938-42) ...... NiB $7500 Ex $5334 Gd $4604

ALL AMERICAN
MODEL 2000 DA PISTOL .... NiB $750 Ex $536 Gd $376
Hammerless semiautomatic w/blued slide and polymer or alloy receiver fitted w/roller-bearing trigger. Caliber: 9mm Para. 15-round magazine, 4.5-inch bbl., 7.5 inches overall. Weight: 29 oz. (Polymer) or 33 oz (Alloy). Fixed blade front sight, square-notch rear w/3-dot system. Matte blued slide w/black polymer or anodized aluminum receiver. Made from 1992 to 1994.

AUTOMATIC .25 PISTOL
As a result of the 1968 Firearms Act restricting the importation of the Colt Pocket Junior that was produced in Spain, Firearms International was contracted by Colt to manufacture a similar blowback action with the same exposed hammer configuration. Both the U.S. and Spanish-made. .25 automatics were recalled to correct an action malfunction. Returned firearms were fitted with a rebounding firing pin to prevent accidental discharges. Caliber: .25 ACP. Six-round magazine, 2.25-inch bbl., 4.5 inches overall. Weight: 12.5 oz. Integral blade front, square-notch rear sight groove. Blued finish. Checkered wood grips w/Colt medallion. Made from 1970 to 1975.
Model as issued................ NiB $365 Ex $293 Gd $157
**Model recalled
& refitted**..................... NiB $364 Ex $293 Gd $157

CHALLENGER
AUTOMATIC PISTOL .... NiB $695 Ex $449 Gd $246
Same basic design as Woodsman Target, Third Issue but lacks some of the refinements. Fixed sights. Magazine catch on butt as in old Woodsman. Does not stay open on last shot. Lacks magazine safety. 4.5- or 6-inch bbl., 9 to 10.5 inches overall. Weight: 30 oz. (4.5-inch bbl.) or 31.5 oz. (6-inch bbl.) Blued finish. Checkered plastic grips. Made from 1950 to 1955.

COMBAT COMMANDER AUTOMATIC PISTOL
Same as Lightweight Commander except has steel frame w/blued or nickel-plated finish. Weight: 36 oz. Made from 1950 to 1976.
9mm Para...................... NiB $696 Ex $567 Gd $402
.38 Super, .45 ACP.............. NiB $802 Ex $652 Gd $461

COMMANDER LIGHTWEIGHT AUTOMATIC PISTOL
Same basic design as Government Model except w/shorter 4.25-inch bbl., and a special lightweight "Coltalloy" receiver and mainspring housing. Calibers: .45 Auto, .38 Super Auto, 9mm Para. Seven-round magazine (.45 cal.), nine-round (.38 Auto and 9mm), 8 inches overall. Weight: 26.5 oz. Fixed sights. Round spur hammer. Improved safety lock. Blued finish. Checkered plastic or walnut grips. Made from 1950 to 1976.
9mm Para...................... NiB $1000 Ex $761 Gd $500
.38 Super, .45 ACP.............. NiB $1100 Ex $835 Gd $575

CONVERSION
UNIT—.22-.45.................. NiB $294 Ex $238 Gd $166
Converts Service Ace .22 to National Match .45 Auto. Unit consists of match-grade slide assembly and bbl., bushing, recoil spring, recoil spring guide and plug, magazine and slide stop. Made from 1938 to 1942.

CONVERSION
UNIT — .45-.22................. NiB $588 Ex $465 Gd $340
Converts Government Model .45 Auto to a .22 LR target pistol. Unit consists of slide assembly, bbl., floating chamber (as in Service Ace), bushing, ejector, recoil spring, recoil spring guide and plug, magazine and slide stop. The component parts differ and are not interchangable between post war, series 70, series 80, ACE I and ACE II units. Made from 1938 to 1984.

DELTA ELITE SEMIAUTO PISTOL

Caliber: 10 mm. Five-inch bbl., 8.5 inches overall. Eight-round magazine, Weight: 38 oz. Checkered Neoprene combat grips w/Delta medallion. Three-dot, high-profile front and rear combat sights. Blued or stainless finish. Made from 1987 to 1996.

First Edition

(500 Ltd. edition)	NiB $925	Ex $748	Gd $510
Blued finish	NiB $875	Ex $567	Gd $409
Matte stainless finish	NiB $925	Ex $748	Gd $510
Ultra stainless finish			Add $80

DELTA GOLD CUP SEMIAUTO PISTOL

Same general specifications as Delta Elite except w/Accro adjustable rear sight. Made 1989 to 1993 and 1995 to 1996.

Blued finish (disc. 1991)	NiB $950	Ex $650	Gd $450
Stainless steel finish	NiB $1000	Ex $700	Gd $500

GOLD CUP MARK III

NATIONAL MATCH . . . . NiB $1195 Ex $982 Gd $676
Similar to Gold Cup National Match .45 Auto except chambered for .38 Special Mid Range. Five-round magazine, Made 1961 to 1974.

GOLD CUP NATIONAL

MATCH .45 AUTO . . . . NiB $1088 Ex $931 Gd $559
Match version of Government Model .45 Auto w/same general specifications except: match grade bbl., w/new design bushing, flat mainspring housing, long wide trigger w/adj. stop, hand-fitted slide w/improved ejection port, adj. rear sight, target front sight, checkered walnut grips w/gold medallions. Weight: 37 oz. Made 1957 to 1970.

GOVERNMENT MODEL 1911/1911A1

See Colt Model 1911.

HUNTSMAN . . . . NiB $650 Ex $425 Gd $320
Same specifications as the Challenger. Made from 1955 to 1976.

MK I & II/SERIES '90 DOUBLE

EAGLE COMBAT COMMANDER . . . NiB $2000 Ex $1755 Gd $1377
Calibers: .40 S&W, .45 ACP. Seven-round magazine, 4.25-inch bbl., 7.75 inches overall. Weight: 36 oz. Fixed blade front sight, square-notch rear. Checkered Xenoy grips. Stainless finish. Made from 1992 to 1996.

MK II/SERIES '90 DOUBLE EAGLE DA SEMIAUTO PISTOL

Calibers: .38 Super, 9mm, .40 S&W, 10mm, .45 ACP. Seven-round magazine. Five-inch bbl., 8.5 inches overall. Weight: 39 oz. Fixed or Accro adj. sights. Matte stainless finish. Checkered Xenoy grips. Made from 1991 to 1996.

.38 Super, 9mm, .40

S&W (fixed sights)	NiB $718	Ex $556	Gd $394
.45 ACP (adjustable sights)	NiB $699	Ex $554	Gd $396
.45 ACP (fixed sights)	NiB $674	Ex $517	Gd $371
10mm (adjustable sights)	NiB $690	Ex $549	Gd $393
10mm (fixed sights)	NiB $676	Ex $528	Gd $378

MK II/SERIES '90 DOUBLE

EAGLE OFFICER'S ACP . . . . NiB $2000 Ex $1554 Gd $1394
Same general specifications as Double Eagle Combat Commander except chambered for .45 ACP only, 3.5-inch bbl., 7.25 inches overall. Weight: 35 oz. Also available in lightweight (25 oz.) w/blued finish (same price). Made from 1990 to 1993.

MK IV/SERIES '70 COMBAT COMMANDER

Same general specifications as the Lightweight Commander except made from 1970 to 1983.

Blued finish	NiB $1050	Ex $835	Gd $674
Nickel finish	NiB $1120	Ex $905	Gd $744

Colt Delta
Gold Cup

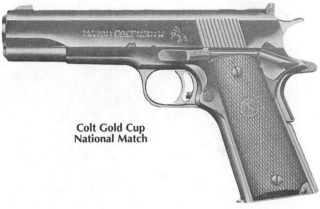

Colt Gold Cup
National Match

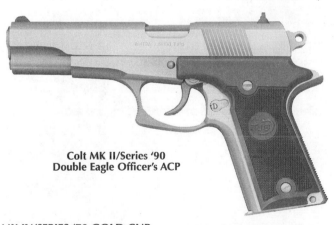

Colt MK II/Series '90
Double Eagle Officer's ACP

MK IV/SERIES '70 GOLD CUP

NATIONAL MATCH .45 AUTO . NiB $1650 Ex $1299 Gd $1094
Match version of MK IV/Series '70 Government Model. Caliber: .45 Auto only. Flat mainspring housing. Accurizor bbl., and bushing. Solid rib, Colt-Elliason adj. rear sight undercut front sight. Adj. trigger, target hammer. 8.75 inches overall. Weight: 38.5 oz. Blued finish. Checkered walnut grips. Made from 1970 to 1984.

MK IV/SERIES '70 GOV'T.

AUTO PISTOL . . . . NiB $1049 Ex $786 Gd $526
Calibers: .45 Auto, .38 Super Auto, 9mm Para. Seven-round magazine in .45, 9-round in .38 and 9mm. Five-inch bbl., 8.38 inches overall. Weight: 38 oz., (.45); 39 oz. in .38 and 9mm. Fixed rear sight and ramp front sight. Blued or nickel-plated finish. Checkered walnut grips. Made from 1970 to 1984.

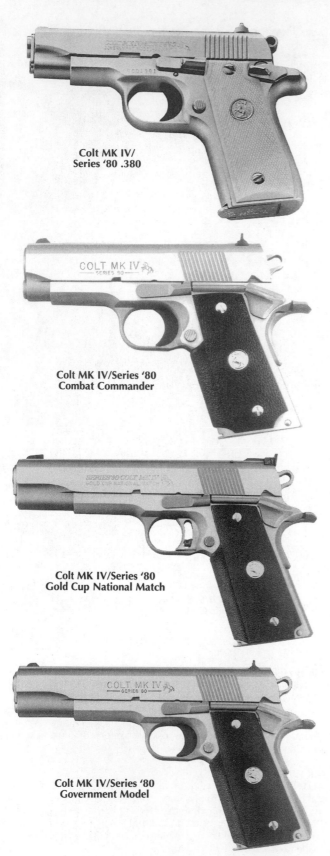

Colt MK IV/
Series '80 .380

Colt MK IV/Series '80
Combat Commander

Colt MK IV/Series '80
Gold Cup National Match

Colt MK IV/Series '80
Government Model

MK IV/SERIES 80 .380 AUTOMATIC PISTOL
Caliber: .380 ACP, 3.29-inch bbl., 6.15 inches overall. Weight: 21.8 oz. Composition grips. Fixed sights. Made since 1983 to 1996.
Blued finish
(disc.1997)................NiB $1050 Ex $852 Gd $648
Bright nickel
(disc.1995).................NiB $1120 Ex $922 Gd $698
Satin nickel
Coltguard (disc.1989) ....NiB $1150 Ex $950 Gd $700
Stainless finish ....NiB $1120 Ex $922 Gd $698

MK IV/SERIES '80 COMBAT COMMANDER
Updated version of the MK IV/Series '70 w/same general specifications. Blued, two-tone or stainless steel w/"pebbled" black Neoprene wraparound grips. Made 1998.
Blued finish
(disc.1996)...................NiB $1100 Ex $865 Gd $766
Satin nickel
(disc.1987)...................NiB $1210 Ex $960 Gd $845
Stainless finish...............NiB $1100 Ex $865 Gd $766
Two-tone finish ....NiB $1275 Ex $1065 Gd $935

MK IV/SERIES '80 COMBAT ELITE
Same general specifications as MK IV/Series '80 Combat Commander except w/Elite enhancements. Calibers: .38 Super, .40 S&W, .45 ACP. Stainless frame w/blued steel slide. Accro adj. sights and beavertail grip safety. Made from 1986 to 1996.
.38 Super,
.45 ACP ....NiB $975 Ex $723 Gd $412
.40 S&W ....NiB $975 Ex $723 Gd $412

MK IV/SERIES '80 GOLD CUP NATIONAL MATCH
Same general specifications as Match '70 version except w/additional finishes and "pebbled" wraparound Neoprene grips. Made from 1983 to 1996.
Blued finish ....NiB $1050 Ex $700 Gd $480
Bright blued
finish........................NiB $1050 Ex $700 Gd $480
Stainless finish................NiB $1125 Ex $850 Gd $625

MK IV/SERIES '80 GOVERNMENT MODEL
Same general specifications as Government Model Series '70 except also chambered in .40 S&W, w/"pebbled" wraparound Neoprene grips, blued or stainless finish. Made 1983 to 1998.
Blued finish ....NiB $950 Ex $650 Gd $400
Bright blued
finish ....NiB $950 Ex $650 Gd $400
Bright stainless
finish ....NiB $950 Ex $650 Gd $400
Matte stainless finish............NiB $950 Ex $650 Gd $400

MK IV/SERIES '80 LIGHT-
WEIGHT COMMANDER .... NiB $1050 Ex $700 Gd $480
Updated version of the MK IV/Series '70 w/same general specifications.

MK IV/SERIES '80
MUSTANG .380 AUTOMATIC
Caliber: .380 ACP. Five- or 6-round magazine, 2.75-inch bbl., 5.5 inches overall. Weight: 18.5 oz. Blued, nickel or stainless finish. Black composition grips. Made from 1983 to 1998.
Blued finish ....NiB $600 Ex $400 Gd $271
Nickel finish
(disc.1994)....................NiB $725 Ex $450 Gd $271
Satin nickel
Coltguard (disc.1988) ....NiB $700 Ex $450 Gd $271
Stainless finish................NiB $650 Ex $362 Gd $271

MK IV/SERIES '80 MUSTANG PLUS II
Caliber: .380 ACP, 7-round magazine, 2.75-inch bbl., 5.5 inches overall. Weight: 20 oz. Blued or stainless finish w/checkered black composition grips. Made from 1988 to 1996.
Blued finish . . . . NiB $650 Ex $378 Gd $282
Stainless finish . . . . NiB $650 Ex $378 Gd $282

MK IV/SERIES '80 MUSTANG POCKETLITE
Same general specifications as the Mustang 30 except weight: 12.5 oz. w/aluminum alloy receiver. Blued, chrome or stainless finish. Optional wood grain grips. Made since 1987.
Blued finish . . . . NiB $625 Ex $375 Gd $290
Lady Elite
(two-tone) finish . . . . NiB $625 Ex $325 Gd $290
Stainless finish . . . . NiB $625 Ex $325 Gd $290
Teflon/stainless finish . . . . NiB $625 Ex $325 Gd $290

MK IV/SERIES '80 OFFICER'S ACP AUTOMATIC PISTOL
Calibers: .40 S&W and .45 ACP, 3.63-inch bbl., 7.25 inches overall. Weight: 34 oz. Made from 1984 to 1997. .40 S&W, disc.1992.
Blued finish
(disc.1996). . . . . NiB $593 Ex $490 Gd $350
Matte finish . . . . NiB $570 Ex $465 Gd $342
Satin nickel finish . . . . NiB $656 Ex $533 Gd $371
Stainless steel . . . . NiB $618 Ex $504 Gd $360

MK IV/SERIES '80
SA LIGHTWEIGHT CONCEALED
CARRY OFFICER . . . . NiB $690 Ex $553 Gd $388
Caliber: .45 ACP. Seven-round magazine, 4.25-inch bbl., 7.75 inches overall. Weight: 35 oz. Aluminum alloy receiver w/stainless slide. Dovetailed low-profile sights w/3-dot system. Matte stainless finish w/blued receiver. Wraparound black rubber grip w/finger grooves. Made in 2000.

MK IV/SERIES '90 DEFENDER
SA LIGHTWEIGHT . . . . NiB $855 Ex $535 Gd $365
Caliber: .45 ACP. Seven-round magazine, 3-inch bbl., 6.75 inches over-all. Weight: 22.5 oz. Aluminum alloy receiver w/stainless slide. Dovetailed low-profile sights w/3-dot system. Matte stainless finish w/Nickel-Teflon receiver. Wraparound black rubber grip w/finger grooves. Made since 1998.

MK IV/SERIES 90
PONY DAO PISTOL . . . . NiB $725 Ex $535 Gd $365
Caliber: .380 ACP. Six-round magazine, 2.75-inch bbl., 5.5 inches overall. Weight: 19 oz. Ramp front sight, dovetailed rear. Stainless finish. Checkered black composition grips. Made 1997 to 1998.

MK IV/SERIES 90
PONY POCKETLITE. . . . . NiB $750 Ex $545 Gd $375
Similar to standard weight Pony Model except w/aluminum frame. Brushed stainless and Teflon finish. Made from 1997 to 1999.

NATIONAL MATCH AUTOMATIC PISTOL
Identical to the Government Model .45 Auto but w/hand-honed action, match-grade bbl., adj. rear and ramp front sights or fixed sights. Made from 1932 to 1940.
W/adjustable
sights . . . . NiB $1650 Ex $1400 Gd $1169
W/fixed sights . . . . NiB $1500 Ex $1235 Gd $1040

NRA CENTENNIAL
.45 GOLD CUP
NATIONAL MATCH . . . . NiB $1295 Ex $1000 Gd $825
Only 2500 produced in 1971.

Colt MK IV/Series
'80 Mustang Plus II

Colt MK IV/Series '80
Mustang Pocketlite

Colt MK IV/Series '80
Officer's ACP

Colt Pocket Junior

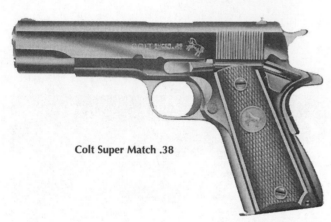

Colt Super Match .38

Colt Targetsman

**Colt Woodsman
Match Target First Issue**

POCKET JUNIOR MODEL
AUTOMATIC PISTOL . . . . **NiB $435 Ex $338 Gd $245**
Made in Spain by Unceta y Cia (Astra). Calibers: .22 Short, .25 Auto. Six-round magazine, 2.25 inch bbl., 4.75 inches overall. Weight: 12 oz. Fixed sights. Checkered walnut grips. Note: In 1980, this model was subject to recall to correct an action malfunction. Returned firearms were fitted with a rebounding firing pin to prevent accidental discharges. Made from 1958 to 1968.

SUPER .38
AUTOMATIC PISTOL
Identical to Government Model .45 Auto except for caliber and magazine capacity. Caliber: .38 Automatic. Nine-round magazine, Made from 1928 to 1970.
Pre-war . . . . **NiB $6000 Ex $4390 Gd $2780**
Post-war. . . . . **NiB $2670 Ex $2170 Gd $1990**

SUPER MATCH .38
AUTOMATIC PISTOL
Identical to Super .38 Auto but w/hand-honed action, match grade bbl., adjustable rear sight and ramp front sight or fixed sights. Made from 1933 to 1946.
W/adjustable sights . . . . **NiB $11,500 Ex $6000 Gd $3000**
W/fixed sights. . . . . **NiB $10,000 Ex $5000 Gd $2000**

TARGETSMAN . . . . **NiB $795 Ex $647 Gd $343**
Similar to Woodsman Target but has "economy" adj. rear sight, lacks automatic slide stop. Made from 1959 to 1976.

WOODSMAN MATCH TARGET
AUTOMATIC PISTOL
FIRST ISSUE. . . . . **NiB $3200 Ex $1830 Gd $999**
Same basic design as other Woodsman models. Caliber: .22 LR. 10-round magazine, 6.5-inch bbl., slightly tapered w/flat sides, 11 inches overall. Weight: 36 oz. Adjustable rear sight. Blued finish. Checkered walnut one-piece grip w/extended sides. Made from 1938 to 1942.

WOODSMAN MATCH
TARGET AUTO PISTOL,
SECOND ISSUE. . . . . **NiB $975 Ex $700 Gd $575**
Same basic design as Woodsman Target Third Issue. Caliber: .22 LR (reg. or high speed). 10-round magazine, Six-inch flat-sided heavy bbl., 10.5 inches overall. Weight: 40 oz. Click adj. rear sight, ramp front. Blued finish. Checkered plastic or walnut grips. Made from 1948 to 1976.

WOODSMAN
MATCH TARGET "4 1/2"
AUTOMATIC PISTOL. . . . . **NiB $650 Ex $400 Gd $275**
Same as Match Target second issue except w/4.5-inch bbl., 9 inches overall. Weight: 36 oz. Made from 1950 to 1976.

WOODSMAN SPORT MODEL
AUTOMATIC PISTOL,
FIRST ISSUE. . . . . **NiB $1023 Ex $840 Gd $575**
Caliber: .22 LR (reg. or high speed). Same as Woodsman Target second issue except has 4.5-inch bbl., adjustable rear sight w/fixed or adjustable front sight. Weight: 27 oz., 8.5 inches overall. Made from 1933 to 1948.

WOODSMAN SPORT
MODEL AUTOMATIC
PISTOL, SECOND ISSUE . . . . . . **NiB $1995 Ex $1355 Gd $1079**
Same as Woodsman Target third Issue but w/4.5-inch bbl., 9 inches overall. Weight: 30 oz. Made from 1948 to 1976.

WOODSMAN TARGET MODEL
AUTOMATIC, FIRST ISSUE . . . . . . **NiB $1600 Ex $750 Gd $482**
Caliber: .22 LR (reg. velocity). 10-round magazine, 6.5-inch bbl., 10.5 inches overall. Weight: 28 oz. Adjustable sights. Blued finish. Checkered walnut grips. Made 1915 to 1932. Note: The mainspring housing of this model is not strong enough to permit safe use of high-speed cartridges. Change to a new heat-treated mainspring housing was made at pistol No. 83,790. Many of the old models were converted by installation of new housings. The new housing may be distinguished from the earlier type by the checkering in the curve under the breech. The new housing is grooved straight across, while the old type bears a diagonally-checkered oval.

WOODSMAN TARGET MODEL
AUTOMATIC, SECOND ISSUE . . . . **NiB $895 Ex $595 Gd $399**
Caliber: .22 LR (reg. or high speed). Same as original model except has heavier bbl., and high-speed mainspring housing. (See note under Woodsman, First Issue). Weight: 29 oz. Made from 1932 to 1948.

WOODSMAN TARGET MODEL
AUTOMATIC, THIRD ISSUE . . . . . . **NiB $795 Ex $475 Gd $295**
Same basic design as previous Woodsman pistols but w/longer grip, magazine catch on left side, larger thumb safety, slide stop, slide stays open on last shot, magazine disconnector thumbrest grips. Caliber: .22 LR (reg. or high speed). 10-round magazine, 6-inch bbl., 10.5 inches overall. Weight: 32 oz. Click adjustable rear sight, ramp front sight. Blued finish. Checkered plastic or walnut grips. Made 1948 to 1976.

WORLD WAR I 50TH ANNIVERSARY
COMMEMORATIVE SERIES
Limited production replica of Model 1911 .45 Auto engraved w/battle scenes, commemorating Battles at Chateau Thierry, Belleau Wood Second Battle of the Marne, Meuse Argonne. In special presentation display cases. Production: 7,400 Standard model, 75 Deluxe, 25 Special Deluxe grade. Match numbered sets offered. Made 1967 to 1969. Values indicated are for commemoratives in new condition.
Standard grade . . . . **NiB $995 Ex $744 Gd $603**
Deluxe grade . . . . **NiB $2095 Ex $1686 Gd $1199**
Special Deluxe grade . . . . **NiB $4500 Ex $3719 Gd $2324**

WORLD WAR II
COMMEMORATIVE
.45 AUTO . . . . **NiB $995 Ex $723 Gd $531**
Limited production replica of Model 1911A1 .45 Auto engraved w/respective names of locations where historic engagements occurred during WW II, as well as specific issue and theater identification. European model has oak leaf motif on slide, palm leaf design frames the Pacific issue. Cased. 11,500 of each model were produced. Made in 1970. Value listed is for gun in new condition.

WORLD WAR II
50TH ANNIVERSARY
COMMEMORATIVE . . . . **NiB $2500 Ex $2220 Gd $1532**
Same general specifications as the Colt World War II Commemorative .45 Auto except slightly different scroll engraving, 24-karat gold-plate trigger, hammer, slide stop, magazine catch, magazine catch lock, safety lock and four grip screws. Made in 1995 only.

WORLD WAR II D-DAY
INVASION COMMEMORATIVE . . . . . . **NiB $1495 Ex $1375 Gd $1090**
High-luster and highly decorated version of the Colt Model 1911A1. Caliber: .45 ACP. Same general specifications as the Colt Model 1911 except for 24-karat gold-plated hammer, trigger, slide stop, magazine catch, magazine catch screw, safety lock and four grip screws. Also has scrolls and inscription on slide. Made in 1991 only.

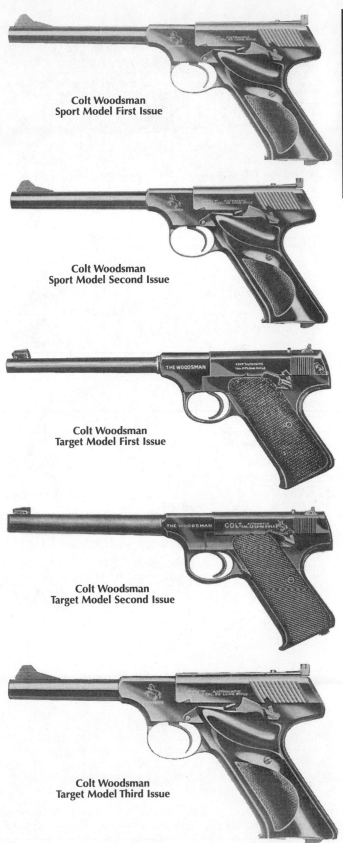

Colt Woodsman
Sport Model First Issue

Colt Woodsman
Sport Model Second Issue

Colt Woodsman
Target Model First Issue

Colt Woodsman
Target Model Second Issue

Colt Woodsman
Target Model Third Issue

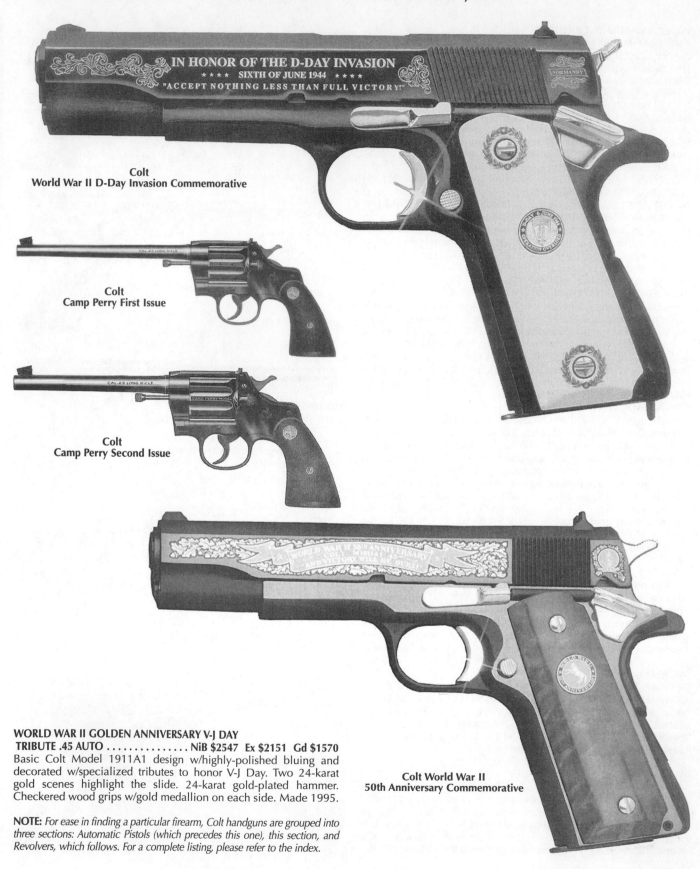

Colt
World War II D-Day Invasion Commemorative

Colt
Camp Perry First Issue

Colt
Camp Perry Second Issue

Colt World War II
50th Anniversary Commemorative

WORLD WAR II GOLDEN ANNIVERSARY V-J DAY
TRIBUTE .45 AUTO . . . . NiB $2547 Ex $2151 Gd $1570
Basic Colt Model 1911A1 design w/highly-polished bluing and decorated w/specialized tributes to honor V-J Day. Two 24-karat gold scenes highlight the slide. 24-karat gold-plated hammer. Checkered wood grips w/gold medallion on each side. Made 1995.

NOTE: *For ease in finding a particular firearm, Colt handguns are grouped into three sections: Automatic Pistols (which precedes this one), this section, and Revolvers, which follows. For a complete listing, please refer to the index.*

SINGLE-SHOT PISTOLS & DERRINGERS

CAMP PERRY MODEL SINGLE-
SHOT PISTOL, FIRST ISSUE . . NiB $1805 Ex $1478 Gd $10427
Built on Officers' Model frame. Caliber: .22 LR (embedded head
chamber for high-speed cartridges after 1930). 10 inch bbl., 13.75
inches overall. Weight: 34.5 oz. Adj. target sights. Hand-finished
action. Blued finish. Checkered walnut grips. Made 1926 to 1934.

CAMP PERRY MODEL
SECOND ISSUE . . . . NiB $1592 Ex $1302 Gd $938
Same general specifications as First Issue except has shorter hammer
fall and 8-inch bbl., 12 inches overall. Weight: 34 oz. Made from
1934 to 1941 (about 440 produced).

CIVIL WAR CENTENNIAL MODEL PISTOL
Single-shot replica of Colt Model 1860 Army Revolver. Caliber: .22 Short. Six-
inch bbl., weight: 22 oz. Blued finish w/gold-plated frame, grip frame, and trig-
ger guard, walnut grips. Cased. 24,114 were produced. Made in 1961.
Single pistol . . . . NiB $315 Ex $254 Gd $188
Pair w/consecutive serial numbers . . . . NiB $644 Ex $515 Gd $389

DERRINGER NO. 4
Replica of derringer No. 3 (1872 Thuer Model). Single-shot w/sideswing
bbl., Caliber: .22 Short, 2.5-inch bbl., 4.9 inches overall. Weight: 7.75
oz. Fixed sights. Gold-plated frame w/blued bbl., and walnut grips or
completely nickel- or gold-plated w/simulated ivory or pearl grips.
Made 1959 to 1963. 112,000 total production. (SN w/D or N suffix)
Single pistol (gun only) . . . . NiB $100 Ex $75 Gd $500
Single pistol (cased w/accessories) . . . . NiB $375 Ex $225 Gd $135

DERRINGER NO. 4 COMMEMORATIVE MODELS
Limited production version of .22 derringers issued, w/appropriate
inscription, to commemorate historical events. Additionally, non-fir-
ing models (w/unnotched bbls.) were furnished in books, picture
frames and encased in plexiglass as singles or in cased pairs.
No. 4 Presentation Derringers
(Non-firing w/accessories) . . . . NiB $375
Ltd. Ed. Book Series
(W/nickel-plated derringers) . . . . NiB $350
1st Presentation Series
(Leatherette covered metal case) . . . . NiB $375
2nd Presentation Series
(Single wooden case) . . . . NiB $175
2nd Presentation Series
(Paired wooden case) . . . . NiB $395
1961 Issue Geneseo, Illinois,
125th Anniversary (104 produced) . . . . NiB $650
1962 Issue Fort McPherson,
Nebraska, Centennial (300 produced) . . . . NiB $650

LORD AND LADY DERRINGERS (NO. 5)
Same as Derringer No. 4. Lord model with blued bbl., w/gold-plated
frame and walnut grips. Lady model is gold-plated w/simulated pearl
grips. Sold in cased pairs. Made from 1970 to 1972. (SN w/Der suffix)
Lord derringer, pair in case . . . . NiB $495 Ex $355 Gd $250
Lady derringer, pair in case . . . . NiB $495 Ex $355 Gd $250
Lord and Lady derringers,
one each, in case . . . . NiB $495 Ex $355 Gd $250

ROCK ISLAND ARSENAL
CENTENNIAL PISTOL . . . . NiB $466 Ex $391 Gd $274
Limited production (550 pieces) version of Civil War Centennial
Model single-shot .22 pistol, made exclusively for Cherry's Sporting
Goods, Geneseo, Illinois, to commemorate the centennial of the
Rock Island Arsenal in Illinois. Cased. Made in 1962.

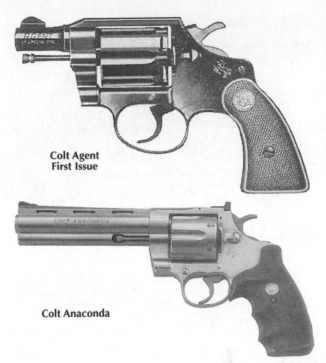

Colt Agent
First Issue

Colt Anaconda

NOTE: *This section of Colt handguns contains only revolvers. For
automatic pistols or single-shot pistols and derringers, please see the
two sections that precede this. For a complete listing, please refer to
the Index.*

REVOLVERS

.38 DS II REVOLVER . . . . NiB $496 Ex $399 Gd $278
Caliber: .38 Special. Six-round cylinder, 2-inch bbl., 7 inches
overall. Weight: 21 oz. Ramp front sight, fixed notch rear. Satin
stainless finish. Black rubber combat grip w/finger grooves. Made
from 1997 to 1998.

AGENT DA REVOLVER,
FIRST ISSUE. . . . . NiB $511 Ex $449 Gd $289
Same as Cobra, first issue except has short-grip frame .38 Special
only, weight: 14 oz. Made from 1955 to 1972.

AGENT (LW) DA REVOLVER,
SECOND ISSUE . . . . NiB $471 Ex $438 Gd $258
Same as Colt Agent, first issue except has shrouded ejector rod and
alloy frame. Made from 1973 to 1986.

ANACONDA DA REVOLVER
Calibers: .44 Mag., .45 Colt., bbl. lengths: 4, 6 or 8 inches; 11.63
inches overall (with 6-inch bbl.). Weight: 53 oz. (6-inch bbl.). Adj.
white outline rear sight, red insert ramp-style front. Matte stainless
or Realtree gray camo finish. Black Neoprene combat grips w/finger
grooves. Made 1990 to 1999 and 2002 to 2006.
Matte stainless . . . . NiB $1050 Ex $680 Gd $450
Realtree gray camo
finish (disc. 1996) . . . . NiB $1595 Ex $1275 Gd $1100
Custom model
(.44 Mag. w/ported bbl.) . . . . NiB $1150 Ex $975 Gd $695
First Edition model
(Ltd. Edition 1000) . . . . NiB $1050 Ex $872 Gd $498
Hunter model
(.44 Mag. w/2x scope) . . . . NiB $1595 Ex $1325 Gd $1095

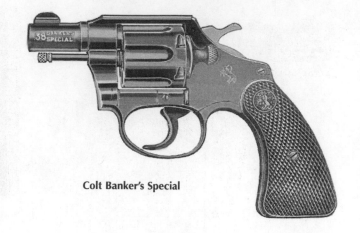

Colt Banker's Special

Colt Bisley

Colt Buntline Special .45

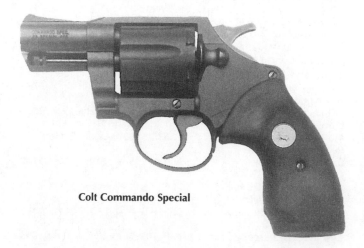

Colt Commando Special

ANACONDA TITANIUM DA REVOLVER
Same general specifications as the standard Anaconda except chambered .44 Mag. only w/titanium-plated finish, gold-plated trigger, hammer and cylinder release. Limited edition of 1,000 distributed by American Historical Foundation w/personalized inscription. Made in 1996.
One of 1000 . . . . NiB $2655 Ex $2130 Gd $1480
Presentation case, add $200

ARMY SPECIAL DA REVOLVER . . . . . . NiB $950 Ex $741 Gd $495
.41-caliber frame. Calibers: .32-20, .38 Special (.41 Colt). Six-round cylinder, right revolution. Bbl., lengths: 4-, 4.5, 5-, and 6-inches, 9.25 inches overall (4-inch bbl.). Weight: 32 oz. (4-inch bbl.). Fixed sights. Blued or nickel-plated finish. Hard rubber grips. Made 1908-27. Note: This model has a somewhat heavier frame than the New Navy, which it replaced. Serial numbers begin w/300,000. The heavy .38 Special High velocity loads should not be used in .38 Special arms of this model.

BANKER'S SPECIAL DA REVOLVER
This is the Police Positive w/a 2-inch bbl., otherwise specifications same as that model, rounded butt intro. in 1933. Calibers: .22 LR (embedded head-cylinder for high speed cartridges intro. 1933), .38 New Police. 6.5 inches overall. Weight: 23 oz. (.22 LR), 19 oz. (.38). Made from 1926 to 1940.
.38 caliber . . . . NiB $1500 Ex $1295 Gd $1050
.22 caliber . . . . NiB $2500 Ex $2275 Gd $2050

BISLEY MODEL SA REVOLVER
Variation of the Single-Action Army, developed for target shooting w/modified grips, trigger and hammer. Calibers: General specifications same as SA Army. Target Model made w/flat-topped frame and target sights. Made 1894 to 1915.
Standard model . . . . NiB $8365 Ex $6732 Gd $4637
Target model (flat-top) . . . . . . NiB $12,151 Ex $9955 Gd $6867

BUNTLINE SPECIAL .45 . . . . NiB $1395 Ex $1095 Gd $775
Same as standard SA Army except has 12-inch bbl., caliber .45 Long Colt. Made from 1957 to 1975.

COBRA DA REVOLVER,
ROUND BUTT, FIRST ISSUE . . . . . . NiB $562 Ex $448 Gd $329
Lightweight Detective Special w/same general specifications as that model except w/Colt-alloy frame. Two-inch bbl., calibers: .38 Special, .38 New Police, .32 New Police. Weight: 15 oz., (.38 cal.). Blued finish. Checkered plastic or walnut grips. Made 1951 to 1973.

COBRA DA REVOLVER,
SECOND ISSUE . . . . NiB $600 Ex $535 Gd $345
Lightweight version of Detective Special, Second Issue has aluminum alloy frame. 16.5 oz. Made from 1973-81.

COBRA DA REVOLVER
SQUARE BUTT . . . . NiB $496 Ex $392 Gd $262
Lightweight Police Positive Special w/same general specifications except has Colt-alloy frame, 4-inch bbl., Calibers: .38 Special, .38 New Police, .32 New Police. Weight: 17 oz. in .38 caliber. Blued finish. Checkered plastic or walnut grips. Made from 1951-73.

COMMANDO SPECIAL
DA REVOLVER . . . . NiB $518 Ex $399 Gd $298
Caliber: .38 Special. Six-round cylinder, 2-inch bbl., 6.88 inches overall. Weight: 21.5 oz. Fixed sights. Low-luster blued finish. Made from 1982-86.

DETECTIVE SPECIAL DA REVOLVER, FIRST ISSUE
Similar to Police Positive Special w/2-inch bbl., otherwise specifications same as that model, rounded butt intro. 1933. .38 Special only in pre-war issue. Blued or nickel-plated finish. Weight: 17 oz. 6.75 inches overall. Made 1926-46.
Blued finish . . . . NiB $500 Ex $435 Gd $321
Nickel finish . . . . NiB $975 Ex $765 Gd $576

**Colt Cobra
Round Butt First Issue**

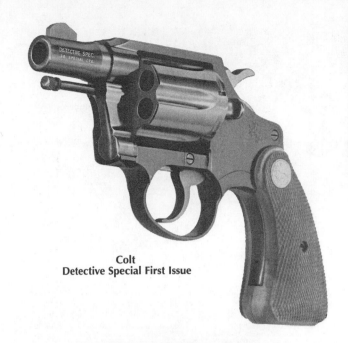

**Colt
Detective Special First Issue**

DETECTIVE SPECIAL DA REVOLVER, 2ND ISSUE

Similar to Detective special first issue except w/2- or 3-inch bbl., and also chambered .32 New Police, .38 New Police. Wood, plastic or over-sized grips. Made from 1947 to 1972.

Blued finish	NiB $527	Ex $425	Gd $309
Nickel finish	NiB $595	Ex $472	Gd $329
W/three-inch bbl., add	. . . . $95		

DETECTIVE SPECIAL DA REVOLVER, 3RD ISSUE

"D" frame, shrouded ejector rod. Caliber: .38 Special. Six-round cylinder, 2-inch bbl., 6.88 inches overall. Weight: 21.5 oz. Fixed rear sight, ramp front. Blued or nickel-plated finish. Checkered walnut wraparound grips. Made from 1973 to 1984.

Blued finish	NiB $530	Ex $414	Gd $310
Nickel finish	NiB $548	Ex $435	Gd $315
W/three-inch bbl., add	. . . . $75		

DETECTIVE SPECIAL DA REVOLVER, 4TH ISSUE

Similar to Detective Special, Third Issue except w/alloy frame. Blued or chrome finish. Wraparound black neoprene grips w/Colt medallion. Made from 1993 to 1995.

Blued finish	NiB $450	Ex $320	Gd $280
Chrome finish	NiB $479	Ex $350	Gd $315
DAO model (bobbed hammer)	NiB $595	Ex $435	Gd $315

**Colt
Detective Special Second Issue**

DIAMONDBACK DA REVOLVER

"D" frame, shrouded ejector rod. Calibers: .22 LR, .22 WRF, .38 Special. Six-round cylinder, 2.5-, 4- or 6-inch bbl., w/vent rib, 9 inches overall (with 4-inch bbl). Weight: 31.75 oz. (.22 cal., 4-inch bbl.), 28.5 oz. (.38 cal.). Ramp front sight, adj. rear. Blued or nickel finish. Checkered walnut grips. Made from 1966 to 1984.

Blued finish	NiB $1260	Ex $1048	Gd $766
Nickel finish	NiB $1495	Ex $1250	Gd $955
.22 Mag. model	NiB $2000	Ex $1859	Gd $1695
W/2.5-inch bbl., add	. . . . $75		

DA ARMY (1878) REVOLVER. . . . NiB $5900 Ex $4375 Gd $3000

Also called DA Frontier. Similar in appearance to the smaller Lightning Model but has heavier frame of different shape, round disc on left side of frame, lanyard loop in butt. Calibers: .38-40, .44-40, .45 Colt. Six-round cylinder, bbl. lengths: 3.5- and 4-inches (w/o ejector), 4.75-, 5.5- and 7.5-inches w/ejector. 12.5 inches overall (7.5-inch bbl.). Weight: 39 oz. (.45 cal., 7.5-inch bbl.). Fixed sights. Hard rubber bird's-head grips. Blued or nickel finish. Made from 1878 to 1905.

**Colt
Diamondback**

Colt Lightning/Thunderer
1877-1912

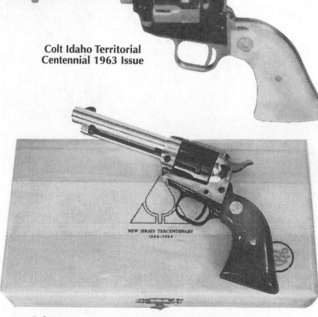

Colt Idaho Territorial
Centennial 1963 Issue

Colt New Jersey Tercentenary — 1964 issue

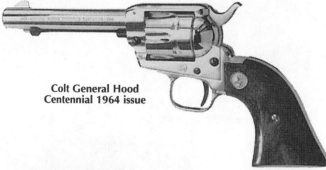

Colt General Hood
Centennial 1964 issue

FRONTIER SCOUT REVOLVER

SA Army replica, scale. Calibers: .22 Short, Long, LR or .22 WMR (interchangeable cylinder available). Six-round cylinder, 4.75-inch bbl., 9.9 inches overall. Weight: 24 oz. Fixed sights. Plastic grips. Originally made w/bright alloy frame. Since 1959 w/steel frame and blued finish or all-nickel finish w/composition, wood or Staglite grips. Made 1958 to 1971.

Blued finish, plastic grips. . . . . NiB $414 Ex $337 Gd $233
Nickel finish, wood grips. . . . . NiB $462 Ex $384 Gd $264
Buntline model, add $60
Extra interchangeable
cylinder, add $75

FRONTIER SCOUT REVOLVER COMMEMORATIVE MODELS

Limited production versions of Frontier Scout issued, w/appropriate inscription, to commemorate historical events. Cased, in new condition.

1961 ISSUES
Kansas Statehood Centennial
(6201 produced) . . . . NiB $495
Pony Express Centennial
(1007 produced) . . . . NiB $595
1962 ISSUES
Columbus, Ohio, Sesquicentennial
(200 produced) . . . . NiB $595
Fort Findlay, Ohio, Sesqui-
centennial (130 produced) . . . . NiB $855
Fort Findlay Cased Pair, .22 Long
Rifle and .22 Magnum (20 produced) . . . . NiB $2500
New Mexico Golden Anniversary . . . . NiB $595
West Virginia Statehood
Centennial (3452 produced) . . . . NiB $5957

1963 ISSUES
Arizona Territorial Centennial
(5355 produced) . . . . NiB $595
Battle of Gettysburg Centennial
(1019 produced) . . . . NiB $595
Carolina Charter Tercentenary
(300 produced) . . . . NiB $2195
Fort Stephenson, Ohio, Sesquicentennial
(200 produced) . . . . NiB $595
General John Hunt Morgan Indiana Raid . . . . NiB $650
Idaho Territorial Centennial (902 produced) . . . . NiB $595

1964 ISSUES
California Gold Rush
(500 produced) . . . . NiB $595
Chamizal Treaty (450 produced) . . . . NiB $595
General Hood Centennial
(1503 produced) . . . . NiB $595
Montana Territorial Centennial
(2300 produced) . . . . NiB $595
Nevada "Battle Born"
(981 produced) . . . . NiB $522
Nevada Statehood Centennial
(3984 produced) . . . . NiB $2595
New Jersey Tercentenary
(1001 produced) . . . . NiB $495
St. Louis Bicentennial
(802 produced) . . . . NiB $495
Wyoming Diamond Jubilee
(2357 produced) . . . . NiB $595
1965 ISSUES
Appomattox Centennial
(1001 produced) . . . . NiB $495
Forty-Niner Miner
(500 produced) . . . . NiB $595
General Meade Campaign
(1197 produced) . . . . NiB $1595
Kansas Cowtown Series—Wichita
500 produced) . . . . NiB $495
Old Fort Des Moines Reconstruction
(700 produced) . . . . NiB $2195
Oregon Trail (1995 produced) . . . . NiB $595
St. Augustine Quadricentennial
(500 produced) . . . . NiB $595

1966 ISSUES
Colorado Gold Rush
(1350 produced) .... NiB $595
Dakota Territory (1000 produced) .... NiB $595
Indiana Sesquicentennial
(1500 produced) .... NiB $595
Kansas Cowtown Series—Abilene
(500 produced) .... NiB $495
Kansas Cowtown Series—Dodge City
(500 produced) .... NiB $495
Oklahoma
Jubilee (1343 produced) .... NiB $595

1967 ISSUES
Alamo (4500 produced) .... NiB $495
Kansas Cowtown Series—Coffeyville
(500 produced)........................... NiB $507
Kansas Trail Series—Chisholm
Trail (500 produced)....................... NiB $517
Lawman Series—
Bat Masterson (3000 produced)................ NiB $528

1968 ISSUES
Kansas Cowtown Series—Santa Fe Trail
(501 produced)........................... NiB $495
Kansas Trail Series—Pawnee Trail
(501 produced)........................... NiB $495
Lawman Series—Pat Garrett
(3000 produced).......................... NiB $595
Nebraska Centennial
(7001 produced).......................... NiB $495

1969 ISSUES
Alabama Sesquicentennial
(3001 produced) .... NiB $495
Arkansas Territory Sesquicentennial
(3500 produced) .... NiB $497
California Bicentennial (5000 produced)............ NiB $481
General Nathan Bedford Forrest
(3000 produced) .... NiB $495
Golden Spike (11,000 produced)................. NiB $495
Kansas Trail Series—Shawnee Trail
(501 produced) .... NiB $495
Lawman Series—Wild Bill Hickock
(3000 produced) .... NiB $595

1970 ISSUES
Kansas Fort Series—Fort Larned
(500 produced) .... NiB $495
Kansas Fort Series—Fort Hays
(500 produced) .... NiB $495
Kansas Fort Series—Fort Riley
(500 produced)........................... NiB $495
Lawman Series—Wyatt Earp
(3000 produced) .... NiB $695
Maine Sesquicentennial
(3000 produced).......................... NiB $495
Missouri Sesquicentennial (3000 produced) .... NiB $495

1971 ISSUES
Kansas Fort Series—Fort Scott (500 produced) .... NiB $495

1972 ISSUES
Florida Territory Sesquicentennial (2001 produced) ... NiB $595
1973 ISSUES Arizona ranger
(3001 produced) .... NiB $595

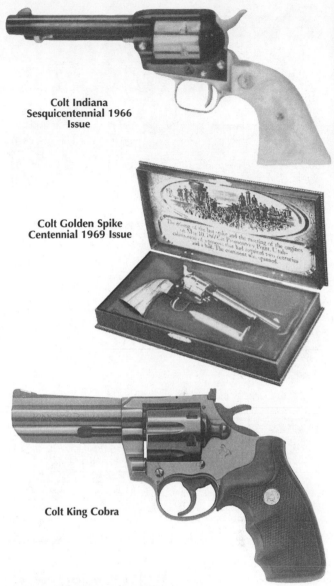

Colt Indiana
Sesquicentennial 1966
Issue

Colt Golden Spike
Centennial 1969 Issue

Colt King Cobra

COLT KING COBRA REVOLVER
Caliber: .357 Mag., bbl. lengths: 2.5-, 4-, 6- or 8-inches, 9 inches overall (with 4-inch bbl.). Weight: 42 oz., average. Matte stainless steel finish. Black Neoprene combat grips. Made 1986 to date. 2.5-inch bbl. and "Ultimate" bright or blued finish. Made from 1988 to 1992.
Matte stainless................. NiB $625   Ex $412   Gd $299
Ultimate bright stainless .... NiB $700   Ex $439   Gd $322
Blued........................ NiB $550   Ex $434   Gd $278

LAWMAN MK III
DA REVOLVER
"J" frame, shrouded ejector rod on 2-inch bbl., only. Caliber: .357 Magnum. Six-round cylinder, bbl. lengths: 2-, 4-inch. 9.38 inches overall (w/4-inch bbl.), Weight: (with 4-inch bbl.), 35 oz. Fixed rear sight, ramp front. Service trigger and hammer or target trigger and wide-spur hammer. Blued or nickel-plated finish. Checkered walnut service or target grips. Made from 1969 to 1982.
Blued finish .... NiB $455   Ex $371   Gd $231
Nickel finish .... NiB $505   Ex $387   Gd $247

**Colt Lawman
MK V**

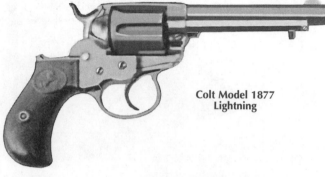

**Colt Model 1877
Lightning**

Colt New Navy

LAWMAN MK V DA REVOLVER
Similar to Trooper MK V. Caliber: .357 Mag. Six-round cylinder, 2- or 4-inch bbl., 9.38 inches overall (4-inch bbl.). Weight: 35 oz. (4-inch bbl.). Fixed sights. Checkered walnut grips. Made 1984 and 1991.
Blued finish . . . . NiB $324 Ex $276 Gd $194
Nickel finish . . . . NiB $355 Ex $289 Gd $206

MAGNUM CARRY DA REVOLVER . . . . NiB $461 Ex $348 Gd $279
Similar to Model DS II except chambered for .357 Magnum. Made from 1998 to date.

MARINE CORPS MODEL (1905) DA REVOLVER
General specifications same as New Navy Second Issue except has round butt, was supplied only in .38 caliber (.38 Short & Long Colt, .38 Special) w/6-inch bbl. (SN range 10,001-10,926) Made 1905 to 1909.
Marine Corps model . . . . . NiB $15,000 Ex $13,750 Gd $12,975
Marked "USMC" . . . . NiB $7500 Ex $5475 Gd $3750

METROPOLITAN MK
III DA REVOLVER . . . . NiB $495 Ex $393 Gd $288
Same as Official Police MK III except has 4-inch bbl. w/service or target grips. Weight: 36 oz. Made from 1969 to 1972.

MODEL 1877
LIGHTNING REVOLVER . . . . . . NiB $4000 Ex $3175 Gd $2895
Also called Thunderer Model. Calibers: .38 and .41 centerfire. Six-round cylinder, bbl. lengths: 2.5-, 3.5-, 4.5- and 6-inch without ejector, 4.5- and 6-inch w/ejector, 8.5 inches overall (3.5-inch bbl.). Weight: 23 oz. (.38 cal., with 3.5-inch bbl.) Fixed sights. Blued or nickel finish. Hard rubber bird's-head grips. Made 1877 to 1909.

NEW FRONTIER BUNTLINE SPECIAL
Same as New Frontier SA Army except has 12-inch bbl.,
Second generation (1962-75) . . NiB $2492 Ex $1933 Gd $1302
Third generation (1976-92) . . . . . . NiB $1070 Ex $956 Gd $681

NEW FRONTIER SA ARMY REVOLVER
Same as SA Army except has flat-top frame, adj. target rear sight, ramp front sight, smooth walnut grips. 5.5- or 7.5-inch bbl., Calibers: .357 Magnum, .44 Special, .45 Colt. Made 1961 to 1992.
Second generation (1961-75) . . NiB $2800 Ex $2550 Gd $2360
Third generation (1976-92) . . . . . NiB $1299 Ex $1061 Gd $801

NEW FRONTIER SA .22 REVOLVER . . . . . . NiB $495 Ex $310 Gd $196
Same as Peacemaker .22 except has flat-top frame, adj. rear sight, ramp front sight. Made from 1971-76; reintro. 1982 to 1986.

NEW NAVY (1889) DA, FIRST ISSUE
Also called New Army. Calibers: .38 Short & Long Colt, .41 Short & Long Colt. Six-round cylinder, left revolution. Bbl. lengths: 3-, 4.5- and 6-inches, 11.25 inches overall (with 6-inch bbl.). Weight: 32 oz. with 6-inch bbl. Fixed sights, knife-blade and V-notch. Blued or nickel-plated finish. Walnut or hard rubber grips. Made 1889 to 1994. Note: This model, which was adopted by both the Army and Navy, was Colt's first revolver of the solid frame, swing-out cylinder type. It lacks the cylinder-locking notches found on later models made on this .41 frame; ratchet on the back of the cylinder is held in place by a double projection on the hand.
First issue. . . . . NiB $1928 Ex $1575 Gd $1111
First issue w/3-inch bbl. . . . . . . NiB $2691 Ex $2183 Gd $1534
Navy contract, marked
"U.S.N.(SN 1-1500) . . . . NiB $3545 Ex $2870 Gd $2007

NEW NAVY (1892) DA, SECOND ISSUE
Also called New Army. General specifications same as First Issue except has double cylinder notches and double locking bolt. Calibers: .38 Special added in 1904 and .32-20 in 1905. Made 1892 to 1907. Note: The heavy .38 Special High Velocity loads should not be used in .38 Special arms of this model.
Second issue . . . . NiB $1686 Ex $1385 Gd $978
Second issue w/3-inch bbl. . . . . . NiB $2444 Ex $1988 Gd $1406
Navy contract, marked "U.S.N" . . . . . . NiB $2766 Ex $2247 Gd $1583

NEW POCKET DA REVOLVER . . . . NiB $720 Ex $591 Gd $426
Caliber: .32 Short & Long Colt. Six-round cylinder. bbl. lengths: 2.5, 3.5- and 6-inches. 7.5 inches overall w/3.5-inch bbl., Weight: 16 oz., with 3.5-inch bbl. Fixed sights, knife-blade and V-notch. Blued or nickel finish. Rubber grips. Made from 1893 to 1905.

NEW POLICE DA REVOLVER . . . . . NiB $950 Ex $559 Gd $387
Built on New Pocket frame but w/larger grip. Calibers: .32 Colt New Police, .32 Short & Long Colt. Bbl. lengths: 2.5-, 4- and 6-inches, 8.5 inches overall (with 4-inch bbl.). Weight: 17 oz., with 4-inch bbl. Fixed knife-blade front sight, V-notch rear. Blued or nickel finish. Rubber grips. Made from 1896 to 1905.

NEW POLICE TARGET DA REVOLVER . . . . . NiB $1200 Ex $1060 Gd $840
Target version of the New Police w/same general specifications. Target sights. Six-inch bbl., blued finish only. Made 1896 to 1905.

NEW SERVICE DA REVOLVER

Calibers: .38 Special, .357 Magnum (intro. 1936), .38-40, .44-40, .44 Russian, .44 Special, .45 Auto, .45 Colt, .450 Eley, .455 Eley, .476 Eley. Six-round cylinder, bbl. lengths: 4-, 5- and 6-inch in .38 Special and .357 Magnum, 4.5-, 5.5- and 7.5 inches in other calibers; 9.75 inches overall (with 4.5-inch bbl.). Weight: 39 oz. (.45 cal. with 4.5-inch bbl.). Fixed sights. Blued or nickel finish. Checkered walnut grips. Made 1898-42. Note: More than 500,000 of this model in caliber .45 Auto (designated "Model 1917 Revolver") were purchased by the U.S. Gov't. during WW I. These arms were later sold as surplus to National Rifle Association members through the Director of Civilian Marksmanship. Price was $16.15 plus packing charge. Supply exhausted during the early 1930s.

Commercial model	NiB $1790	Ex $1453	Gd $1022
Magnum	NiB $1178	Ex $964	Gd $689
1917 Army	NiB $1140	Ex $643	Gd $669

NEW SERVICE TARGET . . . . NiB $1280 Ex $1141 Gd $730

Target version of the New Service. Calibers: Originally chambered for .44 Russian, .450 Eley, .455 Eley and .476 Eley, later models in .44 Special, .45 Colt and .45 Auto. Six- or 7.5-inch bbl., 12.75 inches overall (7.5-inch bbl.). Adj. target sights. Hand-finished action. With blued finish. Checkered walnut grips. Made 1900 to 1940.

OFFICERS' MODEL MATCH . . . . . . NiB $806 Ex $676 Gd $390

Same general design as Officers' Model revolvers. Has tapered heavy bbl., wide hammer spur, Adjustable rear sight ramp front sight, large target grips of checkered walnut. Calibers: .22 LR, .38 Special. Six-inch bbl., 11.25 inches overall. Weight: 43 oz. (in .22 cal.), 39 oz. (.38 cal.). Blued finish. Made from 1953 to 1970.

OFFICERS' MODEL SPECIAL . . . . . . NiB $852 Ex $592 Gd $384

Target version of Officers' Model Second Issue w/similar characters except w/heavier, nontapered bbl. redesigned hammer. Ramp front sight, Colt Officers' Model Special "Coltmaster" rear sight adj. for windage and elevation. Calibers: .22 LR, .38 Special. Six-inch bbl. 11.25 inches overall. Weight: 39 oz. (in .38 cal.), 43 oz., (.22 cal.). Blued finish. Checkered plastic grips. Made from 1949 to 1953.

OFFICERS' MODEL TARGET DA
REVOLVER, FIRST ISSUE . . . . NiB $1291 Ex $1051 Gd $745

Caliber: .38 Special. Six-inch bbl., hand-finished action, adj. target sights. Checkered with walnut grips. General specifications same as New Navy, Second Issue. Made from 1904 to 1908.

OFFICERS' MODEL TARGET, SECOND ISSUE

Calibers: .22 LR (intro. 1930, embedded head-cylinder for high-speed cartridges after 1932), .32 Police Positive (made 1932-1942), .38 Special. Six-round cylinder, bbl. lengths: 4-, 4.5-, 5-, 6- and 7.5-inch (in .38 Special) or 6-inch only (.22 LR and .32 PP), 11.25 inches overall (6-inch bbl. in .38 Special). Adj. target sights. Blued finish. Checkered walnut grips. Hand-finished action. General features same as Army Special and Official Police of same date. Made from 1908 to 1949 (w/exceptions noted).

Second issue (.38 caliber)	NiB $1084	Ex $876	Gd $621
Second issue (.32 caliber)	NiB $1676	Ex $1358	Gd $940
Second issue (.22 caliber)	NiB $1186	Ex $964	Gd $681
W/shorter bbls. (4-, 4.5- or 5-inches), add			40%

OFFICIAL POLICE DA REVOLVER

Calibers: .22 LR (intro. 1930, embedded head-cylinder for high-speed cartridges after 1932), .32-20 (disc. 1942), .38 Special, .41 Long Colt (disc. 1930). Six-round cylinder, bbl. lengths: 4-, 5-, 6-inch or 2-inch and 6-inch heavy bbl. in .38 Special only; .22 LR w/4- and 6-inch bbls. only; 11.25 inches overall. Weight: 36 oz. (standard 6-inch bbl.) in .38 Special. Fixed sights. Blued or nickel-plated finish. Checkered walnut grips on all revolvers of this model except some of postwar production had checkered plastic grips. Made 1927-69. Note: This model is a refined version of the Army Special, which it replaced in 1928 at about serial number 520,000. The Commando .38 Special was a wartime adaptation of the Official Police made to government specifications. Commando can be identified by its sandblasted blued finish. Serial numbers start w/number 1-50,000 (Made 1942 to 1945).

Commercial model (pre-war)	NiB $592	Ex $488	Gd $355
Commercial model (post-war)	NiB $528	Ex $436	Gd $320
Commando model	NiB $624	Ex $514	Gd $373

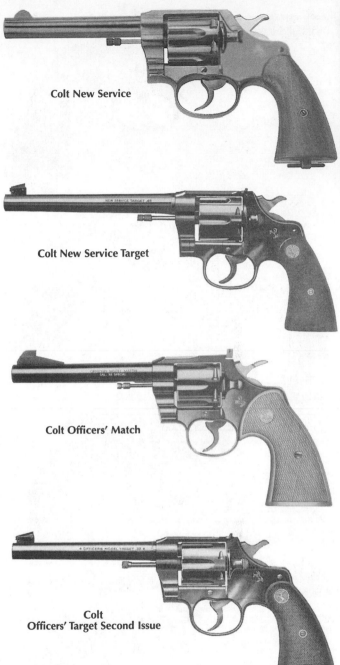

Colt New Service

Colt New Service Target

Colt Officers' Match

Colt
Officers' Target Second Issue

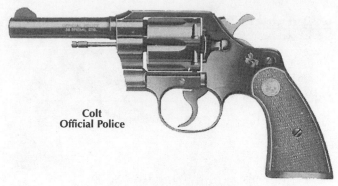

**Colt
Official Police**

**Colt
Peacekeeper**

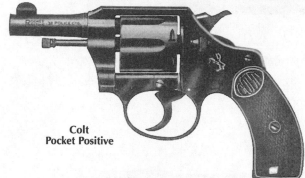

**Colt
Pocket Positive**

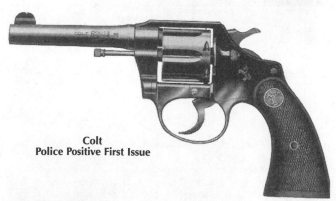

**Colt
Police Positive First Issue**

OFFICIAL POLICE MK III DA REVOLVER . . . . NiB $296 Ex $244 Gd $186

"J" frame, without shrouded ejector rod. Caliber: .38 Special. Six-round cylinder. bbl., lengths: 4-, 5-, 6-inches, 9.25 inches overall w/4-inch bbl., weight: 34 oz. (4-inch bbl.). Fixed rear sight, ramp front. Service trigger and hammer or target trigger and wide-spur hammer. Blued or nickel-plated finish. Checkered walnut service grips. Made 1969 to 1975.

PEACEKEEPER DA REVOLVER . . . . . NiB $464 Ex $391 Gd $199

Caliber: .357 Mag. Six-round cylinder, 4- or 6-inch bbl., 11.25 inches overall (6-inch bbl.). Weight: 46 oz. (with 6-inch bbl.). Adj. white outline rear sight, red insert ramp-style front. Non-reflective matte blued finish. Made from 1985 to 1989.

PEACEMAKER .22 SECOND AMENDMENT COMMEMORATIVE. . . . . NiB $625 Ex $521 Gd $261

Caliber: .22, revolver w/7.5-inch bbl., nickel-plated frame, bbl. ejector rod assembly, hammer and trigger, blued cylinder, backstrap and trigger guard. Black pearlite grips. bbl., inscribed "The Right to Keep and Bear Arms." Presentation case. Limited edition of 3000 issued in 1977. Top value is for revolver in new condition.

PEACEMAKER .22 SA REVOLVER . . NiB $415 Ex $311 Gd $259

Calibers: .22 LR and .22 WMR. Furnished w/cylinder for each caliber, 6-round. Bbl.: 4.38-, 6- or 7.5-inches, 11.25 inches overall (with 6-inch bbl.). Weight: 30.5 oz. (with 6-inch bbl.). Fixed sights. Black composite grips. Made from 1971 to 1976.

POCKET POSITIVE DA REVOLVER. . . . . NiB $601 Ex $539 Gd $367

General specifications same as New Pocket except this model has positive lock feature (see Police Positive). Calibers: .32 Short & Long Colt (disc. 1914), .32 Colt New Police (.32 S&W Short & Long). Fixed sights, flat top and square notch. Blue or nickel finish. Made from 1905 to 1940.

Blue finish . . . . NiB $569 Ex $466 Gd $335
Nickel finish . . . . NiB $673 Ex $549 Gd $401

POLICE POSITIVE DA, FIRST ISSUE

Improved version of the New Police w/the "Positive Lock," which prevents the firing pin coming in contact w/the cartridge except when the trigger is pulled. Calibers: .32 Short & Long Colt (disc. 1915), .32 Colt New Police (.32 S&W Short & Long), .38 New Police (.38 S&W). Six-round cylinder, bbl. lengths: 2.5- (.32 cal. only), 4- 5- and 6-inches; 8.5 inches overall (with 4-inch bbl.). Weight 20 oz. (with 4-inch bbl.). Fixed sights. Blued or nickel finish. Rubber or checkered walnut grips. Made from 1905 to 1947.

Blue finish . . . . NiB $506 Ex $414 Gd $298
Nickel finish . . . . NiB $570 Ex $466 Gd $333

POLICE POSITIVE DA, SECOND ISSUE

Same as Detective Special second issue except has 4-inch bbl., 9 inches overall, weight: 26.5 oz. Intro. in 1977. Note: Original Police Positive (First Issue) has a shorter frame, is not chambered for .38 Special.

Blue finish . . . . NiB $490 Ex $402 Gd $288
Nickel finish . . . . NiB $562 Ex $459 Gd $328

POLICE POSITIVE SPECIAL DA REVOLVER . . . . NiB $562 Ex $459 Gd $328

Based on the Police Positive w/frame lengthened to permit longer cylinder. Calibers: .32-20 (disc. 1942), .38 Special, .32 New Police and .38 New Police (intro. 1946). Six-round cylinder; bbl. lengths: 4-(only length in current production), 5- and 6-inch; 8.75 inches overall (with 4-inch bbl.). Weight: 23 oz. (with 4-inch bbl. in .38 Special). Fixed sights. Checkered grips of hard rubber, plastic or walnut. Made 1907 to 1973.

COLT POLICE POSITIVE TARGET DA REVOLVER. . . . . NiB $850 Ex $695 Gd $497

Target version of the Police Positive. Calibers: .22 LR (intro. 1910, embedded-head cylinder for high-speed cartridges after 1932), .22 WRF (1910-35), .32 Short & Long Colt, (1915), .32 New Police (.32 S&W Short & Long). Six-inch bbl., blued finish only, 10.5 inches overall. Weight: 26 oz. in .22 cal. Adj. target sights. Checkered walnut grips. Made from 1905 to 1940.

PYTHON DA REVOLVER

"I" frame, shrouded ejector rod. Calibers: .357 Magnum, .38 Special. Six-round cylinder, 2.5-, 4-, 6- or 8-inch vent rib bbl., 11.25 inches overall (with 6-inch bbl.). Weight: 44 oz. (6-inch bbl.). Adj. rear sight, ramp front. Blued, nickel or stainless finish. Checkered walnut target grips. Made from 1955 to 1996. Ultimate stainless finish made in 1985.

Blued finish	NiB $1200	Ex $887	Gd $395
Royal blued finish	NiB $1200	Ex $887	Gd $393
Nickel finish	NiB $1200	Ex $887	Gd $395
Stainless finish	NiB $1250	Ex $900	Gd $435
Ultimate stainless finish	NiB $1300	Ex $975	Gd $550
Hunter model (w/2x scope)	NiB $1800	Ex $1413	Gd $867
Silhouette model (w/2x scope)	NiB $2110	Ex $1768	Gd $1019

SHOOTING MASTER DA REVOLVER

Deluxe target arm based on the New Service model. Calibers: Originally made only in .38 Special, .44 Special, .45 Auto and .45 Colt added in 1933, .357 Magnum in 1936. Six-inch bbl., 11.25 inches overall. Weight: 44 oz., in (.38 cal.), adj. target sights. Hand-finished action. Blued finish. Checkered walnut grips. Rounded butt. Made from 1932 to 1941.

Shooting Master .38 Special	NiB $1441	Ex $1285	Gd $869
Shooting Master .357 Mag.	NiB $1488	Ex $1212	Gd $858
Shooting Master .44 Special, .45 ACP, .45LC	NiB $3970	Ex $3658	Gd $2202

SA ARMY REVOLVER

Also called Frontier Six-Shooter and Peacemaker. Available in more than 30 calibers including: .22 Rimfire (Short, Long, LR), .22 WRF, .32 Rimfire, .32 Colt, .32 S&W, .32-20, .38 Colt, .38 S&W, .38 Special, .357 Magnum, .38-40, .41 Colt, .44 Rimfire, .44 Russian, .44 Special, .44-40, .45 Colt, .45 Auto, .450 Boxer, 450 Eley, .455 Eley, .476 Eley. Six-round cylinder. Bbl. lengths: 4.75, 5 .5 and 7.5 inches w/ejector or 3 and 4 inches w/o ejector. 10.25 inches overall (with 4.75-inch bbl.). Weight: 36 oz. (.45 cal. w/4.75-inch bbl.). Fixed sights. Also made in Target Model w/flat top-strap and target sights. Blued finish w/casehardened frame or nickel-plated. One-piece smooth walnut or checkered black rubber grips. Note: S.A. Army Revolvers w/serial numbers above 165,000 (circa 1896) are adapted to smokeless powder and cylinder pin screw was changed to spring catch at about the same time. The "First Generation" of SA Colts included both blackpowder and smokeless configurations and were manufactured from 1873 to 1940. Production resumed in 1955 w/serial number 1001SA and continued through 1975 to complete the second series, which is referred to as the "Second Generation." In 1976, the "Third Generation" of production began and continues to to date. However, several serial number rollovers occurred at 99,999. For example, in 1978 the "SA" suffix became an "SA" prefix and again in 1993, when the serial number SA99,999 was reached, the serialization format was changed again to include both an "S" prefix and an "A" suffix. Although the term "Fourth Generation" is frequently associated with this rollover, no series change actually occurred, therefore, the current production is still a "Third Generation" series. Current calibers: .357 Magnum, .44 Special, .45 Long Colt.

Pinched frame (1873 only)	NiB $82,656	Ex $66,132	Gd $44,983

Colt SA Army

Colt Police Positive Target

Colt Python

Early commercial (1873-77)	NiB $42,576	Ex $34,060	Gd $23,161
Early military (1873-77)	NiB $48,750	Ex $39,000	Gd $26,520
Large bore rimfire (1875-80)	NiB $39,650	Ex $31,720	Gd $21,570
Small bore rimfire (1875-80)	NiB $30,550	Ex $24,440	Gd $16,619
Frontier six-shooter, .44-40 (1878-82)	NiB $46,216	Ex $36,972	Gd $25,141
Storekeeper's model, no ejector (1883-98)	NiB $48,750	Ex $39,000	Gd $26,520
Sheriff's model (1883-98)	NiB $46,150	Ex $36,920	Gd $25,106
Target model, flat top strap, target sights	NiB $25,350	Ex $20,280	Gd $13,790
U.S. Cavalry model, .45 (1873-92)	NiB $44,850	Ex $35,880	Gd $24,398

Colt SA Army — 125th Anniversary

Colt 150th Anniversary Deluxe

Colt 150th Anniversary Engraving Sampler

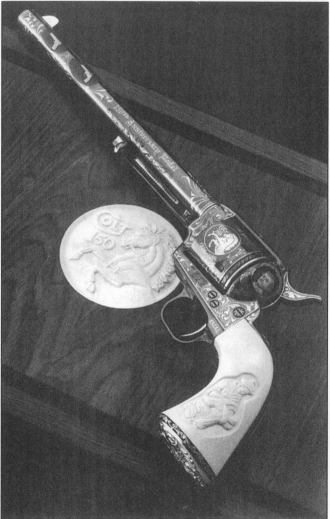

In the previous section the GTG deviates from the observed practice of listing only the value of firearms produced after 1900. This deliberate departure from the standard format is intended to provide a general reference and establish proper orientation for the reader, because the Colt SSA had its origins in the last quarter of the 19th century. Consequently, antique firearms produced prior to 1898 have been listed as a preface and introduction to the first series of production (what is now recognized as "1st Generation") in order to systematically demonstrate the progressive and sequential development of the multi-generation Colt SAA. Therefore, the previous general values have been provided to establish a point of reference to allow a more comprehensive examination of the evolution of the Colt SAA. However, please note that the following values apply only to original models, not to similar S.A.A. revolvers of more recent manufacture.

Standard model, pre-war
(1st generation) . . . . $13,000 to $65,000
Standard model (1955-75)
(2nd generation) . . . . NiB $2438 Ex $1989 Gd $1415
Standard model (1976 to date) . . NiB $1226 Ex $1043 Gd $771

SA ARMY — 125TH ANNIVERSARY . . . NiB $1595 Ex $1375 Gd $1175
Limited production deluxe version of SA Army issued in commemoration of Colt's 125th Anniversary. Caliber: .45 Long Colt., 7.5-inch bbl., cold-plated frame trigger, hammer, cylinder pin, ejector rod tip, and grip medallion. Presentation case w/anniversary medallion. Serial numbers "50AM." 7368 were made in 1961.

HANDGUNS

SA ARMY COMMEMORATIVE MODELS
Limited production versions of SA Army .45 issued, w/appropriate inscription to commemorate historical events. Cased. Note: Values indicated are for commemorative revolvers in new condition.

1963 ISSUES
Arizona Territorial Centennial
(1280 produced)...........................NiB $1595
West Virginia Statehood
Centennial (600 produced).....................NiB $1595

1964 ISSUES
Chamizal Treaty (50 produced) ....NiB $1795
Colonel Sam Colt Sesquicentennial
Presentation (4750 produced).....................NiB $1595
Deluxe Presentation
(200 produced) ....NiB $3500
Special Deluxe Presentation
(50 produced) ....NiB $5500
Montana Territorial Centennial
(851 produced) ....NiB $1650
Nevada "Battle Born"
(100 produced) ....NiB $2595
Nevada Statehood Centennial
(1877 produced) ....NiB $2195
New Jersey Tercentenary
(250 produced) ....NiB $1595
Pony Express Presentation
(1004 produced) ....NiB $1750
St. Louis Bicentennial
(450 produced) ....NiB $1595
Wyatt Earp Buntline
(150 produced) ....NiB $2750

1965 ISSUES
Appomattox Centennial
(500 produced).............................NiB $1595
Old Fort Des Moines Reconstruction (200 produced) ....NiB $1595

1966 ISSUES
Abercrombie & Fitch Trailblazer—Chicago (100 produced) ....NiB $1395
Abercrombie & Fitch Trailblazer—New York (200 produced) ....NiB $1395
Abercrombie & Fitch Trailblazer—San Francisco (100 produced) ....NiB $1395
California Gold Rush
(130 produced) ....NiB $1395
General Meade (200 produced) ....NiB $1595
Pony Express Four Square (4 guns) ....NiB $6595

1967 ISSUES
Alamo (1000 produced) ....NiB $1595
Lawman Series—Bat Masterson
(500 produced)............................NiB $1695

1968 ISSUES
Lawman Series—Pat Garrett (500 produced)...............NiB $1595
1969 ISSUES
Lawman Series—Wild Bill Hickok
(500 produced) ....NiB $1595

1970 ISSUES
Lawman Series—Wyatt Earp
(501 produced) ....NiB $2750

Colt SA Army Flat Top

Missouri Sesquicentennial
(501 produced)............................NiB $1595
Texas Ranger
(1000 produced) ....NiB $2250

1971 ISSUES
NRA Centennial, .357 or .45
(5001 produced) ....NiB $1495

1975 ISSUES
Peacemaker Centennial .45
(1501 produced) ....NiB $1795
Peacemaker Centennial .44-40
(1501 produced)...........................NiB $1795
Peacemaker Centennial Cased
Pair (501 produced) ....NiB $3750

1979 ISSUES
Ned Buntline .45
(3000 produced) ....NiB $1295
1986 ISSUES
Colt 150th Anniversary (standard) ....NiB $1995
Colt 150th Anniversay (engraved).................NiB $3500

COLT SA COWBOY REVOLVER NiB $598......Ex $440......Gd $335
SA variant designed for "Cowboy Action Shooting." Caliber: .45 Colt. Six-round cylinder, 5.5-inch bbl., 11 inches overall. Weight: 42 oz. Blade front sight, fixed V-notch rear. Blued finish w/color casehardened frame. Smooth walnut grips. Made from 1999 to 2003.

SA SHERIFF'S MODEL .45
Limited edition replica of Storekeeper's Model in caliber .45 Colt, made exclusively for Centennial Arms Corp. Chicago, Illinois. Numbered "1SM." Blued finish w/casehardened frame or nickel-plated. Walnut grips. Made in 1961.
Blued finish (478 produced) .... NiB $2000 Ex $2390 Gd $1720
Nickel finish (25 produced) .... NiB $7800 Ex $5502 Gd $3833

THREE-FIFTY-SEVEN DA REVOLVER
Heavy frame. Caliber: .357 Magnum. Six-shot cylinder, 4 or 6-inch bbl. Quickdraw ramp front sight, Accro rear sight. Blued finish. Checkered walnut grips. 9.25 or 11.25 inches overall. Weight: 36 oz. (4-inch bbl.), 39 oz. (6 inch bbl.). Made from 1953 to 1961.
W/standard hammer and service grips .... NiB $659 Ex $547 Gd $394
W/wide-spur hammer and target grips .... NiB $697 Ex $578 Gd $414

TROOPER DA REVOLVER
Same specifications as Officers' Model Match except has 4-inch bbl. w/quick-draw ramp front sight, weight: 34 oz. in .38 caliber. Made from 1953 to 1969.
W/standard hammer and service grips .... NiB $500 Ex $422 Gd $322
W/wide-spur hammer and target grips .... NiB $575 Ex $484 Gd $357

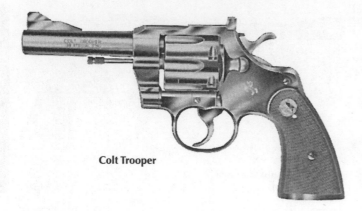

Colt Trooper

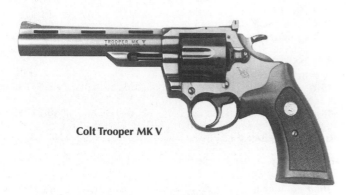

Colt Trooper MK V

Colt U.S. Bicentennial Commemorative Set

TROOPER MK III DA REVOLVER

"J"frame, shrouded ejector rod. Calibers: .22 LR, .22 Magnum, .38 Special, .357 Magnum. Six-round cylinder. bbl. lengths: 4-, 6-inches. 9.5 inches overall (with 4-inch bbl.). Weight: 39 oz. (4-inch bbl.). Adj. rear sight, ramp front. Target trigger and hammer. Blued or nickel-plated finish. Checkered walnut target grips. Made 1969 to 1978.

Blued finish . . . . NiB $550 Ex $390 Gd $192
Nickel finish . . . . NiB $600 Ex $433 Gd $199

TROOPER MK V REVOLVER

Re-engineered Mark III for smoother, faster action. Caliber: .357 Magnum. Six-round cylinder, bbl. lengths: 4-, 6-, 8-inch w/vent rib. Adj. rear sight, ramp front, red insert. Checkered walnut grips. Made from 1982 to 1986.

Blued finish . . . . NiB $500 Ex $485 Gd $322
Nickel finish . . . . NiB $525 Ex $477 Gd $297

VIPER DA REVOLVER . . . . NiB $725 Ex $575 Gd $325

Same as Cobra, Second Issue except has 4-inch bbl., 9 inches overall, weight: 20 oz. Made from 1977 to 1984.

U.S. BICENTENNIAL
COMMEMORATIVE SET . . . . NiB $3175

Replica Colt 3rd Model Dragoon revolver w/accessories, Colt SA Army revolver, and Colt Python revolver. Matching roll-engraved unfluted cylinders, blued finish and rosewood grips w/Great Seal of the United States silver medallion. Dragoon revolver has silver grip frame. Serial numbers 0001 to 1776. All revolvers in set have same number. Deluxe drawer-style presentation case of walnut w/book compartment containing a reproduction of "Armsmear." Issued in 1976. Value is for revolvers in new condition.

COONAN ARMS, INC. — Maplewood, Minnesota *(formerly St. Paul, Minnesota)*

MODEL .357 MAGNUM AUTO PISTOL

Caliber: .357 Mag. Seven-round magazine, 5- or 6-inch bbl., 8.3 inches overall (with 5-inch bbl.). Weight: 42 oz. Front ramp interchangeable sight, fixed rear sight, adj. for windage. Black walnut grips. Made from 1983 to 1999.

Model A Std. grade w/o grip
safety (disc. 1991) . . . . NiB $1170 Ex $1013 Gd $807
Model B Std. grade w/5-inch bbl., ... NiB $895 Ex $655 Gd $475
Model B Std. grade w/6-inch bbl., ... NiB $691 Ex $558 Gd $402
Model B w/5-inch
compensated bbl., (Classic) . . . . NiB $1275 Ex $1060 Gd $880
Model B w/6-inch
compensated bbl. . . . . NiB $950 Ex $756 Gd $533

.357 MAGNUM CADET COMPACT

Similar to the standard .357 Magnum model except w/3.9-inch bbl., on compact frame. Six-round (Cadet), 7- or 8-round magazine (Cadet II). Weight: 39 oz., 7.8 inches overall. Made 1993 to 1999.

Cadet model . . . . NiB $850 Ex $625 Gd $425
Cadet II model . . . . NiB $850 Ex $625 Gd $425

CZ PISTOLS — Uhersky Brod (formerly Strakonice), Czechoslovakia Mfd. by Ceska Zbrojovka-Nardoni Podnik (formerly Bohmische Waffenfabrik A. G.)

Currently imported by CZ-USA, Kansas City, KS. Previously by Magnum Research and Action Arms. Vintage importation is by Century International Arms. Also, see Dan Wesson Firearms listings.

CZ P-01 . . . . **NiB $629 Ex $377 Gd $289**
Caliber: 9mm Para. Based on CZ-75 design but with improved metals, aluminum alloy frame, hammer forged bbl. (3.8 inches), checkered rubber grips, matte black polycoat finish. Imported 2003.

CZ 40 . . . . **NiB $475 Ex $345 Gd $299**
Caliber: .40 S&W. M1911-style frame, CZ-75B operating mechanism; single or double-action; black polycoat finish. Fixed sights; 10-round mag.

MODEL 27 AUTO PISTOL . . . . **NiB $625 Ex $520 Gd $355**
Caliber: .32 Automatic (7.65mm). Eight-round magazine, 4-inch bbl., 6 inches overall. Weight: 23.5 oz. Fixed sights. Blued finish. Plastic grips. Made from 1927 to 1951. Note: After the German occupation (March 1939), Models 27 and 38 were marked w/manufacturer code "fnh." Designation of Model 38 was changed to "Pistole 39(t)."

MODEL .38 AUTO PISTOL (VZ SERIES)
Caliber: .380 Automatic (9mm). Nine-round magazine, 3.75-inch bbl., 7 inches overall. Weight: 26 oz. Fixed sights. Blued finish. Plastic grips. After 1939 designated as T39. Made 1938 to 1945.
CZ DAO model . . . . **NiB $489 Ex $425 Gd $325**
CZ SA/DA model . . . . **NiB $1397 Ex $1099 Gd $784**

MODEL 50 DA AUTO PISTOL . . . . . **NiB $248 Ex $177 Gd $143**
Similar to Walther Model PP except w/frame-mounted safety and trigger guard not hinged. Caliber: .32 ACP (7.65mm), 8-round magazine, 3.13-inch bbl., 6.5 inches overall. Weight: 24.5 oz. Fixed sights. Blued finished. Intro. in 1950. disc. Note: "VZ50" is the official designation of this pistol used by the Czech National Police ("New Model .006" was the export designation but very few were released).

MODEL 52 SA AUTO PISTOL . . . . . . **NiB $235 Ex $185 Gd $124**
Roller-locking breech system. Calibers: 7.62mm or 9mm Para. Eight-round magazine, 4.7-inch bbl., 8.1 inches overall. Weight: 31 oz. Fixed sights. Blued finish. Grooved composition grips. Made 1952 to 1956.

MODEL 70 DA AUTO PISTOL . . . . . . **NiB $494 Ex $389 Gd $277**
Similar to Model 50 but redesigned to improve function and dependability. Made from 1962 to 1983.

MODEL 75 DA/DAO AUTOMATIC PISTOL
Calibers: 9mm Para. or .40 S&W w/selective action mode. 10-, 13- or 15-round magazine, 3.9-inch bbl., (Compact) or 4.75-inch bbl., (Standard), 8 inches overall (Standard). Weight: 35 oz. Fixed sights. Blued, nickel, Two-Tone or black polymer finish. Checkered wood or high-impact plastic grips. Made from 1994 to date.
Black polymer finish . . . . **NiB $435 Ex $359 Gd $260**
High-polish blued finish . . . . **NiB $499 Ex $410 Gd $297**
Matte blued finish . . . . **NiB $470 Ex $378 Gd $277**
Nickel finish . . . . **NiB $489 Ex $399 Gd $290**
Two-tone finish . . . . **NiB $477 Ex $399 Gd $288**
W/.22 Kadet conversion, add $250
Compact model, add $50

82 DA AUTO PISTOL . . . . **NiB $379 Ex $323 Gd $200**
Similar to the standard CZ 83 model except chambered in 9x18 Makarov. This model currently is the Czech military sidearm.

83 DA AUTOMATIC PISTOL
Calibers: .32 ACP, .380 ACP. 15-round (.32 ACP) or 13-round (.380 ACP) magazine, 3.75-inch bbl., 6.75 inches overall. Weight: 26.5 oz. Fixed sights. Blued (standard); chrome and nickel (optional special edition) w/brushed, matte or polished finish. Checkered black plastic grips. Made from 1985 to date.
Standard finish . . . . **NiB $395 Ex $323 Gd $199**
Special edition . . . . **NiB $544 Ex $433 Gd $312**
Engraved . . . . **NiB $1188 Ex $966 Gd $683**

CZ Model 75 Compact

CZ Model 75 Kadet

CZ Model 83

CZ Model 85 Combat

CZ Model 97B

CZ Model 100

Daewoo DH40

85 COMBAT DA AUTOMATIC PISTOL

Similar to the standard CZ 85 model except w/13-round magazine, combat-style hammer, fully adj. rear sight and walnut grips. Made from 1986 to date.

Black polymer
finish . . . . **NiB $525 Ex $452 Gd $277**
High-polished
blued finish . . . . **NiB $554 Ex $452 Gd $322**
Matte blued
finish . . . . **NiB $574 Ex $452 Gd $332**

MODEL 97B DA

AUTOLOADING PISTOL . . . . **NiB $590 Ex $519 Gd $328**
Similar to the CZ Model 75 except chambered for the .45 ACP cartridge. 10-round magazine, Frame-mounted thumb safety that allows single-action, cocked-and-locked carry. Made from 1998 to date.

MODEL 100 DA

AUTOMATIC PISTOL . . . . **NiB $455 Ex $364 Gd $230**
Caliber: 9mm, .40 S&W. 10-round magazine, 3.8-inch bbl., Weight: 25 oz. Polymer grips w/fixed low-profile sights. Made from 1996 to 2007. Reintroduced 2009.

MODEL 1945 DA

POCKET AUTO PISTOL . . . . **NiB $309 Ex $229 Gd $168**
Caliber: .25 Auto (6.35mm). Eight-round magazine, 2.5-inch bbl., 5 inches overall. Weight: 15 oz. Fixed sights. Blued finish. Plastic grips. Intro. 1945. disc.

DUO POCKET

AUTO PISTOL . . . . **NiB $310 Ex $239 Gd $162**
Caliber: .25 Automatic (6.35mm). Six-round magazine, 2.13 inch bbl., 4.5 inches overall. Weight: 14-.5 oz. Fixed sights. Blued or nickel finish. Plastic grips. Made circa 1926 to 1960.

DAEWOO PISTOLS — Seoul, Korea
Mfd. by Daewoo Precision Industries Ltd.

Imported by Daewoo Precision Industries, Southhampton, PA, Previously by Nationwide Sports Distributors and KBI, Inc.

DH40 AUTO PISTOL . . . . **NiB $345 Ex $300 Gd $259**
Caliber: .40 S&W. 12-round magazine, 4.25-inch bbl., 7 inches overall. Weight: 28 oz. Blade front sight, dovetailed rear w/3-dot system. Blued finish. Checkered composition grips. DH/DP series feature a patented "fastfire" action w/5-6 lb. trigger pull. Made from 1994 to 1996.

DH45 AUTO PISTOL . . . . **NiB $325 Ex $300 Gd $259**
Caliber: .45 ACP. 13-round magazine, 5-inch bbl., 8.1 inches over-all. Weight: 35 oz. Blade front sight, dovetailed rear w/3-dot system. Blued finish. Checkered composition grips. Announced 1994, but not imported.

DP51 AUTO PISTOL . . . . **NiB $315 Ex $255 Gd $200**
Caliber: 9mm Para. 13-round magazine, 4.1-inch bbl., 7.5 inches overall. Weight: 28 oz. Blade front and square-notch rear sights. Matte black finish. Checkered composition grips. Made from 1991 to 1996.

DP52 AUTO PISTOL . . . . **NiB $345 Ex $285 Gd $218**
Caliber: .22 LR. 10-round magazine, 3.8-inch bbl., 6.7 inches over-all. Weight: 23 oz. Blade front sight, dovetailed rear w/3-dot system. Blued finish. Checkered wood grips. Made from 1994 to 1996.

DAKOTA/E.M.F. CO. — Santa Ana, California

MODEL 1873 SA REVOLVER
Calibers: .22 LR, .22 Mag., .357 Mag., .45 Long Colt, .30 M1 carbine, .38-40, .32-20, .44-40. Bbl. lengths: 3.5, 4.75, 5.5, 7.5 inches. Blued or nickel finish. Engraved models avail.
Standard model . . . . NiB $325 Ex $280 Gd $215
Nickel finish . . . . Add 30%

MODEL 1875 OUTLAW
SA REVOLVER . . . . NiB $495 Ex $390 Gd $275
Calibers: .45 Long Colt, .357 Mag., .44-40. 7.5-inch bbl. Casehardened frame, blued finish. Walnut grips. This is an exact replica of the Remington Number 3 revolver produced 1875 to 1889.

MODEL 1890 REMINGTON POLICE
Calibers: .357 Mag., .44-40, .45 Long Colt, 5.75-inch bbl., blued or nickel finish. Similar to Outlaw w/lanyard ring and no bbl. web .
Standard model . . . . NiB $531 Ex $420 Gd $304
Nickel model . . . . NiB $610 Ex $491 Gd $353
Engraved model . . . . NiB $699 Ex $563 Gd $402

BISLEY SA REVOLVER
Calibers: .44-40, .45 Long Colt, .357 Mag, 5.5- or 7.5-inch bbl., disc. 1992. Reintroduced 1994.
Standard model . . . . NiB $435 Ex $356 Gd $254
Engraved model . . . . NiB $600 Ex $475 Gd $259

HARTFORD SA REVOLVER
Calibers: .22 LR, .32-20, .357 Mag., .38-40, .44-40, .44 Special, .45 Long Colt. These are exact replicas of the original Colts w/steel backstraps, trigger guards and forged frames. Blued or nickel finish. Imported from 1990 to 2008.
Standard model . . . . NiB $412 Ex $335 Gd $239
Engraved model . . . . NiB $691 Ex $505 Gd $404
Hartford Artillery,
U.S. Cavalry models . . . . NiB $458 Ex $379 Gd $249

SHERIFF'S MODEL
SA REVOLVER . . . . NiB $415 Ex $361 Gd $259
Calibers: .32-20, .357 Mag., .38-40, .44 Special, .44-40, .45 LC. 3.5-inch bbl. Reintroduced 1994.

TARGET SA REVOLVER . . . . NiB $448 Ex $325 Gd $241
Calibers: .45 Long Colt, .357 Mag., .22 LR; 5.5- or 7.5-inch bbl. Polished, blued finish, casehardened frame. Walnut grips. Ramp front, blade target sight, adj. rear sight.

CHARLES DALY HANDGUNS — Currently imported by K.B.I., Harrisburg, PA.

MODEL M1911-A1 FIELD FS AUTOMATIC PISTOL
Caliber: .45 ACP. Eight- or 10-round magazine (Hi-Cap), 5-inch bbl., 8.75 inches overall. Weight: 38 oz. Blade front sight, drift adjustable rear w/3-dot system. Skeletonized tactical hammer and trigger. Extended slide release and beavertail grip safety. Matte blue, stainless or Duo finish. Checkered composition or wood stocks. Imported from 1999 to 2000.
Matte blue (Field FS) . . . . NiB $475 Ex $440 Gd $287
Stainless (Empire EFS) . . . . NiB $525 Ex $460 Gd $325
Duo (Superior FS) . . . . NiB $595 Ex $440 Gd $318
W/.22 conversion kit, add $200

Dakota Hartford

DAVIS INDUSTRIES, INC. — Chino, California

MODEL D DERRINGER
Single-action double derringer. Calibers: .22 LR, .22 Mag., .25 ACP, .32 Auto, .32 H&R Mag., 9mm, .38 Special. Two-round capacity, 2.4-inch or 2.75-inch bbl., 4 inches overall (2.4-inch bbl.). Weight: 9 to 11.5 oz. Laminated wood grips. Black Teflon or chrome finish. Made from 1987 to 2001.
.22 LR or .25 ACP . . . . NiB $159 Ex $92 Gd $73
.22 Mag., .32 H&R Mag., .38 Spec. . . . . NiB 185 Ex $107 Gd $83
.32 Auto. . . . . NiB 195 Ex $102 Gd $80
9mm Para. . . . . NiB $155 Ex $118 Gd $90

LONG BORE DERRINGER. . . . . NiB $185 Ex $107 Gd $83
Similar to Model D except in calibers .22 Mag., .32 H&R Mag., .38 Special, 9mm Para. 3.75-inch bbl., weight: 16 oz. Made from 1995 to 2001.

MODEL P-.32 . . . . NiB $135 Ex $97 Gd $76
Caliber: .32 Auto. Six-round magazine, 2.8-inch bbl., 5.4 inches overall. Weight: 22 oz. Black Teflon or chrome finish. Laminated wood grips. Made from 1987 to 2001.

MODEL P-.380 . . . . NiB $175 Ex $107 Gd $82
Caliber: .380 Auto. Five-round magazine, 2.8-inch bbl., 5.4 inches overall. Weight: 22 oz. Black Teflon or chrome finish. Made from 1990 to 2001.

DESERT INDUSTRIES, INC. — Las Vegas, Nevada (Previously Steel City Arms, Inc.)

DOUBLE DEUCE DA PISTOL . . . . . NiB $359 Ex $266 Gd $209
Caliber: .22 LR. Six-round magazine, 2.5-inch bbl., 5.5 inches overall. Weight: 15 oz. Matte-finish stainless steel. Rosewood grips.

TWO-BIT SPECIAL PISTOL . . . . NiB $385 Ex $295 Gd $210
Similar to the Double Deuce model except chambered in .25 ACP w/5-shot magazine.

DETONICS FIREARMS IND. — Phoenix, Arizona (Previously Detonics Firearms Industries, Bellevue, WA)

COMBATMASTER
Calibers: .45 ACP, .451 Detonics Mag. Six-round magazine, 3.5-inch bbl., 6.75 inches overall. Combat-type w/fixed or adjustable sights. Checkered walnut grip. Stainless steel construction. Disc. 1992.
MK I matte stainless,
fixed sights, (disc. 1981) . . . . NiB $1050 Ex $910 Gd $857
MK II polish finish, (disc. 1979) . . . NiB $1425 Ex $1325 Gd $1095

HANDGUNS

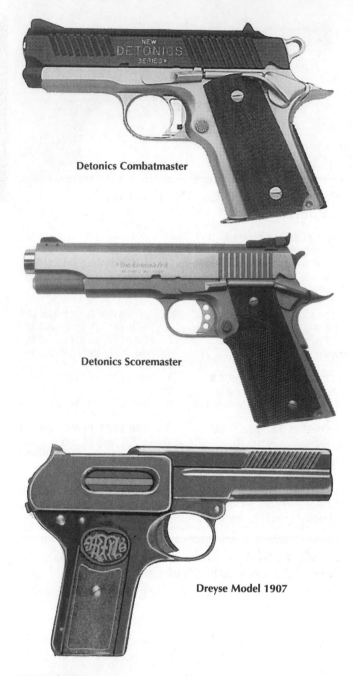

Detonics Combatmaster

Detonics Scoremaster

Dreyse Model 1907

MK III chrome,
(disc. 1980) . . . . NiB $523 Ex $427 Gd $305
MK IV polished blued,
adj. sights, (disc. 1981) . . . . NiB $574 Ex $468 Gd $333
MK V matte stainless,
fixed sights, (disc. 1985) . . . . NiB $733 Ex $598 Gd $424
MK VI polished ptainless, adj.
sights, (disc. 1989). . . . . NiB $789 Ex $643 Gd $456
MK VI in .451 Magnum,
(disc. 1986) . . . . NiB $1161 Ex $954 Gd $677
MK VII matte stainless steel,
no sights, (disc. 1985) . . . . NiB $1017 Ex $825 Gd $580
MK VII in .451 Magnum,
(disc. 1980) . . . . NiB $1350 Ex $1104 Gd $780

POCKET 9 . . . . NiB $645 Ex $522 Gd $397
Calibers: 9mm Para., .380. Six-round magazine, three-inch bbl., 5.88 inches overall. Fixed sights. Double- and single-action trigger mechanism. Disc. 1986.

SCOREMASTER . . . . NiB $1495 Ex $1239 Gd $1086
Calibers: .45 ACP, .451 Detonics Mag. Seven-round magazine. Five- or 6-inch heavyweight match bbl., 8.75 inches overall. Weight: 47 oz. Stainless steel construction, self-centering bbl., system. Disc. 1992.

SERVICEMASTER . . . . NiB $1050 Ex $757 Gd $502
Caliber: .45 ACP. Seven-round magazine, 4.25-inch bbl., weight: 39 oz. Interchangeable front sight, Millett rear sight. Disc. 1986.

SERVICEMASTER II . . . . NiB $1050 Ex $757 Gd $502
Same general specifications as standard Service Master except comes in polished stainless steel w/self-centering bbl., system. Disc. 1992.

DOWNSIZER CORPORATION — Santee, California

MODEL WSP
DAO PISTOL . . . . NiB $415 Ex $360 Gd $248
Single-round, tip-up pistol. Calibers: .22 Mag., .32 Mag., .380 ACP. 9mm Parabellum, .357 Mag., .40 S&W, .45 ACP. Six-round cylinder, 2.10-inch bbl. w/o extractor, 3.25 inches overall. Weight: 11 oz. No sights. Stainless finish. Synthetic grips. Made from 1994 to 2007.

DREYSE PISTOLS — Sommerda, Germany
Mfd. by Rheinische Metallwaren und Maschinenfabrik ("Rheinmetall")

MODEL 1907
AUTOMATIC PISTOL . . . . NiB $250 Ex $202 Gd $160
Caliber: .32 Auto (7.65mm). Eight-round magazine, 3.5-inch bbl., 6.25 inches overall. Weight: About 24 oz. Fixed sights. Blued finish. Hard rubber grips. Made circa 1907 to 1914.

VEST POCKET
AUTOMATIC PISTOL . . . . NiB $325 Ex $279 Gd $192
Conventional Browning type. Caliber: .25 Auto (6.35mm). Six-round magazine, 2-inch bbl., 4.5 inches overall. Weight: About 14 oz. Fixed sights. Blued finish. Hard rubber grips. Made 1909 to 1914.

DWM PISTOL — Berlin, Germany
Mfd. by Deutsche Waffen-und-Munitionsfabriken

POCKET AUTOMATIC PISTOL . . . NiB $1000 Ex $878 Gd $682
Similar to the FN Browning Model 1910. Caliber: .32 Automatic (7.65mm). 3.5-inch bbl., 6 inches overall. Weight: About 21 oz. Blued finish. Hard rubber grips. Made circa 1921 to 1931.

ED BROWN — Perry, Montana

"CLASS A LTD" SA
AUTOMATIC PISTOL . . . . NiB $2248 Ex $2080 Gd $997
Caliber: .38 Super, 9mm, 9x23, .45 ACP. Seven-round magazine, 4.25- or 5-inch bbl., weight: 34-39 oz. Rubber checkered or optional Hogue exotic wood grip. M1911 style single action pistol. Fixed front and rear Novak Lo-mount or fully adjustable sights.

"CLASSIC CUSTOM" SA
AUTOMATIC PISTOL . . . . **NiB $3165 Ex $2505 Gd $1490**
Caliber: .45 ACP. Seven-round magazine, 4.25- or 5-inch bbl., weight: 39 oz. Exotic Hogue wood grip w/modified ramp or post front and rear adjustable sights.

"SPECIAL FORCES" SA
AUTOMATIC PISTOL . . . . **NiB $2199 Ex $1878 Gd $1408**
Caliber: .45 ACP. Seven-round magazine, 4.25- or 5-inch bbl., weight: 34-39 oz. Rubber checkered, optional exotic wood grips. Single action M1911 style pistol.

ENFIELD REVOLVER — Enfield Lock, Middlesex, England
Manufactured by Royal Small Arms Factory

(BRITISH SERVICE) NO. 2
MK 1 REVOLVER . . . . **NiB $345 Ex $254 Gd $192**
Webley pattern. Hinged frame. Double action. Caliber: .380 British Service (.38 S&W w/200-grain bullet). Six-round cylinder, 5-inch bbl., 10.5 inches overall. Weight: About 27.5 oz. Fixed sights. Blued finish. Vulcanite grips. First issued in 1932, this was the standard revolver of the British Army in WW II. Now obsolete. Note: This model also produced w/spurless hammer as No. 2 Mk 1* and Mk 1**.

ENTREPRISE ARMS — Irwindale, California

ELITE SERIES SA
AUTO PISTOL . . . . **NiB $625 Ex $475 Gd $385**
Single action M1911 style pistol. Caliber: .45 ACP. 10-round magazine, 3.25-, 4.25-, 5-inch bbl., (models P325, P425, P500). Weight: 36-40 oz. Ultraslim checkered grips, Tactical 2 high profile sights w/3-dot system. Lightweight adjustable trigger. Blued or matte black oxide finish. Made from 1997 to date.

MEDALIST SA AUTOMATIC PISTOL
Similar to Elite model except machined to match tolerances and target configuration. Caliber: .45 ACP, .40 S&W. 10-round magazine, 5-inch compensated bbl. w/dovetail front and fully adjustable rear Bo-Mar sights. Weight: 40 oz. Made from 1997 to date.
.40 S&W model . . . . **NiB $995 Ex $845 Gd $675**
.45 ACP model . . . . **NiB $875 Ex $725 Gd $555**

TACTICAL SA AUTOMATIC PISTOL
Similar to Elite model except in combat carry configuration. Dehorned frame and slide w/ambidextrous safety. Caliber: .45 ACP. 10-round magazine, 3.25-, 4.25-, 5-inch bbl., weight: 36-40 oz. Tactical 2 Ghost Ring or Novak Lo-mount sights.
Tactical 2 ghost
ring sights . . . . **NiB $875 Ex $700 Gd $550**
Novak Lo-Mount . . . . **NiB $875 Ex $700 Gd $550**
Tactical plus model . . . . **NiB $875 Ex $700 Gd $550**

BOXER SA AUTO-
MATIC PISTOL . . . . **NiB $1197 Ex $1086 Gd $800**
Similar to Medalist model except w/profiled slide configuration and fully adjustable target sights. weight: 42 oz. Made from 1997 to date.

TOURNAMENT SHOOTER MODEL SA AUTOMATIC PISTOL
Similar to Elite model except in IPSC configuration. Caliber: .45 ACP, .40 S&W. 10-round magazine, 5-inch compensated bbl., w/dovetail front and fully adjustable rear Bo-Mar sights. Weight: 40 oz. Made from 1997 to date.

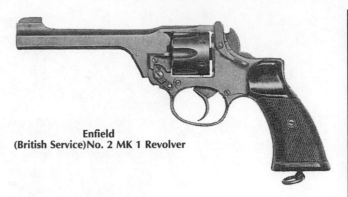

Enfield
(British Service) No. 2 MK 1 Revolver

Erma
Model ER-772 Match Revolver

TSM I model . . . . **NiB $2100 Ex $1950 Gd $1605**
TSM II model. . . . . **NiB $1800 Ex $1650 Gd $1305**
TSM III model . . . . **NiB $2500 Ex $1350 Gd $1605**

ERMA-WERKE — Dachau, Germany

MODEL ER-772
MATCH REVOLVER . . . . **NiB $1100 Ex $1030 Gd $639**
Caliber: .22 LR. Six-round cylinder, 6-inch bbl., 12 inches overall. Weight: 47.25 oz. Adjustable micrometer rear sight and front sight blade. Adjustable trigger. Interchangeable walnut sporter or match grips. Polished blued finish. Made from 1991 to 1994.

MODEL ER-773
MATCH REVOLVER . . . . **NiB $925 Ex $787 Gd $570**
Same general specifications as Model 772 except chambered for .32 S&W. Made from 1991 to 1995.

MODEL ER-777
MATCH REVOLVER . . . . **NiB $875 Ex $750 Gd $600**
Caliber: .357 Magnum. Six-round cylinder. 4- or 5.5-inch bbl., 9.7 to 11.3 inches overall. Weight: 43.7 oz. (with 5.5-inch bbl.). Micrometer adj. rear sight. Checkered walnut sporter or match-style grip (interchangeable). Made from 1991 to 1995.

MODEL ESP-85A COMPETITION PISTOL
Calibers: .22 LR and .32 S&W Wadcutter. Eight- or 5-round magazine, 6-inch bbl., 10 inches overall. Weight: 40 oz. Adj. rear sight, blade front sight. Checkered walnut grip w/thumbrest. Made from 1991 to 1997.
Match model . . . . **NiB $1225 Ex $1097 Gd $696**
Chrome match. . . . . **NiB $1475 Ex $1299 Gd $979**
Sporting model . . . . **NiB $1225 Ex $1025 Gd $713**
Conversion unit .22 LR . . . . **NiB $2205 Ex $1975 Gd $1691**
Conversion unit .32 S&W . . . . . **NiB $2556 Ex $2098 Gd $1736**

**European American Armory
Big Bore Bounty Hunter**

MODEL KGP68
AUTOMATIC PISTOL . . . . NiB $453 Ex $282 Gd $227
Luger type. Calibers: .32 Auto (7.65mm), .380 Auto (9mm Short). Six-round magazine (.32 Auto), 5-round (.380 Auto), 4-inch bbl., 7.38 inches overall. Weight: 22.5 oz. Fixed sights. Blued finish. Checkered walnut grips. Made from 1968 to 1993.

MODEL KGP69
AUTOMATIC PISTOL . . . . NiB $335 Ex $272 Gd $200
Luger type. Caliber: .22 LR. Eight-round magazine, 4-inch bbl., 7.75 inches overall. Weight: 29 oz. fixed sights. Blued finish. Checkered walnut grips. Imported from 1969 to 1993.

**Erma-Werke
Model KGP69**

EUROPEAN AMERICAN ARMORY, Rockledge, Florida
See also listings under Astra Pistols.

EUROPEAN MODEL AUTO PISTOL
Calibers: .32 ACP (SA only), .380 ACP (SA or DA), 3.85-inch bbl., 7.38 overall, 7-round magazine, Weight: 26 oz. Blade front sight, drift-adj. rear. Blued, chrome, blue/chrome, blue/gold, Duo-Tone or Wonder finish. Imported 1991 to date.
Blued .32 ACP (disc. 1995) . . . . NiB $130 Ex $100 Gd $80
Blue/chrome .32 caliber
(disc. 1995) . . . . NiB $185 Ex $101 Gd $74
Chrome .32 caliber
(Disc. 1995). . . . . NiB $130 Ex $100 Gd $80
Blued .380 caliber . . . . NiB $145 Ex $105 Gd $75
Blue/chrome .380 caliber
(disc. 1993) . . . . NiB $185 Ex $121 Gd $75
DA .380 caliber (disc. 1994) . . . . . . NiB $375 Ex $255 Gd $155
Lady .380 caliber (disc. 1995). . . . . NiB $250 Ex $190 Gd $135
Wonder finish .380 caliber . . . . NiB $259 Ex $176 Gd $123

BIG BORE BOUNTY HUNTER SA REVOLVER
Calibers: .357 Mag., .41 Mag., .44-40, .44 Mag., .45 Colt. Bbl. lengths: 4.63, 5.5, 7.5 inches. Blade front and grooved topstrap rear sights. Blued or chrome finish w/color casehardened or gold-plated frame. Smooth walnut grips. Imported 1992.
Blued finish . . . . NiB $365 Ex $245 Gd $180
Blued w/color-
casehardened frame . . . . NiB $365 Ex $245 Gd $180
Blued w/gold-plated frame . . . . NiB $380 Ex $260 Gd $195
Chrome finish . . . . NiB $385 Ex $265 Gd $200
Gold-plated frame, add $100

**Model ESP-85A
Competition Pistol**

BOUNTY HUNTER SA REVOLVER
Calibers: .22 LR, .22 Mag. Bbl. lengths: 4.75, 6 or 9 inches. Blade front and dovetailed rear sights. Blued finish or blued w/gold-plated frame. European hardwood grips. Imported from 1997 to date.

Blued finish (4.75-inch bbl.)	NiB $265	Ex $180	Gd $115
Blued .22 LR/.22 WRF combo (4.75-inch bbl.)	NiB $265	Ex $180	Gd $115
Blued .22 LR/.22 WRF combo (6-inch bbl.)	NiB $265	Ex $180	Gd $115
Blued .22 LR/.22 WRF combo (9-inch bbl.)	NiB $265	Ex $180	Gd $115

EA22 TARGET
EA22 TARGET . . . . NiB $375 Ex $265 Gd $195

Caliber: .22 LR. 12-round magazine, 6-inch bbl., 9.10 inches overall. Weight: 40 oz. Ramp front sight, fully adj. rear. Blued finish. Checkered walnut grips w/thumbrest. Made from 1991 to 1994.

FAB 92 AUTO PISTOL
Similar to the Witness model except chambered in 9mm only w/slide-mounted safety and no cock-and-lock provision. Imported 1992 to 1995.

FAB 92 standard	NiB $397	Ex $321	Gd $211
FAB 92 compact	NiB $397	Ex $321	Gd $211

STANDARD GRADE REVOLVER
Calibers: .22 LR, .22 WRF, .32 H&R Mag., .38 Special. Two-, 4- or 6-inch bbl., blade front sight, fixed or adj. rear. Blued finish. European hardwood grips w/finger grooves. Imported 1991 to date.

.22 LR (4-inch bbl.)	NiB $208	Ex $164	Gd $120
.22 LR (6-inch bbl.)	NiB $221	Ex $174	Gd $127
.22 LR combo (4-inch bbl.)	NiB $285	Ex $225	Gd $162
.22 LR combo (6-inch bbl.)	NiB $321	Ex $255	Gd $182
.32 H&R, .38 Special (2-inch bbl.)	NiB $224	Ex $169	Gd $123
.38 Special (4-inch bbl.)	NiB $228	Ex $179	Gd $129
.357 Mag	NiB $235	Ex $199	Gd $138

TACTICAL GRADE REVOLVER
Similar to the Standard model except chambered in .38 Special only. Two- or 4-inch bbl., fixed sights. Available w/compensator. Imported from 1991-93.

Tactical revolver	NiB $220	Ex $175	Gd $100
Tactical revolver w/compensator	NiB $300	Ex $255	Gd $180

WINDICATOR TARGET REVOLVER
WINDICATOR TARGET REVOLVER . . . . . . NiB $425 Ex $368 Gd $241

Calibers: .22 LR, .38 Special, .357 Magnum. Eight-round cylinder in .22 LR, 6-round in .38 Special and .357 Magnum. Six-inch bbl. w/bbl. weights. 11.8 inches overall. Weight: 50.2 oz. Interchangeable blade front sight, fully adj. rear. Walnut competition-style grips. Imported from 1991-93.

WITNESS DA AUTO PISTOL
Similar to the Brno CZ-75 w/a cocked-and-locked system. Double or single action. Calibers: 9mm Para. .38 Super, .40 S&W, 10mm; .41 AE and .45 ACP. 16-round magazine (9mm), 12 shot (.38 Super/.40 S&W), or 10-round (10mm/.45 ACP), 4.75-inch bbl., 8.10 inches overall. Weight: 35.33 oz. Blade front sight, rear sight adj. for windage w/3-dot sighting system. Steel or polymer frame. Blued, satin chrome, blue/chrome, stainless or Wonder finish. Checkered rubber grips. EA Series imported 1991 to date.

9mm blue	NiB $459	Ex $321	Gd $235
9mm chrome or blue/chrome	NiB $459	Ex $331	Gd $235
9mm stainless	NiB $455	Ex $377	Gd $268
9mm Wonder finish	NiB $470	Ex $341	Gd $255
.38 Super and .40 S&W blued	NiB $459	Ex $321	Gd $229
.38 Super and .40 S&W chrome or blue/chrome	NiB $454	Ex $371	Gd $265
.38 Super and .40 S&W stainless	NiB $525	Ex $399	Gd $279
.38 Super and .40 S&W Wonder finish	NiB $545	Ex $391	Gd $288
10mm, .41 AE and .45 ACP blued	NiB $455	Ex $331	Gd $229

**European American Armory
Windicator Target**

European American Armory Witness

10mm, .41 AE and .45 ACP chrome or blue/chrome	NiB $525	Ex $428	Gd $303
10mm, .41 AE and .45 ACP stainless	NiB $545	Ex $448	Gd $323
10mm, .41 AE and .45 ACP Wonder finish	NiB $551	Ex $433	Gd $307

COMPACT WITNESS DA AUTO PISTOL (L SERIES)
Similar to the standard Witness series except more compact w/ 3.625-inch bbl., and polymer or steel frame. Weight: 30 oz. Matte blued or Wonder finish. EA Compact series imported 1999 to date.

9mm blue	NiB $450	Ex $321	Gd $229
9mm Wonder finish	NiB $450	Ex $321	Gd $229
.38 Super and .40 S&W blued	NiB $450	Ex $321	Gd $229
.38 Super and .40 S&W Wonder finish	NiB $450	Ex $321	Gd $229
10mm, .41 AE and .45 ACP blued	NiB $525	Ex $351	Gd $250
10mm, .41 AE and .45 ACP Wonder fin.	NiB $525	Ex $351	Gd $250
W/ported bbl., add			$30

WITNESS CARRY COMP
Double/Single action. Calibers: .38 Super, 9mm Parabellum, .40 S&W, 10mm, .45 ACP. 10-, 12- or 16-round magazine, 4.25-inch bbl., w/1-inch compensator. Weight: 33 oz., 8.10 inches overall. Black rubber grips. Post front sight, drift adjustable rear w/3-dot system. Matte blue, Duo-Tone or Wonder finish. Imported 1992 to 2004.

9mm, .40 S&W	NiB $425	Ex $347	Gd $264
.38 Super, 10mm, .45 ACP	NiB $425	Ex $347	Gd $264
W/Duo-Tone finish (disc.), add			$20
W/Wonder finish, add			$10

Feather Guardian Angel Derringer

FEG Mark II AP-.22

WITNESS LIMITED
CLASS AUTO PISTOL . . . . NiB $875 Ex $700 Gd $545
Single action. Calibers: .38 Super, 9mm Parabellum, .40 S&W, .45 ACP. 10-round magazine, 4.75-inch bbl., Weight: 37 oz. Checkered competition-style walnut grips. Long slide w/post front sight, fully adj. rear. Matte blue finish. Imported 1994 to 1998.

WITNESS SUBCOMPACT DA AUTO PISTOL
Calibers: 9mm Para., .40 S&W, 41 AK, .45 ACP. 13-round magazine in 9mm, 9-round in .40 S&W, 3.66-inch bbl., 7.25 inches overall. Weight: 30 oz. Blade front sight, rear sight adj. for windage. Blued, satin chrome or blue/chrome finish. Imported from 1995 to 1997.

9mm blue	NiB $386	Ex $351	Gd $325
9mm chrome or blue/chrome	NiB $431	Ex $346	Gd $250
.40 S&W blue	NiB $431	Ex $346	Gd $250
.40 S&W chrome or blue/chrome . .	NiB $469	Ex $376	Gd $270
.41 AE blue	NiB $510	Ex $412	Gd $298
.41 AE chrome or blue/chrome	NiB $530	Ex $427	Gd $305
.45 ACP blued	NiB $514	Ex $412	Gd $295
.45 ACP chrome or blue/chrome. . .	NiB $488	Ex $412	Gd $300

WITNESS TARGET PISTOLS
Similar to standard Witness model except fitted w/2- or 3-port compensator, competition frame and S/A target trigger. Calibers: 9mm Para., 9x21, .40 S&W, 10mm and .45 ACP, 5.25-inch match bbl., 10.5 inches overall. Weight: 38 oz. Square post front sight, fully adj. rear or drilled and tapped for scope. Blued or hard chrome finish. Low-profile competition grips. Imported 1992 to date.

**Silver Team (blued w/2-port
compensator)**. . . . . NiB $855 Ex $740 Gd $535
**Gold Team (chrome
w/3-port compensator)** . . . . NiB $1775 Ex $1500 Gd $1277

FAS PISTOLS — Malino, Italy
Currently imported by Nygord Precision
Products *(Previously by Beeman Precision Arms and Osborne's, Cheboygan, MI)*

OP601 SEMIAUTOMATIC MATCH TARGET PISTOL
Caliber: .22 Short. Five-round top-loading magazine, 5.6-inch ported and ventilated bbl., 11 inches overall. Weight: 41.5 oz. Removable, adj. trigger group. Blade front sight, open-notch fully adj. rear. Stippled walnut wraparound or adj. target grips.
Right-hand model . . . . NiB $1025 Ex $900 Gd $675
Left-hand model . . . . NiB $1100 Ex $955 Gd $720

602 SEMIAUTOMATIC MATCH TARGET PISTOL
Similar to Model FAS 601 except chambered for .22 LR. Weight: 37 oz.
Right-hand model . . . . NiB $895 Ex $675 Gd $550
Left-hand model . . . . NiB $995 Ex $785 Gd $645

CF603 SEMIAUTOMATIC
MATCH TARGET PISTOL. . . . . NiB $975 Ex $755 Gd $610
Similar to Model FAS 601 except chambered for .32 S&W (wadcutter).

SP607 SEMIAUTOMATIC
MATCH TARGET PISTOL. . . . . NiB $985 Ex $755 Gd $610
Similar to Model FAS 601 except chambered for .22 LR, w/removable bbl. weights. Imported 1995 to date.

FEATHER INDUSTRIES — Boulder, Colorado

GUARDIAN ANGEL DERRINGER
Double-action over/under derringer w/interchangeable drop-in loading blocks. Calibers: .22 LR, .22 WMR, 9mm, .38 Spec. Two-round capacity, 2-inch bbl., 5 inches overall. weight: 12 oz. Stainless steel. Checkered black grip. Made from 1988 to 1995.
.22 LR, .22 WMR. . . . . NiB $160 Ex $100 Gd $77
9mm, .38 Special (disc. 1989). . . . . NiB $225 Ex $175 Gd $145

FEG (FEGYVERGYAN) PISTOLS — Budapest, Soroksariut, Hungary *(Currently imported by KBI, Inc. and Century International Arms (Previously by Interarms)*

MARK II AP-.22 DA AUTOMATIC PISTOL . . . . NiB $255 Ex $210 Gd $165
Caliber: .22 LR. Eight-round magazine, 3.4-inch bbl., Weight: 23 oz. Drift-adj. sights. Double action, all-steel pistol. Imported 1997 to 1998.

MARK II AP-.380 DA AUTOMATIC PISTOL . . . NiB $255 Ex $210 Gd $180
Caliber: .380. Seven-round magazine, 3.9-inch bbl., weight 27 oz. Drift-adj. sights. Double action, all-steel pistol. Imported 1997 to 1998.

**MARK II APK-.380 DA
AUTOMATIC PISTOL** . . . . NiB $255 Ex $210 Gd $180
Caliber: .380. Seven-round magazine, 3.4-inch bbl., weight: 25 oz. Drift-adj. sights. Double action, all-steel pistol. Imported 1997 to 1998.

MODEL GKK-9 (92C) AUTO PISTOL . . . . NiB $300 Ex $235 Gd $212
Improved version of the double-action FEG Model MBK. Caliber: 9mm Para. 14-round magazine, 4-inch bbl., 7.4 inches overall. Weight: 34 oz. Blade front sight, rear sight adj. for windage. Checkered wood grips. Blued finish. Imported from 1992 to 1993.

MODEL GKK-.45 AUTO PISTOL
Improved version of the double-action FEG Model MBK. Caliber: .45 ACP. Eight-round magazine, 4.1-inch bbl., 7.75 inches overall. Weight: 36 oz. Blade front sight, rear sight adj. for windage w/3-dot system. Checkered walnut grips. Blued or chrome finish. Imported 1993 to 1996.
Blued model (disc. 1994) . . . . **NiB $310 Ex $255 Gd $200**
Chrome model . . . . **NiB $345 Ex $310 Gd $245**

MODEL MBK-9HP
AUTO PISTOL . . . . **NiB $450 Ex $290 Gd $140**
Similar to the double-action Browning Hi-Power. Caliber: 9mm Para. 14-round magazine, 4.6-inch bbl., 8 inches overall. Weight: 36 oz. Blade front sight, rear sight adj. for windage. Checkered wood grips. Blued finish. Imported from 1992 to 1993.

MODEL PJK-9HP AUTO PISTOL
Similar to the single-action Browning Hi-Power. Caliber: 9mm Para. 13-round magazine, 4.75-inch bbl., 8 inches overall. Weight: 21 oz. Blade front sight, rear sight adj. for windage w/3-dot system. Checkered walnut or rubber grips. Blued or chrome finish. Imported 1992 to 2003.
Blued model . . . . **NiB $455 Ex $365 Gd $245**
Chrome model . . . . **NiB $485 Ex $405 Gd $295**

MODEL PSP-.25 AUTO PISTOL
Similar to the Browning .25. Caliber: .25 ACP. Six-round magazine, 2.1-inch bbl., 4.1 inches overall. Weight: 9.5 oz. Fixed sights. Checkered composition grips. Blued or chrome finish.
Blued model . . . . **NiB $296 Ex $210 Gd $164**
Chrome model . . . . **NiB $296 Ex $210 Gd $164**

MODEL SMC-.22 AUTO PISTOL . . . . **NiB $210 Ex $125 Gd $75**
Same general specifications as FEG Model SMC-.380 except in .22 LR. Eight-round magazine, 3.5-inch bbl., 6.1 inches overall. Weight: 18.5 oz. Blade front sight, rear sight adj. for windage. Checkered composition grips w/thumbrest. Blued finish.

MODEL SMC-.380 AUTO PISTOL. . . . **NiB $215 Ex $125 Gd $75**
Similar to the Walther DA PPK w/alloy frame. Caliber: .380 ACP. Six-round magazine, 3.5-inch bbl., 6.1 inches overall. Weight: 18.5 oz. Blade front sight, rear sight adj. for windage. Checkered composition grips w/ thumbrest. Blued finish. Imported 1993 to 1997.

MODEL SMC-918 AUTO PISTOL. . . . . **NiB $190 Ex $125 Gd $90**
Same general specifications as FEG Model SMC-.380 except chambered in 9x18mm Makarov. Imported from 1994 to 1997.

FIALA OUTFITTERS, INC. — New York
REPEATING PISTOL. . . . . **NiB $660 Ex $465 Gd $355**
Hand-operated, not semi-auto. Caliber: .22 LR. 10-round magazine, bbl. lengths: 3-, 7.5- and 20-inch. 11.25 inches overall (with 7.5-inch bbl.). Weight: 31 oz. (with 7.5-inch bbl.). Target sights. Blued finish. Plain wood grips. Shoulder stock was originally supplied for use w/20-inch bbl. Made from 1920 to 1923. Value shown is for pistol w/one bbl., no shoulder stock. Three bbl. cased sets start at $3,000.

F.I.E. CORPORATION — Hialeah, Florida
The F.I.E. Corporation became QFI (Quality Firearms Corp.) of Opa Locka, Fl., about 1990, when most of F.I.E.'s models were discontinued.

FEG Model PJK-9HP

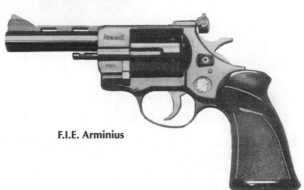

F.I.E. Model A27BW

F.I.E. Arminius

MODEL A27 "THE BEST SEMIAUTO NiB $130 Ex $90 Gd $60**
Caliber: .25 ACP. Six-round magazine, 2.5-inch bbl., 6.75 inches overall. Weight: 13 oz. Fixed sights. Checkered walnut grip. Discontinued in 1990.

ARMINIUS DA STANDARD REVOLVER
Calibers: .22 LR, .22 combo w/interchangeable cylinder, .32 S&W, .38 Special, .357 Magnum. Six, 7 or 8 rounds depending on caliber. Swing-out cylinder. bbl. lengths: 2-, 3-, 4, 6-inch. Vent rib on calibers other than .22, 11 inches overall (with 6-inch bbl.). Weight: 26 to 30 oz. Fixed or micro-adj. sights. Checkered plastic or walnut grips. Blued finish. Made in Germany. Disc.
.22 LR . . . . **NiB $121 Ex $99 Gd $77**
.22 Combo. . . . . **NiB $189 Ex $153 Gd $102**
.32 S&W . . . . **NiB $197 Ex $147 Gd $106**
.38 Special. . . . . **NiB $150 Ex $162 Gd $117**
.357 Magnum . . . . **NiB $229 Ex $184 Gd $138**

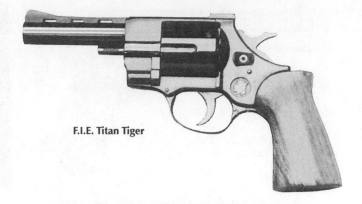

F.I.E. Titan Tiger

F.I.E. Titan II

F.I.E. Model TZ75

BUFFALO SCOUT SA REVOLVER
Calibers: .22 LR, .22 WRF, .22 combo w/interchangeable cylinder. 4.75-inch bbl., 10 inches overall. Weight: 32 oz. Adjustable sights. Blued or chrome finish. Smooth walnut or black checkered nylon grips. Made in Italy. Disc.

Blued standard....................	NiB $75	Ex $55	Gd $35
Blued convertible	NiB $85	Ex $55	Gd $35
Chrome standard.................	NiB $85	Ex $55	Gd $35
Chrome convertible..............	NiB $85	Ex $55	Gd $35

HOMBRE SA REVOLVER
.... NiB $220 Ex $170 Gd $100
Calibers: .357 Magnum, .44 Magnum, .45 Colt. Six-round cylinder. bbl. lengths: 6 or 7.5 inches, 11 inches overall (with - inch bbl.). Weight: 45 oz. (6-inch bbl.). Fixed sights. Blued bbl., w/color-casehardened receiver. Smooth walnut grips. Made from 1979 to 1990.

SUPER TITAN II
Caliber: .32 ACP or .380 ACP, 3.25-inch bbl., weight: 28 oz. Blued or chrome finish. Disc. 1990.

.32 ACP in blue	NiB $130	Ex $90	Gd $65
.32 ACP in chrome	NiB $130	Ex $90	Gd $65
.380 ACP in blue	NiB $130	Ex $90	Gd $65
.380 ACP in chrome	NiB $130	Ex $90	Gd $65

TEXAS RANGER
SINGLE-ACTION REVOLVER
Calibers: .22 LR, .22 WRF, .22 combo w/interchangeable cylinder. bbl., lengths: 4.75-, 6.5-, 9-inch. 10 inches overall (with 4.75-inch bbl.). Weight: 32 oz. (with 4.75-inch bbl.). Fixed sights. Blued finish. Smooth walnut grips. Made from 1983 to 1990.

Standard	NiB $85	Ex $75	Gd $55
Convertible	NiB $100	Ex $90	Gd $70

LITTLE RANGER SA REVOLVER
Same as the Texas Ranger except w/3.25-inch bbl. and bird's-head grips. Made from 1986 to 1990.

Standard	NiB $85	Ex $75	Gd $55
Convertible	NiB $100	Ex $75	Gd $55

TITAN TIGER DOUBLE-
ACTION REVOLVER
.... NiB $60 Ex $40 Gd $25
Caliber: .38 Special. Six-round cylinder, 2- or 4-inch bbl., 8.25 inches overall (with 4-inch bbl.). Weight: 30 oz. (4-inch bbl.). Fixed sights. Blued finish. Checkered plastic or walnut grips. Made in the U.S. Disc. 1990.

TITAN II SEMIAUTOMATIC
Caiibers: .22 LR, .32 ACP, .380 ACP. 10-round magazine, integral tapered post front sight, windage-adjustable rear sight. European walnut grips. Blued or chrome finish. Disc. 1990.

.22 LR in blue	NiB $130	Ex $100	Gd $80
.32 ACP in blued	NiB $196	Ex $162	Gd $118
.32 ACP in chrome	NiB $208	Ex $168	Gd $137
.380 ACP in blue	NiB $215	Ex $175	Gd $138
.380 ACP in chrome	NiB $225	Ex $175	Gd $150

MODEL TZ75 DA SEMIAUTOMATIC
Double action. Caliber: 9mm. 15-round magazine, 4.5-inch bbl., 8.25 inches overall. Weight: 35 oz. Ramp front sight, windage-adjustable rear sight. European walnut or black rubber grips. Imported from 1988 to 1990.

Blued finish....................	NiB $375	Ex $300	Gd $220
Satin chrome...................	NiB $395	Ex $320	Gd $245

YELLOW ROSE SA REVOLVER
Same general specifications as the Buffalo Scout except in .22 combo w/interchangeable cylinder and plated in 24-karat gold. Limited Edition w/scrimshawed ivory polymer grips and American walnut presentation case. Made from 1987 to 1990.

Yellow Rose			
.22 combo......................	NiB $130	Ex $89	Gd $54
Yellow Rose			
Limited Edition	NiB $280	Ex $230	Gd $185

FIREARMS INTERNATIONAL CORP. — Washington, D.C.

MODEL D
AUTOMATIC PISTOL . . . . **NiB $210 Ex $170 Gd $90**
Caliber: .380 Automatic. Six-round magazine, 3.3-inch bbl., 6.13 inches overall. Weight: 19.5 oz. Blade front sight, windage-adjustable rear sight. Blued, chromed, or military finish. Checkered walnut grips. Made from 1974 to 1977.

REGENT DA
REVOLVER. **NiB $175 Ex $122 Gd $102**
Calibers: .22 LR, .32 S&W Long. Eight-round cylinder (.22 LR), or 7-round (.32 S&W). Bbl. lengths: 3-, 4-, 6-inches (.22 LR) or 2.5-, 4-inches (.32 S&W). Weight: 28 oz.(with 4-inch bbl.). Fixed sights. Blued finish. Plastic grips. Made from 1966 to 1972.

**Firearms International
Model D**

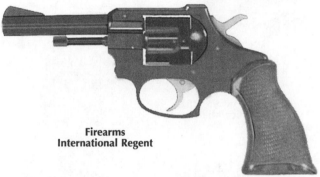

**Firearms
International Regent**

FN BROWNING PISTOLS — Liege, Belgium
Mfd. by Fabrique Nationale Herstal

See also Browning Pistols.

6.35MM POCKET AUTO PISTOL
(See FN Browning Baby Auto Pistol)

MODEL 1900 POCKET
AUTO PISTOL . . . . **NiB $810 Ex $679 Gd $466**
Caliber: .32 Automatic (7.65mm). Seven-round magazine, 4-inch bbl., 6.75 inches overall. Weight: 22 oz. Fixed sights. Blued finish. Hard rubber grips. Made from 1899 to 1910.

MODEL 1903 MILITARY AUTO PISTOL
Caliber: 9mm Browning Long. Seven-round magazine, 5-inch bbl., 8 inches overall. Weight: 32 oz. Fixed sights. Blued finish. Hard rubber grips. Note: Aside from size, this pistol is of the same basic design as the Colt Pocket .32 and .380 Automatic pistols. Made from 1903 to 1939.
Model 190
Standard . . . . **NiB $1200 Ex $1075 Gd $850**
Model 1903
(w/slotted backstrap) . . . . **NiB $1200 Ex $1075 Gd $850**
**Model 1903 (w/slotted
backstrap, shoulder stock
and extended magazine)** . . . . . . **NiB $2400 Ex $2150 Gd $1700**

MODEL 1910
POCKET AUTO PISTOL . . . . **NiB $545 Ex $385 Gd $265**
Calibers: .32 Auto (7.65mm), .380 Auto (9mm). Seven-round magazine (.32 cal.), or 6-round (.380 cal.), 3.5-inch bbl., 6 inches overall. Weight: 20.5 oz. Fixed sights. Blued finish. Hard rubber grips. Made from 1910 to 1954.

MODEL 1922 (10/.22)
POLICE/MILITARY AUTO
Calibers: .32 Auto (7.65mm), .380 Auto (9mm). Nine-round magazine (.32 cal.), or 8-round (.380 cal.), 4.5-inch bbl., 7 inches overall. Weight: 25 oz. Fixed sights. Blued finish. Hard rubber grips. Made from 1922 to 1959.
**Model 1910
commercial** . . . . **NiB $445 Ex $390 Gd $255**
**Model 191
Military contract** . . . . **NiB $550 Ex $400 Gd $325**
**Model 1910 (w/Nazi
proofs 1940-44), add** **25%**

**FN Browning
6.35mm Pocket**

**FN Browning
1900 Pocket**

**FN Browning 1910
Pocket**

**FN Browning 1922
Police/Military**

**FN Browning 1935
Military Hi-Power**

**FN Browning
Baby**

MODEL 1935 MILITARY HI-POWER PISTOL

Variation of the Browning-Colt .45 Auto design. Caliber: 9mm Para.13-round magazine, 4.63-inch bbl., 7.75 inches overall. Weight: About 35 oz. Adjustable rear sight and fixed front, or both fixed. Blued finish (Canadian manufacture Parkerized). Checkered walnut or plastic grips. Note: Above specifications in general apply to both the original FN production and the pistols made by John Inglis Company of Canada for the Chinese government. A smaller version, w/shorter bbl. and slide and 10-round magazine, was made by FN for the Belgian and Rumanian Governments about 1937 to 191940. Both types were made at the FN plant during the German occupation of Belgium.

Pre-war commercial (w/fixed sights)..... NiB $1106 Ex $890 Gd $684
Pre-war commercial
(w/tangent sight only)............... NiB $1992 Ex $1302 Gd $684
Pre-war commercial
(w/tangent sight, slotted backstrap) ... NiB $2931 Ex $2571 Gd $1386
Pre-war Belgian military contract....... NiB $1192 Ex $982 Gd $672
Pre-war Foreign military contract..... NiB $2144 Ex $1733 Gd $1208
War production (w/fixed sights)......... NiB $844 Ex $661 Gd $475
War production (w/tangent sight only).. NiB $1377 Ex $1111 Gd $783
War production
(w/tangent sight and slotted backstrap) ... NiB $3420 Ex $2716 Gd $1876
Post-war/pre-BAC (w/fixed sights) .... NiB $825 Ex $555 Gd $392
Post-war/pre-BAC (w/tangent sight only) .. NiB $875 Ex $555 Gd $392
Post-war/pre-BAC
(w/tangent sight, slotted backstrap) ...... NiB $950 Ex $784 Gd $756
Inglis manufacture
Canadian military (w/fixed sights) .... NiB $995 Ex $743 Gd $560
Canadian military
(w/fixed sight, slotted) .... NiB $1834 Ex $1465 Gd $1021
Canadian military
(w/tangent sight, slotted) .... NiB $1503 Ex $1211 Gd $850
Canadian military
(marked w/Inglis logo) .... NiB $2602 Ex $2107 Gd $1462
Chinese military contract
(w/tangent sight, slotted) .... NiB $3354 Ex $2700 Gd $1876
Canadian military
(w/fixed sight, slotted backstrap) ..... NiB $1842 Ex $1474 Gd $1029
Canadian military
(marked w/Inglis logo) .... NiB $2590 Ex $2105 Gd $1460
W/issue wooden holster, add $400

BABY AUTO PISTOL .... NiB $600 Ex $500 Gd $358
Caliber: .25 Automatic (6.35mm). Six-round magazine, 2.13-inch bbl., 4 inches overall. Weight: 10 oz. Fixed sights. Blued finish. Hard rubber grips. Made from 1931 to 1983.

FOREHAND & WADSWORTH — Worcester, Massachusetts

REVOLVERS
See listings of comparable Harrington & Richardson and Iver Johnson revolvers for values.

FORT WORTH FIREARMS — Fort Worth, TX

MATCH MASTER STANDARD.......... NiB $425 Ex $265 Gd $235
Semi-automatic. Caliber: .22LR. Equipped with 3 7/8-, 4 1/2-, 5 1/2-, 7 1/2- or 10-inch bull bbl., double extractors, includes upper push button and standard magazine release, angled grip, low profile frame. Made from 1995 to 2000.

MATCH MASTER
DOVETAIL. . . . . **NiB $485 Ex $400 Gd $310**
Similar to Match Master except has 3 7/8-, 4 1/2-, or 5 1/2-inch bbl. with dovetail rib.

MATCH MASTER DELUXE. . . . . **NiB $555 Ex $430 Gd $335**
Similar to Match master Standard except has Weaver rib on bbl.
W/10-inch bbl.. . . . . **Add $100**

SPORT KING. . . . . **NiB $565 Ex $295 Gd $260**
Semi-automatic. Caliber: .22 LR. Equipped with 4 1/2- or 5 1/2-inch bbl., blued finish, military grips, drift sights, 10 round magazine. Made from 1995 to 2000.

CITATION. . . . . **NiB $418 Ex $310 Gd $270**
Semi-automatic. Caliber: .22 LR. Equipped with 5 1/2-inch bull bbl. or 7 1/2-inch fluted bbl., military grips, 10-round magazine.

TROPHY. . . . . **NiB $413 Ex $318 Gd $253**
Semi-automatic. Caliber: .22 LR. Equipped with 5 1/2- or 7 1/2-inch bull bbl. blued finish, military grips, 10-round magazine.
W/LH action (5 1/2-inch bbl. only). . . . . **Add $50**

VICTOR. . . . . **NiB $473 Ex $373 Gd $282**
Semi-automatic. Caliber: .22LR. Equipped with 3 7/8-, 4 1/2- (VR or Weaver rib), 8- (Weaver rib) or 10-inch (Weaver rib) bbls.; blued finish, military grips, 10-round magazine.
W/4 1/2- or 4 1/2-inch Weaver rib bbls.. . . . . **Add $80**
W/8- or 10-inch Weaver rib bbls.. . . . . **Add $175**

OLYMPIC. . . . . **NiB $625 Ex $499 Gd $387**
Semi-automatic. Caliber: .22 LR or Short. Equipped with 6 1/2-inch fluted bbl., blued finish, military grips, 10-round magazine.

SHARPSHOOTER. . . . . **NiB $421 Ex $331 Gd $246**
Semi-automatic. Caliber: .22 LR. Equipped with 5 1/2-inch bull bbl.,blued finish, military grips, 10-round magazine.

LE FRANCAIS PISTOLS — St. Etienne, France
Produced by Manufacture Francaise d'Armes et Cycles

ARMY MODEL
AUTOMATIC PISTOL. . . . . **NiB $1693 Ex $1266 Gd $820**
Similar in operation to the Le Francais .25 Automatics. Caliber: 9mm Browning Long. Eight-round magazine, 5-inch bbl., 7.75 inches overall. Weight: About 34 oz. Fixed sights. Blued finish. Checkered walnut grips. Made from 1928 to 1938.

POLICEMAN MODEL
AUTOMATIC PISTOL. . . . . **NiB $957 Ex $886 Gd $375**
DA. Hinged bbl., Caliber: .25 Automatic (6.35mm). Seven-round magazine, 3.5-inch bbl., 6 inches overall. Weight: About 12 oz. Fixed sights. Blued finish. Hard rubber grips. Introduced in 1914. disc.

STAFF OFFICER MODEL
AUTOMATIC PISTOL. . . . . **NiB $355 Ex $280 Gd $199**
Caliber: .25 Automatic. Similar to the "Policeman" model except does not have cocking-piece head, barrel, is about an inch shorter and weight is an ounce less. Introduced in 1914. disc.

FREEDOM ARMS — Freedom, Wyoming

MODEL 97
PREMIER GRADE SA REVOLVER
Calibers: .357 Mag., .41 Mag. or .45 LC. Five- or 6-round cylinder, 4.25, 5, 5.5, 6 or 7.5-inch bbl., removable front blade with adjustable or fixed rear sight. Hardwood or black Micarta grips. Satin stainless finish. Made from 1997 to date.
Premier grade 97. . . . . **NiB $1685 Ex $1375 Gd $845**
For extra cylinder, add. **$200**
For fixed sights, deduct. **$140**

MODEL FA-.44 (83-44) SA REVOLVER
Similar to Model 454 Casull except chambered in .44 Mag. Made from 1988 to date.
Field grade. . . . . **NiB $1480 Ex $1110 Gd $869**
Premier grade. . . . . **NiB $1790 Ex $1327 Gd $812**
Silhouette class (w/10-inch bbl.). **NiB $1477 Ex $1117 Gd $870**
Silhouette pac
(10-inch bbl., access.). . . . . **NiB $1452 Ex $1112 Gd $859**
For fixed sights, deduct. **$95**

MODEL FA-.45 (83-45) SA REVOLVER
Similar to Model 454 Casull except chambered in .45 Long Colt. Made from 1988 to 1990.
Field grade. . . . . **NiB $1326 Ex $1007 Gd $636**
Premier grade. . . . . **NiB $1181 Ex $951 Gd $668**
For fixed sights, deduct. **$95**

MODEL FA-252 (83-22) SA REVOLVER
Calibers: .22 LR w/optional .22 Mag. cylinder. Bbl. lengths: 5.13 and 7.5 (Varmint Class), 10 inches (Silhouette Class). Adjustable express or competition silhouette sights. Brushed or matte stainless finish. Black Micarta (Silhouette) or black and green laminated hardwood grips (Varmint). Made from 1991 to date.
Silhouette class. . . . . **NiB $1976 Ex $1664 Gd $711**
Silhouette class
w/extra .22 Mag. cyl. . . . . **NiB $1550 Ex $1249 Gd $880**
Varmint class. . . . . **NiB $1195 Ex $958 Gd $680**
Varmint class
w/extra .22 Mag. cyl. . . . . **NiB $1479 Ex $1192 Gd $838**

MODEL FA-353 (83-357) SA REVOLVER
Caliber: .357 Mag., bbl. lengths: 4.75, 6, 7.5 or 9 inches. Removable blade front sight, adjustable rear. Brushed or matte stainless finish. Pachmayr Presentation or impregnated hardwood grips.
Field grade. . . . . **NiB $1038 Ex $864 Gd $597**
Premier grade. . . . . **NiB $1678 Ex $1562 Gd $712**
Silhouette class
(w/9-inch bbl.). . . . . **NiB $1059 Ex $862 Gd $612**

MODEL FA-454AS (83-454) REVOLVER
Caliber: .454 Casull (w/optional .45 ACP, .45 LC, .45 Win. Mag. cylinders). Five-round cylinder, bbl. lengths: 4.75, 6, 7.5 or 10 inches. Adjustable express or competition silhouette sights. Pachmayr presentation or impregnated hardwood grips. Brushed or matte stainless steel finish.
Field grade. . . . . **NiB $1687 Ex $1253 Gd $609**
Premier grade. . . . . **NiB $2149 Ex $1803 Gd $722**
Silhouette class (w/10-inch bbl.). **NiB $1079 Ex $869 Gd $614**
For extra cylinder, add. **$250**

MODEL FA-454FS REVOLVER
Same general specifications as Model FA-454AS except w/fixed sight.
Field grade. . . . . **NiB $1717 Ex $1484 Gd $918**
Premier grade. . . . . **NiB $1763 Ex $1510 Gd $918**

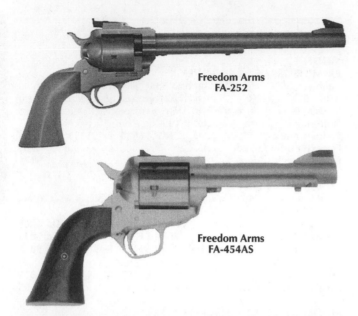

Freedom Arms
FA-252

Freedom Arms
FA-454AS

MODEL FA-454 GAS REVOLVER ...... **NiB $1697 Ex $1494 Gd $918**
Field Grade version of Model FA-454AS except not made w/12-inch bbl., Matte stainless finish, Pachmayr presentation grips. Adj. Sights or fixed sight on 4.75-inch bbl.

MODEL FA-555 REVOLVER
Similar to Model .454 Casull except chambered in .50 AK. Made 1994.
Field grade .... **NiB $1540 Ex $1119 Gd $866**
Premier grade .... **NiB $1903 Ex $1383 Gd $1023**

MODEL FA-BG-22LR
MINI-REVOLVER .... **NiB $225 Ex $160 Gd $125**
Caliber: .22 LR. Three-inch tapered bbl., partial high-gloss stainless steel finish. Disc. 1987.

MODEL FA-BG-22M
MINI-REVOLVER .... **NiB $239 Ex $177 Gd $136**
Same general specifications as model FA-BG-22LR except in caliber .22 WMR. Disc. 1987.

MODEL FA-BG-22P
MINI-REVOLVER .... **NiB $229 Ex $188 Gd $126**
Same general specifications as Model FA-BG-22LR except in .22 percussion. Disc. 1987.

MODEL FA-L-22LR MINI-REVOLVER ... **NiB $196 Ex $155 Gd $98**
Caliber: .22 LR, 1.75-inch contoured bbl., partial high-gloss stainless steel finish. Bird's-head-type grips. Disc. 1987.

MODEL FA-L-22M
MINI-REVOLVER .... **NiB $200 Ex $165 Gd $104**
Same general specifications as Model FA-L-22LR except in caliber .22 WMR. Disc. 1987.

MODEL FA-L-22P MINI-REVOLVER ... **NiB $225 Ex $152 Gd $116**
Same general specifications as Model FA-L-22LR except in .22 percussion. Disc. 1987.

MODEL FA-S-22LR MINI-REVOLVER ... **NiB $200 Ex $175 Gd $98**
Caliber: .22 LR. One-inch contoured bbl., partial high-gloss stainless steel finish. Disc. 1988.

MODEL FA-S-22M MINI-REVOLVER... **NiB $175 Ex $130 Gd $100**
Same general specifications as Model FA-S-22LR except in caliber .22 WMR. Disc. 1988.
MODEL FA-S-22P MINI-REVOLVER ... **NiB $200 Ex $170 Gd $125**
Same general specifications as Model FA-S-22LR except in .22 percussion. Disc. 1988.

FRENCH MILITARY PISTOLS — Cholet, France
Manufactured originally by Société Alsacienne de Constructions Mécaniques (S.A.C.M.). Currently made by Manufacture d'Armes Automatiques, Lotissement Industriel des Pontots, Bayonne

MODEL 1935A AUTOMATIC PISTOL ...... **NiB $350 Ex $261 Gd $134**
Caliber: 7.65mm Long. Eight-round magazine, 4.3-inch bbl., 7.6 inches overall. Weight: 26 oz. Two-lug locking system similar to the Colt U.S. M1911A1. Fixed sights. Blued finish. Checkered grips. Made 1935-45. Note: This pistol was used by French troops during WW II and in Indo-China 1945 to 1954.

MODEL 1935S AUTOMATIC PISTOL ...... **NiB $325 Ex $270 Gd $130 v**
Similar to Model 1935A except shorter (4.1-inch bbl., and 7.4 inches overall) and heavier (28 oz.). Single-step lug locking system.

MODEL 1950 AUTOMATIC PISTOL .... **NiB $465 Ex $371 Gd $265**
Caliber: 9mm Para. Nine-round magazine, 4.4-inch bbl., 7.6 inches overall. Weight: 30 oz. Fixed sights, tapered post front and U-notched rear. Similar in design and function to the U.S. .45 service automatic except no bbl. bushing.

MODEL MAB F1 AUTOMATIC PISTOL ...... **NiB $628 Ex $567 Gd $261**
Similar to Model MAB P-15 except w/6-inch bbl. and 9.6 inches overall. Adjustable target-style sights. Parkerized finish.

MODEL MAB P-8 AUTOMATIC PISTOL ..... **NiB $558 Ex $450 Gd $324**
Similar to Model MAB P-15 except w/8-round magazine,

MODEL MAB P-15 AUTOMATIC PISTOL .... **NiB $600 Ex $450 Gd $370**
Caliber: 9mm Para. 15-round magazine, 4.5-inch bbl., 7.9 inches overall. Weight: 38 oz. Fixed sights, tapered post front and U-notched rear.

FROMMER PISTOLS — Budapest, Hungary
Mfd. by Fémáru-Fegyver-és Gépgyár R.T.
LILIPUT POCKET
AUTOMATIC PISTOL .... **NiB $400 Ex $340 Gd $225**
Caliber: .25 Automatic (6.35mm). Six-round magazine, 2.14-inch bbl., 4.33 inches overall. Weight: 10.13 oz. Fixed sights. Blued finish. Hard rubber grips. Made during early 1920s. Note: Although similar in appearance to the Stop and Baby, this pistol is designed for blowback operation.

STOP POCKET AUTOMATIC PISTOL .. **NiB $395 Ex $290 Gd $155**
Locked-breech action, outside hammer. Calibers: .32 Automatic (7.65mm), .380 Auto (9mm short). Seven-round (.32 cal.) or 6-round (.380 cal.) magazine, 3.88-inch bbl., 6.5 inches overall. Weight: About 21 oz. Fixed sights. Blued finish. Hard rubber grips. Made 1912 to 1920.

BABY POCKET AUTOMATIC PISTOL .. **NiB $300 Ex $253 Gd $136**
Similar to Stop model except has 2-inch bbl., 4.75 inches overall. Weight 17.5 oz. Magazine capacity is one round less than Stop Model. Intro. shortly after WW I.

Galena Industries Inc., — Sturgis, South Dakota

Galena Industries purchased the rights to use the AMT trademark in 1998. Many, but not all, original AMT designs were included in the transaction.

AMT BACKUP . . . . NiB $455 Ex $279 Gd $210
Caliber: .380 (small frame, 2.5-inch bbl. only), .38 Super, .357 Sig, .40 S&W, .400 CorBon, .45 ACP, 9mm; magazine capacity: 5 or 6 rounds. Double action, 3-inch bbl., weight: 18 oz. (in .380), or 23 oz.
.38 Super, .357 Sig, .400 CorBon. . . . . **Add $50**

AUTOMAG II SEMI AUTO . . . . NiB $795 Ex $565 Gd $300
Caliber: .22 WMR, 9-round magazine (except 7-round in 3.38-inch bbl.); 3.38- 4.5- or 6-inch bbls.; weight: About 32 oz.

AUTOMAG III . . . . NiB $530 Ex $479 Gd $367
Similar to Automag II except chambered for the .30 Carbine cartridge, 6.38-inch bbl., stainless steel finish, weight: About 43 oz.

AUTOMAG IV . . . . NiB $530 Ex $415 Gd $325
Caliber: .45 Winchester Magnum; 7-round magazine, 6.5-inch bbl., weight: 46 oz.

AUTOMAG .440 CORBON . . . . . . NiB $785 Ex $650 Gd $540
Semiautomatic, 7.5-inch bbl., 5-round magazine, checkered walnut grips, matte black finish, weight: 46 oz. Intro. in 2000.

HARDBALLER II . . . . NiB $485 Ex $325 Gd $225
Based on the Colt Model 1911 frame. Caliber: .45 ACP, .40 S&W, .400 CorBon, 7-round magazine capacity, 5-inch bbl., weight: About 38 oz.

HARDBALLER II LONGSLIDE . . . . . NiB $510 Ex $400 Gd $320
Similar to Hardballer model except caliber: .45 ACP, 7-inch bbl., 7-round magazine capacity, stainless steel finish, weight: About 46 ounces.

HARDBALLER ACCELERATOR . . . . . NiB $560 Ex $400 Gd $300
Similar to Hardballer model except caliber: .400 CorBon, 7-inch bbl., 7-round magazine capacity, stainless steel finish, weight: About 46 ounces.

COMMANDO . . . . NiB $450 Ex $300 Gd $200
Similar to Hardballer model except caliber: .40 S&W, 4-inch bbl., 8-round magazine capacity, stainless steel finish, weight: About 38 ounces.

GALESI PISTOLS — Collebeato (Brescia), Italy Mfd. by Industria Armi Galesi

MODEL 6
POCKET AUTOMATIC PISTOL . . . . NiB $210 Ex $153 Gd $113
Calibers: .22 Long, .25 Automatic (6.35mm). Six-round magazine, 2.25-inch bbl., 4.38 inches overall. Weight: About 11 oz. Fixed sights. Blued finish. Plastic grips. Made from 1930 to date.

MODEL 9 POCKET
AUTOMATIC PISTOL
Calibers: .22 LR, .32 Auto (7.65mm), .380 Auto (9mm Short). Eight-round magazine, 3.25-inch bbl., 5.88 inches overall. Weight: About 21 oz. Fixed sights. Blued finish. Plastic grips. Made from 1930 to date.

**Galesi
Model 6 Pocket**

AUTOMATIC PISTOL
Note: Specifications vary, but those shown for .32 Automatic are common.
**.22 LR or
.380 Auto.** . . . . NiB $255 Ex $183 Gd $122
.32 Auto. . . . . NiB $235 Ex $173 Gd $106

GLISENTI PISTOL — Carcina (Brescia), Italy Mfd. by Societa Siderurgica Glisenti

MODEL 1910 ITALIAN
SERVICE AUTOMATIC. . . . . NiB $1350 Ex $1170 Gd $975
Caliber: 9mm Glisenti. Seven-round magazine, 4-inch bbl., 8.5 inches overall. Weight: About 32 oz. Fixed sights. Blued finish. Hard rubber or plastic grips. Adopted 1910 and used through WWII.

GLOCK, INC. — Smyrna, Georgia

NOTE: *Models: 17, 19, 20, 21, 22, 23, 24, 31, 32, 33, 34 and 35 were fitted with a redesigned grip-frame in 1998. Models: 26, 27, 29, 30 and all "C" guns (compensated models) retained the original frame design.*

MODEL 17 DA
AUTOMATIC PISTOL
Caliber: 9mm Parabellum. 10-, 17- or 19-round magazine, 4.5-inch bbl., 7.2 inches overall. Weight: 22 oz. w/o magazine, Polymer frame, steel bbl., slide and springs. Fixed or adj. rear sights. Matte, nonglare finish. Made of only 35 components, including three internal safety devices. Imported from 1985 to date.
Model 17 (w/fixed sights) . . . . NiB $485 Ex $379 Gd $275
Model 17C (compensated bbl.) . . . . NiB $650 Ex $525 Gd $375
W/adjustable sights, add $50
W/Meprolight sights, add $90
W/Trijicon sights, add $105

MODEL 17L
COMPETITION
Same general specifications as Model 17 except weight: 23.35 oz. with 6-inch bbl. 8.85 inches overall. Imported 1988 to 1999.
Model 1 L7 (w/fixed sights) . . . . . . .NiB $665 Ex $545 Gd $375
W/ported bbl., (early production), add $50
W/adjustable sights, add $30

**Glock Model 19
Compact**

**Glock
Model 30**

MODEL 19 COMPACT
Same general specifications as Model 17 except smaller version with 4-inch bbl., 6.85 inches overall and weight: 21 oz. Imported from 1988 to date.
Model 19 (w/fixed sights) . . . . NiB $479 Ex $390 Gd $245
Model 19C (compensated bbl.). . . . . NiB $575 Ex $475 Gd $340
W/adjustable sights, add $50
W/Meprolight sights, add $80
W/Trijicon sights, add $105

MODEL 20 DA AUTO PISTOL
Caliber: 10mm. 15-round, hammerless, 4.6-inch bbl., 7.59 inches overall. Weight: 26.3 oz. Fixed or adj. sights. Matte, non-glare finish. Made from 1990 to date.
Model 20 (w/fixed sights) . . . . NiB $500 Ex $355 Gd $260
Model 19C (compensated bbl.) . . . . NiB $600 Ex $455 Gd $360
W/adjustable sights, add $50
W/Meprolight sights, add $80
W/Trijicon sights, add $105

MODEL 21 AUTOMATIC PISTOL
Same general specifications as Model 17 except chambered in .45 ACP. 13-round magazine, 7.59 inches overall. Weight: 25.2 oz. Imported from 1990 to date.
Model 21 (w/fixed sights) . . . . NiB $500 Ex $355 Gd $260
Model 21C (compensated bbl.) . . . . NiB $600 Ex $355 Gd $260
W/adjustable sights, add $50
W/Meprolight sights, add $80
W/Trijicon sights, add $105

MODEL .22 AUTOMATIC PISTOL
Same general specifications as Model 17 except chambered for .40 S&W. 15-round magazine, 7.4 inches overall. Imported from 1990 to date.
Model .22 (w/fixed sights) . . . . NiB $479 Ex $325 Gd $250
Model 22C
(compensated bbl.) . . . . NiB $575 Ex $325 Gd $250
W/adjustable sights, add $50
W/Meprolight sights, add $80
W/Trijicon sights, add $105

MODEL 23 AUTOMATIC PISTOL
Same general specifications as Model 19 except chambered for .40 S&W. 13-round magazine, 6.97 inches overall. Imported from 1990 to date.
Model 23 (w/fixed sights) . . . . NiB $479 Ex $325 Gd $250
Model 23C (compensated bbl.) . . . . NiB $580 Ex $425 Gd $350
W/adjustable sights, add $50
W/Meprolight sights, add $80
W/Trijicon sights, add $105

MODEL 24 AUTOMATIC PISTOL
Caliber: .40 S&W, 10- and 15-round magazines (the latter for law enforcement and military use only), 8.85 inches overall. Weight: 26.5 oz. Manual trigger safety; passive firing block and drop safety. Made from 1994 to 1999.
Model 24 (w/fixed sights) . . . . NiB $675 Ex $500 Gd $380
Model 24C (compensated bbl.) . . . . NiB $775 Ex $610 Gd $480
W/adjustable sights, add $50

MODEL 26 DA AUTOMATIC PISTOL
Caliber: 9mm, 10-round magazine, 3.47-inch bbl., 6.3 inches overall. Weight: 19.77 oz. Imported from 1995 to date.
Model 26 (w/fixed sights) . . . . NiB $475 Ex $325 Gd $285
Model 26C (compensated bbl.) . . . . NiB $619 Ex $519 Gd $368
W/adjustable sights, add $30

MODEL 27 DA AUTO PISTOL
Similar to the Glock Model .22 except subcompact. Caliber: .40 S&W, 10-round magazine, 3.5-inch bbl., Weight: 21.7 oz. Polymer stocks, fixed or fully adjustable sights. Imported from 1995 to date.
Model 27 (w/fixed sights) . . . . NiB $475 Ex $359 Gd $275
W/adjustable sights, add $50
W/Meprolight sights, add $80
W/Trijicon sights, add $105

MODEL 28 COMPACT (LAW ENFORCEMENT ONLY)
Same general specifications as Model .25 except smfrom aller version. .380 ACP with 3.5-inch bbl., weight: 20 oz. Imported 1999 to date.

MODEL 29 DA AUTO PISTOL
Similar to the Glock Model 20 except subcompact. Caliber: 10mm. 10-round magazine, 3.8-inch bbl., weight: 27.1 oz. Polymer stocks, fixed or fully adjustable sights. Imported from 1997 to date.
Model 29 (w/fixed sights) . . . . NiB $520 Ex $350 Gd $250
W/adjustable sights, add $50
W/Meprolight sights, add $80
W/Trijicon sights, add $100

MODEL 30 DA AUTO PISTOL
Similar to the Glock Model 21 except subcompact. Caliber: .45 ACP. 10-round magazine, 3.8-inch bbl., weight: 26.5 oz. Polymer stocks, fixed or fully adjustable sights. Imported from 1997 to date.
Model 30 (w/fixed sights) . . . . NiB $520 Ex $350 Gd $275
W/adjustable sights, add $50
W/Meprolight sights, add $80
W/Trijicon sights, add $105

MODEL 31 DA AUTOMATIC PISTOL

Caliber: .357 Sig., safe action system. 10- 15- or 17-round magazine, 4.49-inch bbl., weight: 23.28 oz. Safe Action trigger system w/3 safeties. Imported from 1998 to date.

Model 31
(w/fixed sights) . . . . **NiB $485 Ex $325 Gd $255**
Model 31C
(compensated bbl.) . . . . **NiB $575 Ex $425 Gd $255**
W/adjustable sights, add $30
W/Meprolight sights, add $80
W/Trijicon sights, add $105

MODEL .32 DA AUTOMATIC PISTOL

Caliber: .357 Sig., safe action system. 10- 13- or 15-round magazine, 4.02-inch bbl., weight: 21.52 oz. Imported from 1998 to date.

Model .32
(w/fixed sights) . . . . **NiB $475 Ex $325 Gd $265**
Model 32C. . . . . **NiB $605 Ex $445 Gd $375**
W/adjustable sights, add $30
W/Meprolight sights, add $80
W/Trijicon Sights, add $105

MODEL 33 DA AUTOMATIC PISTOL

Caliber: .357 Sig., safe action system. Nine- or 11-round magazine, 3.46-inch bbl. Weight: 19.75 oz. Imported from 1998 to date.

Model 33
(w/fixed sights) . . . . **NiB $475 Ex $325 Gd $265**
W/adjustable sights, add $30
W/Meprolight sights, add $80
W/Trijicon sights, add $105

MODEL 34 AUTO PISTOL . . . . NiB $525 Ex $445 Gd $335

Similar to Model 17 except w/redesigned grip-frame and extended slide-stop lever and magazine release. 10-, 17- or 19-round magazine, 5.32- inch bbl. Weight: 22.9 oz. Fixed or adjustable sights. Imported from 1998 to date.

MODEL 35 AUTO PISTOL . . . . NiB $545 Ex $445 Gd $325

Similar to Model 34 except .40 S&W. Imported from 1998 to date.

MODEL 36 DA AUTOMATIC PISTOL

Caliber: .45 ACP., safe action system. Six-round magazine, 3.78-inch bbl., weight: 20.11 oz. Safe Action trigger system w/3 safeties. Imported from 1999 to date.

Model 36
(w/fixed sights) . . . . **NiB $500 Ex $420 Gd $320**
W/adjustable sights, add $50
W/Meprolight sights, add $80
W/Trijicon sights, add $105

DESERT STORM

COMMEMORATIVE. . . . . **NiB $1500 Ex $1350 Gd $1200**
Same specifications as Model 17 except "Operation Desert Storm, January 16-February 27, 1991" engraved on side of slide w/list of coalition forces. Limited issue of 1,000 guns. Made in 1991.

GREAT WESTERN ARMS CO. — North Hollywood, California

NOTE: *Values shown are for improved late model revolvers early Great Westerns are variable in quality and should be evaluated accordingly. It should also be noted that, beginning about July 1956, these revolvers were offered in kit form. Values of guns assembled from these kits will, in general, be of less value than factory-completed weapons.*

Grendel Model P-12

DOUBLE BARREL DERRINGER . . . . NiB $825 Ex $705 Gd $495

Replica of Remington Double Derringer. Caliber: .38 S&W, .38 S&W Spl. . Double bbls. (superposed), 3-inch bbl. Overall length: 5 inches. Fixed sights. Blued finish. Checkered black plastic grips. Made 1953 to 1962 in various configurations.

SA FRONTIER REVOLVER . . . . NiB $670 Ex $495 Gd $359

Replica of the Colt Single Action Army Revolver. Calibers: .22 LR, .22 WMR, .357 Magnum, .38 Special, .44 Special, .44 Magnum .45 Colt. Six-round cylinder, bbl. lengths: 4.75-, 5.5 and 7.5-inches. Weight: 40 oz. in .22 cal. w/5.5-inch bbl. Overall length: 11.13 inches w/5.5-inch bbl. Fixed sights. Blued finish. Imitation stag grips. Made from 1951 to 1962.

GRENDEL, INC. — Rockledge, Florida

MODEL P-10 AUTOMATIC PISTOL

Hammerless, blow-back action. DAO with no external safety. Caliber: .380 ACP. 10-round box magazine integrated in grip. Three-inch bbl., 5.3 inches overall. Weight: 15 oz. Matte blue, nickel or green Teflon finish. Made from 1988 to 1991.

Blued finish . . . . **NiB $200 Ex $150 Gd $95**
Nickel finish . . . . **NiB $215 Ex $165 Gd $110**
Green finish. . . . . **NiB $215 Ex $165 Gd $110**
W/compensated bbl., add $50

MODEL P-12 DA AUTOMATIC PISTOL

Caliber: .380 ACP. 11-round Zytel magazine, 3-inch bbl., 5.3 inches overall. Weight: 13 oz. Fixed sights. Polymer DuPont ST-800 grip. Made from 1991 to 1995.

Standard model . . . . **NiB $200 Ex $125 Gd $90**
Electroless nickel . . . . **NiB $220 Ex $145 Gd $110**

MODEL P-30 AUTOMATIC PISTOL

Caliber: .22 WMR. 30-round magazine, 5-or 8-inch bbl., 8.5 inches overall w/5-inch bbl., weight: 21 oz. Blade front sight, fixed rear sight. Made from 1991 to 1995.

W/5-inch bbl., ... **NiB $315 Ex $230 Gd $190**
W/8-inch bbl., ... **NiB $315 Ex $230 Gd $190**

MODEL P-31

AUTOMATIC PISTOL . . . . **NiB $450 Ex $325 Gd $260**
Caliber: .22 WMR. 30-round Zytel magazine, 11-inch bbl., 17.3 inches overall. Weight: 48 oz. Adjustable blade front sight, fixed rear. Checkered black polymer DuPont ST-800 grip and forend. Made from 1991 to 1995.

Hämmerli Model
33MP Free Pistol

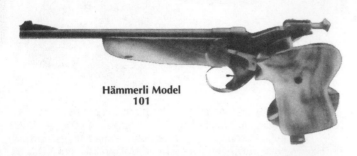

Hämmerli Model
101

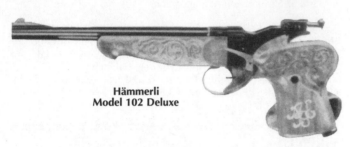

Hämmerli
Model 102 Deluxe

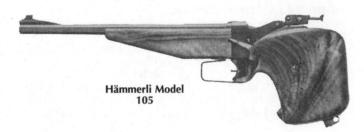

Hämmerli Model
105

GUNSITE — Paulden, Arizona

"ADVANCED TACTICAL" SA AUTO PISTOL

Manufactured w/Colt 1991 or Springfield 1991 parts. Caliber: .45 ACP. Eight-round magazine, 3.5-, 4.25-, 5-inch bbl. Weight: 32-38 oz. Checkered or laser-engraved walnut grips. Fixed or Novak Lo-mount sights.

Stainless finish . . . . NiB $1144 Ex $931 Gd $672
Blued finish . . . . NiB $996 Ex $809 Gd $582

"CUSTOM CARRY" SA AUTO PISTOL

Caliber: .45 ACP. Eight-round magazine, 3.5-, 4.25-, 5-inch bbl., Weight: 32-38 oz. Checkered or laser-engraved walnut grips. Fixed Novak Lo-mount sights. Single action, manufactured based on enhanced colt models.

Stainless finish . . . . NiB $1164 Ex $973 Gd $694
Blued finish . . . . NiB $1116 Ex $913 Gd $654

H&R 1871, INC. — Gardner, Massachusetts

NOTE: In 1991, H&R 1871, Inc. was formed from the residual of the parent company, Harrington & Richardson, and then took over the New England Firearms facility. H&R 1871 produced firearms under both their logo and the NEF brand name until 1999, when the Marlin Firearms Company acquired the assets of H&R 1871. See listings under Harrington & Richardson, Inc.

HÄMMERLI AG JAGD-UND SPORTWAFFE FABRIK — Lenzburg, Switzerland

Currently imported by Sigarms, Inc., Exeter, NH. Previously by Hammerli, USA; Beeman Precision Arms & Mandall Shooting Supplies.

MODEL 33MP FREE PISTOL . . . . . . NiB $925 Ex $830 Gd $546
System Martini single-shot action, set trigger. Caliber: .22 LR. 11.5-inch octagon bbl., 16.5 inches overall. Weight: 46 oz. Micrometer rear sight, interchangeable front sights. Blued finish. Walnut grips, forearm. Imported from 1933 to 1949.

MODEL 100 FREE PISTOL
Same general specifications as Model 33MP. Improved action and sights, redesigned stock. Standard model has plain grips and forearm, deluxe model has carved grips and forearm. Imported 1950 to 1956.
Standard model . . . . NiB $895 Ex $744 Gd $527
Deluxe model . . . . NiB $990 Ex $861 Gd $583

MODEL 101 . . . . NiB $880 Ex $760 Gd $575
Similar to Model 100 except has heavy round bbl. w/matte finish, improved action and sights, adj. grips. Weight: About 49 oz. Imported from 1956 to 1960.

MODEL 102
Same as Model 101 except bbl., has highly polished blued finish. Deluxe model (illustrated) has carved grips and forearm. Made from 1956 to 1960.
Standard model . . . . NiB $885 Ex $750 Gd $575
Deluxe model . . . . NiB $990 Ex $775 Gd $582

MODEL 103 . . . . NiB $935 Ex $800 Gd $514
Same as Model 101 except has lighter octagon bbl. (as in Model 100) w/highly polished blued finish, grips and forearm of select French walnut. Weight: About 46 oz. Imported 1956 to 1960.

MODEL 104 . . . . NiB $775 Ex $650 Gd $420
Similar to Model 102 except has lighter round bbl., improved action redesigned grips and forearm. Weight: 46 oz. Imported 1961 to 1965.

MODEL 105 . . . . NiB $935 Ex $750 Gd $475
Similar to Model 103 except has improved action, redesigned grips and forearm. Imported from 1961 to 1965.

MODEL 106 . . . . NiB $900 Ex $775 Gd $451
Similar to Model 104 except has improved trigger and grips. Made from 1966 to 1971.

MODEL 107
Similar to Model 105 except has improved trigger and stock. Deluxe model (illustrated) has engraved receiver and bbl., carved grips and forearm. Imported from 1966 to 1971.
Standard model . . . . NiB $990 Ex $800 Gd $459
Deluxe model . . . . NiB $1320 Ex $1090 Gd $775

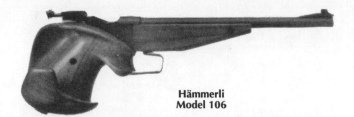

**Hämmerli
Model 106**

**Hämmerli
Model 107 Deluxe**

**Hämmerli
Model 120 Heavy Barrel**

MODEL 120 HEAVY BARREL
Same as Models 120-1 and 120-2 except has 5.7-inch heavy bbl., weight: 41 oz. Avail. w/standard or adj. grips. 1,000 made. Imported from 1972.
W/standard grips . . . . NiB $600 Ex $600 Gd $364
W/adj. grips. . . . . NiB $725 Ex $570 Gd $364

MODEL 120-1 SINGLE-
SHOT FREE PISTOL . . . . NiB $625 Ex $510 Gd $375
Side lever-operated bolt action. Adj. single-stage or two-stage trigger. Caliber: .22 LR, 9.9-inch bbl., 14.75 inches overall. Weight: 44 oz. Micrometer rear sight, front sight on high ramp. Blued finish bbl., and receiver, lever and grip frame anodized aluminum. Checkered walnut thumbrest grips. Imported from 1972 to date.

MODEL 120-2 . . . . NiB $700 Ex $620 Gd $364
Same as Model 120-1 except has hand-contoured grips w/adj. palm rest (available for right or left hand). Imported from 1972 to date.

MODELS 150/151 FREE PISTOLS
Improved Martini-type action w/lateral-action cocking lever. Set trigger adj. for weight, length and angle of pull. Caliber: .22 LR, 11.3-inch round free-floating bbl., 15.4 inches overall. Weight: 43 oz. (w/extra weights, 49.5 oz.). Micrometer rear sight, front sight on high ramp. Blued finish. Select walnut forearm and grips w/adj. palm shelf. Imported from 1972 to 1993.
Model 150 (disc. 1989) . . . . NiB $1850 Ex $1637 Gd $972
Model 151 (disc. 1993) . . . . NiB $1850 Ex $1637 Gd $972

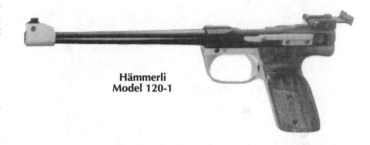

**Hämmerli
Model 120-1**

MODEL 152 ELECTRONIC PISTOL
Same general specifications as Model 150 except w/electronic trigger. Made from 1990 to 1992
Right hand . . . . NiB $1995 Ex $1756 Gd $1128
Adj. Grips. . . . . Add $300

MODELS 160/162 FREE PISTOLS
Caliber: .22 LR. Single-shot. 11.31-inch bbl., 17.5 inches overall. Weight: 46.9 oz. Interchangeable front sight blades, fully adj. match rear. Match-style stippled walnut grips w/adj. palm shelf and poly-carbon fiber forend. Imported from 1993 to 2002.
**Model 160 w/mechanical
set trigger (disc. 2000)** . . . . NiB $1745 Ex $1625 Gd $975
Model 162 w/electronic trigger. . . . . . NiB $1930 Ex $1564 Gd $1094

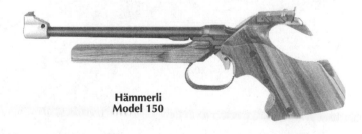

**Hämmerli
Model 150**

MODEL 208 STANDARD
AUTO PISTOL . . . . NiB $1744 Ex $1437 Gd $920
Caliber: .22 LR. Eight-round magazine, 5.9-inch bbl., 10 inches overall. Weight: 35 oz. (bbl. weight adds 3 oz.). Micrometer rear sight, ramp front. Blued finish. Checkered walnut grips w/adj. heel plate. Imported from 1966 to 1988.

MODEL 208S TARGET PISTOL . . . . NiB $2450 Ex $2137 Gd $1993
Caliber: .22 LR. Eight-round magazine, 6-inch bbl., 10.2 inches overall. Weight: 37.3 oz. Micrometer rear sight, ramp front sight. Blued finish. Stippled walnut grips w/adj. heel plate. Imported from 1988 to 2000.

MODEL 211 . . . . NiB $1550 Ex $1406 Gd $804
Same as Model 208 except has standard. Thumbrest grips. Imported from 1966 to 1990.

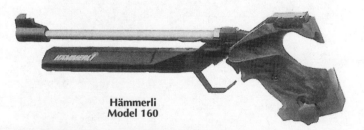

**Hämmerli
Model 160**

**Hämmerli
Model 232 Rapid Fire**

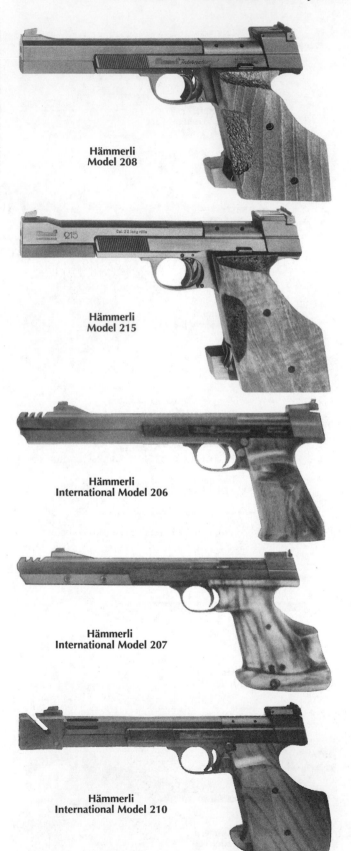

**Hämmerli
Model 208**

**Hämmerli
Model 215**

**Hämmerli
International Model 206**

**Hämmerli
International Model 207**

**Hämmerli
International Model 210**

MODEL 212
HUNTER'S PISTOL . . . . **NiB $2100 Ex $1770 Gd $1395**
Caliber: .22 LR, 4.88-inch bbl., 8.5 inches overall. Weight: 31 oz. Blade front sight, square-notched fully adj. rear. Blued finish. Checkered walnut grips. Imported from 1984 to 1993.

MODEL 215
. . . . **NiB $2320 Ex $1991 Gd $1672**
Similar to the Model 208 except w/heavier bbl. and fewer deluxe features. Imported from 1990 to 1993.

MODEL 230-1 RAPID FIRE
AUTO PISTOL . . . . **NiB $725 Ex $549 Gd $459**
Caliber: .22 Short. Five-round magazine, 6.3-inch bbl., 11.6 inches overall. Weight: 44 oz. Micrometer rear sight, post front. Blued finish. Smooth walnut thumbrest grips. Imported from 1970 to 1983.

MODEL 230-2 RAPID FIRE
AUTO PISTOL . . . . **NiB $755 Ex $576 Gd $424**
Same as Model 230-1 except has checkered walnut grips w/adj. heel plate. Imported from 1970 to 1983.

MODEL 232 RAPID FIRE
AUTO PISTOL . . . . **NiB $1399 Ex $1233 Gd $743**
Caliber: .22 Short. Six-round magazine, 5.1-inch ported bbl., 10.5 inches overall. Weight: 44 oz. Fully adj. target sights. Blued finish. Stippled walnut wraparound target grips. Imported 1984 to 1993.

INTERNATIONAL MODEL 206
AUTO PISTOL . . . . **NiB $675 Ex $450 Gd $295**
Calibers: .22 Short, .22 LR. Six-round (.22 Short) or 8-round (.22 LR) magazine, 7.1-inch bbl. w/muzzle brake, 12.5 inches overall. Weight: 33 oz. (.22 Short), 39 oz. (.22 LR) (supplementary weights add 5 and 8 oz.). Micrometer rear sight, ramp front. Blued finish. Standard thumbrest grips. Imported from 1962 to 1969.

INTERNATIONAL MODEL 207
AUTO PISTOL . . . . **NiB $725 Ex $600 Gd $450**
Same as Model 206 except has grips w/adj. heel plate, weight: 2 oz. more. Made from 1962 to 1969.

INTERNATIONAL MODEL 209
AUTO PISTOL . . . . **NiB $800 Ex $650 Gd $525**
Caliber: .22 Short. Five-round mag., 4.75-inch bbl., w/muzzle brake and gas-escape holes, 11 inches overall. Weight: 39 oz. (interchangeable front weight adds 4 oz.). Micrometer rear sight, post front. Blued finish. Standard thumbrest grips of checkered walnut. Imported from 1966 to 1970.

INTERNATIONAL MODEL 210
. . . . **NiB $800 Ex $650 Gd $500**
Same as Model 209 except has grips w/adj. heel plate, is 0.8-inch longer and weighs 1 ounce more. Made from 1966 to 1970.

MODEL 280 TARGET PISTOL

Carbon-reinforced synthetic frame and bbl., housing. Calibers: .22 LR, .32 S&W Long WC. Six-round (.22 LR) or 5-round (.32 S&W) magazine, 4.5-inch bbl. w/interchangeable metal or carbon fiber counterweights. 11.88 inches overall. Weight: 39 oz. Micro-adj. match sights w/interchangeable elements. Imported from 1988 to 2000.

.22 LR	NiB $1450	Ex $1256	Gd $589
.32 S&W Long WC	NiB $1650	Ex $1450	Gd $800

.22/.32 Conversion kit, add $775

VIRGINIAN SA REVOLVER .... NiB $700 Ex $575 Gd $410

Similar to Colt Single-Action Army except has base pin safety system (SWISSAFE). Calibers: .357 Magnum, .45 Colt. Six-round cylinder. 4.63-, 5.5- or 7.5-inch bbl., 11 inches overall (with 5.5-inch bbl.). Weight: 40 oz. (with 5.5-inch bbl.). Fixed sights. Blued bbl. and cylinder, casehardened frame, chrome-plated grip frame and trigger guard. One-piece smooth walnut stock. Imported from 1973 to 1976 by Interarms, Alexandria, Va.

WALTHER
OLYMPIA MODEL 200
AUTOMATIC PISTOL, 1952-TYPE.... NiB $666 Ex $600 Gd $459

Similar to 1936 Walther Olympia Funfkampf model. Calibers: .22 Short, .22 LR. Six-round (.22 Short) or 10-round (.22 LR) magazine, 7.5-inch bbl., 10.7 inches overall. Weight: 27.7 oz. (.22 Short, light alloy breechblock), 30.3 oz. (.22 LR). Supplementary weights provided. Adj. target sights. Blued finish. Checkered walnut thumbrest grips. Imported 1952 to 1958.

WALTHER
OLYMPIA MODEL 200,1958-TYPE... NiB $715 Ex $600 Gd $493

Same as Model 200 1952 type except has muzzle brake, 8-round magazine (.22 LR). 11.6 inches overall. Weight: 30 oz. (.22 Short), 33 oz. (.22 LR). Imported 1958 to 1963.

WALTHER
OLYMPIA MODEL 201 .... NiB $650 Ex $500 Gd $395

Same as Model 200,1952-Type except has 9.5-inch bbl. Imported from 1955 to 1957.

WALTHER
OLYMPIA MODEL 202 .... NiB $715 Ex $600 Gd $500

Same as Model 201 except has grips w/adjustable heel plate. Imported from 1955 to 1957.

WALTHER
OLYMPIA MODEL 203

Same as corresponding Model 200 (1955 type lacks muzzle brake) except has grips w/adjustable heel plate. Imported 1955 to 1963.

1955 type	NiB $715	Ex $600	Gd $520
1958 type	NiB $770	Ex $625	Gd $550

WALTHER
OLYMPIA MODEL 204

American model. Same as corresponding Model 200 (1956-Type lacks muzzle brake) except in .22 LR only, has slide stop and micrometer rear sight. Imported from 1956 to 1963.

1956-type	NiB $745	Ex $600	Gd $455
1958-type	NiB $800	Ex $680	Gd $545

WALTHER
OLYMPIA MODEL 205

American model. Same as Model 204 except has grips w/adjustable heel plate. Imported from 1956 to 1963.

**Hämmerli-Walther
Olympia Model 203 1958-Type**

**Hämmerli-Walther
Olympia Model 205**

**SIG-Hämmerli
Model P240 Target**

1956-type	NiB $800	Ex $675	Gd $588
1958-type	NiB $855	Ex $700	Gd $530

MODEL P240 TARGET AUTO PISTOL

Calibers: .32 S&W Long (wadcutter), .38 Special (wadcutter). Five-round magazine, 5.9-inch bbl., 10 inches overall. Weight: 41 oz. Micrometer rear sight, post front. Blued finish/smooth walnut thumbrest grips. Accessory .22 LR conversion unit available. Imported from 1975 to 1986.

.32 S&W Long	NiB $1475	Ex $1282	Gd $719
.38 Special	NiB $2500	Ex $2300	Gd $2000

.22 LR conversion unit. .... Add $500

Harrington & Richardson SL .32

Harrington & Richardson USRA
Model Single-Shot Target Pistol

Harrington & Richardson Model 4

Harrington & Richardson Model 5

HARRINGTON & RICHARDSON, INC. —
Gardner, Massachusetts
(Now H&R 1871, Inc., Gardner, Mass.)

Formerly Harrington & Richardson Arms Co. of Worcester, Mass. One of the oldest and most distinguished manufacturers of handguns, rifles and shotguns, H&R suspended operations on January 24, 1986. In 1987, New England Firearms was established as an independent company producing selected H&R models under the NEF logo. In 1991, H&R 1871, Inc., was formed from the residual of the parent company and then took over the New England Firearms facility. H&R 1871 produced firearms under both its logo and the NEF brand name until 1999, when the Marlin Firearms Company acquired the assets of H&R 1871.

NOTE: *For ease in finding a particular firearm, H&R handguns are grouped into Automatic/Single-Shot Pistols, followed by Revolvers. For a complete listing, please refer to the index.*

AUTOMATIC/SINGLE-SHOT PISTOLS

SL .25 PISTOL. . . . . **NiB $565 Ex $395 Gd $285**
Modified Webley & Scott design. Caliber: .25 Auto. Six-round magazine, 2-inch bbl., 4.5 inches overall. Weight: 12 oz. Fixed sights. Blued finish. Black hard rubber grips. Made from 1912 to 1916.

SL .32 PISTOL . . . . **NiB $525 Ex $300 Gd $190**
Modified Webley & Scott design. Caliber: .32 Auto. Eight-round magazine, 3.5-inch bbl., 6.5 inches overall. Weight: About 20 oz. Fixed sights. Blued finish. Black hard rubber grips. Made from 1916 to 1924.

**USRA MODEL SINGLE-
SHOT TARGET PISTOL** . . . . **NiB $527 Ex $481 Gd $277**
Hinged frame. Caliber: .22 LR, bbl. lengths: 7-, 8- and 10-inch. Weight: 31 oz. w/10-inch bbl., Adj. target sights. Blued finish. Checkered walnut grips. Made from 1928 to 1941.

REVOLVERS

**MODEL 4
(1904) DA** . . . . **NiB $240 Ex $175 Gd $80**
Solid frame. Calibers: .32 S&W Long, .38 S&W. Six-round cylinder (.32 cal.), or 5-round (.38 cal.), bbl. Lengths: 2.5-, 4.5- and 6-inch. Weight: About 16 oz. (in .32 cal.) Fixed sights. Blued or nickel finish. Hard rubber grips. Disc. prior to 1942.

MODEL 5 (1905) DA. . . . . **NiB $225 Ex $150 Gd $70**
Solid frame. Caliber: .32 S&W. Five-round cylinder, bbl., lengths: 2.5-,4.5- and 6-inch. Weight: About 11 oz. Fixed sights. Blued or nickel finish. Hard rubber grips. Disc. prior to 1942.

MODEL 6 (1906) DA. . . . . **NiB $185 Ex $110 Gd $70**
Solid frame. Caliber: .22 LR. Seven-round cylinder, bbl. lengths: 2.5, 4.5- and 6-inches. Weight: About 10 oz. Fixed sights. Blued or nickel finish. Hard rubber grips. Disc. prior to 1942.

.22 SPECIAL DA. . . . . **NiB $330 Ex $190 Gd $95**
Heavy hinged frame. Calibers: .22 LR, .22 Mag. Nine-round cylinder, 6-inch bbl., weight: 23 oz. Fixed sights, front gold-plated. Blued finish. Checkered walnut grips. Recessed safety cylinder on later models for high-speed ammunition. Disc. prior to 1942.

MODEL 199 SPORTSMAN
SA REVOLVER . . . . **NiB $324 Ex $274 Gd $146**
Hinged frame. Caliber: .22 LR. Nine-round cylinder, 6-inch bbl., 11 inches overall. Weight: 30 oz. Adj. target sights. Blued finish. Checkered walnut grips. Disc. 1951.

MODEL 504 DA . . . . **NiB $235 Ex $175 Gd $130**
Caliber: .32 H&R Magnum. Five-round cylinder, 4- or 6-inch bbl., (square butt), 3- or 4-inch bbl., round butt. Made 1984 to 1986.

MODEL 532 DA . . . . **NiB $165 Ex $120 Gd $80**
Caliber: .32 H&R Magnum. Five-round cylinder, 2.5- or 4-inch bbl., weight: Approx. 20 and 25 oz. respectively. Fixed sights. American walnut grips. Lustre blued finish. Made 1984 to 1986.

MODEL 586 DA . . . . **NiB $275 Ex $180 Gd $125**
Caliber: .32 H&R Magnum. Five-round cylinder. bbl. lengths: 4.5, 5.5, 7.5, 10 inches. Weight: 30 oz. average. Adj. rear sight, blade front. Walnut finished hardwood grips. Made from 1984 to 1986.

MODEL 603 TARGET . . . . **NiB $210 Ex $150 Gd $110**
Similar to Model 903 except in .22 WMR. Six-round capacity w/unfluted cylinder. Made from 1980 to 1983.

MODEL 604 TARGET . . . . **NiB $210 Ex $150 Gd $110**
Similar to Model 603 except w/6-inch bull bbl., weight: 38 oz. Made from 1980 to 1983.

MODEL 622/623 DA . . . . **NiB $165 Ex $121 Gd $75**
Solid frame. Caliber: .22 Short, Long, LR, 6-round cylinder. bbl., lengths: 2.5-, 4-, 6-inches. Weight: 26 oz. (with 4-inch bbl.). Fixed sights. Blued finish. Plastic grips. Made from 1957 to 1986. Note: Model 623 is same except chrome or nickel finish.

MODEL 632/633
GUARDSMAN DA REVOLVER . . . . **NiB $165 Ex $106 Gd $71**
Solid Frame. Caliber: .32 S&W Long. Six-round cylinder, bbl., lengths: 2.5- or 4-inch. Weight: 19 oz. (with 2.5-inch bbl.). Fixed sights. Blued or chrome finish. Checkered Tenite grips (round butt on 2.5-inch, square butt on 4-inch). Made from 1953 to 1986. Note: Model 633 is the same except for chrome or nickel finish.

MODEL 649/650 DA . . . . **NiB $250 Ex $150 Gd $90**
Solid frame. Side loading and ejection. Convertible model w/two 6-round cylinders. Calibers: .22 LR, .22 WMR. 5.5-inch bbl., Weight: 32 oz. Adj. rear sight, blade front. Blued finish. One-piece, Western-style walnut grip. Made from 1976 to 1986. Note: Model 650 is same except nickel finish.

MODEL 666 DA . . . . **NiB $145 Ex $96 Gd $60**
Solid frame. Convertible model w/two 6-round cylinders. Calibers: .22 LR, .22 WMR. Six-inch bbl., weight: 28 oz. Fixed sights. Blued finish. Plastic grips. Made from 1976 to 1978.

MODEL 676 DA . . . . **NiB $275 Ex $190 Gd $100**
Solid frame. Side loading and ejection. Convertible model w/two 6-round cylinders. Calibers: .22 LR, .22 WMR, bbl. lengths: 4.5, 5.5, 7.5, 12-inches. Weight: 32 oz. (with 5.5-inch bbl.). Adj. rear sight, blade front. Blued finish, color-casehardened frame. One-piece, Western-style walnut grip. Made from 1976 to 1980.

MODEL 686 DA . . . . **NiB $285 Ex $190 Gd $116**
Caliber: .22 LR and .22 WMR. Six-round magazine, 4.5, 5.5, 7.5, 10 or 12-inch bbl. Adj. rear sight, ramp and blade front. Blued, color-casehardened frame. Weight: 31 oz. (with 4.5-inch bbl.). Made from 1980 to 1986.

Harrington & Richardson
Model 6

Harrington & Richardson
.22 Special

Harrington & Richardson
Model 199 Sportsman

Harrington & Richardson
Model 632

Harrington & Richardson
Model 622

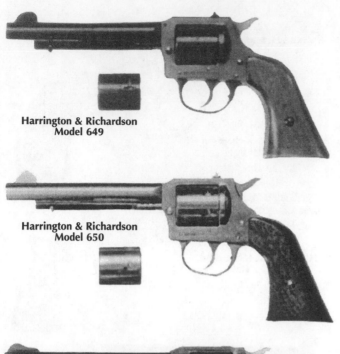

Harrington & Richardson
Model 649

Harrington & Richardson
Model 650

Harrington & Richardson
Model 686

Harrington & Richardson
Model 666

Harrington & Richardson
Model 733

Harrington & Richardson
Model 676

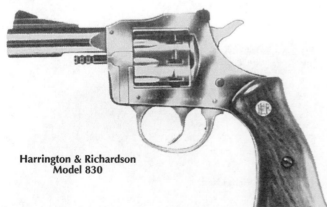

Harrington & Richardson
Model 830

MODEL 732/733 DA . . . . NiB $185 Ex $124 Gd $78
Solid frame, swing-out 6-round cylinder. Calibers: .32 S&W, .32 S&W Long. bbl., lengths: 2.5 and 4-inch. Weight: 26 oz. (with 4-inch bbl.). Fixed sights (windage adj. rear on 4-inch bbl. model). Blued finish. Plastic grips. Made from 1958 to 1986. Note: Model 733 is the same except with nickel finish.

MODEL 826 DA . . . . NiB $190 Ex $129 Gd $83
Caliber: .22 WMR. Six-round magazine, 3-inch bull bbl., ramp and blade front sight, adj. rear. American walnut grips. Weight: 28 oz. Made from 1981 to 1983.

MODEL 829/830 DA
Same as Model 826 except in .22 LR caliber. Nine round capacity. Made from 1981 to 1983.
Model 829, blued . . . . NiB $175 Ex $134 Gd $88
Model 830, nickel . . . . NiB $170 Ex $130 Gd $93

MODEL 832,1833 DA
Same as Model 826 except in .32 SW Long. Blued or nickel finish. Made from 1981 to 1983.
Model 832, blued . . . . NiB $190 Ex $108 Gd $73
Model 833, nickel . . . . NiB $190 Ex $108 Gd $73

MODEL 900/901 DA . . . . NiB $170 Ex $100 Gd $65
Solid frame, snap-out cylinder. Calibers: .22 Short, Long, LR. Nine-round cylinder, bbl. lengths: 2.5, 4, and 6-inches. Weight: 26 oz. (with 6-inch bbl.). Fixed sights. Blued finish. Cycolac grips. Made from 1962 to 1973. Note: Model 901 (disc. in 1963) is the same except has chrome finish and white Tenite grips.

MODEL 903 TARGET . . . . NiB $225 Ex $162 Gd $106
Caliber: .22 LR. Nine round capacity. SA/DA, 6-inch target-weight flat-side bbl., swing-out cylinder. Weight: 35 oz. Blade front sight, adj. rear. American walnut grips. Made from 1980- to 1983.

MODEL 904 TARGET . . . . NiB $245 Ex $160 Gd $106
Similar to Model 903 except 4 or 6-inch bull bbl. Weight: 32 oz. with 4-inch bbl. Made from 1980 to 1986.

**Harrington & Richardson
Model 900**

**Harrington & Richardson
Model 925**

**Harrington & Richardson
Model 903**

**Harrington & Richardson
Model 905**

**Harrington & Richardson
Model 922, First Issue**

**Harrington & Richardson
Model 922, Second Issue**

**Harrington & Richardson
Model 926**

MODEL 905
TARGET . . . . **NiB $255 Ex $172 Gd $129**
Same as Model 904 except w/4-inch bbl. only. Nickel finish. Made from 1981 to 1983.

MODEL 922
DA REVOLVER
FIRST ISSUE . . . . **NiB $215 Ex $172 Gd $131**
Solid frame. Caliber: .22 LR. Nine-round cylinder, 10-inch octagon bbl., (early model) or 6-inches, round bbl. (later production). Weight: 26 oz. (with 6-inch bbl.). Fixed sights. Blued finish. Checkered walnut grips. Safety cylinder on later models. Disc. prior to 1942.

MODEL 922/923
DA REVOLVER,
SECOND ISSUE . . . . **NiB $195 Ex $103 Gd $79**
Solid frame. Caliber: .22 LR. Nine-round cylinder, bbl. lengths: 2.5, 4, and 6-inches. Weight: 24 oz. (with 4-inch bbl.). Fixed sights. Blued finish. Plastic grips. Made 1950 to 1986. Note: Second Issue Model 922 has a different frame from that of the First Issue. Model 923 is same as Model 922, Second Issue except for nickel finish.

MODEL 925
DEFENDER . . . . **NiB $235 Ex $139 Gd $104**
DA. Hinged frame. Caliber: .38 S&W. Five-round cylinder, 2.5-inch bbl., weight: 22 oz. Adj. rear sight, fixed front. Blued finish. One-piece wraparound grip. Made from 1964 to 1978.

MODEL 926 DA . . . . **NiB $225 Ex $145 Gd $100**
Hinged frame. Calibers: .22 LR, .38 S&W. Nine-round (.22 LR) or 5-round (.38) cylinder, 4-inch bbl., weight: 31 oz. Adj. rear sight, fixed front. Blued finish. Checkered walnut grips. Made 1968 to 1978.

Harrington & Richardson
Model 939

Harrington & Richardson
Model 949

Harrington & Richardson
Model 950

Harrington & Richardson
Model 999, First Issue

Harrington & Richardson
Model 999, Second Issue

Harrington & Richardson
Model 929

MODEL 929/930
SIDEKICK DA REVOLVER . . . . NiB $195 Ex $118 Gd $89
Caliber: .22 LR. Solid frame, swing-out 9-round cylinder, bbl. lengths: 2.5-, 4-, 6-inches. Weight: 24 oz. (with 4-inch bbl.). Fixed sights. Blued finish. Checkered plastic grips. Made from 1956 to 1986. Note: Model 930 is same except with nickel finish.

MODEL 939/940
ULTRA SIDEKICK
DA REVOLVER. . . . . NiB $275 Ex $175 Gd $100
Solid frame, swing-out 9-round cylinder. Safety lock. Calibers: .22 Short, Long, LR. Flat-side 6-inch bbl. w/vent rib. Weight: 33 oz. Adj. rear sight, ramp front. Blued finish. Checkered walnut grips. Made 1958 to 1986, reintroduced by H&R 1871 in 1992. Note: Model 940 is same except has round bbl.

MODEL 949/950
FORTY-NINER
DA REVOLVER. . . . . NiB $250 Ex $170 Gd $97
Solid frame. Side loading and ejection. Calibers: .22 Short, Long, LR. Nine-round cylinder, 5.5- or 7.5 inch bbl., weight: 31 to 38 oz. Adj. rear sight, blade front. Blued or nickel finish. One-piece, Western-style walnut grip. Made 1960 to 1986, reintroduced by H&R 1871 in 1992 to 1999. Note: Model 950 is same except has nickel finish.

MODEL 976 DA . . . . NiB $295 Ex $185 Gd $100
Same as Model 949 except has color-casehardened frame, 7.5-inch bbl. Weight: 36 oz. Intro. 1977. Disc.

HARRINGTON & RICHARDSON
MODEL 999 SPORTSMAN
DA REVOLVER, FIRST ISSUE . . . . . . NiB $425 Ex $295 Gd $188
Hinged frame. Calibers: .22 LR, .22 Mag. Same specifications as Model 199 Sportsman Single Action. Disc. before 1942.

MODEL 999 SPORTSMAN
DA REVOLVER
SECOND ISSUE. . . . . NiB $425 Ex $295 Gd $185
Hinged frame. Caliber: .22 LR. Nine-round cylinder, 6-inch bbl. w/vent rib. Weight: 30 oz. Adj. sights. Blued finish. Checkered walnut grips. Made from 1950 to 1986.

(NEW) MODEL 999 SPORTSMAN
DA REVOLVER. . . . . NiB $425 Ex $295 Gd $185
Hinged frame. Caliber: .22 Short, Long, LR. Nine-round cylinder. Six-inch bbl. w/vent rib. Weight: 30 oz. Blade front sight adj. for elevation, square-notched rear adj. for windage. Blued finish. Checkered hardwood grips. Reintroduced by H&R 1871 in 1992.

AMERICAN DA . . . . **NiB $235 Ex $99 Gd $75**
Solid frame. Calibers: .32 S&W Long, .38 S&W. Six-round (.32 cal.) or 5-round (.38 cal.) cylinder, bbl. lengths: 2.5-,4.5- and 6-inches. Weight: About 16 oz. Fixed sights. Blued or nickel finish. Hard rubber grips. Disc. prior to 1942.

AUTOMATIC EJECTING DA REVOLVER . . . . . **NiB $221 Ex $165 Gd $120**
Hinged frame. Calibers: .32 S&W Long, .38 S&W. Six-round (.32 cal.) or 5-round (.38 cal.) cylinder, bbl. lengths: 3.25-, 4-, 5- and 6-inches. Weight: 16 oz. (.32 cal.), 15 oz. (.38 cal.). Fixed sights. Blued or nickel finish. Black hard rubber grips. Disc. prior to 1942.

**Harrington & Richardson
Automatic Ejecting**

BOBBY DA . . . . **NiB $285 Ex $195 Gd $145**
Hinged frame. Calibers: .32 S&W, .38 S&W. Six-round cylinder (.32 cal.) or 5-round (.38 cal.). Four-inch bbl., 9 inches overall. Weight: 23 oz. Fixed sights. Blued finish. Checkered walnut grips. Disc. 1946. Note: Originally designed and produced for use by London's bobbies.

DEFENDER .38 DA . . . . **NiB $325 Ex $200 Gd $100**
Hinged frame. Based on the Sportsman design. Caliber: .38 S&W. Bbl. lengths: 4- and 6-inches, 9 inches overall (with 4-inch bbl.). Weight: 25 oz. with 4-inch bbl. Fixed sights. Blued finish. Black plastic grips. Disc. 1946. Note: This model was manufactured during WW II as an arm for plant guards, auxiliary police, etc.

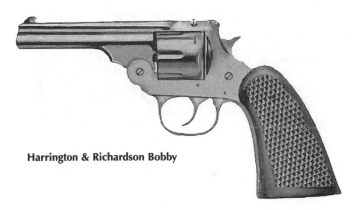

Harrington & Richardson Bobby

EXPERT MODEL DA . . . . **NiB $430 Ex $265 Gd $195**
Same specifications as .22 Special except has 10-inch bbl., weight: 28 oz. Disc. prior to 1942.

HAMMERLESS DA, LARGE FRAME . . . . **NiB $190 Ex $125 Gd $109**
Hinged frame. Calibers: .32 S&W Long 38 S&W. Six-round (.32 cal.), or 5-round (.38 cal.) cylinder, bbl. lengths: 3.25, 4, and 6-inches. Weight: About 17 oz. Fixed sights. Blued or nickel finish. Hard rubber grips. Disc. prior to 1942.

HAMMERLESS DA, SMALL FRAME . . . . **NiB $180 Ex $125 Gd $92**
Hinged frame. Calibers: .22 LR, .32 S&W. Seven-round (.22 cal.) or 5-round (.32 cal.) cylinder, bbl. lengths: 2, 3, 4, 5 and 6-inches. Weight: About 13 oz. Fixed sights. Blued or nickel finish. Hard rubber grips. Disc. prior to 1942.

**Harrington & Richardson
Defender .38**

HUNTER MODEL DA . . . . **NiB $565 Ex $400 Gd $295**
Solid frame. Caliber: .22 LR. Nine-round cylinder, 10-inch octagon bbl., weight: 26 oz. Fixed sights. Blued finish. Checkered walnut grips. Safety cylinder on later models. Note: An earlier Hunter Model was built on the smaller 7-round frame. Disc. prior to 1942.

NEW DEFENDER DA . . . . **NiB $325 Ex $235 Gd $175**
Hinged frame. Caliber: .22 LR. Nine-round cylinder, 2-inch bbl., 6.25 inches overall. Weight: 23 oz. Adj. sights. Blued finish. Checkered walnut grips, round butt. Note: Basically, this is the Sportsman DA w/a short bbl., Disc. prior to 1942.

PREMIER DA . . . . **NiB $285 E $175 Gd $95**
Small hinged frame. Calibers: .22 LR, .32 S&W. Seven-round (.22 LR) or 5-round (.32) cylinder. Bbl. Lengths: 2, 3, 4, 5, and 6-inches. Weight: 13 oz. (in .22 LR), 12 oz. (in .32 S&W). Fixed sights. Blued or nickel finish. Black hard rubber grips. Disc. prior to 1942.

MODEL STR 022 BLANK REVOLVER . . . . **NiB $125 Ex $90 Gd $70**
Caliber: .22 RF blanks. Nine-round cylinder, 2.5-inch bbl. Weight: 19 oz. Satin blued finish.

MODEL STR 032 BLANK REVOLVER . . . . **NiB $140 Ex $95 Gd $75**
Same general specifications as STR 022 except chambered for .32 S&W blank cartridges.

**Harrington & Richardson
Hammerless, Small Frame**

**Harrington & Richardson
Premier**

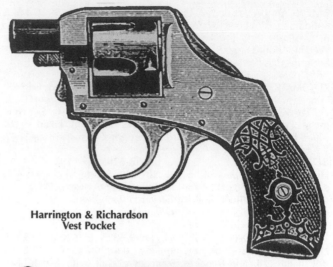

**Harrington & Richardson
Vest Pocket**

**Harrington & Richardson
Target**

**Harrington & Richardson
Young American**

**Harrington & Richardson
Trapper**

**Harrington & Richardson
Ultra Sportsmen**

TARGET MODEL DA . . . . **NiB $210 Ex $157 Gd $114**
Small hinged frame. Calibers: .22 LR, .22 W.R.F. Seven-round cylinder, 6-inch bbl., weight: 16 oz. Fixed sights. Blued finish. Checkered walnut grips. Disc. prior to 1942.

TRAPPER MODEL DA . . . . **NiB $365 Ex $200 Gd $120**
Solid frame. Caliber: .22 LR. Seven-round cylinder, 6-inch octagon bbl., weight: 12.5 oz. Fixed sights. Blued finish. Checkered walnut grips. Safety cylinder on later models. Disc. prior to 1942.

ULTRA SPORTSMAN . . . . **NiB $300 Ex $208 Gd $157**
SA. Hinged frame. Caliber: .22 LR. Nine-round cylinder, 6-inch bbl., weight: 30 oz. Adj. target sights. Blued finish. Checkered walnut grips. This model has short action, wide hammer spur, cylinder is length of a .22 LR cartridge. Disc. prior to 1942.

VEST POCKET DA . . . . **NiB $129 Ex $99 Gd $75**
Solid frame. Spurless hammer. Calibers: .22 Rimfire, .32 S&W. Seven-round (.22 cal.) or 5-round (.32 cal.) cylinder, 1.13-inch bbl., weight: About 9 oz. Blued or nickel finish. Hard rubber grips. Disc. prior to 1942.

YOUNG AMERICA DA . . . . **NiB $235 Ex $100 Gd $75**
Solid frame. Calibers: .22 Long, .32 S&W. Seven-round (.22 cal.) or 5-round (.32 cal.) cylinder. Bbl. lengths: 2-, 4.5- and 6-inches. Weight: About 9 oz. Fixed sights. Blued or nickel finish. Hard rubber grips. Disc. prior to 1942.

HARTFORD ARMS & EQUIPMENT CO. — Hartford, Connecticut

Hartford pistols were the forebearer of the original High Standard line. High Standard Mfg. Corp. acquired Hartford Arms & Equipment Co. in 1932. The High Standard Model B is essentially the same as the Hartford Automatic.

AUTOMATIC TARGET PISTOL.....NiB $610 Ex $505 Gd $405
Caliber. .22 LR. 10-round magazine, 6.75-inch bbl., 10.75 inches overall. Weight: 31 oz. Target sights. Blued finish. Black rubber grips. This gun closely resembles the early Colt Woodsman and High Standard pistols. Made 1929 to 1930.

REPEATING PISTOL.............NiB $750 Ex $553 Gd $324
Check for authenticity. This model is a hand-operated repeating pistol similar to the Fiala and Schall pistols Made from 1929 to 1930.

SINGLE-SHOT TARGET PISTOL....NiB $750 Ex $543 Gd $324
Similar in appearance to the Hartford Automatic. Caliber: .22 LR, 6.75-inch bbl., 10.75 inches overall. Weight: 38 oz. Target sights. Mottled frame and slide, blued bbl., Black rubber or walnut grips. Made from 1929 to 1930.

HASKELL MANUFACTURING — Lima, Ohio
See listings under Hi-Point.

HAWES FIREARMS — Van Nuys, California

DEPUTY MARSHAL SA REVOLVER
Calibers: .22 LR, also .22 WMR in two-cylinder combination. Six-round cylinder, 5.5-inch bbl., 11 inches overall. Weight: 34 oz. Adj. rear sight, blade front. Blued finish. Plastic or walnut grips. Imported 1973 to 1981.
.22 LR (plastic grips).............NiB $200 Ex $110 Gd $70
Combination, .22 LR/.22 WMR (plastic)....NiB $150 Ex $125 Gd $90
Walnut grips, add...................................$10

DEPUTY DENVER MARSHAL
Same as Deputy Marshal SA except has brass frame. Imported 1973 to 1981.
.22 LR (plastic grips)..................NiB $245 Ex $196 Gd $100
Combination, .22 LR/.22 WMR (plastic)...NiB $275 Ex $210 Gd $125
Walnut grips add.......................................$10

DEPUTY MONTANA MARSHAL
Same as Deputy Marshal except has brass grip frame. Walnut grips only. Imported from 1973 to 1981.
.22 LR ....NiB $260 Ex $190 Gd $110
Combination, .22 LR/.22 WMR....NiB $290 Ex $220 Gd $155

DEPUTY SILVER CITY MARSHAL
Same as Deputy Marshal except has chrome-plated frame, brass grip frame, blued cylinder and bbl., Imported from 1973 to 1981.
.22 LR (plastic grips) ....NiB $265 Ex $196 Gd $145
Combination, .22 LR/.22 WMR (plastic)...NiB $295 Ex $220 Gd $110
Walnut grips add $10

DEPUTY TEXAS MARSHAL
Same as Deputy Marshal except has chrome finish. Imported 1973 to 1981.
.22 LR (plastic grips)................NiB $275 Ex $195 Gd $100
Combination, .22 LR/.22 WMR (plastic) ...NiB $295 Ex $175 Gd $100
Walnut grips add.......................................$10

FAVORITE SINGLE-SHOT TARGET PISTOL..NiB $200 Ex $115 Gd $75
Replica of Stevens No. 35. Tip-up action. Caliber: .22 LR. Eight-inch bbl., 12 inches overall. Weight: 24 oz. Target sights. Chrome-plated frame. Blued bbl., Plastic or rosewood grips (add $5). Imported 1972- to 1976.

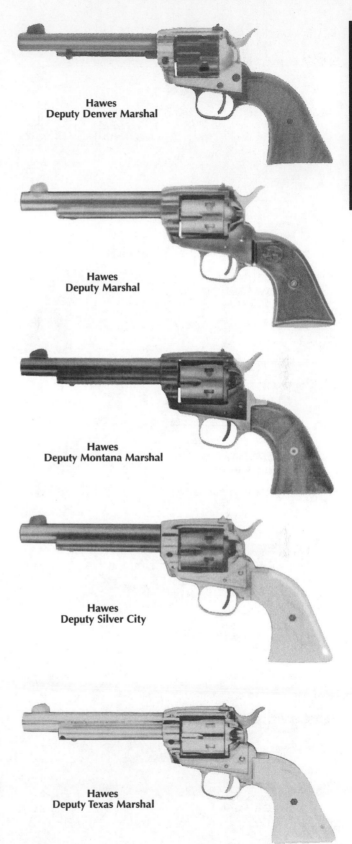

Hawes
Deputy Denver Marshal

Hawes
Deputy Marshal

Hawes
Deputy Montana Marshal

Hawes
Deputy Silver City

Hawes
Deputy Texas Marshal

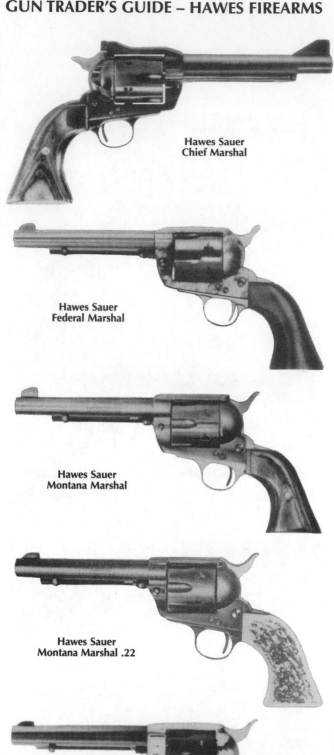

Hawes Sauer
Chief Marshal

Hawes Sauer
Federal Marshal

Hawes Sauer
Montana Marshal

Hawes Sauer
Montana Marshal .22

Hawes Sauer
Silver City Marshal

Hawes Sauer
Texas Marshal

SAUER CHIEF MARSHAL SA TARGET REVOLVER
Same as Western Marshal except has adjustable rear sight and front sight, oversized rosewood grips. Not made in .22 caliber. Imported from 1973 to 1981.

.357 Magnum or .45 Colt . . . . NiB $300 Ex $241 Gd $175
.44 Magnum . . . . NiB $344 Ex $266 Gd $193
Combination .357 Magnum
and 9mm Para.
.45 Colt and .45 Auto . . . . NiB $343 Ex $277 Gd $164
Combination
.44 Magnum and .44-40 . . . . NiB $337 Ex $266 Gd $190

SAUER FEDERAL MARSHAL
Same as Western Marshal except has color-casehardened frame, brass grip frame, one-piece walnut grip. Not made in .22 caliber. Imported from 1973 to 1981.

.357 Magnum or .45 Colt . . . . NiB $287 Ex $226 Gd $164
.44 Magnum . . . . NiB $332 Ex $246 Gd $172
Combination
.357 Magnum and 9mm Para.,
.45 Colt and .45 Auto . . . . NiB $333 Ex $278 Gd $160
Combination .44 Magnum and .44-40 . . . . NiB $328 Ex $257 Gd $152

SAUER MONTANA MARSHAL
Same as Western Marshal except has brass grip frame. Imported from 1973 to 1981.

.357 Magnum or .45 Colt . . . . NiB $298 Ex $241 Gd $176
.44 Magnum . . . . NiB $324 Ex $266 Gd $193
Combination .357 Magnum and 9mm Para.,
.45 Colt and .45 Auto . . . . NiB $349 Ex $285 Gd $206
Combination .44 Magnum and .44-40 . . . . NiB $359 Ex $295 Gd $213
.22 LR . . . . NiB $295 Ex $235 Gd $172
Combination .22 LR and .22 WMR . . . . NiB $304 Ex $250 Gd $182

SAUER SILVER CITY MARSHAL
Same as Western Marshal except has nickel plated frame, brass grip frame, blued cylinder and barrel, pearlite grips. Imported from 1973 to 1981.

.44 Magnum . . . . NiB $359 Ex $288 Gd $209
Combination .357 Magnum and 9mm Para.
.45 Colt and .45 Auto . . . . NiB $343 Ex $252 Gd $170
Combination .44 Magnum and .44-40 . . . . NiB $359 Ex $263 Gd $196

SAUER TEXAS MARSHAL
Same as Western Marshal except nickel plated, has pearlite grips. Imported from 1973 to 1981.

.357 Magnum or .45 Colt . . . . NiB $335 Ex $267 Gd $194
.44 Magnum . . . . NiB $344 Ex $283 Gd $204
Combination .357 Magnum and 9mm Para.,
.45 Colt and .45 Auto . . . . NiB $369 Ex $303 Gd $219
Combination .44 Magnum and .44-40 . . . . NiB $389 Ex $318 Gd $229
.22 LR . . . . NiB $287 Ex $237 Gd $174
Combination .22 LR and .22 WMR . . . . NiB $317 Ex $247 Gd $176

SAUER WESTERN MARSHAL SA REVOLVER

Calibers: .22 LR (disc.), .357 Magnum, .44 Magnum, .45 Auto. Also in two-cylinder combinations: .22 WMR (disc.), 9mm Para., .44-40, .45 Auto. Six-round cylinder, bbl. lengths: 5.5-inch (disc.), 6-inch, 11.75 inches overall (with 6-inch bbl.). Weight: 46 oz. Fixed sights. Blued finish. Originally furnished w/simulated stag plastic grips. Recent production has smooth rosewood grips. Made from 1968 by J. P. Sauer & Sohn, Eckernforde, Germany. Imported from 1973 to 1981.

.357 Magnum or .45 Colt . . . . NiB $325 Ex $242 Gd $177
.44 Magnum . . . . NiB $350 Ex $277 Gd $197
Combination .357 Magnum and 9mm Para.,
.45 Colt and .45 Auto . . . . NiB $355 Ex $257 Gd $191
Combination .44 Magnum
and .44-40 . . . . NiB $375 Ex $283 Gd $204
.22 LR . . . . NiB $265 Ex $191 Gd $151
Combination .22 LR
and .22 WMR . . . . NiB $265 Ex $227 Gd $171

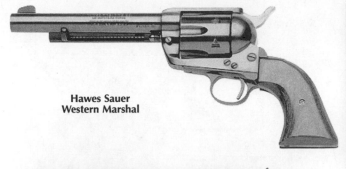

Hawes Sauer Western Marshal

HECKLER & KOCH — Oberndorf am Neckar, West Germany, and Chantilly, Virginia

MODEL HK4 DA AUTO PISTOL

Calibers: .380 Automatic (9mm Short), .22 LR, .25 Automatic (6.35mm), .32 Automatic (7.65mm) w/conversion kits. Seven-round magazine (.380 Auto), 8-round in other calibers, 3.4-inch bbl., 6.19 inches overall. Weight: 18 oz. Fixed sights. Blued finish. Plastic grip. Disc. 1984.

.22 LR or .380 Automatic . . . . NiB $485 Ex $357 Gd $247
.25 ACP or .32 ACP Automatic . . . . NiB $485 Ex $357 Gd $247
.380 Automatic w/.22
conversion unit . . . . NiB $475 Ex $325 Gd $220
.380 Automatic w/.22, .25, .32
conversion units . . . . NiB $475 Ex $325 Gd $220

Heckler & Koch Model HK4

MODEL MARK 23

DA AUTO PISTOL . . . . NiB $2274 Ex $1748 Gd $1217
Short-recoil semiautomatic pistol w/polymer frame and steel slide. Caliber: .45 ACP. 10-round magazine, 5.87-inch bbl., 9.65 inches overall. Weight: 43 oz. Seven interchangeable rear sight adjustment units w/3-dot system. Developed primarily in response to specifications by the Special Operations Command (SOCOM) for a Special Operations Forces Offensive Handgun Weapon System. Imported from 1996 to date.

Heckler & Koch Mark 23

MODEL P7 K3 DA

AUTO PISTOL
Caliber: .380 ACP. Eight-round magazine, 3.8 inch-bbl., 6.3 inches overall. Weight: About 26 oz. Adj. rear sight. Imported 1988 to 1994.
P7K3 in .380 Cal. . . . . NiB $913 Ex $753 Gd $526
.22 LR conversion kit. . . . . NiB $681 Ex $588 Gd $413
.32 ACP conversion kit . . . . NiB $362 Ex $310 Gd $218

MODEL P7 M8 . . . . NiB $1250 Ex $764 Gd $548

Squeeze-cock SA semiautomatic pistol. Caliber: 9mm Para. Eight-round magazine, 4.13-inch bbl., 6.73 inches overall. Weight: 29.9 oz. Matte black or nickel finish. Adjustable rear sight. Imported from 1985 to 2005.

MODEL P7 M10

Caliber: .40 S&W. Nine-round magazine, 4.2-inch bbl., 6.9 inches overall. Weight: 43 oz. Fixed front sight blade, adj. rear w/3-dot system. Imported from 1992 to 1994.
Blued finish . . . . NiB $1125 Ex $863 Gd $621
Nickel finish . . . . NiB $1125 Ex $873 Gd $521

Heckler & Koch Model P7K3

**Heckler & Koch
Model P7M13**

Heckler & Koch USP45

**Heckler & Koch
Model P7 (PSP)**

**Heckler & Koch
Model P9S DA**

MODEL P7 M13 . . . . **NiB $2150 Ex $1792 Gd $1571**
Caliber: 9mm. 13-round magazine, 4.13-inch bbl., 6.65 inches overall. Weight: 34.42 oz. Matte black finish. Adj. rear sight. Imported 1985 to 1994.

**MODEL P7 (PSP)
AUTO PISTOL** . . . . **NiB $850 Ex $677 Gd $481**
Caliber: 9mm Para. Eight-round magazine, 4.13-inch bbl., 6.54 inches overall. DA. Weight: About 33.5 oz. Blued finish. Imported 1983 to 1985 and again in 1990 with limited availability.

**MODEL P9S
DA AUTOMATIC PISTOL**
Calibers: 9mm Para., .45 Automatic. Nine-round (9mm) or 7-round (.45 Auto) magazine. Four-inch bbl., 7.63 inches overall. Weight: 32 ounces. Fixed sights. Blued finish. Contoured plastic grips. This model disc. 1986.
9mm . . . . **NiB $850 Ex $625 Gd $456**
.45 Automatic . . . . **NiB $875 Ex $682 Gd $471**

MODEL P9S TARGET COMPETITION KIT
Same as Model P9S Target except comes w/extra 5.5-inch bbl. and bbl. weights. Also available w/walnut competition grip.
W/standard grip . . . . **NiB $1000 Ex $900 Gd $712**
Competition grip . . . . **NiB $1150 Ex $1063 Gd $750**

MODEL SP89. . . . . **NiB $3944 Ex $3161 Gd $2183**
Semiautomatic, recoil-operated, delayed roller-locked bolt system. Caliber: 9mm Para. 15-round magazine, 4.5-inch bbl., 13 inches overall. Weight: 68 oz. Hooded front sight, adj. rotary-aperture rear. Imported 1989 to 1993.

**MODEL USP
AUTO PISTOL**
Polymer integral grip/frame design w/recoil reduction system. Calibers: 9mm Para., .40 S&W or .45 ACP. 15-round (9mm) or 13-round (.40 S&W and .45ACP) magazine, 4.13- or 4.25-inch bbl., 6.88 to 7.87 inches overall. Weight: 26.5-30.4 oz. Blade front sight, adj. rear w/3-dot system. Matte black or stainless finish. Stippled black polymer grip. Available in SA/DA or DAO. Imported 1993 to date.
Matte
Black finish . . . . **NiB $885 Ex $558 Gd $425**
Stainless. . . . . **NiB $775 Ex $475 Gd $300**
W/Tritium sights, add **$95**
W/ambidextrous decocking lever, add **$20**

Heckler & Koch Model USP45 Compact 50th Anniversary

Heckler & Koch Model USP9 Compact (Stainless)

Heckler & Koch Model USP357 Compact

Heckler & Koch Model USP Expert

Heckler & Koch Model USP Tactical

MODEL USP9 COMPACT
Caliber: 9mm. 10-round magazine, 4.25-inch bbl., 7.64 inches overall. Weight: 25.5 oz. Short recoil w/modified Browning action. 3-dot sighting system. Polymer frame w/integral grips. Imported from 1993 to date.
Blued finish . . . . NiB $1250 Ex $1158 Gd $993
Stainless finish . . . . NiB $1250 Ex $1153 Gd $993
W/ambidextrous
decocking lever, add $50

MODEL USP40 COMPACT
Caliber: .40 S&W. 10-round magazine, 3.58- inch bbl., 6.81 inches overall. Weight: 27 oz. Short recoil w/modified Browning action. 3-dot sighting system. Polymer frame w/integral grips. Imported from 1993 to date.
Blued finish . . . . NiB $815 Ex $594 Gd $398
Stainless finish . . . . NiB $735 Ex $611 Gd $405
W/ambidextrous
decocking lever, add $25

MODEL USP45 COMPACT
Caliber: .45 ACP. Eight-round magazine, 3.8- inch bbl., 7.09 inches overall. Weight: 28 oz. Short recoil w/modified Browning action. 3-dot sighting system. Polymer frame w/integral grips. Imported from 1998 to date.
Blued finish . . . . NiB $885 Ex $594 Gd $398
Stainless finish . . . . NiB $775 Ex $619 Gd $413
W/ambidextrous
decocking lever, add $25
50th Anniversary
(1 of 1,000) . . . . NiB $1150 Ex $903 Gd $675

MODEL
USP EXPERT . . . . NiB $1250 Ex $1082 Gd $804
Caliber: .45 ACP. 10-round magazine, 6.2- inch bbl., 9.65 inches overall. Weight: 30 oz. Adjustable 3-dot target sights. Short recoil modified Browning action w/recoil reduction system. Reinforced polymer frame w/integral grips and match-grade slide. Imported from 1999 to 2009.

MODEL USP
TACTICAL . . . . NiB $1125 Ex $896 Gd $603
SOCOM Enhanced version of the USP Standard Model, w/4.92-inch threaded bbl. Chambered for .45 ACP only. Imported from 1998 to date.

**Heckler & Koch
Model VP 7OZ**

**Heritage
Rough Rider**

**Heritage
Sentry**

MODEL VP 70Z AUTO PISTOL . . . . NiB $750 Ex $484 Gd $355
Caliber: 9mm Para. 18-round magazine, 4.5-inch bbl., 8 inches overall. Weight: 32.5 oz. DA Fixed sights. Blued slide, plastic receiver and grip. Disc. 1986.

HELWAN PISTOLS
See listings under Interarms.

HERITAGE MANUFACTURING — Opa Locka, Florida

MODEL H-25 AUTO PISTOL
Caliber: .25 ACP. Six-round magazine, 2.5-inch bbl., 4.63 inches overall. Weight: 12 oz. Fixed sights. Blued or chrome finish. Made 1995 to 1999.
Blued . . . . NiB $125 Ex $100 Gd $90
Nickel. . . . . Add $10

ROUGH RIDER SA REVOLVER
Calibers: .22 LR, .22 Mag. Six-round cylinder. bbl. lengths: 2.75, 3.75, 4.75, 6.5 or 9 inches. Weight: 31-38 oz. Blade front sight, fixed rear. High-polished blued finish w/gold accents. Smooth walnut grips. Made from 1993 to date.
.22 LR . . . . NiB $230 Ex $100 Gd $70
.22 LR/.22 WRF combo . . . . NiB $255 Ex $133 Gd $102

SENTRY DA REVOLVER
Calibers: .22 LR, .22 Mag., .32 Mag., 9mm or .38 Special. Six- or 8-round (rimfire) cylinder, 2- or 4-inch bbl., 6.25 inches overall (2-inch bbl.). Ramp front sight, fixed rear. Blued or nickel finish. Checkered polymer grips. Made from 1993 to 1997.
Blued . . . . NiB $110 Ex $113 Gd $84
Nickel. . . . . Add $10

STEALTH DA AUTO PISTOL . . . . NiB $225 Ex $165 Gd $95
Calibers: 9mm, .40 S&W. 10-round magazine, 3.9-inch bbl., weight: 20.2 oz. Gas-delayed blowback, double action only. Ambidextrous trigger safety. Blade front sight, drift-adj. rear. Black chrome or stainless slide. Black polymer grip frame. Made from 1996 to 2000.

HI-POINT FIREARMS — Mansfield, Ohio

MODEL JS-9MM
AUTO PISTOL . . . . NiB $140 Ex $112 Gd $81
Caliber: 9mm Para. Eight-round magazine, 4.5-inch bbl., 7.75 inches overall. Weight: 39 oz. Fixed low-profile sights w/3-dot system. Matte blue, matte black or chrome finish. Checkered synthetic grips. Made from 1990 to 2000.

MODEL JS-9MM COMPETITION PISTOL
(STALLARD) . . . . NiB $135 Ex $110 Gd $81
Similar to standard JS-9 except w/4-inch compensated bbl. w/ shortened slide and adj. sights. 10-round magazine, 7.25 inches overall. Weight: 30 oz. Made from 1998 to 2006.

MODEL JS-9MM/C-9MM COMPACT PISTOL
(BEEMILLER) . . . . NiB $125 Ex $100 Gd $82
Similar to standard JS-9 except w/3.5-inch bbl. and shortened slide w/alloy or polymer frame. 6.72 inches overall. Weight: 29 oz. or 32 oz. Three-dot-style sights. Made from 1993 to date.

MODEL CF-.380
POLYMER . . . . NiB $135 Ex $73 Gd $53
Caliber: .380 ACP. Eight-round magazine, 3.5-inch bbl., 6.72 inches overall. Weight: 32 oz. Three-dot sights. Made from 1994 to date.

MODEL JS-.40/JC-.40 AUTO PISTOL
(IBERIA) . . . . NiB $160 Ex $132 Gd $96
Similar to Model JS-9mm except in caliber .40 S&W.

MODEL JS-.45/JH-.45
AUTO PISTOL
(HASKELL) . . . . NiB $135 Ex $142 Gd $102
Similar to Model JS-9mm except in caliber .45 ACP w/7-round magazine and two-tone Polymer finish.

J. C. HIGGINS

See Sears, Roebuck & Company

HIGH STANDARD SPORTING FIREARMS — East Hartford, Connecticut Formerly High Standard Mfg. Co., Hamden, Connecticut

A long-standing producer of sporting arms, High Standard disc. its operations in 1984. See new High Standard models under separate entry, HIGH STANDARD MFG. CO., INC.

NOTE: *For ease in finding a particular firearm, High Standard handguns are grouped into three sections: Automatic pistols (below), derringers and revolvers. For a complete listing, please refer to the Index.*

AUTOMATIC PISTOLS

MODEL A
HAMMERLESS . . . . **NiB $795 Ex $668 Gd $456**
Caliber: .22 LR. 10-round magazine, bbl. lengths: 4.5-, 6.75-inch. 11.5 inches overall (6.75-inch bbl.). Weight: 36 oz. (in 6.75-inch bbl.). Adj. target sights. Blued finish. Checkered walnut grips. Made from 1938 to 1942.

High Standard
Model A

MODEL B
AUTOMATIC PISTOL . . . . **NiB $625 Ex $413 Gd $337**
Original Standard pistol. Hammerless. Caliber: .22 LR. 10-round magazine, bbl. lengths: 4.5-, 6.75-inch, 10.75 inches overall (with 6.75-inch bbl.). Weight: 33 oz. (6.75-inch bbl.). Fixed sights. Blued finish. Hard rubber grips. Made from 1932 to 1942.

High Standard
Model B

MODEL C
AUTOMATIC PISTOL . . . . **NiB $925 Ex $788 Gd $533**
Same as Model B except in .22 Short. Made from 1935 to 1942.

MODEL D
AUTOMATIC PISTOL . . . . **NiB $995 Ex $732 Gd $520**
Same general specifications as Model A but heavier bbl., weight: 40 oz. (6.75-inch bbl.). Made from 1937 to 1942.

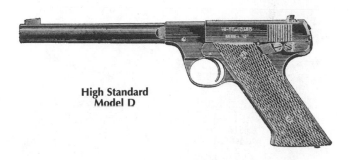

High Standard
Model D

DURA-MATIC
AUTOMATIC PISTOL . . . . **NiB $325 Ex $270 Gd $222**
Takedown. Caliber: .22 LR. 10-round magazine, 4.5 or 6.5 inch interchangeable bbl., 10.88 inches overall (6.5-inch bbl.). Weight: 35 oz. (in 6.5-inch bbl.). Fixed sights. Blued finish. Checkered grips. Made from 1952 to 1970.

MODEL E
AUTOMATIC PISTOL . . . . **NiB $1225 Ex $1017 Gd $916**
Same general specifications as Model A but w/extra heavy bbl. and thumbrest grips. Weight: 42 oz. (6.75-inch bbl.). Made 1937 to 1942.

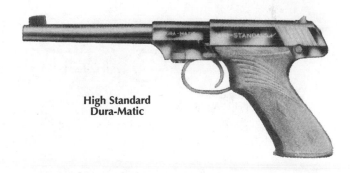

High Standard
Dura-Matic

FIELD-KING
AUTOMATIC PISTOL
FIRST MODEL
Same general specifications as Sport-King but w/heavier bbl. and target sights. Late model 6.75-inch bbls. have recoil stabilizer and lever take-down feature. Weight: 43 oz. (6.75-inch bbl.). Made from 1951 to 1958.
W/one bbl. **NiB $650 Ex $500 Gd $390**
W/both bbls. . . . . **NiB $800 Ex $650 Gd $500**

FIELD-KING AUTOMATIC PISTOL
SECOND MODEL
Same general specifications as First Model Field-King but w/button take-down and marked FK 100 or FK 101.
W/one bbl. **NiB $800 Ex $560 Gd $279**

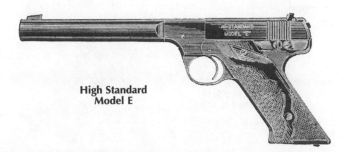

High Standard
Model E

GRADING: **NiB** = New in Box   **Ex** = Excellent or NRA 95%   **Gd** = Good or NRA 68%

**High Standard
G-.380**

**High Standard
Model G-B**

**High Standard
Model G-E**

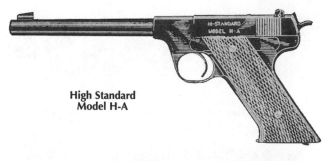

**High Standard
Model H-A**

**High Standard
Model H-B**

FLITE-KING AUTOMATIC PISTOL — FIRST MODEL
Same general specifications as Sport-King except in .22. Short w/aluminum alloy frame and slide and marked FK 100 or FK 101. Weight: 26 oz. (6.5-inch bbl.). Made from 1953 to 1958.
W/one bbl. NiB $625 Ex $447 Gd $318
W/both bbls. . . . . NiB $705 Ex $534 Gd $383

FLITE-KING AUTOMATIC PISTOL — SECOND MODEL
Same as Flite-King—First Model except w/steel frame and marked in the 102 or 103 series. Made from 1958 to 1966.
Model 102 . . . . NiB $525 Ex $375 Gd $245
Model 103 . . . . NiB $525 Ex $375 Gd $245

MODEL G-.380
AUTOMATIC PISTOL . . . . NiB $630 Ex $544 Gd $380
Lever takedown. Visible hammer. Thumb safety. Caliber: .380 Automatic. Six-round magazine, 5-inch bbl., weight: 40 oz. Fixed sights. Blued finish. Checkered plastic grips. Made 1943 to 1950.

MODEL G-B AUTOMATIC PISTOL
Lever takedown. Hammerless. Interchangeable bbls. Caliber: .22 LR. 10-round magazine, bbl. lengths: 4.5, 6.75 inches, 10.75 inches overall (with 6.75-inch bbl.). Weight: 36 oz. (with 6.75-inch bbl.). Fixed sights. Blued finish. Checkered plastic grips. Made 1948 to 1951.
W/one bbl. NiB $650 Ex $467 Gd $345
W/both bbls. . . . . NiB $875 Ex $790 Gd $660

MODEL G-D AUTOMATIC PISTOL
Lever takedown. Hammerless. Interchangeable bbls. Caliber: .22 LR. 10-round magazine, bbl. lengths: 4.5, 6.75 inches. 11.5 inches overall (with 6.75-inch bbl.). Weight: 41 oz. (6.75-inch bbl.). Target sights. Blued finish. Checkered walnut grips. Made 1948 to 1951.
W/one bbl. NiB $1025 Ex $876 Gd $675
W/both bbls. . . . . NiB $1157 Ex $907 Gd $660

MODEL G-E AUTOMATIC PISTOL
Same general specifications as Model G-D but w/extra heavy bbl. and thumbrest grips. Weight: 44 oz. (with 6.75-inch bbl.). Made from 1949 to 1951.
W/one bbl. NiB $1425 Ex $1236 Gd $963
W/both bbls. . . . . NiB $1750 Ex $1550 Gd $1310

MODEL H-A
AUTOMATIC PISTOL . . . . NiB $1325 Ex $1205 Gd $839
Same as Model A but w/visible hammer, no thumb safety. Made from 1939 to 1942.

MODEL H-B
AUTOMATIC PISTOL . . . . NiB $775 Ex $563 Gd $407
Same as Model B but w/visible hammer, no thumb safety. Made from 1940 to 1942.

MODEL H-D
AUTOMATIC PISTOL . . . . NiB $1225 Ex $1075 Gd $756
Same as Model D but w/visible hammer, no thumb safety. Made from 1939 to 1942.

MODEL H-DM
AUTOMATIC PISTOL . . . . NiB $625 Ex $500 Gd $405
Also called H-D Military. Same as Model H-D but w/thumb safety. Made from 1941 to 1951.

MODEL H-E
AUTOMATIC PISTOL . . . . NiB $2200 Ex $2069 Gd $1147
Same as Model E but w/visible hammer, no thumb safety. Made from 1939 to 1942.

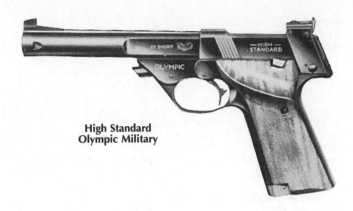

High Standard
Olympic Military

High Standard
Model H-E

High Standard Olympic
Automatic – First Model

High Standard Olympic
Automatic – Second Model

High Standard
Olympic I.S.U.

High Standard Olympic
I.S.U. Military

OLYMPIC AUTOMATIC PISTOL FIRST MODEL (G-O)
Same general specifications as Model G-E but in .22 Short w/light alloy slide. Made from 1950 to 1951.

W/one bbl. . . . . NiB $1725   Ex $1107   Gd $602
W/both bbls. . . . . Add $375

OLYMPIC AUTOMATIC
SECOND MODEL
Same general specifications as Supermatic but in .22 Short w/light alloy slide. Weight: 39 oz. (6.75-inch bbl.). Made 1951 to 1958.

W/one bbl. . . . . NiB $1256   Ex $1029   Gd $704
W/both bbls. . . . . Add $250

OLYMPIC AUTOMATIC PISTOL
THIRD MODEL . . . . NiB $1174   Ex $941   Gd $694
Same as Supermatic Trophy w/bull bbl. except in .22 Short. Made from 1963 to 1966.

OLYMPIC COMMEMORATIVE
Limited edition of Supermatic Trophy Military issued to commemorate the only American-made rimfire target pistol ever to win an Olympic gold medal. Highly engraved w/Olympic rings inlaid in gold. Deluxe presentation case. Two versions issued: In 1972 (.22 LR) and 1980 (.22 Short).

1972 issue . . . . NiB $6345   Ex $5285   Gd $3498
1980 issue . . . . NiB $2164   Ex $1805   Gd $1180

OLYMPIC I.S.U . . . . NiB $1250   Ex $985   Gd $756
Same as Supermatic Citation except caliber .22 Short, 6.75- or 8-inch tapered bbl. w/stabilizer, detachable weights. Made from 1958 to 1977. Eight-inch bbl. disc. in 1966.

OLYMPIC I.S.U. MILITARY . . . . . . NiB $1099   Ex $929   Gd $680
Same as Olympic I.S.U. except has military grip and bracket rear sight. Intro. in 1965. Disc.

OLYMPIC MILITARY . . . . NiB $1132   Ex $917   Gd $721
Same as Olympic — Third Model except has military grip and bracket rear sight. Made in 1965.

SHARPSHOOTER
AUTOMATIC PISTOL . . . . NiB $350   Ex $240   Gd $165
Takedown. Hammerless. Caliber: .22 LR. 10-round magazine, 5.5-inch bull bbl., 9 inches overall. Weight: 42 oz. Micrometer rear sight, blade front sight. Blued finish. Plastic grips. Made from 1971 to 1983.

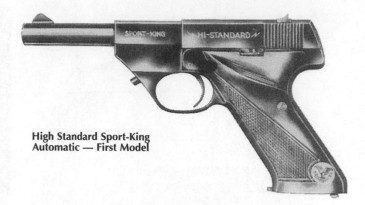

High Standard Sport-King Automatic — First Model

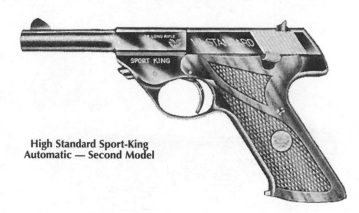

High Standard Sport-King Automatic — Second Model

High Standard Sport-King Automatic — Third Model

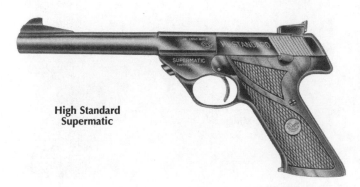

High Standard Supermatic

SPORT-KING AUTOMATIC PISTOL FIRST MODEL

Takedown. Hammerless. Interchangeable barrels. Caliber: .22 LR. 10-round magazine, barrel lengths: 4.5-, 6.75-inches. 11.5 inches overall (with 6.75-inch barrel). Weight: 39 oz. (with 6.75-inch barrel). Fixed sights. Blued finish. Checkered plastic thumbrest grips. Made from 1951 to 1958. Note: 1951 to 1954 production has lever takedown as in "G" series. Later version (illustrated at left) has push-button takedown.

W/one bbl. NiB $350 Ex $275 Gd $200
W/both bbls. . . . . NiB $550 Ex $475 Gd $400

SPORT-KING AUTOMATIC PISTOL
SECOND MODEL . . . . NiB $325 Ex $200 Gd $170
Caliber: .22 LR. 10-round magazine, 4.5- or 6.75 inch interchangeable bbl. 11.25 inches overall (with 6.75-inch barrel). Weight: 42 oz. (with 6.75-inch barrel). Fixed sights. Blued finish. Checkered grips. Made from 1958 to 1970.

SPORT-KING AUTOMATIC PISTOL
THIRD MODEL . . . . NiB $275 Ex $190 Gd 125
Similar to Sport-King — Second Model with same general specifications for weight and length. Blued or nickel finish. Introduced in 1974. Disc.

SPORT-KING LIGHTWEIGHT

Same as standard Sport-King except lightweight has forged aluminum alloy frame. Weight: 30 oz. with 6.75-inch barrel Made from 1954 to 1965.

W/one bbl. NiB $550 Ex $350 Gd $225
W/both bbls. . . . . NiB $750 Ex $550 Gd $425

SUPERMATIC AUTOMATIC PISTOL

Takedown. Hammerless. Interchangeable bbls. Caliber: .22 LR. 10-round magazine, barrel lengths: 4.5-, 6.75-inches. Late model 6.75-inch barrel have recoil stabilizer feature. Weight: 43 oz. (with 6.75-inch barrel) 11.5 inches overall (with 6.75-inch barrel). Target sights. Elevated serrated rib between sights. Adjustable barrel weights add 2 or 3 oz. Blued finish. Checkered plastic thumb-rest grips. Made from 1951 to 1958.

W/one bbl. NiB $825 Ex $650 Gd $475
W/both bbls. . . . . NiB $1025 Ex $850 Gd $675

SUPERMATIC CITATION

Same as Supermatic Tournament except 6.75-, 8- or 10-inch tapered bbl. with stabilizer and two removable weights. Also furnished with Tournament's 5.5-inch bull barrel, adjustable trigger pull, recoil-proof click-adjustable rear sight (barrel-mounted on 8- and 10-inch barrels), checkered walnut thumb-brest grips on bull barrel model. Currently manufactured with only bull barrel. Made from 1958 to 1966.

With 5.5-inch
bull bbl. NiB $850 Ex $575 Gd $345
With 6.75-inch
tapered bbl. . . . . NiB $850 Ex $575 Gd $345
With 8-inch
tapered bbl. . . . . NiB $1000 Ex $725 Gd $495
With 10-inch
tapered bbl. . . . . NiB $1050 Ex $775 Gd $545

**High Standard Victor
Solid Rib Barrel**

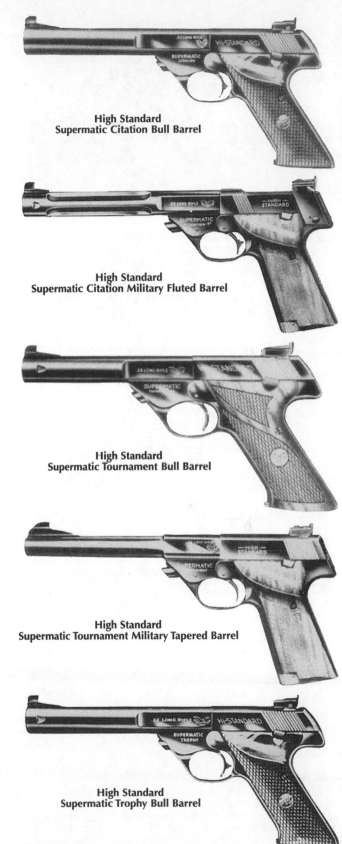

**High Standard
Supermatic Citation Bull Barrel**

**High Standard
Supermatic Citation Military Fluted Barrel**

**High Standard
Supermatic Tournament Bull Barrel**

**High Standard
Supermatic Tournament Military Tapered Barrel**

**High Standard
Supermatic Trophy Bull Barrel**

SUPERMATIC CITATION MILITARY
Same as Supermatic Citation except has military grip and bracket rear sight as in Supermatic Trophy. Made from 1965 to 1973.
W/bull bbl. . . . . NiB $850 Ex $555 Gd $410
W/fluted bbl. . . . . NiB $925 Ex $776 Gd $576

SUPERMATIC
TOURNAMENT . . . . NiB $695 Ex $556 Gd $323
Takedown. Caliber: .22 LR. 10-round magazine, interchangeable 5.5-inch bull or 6.75-inch heavy tapered bbl., notched and drilled for stabilizer and weights. 10 inches overall (with 5.5-inch bbl.). Weight: 44 oz. (5.5-inch bbl.). Click adj. rear sight, undercut ramp front. Blued finish. Checkered grips. Made from 1958 to 1966.

SUPERMATIC
TOURNAMENT
MILITARY . . . . NiB $1245 Ex $955 Gd $795
Same as Supermatic Tournament except has military grip. Made from 1965 to 1971.

SUPERMATIC TROPHY
Same as Supermatic Citation except with 5.5-inch bull bbl., or 7.25-inch fluted bbl., w/detachable stabilizer and weights, extra magazine, High-luster blued finish, checkered walnut thumbrest grips. Made from 1963 to 1966.
W/bull bbl. . . . . NiB $1255 Ex $1028 Gd $589
W/fluted bbl. . . . . NiB $1255 Ex $1028 Gd $589

SUPERMATIC
TROPHY MILITARY
Same as Supermatic Trophy except has military grip and bracket rear sight. Made from 1965 to 1984.
W/bull bbl. . . . . NiB $1300 Ex $1036 Gd $719
W/fluted bbl. . . . . NiB $1350 Ex $1090 Gd $775

THE VICTOR
AUTOMATIC . . . . NiB $3200 Ex $2710 Gd $2488
Takedown. Caliber: .22 LR. 10-round magazine, 4.5-inch solid or vent rib and 5.5-inch vent rib, interchangeable bbl., 9.75 inches overall (with 5.5-inch bbl.). Weight: 52 oz. (with 5.5-inch bbl.). Rib mounted target sights. Blued finish. Checkered walnut thumbrest grips. Standard or military grip configuration. Made from 1972 to 1984 (standard-grip model made from 1974 to 1975).

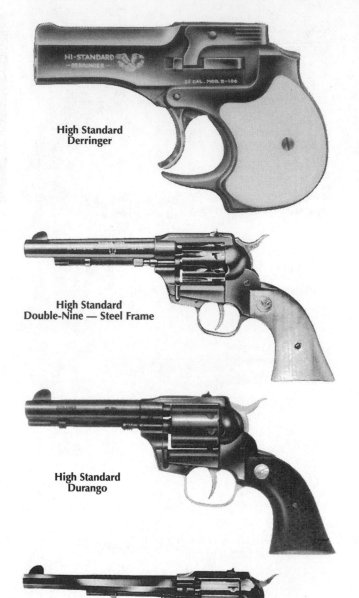

High Standard Derringer

High Standard Double-Nine — Steel Frame

High Standard Durango

High Standard Sierra

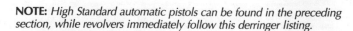

NOTE: *High Standard automatic pistols can be found in the preceding section, while revolvers immediately follow this derringer listing.*

DERRINGERS

DERRINGER
Hammerless, double action, two-round, double bbl. (over/under). Calibers: .22 Short, Long, LR or .22 Magnum Rimfire, 3.5-inch bbls., 5 inches overall. Weight: 11 oz. Standard model has blued or nickel finish w/plastic grips. Presentation model is goldplated in walnut case. Standard model made from 1963 (.22 S-L-LR) and 1964 (.22 MRF) to 1984. Gold model, made from 1965 to 1983.

Gold Presentation One
Derringer . . . . NiB $500 Ex $325 Gd $255
Silver Presentation One
Derringer . . . . NiB $550 Ex $375 Gd $305
Presentation Set, matched
pair, consecutive numbers
(1965 only) . . . . NiB $1300 Ex $1125 Gd $785
Standard model (blue) . . . . NiB $295 Ex $200 Gd $175
Standard model (nickel) . . . . NiB $300 Ex $205 Gd $180
Standard model
(Electroless nickel) . . . . NiB $300 Ex $250 Gd $200

REVOLVERS

NOTE: *Only High Standard revolvers can be found in this section. See the preceding sections for automatic pistols and derringers. For a complete listing of High Standard handguns, please refer to the Index.*

CAMP GUN . . . . NiB $250 Ex $200 Gd $175
Same as Sentinel Mark I/Mark IV except has 6-inch bbl., adj. rear sight, target-style checkered walnut grips. Caliber: .22 LR or .22 WMR. Made from 1976 to 1983.

DOUBLE-NINE DA REVOLVER —ALUMINUM FRAME
Western-style version of Sentinel. Blued or nickel finish w/simulated ivory, ebony or stag grips, 5.5-inch bbl., 11 inches overall. Weight: 27.25 oz. Made from 1959 to 1971.
Blue model . . . . NiB $235 Ex $185 Gd $145

DOUBLE-NINE—STEEL FRAME
Similar to Double-Nine—Aluminum Frame, w/same general specifications except w/steel frame and has extra cylinder for .22 WMR, walnut grips. Intro. in 1971. Disc.
Blue model . . . . NiB $270 Ex $200 Gd $155
Nickel model . . . . NiB $285 Ex $215 Gd $170

DOUBLE-NINE DELUXE . . . . NiB $295 Ex $225 Gd $180
Same as Double-Nine Steel Frame except has adj. target rear sight. Intro. in 1971. Disc.

DURANGO
Similar to Double-Nine—Steel Frame except .22 LR only, available w/4.5- or 5.5-inch bbl. Made from 1971 to 1973.
Blue model . . . . NiB $250 Ex $175 Gd $135
Nickel model . . . . NiB $275 Ex $200 Gd $160

HIGH SIERRA DA REVOLVER
Similar to Double-Nine—Steel Frame except has 7-inch octagon bbl., w/gold-plated grip frame, fixed or adj. sights. Made 1973 to 1983.
W/fixed sights . . . . NiB $320 Ex $265 Gd $200
W/adj. sights . . . . NiB $345 Ex $290 Gd $225

HOMBRE
Similar to Double-Nine—Steel Frame except .22 LR only, lacks single-action type ejector rod and tube, has 4.5-inch bbl. Made from 1971 to 1973.
Blue model . . . . NiB $250 Ex $180 Gd $125
Nickel model . . . . NiB $275 Ex $205 Gd $150

KIT GUN DA REVOLVER . . . . NiB $250 Ex $200 Gd $135
Solid frame, swing-out cylinder. Caliber: .22 LR. Nine-round cylinder, 4-inch bbl., 9 inches overall. Weight: 19 oz. Adj. rear sight, ramp front. Blued finish. Checkered walnut grips. Made from 1970 to 1973.

High Standard Longhorn Steel Frame

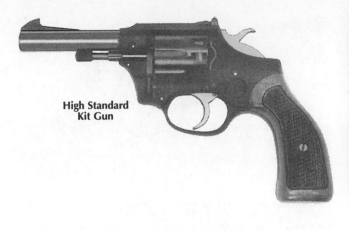

High Standard Kit Gun

High Standard Sentinel

High Standard Longhorn Aluminum Frame

LONGHORN
ALUMINUM FRAME
Similar to Double-Nine—Aluminum Frame except has Longhorn hammer spur, 4.5-, 5.5- or 9.5-inch bbl., Walnut, simulated pearl or simulated stag grips. Blued finish. Made from 1960 to 1971.
W/4.5- or 5.5-inch bbl. . . . . NiB $325 Ex $238 Gd $177
W/9.5-inch bbl . . . . NiB $325 Ex $239 Gd $177

LONGHORN
STEEL FRAME
Similar to Double-Nine — Steel Frame except has 9.5-inch bbl. w/fixed or adj. sights. Made from 1971 to1983
W/fixed sights . . . . NiB $330 Ex $255 Gd $190
W/adj. sights . . . . NiB $355 Ex $280 Gd $215

NATCHEZ . . . . NiB $375 Ex $250 Gd $190
Similar to Double-Nine — Aluminum Frame except 4.5-inch bbl., 10 inches overall, weight: 25.25 oz., blued finish, simulated ivory bird's-head grips. Made 1961-66.

POSSE . . . . NiB $250 Ex $165 Gd $130
Similar to Double-Nine — Aluminum Frame except 3.5-inch bbl., 9 inches overall, weight: 23.25 oz. Blued finish, brass-grip frame and trigger guard, walnut grips. Made from 1961 to 1966.

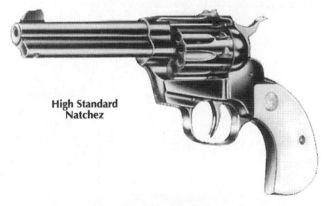

High Standard Natchez

SENTINEL DA REVOLVER
Solid frame, swing-out cylinder. Caliber: .22 LR. Nine-round cylinder, 3- 4- or 6-inch bbl. Nine inches overall (with 4-inch-bbl.). Weight: 19 oz. (with 4-inch bbl.). Fixed sights. Aluminum frame. Blued or nickel finish. Checkered grips. Made from 1955 to 1956.
Blue model . . . . NiB $265 Ex $147 Gd $110
Blue/green model . . . . NiB $525 Ex $400 Gd $295
Gold model . . . . NiB $500 Ex $350 Gd $250
Nickel model . . . . NiB $250 Ex $200 Gd $150
Pink model . . . . NiB $525 Ex $300 Gd $180

SENTINEL DELUXE
Same as Sentinel except w/4- or 6-inch bbl., wide trigger, drift-adj. rear sight, two-piece square-butt grips. Made from 1957 to 1974. Note: Designated Sentinel after 1971.
Blue model . . . . NiB $225 Ex $150 Gd $120
Nickel model . . . . NiB $250 Ex $175 Gd $145

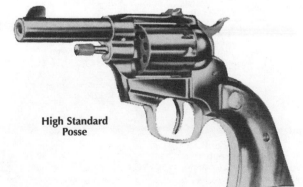

High Standard Posse

**High Standard
Sentinel I**

**High Standard
Sentinel Mark II**

**High Standard
Sentinel Mark III**

**High Standard
Sentinel Snub**

SENTINEL IMPERIAL

Same as Sentinel except has onyx-black or nickel finish, two-piece checkered walnut grips, ramp front sight. Made from 1962 to 1965.
Blue model . . . . NiB $240 Ex $155 Gd $115
Nickel model . . . . NiB $250 Ex $165 Gd $130

SENTINEL MARK 1 DA REVOLVER

Steel frame. Caliber: .22 LR. Nine-round cylinder, bbl. lengths: 2-, 3-, 4-inch, 6.88 inches overall (with 2-inch bbl.). Weight: 21.5 oz. (2-inch bbl.). Ramp front sight, fixed or adj. rear. Blued or nickel finish. Smooth walnut grips. Made from 1974 to 1983.
Blue model . . . . NiB $245 Ex $200 Gd $150
Nickel model . . . . NiB $275 Ex $230 Gd $197
W/adj. sights . . . . NiB $300 Ex $255 Gd $220

SENTINEL MARK II

DA REVOLVER . . . . NiB $300 Ex $225 Gd $160
Caliber: .357 Magnum. Six-round cylinder, bbl. lengths: 2.5-, 4-, 6-inch, 9 inches overall w/4-inch bbl., weight: 38 oz. (with 4-inch bbl.). Fixed sights. Blued finish. Walnut service or combat-style grips. Made from 1974 to 1976.

SENTINEL MARK III . . . . NiB $300 Ex $250 Gd $200

Same as Sentinel Mark II except has ramp front and adj. rear sights. Weight: 40 oz. (with 4-inch bbl.). Blued finish. Made 1974 to 1976.

SENTINEL MARK IV

Same as Sentinel Mark I except in .22 WMR. Made 1974 to 1983.
Blue model . . . . NiB $265 Ex $200 Gd $160
Nickel model . . . . NiB $295 Ex $230 Gd $190
W/adj. sights . . . . NiB $320 Ex $355 Gd $215

SENTINEL SNUB

Same as Sentinel Deluxe except w/2.75-inch bbl., (7.25 inches overall, weight: 15 oz.), checkered bird's head-type grips. Made 1957 to 1974.
Blued finish . . . . NiB $225 Ex $175 Gd $140
Nickel finish . . . . NiB $250 Ex $145 Gd $100

HIGH STANDARD MFG. CO., INC. —
Houston, Texas
Distributed from Hartford, Connecticut

VICTOR 10X AUTO PISTOL . . . . . NiB $1050 Ex $821 Gd $492

Caliber: .22 LR. 10-round magazine, 5.5-inch bbl., 9.5 inches overall. Weight: 45 oz. Checkered walnut grips. Blued finish. Made from 1994 to date.

OLYMPIC I.S.U. AUTOMATIC PISTOL

Same specifications as the 1958 I.S.U. issue. See listing under previous High Standard Section.
Olympic I.S.U. model . . . . NiB $550 Ex $315 Gd $250
Olympic I.S.U. military model. . . . . NiB $750 Ex $515 Gd $275

SPORT KING AUTO PISTOL . . . . NiB $650 Ex $395 Gd $275

Caliber: .22 LR. 10-round magazine, 4.5- or 6.75-inch bbl., 8.5 or 10.75 inches overall. Weight: 44 oz. (with 4.5-inch bbl.), 46 oz. (with 6.75-inch bbl.). Fixed sights, slide mounted. Checkered walnut grips. Parkerized finish. Manufactured in limited quantities.

SUPERMATIC CITATION AUTO PISTOL

Caliber: .22 LR. 10-round magazine, 5.5- or 7.75-inch bbl., 9.5 or 11.75 inches overall. Weight: 44 oz. (with 5.5-inch bbl.), 46 oz. (with 7.75-inch bbl.). Frame-mounted, micro-adj. rear sight, undercut ramp front sight. Blued or Parkerized finish. Made from 1994 to 2003.

Supermatic Citation model . . . . NiB $480 Ex $378 Gd $234
.22 Short conversion . . . . NiB $383 Ex $311 Gd $223

CITATION MS AUTO PISTOL . . . . . NiB $775 Ex $600 Gd $454
Similar to the Supermatic Citation except has 10-inch bbl., 14 inches overall. Weight: 49 oz. Made from 1994 to date.

SUPERMATIC TOURNAMENT . . . . . NiB $695 Ex $350 Gd $250
Caliber: .22 LR. 10-round magazine, bbl. lengths: 4.5, 5.5, or 6.75 inches, overall length: 8.5, 9.5 or 10.75 inches. Weight: 43, 44 or 45 oz. depending on bbl. length. Micro-adj. rear sight, undercut ramp front sight. Checkered walnut grips. Parkerized finish. Made from 1995 to 1997.

SUPERMATIC TROPHY
Caliber: .22 LR. 10-round magazine, 5.5 or 7.25-inch bbl., 9.5 or 11.25 inches overall. Weight: 44 oz. (with 5.5-inch bbl.). Micro-adj. rear sight, undercut ramp front sight. Checkered walnut grips w/thumbrest. Blued or Parkerized finish. Made from 1994 to date.
Supermatic Trophy. . . . . NiB $675 Ex $330 Gd $205
.22 Short Conversion. . . . . NiB $1100 Ex $785 Gd $655

VICTOR AUTOMATIC
Caliber: .22 LR.10-round magazine, 4.5- or 5.5-inch ribbed bbl., 8.5 or 9.5 inches overall. Weight: 45 oz. (with 4.5-inch bbl.), 46 oz. (with 5.5-inch bbl.). Micro-adj. rear sight, post front. Checkered walnut grips. Blued or Parkerized finish. Made from 1994 to date.
Victor Model . . . . NiB $675 Ex $450 Gd $250
.22 Short conversion . . . . NiB $1125 Ex $900 Gd $700

HOPKINS & ALLEN ARMS CO. — Norwich, Connecticut

HOPKINS & ALLEN REVOLVERS
See listings of comparable Harrington & Richardson and Iver Johnson models for values.

INGRAM — Mfd. by Military Armament Corp.

See listings under M.A.C. (Military Armament Corp.)

Note: *Military Armament Corp. ceased production of the select-fire automatic, M10 (9mm & .45 ACP) and M11 (.380 ACP) in 1977. Commercial production resumed on semiautomatic versions under the M.A.C. banner until 1982.*

INTERARMS — Alexandria, Virginia
See also Bersa Pistol.

HELWAN BRIGADIER
AUTO PISTOL . . . . NiB $236 Ex $189 Gd $128
Caliber: 9mm Para. Eight-round magazine, 4.25-inch bbl., 8 inches overall. Weight: 32 oz. Blade front sight, dovetailed rear. Blued finish. Grooved plastic grips. Imported from 1987 to 1995.

VIRGINIAN DRAGOON SA REVOLVER
Calibers: .357 Magnum, .44 Magnum, .45 Colt. Six-round cylinder. Bbls.: 5- (not available in .44 Magnum), 6-, 7.5-, 8.38-inch (latter only in .44 Magnum w/adj. sights), 11.88 inches overall with (6-inch bbl.). Weight: 48 oz. (with 6-inch bbl.). Fixed sights or micrometer rear and ramp front sights. Blued finish w/color-casetreated frame. Smooth walnut grips. SWISSAFE base pin safety system.

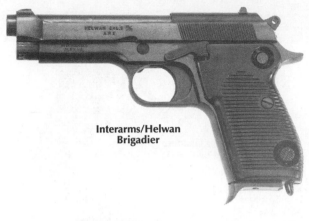

Interarms/Helwan
Brigadier

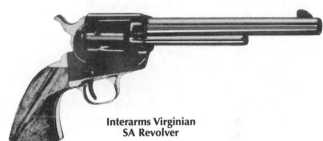

Interarms Virginian
SA Revolver

Mfg. by Interarms Industries Inc., Midland, VA. from 1977 to 1984.
Standard Dragoon. . . . . NiB $350 Ex $250 Gd $191
Engraved Dragoon . . . . NiB $650 Ex $500 Gd $340
Deputy model . . . . NiB $340 Ex $240 Gd $150
Stainless. . . . . NiB $375 Ex $2508 Gd $235

VIRGINIAN REVOLVER
SILHOUETTE MODEL . . . . NiB $350 Ex $255 Gd $225
Same general specifications as regular model except designed in stainless steel w/untapered bull bbl., lengths of 7.5, 8.38 and 10.5 inches. Made from 1985 to 1986.

VIRGINIAN SA REVOLVER . . . . NiB $551 Ex $442 Gd $312
Similar to Colt Single-Action Army except has base pin safety system. Imported from 1973-76. (See also listing under Hämmerli.)

INTRATEC U.S.A., INC. — Miami, Florida

CATEGORY 9 DAO
SEMIAUTOMATIC . . . . NiB $235 Ex $165 Gd $100
Blowback action w/polymer frame. Caliber: 9mm Par Eight-round magazine, 3-inch bbl., 7.7 inches overall. Weight: 18 oz. Textured black polymer grips. Matte black finish. Made from 1993 to 2000.

CATEGORY 40
DAO SEMIAUTOMATIC . . . . NiB $235 Ex $165 Gd $100
Locking-breech action w/polymer frame. Caliber: .40 S&W. Seven-round magazine, 3.25-inch bbl., 8 inches overall. Weight: 21 oz. Textured black polymer grips. Matte black finish. Made from 1994 to 2000.

CATEGORY 45
DAO SEMIAUTOMATIC . . . . NiB $255 Ex $185 Gd $120
Locking-breech action w/polymer frame. Caliber: .45 ACP. Six-round magazine, 3.25-inch bbl., 8 inches overall. Weight: 21 oz. Textured black polymer grips. Matte black finish. Made from 1994 to 2000.

Japanese
Model 14 (1925)

Japanese
Model 26 DAO Revolver

MODEL PROTEC .25 ACP
DA SEMIAUTOMATIC
Caliber: .25 ACP. 10-round magazine, 2.5-inch bbl., 5 inches overall. Weight: 14 oz. Wraparound composition grips. Black Teflon, satin grey or Tec-Kote finish. Disc. 2000..
ProTec .25 standard . . . . NiB $110 Ex $75 Gd $50
ProTec .25 w/satin or Tec-Kote . . . . NiB $115 Ex $80 Gd $55

MODEL TEC-DC9 SEMIAUTOMATIC
Caliber: 9mm Para. 20- or 36-round magazine, 5-inch bbl., weight: 50-51 oz. Open fixed front sight, adj. rear. Military nonglare blued or stainless finish.
Tec-9 w/blued finish . . . . NiB $475 Ex $300 Gd $255
Tec-9 w/Tec Kote finish. . . . . NiB $495 Ex $320 Gd $275
Tec 9S w/stainless finish . . . . NiB $550 Ex $375 Gd $275

MODEL TEC-DC9M SEMIAUTOMATIC
Same specifications as Model Tec-9 except has 3-inch bbl. without shroud and 20-round magazine, blued or stainless finish.
Tec-9M w/blued finish. . . . . NiB $495 Ex $300 Gd $250
Tec-9MS w/stainless finish. . . . . NiB $575 Ex $380 Gd $235

MODEL TEC-22T SEMIAUTOMATIC
Caliber: .22 LR. 10/.22-type 30-round magazine, 4-inch bbl., 11.19 inches overall. Weight: 30 oz. Protected post front sight, adj. rear sight. Matte black or Tec-Kote finish. Made from 1991 to 1994.
Tec-22T standard . . . . NiB $395 Ex $200 Gd $165
Tec-22TK Tec-Kote . . . . Add $25

TEC-38
DERRINGER . . . . NiB $152 Ex $119 Gd $88
Calibers: .22 Mag., .32 H&R Mag., .357 Mag.,.38 Special. Two-round capacity, 3-inch blued bbl., 4.63 inches overall. Weight: 13 oz. Fixed sights. Synth. black frame. Double-action. Made from 1986 to 1988.

ISRAEL ARMS — Kfar Sabs, Israel
Imported by Israel Arms International, Houston TX

MODEL BUL-M5 LOCKED
BREECH (2000) AUTO PISTOL . . . . NiB $360 Ex $295 Gd $200
Similar to the M1911 U.S. Government model. Caliber: .45 ACP. Seven-round magazine, 5-inch bbl., 8.5 inches overall. Weight: 38 oz. Blade front and fixed, low-profile rear sights.

KAREEN MK II (1500) AUTO PISTOL
Single-action only. Caliber: 9mm Para. 10-round magazine, 4.75-inch bbl., 8 inches overall. Weight: 33.6 oz. Blade front sight, rear adjustable for windage. Textured black composition or rubberized grips. Blued, two-tone, matte black finish. Imported from 1997 to 1998.
Blued or matte black finish . . . . NiB $355 Ex $275 Gd $195
Two-tone finish . . . . NiB $510 Ex $335 Gd $275
Meprolite sights, add. $40

KAREEN MK II COMPACT
(1501) AUTO PISTOL . . . . NiB $360 Ex $275 Gd $200
Similar to standard Kareen MKII except w/3.85-inch bbl., 7.1 inches overall. Weight: 32 oz. Imported 1999 to 2000.

GOLAN MODEL (2500) AUTO PISTOL
Single or double action. Caliber: 9mm Para., .40 S&W. 10-round magazine, 3.85-inch bbl., 7.1 inches overall. Weight: 34 oz. Steel slide and alloy frame w/ambidextrous safety and decocking lever. Matte black finish. Imported 1999.
9mm Para. NiB $900 Ex $715 Gd $500
.40 S&W . . . . NiB $900 Ex $715 Gd $500

GAL MODEL
(5000) AUTO PISTOL . . . . NiB $395 Ex $265 Gd $200
Caliber: .45 ACP. Eight-round magazine, 4.25-inch bbl., 7.25 inches overall. Weight: 42 oz. Low profile 3-dot sights. Combat-style black rubber grips. Imported from 1999 to 2001.

JAPANESE MILITARY PISTOLS — Tokyo, Japan
Manufactured by Government Plant

MODEL 14 (1925)
AUTOMATIC PISTOL . . . . NiB $6993 Ex $5555 Gd $3392
Modification of the Nambu Model 1914, changes chiefly intended to simplify mass production. Standard round trigger guard or oversized guard for use w/gloves. Caliber: 8mm Nambu. Eight-round magazine, 4.75-inch bbl., 9 inches overall. Weight: About 29 oz. Fixed sights. Blued finish. Grooved wood grips. Intro. 1925 and mfd. through WW II.

MODEL 26 DAO REVOLVER . . . . NiB $1500 Ex $1000 Gd $700
Top-break frame. Caliber: 9mm. Six-round cylinder w/automatic extractor/ejector, 4.7-inch bbl., adopted by the Japanese Army from 1893 to 1914, replaced by the Model 14 Automatic Pistol but remained in service through World War II.

MODEL 94 (1934)

AUTOMATIC PISTOL . . . . NiB $339 Ex $237 Gd $160
Poorly designed and constructed, this pistol is unsafe and can be fired merely by applying pressure on the sear, which is exposed on the left side. Caliber: 8mm Nambu. Six-round magazine, 3.13-inch bbl., 7.13 inches overall. Weight: About 27 oz. Fixed sights. Blued finish. Hard rubber or wood grips. Intro. in 1934, principally for export to Latin American countries, production continued thru WW II.

NAMBU MODEL

1914 AUTOMATIC PISTOL . . . . NiB $7000 Ex $5525 Gd $4750
Original Japanese service pistol, resembles Luger in appearance and Glisenti in operation. Caliber: 8mm Nambu. Seven-round magazine, 4.5-inch bbl., 9 inches overall. Weight: About 30 oz. Fixed front sight, adj. rear sight. Blued finish. Checkered wood grips. Made from 1914 to 1925.

Japanese Model 94 (1934)

JENNINGS FIREARMS INC. — Currently Mfd. by Bryco Arms, Irvine, California
Previously by Calwestco, Inc. & B.L. Jennings

See additional listings under Bryco Arms.

MODEL J-22 AUTO PISTOL

Calibers: .22 LR, .25 ACP. Six-round magazine, 2.5-inch bbl., about 5 inches overall. Weight: 13 oz. Fixed sights. Chrome, satin nickel or black Teflon finish. Walnut, grooved black Cycolac or resin-impregnated wood grips. Made from 1981-85 under Jennings and Calwestco logos; disc. 1985 by Bryco Arms.

Model J-22 . . . . NiB $65 Ex $50 Gd $40
Model J-25 . . . . NiB $75 Ex $60 Gd $50

Jennings Model J Auto Pistol

IVER JOHNSON ARMS, INC. — Jacksonville, Arkansas.

Operation of this company dates back to 1871, when Iver Johnson and Martin Bye partnered to manufacture metallic cartridge revolvers. Johnson became the sole owner and changed the name to Iver Johnson's Arms & Cycle Works, which it was known as for almost 100 years. Modern management shortened the name, and after several owner changes the firm was moved from Massachusetts, its original base, to Jacksonville, Arkansas. In 1987, the American Military Arms Corporation (AMAC) acquired the operation, which subsequently ceased in 1993.

NOTE: *For ease in finding a particular firearm, Iver Johnson handguns are divided into two sections: Automatic Pistols (below) and Revolvers, which follow. For the complete handgun listing, please refer to the Index.*

AUTOMATIC PISTOLS

9MM DA AUTOMATIC . . . . NiB $432 Ex $336 Gd $239

Caliber: 9mm. Six-round magazine, 3-inch bbl., 6.5 inches overall. Weight: 26 oz. Blade front sight, adj. rear. Smooth hardwood grip. Blued or matte blued finish. Intro. 1986.

COMPACT .25 ACP . . . . NiB $250 Ex $170 Gd $125

Bernardelli V/P design. Caliber: .25 ACP. Five-round magazine, 2.13-inch bbl., 4.13 inches overall. Weight: 9.3 oz. Fixed sights. Checkered composition grips. Blued slide, matte blued frame and color-casehardened trigger. Made from 1991 to 1993.

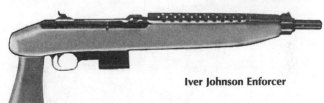

Iver Johnson Enforcer

ENFORCER . . . . NiB $850 Ex $600 Gd $395
Semiautomatic. Caliber: .30 U.S. Carbine. Five-, 15-, or 30-round magazine, 9.5- inch bbl., weight: 5.5 lbs. Adj. sights. Walnut stock. Made 1986.

I.J. SUPER

ENFORCER AUTOMATIC . . . . NiB $850 Ex $600 Gd $395
Caliber: .30 U.S. Carbine. Fifteen- or 30-round magazine, 9.5-inch bbl., 17 inches overall. Weight: 4 pounds. Adj. peep rear sight, blade front. American walnut stock. Made from 1978 to 1993.

PONY AUTOMATIC PISTOL

Caliber: .380 Auto. Six-round magazine, 3.1-inch bbl., 6.1 inches overall. Blue, matte blue, nickel finish or stainless. Weight: 20 oz. Wooden grips. Smallest of the locked breech automatics. Made from 1982-88. Reintroduced from 1989 to 1991.

Blue or matte
blue model . . . . NiB $385 Ex $300 Gd $240
Nickel model . . . . NiB $435 Ex $330 Gd $270
Deluxe model . . . . NiB $439 Ex $352 Gd $259

Iver Johnson
Model 57A Target

Iver Johnson
Model TP

Iver Johnson
Model 55 Target

Iver Johnson
Model 55-S

Iver Johnson
Model 56 Blank Revolver

MODEL TP-22 DA
AUTOMATIC . . . . **NiB $275 Ex $200 Gd $140**
Calibers: .22 LR, Seven-round magazine, 2.85-inch bbl., 5.39 inches overall. Blued finish. Weight: 14.46 oz. Made from 1982 to 1989.

MODEL TP25 DA
POCKET PISTOL . . . . **NiB $250 Ex $170 Gd $125**
Double-action automatic. Caliber: .25 ACP. Seven-round magazine, 3-inch bbl., 5.5 inches overall. Weight: 12 oz. Black plastic grips and blued finish. Made from 1981 to 1982.

TRAILSMAN
AUTOMATIC PISTOL
Caliber: .22 LR. 10-round magazine, 4.5 or 6-inch bbl., 8.75 inches overall (with 4.5-inch bbl.). Weight: 46 oz. Fixed target-type sights. Checkered composition grips. Made from 1985 to 1991.
Standard model . . . . **NiB $275 Ex $200 Gd $145**
Deluxe model . . . . **NiB $295 Ex $220 Gd $165**

REVOLVERS

MODEL 55 TARGET DA REVOLVER . . . . . . **NiB $225 Ex $150 Gd $100**
Solid frame. Caliber: .22 LR. Eight-round cylinder, bbl. lengths: 4.5-, 6-inches. 10.75 inches overall (with 6-inch bbl.). Weight: 30.5 oz. (with 6-inch bbl.). Fixed sights. Blued finish. Walnut grips. Note: Original model designation was 55; changed to 55A when loading gate was added in 1961. Made from 1955 to 1960.

MODEL 55-S REVOLVER . . . . **NiB $225 Ex $150 Gd $100**
Same general specifications as the Model 55 except for 2.5-inch bbl. and small, molded pocket-size grip.

MODEL 56
BLANK REVOLVER . . . . **NiB $120 Ex $80 Gd $55**
Solid frame. Caliber: .22 blanks only. Eight-round cylinder, 2.5-inch solid bbl., 6.75 inches overall. Weight: 10 oz.

MODEL 57A
TARGET DA REVOLVER . . . . **NiB $235 Ex $125 Gd $95**
Solid frame. Caliber: .22 LR. Eight-round cylinder, bbl. lengths: 4.5, and 6-inches. 10.75 inches overall. Weight: 30.5 oz. with 6-inch bbl. Adj. sights. Blued finish. Walnut grips. Note: Original model designation was 57, changed to 57A when loading gate was added in 1961. Made from 1961 to 1978.

TRAILSMAN
DA REVOLVER . . . . **NiB $275 Ex $200 Gd $150**
Hinged frame. Rebounding hammer. Caliber: .22 LR. Eight-round cylinder, 6-inch bbl., 11 inches overall. Weight: 34 oz. Adj. sights. Blued finish. Walnut grips. Made from 1985 to 1991.

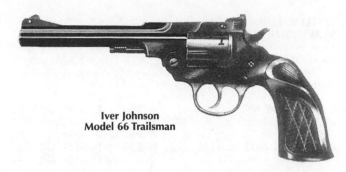

**Iver Johnson
Model 66 Trailsman**

**Iver Johnson
Model 67 Viking**

MODEL 67 VIKING DA REVOLVER . . . . **NiB $250 Ex $150 Gd $100**
Hinged frame. Caliber: .22 LR. Eight-round cylinder, bbl. lengths: 4.5-
and 6-inches, 11 inches overall (with 6-inch bbl.). Weight: 34 oz. (with
6-inch bbl.). Adj. sights. Walnut grips w/thumbrest. Made 1964 to 1978.

**MODEL 67S VIKING
SNUB REVOLVER** . . . . **NiB $260 Ex $175 Gd $200**
DA. Hinged frame. Calibers: .22 LR, .32 S&W Short and Long, .38
S&W. Eight-round cylinder in .22, 5-round in .32 and .38 calibers;
2.75-inch bbl. Weight: 25 oz. Adj. sights. Tenite grips. Made from 1964
to 1978.

MODEL 1900 DA REVOLVER . . . . . . **NiB $140 Ex $100 Gd $80**
Solid frame. Calibers: .22 LR, .32 S&W, .32 S&W Long, .38 S&W.
Seven-round cylinder in .22 cal.,or 6-round (.32 S&W), 5-round (.32
S&W Long, .38 S&W); bbl. lengths: 2.5-, 4.5- and 6-inches. Weight:
12 oz. (in .32 S&W w/2.5-inch bbl.). Fixed sights. Blued or nickel
finish. Hard rubber grips. Made from 1900 to 1941.

**Iver Johnson
Model 67S Viking Snub**

**MODEL 1900
TARGET DA REVOLVER** . . . . **NiB $200 Ex $165 Gd $110**
Solid frame. Caliber: .22 LR. Seven-round cylinder, bbl. lengths: 6-
and 9.5-inches. Fixed sights. Blued finish. Checkered walnut grips.
(This earlier model does not have counterbored chambers as in the
Target Sealed 8. Made from 1925 to 1942.)

AMERICAN BULLDOG DA REVOLVER
Solid frame. Calibers: .22 LR, .22 WMR, .38 Special. Six-round
cylinder in .22, 5-round in .38. Bbl. lengths: 2.5-, 4-inch. 9 inches
overall (with 4-inch bbl.). Weight: 30 oz. (with 4-inch bbl.). Adj.
sights. Blued or nickel finish. Plastic grips. Made from 1974 to 1976.
.38 Special . . . . **NiB $425 Ex $260 Gd $180**
Other calibers . . . . **NiB $425 Ex $260 Gd $180**

**Iver Johnson
Model 1900 Target**

ARMSWORTH MODEL 855 SA . . . . **NiB $425 Ex $275 Gd $145**
Hinged frame. Caliber: .22 LR. Eight-round cylinder, 6-inch bbl., 10.75
inches overall. Weight: 30 oz. Adj. sights. Blued finish. Checkered walnut one-piece grip. Adj. finger rest. Made from 1955 to 1957.

CADET DA REVOLVER . . . . **NiB $225 Ex $140 Gd $100**
Solid frame. Calibers: .22 LR, .22 WMR, .32 S&W Long, .38 S&W, .38
Special. Six- or 8-round cylinder in .22, 5-round in other calibers, 2.5-
inch bbl., 7 inches overall. Weight: 22 oz. Fixed sights. Blued finish or
nickel finish. Plastic grips. Note: Loading gate added in 1961, .22 cylinder capacity changed from 8 to 6 rounds in 1975. Made 1955 to 1977.

CATTLEMAN SA REVOLVER
Patterned after the Colt Army SA revolver. Calibers: .357 Magnum, .44
Magnum, .45 Colt. Six-round cylinder. Bbl. lengths: 4.75-, 5.5- (not available in .44), 6- (.44 only), 7.25-inch. Weight: About 41 oz. Fixed sights.
Blued bbl., and cylinder color-casehardened frame, brass grip frame. One-
piece walnut grip. Made by Aldo Uberti, Brescia, Italy, from 1973 to 1978.
.44 Magnum . . . . **NiB $350 Ex $275 Gd $150**

**Iver Johnson
Cadet**

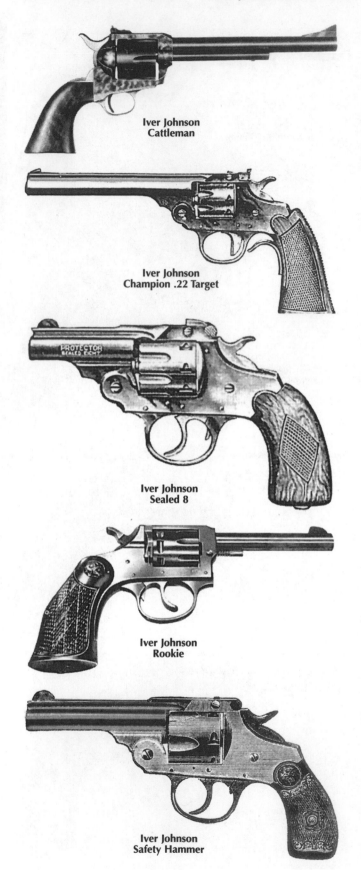

Iver Johnson
Cattleman

Iver Johnson
Champion .22 Target

Iver Johnson
Sealed 8

Iver Johnson
Rookie

Iver Johnson
Safety Hammer

CATTLEMAN BUCKHORN
SA REVOLVER
Same as standard Cattleman except has adj. rear and ramp front sights. Bbl. lengths: 4.75- (.44 only), 5.75- (not available in .44), 6- (.44 only), 7.5- or 12-inches bbl., weight: About 44 oz. Made from 1973 to 1978.

.357 Magnum or .45
Colt w/12-inch bbl. . . . . NiB $400 Ex $295 Gd $195
.357 Magnum or .45
Colt w/5.75- or 7.5-inch bbl. . . . . . NiB $302 Ex $239 Gd $152
.44 Magnum, w/12-inch bbl. . . . . . . NiB $425 Ex $325 Gd $245
.44 Magnum, other bbls. . . . . NiB $400 Ex $310 Gd $245

CATTLEMAN BUNTLINE
SA REVOLVER
Same as Cattleman Buckhorn except has 18-inch bbl., walnut shoulder stock w/brass fittings. Weight: About 56 oz. Made from 1973 to 1978.

.44 Magnum . . . . NiB $400 Ex $325 Gd $225
Other calibers . . . . NiB $400 Ex $325 Gd $225

CATTLEMAN
TRAIL BLAZER. . . . . NiB $350 Ex $255 Gd $155
Similar to Cattleman Buckhorn except .22 caliber has interchangeable .22 LR and .22 WMR cylinders, 5.5- or 6.5-inch bbl., weight: About 40 oz. Made from 1973 to 1978.

CHAMPION 822
.22 TARGET SA . . . . NiB $415 Ex $295 Gd $160
Hinged frame. Caliber: .22 LR. Eight-round cylinder. Single action. Counterbored chambers as in Sealed 8 model, 6-inch bbl., 10.75 inches overall. Weight: 28 oz. Adj. target sights. Blued finish. Checkered walnut grips, adj. finger rest. Made from 1938 to 1948.

DELUXE TARGET . . . . NiB $275 Ex $217 Gd $165
Same as Sportsman except has adj. sights. Made from 1975 to 1976.

PROTECTOR
SEALED 8
DA REVOLVER. . . . . NiB $415 Ex $325 Gd $195
Hinged frame. Caliber: .22 LR. Eight-round cylinder, 2.5-inch bbl., 7.25 inches overall. Weight: 20 oz. Fixed sights. Blued finish. Checkered walnut grips. Made from 1933 to 1949.

ROOKIE
DA REVOLVER. . . . . NiB $240 Ex $190 Gd $80
Solid frame. Caliber: .38 Special. Five-round cylinder, 4-inch bbl., 9-inches overall. Weight: 30 oz. Fixed sights. Blued or nickel finish. Plastic grips. Made from 1975 to 1977.

SAFETY HAMMER
DA REVOLVER. . . . . NiB $290 Ex $140 Gd $100
Hinged frame. Calibers: .22 LR, .32 S&W, .32 S&W Long, .38 S&W. Seven-round cylinder in .22 cal.,or 6-round (.32 S&W Long), 5-round (.32 S&W, .38 S&W). bbl. lengths: 2, 3, 3.25, 4, 5 or 6 inches. Weight w/4-inch bbl.: 15 oz. (.22, .32 S&W), 19.5 oz. (.32 S&W Long) or 19 oz. (.38 S&W). Fixed sights. Blued or nickel finish. Hard rubber, round butt grips or square butt, rubber or walnut grips available. Note: .32 S&W Long and .38 S&W models built on heavy frame. Made from 1892 to 1950.

SAFETY
HAMMERLESS
DA REVOLVER. . . . . NiB $300 Ex $195 Gd $110
Similar to the Safety Hammer Model except w/shrouded hammerless frame. Made from 1895 to 1950.

SIDEWINDER

DA REVOLVER..............**NiB $250 Ex $155 Gd $100**
Solid frame. Caliber: .22 LR. Six- or 8-round cylinder, bbl.
lengths: 4.75, 6 inches; 11.25 inches overall (with 6-inch bbl.).
Weight: 31 oz. (with 6-inch bbl.). Fixed sights. Blued or nickel
finish w/plastic staghorn grips or color-casehardened frame
w/walnut grips. Note: Cylinder capacity changed from 8 to 6
rounds in 1975. Made from1961 to 1978

SIDEWINDER "S" ....**NiB $250 Ex $155 Gd $100**
Same as Sidewinder except has interchangeable cylinders in .22 LR
and .22 WMR, adj. sights. Intro. 1974. Disc.

SPORTSMAN

DA REVOLVER..............**NiB $200 Ex $150 Gd $100**
Solid frame. Caliber: .22 LR. Six-round cylinder. Bbl. lengths: 4.75-, 6-
inches, 10.75 inches overall (with 6-inch bbl.). Weight: 30.5 oz. (with 6-
inch bbl.). Fixed sights. Blued finish. Plastic grips. Made 1974 to 1976.

SUPERSHOT .22 DA REVOLVER....**NiB $250 Ex $195 Gd $125**
Hinged frame. Caliber: .22 LR. Seven-round cylinder, 6-inch bbl.
Fixed sights. Blued finish. Checkered walnut grips. This earlier
model does not have counterbored chambers as in the Supershot
Sealed 8. Made from 1929 to 1949.

SUPERSHOT 9

DA REVOLVER..............**NiB $250 Ex $195 Gd $125**
Same as Supershot Sealed 8 except has nine non-counterbored
chambers. Made from 1929 to 1949.

SUPERSHOT MODEL 844 DA.....**NiB $300 Ex $185 Gd $120**
Hinged frame. Caliber: .22 LR. Eight-round cylinder, bbl. lengths:
4.5- or 6-inch, 9.25 inches overall (with 4.5-inch bbl.). Weight: 27
oz. (4.5-inch bbl.). Adj. sights. Blued finish. Checkered walnut one-
piece grip. Made from 1955 to 1956.

SUPERSHOT SEALED

8 DA REVOLVER..............**NiB $275 Ex $165 Gd $119**
Hinged frame. Caliber: .22 LR. Eight-round cylinder, 6-inch bbl.,
10.75 inches overall. Weight: 24 oz. Adj. target sights. Blued finish.
Checkered walnut grips. Postwar model does not have adj. finger
rest as earlier version. Made from 1931 to 1957.

SWING-OUT DA REVOLVER

Calibers: .22 LR, .22 WMR, .32 S&W Long, .38 Special. Six-round
cylinder in .22, 5-round in .32 and .38. Two, 3-, 4-inch plain bbl., or
4- 6-inch vent rib bbl., 8.75 inches overall (with 4-inch bbl.). Fixed
or adj. sights. Blue or nickel finish. Walnut grips. Made in 1977.
W/plain barrel, fixed sights.......**NiB $202 Ex $152 Gd $110**
W/vent rib, adj. sights...........**NiB $182 Ex $203 Gd $131**

TARGET 9 DA REVOLVER...............**NiB $244 Ex $177 Gd $131**
Same as Target Sealed 8 except has nine non-counterbored chambers. Made from 1929 to 1946.

TARGET SEALED 8 DA REVOLVER.......**NiB $263 Ex $158 Gd $126**
Solid frame. Caliber: .22 LR. Eight-round cylinder, bbl. lengths: 6-
and 10-inches. 10.75 inches overall (with 6-inch bbl.). Weight: 24
oz. (with 6-inch bbl.). Fixed sights. Blued finish. Checkered walnut
grips. Made from 1931 to 1957.

TRIGGER-COCKING SA TARGET........**NiB $296 Ex $225 Gd $168**
Hinged frame. First pull on trigger cocks hammer, second pull releas-
es hammer. Caliber: .22 LR. Eight-round cylinder, counterbored
chambers, 6-inch bbl., 10.75 inches overall. Weight: 24 oz. Adj. target sights. Blued finish. Checkered walnut grips. Made 1940 to 1947.

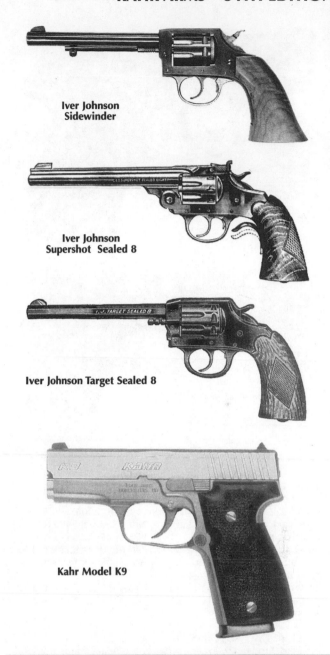

Iver Johnson
Sidewinder

Iver Johnson
Supershot Sealed 8

Iver Johnson Target Sealed 8

Kahr Model K9

KAHR ARMS — Pearl River, New York and Worcester, MA

MODEL K9 DAO AUTO PISTOL
Caliber: 9mm Para. Seven-round magazine, 3.5-inch bbl., 6 inches
overall. Weight: 24 oz. Fixed sights. Matte black, electroless nickel,
Birdsong Black-T or matte stainless finish. Wraparound textured
polymer or hardwood grips. Made from 1994 to 2003.
Duo-Tone finish.................**NiB $560 Ex $440 Gd $300**
Electroless nickel finish..........**NiB $630 Ex $520 Gd $375**
Black-T finish...................**NiB $685 Ex $565 Gd $425**
Matte stainless finish.............**NiB $750 Ex $600 Gd $425**
Kahr Lady K9 model.............**NiB $480 Ex $325 Gd $245**
Elite model.....................**NiB $785 Ex $575 Gd $375**
Tritium Night Sights, add..............................$90

Kel-Tec Model P-11

Kimber Model Classic .45

MODEL K40 DAO AUTO PISTOL
Similar to Model K9 except chambered .40 S&W w/5- or 6-round magazine, Weight: 26 oz. Made from 1997 to 2003.

Matte black finish	NiB $560	Ex $400	Gd $290
Electroless nickel finish	NiB $635	Ex $575	Gd $370
Black-T finish	NiB $690	Ex $525	Gd $320
Matte black stainless finish	NiB $600	Ex $440	Gd $320
Covert model (shorter grip-frame)	NiB $500	Ex $375	Gd $290
Elite model	NiB $785	Ex $575	Gd $400
Tritium Night Sights, add			$90

MODEL K9 DAO AUTO PISTOL
Similar to Model K9 except w/Micro-Compact frame. Six- or 7-round magazine, 3- inch bbl., 5.5 inches overall. Weight: 22 oz. Stainless or Duo-Tone finish. Made from 1993 to 2003.

Duo-Tone finish	NiB $650	Ex $500	Gd $375
Matte stainless finish	NiB $400	Ex $325	Gd $280
Elite model	NiB $795	Ex $500	Gd $390
Tritium Night Sights, add			$90

KBI, INC — Harrisburg, Pennsylvania

MODEL PSP-.25 AUTO PISTOL.... NiB $293 Ex $235 Gd $149
Caliber: .25 ACP. Six-round magazine, 2.13-inch bbl., 4.13 inches overall. Weight: 9.5 oz. All-steel construction w/dual safety system. Made 1994.

KEL-TEC CNC INDUSTRIES, INC. — Cocoa, Florida

MODEL P-11 DAO PISTOL
Caliber: 9mm Parabellum or .40 S&W. 10-round magazine, 3.1-inch bbl., 5.6 inches overall. Weight: 14 oz. Blade front sight, drift adjustable rear. Aluminum frame w/steel slide. Checkered black, gray, or green polymer grips. Matte blue, nickel, stainless steel or Parkerized finish. Made from 1995 to date.

9mm	NiB $275	Ex $200	Gd $145
.40 S&W	NiB $550	Ex $375	Gd $225
Parkerized finish, add			$50
Nickel finish, add (disc. 1995)			$50
Stainless finish, add (1996 to date)			$50
Tritium Night Sights, add			$80
.40 cal. conversion kit, add			$175

KIMBER MANUFACTURING, INC. — Yonkers, New York (Formerly Kimber of America, Inc.)

MODEL CLASSIC .45
Similar to Government 1911 built on steel, polymer or alloy full-size or compact frame. Caliber: .45 ACP. Seven-, 8-, 10- or 14-round magazine, 4- or 5-inch bbl., 7.7 or 8.75 inches overall. Weight: 28 oz. (Compact LW), 34 oz. (Compact or Polymer) or .38 oz. (Custom FS). McCormick low-profile combat or Kimber adj. target sights. Blued, matte black oxide or stainless finish. Checkered custom wood or black synthetic grips. Made from 1994 to date.

Custom (matte black)	NiB $825	Ex $555	Gd $390
Custom Royal (polished blue)	NiB $739	Ex $584	Gd $411
Custom stainless (satin stainless)	NiB $711	Ex $553	Gd $390
Custom Target (matte black)	NiB $713	Ex $563	Gd $396
Target Gold Match (polished blue)	NiB $988	Ex $739	Gd $550
Target stainless Match (polished stainless)	NiB $794	Ex $639	Gd $453
Polymer (matte black)	NiB $794	Ex $639	Gd $453
Polymer Stainless (satin stainless slide)	NiB $936	Ex $755	Gd $536
Polymer Target (matte black slide)	NiB $878	Ex $714	Gd $505
Compact (matte black)	NiB $621	Ex $506	Gd $360
Compact stainless (satin stainless)	NiB $686	Ex $542	Gd $388
Compact LW (matte black w/alloy frame)	NiB $686	Ex $542	Gd $388

KORTH PISTOLS — Ratzeburg, Germany

Currently imported by Keng's Firearms Specialty, Inc. Previously by Beeman Precision Arms; Osborne's and Mandall Shooting Supply

REVOLVERS COMBAT, SPORT, TARGET
Calibers: .357 Mag. and .22 LR w/interchangeable combination cylinders of .357 Mag./9mm Para. or .22 LR/.22 WMR also .22 Jet, .32 S&W and .32 H&R Mag. Bbls: 2.5-, 3-, 4-inch (combat) and 5.25- or 6-inch (target). Weight: 33 to 42 oz. Blued, stainless, matte silver or polished silver finish. Checkered walnut grips. Imported 1967 to date.

Standard rimfire model	NiB $4500	Ex $2699	Gd $1845
Standard centerfire model	NiB $6800	Ex $5025	Gd $3896
ISU Match Target model	NiB $7390	Ex $5397	Gd $3298
Custom stainless finish, add			$450
Matte silver finish, add			$650

SEMIAUTOMATIC PISTOL

Calibers: 30 Luger, 9mm Para., .357 SIG, .40 S&W, 9x21mm. 10- or 14-round magazine, 4- or 5-inch bbl., all-steel construction, recoil-operated. Ramp front sight, adj. rear. Blued, stainless, matte silver or polished silver finish. Checkered walnut grips. Limited import from 1988

.Standard model ....NiB $6400	Ex $4962	Gd $3831
Matte silver finish, add		$300
Polished silver finish, add		$750

Lahti Automatic Pistol

LAHTI PISTOLS — Mfd. by Husqvarna Vapenfabriks A. B. Huskvarna, Sweden, and Valtion Kivaar Tedhas ("VKT") Jyväskyla, Finland

AUTOMATIC PISTOL

Caliber: 9mm Para. Eight-round magazine, 4.75-inch bbl., weight: About 46 oz. Fixed sights. Blued finish. Plastic grips. Specifications given are those of the Swedish Model 40 but also apply in general to the Finnish Model L-35, which differs only slightly. A considerable number of Swedish Lahti pistols were imported and sold in the U.S. The Finnish model, somewhat better made, is rare. Finnish Model L-35 adopted 1935. Swedish Model 40 adopted 1940, mfd. through 1944.

Finnish L-35 model	NiB $4100	Ex $3968	Gd $2355
Swedish 40 model	NiB $600	Ex $438	Gd $294

L.A.R. Mark I Grizzly

L.A.R. MANUFACTURING, INC. — West Jordan, Utah

MARK I GRIZZLY WIN. MAG. AUTOMATIC PISTOL

Calibers: .357 Mag., .45 ACP, .45 Win. Mag. Seven-round magazine, 6.5-inch bbl., 10.5 inches overall. Weight: 48 oz. Fully adj. sights. Checkered rubber combat-style grips. Blued finish. Made from 1983 to date. 8- or 10-inch bbl., Made from 1987 to 1999.

.357 Mag. (6.5 inch barrel)	NiB $875	Ex $605	Gd $405
.45 Win. Mag.(6.5 inch barrel)	NiB $875	Ex $605	Gd $405
8-inch barrel	NiB $1200	Ex $1015	Gd $905
10-inch barrel	NiB $1275	Ex $1080	Gd $1025

MARK 4 GRIZZLY

AUTOMATIC PISTOL	NiB $875	Ex $700	Gd $600

Same general specifications as the L.A.R. Mark I except chambered for .44 Magnum, has 5.5- or 6.5-inch bbl., beavertail grip safety, matte blued finish. Made from 1991 to 1999.

Laseraim Series I

MARK 5 AUTO PISTOL	NiB $1475	Ex $1255	Gd $1095

Similar to the Mark I except chambered in 50 Action Express. Six-round magazine, 5.4- or 6.5-inch bbl., 10.6 inches overall (with 5.4-inch bbl.). Weight: 56 oz. Checkered walnut grips. Made 1993 to 1999.

LASERAIM TECHNOLOGIES, INC. — Little Rock, Arkansas

SERIES I SA AUTO PISTOL

Calibers: .40 S&W, .45 ACP, 10mm. Seven or 8- round magazine, 3.875- or 5.5-inch dual-port compensated bbl., 8.75 or 10.5 inches overall. Weight: 46 or 52 oz. Fixed sights w/Laseraim or adjustable Millet sights. Textured black composition grips. Extended slide release, ambidextrous safety and beveled magazine well. Stainless or matte black Teflon finish. Made from 1993 to 1999.

Series I w/adjustable sights........	NiB $330	Ex $230	Gd $170
Series I w/fixed sights	NiB $330	Ex $230	Gd $170
Series I w/fixed sights (HotDot)	NiB $450	Ex $250	Gd $190
Series I Dream Team (RedDot)	NiB $450	Ex $250	Gd $190
Series I Illusion (Laseraim)	NiB $450	Ex $250	Gd $190

Laseraim Series II

**Laseraim Series III
w/LA93 Illusion III Scope**

**Llama Model IIIA
Deluxe Chrome Engraved First Issue**

**Llama Model IIIA
Deluxe Blue Engraved Second Issue**

SERIES II SA AUTO PISTOL
Similar to Series I except w/stainless finish and no bbl., compensator. Made from 1993 to 1996.

Series II w/adjustable sights . . . . . . NiB $485 Ex $333 Gd $241
Series II w/fixed sights. . . . . NiB $485 Ex $305 Gd $223
Series II Dream Team. . . . . NiB $545 Ex $435 Gd $310
Series II Illusion. . . . . NiB $500 Ex $410 Gd $295

SERIES III SA AUTO PISTOL
Similar to Series II except w/serrated slide and 5-inch compensated bbl., only. Made 1994. Disc.

Series III w/
adjustable sights . . . . NiB $595 Ex $496 Gd $354
Series III w/fixed sights . . . . NiB $596 Ex $455 Gd $325

VELOCITY SERIES SA AUTO PISTOL
Similar to Series I except chambered for .357 Sig. or .400 Cor-Bon, 3.875-inch unported bbl., (compact) or 5.5-inch dual-port compensated bbl. Made from 1993 to 1999. See illustration previous page.

Compact model (unported) . . . . NiB $325 Ex $265 Gd $185
Government model (ported) . . . . . . NiB $325 Ex $265 Gd $185
W/wireless laser
(HotDot), add $150

LIGNOSE PISTOLS — Suhl, Germany
Aktien-Gesellschaft "Lignose" Abteilung

The following Lignose pistols were manufactured from 1920 to the mid-1930s. They were also marketed under the Bergmann name.

EINHAND MODEL 2A
POCKET AUTO PISTOL . . . . NiB $395 Ex $270 Gd $195
As the name implies, this pistol is designed for one-hand operation, pressure on a "trigger" at the front of the guard retracts the slide. Caliber: .25 Auto. (6.35 mm). Six-round magazine, 2-inch bbl., 4.75 inches overall. Weight: About 14 oz. Blued finish. Hard rubber grips.

MODEL 2 POCKET
AUTO PISTOL . . . . NiB $330 Ex $220 Gd $165
Conventional Browning type. Same general specifications as Einhand Model 2A but lacks the one-hand operation.

EINHAND MODEL
3A POCKET AUTO PISTOL . . . . NiB $450 Ex $340 Gd $245
Same as the Model 2A except has longer grip, 9-round magazine, weight: About 16 oz.

LLAMA HANDGUNS — Mfd. by Gabilondo y Cia, Vitoria, Spain (Imported by S.G.S., Wanamassa, New Jersey)

NOTE: *For ease in finding a particular Llama handgun, the listings are divided into two groupings: Automatic Pistols (below) and Revolvers, which follow. For a complete listing of Llama handguns, please refer to the index.*

AUTOMATIC PISTOLS

MODEL IIIA
AUTOMATIC PISTOL . . . . NiB $299 Ex $155 Gd $100
Caliber: .380 Auto. Seven-round magazine, 3.69-inch bbl., 6.5 inches overall. Weight: 23 oz. Adj. target sights. Blued finish. Plastic grips. Intro. 1951. Disc.

MODELS IIIA, XA, XV DELUXE
Same as standard Model IIIA, XA and XV except engraved w/blued
or chrome finish and simulated pearl grips.
Chrome-engraved finish . . . . NiB $350 Ex $290 Gd $200
Blue-engraved finish . . . . NiB $330 Ex $275 Gd $200

MODEL VIII
AUTOMATIC PISTOL . . . . NiB $355 Ex $290 Gd $225
Caliber: .38 Super. Nine-round magazine, 5-inch bbl., 8.5 inches overall.
Weight: 40 oz. Fixed sights. Blued finish. Wood grips. Intro. in 1952. Disc.

MODELS VIII, IXA, XI DELUXE
Same as standard Models VIII, IXA and XI except finish (chrome
engraved or blued engraved) and simulated pearl grips. Disc. 1984.
Chrome-engraved finish . . . . NiB $350 Ex $275 Gd $170
Blue-engraved finish . . . . NiB $350 Ex $275 Gd $170

MODEL IXA AUTOMATIC PISTOL . . . . NiB $350 Ex $275 Gd $170
Same as model VIII except .45 Auto, 7-round magazine,

MODEL XA AUTOMATIC PISTOL . . . . . NiB $350 Ex $275 Gd $170
Same as model IIIA except .32 Auto, 8-round magazine,

MODEL XI AUTOMATIC PISTOL . . . . . NiB $350 Ex $290 Gd $200
Same as model VIII except 9mm Para.

MODEL XV AUTOMATIC PISTOL . . . . . NiB $295 Ex $235 Gd $155
Same as model XA except .22 LR.

MODELS BE-IIIA, BE-XA, BE-XV . . . . . . NiB $495 Ex $300 Gd $220
Same as models IIIA, XA and XV except w/blued-engraved finish. Made
from 1977-84.

MODELS BE-VIII,
BE-IXA, BE-XI DELUXE . . . . NiB $495 Ex $370 Gd $255
Same as models VIII, IXA and XI except w/blued-engraved finish.
Made from 1977 to 1984.

MODELS C-IIIA, C-XA, C-XV . . . . . NiB $375 Ex $340 Gd $235
Same as models IIIA, XA and XV except in satin chrome.

MODELS C-VIII, C-IXA, C-XI . . . . . NiB $448 Ex $341 Gd $234
Same as models VIII, IXA and XI except in satin chrome.

MODELS CE-IIIA,
CE-XA, CE-XV . . . . NiB $478 Ex $402 Gd $280
Same as models IIIA, XA and XV except w/chrome engraved finish.
Made from 1977 to 1984.

MODELS CE-VIII,
CE-IXA, CE-XI . . . . NiB $450 Ex $340 Gd $275
Same as models VIII, IXA and XI, w/except chrome engraved finish.
Made from 1977 to 1984.

COMPACT FRAME
AUTO PISTOL . . . . NiB $320 Ex $255 Gd $195
Calibers: 9mm Para., .38 Super, .45 Auto. Seven-, 8- or 9-round
magazine, 5-inch bbl., 7.88 inches overall. Weight: 34 oz. Blued,
satin-chrome or Duo-Tone finishes. Made from 1986 to 1997. Duo-
Tone disc. 1993.

DUO-TONE LARGE
FRAME AUTO PISTOL . . . . NiB $427 Ex $340 Gd $270
Caliber: .45 ACP. Seven-round magazine, 5-inch bbl., 8.5 inches
overall. Weight: 36 oz. Adj. rear sight. Blued finished w/satin
chrome. Polymer black grips. Made from 1991 to 1993.

Llama Model XA First Issue

Llama Model C-XI

Llama Model CE-IIIA

Llama Model Compact

Llama Duo-Tone Large Frame

Llama M-82 DA Auto

Llama MINI-MAX II

Llama MAX-I

DUO-TONE SMALL

FRAME AUTO PISTOL . . . . NiB $280 Ex $200 Gd $145
Calibers: .22 LR, .32 and .380 Auto. Seven- or 8-round magazine, 3.69 inch bbl., 6.5 inches overall. Weight: 23 oz. Square-notch rear sight, Partridge-type front. Blued finish w/chrome. Made from 1990 to 1993.

MODEL G-IIIA DELUXE . . . . . . NiB $2495 Ex $1926 Gd $1647
Same as Model IIIA except gold damascened w/simulated pearl grips. Disc. 1982.

LARGE-FRAME AUTOMATIC PISTOL (IXA)
Caliber: .45 Auto. Seven-round magazine, 5-inch bbl., weight: 2 lbs., 8 oz. Adj. rear sight, Partridge-type front. Walnut grips or teakwood on satin chrome model. Later models w/polymer grips.
Blued finish . . . . NiB $350 Ex $255 Gd $190
Satin chrome finish . . . . NiB $525 Ex $425 Gd $275

M-82 DA AUTOMATIC PISTOL . . . . NiB $550 Ex $375 Gd $255
Caliber: 9mm Para. 15-round magazine, 4.25-inch bbl., 8 inches overall. Weight: 39 oz. Drift-adj. rear sight. Matte blued finish. Matte black polymer grips. Made from 1988 to 1993.

M-87 COMPETITION PISTOL . . . . . NiB $995 Ex $790 Gd $625
Caliber: 9mm Para. 15-round magazine, 5.5-inch bbl., 9.5 inches overall. Weight: 40 oz. Low-profile combat sights. Satin nickel finish. Matte black grip panels. Built-in ported compensator to minimize recoil and muzzle rise. Made from 1989 to 1993.

MICRO-MAX SA AUTOMATIC PISTOL
Caliber: .380 ACP. Seven-round magazine, 3.125-inch bbl., weight: 23 oz. Blade front sight, drift adjustable rear w/3-dot system. Matte blue or satin chrome finish. Checkered polymer grips. Imported from 1997 to 2005.
Matte blue finish . . . . NiB $265 Ex $200 Gd $175
Satin chrome finish . . . . NiB $270 Ex $220 Gd $195

MINI-MAX SA AUTOMATIC PISTOL
Calibers: 9mm, .40 S&W or .45 ACP. Six- or 8-round magazine, 3.5-inch bbl., 8.3 inches overall. Weight: 35 oz. Blade front sight, drift adjustable rear w/3-dot system. Matte blue, Duo-Tone or satin chrome finish. Checkered polymer grips. Imported 1996 to 2005.
Duo-Tone finish . . . . NiB $275 Ex $200 Gd $145
Matte blue finish . . . . NiB $265 Ex $220 Gd $165
Satin chrome finish . . . . NiB $300 Ex $225 Gd $165
Stainless (disc.) . . . . NiB $335 Ex $270 Gd $215

MINI-MAX II SA AUTOMATIC PISTOL
Cal: .45 ACP only. 10-round mag., 3.625 inch bbl., 7.375 inch overall. Wt: 37 oz. Blade front sight, drift adj. rear w/3-dot system. Shortened barrel and grip. Matte and Satin Chrome finish. Imp. 2005.
Matte blue finish . . . . NiB $265 Ex $220 Gd $165
Satin chrome finish . . . . NiB $285 Ex $240 Gd $185

MAX-I SA AUTOMATIC PISTOL
Calibers: 9mm or .45 ACP. 7- or 9-round magazine, 4.25- to 5.125 inch bbl., weight: 34 or 36 oz. Blade front sight, drift adj. rear w/3-dot system. Matte blue, Duo-Tone or satin chrome finish. Checkered black rubber grips. Imported from 1995 to 1999.
Duo-Tone finish . . . . NiB $275 Ex $230 Gd $185
Matte blue finish . . . . NiB $265 Ex $220 Gd $175
Satin chrome finish . . . . NiB $285 Ex $240 Gd $205

MAX-II SA AUTOMATIC PISTOL
Same as the MAX-I with 4.25 bbl. except w/10-round mag. Weight 40 oz., made 2005.
Matte blue finish . . . . NiB $275 Ex $195 Gd $140
Satin chrome finish . . . . NiB $290 Ex $215 Gd $160

OMNI 45
DOUBLE-ACTION
AUTOMATIC PISTOL . . . . **NiB $395 Ex $265 Gd $200**
Caliber: .45 Auto. Seven-round magazine, 4.25-inch bbl., 7.75 inches overall. Weight: 40 oz. Adj. rear sight, ramp front. Highly polished deep blued finish. Made from 1984-86.

OMNI 9MM
DOUBLE-ACTION
AUTOMATIC . . . . **NiB $445 Ex $330 Gd $280**
Same general specifications as .45 Omni except chambered for 9mm w/13-round magazine. Made from 1983-86.

SINGLE-ACTION
AUTOMATIC PISTOL . . . . **NiB $463 Ex $361 Gd $247**
Calibers: .38 Super, 9mm, .45 Auto. Nine-round magazine (7-round for .45 Auto), 5-inch bbl., 8.5 inches overall. Weight: 2 lbs., 8 oz. Intro. in 1981.

SMALL-FRAME
AUTOMATIC PISTOL
Calibers: .380 Auto (7-round magazine), .22 RF (8-round magazine), 3.69-inch bbl., weight: 23 oz. Partridge-blade front sight, adj. rear. Blued or satin-chrome finish. Disc. 1997.
Blued finish . . . . **NiB $220 Ex $190 Gd $145**
Satin-chrome finish . . . . **NiB $240 Ex $210 Gd $165**

REVOLVERS

MARTIAL DOUBLE-
ACTION REVOLVER . . . . **NiB $225 Ex $160 Gd $110**
Calibers: .22 LR, .38 Special. Six-round cylinder, bbl. lengths: 4-inch (.38 Special only) or 6-inch; 11.25 inches overall (w/6-inch bbl.). Weight: About 36 oz. w/6-inch bbl. Target sights. Blued finish. Checkered walnut grips. Made from 1969 to 1976.

MARTIAL
DOUBLE-ACTION DELUXE
Same as standard Martial except w/satin chrome, chrome-engraved, blued engraved or gold damascened finish. Simulated pearl grips. Made from 1969 to 1976.
Satin-chrome finish . . . . **NiB $275 Ex $200 Gd $145**
Chrome-engraved finish. . . . . **NiB $550 Ex $395 Gd $265**
Blue-engraved finish . . . . **NiB $600 Ex $415 Gd $310**
Gold-damascened finish . . . . **NiB $2775 Ex $2500 Gd $2259**

COMANCHE I
DOUBLE-ACTION
REVOLVER. . . . . **NiB $255 Ex $200 Gd $160**
Same general specifications as Martial .22. Made 1977 to 1982.

COMANCHE II . . . . **NiB $240 Ex $175 Gd $145**
Same general specifications as Martial .38. Made 1977 to 1982.

COMANCHE III
DOUBLE-ACTION
REVOLVER. . . . . **NiB $280 Ex $200 Gd $135**
Caliber: .357 Magnum. Six-round cylinder, 4-inch bbl., 9.25 inches overall. Weight: 36 oz. Adj. rear sight, ramp front. Blued finish. Checkered walnut grips. Made from 1975 to 1995. Note: Prior to 1977, this model was designated "Comanche."

COMANCHE III
CHROME. . . . . **NiB $330 Ex $255 Gd $190**
Same gen. specifications as Comanche III except has satin chrome finish, 4- or 6-inch bbl. Made from 1975 to 1995.

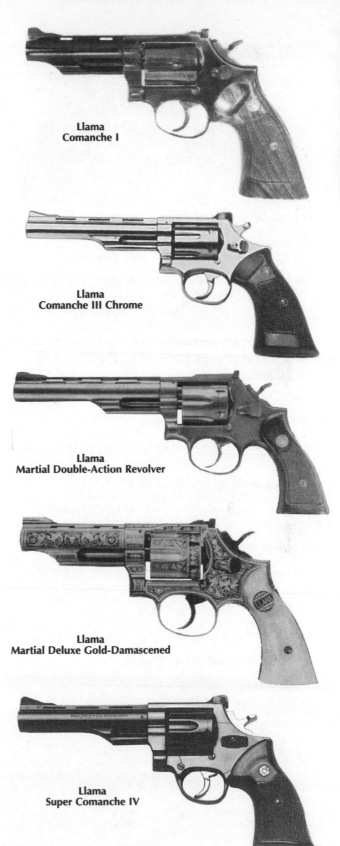

Llama
Comanche I

Llama
Comanche III Chrome

Llama
Martial Double-Action Revolver

Llama
Martial Deluxe Gold-Damascened

Llama
Super Comanche IV

**Luger 1900
American Eagle**

SUPER COMANCHE IV DA REVOLVER . . . NiB $350 Ex $260 Gd $185
Caliber: .44 Magnum. Six-round cylinder, 6-inch bbl., 11.75 inches overall. Weight: 50 oz. Adj. rear sight, ramp front. Polished deep blued finish. Checkered walnut grips. Disc. 1998.

SUPER COMANCHE V DA REVOLVER . . . . NiB $335 Ex $290 Gd $200
Caliber: .357 Mag. Six-round cylinder, 4-, 6- or 8.5-inch bbl., weight: 48 ozs. Ramped front blade sight, click-adj. Rear. Made from 1980 to 1988.

LORCIN ENGINEERING CO., INC. — Mira Loma, California

MODEL L-22 SEMIAUTOMATIC PISTOL . . . . NiB $109 Ex $84 Gd $65
Caliber: 22 LR. Nine-round magazine, 2.5-inch bbl., 5.25 inches overall. Weight: 16 oz. Blade front sight, fixed notch rear w/3-dot system. Black Teflon or chrome finish. Black, pink or pearl composition grips. Made from 1990 to 1998.

MODEL L-25, LT-.25 SEMIAUTOMATIC PISTOL
Caliber: 25 ACP. Seven-round magazine, 2.4-inch bbl., 4.8 inches overall. Weight: 12 oz. (LT-25) or 14.5 oz. (L-25). Blade front sight, fixed rear. Black Teflon or chrome finish. Black, pink or pearl composition grips. Made from 1989-98.
Model L-25 . . . . NiB $75 Ex $50 Gd $35
Model L-25 . . . . NiB $65 Ex $40 Gd $25
Model Lady Lorcin. . . . . NiB $70 Ex $45 Gd $25

MODEL L-32 SEMIAUTOMATIC PISTOL . . . . . NiB $80 Ex $55 Gd $40
Caliber: 32 ACP. Seven-round magazine, 3.5-inch bbl., 6.6 inches overall. Weight: 27 oz. Blade front sight, fixed notch rear. Black Teflon or chrome finish. Black composition grips. Made from 1992 to 1998.

MODEL L-380 SEMIAUTOMATIC PISTOL
Caliber: .380 ACP. Seven- or 10-round magazine, 3.5-inch bbl., 6.6 inches overall. Weight: 23 oz. Blade front sight, fixed notch rear. Matte Black finish. Grooved black composition grips. Made 1994 to 1998.
Model L9MM (7-round) . . . . NiB $125 Ex $90 Gd $60
Model L9MM (10-round). . . . . NiB $125 Ex $90 Gd $60

MODEL L9MM SEMIAUTOMATIC PISTOL
Caliber: 9mm Parabellum. 10- or 13-round magazine, 4.5-inch bbl., 7.5 inches overall. Weight: 31 oz. Blade front sight, fixed notch rear w/3-dot system. Black Teflon or chrome finish. Black composition grips. Made from 1992 to 1998.
Model L-380 (10-round) . . . . NiB $125 Ex $90 Gd $60
Model L-380 (13-round). . . . . NiB $145 Ex $110 Gd $80

O/U DERRINGER . . . . NiB $175 Ex $110 Gd $75
Caliber: .38 Special/.357 Mag., .45LC. Two-round derringer. 3.5-

inch bbls. 6.5 inches overall. Weight: 12 oz. Blade front sight, fixed notch rear. Stainless finish. Black composition grips. Made from 1996-98.

LUGER PISTOLS
Mfd. by Deutsche Waffen und Munitionsfabriken (DWM), Berlin, Germany.

1900 AMERICAN EAGLE . . . . . .NiB $6300 Ex $4800 Gd $3970
Caliber: 7.65 mm. Eight-round magazine; thin, 4.75-inch; tapered bbl.; 9.5 inches overall. Weight: 32 oz. Fixed rear sight, dovetailed front sight. Grip safety. Checkered walnut grips. Early-style toggle, narrow trigger, wide guard, no stock lug. American Eagle over chamber. Estimated 8,000 production.

1900 COMMERCIAL . . . . NiB $5515 Ex $4685 Gd $3463
Same specifications as Luger 1900 American Eagle except DWM on early-style toggle, no chamber markings. Estimated 8000 production.

1900 SWISS. . . . . NiB $6000 Ex $4905 Gd $3589
Same specifications as Luger 1900 American Eagle except Swiss cross in sunburst over chamber. Estimated 9,000 production.

1902 AMERICAN EAGLE
. . . . NiB $15,000 Ex $14,915 Gd $13,795
Caliber: 9mm Para. Eight-round magazine, 4-inch heavy tapered bbl., 8.75 inches overall. Weight: 30 oz. Fixed rear sight, dovetailed front sight. Grip safety. Checkered walnut grips. American Eagle over chamber, DWM on early-style toggle, narrow trigger, wide guard, no stock lug. Estimated 700 production.

1902 CARBINE
Caliber: 7.65mm. Eight-round magazine, 11.75-inch tapered bbl., 16.5 inches overall. Weight: 46 oz. Adj. 4-position rear sight, long ramp front sight. Grip safety. Checkered walnut grips and forearm. DWM on early-style toggle, narrow trigger, wide guard, no chamber markings, stock lug. Estimated 3,200 production.
Model 1902 carbine (gun only) . . . . NiB $11,000 Ex $9825 Gd $6651
Model 1902 carbine
(gun only, American Eagle) . . . . NiB $12,926 Ex $10,542 Gd $9488
W/issued stock and matching numbers. . . . . Add 20%
W/original stock and non-matching numbers . . . . Deduct 20%

1902 CARTRIDGE COUNTER . . . . . . NiB $41,000 Ex $37,160 Gd $28,996
Caliber: 9mm Para. Eight-round magazine, Heavy, tapered 4-inch bbl., 8.75 inches overall. Weight: 30 oz. Fixed rear sight, dovetailed front sight. Grip safety. Checkered walnut grips. DWM on dished toggle w/lock, American Eagle over chamber when marked. No stock lug. Estimated production unknown.

1902 COMMERCIAL . . . . NiB $11,300 Ex $9391 Gd $8250
Same basic specifications as Luger 1902 Cartridge Counter except DWM on early-style toggle, narrow trigger, wide guard, no chamber markings, no stock lug. Estimated 400 production.

1902 AMERICAN EAGLE
. . . . NiB $15,000 Ex $13,391 Gd $11,016
Same basic specifications as Luger 1902 Commercial except American Eagle over chamber, DWM on early-style toggle, narrow trigger, wide guard, no stock lug. Estimated 700 production.

1902 AMERICAN EAGLE
CARTRIDGE COUNTER. . . . . NiB $40,936 Ex $37,160 Gd $29,048
Same basic specifications as Luger 1902 Cartridge Counter except American Eagle over chamber, DWM on early-style toggle, narrow trigger, wide guard, no stock lug. Estimated 700 production.

1904 GL "BABY" . . . . **Nib $195,000 Ex $156,000 Gd $106,080**
Caliber: 9mm Para. Seven-round magazine, 3.25-inch bbl., 7.75 inches overall. Weight: Approx. 20 oz. Serial number 10077B. "GL" marked on rear of toggle. Georg Luger's personal sidearm. Only one made in 1904.

1904 NAVAL (REWORKED) . . . . . . **Nib $13,556 Ex $10,644 Gd $7602**
Caliber: 9mm Para. Eight-round magazine, bbl., length altered to 4 inches., 8.75 inches overall. Weight: 30 oz. Adj. two-position rear sight, dovetailed front sight. Thumb lever safety. Checkered walnut grips. Heavy tapered bbl., DWM on new-style toggle w/lock, 1902 over chamber. W/or without grip safety and stock lug. Estimated 800 production. Untouched original (rare) worth $50,000.

1906 (11.35) . . . . **Nib $117,000 Ex $93,600 Gd $63,648**
Caliber: .45 ACP. Six-round magazine, 5-inch bbl., 9.75 inches overall. Weight: 36 oz. Fixed rear sight, dovetailed front sight. Grip safety. Checkered walnut grips. GL monogram on rear toggle link, larger frame w/altered trigger guard and trigger, no proofs, no markings over chamber. No stock lug. Only two were known to be made. Note: This version of the Luger pistol is the most valuable next to the "GL" Baby Luger.

**1906 AMERICAN EAGLE
(7.65)** . . . . **Nib $4200 Ex $3210 Gd $2118**
Caliber: 7.65mm. Eight-round magazine, thin 4.75-inch tapered bbl., 9.5 inches overall. Weight: 32 oz. Fixed rear sight, dovetailed front sight. Grip safety. Checkered walnut grips. DWM on new-style toggle, American Eagle over chamber. No stock lug. Estimated 8,000 production.

1906 AMERICAN EAGLE (9MM) . . . . . . **Nib $3642 Ex $2371 Gd $1373**
Same basic specifications as the 7.65mm 1906 except in 9mm Para. w/4-inch barrel, 8.75 inches overall, weight: 30 oz. Estimated 3,500 production.

1906 BERN (7.65MM) . . . . **Nib $4350 Ex $2424 Gd $1902**
Same basic specifications as the 7.65mm 1906 American Eagle except checkered walnut grips w/.38-inch borders, Swiss Cross on new-style toggle, Swiss proofs, no markings over chamber, no stock lug. Estimated 17,874 production.

1906 BRAZILIAN (7.65MM) . . . . **Nib $3245 Ex $2987 Gd $1843**
Same general specifications as the 7.65mm 1906 American Eagle except w/Brazilian proofs, no markings over chamber, no stock lug. Estimated 4,500 produced.

1906 BRAZILIAN (9MM) . . . . . . **Nib $1590 Ex $1343 Gd $994**
Same basic specifications as the 9mm 1906 American Eagle except w/Brazilian proofs, no markings over chamber, no stock lug. Production fewer than 4,000 estimated.

1906 COMMERCIAL . . . . **Nib $2937 Ex $2639 Gd $2363**
Calibers: 7.65mm 9mm. Same specifications as the 1906 American Eagle versions (above) except no chamber markings and no stock lug. Estimated production: 6,000 (7.65mm) and 3,500 (9mm).

1906 DUTCH . . . . **Nib $4125 Ex $3602 Gd $2719**
Caliber: 9mm Para. Same specifications as the 9mm 1906 American Eagle except tapered bbl., w/proofs, no markings over chamber, no stock lug. Estimated 3,000 production.

1906 LOEWE AND COMPANY . . . . **Nib $4773 Ex $3839 Gd $2658**
Caliber: 7.65mm. Eight-round magazine, 6-inch tapered bbl., 10.75 inches overall. Weight: 35 oz. Adj. two-position rear sight, dovetailed front sight. Grip safety. Checkered walnut grips. Loewe & Company over chamber, Naval proofs, DWM on new-style toggle, no stock lug. Estimated production unknown.

1906 NAVY
Caliber: 9mm Para. Eight-round magazine, 6-inch tapered bbl., 10.75 inches overall. Weight: 35 oz. Adj. two-position rear sight, dovetailed front sight. Grip safety and thumb safety w/lower marking (1st issue), higher marking (2nd issue). Checkered walnut grips. No chamber markings, DWM on new-style toggle w/o lock, but w/stock lug. Est. production: 9,000 (lst issue); 2,000 (2nd issue).
First issue . . . . **Nib $6850 Ex $5780 Gd $4380**

1906 NAVY COMMERCIAL . . . . **Nib $3980 Ex $3170 Gd $1360**
Same as the 1906 Navy except lower marking on thumb safety, no chamber markings. DWM on new-style toggle, w/stock lug and commercial proofs. Estimated ,3000 production.

1906 PORTUGUESE ARMY . . . . **Nib $3200 Ex $2499 Gd $1599**
Same specifications as the 7.65mm 1906 American Eagle except w/Portuguese proofs, crown and crest over chamber. No stock lug. Estimated 3,500 production.

1906 PORTUGUESE NAVAL . . . . **Nib $10,630 Ex $9120 Gd $7120**
Same as the 9mm 1906 American Eagle except w/Portuguese proofs, crown and anchor over chamber, no stock lug.

1906 RUSSIAN . . . . **Nib $17,200 Ex $14,950 Gd $11,500**
Same general specifications as the 9mm 1906 American Eagle except thumb safety has markings concealed in up position, DWM on new-style toggle, DWM bbl., proofs, crossed rifles over chamber. Estimated production unknown.

1906 SWISS . . . . **Nib $2937 Ex $2637 Gd $2307**
Same general specifications as the 7.65mm 1906 American Eagle Luger except Swiss Cross in sunburst over chamber, no stock lug. Estimated 10,300 production.

1906 SWISS (REWORK) . . . . **Nib $3237 Ex $2847 Gd $2297**
Same basic specifications as the 7.65mm 1906 Swiss except in bbl. lengths of 3.63, 4 and 4.75 inches, overall length 8.38 inches (with 4-inch bbl.). Weight 32 oz. (with 4-inch bbl.). DWM on new-style toggle, bbl., w/serial number and proof marks, Swiss Cross in sunburst or shield over chamber, no stock lug. Estimated production unknown.

1906 SWISS POLICE . . . . **Nib $2907 Ex $2847 Gd $2297**
Same general specifications as the 7.65mm 1906 Swiss except DWM on new-style toggle, Swiss Cross in matted field over chamber, no stock lug. Estimated 10,300 production.

1908 BULGARIAN . . . . **Nib $2907 Ex $2897 Gd $2547**
Caliber: 9mm Para. Eight-round magazine, 4-inch tapered bbl., 8.75 inches overall. Weight: 30 oz. Fixed rear sight dovetailed front sight. Thumb safety w/lower marking concealed. Checkered walnut grips. DWM chamber marking, no proofs, crown over shield on new-style toggle lanyard loop, no stock lug. Estimated production unknown.

1908 COMMERCIAL . . . . **Nib $2400 Ex $1859 Gd $1559**
Same basic specifications as the 1908 Bulgarian except higher marking on thumb safety. No chamber markings, commercial proofs, DWM on new-style toggle, no stock lug. Estimated 4,000 production.

1908 ERFURT MILITARY . . . . . . **Nib $2298 Ex $1954 Gd $1768**
Caliber: 9mm Para. Eight-round magazine, 4-inch tapered bbl., 8.75 inches overall. Weight: 30 oz. Fixed rear sight dovetailed front sight. Thumb safety w/higher marking concealed. Checkered walnut grips. Serial number and proof marks on barrel, crown and Erfurt on new-style toggle, dated chamber, but no stock lug. Estimated production unknown.

Luger 1923 Stoeger

1908 MILITARY
Same general specifications as the 9mm 1908 Erfurt Military Luger except first and second issue have thumb safety w/higher marking concealed, serial number on bbl., no chamber markings, proofs on frame, DWM on new-style toggle but no stock lug. Estimated production: 10,000 (first issue) and 5000 (second issue). Third issue has serial number and proof marks on barrel, dates over chamber, DWM on new-style toggle but no stock lug. Estimated 3,000 production.
First issue . . . . **Nib $2200 Ex $1844 Gd $1580**
Second issue . . . . **Nib $1950 Ex $1544 Gd $1280**
Third issue . . . . **Nib $2200 Ex $1844 Gd $1580**

1908 NAVY . . . . **Nib $8000 Ex $5429 Gd $3371**
Same basic specifications as the 9mm 1908 military Lugers except w/6-inch bbl, adj. two-position rear sight, no chamber markings, DWM on new-style toggle, w/stock lug. Estimated 26,000 production.

1908 NAVY
(COMMERCIAL) . . . . **Nib $4837 Ex $3267 Gd $1707**
Same specifications as the 1908 Naval Luger except no chamber markings or date. Commercial proofs, DWM on new-style toggle, w/stock lug. Estimated 1,900 produced.

1914 ERFURT ARTILLERY . . . . . **Nib $4450 Ex $3920 Gd $2968**
Caliber: 9mm Para. Eight-shot magazine, 8-inch tapered bbl., 12.75 inches overall. Weight: 40 oz. Artillery rear sight, Dovetailed front sight. Thumb safety w/higher marking concealed. Checkered walnut grips. Serial number and proof marks on barrel, crown and Erfurt on new-style toggle, dated chamber, w/stock lug. Estimated production unknown.

1914 ERFURT MILITARY . . . . . . **Nib $1750 Ex $1394 Gd $1082**
Same specifications as the 1914 Erfurt Artillery except w/4-inch bbl., and corresponding length, weight, etc.; fixed rear sight. Estimated 3,000 production.

1914 NAVY . . . . **Nib $4956 Ex $3446 Gd $2146**
Same specifications as 9mm 1914 Lugers except has 6-inch bbl. w/corresponding length and weight, adj. two-position rear sight. Dated chamber, DWM on new-style toggle, w/stock lug. Estimated 40,000 produced.

1914–1918 DWM ARTILLERY . . . . . **Nib $1750 Ex $1565 Gd $1203**
Caliber: 9mm Para. Eight-shot magazine, 8-inch tapered bbl., 12.75 inches overall. Weight: 40 oz. Artillery rear sight, dovetailed front sight. Thumb safety w/higher marking concealed. Checkered walnut grips. Serial number and proof marks on barrel, DWM on new-style toggle, dated chamber, w/stock lug. Estimated 3,000 production.

1914–1918 DWM MILITARY. . . . .Nib $4150 Ex $3898 Gd $2586
Same specifications as the 9mm 1914-1918 DWM Artillery except w/4-inch tapered bbl., and corresponding length, weight, etc., and fixed rear sight. Production unknown.

1920 CARBINE
Caliber: 7.65mm. Eight-round magazine, 11.75-inch tapered bbl., 15.75 inches overall. Weight: 44 oz. Four-position rear sight, long ramp front sight. Grip (or thumb) safety. Checkered walnut grips and forearm. Serial numbers and proof marks on barrel, no chamber markings, various proofs, DWM on new-style toggle, w/stock lug. Estimated production unknown.
**Model 1920 Carbine
(gun only)** . . . . **Nib $6784 Ex $6226 Gd $5738**
**Model 1920 Carbine
(W/shoulder stock), add** **$4000**

1920 NAVY CARBINE . . . . **Nib $4400 Ex $3096 Gd $2148**
Caliber: 7.65mm. Eight-round magazine, 11.75-inch tapered bbl., 15.75 inches overall. Two-position sliding rear sight. Naval military proofs and no forearm. Production unknown.

1920 COMMERCIAL . . . . **Nib $1400 Ex $1250 Gd $1018**
Calibers: 7.65mm, 9mm Para. Eight-round magazine, 3.63-, 3.75-, 4-, 4.75-, 6-, 8-, 10-, 12-, 16-, 18- or 20-inch tapered bbl., overall length: 8.375 to 24.75 inches. Weight: 30 oz. (with 3.63-inch bbl.). Varying rear sight configurations, dovetailed front sight. Thumb safety. Checkered walnut grips. Serial numbers and proof marks on barrel, no chamber markings, various proofs, DWM or crown over Erfurt on new-style toggle, w/stock lug. Production not documented.

1920 POLICE. . . . . **Nib $1328 Ex $1023 Gd $716**
Same specifications as 9mm 1920 DWM w/some dated chambers, various proofs, DWM or crown over Erfurt on new-style toggle, identifying marks on grip frame, w/stock lug. Estimated 3,000 production.

1923 COMMERICAL . . . . **Nib $1444 Ex $1292 Gd $1042**
Calibers: 7.65mm and 9mm Para. Eight-round magazine, 3.63, 3.75, 4, 6, 8, 12 or 16-inch tapered bbl., overall length: 8.38 inches (with 3.63-inch bbl.). Weight: 30 oz. (with 3.63-inch bbl.). Various rear sight configurations, dovetailed front sight. Thumb lever safety. Checkered walnut grips. DWM on new-style toggle, serial number and proofs on barrel, no chamber markings, w/stock lug. Estimated 15,000 production.

1923 DUTCH COMMERICAL . . . . **Nib $2052 Ex $1834 Gd $1502**
Same basic specifications as 1923 Commercial Luger w/same caliber offerings, but only 3.63 or 4-inch bbl. Fixed rear sight, thumb lever safety w/arrow markings. Production unknown.

1923 KRIEGHOFF COMMERCIAL . . . . **Nib $2200 Ex $1930 Gd $1779**
Same specifications as 1923 Commercial Luger, w/same caliber offerings but bbl., lengths of 3.63, 4, 6, and 8 inches. "K" marked on new-style toggle. Serial number, proofs and Germany on barrel. No chamber markings, but w/ stock lug. Production unknown.

1923 SAFE AND LOADED . . . . . **Nib $2200 Ex $1914 Gd $1594**
Same caliber offerings, bbl., lengths and specifications as the 1923 Commercial except thumb lever safety, safe markings, w/stock lug. Estimated 10,000 production.

1923 STOEGER
Same general specifications as the 1923 Commercial Luger with the same caliber offerings and bbl., lengths of 3.75, 4, 6, 8 and up to 24 inches. Thumb lever safety. DWM on new-style toggle, serial number and/or proof marks on barrel. American Eagle over chamber but no stock lug. Estimated production less than 1000 (also see Stoeger listings). Note: Qualified appraisals should be obtained on all Stoeger Lugers with bbl. lengths over 8 inches to ensure accurate values.

3.75-, 4-, or 6-inch bbl. . . . . **Nib $5200 Ex $3650 Gd $2598**
8-inch bbl. . . . . **Nib $6000 Ex $4171 Gd $2191**

1926 "BABY" PROTOTYPE . . **Nib $110,500 Ex $88,400 Gd $60,112**
Calibers: 7.65mm Browning and 9mm Browning (short). Five-round magazine, 2.31-inch bbl., about 6.25 inches overall. Small-sized-frame and toggle assembly. Prototype for a Luger "pocket pistol," but never manufactured commercially. Checkered walnut grips, slotted for safety. Only four known to exist, but as many as a dozen could have been made.

1929 SWISS . . . . **Nib $1886 Ex $1201 Gd $706**
Caliber: 7.65mm. Eight-round magazine, 4.75-inch tapered bbl., 9.5 inches overall. Weight: 32 oz. Fixed rear sight, dovetailed front sight. Long grip safety and thumb lever w/S markings. Stepped receiver and straight grip frame. Checkered plastic grips. Swiss Cross in shield on new-style toggle. Serial numbers and proofs on barrel, no markings over chamber and no stock lug. Estimated 1,900 production.

1934 KRIEGHOFF
COMMERCIAL (SIDE FRAME) . . . . **Nib $4100 Ex $3266 Gd $2714**
Caliber: 7.65mm or 9mm Para. Eight-round magazine, bbl. lengths: 4, 6, and 8 inches, overall length: 8.75 (with 4-inch bbl.). Weight: 30 oz. (with 4-inch bbl.). Various rear sight configurations w/dovetailed front sight. Thumb lever safety. Checkered brown plastic grips. Anchor w/H K Krieghoff Suhl on new-style toggle, but no chamber markings. Tapered bbl., w/serial number and proofs; w/stock lug. Estimated 1,700 production.

1934 KRIEGHOFF S
Caliber: 9mm Para. Eight-round magazine, 4-inch tapered bbl., 8.75 inches overall. Weight: 30 oz. Fixed rear sight, dovetailed front sight. Thumb lever safety. Anchor w/H K Krieghoff Suhl on new-style toggle, S dated chamber, bbl., proofs and stock lug. Early model: Checkered walnut or plastic grips. Estimated 2,500 production. Late model: Checkered brown plastic grips. Estimated 1,200 production.
Early model . . . . **Nib $4100 Ex $3908 Gd $2811**
Late model . . . . **Nib $2631 Ex $2113 Gd $1464**

1934 BYF . . . . **Nib $1308 Ex $996 Gd $580**
Caliber: 9mm Para. Eight-round magazine, 4-inch tapered bbl., 8.75 inches overall. Weight: 30 oz. Fixed rear sight, dovetailed front sight. Thumb lever safety. Checkered walnut or plastic grips. byf on new-style toggle, serial number and proofs on bbl., 41-42 dated chamber and w/stock lug. Estimated 3,000 production.

1934 MAUSER S/42 K . . . . **Nib $6590 Ex $4062 Gd $1670**
Caliber: 9mm Para. Eight-round magazine, 4-inch tapered bbl., 8.75 inches overall. Weight: 30 oz. Fixed rear sight dovetailed front sight. Thumb lever safety. Checkered walnut or plastic grips. 42 on new-style toggle, serial number and proofs on barrel, 1939-.40 dated chamber markings and w/stock lug. Estimated 10,000 production.

1934 MAUSER S/42 (DATED) . . . **Nib $2045 Ex $1852 Gd $1462**
Same specifications as Luger 1934 Mauser 42 except 41 dated chamber markings and w/stock lug. Production unknown.

Luger S42

1934 MAUSER BANNER (MILITARY) . . . . . **Nib $3950 Ex $3349 Gd $2965**
Same specifications as Luger 1934 Mauser 42 except Mauser in banner on new-style toggle, tapered bbl., w/serial number and proofs usually, dated chamber markings and w/stock lug. Production unknown.

1934 MAUSER COMMERCIAL . . . . **Nib $3950 Ex $3349 Gd $2965**
Same specifications as Luger 1934 Mauser 42 except checkered walnut grips. Mauser in banner on new-style toggle, tapered bbl., usually w/serial number and proofs, no chamber markings, but w/stock lug. Production unknown.

1934 MAUSER DUTCH . . . . **Nib $3570 Ex $3252 Gd $2904**
Same specifications as Luger 1934 Mauser 42 except checkered walnut grips. Mauser in banner on new-style toggle, tapered bbl., w/caliber, 1940 dated chamber markings and w/stock lug. Production unknown.

1934 MAUSER LATVIAN . . . . . . **Nib $3059 Ex $2102 Gd $1852**
Caliber: 7.65mm. Eight-round magazine, 4-inch tapered bbl., 8.75 inches overall. Weight: 30 oz. Fixed square-notched rear sight, dovetailed Partridge front sight. Thumb lever safety. Checkered walnut stocks. Mauser in banner on new-style toggle,1937 dated chamber markings and w/stock lug. Production unknown.

1934 MAUSER (OBERNDORF) . . . . **Nib $3030 Ex $2424 Gd $1675**
Same as 1934 Mauser 42 except checkered walnut grips. Oberndorf 1934 on new-style toggle, tapered bbl., w/proofs and caliber, Mauser banner over chamber and w/stock lug (also see Mauser).

1934 SIMSON-S TOGGLE. . . . . . **Nib $4255 Ex $3907 Gd $3629**
Same as 1934 Mauser 42 except checkered walnut grips, S on new-style toggle, tapered bbl., w/serial number and proofs, no chamber markings; w/stock lug. Estimated 10,000 production.

42 MAUSER BANNER (BYF) . . . **Nib $3855 Ex $2986 Gd $2570**
Same specifications as Luger 1934 Mauser 42 except weight: 32 oz. Mauser in banner on new-style toggle, tapered bbl., w/serial number and proofs usually, dated chamber markings and w/stock lug. Estimated 3,500 production.

ABERCROMBIE AND FITCH . . . . **Nib $5250 Ex $4536 Gd $3910**
Calibers: 7.65mm and 9mm Para. Eight-round magazine, 4.75-inch tapered bbl., 9.5 inches overall. Weight: 32 oz. Fixed rear sight, dovetailed front sight. Grip safety. Checkered walnut grips. DWM on new-style toggle Abercrombie & Fitch markings on barrel, Swiss Cross in sunburst over chamber, no stock lug. Est. 100 production.

Luna Model 200
Free Pistol

DUTCH ROYAL AIR FORCE . . . . **Nib $2995 Ex $1841 Gd $703**
Caliber: 9mm Para. Eight-round magazine, 4-inch tapered bbl., 8.75 inches overall. Weight: 30 oz. Fixed rear sight dovetailed front sight. Grip safety and thumb safety w/markings and arrow. Checkered walnut grips. DWM on new-style toggle, bbl., dated w/serial number and proofs, no markings over chamber, no stock lug. Estimated 4,000 production.

DWM (G DATE). . . . . **Nib $2034 Ex $1882 Gd $1514**
Caliber: 9mm Para. Eight-round magazine, 4-inch tapered bbl., 8.75 inches overall. Weight: 30 oz. Fixed rear sight, dovetailed front sight. Thumb lever safety. Checkered walnut grips. DWM on new-style toggle, serial number and proofs on barrel, G (1935 date) over chamber and w/stock lug. Production unknown.

DWM AND ERFURT . . . . **Nib $1230 Ex $977 Gd $679**
Caliber: 9mm Para. Eight-round magazine, 4- or 6-inch tapered bbl., overall length: 8.75 or 10.75 inches. Weight: 30 or 38 oz. Fixed rear sight, dovetailed front sight. Thumb safety. Checkered walnut grips. Serial numbers and proof marks on barrel, double dated chamber, various proofs, DWM or crown over Erfurt on new-style toggle and w/stock lug. Production unknown.

KRIEGHOFF 36 . . . . **Nib $4213 Ex $2560 Gd $1773**
Caliber: 9mm Para. Eight-round magazine, 4-inch tapered bbl., 8.75 inches overall. Weight: 30 oz. Fixed rear sight, dovetailed front sight. Thumb lever safety. Checkered brown plastic grips. Anchor w/H K Krieghoff Suhl on new-style toggle, 36 dated chamber, serial number and proofs on barrel and w/stock lug. Estimated 700 production.

KRIEGHOFF-DATED
1936-1945 . . . . **Nib $3279 Ex $2687 Gd $1127**
Same specifications as Luger Krieghoff 36 except 1936-45 dated chamber, bbl. proofs. Est. 8,600 production.

KRIEGHOFF (GRIP SAFETY) . . . . **Nib $4873 Ex $3894 Gd $2691**
Same specifications as Luger Krieghoff 36 except grip safety and thumb lever safety. No chamber markings, tapered bbl., w/serial number, proofs and caliber, no stock lug. Production unknown.

MAUSER BANNER
(GRIP SAFETY). . . . . **Nib $2794 Ex $1942 Gd $1328**
Caliber: 7.65mm. Eight-round magazine, 4.75-inch tapered bbl., 9.5 inches overall. Weight: 30 oz. Fixed rear sight, dovetailed front sight. Grip safety and thumb lever safety. Checkered walnut grips. Mauser in banner on new-style toggle, serial number and proofs on barrel, 1939 dated chamber markings, but no stock lug. Production unknown.

MAUSER BANNER 42 (DATED). . . . **Nib $1625 Ex $1144 Gd $669**
Caliber: 9mm Para. Eight-round magazine, 4-inch tapered bbl., 8.75 inches overall. Weight: 30 oz. Fixed rear sight, dovetailed front sight. Thumb lever safety. Checkered walnut or plastic grips. Mauser in banner on new-style toggle serial number and proofs on bbl., (usually) 1942 dated chamber markings and stock lug. Production unknown.

MAUSER BANNER
(SWISS PROOF). . . . . **Nib $3353 Ex $2655 Gd $1407**
Same specifications as Luger Mauser Banner 42 except checkered walnut grips and 1939 dated chamber.

MAUSER FREISE. . . . . **Nib $4753 Ex $3819 Gd $2609**
Same specifications as Mauser Banner 42 except checkered walnut grips, tapered bbl. w/proofs on sight block and Freise above chamber. Production unknown.

S/42
Caliber: 9mm Para. Eight-round magazine, 4-inch tapered barrel. 8.75 inches overall. Weight: 30 oz. Fixed rear sight, dovetailed front sight. Thumb lever safety. Checkered walnut grips. S/42 on new-style toggle, serial number and proofs on barrel and w/stock lug. Dated Model: Has dated chamber; estimated 3000 production. G Date: Has G (1935 date) over chamber; estimated 3000 production. K Date: Has K (1934 date) over chamber; production unknown.

Dated model . . . . **Nib $6600 Ex $5845 Gd $4455**
G date model. . . . . **Nib $2580 Ex $2246 Gd $1956**
K date model . . . . **Nib $6600 Ex $5845 Gd $4455**

RUSSIAN
COMMERCIAL. . . . . **Nib $2866 Ex $2306 Gd $1590**
Caliber: 7.65mm. Eight-round magazine, 3.63-inch tapered bbl., 8.38 inches overall. Weight: 30 oz. Fixed rear sight, dovetailed front sight. Thumb lever safety. Checkered walnut grips. DWM on new-style toggle, Russian proofs on barrel, no chamber markings but w/stock lug. Production unknown.

SIMSON AND COMPANY
Calibers: 7.65mm and 9mm Para. Eight-round magazine, Weight: 32 oz. Fixed rear sight, dovetailed front sight. Thumb lever safety. Checkered walnut grips. Simson & Company Suhl on new-style toggle, serial number and proofs on barrel, date over chamber and w/stock lug. Estimated 10,000 production.

Simson and
Company
(9mm w/1925 date). . . . . **Nib $2696 Ex $2166 Gd $788**
Simson and
Company
(undated) . . . . **Nib $1549 Ex $893 Gd $519**
Simson and
Company
(S code) . . . . **Nib $1988 Ex $1426 Gd $626**

VICKERS-DUTCH . . . . **Nib $4120 Ex $3858 Gd $3210**
Caliber: 9mm Para. Eight-round magazine, 4-inch tapered bbl., 8.75 inches overall. Weight: 30 oz. Fixed rear sight, dovetailed front sight. Grip safety and thumb lever w/arrow markings. Checkered walnut grips (coarse). Vickers LTD on new-style toggle, no chamber markings, dated barrel but no stock lug. Estimated 10,000 production.

LUNA FREE PISTOL — Zella-Mehlis, Germany Originally mfd. by Ernst Friedr. Buchel and later by Udo Anschutz

MODEL 200 FREE PISTOL . . . . **Nib $1118 Ex $999 Gd $698**
Single-shot. System Aydt action. Set trigger. Caliber: .22 LR. Eleven-inch bbl., weight: 40 oz. Target sights. Blued finish. Checkered and carved walnut grip and forearm; improved design w/adj. hand base on later models of Udo Anschutz manufacture. Made prior to WWII.

M.A.C. (Military Armament Corp.) — Ducktown, TN

INGRAM MODEL 10 AUTO PISTOL Select fire (NFA-Title II-Class III) SMG based on Ingram M10 blowback system using an open bolt design with or without telescoping stock. Calibers: 9mm or .45 ACP. Cyclic rate: 750 RPM (9mm) or 900 RPM (.45 ACP). 32- or 30-round magazine, 5.75-inch threaded bbl. (to accept muzzle brake) bbl. extension or suppressor, 10.5 inches overall w/o stock or 10.6 (w/tele-scoped stock) and 21.5 (w/extended stock). Weight: 6.25 pounds. Front protected post sight, fixed aperture rear sight.

9mm model	Nib $979	Ex $851	Gd $618.45
ACP model	Nib $960	Ex $851	Gd $617
W/bbl. extension, add			$200
W/suppressor, add			$500

INGRAM MODEL 10A1S SEMIAUTOMATIC
Similar to the Model 10 except (Class I) semiautomatic w/closed bolt design to implement an interchangable component system to easily convert to fire 9mm and .45 ACP.

9mm model	Nib $355	Ex $315	Gd $236
.45 ACP model	Nib $365	Ex $319	Gd $236
W/bbl. extension, add			$150
W/fake suppressor, add			$195

INGRAM MODEL 11 SEMIAUTOMATIC
Similar to the Model 10A1 except (Class I) semiautomatic chambered .380 ACP.

.380 ACP model	Nib $736	Ex $655	Gd $529
W/bbl. extension, add			$150
W/fake suppressor, add			$195

MAGNUM RESEARCH, INC. — Minneapolis, Minnesota

BABY EAGLE SEMIAUTOMATIC . . . . Nib $497 Ex $399 Gd $273
DA. Calibers: 9mm, .40 S&W, .41 AE. 15-shot magazine (9mm), 9-round magazine (.40 S&W), 10-round magazine (.41 AE), 4.75-inch bbl., 8.15 inches overall. Weight: 35.4 oz. Combat sights. Matte blued finish. Imported from 1991-96 and 1999 to 2007.

DESERT EAGLE MK VII SEMIAUTOMATIC
Gas-operated. Calibers: .357 Mag., .41 Mag., .44 Mag., .50 Action Express (AE). Eight- or 9-round magazine, 6-inch w/standard bbl., or 10- and 14-inch w/polygonal bbl., 10.6 inches overall (with 6-inch bbl.). Weight: 52 oz. (w/alum. alloy frame) or 67 oz. (w/steel frame). Fixed or adj. combat sights. Combat-type trigger guard. finish: Military black oxide, nickel, chrome, stainless or blued. Wraparound rubber grips. Made from 1983 to 1995 and 1998 to 2001.

.357 standard (steel) or alloy (6-inch bbl.)	Nib $785	Ex $539	Gd $474
.357 stainless steel (6-inch bbl.)	Nib $830	Ex $626	Gd $465
.41 Mag. standard (steel) or alloy 6-inch bbl.)	Nib $971	Ex $763	Gd $540
.41 Mag. stainless steel (6-inch bbl.)	Nib $1025	Ex $839	Gd $622
.44 Mag. standard (steel) or alloy (6-inch bbl.)	Nib $909	Ex $723	Gd $522
.44 Mag. stainless steel (6-inch bbl.)	Nib $991	Ex $790	Gd $559
.50 AE Magnum standard	Nib $1074	Ex $848	Gd $598
For 10-inch bbl., add	Nib $165	Ex $130	Gd $98
For 14-inch bbl., add	Nib $196	Ex $156	Gd $115

MODEL DESERT EAGLE MARK XIX SEMI-AUTOMATIC PISTOL
Interchangeable component system based on .50-caliber frame. Calibers: .357 Mag., .44 Mag., .50 AE. Nine-, 8-, 7-round magazine, 6- or 10-inch bbl. w/dovetail design and cross slots to accept scope rings. Weight: 70.5

Magnum Research Model Desert Eagle Mark XIX (Shown w/Optional Leupold Scope

Magnum Research Model One Pro .45

oz. (6-inch bbl.) or 79 oz. 10.75 or 14.75 inches overall. Sights: Post front and adjustable rear. Blue, chrome or nickel finish; available brushed, matte or polished. Hogue soft rubber grips. Made from 1995 to 1998..

.357 Mag. (W/6-inch bbl.)	Nib $3900	Ex $3681	Gd $2987
.44 Mag. (W/6-inch bbl.)	Nib $3900	Ex $3681	Gd $2987
.50 AE (W/6-inch bbl.)	Nib $1325	Ex $1098	Gd $933
W/10-inch bbl., add			$40
Two caliber conversion (bbl., bolt & mag.), add			$395
XIX Platform System			
3 caliber-conversion w/6 bbls.)	Nib $3995	Ex $3687	Gd $3157
XIX6 System (two caliber-conversion			
w/2 6-inch bbls.)	Nib $2550	Ex $2085	Gd $1802
XIX10 System			
(two cal.-conv. w/ two 10 inch bbls.)	Nib $2150	Ex $1720	Gd $1196
Custom shop finish, add			15%
24K gold finish, add			35%

(ASAI) MODEL ONE PRO .45 PISTOL
Calibers: .45 ACP or .400 COR-BON, 3.75- inch bbl., 7.04 or 7.83 (IPSC Model) inches overall. Weight: 23.5 (alloy frame) or 31.1 oz. 10-round magazine. Short recoil action. SA or DA mode w/de-cocking lever. Steel or alloy grip-frame. Textured black polymer grips. Imported from 1998.

Model 1P45	Nib $644	Ex $499	Gd $361
Model 1C45/400 (compensator kit), add			$175
Model 1C400NC (400 conversion kit), add			$125

Magnum Research SSP-91 Lone Eagle Pistol
(w/Optional Leupold Scope)

Mauser
Model 80-SA

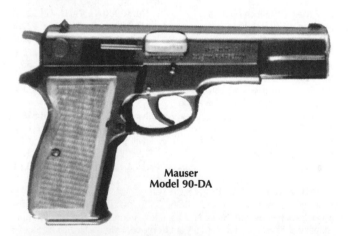

Mauser
Model 90-DA

MOUNTAIN EAGLE SEMIAUTOMATIC

Caliber: .22 LR. 15-round polycarbonate resin magazine, 6.5-inch injection-molded polymer and steel bbl., 10.6 inches overall. Weight: 21 oz. Ramp blade front sight, adj. rear. Injection-molded, checkered and textured grip. Matte black finish. Made 1992 to 1996.
Mountain Eagle (standard, 6.5-inch bbl.) . . NiB $185 Ex $152 Gd $139
Mountain Eagle (compact 4.5-inch bbl.) . . . . NiB $165 Ex $103 Gd $85

SSP-91 LONE EAGLE PISTOL

Single-shot action w/interchangeable rotating breech bbl., assembly. Calibers: .22 LR, .22 Mag., .22 Hornet, .22-250, .223 Rem., .243 Win., 6mm BR, 7mm-08, 7mm BR, .30-06, .30-30, .308 Win., .35 Rem., .357 Mag., .44 Mag., .444 Marlin. 14-inch interchangeable bbl. assembly, 15 inches overall. Weight: 4.5 lbs. Black or chrome finish. Made from 1991 to 2001.
SSP-91 S/S pistol (complete gun w/black finish) . . . . . . NiB $380 Ex $293 Gd $157
SSP-91 S/S pistol (complete gun w/chrome finish) . . NiB $420 Ex $333 Gd $197
Extra 14-inch bbl., action w/black finish . . . . Add $120
Extra 14-inch bbl., action w/chrome finish. . . . . Add $160
Ambidextrous stock assembly, add . . . . Add $200
W/muzzle brake, add . . . . Add $365
W/open sights, add $35

MAUSER PISTOLS — Oberndorf, Germany
Waffenfabrik Mauser of Mauser-Werke A.G.

MODEL 80-SA AUTOMATIC . . . . . . NiB $524 Ex $374 Gd $232
Caliber: 9mm Para. 13-round magazine, 4.66-inch bbl., 8 inches overall. Weight: 31.5 oz. Blued finish. Hardwood grips. Made 1992 to 1996.

MODEL 90 DA AUTOMATIC . . . . . NiB $509 Ex $354 Gd $234
Caliber: 9mm Para. 14-round magazine, 4.66-inch bbl., 8 inches overall. Weight: 35 oz. Blued finish. Hardwood grips. Made 1992 to 1996.

MODEL 90 DAC COMPACT . . . . . . NiB $534 Ex $374 Gd $234
Caliber: 9mm Para. 14-round magazine, 4.13-inch bbl., 7.4 inches overall. Weight: 33.25 oz. Blued finish. Hardwood grips. Made 1992 to 1996.

MODEL 1898 (1896) MILITARY AUTO PISTOL
Caliber: 7.63mm Mauser, but also chambered for 9mm Mauser and 9mm Para. w/the latter being identified by a large red "9" in the grips. 10-round box magazine, 5.25-inch bbl., 12 inches overall. Weight: 45 oz. Adj. rear sight. Blued finish. Walnut grips. Made from 1897 to 1939. Note: Specialist collectors recognize a number of variations at significantly higher values. Price here is for more common commercial and military types with original finish.
Commercial model (pre-war) . . . . NiB $3492 Ex $2692 Gd $1054
Commercial model (wartime) . . . . NiB $1969 Ex $1471 Gd $586
Red 9 Commercial model (fixed sight) . . . . . NiB $1241 Ex $941 Gd $483
Red 9 WWI Contract (tangent sight) . . . . NiB $2099 Ex $1527 Gd $737
W/stock sssembly (matching SN), add $550

MODEL HSC DA AUTO PISTOL
Calibers: .32 Auto (7.65mm), .380 Auto (9mm Short). Eight-round (.32) or 7-round (.380) magazine, 3.4-inch bbl., 6.4 inches overall. Weight: 23.6 oz. Fixed sights. Blued or nickel finish. Checkered walnut grips. Made from 1938 to 1945 and from 1968 to 1996.
Commercial model (low grip screw) . . . . . . NiB $5000 Ex $3904 Gd $2704
Commercial model (wartime) . . . . NiB $460 Ex $372 Gd $202
Nazi military model (pre-war) . . . . NiB $1000 Ex $812 Gd $548
Nazi military model (wartime) . . . . NiB $550 Ex $397 Gd $220
French production (postwar) . . . . NiB $400 Ex $335 Gd $185
Mauser production (postwar) . . . . NiB $450 Ex $340 Gd $189
Recent importation (Armes De Chasse) . . . . . . NiB $445 Ex $375 Gd $253
Recent importation (Interarms) . . . . NiB $350 Ex $249 Gd $189
Recent importation (European Amer. Arms) . . . NiB $270 Ex $170 Gd $104
Recent importation (Gamba, USA) . . . . NiB $395 Ex $276 Gd $162
American Eagle model (1 of 5000) . . . . NiB $500 Ex $400 Gd $284

LUGER LANGE PISTOL 08
Caliber: 9mm Para. Eight-inch bbl., Checkered grips. Blued finish. Accessorized w/walnut shoulder stock, front sight tool, spare magazine, leather case. Currently in production. Commemorative version made in limited quantities w/ivory grips and 14-carat gold monogram plate.

**Mauser Model 1898
(1896) Military**

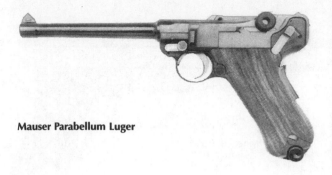

Mauser Parabellum Luger

Commemorative model (100 produced) . . . NiB $2700 Ex $2181 Gd $1527
Commemorative matched pair . . . . NiB $5362 Ex $4323 Gd $2994
Cartridge counter model. . . . . NiB $3491 Ex $2797 Gd $1953
Carbine model (w/matching buttstock) . NiB $6500 Ex $5228 Gd $3624

PARABELLUM LUGER AUTO PISTOL
Current commercial model. Swiss pattern with grip safety. Calibers: 7.65mm
Luger, 9mm Para. Eight-round magazine, bbl. lengths: 4-, 6-inch, 8.75 inches
overall (with 4-inch bbl.). Weight: 30 oz. (with 4-inch bbl.). Fixed sights. Blued
finish. Checkered walnut grips. Made from 1970 to date. Note: Pistols of this
model sold in the U.S. have the American Eagle stamped on the receiver.
Standard model (blue) . . . . NiB $1135 Ex $880 Gd $665

POCKET MODEL 1910 AUTO PISTOL
Caliber: .25 Auto (6.35mm). Nine-round magazine, 3.1-inch bbl.,
5.4 inches overall. Weight: 15 oz. Fixed sights. Blued finish.
Checkered walnut or hard rubber grips. Made from 1910 to 1934.
**Model 1910 (standard) . . . . NiB $650 Ex $446 Gd $280
Model 1910 (w/side latch) . . . . NiB $496 Ex $403 Gd $285**

POCKET MODEL 1914 AUTOMATIC. . . . . NiB $650 Ex $446 Gd $280
Similar to Pocket Model 1910. Caliber: .32 Auto (7.65mm). Eight-
round magazine, 3.4-inch bbl., 6 inches overall. Weight: 21 oz.
Fixed sights. Blued finish. Checkered walnut or hard rubber grips.
Made 1914 to 1934

POCKET MODEL 1934 . . . . NiB $750 Ex $572 Gd $390
Similar to Pocket Models 1910 and 1914 in the respective calibers.
Chief difference is in the more streamlined, one-piece grips. Made
from 1934 to 1939.

WTP MODEL I AUTO PISTOL. . . . . NiB $750 Ex $572 Gd $390
"Westentaschen-Pistole" (Vest Pocket Pistol). Caliber: .25 Automatic
(6.35mm). Six-round magazine, 2.5-inch bbl., 4 inches overall. Weight:
11.5 oz. Blued finish. Hard rubber grips. Made from 1922 to 1937.

WTP MODEL II AUTO PISTOL . . NiB $1345 Ex $1089 Gd $851
Similar to Model I but smaller and lighter. Caliber: .25 Automatic
(6.35mm). Six-round magazine, 2-inch bbl., 4 inches overall. Weight:
9.5 oz. Blued finish. Hard rubber grips. Made from 1938 to 1940.

MERWIN HULBERT & CO. — New York, NY

FIRST MODEL
FRONTIER ARMY . . . . NiB $9624 Ex $7956 Gd $5864
Single action, .44 caliber, 7.5-inch bbl. Square butt, open top,
scoop flutes on cylinder, two screws above trigger guard

SECOND MODEL
FRONTIER ARMY . . . . NiB $8506 Ex $7574 Gd $6042
Similar to First Model except has only one screw above trigger guard.

SECOND MODEL
POCKET ARMY . . . . NiB $7517 Ex $6417 Gd $4949
Similar to Second Model except has bird's-head butt instead of
square butt, 3.5- or 7-inch (scarce) bbl. Some models may be
marked "Pocket Army."

THIRD MODEL
FRONTIER ARMY . . . . NiB $5317 Ex $1417 Gd $949
Caliber: .44, 7-inch round bbl. with no rib, single action. Square
butt, top strap, usually has conventional fluting on cylinder but
some have scoop flutes.

THIRD MODEL
FRONTIER ARMY . . . . NiB $7000 Ex $5254 Gd $4890
Similar to Third Model Frontier Army SA except is double action.

THIRD MODEL POCKET ARMY NiB $7500 Ex $5254 Gd $4890
Caliber: .44, 3.5- or 7.5-inch bbl. with no rib. Single action, bird's-
head butt, top strap.

THIRD MODEL POCKET ARMY NiB $6500 Ex $4960 Gd $3848
Similar to Third Model Pocket Army SA except is double action.

FOURTH MODEL
FRONTIER ARMY . . . . NiB $7898 Ex $5778 Gd $4900
Caliber: .44, 3.5- 5- or 7-inch unique ribbed bbl. Single action,
square butt, top strap, conventional flutes on cylinder.

FOURTH MODEL FRONTIER ARMY
. . . . . NiB $8010 Ex $5750 Gd $5346
Similar to Fourth Model Frontier Army SA except is double action.

*(The following handguns are foreign copies of Merwin Hulbert Co.
guns and may be marked as such, or as "Sistema Merwin Hulbert,"
but rarely with the original Hopkins & Allen markings. These guns
will usually bring half or less of a comparable genuine Merwin
Hulbert product.)*

FIRST POCKET MODEL. . . . . . . NiB $2000 Ex $1635 Gd $1401
Caliber: .38 Special, 5-round cylinder (w/cylinder pin exposed at
front of frame), single action. Spur trigger; round loading hole in
recoil shield, no loading gate.

SECOND POCKET MODEL . . . NiB $1766 Ex. $1554 Gd $1371
Similar to First Pocket Model except has sliding loading gate.

THIRD POCKET MODEL . . . . . .NiB $1559 Ex $1223 Gd $1051
Similar to First Pocket Model except has enclosed cylinder pin.

THIRD POCKET
MODEL W/TRIGGER GUARD. . NiB $1459 Ex $1249 Gd $1077
Similar to First Pocket Model except w/conventional trigger guard.

**Mitchell Arms
Citation II**

**Mitchell Arms
Sharpshooter II**

**MEDIUM FRAME
POCKET MODEL** . . . . **NiB $1195 Ex $894 Gd $644**
Caliber: .38 Spec., 5-round cylinder, DA, may have hammer spur.

**MEDIUM FRAME
POCKET MODEL 32** . . . . **Nib $1355 Ex $1152 Gd $902**
Similar to Medium Frame Pocket Model except .32 caliber, 7-round cylinder, double action.

TIP-UP MODEL 22 . . . . **NiB $1500 Ex $1292 Gd $1022**
Similar to S&W Model One except .22 caliber, 7-round cylinder, spur trigger. Scarce.

MITCHELL ARMS, INC. — Santa Ana, California

MODEL 1911 GOLD SIGNATURE
Caliber: .45 ACP. Eight-round mag, 5-inch bbl., 8.75 inches overall. Weight: 39 oz. Interchangeable blade front sight, drift-adj. combat or fully adj. rear. Smooth or checkered walnut grips. Made 1994 to 1996.
Blued model w/fixed sights . . . . **NiB $467 Ex $375 Gd $281**
Blued model w/adj. sights . . . . **NiB $510 Ex $425 Gd $381**
Stainless model w/fixed sights . . . . . **NiB $675 Ex $520 Gd $435**
Stainless model w/adj. sights . . . . . . **NiB $710 Ex $560 Gd $475**

ALPHA MODEL AUTO PISTOL
Dual action w/interchangeable trigger modules. Caliber: .45 ACP. Eight-round magazine, 5-inch bbl., 8.75 inches overall. Weight: 39 oz. Interchangeable blade front sight, drift-adj. rear. Smooth or checkered walnut grips. Blued or stainless finish. Made in 1994 . Advertised in 1995 but not manufactured.
Blued model w/fixed sights . . . . **NiB $960 Ex $775 Gd $544**
Blued model w/adj. sights . . . . **NiB $994 Ex $803 Gd $563**
Stainless model w/fixed sights . . . . **NiB $994 Ex $803 Gd $563**
Stainless model w/adj. sights . . . . **NiB $1025 Ex $824 Gd $579**

AMERICAN EAGLE PISTOL . . . . **NiB $590 Ex $455 Gd $350**
Stainless-steel re-creation of the American Eagle Parabellum auto pistol. Caliber: 9mm Para. Seven-round magazine, 4-inch bbl., 9.6 inches overall. Weight: 26.6 oz. Blade front sight, fixed rear. Stainless finish. Checkered walnut grips. Made from 1993 to 1994.

CITATION II AUTO PISTOL . . . . . . **NiB $395 Ex $285 Gd $200**
Re-creation of the High Standard Supermatic Citation Military. Caliber: .22 LR. 10-round magazine, 5.5-inch bull bbl. or 7.25 fluted bbl., 9.75 inches overall (5.5-inch bbl.). Weight: 44.5 oz. Ramp front sight, slide-mounted micro-adj. rear. Satin blued or stainless finish. Checkered walnut grips w/thumbrest. Made 1992 to 1996.

**OLYMPIC I.S.U.
AUTO PISTOL** . . . . **NiB $625 Ex $505 Gd $395**
Similar to the Citation II model except chambered in .22 Short, 6.75-inch round tapered bbl. w/stabilizer and removable counterweights. Made from 1992 to 1996.

**SHARPSHOOTER I
AUTO PISTOL** . . . . **NiB $321 Ex $255 Gd $209**
Re-creation of the High Standard Sharpshooter. Caliber: .22 LR. 10-round magazine, 5-inch bull bbl., 10.25 inches overall. Weight: 42 oz. Ramp front sight, slide-mounted micro-adj. rear. Satin blued or stainless finish. Checkered walnut grips w/thumbrest. Made 1992 to 1996.

MODEL SA SPORT KING II . . . . **NiB $270 Ex $206 Gd $156**
Caliber: .22 LR. 10-round magazine, 4.5- or 6.75-inch bbl., 9 or 11.25 inches overall. Weight: 39 or 42 oz. Checkered walnut or black plastic grips. Blade front sight and drift adjustable rear. Made 1993 to 1994.

SA ARMY REVOLVER
Calibers: .357 Mag., .44 Mag., .45 Colt/.45 ACP. Six-round cylinder. bbl., lengths: 4.75, 5.5, 7.5 inches, weight: 40-43 oz. Blade front sight, grooved top strap or adj. rear. Blued or nickel finish w/color-casehardened frame. Brass or steel backstrap/trigger guard. Smooth one-piece walnut grips. Imported from 1987-94 and 1997. Disc.
Standard model w/blued finish . . . . **NiB $395 Ex $300 Gd $220**
Standard model w/nickel finish . . . . **NiB $435 Ex $350 Gd $275**
Standard model w/steel backstrap . . . . **NiB $485 Ex $395 Gd $281**
.45 Combo w/blued finish . . . . **NiB $490 Ex $395 Gd $315**
.45 Combo w/nickel finish . . . . **NiB $545 Ex $450 Gd $375**

**TROPHY II
AUTO PISTOL** . . . . **NiB $425 Ex $315 Gd $245**
Similar to the Citation II model except w/gold-plated trigger and gold-filled markings. Made from 1992 to 1996.

VICTOR II AUTO PISTOL . . . . **NiB $500 Ex $410 Gd $325**
Re-creation of the High Standard Victor w/full-length vent rib. Caliber: .22 LR. 10-round magazine, 4.5- or 5.5-inch bbl., 9.75 inches overall (with 5.5-inch bbl.). Weight: 52 oz. (with 5.5-inch bbl.). Rib-mounted target sights. Satin blued or stainless finish. Checkered walnut grips w/thumbrest. Made from 1992 to 1996.

GUARDIAN ANGEL
DERRINGER . . . . **NiB $125 Ex $100 Gd $90**
Hammerless, double-action O/U derringer w/interchangeable drop-in breech block. Calibers: .22 LR, .22 WRM. Two-round capacity. Two-inch bbl., 5 inches overall. Weight: 12 oz. Blue, nickel or gold finish. Blade front and fixed rear sights. Checkered black grips. Made from 1996 to 1997.

GUARDIAN II . . . . **NiB $299 Ex $221 Gd $159**
Caliber: .38 Special, Six-round cylinder, 2-, 4- or 6-inch bbl., 8.5 inches overall (with 4-inch bbl.). Weight: 32 oz (with 4-inch bbl.). Blade ramp front and fixed rear sights. Checkered combat or target grips. Blued finish. Made in 1995.

GUARDIAN III . . . . **NiB $327 Ex $256 Gd $170**
Same specifications as Guardian II model except w/adjustable rear sights. Made in 1995.

TITAN II DA . . . . **NiB $340 Ex $240 Gd $140**
Caliber: .357 Mag. Six-round cylinder. 2-, 4- or 6-inch bbl., 7.75 inches overall (with 4-inch bbl.). Weight: 38 oz (with 4-inch bbl.). Blade front and fixed rear sights. Crane mounted cylinder release. Blued or stainless finish. Made in 1995.

TITAN III DA . . . . **NiB $260 Ex $190 Gd $105**
Same specification as the Titan II except w/adjustable rear sight. Made in 1995.

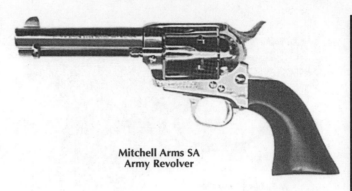

**Mitchell Arms SA
Army Revolver**

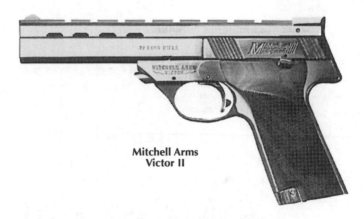

**Mitchell Arms
Victor II**

MKE PISTOL — Ankara, Turkey
Mfd. by Makina ve Kimya Endüstrisi Kurumu

KIRIKKALE DA
AUTOMATIC PISTOL . . . . **NiB $370 Ex $265 Gd $195**
Similar to Walther PP. Calibers: .32 Auto (7.65mm), .380 Auto (9mm Short). Seven-round magazine, 3.9-inch bbl., 6.7 inches overall. Weight: 24 oz. Fixed sights. Blued finish. Checkered plastic grips. Made from 1948 to 1988. Note: This is a Turkish Army standard service pistol.

MOA CORPORATION — Dayton, Ohio

MAXIMUM SINGLE-SHOT PISTOL
Calibers: .22 Hornet to .454 Casull Mag. Armoloy, Chromoloy or stainless falling block action fitted w/blued or stainless 8.75-, 10- or 14-inch Douglas bbl., weight: 60-68 oz. Smooth walnut grips. Made from 1986.
Chromoloy receiver
(blued bbl.) . . . . **NiB $745 Ex $560 Gd $430**
Armoloy receiver (blued bbl.) . . . . . **NiB $896 Ex $789 Gd $437**
Stainless receiver (blued bbl.) . . . . . **NiB $999 Ex $892 Gd $647**
W/stainless bbl., add **$270**
W/extra bbl., add **$340**

MAXIMUM CARBINE PISTOL
Similar to Maximum Pistol except w/18-inch bbl. Made intermittently from 1986-88 and from 1994 to date.
MOA Maximum (blued bbl.) . . . . **NiB $925 Ex $745 Gd $545**
MOA Maximum (stainless bbl.) . . . **NiB $1025 Ex $850 Gd $575**

MKE Kirikkale

**MOA Maximum
Carbine Pistol**

Mossberg Brownie "Pepperbox" Pistol

Navy Arms Model 1875 Schofield

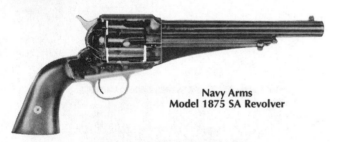

Navy Arms Model 1875 SA Revolver

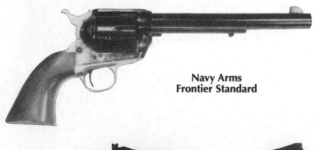

Navy Arms Frontier Standard

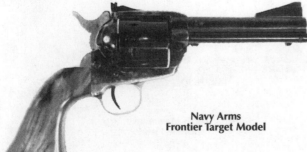

Navy Arms Frontier Target Model

O.F. MOSSBERG & SONS, INC. — North Haven, Connecticut

BROWNIE "PEPPERBOX" PISTOL....... NiB $800 Ex $540 Gd $3756
Hammerless, top-break, double-action, four bbls. w/revolving firing pin. Caliber: .22 LR, 2.5-inch bbls., weight: 14 oz. Blued finish. Serrated grips. Approximately 37,000 made from 1919-.32.

NAMBU PISTOLS
See Listings under Japanese Military Pistols.

NAVY ARMS COMPANY — Martinsburg, West Virginia

MODEL 1873 SA REVOLVER
Calibers: .44-40, .45 Colt. Six-round cylinder, bbl. lengths: 3, 4.75, 5.5, 7.5 inches, 10.75 inches overall (with 5.5-inch bbl.). Weight: 36 oz. Blade front sight, grooved topstrap rear. Blued w/color-case-hardened frame or nickel finish. Smooth walnut grips. Made from 1991 to 2009.
Blued finish w/brass backstrap.... NiB $420 Ex $323 Gd $219
U.S. Artillery model w/5-inch bbl.... NiB $515 Ex $344 Gd $245
U.S. Cavalry model w/7-inch bbl... NiB $515 Ex $344 Gd $245
Bisley model .... NiB $490 Ex $335 Gd $190
Sheriff's model (disc. 1998)....... NiB $395 Ex $313 Gd $189

MODEL 1875 SCHOFIELD REVOLVER
Replica of S&W Model 3, top-break single-action w/auto ejector. Calibers: .44-40 or .45 LC. Six-round cylinder, 5- or 7-inch bbl., 10.75 or 12.75 inches overall. Weight: 39 oz. Blade front sight, square-notched rear. Polished blued finish. Smooth walnut grips. Made from 1999 to 2009.
Cavalry model (7-inch bbl.)....... NiB $615 Ex $500 Gd $289
Deluxe Cavalry model
(engraved) .... NiB $1675 Ex $1350 Gd $1154
Wells Fargo model (5-inch bbl.) ... NiB $715 Ex $555 Gd $389
Deluxe Wells Fargo
model (engraved)........... NiB $1425 Ex $1225 Gd $1050
Hideout model (3.5-inch bbl.)..... NiB $715 Ex $555 Gd $350

MODEL 1875 SA REVOLVER ...... NiB $360 Ex $259 Gd $182
Replica of Remington Model 1875. Calibers: .357 Magnum, .44-40, .45 Colt. Six-round cylinder, 7.5-inch bbl., 13.5 inches overall. Weight: About 48 oz. Fixed sights. Blued or nickel finish. Smooth walnut grips. Made in Italy c.1955-1980 and 1994 to 2000. Originally marketed in the U.S. as Replica Arms Model 1875 (that firm was acquired by Navy Arms Co).

FRONTIER SA REVOLVER .... NiB $360 Ex $270 Gd $194
Calibers: .22 LR, .22 WMR, .357 Mag., .45 Colt. Six-round cylinder, bbl. lengths: 4.5-, 5.5-, 7.5-inches, 10.25 inches overall (with 4.5-inch bbl.). Weight: About 36 oz. (with 4.5-inch bbl.). Fixed sights. Blued bbl., and cylinder, color-casehardened frame, brass grip frame. One-piece smooth walnut grip. Imported from 1975 to 1979.

FRONTIER TARGET MODEL ...... NiB $375 Ex $290 Gd $208
Same as standard Frontier except has adj. rear sight and ramp front sight. Imported from 1975 to 1979.

BUNTLINE FRONTIER.......... NiB $529 Ex $421 Gd $298
Same as Target Frontier except has detachable shoulder stock and 16.5-inch bbl. Calibers: .357 Magnum and .45 Colt only. Made from 1975 to 1979.

LUGER (STANDARD) AUTOMATIC . . . . **NiB $144 Ex $102 Gd $80**
Caliber: .22 LR, standard or high velocity. 10-round magazine, bbl. length: 4.5 inches, 8.9 inches overall. Weight: 1 lb., 13.5 oz. Square blade front sight w/square notch, stationary rear sight. Walnut checkered grips. Non-reflecting black finish. Made 1986 to 1988.

ROLLING BLOCK
SINGLE-SHOT PISTOL . . . . **NiB $390 Ex $322 Gd $203**
Calibers: .22 LR, .22 Hornet, .357 Magnum. Eight-inch bbl., 12 inches overall. Weight: About 40 oz. Adjustable sights. Blued bbl., color-casehardened frame, brass trigger guard. Smooth walnut grip and forearm. Imported from 1965 to 1980.

TT-OLYMPIA PISTOL . . . . **NiB $255 Ex $200 Gd $160**
Reproduction of the Walther Olympia Target Pistol. Caliber: .22 LR. Eight inches overall 4.6-inch bbl., weight: 28 oz. Blade front sight, adj. rear. Blued finish. Checkered hardwood grips. Imported 1992 to 1994.

NEW ENGLAND FIREARMS — Gardner, Massachusetts

In 1987, New England Firearms was established as an independent company producing select H&R models under the NEF logo. In 1991, H&R 1871, Inc. was formed from the residual of the parent company and took over the New England Firearms facility. H&R 1871 produced firearms under both their logo and the NEF brand name until 1999, when the Marlin Firearms Company acquired the assets of H&R 1871.

MODEL R73 REVOLVER . . . . **NiB $125 Ex $85 Gd $50**
Caliber: .32 H&R Mag. Five-round cylinder, 2.5- or 4-inch bbl., 8.5 inches overall (with 4-inch bbl.). Weight: 26 oz. (with 4 inch bbl.). Fixed or adjustable sights. Blued or nickel finish. Walnut-finish hardwood grips. Made from 1988 to 1999.

MODEL R92 REVOLVER . . . . **NiB $125 Ex $85 Gd $50**
Same general specifications as Model R73 except chambered for .22 LR. Nine-round cylinder. Weight: 28 oz. w/4 inch bbl., Made 1988 to 1999.

MODEL 832 STARTER PISTOL . . . . . . **NiB $133 Ex $94 Gd $70**
Calibers: .22 Blank, .32 Blank. Nine- and 5-round cylinders, respectively. Push-pin swing-out cylinder. Solid wood grips w/NEF medallion insert.

ULTRA REVOLVER . . . . **NiB $150 Ex $100 Gd $65**
Calibers: .22 LR, .22 Mag. Nine-round cylinder in .22 LR, 6-round cylinder in .22 Mag., 4- or 6-inch ribbed bull bbl., 10.75 inches overall (with 6-inch bbl.). Weight: 36 oz. (with 6-inch bbl.). Blade front sight, adj. square-notched rear. Blued or nickel finish. Walnut-finish hardwood grips. Made from 1989 to 1999.

LADY ULTRA REVOLVER . . . . **NiB $155 Ex $130 Gd $95**
Same basic specifications as the Ultra except in .32 H&R Mag. w/5-round cylinder and 3-inch ribbed bull bbl., 7.5 inches overall. Weight: 31 oz. Made from 1992 to 1999.

NORTH AMERICAN ARMS — Provo, Utah

MODEL 22LR . . . . **NiB $155 Ex $100 Gd $65**
Same as Model 22S except chambered for .22 LR., is 3.88-inches overall, weight: 4.5 oz. Made from 1975 to date.

MODEL 22S MINI REVOLVER . . . . . . **NiB $155 Ex $100 Gd $65**
Single-Action. Caliber: .22 Short. Five-round cylinder, 1.13-inch bbl., 3.5-inches overall. Weight: 4 oz. Fixed sights. Stainless steel. Plastic grips. Made from 1975 to date.

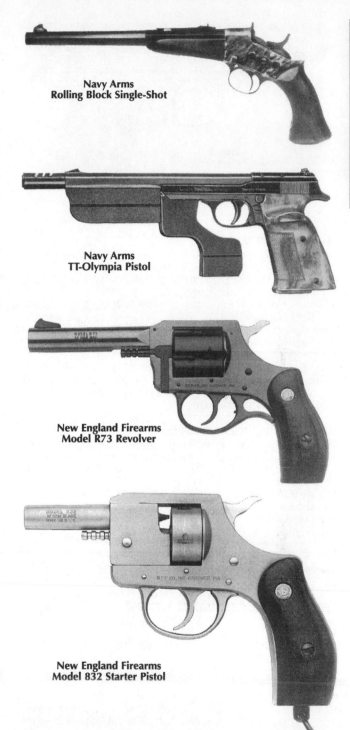

Navy Arms
Rolling Block Single-Shot

Navy Arms
TT-Olympia Pistol

New England Firearms
Model R73 Revolver

New England Firearms
Model 832 Starter Pistol

MODEL 450 MAGNUM EXPRESS
Single-Action. Calibers: .450 Magnum Express, .45 Win. Mag. Five-round cylinder, 7.5- or 10.5-inch bbl., matte or polished stainless steel finish. Walnut grips. Presentation case. Disc. 1984.
Matte stainless model . . . . **NiB $1200 Ex $1037 Gd $782**
Polished stainless model . . . . **NiB $1445 Ex $1199 Gd $937**
W/10-inch bbl., add $250
W/combo cylinder, add $225

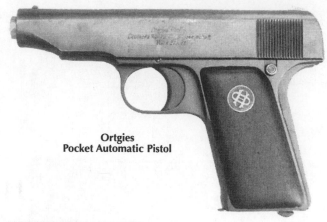

**Ortgies
Pocket Automatic Pistol**

BLACK WIDOW REVOLVER

SA. Calibers: .22 LR., .22 WMR. Five-round cylinder, 2-inch heavy vent bbl., 5.88-inches overall. Weight: 8.8 oz. Fixed or adj. sights. Full-size black rubber grips. Stainless steel brush finish. Made from 1990 to date.

Adj. sight model . . . . NiB $225 Ex $165 Gd $110
Adj. sight combo model . . . . Add $30
Fixed sight model . . . . NiB $225 Ex $165 Gd $110
Fixed sight combo model . . . . Add $35

GUARDIAN DAO PISTOL . . . . NiB $355 Ex $255 Gd $185

Caliber: .32 ACP. Six-round magazine, 2-inch bbl., 4.4 inches overall. Weight: 13.5 oz. Fixed sights. Black synthetic grips. Stainless steel. Made from 1997 to date.

MINI-MASTER TARGET REVOLVER

SA. Calibers: .22 LR., .22 WMR. Five-round cylinder, 4-inch heavy vent rib bbl., 7.75-inches overall. Weight: 10.75 oz. Fixed or adj. sights. Black rubber grips. Stainless steel brush finish. Made from 1990 to date.

Adj. sight model . . . . NiB $240 Ex $200 Gd $155
Adj. sight combo model . . . . Add $30
Fixed sight model . . . . NiB $240 Ex $200 Gd $155
Fixed sight combo model . . . . Add $35

NORWEGIAN MILITARY PISTOLS —
Mfd. by Kongsberg Vaapenfabrikk,
Government Arsenal at Kongsberg, Norway

MODEL 1914
AUTOMATIC PISTOL . . . . NiB $481 Ex $358 Gd $252
Similar to Colt Model 1911 .45 Automatic w/same general specifications except has lengthened slide stop. Made 1919-46.

NORWEGIAN
MODEL 1912 . . . . NiB $2790 Ex $2215 Gd $1508
Same as the model 1914 except has conventional slide stop. Only 500 were made.

OLYMPIC ARMS, INC. —
Olympia, Washington

OA-93 AR SEMIAUTOMATIC PISTOL
AR-15 style receiver with no buffer tube or charging handle. Caliber: .223 Rem. or 7.62x39mm. Five-, 20- or 30-round detachable

magazine, 6-, 9- or 14-inch stainless steel bbl., 15.75 inches overall w/6-inch bbl., weight: 4 lbs., 3 oz. Flattop upper with no open sights. Vortex flash suppressor. A2 stowaway pistol grip and forward pistol grip. Made 1993-94. Note: All post-ban versions of OA-93 style weapons are classified by BATF as "Any Other Weapon" and must be transferred by a Class III dealer. Values listed here are for limited-production, pre-ban guns.

**Model OA-93
(.223 Rem.)** . . . . NiB $1095 Ex $816 Gd $661
**Model OA-93
(7.62x39mm)** . . . . NiB $2200 Ex $1635 Gd $1350

OA-96 AR SEMI-
AUTOMATIC PISTOL . . . . NiB $865 Ex $750 Gd $600
Similar to Model OA-93 AR except w/6.5-inch bbl. only chambered for .223 Rem. Additional compliance modifications include a fixed (nonremovable) well-style magazine and no forward pistol grip. Made from 1996 to 2000.

ORTGIES PISTOLS — Erfurt, Germany
Manufactured by Deutsche Werke A.G.

POCKET AUTO-
MATIC PISTOL . . . . NiB $350 Ex $275 Gd $205
Calibers: .32 Auto (7.65mm), .380 Auto (9mm). Seven-round magazine (.380 cal.), 8-round (.32 cal.), 3.25-inch bbl., 6.5-inches overall. Weight: 22 oz. Fixed sights. Blued finish. Plain walnut grips. Made in 1920's.

VEST POCKET
AUTOMATIC PISTOL . . . . NiB $400 Ex $245 Gd $175
Caliber: .25 Auto (6.35mm). Six-round magazine, 2.75-inch bbl., 5.19 inches overall. Weight: 13.5 oz. Fixed sights. Blued finish. Plain walnut grips. Made in 1920's.

PARA USA, INC. — Pineville, NC

LIMITED EDITION SERIES
Custom-tuned and fully accessorized "Limited Edition" versions of standard "P" Models. Enhanced-grip frame and serrated slide fitted w/match-grade bbl., and full-length recoil spring guide system. Beavertail grip safety and skeletonized hammer. Ambidextrous safety and trigger-stop adjustment. Fully adjustable or contoured low-mount sights. For pricing see individual models.

MODEL P-10 SA
AUTO PISTOL
Super compact. Calibers: .40 S&W, .45 ACP. 10-round magazine, 3-inch bbl., weight: 24 oz. (alloy frame) or 31 oz. (steel frame). Ramp front sight and drift adjustable rear w/3-dot system. Steel or alloy frame. Matte black, Duo-Tone or stainless finish. Made from 1997 to 2002.

Alloy model . . . . NiB $610 Ex $500 Gd $390
Duo-Tone model . . . . NiB $655 Ex $545 Gd $435
Stainless steel model . . . . NiB $660 Ex $550 Gd $440
Steel model . . . . NiB $620 Ex $510 Gd $400
Limited model (tuned & accessorized), add $125

P-12 COMPACT AUTO PISTOL
Calibers: .45 ACP. 11-round magazine, 3.5-inch bbl., 7-inches overall. Weight: 24 oz. (alloy frame). Blade front sight, adj. rear w/3-dot system. Textured composition grips. Matte black alloy or steel finish. Made from 1990 to 2003.

Model P1245 (alloy) .... NiB $750 Ex $585 Gd $430
Model P1245C (steel) .... NiB $825 Ex $645 Gd $491
Limited model (tuned & accessorized), add $125

P-13 AUTO PISTOL
Same general specifications as Model P-12 except w/12-round magazine, 4.5-inch bbl., 8-inches overall. Weight: 25 oz. (alloy frame). Blade front sight, adj. rear w/3-dot system. Textured composition grips. Matte black alloy or steel finish. Made from 1993 to 2003.
Model P1345 (alloy) .... NiB $750 Ex $585 Gd $430
Model P1345C (steel) .... NiB $675 Ex $510 Gd $375
**Limited model
(tuned & accessorized), add** $125

P-14 AUTO PISTOL
Caliber: .45 ACP. 13-round magazine, 5-inch bbl., 8.5 inches overall. Weight: 28 oz. Alloy frame. Blade front sight, adj. rear w/3-dot system. Textured composition grips. Matte black alloy or steel finish. Made from 1990 to 2003.
Model P1445 (alloy) .... NiB $685 Ex $465 Gd $325
Model P1445C (stainless) .... NiB $755 Ex $535 Gd $395
**Limited model (tuned
& accessorized), add.** $125

MODEL P-15 AUTO PISTOL
Caliber: .40 S&W. 10-round magazine, 4.25-inch bbl., 7.75 inches overall. Weight: 28 to 36 oz. Steel, alloy or stainless receiver. Matte black, Duotone or stainless finish. Made 1996 to 1999.
Model P1540 (alloy) .... NiB $625 Ex $505 Gd $435
Model P1540C (steel) .... NiB $635 Ex $515 Gd $445
Duotone stainless model .... NiB $670 Ex $540 Gd $475
Stainless model .... NiB $685 Ex $565 Gd $495

MODEL P-16 SA AUTO PISTOL
Caliber: .40 S&W. 10- or 16-round magazine, 5-inch bbl., 8.5 inches overall. Weight: 40 oz. Ramp front sight and drift adjustable rear w/3-dot system. Carbon steel or stainless frame. Matte black, Duotone or stainless finish. Made from 1995 to 2002.
Blue steel model .... NiB $640 Ex $500 Gd $400
Duotone model .... NiB $675 Ex $535 Gd $435
Stainless model .... NiB $690 Ex $560 Gd $460
**Limited model (tuned
& accessorized), add.** $150

MODEL P-18 SA AUTO PISTOL
Caliber: 9mm Parabellum. 10- or 18-round magazine, 5-inch bbl., 8.5 inches overall. Weight: 40 oz. Dovetailed front sight and fully adjustable rear. Bright stainless finish. Made from 1998 to 2003.
Stainless model .... NiB $800 Ex $652 Gd $523
**Limited model (tuned
& accessorized), add.** $150

PHOENIX ARMS — Ontario, California

MODEL HP22/HP25
SA AUTO PISTOLS. .... NiB $150 Ex $87 Gd $59
Caliber: .22 LR, .25 ACP. 10-round magazine, 3-inch bbl., 5.5 inches overall. Weight: 20 oz. Checkered synthetic grips. Blade front sight, adjustable rear. Blue, chrome or nickel finish. Made from 1994 to date.

**Para-Ordnance
P-12 Compact**

**Para-Ordnance
P-14 Auto Pistol**

MODEL HP
RANGE-MASTER TARGET SA
AUTO PISTOL .... NiB $150 Ex $120 Gd $90
Similar to Model HP .22 except w/5.5-inch target bbl. and extended magazine, Ramp front sight, adjustable notch rear on vent rib. Checkered synthetic grips. Blue or satin nickel finish. Made from 1998 to date.

MODEL HP
RANGE-MASTER DELUXE TARGET
SA AUTO PISTOL .... NiB $185 Ex $150 Gd $100
Similar to Model HP Rangemaster Target model except w/dual-2000 laser sight and custom wood grips. Made from 1998 to date.

RAVEN SA
AUTO PISTOL .... NiB $70 Ex $50 Gd $40
Caliber: .25 ACP. Six-round magazine, 2.5 inch bbl., 4.75 inches overall. Weight: 15 oz. Ivory, pink pearl, or black slotted stocks. Fixed sights. Blue, chrome or nickel finish. Made from 1993 to 1998.

Plainfield Model 71

Plainfield Model 72

Radom P-35

PLAINFIELD MACHINE COMPANY — Dunellen, New Jersey
This firm disc. operation about 1982.

MODEL 71 AUTOMATIC PISTOL
Calibers: .22 LR, .25 Automatic w/conversion kit available. 10-round magazine (.22 LR) or 8-round (.25 Auto), 2.5-inch bbl., 5.13 inches overall. Weight: 25 oz. Fixed sights. Stainless steel frame/slide. Checkered walnut grips. Made from 1970-82.

.22 LR or .25 Auto only . . . . NiB $189 Ex $158 Gd $113
W/conversion kit . . . . NiB $210 Ex $179 Gd $118

MODEL 72 AUTOMATIC PISTOL
Same as Model 71 except has aluminum slide, 3.5-inch bbl., 6 inches overall. Made from 1970 to 1982
.22 LR or .25 Auto only . . . . NiB $199 Ex $164 Gd $960
W/conversion kit . . . . NiB $224 Ex $159 Gd $123

PROFESSIONAL ORDNANCE, INC. — Lake Havasu City, Arizona

MODEL CARBON-15 TYPE 20
SEMIAUTOMATIC PISTOL . . . . NiB $920 Ex $803 Gd $545
Similar to Carbon-15 Type 97 except w/unfluted barrel. Weight: 40 oz. Matte black finish. Made from 1999 to 2000.

MODEL CARBON-15 TYPE 97
SEMIAUTOMATIC PISTOL . . . . NiB $975 Ex $906 Gd $571
AR-15 operating system w/recoil reduction system. Caliber: .223 Rem. 10-round magazine, 7.25-inch fluted bbl., 20 inches overall. Weight: 46 oz. Ghost ring sights. Carbon-fiber upper and lower receivers w/Chromoly bolt carrier. Matte black finish. Checkered composition grip. Made from 1996 to 2003.

RADOM PISTOL — Radom, Poland
Manufactured by the Polish Arsenal

P-35 AUTOMATIC PISTOL
Variation of the Colt Government Model .45 Auto. Caliber: 9mm Para. Eight-round magazine, 4.75-inch bbl., 7.75 inches overall. Weight: 29 oz. Fixed sights. Blued finish. Plastic grips. Made from 1935 thru WWII.
Commercial model
(Polish Eagle) . . . . NiB $3500 Ex $2682 Gd $2345
Nazi military model
(W/slotted backstrap) . . . . NiB $1375 Ex $1046 Gd $842
Nazi military model
(W/takedown lever) . . . . NiB $750 Ex $506 Gd $395
Nazi military model
(No takedown lever or slot) . . . . NiB $436 Ex $334 Gd $213
Nazi military model (Parkerized) . . . . Add $300

RANDALL FIREARMS COMPANY — Sun Valley, California
The short-lived Randall firearms Company (1982 to 1984) was a leader in the production of stainless steel semi-autimatic handguns, particularly in left-handed configurations. Prices shown are for production models. Add 50% for prototype models (t-prefix on serial numbers) and $125 for guns with serial numbers below 2000. Scare models (C311, C332, etc., made in lots of four pieces or less) valued substantially higher to avid collectors.
MODEL A111 . . . . NiB $750 Ex $469 Gd $294
Caliber: .45 Auto. Barrel: 5 inches. Round-slide top; right-hand model. Sights: Fixed. Total production: 3,431 pieces.

MODEL A112 . . . . NiB $895 Ex $619 Gd $519
Calibers: 9mm. Barrel: 5 inches. Round-slide top; right-hand model. Sights: Fixed.

MODEL A121 . . . . NiB $700 Ex $654 Gd $365
Caliber: .45 Auto. Barrel: 5 inches. Flat-slide top; right-hand model. Sights: Fixed.

MODEL A211 . . . . **NiB $750 Ex $543 Gd $468**
Caliber: .45 Auto. Barrel: 4.25 inches. Round-slide top; right-hand model. Sights: Fixed.

MODEL A232 . . . . **NiB $1500 Ex $1338 Gd $1063**
Caliber: 9mm. Barrel: 4.25 inches. Flat-slide top; right-hand model. Sights: Fixed.

MODEL A331 . . . . **NiB $1775 Ex $1526 Gd $1201**
Caliber: .45 Auto. Barrel: 4.25 inches. Flat-slide top; right-hand model. Sights: Fixed.

MODEL B111 . . . . **NiB $1250 Ex $1101 Gd $876**
Caliber: .45 Auto. Barrel: 5 inches. Round-slide top; left-hand model. Sights: Fixed. Toatal production: 297 pieces

MODEL B131 . . . . **NiB $1450 Ex $1280 Gd $1105**
Caliber: .45 Auto. Barrel: 5 inches. Flat-slide top; left-hand model. Sights: Millet. Total production: 225 pieces.

MODEL B311 . . . . **NiB $1575 Ex $1355 Gd $1180**
Caliber: .45 Auto. Barrel: 4.25 inches. Round-slide top; left-hand model. Sights: Fixed. Total production: 52 pieces.

MODEL B312 LEMAY . . . . **NiB $5000 Ex $3500 Gd $2900**
Caliber: 9mm. Barrel: 4.25 inches. Round-slide top; left-hand model. Sights: Fixed. Total production: 9 pieces.

MODEL B331 . . . . **NiB $1775 Ex $1519 Gd $1317**
Caliber: .45 Auto. Barrel: 4.25 inches. Flat-slide top; left-hand model. Sights: Millet. Total production: 45 pieces.

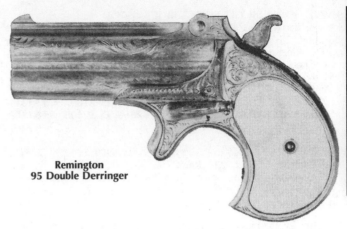

**Remington
95 Double Derringer**

RECORD-MATCH PISTOLS — Zella-Mehlis, Germany, Manufactured by Udo Anschütz

MODEL 200 FREE PISTOL . . . . **NiB $990 Ex $735 Gd $593**
Basically the same as Model 210 except w/different stock design and conventional set trigger, spur trigger guard. Made prior to WW II.

MODEL 210 FREE PISTOL . . . . . . **NiB $1327 Ex $1175 Gd $899**
System Martini action, set trigger w/button release. Caliber: .22 LR. Single-shot, 11-inch bbl., weight: 46 oz. Target sights micrometer rear. Blued finish. Carved and checkered walnut forearm and stock w/adj. hand base. Also made w/dual action (Model 210A); weight 35 oz. Made prior to WWII.

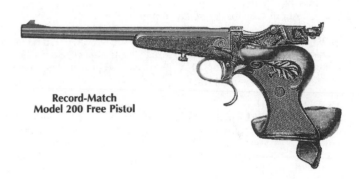

**Record-Match
Model 200 Free Pistol**

REISING ARMS CO. — Hartford, Connecticut

TARGET AUTOMATIC PISTOL. . . . **NiB $1000 Ex $775 Gd $550**
Hinged frame. Outside hammer. Caliber: .22 LR. 12-round magazine, 6.5-inch bbl., fixed sights. Blued finish. Hard rubber grips. Made 1921 to 1924.

REMINGTON ARMS COMPANY — Ilion, New York

MODEL 51 AUTOMATIC PISTOL
Calibers: .32 Auto, .380 Auto. Seven-round magazine, 3.5-inch bbl., 6.63 inches overall. Weight: 21 oz. Fixed sights. Blued finish. Hard rubber grips. Made from 1918 to 1934.
.32 ACP . . . . **NiB $856 Ex $718 Gd $419**
.380 ACP . . . . **NiB $753 Ex $615 Gd $357**

MODEL 95 DOUBLE DERRINGER
SA. Caliber: 41 Short Rimfire. Three-inch double bbls. (superposed), 4.88 inches overall. Early models have long hammer spur and two-armed extractor, but later guns have short hammer spur and sliding extractor (a few have no extractor). Fixed blade front sight and grooved rear. finish: Blued, blued w/nickel-plated frame or fully nickel-plated; also w/factory engraving. Grips: Walnut, checkered hard rubber, pearl, ivory. Weight: 11 oz. Made 1866-1935. Approximately 150,000 were manufactured. Note: During the 70 years of its production, serial numbering of this model was repeated two or three times. Therefore, aside from hammer and extractor differences between the earlier and later models, the best clue to the age of a Double Derringer is the stamping of the company's name on the top of the bbl., or side rib. Prior to 1888, derringers were stamped "E. Remington & Sons, Ilion, N.Y." on one side rib and "Elliot's Patent Dec. 12, 1865" on the other (Type I-early & mid-production) and on the top rib (Type I-late production). In 1888-1911, "Remington Arms Co., Ilion, N.Y." and patent date were stamped on the top rib (Type II) and from 1912-35 "Remington Arms - U.M.C. Co., Ilion, N.Y." and patent date were stamped on the top rib.

**Model 95 (Early Type I,
w/o extractor)** . . . . **NiB $2145 Ex $2083 Gd $796**
**Model 95 (Mid Type I,
w/extractor)** . . . . **NiB $2289 Ex $2135 Gd $894**
**Model 95 (Late Type I,
w/extractor)** . . . . **NiB $2351 Ex $2135 Gd $899**
**Model 95 (Type II
produced 1988-11)** . . . . **NiB $1934 Ex $1512 Gd $688**
**Model 95 (Type III,
produced 1912-35)** . . . . **NiB $968 Ex $789 Gd $560**
**Factory-engraved model w/ivory
or pearl grips, add** **35%**

NEW MODEL SINGLE-SHOT TARGET PISTOL

Also called Model 1901 Target. Rolling-block action. Calibers: .22 Short & Long, .25 Stevens, .32 S&W, .44 S&W Russian. 10-inch half-octagon bbl., 14 inches overall. Weight: 45 oz. (.22 cal.). Target sights. Blued finish. Checkered walnut grips and forearm. Made from 1901 to 1909.

Model 1901 (.22 caliber) . . . . . NiB $2660 Ex $2365 Gd $1065

Model 1901
(.25 Stevens, .32 S&W) . . . . NiB $2339 Ex $1897 Gd $1311

Model 1901 (.44 Russian) . . . . . NiB $2866 Ex $2608 Gd $1166

MODEL XP-100

SINGLE-SHOT PISTOL. . . . . .NiB $900 Ex $387 Gd $279

Bolt action. Caliber: 221 Rem. Fireball. 10.5-inch vent rib bbl., 16.75 inches overall. Weight: 3.75 lbs. Adj. rear sight, blade front, receiver drilled and tapped for scope mounts. Blued finish. One-piece brown nylon stock. Made from 1963 to 1988.

MODEL XP-100 CUSTOM PISTOL . . . . . .NiB $1000 Ex $737 Gd $550

Bolt-action, single-shot, long-range pistol. Calibers: .223 Rem., 7mm-08 or .35 Rem. 14.5-inch bbl., standard contour or heavy. Weight: About 4.25 lbs. Currently in production.

MODEL XP-100 SILHOUETTE . . . . . NiB $900 Ex $578 Gd $335

Same general specifications as Model XP-100 except chambered for 7mm BR Rem. and 35 Rem. 14.75-inch bbl., weight: 4.13 lbs. Made from 1987 to 1992.

MODEL XP-100

VARMINT SPECIAL . . . . NiB $900 Ex $450 Gd $260

Bolt-action, single-shot, long-range pistol. Calibers: .223 Rem., 7mm BR. 14.5-inch bbl., 21.25 inches overall. Weight: About 4.25 lbs. One-piece Du Pont nylon stock w/universal grips. Made from 1986 to 1992.

MODEL XP-100R

CUSTOM REPEATER

Same general specifications as Model XP-100 Custom except 4- or 5- round repeater chambered for .22-250, .223 Rem., .250 Savage, 7mm-08 Rem., .308 Win., .35 Rem. and .350 Rem. Mag. Kevlar-reinforced synthetic or fiberglass stock w/blind magazine and sling swivel studs. Made from 1992-94 and from 1998 to 1999.

Model XP-100R (fiberglass stock) . . . . NiB $900 Ex $599 Gd $425

Model XP-100R KS (kevlar stock) . . . . NiB $900 Ex $599 Gd $425

NOTE: *The following Remington derringers were produced from the mid-1860s through the mid-1930s. The Zig-Zag model is reputed to be the first cartridge handgun ever produced at the Remington plant. Few if any Remington derringers exiswt in "new" or "in box" condition, therefore, guns in 90-percent condition command top price.*

ZIG-ZAG DERRINGER. . . . . NiB $6000 Ex $5828 Gd $4028

Caliber: .22S, L, LR. Six shot, six-barrel (rotating) cluster. 3-inch bbl., blued, ring trigger. Two-piece rubber grips. Fewer than 1,000 pieces produced from 1861 to 1863.

ELIOT'S FIVE-SHOT

DERRINGER .NiB $1812 Ex $916 $741

Caliber: .22S, L, LR. Five shot, five-barrel fixed cluster. 3-inch bbl., ring trigger, blue and/or nickel finish. Two-piece rubber, walnut, ivory or pearl grips.

ELIOT'S FOUR-SHOT

DERRINGER . . . . .NiB $5000 Ex $4275 $3795

Caliber: .32. Four shot, four-barrel fixed cluster. 3-3/8 inch bbl., ring trigger, blue and/or nickel finish. Two-piece rubber, walnut, ivory or pearl grips. Approx. 25,000 pieces (.22 and .32) produced.

VEST POCKET DERRINGER . . . . . . .NiB $3200 Ex $2887 $2512

Caliber: .22, .30, .32, .41 rimfire . Two shot, various bbl. lengths, blue or nickel finish. Two-piece walnut grips. Spur trigger. Made from 1865 to 1888.

OVER AND UNDER DERRINGER . .NiB $6000 Ex $4596 $4321

Caliber: .41 rimfire. Two shot, 3-inch super imposed bbl., spur trigger, blue and/or nickel finish. Two-piece rubber, walnut, ivory or pearl grips. Oscillating firing pin. Produced 1866-1934. Also known as Double Derringer or Model 95. Type 1 and variatitons bear maker's name, patent data stamped between the barrels, with or without extractor. Types Two and Three marked "Remington Arms Company, Ilion, NY." Type Four marked on top of barrel, "Remington Arms-U.M.C. Co. Ilion, NY."

MODEL 1866

ROLLING BLOCK PISTOL . . . . .NiB $6098 Ex $4148 $3048

Caliber: .50 rimfire. Single-shot, 8-1/2 inch round, blue finish. Walnut grip and forearm. Spur trigger. Made from 1866-67. Mistakenly designated as Model 1865 Navy. Top values are for military-marked, pristine pieces. Very few of these guns remain in original condition.

MODEL 1870 NAVY

ROLLING BLOCK PISTOL . . . . .NiB $3145 Ex $2130 $1805

Caliber: .50 centerfire. Single shot, 7-inch round bbl. Standard trigger with trigger guard, walnut grip and forearm. Approx. 6,400 pieces made from 1870-75. Modified for the Navy from Model 1866. Higher values are for 8--inch commercial version without proof marks.

RIDER'S

MAGAZINE PISTOL . . . . .NiB $3500 Ex $2776 $2251

Caliber: .32. Five shot, 3-inch octagon bbl. blued (add 50 percent for case-hardened receiver). Walnut, rosewood, ivory or pearl grips. Spur trigger. Made from 1871 to 1888.

ELIOT'S VEST POCKET

SINGLE-SHOT DERRINGER . . . . . . .NiB $3200 Ex $1018 $833

Caliber: .41 rimfire. Single-shot, 2-1/2-inch round bbl., blue and/or nickel finish. Also known as "Mississippi Derringer." Two-piece walnut grips. Spur trigger. Approx. 10,000 made from 1867 to 1888.

MODEL 1890

SINGLE-ACTION REVOLVER . . . . NiB $11,075 Ex $9325 $6975

Caliber: .41 centerfire . Six shot, 5-3/4 or 7-1/2-inch round bbl., blue or nickel finish. Standard trigger with trigger guard. Two-piece ivory or pearl grips with Remington monogram. nickel finish valued about 15 percent less.

MODEL 51

SEMI-AUTO PISTOL . . . . NiB $800 Ex $583 $358

Caliber: .32 or .380 ACP. Eight shot, (7 in magazine).Two-piece hard rubber grips with company name, flat black finish. Approx. 65,000 pieces made from 1918-26, with another 11 pieces made from spare parts from 1927 to 1934.

MODEL 1911

REMINGTON UMC . . . . .NiB $4790 Ex $2540 $1415

Caliber: .45 ACP. WWII military contract production. Blued finish. Made from 1918 to 1919, with serial numbers 1 to 21,676.

MODEL 1911A1

REMINGTON RAND . . . . .NiB $5950 Ex $3265 $2555

Caliber: .45 ACP. Parkerized finish. Two-piece walnut grips. Made from 1943-45 by Remington Rand Co., not Remington Arms Co.

RG REVOLVERS — Mfg. By Rohm Gmbh, Germany (Imported by R.G. Industries, Miami, Florida)

MODEL 23. . . . . **NiB $95 Ex $75 Gd $60**
SA/DA. 6-round magazine, swing-out cylinder. Caliber: .22 LR. 1.75- or 3.38-inch bbl., Overall length: 5.13 and 7.5 inches. Weight: 16-17 oz. Fixed sights. Blued or nickel finish. Disc. 1986.

MODEL 38S
SA/DA. Caliber: .38 Special. Six-round magazine, swing-out cylinder. Three- or 4-inch bbl., overall length: 8.25 and 9.25 inches. Weight: 32-34 oz. Windage-adj. rear sight. Blued finish. Disc. 1986.
W/plastic grips . . . . **NiB $164 Ex $128 Gd $94**
W/wood grips . . . . **NiB $183 Ex $143 Gd $105**

ROSSI REVOLVERS — São Leopoldo, Brazil Manufactured by Amadeo Rossi S.A. (Imported by Interarms, Alexandria, Virginia)

MODEL 31 DA REVOLVER . . . . **NiB $123 Ex $78 Gd $53**
Caliber: .38 Special. Five-round cylinder, 4-inch bbl., weight: 20 oz. Blued or nickel finish. Disc. 1985.

MODEL 51 DA REVOLVER . . . . **NiB $125 Ex $80 Gd $55**
Caliber: .22 LR. Six-round cylinder, 6-inch bbl., weight: 28 oz. Blued finish. Disc. 1985.

MODEL 68 . . . . **NiB $165 Ex $130 Gd $95**
Caliber: .38 Special. Five-round magazine, 2- or 3 inch bbl., overall length: 6.5 and 7.5 inches. Weight: 21-23 oz. Blued finish. Nickel finish available w/3-inch bbl. Disc. 1998.

MODEL 84 DA REVOLVER . . . . **NiB $190 Ex $155 Gd $105**
Caliber: .38 Special. Six-round cylinder, 3-inch bbl., 8 inches overall. Weight: 27.5 oz. Stainless steel finish. Imported 1984 to 1986.

MODEL 85 DA REVOLVER . . . . **NiB $190 Ex $155 Gd $105**
Same as Model 84 except has vent rib. Imported from 1985 to 1986.

MODEL 88 DA REVOLVER
Caliber: .38 Special. Five-round cylinder, 2- or 3-inch bbl., weight: 21 oz. Stainless steel finish. Imported from 1988 to 1998.
Model 88 (disc.) . . . . **NiB $200 Ex $170 Gd $135**
Model 88 Lady Rossi
(round butt) . . . . **NiB $215 Ex $170 Gd $144**

MODEL 88/2 DA REVOLVER. . . . . . **NiB $200 Ex $170 Gd $124**
Caliber: .38 Special. Five-round cylinder, 2- or 3-inch bbl., 6.5 inches overall. Weight: 21 oz. Stainless steel finish. Imported 1985 to 1987.

MODEL 89 DA REVOLVER . . . . **NiB $175 Ex $100 Gd $70**
Caliber: .32 S&W. Six-round cylinder, 3-inch bbl., 7.5 inches overall. Weight: 17 oz. Stainless steel finish. Imported 1989 to 1990.

MODEL 94 DA REVOLVER . . . .**NiB $160 Ex $103 Gd $77**
Caliber: .38 Special. Six-round cylinder, 3-inch bbl., 8 inches overall. Weight: 29 oz. Imported from 1985 to 1988.

MODEL 95 (951) REVOLVER . . . . . **NiB $190 Ex $163 Gd $134**
Caliber: .38 Special. Six-round magazine, 3-inch bbl., 8 inches overall. Weight: 27.5 oz. Vent rib. Blued finish. Imported 1985 to 1990.

MODEL 351/352 REVOLVERS
Caliber: .38 Special. Five-round cylinder, 2-inch bbl., 6.87 inches overall. Weight: 22 oz. Ramp front and rear adjustable sights. Stainless or matte blued finish. Imported from 1999 to date.
Model 351 (matte blue finish) . . . . . **NiB $335 Ex $234 Gd $163**
Model 352 (stainless finish) . . . . **NiB $395 Ex $290 Gd $235**

MODEL 461/462 REVOLVERS
Caliber: .357 Magnum. Six-round cylinder, 2-inch heavy bbl., 6.87 inches overall. Weight: 26 oz. Rubber grips w/ serrated ramp front sight. Stainless or matte blued finish. Imported 1999 to date.
Model 461 (matte blue finish) . . . . . **NiB $335 Ex $234 Gd $163**
Model 462 (stainless finish) . . . . **NiB $395 Ex $267 Gd $200**

MODEL 511 DA REVOLVER . . . . **NiB $125 Ex $100 Gd $75**
Similar to the Model 51 except in stainless steel. Imported 1986 to 1990.

MODEL 515 DA REVOLVER . . . . **NiB $195 Ex $100 Gd $65**
Calibers: .22 LR, .22 Mag. Six-round cylinder, 4-inch bbl., 9 inches overall. Weight: 30 oz. Red ramp front sight, adj. square-notched rear. Stainless finish. Checkered hardwood grips. Imported from 1994 to 1998.

MODEL 518 DA REVOLVER . . . . **NiB $195 Ex $100 Gd $65**
Similar to the Model 515 except in caliber .22 LR. Imported from 1993 to 1998.

MODEL 677 DA REVOLVER . . . . . . **NiB $215 Ex $180 Gd $154**
Caliber: .357 Mag. Six-round cylinder, 2-inch bbl., 6.87 inches overall. Weight: 26 oz. Serrated front ramp sight, channel rear. Matte blue finish. Contoured rubber grips. Imported from 1997 to 1998.

MODEL 720 DA REVOLVER . . . . . . **NiB $220 Ex $165 Gd $130**
Caliber: .44 Special. Five-round cylinder, 3-inch bbl., 8 inches overall. Weight: 27.5 oz. Red ramp front sight, adj. square-notched rear. Stainless finish. Checkered Neoprene combat-style grips. Imported from 1992 to 1998.

MODEL 841 DA REVOLVER . . . . . **NiB $2940 Ex $198 Gd $144**
Same general specifications as Model 84 except has 4-inch bbl., (9 inches overall), weight: 30 oz. Imported from 1985 to 1986.

MODEL 851 DA REVOLVER . . . . . **NiB $298 Ex $198 Gd $147**
Same general specifications as Model 85 except w/3-or 4-inch bbl., 8 inches overall (with 3-inch bbl.). Weight: 27.5 oz. (with 3-inch bbl.). Red ramp front sight, adj. square-notched rear. Stainless finish. Checkered hardwood grips. Imported from 2001 to 2009 to date.

MODEL 877 DA REVOLVER . . . . . **NiB $220 Ex $155 Gd $105**
Same general specifications as Model 677 except stainless steel. Made from 1996 to date.

MODEL 941 DA REVOLVER . . . . **NiB $190 Ex $100 Gd $70**
Caliber: .38 Special. Six-round cylinder, 4-inch bbl., 9 inches overall. Weight: 30 oz. Blued finish. Imported from 1985-86.

MODEL 951 DA REVOLVER . . . . . . **NiB $190 Ex $135 Gd $100**
Previous designation M95 w/same general specifications.

MODEL 971 DA REVOLVER
Caliber: .357 Magnum. Six-round cylinder, 2.5-, 4- or 6-inch bbl., 9 inches overall (with 4-inch bbl.). Weight: 36 oz. (with 4-inch bbl.). Blade front sight, adj. square-notched rear. Blued or stainless finish. Checkered hardwood grips. Imported from 1988 to 1998.
Blued finish . . . . **NiB $200 Ex $158 Gd $117**
Stainless finish . . . . **NiB $220 Ex $198 Gd $144**
W/compensated bbl., add **$15**

Ruger Mark I Target W/5.5-inch Untapered Bull Barrel

Ruger Mark II

Ruger Mark II .22/.45

MODEL 971 VRC
DA REVOLVER.................. NiB $295 Ex $251 Gd $165
Same general specifications as Model 971 stainless except w/ventilated rib and compensated bbl. Made 1988 to 1998.

CYCLOPS DA REVOLVER .... NiB $385 Ex $343 Gd $259
Caliber: .357 Mag. Six-round cylinder, 6- or 8-inch compensated slab-sided bbl., 11.75 or 13.75 inches overall. Weight: 44 oz. or 51 oz. Undercut blade front sight, fully adjustable rear. B-Square scope mount and rings. Stainless steel finish. Checkered rubber grips. Made from 1997 to 1998.

DA REVOLVER.................. NiB $199 Ex $157 Gd $117
Calibers: .22 LR, .32 S&W Long, .38 Special. Five-round (.38) or 6-round cylinder (other calibers), bbl. lengths: 3-, 6-inches. Weight: 22 oz. (3-inch bbl.). Adj. Rear sight, ramp front. Blued or nickel finish. Wood or plastic grips. Imported from 1965-91.

SPORTSMAN'S .22 .... NiB $265 Ex $210 Gd $153
Caliber: .22 LR. Six-round magazine, 4-inch bbl., 9 inches overall. Weight: 30 oz. Stainless steel finish. Disc. 1991.

RUBY PISTOL — Manufactured by Gabilondo y Urresti, Eibar, Spain and others

7.65MM
AUTOMATIC PISTOL........... NiB $318 Ex $242 Gd $109
Secondary standard service pistol of the French Army in world wars I and II. Essentially the same as the Alkartasuna (see separate listing). Other manufacturers: Armenia Elgoibarresa y Cia., Eceolaza y Vicinai y Cia., Hijos de Angel Echeverria y Cia., Bruno Salaverria y Cia., Zulaika y Cia., all of Eibar, Spain-Gabilondo y Cia., Elgoibar Spain; Ruby Arms Company, Guernica, Spain. Made from 1914 to 1922.

RUGER — Southport, Connecticut Manufactured by Sturm, Ruger & Co.

Rugers made in 1976 are designated "Liberty" in honor of the U.S. Bicentennial and bring a premium of approximately 25 percent in value over regular models.
NOTE: *For ease in finding a particular Ruger handgun, the listings are divided into two groups: Automatic/Single-Shot Pistols (below) and Revolvers, which follow. For a complete listing, please refer to the index.*

AUTOMATIC/SINGLE-SHOT PISTOLS

HAWKEYE SINGLE-SHOT PISTOL ..... NiB $1420 Ex $1204 Gd $689
Built on a SA revolver frame w/cylinder replaced by a swing-out breechblock and fitted w/a bbl., w/integral chamber. Caliber: .256 Magnum. 8.5-inch bbl., 14.5 inches overall. Weight: 45 oz. Blued finish. Ramp front sight, click adj. rear. Smooth walnut grips. Made from 1963 to 1965 (3,300 produced).

MARK I TARGET MODEL AUTOMATIC PISTOL
Caliber: .22 LR. 10-round magazine, 5.25- and 6.88-inch heavy tapered or 5.5-inch untapered bull bbl., 10.88 inches overall (with 6.88-inch bbl.). Weight: 42 oz. (in 5.5- or 6.88-inch bbl.). Undercut target front sight, adj. rear. Blued finish. Hard rubber grips or checkered walnut thumbrest grips. Made from 1952 to 1982.
Standard .... NiB $850 Ex $743 Gd $572
W/red medallion .... NiB $950 Ex $843 Gd $672
Walnut grips, add $15

MARK II AUTOMATIC PISTOL
Caliber: .22 LR, standard or high velocity 10-round magazine, 4.75- or 6-inch tapered bbl., 8.31 inches overall (with 4.75-inch bbl.). Weight: 36 oz. Fixed front sight, square notch rear. Blued or stainless finish. Made from 1982 to 2004.
Blued............................ NiB $225 Ex $185 Gd $132
Stainless .... NiB $295 Ex $235 Gd $200
Bright stainless (ltd. prod. 5,000 in 1982).................. NiB $557 Ex $445 Gd $315

MARK II .22/.45 AUTOMATIC PISTOL

Same general specifications as Ruger Mark II .22 LR except w/blued or stainless receiver and bbl., in four lengths: 4-inch tapered w/adj. sights (P4), 4.75-inch tapered w/fixed sights (KP4), 5.25-inch tapered w/adj. sights (KP 514) and 5.5-inch bull (KP 512). Fitted w/Zytel grip frame of the same design as the Model 1911 45 ACP. Made from 1993 to 2004.

Model KP4 (4.75-inch bbl.) . . . . NiB $225 Ex $162 Gd $124
Model KP512, KP514
(w/5.5- or 5.25-inch bbl.) . . . . NiB $320 Ex $279 Gd $221
Model P4, P512
(Blued w/4- or 5.5-inch bbl.) . . . . NiB $258 Ex $206 Gd $151

MARK II BULL BARREL MODEL

Same as standard Mark II except for bull bbl. (5.5- or 10-inch). Weight: About 2.75 lbs.

Blued finish . . . . NiB $284 Ex $227 Gd $166
Stainless finish (intro. 1985) . . . . . . NiB $250 Ex $165 Gd $113

MARK II GOVERNMENT MODEL AUTO PISTOL

Civilian version of the Mark II used by U.S. Armed Forces. Caliber: .22LR. 10-round magazine, 6.88-inch bull bbl., 11.13 inches overall. Weight: 44 oz. Blued or stainless finish. Made from 1986 to 1999.

Blued model (MK687G commercial) . . . . . NiB $350 Ex $255 Gd $185
Stainless steel model
(KMK678G commercial) . . . . NiB $386 Ex $309 Gd $223
W/U.S. markings (military model) . . . . . . NiB $1000 Ex $856 Gd $5 81

MARK II TARGET MODEL

Caliber: .22 LR. 10-round magazine, 4-, 5.5- and 10-inch bull bbl. or 5.25- and 6.88-inch heavy tappered bbl., weight: 38 oz. to 52 oz. 11.13 inches overall (with 6.88-inch bbl.). Made 1982 to 2004.

Blued . . . . NiB $295 Ex $185 Gd $100
Stainless steel . . . . NiB $355 Ex $290 Gd $180

MODEL P-85 AUTOMATIC PISTOL

Caliber: 9mm. DA, recoil-operated. 15-round capacity, 4.5 inch bbl., 7.84 inches overall. Weight: 32 oz. Fixed rear sight, square-post front. Available w/decocking levers, ambidextrous safety or in DA only. Blued or stainless finish. Made from 1987 to 1992.

Blued finish . . . . NiB $355 Ex $301 Gd $246
Stainless steel finish . . . . NiB $410 Ex $354 Gd $328

MODEL P-89 AUTOMATIC PISTOL

Caliber: 9mm. DA w/slide-mounted safety levers. 15-round magazine, 4.5-inch bbl., 7.84 inches overall. Weight: 32 oz. Square-post front sight, adj. rear w/3-dot system. Blued or stainless steel finish. Grooved black Xenoy grips. Made from 1992 to 2007.

P-89 blued . . . . NiB $380 Ex $290 Gd $200
P-89 stainless . . . . NiB $495 Ex $413 Gd $351

MODEL P-89 DAC/DAO AUTO PISTOLS

Similar to the standard Model P-89 except the P-89 DAC has ambidextrous decocking levers. The P-89 DAO operates in double-action-only mode. Made from 1991 to 2009.

P-89 DAC blued . . . . NiB $380 Ex $285 Gd $200
P-89 DAC/DAO stainless . . . . NiB $490 Ex $399 Gd $299

MODEL P-90, KP90 DA AUTOMATIC PISTOL

Caliber: .45 ACP. Seven-round magazine, 4.5-inch bbl., 7.88 inches overall. Weight: 33.5 oz. Square-post front sight adj. square-notched rear w/3-dot system. Grooved black Xenoy composition grips. Blued or stainless finish. DAC model has ambidextrous decocking levers. Made from 1991 to date.

Model P-90 blued . . . . NiB $475 Ex $320 Gd $225
Model P-90 DAC (decockers) . . . . . NiB $475 Ex $320 Gd $225
Model KP-90 DAC stainless . . . . . . NiB $495 Ex $340 Gd $245
Model KP-90 DAC (decockers) . . . . NiB $495 Ex $340 Gd $245

Ruger P-89
DAC/DAO

Ruger P-90

Ruger P-93
Compact

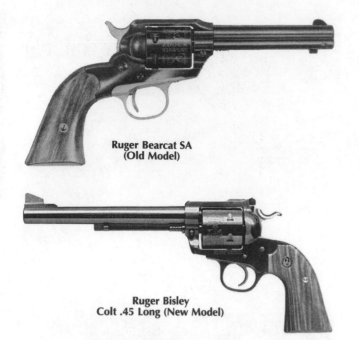

Ruger Bearcat SA
(Old Model)

Ruger Bisley
Colt .45 Long (New Model)

Ruger Bisley
Single-Six Small Frame

Ruger Blackhawk

Ruger Blackhawk
SA .44

Ruger P-97

MODEL KP-91 DA AUTOMATIC PISTOL
Same general specifications as the Model P-90 except chambered for .40 S&W w/12-round double-column magazine, Made 1992 to 1994.

Model P-91 DAC (decockers) . . . . . NiB $395 Ex $272 Gd $207
Model P-91 DAO (DA only) . . . . . . NiB $395 Ex $272 Gd $207

MODEL P-93D AUTO PISTOL
Similar to the standard Model P-89 except w/3.9-inch bbl., (7.3 inches overall) and weight: 31 oz. Stainless steel finish. Made from 1993 to 2004.

Model P-93 DAC (decocker) (disc. 1994) . . . . . . NiB $395 Ex $278 Gd $199
Model P-93 Stainless . . . . NiB $450 Ex $325 Gd $270

MODEL P-94 AUTOMATIC PISTOL
Similar to the Model P-91 except w/4.25-inch bbl., Calibers: 9mm or .40 S&W. Blued or stainless steel finish. Made 1994 to 2004.

Model KP-94 DAC (S/S decocker) . . . . NiB $395 Ex $290 Gd $195
Model KP-94 DAO (S/S dble. action only) . . . . NiB $395 Ex $290 Gd $195
Model P-94 DAC (Blued decocker) . . . . NiB $395 Ex $290 Gd $195
Model P-94 DAO (blued dble. action only) . . . . NiB $395 Ex $290 Gd $195

MODEL P-95PR AUTO PISTOL
Caliber: 9mm Parabellum. 10-round magazine, 3.9-inch bbl., 7.3 inches overall. Weight: 27 oz. Square-post front sight, drift adjustable rear w/3-dot system. Molded polymer grip-frame fitted w/stainless or chrome-moly slide. Ambidextrous decocking levers (P-95D) or double action only (DAO). Matte black or stainless finish. Made from 1997 to date.

P-95 blued . . . . NiB $395 Ex $290 Gd $195
KP-95PR stainless . . . . NiB $345 Ex $265 Gd $175

MODEL P-97D AUTOMATIC PISTOL
Caliber: .45 ACP. Eight-round magazine, 4.5- inch bbl., 7.25 inches overall. Weight: 30.5 oz. Square-post front sight adj. square-notched rear w/3-dot system. Grooved black Xenoy composition grips. Blued or stainless finish. DAC model has ambidextrous decocking levers. Made from 2002 to 2004.

Model KP-97
DAO stainless . . . . NiB $395 Ex $290 Gd $195
Model P-97D
DAC (decockers) . . . . NiB $370 Ex $300 Gd $215

STANDARD MODEL AUTOMATIC PISTOL
Caliber: .22 LR. Nine-round magazine, 4.75- or 6-inch bbl., 8.75 inches overall (with 4.75-inch bbl.). Weight: 36 oz. (with 4.75 inch bbl.). Fixed sights. Blued finish. Hard rubber or checkered walnut grips.

Made from 1949 to date. Note: After the death of Alexander Sturm in 1951, the color of the eagle on the grip medallion was changed from red to black as a memorial. Known as the "Red Eagle Automatic," this early type is now a collector's item. Made from 1951 to 1981.

W/red eagle medallion	NiB $650	Ex $495	Gd $375
W/black eagle medallion	NiB $225	Ex $165	Gd $105
Walnut grips, add			$20

NOTE: *This section contains only Ruger revolvers. Automatic and single-shot pistols may be found on the preceding pages. For a complete listing of Ruger handguns, please refer to the index.*

REVOLVERS

BEARCAT, SUPER (OLD MODEL) .... NiB $550 Ex $340 Gd $237
Same general specifications as Bearcat except has steel frame. Weight: 25 oz. Made from 1971 to 1974.

NEW MODEL BEARCAT REVOLVER
Same general specifications as Super Bearcat except all steel frame and trigger guard. Interlocked mechanism and transfer bar. Calibers: .22 LR and .22WMR. Interchangeable 6-round cylinders (disc. 1996). Smooth walnut stocks w/Ruger medallion. Made from 1994 to date.

Convertible model (disc.
1996 after factory recall)	NiB $425	Ex $342	Gd $247
Standard model (.22 LR only)	NiB $450	Ex $295	Gd $195

BISLEY SA REVOLVER, LARGE FRAME
Calibers: .357 Mag., .41 Mag. .44 Mag., .45 Long Colt. 7.5-inch bbl., 13 inches overall. Weight: 48 oz. Non-fluted or fluted cylinder, no engraving. Ramp front sight, adj. rear. Satin blued or stainless. Made from 1986 to date.

Blued finish	NiB $450	Ex $355	Gd $240
Vaquero/Bisley (blued w/case colored fr.)	NiB $575	Ex $425	Gd $350
Vaquero/Bisley (stainless steel)	NiB $575	Ex $425	Gd $350
W/ivory grips, add			$40

BISLEY SINGLE-SIX REVOLVER, SMALL FRAME
Calibers: .22 LR and .32 Mag. Six-round cylinder, 6.5-inch bbl., 11.5 inches overall. Weight: 41 oz. Fixed rear sight, blade front. Blue finish. Goncalo Alves grips. Made from 1986 to date.

.22 caliber	NiB $450	Ex $355	Gd $240
.32 H&R Mag.	NiB $655	Ex $555	Gd $440

BLACKHAWK SA CONVERTIBLE (OLD MODEL)
Same as Blackhawk except has extra cylinder. Caliber combinations: .357 Magnum and 9mm Para., .45 Colt and .45 Automatic. Made 1967 to 1972.

.357/9mm combo (early w/o prefix SN)	NiB $495	Ex $390	Gd $255
.357/9mm combo (late w/prefix SN)	NiB $495	Ex $390	Gd $255
.45 LC/.45 ACP combo			
(1967-85 & 1999 to date)	NiB $495	Ex $390	Gd $255

BLACKHAWK SA REVOLVER (OLD MODEL)
Calibers: .30 Carbine, .357 Magnum, .41 Magnum, .45 Colt. Six-round cylinder, bbl. lengths: 4.63-inch (.357, .41, .45 caliber), 6.5-inch (.357, .41 caliber), 7.5-inch (.30, .45 caliber). 10.13 inches overall (.357 Mag. w/4.63-inch bbl.). Weight: 38 oz. (.357 w/4.63-inch bbl.). Ramp front sight, adj. rear. Blued finish. Checkered hard rubber or smooth walnut grips. Made from 1955 to 1962.

.30 Carbine, .357 Mag.	NiB $425	Ex $300	Gd $215
.41 Mag.	NiB $425	Ex $300	Gd $215
.45 Colt	NiB $425	Ex $300	Gd $215

BLACKHAWK SA "FLAT-TOP" REVOLVER (OLD MODEL)
Similar to standard Blackhawk except w/"Flat Top" cylinder strap. Calibers: .357 or .44 Magnum. Six-round fluted cylinder, 4.625-, 6.5-, 7.5- or 10-inch bbl., adj. rear sight, ramp front. Blued finish. Black rubber or smooth walnut grips. Made from 1955 to 1962.

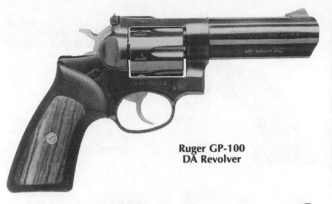

**Ruger GP-100
DA Revolver**

Ruger New Model Blackhawk Convertible

**Ruger Blackhawk High-Gloss Stainless
(New Model) .357 Magnum**

.357 Mag. (w/4.625-inch bbl.)	NiB $1200	Ex $1005	Gd $942
.357 Mag. (w/6.5-inch bbl.)	NiB $450	Ex $295	Gd $165
.357 Mag. (w/10-inch bbl.)	NiB $2000	Ex $1838	Gd $1675
.44 Mag. (w/fluted cylinder/ 4.625-inch bbl.)	NiB $1200	Ex $1005	Gd $942
.44 Mag. (w/fluted cylinder/ 6.5-inch bbl.)	NiB $1000	Ex $666	Gd $408
.44 Mag. (w/fluted cylinder/ 10-inch bbl.)	NiB $2000	Ex $1838	Gd $1674

GP-100 DA REVOLVER
Caliber: .357 Magnum. Three- to 4-inch heavy bbl., or 6-inch standard or heavy bbl., Overall length: 9.38 or 11.38 inches. Cushioned grip panels. Made from 1986 to date.

Blued finish	NiB $515	Ex $375	Gd $245
Stainless steel finish	NiB $540	Ex $375	Gd $245

NEW MODEL BLACKHAWK CONVERTIBLE
Same as New Model Blackhawk except has extra cylinder. Blued finish only. Caliber combinations: .357 Magnum/9mm Para., .44 Magnum/.44-40, .45 Colt/.45 ACP. (Limited Edition Buckeye Special .32-20/.32 H&R Mag. or .38-40/10mm). Made from 1973 to 1985. Reintro. 1999.

**Ruger Single-Six SSM
(New Model)**

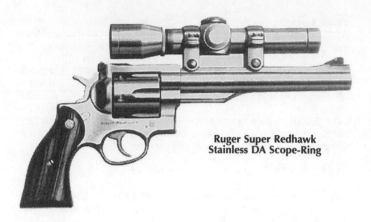

**Ruger Super Redhawk
Stainless DA Scope-Ring**

**Ruger Super Blackhawk
(New Model)**

**Ruger Super Single-Six
Convertible (New Model)**

**Ruger Police Service-Six
Stainless Steel**

Ruger Redhawk

.32-20/.32 H&R Mag. (1989-90) . . . . NiB $495 Ex $350 Gd $225
.38-40/10mm (1990-91) . . . . NiB $495 Ex $329 Gd $225
.357/9mm combo . . . . NiB $495 Ex $350 Gd $225
.44/.44-40 combo (disc.1982) . . . . NiB $495 Ex $381 Gd $225
.45 LC/.45 ACP combo (disc. 1985) . . . . . . NiB $495 Ex $355 Gd $225

NEW MODEL BLACKHAWK SA REVOLVER
Interlocked mechanism. Calibers: .30 Carbine, .357 Magnum,
.357 Maximum, .41 Magnum, .44 Magnum, .44 Special, .45 Colt.
Six-round cylinder, bbl. lengths: 4.63-inch (.357, .41, .45 Colt);
5.5 inch (.44 Mag., .44 Spec.); 6.5-inch (.357, .41, .45 Long Colt);
7.5-inch (.30, .45, .44 Special, .44 Mag.); 10.5-inch in .44 Mag;
10.38 inches overall (.357 Mag. w/4.63-inch bbl.). Weight: 40 oz.
(.357 w/4.63-inch bbl.). Adj. rear sight, ramp front. Blued finish or
stainless steel; latter only in .357 or .45 LC. Smooth walnut grips.
Made from 1973.
Blued finish . . . . NiB $426 Ex $298 Gd $185
High-gloss stainless (.357 Mag., .45 LC) . NiB $420 Ex $329 Gd $239
Satin stainless (.357 Mag., .45 LC) . . . . . NiB $397 Ex $319 Gd $231
.357 Maximum SRM (1984-85) . . . . NiB $452 Ex $350 Gd $226

NEW MODEL SINGLE-
SIX SSM REVOLVER . . . . NiB $363 Ex $327 Gd $198
Same general specifications as standard Single-Six except chambered for .32 H&R Magnum cartridge. Bbl. lengths: 4.63, 5.5, 6.5
or 9.5 inches.

NEW MODEL SUPER BLACKHAWK SA REVOLVER
Interlocked mechanism. Caliber: .44 Magnum. Six-round cylinder, 5.5-inch, 7.5-inch and 10.5-inch bull bbl. 13.38 inches overall. Weight: 48 oz. Adj. rear sight, ramp front. Blued and stainless
steel finish. Smooth walnut grips. Made 1973 to date, 5.5-inch
bbl. made from 1973 to date.
Blued finish . . . . NiB $500 Ex $355 Gd $240
**High-gloss stainless
(1994-96)** . . . . NiB $530 Ex $365 Gd $255
Satin stainless steel . . . . NiB $500 Ex $355 Gd $250

NEW MODEL SUPER SINGLE-SIX CONVERTIBLE REVOLVER
SA w/interlocked mechanism. Calibers: .22 LR and .22 WMR.
Interchangeable 6-round cylinders. Bbl. lengths: 4.63, 5.5, 6.5, 9.5
inches. 10.81 inches overall (with 4.63 inch bbl.). Weight: 33 oz.
(with 4.63-inch bbl.). Adj. rear sight, ramp front. Blued finish or
stainless steel; latter only w/5.5- or 6.5-inch bbl., smooth walnut
grips. Made from 1994 to 2004.
Blued finish . . . . NiB $445 Ex $260 Gd $150
High-gloss stainless (1994-96) . . . NiB $475 Ex $275 Gd $185
Stainless steel . . . . NiB $475 Ex $260 Gd $150

POLICE SERVICE-SIX

Same general specifications as Speed-Six except has square butt. Stainless steel models and 9mm Para. caliber available w/only 4-inch bbl., Made from 1971 to 1988.

.38 Special, blued finish . . . . **NiB $400 Ex $265 Gd $220**
.38 Special, stainless steel . . . . **NiB $325 Ex $279 Gd $253**
.357 Magnum or 9mm Para.,
blued finish . . . . **NiB $400 Ex $265 Gd $220**
.357 Magnum, stainless steel . . . . . **NiB $400 Ex $265 Gd $220**

REDHAWK DA REVOLVER

Calibers: .357 Mag., .41 Mag., .45 LC, .44 Mag. Six-round cylinder, 5.5- and 7.5-inch bbl., 11 and 13 inches overall, respectively. Weight: About 52 oz. Adj. rear sight, interchangeable front sights. Stainless finish. Made from 1979 to date; .357 Mag. disc. 1986. Alloy steel model w/blued finish intro. in 1986 in .41 Mag. and .44 Mag. calibers.

Blued finish . . . . **NiB $560 Ex $386 Gd $241**
Stainless steel . . . . **NiB $596 Ex $473 Gd $391**

**Ruger
Super Redhawk Stainless**

SUPER REDHAWK STAINLESS DA SCOPE-RING REVOLVER

Calibers: .44 Mag., .454 Casull and .45 LC. Six-round cylinder, 7.5- to 9.5- inch bbl., 13 to 15 inches overall. Weight: 53 to 58 oz. Integral scope mounting system w/stainless rings. Adjustable rear sight. Cushioned grip panels. Made from 1987 to date.

Model .44 Mag. 7.5- inch
bbl., stainless . . . . **NiB $740 Ex $500 Gd $395**
Model .44 Mag. 9.5- inch
bbl., stainless . . . . **NiB $795 Ex $525 Gd $400**
Model .454 Casull & 45 LC
Stainless/target gray stainless . . . . . **NiB $785 Ex $555 Gd $435**

**Ruger
Single-Six**

SECURITY-SIX DA REVOLVER

Caliber: .357 Magnum, handles .38 Special. Six-round cylinder, bbl. lengths: 2.25-, 4-, 6-inch, 9.25 inches overall (with 4-inch bbl.). Weight: 33.5 oz. (with 4-inch bbl.). Adj. rear sight, ramp front. Blued finish or stainless steel. Square butt. Checkered walnut grips. Made 1971 to 1985.

Blued finish . . . . **NiB $313 Ex $252 Gd $186**
Stainless steel . . . . **NiB $359 Ex $298 Gd $231**

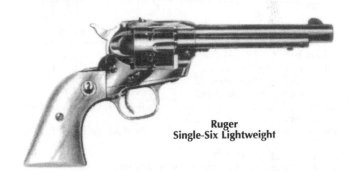

**Ruger
Single-Six Lightweight**

SINGLE-SIX SA REVOLVER (OLD MODEL)

Calibers: .22 LR, .22 WMR. Six-round cylinder. bbl., lengths: 4.63, 5.5, 6.5, 9.5 inches, 10.88 inches overall (with 5.5-inch bbl.). Weight: About 35 oz. Fixed sights. Blued finish. Checkered hard rubber or smooth walnut grips. Made 1953-73. Note: Pre-1956 model w/flat loading gate is worth about twice as much as later version.

Standard . . . . **NiB $850 Ex $575 Gd $395**
Convertible (w/two cylinders,
.22 LR/.22 WMR). . . . . **NiB $500 Ex $355 Gd $240**

SINGLE-SIX — LIGHTWEIGHT . . . **NiB $1000 Ex $755 Gd $450**

Same general specifications as Single-Six except has 4.75-inch bbl., lightweight alloy cylinder and frame, 10 inches overall length, weight: 23 oz. Made in 1956.

**Ruger
Super Single-Six Convertible**

SP101 DA REVOLVER

Calibers: .22 LR, .32 Mag., 9mm, .38 Special+P, .357 Mag. Five- or 6-round cylinder, 2.25-, 3.06- or 4-inch bbl., weight: 25-34 oz. Stainless steel finish. Cushioned grips. Made from 1989 to date.

Standard model . . . .**NiB $490 Ex $295 Gd $175**
DAO model (DA only,
spurless hammer) . . . . **NiB $490 Ex $295 Gd $175**

SPEED-SIX DA REVOLVER

Calibers: .38 Special, .357 Magnum, 9mm Para. Six-round cylinder, 2.75-, 4-inch bbl., (9mm available only w/2.75-inch bbl.). 7.75 inches overall (2.75-inch bbl.). Weight: 31 oz. (with 2.75-inch bbl.).

Ruger Single-Six Fixed Sight

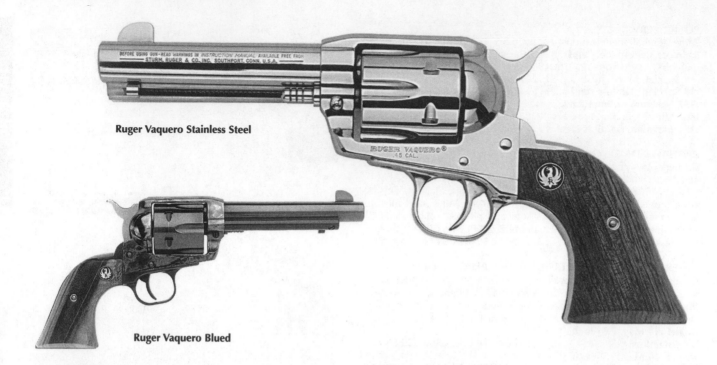

Ruger Vaquero Stainless Steel

Ruger Vaquero Blued

Fixed sights. Blued or stainless steel finish; latter available in .38 Special (with 2.75 inch bbl.), .357 Magnum and 9mm w/either bbl., Round butt. Checkered walnut grips. Made from 1973 to 1987.

.38 Special, blued finish	NiB $400	Ex $255	Gd $180
.38 Special, stainless steel	NiB $425	Ex $280	Gd $195
.357 Magnum or 9mm Para., blued finish	NiB $400	Ex $255	Gd $180
.357 Magnum or 9mm Para., stainless steel	NiB $600	Ex $435	Gd $300

SUPER BLACKHAWK
SA .44 MAGNUM REVOLVER (OLD MODEL)
SA w/heavy frame and unfluted cylinder. Caliber: .44 Magnum. Six-round cylinder. 6.5- or 7.5-inch bbl., Adj. rear sight, ramp front. Steel or brass grip frame w/square-back trigger guard. Smooth walnut grips. Blued finish. Made from 1956 to 1973.

W/6.5-inch bbl.,	NiB $1250	Ex $1095	Gd $875
W/7.5-inch bbl.,	NiB $750	Ex $345	Gd $245
W/brass gripframe	NiB $1550	Ex $1250	Gd $1095

VAQUERO SA REVOLVER
Calibers: .357 Mag., .44-40, .44 Magnum, .45 Colt. Six-round cylinder. Bbl. lengths: 4.625, 5.5, 7.5 inches, 13.63 inches overall (with 7.5-inch bbl.). Weight: 41 oz. (with 7.5-inch bbl.). Blade front sight, grooved topstrap rear. Blued w/color casehardened frame or polished stainless finish. Smooth rosewood grips w/Ruger medallion. Made from 1993 to 2004.

Blued w/color-case hardened frame	NiB $550	Ex $375	Gd $295
Stainless finish	NiB $550	Ex $375	Gd $295
W/ivory grips	NiB $550	Ex $375	Gd $295

RUSSIAN SERVICE PISTOLS Mfd. by Government plants at Tula and elsewhere

Tokarev-type pistols have also been made in Hungary, Poland, Yugoslavia, People's Republic of China, N. Korea.

MODEL TT30 TOKAREV
SERVICE AUTOMATIC
Modified Colt-Browning type. Caliber: 7.62mm Russian Auto (also uses 7.63mm Mauser Auto cartridge). Eight-round magazine, 4.5-inch bbl., 7.75 inches overall. Weight: About 29 oz. Fixed sights. Made from 1930 to mid-1950s. Note: A slightly modified version w/improved locking system and different disconnector was adopted in 1933.

Standard Service Model TT30	NiB $1200	Ex $1095	Gd $875
Standard Service Model TT33	NiB $2400	Ex $2200	Gd $1800
Recent imports (distinguished by importer marks)	NiB $197	Ex $146	Gd $95

MODEL PSM
MAKAROV AUTO PISTOL
NiB $3000 Ex $2445 Gd $2000
Double-action, blowback design. Caliber: 9mm Makarov. Eight-round magazine, 3.8-inch bbl., 6.4 inches overall. Weight: 26 oz. Blade front sight, square-notched rear. Checkered composition grips.

Standard Service Model PM (Pistole Makarov)	NiB $3500	Ex $3050	Gd $2995
Recent imports (distinguished by importer marks)	NiB $400	Ex $280	Gd $155

SAKO HANDGUNS — Riihimaki, Finland Manufactured by Oy Sako Ab

.22-.32 OLYMPIC
PISTOL (TRIACE)
Calibers: .22 LR, .22 Short, .32 S&W Long. Five-round magazine, 6- or 8.85- (.22 Short) inch bbl., weight: About 46 oz. (.22 LR); 44 oz. (.22 Short); 48 oz. (.32). Steel frame. ABS plastic, anatomically designed grip. Non-reflecting matte black upper surface and chromium-plated slide. Equipped w/carrying case and tool set. Limited importation from 1983 to 1989.

Sako .22 or .32 Single pistol	NiB $1310	Ex $1205	Gd $1045
Sako Triace, triple-barrel set w/wooden grip	NiB $2500	Ex $2200	Gd $1995

SAUER HANDGUNS — Mfd. through WW II by J. P. Sauer & Sohn, Suhl, Germany. Now mfd. by J. P. Sauer & Sohn, GmbH, Eckernförde, West Germany

See also listings under Sig Sauer.

MODEL 1913 POCKET
AUTOMATIC PISTOL . . . . **NiB $290 Ex $215 Gd $155**
Caliber: .32 Automatic (7.65mm). Seven-round magazine, 3-inch bbl., 5.88 inches overall. Weight: 22 oz. Fixed sights. Blued finish. Black hard rubber grips. Made from 1913 to 1930.

MODEL 1930 POCKET AUTOMATIC PISTOL
Authority Model (Behorden Model). Successor to Model 1913, has improved grip and safety. Caliber: .32 Auto (7.65mm). Seven-round magazine, 3-inch bbl., 5.75 inches overall. Weight: 22 oz. Fixed sights. Blued finish. Black hard rubber grips. Made from 1930-38. Note: Some pistols made w/indicator pin showing when cocked. Also mfd. w/dual slide and receiver; this type weight: about 7 oz. less than the standard model.
Steel model . . . . **NiB $370 Ex $263 Gd $176**
Dural (alloy) model . . . . **NiB $1350 Ex $1275 Gd $1150**

MODEL 38H DA AUTOMATIC PISTOL
Calibers: .25 Auto (6.35mm), .32 Auto (7.65mm), .380 Auto (9mm). Specifications shown are for .32 Auto model. Seven-round magazine, 3.25-inch bbl., 6.25 inches overall. Weight: 20 oz. Fixed sights. Blued finish. Black plastic grips. Also made in dual model weighing about 6 oz. less. Made 1938-1945. Note: This pistol, designated Model .38, was mfd. during WW II for military use. Wartime models are inferior in design to earlier production, as some lack safety lever.
.22 caliber . . . . **NiB $5500 Ex $3334 Gd $2156**
.32 ACP . . . . **NiB $600 Ex $355 Gd $230**
.32 ACP (w/Nazi proofs) . . . . **NiB $665 Ex $390 Gd $265**
.380 ACP . . . . **NiB $4500 Ex $4255 Gd $3975**

POCKET .25 (1913)
AUTOMATIC PISTOL . . . . **NiB $350 Ex $255 Gd $180**
Smaller version of Model 1913, issued about same time as .32 caliber model. Caliber: .25 Auto (6.35mm). Seven-round magazine, 2.5-inch bbl., 4.25 inches overall. Weight: 14.5 oz. Fixed sights. Blued finish. Black hard rubber grips. Made 1913 to 1930.

SINGLE-ACTION REVOLVERS
See listings under Hawes.

SAVAGE ARMS CO. — Utica, New York

MODEL 101 SA
SINGLE-SHOT PISTOL . . . . **NiB $225 Ex $150 Gd $90**
Barrel integral w/swing-out cylinder. Calibers: .22 Short, Long, LR. 5.5-inch bbl. Weight: 20 oz. Blade front sight, slotted rear, adj. for windage. Blued finish. Grips of compressed, impregnated wood. Made 1960 to 1968.

MODEL 501/502F "STRIKER" SERIES PISTOLS
Calibers: .22 LR., and .22 WMR. 5- or 10- round magazine, 10-inch bbl., 19 inches overall. Weight: 4 lbs. Drilled and tapped sights for scope mount (installed). Ambidextrous rear grip. Made from 2000 to 2005.
Model 501F, .22 LR . . . . **NiB $235 Ex $190 Gd $155**
Model 502F, .22 WMR. . . . . **NiB $295 Ex $190 Gd $155**

MODEL 510/516 "STRIKER" SERIES PISTOLS
Calibers: 223 Rem., .22-250 Rem., .243 Win., 7mm-08 Rem., .260 Rem., and .308 Win. Three-round magazine, 14-inch bbl., .22.5 inches overall. Drilled and tapped for scope mounts. Left hand bolt with right hand ejection. Stainless steel finish. Made from 1998 to 2005.

Model 510F . . . . **NiB $475 Ex $375 Gd $217**
Model 516FSAK . . . . **NiB $495 Ex $435 Gd $365**
Model 516FSS . . . . **NiB $495 Ex $375 Gd $359**
Model 516FSAK . . . . **NiB $650 Ex $435 Gd $375**
Model 516BSS . . . . **NiB $725 Ex $475 Gd $390**

MODEL 1907 AUTOMATIC PISTOL
Caliber: .32 ACP, 10-round magazine, 3.25-inch bbl., 6.5 inches overall. Weight: 19 oz. Checkered hard rubber or steel grips marked "Savage Quality," circling an Indian-head logo. Optional pearl grips. Blue, nickel, silver or gold finish. Made from 1910 to 1917.
Blued model (.32 ACP) . . . . **NiB $550 Ex $335 Gd $150**
Blued model (.380 ACP) . . . . **NiB $650 Ex $455 Gd $295**

Sako Model .22-.32 Olympic

Sauer 1930 Pocket

Savage Model 101

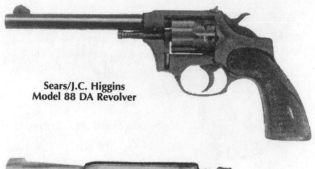

**Sears/J.C. Higgins
Model 88 DA Revolver**

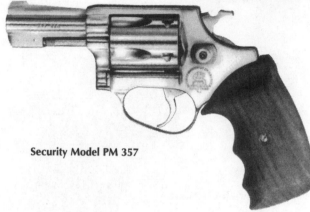

Security Model PM 357

Security Model PPM 357

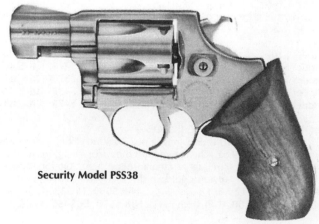

Security Model PSS38

MODEL 1907 AUTOMATIC PISTOL

Calibers: .32 Auto, .380 Auto. 10-round magazine (.32 cal.), 9-round (.380 cal.). 3.75-inch bbl., (.32 cal.), 4.25-inch (.380 cal.). 6.5 inches overall (.32 cal.), 7 inches (.380 cal.). Weight: About 23 oz. Fixed sights. Blued finish. Hard rubber grips. Made in hammerless type w/grip safety or w/exposed hammer spur. Made from 1910 to 1917.
.32 ACP . . . . NiB $550 Ex $325 Gd $250
.380 ACP . . . . NiB $650 Ex $400 Gd $390

MODEL 1915 AUTOMATIC PISTOL

Same general specifications as the Savage Model 1907 except the Model 1915 is hammerless and has a grip safety. It is also chambered for both the .32 and .380 ACP. Made froim 1915 to 1917.
.32 ACP . . . . NiB $900 Ex $690 Gd $470
.380 ACP . . . . NiB $1000 Ex $825 Gd $600

U.S. ARMY TEST MODEL . . . . NiB $10,000 Ex $8730 Gd $6670
Caliber: .45 ACP, Seven-round magazine w/exposed hammer. An enlarged version of the Model 1910 manufactured for military trials between 1907 and 1911. Note: Most "Trial Pistols" were refurbished and resold as commercial models. Values are for original Government Test Issue models.

MODEL 1917 AUTOMATIC PISTOL

Same specifications as 1910 Model except has spur-type hammer and redesigned, heavier grip. Made from 1917 to 1928.
.32 ACP . . . . NiB $425 Ex $300 Gd $245
.380 ACP . . . . NiB $510 Ex $350 Gd $295

SEARS, ROEBUCK & COMPANY — Chicago, Illinois

J.C. HIGGINS MODEL 80
AUTO PISTOL . . . . NiB $255 Ex $150 Gd $100
Caliber: .22 LR. 10-round magazine, 4.5- or 6.5-inch interchangeable bbl., 10.88 inches overall (with 6.5-inch bbl.). Weight: 41 oz. (with 6.5-inch bbl.). Fixed Partridge sights. Blued finish. Checkered grips w/thumbrest.

J.C. HIGGINS MODEL 88
DA REVOLVER. . . . . NiB $195 Ex $100 Gd $75
Caliber: .22 LR. Nine-round cylinder, 4- or 6-inch bbl., 9.5 inches (with 4-inch bbl.). Weight: 23 oz. (with 4-inch bbl.). Fixed sights. Blued or nickel finish. Checkered plastic grips.

J.C. HIGGINS RANGER
DA REVOLVER. . . . . NiB $195 Ex $120 Gd $75
Caliber: .22 LR. Nine-round cylinder, 5.5-inch bbl., 10.75 inches overall. Weight: 28 oz. Fixed sights. Blued or chrome finish. Checkered plastic grips.

SECURITY INDUSTRIES OF AMERICA — Little Ferry, New Jersey

MODEL PM 357 DA REVOLVER . . . . . NiB $225 Ex $200 Gd $150
Caliber: .357 Magnum. Five-round cylinder, 2.5-inch bbl., 7.5 inches overall. Weight: 21 oz. Fixed sights. Stainless steel. Walnut grips. Made 1975. Disc..

MODEL PPM357 DA REVOLVER . . . . . NiB $225 Ex $200 Gd $150
Caliber: .357 Magnum. Five-round cylinder, 2-inch bbl., 6.13 inches overall. Weight: 18 oz. Fixed sights. Stainless steel. Walnut grips. Made in 1975. Note: Spurless hammer (illustrated) was disc. in 1975; this model has the same conventional hammer as other Security revolvers.

MODEL PSS 38
DA REVOLVER................ **NiB $175 Ex $125 Gd $100**
Caliber: .38 Special. Five-round cylinder, 2-inch bbl., 6.5 inches overall. Weight: 18 oz. Fixed sights. Stainless steel. Walnut grips. Intro. 1973. disc.

R. F. SEDGLEY. INC. — Philadelphia, Pennsylvania

BABY HAMMERLESS
EJECTOR REVOLVER........... **NiB $650 Ex $525 Gd $260**
DA. Solid frame. Folding trigger. Caliber: .22 Long. Six-round cylinder, 4 inches overall. Weight: 6 oz. Fixed sights. Blued or nickel finish. Rubber grips. Made 1930 to 1939.

L. W. SEECAMP, INC. — Milford, Connecticut

MODEL LWS .25
DAO PISTOL.................. **NiB $400 Ex $370 Gd $255**
Caliber: .25 ACP. Seven-round magazine, 2-inch bbl., 4.125 inches overall. Weight: 12 oz. Checkered black polycarbonate grips. Matte stainless finish. No sights. Made from 1981 to 1985.

MODEL LWS .32 DAO PISTOL
Caliber: .32 ACP. Six-round magazine, 2-inch bbl., 4.25 inches overall. Weight: 12.9 oz. Ribbed sighting plane with no sights. Checkered black Lexon grips. Stainless steel. Made from 1985 to date. Limited production results in inflated resale values.
Matte stainless finish........... **NiB $425 Ex $355 Gd $255**
Polished stainless finish .... **Add $100**

SHERIDAN PRODUCTS, INC. — Racine, Wisconsin

KNOCKABOUT
SINGLE-SHOT PISTOL .... **NiB $280 Ex $175 Gd $95**
Tip-up type. Caliber: .22 LR, Long, Short; 5-inch bbl., 6.75 inches overall. Weight: 24 oz. Fixed sights. Checkered plastic grips. Blued finish. Made from 1953 to 1960.

SIG PISTOLS — Neuhausen am Rheinfall, Switzerland

See also listings under SIG-Sauer.

MODEL P210-1
AUTOMATIC PISTOL .... **NiB $2770 Ex $2515 Gd $2199**
Calibers: .22 LR, 7.65mm Luger, 9mm Para. Eight-round magazine, 4.75-inch bbl., 8.5 inches overall. Weight: 33 oz. (.22 cal.) or 35 oz. (7.65mm, 9mm). Fixed sights. Polished blued finish. Checkered wood grips. Made from 1949 to 1986.

MODEL P210-2............. **NiB $1680 Ex $1500 Gd $1355**
Same as Model P210-1 except has sandblasted finish, plastic grips. Not avail. in .22 LR. Disc. 2002.

MODEL P210-5
TARGET PISTOL .... **NiB $2265 Ex $2095 Gd $1870**
Same as Model P210-2 except has 6-inch bbl., micrometer adj. rear sight, target front sight, adj. trigger stop, 9.7 inches overall. Weight: About 38.3 oz. Disc. 2007.
MODEL P210-6 TARGET PISTOL ..... **NiB $1850 Ex $1645 Gd $1490**

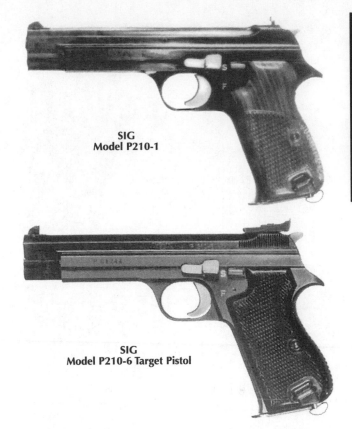

SIG
Model P210-1

SIG
Model P210-6 Target Pistol

Same as Model P210-2 except has micrometer adj. rear sight, target front sight, adj. trigger stop. Weight: About 37 oz. Disc. 1987.

P210 .22 CONVERSION UNIT .... **Add $1480**
Converts P210 pistol to .22 LR. Consists of bbl., w/recoil spring, slide and magazine,

SIG SAUER HANDGUNS
Mfd. by J. P. Sauer & Sohn of West Germany, SIG of Switzerland, and other manufacturers

MODEL P220 DA/DAO AUTOMATIC PISTOL
Calibers: 22LR, 7.65mm, 9mm Para., .38 Super, .45 Automatic. Seven-round in .45, 9-round in other calibers, 4.4-inch bbl., 8 inches overall. Weight: 26.5 oz.(9mm). Fixed sights. Blue, electroless nickel, K-Kote, Duo/nickel or Ilaflon finish. Alloy frame. Checkered plastic grips. Imported from 1976 to date. Note: Also sold in U.S. as Browning BDA.
Blue finish .... **NiB $877 Ex $644 Gd $427**
Duo/nickel finish.............. **NiB $975 Ex $639 Gd $473**
Nickel finish .... **NiB $939 Ex $736 Gd $500**
K-Kote finish .... **NiB $905 Ex $639 Gd $421**
Ilaflon finish .... **NiB $915 Ex $639 Gd $473**
.22 conversion kit, add **$400**
W/Siglite sights, add **$75**

MODEL P220 SPORT AUTOMATIC .... **NiB $1380 Ex $1094 Gd $995**
Similar to Model P220 except .45 ACP only w/4.5-inch compensated bbl., 10-round magazine, adj. target sights. Weight: 46.1 oz. Stainless finish. Made from 1999 to date.

SIG Sauer P220

SIG Sauer P225

SIG Sauer P230

MODEL P225 DA AUTOMATIC

Caliber: 9mm Para. Eight-round magazine, 3.85-inch bbl., 7 inches overall. Weight: 26.1 oz. Blue, nickel, K-Kote, Duo/nickel or Ilaflon finish.

Blued finish . . . . NiB $598 Ex $520 Gd $407
Duo/nickel finish. . . . . NiB $644 Ex $557 Gd $454
Nickel finish . . . . NiB $670 Ex $583 Gd $460
K-Kote finish . . . . NiB $670 Ex $583 Gd $480
W/Siglite sights, add $105

MODEL P226 DA/DAO AUTOMATIC

Caliber: .357 SIG, 9mm Para., .40 S&W, 10- or 15-round magazine, 4.4-inch bbl., 7.75 inches overall. Weight: 29.5 oz. Alloy frame. Blue, electroless nickel, K-Kote, Duo/nickel or Nitron finish. Imported from 1983 to date.

Blued finish . . . . NiB $835 Ex $691 Gd $423
Duo/nickel finish. . . . . NiB $876 Ex $784 Gd $449
Nickel finish . . . . NiB $782 Ex $639 Gd $448
K-Kote finish . . . . NiB $739 Ex $664 Gd $431
Nitron finish
(Blacken stainless) . . . . NiB $756 Ex $609 Gd $434
W/Siglite sights, add $85

MODEL P228 DA AUTOMATIC

Same general specifications as Model P226 except w/3.86-inch bbl., 7.13 inches overall. 10- or 13-round magazine, Imported 1990 to 1997.

Blued finish . . . . NiB $768 Ex $655 Gd $423
Duo/nickel finish. . . . . NiB $820 Ex $697 Gd $466
Electroless nickel finish . . . . NiB $850 Ex $727 Gd $496
K-Kote finish . . . . NiB $815 Ex $702 Gd $470
For Siglite nite sights, add $102

MODEL P229 DA/DAO AUTOMATIC

Same general specifications as Model P228 except w/3.86-inch bbl., 10- or 12-round magazine, weight: 32.5 oz. Nitron or Satin Nickel finish. Imported from 1991 to date.

Nitron finish
(Blackened stainless) . . . . NiB $830 Ex $707 Gd $423
Satin nickel finish . . . . NiB $861 Ex $748 Gd $465
For Siglite nite sights, add $100

MODEL P229

SPORT AUTOMATIC . . . . NiB $1292 Ex $1035 Gd $854
Similar to Model P229 except .357 SIG only w/4.5-inch compensated bbl., adj. target sights. Weight: 43.6 oz. Stainless finish. Made from 1998 to 2003. Reintroduced 2003 to 2005.

MODEL P230 DA AUTOMATIC PISTOL

Calibers: .22 LR, .32 Auto (7.65mm), .380 Auto (9mm Short), 9mm Ultra. 10-round magazine in .22, 8-round in .32, 7-round in 9mm; 3.6-inch bbl., 6.6 inches overall. Weight: 18.2 oz. or 22.4 oz. (steel frame). Fixed sights. Blued or stainless finish. Plastic grips. Imported 1976 to 1996.

Blued finish . . . . NiB $495 Ex $382 Gd $268
Stainless finish (P230SL) . . . . NiB $551 Ex $459 Gd $438

MODEL P232 DA/DAO AUTOMATIC PISTOL

Caliber: .380 ACP. Seven-round magazine, 3.6-inch bbl., 6.6 inches overall. Weight: 16.2 oz. or 22.4 oz. (steel frame). Double/single action or double action only. Blade front and notch rear drift adjustable sights. Alloy or steel frame. Automatic firing pin lock and heelmounted magazine release. Blue, Duo or stainless finish. Stippled black composite stocks. Imported 1997 to date.

Blued finish . . . . NiB $530 Ex $449 Gd $272
Duo finish . . . . NiB $551 Ex $469 Gd $291
Stainless finish . . . . NiB $567 Ex $490 Gd $418
For Siglite nite sights, add $40

MODEL P239 DA/DAO AUTOMATIC PISTOL

Caliber: .357 SIG, 9mm Parabellum or .40 S&W. Seven- or 8-round magazine, 3.6-inch bbl., 6.6 inches overall. Weight: 28.2 oz. Double/single action or double action only. Blade front and notch rear adjustable sights. Alloy frame w/stainless slide. Ambidextrous frame- mounted magazine release. Matte black or Duo finish. Stippled black composite stocks. Made from 1996 to date.

Matte black finish . . . . NiB $562 Ex $500 Gd $274
DAO finish. NiB $601 Ex $490 Gd $348
For Siglite nite sights, add $100

SMITH & WESSON, INC. — Springfield, Massachusetts

NOTE: *For ease in locating a particular S&W handgun, the listings are divided into two groupings: Automatic/Single-Shot Pistols (below) and Revolvers (page 155). For a complete handgun listing, please refer to the index.*

AUTOMATIC/SINGLE-SHOT PISTOLS

35 (1913) AUTOMATIC PISTOL . . . NiB $942 Ex $713 Gd $430
Caliber: 35 S&W Auto. Seven-round magazine, 3.5-inch bbl., (hinged to frame). 6.5 inches overall. Weight: 25 oz. Fixed sights. Blued or nickel finish. Plain walnut grips. Made from 1913 to 1921.

.32 AUTOMATIC PISTOL. . . . . NiB $2990 Ex $2269 Gd $1651
Caliber: .32 Automatic. Same general specifications as .35 caliber model, but barrel is fastened to the receiver instead of hinged. Made from 1924 to 1937.

MODEL .22A SPORT SERIES
Caliber: .22 LR. 10-round magazine, 4-, 5.5- or 7-inch standard (A-series) or bull bbl., (S-series). Single action. Eight, 9.5 or 11 inches overall. Weight: 28 oz. to 33 oz. Partridge front sight, fully adjustable rear. Alloy frame w/stainless slide. Blued finish. Black polymer or Dymondwood grips. Made from 1997 to date.

Model 22A (w/4-inch bbl.)	NiB $230	Ex $175	Gd $100
Model 22A (w/5.5-inch bbl.)	NiB $245	Ex $190	Gd $115
Model 22A (w/7-inch bbl.)	NiB $245	Ex $190	Gd $115
Model 22S (w/5.5-inch bbl.)	NiB $325	Ex $275	Gd $200
Model 22S (w/7-inch bbl.)	NiB $365	Ex $310	Gd $240
W/bull bbl., add $50			
W/Dymondwood grips, add $75			

MODEL 39 9MM DA AUTO PISTOL
Calibers: 9mm Para. Eight-round magazine, 4-inch barrel. Overall length: 7.44-inches. Steel or alloy frames. Weight: 26.5 oz. (w/alloy frame). Click adjustable rear sight, ramp front. Blued or nickel finish. Checkered walnut grips. Made 1954-82. Note: Between 1954 and 1966, 927 pistols were produced w/steel instead of alloy. In 1970, Model 39-1 w/alloy frame and steel slide. In 1971, Model 39-2 was introduced as an improved version of the original Model 39 w/modified extractor.

Model 39 (early production) 1954-70
First series (SN range 1000-2600) . . . . NiB $1495 Ex $1350 Gd $1290
9mm blue(w/steel frame & slide, produced 1966) . . . . NiB $1495 Ex $1350 Gd $1290
9mm blue (w/alloy frame) . . . . NiB $400 Ex $320 Gd $210
Nickel finish, add $35
Models 39-1, 39-2 (late production)
1970-82 9mm blue (w/alloy frame) . . . . . NiB $400 Ex $295 Gd $205
Nickel finish, add $35

MODEL 41 .22 AUTOMATIC PISTOL
Caliber: .22 LR, .22 Short (not interchangeably). 10-round magazine, bbl. lengths: 5-, 5.5-, 7.75-inches; latter has detachable muzzle brake, 12 inches overall (with 7.75-inch bbl.). Weight: 43.5 oz. (with 7.75-inch bbl.). Click adj. rear sight, undercut Partridge front. Blued finish. Checkered walnut grips w/thumbrest. 1957 to date.
.22 LR model . . . . NiB $870 Ex $620 Gd $495
.22 Short model (w/counterweights & muzzle brake) . . . . . NiB $1750 Ex $1245 Gd $1050
W/extended sight, add $100
W/muzzle brake, add $35

**Smith & Wesson
Model 22A Sport Series**

**Smith & Wesson
Model 22S Sport Series
w/Dymondwood Grips**

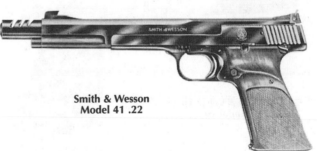

**Smith & Wesson
Model 41 .22**

MODEL 46 .22 AUTO PISTOL. . . . . NiB $725 Ex $500 Gd $325
Caliber: .22 LR. 10-round magazine, bbl. lengths: 5-, 5.5-, 7-inches. 10.56 inches overall (with 7-inch bbl.). Weight: 42 oz. (with 7-inch bbl.). Click adj. rear sight, undercut Partridge front. Blued finish. Molded nylon grips w/thumbrest. Only 4,000 produced. Made from 1957 to 1966.

MODEL 52 .38 MASTER AUTO
Caliber: .38 Special (midrange wadcutter only). Five-round magazine, 5-inch bbl., overall length: 8.63 inches. Weight: 41 oz. Micrometer click rear sight, Partridge front on ramp base. Blued finish. Checkered walnut grips. Made from 1961 to 1963.
Model 52 (1961-63) . . . . NiB $955 Ex $860 Gd $475
Model 52-1 (1963-71) . . . . NiB $950 Ex $860 Gd $475
Model 52-2 (1971-93) . . . . NiB $950 Ex $860 Gd $475
Model 52-A USA Marksman (fewer than 100 mfg.) . . . . NiB $3765 Ex $3390 Gd $3030

GRADING: NiB = New in Box   Ex = Excellent or NRA 95%   Gd = Good or NRA 68%

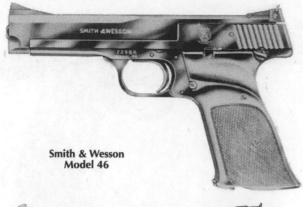

**Smith & Wesson
Model 46**

**Smith & Wesson
Model 439**

**Smith & Wesson
Model 52**

**Smith & Wesson
Model 59**

**Smith & Wesson
Model 422**

MODEL 59
9MM DA AUTO
Similar specifications as Model 39 except has 14-round staggered column magazine, checkered nylon grips. Made 1971 to 1981.

Model 59, blue . . . . NiB $475 Ex $395 Gd $265
Model 59, nickel . . . . NiB $510 Ex $415 Gd $280
Model 59
(early production
w/smooth grip frame) . . . . NiB $625 Ex $545 Gd $320

MODEL 61
ESCORT POCKET AUTOMATIC PISTOL
Caliber: .22 LR. Five-round magazine, 2.13-inch bbl., 4.69 inches overall. Weight: 14 oz. Fixed sights. Blued or nickel finish. Checkered plastic grips. Made from 1970 to 1974.

Model 61, blue . . . . NiB $350 Ex $245 Gd $145
Model 61, nickel . . . . NiB $395 Ex $290 Gd $195

MODEL 410
AUTO PISTOL. . . . . NiB $525 Ex $385 Gd $225
Caliber: .40 S&W. Double action. 10-round magazine, 4-inch bbl., 7.5 inches overall. Weight: 28.5 oz. Alloy frame w/steel slide. Post front sight, fixed rear w/3-dot system. Matte blue finish. Checkered synthetic grips w/straight backstrap. Made from 1996 to 2007.

MODEL 411
AUTO PISTOL . . . . NiB $475 Ex $400 Gd $350
Similar to S&W Model 915 except in caliber .40 S&W. 11-round magazine, made from 1994 to 1996.

MODEL 422 SA
AUTO PISTOL
Caliber: .22 LR. 10-round magazine, 4.5- or 6-inch bbl., 7.5 inches overall (with 4.5-inch bbl.). Weight: 22-23.5 oz. Fixed or adjustable sights. Checkered plastic or walnut grips. Blued finish. Made from 1987 to 1996.

Standard model . . . . NiB $200 Ex $160 Gd $125
Target model . . . . NiB $250 Ex $190 Gd $160

MODEL 439
9MM AUTOMATIC
DA. Caliber: 9mm Para. Two 8-round magazines, 4-inch bbl., 7.44 inches overall. Alloy frame. Weight: 30 oz. Serrated ramp square front sight, square notch rear. Checkered walnut grips. Blued or nickel finish. Made from 1979 to 1988.

Model 439, blue . . . . NiB $475 Ex $350 Gd $275
Model 439, nickel . . . . NiB $505 Ex $380 Gd $275
W/adjustable sights, add $25

Smith & Wesson
Model 645

Smith & Wesson
Model 459

MODEL 457
COMPACT AUTO PISTOL . . . . NiB $525 Ex $395 Gd $235
Caliber: .45 ACP. Double action. Seven-round magazine, 3.75-inch bbl., 7.25 inches overall. Weight: 29 oz. Alloy frame w/steel slide. Post front sight, fixed rear w/3-dot system. Bobbed hammer. Matte blue finish. Wraparound synthetic grip w/straight backstrap. Made from 1996 to 2006.

MODEL 459 DA AUTOMATIC
Caliber: 9mm Para. Two 14-round magazines, 4-inch bbl., 7.44 inches overall. Alloy frame. Weight: 28 oz. Blued or nickel finish. Made from 1979 to 1987.

Model 459, blue	NiB $450	Ex $400	Gd $295
Model 459, nickel	NiB $495	Ex $440	Gd $335
FBI Model (brushed finish)	NiB $700	Ex $575	Gd $410

MODEL 469
(MINI) AUTOMATIC . . . . NiB $475 Ex $375 Gd $270
DA. Caliber: 9mm Para. Two 12-round magazines, 3.5-inch bbl., 6.88 inches overall. Weight: 26 oz. Yellow ramp front sight, dovetail mounted square-notch rear. Sandblasted blued finish. Optional ambidextrous safety. Made from 1982 to 1988.

Smith & Wesson
Model 469

MODEL 539 DA AUTOMATIC
Similar to Model 439 except w/steel frame. Caliber: 9mm Para. Two 8-round magazines, 4-inch bbl., 7.44 inches overall. Weight: 36 oz. Blued or nickel finish. Made from 1980 to 1983.

Model 539, blue	NiB $550	Ex $455	Gd $350
Model 539, nickel	NiB $548	Ex $491	Gd $381
W/adjustable sights, add $50

MODEL 559 DA AUTOMATIC
Similar to Model 459 except w/steel frame. Caliber: 9mm Para. Two 14-round magazines, 4-inch bbl., 7.44 inches overall. Weight: 39.5 oz. Blued or nickel finish. (3750 produced) Made 1980 to 1983.

Model 559, blue	NiB $600	Ex $515	Gd $400
Model 559, nickel	NiB $635	Ex $550	Gd $435
W/adjustable sights, add $30

MODEL 622 SA AUTO PISTOL
Same general specifications as Model 422 except w/stainless finish. Made from 1989 to 1996.

Standard model	NiB $225	Ex $165	Gd $100
Target model	NiB $275	Ex $190	Gd $130

MODEL 639 AUTOMATIC . . . . NiB $475 Ex $355 Gd $280
Caliber: 9mm Para. Stainless. Two 12-round magazines, 3.5-inch bbl., 6.9 inches overall. Weight: 36 oz. Made from 1986 to 1988.

Smith & Wesson
Model 639

Smith & Wesson Model 659

Smith & Wesson Model 745

Smith & Wesson Model 1026

MODEL 645 DA AUTOMATIC
Caliber: .45 ACP. Eight-round. 5-inch bbl., overall length: 8.5 inches. Weight: Approx. 38 oz. Red ramp front, fixed rear sights. Stainless. Made from 1986-88.
Model 645 (w/fixed sights) . . . . NiB $550 Ex $400 Gd $315
Model 645 (w/adjustable sights) . . . NiB $580 Ex $430 Gd $345

MODEL 659 9MM AUTOMATIC
DA. Similar to S&W Model 459 except weight: 39.5 oz. and finish is satin stainless steel finish. Made from 1983-88.
Model 659 (w/fixed sights) . . . . NiB $475 Ex $380 Gd $300
Model 659 (w/adjustable sights) . . . . NiB $500 Ex $405 Gd $325

MODEL 669 AUTOMATIC. . . . . NiB $450 Ex $320 Gd $245
Caliber: 9mm. 12-round magazine, 3.5 inch bbl., 6.9 inches overall. Weight: 26 oz. Serrated ramp front sight w/red bar, fixed rear. Non-glare stainless steel finish. Made from 1986-88.

MODEL 745 AUTOMATIC PISTOL
Caliber: .45 ACP. Eight-round magazine, 5-inch bbl., 8.63 inches overall. Weight: 38.75 oz. Fixed sights. Blued slide, stainless frame. Checkered walnut grips. Similar to the model 645, but w/o DA capability. Made from 1987-90.
W/standard competition features . . . . NiB $700 Ex $525 Gd $395
IPSC Commemorative (first 5,000) . . . . NiB $750 Ex $575 Gd $395

MODEL 908/909/910 AUTO PISTOLS
Caliber: 9mm Parabellum. Double action. Eight-round (Model 908), 9-round (Model 909) or 10-round (Model 910) magazine; 3.5- or 4-inch bbl.; 6.83 or 7.38 inches overall. Weight: 26 oz. to 28.5 oz. Post front sight, fixed rear w/3-dot system. Matte blue steel slide w/alloy frame. Delrin synthetic wrap-around grip w/straight backstrap. Made from 1994 to date.
Model 908 . . . . NiB $495 Ex $355 Gd $240
Model 909 (disc 1996) . . . . NiB $450 Ex $325 Gd $225
Model 910 . . . . NiB $455 Ex $325 Gd $225

MODEL 915 AUTO PISTOL . . . . . . NiB $425 Ex $300 Gd $220
DA. Caliber: 9mm Para. 15-round magazine, 4-inch bbl., 7.5 inches overall. Weight: 28.5 oz. Post front sight, fixed square-notched rear w/3-dot system. Xenoy wraparound grip. Blued steel slide and alloy frame. Made from 1992-94.

MODEL 1000 SERIES DA AUTO
Caliber: 10mm. Nine-round magazine, 4.25- or 5-inch bbl., 7.88 or 8.63 inches overall. Weight: About 38 oz. Post front sight, adj. or fixed square-notched rear w/3-dot system. One-piece Xenoy wrap-around grips. Stainless slide and frame. Made from 1990-94.
Model 1006 (fixed sights, 5 inch bbl.) . . . . NiB $675 Ex $500 Gd $410
Model 1006 (Adj. sights, 5 inch bbl.) . . . . . NiB $700 Ex $525 Gd $435
Model 1026 (fixed sights, 5 inch bbl., decocking lever) . . . . NiB $675 Ex $500 Gd $410
Model 1066 (fixed sights, 4.25 inch bbl.) . . . . NiB $650 Ex $480 Gd $325
Model 1076 (fixed sights, 4.25 inch bbl., frame-mounted decocking lever, straight backstrap) . . . . NiB $700 Ex $500 Gd $400
Model 1076 (same as above w/Tritium night sight) . . . . NiB $700 Ex $500 Gd $400
Model 1086 (same as model 1076 in DA only) . . . . NiB $725 Ex $520 Gd $400

MODEL 2206 SA AUTOMATIC PISTOL
Similar to Model 422 except w/stainless-steel slide and frame, weight: 35-39 oz. Partridge front sight on adj. sight model; post w/white dot on fixed sight model. Plastic grips. Made from 1990-96.
Standard model . . . . NiB $290 Ex $195 Gd $110
Target model . . . . NiB $360 Ex $220 Gd $165

MODEL 2213
SPORTSMAN AUTO . . . . NiB $255 Ex $165 Gd $100
Caliber: .22 LR. Eight-round magazine, 3-inch bbl., 6.13 inches overall. Weight: 18 oz. Partridge front sight, fixed square-notched rear w/3-dot system. Black synthetic molded grips. Stainless steel slide w/alloy frame. Made from 1992-99.

MODEL 2214
SPORTSMAN AUTO . . . . NiB $235 Ex $170 Gd $115
Same general specifications as Model 2214 except w/blued slide and matte black alloy frame. Made from 1990-99.

MODEL 3904/3906 DA AUTO PISTOL

Caliber: 9mm. Eight-round magazine, 4-inch bbl., 7.5 inches overall. Weight: 25.5 oz. (Model 3904) or 34 oz. (Model 3906). Fixed or adj. sights. Delrin one-piece wraparound checkered grips. Alloy frame w/blued carbon steel slide (Model 3904) or satin stainless (Model 3906). Made from 1989 to 1991.

Model 3904 w/adjustable sights . . . . NiB $475 Ex $325 Gd $255
Model 3904 w/fixed sights . . . . NiB $450 Ex $300 Gd $245
Model 3904 w/Novak LC sight . . . . NiB $450 Ex $300 Gd $245
Model 3906 w/adjustable sights . . . . NiB $540 Ex $455 Gd $385
Model 3906 w/Novak LC sight . . . . NiB $510 Ex $425 Gd $340

MODEL 3913/3914 DA AUTOMATIC

Caliber: 9mm Parabellum (Luger). Eight-round magazine, 3.5-inch bbl., 6.88 inches overall. Weight: 25 oz. Post front sight, fixed or adj. square-notched rear. One-piece Xenoy wraparound grips w/straight backstrap. Alloy frame w/stainless or blued slide. Made from 1990 to 1999.

Model 3913 stainless . . . . NiB $535 Ex $400 Gd $320
Model 3913LS Lady Smith stainless
w/contoured trigger guard . . . . NiB $710 Ex $554 Gd $451
Model 3913TSW (intro. 1998) . . . . NiB $690 Ex $549 Gd $451
Model 3914 blued compact
(disc 1995) . . . . NiB $535 Ex $440 Gd $335

**Smith & Wesson
Model 3906**

MODEL 3953/3954 DA AUTO PISTOL

Same general specifications as Model 3913/3914 except double action only. Made from 1990 to 2002.

Model 3953 stainless,
double action only . . . . NiB $535 Ex $400 Gd $350
Model 3954 blued, double
action only (disc. 1992) . . . . NiB $475 Ex $390 Gd $300

**Smith & Wesson
Model 3953**

MODEL 4000 SERIES DA AUTO

Caliber: .40 S&W. 11-round magazine, 4-inch bbl., 7.88 inches overall. Weight: 28-30 oz. w/alloy frame or 36 oz. w/stainless frame. Post front sight, adj. or fixed square-notched rear w/2 white dots. Straight backstrap. One-piece Xenoy wraparound grips. Blued or stainless finish. Made between 1991 to 1993.

Model 4003 stainless w/alloy frame . . . . . . NiB $575 Ex $455 Gd $360
Model 4003 TSW w/
S&W Tactical options . . . . NiB $825 Ex $735 Gd $575
Model 4004 blued w/alloy frame . . . . NiB $540 Ex $420 Gd $355
Model 4006 stainless
frame, fixed sights . . . . NiB $655 Ex $500 Gd $355
Model 4006 stainless
frame, Adj. sights . . . . NiB $700 Ex $600 Gd $455
Model 4006 TSW w/
S&W Tactical options . . . . NiB $825 Ex $724 Gd $431
Model 4013 stainless frame,
fixed sights . . . . NiB $595 Ex $400 Gd $355
Model 4013 TSW w/
S&W Tactical options . . . . NiB $825 Ex $724 Gd $431
Model 4014 blued, fixed sights
(disc. 1993) . . . . NiB $550 Ex $400 Gd $335
Model 4026 w/decocking
Lever (disc. 1994) . . . . NiB $625 Ex $500 Gd $420
Model 4043 DA only, stainless
w/alloy frame . . . . NiB $635 Ex $550 Gd $445
Model 4044 DA only,
blued w/alloy frame . . . . NiB $540 Ex $400 Gd $305
Model 4046 DA only, stainless
frame, fixed sights . . . . NiB $700 Ex $620 Gd $475
Model 4046 TSW w/
S&W Tactical options . . . . NiB $700 Ex $620 Gd $475
Model 4046 DA only, stainless
frame, Tritium night sight . . . . NiB $655 Ex $570 Gd $435

**Smith & Wesson
Model 4013**

**Smith & Wesson
Model 4046**

**Smith & Wesson
Model 4053**

**Smith & Wesson
Model 4586**

**Smith & Wesson Model 5904
w/Adjustable Sights**

MODEL 4013/4014 DA AUTOMATIC
Caliber: .40 S&W. Eight-round capacity, 3.5-inch bbl., 7 inches overall. Weight: 26 oz. Post front sight, fixed Novak LC rear w/3-dot system. One-piece Xenoy wraparound grips. Stainless or blued slide w/alloy frame. Made from 1991 to 1996.

Model 4013 w/stainless slide (disc. 1996) .... NiB $595 Ex $495 Gd $300
Model 4013 Tactical w/stainless slide .... NiB $825 Ex $650 Gd $535
Model 4014 w/blued slide (disc. 1993) ...... NiB $550 Ex $425 Gd $300

MODEL 4053/4054 DA AUTO PISTOL
Same general specifications as Model 4013/4014 except double action only. Alloy frame fitted w/blued steel slide. Made from 1991 to 1997.

Model 4053 DA only w/stainless slide .... NiB $625 Ex $491 Gd $439
Model 4053 TSW w/ S&W Tactical options ... NiB $730 Ex $600 Gd $485
Model 4054 DA only w/blued slide
(disc. 1992) .... NiB $650 Ex $420 Gd $315

MODEL 4500 SERIES DA AUTOMATIC
Caliber: .45 ACP. Six-, 7- or 8-round magazine, bbl. lengths: 3.75, 4.25 or 5 inches; 7.13 to 8.63 inches overall. Weight: 34.5 to 38.5 oz. Post front sight, fixed Novak LC rear w/3-dot system or adj. One-piece Xenoy wraparound grips. Satin stainless finish. Made from 1991 to 1997.

Model 4505 w/fixed sights, 5-inch bbl........ NiB $650 Ex $573 Gd $367
Model 4505 w/Novak LC sight, 5-inch bbl. ... NiB $628 Ex $550 Gd $395
Model 4506 w/fixed sights, 5-inch bbl........ NiB $678 Ex $525 Gd $480
Model 4506 w/Novak LC sight, 5-inch bbl. ... NiB $680 Ex $525 Gd $445
Model 4513T (TSW) w/3.75-inch bbl.
Tactical Combat .... NiB $725 Ex $609 Gd $470
Model 4516 w/3.75-inch bbl. .... NiB $675 Ex $590 Gd $450
Model 4526 w/5-inch bbl., alloy frame,
decocking lever, fixed sights .... NiB $675 Ex $550 Gd $470
Model 4536, decocking lever .... NiB $675 Ex $590 Gd $480
Model 4546, w/3.75-inch bbl., DA only ..... NiB $675 Ex $540 Gd $480
Model 4553T (TSW) w/3.75-inch bbl.
Tactical Combat .... NiB $730 Ex $601 Gd $390
Model 4556, w/3.75-inch bbl., DA only ..... NiB $675 Ex $573 Gd $368
Model 4563 TSW w/4.25-inch bbl.
Tactical Combat .... NiB $750 Ex $609 Gd $470
Model 4566 w/4.25-inch bbl.,
ambidextrous safety, fixed sights .... NiB $650 Ex $500 Gd $420
Model 4566 TSW w/4.25-inch bbl.
Tactical Combat .... NiB $650 Ex $599 Gd $470
Model 4576 w/4.25-inch bbl.,
decocking lever .... NiB $635 Ex $575 Gd $420
Model 4583T TSW w/4.25-inch bbl.
Tactical Combat .... NiB $700 Ex $595 Gd $480
Model 4586 w/4.25-inch bbl., DA only ...... NiB $695 Ex $580 Gd $470
Model 4586 TSW w/4.25-inch bbl.
Tactical Combat .... NiB $700 Ex $595 Gd $480

MODEL 5900 SERIES DA AUTOMATIC
Caliber: 9mm. 15-round magazine, 4-inch bbl., 7.5 inches overall. Weight: 26-38 oz. Fixed or adj. sights. One-piece Xenoy wraparound grips. Alloy frame w/stainless-steel slide (Model 5903) or blued slide (Model 5904) stainless-steel frame and slide (Model 5906). Made from 1990 to 1997.

Model 5903 w/adjustable sights .... NiB $650 Ex $530 Gd $365
Model 5903 w/Novak LC rear sight .... NiB $680 Ex $635 Gd $341
Model 5903 TSW w/4-inch bbl.,
Tactical Combat .... NiB $730 Ex $610 Gd $455
Model 5904 w/adjustable sights .... NiB $535 Ex $415 Gd $353
Model 5904 w/Novak LC rear sight .... NiB $565 Ex $440 Gd $360
Model 5905 w/Adjustable Sights .... NiB $650 Ex $520 Gd $407
Model 5905 w/Novak LC rear sight .... NiB $680 Ex $600 Gd $432
Model 5906 w/adjustable sights .... NiB $615 Ex $500 Gd $400
Model 5906 w/Novak LC rear sight .... NiB $615 Ex $500 Gd $400
Model 5906 w/Tritium night sight........... NiB $730 Ex $615 Gd $515
Model 5906 TSW w/4-inch bbl.,
Tactical Combat .... NiB $806 Ex $708 Gd $528
Model 5924 anodized frame, blued slide ..... NiB $625 Ex $487 Gd $291
Model 5926 Stain. frame, decocking lever .... NiB $600 Ex $505 Gd $410
Model 5943 alloy frame/
stainless slide, DA only .... NiB $550 Ex $410 Gd $320
Model 5943 TSW w/4-inch bbl., DA only .... NiB $625 Ex $510 Gd $395
Model 5944 alloy frame/
blued slide, DA only .... NiB $650 Ex $520 Gd $420
Model 5946 stainless frame/slide, DA only ... NiB $615 Ex $500 Gd $355
Model 5946 TSW w/4-inch bbl., DA only..... NiB $725 Ex $600 Gd $300

MODEL 6900 COMPACT SERIES

Double action. Caliber: 9mm. 12-round magazine, 3.5-inch bbl., 6.88 inches overall. Weight: 26.5 oz. Ambidextrous safety. Post front sight, fixed Novak LC rear w/3-dot system. Alloy frame w/blued carbon steel slide (Model 6904) or stainless steel slide (Model 6906). Made 1989 to 1997.

Model 6904	NiB $550	Ex $400	Gd $330
Model 6906 w/fixed sights	NiB $585	Ex $505	Gd $410
Model 6906 w/Tritium night sight	NiB $796	Ex $586	Gd $450
Model 6926 same as model 6906 w/decocking lever	NiB $650	Ex $554	Gd $351
Model 6944 same as model 6904 in DA only	NiB $600	Ex $498	Gd $302
Model 6946 same as model 6906 in DA only ,fixed sights	NiB $683	Ex $520	Gd $350
Model 6946 w/Tritium night sight	NiB $675	Ex $515	Gd $410

SIGMA SW380 AUTOMATIC PISTOL ..... NiB $475 Ex $320 Gd $260

Caliber: .380 ACP. Double-action only. Six-round magazine, 3-inch bbl., weight: 14 oz. Black integral polymer gripframe w/checkered back and front straps. Fixed channel sights. Polymer frame w/hammerless steel slide. Made from 1994 to 1996.

SIGMA SW9 SERIES AUTOMATIC PISTOL

Caliber: 9mm Parabellum. Double action only. 10-round magazine, 3.25-, 4- or 4.5-inch bbl., weight: 17.9 oz. to 24.7 oz. Polymer frame w/hammerless steel slide. Post front sight and drift adjustable rear w/3-dot system. Gray or black integral polymer gripframe w/checkered back and front straps. Made from 1994 to 1996.

Model SW9C (compact w/3.25-inch bbl.)	NiB $475	Ex $390	Gd $300
Model SW9F (blue slide w/4.5-inch bbl.)	NiB $475	Ex $390	Gd $270
Model SW9M (compact w/3.25-inch bbl.)	NiB $300	Ex $210	Gd $150
Model SW9V (stainless slide w/4-inch bbl.)	NiB $375	Ex $265	Gd $200
Tritium night sight, add			$210

SW40 SERIES AUTOMATIC PISTOL

Same general specifications as SW9 series except chambered for .40 S&W w/4- or 4.5-inch bbl., weight: 24.4 to 26 oz. Made 1994 to 1998.

Model SW40C (compact w/4inch bbl.)	NiB $450	Ex $320	Gd $230
Model SW40F (blue slide w/4.5inch bbl.)	NiB $450	Ex $320	Gd $230
Model SW40V (stainless slide w/4inch bbl.)	NiB $450	Ex $320	Gd $230
Tritium night sight, add			$210

MODEL 1891 SINGLE-SHOT TARGET PISTOL, FIRST MODEL

Hinged frame. Calibers: .22 LR, .32 S&W, .38 S&W. Bbl. lengths: 6-, 8- and 10-inches, approx. 13.5 inches overall (with 10-inch bbl.). Weight: About 25 oz. Target sights, barrel catch rear adj. for windage and elevation. Blued finish. Square butt, hard rubber grips. Made 1893-1905. Note: This model was available also as a combination arm w/accessory .38 revolver bbl. and cylinder enabling conversion to a pocket revolver. It has the frame of the .38 SA revolver Model 1891 w/side flanges, hand and cylinder stop slots.

Single-shot pistol, .22 LR	NiB $2700	Ex $2531	Gd $2397
Single-shot pistol, .32 S&W or .38 S&W	NiB $2200	Ex $1903	Gd $1708
Combination set, revolver and single-shot barrel	NiB $3500	Ex $3010	Gd $2782

MODEL 1891 SINGLE-SHOT TARGET PISTOL, SECOND MODEL ..... NiB $2200 Ex $1861 Gd $1465

Similar to the First Model except side flanges, hand and stop slots eliminated, cannot be converted to revolver, redesigned rear sight. Caliber: .22 LR only, 10-inch bbl. only. Made from 1905 to 1909.

PERFECTED SINGLE-SHOT TARGET PISTOL

Similar to Second Model except has double-action lockwork. Caliber: .22 LR only, 10-inch bbl. Checkered walnut grips, extended

**Smith & Wesson
Model 1**

square-butt target type. Made 1909-23. Note: In 1920 and thereafter, this model was made w/barrels having bore diameter of .223 instead of .226 and tight, short chambering. The first group of these pistols was produced for the U.S. Olympic Team of 1920, thus the designation Olympic Model.

Pre-1920 type	NiB $2210	Ex $1871	Gd $1488
Olympic model	NiB $2550	Ex $2204	Gd $2192

STRAIGHT LINE SINGLE-SHOT
TARGET PISTOL .... NiB $3255 Ex $3100 Gd $2975

Frame shaped like that of an automatic pistol, barrel swings to the left on pivot for extracting and loading, straight-line trigger and hammer movement. Caliber: .22 L.R. 10-inch bbl., 11.25 inches overall. Weight: 34 oz. Target sights. Blued finish. Smooth walnut grips. Supplied in metal case w/screwdriver and cleaning rod. Made from 1925 to 1936.

NOTE: *The following section contains only S&W Revolvers. For a complete listing of S&W handguns, please refer to the index.*

REVOLVERS

MODEL 1 HAND EJECTOR
DA REVOLVER............. NiB $1575 Ex $1325 Gd $1195

First Model. Forerunner of the .32 Hand Ejector and Regulation Police models, this was the first S&W revolver of the solid-frame, swing-out cylinder type. Top strap of this model is longer than those of later models, and it lacks the usual S&W cylinder latch. Caliber: .32 S&W Long. Bbl., lengths: 3.25-, 4.25-, and 6-inches. Fixed sights. Blued or nickel finish. Round butt, hard rubber stocks. Made from 1896 to 1903.

NO. 3 SA FRONTIER .... NiB $5000 Ex $4242 Gd $2909

Caliber: .44-40 WCF. Bbl., lengths: 4-, 5- and 6.5-inch. Fixed or target sights. Blued or nickel finish. Round, hard rubber or checkered walnut grips. Made from 1885 to 1908.

NO. 3 SA (NEW MODEL) ..... NiB $7000 Ex $5908 Gd $4191

Hinged frame. Six-round cylinder. Caliber: .44 S&W Russian. Bbl., lengths: 4-, 5-, 6-, 6.5-, 7.5- and 8-inches. Fixed or target sights. Blued or nickel finish. Round, hard rubber or checkered walnut grips. Made from 1878 to 1908. Note: Value shown is for standard model. Specialist collectors recognize numerous variations w/a range of higher values.

NO. 3 SA TARGET .... NiB $6895 Ex $3707 Gd $3038

Hinged frame. Six-round cylinder. Calibers: .32/.44 S&W, .38/.44 S&W Gallery & Target. 6.5-inch bbl. only. Fixed or target sights. Blued or nickel finish. Round, hard rubber or checkered walnut grips. Made from 1887 to 1910.

**Smith & Wesson
Model 10 (Two-inch Barrel)**

**Smith & Wesson
Model 12 (Two-inch Barrel)**

**Smith & Wesson Model 13
(Heavy Barrel)**

**Smith & Wesson
Model 14**

MODEL 10 .38 MILITARY & POLICE DA
Also called Hand Ejector Model of 1902, Hand Ejector Model of 1905, Model K. Manufactured substantially in its present form since 1902, this model has undergone numerous changes, most of them minor. Round- or square-butt models, the latter intro. in 1904. Caliber: .38 Special. Six-round cylinder, bbl. lengths: 2-(intro. 1933), 4-, 5-, 6- and 6.5-inch (latter disc. 1915) also 4-inch heavy bbl., (intro. 1957); 11.13 inches overall (square-butt model w/6-inch bbl.). Round-butt model is 1/4-inch shorter, weight: About 1/2 oz. less. Fixed sights. Blued or nickel finish. Checkered walnut grips, hard rubber available in round-butt style. Current Model 10 has short action. Made 1902 to date. Note: S&W Victory Model, wartime version of the M & P .38, was produced for the U.S. Government from 1940 to the end of the war. A similar revolver, designated .38/200 British Service Revolver, was produced for the British Government during the same period. These arms have either brush-polish or sandblast blued finish, and most of them have plain, smooth walnut grips, lanyard swivels.

Model of 1902 (1902-05) . . . . NiB $595 Ex $500 Gd $345
Model of 1905 (1905-40) . . . . NiB $1100 Ex $850 Gd $565
.38/200 British Service (1940-45) . . NiB $1100 Ex $850 Gd $565
Victory Model (1942-45) . . . . NiB $585 Ex $480 Gd $375
Model of 1944 (1945-48) . . . . NiB $750 Ex $510 Gd $375
Model 10 (1948 - date) . . . . NiB $595 Ex $400 Gd $300

MODEL 10 .38 MILITARY
& POLICE HEAVY BARREL . . . . NiB $595 Ex $425 Gd $310
Same as standard Model 10 except has heavy 4-inch bbl., weight: 34 oz. Made from 1957 to 1986.

MODEL 12 .38 M
& PAIRWEIGHT . . . . NiB $500 Ex $345 Gd $265
Same as standard Military & Police except has light alloy frame, f8rnished w/2- or 4-inch bbl. only, weight: 18 oz. (w/2-inch bbl.). Made from 1952 to 1986.

MODEL 12/13 (AIR FORCE MODEL)
DA REVOLVER . . . . NiB $500 Ex $410 Gd $245
Special "Air Force" Model designed with alloy cylinder and frame to be used as a "Survival Weapon" for air crews. Athough this weapon was actually a first-series Model 12, the Air Force stamped "M13" on the top strap. Issued 1953 but recalled for function problems in 1954.

MODEL 13 .357
MILITARY/POLICE. . . . . NiB $450 Ex $295 Gd $180
Same as Model 10 .38 Military & Police Heavy Barrel except chambered for .357 Magnum and .38 Special w/3- or 4-inch bbl. Round or square butt configuration. Made from1974 to 1998.

MODELS 14 (K38) AND 16 (K32) MASTERPIECE REVOLVERS
Calibers: .22 LR, .22 Magnum Rimfire, .32 S&W Long, .38 Special. Six-round cylinder. DA/SA. Bbl. lengths: 4- (.22 WMR only), 6-, 8.38-inch (latter not available in K32), 11.13 inches overall (with 6-inch bbl.). Weight: 38.5 oz. (with 6-inch bbl.). Click adj. rear sight, Partridge front. Blued finish. Checkered walnut grips. Made from 1947 to date. (Model 16 disc. 1974; 3,630 produced; reissued 1990 to 1993.)

Model 14 (K-38 double-
action) . . . . NiB $550 Ex $298 Gd $195
Model 14 (K-38 single action,
6-inch bbl.) . . . . NiB $650 Ex $349 Gd $206
Model 14 (K-38 single action,
8.38-inch bbl.). . . . . NiB $428 Ex $335 Gd $236
Model 16 (K-32 double-
action) 1st Issue. . . . . NiB $1371 Ex $1266 Gd $853
Model 16 (K-32 double-
action) . . . . NiB $1350 Ex $1126 Gd $939

MODELS 15 (.38) AND 18 (.22) COMBAT MASTERPIECE DA REVOLVERS

Same as K-.22 and K-.38 Masterpiece but w/2- (.38) or 4-inch bbl., and Baughman quick-draw front sight. 9.13 inches overall w/4-inch bbl., Weight: 34 oz. (.38 cal.). Made from 1950 to 1999.

Model 15 . . . . NiB $775 Ex $549 Gd $428
Model 18 (disc. 1985) . . . . NiB $650 Ex $500 Gd $425
W/target options TH & TT, add $35

MODEL 17 K-.22 MASTERPIECE DA REVOLVER

Caliber: 22LR. Six-round cylinder, Bbl lengths: 4, 6 or 8.38 inches. 11.13 inches overall (with 6-inch bbl.). Weight: 38 oz. (with 6-inch bbl.). Partridge-type front sight, S&W micrometer click rear. Checkered walnut Service grips with S&W momogram. S&W blued finish. Made from 1947-93 and from 1996-98.

Model 17 (4-inch bbl.) . . . . .NiB $595 Ex $430 Gd $315
Model 17 (6-inch bbl.) . . . . NiB $595 Ex $430 Gd $315
Model 17 (8.38-inch bbl.) . . . . NiB $795 Ex $520 Gd $455
W/target options TH & TT, add $35

MODEL 19 .357 COMBAT MAGNUM DA REVOLVER

Caliber: .357 Magnum. Six-round cylinder, bbl. lengths: 2.5 (round butt), 4, or 6 inches, 9.5 inches overall (with 4-inch bbl.). Weight: 35 oz. (with 4-inch bbl.). Click adj. rear sight, ramp front. Blued or nickel finish. Target grips of checkered Goncalo Alves. Made from 1956 to date (2.5- and 6-inch bbls. were disc. in 1991).

Model 19 (2.5-inch bbl.) . . . . NiB $550 Ex $385 Gd $295
Model 19 (4-inch bbl.) . . . . NiB $550 Ex $385 Gd $295
Model 19 (6-inch bbl.) . . . . NiB $550 Ex $385 Gd $295
Model 19 (8.38-inch bbl.) . . . . NiB $550 Ex $385 Gd $295
W/target options TH & TT, add $60

MODEL 20 .38/.44 HEAVY DUTY DA

Caliber: .38 Special. Six-round cylinder, bbl. lengths: 4, 5 and 6.5 inches;10.38 inches overall (with 5-inch bbl.). Weight: 40 oz. (with 5-inch bbl.). Fixed sights. Blued or nickel finish. Checkered walnut grips. Short action after 1948. Made from 1930-56 and from 1957 to 67.

Pre-World War II . . . . NiB $674 Ex $546 Gd $391
Postwar . . . . NiB $441 Ex $335 Gd $195

MODEL 21 1950 .44 MILITARY DA REVOLVER

Postwar version of the 1926 Model 44 Military. Caliber: .44 Special, 6-round cylinder. Bbl. lengths: 4-, 5- and 6.5-inches. 11.75 inches overall (w/6.5-inch bbl.) Weight: 39.5 oz. (w/6.5-inch bbl.). Fixed front sight w/square-notch rear sight; target model has micrometer click rear sight adj. for windage and elevation. Checkered walnut grips w/S&W monogram. Blued or nickel finish. Made 1950 to 1967.

Model 21 (4- or 5-inch bbl.) . . . . NiB $1950 Ex $1718 Gd $765
Model 21 (6.5-inch bbl.) . . . . NiB $2250 Ex $2048 Gd $1919

MODEL .22 1950 ARMY DA . . . . . . NiB $1995 Ex $1718 Gd $765
Postwar version of the 1917 Army w/same general specifications except redesigned hammer. Made from 1950 to 1967.

.22/.32 TARGET DA REVOLVER

Also known as the "Bekeart Model." Design based upon ".32 Hand Ejector." Caliber: .22 LR (recessed head cylinder for high-speed cartridges intro. 1935). Six-round cylinder, 6-inch bbl., 10.5 inches overall. Weight: 23 oz. Adj. target sights. Blued finish. Checkered walnut grips. Made from 1911-53. Note: In 1911, San Francisco gun dealer Phil Bekeart, who suggested this model, received 292 pieces. These are the true "Bekeart Model" revolvers and are marked with separate identification numbers on the base of the wooden grip.

.22/.32 Target model . . . . NiB $825 Ex $602 Gd $479
.22/.32 Target model (early prod. 1-3000) . . . . NiB $850 Ex $675 Gd $595
.22/.32 Target model (Bekeart model). . . . . . . NiB $1204 Ex $988 Gd $293

.22/.32 KIT GUN. . . . . NiB $395 Ex $270 Gd $200
Same as .22/.32 Target except has 2- or 4-inch bbl., round grips, 6 or 8 inches overall, weight: 19-21oz. Made from 1935 to 1953.

**Smith & Wesson
Model 15**

**Smith & Wesson
Model 17 K-22**

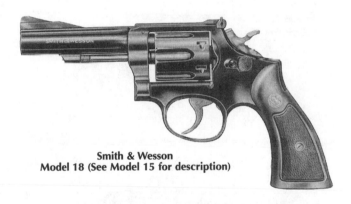

**Smith & Wesson
Model 18 (See Model 15 for description)**

**Smith & Wesson
Model 19 (Round Butt)**

Smith & Wesson
Model 19 (Square Butt)

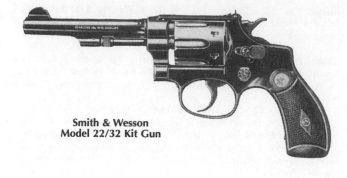

Smith & Wesson
Model 22/32 Kit Gun

Smith & Wesson
Model 20

Smith & Wesson
Model 22/32 Target Revolver

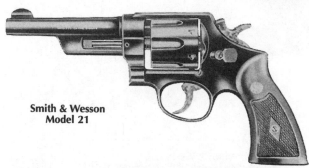

Smith & Wesson
Model 21

Smith & Wesson
Model 23

Smith & Wesson
Model 22

MODEL 23 .38/.44 OUTDOORSMAN DA REVOLVER

Target version of the .38/44 Heavy Duty. 6.5- or 8.75-inch bbl., weight: 41.75 oz. Target sights, micrometer-click rear on postwar models. Blued or nickel finish. 1950 transition model has ribbed barrel, redesigned hammer. Made from 1930 to 1967.

Prewar model (plain bbl.) .... NiB $752 Ex $639 Gd $361
Postwar (ribbed bbl.) .... NiB $886 Ex $753 Gd $419

MODEL 24 1950 .44 TARGET DA REVOLVER

Postwar version of the 1921 Model .44 with 4-, 5- or 6.5-inch ribbed bbl., redesigned hammer, micrometer click rear sight. Matte or polished blue finish. Made from 1950-67. Model 24 reintroduced in 1983 only.

Model 24 (1950)
w/4-inch bbl. .... NiB $1092 Ex $907 Gd $618
Model 24 (1950)
w/5-inch bbl. .... NiB $1099 Ex $922 Gd $634
Model 24 (1950)
w/6.5-inch bbl...................... NiB $794 Ex $660 Gd $454
Model 24 (1950) w/polished
blue finish, add 20%
Model 24 (1950)
w/nickel finish, add..................................... 50%
Model 24
.44 Target reintroduced
(7,500 produced in 1983-84)
Model 24 (w/4-inch bbl.) .... NiB $536 Ex $491 Gd $388
Model 24 (w/6.5-inch bbl.)............. NiB $475 Ex $439 Gd $346
Model 24-3 .44
Lew Horton Special (produced in 1983)
Model 24-3 (w/3-inch bbl.)............. NiB $454 Ex $388 Gd $310

MODEL 25 1955 .45 TARGET DA REVOLVER

Same as 1950 Model .44 Target, but chambered for .45 ACP, .45 Auto Rim or .45 LC w/4-, 6- or 6.5-inch bbl. Made from 1955 to 1991 in several variations. Note: In 1961, the .45 ACP was designated Model .25-2, and in 1978 the .45 LC was designated Model .25-5.

Model 25 1955 .45 Target
Model 25 (.45 ACP w/4- or 6-inch bbl.) . . . . . . NiB $700 Ex $555 Gd $395
Model 25 (.45 ACP w/6.5-inch pinned bbl.) . . . NiB $731 Ex $621 Gd $415
Model 25 (.45 LC early production) . . . . . . NiB $4200 Ex $4000 Gd $3685
Model 25-2 .45 ACP
Model 25 (w/3-inch bbl., Lew Horton Special) NiB $500 Ex $410 Gd $315
Model 25 (w/4-inch bbl.) . . . . NiB $550 Ex $460 Gd $355
Model 24-3 (w/6.5-inch bbl.) . . . . NiB $680 Ex $510 Gd $395
Model 25-5 .45 LC
Model 25 (w/4-inch bbl.) . . . . NiB $550 Ex $460 Gd $355
Model 24-3 (w/6.5-inch bbl.) . . . . NiB $600 Ex $475 Gd $325

MODEL 26 1950 .45 LIGHT TARGET DA REVOLVER

Similar to 1950 Model Target except w/lighter bbl. Note: Lighter profile was not well received. (Only 2,768 produced)
Model 26 (.45 ACP or .45 Auto Rim
w/6.5-inch bbl.) . . . . NiB $4500 Ex $4250 Gd $3938
Model 26 (.45 LC, < 200 produced) . . . . . . NiB $4500 Ex $4250 Gd $3938
W/4- or 5-inch bbl., ... $40

MODEL 27 .357 MAGNUM DA

Caliber: .357 Magnum. Six-round cylinder, bbl. lengths: 3.5-, 4-, 5-, 6-, 6.5-and 8.38-inches, 11.38 inches overall (with 6-inch bbl.). Weight: 44 oz. (with 6-inch bbl.). Adj. target sights, Baughman quick-draw ramp front sight on 3.5-inch bbl., Blued or nickel finish. Checkered walnut grips. Made from 1935-94. Note: Until 1938, the .357 Magnum was custom made in any barrel length from 3.5-inch to 8.75-inch. Each of these revolvers was accompanied by a registration certificate and has its registration number stamped on the inside of the yoke. Postwar magnums have a redesigned hammer w/shortened fall and the new S&W micrometer click rear sight.
Prewar registered model
(Reg number on yoke) . . . . NiB $850 Ex $710 Gd $580
Prewar model without registration number . . . NiB $700 Ex $610 Gd $525
Early model w/pinned bbl., recessed cyl. . . . . . . NiB $850 Ex $710 Gd $580
Late model w/8.38-inch bbl. . . . . NiB $850 Ex $710 Gd $580
Late model, w/3.5-5-inch bbl. . . . . NiB $850 Ex $710 Gd $580
Late model, other bbl. lengths. . . . . NiB $860 Ex $720 Gd $590

MODEL 28 HIGHWAY PATROLMAN

Caliber: .357 Magnum. Six-round cylinder, bbl. lengths: 4- or 6-inches, 11.25 inches overall (with 6-inch bbl.). Weight: 44 oz. (with 6-inch bbl.). Adj.rear sight, ramp front. Blued finish. Checkered walnut grips, Magna or target type. Made from 1954 to 1986.
Prewar registered model
(reg number on yoke) . . . . NiB $850 Ex $710 Gd $580
Prewar model without registration number . . NiB $1150 Ex $945 Gd $675
Early model w/pinned bbl.,
recessed cylinder, 5-screws . . . . NiB $850 Ex $710 Gd $580
Late model, all bbl. lengths . . . . NiB $495 Ex $320 Gd $210

MODEL 29 .44 MAGNUM DA REVOLVER

Caliber: .44 Magnum. Six-round cylinder. bbl., lengths: 4-, 5-, 6.5-, 8.38-inches. 11.88 inches overall (with 6.5-inch bbl.). Weight: 47 oz. (with 6.5-inch bbl.). Click adj. rear sight, ramp front. Blued or nickel finish. Checkered Goncalo Alves target grips. Made from 1956 to 1998. Early Production Standard Series (disc. 1983)
3-Screw model (1962-83) . . . . NiB $550 Ex $425 Gd $350
4-Screw model (1957-61) . . . . NiB $800 Ex $650 Gd $495
5-Screw model (1956-57) . . . . NiB $3455 Ex $2804 Gd $2565
W/5-inch bbl., 3- or 4-screw models, add 95%

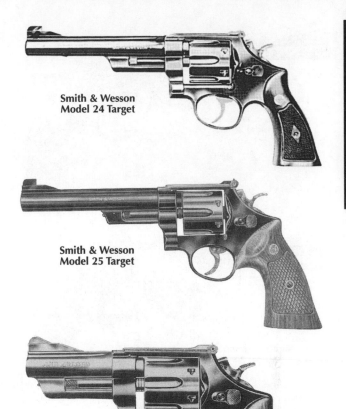

Smith & Wesson
Model 24 Target

Smith & Wesson
Model 25 Target

Smith & Wesson
Model 27

Smith & Wesson
Model 28

Late Production standard series (disc. 1998)
Model 29 (w/4- or 6.5-inch bbl.) . . . . NiB $550 Ex $410 Gd $305
Model 29 (w/3-inch bbl., Lew Horton Special) . . NiB $550 Ex $410 Gd $305
Model 29 (w/8.38-inch bbl.) . . . . NiB $550 Ex $410 Gd $305
Model 29 Classic (w/5- or 6.5-inch bbl.) . . . . . NiB $550 Ex $410 Gd $305
Model 29 Classic (w/8.38-inch bbl.) . . . . NiB $550 Ex $410 Gd $305
Model 29 Classic DX (w/6.5-inch bbl.) . . . . NiB $750 Ex $600 Gd $345
Model 29 Classic DX (w/8.38-inch bbl.) . . . . . NiB $750 Ex $600 Gd $345
Model 29 Magna Classic
(w/7.5-inch ported bbl.) . . . . NiB $900 Ex $795 Gd $480
Model 29 Silhouette (w/10.63-inch bbl.) . . . . . NiB $650 Ex $495 Gd $375

Smith & Wesson
Model 29

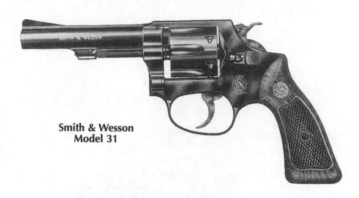

Smith & Wesson
Model 31

Smith & Wesson
Model 32

Smith & Wesson
Model 34

MODEL 30 .32 HAND
EJECTOR DA REVOLVER . . . . **NiB $495 Ex $3155 Gd $215**
Caliber: .32 S&W Long. Six-round cylinder, bbl. lengths: 2-
(intro. 1949), 3-, 4- and 6-inches, 8 inches overall (with 4-inch
bbl.). Weight: 18 oz. (with 4-inch bbl.). Fixed sights. Blued or
nickel finish. Round, checkered walnut or hard rubber grips.
Made from 1903-76.

MODELS 31 & 33 REGULATION POLICE DA REVOLVER
Same basic type as .32 Hand Ejector except has square
buttgrips. Calibers: .32 S&W Long (Model 31) .38 S&W (Model
33). Six-round cylinder in .32 cal., 5-round in .38 caliber. Bbl.,
lengths: 2- (intro. 1949), 3-, 4- and 6-inches in .32 cal., 4-inch
only in .38 cal., 8.5 inches overall (with 4-inch bbl.). Weight:
18 oz. (.38 cal. w/4-inch bbl.), 18.75 oz. (.32 cal. w/4-inch
bbl.). Fixed sights. Blued or nickel finish. Checkered walnut
grips. Made from 1917. Model 33 disc. in 1974; Model 31
disc. in 1992.
Model 31 . . . . **NiB $495 Ex $280 Gd $215**
Model 33 . . . . **NiB $400 Ex $250 Gd $175**

32 DOUBLE-ACTION
REVOLVER . . . . **NiB $489 Ex $432 Gd $190**
Hinged frame. Caliber: .32 S&W. Five-round cylinder, bbl. lengths: 3-
, 3.5- and 6-inches. Fixed sights. Blued or nickel finish. Hard rubber grips. Made from 1880-1919. Note: Value shown applies generally to the several varieties. Exception is the rare first issue of
1880 (identified by squared sideplate and serial no. 1 to 30) valued
up to $2,500.

MODEL 32 TERRIER DA . . . . NiB $450 Ex $300 Gd $210
Caliber: .38 S&W. Five-round cylinder, 2-inch bbl., 6.25 inches
overall. Weight: 17 oz. Fixed sights. Blued or nickel finish.
Checkered walnut or hard rubber grips. Built on .32 Hand Ejector
frame. Made from 1936-74.

.32-20 MILITARY & POLICE DA
. . . .**NiB $2800 Ex $2675 Gd $2475**
Same as M & P 38 except chambered for .32-20 Winchester car-
tridge. First intro. in the 1899 model, M & P revolvers were produced in this caliber until about 1940. Values same as M & P
.38 models.

MODEL 34 1953
.22/.32 KIT GUN. . . . . **NiB $495 Ex $375 Gd $270**
Same general specifications as previous .22/.32 Kit Gun except w/2-
inch or 4-inch bbl. and round or square grips, blued or nickel finish. Made from 1936-91.

MODEL 35 1953
.22/.32 TARGET. . . . . **NiB $725 Ex $550 Gd $325**
Same general specifications as previous model .22/.32 Target except
has micrometer-click rear sight. Magna type target grips. Weight: 25
oz. Made from 1953-74.

MODEL 36 CHIEFS SPECIAL DA
Based on .32 Hand Ejector w/frame lengthened to permit
longer cylinder for .38 Special cartridge. Caliber: .38 Special.
Five-round cylinder, bbl. lengths: 2- or 3-inches, 6.5 inches
overall (with 2-inch bbl.). Weight: 19 oz. Fixed sights. Blued or
nickel finish. Checkered walnut grips, round or square butt.
Made from 1952 to date.
Blued model . . . . **NiB $590 Ex $375 Gd $225**
Nickel model . . . . **NiB $615 Ex $400 Gd $250**
Early model (5-screw, small trigger guard, SN 1-2500)
. . . . **NiB $625 Ex $500 Gd $355**

MODEL 37 AIRWEIGHT

CHIEFS SPECIAL . . . . **NiB $450 Ex $325 Gd $200**
Same general specifications as standard Chiefs Special except has light alloy frame, weight: 12.5 oz. w/2-inch bbl., blued finish only. Made from 1954 to 1995

MODEL 38 BODYGUARD AIRWEIGHT DA REVOLVER

Shrouded hammer. Light alloy frame. Caliber: .38 Special. Five-round cylinder, 2- or 3-inch bbl., 6.38 inches overall (w/2-inch bbl). Weight: 14.5 oz. Fixed sights. Blued or nickel finish. Checkered walnut grips. Made from 1955 to 1998.
Blued model . . . . **NiB $450 Ex $310 Gd $215**
Nickel model . . . . **NiB $465 Ex $325 Gd $230**
Early model (pinned &
recessed, pre-1981) . . . . **NiB $450 Ex $310 Gd $215**

.38 DA REVOLVER . . . . **NiB $900 Ex $675 Gd $500**
Hinged frame. Caliber: .38 S&W. Five-round cylinder, bbl. lengths: 4-, 4.25-, 5-, 6-, 8- and 10-inch. Fixed sights. Blued or nickel finish. Hard rubber grips. Made from 1880-1911. Note: Value shown applies generally to the several varieties. Exceptions are the first issue of 1880 (identified by squared sideplate and serial no. 1 to 4,000) and the 8- and 10-inch bbl. models of the third issue (1884 to 1995).

MODEL .38 HAND EJECTOR DA

Military & Police — First Model. Resembles Colt New Navy in general appearance, lacks bbl., lug and locking bolt common to all later S&W hand ejector models. Caliber: .38 Long Colt. Six-round cylinder, bbl. lengths: 4-, 5-, 6- and 6.5-inch, 11.5 inches overall (with 6.5-inch bbl.). Fixed sights. Blued or nickel finish. Round, checkered walnut or hard rubber grips. Made from 1899 to 1902.
Standard model
(civilian issue) . . . . **NiB $1475 Ex $1290 Gd $1095**
Army Model (marked U.S.
Army Model, 1000 issued) . . . . **NiB $3600 Ex $3350 Gd $2895**
Navy Model (marked USN,
1000 issued) . . . . **NiB $4425 Ex $3721 Gd $3317**

.38 MILITARY &

POLICE TARGET DA . . . . **NiB $3677 Ex $3355 Gd $2695**
Target version of the Military & Police w/standard features of that model. Caliber: .38 Special, six-inch bbl. Weight: 32.25 oz. Adj. target sights. Blued finish. Checkered walnut grips. Made from 1899 to1940. For values, add $175 for corresponding M&P 38 models.

MODEL .38 PERFECTED DA . . . . NiB $1400 Ex $1264 Gd 1125

Hinged frame. Similar to earlier .38 DA Model but heavier frame, side latch as in solid-frame models, improved lockwork. Caliber: .38 S&W. Five-round cylinder, bbl. lengths: 3.25, 4, 5 and 6 inches. Fixed sights. Blued or nickel finish. Hard rubber grips. Made 1909 to 1920.

MODEL 40 CENTENNIAL

DA HAMMERLESS REVOLVER . . . . **NiB $645 Ex $495 Gd $320**
Similar to Chiefs Special but has Safety Hammerless-type mechanism w/grip safety. Two-inch bbl. Weight: 19 oz. Made from 1953 to 1974.

MODEL 42 CENTENNIAL AIRWEIGHT

Same as standard Centennial model except has light alloy frame, weight: 13 oz. Made from 1954 to 1974.
Blued model . . . . **NiB $595 Ex $400 Gd $310**
Nickel model . . . . **NiB $1250 Ex $1062 Gd $850**

MODEL 43 1955 .22/.32

KIT GUN AIRWEIGHT . . . . **NiB $500 Ex $400 Gd $235**
Same as Model 34 Kit Gun except has light alloy frame, square grip. Furnished w/3.5-inch bbl., weight: 14.25 oz. Made 1954 to 1974.

Smith & Wesson
Model 36

Smith & Wesson
Model 37

Smith & Wesson
Model 38 Bodyguard Airweight

MODEL 44 1926 MILITARY DA REVOLVER

Same as the early New Century model with extractor rod casing but lacking the "Triple Lock" feature. Caliber: .44 S&W Special. Six-round cylinder, bbl. lengths: 4, 5 and 6.5 inches, 11.75 inches overall (with 6.5-inch bbl.). Weight: 39.5 oz. (with 6.5-inch bbl.). Fixed sights. Blued or nickel finish. Checkered walnut grips. Made 1926 to 1941.
Standard model . . . . **NiB $3675 Ex $3375 Gd $3095**
Target model w/6.5-inch bbl.,
target sights, blued . . . . **NiB $3675 Ex $3375 Gd $3095**

.38 AND 44 DA REVOLVERS

Also called Wesson Favorite (lightweight model), Frontier (caliber .44-40). Hinged frame. Six-round cylinder. Calibers: .44 S&W Russian, .38-40, .44-40. Bbl. lengths: 4-, 5-, 6- and 6.5-inch. Weight: 37.5 oz. (with 6.5-inch bbl.). Fixed sights. Blued or nickel finish. Hard rubber grips. Made from 1881 to 1913, Frontier disc. 1910.
Standard model, .44 Russian . . **NiB $1900 Ex $1775 Gd $1455**
Standard model, .38-40 . . . . **NiB $1900 Ex $1775 Gd $1455**
Frontier model . . . . **NiB $2500 Ex $2158 Gd $1901**
Favorite model . . . . **NiB $10,375 Ex $8260 Gd $2884**

**Smith & Wesson
Model 48**

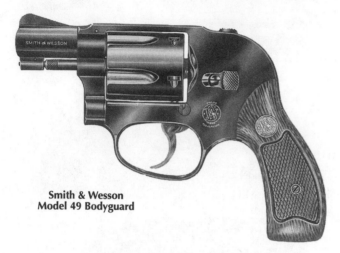

**Smith & Wesson
Model 49 Bodyguard**

**Smith & Wesson
Model 57**

**Smith & Wesson
Model 60**

**Smith & Wesson
Model 63**

**Smith & Wesson
Model 64**

.44 HAND EJECTOR MODEL DA REVOLVER

First Model, New Century, also called "Triple Lock" because of its third cylinder lock at the crane. Six-round cylinder. Calibers: .44 S&W Special, .450 Eley, .455 Mark II. Bbl. lengths: 4-, 5-, 6.5- and 7.5-inch. Weight: 39 oz. (with 6.5-inch bbl.). Fixed sights. Blued or nickel finish. Checkered walnut grips. Made 1907 to 1966.

Second Model is basically the same as New Century except crane lock ("Triple Lock" feature) and extractor rod casing eliminated. Calibers: .44 S&W Special .44-40 Win. .45 Colt. Bbl. lengths: 4-, 5-, 6.5- and 7.5-inch; 11.75 inches overall (with 6.5-inch bbl.). Weight: 38 oz. (with 6.5-inch bbl.). Fixed sights. Blued or nickel finish. Checkered walnut grips. Made from 1915 to 1937.

First Model series w/triple lock (1907-15)
Standard model,
.44 S&W Special . . . . NiB $4655 Ex $4290 Gd $3995
Standard model w/
special calibers . . . . NiB $2750 Ex $2455 Gd $2200
British 455
Target model . . . . NiB $3441 Ex $3173 Gd $994
Second Model series w/o triple lock (1915-37)
Standard model,
.44 S&W Special . . . . NiB $2375 Ex $2054 Gd $1819
Standard model
w/special calibers . . . . NiB $5000 Ex $4075 Gd $3864

.44 HAND EJECTOR, SECOND MODEL
DA REVOLVER. . . . . NiB $2375 Ex $2095 Gd $1855
Basically the same as New Century except crane lock ("Triple Lock" feature) and extractor rod casing eliminated. Calibers: .44 S&W Special .44-40 Win. .45 Colt. Bbl. lengths: 4-, 5-, 6.5- and 7.5-inches, 11.75 inches overall (with 6.5-inch bbl.). Weight: .38 oz. (with 6.5-inch bbl.). Fixed sights. Blued or nickel finish. Checkered walnut grips. Made from 1915 to 1937.

MODEL 48 (K-.22) MASTERPIECE M.R.F. DA REVOLVER
Caliber: .22 Mag. and .22 RF. Six-round cylinder, bbl. lengths: 4, 6 and 8.38 inches, 11.13 inches overall (w/ 6-inch bbl.). Weight: 39 oz. Adj. rear sight, ramp front. Made from 1959 to 1986.

Model 48 (4- or 6-inch bbl.) . . . . NiB $815 Ex $625 Gd $445
Model 48 (8.38-inch bbl.) . . . . NiB $775 Ex $585 Gd $415
W/target options TH & TT, add $50

MODEL 49 BODYGUARD
Same as Model 38 Bodyguard Airweight except has steel frame, weight: 20.5 oz. Made from 1959 to 1996.

Blued model . . . . NiB $450 Ex $300 Gd $210
Nickel model . . . . NiB $475 Ex $325 Gd $235

MODEL 51 1960 .22/.32 KIT GUN . . . . . . NiB $500 Ex $410 Gd $275
Same as Model 34 Kit Gun except chambered for .22 WMR 3.5-inch bbl., weight: 24 oz. Made from 1960 to 1974.

MODEL 53 .22 MAGNUM DA
Caliber: .22 Rem. Jet C.F. Magnum. Six-round cylinder (inserts permit use of .22 Short, Long, or LR cartridges). Bbl. lengths: 4, 6, 8.38 inches, 11.25 inches overall (with 6-inch bbl.). Weight: 40 oz. (with 6-inch bbl.). Micrometer-click rear sight ramp front. Checkered walnut grips. Made from 1960 to 1974.

Model 53 (4- or 6-inch bbl.) . . . . . NiB $900 Ex $725 Gd $600
Model 53 (8.38-inch bbl.) . . . . NiB $990 Ex $800 Gd $665
W/target options TH & TT, add $50

MODEL 57 41 MAGNUM DA REVOLVER
Caliber: 41 Magnum. Six-round cylinder, bbl. lengths: 4-, 6-, 8.38-inch. Weight: 40 oz. (with 6-inch bbl.). Micrometer click rear sight, ramp front. Target grips of checkered Goncalo Alves. Made from 1964 to 1993.

Model 57 (w/4- or 6-inch bbl.) . . . . NiB $650 Ex $500 Gd $395
Model 57 (w/8.63-inch bbl.). . . . . NiB $680 Ex $525 Gd $425
Model 57 (w/pinned bbl., recessed cylinder), add 10%

MODEL 58 41 MILITARY
& POLICE DA REVOLVER . . . . NiB $800 Ex $675 Gd $545
Caliber: 41 Magnum. Six-round cylinder, 4-inch bbl. 9.25 inches overall. Weight: 41 oz. Fixed sights. Checkered walnut grips. Made from 1964 to 1982.

MODEL 60 STAINLESS DA
Caliber: .38 Special or .357 Magnum. Five-round cylinder, bbl. lengths: 2, 2.1 or 3 inches, 6.5 or 7.5 inches overall. Weight: 19 to 23 oz. Square-notch rear sight, ramp front. Satin finish stainless steel. Made from 1965-96 (.38 Special) and from 1996 to date (.357/.38).

.38 Special (disc. 1996) . . . . NiB $425 Ex $303 Gd $241
.357 Mag. . . . . NiB $477 Ex $349 Gd $261
Lady Smith (W/smaller grip) . . . . . . NiB $498 Ex $339 Gd $266

MODEL 63 (1977) KIT GUN DA . . . . NiB $421 Ex $297 Gd $246
Caliber: .22 LR. Six-round cylinder, 2- or 4-inch bbl., 6.5 or 8.5 inches overall. Weight: 19 to 24.5 oz. Adj. rear sight, ramp front. Stainless steel. Checkered walnut or synthetic grips.

MODEL 64 .38 M&P STAINLESS. . . . . NiB $457 Ex $318 Gd $251
Same as standard Model 10 except satin-finished stainless steel, square butt w/4-inch heavy bbl., or round butt w/2-inch bbl. Made from 1970 to date.

MODEL 65 .357 MILITARY/POLICE STAINLESS
Same as Model 13 except satin-finished stainless steel. Made 1974 to 2004.

Model 65 M&P. . . . . NiB $462 Ex $303 Gd $256
Model 65 Lady Smith (W/smaller grip) . . . . . . NiB $498 Ex $354 Gd $277

**Smith & Wesson
Model 66 Combat Magnum**

**Smith & Wesson
Model 67 Combat Masterpiece**

MODEL 66 .357 COMBAT MAGNUM STAINLESS
Same as Model 19 except satin-finished stainless steel. Made from 1971 to date.

Model 66 (2.5-inch bbl.) . . . . NiB $485 Ex $395 Gd $285
Model 66 (3-inch bbl.) . . . . NiB $475 Ex $385 Gd $275
Model 66 (4-inch bbl.) . . . . NiB $475 Ex $385 Gd $275
Model 66 (6-inch bbl.) . . . . NiB $505 Ex $425 Gd $300
W/target options TH & TT, add $48

MODEL 67 .38 COMBAT
MASTERPIECE STAINLESS . . . . NiB $565 Ex $410 Gd $295
Same as Model 15 except satin-finished stainless steel available only w/4-inch bbl. Made from 1972-88 and from 1991 to 1998.

MODEL 68 .38 COMBAT
MASTERPIECE STAINLESS . . . . NiB $750 Ex $625 Gd $575
Same as Model 66 except w/4- or 6-inch bbl., chambered for .38 Special. Made to accommodate CA Highway Patrol because they were not authorized to carry .357 magnums. Made from 1976 yo 1983. (7,500 produced)

125th Anniversary Commemorative
Issued to celebrate the 125th anniversary of the 1852 partnership of Horace Smith and Daniel Baird Wesson. Standard Edition is a Model 25 revolver in .45 Colt w/6.5-inch bbl., bright blued finish, gold-filled bbl., roll mark "Smith & Wesson 125th Anniversary," sideplate marked w/gold-filled Anniversary seal, smooth Goncalo Alves grips, in presentation case w/nickel silver Anniversary medallion and book, "125 Years w/Smith & Wesson," by Roy Jinks. Deluxe Edition is same except revolver is Class A engraved w/gold-filled seal on sideplate, ivory grips, Anniversary medallion is sterling silver and book is leather bound. Limited to 50 units. Total issue is 10,000 units, of which 50 are Deluxe Edition and two are a Custom Deluxe Edition and not for sale. Made in 1977.

Standard edition . . . . NiB $595 Ex $355 Gd $275
Deluxe edition. . . . . NiB $2500 Ex $2300 Gd $1995

Smith & Wesson
Model 629 Classic

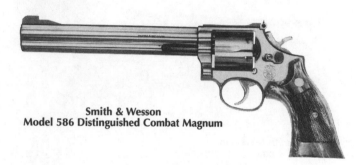

Smith & Wesson
Model 586 Distinguished Combat Magnum

Smith & Wesson
Model 625

Smith & Wesson
Model 629

317 AIRLITE DA REVOLVER

Caliber: .22 LR. Eight-round cylinder, 1.88- or 3-inch bbl., 6.3 or 7.2 inches overall. Weight: 9.9 oz. or 11 oz. Ramp front sight, notched frame rear. Aluminum, carbon fiber, stainless and titanium construction. Brushed aluminum finish. Synthetic or Dymondwood grips. Made from 1997 to date.

Model 317
(w/1.88-inch bbl.) . . . . **NiB $565 Ex $358 Gd $276**
Model 317
(w/3-inch bbl.) . . . . **NiB $630 Ex $425 Gd $335**
Model 317
(w/Dymondwood grips), add. **$75**

MODEL 520

DA REVOLVER. . . . . **NiB $495 Ex $375 Gd $295**
Caliber: .357 Mag. Six-round cylinder. N-Frame w/4-inch bbl. Weight: 40 oz. Fixed sights. In 1980, 3000 pieces were made for the N.Y. State Police but that agency did not purchase those firearms. so they werte sold commercially.

MODEL 547

DA REVOLVER. . . . . **NiB $775 Ex $665 Gd $415**
Caliber: 9mm. Six-round cylinder, bbl. length: 3 or 4 inches, 7.31 inches overall. Weight: 32 oz. Square-notch rear sight, ramp front. Disc. 1986.

MODEL 581 REVOLVER

Caliber: .357 Magnum. Bbl. lengths: 4 inches, weight: 34 oz. Serrated ramp front sight, square notch rear. Checkered walnut grips. Made from 1985 to 1992.
Blued finish. . . . . **NiB $600 Ex $450 Gd $325**
Nickel finish . . . . **NiB $665 Ex $495 Gd $365**

MODEL 586
DISTINGUISHED COMBAT MAGNUM

Caliber: .357 Magnum. Six-round cylinder, bbl. lengths: 4, 6 and 8.38 inches, overall length: 9.75 inches (with 4-inch bbl.). Weight: 42, 46, 53 oz., respectively. Red ramp front sight, micrometer-click adj. rear. Checkered grip. Blued or nickel finish. Made 1980 to 1999.
Model 586
(w/4- or 6-inch bbl.) . . . . **NiB $650 Ex $455 Gd $325**
Model 586
(w/8.63-inch bbl.) . . . . **NiB $675 Ex $475 Gd $345**
Model 586 (w/adjustable
front sight), add. **$35**
Model 586
(w/nickel finish), add. **$45**

MODEL 610 DA REVOLVER . . . . . . NiB $725 Ex $575 Gd $465
Similar to Model 625 except in caliber 10mm. Magna classic grips. Made from 1990 to 1991 and from 1998 to 2004.

MODEL 617 DA REVOLVER

Similar to Model 17 except in stainless. Made from 1990 to date.
Semi-target model w/4- or 6-inch bbl. . . . .**NiB $615 Ex $475 Gd $325**
Target model w/6-inch bbl. . . . .**NiB $615 Ex $475 Gd $325**
Target model w/8.38-inch bbl. . . . .**NiB $615 Ex $475 Gd $325**
W/10-round cylinder, add. **$100**

MODEL 624 DOUBLE-ACTION REVOLVER

Same general specifications as Model 24 except satin finished stainless steel. Limited production of 10,000. Made from 1986 to 1987.
Model 624 w/4-inch bbl. . . . .**NiB $475 Ex $300 Gd $275**
Model 624 w/6 1/2--inch bbl) . . . . **NiB $490 Ex $315 Gd $290**

**Smith & Wesson
Model 642 Centennial Airweight**

**Smith & Wesson
Model 640**

MODEL 625 DA REVOLVER . . . . . . NiB $840 Ex $695 Gd $550
Same general specifications as Model 25 except 3-, 4- or 5-inch bbl., round-butt Pachmayr grips and satin stainless steel finish. Made 1989 to 20087.

MODEL 627 DA REVOLVER . . . . . . NiB $700 Ex $395 Gd $285
Same general specifications as Model 27 except satin stainless steel finish. Made from 1989 to 1991.

MODEL 629 DA REVOLVER
Same as Model 29 in .44 Magnum except in stainless steel. Classic made from 1990 to date.

Model 629 (3-inch bbl., Backpacker)	NiB $745	Ex $545	Gd $390
Model 629 (4- and 6-inch bbl.)	NiB $745	Ex $545	Gd $390
Model 629 (8.38-inch bbl.)	NiB $745	Ex $525	Gd $400
Model 629 Classic (5- and 6.5-inch bbl.) . .	NiB $795	Ex $545	Gd $410
Model 629 Classic (8.38-inch bbl.)	NiB $650	Ex $545	Gd $430
Model 629 Classic DX (6.5-inch bbl.)	NiB $650	Ex $545	Gd $430
Model 629 Classic DX (8.38-inch bbl.) . . .	NiB $650	Ex $545	Gd $430
Model 629 Magna Classic	NiB $900	Ex $625	Gd $495

MODEL 631 DA REVOLVER
Similar to Model 31 except chambered for .32 H&R Mag. Goncalo Alves combat grips. Made in 1991 to 1992.

Fixed sights, 2-inch bbl.	NiB $500	Ex $323	Gd $246
Adjustable sights, 4-inch bbl.	NiB $500	Ex $323	Gd $246
Lady Smith, 2-inch bbl.	NiB $500	Ex $323	Gd $246
Lady Smith, 2-inch bbl. (black stainless). . .	NiB $500	Ex $323	Gd $246

MODEL 632 CENTENNIAL DA
Same general specifications as Model 640 except chambered for .32 H&R Mag. 2- or 3-inch bbl., weight: 15.5 oz. Stainless slide w/alloy frame. Fixed sights. Santoprene combat grips. Made 1991 to 1992.

Model 632 w/2-inch bbl.	NiB $650	Ex $375	Gd $285
Model 632 w/3-inch bbl.	NiB $745	Ex $455	Gd $390

MODEL 637 CHIEFS
SPECIAL AIRWEIGHT DA . . . . NiB $445 Ex $325 Gd $255
Same general specifications as Model 37 except w/clear anodized fuse alloy frame and stainless cylinder. 560 made in 1991 and reintroduced in 1996.

MODEL 638 BODYGUARD
AIRWEIGHT DA . . . . NiB $445 Ex $335 Gd $285
Same general specifications as Model .38 except w/clear anodized fuse alloy frame and stainless cylinder. 1,200 made in 1990 and reintroduced in 1998.

MODEL 640 CENTENNIAL DA . . . . NiB $590 Ex $350 Gd $285
Caliber: .38 Special. Five-round cylinder, 2, 2.1 or 3-inch bbl., 6.31 inches overall. Weight: 20-22 oz. Fixed sights. Stainless finish. Smooth hardwood service grips. Made from 1990 to date.

MODEL 642 CENTENNIAL
AIRWEIGHT DA REVOLVER
Same general specifications as Model 640 except w/stainless steel/aluminum alloy frame and finish. Weight 15.8 oz. Santoprene combat grips. Made from 1990-93 and reintroduced 1996.

Model 642 Centennial.	NiB $445	Ex $340	Gd $265
Model 642 Lady Smith (W/smaller grip)	NiB $595	Ex $440	Gd $365

MODEL 648
DA REVOLVER. . . . . NiB $450 Ex $300 Gd $220
Same general specifications as Models 17/617 except in stainless and chambered for .22 Mag. Made from 1990 to 1993.

MODEL 649
BODYGUARD DA. . . . . NiB $590 Ex $355 Gd $240
Caliber: .38 Special. Five-round cylinder, bbl. length: 2 inches, 6.25 inches overall. Weight: 20 oz. Square-notch rear sight ramp front. Stainless frame and finish. Made from 1986 to date.

MODEL 650
REVOLVER. . . . . NiB $495 Ex $315 Gd $245
Caliber: .22 Mag. Six-round cylinder, 3-inch bbl., 7 inches overall. Weight: 23.5 oz. Serrated ramp front sight, fixed square-notch rear. Round butt, checkered walnut monogrammed grips. Stainless steel finish. Made from 1983 to 1986.

**Smith & Wesson
Model 696**

**Smith & Wesson
Model K-22 Outdoorsman**

**Smith & Wesson
Lady Smith First Model**

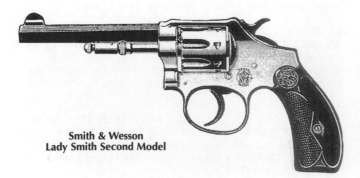

**Smith & Wesson
Lady Smith Second Model**

MODEL 651 STAINLESS DA

Caliber: .22 Mag. Rimfire. Six-round cylinder, bbl. length: 3 and 4 inches, 7 and 8.63 inches, respectively, overall. Weight: 24.5 oz. Adj. rear sight, ramp front. Made from 1983 to 1987 and from 1990 to 1998. Note: .22 LR cylinder available during early production.

Model 651 w/3- or 4-inch bbl. . . . . NiB $500 Ex $345 Gd $230
Model 651 w/extra cylinder . . . . . . NiB $825 Ex $650 Gd $575

MODEL 657 REVOLVER

Caliber: 41 Mag. Six-round cylinder. Bbl. lengths: 4, 6 or 8.4 inches; 9.6, 11.4, and 13.9 inches overall. Weight: 44.2, 48 and 52.5 oz. Serrated black ramp front sight on ramp base click rear, adj. for windage and elevation. Satin finished stainless steel. Made from 1986 to 2008.

W/4- or 6-inch bbl. . . . . NiB $550 Ex $400 Gd $355
W/8.4-inch bbl. . . . . NiB $850 Ex $443 Gd $356

MODEL 681 DSM. . . . . NiB $425 Ex $295 Gd $235
Same as S&W Model 581 except in stainless finish only. Made 1991 to 1993.

MODEL 686

Same as S&W Model 586 Distinguished Combat Magnum except in stainless finish w/additional 2.5-inch bbl. Made from 1991 to date.

Model 686 (w/2.5-inch bbl.) . . . . NiB $615 Ex $400 Gd $310
Model 686 (w/4- or 6-inch bbl.) . . . . NiB $615 Ex $400 Gd $310
Model 686 (w/8.63-inch bbl.) . . . . NiB $615 Ex $400 Gd $310
**Model 686 (w/adjustable
front sight), add.** $35

MODEL 686 PLUS

Same as standard Model 686 Magnum except w/7-round cylinder and 2.5-, 4- or 6-inch bbl. Made from 1996 to date.

Model 686 (w/2.5-inch bbl.) . . . . NiB $655 Ex $580 Gd $395
Model 686 Plus (w/4-inch bbl.) . . . . NiB $650 Ex $570 Gd $385
Model 686 Plus (w/6-inch bbl.) . . . . NiB $655 Ex $580 Gd $395

MODEL 696 . . . . NiB $485 Ex $355 Gd $270
Caliber: .44 S&W Special. L-Frame w/five-round cylinder, 3-inch shrouded bbl., 8.38 inches overall. Weight: 48 oz. Red ramp front sight, micrometer-click adj. rear. Checkered synthetic grip. Satin stainless steel. Made from 1997 to 2002.

MODEL 940 CENTENNIAL DA . . . . NiB $450 Ex $330 Gd $265
Same general specifications as Model 640 except chambered for 9mm. Two- or 3-inch bbl., Weight: 23-25 oz. Santoprene combat grips. Made from 1991 to 1998.

MODEL 1891 SA REVOLVER

Hinged frame. Caliber: .38 S&W. Five-round cylinder, bbl. lengths: 3.25, 4, 5 and 6-inches. Fixed sights. Blued or nickel finish. Hard rubber grips. Made 1891-1911. Note: Until 1906, an accessory single-shot target bbl. (see Model 1891 Single-Shot Target Pistol) was available for this revolver.

Revolver only. . . . . NiB $2695 Ex $2390 Gd $2100
Set w/.22 single-shot bbl. . . . . . . NiB $5250 Ex $4170 Gd $3655

1917 ARMY DA REVOLVER

Caliber: .45 Automatic, using 3-cartridge half-moon clip or .45 Auto Rim, without clip. Six-round cylinder, 5.5-inch bbl., 10.75 inches overall. Weight: 36.25 oz. Fixed sights. Blued finish (blue-black finish on commercial model, brush polish on military). Checkered walnut grips (commercial model, smooth on military). Made under U.S. Government contract 1917-19 and produced commercially 1919-1941. Note: About 175,000 of these revolvers were produced during WW I. The DCM sold these to NRA members during the 1930s at $16.15 each.

Commercial model . . . . NiB $850 Ex $605 Gd $550
Military model. . . . . NiB $975 Ex $775 Gd $60

K-22 MASTERPIECE DA . . . . NiB $4650 Ex $4351 Gd $3688
Improved version of K-22 Outdoorsman w/same specifications but w/micrometer-click rear sight, short action and antibacklash trigger. Fewer than 1,100 manufactured in 1940.

K-22 OUTDOORSMAN DA. . . . NiB $2055 Ex $1858 Gd $1337
Design based on the .38 Military & Police Target. Caliber: .22 LR. Six-round cylinder, 11.13 inches overall. Weight: 35 oz. Adj. target sights. Blued finish. Checkered walnut grip. Made 1931 to 1940.

K32 AND K38 HEAVY MASTERPIECES
Same as K32 and K38 Masterpiece but w/heavy bbl. Weight: 38.5 oz. Made 1950-53. Note: All K32 and K38 revolvers made after September 1953 have heavy bbls. and the "Heavy Masterpiece" designation was disc. Values for Heavy Masterpiece models are the same as shown for Models 14 and 16. (See separate listing).

K-32 TARGET DA REVOLVER . . . . NiB $1350 Ex $1195 Gd $844
Same as .38 Military & Police Target except chambered for .32 S&W Long cartridge, slightly heavier bbl., weight: 34 oz. Only 98 produced. Made from 1938 to 1940.

LADY SMITH (MODEL M HAND EJECTOR) DA REVOLVER
Caliber: .22 LR. Seven-round cylinder, bbl. length: 2.25-, 3-, 3.5- and 6-inch (Third Model only), approximately 7 inches overall w/3.5-inch bbl., weight: About 9.5 oz. Fixed sights, adj. target sights available on Third Model. Blued or nickel finish. Round butt, hard rubber grips on First and Second models; checkered walnut or hard rubber square buttgrips on Third Model. First Model —1902-06: Cylinder locking bolt operated by button on left side of frame, no bbl., lug and front locking bolt. Second Model —1906-11: Rear cylinder latch eliminated, has bbl. lug, forward cylinder lock w/draw-bolt fastening. Third Model —1911-21: Same as Second Model except has square grips, target sights and 6-inch bbl. available. Note: Legend has it that a straight laced D.B. Wesson ordered discontinuance of the Lady Smith when he learned of the little revolver's reputed popularity w/ladies of the evening. The story, which undoubtedly has enhanced the appeal of this model to collectors, is not true: The Lady Smith was disc. because of difficulty of manufacture and high frequency of repairs.

First model . . . . NiB $3052 Ex $2014 Gd $596
Second model . . . . NiB $2200 Ex $1694 Gd $867
Third model, w/fixed sights,
2.25- or 3.5-inch bbl. . . . . NiB $2200 Ex $1684 Gd $887
Third model, w/fixed sights,
6-inch bbl. . . . . NiB $2200 Ex $1658 Gd $867
Third model, w/adj. sights,
6-inch bbl. . . . . NiB $4198 Ex $1807 Gd $887

REGULATION POLICE
DA (I FRAME) . . . . NiB $750 Ex $555 Gd $399
Calibers: .32 S&W (6-round) or .38 S&W (5-round) built on .32 Hand Ejector frames. Two-, 3-, 3.25-, 4-, 4.25- or 6-inch bbl., weight: 20-24 oz. Fixed sights. Blue or nickel finish. Checkered walnut grips. Made 1917-57. Note: After 1957 "J" Frames replaced the older "I" Frames and designations changed to Model 31 and 33 respectively.
Regulation Police, .32 S&W . . . . . . NiB $475 Ex $355 Gd $275
Regulation Police, .38 S&W . . . . . . NiB $475 Ex $355 Gd $275

REGULATION POLICE TARGET DA
Target version of the Regulation Police w/standard features of that model. Calibers: .32 S&W Long or .38 S&W. 6-inch bbl., 10.25 inches overall. Weight: 20 oz. Adjustable target sights. Blue or nickel finish. Checkered walnut grips. Made from about 1917 to 1957.
Regulation Police Target, .32 S&W . . . . . . NiB $1000 Ex $855 Gd $545
Regulation Police Target, .38 S&W . . . . . . NiB $1000 Ex $855 Gd $545

**Smith & Wesson
Regulation Police Target**

**Smith & Wesson
Safety Hammerless**

SAFETY HAMMERLESS
REVOLVER . . . . NiB $1330 Ex $1110 Gd $955
Also called New Departure Double Action. Hinged frame. Calibers: .32 S&W, .38 S&W. Five-round cylinder, bbl. lengths: 2, 3- and 3.5-inch (.32 cal.) or 2-, 3.25-, 4-, 5- and 6-inch (.38 cal.); 6.75 inches overall (.32 cal. w/3-inch bbl.) or 7.5 inches (.38 cal. w/3.25-inch bbl.). Weight: 14.25 oz. (.32 cal. w/3-inch bbl.) or 18.25 oz. (.38 cal. 2.5-inch bbl.). Fixed sights. Blued or nickel finish. Hard rubber grips. Made from 1888 to 1937 (.32 cal.); 1887 to 1941 (.38 cal. w/various minor changes.)

TEXAS RANGER
COMMEMORATIVE. . . . . NiB $595 Ex $325 Gd $250
Issued to honor the 150th anniversary of the Texas Rangers. Model 19 .357 Combat Magnum w/4-inch bbl., sideplate stamped w/Texas Ranger Commemorative Seal, smooth Goncalo Alves grips. Special Bowie knife in presentation case. 8,000 sets made in 1973. Top value is for set in new condition.

SPHINX ENGINEERING S. A. — Matten b. Interlaken, Switzerland

MODEL AT-380 DA PISTOL
Caliber: .380 ACP. 10-round magazine, 3.27- inch bbl., 6.03 inches overall. Weight: 25 oz. Stainless steel frame w/blued slide or Palladium finish. Slide latch w/ambidextrous magazine release. Imported from 1993 to 1996.
Model AT-380 two-tone
(w/blued slide) . . . . NiB $435 Ex $300 Gd $225
Model AT-380
(w/Palladium finish) . . . . NiB $510 Ex $375 Gd $300

NOTE: *The AT-88 pistol series was previously manufactured by ITM in Switzerland and imported by Action Arms before Sphinx-Muller resumed production of these firearms, now designated as the AT-2000 series.*

Springfield Armory
1911-A1 Post '90 Series Trophy Model

Springfield Armory
1911-A1 PDP Series Defender

Springfield Armory
1911-A1 Champion

Springfield Armory
1911-A1 Compact

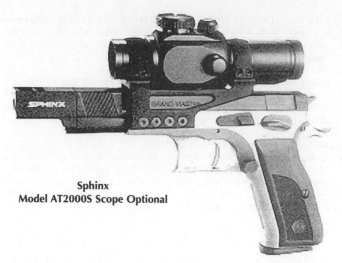

Sphinx
Model AT2000S Scope Optional

MODEL 2000S DA AUTOMATIC PISTOL

Calibers: 9mm Parabellum, .40 S&W. 15- or 11-round magazine respectively, 4.53-inch bbl., (S-standard), 3.66-inch bbl., (P-compact), 3.34-inch bbl., (H-subcompact), 8.25 inches overall. Weight: 36.5 oz. Fixed sights w/3-dot system. Stainless frame w/blued slide or Palladium finish. Ambidextrous safety. Checkered walnut or neoprene grips. Imported 1993 to 1996.

Model AT2000S (standard) . . . . NiB $965	Ex $850	Gd $544
Model AT2000P (compact) . . . . NiB $850	Ex $719	Gd $500
Model AT2000H (subcompact) . . . . NiB $850	Ex $719	Gd $500
.40 S&W, add $40		
For Palladium finish (disc. 1994) . . . . Add $90		

MODEL AT2000C/2000CS COMPETITOR

Similar to the Model AT2000S except also chambered for 9x21mm. 10-round magazine, 5.31-inch compensated bbl., 9.84 inches overall. Weight: 40.56 oz. Fully adjustable BoMar or ProPoint sights. Made 1993 to 1996.

Model 2000C (w/BoMar sight) . . . . NiB $1735	Ex $1383	Gd $950
Model 2000CS (w/ProPoint sight) . . . . Add $290		

MODEL AT2000GM/GMS GRAND MASTER

Similar to the AT2000C except single action only w/square trigger guard and extended beavertail grip. Imported 1993 to 1996.

Model 2000GM (w/BoMar sight) . . . . NiB $1795	Ex $1558	Gd $1362
Model 2000GMS (w/ProPoint sight) . . . . . . NiB $2095	Ex $1850	Gd $1625

SPRINGFIELD, INC. — Geneseo, Illinois (Formerly Springfield Armory)

MODEL M1911 SERIES AUTO PISTOL

Springfield builds the "PDP" (Personal Defense Pistol) Series based on the self-loading M 1911-A1 pistol (military specifications model) as adopted for a standard service weapon by the U.S. Army. With enhancements and modifications they produce a full line of firearms including Ultra-Compacts, Lightweights, Match Grade and Competition Models. For values see specific models.

MODEL 1911-A1 GOVERNMENT

Calibers: 9mm Para., .38 Super, .40 S&W, 10mm or .45 ACP., 7-, 8-, 9- or 10-round magazine, 4- or 5-inch bbl., 8.5 inches overall. Weight: 36 oz. Fixed combat sights. Blued, Parkerized or Duo-Tone finish. Checkered walnut grips. Note: This is an exact duplicate of the Colt M1911-A1 that was used by the U.S. Armed Forces as a service weapon.

Blued finish . . . . NiB $400	Ex $310	Gd $235
Parkerized finish . . . . NiB $400	Ex $310	Gd $235

MODEL 1911-A1 (PRE '90 SERIES)

Calibers: 9mm Parabellum, .38 Super, 10mm, .45 ACP. Seven-, 8-, 9- or 10-round magazine, bbl. length: 3.63, 4, 4.25 or 5 inches, 8.5 inches overall. Weight: 36 oz. Fixed combat sights. Blued, Duo-Tone or Parkerized finish. Checkered walnut stocks. Made 1985 to 1990.

Government model (blued)	NiB $400	Ex $325	Gd $250
Government model (Parkerized)	NiB $575	Ex $414	Gd $333
Bullseye model (wadcutter)	NiB $1415	Ex $1300	Gd $841
Combat Commander model (blued)	NiB $435	Ex $350	Gd $275
Combat Commander model (Parkerized)	NiB $610	Ex $440	Gd $327
Commander model (blued)	NiB $450	Ex $270	Gd $198
Commander model (Duo-Tone)	NiB $530	Ex $450	Gd $368
Commander model (Parkerized)	NiB $620	Ex $470	Gd $338
Compact model (blued)	NiB $450	Ex $390	Gd $295
Compact model (Duo-Tone)	NiB $530	Ex $450	Gd $384
Compact model (Parkerized)	NiB $620	Ex $470	Gd $302
Defender model (blued)	NiB $485	Ex $390	Gd $245
Defender model (Parkerized)	NiB $655	Ex $492	Gd $332
Defender model (Custom Carry)	NiB $485	Ex $390	Gd $295
National Match model (Hardball)	NiB $780	Ex $655	Gd $500
Trophy Master (Competition)	NiB $1300	Ex $1204	Gd $847
Trophy Master (Distinguished)	NiB $2000	Ex $1800	Gd $1137
Trophy Master (Expert)	NiB $1665	Ex $1463	Gd $1292

MODEL 1911-A1 (PDP SERIES)

SA linkless operating system w/steel or alloy frame. Calibers: 9mm Parabellum, .38 Super, .40 S&W, 10mm, .45 ACP. Seven-, 8-, 9- or 10-round magazine, bbl. length: 3.63, 4, 4.25 or 5 inches; 8.5 inches overall. Weight: 28 oz. to 36 oz. Fixed combat sights. Blued, Duo-Tone, Parkerized or stainless finish. Checkered composition or walnut stocks. Made from 1990 to 1998.

Mil-Spec model (blued)	NiB $595	Ex $419	Gd $333
Mil-Spec model (Parkerized)	NiB $765	Ex $595	Gd $395
Standard model (blued)	NiB $850	Ex $645	Gd $395
Standard model (Parkerized)	NiB $1020	Ex $955	Gd $775
Standard model (stainless)	NiB $735	Ex $582	Gd $455
Trophy model (blued)	NiB $1375	Ex $1200	Gd $955
Trophy model (Hi-Tone)	NiB $1385	Ex $1210	Gd $965
Trophy model (stainless)	NiB $675	Ex $550	Gd $395

MODEL 1911-A1 PDP SERIES

PDP Series (Personal Defense Pistol). Calibers: .38 Super, .40 S&W, .45 ACP. Seven-, 8-, 9-, 10-, 13- or 17-round magazine, bbl. length: 4, 5, 5.5 or 5.63 inches, 9 to 11 inches overall w/compensated bbl. Weight: 34.5 oz. to 42.8 oz. Post front sight, adjustable rear w/3-dot system. Blued, Duo-Tone, Parkerized or stainless finish. Checkered composition or walnut stocks. Made from 1991 to 1998.

Defender model (blued)	NiB $850	Ex $725	Gd $519
Defender model (Duo-Tone)	NiB $850	Ex $725	Gd $519
Defender model (Parkerized)	NiB $850	Ex $725	Gd $519
.45 ACP Champion Comp model (blued)	NiB $695	Ex $500	Gd $391
.45 ACP Compact Comp HC model (blued)	NiB $540	Ex $400	Gd $350
.380 Sup Factory Comp model (blued)	NiB $680	Ex $505	Gd $375
.45 ACP Factory Comp model (blued)	NiB $830	Ex $710	Gd $519
.380 Sup Factory Comp HC model (blued)	NiB $680	Ex $505	Gd $375
.45 ACP Factory Comp HC model (blued)	NiB $690	Ex $745	Gd $510

MODEL M1911-A1 CHAMPION

Calibers: .38 ACP, .45 ACP. Six- or 7-round magazine, 4-inch bbl.

**Springfield Armory
M1911-A1 Ultra
Compact Parkerized**

Weight: 26.5 to 33.4 oz. Low profile post front sight and drift adjustable rear w/3-dot sighting system. Commander-style hammer and slide. Checkered walnut grips. Blue, Bi-Tone, Parkerized or stainless finish. Made from 1992 to 2002.

.380 ACP standard (disc. 1995)	NiB $1615	Ex $1395	Gd $1205
.45 ACP Parkerized	NiB $1615	Ex $1395	Gd $1205
.45 ACP blued	NiB $1615	Ex $1395	Gd $1205
.45 ACP Bi-Tone (B/H Model)	NiB $788	Ex $569	Gd $360
.45 ACP stainless	NiB $788	Ex $564	Gd $461
.45 super tuned	NiB $975	Ex $620	Gd $498

MODEL M1911-A1 COMPACT

Similar to the standard M1911 w/champion length slide on a steel or alloy frame w/a shortened grip. Caliber: .45 ACP. Six- or 7-round magazine (10+ law enforcement only), 4-inch bbl. weight: 26.5 to 32 oz. Low profile sights w/3-dot system. Checkered walnut grips. Matte blue, Duo-Tone or Parkerized finish. Made 1991 to 1996.

Compact Parkerized	NiB $415	Ex $335	Gd $265
Compact blued	NiB $415	Ex $335	Gd $265
Compact Duo-Tone	NiB $530	Ex $455	Gd $385
Compact stainless	NiB $495	Ex $335	Gd $255
Compact comp (ported)	NiB $830	Ex $725	Gd $526
High capacity blue	NiB $540	Ex $345	Gd $295
High capacity stainless	NiB $775	Ex $580	Gd $400

MODEL M1911-A1 ULTRA COMPACT

Similar to M1911 Compact except chambered for .380 ACP or .45 ACP. 6- or 7-round magazine, 3.5-inch bbl., weight: 22 oz. to 30 oz. Matte Blue, Bi-Tone, Parkerized (military specs) or stainless finish. Made from 1995 to 2003.

.380 ACP Ultra (disc. 1996)	NiB $680	Ex $560	Gd $345
.45 ACP Ultra Parkerized	NiB $680	Ex $560	Gd $345
.45 ACP Ultra blued	NiB $680	Ex $560	Gd $345
.45 ACP Ultra Bi-Tone	NiB $790	Ex $670	Gd $465
.45 ACP Ultra stainless	NiB $680	Ex $560	Gd $345
.45 ACP ultra high capacity Parkerized	NiB $680	Ex $560	Gd $345
.45 ACP ultra high capacity blue	NiB $735	Ex $585	Gd $455
.45 ACP ultra high capacity stainless	NiB $735	Ex $585	Gd $455
.45 ACP V10 ultra comp Parkerized	NiB $925	Ex $755	Gd $455
.45 ACP V10 ultra comp blue	NiB $925	Ex $755	Gd $455
.45 ACP V10 ultra comp stainless	NiB $925	Ex $755	Gd $455
.45 ACP V10 ultra super tuned	NiB $1027	Ex $884	Gd $517

**Springfield Armory
M1911-A1 Ultra Compact Bi-Tone**

**Springfield Armory
P9 Combat**

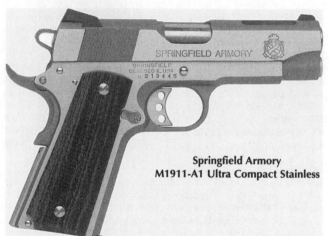

**Springfield Armory
M1911-A1 Ultra Compact Stainless**

Springfield Armory Panther

**Springfield Armory
M1911-A1 Ultra Compact
Super Tuned**

FIRECAT
AUTOMATIC PISTOL
Calibers: 9mm, .40 S&W. Eight-round magazine (9mm) or 7-round magazine (.40 S&W), 3.5-inch bbl., 6.5 inches overall. Weight: 25.75 oz. Fixed sights w/3-dot system. Checkered walnut grip. Matte blued finish. Made from 1991 to 1993.

9mm . . . . NiB $495 Ex $365 Gd $250
.40 S&W . . . . NiB $495 Ex $365 Gd $250

PANTHER
AUTO PISTOL . . . . NiB $540 Ex $410 Gd $300
Calibers: 9mm, .40 S&W. 15-round magazine (9mm) or 11-round magazine (.40 S&W), 3.8-inch bbl., 7.5 inches overall. Weight: 28.95 oz. Blade front sight, rear adj. for windage w/3-dot system. Checkered walnut grip. Matte blued finish. Made from 1991 to 1993.

MODEL P9 DA COMBAT SERIES
Calibers: 9mm, .40 S&W, .45 ACP. Magazine capacity: 15-round (9mm), 11-round (.40 S&W) or 10-round (.45 ACP), 3.66-inch bbl., (Compact and Sub-Compact), or 4.75-inch bbl., (Standard), 7.25 or 8.1 inches overall. Weight: 32 to 35 oz. Fixed sights w/3-dot system. Checkered walnut grip. Matte blued, Parkerized, stainless or Duo-Tone finish. Made from 1990 to 1994.

**Compact model (9mm,
Parkerized)** . . . . NiB $430 Ex $320 Gd $255
**Sub-Compact model (9mm,
Parkerized)** . . . . NiB $395 Ex $290 Gd $200
**Standard model (9mm,
Parkerized)** . . . . NiB $450 Ex $345 Gd $260
W/blued finish, add $25
W/Duo-Tone finish, add $80
W/stainless finish, add $90
.40 S&W, add $20
.45 ACP add $35

MODEL P9 COMPETITION SERIES

Same general specifications as Model P9 except in target config-uration w/5-inch bbl., (LSP Ultra) or 5.25-inch bbl. Factory Comp model w/dual port compensator system, extended safety and magazine release.

**Factory Comp model
(9mm Bi-Tone)** . . . . NiB $595 Ex $400 Gd $300
**Factory Comp model
(9mm stainless)** . . . . NiB $690 Ex $385 Gd $250
**IPSC Ultra model
(9mm Bi-Tone)** . . . . NiB $555 Ex $375 Gd $235
**LSP Ultra model
(9mm stainless)** . . . . NiB $675 Ex $500 Gd $350
.40 S&W, .45 ACP: add $90

STALLARD ARMS — Mansfield, Ohio
See listings under Hi-Point.

STAR PISTOLS — Eibar, Spain
Star, Bonifacio Echeverria, S.A.

MODEL 30M DA AUTO PISTOL . . . NiB $350 Ex $265 Gd $155
Caliber: 9mm Para. 15-round magazine, 4.38-inch bbl., 8 inch-es overall. Weight: 40 oz. Steel frame w/combat features. Adj. sights. Checkered composition grips. Blued finish. Made from 1984 to 1991.

MODEL 30PK DA AUTO PISTOL . . . . NiB $350 Ex $245 Gd $160
Same gen. specifications as Star Model 30M except 3.8-inch bbl., weight: 30 oz. Alloy frame. Made from 1984 to 1989.

MODEL 31P DA AUTO PISTOL
Same general specifications as Model 30M except removable back-strap houses complete firing mechanism. Weight: 39.4 oz. Made from 1990 to 1994.
Blued finish . . . . NiB $350 Ex $225 Gd $140
Starvel finish . . . . Add $30

MODEL 31 PK DA AUTO PISTOL . . . . NiB $350 Ex $225 Gd $140
Same general specifications as Model 31P except w/alloy frame. Weight: 30 oz. Made from 1990 to 1997.

MODEL A AUTOMATIC PISTOL . . . NiB $325 Ex $220 Gd $125
Modification of the Colt Government Model .45 Auto, which it closely resembles, but lacks grip safety. Caliber: .38 Super. Eight-round maga-zine, 5-inch bbl., 8 inches overall. Weight: 35 oz. Fixed sights. Blued finish. Checkered grips. Made from 1934-97. (No longer imported.)

MODELS AS, BS, PS . . . . NiB $445 Ex $340 Gd $235
Same as Models A, B and P except have magazine safety. Made in 1975.

MODEL B . . . . NiB $450 Ex $325 Gd $210
Same as Model A except in 9mm Para. Made from 1934 to 1975.

MODEL BKM . . . . NiB $350 Ex $275 Gd $190
Similar to Model BM except has aluminum frame weight: 25.6 oz. Made from 1976 to 1992.

**MODEL BKS STARLIGHT
AUTOMATIC PISTOL** . . . . NiB $351 Ex $174 Gd $189
Light alloy frame. Caliber: 9mm Para. Eight-round magazine, 4.25-inch bbl., 7 inches overall. Weight: 25 oz. Fixed sights. Blued or chrome finish. Plastic grips. Made from 1970 to 1981.

Star Model 30M

Star Model 30PK

Star Model AS

Star Model BKS

Star Model F

Star Model F Olympic Rapid-Fire

Star Model FS

MODEL BM AUTOMATIC PISTOL
Caliber: 9mm. Eight-round magazine, 3.9-inch bbl., 6.95 inches overall. Weight: 34.5 oz. Fixed sights. Checkered walnut grips. Blued or Starvel finish. Made from 1976 to 1992.
Blued finish . . . . NiB $325 Ex $254 Gd $192
Starvel finish . . . . NiB $345 Ex $275 Gd $225

MODEL CO POCKET
AUTOMATIC PISTOL . . . . NiB $275 Ex $195 Gd $100
Caliber: .25 Automatic (6.35mm), 2.75-inch bbl., 4.5 inches overall. Weight: 13 oz. Fixed sights. Blued finish. Plastic grips. Made from 1941 to 197.

MODEL CU STARLET
POCKET PISTOL . . . . NiB $250 Ex $165 Gd $100
Light alloy frame. Caliber: .25 Auto (6.35mm). Eight-round magazine, 2.38-inch bbl., 4.75 inches overall. Weight: 10.5 oz. Fixed

sights. Blued or chrome-plated slide w/frame anodized in black, blue, green, gray or gold. Plastic grips. Made from 1957 to 1997. (U.S. importation disc. 1968.)

MODEL F
AUTOMATIC PISTOL . . . . NiB $325 Ex $240 Gd $100
Caliber: .22 LR. 10-round magazine, 4.5-inch bbl., 7.5 inches overall. Weight: 25 oz. Fixed sights. Blued finish. Plastic grips. Made from 1942 to 1967.

MODEL F
OLYMPIC RAPID-FIRE . . . . NiB $500 Ex $379 Gd $170
Caliber: .22 Short. Nine-round magazine, 7-inch bbl., 11.06 inches overall. Weight: 52 oz. w/weights. Adj. target sight. Adj. 3-piece bbl. weight. Aluminum alloy slide. Muzzle brake. Plastic grips. Made from 1942 to 1967.

MODEL FM . . . . NiB $325 Ex $260 Gd $140
Similar to Model FR except has heavier frame w/web in front of trigger guard, 4.25-inch heavy bbl., Weight: 32 oz. Made from 1972 to 1991.

MODEL FR . . . . NiB $325 Ex $280 Gd $140
Similar to Model F w/same general specifications but restyled, has slide stop and adj. rear sight. Made from 1967 to 1972.

MODEL FR SPORT . . . . NiB $350 Ex $280 Gd $190
Same as Model FR except has 6-inch bbl., weight: 28 oz. Also avail. in chrome finish. Made from 1967 to 1991.

MODEL FS. . . . . NiB $325 Ex $280 Gd $140
Same as regular Model F but w/6-inch bbl. and adj. sights. Weight: 27 oz. Made from 1942 to 1967.

MODEL HK LANCER
AUTOMATIC PISTOL . . . . NiB $275 Ex $195 Gd $135
Similar to Starfire w/same general specifications except .22 LR. Made from 1955 to 1968.

MODEL HN
AUTOMATIC PISTOL . . . . NiB $375 Ex $260 Gd $195
Caliber: .380 Auto (9mm Short). Six-round magazine, 2.75-inch bbl., 5.56 inches overall. Weight: 20 oz. Fixed sights. Blued finish. Plastic grips. Made from 1934 to 1941.

MODEL H . . . . NiB $350 Ex $275 Gd $165
Same as Model HN except .32 Auto (7.65mm), 7-round magazine, weight: 20 oz. Made from 1934 to 1941.

MODEL I
AUTOMATIC PISTOL . . . . NiB $350 Ex $265 Gd $145
Caliber: .32 Auto (7.65mm). Nine-round magazine, 4.81-inch bbl., 7.5 inches overall. Weight: 24 oz. Fixed sights. Blued finish. Plastic grips. Made from 1934 to 1936.

MODEL IN. . . . . NiB $395 Ex $250 Gd $150
Same as Model I except caliber .380 Auto (9mm Short), 8-round magazine, weight: 24.5 oz. Made from 1934-36.

MODEL M MILITARY
AUTOMATIC PISTOL . . . . NiB $377 Ex $285 Gd $195
Modification of the Model M without grip safety. Calibers: 9mm Bergmann (Largo), .45 ACP, 9mm Para. Eight-round magazine except 7-shot in .45 caliber, 5-inch bbl., 8.5 inches overall. Weight: 36 oz. Fixed sights. Blued finish. Checkered grips. Made from 1934 to 1939.

MODELS M40, M43, M45 FIRESTAR AUTO PISTOLS
Calibers: 9mm, .40 S&W, .45 ACP. Seven-round magazine (9mm) or 6-round (other calibers). 3.4-inch bbl., 6.5 inches overall. Weight: 30.35 oz. Blade front sight, adj. rear w/3-dot system. Checkered rubber grips. Blued or Starvel finish. Made 1990 to 1997.

M40 blued (.40 S&W)	NiB $325	Ex $245	Gd $195
M40 Starvel (.40 S&W)	NiB $345	Ex $265	Gd $125
M43 blued (9mm)	NiB $320	Ex $240	Gd $190
M43 Starvel (9mm)	NiB $345	Ex $265	Gd $125
M45 blued (.45 ACP)	NiB $350	Ex $270	Gd $120
M45 Starvel (.45 ACP)	NiB $370	Ex $290	Gd $140

MEGASTAR AUTOMATIC PISTOL
Calibers: 10mm, .45 ACP. 12-round magazine, 4.6-inch bbl., 8.44 inches overall. Weight: 47.6 oz. Blade front sight, adj. rear. Checkered composition grip. finishes: Blued or Starvel. Made from 1992 to 1997.

Blued finish, 10mm or .45 ACP	NiB $450	Ex $345	Gd $255
Starvel finish, 10mm or .45 ACP	NiB $480	Ex $375	Gd $285

MODEL P . . . . **NiB $425 Ex $320 Gd $240**
Same as Model A except caliber .45 Auto, has 7-round magazine. Made from 1934 to 1975.

MODEL PD AUTOMATIC PISTOL
Caliber: .45 Auto. Six-round magazine, 3.75-inch bbl., 7 inches overall. Weight: 25 oz. Adj. rear sight, ramp front. Blued or Starvel finish. Checkered walnut grips. Made from 1975 to 1992.

Blued finish	NiB $345	Ex $265	Gd $200
Starvel finish	NiB $365	Ex $285	Gd $220

MODEL S . . . . **NiB $275 Ex $200 Gd $138**
Same as Model SI except caliber .380 Auto (9mm), 7-round magazine, weight: 19 oz. Made from 1941 to 1965.

MODEL SI AUTOMATIC PISTOL . . . . **NiB $275 Ex $185 Gd $100**
Reduced-size modification of the Colt Government Model .45 Auto, lacks grip safety. Caliber: .32 Auto (7.65mm). Eight-round magazine, 4-inch bbl., 6.5 inches overall. Weight: 20 oz. Fixed sights. Blued finish. Plastic grips. Made from 1941 to 1965.

STARFIRE DK AUTOMATIC PISTOL . . . . . . **NiB $400 Ex $295 Gd $200**
Light alloy frame. Caliber: .380 Automatic (9mm Short). Seven-round magazine, 3.13-inch bbl.. 5.5 inches overall. Weight: 14.5 oz. Fixed sights. Blued or chrome-plated slide w/frame anodized in black, blue, green, gray or gold. Plastic grips. Made 1957-97. U.S. importation disc. 1968.

MODEL SUPER A AUTOMATIC PISTOL . . . **NiB $460 Ex $378 Gd $200**
Caliber: .38 Super. Improved version of Model A but has disarming bolt permitting easier takedown, cartridge indicator, magazine safety, take-down magazine, improved sights w/luminous spots for aiming in darkness. This is the standard service pistol of the Spanish Armed Forces, adopted 1946.

MODEL SUPER B AUTOMATIC PISTOL
Caliber: 9mm Para. Similar to Model B except w/improvements described under Model Super A. Made 1946 to 1990.

Super blued finish	NiB $393	Ex $297	Gd $185
Starvel finish	NiB $414	Ex $320	Gd $220

MODELS SUPER M, SUPER P . . . . . **NiB $795 Ex $650 Gd $455**
Calibers: .45 ACP, 9mm Parabellum or 9mm Largo, (Super M) and 9mm Parabellum (Super P). Improved versions of the Models M & P w/same general specifications, but has disarming bolt permitting easier takedown, cartridge indicator, magazine safety, take-down magazine, improved sights w/luminous spots for aiming in darkness.

MODELS SUPER SI, SUPER S . . . . . **NiB $275 Ex $200 Gd $155**
Same general specifications as the regular Model SI and S except w/improvements described under Super Star. Made 1946 to 1972.

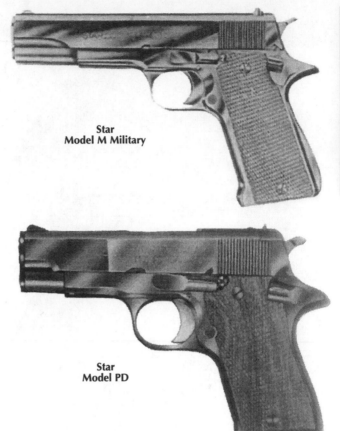

Star
Model M Military

Star
Model PD

MODEL SUPER SM . . . . **NiB $350 Ex $250 Gd $145**
Similar to Model Super S except has adj. rear sight, wood grips. Made from 1973 to 1981.

SUPER TARGET MODEL . . . . . . **NiB $1500 Ex $1345 Gd $1280**
Same as Super Star model except w/adj. target rear sight. (Disc.)

ULTRASTAR DA AUTOMATIC PISTOL . . . . **NiB $325 Ex $255 Gd $135**
Calibers: 9mm Parabellum or .40 S&W. Nine-round magazine, 3.57-inch bbl., 7 inches overall. Weight: 26 oz. Blade front, adjustable rear w/3-dot system. Polymer frame. Blue metal finish. Checkered black polymer grips. Imported from 1994 to 1997.

STENDA-WERKE PISTOL — Suhl, Germany

POCKET AUTOMATIC PISTOL . . . . **NiB $295 Ex $155 Gd $100**
Essentially the same as the Beholla (see listing of that pistol for specifications). Made circa 1920-.25. Note: This pistol may be marked "Beholla" along w/the Stenda name and address.

STERLING ARMS CORPORATION — Gasport, New York

MODEL 283 TARGET 300
AUTO PISTOL . . . . **NiB $150 Ex $100 Gd $85**
Caliber: .22 LR. 10-round magazine, bbl. lengths: 4.5-, 6- 8-inch. 9 inches overall w/4.5-inch bbl., Weight: 36 oz. w/4.52-inch bbl. Adj. sights. Blued finish. Plastic grips. Made from 1970 to 1971.

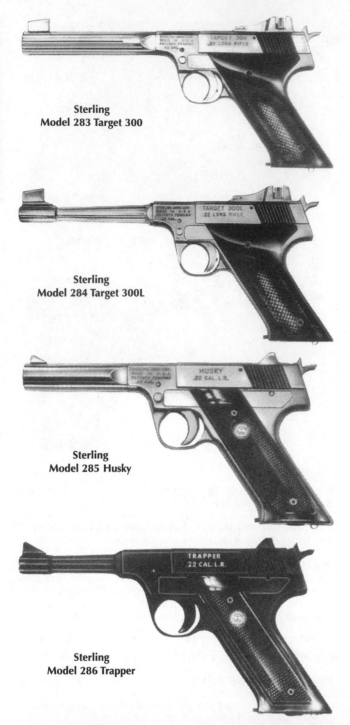

Sterling
Model 283 Target 300

Sterling
Model 284 Target 300L

Sterling
Model 285 Husky

Sterling
Model 286 Trapper

Sterling
Model 300

Sterling
Model 400

MODEL 284 TARGET 300L . . . . **NiB $150 Ex $100 Gd $90**
Same as Model 283 except has 4.5- or 6-inch Luger-type bbl. Made
from 1970 to 1971.

MODEL 285 HUSKY . . . . **NiB $150 Ex $100 Gd $90**
Same as Model 283 except has fixed sights, 4.5-inch bbl only. Made
from 1970 to 1971.

MODEL 286 TRAPPER . . . . **NiB $150 Ex $100 Gd $90**
Same as Model 284 except w/fixed sights. Made from 1970 to 1971.

MODEL 287 PPL-.380
AUTOMATIC PISTOL . . . . **NiB $150 Ex $100 Gd $90**
Caliber: .380 Auto. Six-round magazine, 1-inch bbl., 5.38 inches
overall. Weight: 22.5 oz. Fixed sights. Blued finish. Plastic grips.
Made from 1971- to 1972.

MODEL 300
AUTOMATIC PISTOL . . . . **NiB $150 Ex $90 Gd $75**
Caliber: .25 Auto. Six-round magazine, 2.33-inch bbl., 4.5 inches
overall. Weight: 13 oz. Fixed sights. Blued or nickel finish. Plastic
grips. Made from 1972 to 1983.

MODEL 300S. . . . . **NiB $150 Ex $90 Gd $75**
Same as Model 300 except in stainless steel. Made 1976 to 1983.

MODEL 302 . . . . **NiB $150 Ex $90 Gd $75**
Same as Model 300 except in .22 LR. Made from 1973 to 1983.

MODEL 302S. . . . . **NiB $150 Ex $90 Gd $75**
Same as Model 302 except in stainless steel. Made 1976 to 1983.

MODEL 400 DA
AUTOMATIC PISTOL . . . . **NiB $275 Ex $190 Gd $125**
Caliber: .380 Auto. Seven-round magazine, 3.5-inch bbl., 6.5 inch-
es overall. Weight: 24 oz. Adj. rear sight. Blued or nickel finish.
Checkered walnut grips. Made from 1975 to 1983.

MODEL 400S . . . . **NiB $275 Ex $145 Gd $100**
Same as Model 400 except stainless steel. Made from 1977 to 1983.

MODEL 450 DA
AUTO PISTOL . . . . **NiB $275 Ex $145 Gd $100**
Caliber: .45 Auto. Eight-round magazine, 4-inch bbl., 7.5 inches overall. Weight: 36 oz. Adj. rear sight. Blued finish. Smooth walnut grips. Made from 1977 to 1983.

MODEL PPL-22
AUTOMATIC PISTOL . . . . **NiB $275 Ex $145 Gd $100**
Caliber: .22 LR. 10-round magazine, 1-inch bbl., 5.5 inches overall. Weight: About 24 oz. Fixed sights. Blued finish. Wood grips. Only 382 made in 1970 to 1971.

J. STEVENS ARMS & TOOL CO. — Chicopee Falls, Massachusetts

This firm was established in Civil War era by Joshua Stevens, for whom the company was named. In 1999 Savage Arms began manufacture of Stevens designs..

NO. 10
SINGLE-SHOT
TARGET PISTOL . . . . **NiB $220 Ex $190 Gd $155**
Caliber: .22 LR. 8-inch bbl., 11.5 inches overall. Weight: 37 oz. Target sights. Blued finish. Hard rubber grips. In external appearance this arm resembles an automatic pistol but it has a tip-up action. Made from 1919 to 1939.

NO. 35
OFFHAND MODEL SINGLE-SHOT
TARGET PISTOL . . . . **NiB $350 Ex $285 Gd $235**
Tip-up action. Caliber: .22 LR. Bbl. lengths: 6, 8, 10, 12.25 inches. Weight: 24 oz. w/6-inch bbl. Target sights. Blued finish. Walnut grips. Note: This pistol is similar to the earlier "Gould" model. Made from 1907 to 1939.

OFFHAND
NO. 35 SINGLE-SHOT
PISTOL/SHOTGUN . . . . **NiB $350 Ex $285 Gd $235**
Same general specifications as the standard No. 35 pistol except chambered for the .410 shotshell. Six-, 8-, 10-, or 12-inch half-ocatagonal bbl., iron frame either blued, nickel plated, or case-hardened. BATF Class 3 license required to purchase. Made from 1923 to 1942.

NO. 36
SINGLE-SHOT PISTOL . . . . **NiB $795 Ex $522 Gd $418**
Tip-up action. Calibers: .22 Short and LR, .22 WRF, .25 Stevens, .32 Short Colt, .38 Long Colt, .44 Russian. 10- or 12-inch half-octagonal bbl., iron or brass frame w/nickel plated finish. Blued bbl. Checkered walnut grips. Made from 1880 to 1911.

NO. 37
SINGLE-SHOT PISTOL . . . . **NiB $976 Ex $787 Gd $527**
Similar specifications to the No. 38 except the finger spur on the trigger guard has been omitted. Made from 1889 to 1919.

NO. 38
SINGLE-SHOT PISTOL . . . . **NiB $498 Ex $393 Gd $225**
Tip-up action. Calibers: .22 Short and LR, .22 WRF, .25 Stevens, .32 Stevens, .32 Short Colt. Iron or brass frame. Checkered grips. Made from 1884 to 1903.

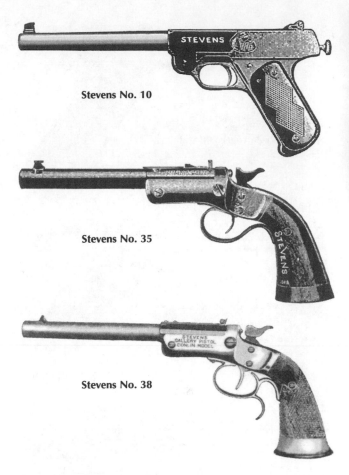

Stevens No. 10

Stevens No. 35

Stevens No. 38

NO. 41 TIP-UP
SINGLE-SHOT PISTOL . . . . **NiB $315 Ex $264 Gd $183**
Tip-up action. Caliber: .22 Short, 3.5-inch half-octagonal bbl. Blued metal parts w/optional nickel frame. Made from 1896 to1915.

STEYR PISTOLS — Steyr, Austria

GB SEMIAUTOMATIC PISTOL
Caliber: 9mm Para. 18-round magazine, 5.4-inch bbl., 8.9 inches overall. Weight: 2.9 lbs. Post front sight, fixed, notched rear. Double, gas-delayed, blow-back action. Made from 1981 to 1988.
Commercial model . . . . **NiB $677 Ex $550 Gd $304**
Military model
(Less than 1000 imported) . . . . **NiB $625 Ex $482 Gd $350**

M12 AUTOMATIC PISTOL
Caliber: 9mm Steyr. Eight-round fixed magazine, charger loaded; 5.1-inch bbl., 8.5 inches overall. Weight: 35 oz. Fixed sights. Blued finish. Checkered wood grips. Made from 1911-19. Adopted by the Austro-Hungarian Army in 1912. Note: Confiscated by the Germans in 1938, an estimated 250,000 of these pistols were converted to 9mm Para. and stamped w/an identifying "08" on the left side of the slide. Mfd. by Osterreichische Waffenfabrik-Gesellschaft.
Commercial model (9mm Steyr) . . . **NiB $512 Ex $445 Gd $363**
Military model (9mm Steyr-
Austro-Hungarian Army) . . . . **NiB $538 Ex $450 Gd $208**
Military model (9mm Parabellum
Conversion marked "08") . . . . **NiB $1002 Ex $847 Gd $477**

**Stoeger
American Eagle Luger P08 Stainless**

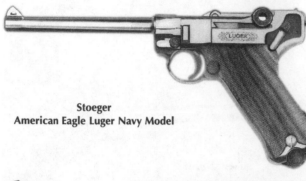

**Stoeger
American Eagle Luger Navy Model**

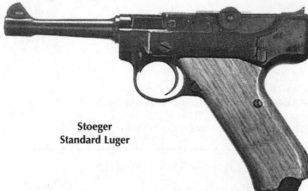

**Stoeger
Standard Luger**

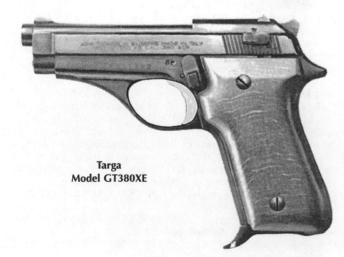

**Targa
Model GT380XE**

STOEGER LUGERS
Formerly mfd. by Stoeger Industries, So. Hackensack, N.J.; later by Classic Arms, Union City, N.J.

AMERICAN EAGLE LUGER
Caliber: 9mm Para. Seven-round magazine, 4- or 6-inch bbl., 8.25 inches overall (with 4-inch bbl.). or 10.25 inches (with 6-inch bbl.). Weight: 30 or 32 oz. Checkered walnut grips. Stainless steel w/brushed or matte black finish. Made from 1994 to date.

**Model P-08
stainless
(4-inch bbl.)** . . . . **NiB $741 Ex $425 Gd $354**
**Navy model
(6-inch bbl.)** . . . . **NiB $741 Ex $425 Gd $354**
**W/matte black
finish, add** **$50**

STANDARD LUGER .22
AUTOMATIC PISTOL . . . . **NiB $192 Ex $126 Gd $95**
Caliber: .22 LR. 10-round magazine, 4.5- or 5.5-inch bbl., 8.88 inches overall (with 4.5-inch bbl.). Weight: 29.5 oz. (with 4.5-inch bbl.). Fixed sights. Black finish. Smooth wood grips. Made 1969 to 1986.

STEEL FRAME LUGER
.22 AUTO PISTOL . . . . **NiB $177 Ex $121 Gd $91**
Caliber: .22 LR. 10-round magazine, 4.5-inch bbl., 8.88 inches overall. Blued finish. Checkered wood grips. Features one piece forged and machined steel frame. Made from 1980 to 1986.

TARGET LUGER
.22 AUTO PISTOL . . . . **NiB $208 Ex $148 Gd $100**
Same as Standard Luger .22 except has target sights 9.38 inches overall w/4.5-inch bbl., Checkered wood grips. Made from 1975 to 1986.

TARGA PISTOLS — Italy
Manufactured by Armi Tanfoglio Guiseppe

MODEL GT26S
AUTO PISTOL . . . . **NiB $140 Ex $90 Gd $75**
Caliber: .25 ACP. Six-round magazine, 2.5-inch bbl., 4.63 inches overall. Weight: 15 oz. fixed sights. Checkered composition grips. Blued or chrome finish. Disc. 1990.

MODEL GT32
AUTO PISTOL
Caliber: .32 ACP. Six-round magazine, 4.88-inch bbl., 7.38 inches overall. Weight: 26 oz. fixed sights. Checkered composition or walnut grips. Blued or chrome finish.
Blued finished . . . . **NiB $150 Ex $100 Gd $75**
Chrome finish . . . . **NiB $170 Ex $110 Gd $85**

MODEL GT380
AUTOMATIC PISTOL
Same as the Targa GT32 except chambered for .380 ACP.
Blued finish . . . . **NiB $170 Ex $100 Gd $75**
Chrome finish . . . . **NiB $185 Ex $130 Gd $90**

MODEL GT380XE
AUTOMATIC PISTOL . . . . **NiB $200 Ex $150 Gd $90**
Caliber: .380 ACP. 11-round magazine, 3.75-inch bbl., 7.38 inches overall. Weight: 28 oz. Fixed sights. Blued or satin nickel finish. Smooth wooden grips. Made from 1980 to 1990.

Taurus Model .44

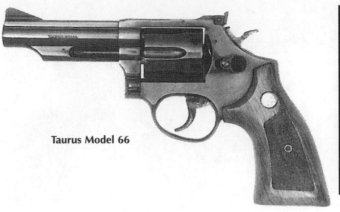

Taurus Model 66

FORJAS TAURUS S.A. — Porto Alegre, Brazil

MODEL 44 DA REVOLVER
Caliber: .44 Mag. Six-round cylinder, 4-, 6.5-, or 8.38-inch bbl. Weight: 44.75 oz., 52.5 or 57.25 oz. Brazilian hardwood grips. Blued or stainless steel finish. Made from 1994 to date.
Blued finish . . . . NiB $400 Ex $305 Gd $200
Stainless. . . . . NiB $550 Ex $455 Gd $255

MODEL 65 DA REVOLVER
Caliber: .357 Magnum. 6-round cylinder, 3- or 4-inch bbl., weight: 32 oz. Front ramp sight, square notch rear. Checkered walnut target grip. Royal blued or satin nickel finish. Imported 1992 to 1997 and from 1999 to date.
Blue . . . . NiB $365 Ex $275 Gd $150
Stainless. . . . . NiB $395 Ex $310 Gd $180

MODEL 66 DA REVOLVER
Calibers: .357 Magnum, .38 Special. Six-round cylinder, 3-, 4- and 6-inch bbl., weight: 35 oz. Serrated ramp front sight, rear click adj. Checkered walnut grips. Royal blued or nickel finish. Imported 1992 1997 and from 1999 to date.
Blue . . . . NiB $395 Ex $310 Gd $180
Stainless. . . . . NiB $460 Ex $370 Gd $215

MODEL 73 DA REVOLVER . . . . NiB $190 Ex $110 Gd $90
Caliber: .32 Long. Six-round cylinder, 3-inch heavy bbl., weight: 20 oz. Checkered grips. Blued or satin nickel finish. Disc. 1993.

MODEL 74 TARGET
GRADE DA REVOLVER . . . . NiB $213 Ex $262 Gd $106
Caliber: .32 S&W Long. Six-round cylinder, 3-inch bbl., 8.25 inches overall. Weight: 20 oz. Adj. rear sight, ramp front. Blued or nickel finish. Checkered walnut grips. Made from 1971 to 1990.

Taurus
Model 74 Target Grade

MODEL 80 DA REVOLVER
Caliber: .38 Special. Six-round cylinder, bbl. lengths: 3, 4 inches, 9.25 inches overall (with 4-inch bbl.). Weight: 30 oz. (with 4-inch bbl.) Fixed sights. Blued or nickel finish. Checkered walnut grips. Made 1996 to 1997.
Blued . . . . NiB $190 Ex $125 Gd $85
Stainless. . . . . NiB $245 Ex $170 Gd $235

MODEL 82 HEAVY BARREL
Same as Model 80 except has heavy bbl., weight: 33 oz. w/4-inch bbl., Made from 1971 to date.
Blued . . . . NiB $345 Ex $270 Gd $200
Stainless. . . . . NiB $385 Ex $310 Gd $240

Taurus Model 80

MODEL 83 HEAVY BARREL TARGET GRADE
Same as Model 84 except has heavy bbl., weight: 34.5 oz. Made from 1977 to date.
Blued . . . . NiB $220 Ex $145 Gd $95
Stainless. . . . . NiB $250 Ex $165 Gd $135

Taurus Model 82

Taurus Model 83

Taurus Model 85 w/Spur Hammer

Taurus Model 84

Taurus Model 85 Concealed Hammer

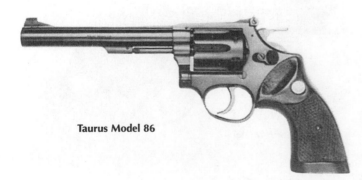

Taurus Model 86

MODEL 84 TARGET
GRADE REVOLVER . . . . **NiB $293 Ex $227 Gd $161**
Caliber: .38 Special. Six-round cylinder, 4-inch bbl., 9.25 inches overall. Weight: 31 oz. Adj. rear sight, ramp front. Blued or nickel finish. Checkered walnut grips. Made from 1971 to 1989.

MODEL 85 DA REVOLVER
Caliber: .38 Special. Five-round cylinder, 2- or 3-inch. bbl., weight: 21 oz. Fixed sights. Checkered walnut grips. Blued, satin nickel or stainless-steel finish. Currently in production. Model 85CH is the same as the standard version except for concealed hammer.
Blued or satin nickel . . . . **NiB $345 Ex $275 Gd $125**
Stainless steel . . . . **NiB $385 Ex $325 Gd $165**

MODEL 86 CUSTOM TARGET
DA REVOLVER. . . . . **NiB $270 Ex $190 Gd $100**
Caliber: .38 Special. Six-round cylinder, 6-inch bbl., 11.25 inches overall. Weight: 34 oz. Adj. rear sight, Partridge-type front. Blued finish. Checkered walnut grips. Made from 1971 to 1994.

MODEL 94 TARGET GRADE
Same as Model 74 except .22 LR. w/9-round cylinder, 3- or 4-inch bbl., weight: 25 oz. Blued or stainless finish. Made from 1971 to date.
Blued finish . . . . **NiB $320 Ex $290 Gd $200**
Stainless finish . . . . **NiB $350 Ex $320 Gd $230**

MODEL 96 TARGET SCOUT . . . . . . **NiB $275 Ex $195 Gd $100**
Same as Model 86 except in .22 LR. Made from 1971 to 1998.

MODEL 431 DA REVOLVER
Caliber: .44 Spec. Five-round cylinder, 3- or 4-inch solid-rib bbl. w/ejector shroud. Weight: 35 oz. w/4-inch bbl., Serrated ramp front sight, notched topstrap rear. Blued or stainless finish. Made 1992 to 1997.
Blued finish . . . . **NiB $220 Ex $180 Gd $130**
Stainless finish . . . . **NiB $285 Ex $245 Gd $175**

MODEL 441 DA REVOLVER
Similar to the Model 431 except w/6-inch bbl. and fully adj. target sights. Weight: 40 oz. Made from 1991 to 1997.
Blued finish . . . . **NiB $273 Ex $212 Gd $130**
Stainless finish . . . . **NiB $394 Ex $287 Gd $295**

MODEL 445 DA REVOLVER
Caliber: .44 Special. Five-round cylinder, 2-inch bbl., 6.75 inches overall. Weight: 28.25 oz. Serrated ramp front sight, notched frame rear. Standard or concealed hammer. Santoprene I grips. Blue or stainless finish. Imported from 1997 to 2003.
Blue model . . . . **NiB $280 Ex $225 Gd $170**
Stainless model . . . . **NiB $310 Ex $255 Gd $200**

MODEL .454 DA RAGING BULL REVOLVER

Caliber: .454 Casull. Five-round cylinder, ported 6.5- or 8.4-inch vent rib bbl., 12 inches overall (w/6.5-inch bbl.). Weight: 53 or 63 oz. Partridge front sight, micrometer adj. rear. Santoprene I or walnut grips. Blue or stainless finish. Imported from 1997 to date.

Blue model	NiB $815	Ex $720	Gd $565
Stainless model	NiB $850	Ex $755	Gd $615

Taurus Model 669

MODEL 669/669VR DA REVOLVER

Caliber: .357 Mag. Six-round cylinder, 4- or 6-inch solid-rib bbl. w/ejector shroud Model 669VR has vent rib bbl., weight: 37 oz. w/4-inch bbl., Serrated ramp front sight, micro-adj. rear. Royal blued or stainless finish. Checkered Brazilian hardwood grips. Made from 1989 to 1998.

Model 669 blued	NiB $260	Ex $200	Gd $155
Model 669 stainless	NiB $325	Ex $270	Gd $230
Model 669VR blued	NiB $270	Ex $210	Gd $165
Model 669VR stainless	NiB $325	Ex $270	Gd $230

MODEL 741/761 DA REVOLVER

Caliber: .32 H&R Mag. Six-round cylinder, 3- or 4-inch solid-rib bbl. w/ejector shroud. Weight: 20 oz. w/3-inch bbl., Serrated ramp front sight, micro-adj. rear. Blued or stainless finish. Checkered Brazilian hardwood grips. Made from 1991 to 1997.

Model 741 blued.	NiB $210	Ex $110	Gd $100
Model 741 stainless	NiB $275	Ex $195	Gd $170
Model 761 (6-inch bbl., blued, 34 oz.)	NiB $250	Ex $175	Gd $120

Taurus Model PT .22

MODEL 941 TARGET REVOLVER

Caliber: .22 Magnum. Eight-round cylinder. Solid-rib bbl. w/ejector shroud. Micro-adj. rear sight. Brazilian hardwood grips. Blued or stainless finish.

Blued finish	NiB $330	Ex $280	Gd $190
Stainless finish	NiB $375	Ex $330	Gd $250

MODEL PT .22 DA

AUTOMATIC PISTOL	NiB $221	Ex $161	Gd $94

Caliber: .22 LR. Nine-round magazine, 2.75-inch bbl., weight: 12.3 oz. Fixed open sights. Brazilian hardwood grips. Blued finish. Made from 1991 to date.

MODEL PT .25 DA

AUTOMATIC PISTOL	NiB $221	Ex $161	Gd $94

Same general specifications as Model PT 22 except in .25 ACP w/eight-round magazine, Made from 1992 to date.

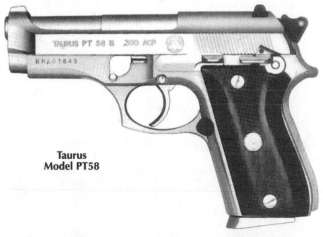

Taurus Model PT58

MODEL PT58 SEMI-

AUTOMATIC PISTOL	NiB $386	Ex $315	Gd $229

Caliber: .380 ACP. Twelve-round magazine, 4-inch bbl., 7.2 inches overall. Weight: 30 oz. Blade front sight, rear adj. for windage w/3-dot sighting system. Blued, satin nickel or stainless finish. Made from 1988 to 1996.

MODEL PT 92AF
SEMIAUTOMATIC PISTOL

Double action. Caliber: 9mm Para. Fifteen-round magazine, 5-inch bbl., 8.5 inches overall. Weight: 24 oz. Blade front sight, notched bar rear. Smooth Brazilian walnut grips. Blued, satin nickel or stainless finish. Made from 1991 to date.

Blued finish	NiB $475	Ex $350	Gd $265
Satin nickel finish	NiB $520	Ex $390	Gd $305
Stainless finish	NiB $495	Ex $370	Gd $285

Taurus Model PT92

**Taurus
Model PT-99AF**

**Taurus
Model PT-908**

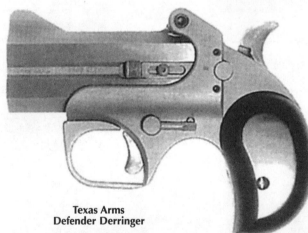

**Texas Arms
Defender Derringer**

MODEL PT-92AFC COMPACT PISTOL
Same general specs as Model PT-92AF except w/13-round magazine, 4.25-inch bbl., 7.5 inches overall. Weight: 31 oz. Made 1991 to 1996
Blued finish . . . . NiB $335 Ex $265 Gd $200
Satin nickel finish . . . . NiB $375 Ex $305 Gd $240
Stainless finish . . . . NiB $400 Ex $320 Gd $200

MODEL PT 99AF SEMI-
AUTOMATIC PISTOL . . . . NiB $495 Ex $400 Gd $275
Same general specifications as Model PT-92AF except rear sight is adj. for elevation and windage, and finish is blued or satin nickel.

MODEL PT 100 DA AUTOMATIC PISTOL
Caliber: .40 S&W. Eleven-round magazine, 5-inch bbl., weight: 34 oz. Fixed front sight, adj. rear w/3-dot system. Smooth hardwood grip. Blued, satin nickel or stainless finish. Made from 1991 to 1997.
Blued finish . . . . NiB $475 Ex $400 Gd $325
Satin finish. . . . . NiB $515 Ex $440 Gd $365
Stainless finish . . . . NiB $495 Ex $420 Gd $345

MODEL PT 101 DA AUTOMATIC PISTOL
Same general specifications as Model 100 except w/micrometer click adj. sights. Made from 1992 to 1996.
Blued finish . . . . NiB $495 Ex $385 Gd $300
Satin nickel finish . . . . NiB $540 Ex $420 Gd $340
Stainless finish . . . . NiB $495 Ex $385 Gd $300

MODEL PT 111 MILLENNIUM DAO PISTOL
Caliber: 9mm Parabellum. 10-round magazine, 3.12-inch bbl., 6 inches overall. Weight: 19.1 oz. Fixed low-profile sights w/3-dot system. Black polymer grip/frame. Blue or stainless slide. Imported from 1998 to 2004.
Blue model . . . . NiB $335 Ex $235 Gd $120
Stainless model . . . . NiB $360 Ex $260 Gd $165

MODEL PT 908 SEMIAUTOMATIC PISTOL
Caliber: 9mm Para. Eight-round magazine, 3.8-inch bbl., 7 inches overall. Weight: 30 oz. Post front sight, drift-adj. combat rear w/3-dot system. Blued, satin nickel or stainless finish. Made 1993 to 1997.
Blued finish . . . . NiB $330 Ex $265 Gd $190
Satin nickel finish . . . . NiB $350 Ex $295 Gd $190
Stainless finish . . . . NiB $385 Ex $290 Gd $245

MODEL PT 911 COMPACT SEMIAUTOMATIC PISTOL
Caliber: 9mm Parabellum. 10-round magazine, 3.75-inch bbl., 7.05 inches overall. Weight: 28.2 oz. Fixed low-profile sights w/3-dot system. Santoprene II grips. Blue or stainless finish. Imported from 1997 to date.
Blue model . . . . NiB $500 Ex $380 Gd $234
Stainless model . . . . NiB $500 Ex $473 Gd $325

MODEL PT 938 COMPACT SEMIAUTOMATIC PISTOL
Caliber: 380 ACP. 10-round magazine, 3.72-inch bbl., 6.75 inches overall. Weight: 27 oz. Fixed low-profile sights w/3-dot system. Santoprene II grips. Blue or stainless finish. Imported 1997 to 2005.
Blue model . . . . NiB $410 Ex $320 Gd $240
Stainless model . . . . NiB $420 Ex $310 Gd $220

MODEL PT 940 COMPACT SEMIAUTOMATIC PISTOL
Caliber: .40 S&W. 10-round magazine, 3.75-inch bbl., 7.05 inches overall. Weight: 28.2 oz. Fixed low-profile sights w/3-dot system. Santoprene II grips. Blue or stainless finish. Imported from 1997 to date.
Blue model . . . . NiB $500 Ex $390 Gd $265
Stainless model . . . . NiB $530 Ex $420 Gd $295

MODEL PT 945 COMPACT SEMIAUTOMATIC PISTOL
Caliber: .45 ACP. Eight-round magazine, 4.25-inch bbl., 7.48 inches overall. Weight: 29.5 oz. Fixed low-profile sights w/3-dot system. Santoprene II grips. Blue or stainless finish. Imported from 1995 to date.
Blue model . . . . NiB $560 Ex $485 Gd $355
Stainless model . . . . NiB $575 Ex $420 Gd $310

TEXAS ARMS — Waco, Texas

DEFENDER DERRINGER . . . . NiB $275 Ex $200 Gd $110
Calibers: 9mm, .357 Mag., .44 Mag., .45 ACP, .45 Colt/.410. Three-inch bbl., 5 inches overall. Weight: 21 oz. Blade front sight, fixed rear. Matte gun-metal gray finish. Smooth grips. Made from 1993 to 1999.

TEXAS LONGHORN ARMS — Richmond, Texas

"THE JEZEBEL" PISTOL . . . . NiB $315 Ex $241 Gd $173
Top-break, single-shot. Caliber: .22 Short, Long or LR. Six-inch half-round bbl., 8 inches overall. Weight: 15 oz. Bead front sight, adj. rear. One-piece walnut grip. Stainless finish. Intro. in 1987.

SA REVOLVER CASED SET
Set contains one each of the Texas Longhorn Single Actions. Each chambered in the same caliber and w/the same serial number. Intro. in 1984.
Standard set . . . . NiB $5780 Ex $4648 Gd $3202
Engraved set . . . . NiB $7509 Ex $6042 Gd $4165

SOUTH TEXAS ARMY LIMITED
EDITION SA REVOLVER . . . . . . NiB $1801 Ex $1347 Gd $1066
Calibers: All popular centerfire pistol calibers. Six-round cylinder, 4.75-inch bbl.,10.25 inches overall. Weight: 40 oz. Fixed sights. Color casehardened frame. One-piece deluxe walnut grips. Blued bbl., Intro. in 1984.

SESQUICENTENNIAL SA REVOLVER . . . . . NiB $2504 Ex $2011 Gd $1393
Same as South Texas Army Limited Edition except engraved and nickel-plated w/one-piece ivory grip. Intro. in 1986.

TEXAS BORDER SPECIAL
SA REVOLVER . . . . NiB $1612 Ex $1288 Gd $898
Same as South Texas Army Limited Edition except w/3.5-inch bbl. and bird's-head grips. Intro. in 1984.

WEST TEXAS FLAT TOP
TARGET SA REVOLVER . . . . NiB $1594 Ex $1244 Gd $861
Same as South Texas Army Limited Edition except w/choice of bbl. lengths from 7 .5 to 15 inches. Same special features w/flat-top style frame and adj. rear sight. Intro. in 1984.

THOMPSON PISTOL — West Hurley, New York Mfd. by Auto-Ordnance Corporation

MODEL 1927A-5
SEMIAUTO PISTOL . . . . .NiB $1050 Ex $855 Gd $655
Similar to Thompson Model 1928A submachine gun except has no provision for automatic firing, does not have detachable buttstock. Caliber: .45 Auto, 20-round detachable box magazine (5-, 15- and 30-round box magazines, 39-round drum also available), 13-inch finned bbl., overall length: 26 inches. Weight: About 6.75 lbs. Adj. rear sight, blade front. Blued finish. Walnut grips. Intro. in 1977. See Auto-Ordnance in Handgun Section.

THOMPSON/CENTER ARMS — Rochester, NH. Acquired by Smith & Wesson in 2006.

CONTENDER SINGLE-SHOT PISTOL
Break frame, underlever action. Calibers: (rimfire) .22 LR. .22 WMR, 5mm RRM; (standard centerfire), .218 Bee, .22 Hornet, .22 Rem. Jet, .221 Fireball, .222 Rem., .25-35, .256 Win. Mag., .30 M1 Carbine, .30-30, .38 Auto, .38 Special .357 Mag./Hot Shot, 9mm Para., .45 Auto, .45 Colt, .44 Magnum/Hot Shot; (wildcat centerfire) .17 Ackley Bee, .17 Bumblebee, .17 Hornet, .17 K Hornet, .17 Mach IV, .17-.222, .17-.223, .22 K Hornet, .30 Herrett, .357 Herrett, .357-4 B&D. Interchangeable bbls.: 8.75- or 10-inch standard octagon (.357 Mag., .44 Mag. and .45 Colt available w/detachable choke for use w/Hot Shot cartridges); 10-inch w/vent rib and detachable internal choke tube for Hot Shots, .357 and .44 Magnum only; 10-inch

**Thompson
Contender Single-Shot Pistol**

**Thompson
Center Contender Bull Barrel**

bull bbl., .30 or .357 Herrett only. 13.5 inches overall w/10-inch bbl., Weight: 43 oz. (w/standard 10-inch bbl.). Adj. rear sight, ramp front; vent rib model has folding rear sight, adj. front; bull bbl., available w/or w/o sights. Lobo 1.5/ scope and mount (add $40 to value). Blued finish. Receiver photoengraved. Checkered walnut thumbrest grip and forearm (pre-1972 model has different grip w/silver grip cap). Made from 1967 to date, w/the following revisions and variations.
Standard model . . . . NiB $380 Ex $300 Gd $185
Vent rib model . . . . NiB $400 Ex $300 Gd $213
Bull bbl. model, w/sights . . . . NiB $385 Ex $305 Gd $188
Bull bbl. model, without sights . . . . NiB $380 Ex $300 Gd $185
Extra standard bbl. . . . . Add $230
Extra vent rib or bull bbl . . . . Add $270

CONTENDER BULL BARREL . . . . . . NiB $380 Ex $300 Gd $185
Caliber offerings of the bull bbl. version expanded in 1973 and 1978, making it the Contender model w/the widest range of caliber options: .22 LR, .22 Win. Mag., .22 Hornet, .223 Rem., 7mm T.C.U., 7x30 Waters, .30 M1 Carbine, .30-30 Win., .32 H&R Mag., .32-20 Win., .357 Rem. Max., .357 Mag., 10mm Auto, .44 Magnum, .445 Super Magnum. 10-inch heavy bbl., Partridge-style iron sights. Contoured Competitor grip. Blued finish.

CONTENDER INTERNAL CHOKE MODEL
Originally made in 1968-69 w/octagonal bbl., this Internal Choke version in .45 Colt/.410 caliber only was reintroduced in 1986 w/10-inch bull bbl. Vent rib also available. Fixed iron rear sight, bead front. Detachable choke screws into muzzle. Blued finish. Contoured American black walnut Competitor grip, also since 1986, has nonslip rubber insert permanently bonded to back of grip.
W/bull bbl . . . . Add $25
W/vent rib . . . . Add $35

CONTENDER OCTAGON BARREL . . . . NiB $355 Ex $275 Gd $195
The original Contender design, this octagonal bbl., version began to see the discontinuance of caliber offerings in 1980. Now it is available in .22 LR only, 10-inch octagonal bbl., Partridge-style iron sights. Contoured Competitor grip. Blued finish.

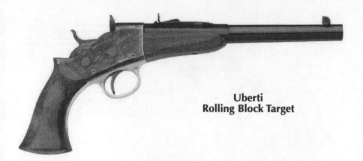

**Uberti
Rolling Block Target**

**Uberti
Model 1873 Cattleman**

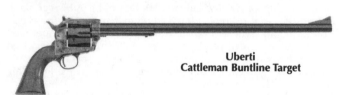

**Uberti
Cattleman Buntline Target**

CONTENDER STAINLESS
Similar to the standard Contender models except stainless steel w/blued sights. Black Rynite forearm and ambidextrous finger-groove grip. Made from 2006 to date.

Standard SS model (10-inch bbl.)	NiB $435	Ex $350	Gd $275
SS Super 14	NiB $360	Ex $265	Gd $135
SS Super 16	NiB $360	Ex $265	Gd $135

CONTENDER SUPER 14/16
Calibers: .22 LR, .222 Rem., .223 Rem., 6mm T.C.U., 6.5mm T.C.U., 7mm T.C.U., 7x30 Waters, .30 Herrett, .30-30 Win., .357 Herrett, .357 Rem. Max., .35 Rem., 10mm Auto, .44 Mag., .445 Super Mag. 14- or 16.25-inch bull bbl., 18 or 20.25 inches overall. Weight: 43-65 oz. Partridge-style ramp front sight, adj. target rear. Blued finish. Made from 1978 to 1997.

Super 14	NiB $360	Ex $280	Gd $185
Super 16	NiB $360	Ex $280	Gd $185

CONTENDER TC ALLOY II
Calibers: .22 LR, .223 Rem., .357 Magnum, .357 Rem. Max., .44 Magnum, 7mm T.C.U., .30-30 Win., .45 Colt/.410 (w/internal choke), .35 Rem. and 7-30 Waters (14-inch bbl.). 10- or 14-inch bull bbl. or 10-inch vent rib bbl. (w/internal choke). All metal parts permanently electroplated w/T/C Alloy II, which is harder than stainless steel, ensuring smoother action, 30 percent longer bbl. life. Other design specifications the same as late model Contenders. Made from 1986 to 1989.

T/C Alloy II 10-inch bull bbl.	NiB $350	Ex $275	Gd $195
T/C Alloy II vent rib bbl. w/choke	NiB $425	Ex $355	Gd $265
T/C Alloy II Super 14	NiB $355	Ex $280	Gd $200

ENCORE SINGLE-SHOT PISTOL
Similar to the standard Contender models except w/10-, 12- or 15-inch bbl., Calibers: .22-250 Rem., .223 Rem., .243 Win., .260 Rem., .270 Win., 7mm BR Rem., 7mm-08 Rem., 7.62x39mm, .308 Win., .30-06 Spfd., .44 Rem. Mag., .444 Marlin, .45-70 Govt., .45 LC/410. Blue or stainless finish. Walnut or composition, ambidextrous finger-groove grip. Hunter Model w/2.5-7x pistol scope. Note: Encore bbls. are not interchangeable with Contenter models. Made from 1998 to date.

Encore model w/10-inch bbl. (blue, disc.)	NiB $535	Ex $420	Gd $250
Encore model w/12-inch bbl. (blue)	NiB $535	Ex $420	Gd $247
Encore model w/15-inch bbl. (blue)	NiB $545	Ex $430	Gd $250
Hunter model w/2.5-7x scope	NiB $730	Ex $510	Gd $345
Encore model (stainless), add			$15

UBERTI HANDGUNS — Mfd. by Aldo Uberti, Ponte Zanano, Italy
(Imported by Uberti USA, Inc.)

MODEL 1871 ROLLING BLOCK
TARGET PISTOL . . . . NiB $387 Ex $295 Gd $213
Single shot. Calibers: .22 LR, .22 Magnum, .22 Hornet and .357 Magnum; 9.5-inch bbl., 14 inches overall. Weight: 44 oz. Ramp front sight, fully adjustable rear. Smooth walnut grip and forearm. Color casehardened frame w/brass trigger guard. Blued half-octagon or full round barrel. Made 2002 to 2006.

MODEL 1873 CATTLEMAN SA REVOLVER
Calibers: .357 Magnum, .38-40, .44-40, .44 Special, .45 Long Colt, .45 ACP. Six-round cylinder, Bbl length: 3.5, 4.5, 4.75, 5.5, 7.5 or 18 inches; 10.75 inches overall (5.5-inch bbl.). Weight: 38 oz. (5.5-inch bbl.). Color casehardened steel frame w/steel or brass back strap and trigger guard. Nickel-plated or blued barrel and cylinder. Imported from 1997 to 2010.

First issue	NiB $422	Ex $366	Gd $228
Bisley	NiB $422	Ex $366	Gd $228
Bisley (flattop)	NiB $422	Ex $366	Gd $228
Buntline (reintroduced 1992)	NiB $475	Ex $366	Gd $228
Quick Draw	NiB $422	Ex $366	Gd $228
Sabre (bird head)	NiB $422	Ex $366	Gd $228
Sheriff's model	NiB $422	Ex $366	Gd $228
Convertible cylinder, add			$51
Stainless steel, add			$125
Steel backstrap and trigger guard, add			$55
Target sights, add			$60

MODEL 1875 REMINGTON OUTLAW
Replica of Model 1875 Remington. Calibers: .357 Mag., .44-40, .45 ACP, .45 Long Colt. Six-round cylinder, 5.5- to 7.5-inch bbl., 11.75 to 13.75 inches overall. Weight: 44 oz. (with 7.5 inch bbl). Color casehardened steel frame w/steel or brass back strap and trigger guard. Blue or nickel finish.

Blue model	NiB $448	Ex $346	Gd $198
Nickel model (disc. 1995)	NiB $530	Ex $473	Gd $315
Convertible cylinder (.45 LC/.45 ACP), add			$92

MODEL 1890 REMINGTON POLICE
Similar to Model 1875 Remington except without the web under the ejector housing.

Blue Model	NiB $455	Ex $346	Gd $198
Nickel Model (disc. 1995)	NiB $825	Ex $655	Gd $310
Convertible Cylinder (.45 LC/.45 ACP), add			$100

ULTRA LIGHT ARMS, INC — Granville, WV.

MODEL 20 SERIES PISTOLS
Calibers: .22-250 thru .308 Win. Five-round magazine, 14-inch bbl., weight: 4 lbs. Composite Kevlar, graphite reinforced stock. Benchrest grade action available in right- or left-hand models. Timney adjustable trigger w/three function safety. Bright or matte finish. Made 1987 to 1999.
Model 20 Hunter's Pistol (disc. 1989)... NiB $1295 Ex $1057 Gd $955
Model 20 Reb Pistol (disc. 1999) ..... NiB $1475 Ex $1310 Gd $1155

UNIQUE PISTOLS — Hendaye, France
Mfd. by Manufacture d'Armes des Pyrénées
Currently imported by Nygord Precision Products (Previously by Beeman Precision Arms)

MODEL B/CF AUTOMATIC PISTOL .... NiB $205 Ex $100 Gd $65
Calibers: .32 ACP, .380 ACP. Nine-round (.32) or 8-round (.38) magazine, 4-inch bbl., 6.6 inches overall. Weight: 24.3 oz. Blued finish. Plain or thumbrest plastic grips. Intro. in 1954. Disc.

MODEL D2 .... NiB $300 Ex $210 Gd $165
Same as Model D6 except has 4.5-inch bbl., 7.5 inches overall, weight: 24.5 oz. Made from 1954. Disc.

MODEL D6 AUTOMATIC PISTOL....... NiB $300 Ex $205 Gd $100
Caliber: .22 LR. 10-round magazine, 6-inch bbl., 9.25 inches overall. Weight: About 26 oz. Adj. sights. Blued finish. Plain or thumbrest plastic grips. Intro. in 1954. Disc.

MODEL DES/32U RAPID FIRE PISTOL
Caliber: .32 S&W Long (wadcutter). Five- or 6-round magazine, 5.9-inch bbl., weight: .40.2 oz. Blade front sight, micro-adj. rear. Trigger adj. for weight and position. Blued finish. Stippled handrest grips. Imported from 1990 to date.
Right-hand model .... NiB $1350 Ex $1240 Gd $1110
Left-hand model .... NiB $1410 Ex $1300 Gd $1170

MODEL DES/69-U STANDARD MATCH PISTOL
Caliber: .22 LR. Five-round magazine, 5.9-inch bbl., w/250 gm counterweight. 10.6 inches overall. Trigger adjusts for position and pull. Weight: 35.3 oz. Blade front sight, micro-adj. rear. Checkered walnut thumbrest grips w/adj. handrest. Blued finish. Imported from 1969 to 1999.
Right-hand model .... NiB $1150 Ex $1094 Gd $879
Left-hand model .... NiB $1180 Ex $1225 Gd $910

MODEL DES 823U RAPID FIRE
MATCH AUTOMATIC PISTOL .... NiB $1100 Ex $950 Gd $820
Caliber: .22 Short. Five-round magazine, 5.9-inch bbl., 10.4 inches overall. Weight: 43 oz. Click adj. rear sight blade front. Checkered walnut thumbrest grips w/adj. handrest. Trigger adj. for length of pull. Made from 1974 to 1998.

KRIEGSMODELL L AUTOMATIC PISTOL..... NiB $325 Ex $225 Gd $145
Caliber: .32 Auto (7.65mm). Nine-round magazine, 3.2-inch bbl., 5.8 inches overall. Weight: 26.5 oz. Fixed sights. Blued finish. Plastic grips. Mfd. during German occupation of France 1940 to 194545. Note: Bears the German military acceptance marks and may have grips marked "7.65m/m 9 SCHUSS."

MODEL L AUTOMATIC PISTOL .... NiB $250 Ex $185 Gd $130
Calibers: .22 LR, .32 Auto (7.65mm), .380 Auto (9mm Short). 10-round magazine in .22, 7 in .32, 6 in .380; 3.3-inch bbl.; 5.8 inches overall. Weight: 16.5 oz. (.380 Auto w/light alloy frame), 23 oz. (w/steel frame).

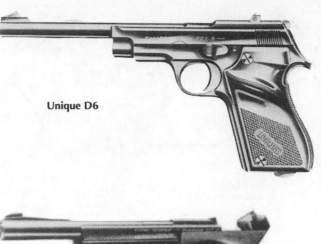
Unique D6

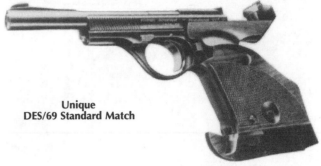
Unique
DES/69 Standard Match

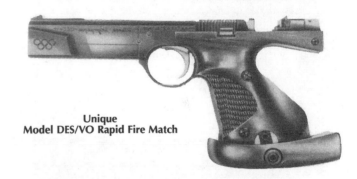
Unique
Model DES/VO Rapid Fire Match

Fixed sights. Blued finish. Plastic grips. Intro. in 1955. Disc.

MODEL MIKROS POCKET
AUTOMATIC PISTOL .... NiB $200 Ex $125 Gd $80
Calibers: .22 Short, .25 Auto (6.35mm). Six-round magazine, 2.25-inch bbl., 4.44 inches overall. Weight: 9.5 oz. (light alloy frame), 12.5 oz. (steel frame.). Fixed sights. Blued finish. Plastic grips. Intro. in 1957. Disc.

MODEL RR
AUTOMATIC PISTOL .... NiB $185 Ex $95 Gd $55
Postwar commercial version of WWII Kriegsmodell w/same general specifications. Intro. in 1951. Disc.

MODEL 2000-U MATCH PISTOL
Caliber: .22 Short. Designed for U.I.T. rapid fire competition. Five-round top-inserted magazine, 5.5-inch bbl., w/five vents for recoil reduction. 11.4 inches overall. Weight: 43.4 oz. Special light alloy frame, solid steel slide and shock absorber. Stippled French walnut w/adj. handrest. Imported from 1990 to 1996.
Right-hand model .... NiB $1305 Ex $1166 Gd $1060
Left-hand model .... NiB $1355 Ex $1215 Gd $1150

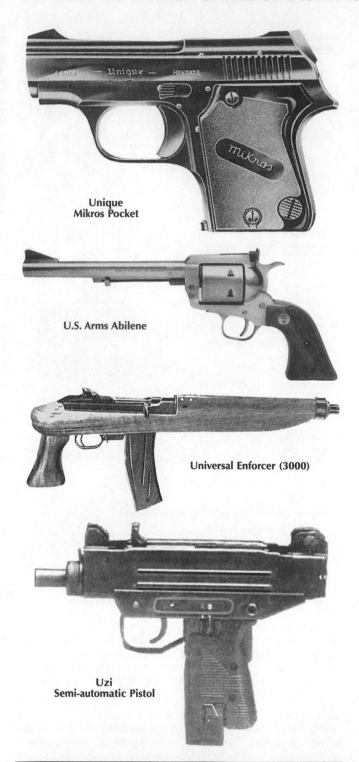

**Unique
Mikros Pocket**

U.S. Arms Abilene

Universal Enforcer (3000)

**Uzi
Semi-automatic Pistol**

UNITED STATES ARMS CORPORATION —
Riverhead, New York

ABILENE SA REVOLVER
Safety Bar action. Calibers: .357 Mag., .41 Mag., .44 Mag., .45 Colt and .357/9mm convertible model w/two cylinders. Six-round cylinder, bbl. lengths: 4.63-, 5.5-, 6.5-inch, 7.5- and 8.5-inches in .44

Mag. only. Weight: About 48 oz. Adj. rear sight, ramp front. Blued finish or stainless steel. Smooth walnut grips. Made 1976 to 1983.

.44 Magnum, blued finish . . . . NiB $346 Ex $275 Gd $208
Magnum, stainless steel . . . . NiB $397 Ex $3076 Gd $244
Other calibers, blued finish . . . . NiB $327 Ex $209 Gd $196
.357 Magnum, stainless steel . . . . . . NiB $391 Ex $300 Gd $231
Convertible, .357 Mag./9mm
Para., blued finish . . . . NiB $346 Ex $295 Gd $208

UNIVERSAL FIREARMS CORPORATION —
Hialeah, Florida
This company was purchased by Iver Johnson Arms in the mid-1980s, when the Enforcer listed below was disc. An improved version was issued under the Iver Johnson name (see separate listing).

ENFORCER (3000)
SEMIAUTOMATIC PISTOL . . . . NiB $450 Ex $320 Gd $220
M-1 Carbine-type action. Caliber: 30 Carbine. Five-, 15- or 30-round clip magazine, 10.25-inch bbl., 17.75 inches overall. Weight: 4.5 lbs. (with 30-round magazine). Adj. rear sight, blade front. Blued finish. Walnut stock w/pistol grip and handguard. Made from 1964 to 1983.

UZI PISTOLS — Mfd. by Israel Military
Industries, Israel
(Currently imported by UZI America)

SEMIAUTOMATIC PISTOL . . . . . . NiB $1005 Ex $828 Gd $624
Caliber: 9mm Para. 20-round magazine, 4.5-inch bbl., about 9.5 inches overall. Weight: 3.8 lbs. Front post-type sight, rear open-type, both adj. Disc. in 1993.

"EAGLE" SERIES
SEMIAUTOMATIC DA PISTOL
Caliber: 9mm Parabellum, .40 S&W, .45 ACP (Short Slide). 10-round magazine, 3.5-, 3.7- and 4.4-inch bbl., weight: 32 oz. to 35 oz. Blade front sight, drift adjustable tritium rear. Matte blue finish. Black synthetic grips. Imported from 1997 to 1998.
Compact model
(DA or DAO) . . . . NiB $485 Ex $375 Gd $290
Polymer compact model . . . . NiB $485 Ex $375 Gd $290
Full-size model . . . . NiB $485 Ex $375 Gd $290
Short slide model . . . . NiB $485 Ex $375 Gd $290

WALTHER PISTOLS — Manufactured by
German, French and Swiss firms
The following Walther pistols were made before and during World War II by Waffenfabrik Walther, Zella-Mehlis (Thür.), Germany.

MODEL 1
AUTOMATIC PISTOL . . . . NiB $750 Ex $552 Gd $283
Caliber: .25 Auto (6.35mm). Six-round. 2.1-inch bbl., 4.4 inches overall. Weight: 12.8 oz. Fixed sights. Blued finish. Checkered hard rubber grips. Intro. in 1908.

MODEL 2
AUTOMATIC PISTOL
Caliber: .25 Auto (6.35mm). Six-round magazine, 2.1-inch bbl., 4.2 inches overall. Weight: 9.8 oz. Fixed sights. Blued finish. Checkered hard rubber grips. Intro. in 1909.
Standard model . . . . NiB $600 Ex $431 Gd $192
Pop-up sight model . . . . NiB $1500 Ex $1305 Gd $1146

MODEL 3 AUTOMATIC PISTOL . . . . . . NiB $3000 Ex $2759 Gd $2438
Caliber: .32 Auto (7.65mm). Six-round magazine, 2.6-inch bbl., 5 inches overall. Weight: 16.6 oz. Fixed sights. Blued finish. Checkered hard rubber grips. Intro. in 1910.

MODEL 4 AUTOMATIC PISTOL . . . . NiB $500 Ex $377 Gd $195
Caliber: .32 Auto (7.65mm). Eight-round magazine, 3.5-inch bbl., 5.9 inches overall. Weight: 18.6 oz. Fixed sights. Blued finish. Checkered hard rubber grips. Made from 1910 to 1918.

MODEL 5 AUTOMATIC PISTOL . . . . NiB $600 Ex $480 Gd $181
Improved version of Model 2 w/same general specifications, distinguished chiefly by better workmanship and appearance. Intro. in 1913.

MODEL 6 AUTOMATIC PISTOL . . . . . . NiB $8500 Ex $7811 Gd $5256
Caliber: 9mm Para. Eight-round magazine, 4.75-inch bbl., 8.25 inches overall. Weight: 34 oz. Fixed sights. Blued finish. Checkered hard rubber grips. Made from 1915-17. Note: The 9mm Para. cartridge is too powerful for the simple blow-back system of this pistol, so firing is not recommended.

MODEL 7 AUTOMATIC PISTOL . . . . NiB $675 Ex $500 Gd $270
Caliber: .25 Auto. (6.35mm). Eight-round magazine, 3-inch bbl., 5.3 inches overall. Weight: 11.8 oz. Fixed sights. Blued finish. Checkered hard rubber grips. Made from 1917 to 1918.

MODEL 8 AUTOMATIC PISTOL . . . . NiB $599 Ex $417 Gd $207
Caliber: .25 Auto. (6.35mm). Eight-round magazine, 2.88-inch bbl., 5.13 inches overall. Weight: 12.38 oz. Fixed sights. Blued finish. Checkered plastic grips. Made from 1920 to 1945.

MODEL 8 LIGHTWEIGHT
AUTOMATIC PISTOL . . . . NiB $700 Ex $470 Gd $390
Same as standard Model Eight except about 25 percent lighter due to use of aluminum alloys.

MODEL 9 VEST POCKET
AUTOMATIC PISTOL . . . . NiB $655 Ex $500 Gd $365
Caliber: .25 Auto (6.35mm). Six-round magazine, 2-inch bbl., 3.94 inches overall. Weight: 9 oz. Fixed sights. Blued finish. Checkered plastic grips. Made from 1921 to 1945.

MODEL HP DOUBLE-ACTION AUTOMATIC
Prewar commercial version of the P38 marked with an "N" proof over an "Eagle" or "Crown." The "HP" is an abbreviation of "Heeres Pistole" (Army Pistol). Caliber: 9mm Para. 8-round magazine, 5-inch bbl., 8.38 inches overall. Weight: About 34.5 oz. Fixed sights. Blued finish. Checkered wood or plastic grips. The Model HP is distinguished by its notably fine material and workmanship. Made from 1937 to 1944. (SN range 1000-25900)
First production (Swedish Trials
model H1000-H2000) . . . . NiB $3500 Ex $2695 Gd $1995
Standard commercial production
(2000-24,000) . . . . NiB $2000 Ex $1720 Gd $1600
War production - marked "P38"
(24,000-26,000) . . . . NiB $1670 Ex $1435 Gd $1245
W/Nazi proof "Eagle/359," add $240

OLYMPIA FUNFKAMPF
MODEL AUTOMATIC . . . . NiB $2500 Ex $2325 Gd $2165
Caliber: .22 LR. 10-round magazine, 9.6-inch bbl., 13 inches overall. Weight: 33 oz., less weight. Set of 4 detachable weights. Adj. target sights. Blued finish. Checkered grips. Intro. in 1936.

OLYMPIA HUNTING
MODEL AUTOMATIC . . . . NiB $2200 Ex $1715 Gd $1532
Same general specifications as Olympia Sport Model but w/4-inch bbl., Weight: 28.5 oz.

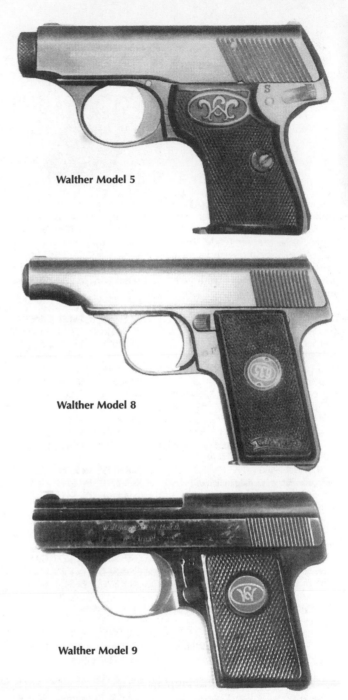

Walther Model 5

Walther Model 8

Walther Model 9

OLYMPIA RAPID FIRE AUTO . . NiB $1610 Ex $1315 Gd $1135
Caliber: .22 Short. Six-round magazine, 7.4-inch bbl., 10.7 inches overall. Weight: (without 12.38 oz. detachable muzzle weight,) 27.5 oz. Adj. target sights. Blued finish. Checkered grips. Made 1936 to 1940.

OLYMPIA SPORT
MODEL AUTOMATIC . . . . NiB $1500 Ex $1325 Gd $1200
Caliber: .22 LR. 10-round magazine, 7.4-inch bbl., 10.7 inches overall. Weight: 30.5 oz., less weight. Adj. target sights. Blued finish. Checkered grips. Set of four detachable weights was supplied at extra cost. Made about 1936 to 1940.

**Walther PP
(Prewar)**

P38 MILITARY DA AUTOMATIC
Modification of the Model HP adopted as an official German Service arm in 1938 and produced throughout WW II by Walther (code "ac"), Mauser (code "byf") and a few other manufacturers. General specifications and appearance same as Model HP, but w/a vast difference in quality, the P38 being a mass-produced military pistol. Some of the late wartime models were very roughly finished and tolerances were quite loose.

War Production w/Walther banner (1940)
Zero Ser. 1st Iss. (SN 01-01,000) .... NiB $8005 Ex $6151 Gd $2340
Zero Ser. 2nd Iss. (SN 01,000-03,500) .... NiB $6438 Ex $5038 Gd $2215
Zero Ser. 3rd Iss. (SN 03,500-013,000) ...... NiB $2982 Ex $2010 Gd $974

WALTHER CONTRACT PISTOLS (LATE 1940-44)
"480" code Series (SN 1-7,600) .... NiB $5667 Ex $3865 Gd $1496
"ac" code Ser. w/no date (SN 7,350-9,700)... NiB $5925 Ex $4286 Gd $2114
"ac" code Ser. w/.40 below
code (SN 9,700-9,900A) .... NiB $4359 Ex $3844 Gd $1784
"ac40" code inline Ser. (SN 1-9,900B)....... NiB $2245 Ex $1833 Gd $783
"ac" code Ser. w/41 below code (SN 1-4,5001) .. NiB $1701 Ex $1546 Gd $877
"ac" code Ser. w/42 below code
(SN 4,500I-9,300K) .... NiB $1439 Ex $1285 Gd $667
"ac" code Ser. w/43 date (inline or below)..... NiB $718 Ex $593 Gd $409
"ac" code Ser. w/45 (inline or below)........ NiB $666 Ex $533 Gd $383

MAUSER CONTRACT PISTOLS (LATE 1942-44)
"byf" code Ser. w/42 date (19,000 prod.) ...... NiB $1255 Ex $952 Gd $740
"bcf" code Ser. w/43, 44 or 45 date
(inline or below) .... NiB $899 Ex $696 Gd $541
"svw" code Ser. (French prod. w/Nazi proofs)... NiB $1219 Ex $939 Gd $549
"svw" code Ser. (French prod. w/star proof) .... NiB $518 Ex $431 Gd $312

SPREEWERKE CONTRACT PISTOLS (LATE 1942-45)
"cyq" code 1st Ser. w/Eagle over
359 (500 prod.) .... NiB $1761 Ex $1447 Gd $1020
"cyq" code Standard Ser. (300,000 prod.) ..... NiB $894 Ex $508 Gd $405
"cyq" code "0" Ser. (5,000 prod.)............. NiB $1132 Ex $726 Gd $540

MODEL PP DA AUTOMATIC PISTOL
Polizeipistole (Police Pistol). Calibers: .22 LR (5.6mm), .25 Auto (6.35mm), .32 Auto (7.65mm), .380 Auto (9mm). Eight-round magazine, (7-round in .380), 3.88-inch bbl., 6.94 inches overall. Weight: 23 oz. Fixed sights. Blued finish. Checkered plastic grips. 1929-45. Post-War production and importation 1963 to 2000.

NOTE: Wartime models are inferior in quality to prewar commercial pistols.

COMMERCIAL MODEL W/CROWN "N" PROOF
.22 cal. (w/comm. Crown "N" proof)....... NiB $1230 Ex $980 Gd $662
.25 cal. (w/comm. Crown "N" proof)....... NiB $3755 Ex $3324 Gd $1676
.32 cal. (w/comm. Crown "N" proof)......... NiB $700 Ex $512 Gd $321

.32 cal. (w/Dural (alloy) frame)............. NiB $570 Ex $4568 Gd $360
.32 cal. (w/Verchromt Fin., pre-war).......... NiB $1175 Ex $987 Gd $645
.32 cal. (A.F.Stoeger Contract, pre-war) ...... NiB $1844 Ex $1381 Gd $583
.32 cal. (Allemagne French contract,
pre-war) .... NiB $1381 Ex $1075 Gd $583
.380 cal. (w/Comm. Crown "N" proof) ×....... NiB $1432 Ex $1170 Gd $686
.380 cal. (w/Verchromt Fin., pre-war)........ NiB $2644 Ex $2235 Gd $911

WARTIME MODEL WITH EAGLE "N" PROOF
.32 cal. (w/Waffenampt proofs)............... NiB $644 Ex $507 Gd $326
.32 cal. (w/Eagle "C" Nazi Police markings)..... NiB $935 Ex $701 Gd $456
.32 cal. (w/Eagle "F" Nazi Police markings) ..... NiB $938 Ex $701 Gd $456
.32 cal. (w/NSKK markings) .... NiB $3158 Ex $2308 Gd $918
.32 cal. (w/NSDAP Gruppe markings)........ NiB $2535 Ex $2175 Gd $861
.380 cal. (w/Waffenampt proofs)............ NiB $1384 Ex $1122 Gd $762

COMMERCIAL MODEL (POST-WAR)
.22 cal. (German manufacture) .... NiB $1040 Ex $911 Gd $499
.32 cal. (German manufacture) .... NiB $937 Ex $576 Gd $404
.380 cal. (German manufacture) .... NiB $1065 Ex $911 Gd $370
.22 cal. (French manufacture) .... NiB $529 Ex $433 Gd $236
.32 cal. (French manufacture) .... NiB $529 Ex $433 Gd $236
.380 cal. (French manufacture) .... NiB $576 Ex $513 Gd $252
.22, .32 or .380 Cal. (other foreign manuf.) ..... NiB $399 Ex $300 Gd $212

MODEL PP SPORT DA AUTOMATIC PISTOL
Target version of the Model PP. Caliber: .22 LR. Eight-round magazine, 5.75- to 7.75 inch bbl. w/adjustable sights. Blue or nickel finish. Checkered plastic grips w/thumbrest. Made from 1953 to 1970.
PP Sport (Walther manufacture) .... NiB $986 Ex $683 Gd $426
PP Sport (Manurhin manufacture)........... NiB $906 Ex $754 Gd $528
PP Sport C model (comp./single act.)........ NiB $1007 Ex $824 Gd $626
W/nickel finish, add $170
W/matched bbl., weights, add $75

MODEL PP DELUXE ENGRAVED
These elaborately engraved models are available in blued finish, silver- or gold-plated.
Blued finish .... NiB $1593 Ex $1368 Gd $1162
Silver-plated. .... NiB $1883 Ex $1461 Gd $1265
Gold-plated .... NiB $2094 Ex $1770 Gd $1368
W/ivory grips, add................................... $250
W/presentation case, add $700
.22 caliber, add $50
.380 caliber, add 95%

MODEL PP LIGHTWEIGHT
Same as standard Model PP except about 25 percent lighter due to use of aluminum alloys (Dural). Values 40 percent higher. (See individual listings).

WALTHER MODEL PP
SUPER DA PISTOL. .... NiB $992 Ex $764 Gd $550
Caliber: 9x18mm. Seven-round magazine, 3.6-inch bbl., 6.9 inches overall. Weight: 30 oz. Fixed sights. Blued finish. Checkered plastic grips. Made from 1973 to 1979.

MODEL PP 7.65MM
PRESENTATION. .... NiB $1993 Ex $1519 Gd $1142
Made of soft aluminum alloy in green-gold color, these pistols were not intended to be fired.

MODEL PPK DOUBLE-ACTION AUTOMATIC PISTOL
Polizeipistole Kriminal (Detective Pistol). Calibers: .22 LR (5.6mm), .25 Auto (6.35mm), .32 Auto (7.65mm), .380 Auto (9mm). Seven-round magazine, (6-round in .380), 3.25-inch bbl., 5.88 inches overall. Weight: 19 oz. Fixed sights. Blued finish. Checkered plastic grips. **Note: Wartime models are inferior in workmanship to prewar commercial pistols. Made 1931 to 1945.**

NOTE: *After both World Wars, the Walther manufacturing facility was required to cease the production of "restricted" firearms as part of the armistice agreements. Following WW II, Walther moved its manufacturing facility from the original location in Zella/Mehilis, Germany to Ulm/Donau. In 1950, the firm Manufacture de Machines du Haut Rhine at Mulhouse, France was licensed by Walther and started production of PP and PPK models at the Manurhin facility in 1952. The MK II Walthers as produced at Manurhin were imported into the U.S. until 1968 when CGA importation requirements restricted the PPK firearm configuration from further importation. As a result, Walther developed the PPK/S to conform to the new regulations and licensed Interarms to produce the firearm in the U.S. from 1986-99. From 1984-86, Manurhin imported PP and PPK/S type firearms under the Manurhin logo. Additional manufacturing facilities (both licensed & unlicensed) that produced PP and PPK type firearms were established after WW II in various locations and other countries including: China, France, Hungary, Korea, Romania and Turkey. In 1996, Walther was sold to Umarex Sportwaffen GmbH and manufacturing facilities were relocated in Arnsberg, Germany. In 1999, Walther formed a partnership with Smith and Wesson and selected Walther firearms were licensed for production in the U.S.*

**Walther PPK
(WW II)**

**Walther PPK
Silver-Plated**

COMMERCIAL MODEL W/EAGLE "N" PROOF (PREWAR)
.22 cal. (w/Comm. Eagle "N" proof) .... NiB $2250 Ex $1674 Gd $1425
.25 cal. (w/Comm. Eagle "N" proof) ..... NiB $7500 Ex $6278 Gd $4866
.32 cal. (w/Comm. Eagle "N" proof) ..... NiB $950 Ex $736 Gd $533
.380 cal. (w/Comm. Eagle "N" proof) ... NiB $4500 Ex $3514 Gd $3278

WARTIME MODEL W/EAGLE "N" PROOF
.22 cal. (w/Comm. Eagle "N" proof) ..... NiB $1800 Ex $1665 Gd $1335
.22 cal. (w/Dural frame) .... NiB $1800 Ex $1665 Gd $1274
.32 cal. (w/Comm. Eagle "N" proof)...... NiB $1100 Ex $926 Gd $720
.32 cal. (w/Dural frame)............... NiB $1100 Ex $926 Gd $720
.32 cal. (w/Verchromt Fin., Pre-War) ...... NiB $1100 Ex $926 Gd $720
.380 cal. (w/Comm. Eagle "N" proof) ... NiB $3750 Ex $2240 Gd $1990
.380 cal. (w/Dural frame)............ NiB $3750 Ex $2240 Gd $1990
.380 cal. (w/Verchromt Fin., Pre-War) .... NiB $3750 Ex $2240 Gd $1990
.22 cal. (w/Comm. Eagle "N" proof) .... NiB $801 Ex $791 Gd $569
.32 cal. (w/Waffenampt proofs) .... NiB $1040 Ex $756 Gd $396
.32 cal. (w/Eagle "C" Nazi Police markings) . NiB $1040 Ex $756 Gd $355
.32 cal. (w/Eagle "F" Nazi Police markings) .... NiB $1396 Ex $1036 Gd $495
.32 cal. (w/NSKK markings)............. NiB $2222 Ex $1811 Gd $1286
.32 cal. (w/NSDAP Gruppe markings) ... NiB $2123 Ex $1608 Gd $1170
.380 cal. (w/Waffenampt proofs) .... NiB $1378 Ex $1069 Gd $811

COMMERCIAL MODEL (POST-WAR)
.22 cal. (German manufacture)............ NiB $1055 Ex $926 Gd $411
.32 cal. (German manufacture)............ NiB $950 Ex $589 Gd $383
.380 cal. (German manufacture).......... NiB $1070 Ex $591 Gd $488
.22 cal. (French manufacture) .... NiB $2212 Ex $924 Gd $538
.32 cal. (French manufacture) .... NiB $857 Ex $651 Gd $420
.380 cal. (French manufacture) .... NiB $1173 Ex $839 Gd $452
.22, .32 or .380 cal. (other foreign manuf.) .. NiB $332 Ex $275 Gd $201

COMMERCIAL MODEL (U.S. PRODUCTION)
.380 cal. (w/blue finish).................... NiB $544 Ex $431 Gd $385
.380 cal. (w/nickel finish) .... NiB $544 Ex $431 Gd $385
.32 or .380 Cal. (stainless steel)............. NiB $544 Ex $431 Gd $385

MODEL PPK DELUXE ENGRAVED
These elaborately engraved models are available in blued finish, chrome-, silver- or gold-plated.
Blued finish .... NiB $1848 Ex $1488 Gd $1153
Chrome-plated .... NiB $2946 Ex $1555 Gd $1190
Silver-plated .... NiB $2141 Ex $1600 Gd $1236

Gold-plated .... NiB $2489 Ex $1897 Gd $1411
W/ivory grips, add $250
W/Presentation case, add $700
.22 cal, add $50
.25 cal, add $100
.380 cal, add $95

MODEL PPK LIGHTWEIGHT
Same as standard Model PPK except about 25 percent lighter due to aluminum alloys. Values 50 percent higher.

MODEL PPK 7.65MM
PRESENTATION.............. NiB $1770 Ex $1312 Gd $817
Made of soft aluminum alloy in green-gold color, these pistols were not intended to be fired.

MODEL PPK/S DA AUTOMATIC PISTOL
Designed to meet the requirements of the U.S. Gun Control Act of 1968, this model has the frame of the PP and the shorter slide and bbl., of the PPK. Overall length: 6.1 inches. Weight: 23 oz. Other specifications are the same as those of standard PPK except steel frame only. German, French and U.S. production 1971 to date. U.S. version made by Interarms 1978 1999.
.22 cal. (German manufacture) ... NiB $1223 Ex $914 Gd $528
.32 cal. (German manufacture) ... NiB $907 Ex $701 Gd $439
.380 cal. (German manufacture) .. NiB $1223 Ex $889 Gd $451
.22 cal. (French manufacture) ..... NiB $842 Ex $610 Gd $455
.32 cal. (French manufacture) ..... NiB $847 Ex $533 Gd $393
.380 cal. (French manufacture) .... NiB $893 Ex $584 Gd $440
.22, .32 or .380 cal., blue
(U.S. manufacture) .... NiB $575 Ex $462 Gd $343
.22, .32 or .380 cal., stainless
(U.S. manuf.) .... NiB $575 Ex $462 Gd $421

NOTE: *Interarms (Interarmco) acquired a license from Walther in 1978 to manufacturer PP and PPK models at the Ranger Manufacturing Co., Inc. in Gadsden, Alabama. In 1988 the Ranger facility was licensed as EMCO and continued to produce Walther firearms for Interarms until 1996. From 1996-99, Black Creek in Gadsden, Alabama produced Walther pistols for Interarms. In 1999, Smith & Wesson acquired manufacturing rights for Walther firearms at the Black Creek facility.*

Walther Free Pistol

MODELS PPK/S DELUXE ENGRAVED
These elaborately engraved models are available in blued finish, chrome-, silver- or gold-plated.

Blued finish . . . . NiB $1561 Ex $1149 Gd $997
Chrome-plated . . . . NiB $1446 Ex $1147 Gd $838
Silver-plated. . . . . NiB $1612 Ex $1200 Gd $894
Gold-plated . . . . NiB $1790 Ex $1456 Gd $930

NOTE: *The following Walther pistols are now manufactured by Carl Walther, Waffenfabrik, Ulm/Donau, Germany.*

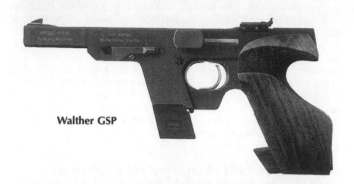

Walther GSP

SELF-LOADING
SPORT PISTOL . . . . NiB $791 Ex $739 Gd $508
Caliber: .22 LR. 10-round magazine, bbl. lengths: 6- and 9-inch, 9.88 inches overall w/6-inch bbl. Target sights. Blued finish. One-piece, wood or plastic grips, checkered. Intro. in 1932.

MODEL FREE PISTOL . . . . NiB $1476 Ex $1279 Gd $1025
Single-Shot. Caliber: .22 LR. 11.7-inch heavy bbl., Weight: 48 oz. Adj. grips and target sights w/electronic trigger. Importation disc. 1991.

MODEL GSP TARGET AUTOMATIC PISTOL
Calibers: .22 LR, .32 S&W Long Wadcutter. Five-round magazine, 4.5-inch bbl., 11.8 inches overall. Weights: 44.8 oz. (.22 cal.) or 49.4 oz. (.32 cal.). Adj. target sights. Black finish. Walnut thumbrest grips w/adj. handrest. Made from 1969 to 1994.
.22 LR . . . . NiB $1470 Ex $1345 Gd $795
.32 S&W Long
Wadcutter . . . . NiB $2652 Ex $2442 Gd $2000
Conversion unit.
.22 Short
or .22 LR . . . . Add $995

MODEL OSP RAPID
FIRE TARGET PISTOL. . . . . NiB $1680 Ex $1455 Gd $1275
Caliber: .22 Short. Five-round magazine, 4.5-inch bbl., 11.8 inches overall. Weight: 42.3 oz. Adj. target sights. Black finish. Walnut thumbrest grips w/adj. handrest. .22 LR conversion unit available (add $275). Made from 1968 to 1994.

MODEL P4 (P38-LV)
DA PISTOL . . . . NiB $756 Ex $653 Gd $339
Similar to P38 except has an uncocking device instead of a manual safety. Caliber: 9mm Para. 4.3-inch bbl., 7.9 inches overall. Other general specifications same as for current model P38. Made from 1974 to 1982.

MODEL P5 DA PISTOL . . . . NiB $838 Ex $709 Gd $478
Alloy frame w/frame-mounted decocking levers. Caliber: 9mm Para. Eight-round magazine, 3.5-inch bbl., 7 inches overall. Weight: 28 oz. blued finish. Checkered walnut or synthetic grips. Made from 1997 to date.

MODEL P5
COMPACT PISTOL . . . . NiB $1018 Ex $890 Gd $452
Similar to model P5 except w/3.1-inch bbl. and weight: 26 oz. Imported from 1987.

Walther P5

MODEL P38 (P1) DA AUTOMATIC
Postwar commercial version of the P38, has light alloy frame. Calibers: .22 LR, 7.65mm Luger, 9mm Para. Eight-round magazine, bbl., lengths: 5.1-inch in .22 caliber, 4.9- inch in 7.65mm and 9mm, 8.5 inches overall. Weight: 28.2 oz. Fixed sights. Nonreflective black finish. Checkered plastic grips. Made from 1957 to 1989. Note: The "P1" is W. German Armed Forces official pistol.
.22 LR . . . . NiB $761 Ex $608 Gd $400
Other calibers . . . . NiB $709 Ex $560 Gd $344

MODEL P38 DELUXE ENGRAVED PISTOL
Elaborately engraved, available in blued or chrome-, silver- or gold-plated finish.
Blued finish . . . . NiB $1963 Ex $1474 Gd $903
Chrome-plated . . . . NiB $1646 Ex $1311 Gd $874
Silver-plated . . . . NiB $1620 Ex $1311 Gd $919

MODEL P38K . . . . **NiB $786 Ex $688 Gd $354**
Short-barreled version of current P38, the "K" standing for "kurz" (meaning short). Same general specifications as standard model except 2.8-inch bbl., 6.3 inches overall, weight: 27.2 oz. Front sight is slide mounted. Caliber: 9mm Para. Made from 1974 to 1980.

MODEL P 88
DA AUTOMATIC
PISTOL . . . . **NiB $1067 Ex $812 Gd $676**
Caliber: 9mm Para. 15-round magazine, 4-inch bbl., 7.38 inches overall. Weight: 31.5 oz. Blade front sight, adj. rear. Checkered black synthetic grips. External hammer w/ambidextrous decocking levers. Alloy frame w/matte blued steel slide. Made 1987 to 1993.

MODEL P 88 DA COMPACT
Similar to the standard P 88 Model except w/10- or 13-round magazine, 3.8-inch bbl., 7.1 inches overall. Weight: 29 oz. Imported from 1993 to 2003.
Model P88
(early importation) . . . . **NiB $980 Ex $828 Gd $570**
Model P88
(post 1994 importation) . . . . **NiB $980 Ex $828 Gd $570**

MODEL P99 DA
AUTOMATIC PISTOL . . . . **NiB $695 Ex $500 Gd $430**
Calibers: 9mm Para., .40 S&W or 9x21mm. 10-round magazine, 4-inch bbl., 7.2 inches overall. Weight: 22-25 oz. Ambidextrous magazine release, decocking lever and 3-function safety. Interchangeable front post sight, micro-adj. rear. Polymer gripframe w/blued slide. Imported from 1995 to date.

MODEL TPH DA POCKET PISTOL
Light alloy frame. Calibers: .22 LR, .25 ACP (6.35mm). Six-round magazine, 2.25-inch bbl., 5.38 inches overall. Weight: 14 oz. Fixed sights. Blued finish. Checkered plastic grips. Made 1968 to date. Note: Few Walther-made models reached the U.S. because of import restrictions. A U.S.-made version was mfd. by Interarms from 1986 to 1999.
German model . . . . **NiB $875 Ex $729 Gd $565**
U.S. model . . . . **NiB $425 Ex $360 Gd $275**

NOTE: The Walther Olympia Model pistols were manufactured 1952-1963 by Hämmerli AG Jagd-und Sportwaffenfabrik, Lenzburg, Switzerland, and marketed as "Hämmerli-Walther." See Hämmerli listings for specific data.

OLYMPIA MODEL
200 AUTO PISTOL,
1952 TYPE . . . . **NiB $715 Ex $600 Gd $445**
Similar to 1936 Walther Olympia Funfkampf Model.

For the following Hammerli-Walther Models
(200, 201, 202, 203, 204, and 205)
See listings under Hammerli Section.

WARNER PISTOL — Norwich, Connecticut Warner Arms Corp. (or Davis-Warner Arms Co.)

INFALLIBLE POCKET
AUTOMATIC PISTOL . . . . **NiB $450 Ex $310 Gd $225**
Caliber: .32 Auto. Seven-round magazine, 3-inch bbl., 6.5 inches overall. Weight: About 24 oz. Fixed sights. Blued finish. Hard rubber grips. Made from 1917 to 1919.

Walther P38

Walther P38K

Walther P88

Walther TPH
(Current)

**Webley 9MM
Military Police Revolver**

**Webley Mark III
38 Military & Police Revolver**

WEBLEY & SCOTT LTD. — London and Birmingham, England

**MODEL 9MM MILITARY
& POLICE AUTOMATIC** ...... NiB $1500 Ex $1395 Gd $1190
Caliber: 9mm Browning Long. Eight-round magazine, 8 inches overall. Weight: 32 oz. Fixed sights. Blued finish. Checkered Vulcanite grips. Made from 1909 to 1930.

**MODEL 25
HAMMER AUTOMATIC** .... NiB $465 Ex $301 Gd $152
Caliber: .25 Automatic. Six-round magazine, overall length: 4.75 inches. Weight: 11.75 oz. No sights. Blued finish. Checkered Vulcanite grips. Made from 1906 to 1940.

**MODEL 25 HAMMERLESS
AUTOMATIC** .... NiB $460 Ex $276 Gd $173
Caliber: .25 Automatic. Six-round magazine, overall length: 4.25 inches, weight: 9.75 oz. Fixed sights. Blued finish. Checkered Vulcanite grips. Made from 1909 to 1940.

**MARK I 455
AUTOMATIC PISTOL** .... NiB $1000 Ex $845 Gd $595
Caliber: .455 Webley Auto. Seven-round magazine, 5-inch bbl., 8.5 inches overall. Weight: About 39 oz. Fixed sights. Blued finish. Checkered Vulcanite grips. Made 1913-31. Reissued during WWII. Total production about 9,300. Note: Mark I No. 2 is same pistol w/adj. rear sight and modified manual safety.

**MARK III 38 MILITARY
& POLICE REVOLVER** .... NiB $900 Ex $735 Gd $585
Hinged frame. DA. Caliber: .38 S&W. Six-round cylinder, bbl. lengths: 3- and 4-inches. 9.5 inches overall (with 4-inch bbl.). Weight: 21 oz. (with 4-inch bbl.). Fixed sights. Blued finish. Checkered walnut or Vulcanite grips. Made from 1897 to 1945.

**MARK IV 22 CALIBER
TARGET REVOLVER** .... NiB $755 Ex $632 Gd $272
Same frame and general appearance as Mark IV .38. Caliber: .22 LR. Six-round cylinder, 6-inch bbl., 10.13 inches overall. Weight: 34 oz. Target sights. Blued finish. Checkered grips. Disc. in 1945.

**MARK IV 38 MILITARY
& POLICE REVOLVER** .... NiB $750 Ex $632 Gd $272
Identical in appearance to the double-action Mark IV .22 w/hinged frame except chambered for .38 S&W. Six-round cylinder, bbl. length: 3-, 4- and 5-inches; 9.13 inches overall (with 5-inch bbl.). Weight: 27 oz. (with 5-inch bbl.). Fixed sights. Blued finish. Checkered grips. Made from 1929 to 1957.

**MARK VI NO. 1 BRITISH
SERVICE REVOLVER** .... NiB $600 Ex $510 Gd $435
DA. Hinged frame. Caliber: 455 Webley. Six-round cylinder, bbl. lengths: 4-, 6- and 7.5-inches; 11.25 inches overall (with 6-inch bbl.). Weight: 38 oz. (with 6-inch bbl.). Fixed sights. Blued finish. Checkered walnut or Vulcanite grips. Made from 1915 to 1947.

**MARK VI 22
TARGET REVOLVER** .... NiB $1200 Ex $1010 Gd $830
Same frame and general appearance as the Mark VI 455. Caliber: .22 LR. Six-round cylinder, 6-inch bbl., 11.25 inches overall. Weight: 40 oz. Target sights. Blued finish. Checkered walnut or Vulcanite grips. Disc. in 1945.

**METROPOLITAN POLICE
AUTOMATIC PISTOL** .... NiB $1508 Ex $1454 Gd $1215
Calibers: .32 Auto, .380 Auto. Eight-round (.32) or 7-round (.380) magazine, 3.5-inch bbl., 6.25 inches overall. weight: 20 oz. Fixed sights. Blued finish. Checkered Vulcanite grips. Made from 1906-40 (.32) and 1908 to 1920 (.380).

RIC MODEL DA REVOLVER ...... NiB $345 Ex $298 Gd $154
Royal Irish Constabulary or Bulldog Model. Solid frame. Caliber: .455 Webley. Five-round cylinder, 2.25-inch bbl., weight: 21 oz. Fixed sights. Blued finish. Checkered walnut or vulcanite grips. Disc.

**SEMIAUTOMATIC
SINGLE-SHOT PISTOL** .... NiB $1020 Ex $861 Gd $578
Similar in appearance to the Webley Metropolitan Police Automatic, this pistol is "semiautomatic" in the sense that the fired case is extracted and ejected and the hammer cocked as in a blow-back automatic pistol; it is loaded singly and the slide manually operated in loading. Caliber: .22 Long, 4.5- or 9-inch bbl., 10.75 inches overall (with 9-inch bbl.). Weight: 24 oz. (with 9-inch bbl.). Adj. sights. Blued finish. Checkered Vulcanite grips. Made from 1911 to 1927.

SINGLE-SHOT TARGET PISTOL ... NiB $1520 Ex $1390 Gd $1147
Hinge frame. Caliber: .22 LR. 10-inch bbl., 15 inches overall. Weight: 37 oz. Fixed sights on earlier models, current production has adj. rear sight. Blued finish. Checkered walnut or Vulcanite grips. Made from 1909.

FOSBERY AUTOMATIC REVOLVER
Hinged frame. Recoil action revolves cylinder and cocks hammer. Caliber: 455 Webley. Six-round cylinder, 6-inch bbl., 12 inches overall. Weight: 42 oz. Fixed or adjustable sights. Blued finish. Checkered walnut grips. Made 1901-1939. Note: A few were produced in caliber .38 Colt Auto w/an 8-shot cylinder (very rare).
1901 model .... NiB $8000 Ex $5905 Gd $3310
1902 model .... NiB $20,000 Ex $17,985 Gd $15,450
1903 model .... NiB $6500 Ex $5190 Gd $3757
.38 Colt (8-round), add 100%
Target model w/adjustable sights, add 20%

WESSON FIREARMS CO., INC. — Palmer, Massachusetts Formerly Dan Wesson Firearms, Inc. Acquired by CZ-USA in 2005.

MODEL 8 SERVICE
Same general specifications as Model 14 except caliber .38 Special. Made from 1971 to 1975. Values same as for Model 14.

MODEL 8-2 SERVICE
Same general specifications as Model 14-2 except caliber .38 Special. Made from 1975 to date. Values same as for Model 14-2.

MODEL 9 TARGET
Same as Model 15 except caliber .38 Special. Made from 1971 to 1975. Values same as for Model 15.

MODEL 9-2 TARGET
Same as Model 15-2 except caliber .38 Special. Made from 1975 to date. Values same as for Model 15-2.

MODEL 9-2H HEAVY BARREL
Same general specifications as Model 15-2H except caliber .38 Special. Made from 1975 to date. Values same as for Model 15-2H. Disc. 1983.

MODEL 9-2HV VENT RIB HEAVY BARREL
Same as Model 15-2HV except caliber .38 Special. Made from 1975 to date. Values same as for Model 15-2HV.

MODEL 9-2V VENT RIB
Same as Model 15-2V except caliber .38 Special. Made from 1975 to date. Values same as for Model 15-2H.

MODEL 11 SERVICE DA REVOLVER
Caliber: .357 Magnum. Six-round cylinder. bbl. lengths: 2.5-, 4-, 6-inches interchangeable bbl. assemblies, 9 inches overall (with 4-inch bbl.). Weight: 38 oz. (with 4-inch bbl.). Fixed sights. Blued finish. Interchangeable grips. Made from 1970-71. Note: The Model 11 has an external bbl. nut.
W/one bbl. assembly and grip . . . . . . **NiB $200 Ex $145 Gd $85**
Extra bbl. assembly, add $60
Extra grip, add $45

MODEL 12 TARGET
Same general specifications as Model 11 except has adj. sights. Made from 1970-71.
W/one-bbl. assembly and grip . . . . . . **NiB $245 Ex $160 Gd $95**
Extra bbl. assembly, add $60
Extra grip, add $25

MODEL 14 SERVICE DA REVOLVER
Caliber: .357 Magnum. Six-round cylinder, bbl. length: 2.25-, 3.75-, 5.75-inches; interchangeable bbl. assemblies, 9 inches overall (with 3.75-inch bbl.). Weight: 36 oz. (with 3.75-inch bbl.). Fixed sights. Blued or nickel finish. Interchangeable grips. Made from 1971 to 1975. Note: Model 14 has recessed bbl. nut.
W/one-bbl. assembly and grip . . . . . **NiB $225 Ex $155 Gd $100**
Extra bbl. assembly, add $60
Extra grip, add $25

MODEL 14-2 SERVICE DA REVOLVER
Caliber: .357 Magnum. Six-round cylinder, bbl. lengths: 2.5-, 4-, 6-, 8-inch; interchangeable bbl. assemblies, 9.25 inches overall (with 4-inch bbl.) Weight: 34 oz. (with 4-inch bbl.). Fixed sights. Blued finish. Interchangeable grips. Made from 1975 to 1995. Note: Model 14-2 has recessed bbl. nut.

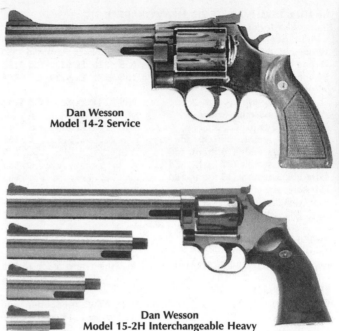

Dan Wesson
Model 14-2 Service

Dan Wesson
Model 15-2H Interchangeable Heavy

**W/one bbl. assembly
(8 inch) and grip** . . . . **NiB $225 Ex $199 Gd $148**
**W/one bbl. assembly
(other lengths) and grip** . . . . **NiB $225 Ex $199 Gd $148**
Extra bbl. assembly, 8 inch, add $65
**Extra bbl. assembly,
other lengths, add** $50
Extra grip, add $25

MODEL 15 TARGET
Same general specifications as Model 14 except has adj. sights. Made from 1971 to 1975.
**W/one bbl. assembly
and grip** . . . . **NiB $275 Ex $200 Gd $155**
Extra bbl. assembly, add $60
Extra grip, add $25

MODEL 15-2 TARGET
Same general specifications as Model 14-2 except has adj. rear sight and interchangeable blade front; also avail. w/10-, 12- or 15-inch bbl., Made from 1975 to 1995.
W/one bbl. assembly (8 inch) and grip   NiB $315 Ex $264 Gd $156
W/one bbl. assembly (10 inch) and grip . . . **NiB $315 Ex $264 Gd $156**
**W/one bbl. assembly
(12 inch)/grip. Disc.** . . . . **NiB $315 Ex $264 Gd $156**
**W/one bbl. assembly
(15 inch)/grip. Disc.** . . . . **NiB $315 Ex $264 Gd $156**
**W/one-bbl. assembly
(other lengths)/grip** . . . . **NiB $204 Ex $139 Gd $103**
Extra bbl. assembly, add $65
Extra grip, add $25

MODEL 15-2H HEAVY BARREL
Same as Model 15-2 except has heavy bbl., assembly weight: with 4-inch bbl., 38 oz. Made from 1975 to 1983.
W/one bbl. assembly . . . . **NiB $445 Ex $310 Gd $195**
Extra bbl. assembly, add $65
Extra grip, add $25

MODEL 15-2HV VENT RIB HEAVY BARREL

Same as Model 15-2 except has vent rib heavy bbl. assembly; weight: (w/4-inch bbl.) 37 oz. Made from 1975 to 1995.

W/one bbl. assembly (8 inch) and grip NiB $276	Ex $230	Gd $153
W/one bbl. assembly (10 inch) and grip NiB $276	Ex $230	Gd $153
W/one bbl. assembly (12 inch) and grip NiB $276	Ex $230	Gd $153
W/one bbl. assembly (15 inch) and grip .... NiB $291	Ex $266	Gd $189
W/one bbl. assembly (other lengths) and grip .... NiB $275	Ex $199	Gd $143
Extra bbl. assembly (8 inch), add $65		
Extra bbl. assembly (10 inch), add $65		
Extra bbl. assembly (12 inch), add $65		
Extra bbl. assembly (15 inch), add $65		
Extra bbl. assembly (other lengths), add.................................... $65		
Extra grip, add.. $25		

MODEL 15-2V VENT RIB

Same as Model 15-2 except has vent rib bbl. assembly, weight: 35 oz. (with 4-inch bbl.). Made from 1975 to date. Values same as for 15-2H.

HUNTER PACS

Dan Wesson Hunter Pacs are offered in all Magnum calibers and include heavy vent rib 8-inch shrouded bbl., Burris scope mounts, bbl. changing tool in a case.

HP22M-V .... NiB $845	Ex $646	Gd $447	
HP22M-2 .... NiB $698	Ex $575	Gd $417	
HP722M-V .... NiB $800	Ex $656	Gd $472	
HP722M-2 .... NiB $775	Ex $635	Gd $458	
HP32-V .... NiB $749	Ex $602	Gd $444	
HP32-2 .... NiB $660	Ex $544	Gd $395	
HP732-V .... NiB $782	Ex $641	Gd $461	
HP732-2 .... NiB $737	Ex $605	Gd $437	
HP15-V .... NiB $737	Ex $605	Gd $437	
HP15-2 .... NiB $686	Ex $564	Gd $409	
HP715-V .... NiB $788	Ex $646	Gd $465	
HP715-2 .... NiB $737	Ex $605	Gd $437	
HP41-V .... NiB $654	Ex $539	Gd $392	
HP741-V .... NiB $841	Ex $689	Gd $495	
HP741-2 .... NiB $739	Ex $607	Gd $439	
HP44-V .... NiB $828	Ex $689	Gd $488	
HP44-2 .... NiB $739	Ex $607	Gd $439	
HP744-V .... NiB $901	Ex $740	Gd $530	
HP744-2 .... NiB $879	Ex $719	Gd $515	
HP40-V .... NiB $584	Ex $483	Gd $354	
HP40-2 .... NiB $800	Ex $656	Gd $472	
HP740-V .... NiB $947	Ex $774	Gd $554	
HP740-2 .... NiB $879	Ex $719	Gd $515	
HP375-V .... NiB $571	Ex $473	Gd $347	
HP375-2 .... NiB $921	Ex $754	Gd $540	
HP45-V .... NiB $711	Ex $585	Gd $424	

WHITNEY FIREARMS COMPANY —
Hartford, Connecticut

WOLVERINE AUTOMATIC PISTOL

Dural frame/shell contains all operating components. Caliber: .22 LR. 10-round magazine, 4.63-inch bbl., 9 inches overall. Weight: 23 oz. Partridge-type sights. Blued or nickel finish. Plastic grips. Made from 1955 to 1962.

Wolverine model, blue .... NiB $575	Ex $405	Gd $256
Wolverine model, nickel ...... NiB $1075	Ex $800	Gd $650

WICHITA ARMS — Wichita, Kansas

CLASSIC PISTOL

Caliber: Chambered to order. Bolt-action, single-shot. 11.25-inch octagonal bbl., 18 inches overall. Weight: 78 oz. Open micro sights. Custom-grade checkered walnut stock. Blued finish. Made from 1980 to 1997.

Standard .... NiB $3251	Ex $2490	Gd $2223
Presentation grade (engraved) .... NiB $5300	Ex $3841	Gd $2097

HIUNTER PISTOL .... NiB $1388 Ex $1002 Gd $822
Bolt-action, single-shot. Calibers: .22 LR, .22 WRF, 7mm Super Mag., 7-30 Waters, .30-30 Win., .32 H&R Mag., .357 Mag., .357 Super Mag. 10.5-inch bbl., 16.5 inches overall, weight: 60 oz. No sights (scope mount only). Stainless steel finish. Walnut stock. Made from 1983 to 1994.

INTERNATIONAL PISTOL ...... NiB $690 Ex $541 Gd $423
Top-break, single-shot. SA. Calibers: 7-30 Waters, 7mm Super Mag., 7R (.30-30 Win. necked to 7mm), .30-30 Win. .357 Mag., .357 Super Mag., .32 H&R Mag., .22 Mag., .22 LR. 10- and 14-inch bbl. (10.5 inch for centerfire calibers). Weight: 50-71 oz. Partridge front sight, adj. rear. Walnut forend and grips.

MK-40 SILHOUETTE PISTOL . NiB $1540 Ex $1358 Gd $1152
Calibers: .22-250, 7mm IHMSA, .308 Win. Bolt-action, single-shot. 13-inch bbl., 19.5 inches overall. Weight: 72 oz. Wichita Multi-Range sight system. Aluminum receiver w/blued bbl., gray Fiberthane glass stock. Made from 1981 to 1994.

SILHOUETTE
PISTOL (WSP) .... NiB $1520 Ex $1400 Gd $1275
Calibers: .22-250, 7mm IHMSA 308 Win. Bolt-action, single-shot. 14.94-inch bbl., 21.38 inches overall. Weight: 72 oz. Wichita Multi-Range sight system. Blued finish. Walnut or gray Fiberthane glass stock. Walnut center or rear grip. Made from 1979 to 1994.

WILKINSON ARMS — Parma, Idaho

LINDA SEMI-
AUTOMATIC CARBINE ...... NiB $1300 Ex $1190 Gd $995
Caliber: 9mm Para. Luger. 31-round magazine, 8.25-inch bbl., 12.25 inches overall. Weight: 77 oz. Rear peep sight w/blade front. Blued finish. Checkered composition grips.

"SHERRY" SEMI-
AUTOMATIC PISTOL......... NiB $245 Ex $160 Gd $110
Caliber: .22 LR. Eight-round magazine, 2.13-inch bbl., 4.38 inches overall. Weight: 9.25 oz. Crossbolt safety. Fixed sights. Blued or blue-gold finish. Checkered composition grips.

34th Edition
GUN TRADER'S GUIDE

Rifles

Action Arms Timber Wolfe

Alpha Arms Custom

Alpha Arms Alaskan

Alpha Arms Jaguar

AA ARMS — Monroe, North Carolina

AR-9 SEMIAUTOMATIC CARBINE. . . NiB $770 Ex $594 Gd $400
Semiautomatic recoil-operated rifle w/side-folding metal stock design. Fires from a closed bolt. Caliber: 9mm Parabellum. 20-round magazine. 16.25-inch bbl., 33 inches overall. Weight: 6.5 lbs. Fixed blade, protected postfront sight adjustable for elevation, winged square notched rear. Matte phosphate/blue or nickel finish. Checkered polymer grip/frame. Made 1991 to 1994 (banned)

ACTION ARMS — Philadelphia, Pennsylvania

MODEL B SPORTER
SEMI-AUTOMATIC CARBINE . . . . . NiB $602 Ex $530 Gd $352
Similar to Uzi Carbine (see separate listing) except w/thumbhole stock. Caliber: 9mm Parabellum, 10-round magazine. 16-inch bbl. Weight: 8.75 lbs. Post front sight; adj. rear. Imported 1994.

TIMBERWOLF REPEATING RIFLE
Calibers: .357 Mag./.38 Special and .44 Mag. slide-action. Tubular magazine holds 10 and 8 rounds, respectively. 18.5-inch bbl. 36.5 inches overall. Weight: 5.5 lbs. Fixed blade front sight; adj. rear. Receiver w/integral scope mounts. Checkered walnut stock. Imported from 1989 to 1993, later by I.M.I. Israel.

Blued model	NiB $317 Ex $260 Gd $184
Chrome model, add.	$50
.44 Mag., add	$100

ALPHA ARMS, INC. — Dallas, Texas

CUSTOM BOLT-ACTION RIFLE . . . . NiB $1627 Ex $1296 Gd $837
Calibers: .17 Rem. thru .338 Win. Mag. Right or left-hand action in three action lengths w/three-lug locking system and 60-degree bolt rotation. 20- to 24-inch round or octagonal bbl. Weight: 6 to 7 lbs. No sights. Presentation-grade California Claro walnut stock w/hand-rubbed oil finish, custom inletted sling swivels and ebony forend tip. Made from 1984 to 1987.

ALASKAN BOLT-ACTION RIFLE . . . . . . NiB $1632 Ex $1301 Gd $842
Similar to Custom model but w/stainless-steel bbl. and receiver w/all other parts coated w/Nitex. Weight: 6.75 to 7.25 lbs. Open sights w/bbl-band sling swivel. Classic-style Alpha wood stock w/Niedner-style steel grip cap and solid recoil pad. Made from 1985 to 1987.

GRAND SLAM
BOLT-ACTION RIFLE. . . . . NiB $1284 Ex $1029 Gd $723
Same as Custom model but has Alphawood (fiberglass and wood) classic-style stock featuring Niedner-style grip cap. Wt: 6.5 lbs. Left-hand models same value. Made 1985 to 1987.

CUSTOM BOLT-ACTION RIFLE

Same as Custom Rifle except designed on Mauser-style action w/claw extractor drilled and tapped for scope. Originally designated Alpha Model 1. Calibers: .243, 7mm-08, .308 original chambering (1984 to 1985) up to .338 Win. Mag. in standard model; .338 thru .458 Win. Mag. in Big Five model (1987). Teflon-coated trigger guard/floorplate assembly. Made from 1984 to 1987.

Jaguar Grade I	NiB $1009	Ex $805	Gd $591
Jaguar Grade II	NiB $1231	Ex $619	Gd $568
Jaguar Grade III	NiB $1282	Ex $1027	Gd $721
Jaguar Grade IV	NiB $1389	Ex $1032	Gd $726
Big Five model	NiB $1648	Ex $1159	Gd $934

AMERICAN ARMS — N. Kansas City, Missouri

1860 HENRY . . . . NiB $893 Ex $678 Gd $398
Replica of 1860 Henry rifle. Calibers: .44-40 or .45 LC. 24.25-inch half-octagonal bbl. 43.75 inches overall. Weight: 9.25 lbs. Brass frame and appointments. Straight-grip walnut buttstock.

1866 WINCHESTER
Replica of 1866 Winchester. Calibers: .44-40 or .45 LC. 19-inch round tapered bbl. (carbine) or 24.25-inch tapered octagonal bbl. (rifle). 38 to 43.25 inches overall. Weight: 7.75 or 8.15 lbs. Brass frame, elevator and buttplate. Walnut buttstock and forend.

Carbine	NiB $701	Ex $599	Gd $380
Rifle	NiB $701	Ex $599	Gd $380

1873 WINCHESTER
Replica of 1873 Winchester rifle. Calibers: .44-40 or .45 LC. 24.25-inch tapered octagonal bbl. w/tubular magazine. Color casehardened steel frame w/brass elevator and ejection port cover. Walnut buttstock w/steel buttplate.

Standard model	NiB $841	Ex $688	Gd $408
Deluxe model	NiB $1085	Ex $879	Gd $614

AMERICAN SPIRIT ARMS CORP.— Scottsdale, Arizona

ASA BULL BARREL FLATTOP RIFLE . . . NiB $999 Ex $674 Gd $497
Semi-automatic. Caliber: ..223 Rem. Patterned after AR-15. Forged steel lower receiver, aluminum flattop upper receiver, 24-inch stainless bull barrel, free-floating aluminum hand guard, includes Harris bipod.

ASA BULL BARREL A2 RIFLE . . . . NiB $924 Ex $699 Gd $499
Similar to Flattop Rifle except has A2 upper receiver with carrying handle and sights. Introduced 1999.

OPEN MATCH RIFLE . . . . NiB $1411 Ex $1011 Gd $711
Caliber: .223 Rem. Bbl.: 16-inch fluted and ported stainless steel match with round shroud. Flattop without sights, forged upper and lower receiver, match trigger. Introduced 2001.

LIMITED MATCH RIFLE . . . . NiB $1361 Ex $885 Gd $586
Caliber: .223 Rem. Bbl.: 16-inch fluted stainless steel match with round shroud. National Match front and rear sights; match trigger.

DCM SERVICE RIFLE . . . . NiB $1361 Ex $870 Gd $586
Caliber: .223 Rem. Bbl.: 20-inch stainless steel match type with free-floating shroud. National Match front and rear sights; match trigger; pistol grip.

ASA M4 RIFLE . . . . NiB $900 Ex $645 Gd $450

Caliber: .223 Rem. Non-collapsible stock, M4 hand guard, 16-inch bbl. w/muzzle brake; aluminum flattop upper receiver.

ASA A2 RIFLE . . . . NiB $870 Ex $600 Gd $475
Caliber: .223 Rem. A2 receiver; 20-inch National Match barrel. Intro. 1999.

ASA CARBINE . . . . NiB $1022 Ex $677 Gd $577
Caliber: .223 Rem. or Short. Side-charging, flattop receiver; M4 hand guard; 16-inch National Match bbl. w/slotted muzzle brake.

POST-BAN CARBINE . . . . NiB $880 Ex $618 Gd $463
Caliber: .223 Rem. Wilson 16-inch National Match bbl.; non-collapsible stock. Introduced 1999.

BULL BARREL A2 INVADER . . . . NiB $1007 Ex $697 Gd $517
Caliber: .223 Rem. Similar to ASA 24-inch bull bbl. rifle except has 16-inch stainless steel bbl.. Introduced 1999.

A2 CAR CARBINE . . . . NiB $1002 Ex $697 Gd $527
Caliber: 9mm Parabellum. Forged receiver, non-collapsible stock. Bbl.: 16-inch Wilson w/o muzzle brake, bird cage flash hider (pre-ban) or muzzle brake (post-ban).

FLATTOP CAR RIFLE . . . . NiB $1002 Ex $777 Gd $577
Caliber: 9mm Parabellum. Similar to A2 CAR Rifle except flattop design w/o sights. Introduced 2002.

ASA TACTICAL RIFLE . . . . NiB $1746 Ex $1066 Gd $746
Caliber: .308 Win. Bbl.: 16-inch stainless steel regular or match; side-charging handle; pistol grip.
Match model (w/fluted bbl. match trigger, chrome finish) Add $525

ASA 24-INCH MATCH RIFLE . . . . . . NiB $1746 Ex $1066 Gd $746
Caliber: .308 Win. Bbl.: 24-inch stainless steel match with or w/o fluting/porting. Side-charging handle; pistol grip. Introduced 2002.

AMT (ARCADIA MACHINE & TOOL) — Irwindale, California (1998)

BOLT-ACTION REPEATING RIFLE
Winchester-type push-feed or Mauser-type controlled-feed short-, medium- or long-action. Calibers: .223 Remington, .22-250 Remington, .243 A, .243 Winchester, 6mm PPC, .25-06 Remington, 6.5x08, .270 Winchester, 7x57 Mauser, 7mm-08 Remington, 7mm Remington Mag., 7.62x39mm, .308 Winchester, .30-06, .300 Winchester Mag., .338 Winchester Mag., .375 H&H, .416 Remington, .416 Rigby, .458 Winchester Mag. 22- to 28-inch number 3 contour bbl. Weight: 7.75 to 8.5 lbs. Sights: None furnished; drilled and tapped for scope mounts. Classic composite or Kevlar stock. Made from 1996 to 1997.

Standard model	NiB $850	Ex $684	Gd $496
Deluxe model	NiB $1025	Ex $795	Gd $475

BOLT-ACTION SINGLE-SHOT RIFLE
Winchester-type cone breech push-feed or Mauser-type controlled-feed action. Calibers: .22 Hornet, .22 PPC, .222 Remington, .223 Remington, .22-250 Remington, .243 A, .243 Winchester, 6mm PPC, 6.5x08, .270 Win., 7mm-08 Remington, .308 Winchester 22- to 28-inch #3 contour bbl. Weight: 7.75 to 8.5 lbs. Sights: None furnished; drilled and tapped for scope mounts. Classic composite or Kevlar stock. Made from 1996.

Standard model	NiB $825	Ex $700	Gd $495
Deluxe model	NiB $1020	Ex $679	Gd $475

RIFLES

Anschutz Model 54.18MS-REP

CHALLENGE AUTOLOADING TARGET RIFLE SERIES I, II & III
Similar to Small Game Hunter except w/McMillan target fiberglass stock. Caliber: .22 LR. 10-round magazine. 16.5-, 18-, 20- or 22-inch bull bbl. Drilled and tapped for scope mount; no sights. Stainless steel finish. Made from 1994 to 1998.

Challenger I Standard . . . . NiB $757 Ex $553 Gd $374
Challenger II w/muzzle brake . . . . . NiB $891 Ex $731 Gd $527
Challenger III w/bbl extension . . . . NiB $925 Ex $555 Gd $425
W/jeweled trigger, add $200

LIGHTNING 25/22
AUTOLOADING RIFLE . . . . NiB $293 Ex $217 Gd $151
Caliber: .22 LR. 25-round magazine. 18-inch tapered or bull bbl. Weight: 6 lbs. 37 inches overall. Sights: Adj. rear; ramp front. Folding stainless-steel stock w/matte finish. Made 1986 to 1993.

SMALL GAME HUNTER SERIES
Similar to AMT 25/22 except w/conventional matte black fiberglass/nylon stock. 10-round rotary magazine. 22-inch bbl. 40.5 inches overall. Weight: 6 lbs. Grooved for scope; no sights. Made from 1986 to 1994 (Series I), and 1993 (Series II).

Hunter I. . . . . NiB $300 Ex $195 Gd $134
**Hunter II (w/22-inch
heavy target bbl.)** . . . . NiB $251 Ex $206 Gd $144

MAGNUM HUNTER AUTO RIFLE . . . . NiB $445 Ex $320 Gd $227
Similar to Lightning Small Game Hunter II model except chambered in .22 WRF w/22-inch match-grade bbl. Made from 1995 to 1998.

ANSCHUTZ RIFLES — Ulm, Germany

Currently imported by Merkel USA.

Anschutz models 1407 ISU, 1408-ED, 1411, 1413, 1418, 1432, 1433, 1518 and 1533 were marketed in the U.S by Savage Arms. Further, Anschutz models 1403, 1416, 1422D, 1441, 1516 and 1522D were sold as Savage/Anschutz with Savage model designations (see also listings under Savage Arms

MODEL 54.18MS . . . . NiB $700 Ex $545 Gd $436
Bolt-action, single-shot, Caliber: .22 LR. 22-inch bbl. European hardwood stock w/cheekpiece. Stipple-checkered forend and Wundhammer swell pistol-grip. Receiver grooved, drilled and tapped for scope blocks. Weight: 8.4 lbs. Imported 1982 to 1997.

MODEL 54.18MS-REP REPEATING RIFLE
Same as model 54.18MS except w/repeating action and 5-round magazine. 22- to 30-inch bbl. 41-49 inches overall. Avg. weight: 7 lbs., 12 oz. Hardwood or synthetic gray thumbhole stock. Imported from 1989 to 1997.

Standard MS-REP model . . . . NiB $700 Ex $550 Gd $398
Left-hand model . . . . NiB $710 Ex $565 Gd $400

MODEL 64S BOLT-ACTION SINGLE-SHOT RIFLE
Bolt-action, single-shot. Caliber: .22 LR. 26-inch bbl. Checkered European hardwood stock w/Wundhammer swell pistol-grip and adj. buttplate. Single-stage trigger. Aperture sights. Weight: 8.25 lbs. Imported from 1963 to 1981.

Standard . . . . NiB $1353 Ex $699 Gd $495
Left-hand model . . . . NiB $1353 Ex $699 Gd $495

MODEL 64MS BOLT-ACTION SINGLE-SHOT RIFLE
Bolt-action, single-shot. Caliber: .22 LR. 21.25-inch bbl. European hardwood silhouette-style stock w/cheekpiece. Forend base and Wundhammer swell pistol-grip, stipple-checkered. Adj. two-stage trigger. Receiver grooved, drilled and tapped for scope blocks. Weight: 8 lbs. Imported from 1982 to 1996.

**Standard or Featherweight
(disc. 1988)** . . . . NiB $1100 Ex $636 Gd $475
Left-hand model . . . . NiB $1100 Ex $641 Gd $494

MODEL 64MSR BOLT-ACTION REPEATER
Similar to Anschutz Model 64MS except repeater w/5-round magazine. Imported from 1996.

Standard model . . . . NiB $1000 Ex $736 Gd $575
Left-hand model . . . . NiB $1000 Ex $736 Gd $553

MODEL 520/61 SEMIAUTOMATIC. . . . . . NiB $300 Ex $245 Gd $141
Caliber: .22 LR. 10-round magazine. 24-inch bbl. Sights: Folding leaf rear, hooded ramp front. Receiver grooved for scope mounting. Rotary-style safety. Monte Carlo stock and beavertail forend, checkered. Weight: 6.5 lbs. Imported from 1982 to 1983.

MODEL 525 AUTOLOADER
Caliber: .22 LR. 10-round magazine. 20- or 24-inch bbl. 39 to 43 inches overall. Weight: 6.1 to 6.5 lbs. Adj. folding rear sight; hooded ramp front. Checkered European hardwood Monte Carlo style buttstock and beavertail forend. Sling swivel studs. Imported 1984 to 1995.

**Carbine model
(disc. 1986)** . . . . NiB $427 Ex $293 Gd $190
Rifle model (24-inch bbl.) . . . . NiB $519 Ex $422 Gd $299

MODEL 1403B . . . . NiB $900 Ex $710 Gd $407
A lighter-weight model designed for Biathlon competition. Caliber: .22 LR. 21.5-inch bbl. Adj. two-stage trigger. Adj. grooved wood buttplate, stipple-checkered deep thumb-rest flute and straight pistol-grip. Weight: 9 lbs. w/sights. Imported from 1990 to 1992.

MODEL 1403D MATCH SINGLE-SHOT TARGET RIFLE
Caliber: .22 LR. 25-inch bbl. 43 inches overall. Weight: 8.6 lbs. No sights, receiver grooved for Anschutz target sights. Walnut-finished hardwood target stock w/adj. buttplate. Importation disc. 1992.

Standard model . . . . NiB $683 Ex $555 Gd $392
W/match sights . . . . NiB $942 Ex $763 Gd $534

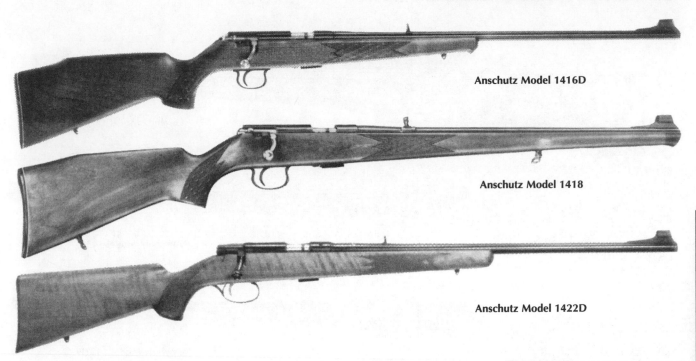

Anschutz Model 1416D

Anschutz Model 1418

Anschutz Model 1422D

MODEL 1407 ISU MATCH 54 RIFLE

Bolt-action, single-shot, caliber: .22 LR. 26.88-inch bbl. Scope bases. Receiver grooved for Anschutz sights. Single-stage adj. trigger. Select walnut target stock w/deep forearm for position shooting, adj. buttplate, hand stop and swivel. Weight: 10 lbs. Imported 1970 to 1981.

Standard model	NiB $604	Ex $527	Gd $270
Left-hand model	NiB $604	Ex $527	Gd $270
W/international sights, add			$65

MODEL 1408 . . . . NiB $450 Ex $398 Gd $347

Bolt-action, single-shot, caliber: .22 LR. 23.5-inch bbl. w/sliding weights. No metallic sights. Receiver drilled and tapped for scope-sight bases. Single-stage adj. trigger. Oversize bolt knob. Select walnut stock w/thumbhole, adj. comb and buttplate. Weight: 9.5 lbs. Intro. 1976. Disc. Add $175 for ED model.

MODEL 1411 MATCH 54 RIFLE

Bolt-action, single-shot. Caliber: .22 LR. 27.5-inch extra heavy bbl. w/mounted scope bases. Receiver grooved for Anschutz sights. Single-stage adj. trigger. Select walnut target stock w/cheekpiece (adj. in 1973 and later production), full pistol-grip, beavertail forearm, adj. buttplate, hand stop and swivel. Model 1411-L has left-hand stock. Weight: 11 lbs. Disc.

W/Non-adj. cheekpiece	NiB $650	Ex $398	Gd $244
W/adj. cheekpiece	NiB $675	Ex $501	Gd $353
with Anschutz			
International Sight set, add			$275

MODEL 1413 SUPER MATCH 54 RIFLE

Freestyle international target rifle w/specifications similar to those of Model 1411, except w/special stock w/thumbhole, adj. pistol grip, adj. cheekpiece in 1973 and later production, adj. hook buttplate, adj. palmrest. Model 1413-L has left-hand stock. Weight: 15.5 lbs. Disc.

W/Non-adj. cheekpiece	NiB $789	Ex $711	Gd $382
W/Adj. cheekpiece	NiB $666	Ex $542	Gd $351
With Anschutz			
International Sight set, add			$275

MODEL 1416D . . . . NiB $572 Ex $553 Gd $347

Bolt-action sporter. Caliber: .22 LR. 22.5-inch bbl. Sights: Folding leaf rear; hooded ramp front. Receiver grooved for scope mounting. Select European stock w/cheekpiece, skip-checkered pistol grip and forearm. Weight: 6 lbs. Imported 1982 to 2007.

MODEL 1416D CLASSIC/CUSTOM SPORTERS

Same as Model 1416D except w/American classic-style stock (Classic) or modified European-style stock w/Monte Carlo roll-over cheekpiece and Schnabel forend (Custom). Weight: 5.5 lbs. (Classic); 6 lbs. (Custom). Imported 1986 to 2007.

Model 1416D Classic	NiB $934	Ex $516	Gd $364
Model 1416D Classic, "True" left-hand	NiB $980	Ex $552	Gd $389
Model 1416D Custom	NiB $915	Ex $500	Gd $345
Model 1416D fiberglass (1991-92)	NiB $943	Ex $603	Gd $424

MODEL 1418 BOLT-ACTION

SPORTER . . . . NiB $391 Ex $314 Gd $185

Caliber: .22 LR. 5- or 10-round magazine. 19.75-inch bbl. Sights: Folding leaf rear; hooded ramp front. Receiver grooved for scope mounting. Select walnut stock, Mannlicher type w/cheekpiece, pistol-grip and forearm skip checkered. Weight: 5.5 lbs. Intro. 1976. Disc.

MODEL 1418D BOLT-ACTION

SPORTER . . . . NiB $973 Ex $860 Gd $514

Caliber: .22 LR. 5- or 10-round magazine. 19.75-inch bbl. European walnut Monte Carlo stock, Mannlicher type w/cheekpiece, pistol-grip and forend skip-line checkered, buffalo horn Schnabel tip. Weight: 5.5 lbs. Imported from 1982 to 1995 and 1998 to 2003.

MODEL 1422D CLASSIC/CUSTOM RIFLE

Bolt-action sporter. Caliber: .22 LR. Five-round removable straight-feed clip magazine. 24-inch bbl. Sights: Folding leaf rear; hooded ramp front. Select European walnut stock, classic type (Classic); Monte Carlo w/hand-carved rollover cheekpiece (Custom). Weight: 7.25 lbs. (Classic) 6.5 lbs. (Custom). Imported 1982 to 1989.

Model 1422D Classic	NiB $792	Ex $637	Gd $405
Model 1422D Custom	NiB $869	Ex $792	Gd $457

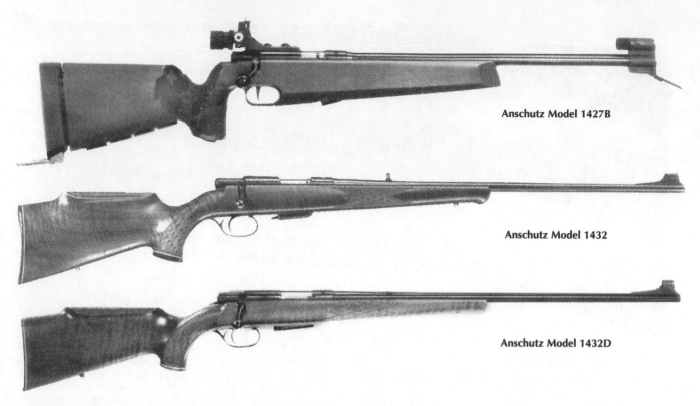

Anschutz Model 1427B

Anschutz Model 1432

Anschutz Model 1432D

MODEL 1827B BIATHLON RIFLE   NiB $1895 Ex $1355 Gd$ 900
Bolt-action clip repeater. Caliber: .22 LR. 21.5-inch bbl. Two-stage trigger w/wing-type safety. Hardwood stock w/deep fluting, pistol grip and deep forestock with adj. hand stop rail. Target sights w/adjustable weights. Advertised in 1981 but imported from 1982 to date as Model 1827B.

MODEL 1430D MATCH . . . . NiB $937 Ex $608 Gd $382
Improved version of Model 64S. Bolt-action, single-shot. Caliber: .22 LR. 26-inch medium-heavy bbl. Walnut Monte Carlo stock w/cheekpiece, adj. buttplate, deep midstock tapered to forend. Pistol-grip and contoured thumb groove w/stipple checkering. Single-stage adj. trigger. Target sights. Weight: 8.38 lbs. Imported from 1982 to 1990.

MODEL 1432 BOLT-ACTION SPORTER
Caliber: .22 Hornet. 5-round box magazine. 24-inch bbl. Sights: Folding leaf rear, hooded ramp front. Receiver grooved for scope mounting. Select walnut stock w/Monte Carlo comb and cheekpiece, pistol-grip and forearm skip-checkered. Weight: 6.75 lbs. Imported from 1974 to 1987. (Reintroduced as 1700/1730 series)
Early model
(1974-85). NiB $1296 Ex $945 Gd $688
Late model
(1985-87). NiB $1112 Ex $890 Gd $607

MODEL 1432D CLASSIC/CUSTOM RIFLE
Bolt-action sporter similar to Model 1422D except chambered for Caliber: .22 Hornet. 4-round magazine. 23.5-inch bbl. Weight: 7.75 lbs. (Classic); 6.5 lbs. (Custom). Classic stock on Classic model; fancy-grade Monte Carlo w/hand-carved rollover cheekpiece (Custom). Imported from 1982 to 1987. (Reintroduced as 1700/1730 series)
Model 1432D Classic . . . . NiB $1297 Ex $946 Gd $689
Model 1432D Custom. . . . . NiB $1126 Ex $895 Gd $612
MODEL 1433 BOLT-ACTION SPORTER . . . . . NiB $1103 Ex $892 Gd $634

Caliber: .22 Hornet. 5-round box magazine. 19.75-inch bbl. Sights: Folding leaf rear, hooded ramp front. Receiver grooved for scope mounting. Single-stage or double-set trigger. Select walnut Mannlicher stock; cheekpiece, pistol-grip and forearm skip-checkered. Weight: 6.5 lbs. Imported from 1976 to 1986.

MODEL 1448D . . . . NiB $334 Ex $303 Gd $215
Similar to Model 1449 except chambered for Caliber: .22 LR. w/22.5-inch smooth bore bbl. and no sights. Walnut-finished hardwood stock. Imported from 1999 to 2001.

MODEL 1449D YOUTH SPORTER . . . . NiB $267 Ex $221 Gd $159
Bolt-action sporter version of Model 2000. Caliber: .22 LR. 5-round box magazine. 16.25-inch bbl. Weight: 3.5 lbs. Hooded ramp front sight, addition. Walnut-finished hardwood stock. Imported from 1990 to 1991.

MODEL 1450B TARGET RIFLE . . . . NiB $686 Ex $505 Gd $351
Biathlon rifle developed on 2000 Series action. 19.5-inch bbl. Weight: 5.5 lbs. Adj. buttplate. Target sights. Imported 1993 to 1994.

MODEL 1451 E/R SPORTER/TARGET
Bolt-action, single-shot (1451E) or repeater (1451R). Caliber: .22 LR. 22- or 22.75-inch bbl. w/o sights. Select hardwood stock w/stippled pistolgrip and vented forearm. beavertail forend, adj. cheekpiece, and deep thumb flute. Weight: 6.5 lbs. Imported from 1996 to 2001.
Model 1451E (disc. 1997) . . . . NiB $447 Ex $344 Gd $241
Model 1451R . . . . NiB $463 Ex $430 Gd $275

MODEL 1451D CLASSIC/CUSTOM RIFLE
Same as Model 1451R except w/walnut-finished hardwood stock (Classic) or modified European-style walnut stock w/Monte Carlo rollover cheekpiece and Schnabel forend (Custom). Weight: 5 lbs. Imported from 1998 to 2001.
Model 1451D Classic (Super) . . . . . NiB $340 Ex $263 Gd $185
Model 1451D Custom. . . . . NiB $479 Ex $438 Gd $299

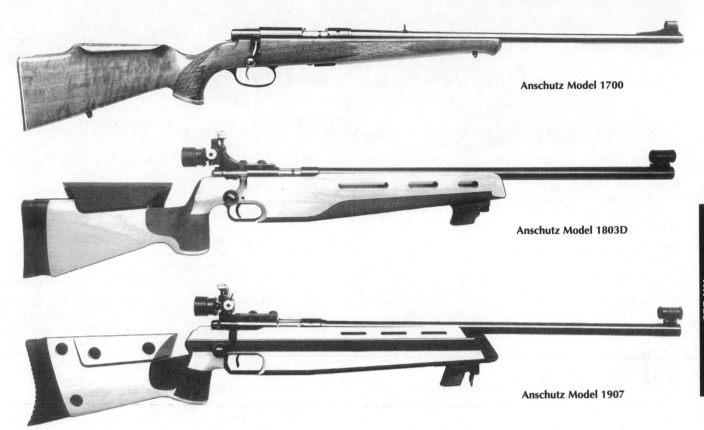

Anschutz Model 1700

Anschutz Model 1803D

Anschutz Model 1907

MODEL 1451 ST- R RIFLE . . . . NiB $467 Ex $427 Gd $312
Same as Model 1451R except w/two-stage trigger and walnut-finished hardwood uncheckered stock. Imported 1996 to 2001.

MODEL 1516D CLASSIC/CUSTOM RIFLE
Same as Model 1416D except chambered for Caliber: .22 Magnum RF, with American classic-style stock (Classic) or modified European-style stock w/Monte Carlo rollover cheekpiece and Schnabel forend (Custom). Weight: 5.5 lbs. (Classic), 6 lbs. (Custom). Imported from 1986 to 2003.
Model 1516D Classic . . . . NiB $688 Ex $538 Gd $363
Model 1516D Custom . . . . NiB $713 Ex $588 Gd $388

MODELS 1516D/1518D LUXUS RIFLES
The alpha designation for these models was changed from Custom to Luxus in 1996 to 1998. (See Custom listings for Luxus values.)

MODELS 1518/1518D SPORTING RIFLES
Same as Model 1418 except chambered for .22 Magnum RF, 4-round box magazine. Model 1518 intro. 1976. Disc. Model 1518D has full Mannlicher-type stock. Imported from 1982 to 2001.
Model 1518 . . . . NiB $741 Ex $621 Gd $391
Model 1518D . . . . NiB $936 Ex $746 Gd $513
W/set trigger, add $125

MODEL 1522D CLASSIC/CUSTOM RIFLE
Same as Model 1422D except chambered for .22 Magnum RF, 4-round magazine. Weight: 6.5 lbs. (Custom). Fancy-grade Classic or Monte Carlo stock w/hand-carved rollover cheekpiece. Imported 1982 to 1989. (Reintroduced as 1700D/1730D series)
Model 1522D Classic . . . . NiB $1056 Ex $866 Gd $616
Model 1522D Custom . . . . NiB $1056 Ex $866 Gd $616

MODEL 1532D CLASSIC/CUSTOM RIFLE
Same as Model 1432D except chambered for .222 Rem. Three-round mag. Weight: 6.5 lbs. (Custom). Classic stock on Classic Model; fancy-grade Monte Carlo stock w/handcarved rollover cheekpiece (Custom). Imported from 1982 to 1989. (Reintroduced as 1700D/174 D0 series)
Model 1532D Classic . . . . NiB $955 Ex $761 Gd $411
Model 1532D Custom . . . . NiB $1251 Ex $961 Gd $661

MODEL 1533 . . . . NiB $1065 Ex $815 Gd $565
Same as Model 1433 except chambered for .222 Rem. Three-shot box magazine. Imported from 1976 to 1994.

MODEL 1700 SERIES BOLT-ACTION REPEATER
Match 54 Sporter. Calibers: .22 LR., .22 Magnum, .22 Hornet, .222 Rem. Five-shot removable magazine 24-inch bbl. 43 inches overall. Weight: 7.5 lbs. Folding leaf rear sight, hooded ramp front. Select European walnut stock w/cheekpiece and Schnabel forend tip. Imported from 1989 to 2001.
Standard Model 1700
Bavarian — rimfire cal. . . . . NiB $971 Ex $911 Gd $551
Standard Model 1700
Bavarian — centerfire cal. . . . . NiB $1292 Ex $1018 Gd $668
Model 1700D Classic (Classic
stock, 6.75 lbs.) rimfire cal. . . . . NiB $1143 Ex $953 Gd $668
Model 1700D Classic — centerfire cal. . . NiB $1256 Ex $1018 Gd $714
Model 1700D Custom — rimfire cal. . . . . . . NiB $1062 Ex $863 Gd $609
Model 1700D Custom — centerfire cal. . . . NiB $1291 Ex $1047 Gd $735
Model 1700D Graphite Cust. (McMillan graphite
reinforced stock, 22-inch bbl., intro. 1991) . . NiB $1120 Ex $945 Gd $620
Select walnut and gold trigger, add $181
Model 1700 FWT Feather-
weight (6.5 lbs.) rimfire calibers . . . . NiB $1097 Ex $891 Gd $627
Model 1700 FWT — centerfire cal. . . . . . . NiB $1258 Ex $1106 Gd $6718

Anschutz Model 2013

MODEL 1733D MANNLICHER....... NiB $1349 Ex $1147 Gd $838
Same as Model 1700D except w/19-inch bbl. and Mannlicher-style stock. 39 inches overall. Weight: 6.25 lbs. Imported from 1993 to 1995 (Reintroduced in 1998, disc. 2001).

MODEL 1740 MONTE CARLO SPORTER
Caliber: .22 Hornet or .222 Rem. Three and 5-round magazines respectively. 24-inch bbl. 43.25 inches overall. Weight: 6.5 lbs. Hooded ramp front, folding leaf rear. Drilled and tapped for scope mounts. Select European walnut stock w/roll-over cheekpiece, checkered grip and forend. Imported from 1998 to 2006.
Model 1740 Custom .... NiB $1313 Ex $1047 Gd $687
Model 1740 Classic
(Meistergrade) .... NiB $1481 Ex $1199 Gd $838

MODEL 1743 MONTE CARLO
SPORTER.................. NiB $1331 Ex $1099 Gd $738
Similar to Model 1740 except w/Mannlicher full stock. Imported from 1997 to 2001.

MODEL 1803D MATCH SINGLE-SHOT TARGET RIFLE
Caliber: .22 LR. 25.5-inch bbl. 43.75 inches overall. Weight: 8.5 lbs. No sights; receiver grooved, drilled and tapped for scope mounts. Blonde or walnut-finished hardwood stock w/adj. cheekpiece, stippled grip and forend. Left-hand version. Imported 1987 to 1993.
Right-hand model
(Reintroduced as 1903D) .... NiB $979 Ex $814 Gd $505
Left-hand model .... NiB $1040 Ex $840 Gd $585

MODEL 1807 ISU
STANDARD MATCH .... NiB $1324 Ex $1050 Gd $680
Bolt-action single-shot. Caliber: 22 LR. 26-inch bbl. Improved Super Match 54 action. Two-stage match trigger. Removable cheekpiece, adj. buttplate, thumbpiece and forestock w/stipple-checkered. Weight: 10 lbs. Imported 1982 to 1988. (Reintroduced as 1907 ISU)

MODEL 1808ED SUPER RUNNING TARGET
Bolt-action single-shot. Caliber: .22 LR. 23.5-inch bbl. w/sliding weights. Improved Super Match 54 action. Heavy beavertail forend w/adj.cheekpiece and buttplate. Adj. single-stage trigger. Weight: 9.5 lbs. Imported from 1982 to 1998.
Right-hand model .... NiB $1608 Ex $1309 Gd $845
Left-hand model .... NiB $1650 Ex $1335 Gd $931

MODEL 1808MS-R
METALLIC SILHOUETTE .... NiB $1983 Ex $1520 Gd $902
Bolt-action repeater. Caliber: .22 LR. 19.2-inch bbl. w/o sights. Thumbhole Monte Carlo stock w/grooved forearm enhanced w/ "Anschutz" logo. Weight: 8.2 lbs. Imported from 1998 to date.

MODEL 1810 SUPER MATCH II .... NiB $1958 Ex $1417 Gd $902
A less detailed version of the Super Match 1813 model. Tapered forend w/deep receiver area. Select European hardwood stock. Weight: 13.5

lbs. Imported from 1982 to 1988 (reintroduced as 1910 series).

MODEL 1811 PRONE MATCH .... NiB $1803 Ex $1592 Gd $835
Bolt-action single-shot. Caliber: .22 LR. 27.5-inch bbl. Improved Super Match 54 action. Select European hardwood stock w/beavertail forend, adj. cheekpiece, and deep thumb flute. Thumb groove and pistol grip w/stipple checkering. Adj. buttplate. Weight: 11.5 lbs. Imported 1982 to 1988. (Reintroduced as 1911 Prone Match)

MODEL 1813 SUPER MATCH........ NiB $2281 Ex $1951 Gd $869
Bolt-action single-shot. Caliber: .22 LR. 27.5-inch bbl. Improved Super Match 54 action w/light firing pin, one-point adj. trigger. European walnut thumbhole stock, adj. palm rest, forend and pistol grip stipple checkered. Adj. cheekpiece and hook buttplate. Weight: 15.5 lbs. Imported from 1979 to 1988. (Reintroduced as 1913 Super Match)

MODEL 1827B BIATHLON RIFLE
Bolt-action clip repeater. Caliber: .22 LR. 21.5-inch bbl. 42.5 inches overall. Weight: 8.5 to 9 lbs. Slide safety. Adj. target sight set w/snow caps. European walnut stock w/cheekpiece, stippled pistol grip and forearm w/adj. weights. Fortner straight pull bolt option offered in 1986. Imported from 1982 to date.
Mdl. 1827B w/Sup. Mat. 54 action ... NiB $2359 Ex $2153 Gd $1020
Model 1827B, left-hand .... NiB $2101 Ex $1716 Gd $1224
Model 1827BT w/Fortner
Option, right-hand .... NiB $2467 Ex $2261 Gd $1022
Model 1827BT, left-hand .... NiB $2604 Ex $2127 Gd $1513
Model 1827BT w/laminated stock, add $175
W/stainless steel bbl., add $205

MODEL 1907 ISU INTERNATIONAL MATCH RIFLE
Updated version of Model 1807 w/same general specifications as Model 1913 except w/26-inch bbl. 44.5 inches overall. Weight: 11 lbs. Designed for ISU 3-position competition. Fitted w/vented beechwood or walnut, blonde or color-laminated stock. Imported from 1989 to date.
Right-hand model .... NiB $1544 Ex $1353 Gd $838
Left-hand model .... NiB $1730 Ex $1415 Gd $1012
W/laminated stock, add $135
W/walnut stock, add $100
W/stainless steel bbl., add $130

MODEL 1910 INTERNATIONAL SUPER MATCH RIFLE
Updated version of Model 1810 w/same general specifications Model 1913 except w/less-detailed hardwood stock w/tapered forend. Weight: 13.5 lbs. Imported from 1989 to 1998.
Right-hand model .... NiB $2566 Ex $2077 Gd $1103
Left-hand model .... NiB $2560 Ex $2097 Gd $1506

MODEL 1911 PRONE MATCH RIFLE
Updated version of Model 1811 w/same general specifications Model 1913 except w/specialized prone match hardwood stock w/beavertail forend. Weight: 11.5 lbs. Imported from 1989 to date.
Right-hand model .... NiB $1854 Ex $1764 Gd $849

Anschutz Achiever

MODEL 1912
LADIES' SPORT RIFLE . . . . **NiB $1810 Ex $1594 Gd $842**
Similar to the Model 1907 designed for ISU 3-position competition w/same general U.I.T. specifications except w/shorter dimensions to accomodate smaller competitors. Weight: 11.4 lbs. Imported from 1999 to date.

MODEL 1913 STANDARD RIFLE . . . . . . **NiB $1572 Ex $1203 Gd $842**
Similar to 1913 Super Match w/economized appointments. Imported from 1997 to date.

MODEL 1913 SUPER MATCH RIFLE
Bolt-action single-shot Super Match (updated version of Model 1813). Caliber: .22 LR. 27.5-inch bbl. Weight: 14.2 lbs. Adj. two-stage trigger. Vented International thumbhole stock w/adj. cheekpiece, hand and palm rest, fitted w/10-way butthook. Imported from 1989 to date.
Right-hand model . . . . **NiB $2269 Ex $1940 Gd $858**
Left-hand model . . . . **NiB $2340 Ex $1885 Gd $1312**
W/laminated stock, add **$130**
W/stainless steel bbl., add **$140**

MODEL 2007 ISU STANDARD RIFLE
Bolt-action single-shot. Caliber: .22 LR. 19.75-inch bbl. 43.5 to 44.5 inches overall. Weight: 10.8 lbs. Two-stage trigger. Standard ISU stock w/adj. cheekpiece. Imported from 1992 to date.
Right-hand model . . . . **NiB $1960 Ex $1496 Gd $883**
Left-hand model . . . . **NiB $2067 Ex $1687 Gd $1201**
W/stainless steel bbl., add **$140**

MODEL 2013
LADIES' SPORT RIFLE . . . . **NiB $2166 Ex $1985 Gd $894**
Similar to the Model 2007 designed for ISU 3-position competition w/same general U.I.T. specifications except w/shorter dimensions to accomodate smaller competitors. Weight: 11.4 lbs. Imported from 1999 to date.

MODEL 2013
BENCHREST RIFLE (BR-50) . . . . . **NiB $1758 Ex $1593 Gd $846**
Bolt-action single-shot. Caliber: .22 LR. 19.6-inch bbl. 43 inches overall. Weight: 10.3 lbs. Adjustable trigger for single or two-stage function. Benchrest-configuration stock. Imported from 1999 to date.

MODEL 2013 SILHOUETTE RIFLE . . . . **NiB $2150 Ex $1625 Gd $904**
Bolt-action single-shot. Caliber: .22 LR. 20-inch bbl. 45.5 inches overall. Weight: 11.5 lbs. Two-stage trigger. Thumbhole black synthetic or laminated stock w/adj. cheekpiece, hand and palm rest. Imported from 1994 to date.

MODEL 2013 SUPER MATCH RIFLE
Bolt-action single-shot. Caliber: .22 LR. 19.75- or 27.1-inch bbl. 43 to 50.1 inches overall. Weight: 15.5 lbs. Two-stage trigger. International thumbhole, black synthetic or laminated stock w/adj. cheekpiece, hand and palm rest; fitted w/10-way butthook. Imported from 1992 to date.
Right-hand model . . . . **NiB $2514 Ex $2278 Gd $1124**

Left-hand model . . . . **NiB $2493 Ex $1230 Gd $1439**
W/laminated stock, add **$180**

ACHIEVER BOLT-ACTION RIFLE. . . . . **NiB $391 Ex $314 Gd $185**
Caliber: .22 LR. 5-round magazine. Mark 2000-type repeating action. 19.5-inch bbl. 36.5 inches overall. Weight: 5 lbs. Adj. open rear sight; hooded ramp front. Plain European hardwood target-style stock w/vented forend and adj. buttplate. Imported 1987 to 1995.

ACHIEVER ST-SUPER TARGET . . . . . **NiB $523 Ex $394 Gd $240**
Same as Achiever except single-shot w/22-inch bbl. and adj. stock. 38.75 inches overall. Weight: 6.5 lbs. Target sights. Imported since 1994 to 1995.

BR-50 BENCH REST RIFLE. . . . . . **NiB $2078 Ex $1641 Gd $997**
Single-shot. Caliber: .22 LR. 19.75-inch bbl. (23 inches w/muzzle weight). 37.75-42.5 inches overall. Weight: 11 lbs. Grooved receiver, no sights. Walnut-finished hardwood or synthetic benchrest stock w/adj. cheekpiece. Imported from 1994 to 1997. (Reintroduced as Model 2013 BR-50)

KADETT BOLT-ACTION
REPEATING RIFLE . . . . **NiB $333 Ex $230 Gd $153**
Caliber: .22 LR. 5-round detachable box magazine. 22-inch bbl. 40 inches overall. Weight: 5.5 lbs. Adj. folding leaf rear sight; hooded ramp front. Checkered European hardwood stock w/walnut-finish. Imported 1987.

MARK 2000 MATCH . . . . **NiB $431 Ex $323 Gd $204**
Takedown, bolt-action single-shot. Caliber: .22 LR. 26-inch heavy bbl. Walnut stock w/deep-fluted thumb-groove, Wundhammer swell pistol grip, beavertail forend. Adj. buttplate, single-stage adj. trigger. Weight: 8 lbs. Imported from 1982 to 1988.

ARMALITE, INC. — Geneseo, Illinois (Formerly Costa Mesa, California)
Armalite was in Costa Mesa, California from 1959-73. Following the acquisition by Eagle Arms in 1995, production resumed under the Armalite, Inc. Logo in Geneseo, Illinois.
Production by ARMALITE

AR-7 EXPLORER SURVIVAL RIFLE. . . **NiB $159 Ex $133 Gd $82**
Takedown. Semiautomatic. Caliber: .22 LR. Eight-round box magazine. 16-inch cast aluminum bbl. w/steel liner. Sights: Peep rear; blade front. Brown plastic stock, recessed to stow barrel, action, and magazine. Weight: 2.75 lbs. Will float stowed or assembled. Made from 1959-1973 by Armalite; from 1974-90 by Charter Arms; from 1990-97 by Survival Arms, Cocoa, FL.; from 1997 to date by Henry Repeating Arms Co., Brooklyn, NY.

AR-7 EXPLORER CUSTOM RIFLE . . . **NiB $211 Ex $175 Gd $97**
Same as AR-7 Survival Rifle except w/deluxe walnut stock w/cheekpiece and pistol grip. Weight: 3.5 lbs. Made from 1964 to 1970.

RIFLES

Armalite AR-10

Armalite AR-10 (T) Target Carbine

Armalite M-15A2 National Match

Armalite M-15A2 HBAR

AR-180 SEMIAUTOMATIC RIFLE
Commercial version of full automatic AR-18 Combat Rifle. Gas-operated semiautomatic. Caliber: .223 Rem. (5.56mm). 5-, 20-, 30-round magazines. 18.25-inch bbl. w/flash hider/muzzle brake. Sights: Flip-up "L" type rear, adj. for windage; post front, adj. for elevation. Accessory: 3x scope and mount (add $60 to value). Folding buttstock of black nylon, rubber buttplate and pistol grip, heat dissipating fiberglass forend (hand guard), swivels, sling. 38 inches overall, 28.75 inches folded. Weight: 6.5 lbs. Note: Made by Armalite Inc. 1969 to 1972, manufactured for Armalite by Howa Machinery Ltd., Nagoya, Japan, from 1972 to 1973; by Sterling Armament Co. Ltd., Dagenham, Essex, England, from 1976 to 1994. Importation disc.

Armalite AR-180 (Mfg. by
Armalite-Costa Mesa) . . . . NiB $2105 Ex $1499 Gd $990
Armalite AR-180 (Mfg. by Howa) . . . . . . NiB $2179 Ex $1496 Gd $936

Armalite AR-180 (Mfg. by Sterling) . . . . . NiB $1789 Ex $1374 Gd $912
W/3x scope and mount, add $225

AR-10 SEMIAUTOMATIC SERIES
Gas-operated semiautomatic action. Calibers: .243 Win. or .308 Win. (7.62 x 51mm). 10-round magazine. 16- or 20-inch bbl. 35.5 or 39.5 inches overall. Weight: 9 to 9.75 lbs. Post front sight, adj. aperature rear. Black or green composition stock. Made from 1995 to date.
AR-10 A2 (Std. carbine) . . . . NiB $2560 Ex $1651 Gd $998
AR-10 A2 (Std. rifle) . . . . NiB $2586 Ex $1101 Gd $968
AR-10 A4 (S.P. carbine) . . . . NiB $2538 Ex $1101 Gd $968
AR-10 A4 (S.P. rifle) . . . . NiB $2538 Ex $1101 Gd $968
W/stainless steel bbl., add $120

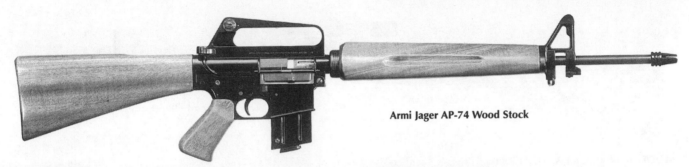

Armi Jager AP-74 Wood Stock

AR-10 (T) TARGET
Similar to Armalite Model AR-10A except in National Match configuration w/three-slot short Picatinny rail system and case deflector. 16- or 24-inch bbl. Weight: 8.25 to 10.4 lbs. Composite stock and handguard. No sights. Optional National Match carry handle and detachable front sight. Made from 1995 to 2004.

AR-10 T (Rifle) . . . . NiB $2551 Ex $1742 Gd $998
AR-10 T (Carbine) . . . . NiB $2551 Ex $1742 Gd $998

MODEL AR-50 SS BOLT-ACTION
RIFLE . . . . NiB $2566 Ex $1995 Gd $1323
Caliber: .50 BMG. 31-inch bbl. w/muzzle brake. 59 inches overall. Weight: 41 lbs. Modified octagonal-form receiver, drilled and slotted for scope rail. Single-stage trigger. Triple front-locking bolt lug w/spring-loaded plunger for automatic ejection. Magnesium phosphate steel, hard-anodized aluminum finish. Made from 1999 to date.

M15 SERIES
Gas-operated semiautomatic w/A2-style forward-assist mechanism and push-type pivot pin for easy takedown. Caliber: .223. 7-round magazine. 16-, 20- or 24-inch bbl. Weight: 7-9.2 lbs. Composite or retractable stock. Fully adj. sights. Black anodized finish. Made from 1995 to date.

M-15A2 (Carbine) . . . . NiB $901 Ex $773 Gd $617
M-15A2 (Service Rifle) . . . . NiB $952 Ex $823 Gd $628
M-15A2 (National Match) . . . . NiB $1325 Ex $1088 Gd $732
M-15A2
(Golden Eagle heavy bbl.) . . . . NiB $1299 Ex $1052 Gd $692
M-15A2 M4C
(retractable stock, disc. 1997) . . . . NiB $1247 Ex $980 Gd $659
M-15A4 (Action Master, disc. 1997) . . . . . NiB $1119 Ex $907 Gd $635
M-15A4 (Predator) . . . . NiB $952 Ex $823 Gd 628
M-15A4 (S.P. Rifle) . . . . NiB $926 Ex $772 Gd $514
M-15A4 (S.P. Carbine) . . . . NiB $875 Ex $720 Gd $463
M-15A4T (Eagle Eye Carbine) . . . . NiB $1299 Ex $1041 Gd $732
M-15A4T (Eagle Eye Rifle) . . . . NiB $1350 Ex $1016 Gd $732

ARMI JAGER — Turin, Italy

AP-74 COMMANDO . . . . NiB $281 Ex $220 Gd $148
Similar to standard AP-74 but styled to resemble original version of Uzi 9mm submachine gun w/wood buttstock. Lacks carrying handle and flash suppressor. Has different type front sight mount and guards, wood stock, pistol grip and forearm. Intro. 1976. Disc.

AP-74 SEMIAUTOMATIC RIFLE
Styled after U.S. M16 military rifle. Caliber: .22 LR, .32 Auto (pistol cartridge). Detachable clip magazine; capacity: 14 rounds caliber .22 LR, 9 rounds .32 ACP. 20-inch bbl. w/flash suppressor. Weight: 6.5 lbs. M16 type sights. Stock, pistol-grip and forearm of black plastic, swivels and sling. Intro. 1974. Disc.

.22 LR . . . . NiB $333 Ex $281 Gd $178
.32 Auto . . . . NiB $359 Ex $307 Gd $189

AP-74 WOOD STOCK MODEL
Same as standard AP-74 except w/wood stock, pistol-grip and forearm weight: 7 lbs. Disc.

.22 LR . . . . NiB $412 Ex $335 Gd $222
.32 Auto . . . . NiB $438 Ex $335 Gd $222

ARMSCOR (Arms Corp.) — Manila, Philippines
(Imported BY Armscor Precision Int'l.)

MODEL 20 AUTO RIFLE
Caliber: .22 LR. 15-round magazine. 21-inch bbl. 39.75 inches overall. Weight: 6.5 lbs. Sights: Hooded front; adj. rear. Checkered or plain walnut finished mahogany stock. Blued finish. Imported 1990 to 1991. (Reinstated by Ruko in the M series.)

Model 20 (checkered stock) . . . . NiB $142 Ex $118 Gd $87
Model 20C (carbine-style stock) . . . . NiB $129 Ex $108 Gd $80
Model 20P (plain stock) . . . . NiB $117 Ex $97 Gd $73

MODEL 1600 AUTO RIFLE
Caliber: .22 LR. 15-round magazine. 19.5-inch bbl. 38 inches overall. Weight: 6 lbs. Sights: Post front; aperture rear. Plain mahogany stock. Matte black finish. Imported 1987 to 1991. (Reinstated by Ruko in the M series.)

Standard model . . . . NiB $164 Ex $123 Gd $92
Retractable stock model . . . . NiB $174 Ex $138 Gd $97

MODEL AK22 AUTO RIFLE
Caliber: .22 LR. 15- or 30-round magazine. 18.5-inch bbl. 36 inches overall. Weight: 7 lbs. Sights: Post front; adj. rear. Plain mahogany stock. Matte black finish. Imported 1987 to 1991.

Standard model . . . . NiB $210 Ex $189 Gd $123
Folding stock model . . . . NiB $225 Ex $194 Gd $148

MODEL M14 SERIES BOLT-ACTION RIFLE
Caliber: .22 LR. 10-round magazine. 23-inch bbl. Weight: 6.25 lbs. Open sights. Walnut or mahogany stock. Imported 1991 to 1997.

M14P Standard model . . . . NiB $118 Ex $92 Gd $68
M14D Deluxe model
(checkered stock, disc. 1995) . . . . NiB $104 Ex $87 Gd $76

MODEL M20 SERIES SEMIAUTOMATIC RIFLE
Caliber: .22 LR. 10- or 15-round magazine. 18.25- or 20.75-inch bbl. Weight: 5.5 to 6.5 lbs. 38 to 40.5 inches overall. Hooded front sight w/windage adj. rear. Walnut finished mahogany stock. Imported 1990 to 1997.

M20C carbine model . . . . NiB $123 Ex $103 Gd $72
M20P standard model . . . . NiB $115 Ex $92 Gd $72
M20S Sporter Deluxe (checkered
mahogany stock) . . . . NiB $148 Ex $132 Gd $82
M20SC Super Classic (checkered
walnut stock) . . . . NiB $281 Ex $225 Gd $108

RIFLES

A-Square — Hannibal

MODEL M1400 BOLT-ACTION RIFLE
Similar to Model 14P except w/checkered stock w/Schnabel forend. Weight: 6 lbs. Imported from 1990 to 1997.
M1400LW (Lightweight, disc. 1992)...... NiB $219 Ex $188 Gd $127
M1400S (Sporter) .... NiB $152 Ex $127 Gd $96
M1400SC (Super Classic) .... NiB $274 Ex $224 Gd $161

MODEL M1500 BOLT-ACTION RIFLE
Caliber: .22 Mag. 5-round magazine. 21.5-inch bbl. Weight: 6.5 lbs. Open sights. Checkered mahogany stock. Imported 1991 to 1997.
M1500 (standard) .... NiB $152 Ex $127 Gd $96
M1500LW (Euro-style walnut
stock, disc. 1992) .... NiB $203 Ex $178 Gd $126
M1500SC (Monte Carlo stock) .... NiB $209 Ex $178 Gd $137

MODEL M1600 AUTO RIFLE
Rimfire replica of Armalite Model AR 180 (M16) except chambered for Caliber .22 LR. 15-round magazine. 18-inch bbl. Weight: 5.25 lbs. Composite or retractable buttstock w/composite handguard and pistol grip. Carrying handle w/adj. aperture rear sight and protected post front. Black anodized finish. Imported from 1991 to 1997.
M-1600 (standard w/fixed stock) ..... NiB $171 Ex $141 Gd $104
M-1600R (retractable stock) .... NiB $183 Ex $151 Gd $111

MODEL M1800 BOLT-ACTION RIFLE
Caliber: .22 Hornet. 5-round magazine. 22-inch bbl. Weight: 6.6 lbs. Checkered hardwood or walnut stock. Sights: Post front; adj. rear. Imported from 1996 to 1997.
M-1800 (standard) .... NiB $282 Ex $211 Gd $154
M-1800SC (checkered walnut stock) ... NiB $384 Ex $313 Gd $231

MODEL M2000 AUTO RIFLE
Similar to Model 20P except w/checkered mahogany stock and adj. sights. Imported from 1991 to 1997.
M2000S (standard) .... NiB $151 Ex $126 Gd $92
M2000SC (checkered walnut stock) ...... NiB $260 Ex $213 Gd $152

ARNOLD ARMS — Arlington, Washington

AFRICAN SAFARI
Calibers: .243 to .458 Win. Magnum. 22- to 26-inch bbl. Weight: 7-9 lbs. Scope mount standard or w/optional M70 Express sights. Chrome-moly in four finishes. "A" and "AA" Fancy Grade English walnut stock with number 5 standard wraparound checkering pattern. Ebony forend tip. Made from 1994 to 2001.
With "A" Grade English
walnut: matte blue .... NiB $4689 Ex $3798 Gd $2658
Std. polish....................... NiB $4944 Ex $3972 Gd $2796
Hi-Luster......................... NiB $5159 Ex $4167 Gd $2920
Stainless steel matte .... NiB $4696 Ex $3805 Gd $2664
With "AA" Grade English
Walnut: C-M matte blue........... NiB $4671 Ex $3784 Gd $2650
Std. polish....................... NiB $4951 Ex $4009 Gd $2803
Hi-Luster......................... NiB $5159 Ex $4177 Gd $2920
Stainless steel matte .... NiB $4696 Ex $3804 Gd $2665
ALASKAN TROPHY

Calibers: .300 Magnum to .458 Win. Magnum. 24- to 26-inch bbl. Weight: 7-9 lbs. Scope mount w/Express sights standard. Stainless steel or chrome-moly Apollo action w/fibergrain or black synthetic stock. Barrel band on 357 H&H and larger magnums. Made from 1996 to 2000.
Matte finish .... NiB $3253 Ex $2643 Gd $1862
Std. polish .... NiB $3509 Ex $2846 Gd $2000
Stainless steel .... NiB $3324 Ex $2699 Gd $1899

A-SQUARE COMPANY INC. — Glenrock, WY

CAESAR BOLT-ACTION RIFLE
Custom rifle built on Remington's 700 receiver. Calibers: Same as Hannibal, Groups I, II and III. 20- to 26-inch bbl. Weight: 8.5 to 11 lbs. Express 3-leaf rear sight, ramp front. Synthetic or classic Claro oil-finished walnut stock w/flush detachable swivels and Coil-Chek recoil system. Three-way adj. target trigger; 3-position safety. Right- or left-hand. Made from 1986 to date.

Synthetic stock model .... NiB $3359 Ex $2740 Gd $1917
Walnut stock model.......... NiB $2998 Ex $2329 Gd $1711

GENGHIS KHAN BOLT-ACTION RIFLE
Custom varmint rifle developed on Winchester's M70 receiver; fitted w/heavy tapered bbl. and Coil-Chek stock. Calibers: .22-250 Rem., .243 Win., .25-06 Rem., 6mm Rem. Weight: 8-8.5 lbs. Made from 1995 to date.
Synthetic stock model .... NiB $3500 Ex $2266 Gd $1997
Walnut stock model.......... NiB $3430 Ex $2812 Gd $1988

HAMILCAR BOLT-ACTION RIFLE
Similar to Hannibal Model except lighter. Calibers: .25-06, .257 Wby., 6.5x55 Swedish, .270 Wby., 7x57, 7mm Rem., 7mm STW, 7mm Wby., .280 Rem., .30-06, .300 Win., .300 Wby., .338-06, 9.3x62. Weight: 8-8.5 lbs. Made from 1994 to date.
Synthetic stock model .... NiB $3515 Ex $2868 Gd $1994
Walnut stock model.......... NiB $3470 Ex $2812 Gd $1972

HANNIBAL BOLT-ACTION RIFLE
Custom rifle built on reinforced P-17 Enfield receiver. Calibers: Group I: 30-06; Group II: 7mm Rem. Mag., .300 Win. Mag., .416 Taylor, .425 Express, .458 Win. Mag.; Group III: .300 H&H, .300 Wby. Mag., 8mm Rem. Mag., .340 Wby. Mag., .375 H&H, .375 Wby. Mag., .404 Jeffery, .416 Hoffman, .416 Rem Mag., .450 Ackley, .458 Lott; Group IV: .338 A-Square Mag., .375 A-Square Mag., .378 Wby. Mag., .416 Rigby, .416 Wby. Mag., .460 Short Square Mag., .500 A-Square Mag. 20- to 26-inch bbl. Weight: 9 to 11.75 lbs. Express 3-leaf rear sight, ramp front. Classic Claro oil-finished walnut stock or synthetic stock w/flush detachable swivels and Coil-Chek recoil system. Adj. trigger w/2-position safety. Made from 1986 to date.
Synthetic stock model .... NiB $3559 Ex $2825 Gd $1886
Walnut stock model.......... NiB $3460 Ex $2766 Gd $1988

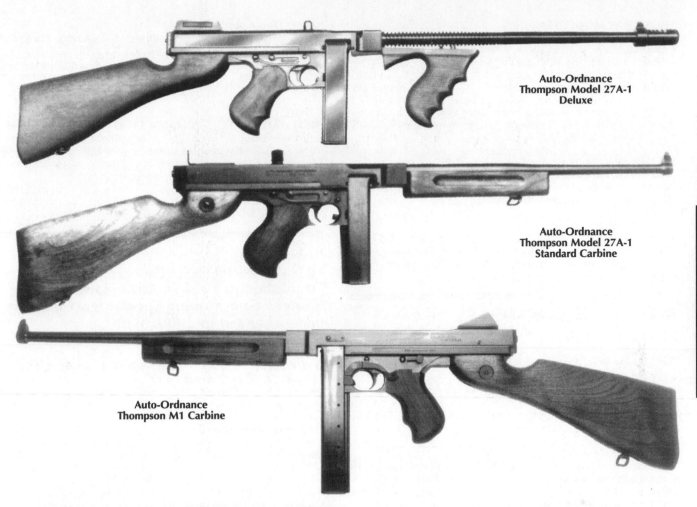

**Auto-Ordnance
Thompson Model 27A-1
Deluxe**

**Auto-Ordnance
Thompson Model 27A-1
Standard Carbine**

**Auto-Ordnance
Thompson M1 Carbine**

AUSTRIAN MILITARY RIFLES — Steyr, Austria
Manufactured at Steyr Armory

MODEL 90
STEYR-MANNLICHER RIFLE....... NiB $302 Ex $179 Gd $126
Straight-pull bolt action. Caliber: 8mm. 5-round magazine. Open sights. 10-inch bayonet. Cartridge clip forms part of the magazine mechanism. Some of these rifles were provided with a laced canvas hand guard, others were of wood.

MODEL 90
STEYR-MANNLICHER CARBINE ... NiB $304 Ex $208 Gd $127
Same general specifications as Model 90 rifle except w/19.5-inch bbl., weight 7 lbs. No bayonet stud or supplemental forend grip.

MODEL 95
STEYR-MANNLICHER CARBINE ... NiB $304 Ex $209 Gd $126
Same general specifications as Model 95 rifle except w/19.5-inch bbl., weight 7 lbs. Post front sight; adj. rear carbine sight.

MODEL 95
**STEYR-MANNLICHER
SERVICE RIFLE.................** NiB $279 Ex $157 Gd $121
Straight-pull bolt action. Caliber: 8x50R Mannlicher (many of these rifles were altered during World War II to use the 7.9mm German service ammunition). 5-round Mannlicher-type box magazine. 30-inch bbl. Weight: 8.5 lbs. Sights: Blade front; rear adj. for elevation. Military-type full stock.

AUTO-ORDNANCE CORPORATION —
Worcester, Massachusetts

THOMPSON
MODEL 22-27A-3 .... NiB $762 Ex $638 Gd $458
Same-bore version of Deluxe Model 27A-1. Same general specifications except 22 LR w/lightweight alloy receiver, weight 6.5 lbs. Magazines include 5-, 20-, 30- and 50-round box types, 80-round drum. Made from 1977 to 1994.

THOMPSON
MODEL 27A-1 DELUXE
Same as Standard Model 27A-1 except w/finned bbl. w/compensator, adj. rear sight, pistol-grip forestock. Caliber: .22 LR, l0mm (1991 to 1993) or 45 ACP. Weight: 11.5 lbs. Made from 1976 to 1999.
.22 LR (Limited production) .... NiB $1340 Ex $1084 Gd $756
10mm or 45 ACP............... NiB $767 Ex $644 Gd $515
50-round drum magazine, add $250
100-round drum magazine, add $450
Violin carrying case, add............................ $100

THOMPSON MODEL 27A-1
STANDARD SEMIAUTO
CARBINE. . . . . **NiB $668 Ex $616 Gd $410**
Similar to Thompson submachine gun ("Tommy Gun") except has no provision for automatic firing. Caliber: .45 Auto. 20-round detachable box magazine (5-,15- and 30-round box magazines, 39-round drum also available). 16-inch plain bbl. Weight: 14 lbs. Sights: Aperture rear; blade front. Walnut buttstock, pistol grip and grooved forearm, sling swivels. Made from 1976-86.

THOMPSON 27A-1C
LIGHTWEIGHT CARBINE. . . . . . **NiB $806 Ex $647 Gd $458**
Similar to Model 27A-1 except w/lightweight alloy receiver. Weight: 9.25 lbs. Made 1984 to date.

THOMPSON M1
SEMI-AUTOMATIC CARBINE . . . **NiB $770 Ex $647 Gd $467**
Similar to Model 27A-1 except in M-1 configuration w/side cocking lever and horizontal forearm. Weight: 11.5 lbs. Made from 1986 to date.

BALLARD RIFLE LLC —
Cody, Wyoming

Firearms manufactured since 1996.
BALLARD 1-1/2
HUNTER'S RIFLE . . . . **NiB $3144 Ex $2394 Gd $1794**
Calibers: Seven calibers from .22 LR to .50-70. Single trigger, S-style lever action; uncheckered stock. Weight: 10.5 lbs.

BALLARD 1-3/4
FAR WEST RIFLE . . . . **NiB $2844 Ex $1994 Gd $1419**
Calibers: Eight calibers from .32-40 WCF to .50-90 SS. Patterned after original Ballard Far West model. 30 or 32-inch bbl., standard or heavyweight octagon; double set triggers; ring-style lever. Weight: 9.75 to 10.5 lbs.

BALLARD NO. 5
PACIFIC . . . . **NiB $3151 Ex $2426 Gd $1951**
Calibers: Nine calibers between .32-40 WCF and .50-90 SS. Similar to No. 1-3/4 Far West model but with under-barrel wiping rod.

BALLARD NO. 4-1/2
MID-RANGE RIFLE . . . . **NiB $2846 Ex $2046 Gd $1721**
Calibers: .Five calibers between .32-40 WCF and .45-110. Designed for black powder silhouette shooting. 30 or 32-inch bbl., half-octagonal heavyweight; single or double set triggers; pistol grip stock; full loop lever; hard rubber Ballard buttplate; Vernier tang sight. Weight: 10.75 to 11.5 lbs.

BALLARD NO. 7
LONG-RANGE RIFLE . . . . . . **NiB $3346 Ex $2271 Gd $1446**
Caliber: Five calibers between .40-65 Win. and .45-110. Similar to No. 4-1/2 Mid-Range Rifle; designed for long-range shooting. 32 or 34-inch half-octagon standard or heavyweight bbl.

MODEL 1885
HIGH WALL RIFLE . . . . **NiB $3135 Ex $2390 Gd $1915**
Calibers: Various. Exact replica of Winchester Model 1885 (parts are interchangeable). 30 or 32-inch bbl., octagon; case-colored receiver, uncheckered straight-grip stock and forearm. Weight: Approx. 9 lbs. Introduced 2001.
Deluxe model, add **$1500**
Sporting model, add. **$200**
Shuetzen model, add. **$325**

BANSNER'S
ULTIMATE RIFLES, LLC —
Established in 1981 in Adamstown, PA as Basner's Gunsmithing Specialties. Company name changed in 2000.

ULTIMATE
ONE RIFLE . . . . **NiB $5430 Ex $3690 Gd $2965**
Calibers: Various. Bolt-action, modeled on Winchester M70 and Remington 700 actions. Various metal finishes; muzzle brake; custom trigger; custom stock; Pachmayer decelerator pad; custom scope mounts and bases.
Three-position safety, add **$250**

HIGH TECH
SERIES RIFLE . . . . **NiB $981 Ex $756 Gd $600**
Calibers: Various. Steel or stainless steel action with factory bbl. Bansner's synthetic stock and Pachmayer decelerator pad.
Stainless steel model, add **$150**

SAFARI
HUNTER RIFLE . . . . **NiB $6081 Ex $4306 Gd $2331**
Calibers: Various dangerous game calibers. Based on Model 70 Classic action; muzzle brake; Lilja Precision stainless steel barrel; synthetic stock; matte black Teflon metal finish. Introduced 2003.

WORLD SLAM
LIMITED EDITION
RIFLE . . . . **NiB $5283 Ex $3733 Gd $2258**
Calibers: Various. Customized Model 700 action; fluted bold body. jeweled trigger. three-position safety; synthetic stock. Only 25-50 of limited edition models were made beginning in 2003.

BARRETT FIREARMS MFG., INC. — Murfreesboro, Tennessee

MODEL 82 A-1
SEMI-AUTOMATIC RIFLE.... NiB $9055 Ex $7559 Gd $4499
Caliber: .50 BMG. 10-round detachable box magazine. 29-inch recoiling bbl. w/muzzle brake. 57 inches overall. Weight: 28.5 lbs. Open iron sights and 10x scope. Composit stock w/Sorbothance recoil pad and self-leveling bipod. Blued finish. Made in various configurations from 1985 to date.

MODEL 90
BOLT-ACTION RIFLE....... NiB $3497 Ex $2982 Gd $1998
Caliber: .50 BMG. Five round magazine. 29-inch match bbl. 45 inches overall. Weight: 22 lbs. Composite stock w/retractable bipod. Made from 1990 to 1995.

MODEL 95 BOLT-ACTION... NiB $6583 Ex $4727 Gd $3490
Similar to Model 90 bullpup design chambered for .50 BMG except w/improved muzzle brake and extendable bipod. Made from 1995 to date.

BEEMAN PRECISION ARMS INC. — Santa Rosa, California

Since 1993 all European firearms imported by Beeman have been distributed by Beeman Outdoor Sports, Div., Roberts Precision Arms, Inc., Santa Rosa, CA.

WEIHRAUCH HW MODELS 60J AND 60J-ST
BOLT-ACTION RIFLES
Calibers: .22 LR (60J-ST), .222 Rem. (60J). 22.8-inch bbl. 41.7 inches overall. Weight: 6.5 lbs. Sights: Hooded blade front; open adj. rear. Blued finish. Checkered walnut stock w/cheekpiece. Made from 1988 to 1994.
Model 60J .... NiB $509 Ex $746 Gd $612
Model 60J-ST............... NiB $626 Ex $509 Gd $361

WEIHRAUCH HW MODEL 60M
SMALL BORE RIFLE........... NiB $664 Ex $561 Gd $374
Caliber: .22 LR. Single-shot. 26.8-inch bbl. 45.7 inches overall. Weight: 10.8 lbs. Adj. trigger w/push-button safety. Sights: Hooded blade front on ramp, precision aperture rear. Target-style stock w/stippled forearm and pistol grip. Blued finish. Made from 1988 to 1994.

WEIHRAUCH HW
MODEL 660 MATCH RIFLE..... NiB $933 Ex $805 Gd $418
Caliber: .22 LR. 26-inch bbl. 45.3 inches overall. Weight: 10.7 lbs. Adj. match trigger. Sights: globe front, precision aperture rear. Match-style walnut stock w/adj. cheekpiece and buttplate. Made from 1988 to 1994.

FEINWERKBAU MODEL 2600 SERIES TARGET RIFLE
Caliber: .22 LR. Single-shot. 26.3-inch bbl. 43.7 inches overall. Weight: 10.6 lbs. Match trigger w/fingertip weight adjustment dial. Sights: Globe front; micrometer match aperture rear. Laminated hardwood stock w/adj. cheekpiece. Made from 1988 to 1994.
Standard Model 2600 (left-hand) .... NiB $1690 Ex $1309 Gd $897
Standard Model 2600
(right-hand) .... NiB $1515 Ex $1206 Gd $794
Free Rifle Model 2602
(left-hand) .... NiB $2133 Ex $1724 Gd $1000
Free Rifle Model 2602
(right-hand) .... NiB $2124 Ex $1721 Gd $1000

BELGIAN MILITARY RIFLES
Mfd. by Fabrique Nationale D'Armes de Guerre, Herstal, Belgium; Fabrique D'Armes de L'Etat, Lunich, Belgium

Hopkins & Allen Arms Co. of Norwich, Conn., as well as contractors in Birmingham, England, also produced these guns during World War I.

MODEL 1889 MAUSER
MILITARY RIFLE .... NiB $246 Ex $196 Gd $134
Caliber: 7.65mm Belgian Service (7.65mm Mauser). 5-round projecting box magazine. 30.75-inch bbl. w/jacket. Weight: 8.5 lbs. Adj. rear sight, blade front. Straight-grip military stock. This, and the carbine version, was the principal weapon of the Belgian Army at the start of WWII. Made from 1889 to c.1935.

MODEL 1916
MAUSER CARBINE .... NiB $271 Ex $220 Gd $174
Same as Model 1889 Rifle except w/20.75-inch bbl. Weighs 8 lbs. and has minor differences in the rear sight graduations, lower band closer to the muzzle and swivel plate on side of buttstock.

MODEL 1935 MAUSER
MILITARY RIFLE .... NiB $348 Ex $271 Gd $159
Same general specifications as F.N. Model 1924; minor differences. Caliber: 7.65mm Belgian Service. Mfd. by Fabrique Nationale D'Armes de Guerre.

MODEL 1936 MAUSER
MILITARY RIFLE .... NiB $251 Ex $206 Gd $146
An adaptation of Model 1889 w/German M/98-type bolt, Belgian M/89 protruding box magazine. Caliber: 7.65mm Belgian Service. Mfd. by Fabrique Nationale D'Armes de Guerre.

BENTON & BROWN FIREARMS, INC. — Fort Worh, Texas

MODEL 93
BOLT-ACTION RIFLE
Similar to Blaser Model R84 (the B&B rifle is built on the Blaser action, see separate listing) with an interchangeable bbl. system. Calibers: .243 Win., 6mm Rem., .25-06, .257 Wby., .264 Win., .270 Win., .280 Rem., 7mm Rem Mag., .30-06, .308, .300 Wby., .300 Win. Mag., .338 Win., .375 H&H. 22- or 24-inch bbl. 41 or 43 inches overall. Bbl.-mounted scope rings and one-piece base; no sights. Two-piece walnut or fiberglass stock. Made from 1993 to 1996.
Walnut stock model......... NiB $1864 Ex $1710 Gd $979
Fiberglass stock model .... add $200
Extra bbl. assembly, add $475
Extra bolt assembly, add $425

RIFLES

Beretta 501
Bolt-Action Sporter

Beretta AR-70

BERETTA U.S.A. CORP. — Accokeek, Maryland, Manufactured by Fabbrica D'Armi Pietro Beretta, S.P.A., Gardone Val Trompia (Brescia), Italy

455 SxS EXPRESS DOUBLE RIFLE
Sidelock action w/removable sideplates. Calibers: .375 H&H, .458 Win. Mag., .470 NE, .500 NE (3 inches), .416 Rigby. Bbls.: 23.5 or 25.5-inch. Weight: 11 lbs. Double triggers. Sights: Blade front; V-notch folding leaf rear. Checkered European walnut forearm and buttstock w/recoil pad. Color casehardened receiver w/blued bbls. Made from 1990 to date.
Model 455 . . . . NiB $40,938 Ex $32,750 Gd $22,270
Model 455EELL. . . . . NiB $51,875 Ex $41,500 Gd $28,220

500 BOLT-ACTION SPORTER
Centerfire bolt-action rifle w/Sako A I short action. Calibers: .222 Rem., .223 Rem. Five round magazine. 23.63-inch bbl. Weight: 6.5 lbs. Available w/ or w/o iron sights. Tapered dovetailed receiver. European walnut stock. Disc. 1998.
Standard . . . . NiB $659 Ex $561 Gd $406
DL Model . . . . NiB $1548 Ex $1251 Gd $872
500 EELL
Engraved . . . . NiB $1608 Ex $1406 Gd $943
W/iron sights, add 10%

501 BOLT-ACTION SPORTER
Same as Model 500 except w/Sako A II medium action. Calibers: .243 Win., .308 Win. Weight: 7.5 lbs. Disc. 1986.
Standard . . . . NiB $595 Ex $456 Gd $393
Standard
w/iron sights . . . . NiB $659 Ex $612 Gd $406
DL model. . . . . NiB $1350 Ex $1061 Gd $901
501 EELL (engraved) . . . . NiB $1573 Ex $1316 Gd $952
W/iron sights, add 10%

502 BOLT-ACTION SPORTER
Same as Model 500 except w/Sako A III long action. Calibers: .270 Win., 7mm Rem. Mag., .30/06, 375 H&H. Weight: 8.5 lbs. Disc. 1986.
Standard model . . . . NiB $657 Ex $517 Gd $438
DL model. . . . . NiB $1526 Ex $1265 Gd $953
502 EELL (engraved) . . . . NiB $1576 Ex $1317 Gd $1052
W/iron sights, add 10%

AR-70 SEMIAUTOMATIC RIFLE . . . . . . NiB $1985 Ex $1754 Gd $1058
Caliber: .223 Rem. (5.56mm). 30-round magazine. 17.75-inch bbl. Weight: 8.25 lbs. Sights: Rear peep adj. for windage and elevation; blade front. High-impact synthetic buttstock. Imported 1984 to 1989.

EXPRESS S686/S689 SILVER SABLE O/U RIFLE
Calibers: .30-06 Spfld., 9.3x74R, and .444 Marlin. 24-inch bbl. Weight: 7.7 lbs. Drilled and tapped for scope mount. European-style cheek rest and ventilated rubber recoil pad. Imported 1995.
Model S686/S689 Silver Sable II. . . . . . NiB $4665 Ex $3708 Gd $2163
Model S689 Gold Sable . . . . NiB $6290 Ex $5260 Gd $3097
Model S686/S689 EELL
Diamond Sable. . . . . NiB $12,840 Ex $9235 Gd $6145
W/extra bbl. set, add $325
W/detachable claw mounts, add $595

EXPRESS SSO O/U EXPRESS DOUBLE RIFLE
Sidelock. Calibers: .375 H&H Mag., .458 Win. Mag., 9.3 x 74R. 23-24- or 25.5-inch blued bbls. Weight: 11 lbs. Double triggers. Express sights w/blade front and V-notch folding leaf rear. Optional Zeiss scope w/claw mounts. Color casehardened receiver w/scroll engraving, game scenes and gold inlays on higher grades. Checkered European walnut forearm and buttstock w/cheekpiece and recoil pad. Imported 1985 to 1989.
Model SS0 (disc. 1989) . . . . NiB $9380 Ex $8247 Gd $5260
Model SS05 (disc. 1990) . . . . NiB $10,410 Ex $8865 Gd $6290
Model SS06 Custom . . . . NiB $26,265 Ex $20,085 Gd $12,360
Model SS06 EELL Gold Custom . . . . NiB $29,767 Ex $26,265 Gd $14,935
Extra bbl. assembly, add $6250
Claw mounts, add $550

Blaser Model R84

MATO
Calibers: .270 Win., .280 Rem., 7mm Rem. Mag., .300 Win. Mag., .338 Win. Mag., .375 H&H. 23.6-inch bbl. Weight: 8 lbs. Adjustable trigger. Drop-out box magazine. Drilled and tapped for scope w/ or w/o adj. sights. Walnut or synthetic stock. Manufactured based on Mauser 98 action. Made from 1997 to 2002.
Standard model . . . . **NiB $976 Ex $697 Gd $488**
Deluxe model . . . . **NiB $1975 Ex $1615 Gd $894**
.375 H&H w/iron sights, add **$300**

SMALL BORE SPORTING CARBINE/TARGET RIFLE
Semiautomatic w/bolt handle in raised or conventional single-shot bolt-action w/handle in lowered position. Caliber: .22 LR. Four, 5-, 8-, 10- or 20-round magazines. 20.5-inch standard or heavy bbl. Sights: 3-leaf folding rear, partridge front. Target or sporting stock w/checkered pistol grip and forend and sling swivels. Weight: 5.5 to 6 lbs.
Sporter model (Super Sport X) . . . . **NiB $420 Ex $343 Gd $235**
Target model (Olympia X) . . . . **NiB $294 Ex $472 Gd $317**

BERNARDELLI, VINCENZO — Brescia, Italy

Currently headquartered in Brescia, Italy, Bernardelli arms were manufactured from 1721 to 1997 in Gardone, Italy. Imported and distributed by Armsport, Inc., Miami, Florida. Also handled by Magnum Research, Inc., Quality Arms, Inc., Armes De Chasse, Stoeger and Action Arms.

EXPRESS VB . . . . **NiB $5680 Ex $4680 Gd $3630**
Double barrel. Calibers: Various. Side-by-side sidelock action. Ejectors, double triggers. Imported from 1990 to1997.
Deluxe model (w/double triggers), add **$1000**

EXPRESS 2000 . . . . **NiB $2625 Ex $1975 Gd $1515**
Calibers: .30-06, 7x65R, 8x57JRS, 9.3x74R. Over/under boxlock design. Single or double triggers, extractors. Checkered walnut stock and forearm. Imported from 1994 to 1997.
Single trigger, add **$150**

MINERVA EXPRESS . . . . **NiB $5000 Ex $3830 Gd $3925**
Caliber: Various. Exposed hammers. Extractors, double triggers. Moderate engraving. Imported from 1995 to 1997.

CARBINA .22 . . . . **NiB $579 Ex $379 Gd $254**
Semi-auto. Caliber: .22 rimfire. Blow-back action. Imported from 1990 to 1997.

MODEL 120 . . . . **NiB $1973 Ex $1508 Gd $1058**
Combination gun; over-under boxlock; 12 gauge over .22 Hornet, .222 Rem., 5.6x50R Mag., .243 Win., 6.5x57R, .270 Win., 7x57R, .308 Win., .30-06, 6.5x55, 7x65R, 8x57JRS, 9.3x74R. Iron sights. Checkered walnut stock and forearm. Double triggers, automatic ejectors or extractors. Ventilated recoil pad. Engraved action. Made in Italy. Discontinued.

MODEL 190 . . . . **NiB $1417 Ex $1092 Gd $1037**
Combination gun; over-under boxlock. Calibers: 12, 16 or 20 ga. Over .222 Rem., .243 Win., .30-06, .308 Win., 5.6x50R Mag., .5.6x57R, 6.5x55, 6.5x57R, 7x57R, 7x65R, 8x57JRS, 9.3x74R. Iron

sights. Checkered walnut stock. Double triggers; extractors. Made in Italy. Introduced in 1969, discontinued 1989.

MODEL 2000 . . . . **NiB $2644 Ex $1816 Gd $1341**
Combination gun; over-under boxlock action. Calibers: 12, 16 or 20 ga. Over .222 Rem., .22 Hornet, 5.6x50R Mag., .243 Win., 6.5x55, 6.5x57R, .270 Win., 7x57R, .308 Win., .30-06, 8x57JRS, 9.3x74R. Bbl: 23 inches. Sights: Blade front, open rear. Hand checkered, oil-finished select European walnut stock, double-set triggers, auto ejectors. Silvered, engraved action. Made in Italy. Introduced in 1990, discontinued 1991.
Extra bbl. assembly, add **$500**

BLASER U.S.A., INC. — Fort Worth, Texas Mfd. by Blaser Jagdwaffen GmbH, Germany *(Imported by Sigarms, Exeter, NH; Autumn Sales, Inc., Fort Worth, TX)*

MODEL R84 BOLT-ACTION RIFLE
Calibers: .22-250, .243, 6mm Rem., .25-06, .270, .280 Rem., .30-06- .257 Wby. Mag., .264 Win. Mag., 7mm Rem Mag., .300 Win. Mag., .300 Wby. Mag., .338 Win. Mag., .375 H&H. Interchangeable bbls. w/standard or Magnum bolt assemblies. Bbl. length: 23 inches (standard); 24 inches (Magnum). 41 to 42 inches overall. Weight: 7 to 7.25 lbs. No sights. Bbl.-mounted scope system. Two-piece Turkish walnut stock w/solid black recoil pad. Imported from 1989 to 1994.
Model R84 Standard . . . . **NiB $2153 Ex $1638 Gd $1115**
Model R84 Deluxe
(game scene) . . . . **NiB $2398 Ex $1978 Gd $1337**
Model R84 Super Deluxe
(Gold and silver inlays) . . . . **NiB $2328 Ex $1900 Gd $1472**
Left-hand model, add **$125**
Extra bbl. assembly, add **$650**

MODEL R93 SAFARI SERIES BOLT-ACTION REPEATER
Similar to Model R84 except restyled action w/straight-pull bolt, unique safety and searless trigger mechanism. Additional chamberings: 6.5x55, 7x57, .308, .416 Rem. Optional open sights. Imported 1994 to 1998.
Model R93 Safari . . . . **NiB $3511 Ex $2219 Gd $1786**
Model R93 Safari Deluxe . . . . **NiB $3870 Ex $4064 Gd $3240**
Model R84 Safari
Super Deluxe . . . . **NiB $4789 Ex $4274 Gd $3398**
Extra bbl. assembly, add **$525**

MODEL R93 CLASSIC SERIES BOLT-ACTION REPEATER
Similar to Model R93 Safari except w/expanded model variations. Imported from 1998 to 2002.
Model R93 Attache
(Premium wood, fluted bbl.) . . . . **NiB $3478 Ex $3810 Gd $3038**
Model R93 Classic
(.22-250 to .375 H&H) . . . . **NiB $3465 Ex $2797 Gd $1942**
Model R93 Classic Safari (.416 Rem.) . . . . . **NiB $3456 Ex $3110 Gd $2156**
Model R93 LX (.22-250 to .416 Rem.) . . . . . **NiB $1719 Ex $1385 Gd $958**
Model R93 Synthetic (.22-250
to .375 H&H) . . . . **NiB $1859 Ex $1103 Gd $775**
Extra bbl. assembly, add **$550**

RIFLES

Brno Model II

Brno Model 21H
Bolt-Action Sporting Rifle

Brno Model 22F

Brno Hornet
Bolt-Action Sporting Rifle

BRITISH MILITARY RIFLES —
Mfd. at Royal Small Arms Factory, Enfield Lock, Middlesex, England, private contractors.

RIFLE NO. 1 MARK III. . . . . NiB $286 Ex $184 Gd $133
Short magazine Lee-Enfield (S.M.L.E.). Bolt action. Caliber: .303 British. 10-round box magazine. 25.25-inch bbl. Weight: 8.75 lbs. Sights: Adj. rear; blade front w/guards. Two-piece, full-length military stock. Note: The earlier Mark III (approved 1907) is virtually the same as Mark III (adopted 1918) except for sights and different magazine cut-off that was eliminated on the latter.

RIFLE NO. 3 MARK I (PATTERN 14) . . . . . . NiB $311 Ex $235 Gd $133
Modified Mauser-type bolt action. Except for caliber .303 British and long-range sight, this rifle is the same as U.S. Model 1917 Enfield. See listing of the latter for general specifications.

RIFLE NO. 4 MARK I . . . . NiB $260 Ex $209 Gd $133
Post-World War I modification of the S.M.L.E. intended to simplify mass production. General specifications same as Rifle No. 1 Mark III except w/aperture rear sight and minor differences in construction and weighs 9.25 lbs.

LIGHT RIFLE NO. 4 MARK I . . . . . . NiB $209 Ex $158 Gd $123
Modification of the S.M.L.E. Caliber: .303 British. 10-round box magazine. 23-inch bbl. Weight: 6.75 lbs. Sights: Micrometer click rear peep; blade front. One-piece military-type stock w/recoil pad. Made during WWII.

RIFLE NO. 5 MARK I . . . . NiB $337 Ex $235 Gd $158
Jungle Carbine. Modification of the S.M.L.E. similar to Light Rifle No. 4 Mark I except w/20.5-inch bbl. w/flash hider, carbine-type stock. Made during WWII, originally designed for use in the Pacific Theater.

BRNO SPORTING RIFLES — Brno, Czech Republic, Manufactured by Ceska Zbrojovka
Imported by Euro-Imports, El Cajon, CA (Previously by Bohemia Arms & Magnum Research)

See also CZ rifles.

**MODEL I BOLT-ACTION
SPORTING RIFLE.** . . . . NiB $662 Ex $595 Gd $404
Caliber: .22 LR. Five round detachable magazine. 22.75-inch bbl. Weight: 6 lbs. Sights: three-leaf open rear; hooded ramp front. Sporting stock w/checkered pistol grip, swivels. Made 1946 to 1973.

**MODEL II BOLT-ACTION
SPORTING RIFLE.** . . . . NiB $613 Ex $510 Gd $404
Same as Model I except w/deluxe grade stock. Made 1949 to 1957.

**MODEL III BOLT-ACTION
TARGET RIFLE** . . . . NiB $668 Ex $516 Gd $459
Same as Model I except w/heavy bbl. and target stock. Made from 1948-56.

**MODEL IV BOLT-ACTION
TARGET RIFLE** . . . . NiB $720 Ex $555 Gd $460
Same as Model III except w/improved target trigger mechanism. Made 1956 to 1962.

**MODEL V BOLT-ACTION
SPORTING RIFLE.** . . . . NiB $768 Ex $593 Gd $404
Same as Model I except w/improved trigger mechanism. Made from 1956 to 1973.

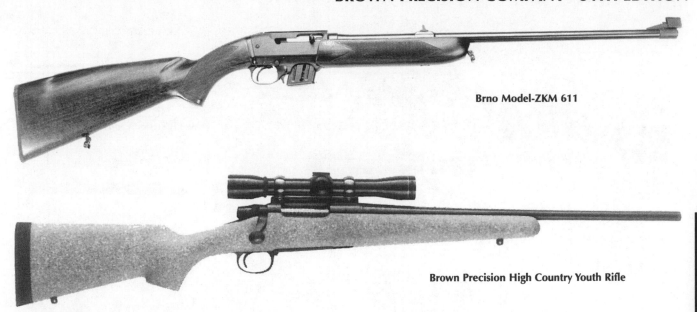

Brno Model-ZKM 611

Brown Precision High Country Youth Rifle

MODEL 21H BOLT-ACTION
SPORTING RIFLE. . . . . **NiB $1500 Ex $1264 Gd $958**
Mauser-type action. Calibers: 6.5x57mm, 7x57mm 8x57mm. Five round box magazine. 20.5-inch bbl. Double set trigger. Weight: 6.75 lbs. Sights: Two-leaf open rear-hooded ramp front. Half-length sporting stock w/cheekpiece, checkered pistol-grip and forearm, swivels. Made from 1946 to 1955.

MODEL 22F. . . . . NiB 1381 Ex $976 Gd $614
Same as Model 21H except w/full-length Mannlicher-type stock, weight: 6 lbs., 14 oz. Disc.

MODEL 98 STANDARD
Calibers: .243 Win., .270 Win., .30-06, .308 Win., .300 Win. Mag., 7x57mm, 7x64mm, or 9.3x62mm. 23.8-inch bbl. Overall 34.5 inches. Weight: 7.25 lbs. Checkered walnut stock w/Bavarian cheekpiece. Imported from 1998. Disc.
Standard calibers . . . . NiB $525 Ex $392 Gd $279
Calibers .300 Win., Mag., 9.3x62mm . . . . . NiB $552 Ex $484 Gd $357
W/single set trigger, add $100

MODEL 98 MANNLICHER
Similar to Model 98 Standard except full length stock and set triggers. Imported from 1998. Disc.
Standard calibers . . . . NiB $685 Ex $515 Gd $359
Calibers .300 Win. Mag., 9.3x62mm. . . . . . NiB $714 Ex $579 Gd $406

ZKB-110 SINGLE-SHOT
Calibers: .22 Hornet, .222 Rem., 5.6x52R, 5.6x50 Mag., 6.5x57R, 7x57R, and 8x57JRS. 23.8-inch bbl. Weight: 6.1 lbs. Walnut checkered buttstock and forearm w/Bavarian cheekpiece. Imported from 1998 to 2003.
Standard model. NiB $254 Ex $197 Gd $146
Lux model . . . . NiB $408 Ex $279 Gd $203
Calibers 7x57R and 8x57 JRS, add $25
W/interchangeable 12 ga.
shotgun bbl., add $132

HORNET BOLT-ACTION
SPORTING RIFLE. . . . . **NiB $1225 Ex $997 Gd $610**
Miniature Mauser action. Caliber: .22 Hornet. Five-round detachable box magazine. 23-inch bbl. Double set trigger. Weight: 6.25 lbs.

Sights: Three-leaf open rear hooded ramp front. Sporting stock w/checkered pistol grip and forearm, swivels. Made 1949-74. Note: This rifle was also marketed in U.S. as "Z-B Mauser Varmint Rifle." (Reintroduced as Model ZKB 680)

MODEL ZKB 680
BOLT-ACTION RIFLE. . . . . **NiB $444 Ex $317 Gd $294**
Calibers: .22 Hornet, .222 Rem. Five-round detachable box magazine. 23.5-inch bbl. Weight: 5.75 lbs. Double-set triggers. Adj. open rear sight, hooded ramp front. Walnut stock. Imported from 1985 to 1992.

MODEL ZKM 611 SEMIAUTOMATIC RIFLE
Caliber: .22 WMR. Six-round magazine. 20-inch bbl. 37 inches overall. Weight: 6.2 lbs. Hooded front sight; mid-mounted rear sight. Checkered walnut or beechwood stock. Single thumbscrew takedown. Grooved receiver for scope mounting. Imported from 2006 to date.
Standard beechwood model . . . . . . NiB $449 Ex $366 Gd $259
Deluxe walnut model . . . . NiB $551 Ex $443 Gd $288

BROWN PRECISION COMPANY — Los Molinos, California

MODEL 7 SUPER LIGHT SPORTER . . . . **NiB $1073 Ex $1015 Gd $717**
Lightweight sporter built on a Remington Model 7 barreled action w/18-inch factory bbl. Weight: 5.25 lbs. Kevlar stock. Made from 1984 to 1992.

HIGH COUNTRY BOLT-ACTION SPORTER
Custom sporting rifles built on Blaser, Remington 700, Ruger 77 and Winchester 70 actions. Calibers: .243 Win., .25-06, .270 Win., 7mm Rem. Mag., .308 Win., .30-06. Five-round magazine (4-round in 7mm Mag.). 22- or 24-inch bbl. Weight: 6.5 lbs. Fiberglass stock w/recoil pad, sling swivels. No sights. Made from 1975 to 1992.
Standard High Country . . . . NiB $1550 Ex $952 Gd $795
Custom High Country . . . . NiB $4407 Ex $3052 Gd $1795
Left-hand action, add. $200
Stainless bbl., add $200
70, 77 or Blaser actions, add. $125
70 SG action, add $350

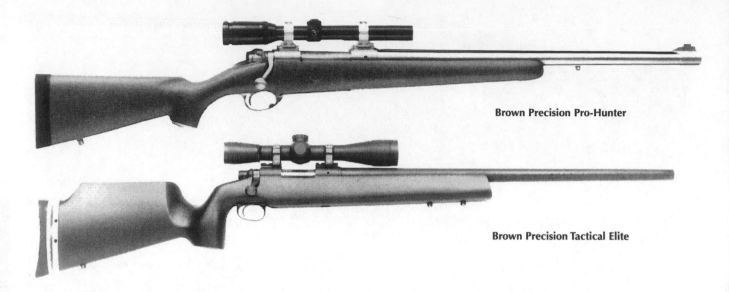

Brown Precision Pro-Hunter

Brown Precision Tactical Elite

HIGH COUNTRY YOUTH RIFLE . . . . NiB $1289 Ex $980 Gd $671
Similar to standard Model 7 Super Light except w/Kevlar or graphite stock, scaled-down to youth dimensions. Calibers: .223, .243, 6mm, 7mm-08, .308. Made from 1993 to 2000.

PRO-HUNTER BOLT-ACTION RIFLE
Custom sporting rifle built on Remington 700 or Winchester 70 SG action fitted w/match-grade Shilen bbl. chambered in customer's choice of caliber. Matte blued, nickel or Teflon finish. Express-style rear sight hooded ramp front. Synthetic stock. Made from 1989 to date
Standard Pro-Hunter . . . . NiB $44752 Ex $3120 Gd $2245
Pro-Hunter Elite (1993 to date) . . . . . . NiB $5962 Ex $3790 Gd $2014

PRO-VARMINTER BOLT-ACTION RIFLE
Custom varminter built on a Remington 700 or 40X action fitted w/Shilen stainless steel benchrest bbl. Varmint or benchrest-style stock. Made from 1993 to date.
Standard Pro-Varminter . . . . NiB $3626 Ex $1972 Gd $909
Pro-Hunter w/Rem 40X action . . . . Add $600

SELECTIVE TARGET MODEL . . . . . . NiB $999 Ex $780 Gd $545
Tactical law-enforcement rifle built on a Remington 700V action. Caliber: .308 Win. 20-, 22- or 24-inch bbl. Synthetic stock. Made from 1989 to 1992.

TACTICAL ELITE RIFLE . . . . . . NiB $4400 Ex $3170 Gd $19 30
Similar to Selective Target Model except fitted w/select match-grade Shilen benchrest heavy stainless bbl. Calibers: .223, .308, .300 Win. Mag. Black or camo Kevlar/graphite composite fiberglass stock w/adj. buttplate. Non-reflective black Teflon metal finish. Made from 1997 to date.

**BROWNING RIFLES — Morgan, Utah
Mfd. for Browning by Fabrique Nationale
d'Armes de Guerre (now Fabrique Nationale
Herstal), Herstal, Belgium; Miroku Firearms
Mfg. Co., Tokyo, Japan; A.T.I., Salt Lake City,
Ut; Oy Sako Ab, Riihimaki, Finland**

.22 AUTOMATIC RIFLE, GRADE I
Similar to discontinued Remington Model 241A. Autoloading. Take-down. Calibers: .22 LR. .22 Short (not interchangeably). Tubular magazine in butt-stock holds 11 LR. 16 Short. Bbl. lengths: 19.25 inches (.22 LR), 22.25 inches (.22 Short). Weight: 4.75 lbs. (.22 LR); 5 lbs. (.22 Short). Receiver scroll engraved. Open rear sight, bead front. Checkered pistol-grip buttstock, semibeavertail forearm. Made from 1956 to 1972 by FN; from 1972 to date by Miroku. Note: Illustrations are of rifles manufactured by FN.
FN manufacture . . . . NiB $832 Ex $452 Gd $246
Miroku manufacture . . . . NiB $544 Ex $341 Gd $289

.22 AUTOMATIC RIFLE, GRADE II
Same as Grade I except satin chrome-plated receiver engraved w/small game animal scenes, gold-plated trigger select walnut stock and forearm. .22 LR only. Made from 1972 to 1984.
FN manufacture . . . . NiB $1060 Ex $720 Gd $519
Miroku manufacture . . . . NiB $456 Ex $380 Gd $250

.22 AUTOMATIC RIFLE, GRADE III
Same as Grade I except satin chrome-plated receiver elaborately hand-carved and engraved w/dog and game-bird scenes, scrolls and leaf clusters: gold-plated trigger, extra-fancy walnut stock and forearm, skip-checkered. .22 LR only. Made from 1972 to 1984.
FN manufacture . . . . NiB $1432 Ex $1020 Gd $796
Miroku manufacture . . . . NiB $772 Ex $553 Gd $455

.22 AUTOMATIC, GRADE VI . . . . . NiB $1163 Ex $757 Gd $577
Same general specifications as standard .22 Automatic except for engraving, high-grade stock w/checkering and glossy finish. Made by Miroku from 1986 to date.

MODEL 52 BOLT-ACTION RIFLE . . . . NiB $763 Ex $608 Gd $402
Limited edition of Winchester Model 52C Sporter. Caliber: .22 LR. Five-round magazine. 24-inch bbl. Weight: 7 lbs. Micro-Motion trigger. No sights. Checkered select walnut stock w/rosewood forend and metal grip cap. Blued finish. 5000 made from 1991 to 1992.

MODEL 53 LEVER-ACTION RIFLE . . . . NiB $790 Ex $662 Gd $446
Limited edition of Winchester Model 53. Caliber: .32-20. Seven-round tubular half-magazine. 22-inch bbl. Weight: 6.5 lbs. Adj. rear sight, bead front. Select walnut checkered pistol-grip stock w/high-gloss finish. Classic-style forearm. Blued finish. 5000 made in 1990.

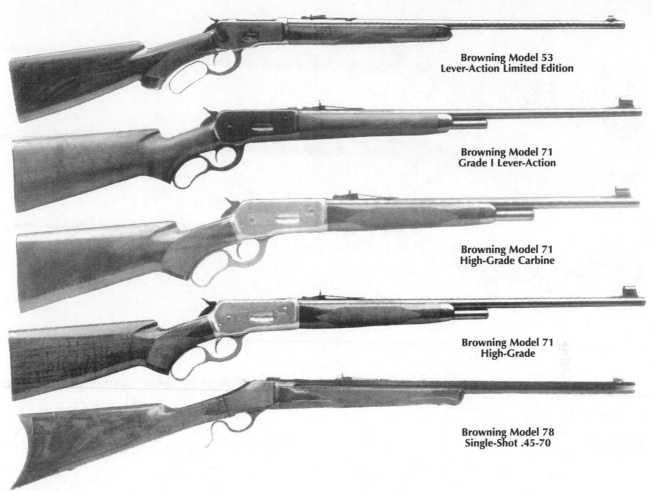

**Browning Model 53
Lever-Action Limited Edition**

**Browning Model 71
Grade I Lever-Action**

**Browning Model 71
High-Grade Carbine**

**Browning Model 71
High-Grade**

**Browning Model 78
Single-Shot .45-70**

MODEL 65 GRADE I
LEVER-ACTION RIFLE . . . . **NiB $575 Ex $417 Gd $314**
Caliber: .218 Bee. 7-round tubular half-magazine. 24-inch bbl. Weight: 6.75 lbs. Sights: Adj. buckhorn-style rear, hooded bead front. Select walnut pistol-grip stock w/high-gloss finish. Semibeavertail forearm. Limited edition of 3500 made in 1989.

MODEL 65 HIGH GRADE RIFLE . . . . **NiB $876 Ex $701 Gd $492**
Same general specifications as Model 65 Grade I except w/engraving and gold-plated animals on grayed receiver. Cut checkering on pistol grip and forearm. Limited edition of 1500 made in 1989.

MODEL 71 GRADE I CARBINE . . . . **NiB $773 Ex $593 Gd $412**
Same general specifications as Model 71 Grade I Rifle except carbine w/20-inch round bbl. and weighs 8 lbs. Limited edition of 4000 made in 1986 to 1987.

MODEL 71 GRADE I
LEVER-ACTION RIFLE . . . . **NiB $872 Ex $676 Gd $470**
Caliber: .348 Win. 4-round magazine. 24-inch round bbl. Weight: 8 lbs., 2 oz. Open buckhorn sights. Select walnut straight grip stock w/satin finish. Classic-style forearm, flat metal buttplate. Limited edition of 3000 made in 1986 to 1987.

MODEL 71 HIGH-GRADE CARBINE . . . . . **NiB $1256 Ex $1080 Gd $638**
Same general specifications as Model 71 High Grade Rifle, except carbine w/20-inch round bbl. Limited edition of 3000 made 1986 to 1988.

MODEL 71 HIGH-GRADE RIFLE . . . . . . **NiB $1338 Ex $1054 Gd $771**
Caliber: .348 Win. Four round magazine. 24-inch round bbl. Weight: 8 lbs., 2 oz. Engraved receiver. Open buckhorn sights. Select walnut checkered pistol-grip stock w/high-gloss finish. Classic-style forearm, flat metal buttplate. Limited edition of 3000 made in 1987.

M-78 BICENTENNIAL SET . . . . . **NiB $3730 Ex $3086 Gd $2082**
Special Model 78 .45-70 w/same specifications as standard type, except sides of receiver engraved w/bison and eagle, scroll engraving on top of receiver, lever, both ends of bbl. and buttplate; high-grade walnut stock and forearm. Accompanied by an engraved hunting knife and stainless steel commemorative medallion, all in an alder wood presentation case. Each item in set has matching serial number beginning with "1776" and ending with numbers 1 to 1,000. Edition limited to 1,000 sets. Made in 1976.

MODEL 78 SINGLE-SHOT RIFLE
Falling-block lever-action similar to Winchester 1885 High Wall single-shot rifle. Calibers: .22-250, 6mm Rem., .243 Win., .25-06, 7mm Rem. Mag., .30-06, .45-70 Govt. 26-inch octagon or heavy round bbl.; 24-inch octagon bull bbl. on .45-70 model. Weight: 7.75 lbs. w/octagon bbl.; w/round bbl., 8.5 lbs.; .45-70, 8.75 lbs. Furnished w/o sights except .45-70 model w/open rear sight, blade front. Checkered fancy walnut stock and forearm. .45-70 model w/straight-grip stock and curved buttplate; others have Monte Carlo comb and cheekpiece, pistol-grip w/cap, recoil pad. Made from 1973 to 1983 by Miroku. Reintroduced in 1985 as Model 1885.
All calibers except .45-70 . . . . . . **NiB $1430 Ex $1202 Gd $960**
.45-70 . . . . **NiB $908 Ex $727 Gd $480**

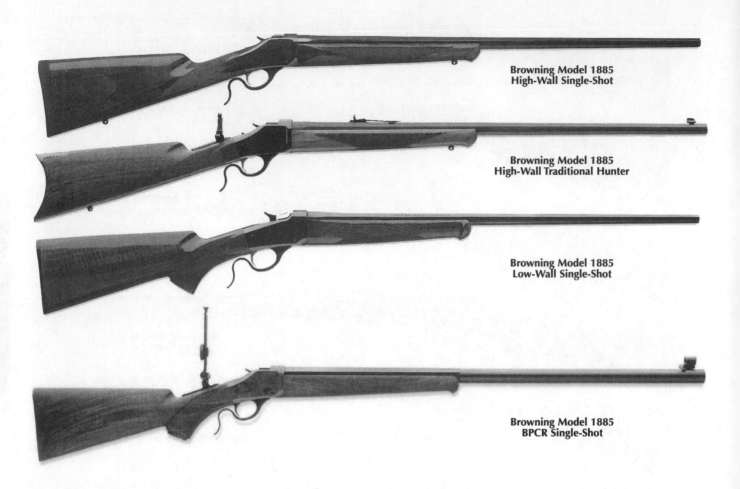

Browning Model 1885
High-Wall Single-Shot

Browning Model 1885
High-Wall Traditional Hunter

Browning Model 1885
Low-Wall Single-Shot

Browning Model 1885
BPCR Single-Shot

MODEL 1885 SINGLE-SHOT RIFLE

Calibers: .22 Hornet, .223, .243, (Low Wall); .357 Mag., .44 Mag., .45 LC (L/W Traditional Hunter); .22-250, .223 Rem., .270 Win., 7mm Rem. Mag., .30-06, .454 Casull Mag., .45.70 (High Wall); .30.30 Win., .38-55 WCF, .45 Govt. (H/W Traditional Hunter); .40-65, .45 Govt. and .45.90 (BPCR). 24-, 28-, 30 or 34-inch round, octagonal or octagonal and round bbl. 39.5, 43.5, 44.25 or 46.125 inches overall. Weight: 6.25, 8.75, 9, 11, or 11.75 lbs. respectively. Blued or color casehardened receiver. Gold-colored adj. trigger. Drilled and tapped for scope mounts w/no sights or vernier tang rear sight w/globe front and open sights on .45-70 Govt. Walnut straight-grip stock and Schnabel forearm w/cut checkering and high-gloss or oil finish. Made from 1985 to 2001.

Low Wall model w/o sights (Intro. 1995)   NiB $1450 Ex $919 Gd $488
Traditional Hunter model (Intro. 1998) .. NiB $1375 Ex $925 Gd $539
High Wall model w/o sights (Intro. 1985) .. NiB $1325 Ex $916 Gd $6462
Traditional Hunter model (Intro. 1997) .. NiB $1325 Ex $979 Gd $744
BPCR model w/no
ejector (Intro. 1996) .... NiB $1679 Ex $1370 Gd $996
BPCR Creedmoor Model .45-90
(Intro. 1998) .... NiB $1679 Ex $1306 Gd $958

MODEL 1886 MONTANA

CENTENNIAL RIFLE .... NiB $1997 Ex $1627 Gd $1045
Same general specifications as Model 1886 High Grade lever-action except w/specially engraved receiver designating Montana Centennial; also different stock design. Made in 1986 in limited issue by Miroku.

MODEL 1886 GRADE I

LEVER-ACTION RIFLE .... NiB $995 Ex $677 Gd $445
Caliber: .45-70 Govt., 8-round magazine. 26-inch octagonal bbl. 45 inches overall. Weight: 9 lbs., 5 oz. Deep blued finish on receiver. Open buckhorn sights. Straight-grip walnut stock. Classic-style forearm. Metal buttplate. Satin finish. Made in 1986 in limited issue 7000 by Miroku.

MODEL 1886 HIGH-

GRADE LA RIFLE .... NiB $1671 Ex $1311 Gd $897
Same general specifications as the Model 1886 Grade I except receiver is grayed, steel embellished w/scroll; elk and American bison engraving. High-gloss stock. Made in 1986 in limited issue of 3000 by Miroku.

MODEL 1895 GRADE I LA RIFLE .... NiB $1600 Ex $967 Gd $715

Caliber: .30-06, .30-40 Krag. Four round magazine. 24-inch round bbl. 42 inches overall. Weight: 8 lbs. French walnut stock and Schnabel forend. Sights: Rear buckhorn; gold bead on elevated ramp front. Made in 1984 in limited issue of 8,000 (2,000 chambered for .30-40 Krag and 6,000 chambered for .30-06). Mfd. by Miroku.

MODEL 1895 HIGH-

GRADE LA RIFLE............. NiB $1458 Ex $1306 Gd $945
Same general specifications as Model 1895 Grade I except engraved receiver and Grade III French walnut stock and forend w/fine checkering. Made in 1985 in limited issue of 1000 in each caliber by Miroku.

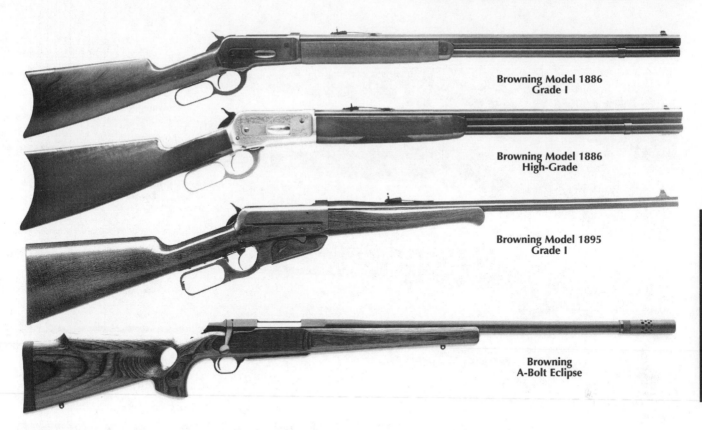

Browning Model 1886
Grade I

Browning Model 1886
High-Grade

Browning Model 1895
Grade I

Browning
A-Bolt Eclipse

MODEL A-BOLT .22 RIFLE

Calibers: .22 LR. .22 Magnum. Five- and 15-round magazines. 22-inch round bbl. 40.25 inches overall. Weight: 5 lbs., 9 oz. Gold-colored adj. trigger. Laminated walnut stock w/checkering. Rosewood forend grip cap; pistol grip. With or w/o sights. Ramp front and adj. folding leaf rear on open sight model. 22 LR made 1985 to 1996; 22 Magnum, 1990 to 1996.

Grade I .22 LR	NiB $496	Ex $310	Gd $226
Grade I .22 Magnum	NiB $473	Ex $390	Gd $241
Deluxe Grade			
Gold Medallion	NiB $576	Ex $447	Gd $334

MODEL A-BOLT ECLIPSE BOLT RIFLE

Same general specifications as Hunter Grade except fitted w/gray and black laminated thumbhole stock. Available in both short and long action w/two bbl. configurations w/BOSS. Mfd. by Miroku 1996 to 2006.

Eclipse w/standard bbl.	NiB $917	Ex $789	Gd $650
Eclipse Varmint w/heavy bbl.	NiB $1077	Ex $927	Gd $799
Eclipse M-1000			
(Target .300 Win. Mag.)	NiB $1234	Ex $969	Gd $721

MODEL A-BOLT EURO-BOLT RIFLE

Same general specifications as Hunter Grade except w/checkered satin-finished walnut stock. W/continental-style cheekpiece, palm-swell grip and Schnabel forend. Mannlicher-style spoon bolt handle and contoured bolt shroud. 22- or 26-inch bbl. w/satin blued finish. Weight: 6.8 to 7.4 lbs. Calibers: .22-250 Rem., .243 Win., .270 Win., .30.06, .308 Win., 7mm Rem. Mag. Mfd. by Miroku 1993 to 1994; 1994 to 1996 (Euro-Bolt II).

Euro-Bolt	NiB $646	Ex $501	Gd $340
Euro-Bolt II	NiB $682	Ex $604	Gd $445
BOSS option, add			$90

MODEL A-BOLT HUNTER GRADE RIFLE

Calibers: .22 Hornet, .223 Rem., .22-250 Rem., .243 Win., .257 Roberts, 7mm-08 Rem., .308 Win., (short action) .25-06 Rem., .270 Win., .280 Rem., .284 Win., .30-06, 7mm Rem. Mag., .300 Win. Mag., .338 Win. Mag. Four-round magazine (standard), 3-round (magnum). 22-inch bbl. (standard), 24-inch (magnum). Weight: 7.5 lbs. (standard), 8.5 lbs. (magnum). With or w/o sights. Classic-style walnut stock. Produced in two action lengths w/nine locking lugs, fluted bolt w/60 degree rotation. Mfd. by Miroku from 1985 to 1993; from 1994 to 2007 (Hunter II).

Hunter	NiB $456	Ex $304	Gd $240
Hunter II	NiB $554	Ex $353	Gd $276
Hunter Micro	NiB $559	Ex $404	Gd $301
BOSS option, add			$90
Open sights, add			$50

MODEL A-BOLT MEDALLION GRADE RIFLE

Same as Hunter Grade except w/high-gloss deluxe stock rosewood grip cap and forend; high-luster blued finish. Also in .375 H&H w/open sights. Left-hand models available in long action only. Mfd. by Miroku from 1988 to 1993; from 1994 to 2009 (Medallion II). Bighorn Sheep Ltd. Ed.

(600 made 1986, .270 Win.)	NiB $1357	Ex $1048	Gd $739
Gold Medallion Deluxe Grade	NiB $644	Ex $479	Gd $306
Gold Medallion II Deluxe Grade	NiB $639	Ex $499	Gd $320
Medallion, Standard Grade	NiB $579	Ex $451	Gd $321
Medallion II, Standard Grade	NiB $585	Ex $476	Gd $336
Medallion, .375 H&H	NiB $957	Ex $735	Gd $452
Medallion II, .375 H&H	NiB $967	Ex $709	Gd $503
Micro Medallion	NiB $654	Ex $526	Gd $347
Micro Medallion II	NiB $656	Ex $534	Gd $373
Pronghorn Antelope Ltd. Ed.			
(500 made 1987, .243 Win.)	NiB $1210	Ex $1062	Gd $882
BOSS option, add			$90
Open sights, add			$50

Browning A-Bolt .22

Browning A-Bolt
Euro-Bolt

Browning A-Bolt
Hunter

Browning A-Bolt
Hunter with BOSS

Browning A-Bolt
Medallion Custom Trophy

Browning A-Bolt
Medallion White Gold

Browning A-Bolt
Medallion

Browning A-Bolt
Medallion (Left-Handed)

Browning A-Bolt Composite Stalker

Browning A-Bolt Stalker

Browning BAR, Grade IV

Browning BAR, Grade V

MODEL A-BOLT STALKER RIFLE

Same general specifications as Model A-Bolt Hunter Rifle except w/checkered graphite-fiberglass composite stock and matte blued or stainless metal. Non-glare matte finish of all exposed metal surfaces. 3 models: Camo Stalker orig. w/multi-colored laminated wood stock, matte blued metal; Composite Stalker w/graphite-fiberglass stock, matte blued metal; w/composite stock, stainless metal. Made by Miroku from 1987 to 1993; 1994 to date. (Stalker II).

Camo Stalker (orig. laminated stock)	NiB $916	Ex $657	Gd $282
Composite Stalker.	NiB $958	Ex $613	Gd $385
Composite Stalker II	NiB $958	Ex $613	Gd $385
Stainless Stalker	NiB $994	Ex $691	Gd $488
Stainless Stalker II.	NiB $819	Ex $616	Gd $513
Stainless Stalker, .375 H&H	NiB $868	Ex $745	Gd $616
BOSS option, add			$90
Left-hand model, add			$90

MODEL A-BOLT

VARMINT II RIFLE . . . . NiB $771 Ex $719 Gd $560
Same general specifications as Stalker model except w/22-inch heavy bbl. w/BOSS system and varmint-style black laminated wood stock. Calibers: .22-250, .223 or .308. No sights. Bright blue or satin finish. Made by Miroku from 2002 to 2008.

MODEL B-92 LEVER-ACTION RIFLE

MODEL B-92 LEVER-ACTION RIFLE . . . . . NiB $501 Ex $440 Gd $244
Calibers: .357 Mag. and .44 Rem. Mag. 11-round magazine. 20-inch round bbl. 37.5 inches overall. Weight: 5.5 to 6.4 lbs. Seasoned French walnut stock w/high gloss finish. Cloverleaf rear sight; steel post front. Made from 1979 to 1989 by Miroku.

BAR AUTOMATIC RIFLE,

GRADE I, STANDARD CALIBERS. . . . . NiB $761 Ex $591 Gd $436
Gas-operated semiautomatic. Calibers: .243 Win., .270 Win., .280 Rem., .308 Win., .30-06. Four-round box magazine. 22-inch bbl. Weight: 7.5 lbs. Folding leaf rear sight, hooded ramp front. French walnut stock and forearm checkered, QD swivels. Made from 1967 to 1992 by FN.

BAR, GRADE I, MAGNUM CALIBERS . . . . NiB $771 Ex $719 Gd $555
Same as BAR in standard calibers, except w/24-inch bbl. 7mm Rem. Mag. or .300 Win. Mag. .338 Win. Mag. w/3-round box magazine and recoil pad. Weight: 8.5 lbs. Made 1969 to 1992 by FN.

BAR, GRADE II

Same as Grade I except receiver engraved w/big-game heads (deer and antelope on standard-caliber rifles, ram and grizzly on Magnum-caliber) and scrollwork, higher grade wood. Made 1967 to 1974 by FN.

Standard calibers.	NiB $1185	Ex $840	Gd $634
Magnum calibers.	NiB $1293	Ex $815	Gd $578

BAR, GRADE III

Same as Grade I except receiver of grayed steel engraved w/big-game heads (deer and antelope on standard-caliber rifles, moose and elk on Magnum-caliber) framed in fine-line scrollwork, gold-plated trigger, stock and forearm of highly figured French walnut, hand-checkered and carved. Made from 1971 to 1974 by FN.

Standard calibers.	NiB $1554	Ex $993	Gd $591
Magnum calibers.	NiB $1617	Ex $1230	Gd $725

BAR, GRADE IV

Same as Grade I except receiver of grayed steel engraved w/full detailed rendition of running deer and antelope on standard-caliber rifles, moose and elk on Magnum-caliber gold-plated trigger, stock and forearm of highly figured French walnut, hand checkered and carved. Made frm 1971 to 1986 by FN.

Standard calibers.	NiB $2400	Ex $1552	Gd $1066
Magnum calibers.	NiB $2560	Ex $1686	Gd $1209

BAR, GRADE V

Same as Grade I except receiver w/complete big-game scenes executed by a master engraver and inlaid w/18K gold (deer and antelope on standard-caliber rifles, moose and elk on Magnum caliber), gold-plated trigger, stock and forearm of finest French walnut, intricately hand-checkered and carved. Made from 1971 to 1974 by FN.

Standard calibers.	NiB $6372	Ex $4641	Gd $2834
Magnum calibers.	NiB $6723	Ex $5053	Gd $3126

GRADING: **NiB** = New in Box   **Ex** = Excellent or NRA 95%   **Gd** = Good or NRA 68%

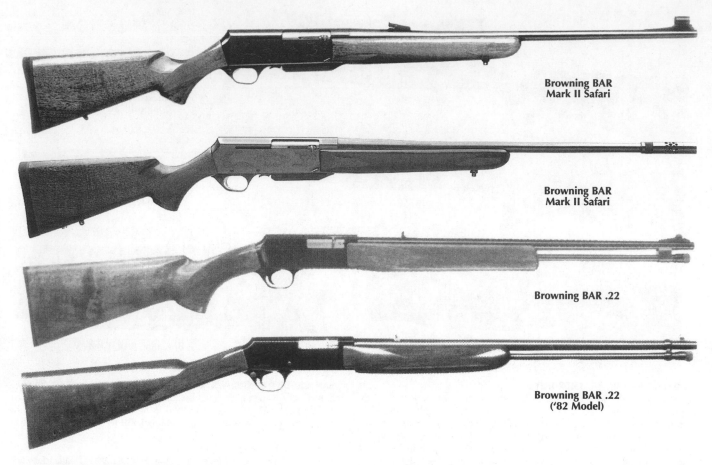

Browning BAR
Mark II Safari

Browning BAR
Mark II Safari

Browning BAR .22

Browning BAR .22
('82 Model)

BAR MARK II SAFARI AUTOMATIC RIFLE
Same general specifications as standard BAR semiautomatic rifle, except w/redesigned gas and buffer systems, new bolt release lever, and engraved receiver. Made from 1993 to date.

Standard calibers . . . . NiB $959 Ex $648 Gd $452
Magnum calibers. . . . . NiB $1010 Ex $784 Gd $578
Lightweight (Alloy receiver
w/20-inch bbl.) . . . . NiB $720 Ex $545 Gd $349
BAR Mk II Grade III (intro. 1996). . . . NiB $3465 Ex $22085 Gd $1235
BAR Mk II Grade IV (intro. 1996). . . . . NiB $3566 Ex $2227 Gd $1789
W/BOSS option, add $60
W/open sights, add $15

BAR .22 AUTOMATIC RIFLE
Semiautomatic. Caliber: .22 LR. Tubular magazine holds 15 rounds. 20.25-inch bbl. Weight: 6.25 lbs. Sights: Folding-leaf rear, gold bead front on ramp. Receiver grooved for scope mounting. French walnut pistol-grip stock and forearm checkered. Made from 1977 to 1985.
Grade I . . . . NiB $595 Ex $333 Gd $299
Grade II . . . . NiB $972 Ex $536 Gd $340

BBR LIGHTNING BOLT-ACTION RIFLE . . . NiB $575 Ex $472 Gd $358
Bolt-action rifle w/short bolt throw of 60 degrees. Calibers: .25-06 Rem., .270 Win., .30-06, 7mm Rem. Mag., .300 Win. Mag. 24-inch bbl. Weight: 8 lbs. Made from 1979 to 1984.

BL-.22 LEVER-ACTION REPEATING RIFLE
Short-throw lever-action. Caliber: .22 LR, Long, Short. Tubular magazine holds 15 LR, 17 Long 22 Short rounds. 20-inch bbl. Weight: 5 lbs. Sights: Folding leaf rear; bead front. Receiver grooved for scope

mounting. Walnut straight-grip stock and forearm, bbl. band. Made from 1970 to date by Miroku.
Grade I . . . . NiB $424 Ex $330 Gd $263
Grade I7
w/scroll engraving . . . . NiB $479 Ex $361 Gd $275

BLR LEVER-ACTION
REPEATING RIFLE
Calibers: (short action only) .243 Win., .308 Win., .358 Win. Four round detachable box magazine. 20-inch bbl. Weight: 7 lbs. Sights: Windage and elevation adj. open rear; hooded ramp front. Walnut straight-grip stock and forearm, checkered, bbl. band, recoil pad. Made in 1966 by BAC/USA; from 1969 to 1973 by FN; from 1974 to 1980 by Miroku. Note: USA manufacture of this model was limited to prototypes and pre-production guns only and may be identified by the "MADE IN USA" roll stamp on the bbl.
FN model. . . . . NiB $960 Ex $633 Gd $479
Miroku model . . . . NiB $650 Ex $451 Gd $348
USA model . . . . NiB $1199 Ex $1036 Gd $624

BLR LIGHTNING MODEL
Lightweight version of the Browning BLR '81 w/forged alloy receiver and redesigned trigger group. Calibers: Short Action— .22-250 Rem., .223 Rem., .243 Win., 7mm-08 Rem., .308 Win.; Long Action— .270 Win., 7mm Rem. Mag., .30-06, .300 Win. Mag. Three or 4-round detachable box magazine. 20-, 22- or 24-inch bbl. Weight: 6.5 to 7.75 lbs. Pistol-grip style walnut stock and forearm, cut checkering and recoil pad. Made by Miroku from 1995 to 2002.
BLR Lightning model short action . . . . NiB $640 Ex $436 Gd $340
BLR Lightning model long action . . . . NiB $650 Ex $472 Gd $317

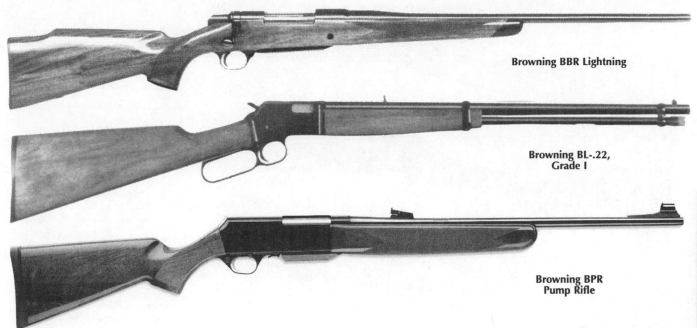

Browning BBR Lightning

Browning BL-.22,
Grade I

Browning BPR
Pump Rifle

BLR MODEL '81

Redesigned version of the Browning BLR. Calibers: .222-50 Rem., .243 Win., .308 Win., .358 Win; Long Action— .270 Win., 7mm Rem. Mag., .30-06. Fourround detachable box magazine. 20-inch bbl. Weight: 7 lbs. Walnut straight-grip stock and forearm, cut checkering, recoil pad. Made by Miroku from 1981 to 1995; Long Action intro. 1991.

BLR Model '81 short action . . . . . . NiB $656 Ex $447 Gd $297
BLR Model '81 long action . . . . NiB $758 Ex $452 Gd $339

BPR-22 PUMP RIFLE

Hammerless slide-action repeater. Specifications same as for BAR-.22, except also available chambered for .22 Magnum RF; magazine capacity, 11 rounds. Made from 1977 to 1982 by Miroku.

Model I . . . . NiB $355 Ex $274 Gd $200
Model II . . . . NiB $425 Ex $437 Gd $262

BPR PUMP RIFLE

Slide-action repeater based on proven BAR designs w/forged alloy receiver and slide that cams down to clear bbl. and receiver. Calibers: .243 Win., .308 Win., .270 Win., .30-06, 7mm Rem. Mag. .300 Win. Mag. Three or 4-round detachable box magazine. 22- or 24-inch bbl. w/ramped front sight and open adj. rear. Weight: 7.2 to 7.4 lbs. Made from 1997 to 2001 by Miroku.

BPR Model standard calibers . . . . . . NiB $695 Ex $498 Gd $371
BPR Model magnum calibers . . . . Add $60

HIGH-POWER BOLT-ACTION
RIFLE, MEDALLION GRADE . . . . NiB $1771 Ex $1612 Gd $994

Same as Safari Grade except receiver and bbl. scroll engraved, ram's head engraved on floorplate; select walnut stock w/rosewood forearm tip, grip cap. Made from 1961 to 1974.

HIGH-POWER BOLT-ACTION
RIFLE, OLYMPIAN GRADE . . . . NiB $3831 Ex $3435 Gd $1925

Same as Safari Grade except bbl. engraved; receiver, trigger guard and floorplate satin chrome-plated and engraved w/game scenes appropriate to caliber; finest figured walnut stock w/rosewood forearm tip and grip cap, latter w/18K-gold medallion. Made from 1961 to 1974.

HIGH-POWER BOLT-ACTION RIFLE,
SAFARI GRADE, MEDIUM ACTION . . . . . NiB $1382 Ex $929 Gd $698

Same as Standard except medium action. Calibers: .22-250, .243 Win., .264 Win. Mag., .284 Win. Mag., .308 Win. Bbl.: 22-inch lightweight bbl.; .22-250 and .243 also available w/24-inch heavy bbl. Weight: 6 lbs., 12 oz. w/lightweight bbl.; 7 lbs. 13 oz. w/heavy bbl. Made 1963 to 1974 by Sako.

HIGH-POWER BOLT-ACTION RIFLE,
SAFARI GRADE, SHORT ACTION . . . . NiB $1682 Ex $899 Gd $698

Same as Standard except short action. Calibers: .222 Rem., .222 Rem. Mag. 22-inch lightweight or 24-inch heavy bbl. No sights. Weight: 6 lbs., 2 oz. w/lightweight bbl.; 7.5 lbs. w/heavy bbl. Made from 1963 to 1974 by Sako.

HIGH-POWER BOLT-ACTION RIFLE,
SAFARI GRADE, STANDARD ACTION . . NiB $1476 Ex $1088 Gd $882

Mauser-type action. Calibers: .270 Win., .30-06, 7mm Rem. Mag., .300 H&H Mag., .300 Win. Mag., .308 Norma Mag. .338 Win. Mag., .375 H&H Mag., .458 Win. Mag. Cartridge capacity: 6 rounds in .270, .30-06; 4 in Magnum calibers. Bbl. length: 22 in., in .270, .30-06; 24 in., in Magnum calibers. Weight: 7 lbs., 2 oz., in .270, .30-06; 8.25 lbs. in Mag. calibers. Folding leaf rear sight, hooded ramp front. Checkered stock w/pistol grip, Monte Carlo cheekpiece, QD swivels; recoil pad on Magnum models. Made from 1959 to 1974 by FN.

T-BOLT T-1 .22 REPEATING RIFLE

Straight-pull bolt action. Caliber: .22 LR. Five round clip magazine. 24-inch bbl. Peep rear sight w/ramped blade front. Plain walnut stock w/pistol grip and laquered finish. Weight: 6 lbs. Also left-hand model. Made from 1965 to 1974 by FN.

Right-hand model . . . . NiB $599 Ex $438 Gd $268
Left-hand model . . . . NiB $625 Ex $482 Gd $368

T-BOLT T-2

Same as T-1 Model except w/checkered fancy figured walnut stock. Made from 1966-74 by FN. (Reintroduced briefly during the late 1980's with oil-finished stock)

Original model . . . . NiB $875 Ex $543 Gd $268
Reintroduced model . . . . .NiB $550 Ex $396 Gd $242

Browning
BL-22 II

Browning
BLR Model '81

Browning High-Power
Bolt-Action Rifle, Medallion Grade

Browning High-Power
Safari Grade Medium Action, Heavy Barrel

Browning High-Power
Safari Grade Short Action, Heavy Barrel

Browning High-Power
Safari Grade Standard Action

F.N. BROWNING FAL SEMIAUTOMATIC RIFLE
Same as F.N. FAL Semiautomatic Rifle. See F.N. listing for specifications. Sold by Browning for a brief period c. 1960.
F.N. FAL standard
model (G-series)......................NiB $4850 Ex $3517 Gd $2819
F.N. FAL lightweight
model (G-series)......................NiB $5200 Ex $4310 Gd $2970
F.N. FAL heavy bbl..
model (G-series) ....NiB $7000 Ex $6133 Gd $4836
BAC FAL model.......................NiB $5200 Ex $4801 Gd $2813

BSA GUNS LTD. — Birmingham, England (Previously Imported by Samco Global Arms, BSA Guns Ltd and Precision Sports)

NO. 12 MARTINI SINGLE-SHOT
TARGET RIFLE.................NiB $725 Ex $510 Gd $382
Caliber .22 LR. 29-inch bbl. Weight: 8.75 lbs. Parker-Hale Model 7 rear sight and Model 2 front sight. Straight-grip stock, checkered forearm. Note: This model was also available w/open sights or w/BSA No. 20 and 30 sights. Made before WWII.

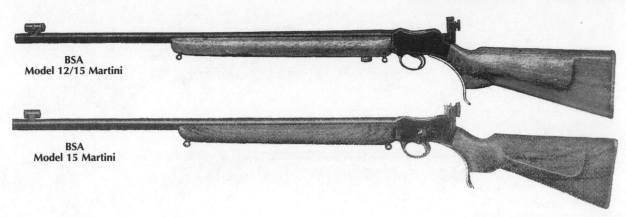

BSA
Model 12/15 Martini

BSA
Model 15 Martini

MODEL 12/15 MARTINI HEAVY . . . . NiB $726 Ex $506 Gd $342
Same as Standard Model 12/15 except w/extra heavy bbl., weighs 11 lbs.

MODEL 12/15 MARTINI
SINGLE-SHOT TARGET RIFLE . . . . . NiB $584 Ex $450 Gd $328
Caliber: .22 LR. 29-inch bbl. Weight: 9 lbs. Parker-Hale No. PH-7A rear sight and No. FS-22 front sight. Target stock w/high comb and cheekpiece, beavertail forearm. Note: This is a post-WWII model; however, a similar rifle, the BSA-Parker Model 12/15, was produced c. 1938.

NO. 13 MARTINI SINGLE-SHOT
TARGET RIFLE . . . . NiB $725 Ex $550 Gd $395
Caliber: .22 LR. Lighter version of the No.12 w/same general specifications except w/25-inch bbl., weighs 6.5lbs. Made before WWII.

NO. 13 SPORTING RIFLE
Same as No. 13 Target except fitted w/Parker-Hale "Sportarget" rear sight and bead front sight. Also available in .22 Hornet. Made before WWII.
.22 Long Rifle . . . . NiB $725 Ex $458 Gd $399
.22 Hornet. NiB $950 Ex $769 Gd $564

MODEL 15 MARTINI
SINGLE-SHOT TARGET RIFLE. . . . . NiB $730 Ex $550 Gd $300
Caliber: .22 LR. 29-inch bbl. Weight: 9.5 lbs. BSA No. 30 rear sight and No. 20 front sight. Target stock w/cheekpiece and pistol-grip, long, semi-beavertail forearm. Made before WWII.

CENTURION MODEL
MATCH RIFLE . . . . NiB $495 Ex $399 Gd $290
Same general specifications as Model 15 except w/Centurion match bbl. Made before WWII.

CF-2 BOLT-ACTION
HUNTING RIFLE . . . . NiB $491 Ex $374 Gd $240
Mauser-type action. Calibers: 7mm Rem. Mag., .300 Win. Mag. Three-round magazine. 23.6-inch bbl. Weight: 8 lbs. Sights: Adj. rear; hooded ramp front. Checkered walnut stock w/Monte Carlo comb, rollover cheekpiece, rosewood forend tip, recoil pad, sling swivels. Made 1975 to 1987.

CF-2 STUTZEN RIFLE . . . . NiB $553 Ex $403 Gd $300
Calibers: .222 Rem., .22-250, .243 Win., .270 Win., .308 Win. .30-06. Four round capacity (5 in 222 Rem.). 20.6-inch bbl. 41.5 inches (approx.) overall length. Weight: 7.5 to 8 lbs. Williams front and rear sights. Hand-finished European walnut stock. Monte Carlo cheekpiece and Wundhammer palm swell. Double-set triggers. Importation disc. 1987.

CFT TARGET RIFLE . . . . NiB $882 Ex $697 Gd $502
Single-shot bolt action. Caliber: 7.62mm. 26.5-inch bbl. About 47.5 inches overall. Weight: 11 lbs., incl. accessories. Bbl. and action weight: 6 lbs., 12 oz. Importation disc. 1987.

MAJESTIC DELUXE FEATHERWEIGHT BOLT-ACTION HUNTING RIFLE
Mauser-type action. Calibers: .243 Win., .270 Win., .308 Win., .30-06, .458 Win. Mag. Four round magazine. 22-inch bbl. w/BESA recoil reducer. Weight: 6.25 lbs.; 8.75 lbs. in 458. Folding leaf rear sight, hooded ramp front. Checkered European-style walnut stock w/cheekpiece, pistol-grip, Schnabel forend, swivels, recoil pad. Made from 1959 to 1965.
.458 Win. Mag. caliber . . . . NiB $606 Ex $478 Gd $323
Other calibers . . . . NiB $475 Ex $400 Gd $272

BSA MAJESTIC DELUXE
STANDARD WEIGHT . . . . NiB $473 Ex $292 Gd $220
Same as Featherweight model except heavier bbl. w/o recoil reducer. Calibers: .22 Hornet, .222 Rem., .243 Win., 7x57mm, .308 Win., .30-06. Weight: 7.25 to 7.75 lbs. Disc.

MARTINI-INTERNATIONAL
ISU MATCH RIFLE . . . . NiB $900 Ex $679 Gd $537
Similar to MK III, but modified to meet International Shooting Union "Standard Rifle" specifications. 28-inch standard weight bbl. Weight: 10.75 lbs. Redesigned stock and forearm, latter attached to bbl. w/"V" section alloy strut. Intro. 1968. Disc.

MARTINI-INTERNATIONAL
MARK V MATCH RIFLE . . . . NiB $1038 Ex $807 Gd $570
Same as ISU model except w/heavier bbl. Weight: 12.25 lbs. Intro. 1976. Disc.

MARTINI-INTERNATIONAL MATCH
RIFLE SINGLE-SHOT HEAVY PATTERN. . . . NiB $799 Ex $587 Gd $481
Caliber: .22 LR. 29-inch heavy bbl. Weight: 14 lbs. Parker-Hale "International" front and rear sights. Target stock w/full cheekpiece and pistol-grip, broad beavertail forearm, handstop, swivels. Right- or left-hand models. Made from 1950 to 1953.

MARTINI-INTERNATIONAL
MATCH RIFLE — LIGHT PATTERN. . . . . NiB $775 Ex $584 Gd $455
Same general specifications as Heavy Pattern except w/26-inch lighter weight bbl. Weight: 11 lbs. Disc.

MARTINI-INTERNATIONAL
MK II MATCH RIFLE . . . . NiB $960 Ex $675 Gd $595
Same general specifications as original model. Heavy and Light Pattern. Improved trigger mechanism and ejection system. Redesigned stock and forearm. Made from 1953 to 1959.

MARTINI-INTERNATIONAL
MK III MATCH RIFLE . . . . NiB $995 Ex $754 Gd $566
Same general specifications as MK II Heavy Pattern. Longer action frame w/I-section alloy strut to which forearm is attached; bbl. is fully floating. Redesigned stock and forearm. Made 1959 to 1967.

BSA CFT Target

BSA Martini-International ISU Match

BSA Martini-International Mark V Match

BSA Martini-International MK III Match

BSA Monarch Deluxe Varmint

MONARCH DELUXE BOLT-ACTION
HUNTING RIFLE . . . . **NiB $675 Ex $328 Gd $230**
Same as Majestic Deluxe Standard Weight model except w/redesigned stock of U.S. style w/contrasting hardwood forend tip and grip cap. Calibers: .222 Rem., .243 Win., .270 Win., 7mm Rem. Mag., .308 Win., .30-06. 22-inch bbl. Weight: 7 to 7.25 lbs. Made 1965 to 1974.

MONARCH DELUXE
VARMINT RIFLE . . . . **NiB $675 Ex $390 Gd $262**
Same as Monarch Deluxe except w/24-inch heavy bbl. and weighs 9 lbs. Calibers: .222 Rem., .243 Win.

BUSHMASTER FIREARMS —
(Quality Parts Company), Windham, Maine

M17S BULLPUP . . . . **NiB $703 Ex $569 Gd $442**
Caliber: .223. 21.5-inch bbl. Weight: 8.2 lbs. Polymer stocks. Handle w/fixed open sights w/Weaver-type rail for any optics. Semi-auto, self-compensating short stroke gas piston. Forward trigger/grip w/rear chamber. Bullpup style. Alloy receiver. Synthetic lower receiver is hinged to upper w/hinged takedown system. Accepts M-16 type magazines. Made from 1992 to 2005.

MODEL XM15 E2S SERIES
Caliber: .223. 16-, 20-, 24- or 26-inch bbl. Weight: 7 to 8.6 lbs. Polymer stocks. Adjustable sights w/dual flip-up aperture; optional flattop rail accepts scope. Direct gas-operated w/rotating bolt. Forged alloy receiver. All steel-coated w/manganese phosphate. Accepts M-16 type magazines. Made from 1989 to date.
XM15 E2S Carbine . . . . **NiB $1146 Ex $966 Gd $721**
XM15 E2S Target Rifle . . . . **NiB $1198 Ex $915 Gd $659**

CABELA'S, INC. — Sidney, Nebraska

Cabela's is a sporting goods dealer and catalog company head-quartered in Sidney, Nebraska. Cabela's imports black powder cartridge Sharps replicas, revolvers and other reproductions and replicas manufactured in Italy by A. Uberti, Pedersoli, Pietta and others.

1858 HENRY REPLICA . . . . **NiB $649 Ex $572 Gd $499**
Lever-action. Modeled after the original Henry rifle. Caliber: .44-40. Thirteen-round magazine; Bbl: 24 inches. Overall length: 43 inches. Weight: 9 pounds. European walnut stock. Sights: Bead front, open adjustable rear. Brass receiver and buttplate. Introduced 1994.

1866 WINCHESTER REPLICA . . . . . **NiB $549 Ex $499 Gd $424**
Lever-action modeled after the original Model 1866 rifle. Caliber: .44-40. Thirteen-round magazine. Bbl: 24 inches, octagonal; overall length: 43 inches. Weight: 9 pounds. European walnut stock, brass receiver, butt plate and forend cap. Sights: Bead front, open adjustable rear.

1873 WINCHESTER REPLICA . . . . . **NiB $499 Ex $434 Gd $374**
Lever-action modeled after the original Model 1873 rifle. Caliber: .44-40, .45 Colt. Thirteen-round magazine. Bbl: 30 inches. Overall length: 43 inches. Weight: 8 pounds. European walnut stock. Sights: Bead front, open adjustable rear or globe front and tang rear. Color case-hardened steel receiver. Introduced 1994.
W/tang rear sight, globe front, add **$150**

1873 SPORTING
MODEL REPLICA. . . . . **NiB $628 Ex $543 Gd $483**
Same as 1873 Winchester except with 30-inch bbl.
W/half-round, half-octagonal bbl., half magazine, add **$100**

CATTLEMAN CARBINE . . . . **NiB $322 Ex $282 Gd $222**
Revolver with shoulder stock. Caliber: .44-40; six-round cylinder. Bbl: 18 inches. Overall length: 34 inches. Weight: 4 pounds. European walnut stock. Sights: Blade front, notch rear. Color case-hardened frame, remainder blued. Introduced 1994.

SHARPS SPORTING RIFLE . . . . **NiB $834 Ex $759 Gd $534**
Single-shot. Caliber: .45-70. Bbl: Tapered octagon, 32 inches. Overall length: 47 inches. Weight: 9 pounds. Checkered walnut stock. Sights: Blade front, open adjustable rear. Color case-hardened receiver and hammer; remainder blued. Introduced 1995.

CALICO LIGHT WEAPONS SYSTEMS — Bakersville, California

LIBERTY 50/100 SEMIAUTOMATIC RIFLE
Retarded blowback action. Caliber: 9mm. 50- or 100-round helical-feed magazine. 16.1-inch bbl. 34.5 inches overall. Weight: 7 lbs. Adjustable post front sight and aperture rear. Ambidextrous rotating safety. Glass-filled polymer or thumbhole-style wood stock. Made 1995 to 2001; reintro. 2007.
Model Liberty 50. . . . . **NiB $783 Ex $630 Gd $375**
Model Liberty 100. . . . . **NiB $860 Ex $834 Gd $452**

MODEL M-100 SEMIAUTOMATIC SERIES
Similar to the Liberty 100 Model except chambered for .22 LR. Weight: 5 lbs. 34.5 inches overall. Folding or glass-filled polymer stock and forearm. Made from 1986 to 1994; reintro. 2007.
Model M-100 w/folding
stock (disc. 1994). . . . . **NiB $565 Ex $328 Gd $285**

Model M-100 FS w/fixed
stock (1996) . . . . **NiB $565 Ex $328 Gd $285**

MODEL M-105
SEMI-AUTOMATIC
SPORTER. **NiB $650 Ex $461 Gd $285**
Similar to the Liberty 100 Model except fitted w/walnut buttstock and forearm. Made from 1989 to 1994.

MODEL M-900
SEMIAUTOMATIC CARBINE
Caliber: 9mm Parabellum. 50- or 100-round magazine. 16.1-inch bbl. 28.5 inches overall. Weight: 3.7 lbs. Post front sight adj. for windage and elevation, fixed notch rear. Collapsible steel buttstock and glass-filled polymer grip. Matte black finish. Made from 1989 to 1990, 1992 to 1993 and 2007.
Model M-100 w/folding
stock (disc. 1994) . . . . **NiB $775 Ex $445 Gd $292**
Model M-100 FS w/fixed
stock (Intro. 1996) . . . . **NiB $642 Ex $494 Gd $366**

MODEL M-951
TACTICAL CARBINE
Similar to Model 900 except w/long compensator and adj. forward grip. Made from 1990 to 1994.
Model 951. **NiB $650 Ex $494 Gd $397**
Model 951-S . . . . **NiB $650 Ex $494 Gd $397**

CANADIAN MILITARY RIFLES — Quebec, Canada, Manufactured by Ross Rifle Co.

MODEL 1907 MARK II
ROSS MILITARY RIFLE . . . . **NiB $357 Ex $255 Gd $225**
Straight-pull bolt action. Caliber: .303 British. Five-round box magazine. 28-inch bbl. Weight: 8.5 lbs. Sights: adj. rear; blade front. Military-type full stock. Note: The Ross was originally issued as a Canadian service rifle in 1907. There were several variations; it was the official weapon at the start of WWI, but has been obsolete for many years. For Ross sporting rifle, see listing under Ross Rifle company.

CENTURY INTERNATIONAL ARMS, INC. — Delray Beach, Florida

CENTURION M38/M96
BOLT-ACTION SPORTER
Sporterized Swedish M38/96 Mauser action. Caliber: 6.5x55mm. Five-round magazine. 24-inch bbl. 44 inches overall. Adj. rear sight. Blade front. Black synthetic or checkered European hardwood Monte Carlo stock. Holden Ironsighter see-through scope mount. Imported from 1987 to date.
W/hardwood stock . . . . **NiB $209 Ex $148 Gd $103**
W/synthetic stock . . . . **NiB $215 Ex $174 Gd $123**

CENTURION M98
BOLT-ACTION SPORTER
Sporterized VZ24 or 98 Mauser action. Calibers: .270 Win., 7.62x39mm, .308 Win., .30-06. Five round magazine. 22-inch bbl. 44 inches overall. Weight: 7.5 lbs. W/Millet or Weaver scope base(s), rings and no iron sights. Classic or Monte Carlo laminated hardwood, black synthetic or checkered European hardwood stock. Imported from 1992 to date.
M98 Action W/black
synthetic stock (w/o rings). . . . . **NiB $270 Ex $199 Gd $142**
M98 Action W/hardwood Stock(w/o rings). . . .**NiB $250 Ex $174 Gd $113**

RIFLES

**VZ24 Action W/laminated
Hardwood Stock (Elite)** . . . . NiB $326 Ex $254 Gd $178
**VZ24 Action W/black
synthetic stock.** . . . . NiB $312 Ex $254 Gd $181
W/Millet base and rings, add $25

CENTURION P-14 SPORTER
Sporterized P-14 action. Caliber: 7mm Rem. Mag., .300 Win. Mag. Five-round magazine. 24-inch bbl. 43.4 inches overall. Weight: 8.25 lbs. Weaver-type scope base. Walnut stained hardwood or fiberglass stock. Imported from 1987 to date.
W/hardwood stock . . . . NiB $244 Ex $203 Gd $142
W/fiberglass stock . . . . NiB $280 Ex $203 Gd $142

ENFIELD SPORTER 4 BOLT-ACTION RIFLE
Sporterized Lee-Enfield action. Caliber: .303 British. 10-round magazine. 25.25-inch bbl. 44.5 inches overall. Blade front sight, adj. aperture rear. Sporterized beechwood military stock or checkered walnut Monte Carlo stock. Blued finish. Imported from 1987 to date.
W/sporterized military stock . . . . NiB $148 Ex $118 Gd $77
W/checkered walnut stock . . . . NiB $199 Ex $174 Gd $118

L1A1 FAL SPORTER . . . . NiB $896 Ex $698 Gd $540
Sporterized L1A1 FAL semiautomatic. Caliber: .308 Win. 20.75-inch bbl. 41 inches overall. Weight: 9.75 lbs. Protected front post sight, adj. aperture rear. Matte blued finish. Black or camo Bell & Carlson thumbhole sporter stock w/rubber buttpad. Imported from 1988-98.

M-14 SPORTER . . . . NiB $432 Ex $311 Gd $208
Sporterized M-14 gas operated semiautomatic action. Caliber: .308 Win. 10-round magazine. 22-inch bbl. 41 inches overall. Weight: 8.25 lbs. Blade front sight, adj. aperture rear sight. Parkerized finish. Walnut stock w/rubber recoil pad. Forged receiver. Imported from 1991 to date.

TIGER DRAGUNOV . . . . NiB $975 Ex $765 Gd $488
Russian SVD semiautomatic sniper rifle. Caliber: 7.62x54R. Five-round magazine. 21-inch bbl. 43 inches overall. Weight: 8.5 lbs. Blade front sight, open rear adj. for elevation. Blued finish. European laminated hardwood thumbhole stock. 4x range-finding scope w/lighted reticle and sunshade. Quick detachable scope mount. Imported from 1994 to 1995.

CHARTER ARMS CORPORATION — Shelton, Connecticut

AR-7 EXPLORER
SURVIVAL RIFLE . . . . NiB $127 Ex $112 Gd $81
Same as Armalite AR-7, except w/black, instead of brown, "wood grain" plastic stock. See listing of that rifle for specifications. Made from 1973 to 1990.

CHIPMUNK RIFLES — Prospect, Oregon Mfd. by Rogue Rifle Company (Formerly Oregon Arms Company and Chipmunk Manufacturing, Inc.)

BOLT-ACTION SINGLE-SHOT RIFLE
Calibers: .22 LR. or .22 WMR. 16.13-inch standard or 18.13-inch bull bbl. Weight: 2.5 lbs. (standard) or 4 lbs. (Bull bbl.) Peep sight rear; ramp front. Plain or checkered American walnut, laminated or black hardwood stock. Made from 1982 to 2007.

**Standard model
w/plain walnut stock** . . . . NiB $191 Ex $135 Gd $89
**Standard model
w/black hardwood stock** . . . . NiB $171 Ex $125 Gd $89
**Standard model
w/camouflage stock** . . . . NiB $201 Ex $155 Gd $104
**Standard model
w/laminated stock** . . . . NiB $187 Ex $155 Gd $115
**Deluxe grade
w/checkered walnut stock** . . . . NiB $257 Ex $201 Gd $132
.22 WMR, add $20

CHURCHILL RIFLES — Mfd. in High Wycombe, England.

HIGHLANDER
BOLT-ACTION RIFLE . . . . . . .NiB $400 Ex $340 Gd $275
Calibers: .243 Win., .25-06 Rem., .270 Win., .308 Win., .30-06, 7mm Rem. Mag., .300 Win. Mag. Four round magazine (standard); 3-round (magnum). Bbl. length: 22-inch (standard); 24-inch (magnum). 42.5 to 44.5 inches overall. Weight: 7.5 lbs. Adj. rear sight, blade front. Checkered European walnut pistol-grip stock. Imported from 1986 to 1991.

"ONE OF ONE THOUSAND" RIFLE
. . . . NiB $3995 Ex $2468 Gd $1920
Made for Interarms to commemorate that firm's 20th anniversary. Mauser-type action. Calibers: .270, 7mm Rem. Mag., .308, .30-06, .300 Win. Mag., .375 H&H Mag., .458 Win. Mag. Five round magazine (3-round in Magnum calibers). 24-inch bbl. Weight: 8 lbs. Classic-style French walnut stock w/cheekpiece, black forend tip, checkered pistol grip and forearm, swivel-mounted recoil pad w/cartridge trap, pistol-grip cap w/trap for extra front sight, barrel-mounted sling swivel. Limited issue of 1,000 rifles made in 1973. See illustration next page.

REGENT
BOLT-ACTION RIFLE . . . . NiB $555 Ex $387 Gd $263
Calibers: .243 Win., .25-06 Rem., .270 Win., .308 Win., .30-06, 7mm Rem. Mag., .300 Win. Mag. Four round magazine. 22-inch round bbl. 42.5 inches overall. Weight: 7.5 lbs. Ramp front sight w/gold bead; adj. rear. Hand-checkered Monte Carlo-style stock of select European walnut; recoil pad. Made from 1986 to 1988.

CIMARRON ARMS — Fredericksburg, Texas

1860 HENRY
LEVER-ACTION REPLICA
Replica of 1860 Henry w/original Henry loading system.Calibers: .44-40, .44 Special, .45 Colt. 13-round magazine. 22-inch bbl. (carbine) or 24.25-inch bbl. (rifle). 43 inches overall (rifle). Weight: 9.5 lbs. (rifle). Bead front sight, open adj. rear. Brass receiver and buttplate. Smooth European walnut buttstock. Imported from 1991.
Carbine model. . . . . NiB $1275 Ex $967 Gd $489
Rifle model . . . . NiB $1275 Ex $695 Gd $514
**Civil War model
(U.S. issue martially marked)** . . . . . NiB $1395 Ex $987 Gd $640
W/A-engraving, add. $1000
W/B-engraving, add. $1290
W/C-engraving, add. $725

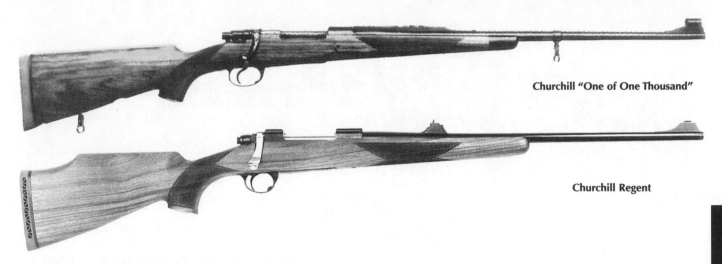

Churchill "One of One Thousand"

Churchill Regent

1866 YELLOWBOY LEVER-ACTION
Replica of 1866 Winchester. Calibers: .22 LR, 22WMR, .38 Special, .44-40, .45 Colt. 16-inch round bbl. (Trapper), 19-inch round bbl. (Carbine) or 24.25-inch ocatagonal bbl. (rifle). 43 inches overall (rifle). Weight: 9 lbs. (rifle). Bead front sight, open adj. rear. Brass receiver, buttplate and forend cap. Smooth European walnut stock. Imported 1991 to date.

Carbine	NiB $1075	Ex $787	Gd $581
Rifle	NiB $1050	Ex $612	Gd $406
Indian model (disc.)	NiB $895	Ex $585	Gd $379
Trapper Model (.44-40 WCF only, disc.)	NiB $995	Ex $756	Gd $502
W/A-engraving, add			$2025
W/B-engraving, add			$2500
W/C-engraving, add			$3000

1873 LEVER-ACTION
Replica of 1873 Winchester. Calibers: .22 LR. .22WMR, .357 Magnum, .44-40 or .45 Colt. 16-inch round bbl. (Trapper), 19-inch round bbl. (SRC), 20-inch octagonal bbl. (short rifle), 24.25-inch octagonal bbl. (sporting rifle) and 30-inch octagonal bbl. (express rifle). 43 inches overall (sporting rifle). Weight: 8 lbs. Fixed blade front sight, adj. semi-buckhorn rear or tang peep sight. Walnut stock and forend. Color case-hardened receiver. Imported from 1989 to date.

Express Rifle	NiB $1175	Ex $905	Gd $604
Short Rifle (disc.)	NiB $1175	Ex $953	Gd $663
Sporting Rifle	NiB $1175	Ex $921	Gd $636
SRC Carbine	NiB $1175	Ex $921	Gd $641
Trapper (disc.)	NiB $1195	Ex $844	Gd $554
One of 1000 engraved model	NiB $2327	Ex $1945	Gd $1246

1874 FALLING BLOCK SPORTING RIFLE
Replica of 1874 Sharps Sporting Rifle. Calibers: .45-65, .45-70, .45-90 or .45-120. 32- or 34-inch round or octagonal bbl. Weight: 9.5 to 10 lbs. Blade or globe front sight w/adj. open rear or sporting tang peep sight. Single or double set triggers. Checkered walnut stock and forend w/nose cap. Color case-hardened receiver. Imported from 1997 to date.

1874 Sporting Rifle - Billy Dixon Model	NiB $1653	Ex $1250	Gd $1014
1874 Sporting Rifle - Quigley Model	NiB $1265	Ex $1085	Gd $844
Sharps Sporting No. 1 Rifle	NiB $1497	Ex $1070	Gd $813

CLERKE RECREATION PRODUCTS — Santa Monica, California

DELUXE HI-WALL	NiB $300	Ex $273	Gd $196

Same as standard model, except w/adj. trigger, half-octagon bbl., select wood, stock w/cheekpiece and recoil pad. Made 1972 to 1974.

HI-WALL

SINGLE-SHOT RIFLE	NiB $250	Ex $174	Gd $121

Falling-block lever-action similar to Winchester 1885 High Wall S.S. Color casehardened investment-cast receiver. Calibers: .222 Rem., .22-250, .243 Rem., 6mm Rem., .25-06, .270 Win., 7mm Rem. Mag., .30-06, .45-70 Govt. 26-inch medium-weight bbl. Weight: 8 lbs. Furnished w/o sights. Checkered walnut pistol-grip stock and Schnabel forearm. Made from 1972 to 1974.

CLIFTON ARMS — Medina, Texas

SCOUT BOLT-ACTION RIFLE
Custom rifle built on the Dakota .76, Ruger .77 or Winchester .70 action. Shilen match-grade barrel cut and chambered to customer's specification. Clifton composite stock fitted and finished to customer's preference. Made from 1992 to 1997.

African Scout	NiB $3065	Ex $2595	Gd $1721
Pseudo Scout	NiB $3036	Ex $2215	Gd $1422
Standard Scout	NiB $3010	Ex $2438	Gd $1396
Super Scout	NiB $3039	Ex $2018	Gd $1473

COLT'S MFG. CO., INC. — West Hartford, Connecticut

NOTE: *Add $200 to pre-ban models made prior to 10/13/94.*

AR-15 A2 DELTA

MATCH H-BAR RIFLE	NiB $1723	Ex $1646	Gd $1414

Similar to AR-15A2 Government Model except w/standard stock and heavy refined bbl. Furnished w/3-9x rubber armored scope and removeable cheekpiece. Made from 1986 to 1991.

AR-15 A2 GOVERNMENT

MODEL CARBINE	NiB $1884	Ex $949	Gd $720

Caliber: .223 Rem., Five-round magazine. 16-inch bbl. w/flash suppressor. 35 inches overall. Weight: 5.8 lbs. Telescoping aluminum buttstock; sling swivels. Made from 1985 to 1991.

Colt AR-15 A2

Colt AR-15 A2 Delta Match H-BAR

Colt AR-15 A2 Government Model

Colt AR-15 Sporter Competition H-BAR

AR-15 A2 SPORTER II . . . . NiB $1874 Ex $1289 Gd $1091
Same general specifications as standard AR-15 Sporter except heavier bbl., improved pistol-grip. Weight 7.5 lbs.; optional 3x or 4x scope. Made from 1985 to 1989.

AR-15 COMPACT 9MM CARBINE . . . . NiB $1972 Ex $1515 Gd $1103
Semiautomatic. Caliber: 9mm NATO. 20-round detachable magazine. Bbl.: 16-inch round. Weight: 6.3 lbs. Adj. rear and front sights. Adj. buttstock. Ribbed round handguard. Made from 1985 to 1986.

Colt Stagecoach

Colteer 1-.22

Colteer .22 Autoloader

Coltsman Deluxe

Coltsman 1957 Standard

AR-15 SEMIAUTOMATIC SPORTER

Commercial version of U.S. M16 rifle. Gas-operated. Takedown. Caliber: .223 Rem. (5.56mm). 20-round magazine w/spacer to reduce capacity to 5 rounds. 20-inch bbl. w/flash suppressor. Sights: Rear peep w/windage adjustment in carrying handle; front adj. for windage. 3x scope and mount optional. Black molded buttstock of high-impact synthetic material, rubber buttplate. Barrel surrounded by handguard of black fiberglass w/heat-reflecting inner shield. Swivels, black web sling strap. Weight: w/o accessories, 6.3 lbs. Made from 1964 to 1994.

Standard Sporter . . . . NiB $1870 Ex $1384 Gd $1056
**W/adj. stock, redesigned
forearm (disc. 1988), add** $200
W/3x scope and mount, add $100

AR-15 SPORTER
COMPETITION

H-BAR RIFLE . . . . NiB $1946 Ex $1084 Gd $703
Similar to AR-15 Sporter Target model except w/integral Weaver-type mounting system on a flat-top receiver. 20-inch bbl. w/counter-bored muzzle and 1:9 rifling twist. Made from 1991 to date.

AR-15 SPORTER

COMPETITION H-BAR (RS) . . . . NiB $1942 Ex $1097 Gd $887
Similar to AR-15 Sporter Competition H-BAR Model except "Range Selected" for accuracy w/3x9 rubber-clad scope w/mount. Carrying handle w/iron sights. Made from 1992 to 1994.

AR-15 SPORTER MATCH TARGET LIGHTWEIGHT

Calibers: .223 Rem., 7.62x39mm, 9mm. Five-round magazine. 16-inch bbl. (non-threaded after 1994). 34.5-35.5 inches overall. Weight: 7.1 lbs. Redesigned stock and shorter handguard. Made from 1991 to 2002.

Standard LW Sporter (except 9mm) . . . . . . NiB $930 Ex $724 Gd $577
Standard LW Sporter, 9mm . . . . NiB $1005 Ex $723 Gd $515
.22 LR conversion (disc. 1994), add $175

AR-15 SPORTER TARGET RIFLE

Caliber: .223 Rem. Five-round magazine. 20-inch bbl. w/flash suppressor (non-threaded after 1994). 39 inches overall. Weight: 7.5 lbs. Black composition stock, grip and handguard. Sights: post front; adj. aperture rear. Matte black finish. Made from 1993 to date.

Sporter Target Rifle . . . . NiB $1190 Ex $1010 Gd $675
.22 LR conversion (disc. 1994), add $200

LIGHTNING MAGAZINE RIFLE - LARGE FRAME

Similar to Medium Frame model except w/large frame to accommodate larger calibers: .38-56, .44-60, .45-60, .45-65, .45-85, or .50-95 Express. Standard 22-inch (carbine & baby carbine) or 28-inch round or octagonal bbl. (rifle). Note: Additional bbl. lengths optional. Weight: 8 to 10.5 lbs. Sights: Open rear; bead or blade front. Walnut stock and checkered forearm. Made 1887 to 1994. (6,496 produced)

Rifle . . . . NiB $11,000 Ex $7294 Gd $3393
Carbine . . . . NiB $10,392 Ex $7435 Gd $4375
Baby Carbine . . . . NiB $13,393 Ex $8334 Gd $5700
.50-95 Express, add 35%

Coltsman 1961 Custom

Coltsman 1961 Standard

Colt-Sauer Grand African

LIGHTNING MAGAZINE RIFLE - MEDIUM FRAME
Slide-action w/12-round tubular magazine Carbine & Baby Carbine) or 15-round tubular magazine (rifle). Calibers: .32-20, .38-40, .44-40. Standard 20-inch (Carbine & Baby Carbine) or 26-inch round or octagonal bbl.(rifle). Note: Additional bbl. lengths optional. Weight: 5.5 lbs. (Baby Carbine), 6.25 lbs. (carbine) or 7 to 9 lbs. (rifle). Sights: Open rear; bead or blade front. Walnut stock and checkered forearm. Blue finish w/color casehardened hammer. Made from 1884 to 1902. (89,777 produced)

Rifle	NiB $6061	Ex $3794	Gd $2228
Carbine	NiB $7725	Ex $4885	Gd $2900
Baby Carbine	NiB $9310	Ex $5187	Gd $3951

Military model
w/bayonet
lug & sling swivels . . . . NiB $5152 Ex $3748 Gd $2611

LIGHTNING MAGAZINE RIFLE - SMALL FRAME
Similar to Medium Frame model except w/smaller frame and chambered for .22 caliber only. Standard 24-inch round or octagonal bbl. w/half magazine. Note: Additional bbl. lengths optional. Weight: 6 lbs. Sights: Open rear; bead or blade front. Walnut stock and checkered forearm. Made from 1884 to 1902. (89,912 produced)

Standard Rifle model. . . . . NiB $5515 Ex $4086 Gd $2756
W/Deluxe or optional features, add 20%

STAGECOACH .22 AUTOLOADER . . . . NiB $325 Ex $318 Gd $189
Same as Colteer .22 Autoloader except w/engraved receiver, saddle ring, 16.5-inch bbl. Weight: 4 lbs., 10 oz. Made from 1965 to 1975.

COLTEER 1-.22 SINGLE-SHOT
BOLT-ACTION RIFLE. . . . . NiB $274 Ex $167 Gd $139
Caliber: .22 LR. Long, Short. 20- or 22-inch bbl. Sights: Open rear; ramp front. Pistol-grip stock w/Monte Carlo comb. Weight: 5 lbs. Made from 1957 to 1967.

.22 AUTOLOADER . . . . NiB $343 Ex $267 Gd $189
Caliber: .22 LR. 15-round tubular magazine. 19.38-inch bbl. Sights: Open rear; hooded ramp front. Straight-grip stock, Western carbine-style forearm w/bbl. band. Weight: 4.75 lbs. Made 1964 to 1975.

CUSTOM BOLT-ACTION
SPORTING RIFLE. . . . . NiB $556 Ex $448 Gd $298
FN Mauser action, side safety, engraved floorplate. Calibers: .30-06, .300 H&H Mag. Five round box magazine. 24-inch bbl., rampfront sight. Fancy walnut stock. Monte Carlo comb, cheekpiece, pistol-grip, checkered, QD swivels. Weight: 7.25 lbs. Made 1957 to 1961.

DELUXE RIFLE. . . . . NiB $926 Ex $720 Gd $514
FN Mauser action. Same as Custom model, except plain floorplate, plainer wood and checkering. Made from 1957-61. Value shown is for rifle as furnished by manufacturer w/o rear sight.

MODELS OF 1957 RIFLES
Sako medium action. Calibers: .243, .308. Weight: 6.75 lbs. Other specifications similar to those of models w/FN actions. Made from 1957 to 1961.

Custom	NiB $875	Ex $669	Gd $463
Deluxe	NiB $875	Ex $695	Gd $463
Standard	NiB $719	Ex $462	Gd $385

MODEL OF 1961,
CUSTOM RIFLE. NiB $682 Ex $537 Gd $357
Sako action. Calibers: .222, .222 Mag., .223, .243, .264, .270, .308, .30-06, .300 H&H. 23-, 24-inch bbl. Sights: Folding leaf rear; hooded ramp front. Fancy French walnut stock w/Monte Carlo comb, rosewood forend tip and grip cap skip checkering, recoil pad, sling swivels. Weight: 6.5 - 7.5 lbs. Made from 1963 to 1965.

MODEL OF 1961,
STANDARD RIFLE . . . . NiB $692 Ex $563 Gd $382
Same as Custom model except plainer, American walnut stock. Made from 1963 to 1965.

STANDARD RIFLE . . . . NiB $666 Ex $511 Gd $357
FN Mauser action. Same as Deluxe model except in .243, .30-06, .308, .300 Mag. and stock w/o cheekpiece, bbl. length 22 inches. Made from 1957 to 1961. Value shown is for rifle as furnished by manufacturer w/o rear sight.

COLT-SAUER DRILLINGS See Colt shotgun listings.

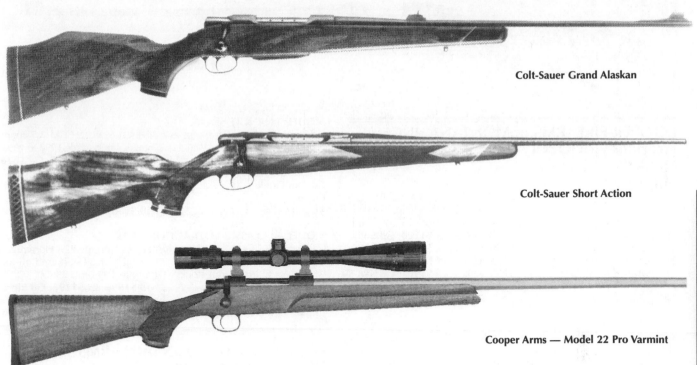

Colt-Sauer Grand Alaskan

Colt-Sauer Short Action

Cooper Arms — Model 22 Pro Varmint

RIFLES

GRAND AFRICAN . . . . **NiB $1930 Ex $1518 Gd $1029**
Same specifications as standard model except .458 Win. Mag., weight: 9.5 lbs. Sights: Adj. leaf rear; hooded ramp front. Magnum-style stock of Bubinga. Made from 1973 to 1985.

GRAND ALASKAN . . . . **NiB $1930 Ex $1338 Gd $900**
Same specifications as standard model except .375 H&H, weight: 8.5 lbs. Sights: Adj. leaf rear; hooded ramp front. Magnum-style stock of walnut.

MAGNUM . . . . **NiB $1461 Ex $1051 Gd $743**
Same specifications as standard model except calibers 7mm Rem. Mag., .300 Win. Mag., .300 Weatherby. Weight: 8.5 lbs. Made from 1973 to 1985.

SHORT ACTION . . . . **NiB $1303 Ex $1020 Gd $711**
Same specifications as standard model except shorter action chambered for the following calibers: .22-250, .243 Win., .308 Win. and similar length cartridges. Weight: 7.5 1bs.; 8.25 lbs. (.22-250). Drilled and tapped for scope mount. No front or rear open sights. Made from 1973 to 1988.

SPORTING RIFLE,
STANDARD MODEL . . . . **NiB $1331 Ex $1047 Gd $738**
Sauer 80 non-rotating bolt action. Calibers: .25-06, .270 Win., .30-06. Three-round detachable box magazine. 24-inch bbl. Weight: 7.75 lbs., 8.5 lbs. (.25-06). Furnished w/o sights. American walnut stock w/Monte Carlo cheekpiece, checkered pistol grip and forearm, rosewood forend tip and pistol-grip cap, recoil pad. Made from 1973 to 1988.

COMMANDO CARBINES — Knoxville, Tennessee, (Formerly Volunteer Enterprises, Inc.)

MARK III
SEMIAUTOMATIC CARBINE
Blow-back action, fires from closed bolt. Caliber: .45 ACP. 15- or 30-round magazine. 16.5-inch bbl. w/cooling sleeve and muzzle brake. Weight: 8 lbs. Sights: peep rear; blade front. "Tommy Gun" style stock and forearm or grip. Made from l969 to 1976.
W/horizontal forearm . . . . **NiB $474 Ex $371 Gd $268**

MARK 9
Same specifications as Mark III and Mark 45 except caliber 9mm Luger. Made from 1976 to 1981.
W/horizontal forearm . . . . **NiB $499 Ex $407 Gd $288**
W/vertical foregrip . . . . **NiB $519 Ex $422 Gd $299**

MARK 45
Same specifications as Mark III. Has redesigned trigger housing and magazines. Made from 1976 to 1988.
W/horizontal forearm . . . . **NiB $499 Ex $438 Gd $293**
W/vertical foregrip . . . . **NiB $596 Ex $484 Gd $341**

CONTINENTAL RIFLES — Manufactured in Belgium for Continental Arms, Corp., New York, N.Y.

DOUBLE RIFLE
Calibers: .270, .303 Sav., .30-40, .348 Win., .30-06, .375 H&H, .400 Jeffrey, .465, .470, .475 No. 2, .500, .600. Side-by-side. Anson-Deeley reinforced boxlock action w/triple bolting lever work. Two triggers. Non-automatic safety. 24- or 26-inch bbls. Sights: Express rear; bead front. Checkered cheekpiece stock and forend. Weight: From 7 lbs., depending on caliber. Imported from 1956 to 1975.
Calibers: .270 to .348 Win. . . . . **NiB $4956 Ex $3832 Gd $3022**
Calibers: .375 H&H & larger . . . . **Add 50%**

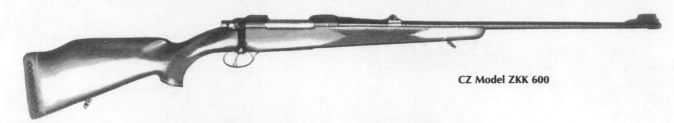

CZ Model ZKK 600

COOPER FIREARMS of MONTANA, INC. — (Previously COOPER ARMS), Stevensville, Montana

MODEL 21
Similar to Model 36C except in calibers .17 Rem., .17 Mach IV, .221 Fireball, .222, .223, 6x45, 6x47. 24-inch stainless or chrome-moly bbl. 43.5 inches overall. Weight: 8.75 lbs. Made from 1994 to date.
21 Benchrest . . . . NiB $1477 Ex $1168 Gd $897
21 Classic . . . . NiB $2150 Ex $1690 Gd $935
21 Custom Classic . . . . NiB $2123 Ex $1805 Gd $987
21 Western Classic . . . . NiB $2923 Ex $1905 Gd $987
21 Varminter . . . . NiB $1357 Ex $911 Gd $727
21 Varmint Extreme . . . . NiB $1873 Ex $1187 Gd $919

MODEL 22
Bolt-action, single-shot. Calibers: .22 BR. .22-250 Rem., 220 Swift, .243 Win., 6mm PPC, 6.5x55mm, 25-06 Rem., 7.62x39mm 26-inch bbl, 45.63 inches overall. Weight: 8 lbs., 12 oz. Single-stage trigger. AAA Claro walnut stock. Made from 1999 to date.
22 Benchrest . . . . NiB $1474 Ex $1540 Gd $1046
22 Classic . . . . NiB $2123 Ex $1267 Gd $689
22 Custom Classic . . . . NiB $1306 Ex $1203 Gd $842
22 Western Classic . . . . NiB $2175 Ex $1306 Gd $900
22 Varminter . . . . NiB $1400 Ex $889 Gd $585
22 Pro-Varmint Extreme . . . . NiB $1953 Ex $1097 Gd $793
22 Black Jack . . . . NiB $1813 Ex $1097 Gd $793

MODEL 36 RF/BR 50 . . . . NiB $1549 Ex $1205 Gd $820
Caliber: .22 LR. Bolt-action. Single-shot. 22-inch bbl. 40.5 inches overall. Weight: 6.8 lbs. No sights. Fully-adj. match-grade trigger. Stainless barrel. McMillan benchrest stock. Three mid-bolt locking lugs. Made from 1993 to 1999.

MODEL 36 CF BOLT-ACTION RIFLE
Calibers: .17 CCM, .22 CCM, .22 Hornet. Four-round mag. 23.75 inch bbl. 42.5 inch overall. Weight: 7 lbs. Walnut or synthetic stock. Made from 1992 to 1994.
Marksman . . . . NiB $1518 Ex $786 Gd $575
Sportsman . . . . NiB $675 Ex $509 Gd $303
Classic Grade . . . . NiB $1818 Ex $1102 Gd $824
Custom Grade . . . . NiB $1698 Ex $892 Gd $634
Custom Classic Grade . . . . NiB $1628 Ex $1210 Gd $849

MODEL 36 RF BOLT-ACTION RIFLE
Similar to Model 36CF except in caliber .22 LR. Five round magazine. Weight: 6.5-7 lbs. Made from 1992 to 1994.
BR-50 (22-inch stainless bbl.) . . . NiB $1708 Ex $1097 Gd $738
Custom Grade . . . . NiB $1697 Ex $871 Gd $608
Custom Classic Grade . . . . NiB $1600 Ex $891 Gd $633
Featherweight . . . . NiB $1562 Ex $943 Gd $662

MODEL 36 TRP-1 SERIES
Similar to Model 36RF except in target configuration w/ ISU or silhouette-style stock. Made from 1992 to 1993.
TRP-1 (ISU single-shot) . . . . NiB $895 Ex $755 Gd $493
TRP-1S (Silhouette) . . . . NiB $895 Ex $755 Gd $493

MODEL 38 SINGLE SHOT
Similar to Model 36CF except in calibers .17 or .22 CCM w/3-round magazine. Weight: 8 lbs. Walnut or synthetic stock. Made 1992 to 1993.
Sporter Standard . . . . NiB $1489 Ex $983 Gd $628
Classic Grade. . . . . NiB $2187 Ex $1781 Gd $928
Custom Grade . . . . NiB $2927 Ex $1946 Gd $934
Custom
Classic Grade . . . . NiB $1507 Ex $1208 Gd $822

MODEL 40 CLASSIC BOLT-ACTION RIFLE
Calibers: .17 CCM, .17 Ackley Hornet, .22 Hornet, .22K Hornet, .22 CCM, 4- or 5-round magazine. 23.75-inch bbl. Checkered oil-finished AAA Claro walnut stock. Made from 1995 to 1996.
Classic. NiB $1596 Ex $1197 Gd $811
Custom Classic . . . . NiB $1799 Ex $1395 Gd $1100
Classic Varminter . . . . NiB $1799 Ex $1395 Gd $1100

CUMBERLAND MOUNTAIN ARMS — Winchester, Tennessee

PLATEAU RIFLE
Falling block action w/underlever. Calibers: .40-65, and .45-70. 32-inch round bbl. 48 inches overall. Weight: 10.5 lbs. American walnut stock. Bead front sight, adj. buckhorn rear. Blued finish. Lacquer finish walnut stock w/crescent buttplate. Made from 1993 to 1999.
Standard model . . . . NiB $1077 Ex $797 Gd $565
Deluxe model . . . . Add $350

CZ RIFLES — Strankonice, Czechoslovakia (Currently Czechpoint, Inc.

See also listings under Brno Sporting Rifles and Springfield, Inc.

ZKK 600 BOLT-ACTION RIFLE
Calibers: .270 Win., 7x57, 7x64, .30-06. Five round magazine. 23.5- inch bbl. Weight: 7.5 lbs. Adj. folding-leaf rear sight, hooded ramp front. Pistol-grip walnut stock. Imported from 1990 to 1995.
Standard model . . . . NiB $574 Ex $466 Gd $327
Deluxe model . . . . NiB $663 Ex $539 Gd $376

ZKK 601 BOLT-ACTION RIFLE
Similar to Model ZKK 600 except w/short action in calibers .223 Rem., .243 Win., .308 Win. 43 inches overall. Weight: 6 lbs., 13 oz. Checkered walnut pistol-grip stock w/Monte Carlo cheekpiece. Imported from 1990 to 1995.
Standard model . . . . NiB $542 Ex $465 Gd $389
Deluxe model . . . . NiB $593 Ex $532 Gd $389

ZKK 602 BOLT-ACTION RIFLE
Similar to Model ZKK 600 except w/Magnum action in calibers .300 Win. Mag., 8x68S, .375 H&H, .458 Win. Mag. 25-inch bbl. 45.5 inches overall. Weight: 9.25 lbs. Imported from 1990 to 1997.
Standard model . . . . NiB $677 Ex $595 Gd $437
Deluxe model . . . . NiB $855 Ex $702 Gd $471

CA Model ZKM 452 LUX Model

CZ 511

CZ Model ZKM 527

CZ 550 LUX Model

ZKM 452 BOLT-ACTION REPEATING RIFLE

Calibers: .22 LR. or .22 WMR. Five, 6- or 10-round magazine. 25-inch bbl. 43.5 inches overall. Weight: 6 lbs. Adj. rear sight, hooded bead front. Oil-finished beechwood or checkered walnut stock w/Schnabel forend. Imported 1995 and 2007.

Standard model (22 LR)	NiB $425	Ex $315	Gd $165
Deluxe model (22 LR)	NiB $427	Ex $284	Gd $197
Varmint model (22 LR)	NiB $430	Ex $354	Gd $207
.22 WMR, add			$35

ZKM 527 BOLT-ACTION RIFLE

Calibers: .22 Hornet, .222 Rem., .223 Rem., 7.62x39mm. Five round magazine. 23.5-inch bbl. 42.5 inches overall. Weight: 6.75 lbs. Adj. rear sight, hooded ramp front. Grooved receiver. Adj. double-set triggers. Oil-finished beechwood or checkered walnut stock . Imported 1995.

Standard model	NiB $598	Ex $431	Gd $315
Classic model	NiB $625	Ex $433	Gd $315
Carbine model (shorter configuration)	NiB $570	Ex $438	Gd $315
Deluxe model	NiB $627	Ex $535	Gd $341

ZKM 537 SPORTER BOLT-ACTION RIFLE

Calibers: .243 Win., .270 Win., 7x57mm, .308 Win., .30-06. Four or 5-round magazine. 19- or 23.5-inch bbl. 40.25 or 44.75 inches overall. Weight: 7 to 7.5 lbs. Adj. folding leaf rear sight, hooded ramp front. Shrouded bolt. Standard or Mannlicher-style checkered walnut stock. Imported 1995.

Standard model	NiB $500	Ex $434	Gd $315
Mannlicher model			Add $100
Mountain Carbine model	NiB $525	Ex $413	Gd $290

511 SEMI-AUTO RIFLE .... NiB $320 Ex $224 Gd $128

Caliber: .22 LR. 8-round magazine. 22- inch bbl., 38.6 inches overall. Weight: 5.39 lbs. Receiver top fitted for telescopic sight mounts. Walnut wood-lacquered checkering stock. Imported 1996, 1998 to 2001, 2005 to 2006.

550 BOLT-ACTION SERIES

Calibers: .243 Win., 6.5x55mm, .270 Win., 7mm Mag., 7x57, 7x64, .30-06, .300 Win Mag., .375 H&H, .416 Rem., .416 Rigby, .458 Win. Mag., 9.3x62. Four or 5-round detachable magazine. 20.5- or 23.6-inch bbl. Weight: 7.25 to 8 lbs. No sights or Express sights on magnum models. Receiver drilled and tapped for scope mount. Standard or Mannlicher-style checkered walnut stock w/buttpad. Imported 1995 to 2000.

Standard	NiB $475	Ex $399	Gd $292
Magnum	NiB $821	Ex $599	Gd $441
Lux	NiB $495	Ex $352	Gd $285
Mannlicher	NiB $775	Ex $568	Gd $341
Calibers .416 Rem., .416 Rigby, .458 Win. Mag., add			$70

CZECHOSLOVAKIAN MILITARY RIFLES — Brno, Czechoslovakia, Manufactured by Ceska Zbrojovka

MODEL 1924 (VZ24)

MAUSER MILITARY RIFLE .... NiB $279 Ex $218 Gd $151
Basically same as German Kar., 98k and F.N. (Belgian Model 1924.) Caliber: 7.9mm Mauser. Five round box magazine. 23.25-inch bbl. Weight: 8.5 lbs. Sights: Adj. rear; blade front w/guards. of Belgian-type military stock, full handguard. Made from 1924 thru WWII. Many of these rifles were made for export. As produced during the German occupation, this model was known as Gewehr 24t.

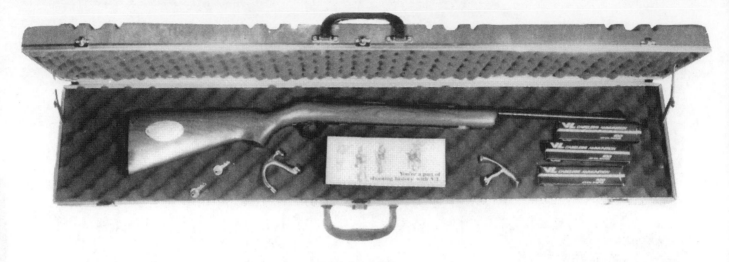

Daisy V/L Collector's Kit

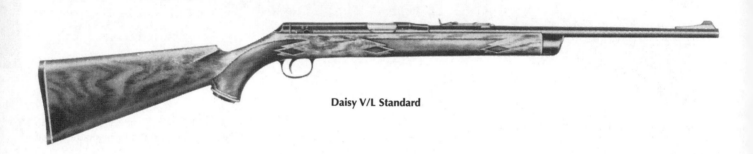

Daisy V/L Standard

MODEL 1933 (VZ33) MAUSER
MILITARY CARBINE . . . . **NiB $363 Ex $285 Gd $208**
Modification of German M/98 action w/smaller receiver ring. Caliber: 7.9mm Mauser. 19.25-inch bbl. Weight: 7.5 lbs. Sights: Adj. rear; blade front w/guards. Military-type full stock. Mfd. 1933 thru WWII. A similar model, produced during the German occupation, was designated Gew. 33/40.

DAEWOO PRECISION INDUSTRIES — Manufactured in Korea (Previously Imported by Kimber of America; Daewoo Precision Industries; Nationwide Sports and KBI, Inc.)

DR200 SA SEMIAUTOMATIC SPORTER
Caliber: .223 Rem. (5.56mm). Six or 10-round magazine. 18.4-inch bbl. 39.25 inches overall. Weight: 9 lbs. Protected post front sight, fully-adj. aperture rear. Forged aluminum receiver w/rotating locking bolt assembly. Synthetic sporterized thumbhole stock. Imported from 1994 to 1996.
Sporter model . . . . **NiB $660 Ex $529 Gd $429**
Varmint model . . . . **NiB $610 Ex $559 Gd $327**

DR300 SA SEMIAUTO-
MATIC SPORTER . . . . **NiB $636 Ex $549 Gd $379**
Similar to Model Daewoo DR200 except chambered for 7.62x39mm. Imported from 1994 to 1996.

DAISY RIFLES — Rogers, Arkansas

Daisy V/L rifles carry the first and only commercial caseless cartridge system. These rifles are expected to appreciate considerably in future years. The cartridge, no longer made, is also a collector's item. Production was discontinued following BATF ruling the V/L model to be a firearm.

COLLECTOR'S KIT. . . . . **NiB $558 Ex $375 Gd $268**
Presentation-grade rifle w/gold plate inscribed w/owner's name and gun serial number mounted on the stock. Also includes a special gun case, pair of brass gun cradles for wall-hanging, 300 rounds of 22 V/L ammunition and a certificate signed by Daisy president Cass S. Hough. Approx. 1,000 manufactured from 1968 to 1969.

PRESENTATION
GRADE . . . . **NiB $337 Ex $270 Gd $236**
Same specifications as standard model except w/walnut stock. Approx. 4,000 manufactured from 1968 to 1969.

STANDARD RIFLE . . . . **NiB $250 Ex $218 Gd $162**
Single-shot under-lever action. Caliber: .22 V/L (caseless cartridge, propellant ignited by jet of hot air). 18-inch bbl. Weight: 5 lbs. Sights: Adj. open rear, ramp w/blade front. Wood-grained Lustran stock (foam-filled). About 19,000 manufactured from 1968 to 1969.

Dakota Model 10 Single-Shot Rifle

Dakota Arms Model 76
African Grade

Dakota Arms Model 76
Classic Grade

Dakota Arms Model 97
Hunter

DAKOTA ARMS, INC. — Sturgis, South Dakota

MODEL 10 SINGLE-SHOT RIFLE
Chambered for most commercially-loaded calibers. 23-inch bbl. 39.5 inches overall. Weight: 5.5 lbs. Top tang safety. No sights. Checkered pistol-grip buttstock and semi-beavertail forearm, QD swivels, rubber recoil pad. Made from 1992 to date.
Standard calibers. . . . . **NiB $4200 Ex $2984 Gd $1903**
Deluxe model . . . . **Add $1,300**

MODEL 22 BOLT-ACTION
SPORTER RIFLE . . . . **NiB $2670 Ex $1152 Gd $783**
Calibers: .22 LR. .22 Hornet. Five round magazine. 22-inch bbl. Weight: 6.5 lbs. Adj. trigger. Checkered classic-style Claro or English walnut stock w/black recoil pad. Made from 2003 to 2004.

MODEL 76 AFRICAN
BOLT-ACTION RIFLE . . . . **NiB $7611 Ex $3968 Gd $2526**
Same general specifications as Model 76 Safari. Calibers: .404 Jeffery, .416 Rigby, .416 Dakota, .450 Dakota. 24-inch bbl. Weight: 8 lbs. Checkered select walnut stock w/two cross bolts. "R" prefix on ser. nos. Intro. 1989.

MODEL 76 ALPINE
BOLT-ACTION RIFLE . . . . **NiB $4753 Ex $2688 Gd $1958**
Same general specifications as Model 76 Classic except short action w/blind magazine. Calibers: .22-250, .243, 6mm Rem., .250-3000, 7mm-08, .308. 21-inch bbl. Weight: 7.5 lbs. Made from 1989 to 1992.

MODEL 76 CLASSIC
BOLT-ACTION RIFLE . . . . **NiB $4622 Ex $3363 Gd $2147**
Calibers: .257 Roberts, .270 Win., .280 Rem., .30-06, 7mm Rem. Mag., .300 Win. Mag., .338 Win. Mag., .375 H&H Mag., .458 Win.

Mag. 21- or 23-inch bbl. Weight: 7.5 lbs. Receiver drilled and tapped for sights. Adj. trigger. Classic-style checkered walnut stock w/steel grip cap and solid recoil pad. Right- and left-hand models. Made from 1987 to date.

MODEL 76 LONGBOW TACTICAL
BOLT-ACTION RIFLE . . . . **NiB $4347 Ex $3364 Gd $2334**
Calibers: .300 Dakota Mag., .330 Dakota Mag., .338 Lapua Mag. Blind magazine. Ported 28-inch bbl. 50 to 51 inches overall. Weight: 13.7 lbs. Black or oliver green fiberglass stock w/adj. cheekpiece and buttplate. Receiver drilled and tapped w/one-piece rail mount and no sights. Made from 1997 to 2009.

MODEL 76 SAFARI
BOLT-ACTION RIFLE . . . . **NiB $6376 Ex $3346 Gd $2265**
Calibers: .300 Win. Mag., .338 Win. Mag., .375 H&H Mag. .458 Win. Mag. 23-inch bbl. w/bbl. band swivel. Weight: 8.5 lbs. Ramp front sight, standing leaf rear. Checkered fancy walnut stock w/ebony forend tip and solid recoil pad. Made from 1987 to date.

MODEL 76 TRAVELER SERIES RIFLES
Threadless take-down action w/interchangeable bbl. capability based on the Dakota 76 design. Calibers: .257 through .458 Win (Standard-Classic & Safari) and .416 Dakota, .404 Jeffery, .416 Rigby, .338 Lapua and .450 Dakota Mag. (E/F Family-African Grade). 23- to 24- inch bbl. Weight: 7.5 to 9.5 lbs. Right or left-hand action. X grade (Classic) or XXX grade (Safari or African) oil finish English Bastogne or Claro walnut stock. Made from 1999 to date.
Classic Grade. . . . . **NiB $5543 Ex $3388 Gd $2327**
Safari Grade . . . . **NiB $6418 Ex $3413 Gd $2785**
African Grade . . . . **NiB $7191 Ex $4450 Gd $3129**
Interchangeable bbl. assemblies
Classic Grade, add. **$1150**
Safari Grade, add. **$1450**
African Grade, add **$1595**

MODEL 76 VARMINT
BOLT-ACTION RIFLE......... NiB $2430 Ex $1915 Gd $1112
Similar to Model 76 Classic except single-shot action w/ heavy bbl. chambered for .17 Rem. to 6mm PPC. Weight: 13.7 lbs. Checkered walnut or synthetic stock. Receiver drilled and tapped for scope mounts and no sights. Made from 1994 to 1998.

MODEL 97 HUNTER BOLT-ACTION SERIES
Calibers: .22-250 Rem. to .330 Dakota Mag.(Lightweight), .25-06 to .375 Dakota Mag. (Long Range). 22-, 24- or 26-inch bbl. 43 to 46 inches overall. Weight: 6.16 lbs. to 7.7 lbs. Black composite fiberglass stock w/recoil pad. Fully adj. match trigger. Made from 1997 to 2004.
Lightweight .... NiB $2650 Ex $1571 Gd $892
Long Range .... NiB $2650 Ex $1571 Gd $892

MODEL 97 VARMINT HUNTER
BOLT-ACTION RIFLE......... NiB $3650 Ex $2494 Gd $1850
Similar to Model 97 Hunter except single-shot action w/ heavy bbl. chambered .22-250 Rem. to .308 Win. Checkered walnut stock. Receiver drilled and tapped for scope mounts and no sights. Made from 1998 to 2004.

CHARLES DALY RIFLE — Harrisburg, Pennsylvania, *Imported by K.B.I., Inc., Harrisburg, PA, (Previously by Outdoor Sports Headquarters, Inc.)*

EMPIRE GRADE BOLT-ACTION RIFLE (RF)
Similar to Superior Grade except w/checkered California walnut stock w/rosewood grip cap and forearm cap. High polished blued finish and damascened bolt. Made from 1998. Disc.
Empire Grade (.22 LR)........... NiB $342 Ex $280 Gd $200
Empire Grade (.22WMR)......... NiB $368 Ex $300 Gd $214
Empire Grade (.22 Hornet) .... NiB $508 Ex $412 Gd $290

FIELD GRADE BOLT-ACTION RIFLE (RF)
Caliber: .22 LR. 16.25-, 17.5- or 22.63-inch bbl. 32 to 41 inches overall. Single-shot (True Youth) and 6- or 10-round magazine. Plain walnut-finished hardwood or checkered polymer stock. Blue or stainless finish. Imported from 1998. Disc.
Field Grade (Standard w/22.63-inch bbl.)... NiB $134 Ex $113 Gd $85
Field Grade (Youth w/17.5-inch bbl.) ...... NiB $141 Ex $118 Gd $88
**Field Grade (True Youth
w/16.25-inch bbl.) ....** NiB $178 Ex $147 Gd $109
Field Grade (Polymer w/stainless action) ... NiB $147 Ex $123 Gd $92

FIELD GRADE HUNTER BOLT-ACTION RIFLE
Calibers: .22 Hornet, .223 Rem., .243 Win., .270 Win., 7mm Rem. Mag. .308 Win., .30-06, .300 Win. Mag., .300 Rem. Ultra Mag., .338 Win. Mag. Three, 4-, or 5-round magazine. 22- or 24-inch bbl. w/o sights. Weight: 7.2 to 7.4 lbs. Checkered walnut or black polymer stock. Receiver drilled and tapped. Blue or stainless finish. Imported from 1998. Disc.
Field Grade Hunter (walnut stock) .... NiB $529 Ex $432 Gd $308
Field Grade Hunter (polymer stock) ...... NiB $549 Ex $448 Gd $319
w/Left-hand model, add $35

HAMMERLESS DRILLING
See listing under Charles Daly shotguns.

HORNET RIFLE ....** NiB $1278 Ex $1025 Gd $725
Same as Herold Rifle. See listing of that rifle for specifications. imported during the 1930s. Disc.

MAUSER 98
Calibers: .243 Win., .270 Win., 7mm Rem. Mag. .308 Win., .30-06, .300 Win. Mag., .375 H&H, or .458 Win. Mag. Three, 4-, or 5-round magazine. 23-inch bbl. 44.5 inches overall. Weight: 7.5 lbs. Checkered European walnut (Superior) or fiberglass/graphic (Field) stock w/recoil pad. Ramped front sight, adj. rear. Receiver drilled and tapped w/side saftey. Imported from 1998. Disc.
Field Grade (standard calibers) Disc...... NiB $432 Ex $382 Gd $132
**Field Grade (375 H&H
and 458 Win. Mag.) ....** NiB $637 Ex $535 Gd $331
Superior Grade (standard calibers) Disc. ... NiB $637 Ex $489 Gd $331
Superior Grade (magnum calibers) Disc. ... NiB $865 Ex $739 Gd $578

MINI-MAUSER 98
Similar to Mauser 98 except w/19.25-inch bbl. chambered for .22 Hornet, .22-250 Rem., .223 Rem., or 7.62x39mm. Five round magazine. Imported from 1998. Disc.
Field Grade .... NiB $387 Ex $336 Gd $219
Superior Grade .... NiB $499 Ex $412 Gd $234

SUPERIOR GRADE BOLT-ACTION RIFLE
Calibers: .22 LR. .22 WMR, .22 Hornet. 20.25- to 22.63-inch bbl. 40.5 to 41.25 inches overall. Five, 6-, or 10-round magazine. Ramped front sight, adj. rear w/grooved receiver. Checkered walnut stock. Made from 1998. Disc.
Superior Grade (.22 LR) .... NiB $166 Ex $146 Gd $95
Superior Grade (.22WMR) .... NiB $202 Ex $162 Gd $116
Superior Grade (.22 Hornet) ...... NiB $369 Ex $317 Gd $204

SEMIAUTOMATIC RIFLE
Caliber: .22 LR. 20.75-inch bbl. 40.5 inches overall. 10-round magazine. Ramped front sight, adj. rear w/grooved receiver. Plain walnut-finished hardwood stock (Field), checkered walnut (Superior), checkered polymer stock or checkered California walnut stock w/rosewood grip cap and forearm cap (Empire). Blue or stainless finish. Imported from 1998. Disc.
Field Grade .... NiB $136 Ex $116 Gd $80
**Field Grade (Polymer
w/stainless action)...............** NiB $148 Ex $126 Gd $85
Superior Grade .... NiB $203 Ex $177 Gd $116
Empire Grade .... NiB $320 Ex $253 Gd $177

BOLT ACTION RIFLE.............** NiB $883 Ex $633 Gd $523
Calibers: .22 Hornet. Bbl.: 24 inches. Five round box magazine, hinged floorplate. Sights: Ramp front, leaf rear. Walnut stock, checkered grip and forearm. Early version rifle, introduced 1931 by Franz Jaeger Co. Discontinued 1939. Imported by Charles Daly but same model was imported by A. F. Stoeger as Herold Rifle.

SUPERIOR
COMBINATION GUN......... NiB $1312 Ex $1107 Gd $962
Calibers: 12-guage shotgun over .22 Hornet, .223 Remington, .22-250, .243 Win., .270 Win., or .30-06. Barrels: 23 1/2 inches. Shotgun choked Imp. Cyl. Weight: About 7.5 pounds. Checkered walnut, pistol grip, semi-beavertail forend. Silvered, engraved receiver. Chrome-moly steel barrels, double triggers, extractors. Gold bead front sight. Introduced 1997, imported by K.B.I.

EMPIRE COMBINATION GUN . NiB $1712 Ex $1502 Gd $1162
Similar to Superior Combination Gun but with fancy grade wood, European style comb and cheekpiece, slimmer forend. Introduced 1997, imported by K.B.I.

FIELD GRADE AUTO RIFLE........** NiB $140 Ex $100 Gd $85
Calibers: .22 LR. Semiautomatic, 10-round magazine, shell deflector. Bbl.: 20 3/4 inches. Weight: 6.5 pounds. Overall length: 40.5

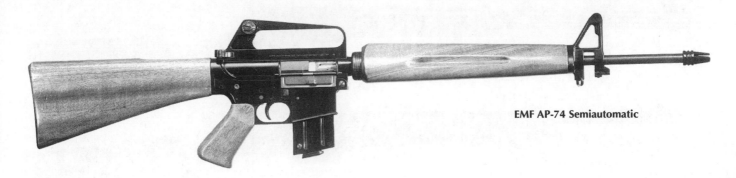

EMF AP-74 Semiautomatic

inches. Stock: Hardwood, walnut-finished, Monte Carlo style. Sights: Hooded front, adjustable open rear. Grooved for scope mounting. Blued finish. Introduced 1998. Imported by K. B. I.

EMPIRE GRADE AUTO RIFLE..... NiB $180 Ex $145 Gd $115
Similar to Field Grade Auto Rifle but with select California walnut stock, hand checkering. Contrasting forend and grip caps. Damascened bolt, high-polish blued finish. Introduced 1998; discontinued.

TRUE YOUTH
BOLT-ACTION RIFLE .... NiB $125 Ex $95 Gd $65
Caliber: .22 LR. Single-shot., bolt-action. Bbl.: 16.25 inches. Weight: 3 pounds. Overall length: 32 inches. Walnut-finished hardwood stock. Sights: Blade front, adjustable rear. Blued finish. Introduced 1998. Imported by K. B. I.

EAGLE ARMS INC. — Geneseo, Illinois (Previously Coal Valley, Illinois)

In 1995, Eagle Arms Inc., became a division of ArmaLite and reintroduced that logo. For current ArmaLite production see models under that listing.

MODEL EA-15 CARBINE
Caliber: .223 Rem. (5.56mm). 30-round magazine. 16-inch bbl. and collapsible buttstock. Weight: 5.75 lbs. (E1); 6.25 lbs. (E2 w/heavy bbl. & National Match sights). Made 1990 to 1995; reintro. 2002 to 2005.
E1 Carbine .... NiB $925 Ex $694 Gd $488
E2 Carbine .... NiB $925 Ex $645 Gd $523

MODEL EA-15 GOLDEN
EAGLE MATCH RIFLE......... NiB $1194 Ex $941 Gd $632
Same general specifications as EA-15 Standard, except w/E2-style National Match sights. 20-inch Douglas Heavy Match bbl. NM trigger and bolt-carrier group. Weight: 12.75 lbs. Made 1991 to 1995, reintro. 2002.
MODEL EA-15 SEMIAUTOMATIC RIFLE . NiB $1172 Ex $697 Gd $470
Same as EA-15 Carbine except 20-inch bbl., 39 inches overall and weighs 7 lbs. Made from 1990 to 1993; reintro. 2002 to 2005.

EMF COMPANY, INC. — Santa Ana, California

MODEL AP-74
SEMI-AUTOMATIC CARBINE..... NiB $353 Ex $286 Gd $189
Calibers: .22 LR or .32 ACP, 15-round magazine. 20-inch bbl. w/flash reducer. 38 inches overall. Weight: 6.75 lbs. Protected pin

front sight; protected rear peep sight. Lightweight plastic buttstock; ventilated snap-out forend. Importation disc. 1989.

MODEL AP74-W
SPORTER CARBINE .... NiB $375 Ex $297 Gd $183
Sporterized version of AP-74 w/wood buttstock and forend. Importation disc. 1989.

MODEL AP74 PARATROOPER ... NiB $395 Ex $230 Gd $209
Same general specifications as Model AP74-W except w/folding tubular buttstock. Made in .22 LR. only. Importation disc. 1987.

MODEL 1860 HENRY RIFLE
Calibers: .44-40 and .45 LC. 24.25-inch bbl.; upper-half octagonal w/magazine tube in one-piece steel. 43.75-inches overall. Weight: 9.25 lbs. Varnished American walnut wood stock. Polished brass frame and brass buttplate. Original rifle was patented by B. Tyler Henry and produced by the New Haven Arms Company, when Oliver Winchester was president. Imported 1987 to 2008.
Deluxe model.................. NiB $925 Ex $660 Gd $320
Engraved model .... NiB $1067 Ex $789 Gd $531

MODEL 1866
YELLOW BOY RIFLE .... NiB $725 Ex $543 Gd $332
Calibers: .44-40, .45 LC and .38 Special. Lever-action. Bbl: 24 inches, 43 inches overall. Bead front sight. Offered w/blued finish, walnut stock and brass frame 2005 to 2008.

MODEL 1866 YELLOW BOY CARBINE
Same features as 1866 Yellow Boy Rifle except carbine.
Standard carbine .... NiB $875 Ex $435 Gd $290
Engraved carbine .... NiB $875 Ex $522 Gd $316

MODEL 1873 SPORTING RIFLE
Calibers: .22 LR. .22 WMR, .357 Mag., .44-40 and .45 LC. 24.25-inch octagonal bbl. 43.25 inches overall. Weight: 8.16 lbs. Color casehardened frame w/blued steel magazine tube. Walnut stock and forend.
Standard Rifle .... NiB $875 Ex $658 Gd $426
Engraved Rifle .... NiB $943 Ex $634 Gd $444
Boy's Rifle
(Youth Model, .22 LR)............... NiB $644 Ex $525 Gd $345

MODEL 1873
SPORTING RIFLE CARBINE
Same features as 1873 sporting rifle except w/19-inch bbl. Overall length: 38.25 inches. Weight: 7.38 lbs. Color casehardened or blued frame. Made 1988 to 1989.
Standard carbine .... NiB $860 Ex $658 Gd $426

Erma — EG712

Erma — EGM1

Erma — EM1 22

ERMA-WERKE — Dachau, Germany
(Previously imported by Precision Sales International; Nygord Precision Products; Mandall's Shooting Supplies)

MODEL EG72
PUMP-ACTION REPEATER . . . . **NiB $131 Ex $101 Gd $95**
Visible hammer. Caliber: .22 LR. 15-round magazine. 18.5-inch bbl. Weight: 5.25 lbs. Sights: open rear; hooded ramp front. Receiver grooved for scope mounting. Straight-grip stock, grooved slide handle. Imported from 1970 to 1976.

MODEL EG73 . . . . **NiB $264 Ex $209 Gd $151**
Same as Model EG712 except chambered for .22 WMR w/12-round tubular magazine, 19.3-inch bbl. Imported from 1973 to 1997.

MODEL EG712 LEVER-ACTION
REPEATING CARBINE . . . . **NiB $260 Ex $209 Gd $145**
Styled after Winchester Model 94. Caliber: .22 LR. Long, Short. Tubul33 magazine holds 15 LR, 17 Long, 21 Short. 18.5-inch bbl. Weight: 5.5 lbs. Sights: Open rear; hooded ramp front. Receiver grooved for scope mounting. Western carbine-style stock and forearm w/bbl. band. Imported 1976 to 1997. Note: A similar carbine of Erma manufacture is marketed in U.S. as Ithaca Model 72 Saddle Gun.

MODEL EGM1 . . . . **NiB $264 Ex $223 Gd $151**
Same as Model EM1 except w/unslotted buttstock, ramp front sight, 5-round magazine standard. Imported from 1970 to 1995.

MODEL EM1 .22
SEMIAUTOMATIC CARBINE . . . . . . **NiB $363 Ex $306 Gd $204**
Styled after U.S. Carbine cal. 30 M1. Caliber: .22 LR. 10- or 15-round magazine. 18-inch bbl. Weight: 5.5 lbs. Carbine-type sights. Receiver grooved for scope mounting. Military stock/handguard. Imported 1966 to 1997.

EUROPEAN AMERICAN ARMORY — Sharpes, Florida

MODEL HW 660 BOLT-ACTION
SINGLE-SHOT RIFLE . . . . **NiB $865 Ex $715 Gd $458**
Caliber: .22 LR. 26.8-inch bbl., 45.7 inches overall. Weight: 10.8 lbs. Match-type aperture rear sight; Hooded ramp front. Stippled walnut stock. Imported from 1992 to 1996.

MODEL HW BOLT-ACTION
SINGLE-SHOT TARGET RIFLE . . . . . **NiB $860 Ex $705 Gd $509**
Same general specification as Model HW 660 except equipped w/ target stock. Imported from 1995 to 1996.

MODEL SABITTI SP1822
Caliber: .22 LR. 10-round detachable magazine. 18.5 inch bbl. 37.5 inches overall. Weight: 5.25 to 7.15 lbs. No sights. Hammer-forged heavy non-tapered bbl. Scope-mounted rail. Flush-mounted magazine release. Alloy receiver w/non-glare finish. Manual bolt lock. Wide claw extractor. Blowback action. Cross-trigger safety. Imported 1994 to 1996.
Traditional Sporter model . . . . **NiB $232 Ex $192 Gd $140**
Thumbhole Sporter
model (synthetic stock) . . . . **NiB $354 Ex $289 Gd $207**

FABRIQUE NATIONALE HERSTAL — Herstal & Liege, Belgium, (Formerly Fabrique Nationale d'Armes de Guerre)

MODELS 1924, 1934/30 AND
1930 MAUSER MILITARY RIFLES . . . . **NiB $413 Ex $311 Gd $209**
Similar to German Kar. 98k w/straight bolt handle. Calibers: 7mm, 7.65mm and 7.9mm Mauser. Five round box magazine. 23.5-inch bbl. Weight: 8.5 lbs. Sights: Adj. rear; blade front. Military stock of M/98 pattern w/slight modification. Model differences are minor. Also produced in a short carbine model w/17.25-inch bbl. Note: These rifles were manufactured under contract for Abyssinia, Argentina, Belgium, Bolivia, Brazil, Chile, China, Colombia, Ecuador, Iran, Luxembourg, Mexico, Peru, Turkey, Uruguay and Yugoslavia. Such arms usually bear the coat of arms of the country for which they were made together with the contractor's name and date of manufacture. Also sold commercially and exported to all parts of the world.

F.N. Model 1949

F.N. Model 1950 Mauser

F.N. Deluxe Mauser

F.N. Supreme Mauser

F.N. FAL Semiautomatic

MODEL 1949 SEMIAUTOMATIC
MILITARY RIFLE . . . . **NiB $752 Ex $624 Gd $293**
Gas-operated. Calibers: 7mm, 7.65mm, 7.92mm, .30-06. 10-round box magazine, clip fed or loaded singly. 23.2-inch bbl. Weight: 9.5 lbs. Sights: Tangent rear-shielded post front. Pistol-grip stock, handguard. Note: Adopted by Belgium in 1949; also by Belgian Congo, Brazil, Colombia, Luxembourg, Netherlands, East Indies, and Venezuela. Approx. 160,000 were made.

MODEL 1950 MAUSER
MILITARY RIFLE . . . . **NiB $489 Ex $336 Gd $259**
Same as previous F.N. models of Kar. 98k type except chambered for .30-06.

DELUXE MAUSER BOLT-ACTION
SPORTING RIFLE. . . . . **NiB $747 Ex $650 Gd $395**
American calibers: .220 Swift, .243 Win., .244 Rem., .250/3000, .257 Roberts, .270 Win., 7mm, .300 Sav., .308 Win. European calibers: 7x57, 8x57JS, 8x60S, 9.3x62, 9.5x57, 10.75x68mm. Five round box magazine. 24-inch bbl. Weight: 7.5-8.25 lbs. American model is standard w/hooded ramp front sight and Tri-Range rear; Continental model w/two-leaf rear. Checkered stock w/cheekpiece, pistol-grip, swivels. Made from 1947 to 1963.

DELUXE MAUSER —
PRESENTATION GRADE . . . . **NiB $1274 Ex $1007 Gd $713**
Same as regular model except w/select grade stock; engraving on receiver, trigger guard, floorplate and bbl. breech. Disc. 1963.

FAL/FNC/LAR SEMIAUTOMATIC
Same as standard FAL military rifle except w/o provision for automatic firing. Gas-operated. Calibers: 7.62mm NATO (.308 Win.) or 5.56mm (.223 Rem.). 10- or 20-round box magazine. 25.5-inch bbl. (including flash hider). Weight: 9 lbs. Sights: Post front; aperture rear. Fixed wood or folding buttstock, pistol-grip, forearm/handguard w/carrying handle and sling swivels. Disc. 1988.
F.N. FAL/LAR model (Light Automatic Rifle) . . . . **NiB $2508 Ex $2177 Gd $1361**
F.N. FAL/HB model (heavy bbl.) . . . . . . **NiB $2830 Ex $2281 Gd $1579**
F.N. FAL/PARA (Paratrooper) . . . . **NiB $3472 Ex $2809 Gd $1789**
F.N. FNC Carbine model (.223 cal.) . . . . **NiB $2648 Ex $1924 Gd $1261**
F.N. FNC Carbine model w/flash suppresser (.223 cal.) . . . . **NiB $2745 Ex $1980 Gd $1316**

SUPREME MAUSER BOLT-ACTION
SPORTING RIFLE. . . . . **NiB $770 Ex $923 Gd $413**
Calibers: .243, .270, 7mm, .308, .30-06. Four round magazine in .243 and .308; 5-round in other calibers. 22-inch bbl. in .308; 24-inch in other calibers. Sights: Hooded ramp front, Tri-Range peep rear. Checkered stock w/ Monte Carlo cheekpiece, pistol-grip, swivels. Weight: 7.75 lbs. Made from 1957 to 1975.

SUPREME MAGNUM MAUSER . . . . **NiB $821 Ex $668 Gd $438**
Calibers: .264 Mag., 7mm Mag., .300 Win. Mag. Specifications same as for standard caliber model except 3-round magazine capacity.

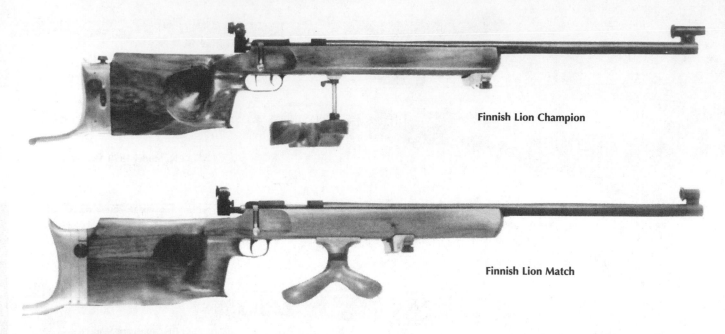

Finnish Lion Champion

Finnish Lion Match

FEATHER INDUSTRIES, INC. — Boulder, Colorado

See MITCHELL ARMS. For current production.

MODEL AT-9 SEMIAUTOMATIC RIFLE
Caliber: 9mm Parabellum. 10-, 25-, 32-, or 100-round magazine. 17-inch bbl. 35 inches overall (extended). Hooded post front sight, adj. aperture rear. Weight: 5 lbs. Telescoping wire stock w/composition pistol-grip and barrel-shroud handguard. Matte black finish. Made from 1988 to 1995.
Model AT-9 . . . . NiB $859 Ex $682 Gd $450
W/32-round magazine, add. $75
W/100-round drum magazine, add $250

MODEL AT-22 . . . . NiB $325 Ex $204 Gd $148
Caliber: .22 LR. 20-round magazine. 17-inch bbl. 35 inches overall (extended). Hooded post front sight; adj. aperture rear. Weight: 3.25 lbs. Telescoping wire stock w/composition pistol-grip and barrel shroud handguard. Matte black finish.

MODEL F2 SA CARBINE . . . . NiB $295 Ex $220 Gd $137
Similar to AT-22, except w/fixed Polymer stock and pistol-grip. Made from 1992 to 1995.

MODEL F9 SA CARBINE . . . . NiB $725 Ex $574 Gd $368
Similar to AT-9, except w/fixed Polymer stock and pistol-grip. Made from 1992 to 1995.

FINNISH LION RIFLES — Jyväkylylä, Finland
Manufactured by Valmet Oy, Tourula Works

CHAMPION FREE RIFLE . . . . NiB $645 Ex $522 Gd $366
Bolt-action single-shot target rifle. Double-set trigger. Caliber: .22 LR. 28.75-inch heavy bbl. Weight: 16 lbs. Sights: Extension rear peep; aperture front. Walnut free-rifle stock w/full pistol-grip, thumbhole, beavertail forend, hook buttplate, palm rest, hand stop, swivel. Made from 1965 to 1972.

STANDARD ISU
TARGET RIFLE . . . . NiB $388 Ex $311 Gd $182
Bolt-action, single-shot. Caliber: .22 LR. 27.5-inch bbl. Weight: 10.5 lbs. Sights: extension rear peep; aperture front. Walnut target stock w/full pistol-grip, checkered beavertail forearm, adj. buttplate, sling swivel. Made from 1966 to 1977.

MATCH RIFLE . . . . NiB $542 Ex $480 Gd $310
Bolt-action, single-shot. Caliber: .22 LR. 28.75-inch heavy bbl. Weight: 14.5 lbs. Sights: Extension rear peep; aperture front. Walnut free-rifle stock w/full pistol-grip, thumbhole, beavertail forearm, hook buttplate, palm rest, hand stop, swivel. Made from 1937 to 1972.

STANDARD
TARGET RIFLE
Bolt-action, single-shot. Caliber: .22 LR. 27.5-inch bbl. 44.5 inches overall. Weight: 10.5 lbs. No sights; micrometer rear and globe front International-style sights available. Select walnut stock in target configuration. Made 1966 to 1997..
Standard
model . . . . NiB $782 Ex $651 Gd $424
Thumbhole
stock model . . . . NiB $842 Ex $682 Gd $476
Standard
model . . . . NiB $391 Ex $288 Gd $185
Deluxe model . . . . NiB $414 Ex $337 Gd $234

LUIGI FRANCHI, S.P.A. — Brescia, Italy

CENTENNIAL AUTOMATIC RIFLE
Commemorates Franchi's 100th anniversary (1868-1968). Centennial seal engraved on receiver. Semiautomatic. Take-down. Caliber: .22 LR. 11-round magazine in buttstock. 21-inch bbl. Weight: 5.13 lbs. Sights: Open rear; gold bead front on ramp. Checkered walnut stock and forend. Deluxe model w/fully engraved receiver, premium grade wood. Made in 1968.
Standard model . . . . NiB $385 Ex $293 Gd $206
Engraved model . . . . NiB $451 Ex $359 Gd $251

Franchi Deluxe Centennial

Francotte Sidelock Double Rifle

Galil .223 AR Semiautomatic Rifle

Francotte Boxlock Mountain Rifle
w/claw mounts and scope

FRANCOTTE RIFLES — Leige, Belgium
Imported by Armes de Chasse, Hertford, NC (Previously by Abercrombie & Fitch)

BOLT-ACTION RIFLE

Custom rifle built on Mauser style bolt action. Available in three action lengths. Calibers: .17 Bee to .505 Gibbs. Barrel length: 21- to 24.5-inches. Weight: 8 to 12 lbs. Stock dimensions, wood type and style to customer's specifications. Engraving, appointments and finish to customer's preference. Note: Deduct 25% for models w/o engraving.

Short action. . . . . NiB $9570 Ex $7520 Gd $4660
Standard action . . . . NiB $7810 Ex $6185 Gd $3785
Magnum Francotte action . . . . . NiB $13,750 Ex $10,800 Gd $7000

BOXLOCK MOUNTAIN RIFLE

Custom single-shot rifle built on Anson & Deeley style boxlock or Holland & Holland style sidelock action. 23- to 26-inch barrels chambered to customer's specification. Stock dimensions, wood type and style to customer's specifications. Engraving, appointments and finish to customer's preference. Note: Deduct 30% for models w/o engraving.

Boxlock . . . . NiB $13,900 Ex $11,700 Gd $7500
Sidelock . . . . NiB $22,438 Ex $17,950 Gd $12,206

DOUBLE RIFLE

Custom side-by-side rifle. Built on Francotte system boxlock or back-action sidelock. 23.5- to 26-inch barrels chambered to customer's specification. Stock dimensions, wood type and style to customer's specifications. Engraving, appointments and finish to customer's preference. Note: Deduct 30% for models w/o engraving.

Boxlock . . . . NiB $25,500 Ex $15,500 Gd $9500
Sidelock . . . . NiB $29,430 Ex $25,000 Gd $15,700

FRENCH MILITARY RIFLE — Saint Etienne, France

MODEL 1936
MAS MILITARY RIFLE . . . . NiB $175 Ex $134 Gd $83

Bolt-action. Caliber: 7.5mm MAS. Five-round box magazine. 22.5-inch bbl. Weight: 8.25 lbs. Sights: Adj. rear; blade front. Two-piece military-type stock. Bayonet carried in forend tube. Made from 1936 to 1940 by Manufacture Francaise d'Armes et de Cycles de St. Etienne (MAS).

GALIL RIFLES — Manufactured by Israel Military Industries, Israel, *Imported by UZI America Inc., North Haven, CT (Previously by Action Arms, Springfield Armory and Magnum Research, Inc.)*

AR SEMIAUTOMATIC RIFLE

Calibers: .308 Win. (7.62 NATO), .223 Rem. (5.56mm). 25-round (.308) or 35-round (.223) magazine. 16-inch (.223) or 18.5-inch (.308) bbl. w/flash suppressor. Weight: 9.5 lbs. Folding aperture rear sight, post front. Folding metal stock w/carrying handle. Imported 1982 to 1994. Currently select fire models available to law enforcement only.

Model .223 AR . . . . NiB $3163 Ex $1909 Gd $1137
Model .308 AR . . . . NiB $3163 Ex $1909 Gd $1137
Model .223 ARM . . . . NiB $3111 Ex $2167 Gd $1565
Model 308 ARM . . . . NiB $3111 Ex $2167 Gd $1565

GRADING: **NiB** = New in Box   **Ex** = Excellent or NRA 95%   **Gd** = Good or NRA 68%

SPORTER SEMIAUTOMATIC RIFLE...... NiB $1652 Ex $981 Gd $646
Same general specifications as AR Model except w/hardwood thumbhole stock and 5-round magazine. Weight: 8.5 lbs. Imported 1991 to 1994.

GARCIA CORPORATION — Teaneck, New Jersey

BRONCO 22 SINGLE-SHOT RIFLE........ NiB $121 Ex $101 Gd $77
Swing-out action. Takedown. Caliber: .22 LR. Long, Short. 16.5-inch bbl. Weight: 3 lbs. Sights: Open rear-blade front. One-piece stock and receiver, crackle finish. Intro. 1967. Discontinued.

GERMAN MILITARY RIFLES — Mfd. by Ludwig Loewe & Co., Berlin, other contractors and by German arsenals and various plants under German government control

MODEL 24T (GEW. 24T) MAUSER RIFLE .... NiB $550 Ex $395 Gd $267
Same general specifications as Czech Model 24 (VZ24) Mauser Rifle w/minor modification and laminated wood stock. Weight: 9.25 lbs. Made in Czechoslovakia during German occupation; adopted 1940.

MODEL 29/40 (GEW. 29/40)
MAUSER RIFLE .... NiB $395 Ex $292 Gd $189
Same general specifications as Kar. 98K w/minor differences. Made in Poland during German occupation; adopted 1940.

MODEL 33/40 (GEW. 33/40)
MAUSER RIFLE .... NiB $1030 Ex $799 Gd $515
Same general specifications as Czech Model 33 (VZ33) Mauser Carbine w/minor modifications and laminated wood stock as found in war-time Model 98K carbines. Made in Czechoslovakia during German occupation; adopted 1940.

MODELS 41 AND 41-W (GEW. 41, GEW. 41-W)
SEMIAUTOMATIC MILITARY RIFLES
Gas-operated, muzzle cone system. Caliber: 7.9mm Mauser. Ten-round box magazine. 22.5-inch bbl. Weight: 10.25 lbs. Sights: Adj. leaf rear; blade front. Military-type stock w/semi-pistol grip, plastic handguard. Note: Model 41 lacks bolt release found on Model 41-W; otherwise, the models are the same. These early models were mfd. in Walther's Zella-Mehlis plant. Made c.1941 to 1943.
Model 41................. NiB $4317 Ex $3479 Gd $2408
Model 41-W .... NiB $3339 Ex $2696 Gd $1874

MODEL 43 (GEW. 43, KAR. 43)
SEMIAUTO MILITARY RIFLES........ NiB $1278 Ex $1032 Gd $719
Gas-operated, bbl. vented as in Russian Tokarev. Caliber: 7.9mm Mauser. 10-round detachable box magazine. 22- or 24-inch bbl. Weight: 9 lbs. Sights: Adj. rear; hooded front. Military-type stock w/semi-pistol-grip, wooden handguard. Note: These rifles are alike except for minor details, have characteristic late WWII mfg. short cuts: cast receiver and bolt cover, stamped steel parts, etc. Gew. 43 may have either 22- or 24-inch bbl. The former length was standardized in late 1944, when weapon designation was changed to "Kar. 43." Made from 1943 to 1945.

MODEL 1888 (GEW. 88) MAUSER-
MANNLICHER SERVICE RIFLE .... NiB $390 Ex $236 Gd $184
Bolt-action w/straight bolt handle. Caliber: 7.9mm Mauser (8x57mm). Five round Mannlicher box magazine. 29-inch bbl. w/jacket. Weight: 8.5 lbs. Fixed front sight, adj. rear. Military-type full stock. Mfd. by Ludwig Loewe & Co., Haenel, Schilling and other contractors.

MODEL 1888 (KAR. 88) MAUSER-
MANNLICHER CARBINE......... NiB $283 Ex $232 Gd $210
Same general specifications as Gew. 88 except w/18-inch bbl., w/o jacket, flat turned-down bolt handle, weight: 6.75 lbs. Mfd. by Ludwig Loewe & Co., Haenel, Schilling and other contractors.

MODEL 1898 (GEW. 98)
MAUSER MILITARY RIFLE........ NiB $526 Ex $397 Gd $243
Bolt action with straight bolt handle. Caliber: 7.9mm Mauser (8x57mm). Five round box magazine. 29-inch stepped bbl. Weight: 9 lbs. Sights: Blade front; adj. rear. Military-type full stock w/rounded bottom pistol grip. Adopted 1898.

MODEL 1898A (KAR. 98A)
MAUSER CARBINE .... NiB $444 Ex $397 Gd $191
Same general specifications as Model 1898 (Gew.98) Rifle except has turned-down bolt handle, smaller receiver ring, light 23.5-inch-straight taper bbl., front sight guards, sling is attached to left side of stock, weight: 8 lbs. Note: Some of these carbines are marked "Kar. 98;" the true Kar. 98 is the earlier original M/98 carbine w/17-inch bbl. and is rarely encountered.

MODEL 1898B (KAR. 98B)
MAUSER CARBINE .... NiB $475 Ex $397 Gd $294
Same general specifications as Model 1898 (Gew.98) Rifle except has turned-down bolt handle and sling attached to left side of stock. This is post-WWI model.

MODEL 1898K (KAR. 98K)
MAUSER CARBINE .... NiB $475 Ex $397 Gd $294
Same general specifications as Model 1898 (Gew.98) Rifle except has turned-down bolt handle, 23.5-inch bbl., may have hooded front sight, sling attached to left side of stock, weighs about 8.5 lbs. Adopted in 1935, this was the standard German service rifle of WWII. Note: Late-war models had stamped sheet steel trigger guards and many of the Model 98K carbines made during WWII had laminated wood stocks These weigh .5 to .75 pound more than the previous Model 98K. Value shown is for earlier type.

MODEL VK 98
PEOPLE'S RIFLE ("VOLKSGEWEHR").. NiB $248 Ex $202 Gd $145
Kar. 98K-type action. Caliber: 7.9mm. Single-shot or repeater (latter w/rough hole-in-the-stock 5-round "magazine" or fitted w/10-round clip of German Model 43 semiauto rifle). 20.9-inch bbl. Weight: 7 lbs. Fixed V-notch rear sight dovetailed into front receiver ring; front blade welded to bbl. Crude, unfinished, half-length stock w/o buttplate. Last ditch weapon made in 1945 for issue to German civilians. Note: Of value only as a military arms collector's item, this hastily-made rifle should be regarded as unsafe to shoot.

GÉVARM RIFLE — Saint Etienne, France
Manufactured by Gevelot

E-1 AUTOLOADING RIFLE .... NiB $199 Ex $174 Gd $123
Caliber: .22 LR. Eight-round clip magazine. 19.5-inch bbl. Sights: Open rear; post front. Pistol-grip stock and forearm of French walnut.

GOLDEN EAGLE RIFLES — Houston, Texas
Mfd. by Nikko Firearms Ltd., Tochigi, Japan

MODEL 7000 GRADE I AFRICAN .... NiB $707 Ex $553 Gd $445
Same as Grade I Big Game except: Caliber: .375 H&H Mag. and .458 Win. Mag. Two-round magazine in .458, weight: 8.75 lbs. in .375 and 10.5 lbs. in .458, furnished w/sights. Imported 1976 to 1981.

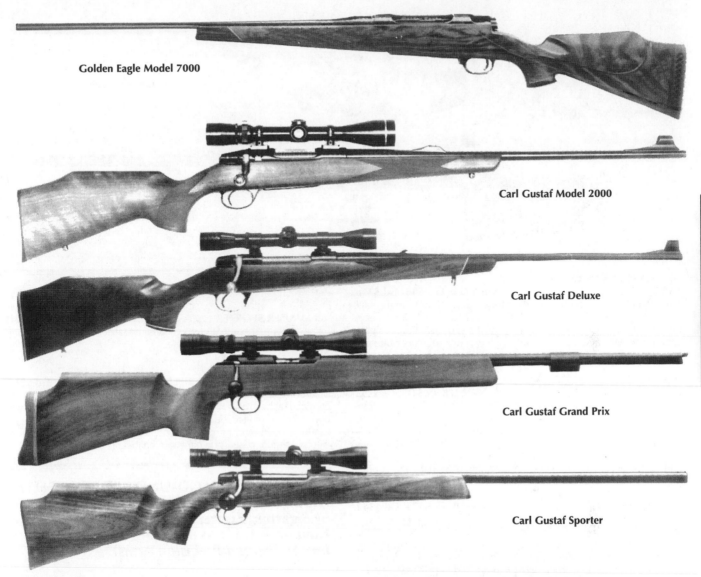

Golden Eagle Model 7000

Carl Gustaf Model 2000

Carl Gustaf Deluxe

Carl Gustaf Grand Prix

Carl Gustaf Sporter

RIFLES

MODEL 7000 BIG GAME SERIES
Bolt action. Calibers: .22-250, .243 Win., .25-06, .270 Win., Weatherby Mag., 7mm Rem. Mag., .30-06, .300 Weatherby Mag., .300 Win. Mag., .338 Win. Mag. Magazine capacity: 4 rounds in .22-250, 3 rounds in other calibers. 24- or 26-inch bbl. (26-inch only in 338). Weight: 7 lbs., .22-250; 8.75, lbs., other calibers. Furnished w/o sights. Fancy American walnut stock, skip checkered, contrasting wood forend tip and grip cap w/gold eagle head, recoil pad. Imported 1976 to 1981.

Model 7000 Grade I . . . . NiB $659 Ex $599 Gd $420
Model 7000 Grade II . . . . NiB $704 Ex $651 Gd $455

GREIFELT & CO. — Suhl, Germany

SPORT MODEL 22 HORNET
BOLT-ACTION RIFLE . . . . NiB $2298 Ex $1861 Gd $1303
Caliber: .22 Hornet. Five round box magazine. 22-inch Krupp steel bbl. Weight: 6 lbs. Sights: Two-leaf rear; ramp front. Walnut stock, checkered pistol-grip and forearm. Made before WWII.

CARL GUSTAF RIFLES — Eskilstuna, Sweden
Mfd. by Carl Gustaf Stads Gevärsfaktori

MODEL 2000 BOLT-ACTION RIFLE
Calibers: .243, 6.5x55, 7x64, .270, .308 Win., .30-06, 7mm Rem. Mag., .300 Win. Mag. Three round magazine. 24-inch bbl. 44 inches overall. Weight: 7.5 lbs. Receiver drilled and tapped. Hooded ramp front sight, open rear. Adj. trigger. Checkered European walnut stock w/Monte Carlo cheekpiece and Wundhammer palmswell grip. Imported 1991 to 1995

Model 2000
w/o sights . . . . NiB $1378 Ex $1196 Gd $835
Model 2000 w/sights . . . . NiB $1678 Ex $1355 Gd $943
Model 2000 LUXE . . . . NiB $1695 Ex $1613 Gd $995

DELUXE . . . . NiB $677 Ex $538 Gd $449
Same specifications as Monte Carlo Standard. Calibers: 6.5x55, 308 Win., .30-06, 9.3x62. Four round magazine in 9.3x62. Jeweled bolt. Engraved floorplate and trigger guard. Deluxe French walnut stock w/rosewood forend tip. Imported 1970 to 1977.

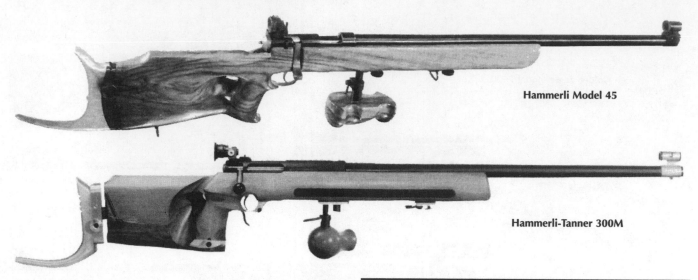

Hammerli Model 45

Hammerli-Tanner 300M

GRAND PRIX SINGLE-SHOT
TARGET RIFLE . . . . **NiB $551 Ex $548 Gd $378**
Special bolt action with "world's shortest lock time." Single-stage trigger adjusts down to 18 oz. Caliber: .22 LR. 26.75-inch heavy bbl. w/adj. trim weight. Weight: 9.75 lbs. Furnished w/o sights. Target-type Monte Carlo stock of French walnut, adj. cork buttplate. Imported from 1970 to 1977.

MONTE CARLO STANDARD
BOLT-ACTION SPORTING RIFLE . . . . **NiB $478 Ex $442 Gd $395**
Carl Gustaf 1900 action. Calibers: 6.5x55, 7x64, .270 Win., 7mm Rem. Mag., .308 Win., .30-06, 9.3x62. Five round magazine, except 4-round in 9.3x62 and 3-round in 7mm Rem. Mag. 23.5-inch bbl. Weight: 7 lbs. Sights: Folding leaf rear; hooded ramp front. French walnut Monte Carlo stock w/cheekpiece, checkered forearm and pistol grip, sling swivels. Also available in left-hand model. Imported from 1970 to 1977.

SPECIAL . . . . **NiB $550 Ex $473 Gd $342**
Also designated "Grade II" in U.S. and "Model 9000" in Canada. Same specifications as Monte Carlo Standard. Calibers: .22-250, .243 Win., .25-06, .270 Win., 7mm Rem. Mag., .308 Win., .30-06, .300 Win. Mag. Three round magazine in magnum calibers. Select wood stock w/rosewood forend tip. Left-hand model avail. Imported from 1970 to 1977.

SPORTER . . . . **NiB $475 Ex $327 Gd $251**
Also designated "Varmint-Target" in U.S. Fast bolt action w/large Bakelite bolt knob. Trigger pull adjusts down to 18 oz. Calibers: .222 Rem., .22-250, .243 Win., 6.5x55. Five round magazine except 6-round in .222 Rem. 26.75-inch heavy bbl. Weight: 9.5 lbs. Furnished w/o sights. Target-type Monte Carlo stock of French walnut. Imported from 1970 to 1977.

STANDARD . . . . **NiB $475 Ex $298 Gd $244**
Same specifications as Monte Carlo Standard. Calibers: 6.5x55, 7x64, .270 Win., .308 Win., .30-06, 9.3x62. Classic-style stock w/o Monte Carlo. Imported from 1970 to 1977.

TROFÉ . . . . **NiB $564 Ex $454 Gd $368**
Also designated "Grade III" in U.S. and "Model 8000" in Canada. Same specifications as Monte Carlo Standard. Calibers: .22-250, .25-06, 6.5x55, .270 Win., 7mm Rem. Mag., .308 Win., .30-06, .300 Win. Mag. Three round magazine in magnum calibers. Furnished w/o sights. Fancy wood stock w/rosewood forend tip, high-gloss lacquer finish. Imported from 1970 to 1977.

C.G. HAENEL — Suhl, Germany

'88 MAUSER SPORTER . . . . **NiB $777 Ex $459 Gd $345**
Same general specifications as Haenel Mauser-Mannlicher except w/Mauser 5-round box magazine.

MAUSER-MANNLICHER
BOLT-ACTION SPORTING RIFLE . . **NiB $775 Ex $522 Gd $367**
Mauser M/88-type action. Calibers: 7x57, 8x57, 9x57mm. Mannlicher clip-loading box magazine, 5-round. 22- or 24-inch half or full octagon bbl. w/raised matted rib. Double-set trigger. Weight: 7.5 lbs. Sights: Leaf-type open rear; ramp front. Sporting stock w/cheekpiece, checkered pistol-grip, raised side-panels, Schnabel tip, swivels.

HÄMMERLI AG JAGD-UND-SPORTWAFFEN-FABRIK — Lenzburg, Switzerland, *Imported by Sigarms, Exetre, NH, (Previously by Hammerli USA; Mandall Shooting Supplies, Inc. & Beeman Precision Arms)*

MODEL 45 SMALLBORE BOLT-ACTION
SINGLE-SHOT MATCH RIFLE . . . . **NiB $725 Ex $611 Gd $405**
Calibers: .22 LR. 22 Extra Long. 27.5-inch heavy bbl. Weight: 15.5 lbs. Sights: Micrometer peep rear; globe front. Free-rifle stock w/cheekpiece, full pistol-grip, thumbhole, beavertail forearm, palm-rest, Swiss-type buttplate, swivels. Made from 1945 to 1957.

MODEL 54 SMALLBORE
MATCH RIFLE . . . . **NiB $675 Ex $511 Gd $380**
Bolt-action, single-shot. Caliber: .22 LR. 27.5-inch heavy bbl. Weight: 15 lbs. Sights: Micrometer peep rear; globe front. Free-rifle stock w/cheekpiece, thumbhole, adj. hook buttplate, palm rest, swivel. Made from 1954 to 1957.

MODEL 503 FREE RIFLE . . . . **NiB $660 Ex $511 Gd $380**
Bolt-action, single-shot. Caliber: .22 LR. 27.5-inch heavy bbl. Weight: 15 lbs. Sights: Micrometer peep rear; globe front. Free-rifle stock w/cheekpiece, thumbhole, adj. hook buttplate, palm rest, swivel. Made from 1957 to 1962.

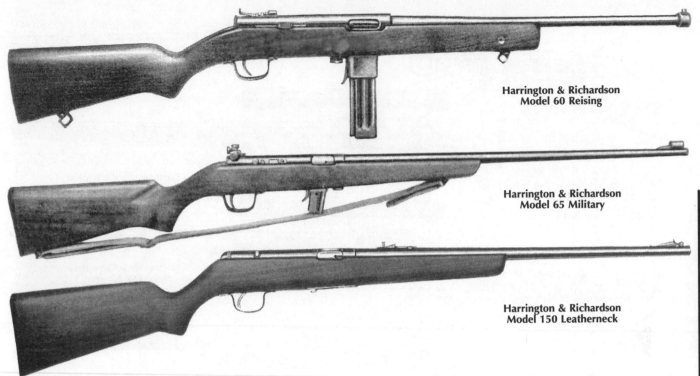

Harrington & Richardson Model 60 Reising

Harrington & Richardson Model 65 Military

Harrington & Richardson Model 150 Leatherneck

RIFLES

MODEL 506 SMALLBORE MATCH RIFLE . . . . NiB $740 Ex $611 Gd $405
Bolt-action, single-shot. Caliber: .22 LR. 26.75-inch heavy bbl. Weight: 16.5 lbs. Sights: Micrometer peep rear; globe front. Free-rifle stock w/cheekpiece, thumbhole adj. hook buttplate, palmrest, swivel. Made from 1963 to 1966.

MODEL OLYMPIC 300 METER BOLT-ACTION
SINGLE-SHOT FREE RIFLE. . . . . NiB $883 Ex $724 Gd $515
Calibers: .30-06, .300 H&H Magnum for U.S.A.; ordinarily produced in 7.5mm, other calibers available on special order. 29.5-inch heavy bbl. Double-pull or double-set trigger. Sights: Micrometer peep rear, globe front. Free-rifle stock w/cheekpiece, full pistol grip, thumbhole, beavertail forend, palmrest, Swiss-type buttplate, swivels. Made 1945 to 1959.

TANNER 300 METER FREE RIFLE . . . . NiB $899 Ex $702 Gd $515
Bolt-action, single-shot. Caliber: 7.5mm standard, available in most popular centerfire calibers. 29.5-inch heavy bbl. Weight: 16.75 lbs. Sights: Micrometer peep rear; globe front. Free-rifle stock w/cheekpiece, thumbhole, adj. hook buttplate, palmrest, swivel. Intro. 1962. Disc. See Illustration previous page.

HARRINGTON & RICHARDSON, INC. —
Gardner, Massachusetts (Now H&R 1871, INC., Gardner, Massachusetts)

Formerly Harrington & Richardson Arms Co. of Worcester, Mass. One of the oldest and most distinguished manufacturers of handguns, rifles and shotguns, H&R suspended operations on January 24, 1986. In 1987, New England Firearms was established as an independent company producing selected H&R models under the NEF logo. In 1991, H&R 1871, Inc. was formed from the residual of the parent company and that took over the New England Firearms facility. H&R 1871 produced firearms under both its logo and the NEF brand name until 1999, when the Marlin Firearms Company acquired the assets of H&R 1871.

MODEL 60 REISING SEMI-
AUTOMATIC RIFLE . . . . NiB $1200 Ex $818 Gd $561
Caliber: .45 Automatic. 12- and 20-round detachable box magazines. 18.25-inch bbl. Weight: 7.5 lbs. Sights: Open rear; blade front. Plain pistol-grip stock. Made from 1944 to 1946.

MODEL 65 MILITARY
AUTOLOADING RIFLE . . . . NiB $450 Ex $276 Gd $168
Also called "General." Caliber: .22 LR. 10-round detachable box magazine. 23-inch heavy bbl. Weight: 9 lbs. Sights: Redfield 70 rear peep, blade front w/protecting "ears." Plain pistol-grip stock, "Garand" dimensions. Made from 1944 to 1946. Note: This model was used as a training rifle by the U.S. Marine Corps.

MODEL 150
LEATHERNECK AUTOLOADER . . . . NiB $300 Ex $205 Gd $98
Caliber: .22 LR. only. Five round detachable box magazine. 22-inch bbl. Weight: 7.25 lbs. Sights: Open rear; blade front, on ramp. Plain pistol-grip stock. Made from 1949 to 1953.

MODEL 151 . . . . NiB $300 Ex $205 Gd $98
Same as Model 150 except w/Redfield 70 rear peep sight.

MODEL 155
SINGLE-SHOT RIFLE. . . . . NiB $251 Ex $160 Gd $108
Model 158 action. Calibers: .44 Rem. Mag., .45-70 Govt. 24- or 28-inch bbl. (latter in .44 only). Weight: 7 or 7.5 lbs. Sights: Folding leaf rear; blade front. Straight-grip stock, forearm w/bbl. band, brass cleaning rod. Made from 1972 to 1982.

MODEL 157
SINGLE-SHOT RIFLE. . . . . NiB $295 Ex $129 Gd $98
Model 158 action. Calibers: .22 WMR, .22 Hornet, .30-30. 22-inch bbl. Weight: 6.25 lbs. Sights: Folding leaf rear; blade front. Pistol-grip stock, full-length forearm, swivels. Made from 1976 to 1986.

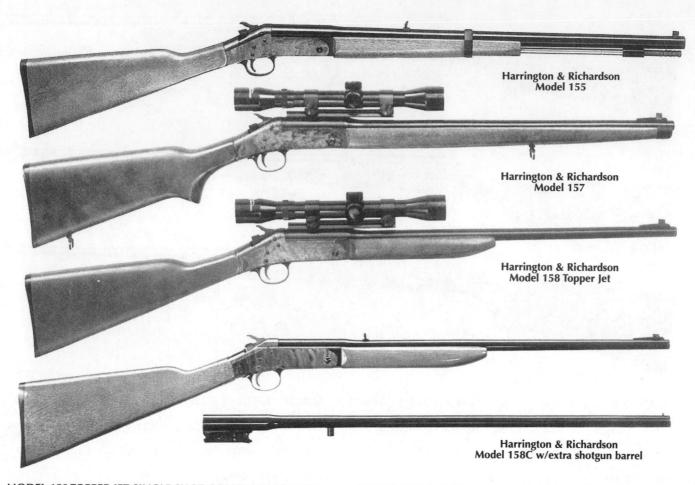

Harrington & Richardson Model 155

Harrington & Richardson Model 157

Harrington & Richardson Model 158 Topper Jet

Harrington & Richardson Model 158C w/extra shotgun barrel

MODEL 158 TOPPER JET SINGLE-SHOT COMBINATION RIFLE
Shotgun-type action w/visible hammer, side lever, auto ejector. Caliber: .22 Rem. Jet. 22-inch bbl. (interchanges with .30-30, .410 ga., 20 ga. bbls.). Weight: 5 lbs. Sights: Lyman folding adj. open rear; ramp front. Plain pistol-grip stock and forearm, recoil pad. Made from 1963 to 1967.
Rifle only . . . . NiB $225 Ex $154 Gd $107
Interchangeable bbl.
.30-30, shotgun, Add $50

MODEL 158C . . . . NiB $225 Ex $154 Gd $107
Same as Model 158 Topper Jet except calibers .22 Hornet, .30-30, .357 Mag., .357 Mag., .44 Mag. Straight-grip stock. Made 1963 to 1986.

MODEL 163 MUSTANG
SINGLE-SHOT RIFLE . . . . NiB $225 Ex $159 Gd $102
Same as Model 158 Topper except w/gold-plated hammer and trigger, straight-grip stock and contoured forearm. Made 1964 to 1967.

MODEL 165 LEATHERNECK AUTOLOADER . . NiB $225 Ex $158 Gd $102
Caliber: .22 LR. 10-round detachable box magazine. 23-inch bbl. Weight: 7.5 lbs. Sights: Redfield 70 rear peep; blade front, on ramp. Plain pistol-grip stock, swivels, web sling. Made from 1945 to 1961.

MODEL 171 . . . . NiB $600 Ex $439 Gd $226
Model 1873 Springfield Cavalry Carbine replica. Caliber: .45-70. 22-inch bbl. Weight: 7 lbs. Sights: Leaf rear; blade front. Plain walnut stock. Made from 1972 to 1981.

MODEL 171 DELUXE . . . . NiB $750 Ex $492 Gd $287
Same as Model 171 except engraved action and different sights. Made from 1972-86. See illustration next page.

MODEL 172 . . . . NiB $738 Ex $688 Gd $533
Same as Model 171 Deluxe except silver-plated, w/fancy walnut stock, checkered, w/grip adapter; tang-mounted aperture sight. Made from 1972 to 1986.

MODEL 173 . . . . NiB $1663 Ex $963 Gd $538
Model 1873 Springfield Officer's Model replica, same as 100th Anniversary Commemorative except w/o plaque on stock. Made from 1972 to 1986.

MODEL 174 . . . . NiB $1244 Ex $992 Gd $589
Little Big Horn Commemorative Carbine. Same as Model 171 Deluxe except w/tang-mounted aperture sight, grip adapter. Made from 1972 to 1984.

MODEL 178 . . . . NiB $700 Ex $392 Gd $289
Model 1873 Springfield Infantry Rifle replica. Caliber: .45-70. 32-inch bbl. Weight: 8 lbs. 10 oz. Sights: Leaf rear; blade front. Full-length stock w/bbl. bands, swivels, ramrod. Made 1973 to 1986.

MODEL 250 SPORTSTER BOLT-ACTION
REPEATING RIFLE . . . . NiB $194 Ex $103 Gd $77
Caliber: .22 LR. Five-round detachable box magazine. 23-inch bbl. Weight: 6.5 lbs. Sights: Open rear; blade front, on ramp. Plain pistol-grip stock. Made from 1948 to 1961.

Harrington & Richardson
Model 171

Harrington & Richardson
Model 171 Deluxe

Harrington & Richardson
Model 172

Harrington & Richardson
Model 173

Harrington & Richardson
Model 174 Little Big Horn Commemorative

Harrington & Richardson
Model 178

MODEL 251 . . . . **NiB $225 Ex $116 Gd $88**
Same as Model 250 except w/Lyman No. 55H rear sight.

**MODEL 265 "REG'LAR" BOLT-
ACTION REPEATING RIFLE** . . . . **NiB $285 Ex $110 Gd $84**
Caliber: .22 LR. 10-round detachable box magazine. 22-inch bbl.
Weight: 6.5 lbs. Sights: Lyman No. 55 rear peep; blade front, on
ramp. Plain pistol-grip stock. Made from 1946 to 1949.

**MODEL 300 ULTRA
BOLT-ACTION RIFLE** . . . . **NiB $533 Ex $486 Gd $280**
Mauser-type action. Calibers: .22-250, .243 Win., .270 Win., .30-06,
.308 Win., 7mm Rem. Mag., .300 Win. Mag. Three round magazine
in 7mm and .300 Mag. calibers, 5-round in others. 22- or 24-inch bbl.
Sights: Open rear; ramp front. Checkered stock w/rollover cheekpiece
and full pistol grip, contrasting wood forearm tip and pistol grip, rubber buttplate, sling swivels. Weight: 7.25 lbs. Made 1965 to 1982.

Harrington & Richardson
Model 300

Harrington & Richardson
Model 301 Carbine

Harrington & Richardson
Model 317P

Harrington & Richardson
Model 330

Harrington & Richardson
Model 360 Ultra

Harrington & Richardson
Model 370 Ultra Medalist

MODEL 301 CARBINE . . . . **NiB $488 Ex $390 Gd $262**
Same as Model 300 except w/18-inch bbl., Mannlicher-style stock, weighs 7.25 lbs.; not available in caliber .22-250. Made 1967 to 1982.

MODEL 308 AUTOMATIC RIFLE. . . NiB $488 Ex $365 Gd $258
Original designation of the Model 360 Ultra. Made 1965 to 1967.

MODEL 317 ULTRA WILDCAT
BOLT-ACTION RIFLE . . . . **NiB $610 Ex $599 Gd $368**
Sako short action. Calibers: .17 Rem. 17/.223 (handload), .222 Rem.,

.223 Rem. Six round magazine. 20-inch bbl. No sights, receiver dovetailed for scope mounts. Checkered stock w/cheekpiece and full pistol grip, contrasting wood forearm tip and pistol-grip cap, rubber buttplate. Weight: 5.25 lbs. Made from 1968 to 1976.

MODEL 317P
PRESENTATION GRADE . . . . **NiB $675 Ex $536 Gd $456**
Same as Model 317 except w/select grade fancy walnut stock w/basket weave carving on forearm and pistol-grip. Made from 1968 to 1976.

Harrington & Richardson
Model 700 Deluxe

Harrington & Richardson
Model 750 Pioneer

Harrington & Richardson
"New" Model 750

Harrington & Richardson
Model 755

RIFLES

MODEL 330 HUNTER'S RIFLE . . . . NiB $400 Ex $296 Gd $210
Similar to Model 300, but w/plainer stock. Calibers: .243 Win., .270 Win., .30-06, .308 Win., 7mm Rem. Mag., .300 Win. Mag. Weight: 7.13 lbs. Made from 1967 to 1972.

MODEL 333 . . . . NiB $400 Ex $296 Gd $210
Plainer version of Model 300 w/uncheckered walnut-finished hardwood stock. Calibers: 7mm Rem. Mag. and .30-06. 22-inch bbl. Weight: 7.25 lbs. No sights. Made in 1974.

MODEL 340 . . . . NiB $415 Ex $338 Gd $230
Mauser-type action. Calibers: .243 Win., .308 Win., .270 Win., .30-06, 7x57. 22-inch bbl. Weight: 7.25 lbs. Hand-checkered American walnut stock. Made from 1982 to 1984.

MODEL 360
ULTRA AUTOMATIC RIFLE . . . . NiB $497 Ex $365 Gd $262
Gas-operated semiautomatic. Calibers: .243 Win., .308 Win. Three round detachable box magazine. 22-inch bbl. Sights: Open rear; ramp front. Checkered stock w/rollover cheekpiece, full pistol grip, contrasting wood forearm tip and pistol-grip cap, rubber buttplate, sling swivels. Weight: 7.25 lbs. Made from 1967 to 1978.

MODEL 361 . . . . NiB $523 Ex $426 Gd $297
Same as Model 360 except w/full rollover cheekpiece for right- or left-hand shooters. Made from 1970 to 1973.

MODEL 365 ACE BOLT-ACTION
SINGLE-SHOT RIFLE . . . . NiB $145 Ex $134 Gd $87
Caliber: .22 LR. 22-inch bbl. Weight: 6.5 lbs. Sights: Lyman No. 55 rear peep, blade front, on ramp. Plain pistol-grip stock. Made 1946 to 1947.

MODEL 370 ULTRA MEDALIST . . . NiB $529 Ex $503 Gd $306
Varmint and target rifle based on Model 300. Calibers: .22-250, .243 Win., 6mm Rem. Three round magazine. 24-inch varmint weight bbl. No sights. Target-style stock w/semibeavertail forearm. Weight: 9.5 lbs. Made from 1968 to 1973.

MODEL 422 SLIDE-ACTION
REPEATER. . . . . NiB $325 Ex $194 Gd $103
Caliber: .22 LR. Long, Short. Tubular magazine holds 21 Short, 17 Long, 15 LR. 24-inch bbl. Weight: 6 lbs. Sights: Open rear; ramp front. Plain pistol-grip stock grooved slide handle. Made 1956 to 1958.

MODEL 450 . . . . NiB $375 Ex $194 Gd $100
Same as Model 451 except w/o front and rear sights.

MODEL 451 MEDALIST
BOLT-ACTION TARGET RIFLE . . . . . NiB $400 Ex $192 Gd $108
Caliber: .22 LR. Five round detachable box magazine. 26-inch bbl. Weight: 10.5 lbs. Sights: Lyman No. 524F extension rear; Lyman No. 77 front, scope bases. Target stock w/full pistol-grip and forearm, swivels and sling. Made from 1948 to 1961.

Harrington & Richardson
Model 760

Harrington & Richardson
Model 866

Harrington & Richardson
Model 1873 — 100th Anniversary

Harrington & Richardson
Model 5200 Sporter

Harrington & Richardson
Ultra Varmint

MODEL 465 TARGETEER SPECIAL
BOLT-ACTION REPEATER . . . . **NiB $395 Ex $195 Gd $108**
Caliber: .22 LR. 10-round detachable box magazine. 25-inch bbl. Weight: 9 lbs. Sights: Lyman No. 57 rear peep; blade front, on ramp. Plain pistol-grip stock, swivels, web sling strap. Made from 1946 to 1947.

MODEL 700
AUTOLOADER . . . . **NiB $4253 Ex $295 Gd $159**
Caliber: .22 WMR. Five-round magazine. 22-inch bbl. Weight: 6.5 lbs. Sights: Folding leaf rear; blade front, on ramp. Monte Carlo-style stock of American walnut. Made from 1977 to 1986.

MODEL 700 DELUXE . . . . NiB $475 Ex $378 Gd $300
Same as Model 700 Standard except w/select custom polished and blued finish, select walnut stock, hand checkering, and no iron sights. Fitted w/H&R Model 432 4x scope. Made from 1980 to 1986.

MODEL 750 PIONEER BOLT-ACTION
SINGLE-SHOT RIFLE . . . . **NiB $129 Ex $98 Gd $77**
Caliber: .22 LR. Long, Short. 22- or 24-inch bbl. Weight: 5 lbs. Sights: Open rear; bead front. Plain pistol-grip stock. Made from 1954 to 1981; redesigned 1982; disc. 1985.

MODEL 751 SINGLE-SHOT RIFLE . . . . NiB $155 Ex $80 Gd $59
Same as Model 750 except w/Mannlicher-style stock. Made in 1971.

MODEL 755 SAHARA
SINGLE-SHOT RIFLE . . . . **NiB $150 Ex $80 Gd $59**
Blow-back action, automatic ejection. Caliber: .22 LR. Long, Short. 18-inch bbl. Weight: 4 lbs. Sights: Open rear; military-type front. Mannlicher-style stock. Made from 1963 to 1971.

MODEL 760 SINGLE-SHOT . . . . NiB $170 Ex $98 Gd $77
Same as Model 755 except w/conventional sporter stock. Made from 1965 to 1970.

MODEL 765 PIONEER BOLT-ACTION
SINGLE-SHOT RIFLE . . . . **NiB $175 Ex $90 Gd $59**
Caliber: .22 LR. Long, Short. 24-inch bbl. Weight: 5 lbs. Sights: Open rear; hooded bead front. Plain pistol-grip stock. Made 1948 to 1954.

MODEL 800 LYNX
AUTOLOADING RIFLE . . . . **NiB $375 Ex $198 Gd $100**
Caliber: .22 LR. Five or 10-round clip magazine. 22-inch bbl. Open sights. Weight: 6 lbs. Plain pistol-grip stock. Made 1958 to1960.

MODEL 852 FIELDSMAN
BOLT-ACTION REPEATER . . . . **NiB $178 Ex $82 Gd $87**
Caliber: .22 LR. Long, Short. Tubular magazine holds 21 Short, 17 Long, 15 LR. 24-inch bbl. Weight: 5.5 lbs. Sights: Open rear; bead front. Plain pistol-grip stock. Made from 1952 to 1953.

MODEL 865 PLAINSMAN
BOLT-ACTION REPEATER . . . . **NiB $140 Ex $107 Gd $76**
Caliber .22 LR. Long, Short. Five round detachable box magazine. 22- or 24-inch bbl. Weight: 5.25 lbs. Sights: Open rear, bead front. Plain pistol-grip stock. Made from 1949 to 1986.

MODEL 866
BOLT-ACTION REPEATER . . . . **NiB $175 Ex $107 Gd $76**
Same as Model 865, except w/Mannlicher-style stock. Made 1971.

MODEL 1873 100TH ANNIVERSARY
(1871-1971) COMMEMORATIVE
OFFICER'S SPRINGFIELD REPLICA . . . **NiB $815 Ex $609 Gd $429**
Model 1873 "trap door" single-shot action. Engraved breech block, receiver, hammer, lock, band and buttplate. Caliber: .45-70. 26-inch bbl. Sights: Peep rear; blade front. Checkered walnut stock w/anniversary plaque. Ramrod. Weight: 8 lbs. 10,000 made in 1971.

MODEL 5200 SPORTER . . . . **NiB $650 Ex $358 Gd $260**
Turn-bolt repeater. Caliber: .22 LR. 24-inch bbl. Classic-style American walnut stock. Adj. trigger. Sights: Peep receiver; hooded ramp front. Weight: 6.5 lbs. Disc. 1983.

MODEL 5200 MATCH RIFLE . . . . . . **NiB $550 Ex $447 Gd $349**
Same action as 5200 Sporter. Caliber: .22 LR. 28-inch target weight bbl. Target stock of American walnut. Weight: 11 lbs. Made 1982 to 1986.

CUSTER MEMORIAL ISSUE
Limited Edition Model 1873 Springfield Carbine replica, richly engraved and inlaid w/gold, fancy walnut stock, in mahogany display case. Made in 1973.
Officers' Model
Limited to 25 pieces . . . . **NiB $3995 Ex $2843 Gd $1360**
Enlisted Men's model,
limited to 243 pieces. . . . . **NiB $1995 Ex $975 Gd $651**

TARGETEER JR. BOLT-ACTION RIFLE . . . . **NiB $182 Ex $156 Gd $120**
Caliber: .22 LR. Five-round detachable box magazine. 20-inch bbl. Weight: 7 lbs. Sights: Redfield 70 rear peep; Lyman No. 17A front. Target stock, junior-size w/pistol grip, swivels and sling. Made 1948 to 1951.

ULTRA SINGLE-SHOT RIFLE
Side-lever single-shot. Calibers: .22-250 Rem., .223 Rem., .25-06 Rem., .308 Win. 22- to 26-inch bbl. Weight: 7-8 lbs. Curly maple or laminated stock. Barrel-mounted scope mount, no sights. Made from 1993 to date.
Ultra Hunter (.25-06, .308) . . . . **NiB $224 Ex $157 Gd $131**
Ultra Varmint. . . . . **NiB $260 Ex $208 Gd $157**

HARRIS GUNWORKS — Phoenix, Arizona (Formerly McMillan Gun Works)

Sporting line of firearms discontinued, now specializes in sniper and tactical arms.

SIGNATURE ALASKAN
BOLT-ACTION RIFLE . . . . **NiB $3462 Ex $2941 Gd $2014**
Same general specifications as Classic Sporter except w/match-grade bbl. Rings and mounts. Sights: Single-leaf rear, bbl. band front. Checkered Monte Carlo stock w/palmswell and solid recoil pad. Nickel finish. Calibers: LA (long): .270 Win., .280 Rem., .30-06, MA (Magnum): 7mm Rem. Mag., .300 Win. Mag., .300 Wby. Mag., .340 Wby. Mag., .358 Win., .375 H&H Mag. Made from 1990. Disc.

SIGNATURE CLASSIC SPORTER
The prototype for Harris' Signature Series, this bolt-action rifle is available in three lengths: SA (standard/ short) — from .22-250 to .350 Rem Mag.; LA (long) — .25-06 to .30-06; MA (Magnum) — 7mm STW to .416 Rem. Mag. Four-round or 3-round (Magnum) magazine. Bbl. lengths: 22, 24 or 26 inches. Weight: 7 lbs. (short action). No sights; rings and bases provided. Harris fiberglass stock, Fibergrain or wood stock optional. Stainless, matte black or black chrome sulfide finish. Available in right- and left-hand models. Made from 1987. Disc. Has pre-64 Model 70-style action for dangerous game.
Classic Sporter Standard . . . . . **NiB $2507 Ex $2298 Gd $1371**
Classic Sporter Stainless. . . . . . **NiB $2503 Ex $2320 Gd $1377**
Talon Sporter . . . . **NiB $2613 Ex $2092 Gd $1474**

SIGNATURE MOUNTAIN RIFLE. . . . . **NiB $2950 Ex $2840 Gd $1557**
Same general specifications as Harris (McMillan) Classic Sporter except w/titanium action and graphite-reinforced fiberglass stock. Weight: 5.5 lbs. Calibers: .270 Win., .280 Rem., .30-06, 7mm Mag., .300 Win. Mag. Other calibers on special order. Made from 1995. Disc.

SIGNATURE SUPER VARMINTER . . . . . **NiB $2450 Ex $2197 Gd $1373**
Same general specifications as Harris (McMillan) Classic Sporter except w/heavy, contoured bbl., adj. trigger, fiberglass stock and field bipod. Calibers: .223, .22-250, .220 Swift, .244 Win., 6mm Rem., .25-06, 7mm-08, .308 Win., .350 Win. Mag. Made from 1995. Disc.

TALON SAFARI RIFLE
Same general specifications as Harris (McMillan) Classic Sporter except w/Harris Safari-grade action, match-grade bbl. and "Safari" fiberglass stock. Calibers: Magnum — .300 H&H Mag., .300 Win Mag., .300 Wby. Mag., .338 Win. Mag., .340 Wby. Mag., .375 H&H Mag., .404 Jeffrey, .416 Rem. Mag., .458 Win., Super Mag. — .300 Phoenix, .338 Lapua, .378 Wby. Mag., .416 Rigby, .416 Wby. Mag., .460 Wby. Mag. Matte black finish. Other calibers available on special order, and at a premium, but the "used gun" value remains the same. Imported 1989. Disc.
Safari Magnum . . . . **NiB $3650 Ex $3085 Gd $2065**
Safari Super Magnum . . . . **NiB $4322 Ex $3561 Gd $2574**

HECKLER & KOCH, GMBH — Oberndorf am Neckar, Germany
Imported by Heckler & Koch, Inc., Sterling, VA

MODEL 911 SEMIAUTO RIFLE. . . . . . . **NiB $1900 Ex $1671 Gd $950**
Caliber: .308 (7.62mm). Five-round magazine. 19.7-inch bull bbl. 42.4 inches overall. Sights: Hooded post front; adj. aperture rear. Weight: 11 lbs. Kevlar-reinforced fiberglass thumbhole-stock. Imported 1989 to 1993.

MODEL HK91 A-2 SEMIAUTO . . . . **NiB $25 52 Ex $2043 Gd $1312**
Delayed roller-locked blow-back action. Caliber: 7.62mmx51 NATO (308 Win.) 5- or 20-round box magazine. 19-inch bbl. Weight: W/o magazine, 9.37 lbs. Sights L "V" and aperture rear, post front. Plastic buttstock and forearm. Disc. 1991.

**Heckler & Koch
Model HK91 A-2**

**Heckler & Koch
Model HK91 A-3**

**Heckler & Koch
Model HK93 A-2**

**Heckler & Koch
Model HK940 Carbine**

MODEL HK91 A-3 . . . . **NiB $2662 Ex $2404 Gd $1529**
Same as Model HK91 A-2 except w/retractable metal buttstock, weighs 10.56 lbs. Disc. 1991.

MODEL HK93 SEMIAUTOMATIC
Delayed roller-locked blow-back action. Caliber: 5.56mm x 45 (.223 Rem.). 5- or 20-round magazine. 16.13-inch bbl. Weight: W/o magazine, 7.6 lbs. Sights: "V" and aperture rear; post front. Plastic buttstock and forearm. Disc. 1991.
HK93 A-2 . . . . **NiB $2761 Ex $2098 Gd $1109**
HK93 A-3 w/retractable stock . . . . **NiB $3504 Ex $2747 Gd $1991**

MODEL HK94 SEMIAUTOMATIC CARBINE
Caliber: 9mm Para. 15-round magazine. 16-inch bbl. Weight: 6.75 lbs. Aperture rear sight, front post. Plastic buttstock and forend or retractable metal stock. Imported from 1983 to 1991.

HK94-A2 w/standard stock . . . . **NiB $3959 Ex $3147 Gd $2694**
HK94-A3 w/retractable stock . . . . **Add 10%**

MODEL HK300
SEMIAUTOMATIC . . . . **NiB $1356 Ex $899 Gd $557**
Caliber: .22 WMR. Five- or 15-round box magazine. 19.7-inch bbl. w/polygonal rifling. Weight: 5.75 lbs. Sights: V-notch rear; ramp front. High-luster polishing and bluing. European walnut stock w/cheekpiece, checkered forearm and pistol-grip. Disc. 1989.

MODEL HK630
SEMIAUTOMATIC . . . . **NiB $1674 Ex $1242 Gd $956**
Caliber: .223 Rem. Four- or 10-round magazine. 24-inch bbl. Overall length: 42 inches. Weight: 7 lbs. Sights: Open rear; ramp front. European walnut stock w/Monte Carlo cheekpiece. Imported from 1983 to 1990.

Heckler & Koch
Model HK PSG-1

Heckler & Koch
Model SL-8

Heckler & Koch
Model USC Carbine

MODEL HK770 SEMIAUTOMATIC . . . . . . NiB $2163 Ex $1628 Gd $1007
Caliber: .308 Win. Three- or 10-round magazine. Overall length: 44.5 inches. Weight: 7.92 lbs. Sights: Open rear; ramp front. European walnut stock w/Monte Carlo cheekpiece. Imported from 1983 to 1986.

MODEL HK940 SEMIAUTOMATIC . . . . . . NiB $1995 Ex $1789 Gd $1040
Caliber: .30-06 Springfield. Three- or 10-round magazine. Overall length: 47 inches. Weight: 8.8 lbs. Sights: Open rear; ramp front. European walnut stock w/Monte Carlo cheekpiece. Imported from 1983 to 1986.

MODEL HK PSG-1
MARKSMAN'S RIFLE . . . . . . NiB $12,672 Ex $10,547 Gd $8828
Caliber: .308 (7.62mm). Five- and 20-round magazine. 25.6-inch bbl. 47.5 inches overall. Hensoldt 6x42 telescopic sight. Weight: 17.8 lbs. Matte black composite stock w/pistol-grip. Imported from 1988 to 1998.

MODEL SL8-1 RIFLE . . . . NiB $1950 Ex $1359 Gd $947
Caliber: .223 Win. Ten-round magazine. 20.80- inch bbl. 38.58 inches overall. Weight: 8.6 lbs. Gas-operated, short-stroke piston w/rotary locking bolt. Rear adjustable sight w/ambidextrous safety selector lever.

Polymer receiver w/adjustable buttstock. Introduced in 1999.

MODEL SR-9
SEMIAUTO RIFLE . . . . NiB $2075 Ex $1722 Gd $1001
Caliber: .308 (7.62mm). Five round magazine. 19.7-inch bull bbl. 42.4 inches overall. Hooded post front sight; adj. aperture rear. Weight: 11 lbs. Kevlar-reinforced fiberglass thumbhole-stock w/wood grain finish. Imported from 1989 to 1993.

MODEL SR-9
TARGET RIFLE. NiB $2795 Ex $2104 Gd $1435
Same general specifications as standard SR-9 except w/ PSG-1 trigger group and adj. buttstock. Imported from 1992 to 1994.

MODEL USC
CARBINE RIFLE. NiB $1595 Ex $1087 Gd $731
Caliber: 45 ACP. 10-round magazine. 16- inch bbl., 35.43 inches overall. Weight: 6 lbs. Blow-back operating system. Polymer receiver w/integral grips. Rear adjustable sight w/ambidextrous safety selector lever. Introduced in 1999.

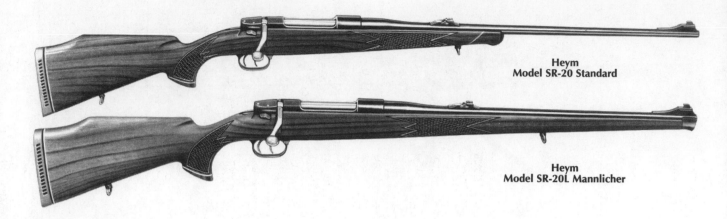

**Heym
Model SR-20 Standard**

**Heym
Model SR-20L Mannlicher**

HEROLD RIFLE — Suhl, Germany
Made by Franz Jaeger & Company

BOLT-ACTION REPEATING
SPORTING RIFLE. . . . . NiB $999 Ex $787 Gd $606
"Herold-Repetierbüchse." Miniature Mauser-type action w/unique 5-round box magazine on hinged floorplate. Double-set triggers. Caliber: .22 Hornet. 24-inch bbl. Sights: Leaf rear; ramp front. Weight: 7.75 lbs. Fancy checkered stock. Made before WWII. Note: These rifles were imported by Charles Daly and A.F. Stoeger Inc. of New York City and sold under their names.

HEYM RIFLES AMERICA, INC. — Mfd. By Heym, GmbH & Co JAGWAFFEN KD., Gleichamberg, Germany, *(Previously imported by Heym America, Inc.; Heckler & Koch; JagerSport, Ltd.)*

MODEL 55B O/U DOUBLE RIFLE
Kersten boxlock action w/double cross bolt and cocking indicators. Calibers: .308 Win., .30-06, .375 H&H, .458 Win. Mag., .470 N.E. 25-inch bbl. 42 inches overall. Weight: 8.25 lbs. Sights: fixed V-type rear; front ramp w/silver bead. Engraved receiver w/optional sidelocks, interchangeable bbls. and claw mounts. Checkered European walnut stock. Imported from Germany.
Model 55 (boxlock) . . . . NiB $6525 Ex $6325 Gd $5725
Model 55 (sidelock . . . . NiB $9338 Ex $7750 Gd $6694
W/Extra rifle bbls., add $5500
W/Extra shotgun bbls., add $2800

MODEL 88B DOUBLE RIFLE
Modified Anson & Deeley boxlock action w/standing gears, double underlocking lugs and Greener extension w/crossbolt. Calibers: 8x57 JRS, 9.3x74R, .30-06, .375 H&H, .458 Win. Mag., .470 Nitro Express, .500 Nitro Express. Other calibers available on special order. Weight: 8 to 10 lbs. Top tang safety and cocking indicators. Double triggers w/front set. Fixed or 3-leaf express rear sight, front ramp w/silver bead. Engraved receiver w/optional sidelocks. Checkered French walnut stock. Imported from Germany.
Model 88B Boxlock . . . . NiB $11,669 Ex $8875 Gd $6067
Model 88B/SS Sidelock . . . . NiB $15,538 Ex $10,850 Gd $7410
Model 88B Safari (Magnum) . . . . . . NiB $15,038 Ex $12,050 Gd $8226

EXPRESS BOLT-ACTION RIFLE
Same general specifications as Model SR-20 Safari except w/modified magnum Mauser action. Checkered AAA-grade European walnut stock w/cheekpiece, solid rubber recoil pad, rosewood forend tip and grip cap. Calibers: .338 Lapua Magnum, .375 H&H, .378 Wby. Mag., .416 Rigby .450 Ackley, .460 Wby. Mag., .500 A-Square, .500 Nitro Express, .600 Nitro Express. Other calibers available on special order, but no change in used gun value. Imported from Germany 1989 to 1995.
Standard Express Magnum . . . . NiB $5584 Ex $4436 Gd $3118
600 Nitro Express . . . . NiB $5796 Ex $5096 Gd $3096
Left-hand models, add $600

SR-20 BOLT-ACTION RIFLE
Calibers: .243 Win., .270 Win., .308 Win., .30-06, 7mm Rem. Mag., .300 Win. Mag., .375 H&H. Five round (standard) or 3-round (Magnum) magazine. Bbl. length: 20.5-inch (SR-20L); 24-inch (SR-20N); 26-inch (SR-20G). Weight: 7.75 lbs. Adj. rear sight, blade front. Checkered French walnut stock in Monte Carlo style (N&G Series) or full Mannlicher (L Series). Imported from Germany. Disc. 1992.
SR-20L . . . . NiB $2266 Ex $1664 Gd $1100
SR-20N . . . . NiB $2236 Ex $1829 Gd $1174
SR-20G . . . . NiB $2774 Ex $2207 Gd $1512

SR-20 CLASSIC BOLT-ACTION RIFLES
Same as SR-20 except w/.22-250 and .338 Win. Mag. plus metric calibers on request. 24-inch (standard) or 25-inch (Magnum) bbl. Checkered French walnut stock. Left-hand models. Imported from Germany since 1985; Sporter version 1989 to 1993.
Classic (Standard) . . . . NiB $1803 Ex $1922 Gd $1370
Classic (Magnum) . . . . NiB $2293 Ex $2114 Gd $1400
Left-hand models, add $300
Classic Sporter (Std.
w/22-inch bbl.) . . . . NiB $2507 Ex $2146 Gd $1455
Classic Sporter (Mag.
w/24-inch bbl.) . . . . NiB $1852 Ex $2242 Gd $1589

SR-20 ALPINE, SAFARI AND TROPHY SERIES
Same general specifications as Model SR-20 Classic Sporter except Alpine Series w/20-inch bbl., Mannlicher stock, chambered in standard calibers only; Safari Series w/24-inch bbl., 3-leaf express sights and magnum action in calibers .375 H & H, .404 Jeffrey, .425 Express, .458 Win. Mag.; Trophy Series w/Krupp-Special tapered octagon bbl. w/quarter rib and open sights, standard and Magnum calibers. Imported from Germany from 1989 to 1993.
Alpine Series . . . . NiB $1907 Ex $1746 Gd $1455
Safari Series . . . . NiB $2254 Ex $2083 Gd $1480
Trophy Series (Stand. calibers) . . . . NiB $2528 Ex $2025 Gd $1854
Trophy Series
(Magnum calibers) . . . . NiB $2688 Ex $2041 Gd $1701

High Standard
Flite-King Pump

High Standard
Hi-Power Deluxe

High Standard
Sport-King Autoloading Carbine

High Standard
Sport-King Deluxe Auto

High Standard
Sport-King Field Auto

High Standard
Sport-King Special Auto

RIFLES

J.C. HIGGINS RIFLES

See Sears, Roebuck & Company.

HI-POINT FIREARMS — Dayton, Ohio

MODEL 995 CARBINE

Semiautomatic recoil-operated carbine. Calibers: 9mm Parabellum or 40 S&W. 10-round magazine. 16.5-inch bbl. 31.5 inches overall. Protected post front sight, aperture rear w/integral scope mount. Matte blue, chrome or Parkerized finish. Checkered polymer grip/frame. Made from 1996 to date.

Model 995, 9mm (blue or Parkerized) .... NiB $187 Ex $155 Gd $114
Model 995, .40 S&W (blue or Parkerized) ... NiB $220 Ex $180 Gd $131
W/laser sights, add $35
W/chrome finish, add $15

HIGH STANDARD SPORTING FIREARMS — East Hartford, Connecticut, (Formerly High Standard Mfg. Co., Hamden, CT)

A long-standing producer of sporting arms, High Standard discontinued its operations in 1984.

SPORT-KING PUMP RIFLE . . . . NiB $180 Ex $129 Gd $88
Hammerless slide-action. Caliber: .22 LR. .22 Long, .22 Short. Tubular mag. holds 17 LR, 19 Long, or 24 Short. 24-inch bbl. Weight: 5.5 lbs. Sights: Partridge rear; bead front. Monte Carlo stock w/pistol grip, serrated semibeavertail forearm. Made from 1963 to 1976.

HI-POWER DELUXE RIFLE . . . NiB $405 Ex $288 Gd $192
Mauser-type bolt action, sliding safety. Calibers: .270, .30-06. Four round magazine. 22-inch bbl. Weight: 7 lbs. Sights: Folding open rear; ramp front. Walnut stock w/checkered pistol-grip and forearm, Monte Carlo comb, QD swivels. Made from 1962 to 1965

Holland & Holland
Best Quality Magazine

Holland & Holland
Royal Deluxe Double

Howa
Model 1500 Hunter

Howa
Model 1500 Lightning

HI-POWER FIELD BOLT-ACTION RIFLE.....NiB $215 Ex $155 Gd $102
Same as Hi-Power Deluxe except w/plain field style stock. Made from 1962 to 1966.

SPORT-KING AUTO-
LOADING CARBINE . . . . NiB $355 Ex $301 Gd $193
Same as Sport-King Field Autoloader except w/18.25-inch bbl., Western-style straight-grip stock w/bbl. band, sling and swivels. Made from 1964 to 1973.

SPORT-KING DELUXE AUTOLOADER . . . . NiB $253 Ex $201 Gd $98
Same as Sport-King Special Autoloader except w/checkered stock. Made from 1966 to 1975.

SPORT-KING FIELD AUTOLOADER . . . . NiB $164 Ex $114 Gd $78
Calibers: .22 LR. .22 Long, .22 Short (high speed). Tubular magazine holds 15 LR, 17 Long, or 21 Short. 22.25-inch bbl. Weight: 5.5 lbs. Sights: Open rear; beaded post front. Plain pistol-grip stock. Made from 1960 to 1966.

SPORT-KING SPECIAL AUTOLOADER . . . . NiB $185 Ex $155 Gd $98
Same as Sport-King Field except stock w/Monte Carlo comb and semibeavertail forearm. Made from 1960 to 1966.

HOLLAND & HOLLAND, LTD. — London, England, *Imported by Holland & Holland, NY, NY*

NO. 2 MODEL HAMMERLESS
EJECTOR DOUBLE RIFLE . . . . NiB $14,943 Ex $11,955 Gd $8131
Same general specifications as Royal Model except plainer finish. Disc. 1960.

BEST QUALITY MAGAZINE RIFLE . . . . NiB $14,380 Ex $11,505 Gd $7825
Mauser or Enfield action. Calibers: .240 Apex, .300 H&H Mag., .375 H&H Magnum. Four round box magazine. 24-inch bbl. Weight: 7.25 lbs., 240 Apex; 8.25 lbs., .300 Mag. and .375 Mag. Sights: Folding leaf rear; hooded ramp front. Detachable French walnut stock w/cheekpiece, checkered pistol-grip and forearm, swivels. Currently mfd. Specifications given apply to most models.

DELUXE MAGAZINE RIFLE. . . . . . . NiB $15,943 Ex $12,755 Gd $8675
Same specifications as Best Quality except w/exhibition-grade stock and special engraving. Currently mfd.

ROYAL HAMMERLESS
EJECTOR RIFLE . . . . NiB $40,630 Ex $32,505 Gd $22,105
Sidelock. Calibers: .240 Apex, 7mm H&H Mag., .300 H&H Mag., .300 Win. Mag., .30-06, .375 H&H Mag., .458 Win. Mag., .465 H&H Mag. 24- to 28-inch bbls. Weight: From 7.5 lbs. Sights: Folding leaf rear, ramp front. Cheekpiece stock of select French walnut, checkered pistol-grip and forearm. Currently mfd. Same general specifications apply to prewar model.

ROYAL DELUXE DOUBLE RIFLE . . . . NiB $56,880 Ex $45,505 Gd $30,945
Formerly designated "Modele Deluxe." Same specifications as Royal Model except w/exhibition-grade stock and special engraving. Currently mfd.

Husqvarna
Series 1100 Deluxe

Husqvarna
1951 Hi-Power

HOWA RIFLES — Tokyo, Japan, *Imported by Legacy Sports Int., Reno, NV*

See also Mossberg (1500) Smith & Wesson (1500 & 1700) and Weatherby (Vanguard).

MODEL 1500 HUNTER
Similar to Trophy Model except w/standard walnut stock. No Monte Carlo cheekpiece or grip cap. Imported from 1988 to 1989.

Standard calibers . . . . NiB $463 Ex $401 Gd $312
Magnum calibers . . . . NiB $473 Ex $389 Gd $282
Stainless steel, add $85

MODEL 1500 LIGHTNING BOLT-ACTION RIFLE
Similar to Hunter Model except fitted w/black Bell & Carlson Carbelite stock w/checkered grip and forend. Weight: 7.5 lbs. Imported 1988.

Standard calibers . . . . NiB $435 Ex $309 Gd $230
Magnum calibers . . . . NiB $452 Ex $389 Gd $282

MODEL 1500 PCS BOLT-ACTION RIFLE
Similar to Hunter Model except in Police Counter Sniper configuration and chambered for .308 Win. only. Walnut or synthetic stock w/checkered grip and forend. Receiver drilled and tapped but w/o sights. Weight: 8.5 to 9.3 lbs. Imported from 1999 to 2000.

PCS Model w/walnut stock . . . . . . NiB $385 Ex $309 Gd $230
PCS Model w/synthetic stock . . . . . NiB $435 Ex $364 Gd $273
Stainless steel, add $85

MODEL 1500 REALTREE
CAMO RIFLE . . . . NiB $508 Ex $441 Gd $312
Similar to Trophy Model except fitted w/Camo Bell & Carlson Carbelite stock w/checkered grip and forend. Weight: 8 lbs. Stock, action and barrel finished in Realtree camo. Available in standard calibers only. Imported 1993 to 1994.

MODEL 1500 TROPHY/VARMINT BOLT-ACTION RIFLE
Calibers: .22-250, .223, .243 Win., .270 Win., .308 Win., .30-06, 7mm Mag., .300 Win. Mag.,. .338 Win. Mag. 22-inch bbl. (standard); 24-inch bbl. (Magnum). 42.5 inches overall (standard). Weight: 7.5 lbs. Adj. rear sight hooded ramp front. Checkered walnut stock w/Monte Carlo cheekpiece. Varmint Model w/24-inch heavy bbl., weight of 9.5 lbs. in calibers .22-250, .223 and .308 only. Imported 1988 to 1992 and 2001 to 2008.

Trophy Standard . . . . NiB $530 Ex $481 Gd $336
Trophy Magnum . . . . NiB $553 Ex $486 Gd $352
Varmint (Parkerized finish) . . . . NiB $571 Ex $459 Gd $354
Stainless steel, add $85

MODEL 1500 WOODGRAIN LIGHTNING RIFLE
Calibers: .243, .270, 7mm Rem. Mag., .30-06. Mag. Five round magazine 22-inch. 42 inches overall. Weight: 7.5 lbs. Receiver drilled and tapped for scope mount, no sights. Checkered woodgrain synthetic polymer stock. Imported from 1993 to 1994.

Standard calibers . . . . NiB $450 Ex $401 Gd $361
Magnum calibers . . . . NiB $460 Ex $420 Gd $380

H-S PRECISION — Rapid City, South Dakota

PRO-SERIES
Custom rifle built on Remington 700 bolt action. Calibers: .22 to .416, 24- or 26-inch bbl. w/fluted option. Aluminum bedding block system w/take-down option. Kevlar/carbon fiber stock to customer's specifications. Appointments and options to customer's preference. Made from 1990 to date.

Sporter model . . . . NiB $2119 Ex $1784 Gd $1063
Pro-Hunter model (PHR) . . . . NiB $2784 Ex $1943 Gd $1006
Long-Range Model . . . . NiB $4509 Ex $3700 Gd $1979
Long-Range
takedown model . . . . NiB $2894 Ex $1892 Gd $1316
Marksman model . . . . NiB $2824 Ex $1789 Gd $1068
Marksman takedown model . . . . NiB $2854 Ex $1975 Gd $1331
Varmint takedown model (VTD) . . . . . . NiB $4295 Ex $2761 Gd $1940
Left-hand models, add $200

HUNGARIAN MILITARY RIFLES — Budapest, Hungary. Manufactured at government arsenal

MODEL 1935M MANN-
LICHER MILITARY RIFLE . . . . NiB $323 Ex $260 Gd $157
Caliber: 8x52mm Hungarian. Bolt action, straight handle. Five round projecting box magazine. 24-inch bbl. Weight: 9 lbs. Adj. leaf rear sight, hooded front blade. Two-piece military-type stock. Made from 1935 to 1940.

MODEL 1943M (GERMAN GEW 98/40) MANNLICHER
MILITARY RIFLE . . . . NiB $363 Ex $283 Gd $182
Modification, during German occupation, of Model 1935M. Caliber: 7.9mm Mauser. Turned-down bolt handle and Mauser M/98-type box magazine; other differences are minor. Made from 1940 to end of war in Europe.

Husqvarna 3000
Crown Grade

Husqvarna 4100
Lightweight

Husqvarna 6000
Imperial Custom

HUSQVARNA VAPENFABRIK A.B. —
Husqvarna, Sweden

MODEL 456 LIGHTWEIGHT
FULL-STOCK SPORTER . . . . **NiB $675 Ex $442 Gd $313**
Same as Series 4000/4100 except w/sporting style full stock w/slope-away cheekrest. Weight: 6.5 lbs. Made from 1959 to 1970.

SERIES 1000 SUPER GRADE . . . . . . **NiB $539 Ex $437 Gd $307**
Same as 1951 Hi-Power except w/European walnut sporter stock w/Monte Carlo comb and cheekpiece. Made from 1952 to 1956.

SERIES 1100 DELUXE MODEL HI-POWER
BOLT-ACTION SPORTING RIFLE . . . . **NiB $525 Ex $442 Gd $310**
Same as 1951 Hi-Power, except w/jeweled bolt, European walnut stock. Made from 1952 to 1956.

1950 HI-POWER SPORTING RIFLE . . . . . . **NiB $500 Ex $390 Gd $275**
Mauser-type bolt action. Calibers: .220 Swift, .270 Win. .30-06 (see note below), 5-round box magazine. 23.75-inch bbl. Weight: 7.75 lbs. Sights: Open rear; hooded ramp front. Sporting stock of Arctic beech, checkered pistol grip and forearm, swivels. Note: Husqvarna sporters were first intro. in U.S. about 1948; earlier models were also available in calibers 6.5x55, 8x57 and 9.3x57. Made from 1946 to 1951.

1951 HI-POWER RIFLE . . . . **NiB $500 Ex $416 Gd $293**
Same as 1950 Hi-Power except w/high-comb stock, low safety.

SERIES 3000 CROWN GRADE . . . . **NiB $575 Ex $390 Gd $262**
Same as Series 3100, except w/Monte Carlo comb stock.

SERIES 3100 CROWN GRADE . . . . **NiB $575 Ex $390 Gd $262**
HVA improved Mauser action. Calibers: .243, .270, 7mm, .30-06, .308 Win. Five round box magazine. 23.75-inch bbl. Weight: 7.75 lbs. Sights: Open rear; hooded ramp front. European walnut stock, checkered, cheekpiece, pistol-grip cap, black forend tip, swivels. Made from 1954 to 1972.

SERIES 4000 LIGHTWEIGHT RIFLE . . . . . . **NiB $660 Ex $390 Gd $262**
Same as Series 4100 except w/Monte Carlo comb stock and no rear sight.

SERIES 4100 LIGHTWEIGHT RIFLE . . . . . . **NiB $575 Ex $390 Gd $236**
HVA improved Mauser action. Calibers: .243, .270, 7mm, .30-06, .308 Win. Five round box magazine. 20.5-inch bbl. Weight: 6.25 lbs. Sights: Open rear; hooded ramp front. Lightweight walnut stock w/cheekpiece, pistol grip, Schnabel forend tip, checkered, swivels. Made from 1954 to 1972.

SERIES 6000 IMPERIAL CUSTOM GRADE   **NiB $795 Ex $552 Gd $371**
Same as Series 3100 except fancy-grade stock, 3-leaf folding rear sight, adj. trigger. Calibers: .243, .270, 7mm Rem. Mag. .308, .30-06. Made from 1968 to 1970.

SERIES 7000 IMPERIAL
MONTE CARLO LIGHTWEIGHT. . . **NiB $850 Ex $551 Gd $371**
Same as Series 4000 Lightweight except fancy-grade stock, 3-leaf folding rear sight, adj. trigger. Calibers: .243, .270, .308, .30-06. Made from 1968 to 1970.

MODEL 8000
IMPERIAL GRADE RIFLE . . . . **NiB $755 Ex $551 Gd $371**
Same as Model 9000 except w/jeweled bolt, engraved floorplate, deluxe French walnut checkered stock, no sights. Made 1971 to 1972.

MODEL 9000 CROWN GRADE RIFLE . . . . **NiB $575 Ex $442 Gd $339**
New design Husqvarna bolt action. Adj. trigger. Calibers: .270, 7mm Rem. Mag., .30-06, .300 Win. Mag. Five round box magazine, hinged floorplate. 23.75-inch bbl. Sights: Folding leaf rear; hooded ramp front. Checkered walnut stock w/Monte Carlo cheekpiece, rosewood forend tip and pistol-grip cap. Weight: 7 lbs. 3 oz. Made from 1971 to 1972.

SERIES P-3000 PRESENTATION RIFLE . . . **NiB $1100 Ex $801 Gd $570**
Same as Crown Grade Series 3000 except w/selected stock, engraved action, adj. trigger. Calibers: .243, .270, 7mm Rem. Mag., .30-06. Made from 1968 to 1970.

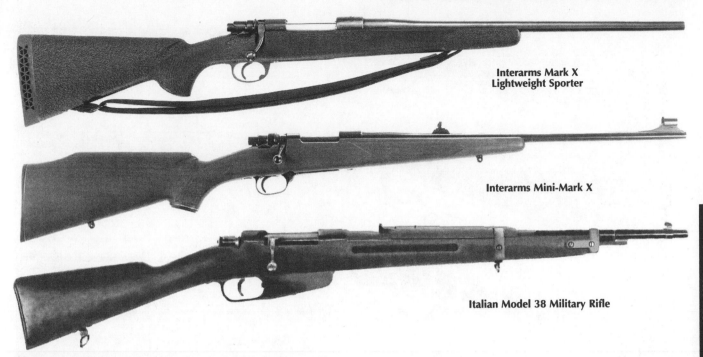

Interarms Mark X Lightweight Sporter

Interarms Mini-Mark X

Italian Model 38 Military Rifle

INTERARMS RIFLES — Alexandria, Virginia

The following Mark X rifles are manufactured by Zavodi Crvena Zastava, Belgrade, Yugoslavia.

MARK X ALASKAN . . . . **NiB $650 Ex $390 Gd $288**
Same specs as Mark X Sporter, except chambered for .375 H&H Mag. and .458 Win. Mag. w/3-round magazine. Stock w/recoil-absorbing cross bolt and heavy duty recoil pad. Weighs 8.25 lbs. Made from 1976 to 1984.

MARK X BOLT-ACTION SPORTER SERIES
Mauser-type action. Calibers: .22-250, .243, .25-06, .270, 7x57, 7mm Rem. Mag., .308, .30-06, .300 Win. Mag. Five round magazine (3-round in magnum calibers). 24-inch bbl. Weight: 7.5 lbs. Sights: Adj. leaf rear; ramp front, w/hood. Classic-style stock of European walnut w/Monte Carlo comb and cheekpiece, checkered pistol grip and forearm, black forend tip, QD swivels. Made from 1972 to 1997.

Mark X Standard	NiB $456	Ex $331	Gd $235
Mark X Camo (Realtree)	NiB $460	Ex $412	Gd $290
American Field, std. (rubber recoil pad)	NiB $526	Ex $507	Gd $355
American Field, Magnum (rubber recoil pad)	NiB $669	Ex $540	Gd $379

MARK X CAVALIER . . . . **NiB $425 Ex $336 Gd $234**
Same specifications as Mark X Sporter except w/contemporary-style stock w/rollover cheekpiece, rosewood forend tip/grip cap, recoil pad. Intro. 1974; Disc.

MARK X CONTINENTAL
MANNLICHER STYLE CARBINE . . . . **NiB $600 Ex $387 Gd $259**
Same specifications as Mark X Sporter except straight European-style comb stock w/sculptured cheekpiece. Precise double-set triggers and classic "butterknife" bolt handle. French checkering. Weight: 7.25 lbs. Disc.

MARK X LIGHTWEIGHT SPORTER . . . . . . **NiB $395 Ex $326 Gd $234**
Calibers: .22-250 Rem., .270 Win., 7mm Rem. Mag., .30-06 or 7mm Mag. Four- or 5-round magazine. 20-inch bbl. Synthenic Carbolite stock Weight: 7 lbs. Imported from 1988-90. (Reintroduced 1994-97.)

MARK X MARQUIS
MANNLICHER STYLE CARBINE . . . . **NiB $550 Ex $382 Gd $270**
Same specifications as Mark X Sporter except w/20-inch bbl., full-length Mannlicher-type stock w/metal forend/muzzle cap. Calibers: .270, 7x57, .308, .30-06. Imported 1976 to 1984.

MINI-MARK X BOLT-ACTION RIFLE . . . . . **NiB $412 Ex $331 Gd $234**
Miniature M98 Mauser action. Caliber: .223 Rem. Five round magazine. 20-inch bbl. 39.75 inches overall. Weight: 6.25 lbs. Adj. rear sight, hooded ramp front. Checkered hardwood stock. Imported from 1987 to 1994.

MARK X VISCOUNT . . . . **NiB $395 Ex $336 Gd $234**
Same specifications as Mark X Sporter except w/plainer field grade stock. Imported from 1974 to 1987.

AFRICAN SERIES . . . . **NiB $995 Ex $584 Gd $390**
Mauser-type bolt-action. Calibers: .375 H&H Mag., .458 Win. Mag. Three round magazine. 24-inch bbl. Weight: 8 lbs. Sights: 3-leaf express open rear, ramp front w/hood. English-style stock of European walnut, w/cheekpiece, black forend tip, checkered pistol grip and forearm, recoil pad, QD swivels. Imported from 1974 to 1996 by Whitworth Rifle Co., England.

ITALIAN MILITARY RIFLES
Manufactured by government plants at Brescia, Gardone, Terni and Turin, Italy

MODEL 38 MILITARY RIFLE . . . . **NiB $123 Ex $113 Gd $72**
Modification of Italian Model 1891 Mannlicher-Carcano Military Rifle w/turned-down bolt handle, detachable folding bayonet. Caliber: 7.35mm Italian Service (many arms of this model were later converted to the old 6.5mm caliber). Six round box magazine. 21.25-inch bbl. Weight: 7.5 lbs. Sights: Adj. rear-blade front. Military straight-grip stock. Adopted 1938.

Ithaca Model 49

Ithaca Model 49
Presentation

Ithaca Model 49R
Sporter

Ithaca Model 72
Saddlegun

Ithaca Model 72
Saddlegun Deluxe

ITHACA GUN COMPANY, INC. — King Ferry, New York, (Formerly Ithaca, NY)

MODEL 49
SADDLEGUN LEVER ACTION
SINGLE-SHOT RIFLE . . . . **NiB $149   Ex $119   Gd $87**
Martini-type action. Hand-operated rebounding hammer. Caliber: .22 LR. Long, Short. 18-inch bbl. Open sights. Western carbine-style stock. Weight: 5.5 lbs. Made from 1961 to 1978.

MODEL 49 SADDLEGUN — DELUXE . . . . **NiB $184   Ex $153   Gd $102**
Same as standard Model 49 except w/gold-plated hammer and trigger, figured walnut stock, sling swivels. Made from 1962 to 1975.

MODEL 49 SADDLEGUN — MAGNUM . . **NiB $189   Ex $179   Gd $118**
Same as standard Model 49 except chambered for .22 WMR cartridge. Made from 1962 to 1978.

MODEL 49 SADDLEGUN
—PRESENTATION . . . . **NiB $295   Ex $218   Gd $150**
Same as standard Model 49 Saddlegun except w/gold-plated hammer and trigger, engraved receiver, full fancy-figured walnut stock w/gold nameplate. Available in .22 LR or .22 WMR. Made from 1962 to 1974.

MODEL 49 SADDLEGUN
— ST. LOUIS BICENTENNIAL . . . . . **NiB $324   Ex $308   Gd $150**
Same as Model 49 Deluxe except w/commemorative inscription. 200 made in 1964. Top value is for rifle in new, unfired condition.

MODEL 49R SADDLEGUN
REPEATING RIFLE . . . . **NiB $265   Ex $228   Gd $130**
Similar in appearance to Model 49 Single-Shot. Caliber: .22 LR. Long, Short. Tubular magazine holds 15 LR, 17 Long, 21 Short. 20-inch bbl. Weight: 5.5 lbs. Sights: Open rear-bead front. Western-style stock, checkered grip. Made from 1968 to 1971.

Ithaca
Model LSA-65 Standard

Ithaca
Model X5-T

Ithaca
Model X-15

Ithaca
BSA CF-2

MODEL 49 YOUTH SADDLEGUN . . . . **NiB $150 Ex $128 Gd $97**
Same as standard Model 49 except shorter stock for young shooters.
Made from 1961 to 1978.

REPEATING CARBINE . . . . **NiB $359 Ex $283 Gd $181**
Caliber: .22 LR. Long, Short. Tubular magazine holds 15 LR, 17
Long, 21 Short. 18.5-inch bbl. Weight: 5.5 lbs. Sights: Open rear;
hooded ramp front. Receiver grooved for scope mounting. Western
carbine stock and forearm of American walnut. Made 1973 to 1978.

MODEL 72 SADDLEGUN — DELUXE . . . . **NiB $413 Ex $337 Gd $225**
Same as standard Model 72 except w/silver-finished and engraved
receiver, octagon bbl., higher grade walnut stock and forearm.
Made from 1974 to 1976.

**MODEL LSA-65 BOLT
ACTION STANDARD GRADE** . . . . . **NiB $461 Ex $413 Gd $283**
Same as Model LSA-55 Standard Grade except calibers .25-06,
.270, .30-06; 4-round magazine, 23-inch bbl., weight: 7 lbs. Made
from 1969 to 1977.

MODEL LSA-65 DELUXE . . . . **NiB $543 Ex $492 Gd $313**
Same as Model LSA-65 Standard Grade except w/special features of
Model LSA-55 Deluxe. Made from 1969 to 1977.

**MODEL X5-C LIGHTNING
AUTOLOADER** . . . . **NiB $195 Ex $153 Gd $102**
Takedown. Caliber: .22 LR. Seven round clip magazine. 22-inch
bbl. Weight: 6 lbs. Sights: Open rear; Ray-bar front. Pistol-grip stock,
grooved forearm. Made from 1958 to 1964.

**MODEL X5-T LIGHTNING
AUTOLOADER TUBULAR
REPEATING RIFLE** . . . . **NiB $195 Ex $153 Gd $102**
Same as Model X5-C except w/16-round tubular magazine, stock
w/plain forearm.

**MODEL X-15 LIGHTNING
AUTOLOADER** . . . . **NiB $195 Ex $169 Gd $102**
Same general specifications as Model X5-C except forend is not
grooved. Made from 1964 to 1967.

**BSA CF-2 BOLT-ACTION
REPEATING RIFLE** . . . . **NiB $475 Ex $330 Gd $253**
Mauser-type action. Calibers: 7mm Rem. Mag., .300 Win. Mag. Three
round magazine. 23.6-inch bbl. Weight: 8 lbs. Sights: Adj. rear; hooded ramp front. Checkered walnut stock w/Monte Carlo comb, rollover
cheekpiece, rosewood forend tip, recoil pad, sling swivels. Imported
from 1976 to 1977. Mfd. by BSA Guns Ltd., Birmingham, England.

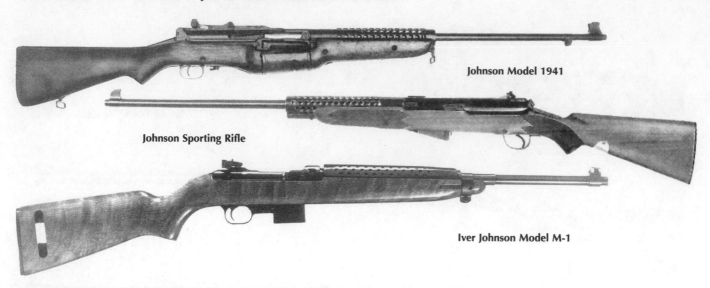

Johnson Model 1941

Johnson Sporting Rifle

Iver Johnson Model M-1

JAPANESE MILITARY RIFLES — Tokyo, Japan Manufactured by Government Plant

MODEL 38 ARISAKA SERVICE RIFLE . . . . . NiB $625 Ex $361 Gd $208
Mauser-type bolt action. Caliber: 6.5mm Japanese. Five round box magazine. Bbl. lengths: 25.38 and 31.25 inches. Weight: 9.25 lbs. w/long bbl. Sights: fixed front, adj. rear. Military-type full stock. Adopted in 1905, the 38th year of the Meiji reign hence, the designation "Model 38."

MODEL 38 ARISAKA CARBINE. . . . NiB $625 Ex $364 Gd $211
Same general specifications as Model 38 Rifle except w/19-inch bbl., heavy folding bayonet, weight 7.25 lbs.

MODEL 44 CAVALRY CARBINE . . NiB $1150 Ex $619 Gd $339
Same general specifications as Model 38 Rifle except w/19-inch bbl., heavy folding bayonet, weight 8.5 lbs. Adopted in 1911, the 44th year of the Meiji reign, hence the designation, "Model 44."

MODEL 99 SERVICE RIFLE . . . . . . NiB $500 Ex $234 Gd $183
Modified Model 38. Caliber: 7.7mm Japanese. Five round box magazine. 25.75-inch bbl. Weight: 8.75 lbs. Sights: Fixed front; adj. aperture rear; anti-aircraft sighting bars on some early models; fixed rear sight on some late WWII rifles. Military-type full stock, may have bipod. Takedown paratroop model was also made during WWII. Adopted in 1939, (Japanese year 2599) from which the designation "Model 99" is taken. Note: The last Model 99 rifles made were of poor quality; some with cast steel receivers. Value shown is for earlier type.

JARRETT CUSTOM RIFLES — Jackson, South Carolina

MODEL NO. 2 WALK ABOUT
BOLT-ACTION RIFLE. . . . . NiB $4625 Ex $2933 Gd $1903
Custom lightweight rifle built on Remington M700 action. Jarrett match- grade barrel cut and chambered to customer's specification in short action calibers only. McMillan fiberglass stock pillar-bedded to action. Made 1995 to 2003.

MODEL NO. 3 CUSTOM
BOLT-ACTION RIFLE. . . . . NiB $4650 Ex $2579 Gd $1624
Custom rifle built on Remington M700 action. Jarrett match grade barrel cut and chambered to customer's specification. McMillan classic fiberglass stock pillar-bedded to action and finished to customer's preference. Made from 1989 to date.

MODEL NO. 4 PROFESSIONAL
HUNTER BOLT-ACTION RIFLE . . . . . . NiB $6833 Ex $5752 Gd $4413
Custom magnum rifle built on Winchester M70 "controlled feed" action. Jarrett match grade barrel cut and chambered to customer's specification in magnum calibers only. Quarter rib w/iron sights and two Leupold scopes w/Q-D rings and mounts. McMillan classic fiberglass stock fitted and finished to customer's preference.

JOHNSON AUTOMATICS, INC. — Providence, Rhode Island

MODEL 1941 SEMIAUTO
MILITARY RIFLE . . . . NiB $7379 Ex $5654 Gd $3279
Short-recoil operated. Removable, air-cooled, 22-inch bbl. Caliber: .30-06, 7mm Mauser. 10-round rotary magazine. Two-piece wood stock, pistol grip, perforated metal radiator sleeve over rear half of bbl. Sights: Receiver peep; protected post front. Weight: 9.5 lbs. Note: The Johnson M/1941 was adopted by the Netherlands government in 1940-41 and the major portion of the production of this rifle, 1941-43, was on Dutch orders. A quantity was also bought by the U.S. government for use by Marine Corps parachute troops (1943) and for Lend Lease. All these rifles were caliber .30-06; the 7mm Johnson rifles were made for the South American government.

SPORTING RIFLE PROTOTYPE. . . . NiB $13,750 Ex $11,000 Gd $7480
Same general specifications as military rifle except fitted w/sporting stock, checkered grip and forend. Blade front sight; receiver peep sight. Less than a dozen made prior to World War II.

IVER JOHNSON ARMS, INC. — Jacksonville, Arkansas, (Formerly of Fitchburg, Massachusetts, and Middlesex, New Jersey)

LI'L CHAMP BOLT-ACTION RIFLE . . NiB $175 Ex $107 Gd $71
Caliber: .22 S. L. LR. Single-shot. 16.25-inch bbl. 32.5 inches overall. Weight: 3.25 lbs. Adj. rear sight, blade front. Synthetic composition stock. Made from 1986 to 1988.

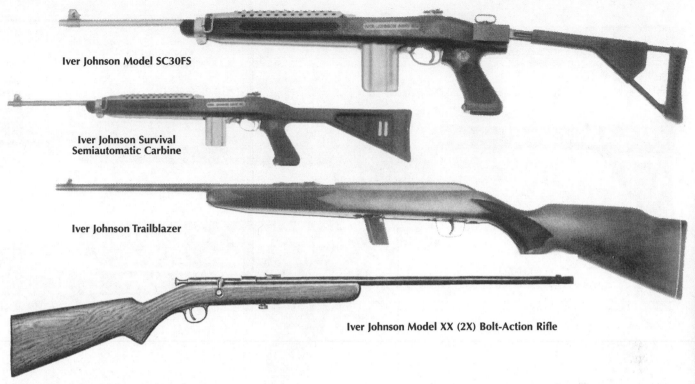

Iver Johnson Model SC30FS

Iver Johnson Survival Semiautomatic Carbine

Iver Johnson Trailblazer

Iver Johnson Model XX (2X) Bolt-Action Rifle

MODEL M-1 SEMIAUTOMATIC CARBINE
Similar to U.S. M-1 Carbine. Calibers: 9mm Parabellum 30 U.S. Carbine. 15- or 30-round magazine. 18-inch bbl. 35.5 inches overall. Weight: 6.5 lbs. Sights: blade front, w/guards; adj. peep rear. Walnut, hardwood or collapsible wire stock. Parkerized finish.

Model M-1 (30 cal. w/hardwood). . . . . . . NiB $365 Ex $287 Gd $184
Model M-1 (30 cal. w/walnut) . . . . NiB $392 Ex $300 Gd $197
Model M-1 (30 cal. w/wire) . . . . NiB $444 Ex $367 Gd $202
Model M-1 (9mm w/hardwood) . . . . NiB $272 Ex $257 Gd $221
Model M-1 (9mm w/walnut). . . . . NiB $336 Ex $289 Gd $228
Model M-1 (9mm w/wire) . . . . NiB $393 Ex $331 Gd $217

MODEL PM.30
SEMIAUTOMATIC CARBINE . . . . . . NiB $372 Ex $289 Gd $186
Similar to U.S. Carbine, Cal. 30 M1. 18-inch bbl. Weight: 5.5 lbs. 15- or 30-round detachable magazine. Both hardwood and walnut stock.

MODEL SC30FS
SEMIAUTOMATIC CARBINE . . . . . . NiB $444 Ex $367 Gd $202
Similar to Survival Carbine except w/folding stock. Made from 1983 to 1989.

SURVIVAL SEMIAUTOMATIC CARBINE . . NiB $418 Ex $392 Gd $212
Similar to Model PM.30 except in stainless steel. Made from 1983 to 1989. W/folding high-impact plastic stock add $35.

TRAILBLAZER SEMIAUTO RIFLE . . . NiB $250 Ex $134 Gd $114
Caliber: .22 LR. 18-inch bbl. Weight: 5.5 lbs. Sights: Open rear, blade front. Hardwood stock. Made from 1983 to 1985

MODEL X BOLT-ACTION RIFLE . . . NiB $255 Ex $179 Gd $108
Takedown, Single-shot. Caliber: .22 Short, Long and LR. 22-inch bbl. Weight: 4 lbs. Sights: Open rear; blade front. Pistol-grip stock w/knob forend tip. Made from 1928 to 1932.
MODEL XX (2X) BOLT-ACTION RIFLE. . . . . NiB $285 Ex $154 Gd $93

Improved version of Model X w/heavier 24-inch bbl. larger stock (w/o knob tip), weight: 4.5 lbs. Made from 1932 to 1955.

K.B.I., INC. — Harrisburg, Pennsylvania

See listing under Armscor; Charles Daly; FEG; Liberty and I.M.I.
SUPER CLASSIC
Calibers: .22 LR, .22 Mag., RF, .22 Hornet. Five- or 10-round capacity. Bolt and semiauto action. 22.6- or 20.75-inch bbl. 41.25 or 40.5 inches overall. Weight: 6.4 to 6.7 lbs. Blue finish. Oil-finished American walnut stock w/hardwood grip cap and forend tip. Checkered Monte Carlo comb and cheekpiece. High polish blued barreled action w/damascened bolt. Dovetailed receiver and iron sights. Recoil pad. QD swivel posts.
.22 Long Rifle (M-1500 SC). . . . . NiB $450 Ex $208 Gd $153
.22 Magnum Rimfire (M-1500 SC) . . . . NiB $276 Ex $229 Gd $168
.22 Hornet (M-1800-S) . . . . NiB $418 Ex $342 Gd $245
.22 Long Rifle Semiauto (M-2000 SC). . . . . NiB $276 Ex $229 Gd $168

K.D.F. INC. — Sequin, Texas

MODEL K15
BOLT-ACTION RIFLE
Calibers: (Standard) .22-250, .243 Win., 6mm Rem., .25-06, .270 Win., .280 Rem., 7mm Mag., .30-60; (Magnum) .300 Wby., .300 Win., .338 Win., .340 Wby., .375 H&H, .411 KDF, .416 Rem., .458 Win. Four round magazine (standard), 3-shot (magnum). 22-inch (standard) or 24-inch (magnum) bbl. 44.5 to 46.5 inches overall. Weight: 8 lbs. Sights optional. Kevlar composite or checkered walnut stock in Classic, European or thumbhole-style. Note: U.S. Manufacture limited to 25 prototypes and pre-production variations.
Standard model . . . . NiB $1754 Ex $1673 Gd $953
Magnum model . . . . NiB $1795 Ex $1519 Gd $1004

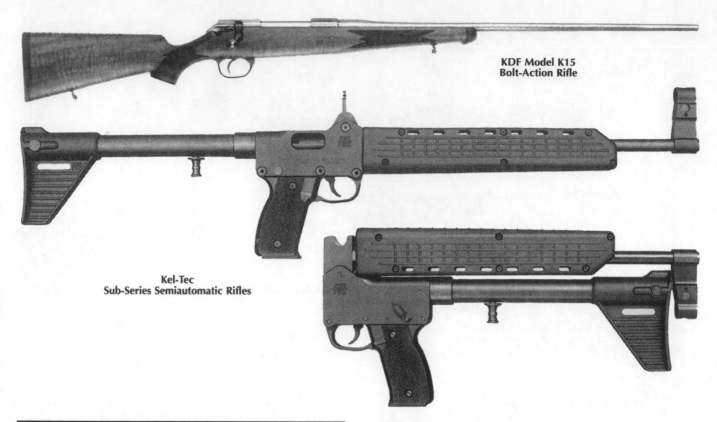

**KDF Model K15
Bolt-Action Rifle**

**Kel-Tec
Sub-Series Semiautomatic Rifles**

KEL-TEC CNC INDUSTRIES, INC. — Cocoa, Florida

SUB-SERIES SEMIAUTOMATIC RIFLES
Semiautomatic blow-back action w/pivoting bbl., takedown. 9mm Parabellum or 40 S&W. Interchangeable grip assembly accepts most double column, high capacity handgun magazines. 16.1-inch bbl. 31.5 inches overall. Weight: 4.6 lbs. Hooded post front sight, flip-up rear. Matte black finish. Tubular buttstock w/grooved polymer buttplate and vented handguard. Made from 1997 to 2000.

Sub-9 Model (9mm)............ **NiB $365 Ex $303 Gd $236**
Sub-40 Model (40 S&W)......... **NiB $365 Ex $302 Gd $287**

KIMBER RIFLES — Mfd. By Kimber Manufacturing, Inc., Yonkers, NY (Formerly Kimber of America, Inc.; Kimber of Oregon, Inc.)

Note: From 1980-91, Kimber of Oregon produced Kimber firearms. A redesigned action designated by serialization with a "B" suffix was introduced 1986. Pre-1986 production is recognized as the "A" series but is not so marked. These early models in rare configurations and limited-run calibers command premium prices from collectors. Kimber of America, in Clackamas, Oregon, acquired the Kimber trademark and resumed manufactured of Kimber rifles. During this transition, Nationwide Sports Distributors, Inc. in Pennsylvania and Nevada became exclusive distributors of Kimber products. In 1997, Kimber Manufacturing acquired the trademark with manufacturing rights and expanded production to include a 1911-A1-style semiautomatic pistol, the Kimber Classic 45.

Rifle production resumed in late 1998 with the announcement of an all-new Kimber .22 rifle and a refined Model 84 in both single-shot and repeater configurations.

MODEL 82 BOLT-ACTION RIFLE
Small action based on Kimber's "A" Model 82 rimfire receiver w/twin rear locking lugs. Calibers: .22 LR. .22 WRF, .22 Hornet, .218 Bee, .25-20. 5- or 10-round magazine (.22 LR); 5-round magazine (22WRF); 3-round magazine (.22 Hornet). .218 Bee and .25-20 are single-shot. 18- to 25-inch bbl. 37.63 to 42.5 inches overall. Weight: 6 lbs. (Light Sporter), 6.5 lbs. (Sporter), 7.5 lbs. (Varmint); 10.75 lbs. (Target). Right- and left-hand actions are available in distinctive stock styles.

Cascade (disc. 1987)........... **NiB $775 Ex $546 Gd $363**
Classic (disc. 1988)............ **NiB $775 Ex $546 Gd $363**
Continental .... **NiB $1414 Ex $1143 Gd $797**
Custom Classic
(disc. 1988) .... **NiB $981 Ex $795 Gd $556**
Mini Classic.................. **NiB $634 Ex $527 Gd $366**
Super America............... **NiB $1264 Ex $1072 Gd $814**
Super Continental .... **NiB $1203 Ex $1355 Gd $840**
1990 Classifications
All-American Match .... **NiB $1947 Ex $818 Gd $587**
Deluxe Grade
(disc. 1990) .... **NiB $1346 Ex $1063 Gd $857**
Hunter
(Laminated stock) .... **NiB $875 Ex $720 Gd $489**
Super America............... **NiB $1675 Ex $1058 Gd $704**
Target
(Government Match)........... **NiB $900 Ex $843 Gd $669**

MODEL 82C CLASSIC BOLT-ACTION RIFLE
Caliber: .22 LR. Four- or 10-round magazine. 21-inch air-gauged bbl. 40.5 inches overall. Weight: 6.5 lbs. Receiver drilled and tapped for Warne scope mounts; no sights. Single-set trigger. Checkered Claro walnut stock w/red buttpad and polished steel grip cap. Reintroduced 1993.

Classic model .... **NiB $775 Ex $659 Gd $460**
Left-hand model, add................................ **$75**

Kimber Model 82 Rimfire Classic

Kimber Model 82C Rimfire Classic

Kimber Model 84 Classic

Kimber Model 89 Big Game 375 Caliber

Kimber Model 89 Big Game 375 H&H Caliber

MODEL 84 BOLT-ACTION RIFLE

Classic (disc. 1988) Compact-medium action based on a scaled-down Mauser-type receiver, designed to accept small base centerfire cartridges. Calibers: .17 Rem., .221 Fireball, .222 Rem., .223 Rem. Five round magazine. Same general barrel and stock specifications as Model 82.

Classic (discontinued 1988)	NiB $898	Ex $773	Gd $540
Continental	NiB $1291	Ex $1045	Gd $732
Custom Classic (disc. 1988)	NiB $1173	Ex $953	Gd $670
Super America (disc. 1988)	NiB $1925	Ex $1078	Gd $757
Super Continental (disc. 1988)	NiB $1393	Ex $1125	Gd $789
1990 Classifications			
Deluxe Grade (disc. 1990)	NiB $1225	Ex $994	Gd $699
Hunter/Sporter (laminated stock)	NiB $1096	Ex $891	Gd $624
Super America (disc. 1991)	NiB $1925	Ex $1107	Gd $779
Super Varmint (disc. 1991)	NiB $1096	Ex $1138	Gd $799
Ultra Varmint (disc. 1991)	NiB $1150	Ex $1056	Gd $740

MODEL 89 BIG-GAME RIFLE

Large action combining the best features of the pre-64 Model 70 Winchester and the Mauser 98. Three action lengths are offered in three stock styles. Calibers: .257 Roberts, .25-06, 7x57, .270 Win. .280 Win., .30-06, 7mm Rem. Mag., .300 Win. Mag., .300 H&H, .330 Win., 35 Whelen, .375 H&H, .404 Jeffrey, .416 Rigby, .460

Wby., .505 Gibbs (.308 cartridge family to follow). Five round magazine (standard calibers); 3-round magazine (Magnum calibers). 22- to 24-inch bbl. 42 to 44 inches overall. Weight: 7.5 to 10.5 lbs. Model 89 African features express sights on contoured quarter rib, banded front sight. Barrel-mounted recoil lug w/integral receiver lug and twin recoil crosspins in stock.

BGR Long Action			
Classic (disc. 1988)	NiB $875	Ex $772	Gd $543
Custom Classic (disc. 1988)	NiB $1221	Ex $990	Gd $695
Super America	NiB $1486	Ex $1204	Gd $843
1990 Classifications			
Deluxe Grade: Featherweight	NiB $1957	Ex $1420	Gd $996
Medium	NiB $1786	Ex $153	Gd $1015
.375 H&H	NiB $1885	Ex $1526	Gd $1066
Hunter Grade (laminated stock)			
.270 and .30-06	NiB $1327	Ex $1059	Gd $748
.375 H&H	NiB $1594	Ex $1286	Gd $893
Super America: Featherweight	NiB $2037	Ex $1642	Gd $1149
Medium	NiB $2127	Ex $1723	Gd $1206
.375 H&H	NiB $2699	Ex $2184	Gd $1524
African — All calibers	NiB $5565	Ex $3838	Gd $2654

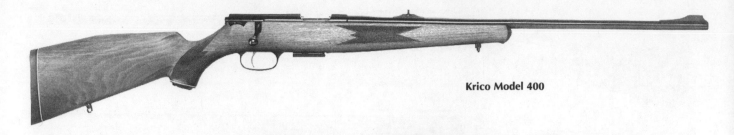

Krico Model 400

KNIGHT'S MANUFACTURING COMPANY — Vero Beach, Florida

SR-15 SEMIAUTOMATIC
MATCH RIFLE . . . . NiB $1675 Ex $1469 Gd $1006
AR-15 configuration. Caliber: .223 Rem. (5.56mm). Five- or 10-round magazine. 20-inch w/free-floating, match-grade bbl., 38 inches overall. Weight: 7.9 lbs. Integral Weaver-style rail. Two-stage target trigger. Matte black oxide finish. Black synthetic AR-15A2-style stock and forearm. Made from 1997 to 2008.

SR-15 M-4 SEMIAUTOMATIC CARBINE
Similar to SR-15 rifle except w/16-inch bbl. Sights and mounts optional. Fixed synthetic or collapsible buttstock. Made from 1997 to 2008.
Model SR-15 Carbine
(w/collapsible stock) . . . . NiB $1440 Ex $1307 Gd $946

SR-15 M-5
SEMIAUTOMATIC RIFLE . . . . . . NiB $1675 Ex $1385 Gd $1050
Caliber: .223 Rem. (5.56mm). Five- or 10-round magazine. 20-inch bbl. 38 inches overall. Weight: 7.6 lbs. Integral Weaver-style rail. Two-stage target trigger. Matte black oxide finish. Black synthetic AR-15A2-style stock and forearm. Made from 1997 to 2008.

SR-25 MATCH RIFLE
Similar to SR-25 Sporter except w/free floating 20- or 24-inch match bbl. 39.5-43.5 inches overall. Weight: 9.25 and 10.75 lbs., respectively. Integral Weaver-style rail. Sights and mounts optional. 1 MOA guaranteed. Made from 1993 to 2008.
Model SR-25 LW Match (w/20-inch bbl.) . . . . . NiB $5675 Ex $3224 Gd $2575
W/RAS (Rail Adapter System), add $300

SR-25 SEMIAUTOMATIC CARBINE
Similar to SR-25 Sporter except w/free floating 16-inch bbl. 35.75 inches overall. Weight: 7.75 lbs. Integral Weaver-style rail. Sights and mounts optional. Made from 1995 to 2008.
Model SR-25 Carbine (w/o sights) . . . . NiB $6000 Ex $3927 Gd $1949
W/RAS (Rail Adapter System), add $300

SR-25 SEMIAUTOMATIC
SPORTER RIFLE . . . . NiB $2688 Ex $2373 Gd $1652
AR-15 configuration. Caliber: .308 Win. (7.62 NATO). Five, 10- or 20-round magazine. 20-inch bbl. 39.5 inches overall. Weight: 8.75 lbs. Integral Weaver-style rail. Protected post front sight adjustable for elevation, detachable rear adjustable for windage. Two-stage target trigger. Matte black oxide finish. Black synthetic AR-15A2-style stock and forearm. Made from 1993 to 1997.

SR-50 SEMIAUTOMATIC LONG
RANGE PRECISION RIFLE . . . . . NiB $6737 Ex $5913 Gd $3544
Gas-operated semiautomatic action. Caliber: .50 BMG. 10-round magazine. 35.5-inch bbl. 58.5 inches overall. Weight: 31.75 lbs. Integral Weaver-style rail. Two-stage target trigger. Matte black oxide finish. Tubular-style stock. Limited production from 1996 to 2008.

KONGSBERG RIFLES — Kongsberg, Norway
(Imported by Kongsberg America L.L.C., Fairfield, CT)

MODEL 393 CLASSIC SPORTER
Calibers: .22-250 Rem., .243 Win., 6.5x55, .270 Win., 7mm Rem. Mag., .30-06, .308 Win. .300 Win. Mag., .338 Win. Mag. Three- or 4-round rotary magazine. 23-inch bbl. (Standard) or 26-inch bbl. (magnum). Weight: 7.5 to 8 lbs. 44 to 47 inches overall. No sights w/ dovetailed receiver or optional hooded blade front sight, adjustable rear. Blue finish. Checkered European walnut stock w/rubber buttplate. Imported from 1994 to 1998.
Standard calibers . . . . NiB $898 Ex $735 Gd $550
Magnum calibers . . . . NiB $1241 Ex $1029 Gd $757
Left-hand model, add $135
W/optional sights, add $50

MODEL 393 DELUXE SPORTER
Similar to Classic Model except w/deluxe European walnut stock. Imported from 1994 to 1998.
Standard calibers . . . . NiB $950 Ex $806 Gd $546
Magnum calibers . . . . NiB $1274 Ex $1055 Gd $775
Left-hand model, add. $135
W/optional sights, add $50

MODEL 393 THUMBHOLE SPORTER
Calibers: 22-250 Rem. or 308 Win. Four round rotary magazine. 23-inch heavy bbl. Weight: 8.5 lbs. 44 inches overall. No sights, dovetailed receiver. Blue finish. Stippled American walnut thumbhole stock w/adjustable cheekpiece. Imported from 1993 to 1998.
Right-hand model . . . . NiB $1355 Ex $1275 Gd $580
Left-hand model . . . . NiB $1475 Ex $1330 Gd $740

KRICO RIFLES — Stuttgart-Hedelfingen, Germany, Mfd. by Sportwaffenfabrik, Kriegeskorte GmbH

Imported by Northeast Arms, LLC, Ft. Fairfield, Maine. (Previously by Beeman Precision Arms, Inc and Mandell Shooting Supplies)

MODEL 260
SEMIAUTOMATIC RIFLE . . . . NiB $676 Ex $614 Gd $408
Caliber: .22 LR. 10-round magazine. 20-inch bbl. 38.9 inches overall. Weight: 6.6 lbs. Hooded blade front sight; adj. rear. Grooved receiver. Beech stock. Blued finish. Introduced 1989. Disc.

MODEL 300 BOLT-ACTION RIFLE
Calibers: .22 LR. .22 WMR, .22 Hornet. 19.6-inch bbl. (22 LR), 23.6-inch (22 Hornet). 38.5 inches overall. Weight: 6.3 lbs. Double-set triggers. Sights: Ramped blade front, adj. open rear. Checkered walnut-finished hardwood stock. Blued finish. Introduced 1989. Disc.
Model 300 Standard . . . . NiB $694 Ex $539 Gd $385
Model 300 Deluxe . . . . NiB $720 Ex $565 Gd $410
Model 300 SA (Monte Carlo walnut stock) . . . . NiB $837 Ex $691 Gd $505
Model 300 Stutzen (full-length walnut stock) . . . . . NiB $959 Ex $830 Gd $573

Krico Model 420

Krico 640 Varmint

MODEL 311 SMALL-BORE RIFLE
Bolt action. Caliber: .22 LR. Five or 10-round clip magazine. 22-inch bbl. Weight: 6 lbs. Single- or double-set trigger. Sights: Open rear; hooded ramp front; available w/factory-fitted Kaps 2.5x scope. Checkered stock w/cheekpiece, pistol-grip and swivels. Disc. 1962.
W/scope sight . . . . **NiB $330 Ex $299 Gd $195**
W/iron sights only . . . . **NiB $302 Ex $290 Gd $239**

MODEL 320 BOLT-ACTION SPORTER . . . . **NiB $850 Ex $579 Gd $398**
Caliber: .22 LR. Five round detachable box magazine. 19.5-inch bbl. 38.5 inches overall. Weight: 6 lbs. Adj. rear sight, blade ramp front. Checkered European walnut Mannlicher-style stock w/low comb and cheekpiece. Single or double-set triggers. Imported from 1986 to 1988.

**MODEL 340 METALLIC
SILHOUETTE
BOLT-ACTION RIFLE** . . . . **NiB $749 Ex $630 Gd $440**
Caliber: .22 LR. Five round magazine. 21-inch heavy, bull bbl. 39.5 inches overall. Weight: 7.5 lbs. No sights. Grooved receiver for scope mounts. European walnut stock in off-hand, match-style configuration. Match or double-set triggers. Imported from 1983 to 1988. Disc.

MODEL 360S BIATHLON RIFLE . . . . . . **NiB $1376 Ex $1138 Gd $649**
Caliber: .22 LR. Five 5-round magazines. 21.25-inch bbl. w/snow cap. 40.5 inches overall. Weight: 9.25 lbs. Straight-pull action. Match trigger w/17-oz. pull. Sights: Globe front, adj. match peep rear. Biathlon-style walnut stock w/high comb and adj. butt-plate. Imported from 1991. Disc.

MODEL 360 S2 BIATHLON RIFLE . . . . . **NiB $1300 Ex $1087 Gd $623**
Similar to Model 360S except w/pistol-grip activated action. Biathlon-style walnut stock w/black epoxy finish. Imported from 1991. Disc.

MODEL 400 BOLT-ACTION RIFLE . . . . **NiB $845 Ex $737 Gd $515**
Caliber: .22 Hornet. Five round detachable box magazine. 23.5-inch bbl. Weight: 6.75 lbs. Adj. open rear sight, ramp front. European walnut stock. Disc. 1990.

MODEL 420 BOLT-ACTION RIFLE . . . . **NiB $975 Ex $763 Gd $531**
Same as Model 400 except w/full-length Mannlicher-style stock and double-set triggers. Scope optional, extra. Disc. 1989.

MODEL 440 S BOLT-ACTION RIFLE . . . . . . **NiB $846 Ex $717 Gd $500**
Caliber: .22 Hornet. Detachable box magazine. 20-inch bbl. 36.5 inches overall. Weight: 7.5 lbs. No sights. French walnut stock w/ventilated forend. Disc. 1988.

MODEL 500 MATCH RIFLE . . . . **NiB $3555 Ex $2872 Gd $999**
Caliber: .22 LR. Single-shot. 23.6-inch bbl. 42 inches overall. Weight: 9.4 lbs. Kricotronic electronic Ignition system. Sights: Globe front; match micrometer aperture rear. Match-style European walnut stock w/adj. butt.

MODEL 600 BOLT-ACTION RIFLE . . . . . . **NiB $1135 Ex $989 Gd $694**
Same general specifications as Model 700 except w/short action. Calibers: .17 Rem., .222, .223, .22-250, .243, 5.6x50 Mag. and 308. Introduced 1983. Disc.

MODEL 620 BOLT-ACTION RIFLE . . . . . **NiB $1167 Ex $1081 Gd $700**
Same as Model 600 except w/short-action-chambered for .308 Win. only and full-length Mannlicher-style stock w/Schnabel forend tip. 20.75-inch bbl. Weight: 6.5 lbs. No longer imported.

**MODEL 640 SUPER SNIPER
BOLT-ACTION REPEATING RIFLE** . . **NiB $1792 Ex $1210 Gd $850**
Calibers: .223 Rem., .308 Win. Three round magazine. 26-inch bbl. 44.25 inches overall. Weight: 9.5 lbs. No sights drilled and tapped for scope mounts. Single or double-set triggers. Select walnut stock w/adj. cheekpiece and recoil pad. Disc. 1989.

MODEL 640 VARMINT RIFLE . . . . **NiB $941 Ex $812 Gd $503**
Caliber: .222 Rem. Four round magazine. 23.75-inch bbl. Weight: 9.5 lbs. No sights. European walnut stock. No longer imported.

MODEL 700 BOLT-ACTION RIFLE
Calibers: .17 Rem., .222, .222 Rem. Mag., .223, .22-250, 5.6x50 Mag., .243, 5.6x57 RSW, 6x62, 6.5x55, 6.5x57, 6.5x68 .270 Win., 7x64, 7.5 Swiss, 7mm Mag., .30-06, .300 Win., 8x68S, 9.3x64. 24-inch (standard) or 26-inch (magnum) bbl. 44 inches overall (standard). Weight: 7.5 lbs. Adj. rear sight; hooded ramp front. Checkered European-style walnut stock w/Bavarian cheekpiece and rosewood Schnabel forend tip. Imported from 1983 to date.
Model 700 . . . . **NiB $1074 Ex $934 Gd $654**
Model 700 Deluxe . . . . **NiB $1155 Ex $981 Gd $686**
Model 700 Deluxe S . . . . **NiB $1153 Ex $1190 Gd $830**
Model 700 Stutzen . . . . **NiB $1227 Ex $1041 Gd $728**

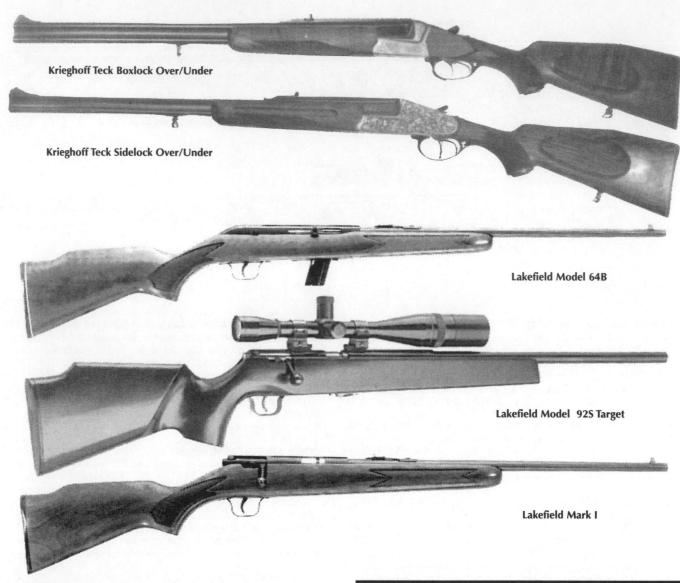

Krieghoff Teck Boxlock Over/Under

Krieghoff Teck Sidelock Over/Under

Lakefield Model 64B

Lakefield Model 92S Target

Lakefield Mark I

MODEL 720 BOLT-ACTION RIFLE
Same general specifications as Model 700 except in calibers .270 Win. and .30-06 w/full-length Mannlicher-style stock and Schnabel forend tip. 20.75-inch bbl. Weight: 6.75 lbs. Disc. importing 1990.
Sporter Model . . . . NiB $1110 Ex $989 Gd $684
Ltd. Edition . . . . NiB $2355 Ex $2136 Gd $1116

BOLT-ACTION SPORTING RIFLE . . . . NiB $705 Ex $606 Gd $426
Miniature Mauser action. Single- or double-set trigger. Calibers: .22 Hornet, .222 Rem. Four round clip magazine. 22-24- or 26-inch bbl. Weight: 6.25 lbs. Sights: Open rear; hooded ramp front. Checkered stock w/cheekpiece, pistol-grip, black forend tip, sling swivels. Imported from 1956 to 1962. Disc.

CARBINE . . . . NiB $709 Ex $581 Gd $400
Same as Krico Sporting Rifle except w/20- or 22-inch bbl., full-length Mannlicher-type stock. Disc. 1962.

SPECIAL VARMINT RIFLE . . . . NiB $709 Ex $581 Gd $400
Same as Krico Rifle except w/heavy bbl., no sights, weight: 7.25 lbs. Caliber: .222 Rem. only. Disc. 1962.

KRIEGHOFF RIFLES — Ulm (Donau), Germany, Mfd. by H. Krieghoff Jagd und Sportwaffenfabrik

See also Combination Guns under Krieghoff shotgun listings.

TECK OVER/UNDER RIFLE
Kersten action, double crossbolt, double underlugs. Boxlock. Calibers: 7x57r5, 7x64, 7x65r5, .30-30, .308 Win. .30-06, .300 Win. Mag., 9.3x74r5, .375 H&H Mag. .458 Win. Mag. 25-inch bbls. Weight: 8 to 9.5 lbs. Sights: Express rear; ramp front. Checkered walnut stock and forearm. Made from 1967. Disc.
Standard calibers . . . . NiB $8725 Ex $6832 Gd $5390
.375 H&H Mag.
(Disc. 1988)
.458 Win. Mag . . . . NiB $10,125 Ex $7346 Gd $6725

ULM OVER/
UNDER RIFLE . . . . NiB $14,329 Ex $10,609 Gd $6180
Same general specifications as Teck model except w/sidelocks w/leaf Arabesque engraving. Made from 1963. Disc.

**Magnum Research Mountain Eagle
Bolt-Action Rifle**

ULM-PRIMUS OVER/UNDER RIFLE. . . NiB $19,485 Ex $15,587 Gd $9879
Delux version of Ulm model, w/detachable sidelocks, higher grade engraving and stock wood. Made from 1963. Disc.

LAKEFIELD ARMS LTD. — Ontario, Canada

See also listing under Savage for production since 1994.

MODEL 64B SEMIAUTOMATIC RIFLE . . . . . NiB $125 Ex $104 Gd $83
Caliber: .22 LR. 10-round magazine. 20-inch bbl. Weight: 5.5 lbs. 40 inches overall. Bead front sight, adj. rear. Grooved receiver for scope mounts. Stamped checkering on walnut-finished hardwood stock w/Monte Carlo cheekpiece. Imported from 1990 to 1994.

**MODEL 90B
BOLT-ACTION TARGET RIFLE . . . . . NiB $431 Ex $334 Gd $207**
Caliber: .22 LR. Five round magazine. 21-inch bbl. w/snow cap. 39.63 inches overall. Weight: 8.25 lbs. Adj. receiver peep sight; globe front w/colored inserts. Receiver drilled and tapped for scope mounts. Biathlon-style natural finished hardwood stock w/shooting rails, hand stop and butthook. Made from 1991 to 1994.

MODEL 91T/91TR BOLT-ACTION TARGET RIFLE
Calibers: .22 Short, Long, LR. 25-inch bbl. 43.63 inches overall. Weight: 8 lbs. Adj. rear peep sight; globe front w/inserts. Receiver drilled and tapped for scope mounts. Walnut-finished hardwood stock w/shooting rails and hand stop. Model 91TR is a 5-round clip-fed repeater. Made from 1991 to 1994.
Model 91T single-shot. . . . . NiB $345 Ex $288 Gd $130
Model 91TR repeater (.22 LR only). . . . . . . NiB $385 Ex $232 Gd $140

MODEL 92S TARGET RIFLE. . . . . . NiB $300 Ex $257 Gd $184
Same general specifications as Model 90B except w/conventional target-style stock. 8 lbs. No sights, but drilled and tapped for scope mounts. Made from 1993 to 1995.

MODEL 93M BOLT ACTION. . . . . . NiB $165 Ex $136 Gd $100
Caliber: .22 WMR. Five round magazine. 20.75-inch bbl. 39.5 inches overall. Weight: 5.75 lbs. Bead front sight, adj. open rear. Receiver grooved for scope mount. Thumb-operated rotary safety. Checkered walnut-finished hardwood stock. Blued finish. Made in 1995.

MARK I BOLT-ACTION RIFLE . . . . NiB $112 Ex $93 Gd $71
Calibers: .22 Short, Long, LR. Single-shot. 20.5-inch bbl. (19-inch Youth Model); available in smoothbore. Weight: 5.5 lbs. 39.5 inches overall. Bead front sight; adj. rear. Grooved receiver for scope mounts. Checkered walnut-finished hardwood stock w/Monte Carlo and pistol-grip. Blued finish. Made from 1990 to 1994.

MARK II BOLT-ACTION RIFLE
Same general specifications as Mark I except has repeating action w/10-round detachable box magazine. .22 LR. only. Made 1992 to 1994.

Mark II Standard . . . . NiB $120 Ex $101 Gd $76
Mark II Youth (19-inch barrel). . . . . . NiB $132 Ex $111 Gd $83
Mark II left-hand . . . . NiB $158 Ex $131 Gd $96

LAURONA RIFLES — Mfg. in Eibar, Spain
Imported by Galaxy Imports, Victoria, TX

MODEL 2000X O/U EXPRESS RIFLE
Calibers: .30-06, 8x57 JRS, 8x75 JR, .375 H&H, 9.3x74R Five round magazine. 24-inch separated bbls. Weight: 8.5 lbs. Quarter rib drilled and tapped for scope mount. Open sights. Matte black chrome finish. Monte Carlo-style checkered walnut buttstock; tulip forearm. Custom orders only. Imported from 1993 to date.
Standard calibers. . . . . NiB $3110 Ex $2430 Gd $1689
Magnum calibers. . . . . NiB $3718 Ex $2996 Gd $2077

L.A.R. MANUFACTURING, INC. — West Jordan, Utah

**BIG BOAR COMPETITOR
BOLT-ACTION RIFLE. . . . . NiB $2178 Ex $1901 Gd $1389**
Single-shot, bull-pup action. Caliber: .50 BMG. 36-inch bbl. 45.5 inches overall. Weight: 28.4 lbs. Made from 1994 to date.

LUNA RIFLE — Mehlis, Germany
Mfg. by Ernst Friedr. Büchel

SINGLE-SHOT TARGET RIFLE . . . . . NiB $992 Ex $737 Gd $528
Falling block action. Calibers: .22 LR. .22 Hornet. 29-inch bbl. Weight: 8.25 lbs. Sights: Micrometer peep rear tang; open rear; ramp front. Cheekpiece stock w/full pistol-grip, semibeavertail forearm, checkered, swivels. Made before WWII.

MAGNUM RESEARCH, INC. — Minneapolis, Minnesota

MOUNTAIN EAGLE BOLT-ACTION RIFLE SERIES
Calibers: .222 Rem., .223 Rem., .270 Win., .280 Rem., 7mm Rem. Mag., 7mm STW, .30-06, .300 Win. Mag., .338 Win. Mag., .340 Wby. Mag., .375 H&H, .416 Rem. Mag. Five round (std.) or 4-round (Mag.). 24- or 26-inch bbl. 44 to 46 inches overall. Weight: 7.75 to 9.75 lbs. Receiver drilled and tapped for scope mount; no sights. Blued finish. Fiberglass composite stock. Made from 1994 to 2000.
Standard model. . . . . NiB $1333 Ex $1172 Gd $683
Magnum model. . . . . NiB $1933 Ex $1150 Gd $683
Varmint model (Intro. 1996). . . . . NiB $1433 Ex $1159 Gd $683
Calibers .375 H&H, .416 Rem. Mag., add. $300
Left-hand model, add $95

RIFLES

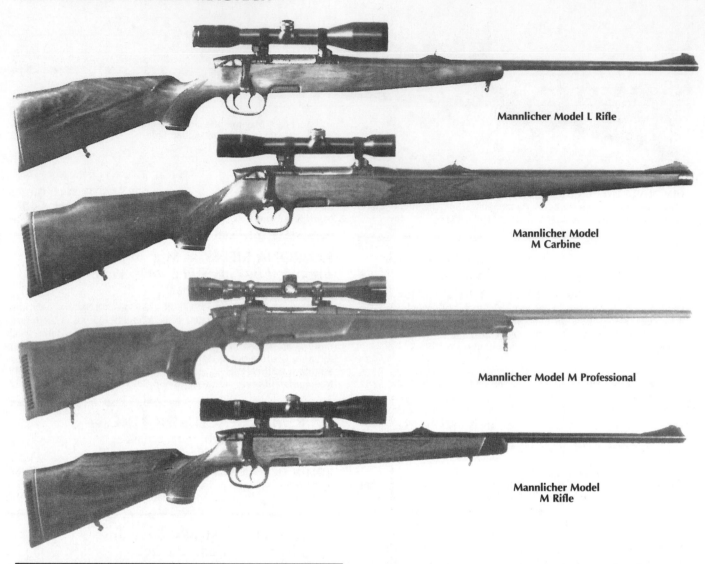

Mannlicher Model L Rifle

Mannlicher Model
M Carbine

Mannlicher Model M Professional

Mannlicher Model
M Rifle

MAGTECH — Las Vegas, Nevada
Mfg. by CBC, Brazil

MODEL MT 122.2/S BOLT-ACTION RIFLE . . NiB $125 Ex $118 Gd $77
Calibers: .22 Short, Long, Long Rifle. Six- or 10-round clip. Bolt
action. 25-inch free-floating bbl. 43 inches overall. Weight: 6.5 lbs.
Double locking bolt. Red cocking indicator. Safety lever. Brazilian
hardwood finish. Double extractors. Beavertail forearm. Sling
swivels. Imported from 1994. Disc.

MODEL MT 122.2/R BOLT-ACTION RIFLE . . NiB $134 Ex $113 Gd $85
Same as Model MT 122.2/S except adj. rear sight and post front sight.
Introduced 1994. Disc.

MODEL MT 122.2T BOLT-ACTION RIFLE . . NiB $145 Ex $118 Gd $88
Same as Model MT 122.2/S except w/adj. micrometer-type rear
sight and ramp front sight. Introduced 1994. Disc.

MANNLICHER SPORTING RIFLES — Steyr,
Austria, Mfg. by Steyr-Daimler-Puch, A.-G.

NOTE: *Certain Mannlicher-Schoenauer models were produced before WWII. Manufacture of sporting rifles and carbines was resumed at the Steyr-Daimler-Puch plant in Austria
in 1950 during which time the Model 1950 rifles and carbines
were introduced.*

*In 1967, Steyr-Daimler-Puch introduced a series of sporting
rifles with a bolt action that is a departure from the Mannlicher-
Schoenauer system of earlier models. In the latter, the action is
locked by lugs symmetrically arranged behind the bolt head as
well as by placing the bolt handle ahead of the right flank of the
receiver, the rear section of which is open on top for backward
movement of the bolt handle. The current action, made in four
lengths to accommodate different ranges of cartridges, has a
closed-top receiver; the bolt locking lugs are located toward the
rear of the bolt (behind the magazine). The Mannlicher-
Schoenauer rotary magazine has been redesigned as a detachable box type made of Makrolon. Imported by Gun South, Inc.
Trussville, AL*

MODEL L CARBINE . . . . NiB $1411 Ex $1139 Gd $794
Same general specifications as Model SL Carbine except w/type "L" action,
weight: 6.2 lbs. Calibers same as for Model L Rifle. Imported 1968 to 1996.

**Mannlicher Model SL
Rifle w/Single-Set Trigger**

MODEL L RIFLE . . . . NiB $2000 Ex $1459 Gd $893
Same general specifications as Model SL Rifle except w/type "L" action, weighs 6.3 lbs. Calibers: .22-250, 5.6x57 (disc. 1991), ..243 Win., 6mm Rem. .308 Win. Imported 1968 to 1996.

MODEL L VARMINT RIFLE . . . . . NiB $2026 Ex $1501 Gd $883
Same general specs as Model SL Varmint Rifle except w/type "L" action. Calibers: .22-250, .243 Win., .308 Win. Imported 1969 to 1996.

MODEL LUXUS BOLT-ACTION RIFLE
Same general specifications as Models L and M except w/3-round detachable box magazine and single-set trigger. Full or half-stock w/low-luster oil or high-gloss lacquer finish. Disc. 1996.
Full stock . . . . NiB $2078 Ex $1719 Gd $1259
Half stock . . . . NiB $2652 Ex $1904 Gd $885

MODEL M CARBINE
Same general specifications as Model SL Carbine except w/type "M" action, stock w/recoil pad, weighs 6.8 lbs. Left-hand version w/additional 6.5x55 and 9.3x62 calibers intro. 1977. Imported 1969 to 1996.
Right-hand carbine . . . . NiB $2130 Ex $1518 Gd $848
Left-hand carbine . . . . NiB $2284 Ex $1924 Gd $1465

MODEL M PROFESSIONAL RIFLE . . . . . NiB $2027 Ex $1460 Gd $791
Same as standard Model M Rifle except w/synthetic (Cycolac) stock, weighs 7.5 lbs. Calibers: 6.5x55, 6.5x57, .270 Win., 7x57, 7x64, 7.5 Swiss, .30-06, 8x57JS, 9.3x62. Imported 1977 to 1993.

MODEL M RIFLE
Same general specifications as Model SL Rifle except w/type "M" action, stock w/forend tip and recoil pad; weighs 6.9 lbs. Calibers: 6.5x57, .270 Win., 7x57, 7x64, .30-06, 8x57JS, 9.3x62. Made 1969 to date. Left-hand version also in calibers 6.5x55 and 7.5 Swiss. Imported 1977 to 1996.
Right-hand rifle . . . . NiB $1613 Ex $1149 Gd $789
Left-hand rifle . . . . NiB $2282 Ex $1922 Gd $1463

MODEL S RIFLE . . . . NiB $1613 Ex $1149 Gd $789
Same general specs as Model SL Rifle except w/type "S" action, 4-round magazine, 25.63-inch bbl., stock w/forend tip and recoil pad, weighs 8.4 lbs. Calibers: 6.5x68, .257 Weatherby Mag., .264 Win. Mag., 7mm Rem. Mag., .300 Win. Mag., .300 H&H Mag., .308 Norma Mag., 8x68S, .338 Win. Mag., 9.3x64, .375 H&H Mag. Imported 1970 to 1996.

MODEL SL CARBINE . . . . NiB $1613 Ex $1149 Gd $789
Same general specifications as Model SL Rifle except w/20-inch bbl. and full-length stock, weight: 6 lbs. Imported 1968 to 1996.

MODEL SL RIFLE . . . . NiB $1613 Ex $1149 Gd $789
Steyr-Mannlicher SL bolt action. Calibers: .222 Rem., .222 Rem., .222 Rem. Mag., .223 Rem. Five round rotary magazine, detachable. 23.63-inch bbl. Weight: 6 lbs. Single- or double-set trigger (mechanisms interchangeable). Sights: Open rear; hooded ramp front. Half stock of European walnut w/Monte Carlo comb and cheekpiece, skip-checkered forearm and pistol grip, rubber buttpad, QD swivels. Imported 1967 to 1996.

**MODEL SL
VARMINT RIFLE . . . . NiB $1195 Ex $1169 Gd $809**
Same general specifications as Model SL Rifle except caliber .222 Rem. only, w/25.63-inch heavy bbl., no sights, weighs 7.92 lbs. Imported 1969 to 1996.

MODEL SSG MATCH TARGET RIFLE
Type "L" action. Caliber: .308 Win. (7.62x51 NATO). Five- or 10-round magazine, single-shot plug. 25.5-inch heavy bbl. Weight: 10.25 lbs. Single trigger. Sights: Micrometer peep rear; globe front. Target stock, European walnut or synthetic, w/full pistol-grip, wide forearm w/swivel rail, adj. rubber buttplate. Imported 1969 to date.
W/walnut stock . . . . NiB $2354 Ex $1890 Gd $1223
W/synthetic stock . . . . NiB $1423 Ex $1089 Gd $662

MODEL S/T RIFLE . . . . NiB $2135 Ex $1532 Gd $701
Same as Model S Rifle except w/heavy 25.63-inch bbl., weight: 9 lbs. Calibers: 9.3x64, .375 H&H Mag., .458 Win. Mag. Option of 23.63-inch bbl. in latter caliber. Imported 1975 to 1996.

**MODEL 1903
BOLT-ACTION
SPORTING CARBINE . . . . NiB $2500 Ex $1048 Gd $649**
Caliber: 6.5x53mm (referred to in some European gun catalogs as 6.7x53mm, following the Austrian practice of designating calibers by bullet diameter). Five round rotary magazine. 450mm (17.7-inch) bbl. Weight: 6.5 lbs. Double-set trigger. Sights: Two-leaf rear; ramp front. Full-length sporting stock w/cheekpiece, pistol-grip, trap buttplate, swivels. Pre-WWII.

MODEL 1905 CARBINE . . . . NiB $1905 Ex $866 Gd $584
Same as Model 1903 except w/19.7-inch bbl.chambered 9x56mm and weight: 6.75 lbs. Pre-WWII.

MODEL 1908 CARBINE . . . . NiB $1904 Ex $1202 Gd $893
Same as Model 1905 except calibers 7x57mm and 8x56mm Pre-WWII.

MODEL 1910 CARBINE . . . . NiB $1577 Ex $1307 Gd $638
Same as Model 1905 except in 9.5x57mm. Pre-WWII.

MODEL 1924 CARBINE . . . . . . NiB $1722 Ex $1516 Gd $1001
Same as Model 1905 except caliber .30-06 (7.62x63mm). Pre-WWII.

**MODEL 1950
BOLT-ACTION
SPORTING RIFLE . . . . NiB $1905 Ex $1411 Gd $535**
Calibers: .257 Roberts, .270 Win., .30-06. Five round rotary magazine. 24-inch bbl. Weight: 7.25 lbs. Single trigger or double-set trigger. Redesigned low bolt handle, shotgun-type safety. Sights: Folding leaf open rear; hooded ramp front. Improved half-length stock w/cheekpiece, pistol grip, checkered, ebony forend tip, swivels. Made from 1950 to 1952.

GRADING: NiB = New in Box   **Ex** = Excellent or NRA 95%   **Gd** = Good or NRA 68%

269

Mannlicher-Schoenauer
Model 1950 Carbine

Mannlicher-Schoenauer
Model 1950 Carbine

Mannlicher-Schoenauer
Model 1950 Carbine

Mannlicher-Schoenauer
Model 1950 Carbine

Mannlicher-Schoenauer
Model 1950 Carbine

MODEL 1950 CARBINE . . . . NiB $2004 Ex $1515 Gd $948
Same general specifications as Model 1950 Rifle except w/20-inch bbl., full-length stock, weighs 7 lbs. Made from 1950 to 1952.

MODEL 1950
6.5 CARBINE . . . . NiB $2000 Ex $1721 Gd $990
Same as other Model 1950 Carbines except caliber 6.5x53mm, w/18.25-inch bbl., weighs 6.75 lbs. Made from 1950 to 1952.

MODEL 1952
IMPROVED CARBINE . . . . NiB $1837 Ex $1414 Gd $883
Same as Model 1950 Carbine except w/swept-back bolt handle, redesigned stock. Calibers: .257, .270, 7mm, .30-06. Made 1952 to 1956.

MODEL 1952 IMPROVED
6.5 CARBINE . . . . NiB $2045 Ex $1042 Gd $579
Same as Model 1952 Carbine except caliber 6.5x53mm, w/18.25-inch bbl. Made from 1952 to 1956.

MODEL 1952 IMPROVED
SPORTING RIFLE . . . . NiB $1812 Ex $1306 Gd $842
Same as Model 1950 except w/swept-back bolt handle, redesigned stock. Calibers: .257, .270, .30-06, 9.3x62mm. Made from 1952 to 1956 and imported exclusively by Stoeger Arms Corp.

MODEL 1956 CUSTOM CARBINE . . . . . . NiB $1995 Ex $765 Gd $533
Same general specifications as Models 1950 and 1952 Carbines except w/redesigned stock w/high comb. Drilled and tapped for scope mounts. Calibers: .243, 6.5mm, .257, .270, 7mm, .30-06, .308. Made 1956 to 1960.

CARBINE, MODEL 1961-MCA   NiB $1845 Ex $1990 Gd $1600
Same as Model 1956 Carbine except w/universal Monte Carlo design stock. Calibers: .243 Win., 6.5mm, .270, .308, .30-06. Made from 1961 to 1971.

RIFLE, MODEL 1961-MCA . . . . . NiB $2999 Ex $1314 Gd $644
Same as Model 1956 Rifle except w/universal Monte Carlo design stock. Calibers: .243, .270, .30-06. Made from 1961 to 1971.

HIGH VELOCITY
BOLT-ACTION SPORTING RIFLE . . NiB $6500 Ex $4041 Gd $1985
Calibers: 7x64 Brenneke, .30-06 (7.62x63), 8x60 Magnum, 9.3x62, 10.75x68mm. 23.6-inch bbl. Weight: 7.5 lbs. Sights: British-style 3-leaf open rear; ramp front. Half-length sporting stock w/cheekpiece, pistol grip, checkered, trap buttplate, swivels. Also produced in a takedown model. Pre-WWII. See illustration next page.

M72 MODEL L/M CARBINE . . . . . . NiB $971 Ex $703 Gd $456
Same general specifications as M72 Model L/M Rifle except w/20-inch bbl. and full-length stock, weight: 7.2 lbs. Imported from 1972 to date.

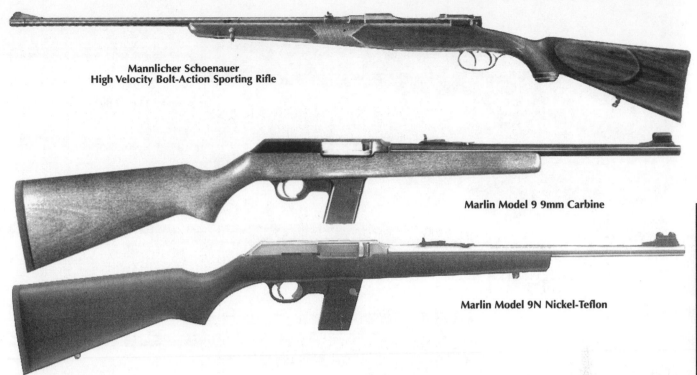

**Mannlicher Schoenauer
High Velocity Bolt-Action Sporting Rifle**

Marlin Model 9 9mm Carbine

Marlin Model 9N Nickel-Teflon

M72 MODEL L/M RIFLE . . . . **NiB $864 Ex $787 Gd $555**
M72 bolt-action, type L/M receiver front-locking bolt internal rotary magazine (5-round). Calibers: .22-250, 5.6x57, 6mm Rem., .243 Win., 6.5x57, .270 Win., 7x57, 7x64, .308 Win., .30-06. 23.63-inch bbl. Weight: 7.3 lbs. Single- or double-set trigger (mechanisms interchangeable). Sights: Open rear; hooded ramp front. Half stock of European walnut, checkered forearm and pistol-grip, Monte Carlo cheekpiece, rosewood forend tip, recoil pad QD swivels. Imported 1972 to 1981.

M72 MODEL S RIFLE . . . . **NiB $838 Ex $735 Gd $503**
Same general specifications as M72 Model L/M Rifle except w/magnum action, 4-round magazine, 25.63-inch bbl., weighs 8.6 lbs. Calibers: 6.5x68, 7mm Rem. Mag., 8x68S, 9.3x64, .375 H&H Mag. Imported from 1972 to 1981.

M72 MODEL S/T RIFLE . . . . **NiB $1421 Ex $1112 Gd $756**
Same as M72 Model S Rifle except w/heavy 25.63-inch bbl., weighs 9.3 lbs. Calibers: .300 Win. Mag. 9.3x64, .375 H&H Mag., .458 Win. Mag. Option of 23.63-inch bbl. in latter caliber. Imported from 1975 to 1981.

MODEL SBS FORESTER RIFLE
Calibers: .243 Win., .25-06 Rem., .270 Win., .6.5x55mm, 6.5x57mm, 7x64mm, 7mm-08 Rem., .30-06, .308 Win. 9.3x64mm. Four round detachable magazine. 23.6-inch bbl. 44.5 inches overall. Weight: 7.5 lbs. No sights w/drilled and tapped for Browning A-Bolt configuration. Checkered American walnut stock w/Monte Carlo cheekpiece and Pachmayr swivels. Polished or matte blue finish. Imported from 1997 to date.
SBS Forester Rifle (standard calibers) . . . . . **NiB $854 Ex $684 Gd $447**
SBS Forester Mountain Rifle (20-inch bbl.) . . . . **NiB $819 Ex $658 Gd $442**
For magnum calibers, add. $25
For metric calibers, add $100

MODEL SBS PRO-HUNTER RIFLE
Similar to the Forester Model, except w/ASB black synthetic stock. Matte blue finish. Imported from 1997 to date.

SBS Pro-Hunter Rifle (standard calibers). . . . . **NiB $802 Ex $658 Gd $442**
SBS Pro-Hunter Rifle
Mountain Rifle (20-inch bbl.) . . . . **NiB $854 Ex $650 Gd $457**
SBS Pro-Hunter Rifle (.376 Steyr) . . . . **NiB $844 Ex $684 Gd $478**
SBS Pro-Hunter Youth/Ladies Rifle . . . . **NiB $854 Ex $684 Gd $447**
For magnum calibers, add. $25
For metric calibers, add. $100
W/walnut stock . . . . **NiB $2307 Ex $1896 Gd $1371**
W/synthetic stock . . . . **NiB $1839 Ex $1505 Gd $1078**

MARLIN FIREARMS CO. — North Haven, Connecticut

MODEL 9
SEMIAUTOMATIC CARBINE
Calibers: 9mm Parabellum. 12-round magazine. 16.5-inch bbl. 35.5 inches overall. Weight: 6.75 lbs. Manual bolt hold-open. Sights: Hooded post front; adj. open rear. Walnut-finished hardwood stock w/rubber buttpad. Blued or nickel-Teflon finish. Made 1985 to 1999.
Model 9 . . . . **NiB $475 Ex $365 Gd $191**
Model 9N, Nickel-Teflon (disc. 1994) . . . . **NiB $475 Ex $390 Gd $146**

MODEL 15Y/15YN
Bolt-action, single-shot "Little Buckaroo" rifle. Caliber: .22 Short, Long or LR. 16.25-inch bbl. Weight: 4.25 lbs. Thumb safety. Ramp front sight; adj. open rear. One-piece walnut Monte Carlo stock w/full pistol-grip. Made 1984 to 1988. Reintroduced in 1989 as Model 15YN.
Model 15Y. . . . . **NiB $175 Ex $117 Gd $81**
Model 15YN. . . . .**NiB $195 Ex $122 Gd $86**

MODEL 18 BABY SLIDE-ACTION
REPEATER . . . . **NiB $750 Ex $413 Gd $284**
Exposed hammer. Solid frame. Caliber: .22 LR, Long Short. Tubular magazine holds 14 Short cartridges. 20-inch bbl., round or octagon. Weight: 3.75 lbs. Sights: Open rear; bead front. Plain straight-grip stock and slide handle. Made from 1906 to 1909.

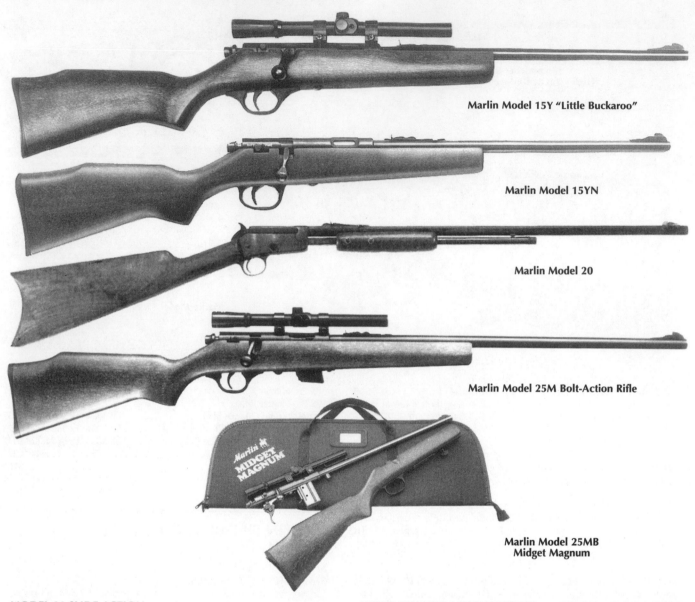

Marlin Model 15Y "Little Buckaroo"

Marlin Model 15YN

Marlin Model 20

Marlin Model 25M Bolt-Action Rifle

Marlin Model 25MB
Midget Magnum

MODEL 20 SLIDE-ACTION
REPEATING RIFLE . . . . **NiB $750 Ex $517 Gd $383**
Exposed hammer. Takedown. Caliber: .22 LR. Long, Short. Tubular magazine: Half-length holds 15 Short, 12 Long, 10 LR; full-length holds 25 Short, 20 Long, 18 LR. 24-inch octagon bbl. Weight: 5 lbs. Sights: Open rear; bead front. Plain straight-grip stock, grooved slide handle. Made from 1907 to 1922. Note: After 1920 was designated "Model 20-S."

MODEL MB 25 BOLT-ACTION RIFLE . . . . . . **NiB $150 Ex $105 Gd $93**
Caliber: .22 Short, Long or LR; 7-round clip. 22-inch bbl. Weight: 5.5 lbs. Ramp front sight, adj. open rear. One-piece walnut Monte Carlo stock w/full pistol-grip Mar-Shield finish. Made 1984 to 1988.

MODEL 25
SLIDE-ACTION REPEATER . . . . **NiB $850 Ex $521 Gd $393**
Exposed hammer. Takedown. Caliber: .22 Short (also handles 22 CB caps). Tubular magazine holds 15 Short. 23-inch bbl. Weight: 4 lbs. Sights: Open rear; beaded front. Plain straight-grip stock and slide handle. Made from 1909 to 1910.

MODEL 25M BOLT ACTION W/SCOPE . . . . **NiB $144 Ex $104 Gd $86**
Caliber: .22 WMR. 7-round clip. 22-inch bbl. Weight: 6 lbs. Ramp front sight w/brass bead, adj. open rear. Walnut-finished stock w/Monte Carlo styling and full pistol-grip. Sling swivels. Made 1986 to 1988.

MODEL 25MB MIDGET MAGNUM . . . . **NiB $140 Ex $104 Gd $93**
Bolt action. Caliber: .22 WMR. Seven round capacity.16.25-inch bbl. Weight: 4.75 lbs. Walnut-finished Monte Carlo-style stock w/full pistol grip and abbreviated forend. Sights: Ramp front w/brass bead, adj. open rear. Thumb safety. Made from 1986 to 1988.

MODEL 25MG/25MN/25N/25NC BOLT-ACTION RIFLE
Caliber: .22 WMR (Model 25MN) or .22 LR. (Model 25N). Seven round clip magazine. 22-inch bbl. 41 inches overall. Weight: 5.5 to 6 lbs. Adj. open rear sight, ramp front; receiver grooved for scope mounts. One piece walnut-finished hardwood Monte Carlo stock w/pistol grip. Made from 1989 to 2003.
Marlin Model 25MG (Garden Gun) . . . . . . **NiB $185 Ex $160 Gd $117**
Marlin Model 25MN . . . . **NiB $174 Ex $144 Gd $105**
Marlin Model 25N . . . . **NiB $161 Ex $134 Gd $99**
Marlin Model 25NC (camouflage stock) . . . . **Add $40**

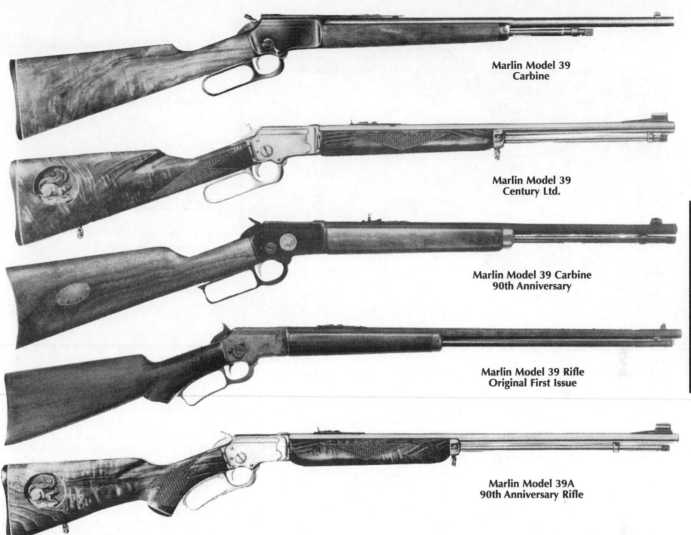

Marlin Model 39
Carbine

Marlin Model 39
Century Ltd.

Marlin Model 39 Carbine
90th Anniversary

Marlin Model 39 Rifle
Original First Issue

Marlin Model 39A
90th Anniversary Rifle

MODEL 27 SLIDE-ACTION
REPEATING RIFLE . . . . **NiB $1125 Ex $869 Gd $591**
Exposed hammer. Takedown. Calibers: .25-20, .32-20. Magazine (tubular) holds 7 rounds. 24-inch octagon bbl. Weight: 5.75 lbs. Sights: Open rear; bead front. Plain, straight-grip stock, grooved slide handle. Made from 1910 to 1916.

MODEL 27S. . . . . **NiB $875 Ex $551 Gd $366**
Same as Model 27 except w/round bbl., also chambered for .25 Stevens rimfire Made from 1920 to 1932.

MODEL 29 SLIDE-ACTION REPEATER . . . . **NiB $625 Ex $369 Gd $266**
Similar to Model 20 w/23-inch round bbl., half magazine only, weight 5.75 lbs. Made from 1913 to 1916.

MODEL 30/30A AND 30AS LEVER-ACTION
Caliber: .30/30 Win. Six-round tubular magazine. 20-inch bbl. w/Micro-Groove rifling. 38.25 inches overall. Weight: 7 lbs. Brass bead front sight, adj. rear. Solid top receiver, offset hammer spur for scope use. Walnut-finished hardwood stock w/pistol-grip. Mar-Shield finish. Made from 1964 to 2000.
Model 30/30A . . . . **NiB $259 Ex $186 Gd $136**
Model 30AS . . . . **NiB $259 Ex $186 Gd $135**
Model 30AS w/4x scope, add **$10**

MODEL 32 SLIDE-ACTION REPEATER . . . NiB $1100 Ex $662 Gd $482
Hammerless. Takedown. Caliber: .22 LR, Long, Short. Tubular magazine holds 15 Short, 12 Long, 10 LR; full magazine, 25 Short, 20 Long, 18 LR. 24-inch octagon bbl. Weight: 5.5 lbs. Sights: Open rear; bead front. Plain pistol-grip stock, grooved slide handle. Made from 1914 to 1915.

MODEL 36 LEVER-ACTION REPEATING CARBINE
Calibers: .30-30, .32 Special. Seven-round tubular magazine. 20-inch bbl. Weight: 6.5 lbs. Sights: Open rear; bead front. Pistol-grip stock, semibeavertail forearm w/carbine bbl. band. Early production w/receiver, lever and hammer color casehardened and the remaining metal blued. Late production w/blued receiver. Made 1936 to 1948. Note: In 1936, this was designated "Model 1936" and was so marked on the upper tang. In 1937, the model designation was shortened to "36". An "RC" serial number suffix identifies a "Regular/Carbine".
Model 1936 (CC receiver,
w/long tang, w/o SN prefix) . . . . **NiB $826 Ex $698 Gd $466**
Model 1936 (CC receiver,
w/short tang, w/o SN prefix) . . . . **NiB $597 Ex $487 Gd $348**
Model 1936 (CC receiver, w/SN prefix) . . . **NiB $489 Ex $408 Gd $293**
Model 36 (CC receiver, w/SN prefix) . . . . . **NiB $466 Ex $383 Gd $276**
Model 36 (blued receiver, w/SN prefix) . . . **NiB $422 Ex $346 Gd $249**

Marlin Model 39 — ADL

Marlin Model 39AS

MODEL 36 SPORTING CARBINE
Same as M36 carbine except w/6-round, (2/3 magazine) and weighs 6.25 lbs.
**Model 1936 (CC receiver,
w/long tang, w/o SN prefix)** . . . . NiB $829 Ex $675 Gd $469
**Model 1936 (CC receiver,
w/short tang, w/o SN prefix)** . . . . NiB $623 Ex $546 Gd $366
Model 1936 (CC receiver, w/SN prefix) . . . NiB $561 Ex $460 Gd $329
Model 36 (CC receiver, w/SN prefix) . . . . . NiB $510 Ex $418 Gd $299
Model 36 (blued receiver, w/SN prefix) . . . NiB $465 Ex $382 Gd $275

MODEL 36A/36A-DL LEVER-ACTION REPEATING RIFLE
Same as Model 36 Carbine except has 24-inch bbl. w/hooded front
sight and 2/3 magazine holding 6 cartridges. Weight: 6.75 lbs. Note:
An "A" serial number suffix identifies a Rifle while an "A-DL" suffix
designates a Deluxe Model w/checkered stock, semibeavertail fore-
arm, swivels and sling. Made from 1936 to 1948.
**Model 1936 (CC receiver,
w/long tang, w/o SN prefix)** . . . . NiB $1155 Ex $1101 Gd $380
**Model 1936 (CC receiver,
w/short tang, w/o SN prefix)** . . . . NiB $750 Ex $526 Gd $346
Model 1936 (CC receiver, w/SN prefix) . . . NiB $775 Ex $475 Gd $335
Model 36 (CC receiver, w/SN prefix) . . . . . NiB $750 Ex $423 Gd $300
Model 36 (blued receiver, w/SN prefix) . . . NiB $700 Ex $397 Gd $282
For ADL model, add 25%

MODEL 37 SLIDE-ACTION
REPEATING RIFLE . . . . NiB $600 Ex $397 Gd $191
Similar to Model 29 except w/24-inch bbl. and full magazine.
Weight: 5.25 lbs. Made from 1913 to 1916.

MODEL 38 SLIDE-ACTION
REPEATING RIFLE . . . . NiB $700 Ex $389 Gd $296
Hammerless. Takedown. Caliber: .22 LR. Long, Short. 2/3 magazine (tubular) holds 15 Short, 12 Long, 10 LR. 24-inch octagon or round bbls. Weight:
5.5 lbs. Sights: Open rear; bead front. Plain shotgun-type pistol-grip buttstock w/hard rubber buttplate, grooved slide handle. Ivory bead front sight;
adj. rear. About 20,000 Model 38 rifles were made 1920 to 1930.

MODEL 39 CARBINE
. . . . NiB $500 Ex $303 Gd $252
Same as 39M except w/lightweight bbl., 3/4 magazine (capacity: 18 Short,
14 Long, 12 LR), slimmer forearm. Weight: 5.25 lbs. Made 1963 to 1967.

MODEL 39 90TH
ANNIVERSARY CARBINE . . . . NiB $1188 Ex $911 Gd $769
Carbine version of 90th Anniversary Model 39A. 500 made in 1960.
Top value is for carbine in new, unfired condition.

MODEL 39 CENTURY LTD.
. . . . NiB $625 Ex $339 Gd $226
Commemorative version of Model 39A. Receiver inlaid w/brass
medallion, "Marlin Centennial 1870-1970." Square lever. 20-
inch octagon bbl. Fancy walnut straight-grip stock and forearm;
brass forend cap, buttplate, nameplate in buttstock. 35,388
made in 1970.

MODEL 39 LEVER-ACTION
REPEATER . . . . NiB $2975 Ex $1096 Gd $922
Takedown. Casehardened receiver. Caliber: .22 LR. Long, Short.
Tubular magazine holds 25 Short, 20 Long, 18 LR. 24-inch octagon
bbl. Weight: 5.75 lbs. Sights: Open rear; bead front. Plain pistol-grip
stock and forearm. Made from 1922 to 1938.

MODEL 39A
General specifications same as Model 39 except w/blued receiver,
round bbl., heavier stock w/semibeavertail forearm, weight 6.5 lbs.
Made from 1939 to 1960.
Early model (no prefix) . . . . NiB $1455 Ex $1017 Gd $712
Late model ("B" prefix) . . . . NiB $1125 Ex $831 Gd $584

MODEL 39A 90TH
ANNIVERSARY RIFLE . . . . NiB $1196 Ex $1040 Gd $773
Commemorates Marlin's 90th anniversary. Same general specifications as Golden 39A except w/chrome-plated bbl. and action, stock
and forearm of select walnut-finely checkered, carved figure of a
squirrel on right side of buttstock. 500 made in 1960. Top value is
for rifle in new, unfired condition.

MODEL 39A
ARTICLE II RIFLE . . . . NiB $450 Ex $391 Gd $289
Commemorates National Rifle Association Centennial 1871-1971.
"The Right to Bear Arms" medallion inlaid in receiver. Similar to
Model 39A. Magazine capacity: 26 Short, 21 Long, 19 LR. 24-inch
octagon bbl. Fancy walnut pistol-grip stock and forearm; brass
forend cap, buttplate. 6,244 made in 1971.

Marlin Model 56

Marlin Model 57

Marlin Model 60C

Marlin Model 60SS

Marlin Model 62

GOLDEN 39A/39AS RIFLE
Same as Model 39A except w/gold-plated trigger, hooded ramp front sight, sling swivels. Made from 1960-87 (39A); Model 39AS from 1988 to date.
Golden 39A. . . . . **NiB $450 Ex $286 Gd $158**
Golden 39AS (W/hammer block safety) . . **NiB $450 Ex $269 Gd $142**

MODEL 39A "MOUNTIE" LEVER-
ACTION REPEATING RIFLE. . . . . **NiB $450 Ex $338 Gd $209**
Same as Model 39A except w/lighter, straight-grip stock, slimmer forearm. Weight: 6.25 lbs. Made from 1953 to 1960.

MODEL 39A OCTAGON . . . . **NiB $595 Ex $546 Gd $340**
Same as Golden 39A except w/oct. bbl., plain bead front sight, slimmer stock and forearm, no pistol-grip cap or swivels. Made in 1973. (2551 produced).

MODEL 39D . . . . **NiB $395 Ex $214 Gd $158**
Same as Model 39M except w/pistol-grip stock, forearm w/bbl. band. Made from 1970 to 1974.

39M ARTICLE II CARBINE. . . . . . . **NiB $452 Ex $436 Gd $261**
Same as 39A Article II Rifle except w/straight-grip buttstock, square lever, 20-inch octagon bbl., reduced magazine capacity. 3,824 units, made in 1971.

GOLDEN 39M
Calibers: .22 Short, Long and LR. Tubular magazine holds 21 Short, 16 Long or 15 LR cartridges. 20-inch bbl. 36 inches overall. Weight: 6 lbs. Gold-plated trigger. Hooded ramp front sight, adj. folding semi-buckhorn rear. Two-piece, straight-grip American black walnut stock. Sling swivels. Mar-Shield finish. Made from 1960 to 1987.
Model Golden 39M . . . . **NiB $398 Ex $288 Gd $236**
Model 39M
Octagon
(octagonal bbl.
made 1973 only) . . . . **NiB $468 Ex $437 Gd $339**

MODEL 39M
"MOUNTIE" CARBINE
Same as Model 39A "Mountie" Rifle except w/20-inch bbl. Weight: 6 lbs. 500 made in 1960. (For values See Marlin 39 90th Anniversary Carbine)

MODEL 39TDS
CARBINE . . . . **NiB $500 Ex $331 Gd $254**
Same general specifications as Model 39M except takedown style w/16.5-inch bbl. and reduced magazine capacity. 32.63 inches overall. Weight: 5.25 lbs. Made from 1988 to 1995.

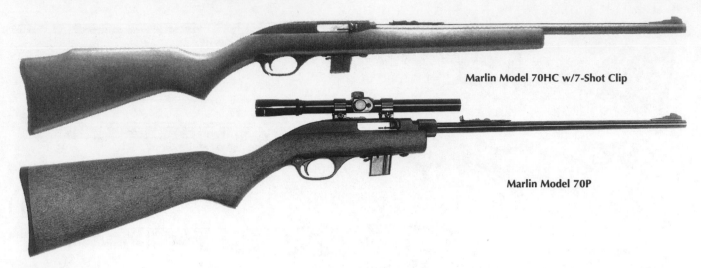

Marlin Model 70HC w/7-Shot Clip

Marlin Model 70P

MODEL 45 . . . . **NiB $345 Ex $259 Gd $156**
Semiautomatic action. Caliber: .45 Auto. Seven round clip.16.5-inch bbl. 35.5 inches overall. Weight: 6.75 lbs. Manual bolt hold-open. Sights: Ramp front sight w/brass bead, adj. folding rear. Receiver drilled and tapped for scope mount. Walnut-finished hardwood stock. Made from 1986 to 1999.

MODEL 49/49DL AUTOLOADING RIFLE
Same as Model 99C except w/two-piece stock, checkered after 1970. Made 1968-71. Model 49DL w/scrollwork on sides of receiver, checkered stock and forearm; made from 1971 to 1978.
Model 49 . . . . **NiB $179 Ex $149 Gd $109**
Model 49DL . . . . **NiB $186 Ex $154 Gd $113**

MODEL 50/50E AUTOLOADING RIFLE
Takedown. Cal: .22 LR. Six round detachable box mag. 22 inch bbl. Wt: 6 lbs. Sights: Open rear; bead front; Mdl. 50E w/peep rear sight, hooded front. Plain pistol-grip stock, forearm w/finger grooves. Made from 1931 to 1934.
Model 50 . . . . **NiB $195 Ex $154 Gd $103**
Model 50E . . . . **NiB $205 Ex $154 Gd $107**

MODEL 56 LEVERMATIC RIFLE . . . **NiB $300 Ex $225 Gd $132**
Same as Model 57 except clip-loading. Magazine holds eight rounds. Weight: 5.75 lbs. Made from 1955 to 1964.

MODEL 57 LEVERMATIC RIFLE . . . **NiB $375 Ex $225 Gd $132**
Lever-action. Cal: .22 LR. 22 Long, 22 Short. Tubular mag. holds 19 LR, 21 Long, 27 Short. 22 inch bbl. Wt: 6.25 lbs. Sights: Open rear, adj. for windage and elevation; hooded ramp front. Monte Carlo-style stock w/pistol-grip. Made from 1959 to 1965.

MODEL 57M LEVERMATIC . . . . **NiB $399 Ex $216 Gd $133**
Same as Model 57 except chambered for 22 WMR cartridge, w/24-inch bbl., 15-round magazine. Made from 1960 to 1969.

MODEL 60 SEMIAUTOMATIC RIFLE . . . . . . **NiB $156 Ex $100 Gd $74**
Caliber: .22 LR. 14-round tubular magazine. 22-inch bbl. 40.5 inches overall. Weight: 5.5 lbs. Grooved receiver. Ramp front sight w/removable hood; adj. open rear. Anodized receiver w/blued bbl. Monte Carlo-style walnut-finished hardwood stock w/Mar-Shield finish. Made 1981 to date. Note: Marketed 1960 to 1980 under Glenfield promotion logo and w/slightly different stock configuration.

MODEL 60C SELF-LOADING RIFLE . . . . . . **NiB $170 Ex $121 Gd $95**
Caliber: .22 LR. 14- round tubular mag. 22 inch Micro-Groove bbl., 40.5 inch overall. Wt: 5.5 lbs. Screw-adjustable open rear and ramp front sights. Aluminum receiver, grooved for scope mount. Hardwood Monte Carlo stock w/Mossy Oak "Break-Up" camouflage pattern. Made from 2000 to date.

MODEL 60SS
SEMIAUTOMATIC RIFLE
Same general specifications as Model 60 except w/stainless bbl. and magazine tube. Synthetic, uncheckered birch or laminated black/gray birch stock w/nickel-plated swivel studs. Made from 1993 to date.
Model 60SB w/uncheckered
birch stock . . . . **NiB $245 Ex $181 Gd $120**
Model 60SS w/laminated
birch stock . . . . **NiB $243 Ex $181 Gd $120**
Model 60SSK w/fiberglass stock . . . . **NiB $233 Ex $181 Gd $120**

MODEL 62
LEVERMATIC RIFLE . . . . **NiB $500 Ex $392 Gd $264**
Lever-action. Calibers: .256 Magnum, .30 Carbine. Four round clip magazine. 23-inch bbl. Weight: 7 lbs. Sights: Open rear; hooded ramp front. Monte Carlo-style stock w/pistol-grip, swivels and sling. Made in .256 Magnum 1963 to 1966; in .30 Carbine 1963 to 1969.

MODEL 65 BOLT-ACTION
SINGLE-SHOT RIFLE . . . . **NiB $115 Ex $683 Gd $61**
Takedown. Caliber: .22 LR. Long, Short. 24-inch bbl. Weight: 5 lbs. Sights: Open rear; bead front. Plain pistol-grip stock w/grooved forearm. Made 1932-38. Model 65E is same as Model 65 except w/rear peep sight and hooded front sight.

MODEL 70HC SEMIAUTOMATIC
Caliber: .22 LR. Seven and 15-round magazine. 18-inch bbl. Weight: 5.5 lbs. 36.75 inches overall. Ramp front sight; adj. open rear. Grooved receiver for scope mounts. Walnut-finished hardwood stock w/Monte Carlo and pistol-grip. Made from 1988 to 1996.
Marlin model . . . . **NiB $171 Ex $146 Gd $119**
Glenfield model . . . . **NiB $125 Ex $104 Gd $73**

MODEL 70P
SEMIAUTOMATIC . . . . **NiB $176 Ex $151 Gd $94**
"Papoose" takedown. Caliber: .22 LR. Seven round clip. 16.25-inch bbl. 35.25 inches overall. Weight: 3.75 lbs. Sights: Ramp front, adj. open rear. Side ejection, manual bolt hold-open. Cross-bolt safety. Walnut-finished hard-wood stock w/abbreviated forend, pistol-grip. Made 1984 to 1994.

MODEL 70PSS
SELF-LOADING CARBINE . . . . **NiB $245 Ex $151 Gd $99**
"Papoose" takedown carbine. Caliber: .22 LR. Seven round clip. 16.25- inch bbl., 35.25 inches overall. Weight: 3.25 lbs. Ramp front and adjustable open rear sights. Automatic last-shot hold open (1996). Black fiberglass synthetic stock. Made from 1995 to date.

Marlin Model 75C

Marlin Model 80C

Marlin Model 80DL

RIFLES

Marlin Model 81DL

MODEL 75C
SEMIAUTOMATIC . . . . **NiB $176 Ex $125 Gd $99**
Caliber: .22 LR. 13-round tubular magazine.18-inch bbl. 36.5 inches overall. Weight: 5 lbs. Side ejection. Cross-bolt safety. Sights: Ramp-mounted blade front; adj. open rear. Monte Carlo-style walnut-finished hardwood stock w/pistol-grip. Made 1975 to 1992.

MODEL 80 BOLT-ACTION REPEATING RIFLE
Takedown. Caliber: .22 LR. Long, Short. Eight round detachable box magazine. 24-inch bbl. Weight: 6 lbs. Sights: Open rear; bead front. Plain pistol-grip stock. Made from 1934 to 1939. Model 80E, w/peep rear sight; hooded front, made from 1934 to 1940.
Model 80 Standard . . . . **NiB $146 Ex $115 Gd $84**
Model 80E . . . . **NiB $135 Ex $99 Gd $79**

MODEL 80C/80DL
BOLT-ACTION REPEATER
Improved version of Model 80. Model 80C w/bead from sight, semi-beavertail forearm; made 1940-70. Model 80DL w/peep rear sight; hooded blade front sight on ramp, swivels; made 1940 to 1965.
Model 80C. . . . . **NiB $146 Ex $115 Gd $84**
Model 80DL . . . . **NiB $120 Ex $99 Gd $84**

MODEL 81/81E BOLT-ACTION REPEATER
Takedown. .22 LR. Long, Short. Tubular magazine holds 24 Short, 20 Long, 18 LR. 24-inch bbl. Weight: 6.25 lbs. Sights: Open rear, bead front. Plain pistol-grip stock. Made from 1937 to 1940. Model 81E w/peep rear sight; hooded front w/ramp.
Model 81 . . . . **NiB $156 Ex $153 Gd $84**
Model 81E . . . . **NiB $176 Ex $125 Gd $115**

MODEL 81C/81DL BOLT-ACTION REPEATER
Improved version of Model 81 w/same general specifications. Model 81C w/bead front sight, semibeavertail forearm; made 1940 to 1970. Model 81 DL w/peep rear sight, hooded front, swivels; disc. 1965.
Model 81C. . . . . **NiB $176 Ex $151 Gd $84**
Model 81DL . . . . **NiB $192 Ex $156 Gd $99**

MODEL 88-C/88-DL AUTOLOADING
Takedown. Caliber: .22 LR. Tubular magazine in buttstock holds 14 cartridges. 24-inch bbl. Weight: 6.75 lbs. Sights: Open rear; hooded front. Plain pistol-grip stock. Made from 1947-56. Model 88-DL w/received peep sight, checkered stock and sling swivels, made 1953 to 1956.
Model 88-C. . . . . **NiB $150 Ex $106 Gd $75**
Model 88-DL . . . . **NiB $150 Ex $107 Gd $70**

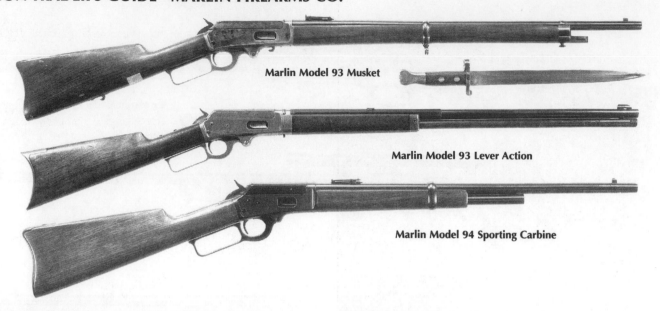

Marlin Model 93 Musket

Marlin Model 93 Lever Action

Marlin Model 94 Sporting Carbine

MODEL 89-C/89-DL AUTOLOADING RIFLE

Clip magazine version of Model 88-C. Seven round clip (12-round in later models); other specifications same. Made from 1950 to 1961. Model 89-DL w/receiver peep sight, sling swivels.
Model 89-C . . . . **NiB $154 Ex $108 Gd $80**
Model 89-DL . . . . **NiB $159 Ex $108 Gd $80**

MODEL 92 LEVER-ACTION REPEATING RIFLE

Calibers: .22 Short, Long, LR. .32 Short, Long (rimfire or centerfire by changing firing pin). Tubular magazines holding 25 Short, 20 Long, 18 LR (.22); or 17 Short, 14 Long (.32); 16-inch bbl. model w/shorter magazine holding 15 Short, 12 Long, 10 LR. Bbl. lengths: 16 (.22 cal. only) 24, 26, 28 inches. Weight: 5.5 lbs. w/24-inch bbl. Sights: open rear; blade front. Plain straight-grip stock and forearm. Made 1892 to 1916. Note: Originally designated "Model 1892."
Model 92 (.22 caliber) . . . . **NiB $1527 Ex $1360 Gd $742**
Model 92 (.32 caliber) . . . . **NiB $1501 Ex $1202 Gd $872**

MODEL 93/93SC CARBINE

Same as Standard Model 93 Rifle except in calibers .30-30 and .32 Special only. Model 93 w/7-round magazine. 20-inch round bbl., carbine sights, weight: 6.75 lbs. Model 93SC magazine capacity 5 rounds, weight 6.5 lbs.
Model 93 Carbine
(w/saddle ring) . . . . **NiB $1615 Ex $1357 Gd $1074**
Model 93 Carbine ("Bullseye"
w/o saddle ring) . . . . **NiB $1395 Ex $982 Gd $631**
Model 93SC Sporting Carbine . . . . **NiB $1321 Ex $1012 Gd $875**

MODEL 93
LEVER-ACTION
REPEATING RIFLE . . . . **NiB $2768 Ex $1956 Gd $1333**
Solid frame or takedown. Calibers: .25-36 Marlin, .30-30, .32 Special, .32-40, .38-55. Tubular magazine holds 10 cartridges. 26-inch round or octagon bbl. standard; also made w/28-, 30- and 32-inch bbls. Weight: 7.25 lbs. Sights: Open rear; bead front. Plain straight-grip stock and forearm. Made from 1893 to 1936. Note: Before 1915 designated "Model 1893."

MODEL 93 MUSKET . . . . **NiB $5558 Ex $3718 Gd $2779**
Same as Standard Model 93 except w/30-inch bbl., angular bayonet, ramrod under bbl., musket stock, full-length military-style forearm. Weight: 8 lbs. Made from 1893 to 1915.

MODEL 94 LEVER-ACTION
REPEATING RIFLE . . . . **NiB $2550 Ex $1765 Gd $936**
Solid frame or takedown. Calibers: .25-20, .32-20, .38-40, .44-40. 10-round tubular magazine. 24-inch round or octagon bbl. Weight: 7 lbs. Sights open rear; bead front. Plain straight-grip stock and forearm (also available w/pistol-grip stock). Made from 1894 to 1934. Note: Before 1906 designated "Model 1894."

MODEL 94 LEVER-ACTION COWBOY SERIES

Calibers: .357 Mag., .44-40, .44 Mag., .45 LC. 10-round magazine. 24-inch tapered octagon bbl. Weight: 7.5 lbs. 41.5 inches overall. Marble carbine front sight, adjustable semi-buckhorn rear. Blue finish. Checkered, straight-grip American black walnut stock w/hard rubber buttplate. Made from 1996 to date. Cowboy II introduced in 1997.
Cowboy model (.45 LC) . . . . **NiB $760 Ex $600 Gd $433**
Cowboy II model (.357 Mag.,
.44-40, .44 Mag) . . . . **NiB $800 Ex $621 Gd $493**

MODEL 97 LEVER-ACTION
REPEATING RIFLE . . . . **NiB $2514 Ex $20 b30 Gd $1244**
Takedown. Caliber: .22 LR. Long, Short. Tubular magazine; full length holds 25 Short, 20 Long, 18 LR; half length holds 16 Short, 12 Long and 10 LR. Bbl. lengths: 16, 24, 26, 28 inches. Weight: 6 lbs. Sights: Open rear; bead front. Plain, straight-grip stock and forearm (also avail. w/pistol-grip stock). Made from 1897 to 1922. Note: Before 1905 designated "Model 1897."

MODEL 98 AUTOLOADING RIFLE . . . . **NiB $174 Ex $118 Gd $97**
Solid frame. Caliber: .22 LR. Tubular magazine holds 15 cartridges. 22-inch bbl. Weight: 6.75 lbs. Sights: Open rear; hooded ramp front. Monte Carlo stock w/cheekpiece. Made from 1950 to 1961.

MODEL 99 AUTOLOADING RIFLE . . . . **NiB $174 Ex $118 Gd $97**
Caliber: .22 LR. Tubular magazine holds 18 cartridges. 22-inch bbl. Weight: 5.5 lbs. Sights: Open rear; hooded ramp front. Plain pistol-grip stock. Made from 1959 to 1961.

MODEL 99C . . . . **NiB $187 Ex $151 Gd $104**
Same as Model 99 except w/gold-plated trigger, receiver grooved for tip-off scope mounts, Monte Carlo stock (checkered in later production). Made from 1962 to 1978.

MODEL 99DL . . . . **NiB $230 Ex $205 Gd $122**
Same as Model 99 except w/gold-plated trigger, jeweled breech bolt, Monte Carlo stock w/pistol-grip, swivels and sling. Made 1960 to 1965.

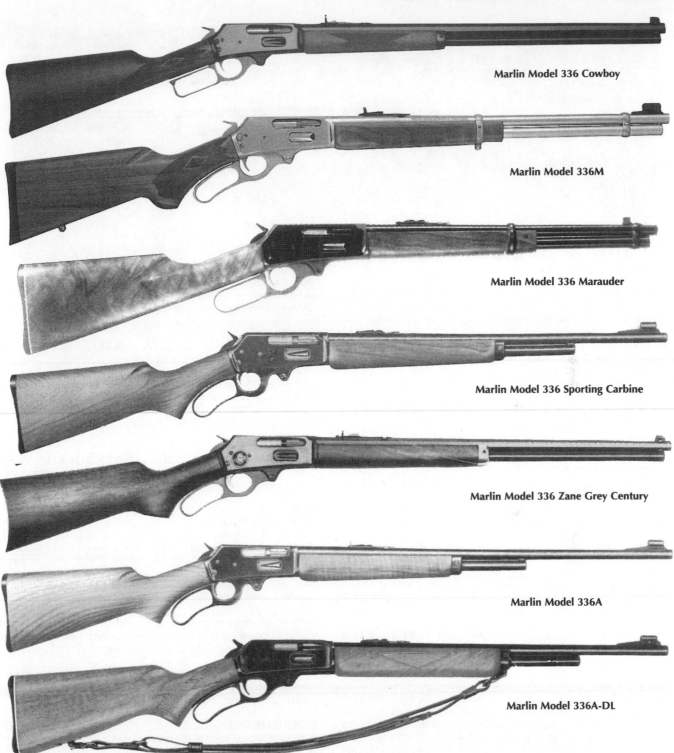

Marlin Model 336 Cowboy

Marlin Model 336M

Marlin Model 336 Marauder

Marlin Model 336 Sporting Carbine

Marlin Model 336 Zane Grey Century

Marlin Model 336A

Marlin Model 336A-DL

MODEL 100 BOLT-ACTION
SINGLE-SHOT RIFLE . . . . **NiB $150 Ex $90 Gd $75**
Takedown. Caliber: .22 LR, Long, Short. 24-inch bbl. Weight: 4.5 lbs. Sights: Open rear; bead front. Plain pistol-grip stock. Made 1936 to 1960.

MODEL 100SB . . . . **NiB $95 Ex $88 Gd $45**
Same as Model 100 except smoothbore for use w/22 shot car-

tridges, shotgun sight. Made from 1936 to 1941.

MODEL 99M1 CARBINE . . . . **NiB $150 Ex $93 Gd $75**
Same as Model 99C except styled after U.S. .30 M1 Carbine; 9-round tubular magazine, 18-inch bbl. Sights: Open rear; military-style ramp front; carbine stock w/handguard and bbl. band, sling swivels. Weight: 4.5 lbs. Made 1966 to 1979.

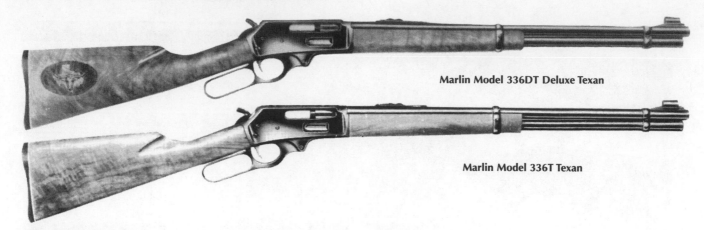

Marlin Model 336DT Deluxe Texan

Marlin Model 336T Texan

MODEL 100 TOM MIX SPECIAL........ **NiB $275 Ex $195 Gd $140**
Same as Model 100 except w/peep rear sight; hooded front; sling. Made from 1936 to 1946.

MODEL 101 .... **NiB $85 Ex $66 Gd $50**
Improved version of Model 100 w/same general specifications, except w/stock w/beavertail forearm, weighs 5 lbs. Intro. 1951. Disc.

MODEL 101 DL................. **NiB $100 Ex $81 Gd $65**
Same as Model 101 except has peep rear sight; hooded front, swivels. Disc.

MODEL 122 SINGLE-SHOT
JUNIOR TARGET RIFLE............. **NiB $96 Ex $70 Gd $55**
Bolt action. Caliber: .22 LR, .22 Long, .22 Short. 22-inch bbl. Weight: 5 lbs. Sights: Open rear; hooded ramp front. Monte Carlo stock w/pistol-grip, swivels, sling. Made from 1961 to 1965.

MODEL 322 BOLT-ACTION
VARMINT RIFLE .... **NiB $550 Ex $351 Gd $240**
Sako short Mauser action. Caliber: .222 Rem. Three round clip magazine. 24-inch medium weight bbl. Checkered stock. Sights: Two-position peep rear; hooded ramp front. Weight: 7.5 lbs. Made from 1954-57.

MODEL 336A
LEVER-ACTION RIFLE .... **NiB $500 Ex $350 Gd $293**
Improved version of Model 36A Rifle w/same general specifications except w/improved action w/round breech bolt. Calibers: .30-30, .32 Special (disc. 1963), .35 Rem. (intro. 1952). Made from 1948-63; reintroduced 1973, disc. 1980.

MODEL 336A-DL .... **NiB $625 Ex $495 Gd $316**
Same as Model 336A Rifle except w/deluxe checkered stock and forearm, swivels and sling. Made from 1948-63.

MODEL 336AS
LEVER-ACTION RIFLE .... **NiB $475 Ex $291 Gd $139**
Similar to Model 30AS. Caliber: .30-30 Win., Six round tubular magazine. 20- inch Micro-Groove bbl. 38.25 inches overall. Weight: 7 lbs. Maine birch pistol grip stock w/swivel studs and hard rubber butt plate. Tapped for scope mount and receiver sight. Screw-adjustable open rear and ramp front sight. Checkered walnut finish. Made from 1999 to date.

MODEL 336C
LEVER-ACTION CARBINE .... **NiB $495 Ex $353 Gd $278**
Improved version of Model 36 Carbine w/same general specifications except w/improved action w/round breech bolt. Original calibers: .30-30 and .32 Win. Spec. Made from 1948-83. Note: Caliber .35 Rem. intro. 1953. Caliber .32 Winchester Special disc. 1963.

MODEL 336 COWBOY
LEVER-ACTION RIFLE .... **NiB $550 Ex $409 Gd $320**
Calibers: .30-30 Win., or .38-55 Win., 6- round tubular magazine. 24- inch tapered octagon bbl. 42.5 inches overall. Weight: 7.5 lbs. American black walnut checkering stock. Marble carbine front sight w/solid top receiver drilled and tapped for scope mount. Mar-Shield finish. Made from 1998 to date.

MODEL 336CS
W/SCOPE .... **NiB $435 Ex $282 Gd $184**
Lever-action w/hammer block safety. Caliber: .30/30 Win. or .35 Rem. Six round tubular magazine. 20-inch round bbl. w/Micro-Groove rifling. 38.5 inches overall. Weight: 7 lbs. Ramp front sight w/hood, adj. semi-buckhorn folding rear. Solid top receiver drilled and tapped for scope mount or receiver sight; offset hammer spur for scope use. American black walnut stock w/pistol-grip, fluted comb. Mar-Shield finish. Made from 1984 to date.

MODEL 336DT
DELUXE TEXAN................ **NiB $450 Ex $437 Gd $339**
Same as Model 336T except w/select walnut stock and forearm, hand-carved longhorn steer and map of Texas on buttstock. Made 1962 to 1964.

MODEL 336M
LEVER-ACTION RIFLE .... **NiB $550 Ex $447 Gd $318**
Calibers: .30-30 Win., 6- round tubular magazine. 20- inch stainless steel Micro Groove bbl., 38.5 inches overall. Weight: 7 lbs. American black walnut w/checkered pistol-grip stock. Adjustable folding semi-buckhorn rear and ramp front sight w/brass bead and removable Wide-Scan hood. Tapped for receiver sight and scope mount. Mar-Shield finish. Made from 1999 to date.

MODEL 336 MARAUDER .... **NiB $550 Ex $447 Gd $261**
Same as Model 336 Texan Carbine except w/16.25-inch bbl., weight: 6.25 lbs. Made from 1963 to 1964.

MODEL 336-MICRO GROOVE ZIPPER ... **NiB $800 Ex $598 Gd $339**
General specifications same as Model 336 Sporting Carbine except caliber .219 Zipper. Made from 1955 to 1961.

MODEL 336 OCTAGON .... **NiB $500 Ex $483 Gd $220**
Same as Model 336T except chambered for .30-30 only w/22-inch octagon bbl. Made in 1973.

MODEL 336 SPORTING CARBINE....... **NiB $800 Ex $541 Gd $386**
Same as Model 336A rifle except w/20-inch bbl., weight: 6.25 lbs. Made from 1948 to 1963.

MODEL 336T TEXAN CARBINE .... **NiB $324 Ex $233 Gd $207**
Same as Model 336 Carbine except w/straight-grip stock and is not available in caliber .32 Special. Made 1953-83. Caliber .44 Magnum made 1963 to 1967.

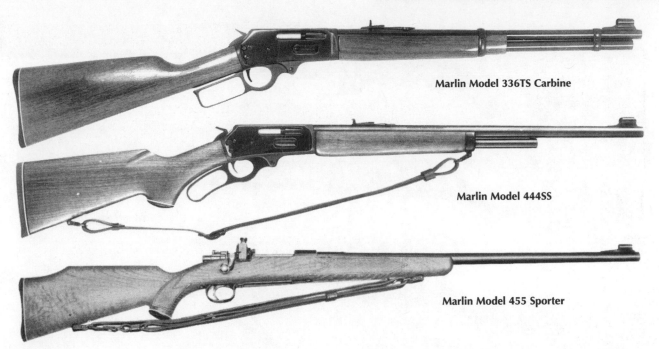

Marlin Model 336TS Carbine

Marlin Model 444SS

Marlin Model 455 Sporter

MODEL 336TS. . . . . **NiB $363 Ex $311 Gd $157**
Lever-action w/hammer-block safety. Caliber: .30-30 Win. Six round tubular magazine. 18.5-inch Micro-Groove bbl. 37 inches overall. Weight: 6.5 lbs. Ramp front sight, adj. semi-buckhorn folding rear. Straight-grip American black walnut stock. Made 1983 to 1987.

**MODEL 336 ZANE
GREY CENTURY** . . . . **NiB $453 Ex $390 Gd $262**
Similar to Model 336A except w/22-inch octagonal bbl., caliber .30-30, Zane Grey Centennial 1872-1972 medallion inlaid in receiver; select walnut stock w/classic pistol-grip and forearm; brass buttplate, forend cap. Weight: 7 lbs. 10,000 produced (numbered ZG1 through ZG10,000). Made in 1972.

**MODEL 444 LEVER-ACTION
REPEATING RIFLE** . . . . **NiB $430 Ex $365 Gd $184**
Action similar to Model 336. Caliber: .444 Marlin. Four round tubular magazine. 24-inch bbl. Weigh: 7.5 lbs. Sights: Open rear; hooded ramp front. Monte Carlo stock w/straight grip, recoil pad. Carbine-style forearm w/bbl. band. Swivels, sling. Made from 1965 to 1971.

MARLIN MODEL 444 SPORTER . . . . **NiB $525 Ex $390 Gd $195**
Same as Model 444 Rifle except w/22-inch bbl., pistol-grip stock and forearm as on Model 336A, recoil pad, QD swivels and sling. Made from 1972 to 1983.

**MODEL 444P (OUTFITTER)
LEVER-ACTION RIFLE** . . . . **NiB $495 Ex $390 Gd $210**
Caliber: .444 Marlin. Five round tubular magazine. 18.5-inch ported bbl., 37 inches overall. Weight: 6.75 lbs. Ramp front and adjustable folding rear sights. Black walnut straight grip stock w/cut checkering and Mar-Shield finish. Made from 1999 to 2002.

MODEL 444SS. . . . . **NiB $525 Ex $390 Gd $210**
Same general specifications as Model 444 except w/hammer safety. Made from 1984-2002. (Changed to M444 in 2001.)

MODEL 455 BOLT-ACTION SPORTER
FN Mauser action w/Sako trigger. Calibers: .30-06 or .308. Five round box magazine. 24-inch medium weight stainless-steel bbl. Monte Carlo stock w/cheekpiece, checkered pistol grip and forearm. Lyman No. 48 receiver sight; hooded ramp front. Weight: 8.5 lbs. Made from 1957 to 1959.
**Model 455 (chambered for .30-06,
1079 produced)** . . . . **NiB $657 Ex $479 Gd $273**
Model 455 (chambered for .308, 59 produced) . . . . **NiB $757 Ex $499 Gd $373**

MODEL 780 BOLT-ACTION REPEATER SERIES
Caliber: .22 LR. Long, Short. Seven round clip magazine. 22-inch bbl. Weight: 5.5 to 6 lbs. Sights: Open rear; hooded ramp front. Receiver grooved for scope mounting. Monte Carlo stock w/checkered pistol-grip and forearm. Made from 1971 to 1988.
Model 780 Standard . . . . **NiB $116 Ex $95 Gd $80**
Model 781 (w/17-round tubular magazine) . . **NiB $116 Ex $95 Gd $80**
Model 782 (.22 WMR, w/swivels, sling) . . . **NiB $116 Ex $95 Gd $80**
Model 783 (w/12-round tubular magazine) . . **NiB $116 Ex $95 Gd $80**

MODEL 795 SELF-LOADING RIFLE . . . . . . **NiB $135 Ex $126 Gd $105**
Caliber: .22 LR. 10- round clip. 18- inch Micro-Groove bbl., 37 inches overall. Weight: 5 lbs. Screw-adjustable open rear and ramp front sight. Monte Carlo synthetic stock with checkering swivel studs. Made from 1999 to date.

MODEL 880 BOLT-ACTION REPEATER SERIES
Caliber: .22 rimfire. Seven round magazine. 22-inch bbl. 41 inches overall. Weight: 5.5 to 6 lbs. Hooded ramp front sight; adj. folding rear. Grooved receiver for scope mounts. Checkered Monte Carlo-style walnut stock w/QD studs and rubber recoil pad. Made from 1989 to 1997.
Model 880 (.22 LR) . . . . **NiB $185 Ex $162 Gd $105**
Model 880SS (Stainless .22 LR) . . . . **NiB $240 Ex $192 Gd $140**
Model 880SQ (Squirrel .22 LR) . . . . **NiB $247 Ex $203 Gd $147**
Model 881 (w/7-round tubular magazine) **NiB $218 Ex $167 Gd $105**
Model 882 (.22 WMR) . . . . **NiB $208 Ex $172 Gd $126**
Model 882L (w/laminated hardwood stock) . . . .**NiB $240 Ex $167 Gd $105**
Model 882SS (Stainless w/fire sights) . . . . . **NiB $254 Ex $208 Gd $151**
Model 882SSV (Stainless .22 LR) . . . . **NiB $251 Ex $208 Gd $151**
**Model 883 (.22 WMR w/12-
round tubular magazine)** . . . . **NiB $213 Ex $162 Gd $105**
Model 883N (w/nickel-Teflon finish) . . . . . **NiB $250 Ex $206 Gd $154**
Model 883SS (stainless w/laminated stock) . . . .**NiB $269 Ex $188 Gd $166**

Marlin Model 780

Marlin Model 781

Marlin Model 783

Marlin Model 882L

Marlin Model 883N

MODEL 922 MAGNUM
SELF-LOADING RIFLE...........**NiB $360 Ex $213 Gd $132**
Similar to Model 9 except chambered for .22 WMR. Seven round magazine. 20.5-inch bbl. 39.5 inches overall. Weight: 6.5 lbs. American black walnut stock w/Monte Carlo. Blued finish. Made from 1993 to 2001.

MODEL 980 .22 MAGNUM ......**NiB $250 Ex $137 Gd $101**
Bolt action. Caliber: .22 WMR. Eight round clip magazine. 24-inch bbl. Weight: 6 lbs. Sights: Open rear; hooded ramp front. Monte Carlo stock, swivels, sling. Made from 1962 to 1970.

MODEL 989 AUTOLOADING RIFLE......**NiB $168 Ex $122 Gd $96**
Caliber: .22 LR. Seven round clip magazine. 22-inch bbl. Weight: 5.5 lbs. Sights: Open rear; hooded ramp front. Monte Carlo walnut stock w/pistol grip. Made from 1962 to 1966.

MODEL 989M2
CARBINE.....................**NiB $225 Ex $117 Gd $92**
Same as Model 99M1 except clip-loading, 7-round magazine. Made from 1966- to 199.

MODEL 990
SEMIAUTOMATIC
Caliber: .22 LR. 17-round tubular magazine. 22-inch bbl. 40.75 inches overall. Weight: 5.5 lbs. Side ejection. Cross-bolt safety. Ramp front sight w/brass bead; adj. semi-buckhorn folding rear. Receiver grooved for scope mount. Monte Carlo-style American black walnut stock w/checkered pistol grip and forend. Made from 1979 to 1987.
Model 990 Semiautomatic ....**NiB $115 Ex $97 Gd $76**
Model 990L (w/14 rounds,
laminated hardwood stock, QD studs,
black recoil pad; 1992 to date)............**NiB $53 Ex $122 Gd $96**

Marlin Model 980

Marlin Model 989

Marlin Model 989M2

Marlin Model 990

Marlin Model 990L

Marlin Model 995

MODEL 995 SEMIAUTOMATIC . . . . NiB $159 Ex $128 Gd $91
Caliber: .22 LR. Seven round clip magazine.18-inch bbl. 36.75 inches overall. Weight: 5 lbs. Cross-bolt safety. Sights: Ramp front w/brass bead; adj. folding semi-buckhorn rear. Monte Carlo-style American black walnut stock w/checkered pistol grip and forend. Made from 1979 to 1994.

MODEL 1870-1970
CENTENNIAL MATCHED
PAIR, MODELS 336 AND 39 . . . . NiB $2115 Ex $1680 Gd $1114
Presentation-grade rifles in luggage-style case. Matching serial numbers. Fancy walnut straight-grip buttstock and forearm brass buttplate and forend cap. Engraved receiver w/inlaid medallion; square lever. 20-inch octagon bbl. Model 336: .30-30, 7-round

capacity; weight: 7 lbs. Model 39: .22 Short, Long, LR, tubular magazine holds 21 Short, 16 Long, 15 LR. 1,000 sets produced. Made in 1970. Top value is for rifles in new, unfired condition. See illustration on page 284.

MODEL 1892 LEVER-ACTION RIFLE
See Marlin Model 92 listed previously under this section.

MODEL 1893 LEVER-ACTION RIFLE
See Marlin Model 93 listed previously under this section.

MODEL 1894 LEVER-ACTION RIFLE
See Marlin Model 94 Lever-Action Rifle listed previously under this section.

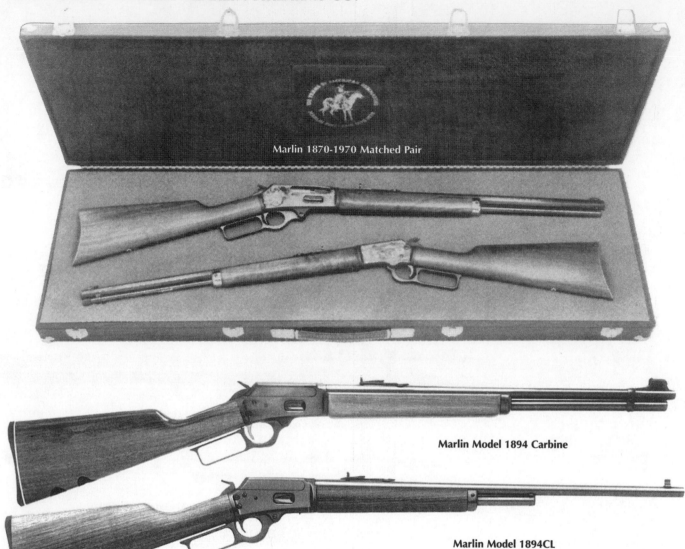

Marlin 1870-1970 Matched Pair

Marlin Model 1894 Carbine

Marlin Model 1894CL

MODEL 1894 CARBINE

Replica of original Model 94. Caliber: .44 Rem. 10-round magazine. 20-inch round bbl. Weight: 6 lbs. Sight: Open rear; ramp front. Straight-grip stock. Made from 1969 to 1984.

Standard Model

1894 Carbine . . . . **NiB $375 Ex $290 Gd $213**

Model 1894 Octagon

(made 1973) . . . . **NiB $475 Ex $368 Gd $218**

Model 1894 Sporter (w/22-inch bbl.,

made 1973) . . . . **NiB $500 Ex $290 Gd $265**

MODEL 1894CL

CLASSIC . . . . **NiB $688 Ex $470 Gd $325**

Calibers: .218 Bee, .25-20 Win., .32-20 Win. Six round tubular magazine. 22-inch bbl. 38.75 inches overall. Weight: 6.25 lbs. Adj. semibuckhorn folding rear sight, brass bead front. Receiver tapped for scope mounts. Straight-grip American black walnut stock w/Mar-Shield finish. Made from 1988 to 1994.

MODEL 1894CS LEVER-ACTION . . . . NiB $700 Ex $495 Gd $289

Caliber: .357 Magnum, .38 Special. Nine round tubular magazine. 18.5-inch bbl. 36 inches overall. Weight: 6 lbs. Side ejection. Hammer block safety. Square finger lever. Bead front sight, adj. semi-buckhorn folding rear. Offset hammer spur for scope use. Two-piece straight grip American black walnut stock w/white buttplate spacer. Mar-Shield finish. Made from 1984 to 2002.

MODEL 1894M LEVER-ACTION . . . . NiB $450 Ex $391 Gd $188

Caliber: .22 WMR.11-round tubular magazine. 20-inch bbl. Weight: 6.25 lbs. Sights: Ramp front w/brass bead and Wide-Scan hood; adj. semi-buckhorn folding rear. Offset hammer spur for scope use. Straight-grip American black walnut stock w/white buttplate spacer. Squared finger lever. Made from 1986 to 1988.

MODEL 1894S LEVER-ACTION . . . . NiB $450 Ex $317 Gd $214

Calibers: .41 Mag., .44 Rem. Mag., .44 S&W Special, .45 Colt.10-shot tubular magazine. 20-inch bbl.37.5 inches overall. Weight: 6 lbs. Sights and stock same as Model 1894M. Made 1984 to 2002.

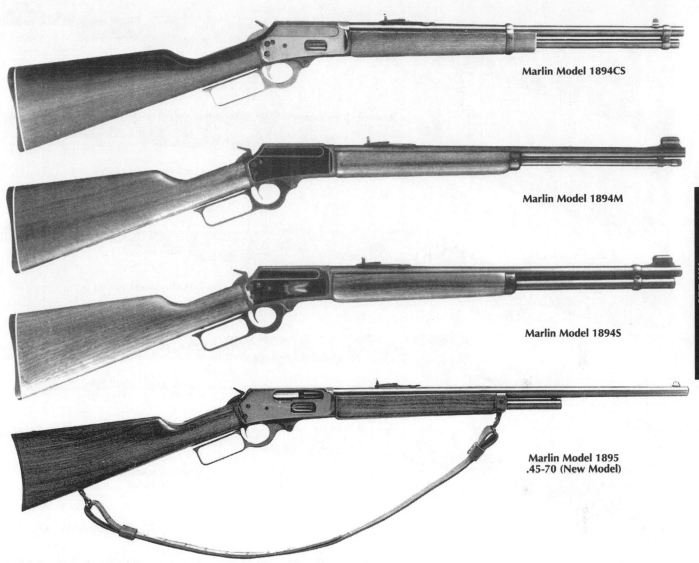

Marlin Model 1894CS

Marlin Model 1894M

Marlin Model 1894S

Marlin Model 1895
.45-70 (New Model)

MODEL 1895 .45-70 REPEATER . . . NiB $398 Ex $349 Gd $194
Model 336-type action. Caliber: .45-70 Government. Four round magazine. 22-inch bbl. Weight: 7 lbs. Sights: Open rear; bead front. Straight-grip stock, forearm w/metal end cap, QD swivels, leather sling. Made 1972 to 1979.

MODEL 1895
LEVER-ACTION REPEATER . . . . NiB $399 Ex $318 Gd $246
Solid frame or takedown. Calibers: .33 WCF, .38-56, .40-65, .40-70, .40-82, .45-70. Nine round tubular magazine. 24-inch round or octagongon bbl. standard (other lengths available). Weight: 8 lbs. Sights: Open rear; bead front. Plain stock and forearm (also available w/pistol-grip stock). Made 1895 to 1915.

MODEL 1895G (GUIDE GUN)
LEVER-ACTION RIFLE . . . . NiB $550 Ex $353 Gd $256
Caliber: .45-70 Govt., 4- round magazine. 18.5-inch ported bbl., 37 inches overall. Weight: 6.75 lbs. Ramp front and adjustable folding rear sights. Black walnut straight grip stock w/cut checkering and Mar-Shield finish. 2,500 made starting in 1998.

MODEL 1895M
LEVER-ACTION RIFLE . . . . NiB $395 Ex $259 Gd $119
Caliber: .450 Marlin. Four round tubular magazine., 18.5- inch ported bbl. w/Ballard-type rifling. 37 inches overall. Weight: 6.75 lbs. Genuine American black walnut straight-grip stock w/checkering. Ventilated recoil pad. Adjustable folding semi-buckhorn rear and ramp front sights. Mar-Shield finish. Made 2000 to date.

MODEL 1895SS
LEVER-ACTION . . . . NiB $550 Ex $397 Gd $290
Caliber: .45-70 Govt. Four round tubular magazine. 22-inch bbl. w/Micro-Groove rifling. 40.5 inches overall. Weight: 7.5 lbs. Ramp front sight w/brass bead and Wide-Scan hood; adj. semi-buckhorn folding rear. Solid top receiver tapped for scope mount or receiver sight. Off-set hammer spur for scope use. Two-piece American black walnut stock w/fluted comb, pistol-grip, sling swivels. Made 1984 to date. (Changed to M1895 in 2001.)

MODEL 1897 LEVER-ACTION RIFLE
See Marlin Model 97 listed previously under this section.

Marlin Model 1895G

Marlin Model 1895M

Marlin Model 1895SS

Marlin Model 1895 Rifle
(Old Model — 1895-1915)

Marlin Model 1897
Cowboy

MODEL 1897 COWBOY
LEVER-ACTION RIFLE . . . . **NiB $575 Ex $455 Gd $323**
Caliber: .22 LR., capacity: 19 LR, 21 L, or 26 S, tubular magazine. 24-inch tapered octagon bbl., 40 inches overall. Weight: 6.5 lbs. Marble front and adjustable rear sight, tapped for scope mount. Black walnut straight grip stock w/cut checkering and Mar-Shield finish. Made from 1999 to 2001.

MODEL 1936 LEVER-ACTION CARBINE
See Marlin Model 36 listed previously under this section.

MODEL 2000 TARGET RIFLE
Bolt-action single-shot. Caliber: .22 LR. Optional 5-round adapter kit available. 22-inch bbl. 41 inches overall. Weight: 8 lbs. Globe front sight, adj. peep or aperture rear. two-stage target trigger. Textured composite Kevlar or black/gray laminated stock. Made from 1991 to 1995.
Model 2000 (disc. 1995) . . . . **NiB $550 Ex $455 Gd $295**
Model 2000A w/Adj. comb
(Made 1994 only) . . . . **NiB $579 Ex $476 Gd $295**
Model 2000L w/laminated
stock (intro. 1996) . . . . **NiB $609 Ex $501 Gd $365**

MODEL 7000 . . . . **NiB $215 Ex $183 Gd $147**
Caliber: .22 LR. 10-round magazine. 18-inch bbl. Weight: 5.5 lbs. Synthetic stocks. No sights; receiver grooved for scope. Semi-auto. Side ejection. Manual bolt hold-open. Cross-bolt safety. Matte finish. Made from 1997 to 2001.
Model 7000 . . . . **NiB $210 Ex $183 Gd $147**
Model 7000T . . . . **NiB $365 Ex $302 Gd $290**

MODEL A-1
AUTOLOADING RIFLE . . . . **NiB $155 Ex $100 Gd $75**
Takedown. Caliber: .22 LR. Six round detachable box magazine. 24-inch bbl. Weight: 6 lbs. Open rear sight. Plain pistol-grip stock. Made from 1935 to 1946.

MODEL A-1C
AUTOLOADING RIFLE . . . . **NiB $155 Ex $100 Gd $79**
Improved version of Model A-1 w/same general specifications, stock w/semibeavertail forend. Made from 1940 to 1946.

MODEL A-1DL . . . . **NiB $155 Ex $100 Gd $89**
Same as Model A-1C above, except w/peep rear sight; hooded front, swivels.

Marlin Model 2000

Marlin Model 2000L

Marlin Model 7000

Marlin Model 7000T

MODEL A-1E . . . . NiB $160 Ex $117 Gd $85
Same as Model A-1 except w/peep rear sight; hooded front.

MODEL MR-7 BOLT-ACTION RIFLE
Calibers: .25-06 Rem., .270 Win., .280 Rem., .308 Win. or .30-06.
Four round magazine. 22-inch bbl. w/ or w/o sights. 43.31 inches
overall. Weight: 7.5 lbs. Checkered American walnut or birch stock
w/recoil pad and sling-swivel studs. Jeweled bolt w/cocking indica-
tor and 3-position safety. Made from 1996 to 1999.
Model MR-7 . . . . NiB $525 Ex $366 Gd $262
**Model MR7B w/birch
stock (Intro. 1998)** . . . . NiB $425 Ex $355 Gd $224
Open sights, add $35

MODEL 10 . . . . NiB $127 Ex $106 Gd $80
Same as Marlin Model 101 except w/walnut-finished hardwood
stock. Made 1966-79. Note: Later production featuring hot-
ironstamped wood pistol grip to simulate checkering/carving;
plain forend.

MODEL 20 . . . . NiB $750 Ex $406 Gd $280
Same as Marlin Model 80/780 except w/bead front sight, walnut-
finished hardwood stock. Made 1966 to 1982. Note: Recent production has stamped pistol grip; plain forend.

MODEL 30 . . . . NiB $250 Ex $117 Gd $86
Same as Marlin Model 336C except chambered for .30-30 only,
w/4-round magazine, plainer stock and forearm of walnut-finished
hardwood. Made 1966 to 1968.

MODEL 30A . . . . NiB $250 Ex $182 Gd $131
Same as Marlin Model 336C but chambered for .30-30 only,
w/checkered walnut-finished hardwood stock. Made 1969 to 1983.

MODEL 36G . . . . NiB $825 Ex $582 Gd $225
Same as Marlin Model 336C except chambered for .30-30 only,
w/5-round magazine, plainer stock. Made 1960 to 1965.

MODEL 60 . . . . NiB $155 Ex $94 Gd $69
Same as Marlin Model 99C except w/walnut-finished hardwood
stock. Made 1960 to 1980.

MODEL 70 . . . . NiB $170 Ex $95 Gd $64
Same as Marlin Model 989M2 except w/walnut-finished hardwood
stock; no handguard. Made 1966 to 1969.

MODEL 80G . . . . NiB $80 Ex $55 Gd $45
Same as Marlin Model 80C except w/plain stock, bead front sight.
Made 1960 to 1965.

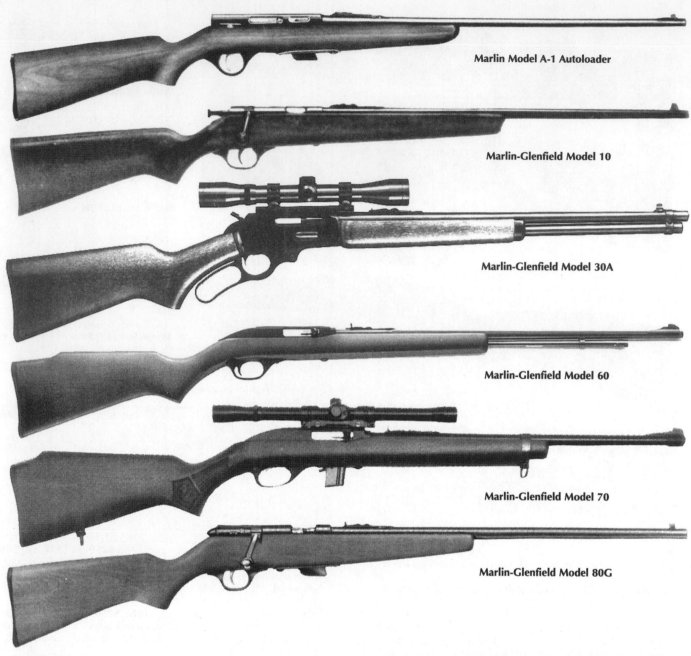

Marlin Model A-1 Autoloader

Marlin-Glenfield Model 10

Marlin-Glenfield Model 30A

Marlin-Glenfield Model 60

Marlin-Glenfield Model 70

Marlin-Glenfield Model 80G

MODEL 81G . . . . **NiB $98 Ex $72 Gd $62**
Same as Marlin Model 81C except w/plain stock, bead front sight.
Made from 1960 to 1965.

MODEL 99G . . . . **NiB $150 Ex $88 Gd $55**
Same as Marlin Model 99C except w/plain stock, bead front sight.
Made from 1960 to 1965.

MODEL 101G . . . . **NiB $80 Ex $71 Gd $45**
Same as Marlin Model 101 except w/plain stock. Made 1960 to 1965.

MODEL 989G
AUTOLOADING RIFLE . . . . **NiB $150 Ex $99 Gd $75**
Same as Marlin Model 989 except w/plain stock, bead front sight.
Made from 1962 to 1964.

MAUSER SPORTING RIFLES — Oberndorf am Neckar, Germany, Mfg. by Mauser-Werke GmbH, *Imported by Brolin Arms, Pomona, CA, (Previously by Gun South, Inc.; Gibbs Rifle Co.; Precision Imports, Inc. and KDF, Inc.)*

Before the end of WWI the name of the Mauser firm was "Waffenfabrik Mauser A.-G." Shortly after WWI it was changed to "Mauser-Werke A.-G." This information may be used to determine the age of genuine original Mauser sporting rifles made before WWII because all bear either of these firm names as well as the Mauser banner trademark.

Mauser Model ES340

Mauser Model ES350

The first four rifles listed were manufactured before WWI. Those that follow were produced between World Wars I and II. The early Mauser models can generally be identified by the pistol grip, which is rounded instead of capped, and the M/98 military-type magazine floorplate and catch. The later models have hinged magazine floorplates with lever or button release.

NOTE: The "B" series of Mauser .22 rifles (Model ES340B, MS350B, etc.) were improved versions of their corresponding models and were introduced about 1935.

PRE-WORLD WAR I MODELS

BOLT-ACTION SPORTING CARBINE
Calibers: 6.5x54, 6.5x58, 7x57, 8x57, 957mm. 19.75-inch bbl. Weight: 7 lbs. Full-stocked to muzzle. Other specifications same as for standard rifle.
Sporting Carbine w/20-inch
bbl. (Type M). NiB $2422 Ex $1960 Gd $1369
Sporting Carbine w/20
or 24-inch bbl. (Type S). . . . . NiB $2492 Ex $2016 Gd $1407

BOLT-ACTION SPORTING RIFLE
Calibers: 6.5x55, 6.5x58, 7x57, 8x57, 9x57, 9.3x62 10.75x68. Five-round box magazine, 23.5-inch bbl. Weight: 7 to 7.5 lbs. Pear-shaped bolt handle. Double-set or single trigger. Sights: Tangent curve rear; ramp front. Pistol-grip stock, forearm w/Schnabel tip and swivels.
Sporting Rifle (Type A, English export) . NiB $2570 Ex $2169 Gd $1513
Sporting Rifle (Type B) . . . . NiB $1730 Ex $1394 Gd $969

BOLT-ACTION SPORTING RIFLE,
MILITARY MODEL TYPE C . . . . NiB $750 Ex $608 Gd $427
So called because of stepped M/98-type bbl., military front sight and double-pull trigger. Calibers: 7x57, 8x57, 9x57mm. Other specifications same as for standard rifle.

BOLT-ACTION SPORTING RIFLE
SHORT MODEL TYPE K . . . . NiB $3764 Ex $3044 Gd $2115
Calibers: 6.5x54, 8x51mm. 19.75-inch bbl. Weight: 6.25 lbs. Other specifications same as for standard rifle.

PRE-WORLD WAR II MODELS

MODEL DSM34 BOLT-ACTION
SINGLE-SHOT SPORTING RIFLE . . . . NiB $625 Ex $416 Gd $293
Also called "Sport-model." Caliber: .22 LR. 26-inch bbl. Weight: 7.75 lbs. Sights: Tangent curve open rear; Barleycorn front. M/98 military-type stock, swivels. Intro. c. 1935.

MODEL EL320 BOLT-ACTION
SINGLE-SHOT SPORTING RIFLE . . . . NiB $493 Ex $401 Gd $282
Caliber: .22 LR. 23.5-inch bbl. Weight: 4.25 lbs. Sights: Adj. open rear; bead front. Sporting stock w/checkered pistol grip, swivels.

MODEL EN310 BOLT-ACTION
SINGLE-SHOT SPORTING RIFLE . . . . NiB $448 Ex $365 Gd $258
Caliber: .22 LR. ("22 Lang fur Buchsen.") 19.75-inch bbl. Weight: 4 lbs. Sights: Fixed open rear, blade front. Plain pistol-grip stock.

MODEL ES340 BOLT-ACTION
SINGLE-SHOT TARGET RIFLE . . . . NiB $725 Ex $416 Gd $293
Caliber: .22 LR. 25.5-inch bbl. Weight: 6.5 lbs. Sights: Tangent curve rear; ramp front. Sporting stock w/checkered pistol-grip and grooved forearm, swivels.

MODEL ES340B
BOLT-ACTION SINGLE-SHOT
TARGET RIFLE . . . . NiB $725 Ex $416 Gd $293
Caliber: .22 LR. 26.75-inch bbl. Weight: 8 lbs. Sights: Tangent curve open rear; ramp front. Plain pistol-grip stock, swivels.

MODEL ES350 BOLT-ACTION SINGLE-SHOT
TARGET RIFLE . . . . NiB $925 Ex $744 Gd $504
"Meistershaftsbuchse" (Championship Rifle). Caliber: .22 LR. 27.5-inch bbl. Weight: 7.75 lbs. Sights: Open micrometer rear; ramp front. Target stock w/checkered pistol-grip and forearm, grip cap, swivels.

MODEL ES350B BOLT-ACTION SINGLE-SHOT
TARGET RIFLE . . . . NiB $925 Ex $625 Gd $469
Same general specifications as Model MS350B except single-shot, weight: 8.25 lbs.

MODEL KKW BOLT-ACTION
SINGLE-SHOT TARGET RIFLE . . . . NiB $900 Ex $622 Gd $499
Caliber: .22 LR. 26-inch bbl. Weight: 8.75 lbs. Sights: Tangent curve open rear; Barleycorn front. M/98 military-type stock, swivels. Note: This rifle has an improved design Mauser 22 action w/separate nonrotating bolt head. In addition to being produced for commercial sale, this model was used as a training rifle by the German armed forces; it was also made by Walther and Gustoff. Intro. just before WWII.

MODEL MM410 BOLT-ACTION
REPEATING SPORTING RIFLE . . . . NiB $2000 Ex $1540 Gd $918
Caliber: .22 LR. Five round detachable box magazine. 23.5-inch bbl. Weight: 5 lbs. Sights: Tangent curve open rear; ramp front. Sporting stock w/checkered pistol-grip, swivels.

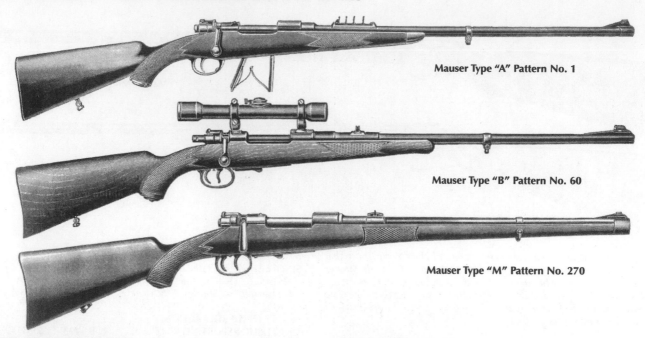

Mauser Type "A" Pattern No. 1

Mauser Type "B" Pattern No. 60

Mauser Type "M" Pattern No. 270

MODEL MM410B BOLT-ACTION
REPEATING SPORTING RIFLE . . . . **NiB $2000 Ex $1558 Gd $929**
Caliber: .22 LR. Five round detachable box magazine. 23.5-inch bbl. Weight: 6.25 lbs. Sights: Tangent curve open rear; ramp front. Lightweight sporting stock w/checkered pistol-grip, swivels.

MODEL MS350B BOLT-ACTION
REPEATING TARGET RIFLE . . . . **NiB $1200 Ex $758 Gd $529**
Caliber: .22 LR. Five round detachable box magazine. Receiver and bbl. grooved for detachable rear sight or scope. 26.75-inch bbl. Weight: 8.5 lbs. Sights: Micrometer open rear; ramp front. Target stock w/checkered pistol grip and forearm, grip cap, sling swivels.

MODEL MS420 BOLT-ACTION
REPEATING SPORTING RIFLE . . . . **NiB $1108 Ex $814 Gd $567**
Caliber: .22 LR. Five round detachable box magazine. 25.5-inch bbl. Weight: 6.5 lbs. Sights: Tangent curve open rear; ramp front. Sporting stock w/checkered pistol grip, grooved forearm swivels.

MODEL MS420B BOLT-ACTION
REPEATING TARGET RIFLE . . . . **NiB $1110 Ex $886 Gd $580**
Caliber: .22 LR. Five round detachable box magazine. 26.75-inch bbl. Weight: 8 lbs. Sights: Tangent curve open rear; ramp front. Target stock w/checkered pistol grip, grooved forearm, swivels.

STANDARD MODEL RIFLE . . . . **NiB $285 Ex $181 Gd $108**
Refined version of German Service Kar. 98k. Straight bolt handle. Calibers: 7mm Mauser (7x57mm), 7.9mm Mauser (8x57mm). Five round box magazine. 23.5-inch bbl. Weight: 8.5 lbs. Sights: Blade front; adj. rear. Walnut stock of M/98 military-type. Note: These rifles were made for commercial sale and are of the high quality found in the Oberndorf Mauser sporters. They bear the Mauser trademark on the receiver ring.

TYPE "A" BOLT-ACTION
SPORTING RIFLE . . . . **NiB $5505 Ex $3151 Gd $1894**
Special British Model. 7x57, 30-06 (7.62x63), 8x60, 9x57, 9.3x62mm. Five round box mag. 23.5-inch round bbl. Weight: 7.25 lbs. Mil.-type single trigger. Sights: Express rear; hooded ramp front. Circassian walnut sporting stock w/checkered pistol-grip and forearm, w/ or w/o cheekpiece, buffalo horn forend tip and grip cap, detachable swivels. Variations: Octagon bbl., double-set trigger, shotgun-type safety, folding peep rear sight, tangent curve rear sight, three-leaf rear sight.

TYPE "A" BOLT-ACTION
SPORTING RIFLE,
MAGNUM MODEL . . . . **NiB $5500 Ex $3360 Gd $2668**
Same general specifications as standard Type "A" except w/Magnum action, weighs 7.5 to 8.5 lbs. Calibers: .280 Ross, .318 Westley Richards Express, 10.75x68mm, .404 Nitro Express.

TYPE "A" BOLT-ACTION
SPORTING RIFLE,
SHORT MODEL . . . . **NiB $6000 Ex $3948 Gd $2358**
Same as standard Type "A" except w/short action, 21.5-inch round bbl., weight 6 lbs. Calibers: .250-3000, 6.5x54, 8x51mm.

TYPE "B" BOLT-ACTION
SPORTING
RIFLE . . . . **NiB $4750 Ex $2461 Gd $1917**
Normal Model. Calibers: 7x57, .30-06 (7.62x63), 8x57, 8x60, 9x57, 9.3x62, 10.7568mm. Five round box magazine. 23.5-inch round bbl. Weight: 7.25 lbs. Double-set trigger. Sights: Three-leaf rear, ramp front. Fine walnut stock w/checkered pistol-grip, Schnabel forend tip, cheekpiece, grip cap, swivels. Variations: Octagon or half-octagon bbl., military-type single trigger, shotgun-type safety, folding peep rear sight, tangent curve rear sight, telescopic sight.

TYPE "K"
BOLT-ACTION
SPORTING RIFLE. . . . . **NiB $5999 Ex $3251 Gd $2722**
Light Short Model. Same specifications as Normal Type "B" model except w/short action, 21.5-inch round bbl., weight: 6 lbs. Calibers: .250-3000, 6.5x54, 8x51mm.

TYPE "M"
BOLT-ACTION
SPORTING CARBINE . . . . **NiB $5500 Ex $3936 Gd $2345**
Calibers: 6.5x54, 7x57, .30-06 (7.62x63), 8x51, 8x60, 9x57mm. Five round box magazine. 19.75-inch round bbl. Weight: 6 to 6.75 lbs. Double-set trigger, flat bolt handle. Sights: Three-leaf rear; ramp front. Stocked to muzzle, cheekpiece, checkered pistol-grip and forearm, grip cap, steel forend cap, swivels. Variations: Military-type single trigger, shotgun-type trigger, shotgun-type safety, tangent curve rear sight, telescopic sight.

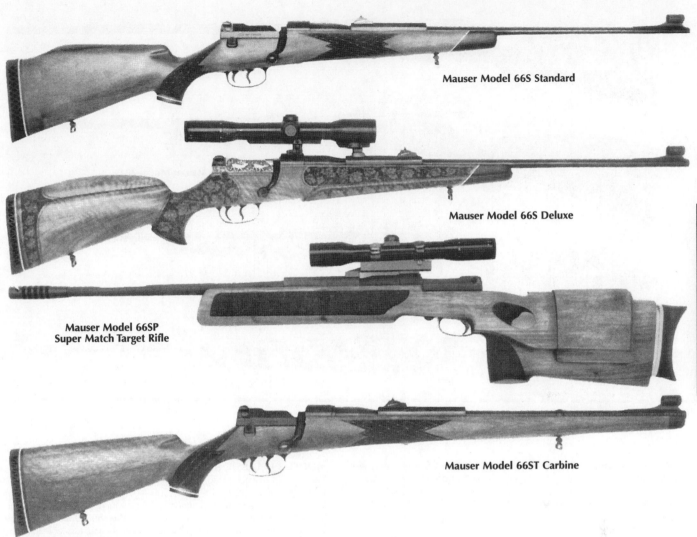

Mauser Model 66S Standard

Mauser Model 66S Deluxe

Mauser Model 66SP
Super Match Target Rifle

Mauser Model 66ST Carbine

TYPE "S" BOLT-ACTION

SPORTING CARBINE .... **NiB $4253 Ex $2296 Gd $1950**
Calibers: 6.5x54 7x57, 8x51, 8x60, 9x57mm. Five-round box magazine. 19.75-inch round bbl. Weight: 6 to 6.75 lbs. Double-set trigger. Sights: Three-leaf rear; ramp front. Stocked to muzzle, Schnabel forend tip, cheekpiece, checkered pistol-grip w/cap, swivels. Variations: Same as listed for Normal Model Type "B."

POST-WORLD WAR II MODELS

NOTE: *Production of original Mauser sporting rifles (66 series) resumed at the Oberndorf plant in 1965 by Mauser-Jagdwaffen GmbH, now Mauser-Werke Oberndorf GmbH. The Series 2000-3000-4000 rifles, however, were made for Mauser by Friedrich Wilhelm Heym Gewehrfabrik, Muennerstadt, West Germany.*

MODEL 66S BOLT-ACTION STANDARD SPORTING RIFLE
Telescopic short action. Bbls. interchangeable within cal. group. Single- or double-set trigger (interchangeable). Cal: .243 Win., 6.5x57, .270 Win., 7x64, .308 Win., .30-06. Three round mag. 23.6 inch bbl. (25.6inch in 7x64). Wt: 7.3 lbs. (7.5 lbs. in 7x64). Sights: Adj. open rear, hooded ramp front. Select Eur. walnut stock, Monte Carlo w/cheekpiece, rosewood forend tip and pistol-grip cap, skip checkering, recoil pad, sling swivels. Made from 1974 to 1995, export to U.S. disc. 1974. Note: U.S. designation, 1971 to 1973,

was "Model 660."
Model 66S .... **NiB $4650 Ex $2940 Gd $1910**
W/extra bbl. assembly, add **$550**

MODEL 66S DELUXE SPORTER
Limited production special order. Model 66S rifles and carbines are available with /elaborate engraving, gold and silver inlays and carved select walnut stocks. Added value is upward of $4500.

MODEL 66S ULTRA
Same general specifications as Model 66S Standard except with 20.9-inch bbl., weight: 6.8 lbs.
Model 66S Ultra .... **NiB $1683 Ex $1596 Gd $1039**
W/extra bbl. assembly, add **$550**

MODEL 66SG BIG GAME
Same general specifications as Model 66S Standard except w/25.6-inch bbl., weight 9.3 lbs. Calibers: .375 H&H Mag., .458 Win. Mag. Note: U.S. designation, 1971-73, was "Model 660 Safari."
Model 66SG .... **NiB $2992 Ex $2036 Gd $1279**
W/ extra bbl. assembly, add **$550**

Mauser Model 99

Mauser Model 201

Mauser Model 3000

Mauser Model 4000

MODEL 66SH HIGH PERFORMANCE NiB $1640 Ex $1465 Gd $1040
Same general specifications as Model 66S Standard except w/25.6-inch bbl., weighs 7.5 lbs. (9.3 lbs. in 9.3x64). Calibers: 6.5x68, 7mm Rem. Mag., 7mm S.E.v. Hoffe, .300 Win. Mag., 8x68S, 9.3x64.

MODEL 66SP SUPER MATCH
BOLT-ACTION TARGET RIFLE. . . . . . . NiB $4145 Ex $3627 Gd $1927
Telescopic short action. Adj. single-stage trigger. Caliber: .308 Win. (chambering for other cartridges available on special order). Three round magazine. 27.6-inch heavy bbl. w/muzzle brake, dovetail rib for special scope mount. Weight: 12 lbs. Target stock w/wide and deep forearm, full pistol-grip, thumbhole adj. cheekpiece, adj. rubber buttplate.

MODEL 66ST CARBINE
Same general specifications as Model 66S Standard except w/20.9-inch bbl., full-length stock, weight: 7 lbs.
Model 66ST. . . . . NiB $2522 Ex $1639 Gd $1201
W/extra bbl. assembly, add $550

MODEL 83 BOLT-ACTION RIFLE . . . . . NiB $2177 Ex $2100 Gd $1328
Centerfire single-shot, bolt-action rifle for 300-meter competition. Caliber: .308 Win. 25.5-inch fluted bbl. Weight: 10.5 lbs. Adj. micrometer rear sight globe front. Fully adj. competition stock. Disc. 1988.

MODEL 96 . . . . NiB $628 Ex $583 Gd $410
Calibers: .25-06, .270 Win., 7x64, .308 Win., .30-06, 7mm Rem. Mag., .300 Win. Mag. 22-inch bbl.; magnums 24-inch. Weight: 6.25 lbs. No sights; drilled and tapped for scope. Walnut stock. Five-round top-loading magazine. 3-position safety.

MODEL 99 CLASSIC BOLT-ACTION RIFLE
Calibers: .243 Win., .25-06, .270 Win., .30-06, .308 Win., .257 Wby., .270 Wby., 7mm Rem. Mag., .300 Win., .300 Wby. .375 H&H. Four round magazine (standard), 3-round (Magnum). Bbl.: 24-inch (standard) or 26-inch (Magnum). 44 inches overall (standard). Weight: 8 lbs. No sights. Checkered European walnut stock w/rosewood grip cap available in Classic and Monte Carlo styles w/High-Luster or oil finish. Disc. importing 1994.
Standard Classic or
Monte Carlo (oil finish). . . . . NiB $1122 Ex $1022 Gd $686
Magnum Classic or
Monte Carlo (oil finish). . . . . NiB $1212 Ex $1067 Gd $754
Standard Classic or
Monte Carlo (H-L finish). . . . . NiB $1152 Ex $1046 Gd $703
Magnum Classic or
Monte Carlo (H-L finish). . . . . NiB $1282 Ex $1087 Gd $770

MODEL 107 BOLT-ACTION RIFLE . . . . NiB $305 Ex $242 Gd $199
Caliber: .22 LR. Mag. Five round magazine. 21.5-inch bbl. 40 inches overall. Weight: 5 lbs. Receiver drilled and tapped for rail scope mounts. Hooded front sight, adj. rear. Disc. importing 1994.

MODEL 201/201 LUXUS BOLT-ACTION RIFLE
Calibers: .22 LR. .22 Win. Mag. Five round magazine. 21-inch bbl. 40 inches overall. Weight: 6.5 lbs. Receiver drilled and tapped for scope mounts. Sights optional. Checkered walnut-stained beech stock w/Monte Carlo. Model 201 Luxus w/checkered European walnut stock QD swivels, rosewood forend and rubber recoil pad. Made from 1989 to 1997.
Model 201 Standard . . . . NiB $635 Ex $519 Gd $363
Model 201 Magnum . . . . NiB $665 Ex $549 Gd $393
Model 201 Luxus Standard . . . . NiB $710 Ex $519 Gd $436
Model 201 Luxus Magnum . . . . NiB $797 Ex $544 Gd $539

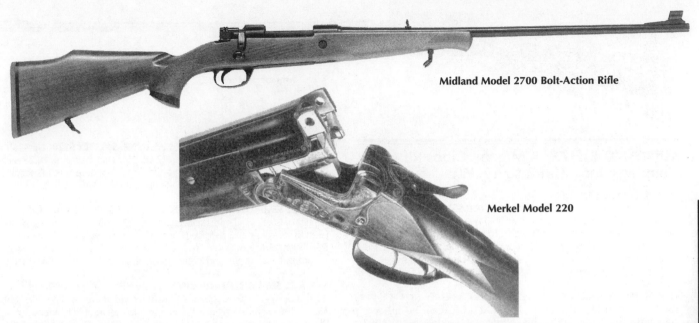

Midland Model 2700 Bolt-Action Rifle

Merkel Model 220

RIFLES

MODEL 2000 BOLT-ACTION
SPORTING RIFLE. . . . . **NiB $499 Ex $321 Gd $241**
Modified Mauser-type action. Calibers: .270 Win., .308 Win., .30-06.
Five-round magazine. 24-inch bbl. Weight: 7.5 lbs. Sights: Folding
leaf rear; hooded ramp front. Checkered walnut stock w/Monte Carlo
comb and cheekpiece, forend tip, sling swivels. Made from 1969 to
1971. Note: Model 2000 is similar in appearance to Model 3000.

MODEL 2000 CLASSIC BOLT-ACTION SPORTING RIFLE
Calibers: .22-250 Rem., .234 Win., .270 Win., 7mm Mag., .308 Win.,
.30-06, .300 Win. Mag. Three or 5-round magazine. 24-inch bbl.
Weight: 7.5 lbs. Sights: Folding leaf rear; hooded ramp front.
Checkered walnut stock w/Monte Carlo comb and cheekpiece, forend
tip, sling swivels. Imported 1998. Note: The Model 2000 Classic is
designed to interchange bbl. assemblies within a given caliber group.
Model 2000 Classic. . . . . **NiB $1645 Ex $1330 Gd $926**
Model 2000 Professional
w/Recoil Compensator . . . . **NiB $3194 Ex $2661 Gd $1939**
Model 2000 Sniper . . . . **NiB $1966 Ex $1508 Gd $1037**
Model 2000 Varmint . . . . **NiB $1909 Ex $1460 Gd $1016**
Extra bbl. assembly, add **$895**

MODEL 3000 BOLT-ACTION
SPORTING RIFLE. . . . . **NiB $525 Ex $401 Gd $368**
Modified Mauser-type action. Calibers: .243 Win., .270 Win., .308
Win., .30-06. Five round magazine. 22-inch bbl. Weight: 7 lbs. No
sights. Select European walnut stock, Monte Carlo style w/cheek-
piece, rosewood forend tip and pistol-grip cap, skip checkering,
recoil pad, sling swivels. Made from 1971 to 1974.

MODEL 3000 MAGNUM . . . . **NiB $575 Ex $453 Gd $350**
Same general specifications as standard Model 3000, except w/3-
round magazine, 26-inch bbl., weight: 8 lbs. Calibers: 7mm Rem.
Mag., .300 Win. Mag., .375 H&H Mag.

MODEL 4000 VARMINT RIFLE . . . . **NiB $425 Ex $350 Gd $237**
Same general specifications as standard Model 3000, except
w/smaller action, folding leaf rear sight; hooded ramp front, rubber
buttplate instead of recoil pad, weight 6.75 lbs. Calibers: .222 Rem.,
.223 Rem. 22-inch bbl. Select European walnut stock w/rosewood
forend tip and pistol-grip cap. French checkering and sling swivels.

McMILLAN GUN WORKS — Phoenix, Arizona
Harris Gunworks
See Harris Gunworks.

GEBRÜDER MERKEL — Suhl, Germany

For Merkel combination guns and drillings, see listings under Merkel shotguns.

OVER/UNDER RIFLES ("BOCK-DOPPELBÜCHSEN")
Calibers: 5.6x35 Vierling, 6.5x58r5, 7x57r5, 8x57JR, 8x60R
Magnum, 9.3x53r5, 9.3x72r5, 9.3x74r5, 10.3x60R as well as
most of the British calibers for African and Indian big game.
Various bbl. lengths, weights. In general, specifications correspond to those of Merkel over/under shotguns. Values of these
over/under rifles (in calibers for which ammunition is obtainable)
are about the same as those of comparable shotgun models cur-
rently manufactured. For more specific data, see Merkel shotgun
models indicated below.
Model 210 . . . . **NiB $5700 Ex $4400 Gd $3000**
Model 210E . . . . **NiB $6575 Ex $4400 Gd $2400**
Model 213 . . . . **NiB $13,438 Ex $9950 Gd $7046**
Model 240E1 . . . . **NiB $6813 Ex $4850 Gd $3338**
Model 313E . . . . **NiB $19,125 Ex $16,500 Gd $9420**
Model 320E . . . . **NiB $15,000 Ex $12,000 Gd $8160**
Model 321 . . . . **NiB $16,563 Ex $13,250 Gd $9010**
Model 321E . . . . **NiB $17,500 Ex $14,000 Gd $9520**
Model 322 . . . . **NiB $18,125 Ex $14,500 Gd $9860**
Model 323E . . . . **NiB $23,125 Ex $18,500 Gd $12,580**
Model 324 . . . . **NiB $26,875 Ex $21,500 Gd $14,620**

MEXICAN MILITARY RIFLE
Mfd. by Government Arsenal, Mexico, D.F.

MODEL 1936 MAUSER MILITARY RIFLE . . . **NiB $221 Ex $169 Gd $95**
Same as German Kar.98k w/minor variations and U.S. M/1903
Springfield-type knurled cocking piece.

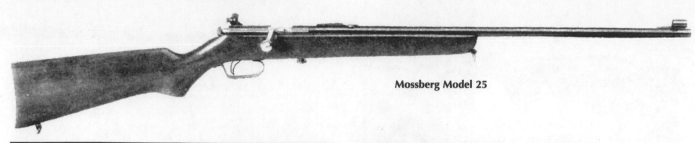

Mossberg Model 25

MIDLAND RIFLES — Mfg. by Gibbs Rifle Company, Inc., Martinsburg, WV

MODEL 2100 BOLT-ACTION

RIFLE .... NiB $374 Ex $306 Gd $218
Calibers: .22-250, .243 Win., 6mm Rem., .270 Win., 6.5x55, 7x57, 7x64, .308 Win., and .30-06. Springfield 1903 action. Four-round magazine. 22-inch bbl. 43 inches overall. Weight: 7 lbs. Flip-up rear sight; hooded ramp front. Finely finished and checkered walnut stock w/pistol-grip cap and sling swivels. Steel recoil bar. Action drilled and tapped for scope mounts. Production disc.1997.

MODEL 2600 BOLT-ACTION RIFLE ...... NiB $393 Ex $321 Gd $198
Same general specifications as Model 2100 except no pistol-grip cap, and stock is walnut-finished hardwood. Made 1992 to 1997.

MODEL 2700 BOLT-ACTION RIFLE ...... NiB $393 Ex $216 Gd $213
Same general specifications as Model 2100 except the weight of this rifle as been reduced by utilizing a tapered bbl., anodized aluminum trigger housing and lightened stock. Weight: 6.5 lbs. Disc.

MODEL 2800 LIGHTWEIGHT RIFLE ..... NiB $400 Ex $327 Gd $233
Same general specifications as Model 2100 except w/laminated birch stock. Made from 1992 to 1994 and from 1996 to 1997.

MITCHELL ARMS. INC. — Fountain Valley, California, (Formerly Santa Ana, CA)

MODEL 15/22 SEMIAUTOMATIC
High Standard-style action. Caliber: .22 LR. 15-round magazine (10-round after 10/13/94). 20.5-inch bbl. 37.5 inches overall. Weight: 6.25 lbs. Ramp front sight; adj. open rear. Blued finish. Mahogany stock; Monte Carlo-style American walnut stock on Deluxe model. Made from 1994 to 1996.
Model 15/22 SP (Special)
w/plastic buttplate .... NiB $225 Ex $106 Gd $72
Model 15/22 Carbine .... NiB $225 Ex $107 Gd $72
Model 15/22D Deluxe .... NiB $230 Ex $148 Gd $107

MODEL 9300 SERIES BOLT-ACTION RIFLE
Calibers: .22 LR. .22 Mag. Five or 10-round magazine. 22.5-inch bbl. 40.75 inches overall. Weight: 6.5 lbs. Beaded ramp front sight; adj. open rear. Blued finish. American walnut stock. Made 1994 to 1995.
Model 9302 (.22 LR,
checkered, rosewood caps) .... NiB $277 Ex $220 Gd $159
Model 9302 (.22 Mag.,
checkered, rosewood caps) .... NiB $275 Ex $230 Gd $166
Model 9303 (.22 LR, plain stock) .... NiB $275 Ex $178 Gd $131
Model 9304 (.22 Mag.,
checkered, No rosewood caps) .... NiB $249 Ex $189 Gd $137
Model 9305 (.22 LR, special stock) ...... NiB $188 Ex $156 Gd $215

AK-22 SEMIAUTOMATIC RIFLE .... NiB $325 Ex $220 Gd $159
Replica of AK-47 rifle. .22 LR. .22 WMR., 20-round magazine (.22 LR), 10-round (.22 WMR). 18-inch bbl. 36 inches overall. Weight: 6.5 lbs. Sights: Post front; open adj. rear. European walnut stock and forend. Matte black finish. Made from 1985 to 1994.

CAR-15 .... Nib $495 Ex $320 Gd $259
Replica of AR-15 CAR rifle. Caliber: .22 LR. 15-round magazine.16.25-inch bbl. 32 inches overall. Sights: Adj. post front; adj. aperture rear. Telescoping buttstock and ventilated forend. Matte black finish. Made 1990 to 1994.

GALIL 22 SEMIAUTOMATIC RIFLE. ..... NiB $395 Ex $261 Gd $173
Replica of Israeli Galil rifle. Calibers: .22 LR. .22 WMR., 20-round magazine (.22 LR), 10-round (.22 WMR). 18-inch bbl. 36 inches overall. Weight: 6.5 lbs. Sights: Adj. post front; rear adj. for windage. Folding metal stock w/European walnut grip and forend. Matte black finish. Made 1987 to 1993.

M-16A 22 SEMIAUTOMATIC RIFLE ..... NiB $450 Ex $290 Gd $159
Replica of AR-15 rifle. Caliber: .22 LR. 15-round magazine. 20.5-inch bbl. 38.5 inches overall. Weight: 7 lbs. Sights: Adj. post front, adj. aperture rear. Black composite stock and forend. Matte black finish. Made 1990 to 1994.

MAS 22 SEMIAUTOMATIC RIFLE .... NiB $399 Ex $256 Gd $182
Replica of French MAS bullpup rifle. Caliber: .22 LR. 20-round magazine. 18-inch bbl. 28 inches overall. Weight: 7.5 lbs. Sights: Adj. post front, folding aperture rear. European walnut buttstock and forend. Matte black finish. Made from 1987 to 1993.

PPS SEMIAUTOMATIC RIFLE
Caliber: .22 LR. 20-round magazine, 50-round drum. 16.5-inch bbl. 33.5 inches overall. Weight: 5.5 lbs. Sights: Blade front; adj. rear. European walnut stock w/ventilated bbl. shroud. Matte black finish. Made 1989 to 1994.
Model PPS (20-round) .... NiB $325 Ex $235 Gd $169
Model PPS/50 (50-round drum) ... NiB $475 Ex $370 Gd $263

O.F. MOSSBERG & SONS, INC. — North Haven, Connecticut, (Formerly New Haven, CT)

MODEL 10 BOLT-ACTION
SINGLE-SHOT RIFLE .... NiB $300 Ex $131 Gd $105
Takedown. Caliber: .22 LR, Long, Short. 22-inch bbl. Weight: 4 lbs. Sights: Open rear; bead front. Plain pistol-grip stock w/swivels, sling. Made 1933 to 1935.

MODEL 14 BOLT-ACTION
SINGLE-SHOT RIFLE .... NiB $300 Ex $131 Gd $105
Takedown. Caliber: .22 LR. Long, Short. 24-inch bbl. Weight: 5.25 lbs. Sights: Peep rear; hooded ramp front. Plain pistol-grip stock w/semi-beavertail forearm, 1.25-inch swivels. Made 1934 to 1935.

MODEL 20 BOLT-ACTION
SINGLE-SHOT RIFLE .... NiB $300 Ex $131 Gd $105
Takedown. Caliber: .22 LR. Long, Short. 24-inch bbl. Weight: 4.5 lbs. Sights: Open rear; bead front. Plain pistol-grip stock and forearm w/finger grooves, sling and swivels. Made from 1933 to 1935.

MODEL 25/25A BOLT-ACTION SINGLE-SHOT RIFLE
Takedown. Caliber: .22 LR. Long, Short. 24-inch bbl. Weight: 5 lbs. Sights: Peep rear; hooded ramp front. Plain pistol-grip stock w/semi-beavertail forearm. 1.25-inch swivels. Made from 1935 to 1936.
Model 25. .... NiB $300 Ex $131 Gd $105
Model 25A (Improved Model 25, 1936-38) .... NiB $300 Ex $131 Gd $105

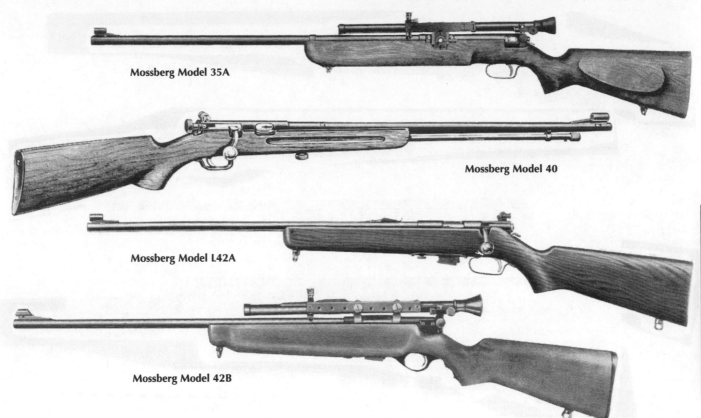

Mossberg Model 35A

Mossberg Model 40

Mossberg Model L42A

Mossberg Model 42B

MODEL 26B/26C BOLT-ACTION SINGLE-SHOT
Takedown. Caliber: .22 LR. Long, Short. 26-inch bbl. Weight: 5.5 lbs. Sights; Rear, micrometer click peep or open; hooded ramp front. Plain pistol-grip stock swivels. Made from 1938 to 1941.
Model 26B . . . . NiB $300 Ex $163 Gd $101
Model 26C
(No rear sight/swivels) . . . . NiB $250 Ex $132 Gd $91

MODEL 30 BOLT-ACTION
SINGLE-SHOT RIFLE . . . . NiB $300 Ex $132 Gd $101
Takedown. Caliber: .22 LR. Long, Short. 24-inch bbl. Weight: 4.5 lbs. Sights: Peep rear; bead front, on hooded ramp. Plain pistol-grip stock, forearm w/finger grooves. Made from 1933 to 1935.

MODEL 34 BOLT-ACTION
SINGLE-SHOT RIFLE . . . . NiB $300 Ex $132 Gd $101
Takedown. Caliber: .22 LR. Long, Short. 24-inch bbl. Weight: 5.5 lbs. Sights: Peep rear; hooded ramp front. Plain pistol-grip stock w/semibeavertail forearm, 1.25-inch swivels. Made 1934 to 1935.

MODEL 35 TARGET GRADE
BOLT-ACTION SINGLE-SHOT RIFLE . . . . . . NiB $400 Ex $259 Gd $116
Caliber: .22 LR. 26-inch heavy bbl. Weight: 8.25 lbs. Sights: Micrometer click rear peep; hooded ramp front. Large target stock w/full pistol grip, cheekpiece, full beavertail forearm, 1.25-inch swivels. Made from 1935 to 1937.

MODEL 35A BOLT-ACTION
SINGLE-SHOT RIFLE . . . . NiB $400 Ex $258 Gd $114
Caliber: .22 LR. 26-inch heavy bbl. Weight: 8.25 lbs. Sights: Micrometer click peep rear; hooded front. Target stock w/cheekpiece full pistol grip and forearm, 1.25-inch sling swivels. Made from 1937 to 1938.

MODEL 35A-LS . . . . NiB $400 Ex $293 Gd $205
Caliber .22 LR. Same as Model 35A but w/Lyman No. 57 rear sight, 17A front. Target stock w/checkpiece, full pistol-grip and forearm.

MODEL 35B . . . . NiB $400 Ex $282 Gd $200
Same specifications as Model 44B except single-shot. Made from 1938 to 1940.

MODEL 40 BOLT-ACTION REPEATER. . . . . NiB $180 Ex $129 Gd $98
Takedown. Caliber: .22 LR. Long, Short, 16-round tubular magazine. 24-inch bbl. Weight: 5 lbs. Sights: Peep rear; bead front, on hooded ramp. Plain pistol-grip stock, forearm w/finger grooves. Made 1933 to 1935.

MODEL 42 BOLT-ACTION REPEATER. . . . . NiB $250 Ex $129 Gd $98
Takedown. Caliber: .22 LR. Long, Short. Seven-round detachable box magazine. 24-inch bbl. Weight: 5 lbs. Sights: Receiver peep, open rear; hooded ramp front. Pistol-grip stock. 1.25-inch swivels. Made 1935 to 1937.

MODEL 42A/L42A BOLT-ACTION REPEATERS
Takedown. Caliber: .22 LR. Long, Short. Seven-round detachable box magazine. 24-inch bbl. Weight: 5 lbs. Sights: Receiver peep, open rear; ramp front. Plain pistol-grip stock. Made from 1937-38. Model L42A (left-hand action) made from 1937 to 1941.
Model 42A. NiB $250 Ex $150 Gd $110
Model L42A. NiB $260 Ex $221 Gd $160

MODEL 42B/42C BOLT-ACTION REPEATERS
Takedown. Caliber: .22 LR. Long, Short. Five-round detachable box magazine. 24-inch bbl. Weight: 6 lbs. Sights: Micrometer click receiver peep, open rear hooded ramp front. Plain pistol-grip stock, swivels. Made from 1938 to 1941.
Model 42B. NiB $250 Ex $155 Gd $88
Model 42C (No rear peep sight) . . . . NiB $200 Ex $124 Gd $93

Mossberg Model 42C

Mossberg Model L-43

Mossberg Model 43B

Mossberg Model 44US

Mossberg Model L45A
Left-Hand Model

Mossberg Model 45B

Mossberg Model L46A-LS

Mossberg Model 46B

MODEL 42M BOLT-ACTION
REPEATER . . . . **NiB $300 Ex $182 Gd $110**
Caliber: .22 LR. Long, Short. Seven-round detachable box magazine. 23-inch bbl. Weight: 6.75 lbs. Sights: Microclick receiver peep, open rear; hooded ramp front. Two-piece Mannlicher-type stock w/cheekpiece and pistol-grip, swivels. Made from 1940 to 1950.

MODEL 43/L43 BOLT-ACTION
REPEATERS . . . . **NiB $353 Ex $370 Gd $261**

Speedlock, adj. trigger pull. Caliber: .22 LR. Seven-round detachable box magazine. 26-inch heavy bbl. Weight: 8.25 lbs. Sights: Lyman No. 57 rear; selective aperture front. Target stock w/cheekpiece, full pistol-grip, beavertail forearm, adj. front swivel. Made from 1937-38. Model L43 is same as Model 43 except w/left-hand action.

MODEL 43B . . . . **NiB $350 Ex $286 Gd $127**
Same as Model 44B except w/Lyman No. 57 receiver sight and No. 17A front sight. Made from 1938 to 1939.

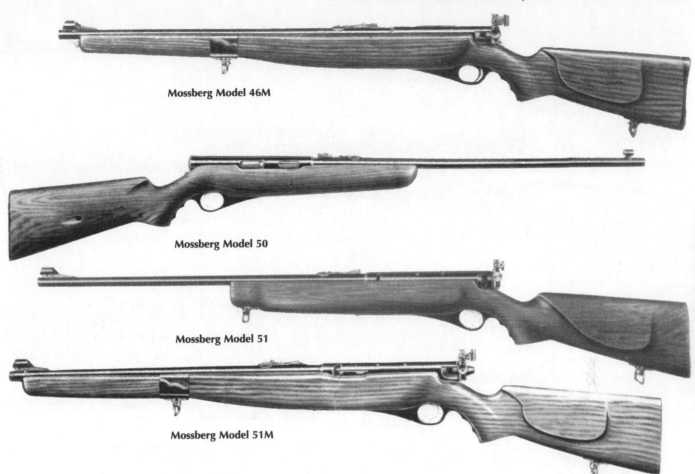

Mossberg Model 46M

Mossberg Model 50

Mossberg Model 51

Mossberg Model 51M

MODEL 44 BOLT-ACTION REPEATER..... NiB $350 Ex $244 Gd $131
Takedown. Caliber: .22 LR. Long, Short. Tubular magazine holds 16 LR. 24-inch bbl. Weight: 6 lbs. Sights: Peep rear; hooded ramp front. Plain pistol-grip stock w/semi-beavertail forearm, 1.25-inch swivels. Made from 1934 to 1935. Note: Do not confuse this rifle w/later Models 44B and 44US, which are clip repeaters.

**MODEL 44B BOLT-ACTION
TARGET RIFLE.................** NiB $359 Ex $237 Gd $134
Caliber: .22 LR. Seven-round detachable box magazine. Made from 1938 to 1941.

MODEL 44US BOLT-ACTION REPEATER
Caliber: .22 LR. Seven round detachable box magazine. 26-inch heavy bbl. Weight: 8.5 lbs. Sights: Micrometer click receiver peep, hooded front. Target stock, swivels. Made from 1943-48. Note: This model was used as a training rifle by the U.S. Armed Forces during WWII.
Model 44US .... NiB $350 Ex $260 Gd $121
Model 44US (marked U.S. Property) ..... NiB $350 Ex $311 Gd $234

MODEL 45 BOLT-ACTION REPEATER..... NiB $254 Ex $178 Gd $117
Takedown. Caliber: .22 LR. Long, Short. Tubular magazine holds 15 LR. 18 Long, 22 Short. 24-inch bbl. Weight: 6.75 lbs. Sights: Rear peep; hooded ramp front. Plain pistol-grip stock, 1.25-inch swivels. Made 1935 to 1937.

MODEL 45A, L45A, 45AC BOLT-ACTION REPEATERS
Takedown. Caliber: .22 LR. Long, Short. Tubular magazine holds 15 LR, 18 Long, 22 Short. 24-inch bbl. Weight: 6.75 lbs. Sights: Receiver peep, open rear; hooded blade front sight mounted on ramp. Plain pistol-grip stock, 1.25-inch sling swivels. Made 1937 to 1938.
Model 45A .... NiB $254 Ex $168 Gd $122
Model L45A (Left-hand action).......... NiB $600 Ex $309 Gd $250
Model 45AC (No receiver peep sight)..... NiB $189 Ex $148 Gd $106

MODEL 45B/45C BOLT-ACTION REPEATERS
Takedown. Caliber: .22 LR. Long, Short. Tubular magazine holds 15 LR, 18 Long, 22 Short. 24-inch bbl. Weight: 6.25 lbs. Open rear sight; hooded blade front sight mounted on ramp. Plain pistol-grip stock w/sling swivels. Made from 1938 to 1940.
Model 45B .... NiB $300 Ex $152 Gd $112
Model 45C (No sights, made 1935 to 1937). NiB $300 Ex $137 Gd $91

MODEL 46 BOLT-ACTION REPEATER..... NiB $300 Ex $209 Gd $117
Takedown. Caliber: .22 LR. Long, Short. Tubular magazine holds 15 LR, 18 Long, 22 Short. 26-inch bbl. Weight: 7.5 lbs. Sights: Micrometer click rear peep; hooded ramp front. Pistol-grip stock w/cheekpiece, full beavertail forearm, 1.25-inch swivels. Made from 1935 to 1937.

MODEL 46A, 46A-LS, L46A-LS BOLT-ACTION REPEATERS
Takedown. Caliber: .22 LR. Long, Short. Tubular magazine holds 15 LR, 18 Long, 22 Short. 26-inch bbl. Weight: 7.25 lbs. Sights: Micrometer click receiver peep, open rear; hooded ramp front. Pistol-grip stock w/cheekpiece and beavertail forearm, quick-detachable swivels. Made from 1937 to 1938.
Model 46A......................... NiB $300 Ex $175 Gd $128
Mdl. 46A-LS (w/Lyman No. 57 receiver sight) .... NiB $350 Ex $231 Gd $167
Model L46A-LS (Left-hand action) .... NiB $600 Ex $324 Gd $230

Mossberg Model 140B

Mossberg Model 140K

Mossberg Model 144LS

Mossberg Model 146B

MODEL 46B BOLT-ACTION
REPEATER . . . . NiB $250 Ex $143 Gd $105
Takedown. Caliber: .22 LR. Long, Short. Tubular magazine holds 15 LR, 18 Long, 22 Short. 26-inch bbl. Weight: 7 lbs. Sights: Micrometer click receiver peep, open rear, hooded front. Plain pistol-grip stock w/cheekpiece, swivels. Note: Postwar version of this model has full magazine holding 20 LR, 23 Long, 30 Short. Made 1938 to 1950.

MODEL 46BT . . . . NiB $300 Ex $197 Gd $142
Same as Model 46B except w/heavier bbl. and stock. Weight: 7.75 lbs. Made from 1938 to 1939.

MODEL 46C . . . . NiB $300 Ex $181 Gd $120
Same as Model 46 except w/a heavier bbl. and stock than that model. Weight: 8.5 lbs. Made from 1936 to 1937.

MODEL 46M
BOLT-ACTION REPEATER . . . . NiB $300 Ex $181 Gd $120
Caliber: .22 LR. Long, Short. Tubular magazine holds 22 Short, 18 Long, 15 LR. 23-inch bbl. Weight: 7 lbs. Sights: Microclick receiver peep, open rear; hooded ramp front. Two-piece Mannlicher-type stock w/cheekpiece and pistol-grip, swivels. Made 1940 to 1952.

MODEL 50
AUTOLOADING RIFLE . . . . NiB $250 Ex $171 Gd $125
Same as Model 51 except w/plain stock w/o beavertail cheekpiece, swivels or receiver peep sight. Made from 1939 to 1942.

MODEL 51 AUTOLOADING RIFLE . . . . . . NiB $250 Ex $154 Gd $123
Takedown. Caliber: .22 LR. Fifteen-round tubular magazine in butt-stock. 24-inch bbl. Weight: 7.25 lbs. Sights: Micrometer click receiver peep, open rear; hooded ramp front. Cheekpiece stock w/full pistol grip and beavertail forearm, swivels. Made in 1939 only.

MODEL 51M AUTOLOADING RIFLE . . . . . NiB $275 Ex $154 Gd $123
Caliber: .22 LR. Fifteen-round tubular magazine. 20-inch bbl. Weight: 7 lbs. Sights: Microclick receiver peep, open rear; hooded ramp front. Two-piece Mannlicher-type stock w/pistol-grip and cheekpiece, hard-rubber buttplate and sling swivels. Made from 1939 to 1946.

MODEL 140B SPORTER-TARGET RIFLE . . . NiB $200 Ex $154 Gd $123
Same as Model 140K except w/peep rear sight, hooded ramp front sight. Made from 1957 to 1958.

MODEL 140K BOLT-ACTION REPEATER . . . NiB $200 Ex $149 Gd $109
Caliber: .22 LR. .22 Long, .22 Short. Seven-round clip magazine. 24.5-inch bbl. Weight: 5.75 lbs. Sights: Open rear; bead front. Monte Carlo stock w/cheekpiece and pistol-grip, sling swivels. Made 1955 to 1958.

MODEL 142-A BOLT-ACTION
REPEATING CARBINE . . . . NiB $225 Ex $179 Gd $130
Caliber: .22 Short Long, LR. Seven-round detachable box magazine. 18-inch bbl. Weight: 6 lbs. Sights: Peep rear, military-type front. Monte Carlo stock w/pistol-grip, hinged forearm pulls down to form hand grip; sling swivels mounted on left side of stock. Made from 1949 to 1957.

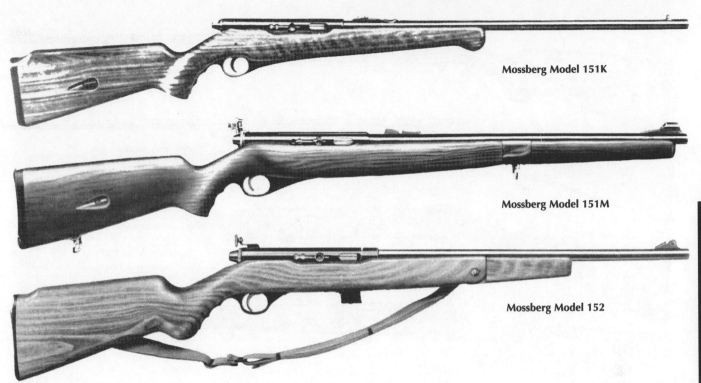

Mossberg Model 151K

Mossberg Model 151M

Mossberg Model 152

MODEL 142K . . . . **NiB $200 Ex $129 Gd $94**
Same as Model 142 except w/open rear sight. Made 1953 to 1957.

MODEL 144 BOLT-ACTION
TARGET RIFLE . . . . **NiB $359 Ex $365 Gd $210**
Caliber: .22 LR. Seven-round detachable box magazine. 26-inch heavy bbl. Weight: 8 lbs. Sights: Microclick receiver peep; hooded front. Pistol-grip target stock w/beavertail forearm, adj. hand stop, swivels. Made from 1949 to 1954. Note: This model designation was resumed c.1973 to replace Model 144LS, and then disc. again in 1985.

MODEL 144LS . . . . **NiB $350 Ex $433 Gd $200**
Same as Model 144 except w/Lyman No. 57MS or Mossberg S331 receiver sight and Lyman 17A front sight. Made from 1954 to date. Note: Since 1973, this model has been marketed as Model 144.

MODEL 146B BOLT-ACTION REPEATER . . **NiB $300 Ex $178 Gd $127**
Takedown. Caliber: .22 LR. Long, Short. Tubular magazine holds 30 Short, 23 Long, 20 LR. 26-inch bbl. Weight: 7 lbs. Sights: Micrometer click rear peep, open rear; hooded front. Plain stock w/pistol-grip, Monte Carlo comb and cheekpiece, knob forend tip, swivels. Made from 1949 to 1954.

MODEL 151K . . . . **NiB $259 Ex $168 Gd $117**
Same as Model 151M except w/24-inch bbl., weight: 6 lbs., w/o peep sight, plain stock w/Monte Carlo comb and cheekpiece, pistol-grip knob, forend tip, w/o swivels. Made from 1950 to 1951.

MODEL 151M AUTOLOADING RIFLE . . . . **NiB $300 Ex $169 Gd $117**
Improved version of Model 51M w/same general specifications, complete action is instantly removable w/o use of tools. Made 1946 to 1958.

MODEL 152 AUTOLOADING CARBINE . . **NiB $229 Ex $168 Gd $117**
Caliber: .22 LR. Seven-round detachable box magazine. 18-inch bbl. Weight: 5 lbs. Sights: Peep rear; military-type front. Monte Carlo stock w/pistol-grip, hinged forearm pulls down to form hand grip, sling mounted on swivels on left side of stock. Made 1948 to 1957.

MODEL 152K . . . . **NiB $200 Ex $152 Gd $105**
Same as Model 152 except w/open instead of peep rear sight. Made from 1950 to 1957.

MODEL 320B BOY SCOUT TARGET RIFLE . . . . **NiB $200 Ex $157 Gd $114**
Same as Model 340K except single-shot w/auto. safety. Made 1960 to 1971.

MODEL 320K HAMMERLESS
BOLT-ACTION SINGLE-SHOT . . . . . . **NiB $200 Ex $123 Gd $90**
Same as Model 346K except single-shot, w/drop-in loading platform, automatic safety. Weight: 5.75 lbs. Made from 1958 to 1960.

MODEL 321B . . . . **NiB $300 Ex $138 Gd $100**
Same as Model 321K except w/receiver peep sight. Made 1972 to 1975.

MODEL 321K BOLT-ACTION
SINGLE-SHOT . . . . **NiB $300 Ex $144 Gd $104**
Same as Model 341 except single-shot. Made from 1972 to 1980.

MODEL 333 AUTOLOADING CARBINE . . **NiB $225 Ex $149 Gd $123**
Caliber: .22 LR. 15-round tubular magazine. 20-inch bbl. Weight: 6.25 lbs. Sights: Open rear; ramp front. Monte Carlo stock w/checkered pistol grip and forearm, bbl. band, swivels. Made 1972 to 1973.

MODEL 340B TARGET SPORTER . . . . **NiB $208 Ex $177 Gd $126**
Same as Model 340K except w/peep rear sight, hooded ramp front sight. Made from 1958 to 1981.

MODEL 340K HAMMERLESS
BOLT-ACTION REPEATER . . . . **NiB $200 Ex $152 Gd $126**
Same as Model 346K except clip type, 7-round magazine. Made from 1958 to 1971.

MODEL 340M . . . . **NiB $600 Ex $365 Gd $189**
Same as Model 340K except w/18.5-inch bbl., Mannlicher-style stock w/swivels and sling. Weight: 5.25 lbs. Made from 1970 to 1971.

Mossberg Model 320B

Mossberg Model 320K

Mossberg Model 333

Mossberg Model 340B

Mossberg Model 340K

Mossberg Model 341

Mossberg Model 342K

Mossberg Model 346B

Mossberg Model 346K

Mossberg Model 350K
Autoloading — Clip Type

Mossberg Model 351K
Automatic Sporter

Mossberg Model 352K
Carbine

Mossberg Model 353
Carbine

Mossberg Model 377
Plinkster

MODEL 341 BOLT-ACTION REPEATER.... NiB $250 Ex $121 Gd $95
Caliber: .22 Short. Long, LR. Seven-round clip magazine. 24-inch bbl. Weight: 6.5 lbs. Sights: Open rear, ramp front. Monte Carlo stock w/checkered pistol-grip and forearm, sling swivels. Made 1972 to 1985.

**MODEL 342K HAMMERLESS
BOLT-ACTION CARBINE......... NiB $200 Ex $152 Gd $116**
Same as Model 340K except w/18-inch bbl., stock w/no cheekpiece, extension forend is hinged, pulls down to form hand grip; sling swivels and web strap on left side of stock. Weight: 5 lbs. Made 1958 to 1974.

MODEL 346B .... NiB $250 Ex $152 Gd $116
Same as Model 346K except w/peep rear sight, hooded ramp front sight. Made from 1958 to 1967.

**MODEL 346K HAMMERLESS
BOLT-ACTION REPEATER .... NiB $200 Ex $141 Gd $103**
Caliber: .22 Short. Long, LR. Tubular magazine holds 25 Short, 20 Long, 18 LR. 24-inch bbl. Weight: 6.5 lbs. Sights: Open rear; bead front. Walnut stock w/Monte Carlo comb, cheekpiece, pistol-grip, sling swivels. Made from 1958 to 1971.

**MODEL 350K AUTOLOADING
RIFLE — CLIP TYPE .... NiB $200 Ex $121 Gd $95**
Caliber: .22 Short (High Speed), Long, LR. Seven round clip magazine.

23.5-inch bbl. Weight: 6 lbs. Sights: Open rear; bead front. Monte Carlo stock w/pistol-grip. Made from 1958 to 1971.

MODEL 351C AUTOLOADING CARBINE . NiB $200 Ex $158 Gd $117
Same as Model 351K except w/18.5-inch bbl., Western carbine-style stock w/barrel band and sling swivels. Weight: 5.5 lbs. Made from 1965 to 1971.

**MODEL 351K AUTOLOADING
SPORTER.......................... NiB $200 Ex $158 Gd $117**
Caliber: .22 LR. Fifteen-round tubular magazine in buttstock. 24-inch bbl. Weight: 6 lbs. Sights: Open rear; bead front. Monte Carlo stock w/pistol-grip. Made from 1960 to 1971.

MODEL 352K AUTOLOADING CARBINE..... NiB $200 Ex $158 Gd $117
Caliber: .22 Short, Long, LR. Seven-round clip magazine. 18-inch bbl. Weight: 5 lbs. Sights: Open rear; bead front. Monte Carlo stock w/pistol grip; extension forend of Tenite is hinged, pulls down to form hand grip; sling swivels, web strap. Made from 1958 to 1971.

MODEL 353 AUTOLOADING CARBINE . . .NiB $200 Ex $158 Gd $117
Caliber: .22 LR. Seven round clip magazine. 18-inch bbl. Weight: 5 lbs. Sights: Open rear; ramp front. Monte Carlo stock w/checkered pistol-grip and forearm; black Tenite extension forend pulls down to form hand grip. Made 1972 to 1985.

Mossberg Model 400

Mossberg Model 402

Mossberg Model 472
Brush Gun

Mossberg Model 472
Carbine (Pistol Grip)

Mossberg Model 472
Carbine (Straight Grip)

Mossberg Model 472
"One in Five Thousand"

MODEL 377 PLINKSTER AUTOLOADER . . NiB $250 Ex $190 Gd $144
Caliber: .22 LR. Fifteen-round tubular magazine. 20-inch bbl. Weight: 6.25 lbs. 4x scope sight. Thumbhole stock w/rollover cheekpiece, Monte Carlo comb, checkered forearm; molded of modified polystyrene foam in walnut-finish; sling swivel studs. Made 1977 to 1979.

MODEL 380 SEMIAUTOMATIC RIFLE . . . . NiB $250 Ex $150 Gd $110
Caliber: .22 LR. Fifteen-round buttstock magazine. 20-inch bbl. Weight: 5.5 lbs. Sights: Open rear; bead front. Made 1980 to 1985.

MODEL 400 PALOMINO LEVER-ACTION. . . . . NiB $355 Ex $224 Gd $131
Hammerless. Caliber: .22 Short, Long, LR. Tubular magazine holds 20 Short, 17 Long, 15 LR. 24-inch bbl. Weight: 5.5 lbs. Sights: Open rear; bead front. Monte Carlo stock w/checkered pistol-grip; beavertail forearm. Made 1959 to 1964.

MODEL 402 PALOMINO CARBINE . . . . . . NiB $355 Ex $234 Gd $208
Same as Model 400 except w/18.5-inch (1961-64) or 20-inch bbl. (1964-71), forearm w/bbl. band, swivels; magazine holds two fewer rounds. Weight: 4.75 lbs. Made from 1961 to 1971.

MODEL 430 AUTOLOADING RIFLE. . . . . . NiB $300 Ex $140 Gd $102
Caliber: .22 LR. Eighteen-round tubular magazine. 24-inch bbl. Weight: 6.25 lbs. Sights: Open rear; bead front. Monte Carlo stock w/checkered pistol grip; checkered forearm. Made 1970 to 1971.

MODEL 432 WESTERN-STYLE AUTO . . . . . NiB $300 Ex $195 Gd $109
Same as Model 430 except w/plain straight-grip carbine-type stock and forearm, bbl. band, sling swivels. Magazine capacity: 15 cartridges. Weight: 6 lbs. Made from 1970 to 1971.

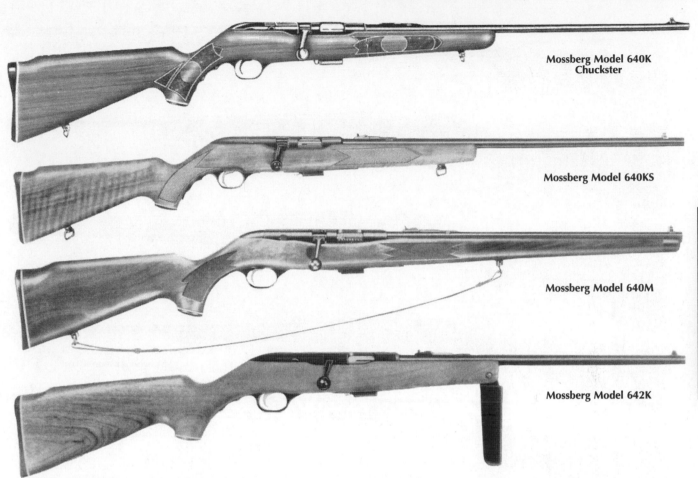

Mossberg Model 640K Chuckster

Mossberg Model 640KS

Mossberg Model 640M

Mossberg Model 642K

MODEL 472 BRUSH GUN . . . . **NiB $300 Ex $206 Gd $129**
Same as Model 472 Carbine w/straight-grip stock except w/18-inch bbl., weight: 6.5 lbs. Caliber: .30-30. Magazine capacity: 5 rounds. Made from 1974 to 1976.

MODEL 472 LEVER-ACTION CARBINE . . . **NiB $300 Ex $180 Gd $129**
Calibers: .30-30, .35 Rem. Six round tubular magazine. 20-inch bbl. Weight: 6.75 to 7 lbs. Sights: Open rear; ramp front. Pistol-grip or straight-grip stock, forearm w/bbl. band; sling swivels on pistol-grip model saddle ring on straight-grip model. Made from 1972 to 1979.

MODEL 472 ONE IN FIVE THOUSAND . . . **NiB $600 Ex $351 Gd $186**
Same as Model 472 Brush Gun except w/Indian scenes etched on receiver; brass buttplate, saddle ring and bbl. bands, gold-plated trigger, bright blued finish, select walnut stock and forearm. Limited edition of 5,000; serial numbered 1 to 5,000. Made in 1974.

MODEL 472 RIFLE. . . . . **NiB $300 Ex $207 Gd $130**
Same as Model 472 Carbine w/pistol-grip stock except w/24-inch bbl., 5-round magazine, weight: 7 lbs. Made from 1974 to 1976.

MODEL 479
Caliber: .30-30. Six-round tubular magazine. 20-inch bbl. Weight: 6.75 to 7 lbs. Sights: Open rear; ramp front. Made 1983 to 1985.
Model 479 Rifle . . . . **NiB $300 Ex $207 Gd $151**
Model 479PCA
(Carbine w/20-inch bbl.). . . . . **NiB $300 Ex $207 Gd $151**
Model 479RR
(Roy Rogers, 5000 Ltd. Edition) . . . . **NiB $600 Ex $412 Gd $253**

**MODEL 620K HAMMERLESS SINGLE-SHOT
BOLT-ACTION RIFLE** . . . . **NiB $250 Ex $167 Gd $121**
Single shot. Caliber: .22 WMR. 24-inch bbl. Weight: 6 lbs. Sights: Open rear; bead front. Monte Carlo stock w/cheekpiece, pistol-grip, sling swivels. Made from 1959 to 1960.

MODEL 620K-A. . . . . **NiB $250 Ex $152 Gd $111**
Same as Model 640K except w/sight modification. Made 1960 to 1968.

**MODEL 640K CHUCKSTER HAMMERLESS
BOLT-ACTION RIFLE** . . . . **NiB $300 Ex $197 Gd $121**
Caliber: .22 WMR. Five-round detachable clip magazine. 24-inch bbl. Weight: 6 lbs. Sights: Open rear; bead front. Monte Carlo stock w/cheekpiece, pistol grip, sling swivels. Made from 1959 to 1984.

MODEL 640KS . . . . **NiB $300 Ex $177 Gd $126**
Deluxe version of Model 640K w/select walnut stock hand checkering; gold-plated front sight, rear sight elevator, and trigger. Made 1960 to 1964.

MODEL 640M . . . . **NiB $600 Ex $410 Gd $307**
Similar to Model 640K except w/heavy receiver and jeweled bolt. 20-inch bbl., full length Mannlicher-style stock w/Monte Carlo comb and cheekpiece, swivels and leather sling. 40.75 inches overall. Weight: 6 lbs. Made from 1971 to 1973.

MODEL 642K CARBINE . . . . **NiB $355 Ex $247 Gd $156**
Caliber: .22 WMR. Five-round detachable clip magazine. 18-inch bbl. Weight: 5 lbs. 38.25 inches overall. Sights: Open rear; bead front. Monte Carlo walnut stock w/black Tenite forearm extension that pulls down to form hand grip. Made from 1961 to 1968.

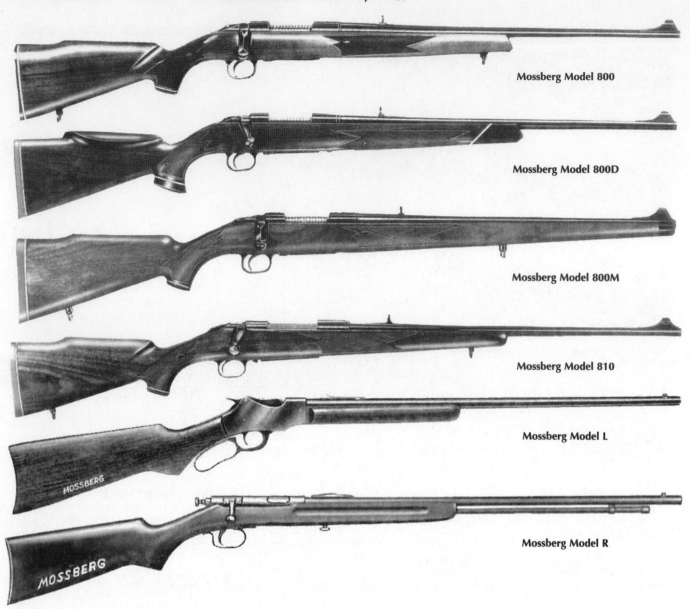

Mossberg Model 800

Mossberg Model 800D

Mossberg Model 800M

Mossberg Model 810

Mossberg Model L

Mossberg Model R

MODEL 800 BOLT-ACTION
CENTERFIRE RIFLE . . . . **NiB $400 Ex $257 Gd $150**
.222 Rem., .22-250, .243 Win., .308 Win. Four-round mag., 3-round in .222. 22-inch bbl. Weight: 7.5 lbs. Sights: Folding leaf rear; ramp front. Monte Carlo stock w/cheekpiece, checkered pistol-grip and forearm, sling swivels. Made from 1967 to 1979.

MODEL 800D SUPER GRADE . . . . . **NiB $400 Ex $321 Gd $227**
Deluxe version of Model 800 except w/stock w/rollover comb and cheekpiece, rosewood forend tip and pistol-grip cap. Weight: 6.75 lbs. Chambered for all calibers listed for the Model 800 except for .222 Rem. Sling swivels. Made from 1970 to 1973.

MODEL 800M . . . . **NiB $600 Ex $284 Gd $181**
Same as Model 800 except w/flat bolt handle, 20-inch bbl., Mannlicher-style stock. Weight: 6.5 lbs. Calibers: .22-250, .243 Win., .308 Win. Made from 1969 to 1972.

MODEL 800VT VARMINT/TARGET . . . . . . **NiB $400 Ex $277 Gd $197**
Similar to Model 800 except w/24-inch heavy bbl., no sights. Weight: 9.5 lbs. Calibers: .222 Rem., .22-250, .243 Win. Made 1968 to 1979.

MODEL 810 BOLT-ACTION CENTERFIRE RIFLE
Calibers: .270 Win., .30-06, 7mm Rem. Mag., .338 Win. Mag. Detachable box magazine (1970-75) or internal magazine w/hinged floorplate (1972 to date). Capacity: Four-round in .270 and .30-06, 3-round in Magnums. 22-inch bbl. in .270 and .30-06, 24-inch in Magnums. Weight: 7.5 to 8 lbs. Sights: Leaf rear; ramp front. Stock w/Monte Carlo comb and cheekpiece, checkered pistol-grip and forearm, grip cap, sling swivels. Made from 1970 to 1979.
Standard calibers . . . . **NiB $355 Ex $298 Gd $212**
Magnum calibers . . . . **NiB $370 Ex $313 Gd $226**

MODEL 1500
MOUNTAINEER
GRADE I CENTERFIRE RIFLE . . . . . . **NiB $385 Ex $300 Gd $265**
Calibers: .223, .243, .270, .30-06, 7mm Mag. 22-inch or 24-inch (7mm Mag.) bbl. Weight: 7 lbs. 10 oz. Hardwood walnut-finished checkered stock. Sights: Hooded ramp front w/gold bead; fully adj. rear. Drilled and tapped for scope mounts. Sling swivel studs. Imported from 1986 to 1987.

Musgrave Premier NR5

Musgrave RSA NR1

Musgrave Valiant NR6

Musketeer Mauser Sporter

MODEL 1500 VARMINT BOLT-ACTION RIFLE
Same as Model 1500 Grade I except w/22-inch heavy bbl. Chambered in .222, .22-250, .223 only. High-luster blued finish or Parkerized satin finished stock. Imported from Japan 1986 to 1987.
High-luster blue. . . . . NiB $385 Ex $309 Gd $262
Parkerized satin finish . . . . NiB $395 Ex $319 Gd $275

MODEL 1700LS CLASSIC
HUNTER BOLT-ACTION RIFLE . . . . NiB $450 Ex $390 Gd $262
Same as Model 1500 Grade I except w/checkered classic-style stock and Schnabel forend. Chambered in 243, 270, 30-06 only. Imported from Japan 1986 to 1987.

MODEL B BOLT-ACTION RIFLE . . . . NiB $300 Ex $175 Gd $93
Takedown. Caliber: .22 LR. Long, Short. Single-shot. 22-inch bbl. Sights: Open rear; bead front. Plain pistol-grip stock. Made from 1930 to 1932.

MODEL K SLIDE-ACTION REPEATER . . . . . NiB $500 Ex $350 Gd $193
Hammerless. Takedown. Caliber: .22 LR. Long, Short. Tubular magazine holds 20 Short, 16 Long, 14 LR. 22-inch bbl. Weight: 5 lbs. Sights: Open rear; bead front. Plain, straight-grip stock. Grooved slide handle. Made from 1922 to 1931.

MODELS L42A, L43, L45A, L46A-LS
See Models 42A, 43, 45A and 46A-LS respectively; "L" refers to a left-hand version of those rifles.

MODEL L SINGLE-SHOT RIFLE . . . . NiB $800 Ex $485 Gd $372
Martini-type falling-block lever-action. Takedown. Caliber: .22 LR, Long, Short. 24-inch bbl. Weight: 5 lbs. Sights: Open rear; bead front. Plain pistol-grip stock and forearm. Made from 1929 to 1932.

MODEL M SLIDE-ACTION REPEATER . . . . NiB $500 Ex $298 Gd $184
Specifications same as for Model K except w/24-inch octagon bbl., pistol-grip stock, weighs 5.5 lbs. Made from 1928 to 1931.

MODEL R BOLT-ACTION REPEATER . . . . . NiB $350 Ex $247 Gd $176
Takedown. Caliber: .22 LR, Long, Short. Tubular magazine. 24-inch bbl. Sights: Open rear; bead front. Plain pistol-grip stock. Made from 1930 to 1932.

MUSGRAVE RIFLES, MUSGRAVE MFRS. & DIST. (PTY) LTD. — Bloemfontein, South Africa

PREMIER NR5 BOLT-
ACTION HUNTING RIFLE . . . . NiB $425 Ex $395 Gd $267
Calibers: .243 Win., .270 Win., .30-06, .308 Win., 7mm Rem. Mag. Five-round magazine. 25.5-inch bbl. Weight: 8.25 lbs. Furnished w/o sights, but drilled and tapped for scope mount. Select walnut Monte Carlo stock w/cheekpiece, checkered pistol-grip and forearm, contrasting pistol-grip cap and forend tip, recoil pad, swivel studs. Musgrave or Mauser action. Made from 1971 to 1976.

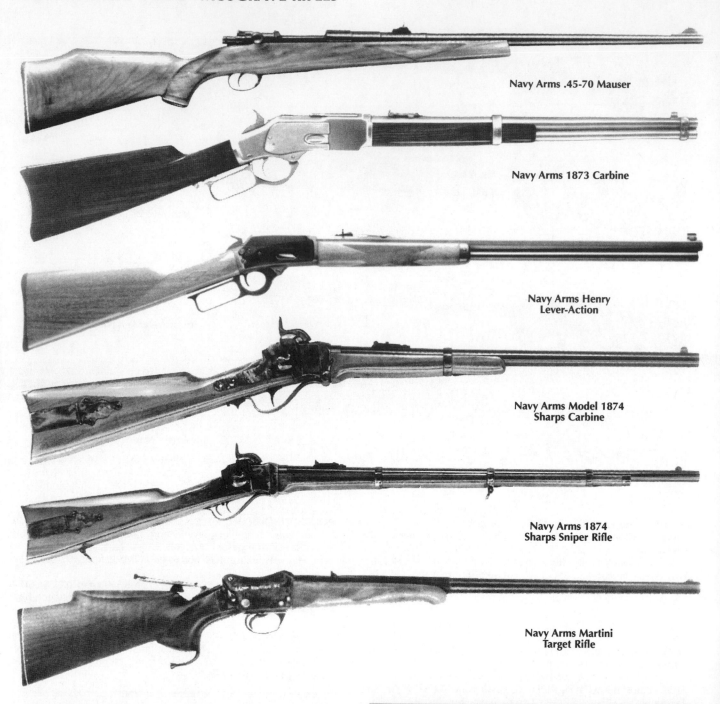

Navy Arms .45-70 Mauser

Navy Arms 1873 Carbine

Navy Arms Henry
Lever-Action

Navy Arms Model 1874
Sharps Carbine

Navy Arms 1874
Sharps Sniper Rifle

Navy Arms Martini
Target Rifle

RSA NR1 BOLT-ACTION
SINGLE-SHOT TARGET RIFLE . . . . . NiB $429 Ex $390 Gd $277
Caliber: .308 Win. (7.62mm NATO). 26.4-inch heavy bbl. Weight:
10 lbs. Sights: Aperture receiver; tunnel front. Walnut target stock
w/beavertail forearm, handguard, bbl. band, rubber buttplate, sling
swivels. Made from 1971 to 1976.

VALIANT NR6 HUNTING RIFLE. . . NiB $375 Ex $344 Gd $236
Similar to Premier except w/24-inch bbl.; stock w/straight
comb, skip French-style checkering, no grip cap or forend tip.
Sights: Leaf rear; hooded ramp front bead sight. Weight: 7.7 lbs.
Made from 1971 to 1976.

MUSKETEER RIFLES — Washington, D.C. Mfd. by Firearms International Corp.

MAUSER SPORTER
FN Mauser bolt action. .243, .25-06, .270, .264 Mag., .308, .30-06,
7mm Mag., .300 Win. Mag. Magazine holds 5 standard, 3 Magnum
cartridges. 24-inch bbl. Weight: 7.25 lbs. No sights. Monte Carlo stock
w/checkered pistol-grip and forearm, swivels. Made 1963 to 1972.
Standard Sporter . . . . NiB $375 Ex $270 Gd $236
Deluxe Sporter . . . . NiB $425 Ex $355 Gd $241
Standard Carbine. . . . . NiB $375 Ex $324 Gd $236

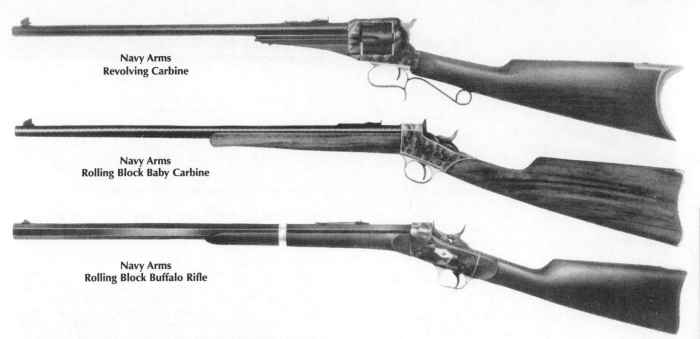

Navy Arms
Revolving Carbine

Navy Arms
Rolling Block Baby Carbine

Navy Arms
Rolling Block Buffalo Rifle

NAVY ARMS — Ridgefield, New Jersey

.45-70 MAUSER CARBINE........ NiB $257 Ex $206 Gd $150
Same as .45-70 Mauser Rifle except w/18-inch bbl., straight-grip stock w/low comb, weight: 7.5 lbs. Disc.

.45-70 MAUSER RIFLE.......... NiB $232 Ex $191 Gd $139
Siamese Mauser bolt action. Caliber: .45-70 Govt. Three-round magazine. 24- or 26-inch bbl. Weight: 8.5 lbs. w/26-inch bbl. Sights: Open rear; ramp front: Checkered stock w/Monte Carlo comb. Intoduced 1973. Disc.

MODEL 1873 WINCHESTER
BORDER RIFLE .... NiB $1027 Ex $800 Gd $338
Replica of Winchester Model 1873 Short Rifle. Calibers: .357 Mag., .44-40, and .45 Colt. 20- inch bbl., 39.25 inches overall. Weight: 7.6 lbs. Blued full octagonal barrel, color casehardened receiver w/walnut stocks. Made from 1999 to 2009.

MODEL 1873 CARBINE .... NiB $950 Ex $700 Gd $368
Similar to Model 1873 Rifle except w/blued receiver, 10-round magazine, 19-inch round bbl. carbine-style forearm w/bbl. band, weighs 6.75 lbs. Disc. Reissued in 1991 in .44-40 or .45 Colt.

MODEL 1873 LEVER-ACTION RIFLE ..... NiB $950 Ex $725 Gd $394
Replica of Winchester Model 1873. Casehardened receiver. Calibers: .22 LR. .357 Magnum, .44-40. 15-round magazine. 24-inch octagon bbl. Weight: 8 lbs. Sights: Open rear; blade front. Straight-grip stock, forearm w/end cap. Disc. Reissued in 1991 in .44-40 or .45 Colt w/12-round magazine. Disc. 1994.

MODEL 1873 TRAPPER......... NiB $700 Ex $519 Gd $382
Same as Model 1873 Carbine, except w/16.5-inch bbl., 8-round magazine, weighs 6.25 lbs. Disc.

MODEL 1873 SPORTING CARBINE/RIFLE
Replica of Winchester Model 1873 Sporting Rifle. Calibers: .357 Mag. (24.25-inch bbl. only), .44-40 and .45 Colt. 24.25-inch bbl. (Carbine) or 30-inch bbl. (Rifle). 48.75 to 53 inches overall. Weight: 8.14 to 9.3 lbs. Octagonal barrel, case-hardened receiver and checkered walnut pistol-grip. Made from 1999 to 2003.
Carbine model................ NiB $9500 Ex $781 Gd $424
Rifle model .... NiB $995 Ex $883 Gd $475

MODEL 1874 SHARPS
CAVALRY CARBINE............ NiB $975 Ex $704 Gd $551
Replica of Sharps 1874 Cavalry Carbine. Similar to Sniper Model, except w/22-inch bbl. and carbine stock. Caliber: .45-70. Imported from 1997 to 2009.

MODEL 1874 SHARPS SNIPER RIFLE
Replica of Sharps 1874 Sharpshooter's Rifle. Caliber: .45-70. Falling breech, single-shot. 30-inch bbl. 46.75 inches overall. Weight: 8.5 lbs. Double-set triggers. Color casehardened receiver. Blade front sight; rear sight w/elevation leaf. Polished blued bbl. Military three-band stock w/patch box. Imported from 1994 to 2000.
Infantry model (single trigger) .... NiB $896 Ex $758 Gd $600
Sniper model (double set trigger) ...... NiB $1950 Ex $1058 Gd $900

ENGRAVED MODELS
Yellowboy and Model 1873 rifles are available in deluxe models w/select walnut stocks and forearms and engraving in three grades. Grade "A" has delicate scrollwork in limited areas. Grade "B" is more elaborate with 40 percent coverage. Grade "C" has highest grade engraving. Add to value:
Grade "A" .... NiB $962 Ex $717 Gd $560
Grade "B" .... NiB $1088 Ex $938 Gd $775
Grade "C" .... NiB $1510 Ex $944 Gd $683

HENRY LEVER-ACTION RIFLE
Replica of the Winchester Model 1860 Henry Rifle. Caliber: .44-40. Twelve round magazine. 16.5-, 22- or 24.25-inch octagon bbl. Weight: 7.5 to 9 lbs. 35.4 to 43.25 inches overall. Sights: Blade front, adjustable ladder rear. European walnut straight grip buttstock w/bbl. and side stock swivels. Imported from 1985 to date. Brass or steel receiver. Blued or color casehardened metal.
Carbine model w/22-inch bbl.,
introduced 1992) .... NiB $685 Ex $459 Gd $329
Military rifle model (w/brass frame) ...... NiB $925 Ex $659 Gd $429
Trapper model (w/brass frame).......... NiB $685 Ex $559 Gd $429
Trapper model (w/iron frame).......... NiB $1000 Ex $786 Gd $450
W/"A" engraving, add....................................$300
W/"B" engraving, add....................................$500
W/"C" engraving, add....................................$900

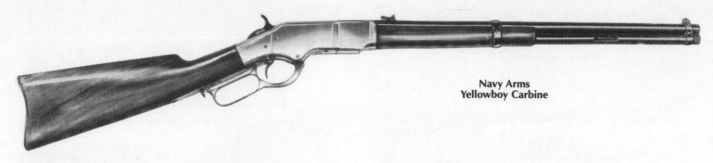

**Navy Arms
Yellowboy Carbine**

MARTINI TARGET RIFLE . . . . **NiB $480 Ex $344 Gd $281**
Martini single-shot action. Calibers: .444 Marlin, .45-70. 26- or 30-inch half-octagon or full-octagon bbl. Weight: 9 lbs. w/26-inch bbl. Sights: Creedmoor tang peep, open middle, blade front. Stock w/cheekpiece and pistol-grip, forearm w/Schnabel tip, both checkered. Intro. 1972. Disc.

REVOLVING CARBINE . . . . **NiB $575 Ex $490 Gd $367**
Action resembles that of Remington Model 1875 Revolver. Casehardened frame. Calibers: .357 Magnum, .44-40, .45 Colt. Six round cylinder. 20-inch bbl. Weight: 5 lbs. Sights: Open rear; blade front. Straight-grip stock brass trigger guard and buttplate. Intro. 1968. Disc.

ROLLING BLOCK BABY CARBINE . . . . **NiB $215 Ex $184 Gd $147**
Replica of small Remington Rolling Block single-shot action. Casehardened frame, brass trigger guard. Calibers: .22 LR. .22 Hornet, .357 Magnum, .44-40. 20-inch octagon or 22-inch round bbl. Weight: 5 lbs. Sights: Open rear; blade front. Straight-grip stock, plain forearm, brass buttplate. Imported from 1968 to 1981.

ROLLING BLOCK BUFFALO CARBINE. . . . **NiB $385 Ex $290 Gd $199**
Same as Buffalo Rifle except w/18-inch bbl., weight: 10 lbs

ROLLING BLOCK BUFFALO RIFLE. . . . . . . **NiB $655 Ex $532 Gd $278**
Replica Remington Rolling Block single-shot action. Casehardened frame, brass trigger guard. Calibers: .444 Marlin, .45-70, .50-70. 26- or 30-inch heavy half-octagon or full-octagon bbl. Weight: 11 to 12 lbs. Sights: Open rear; blade front. Straight-grip stock w/brass buttplate, forearm w/brass bbl. band. Made from 1971 to 2003.

ROLLING BLOCK CREEDMOOR RIFLE
Same as Buffalo Rifle except calibers .45-70 and .50-70 only, 28- or 30-inch heavy half-octagon or full-octagon bbl., Creedmoor tang peep sight.
Target model . . . . **NiB $1450 Ex $918 Gd $648**
Deluxe target model (disc. 1998) . . . . . **NiB $1625 Ex $1284 Gd $1054**

YELLOWBOY CARBINE. . . . . **NiB $800 Ex $566 Gd $428**
Similar to Yellowboy Rifle except w/19-inch bbl., 10-round magazine (14-round in 22 Long Rifle), carbine-style forearm. Weight: 6.75 lbs. Disc. Reissued 1991 in .44-40 only.

YELLOWBOY LEVER-ACTION REPEATER . . . . . **NiB $950 Ex $542 Gd $339**
Replica of Winchester Model 1866. Calibers: .38 Special, .44-40. 15-round magazine. 24-inch octagon bbl. Weight: 8 lbs. Sights: Folding leaf rear; blade front. Straight-grip stock, forearm w/end cap. Intro. 1966. Disc. Reissued 1991 in .44-40 only w/12-round magazine and adj. ladder-style rear sight.

YELLOWBOY TRAPPER'S MODEL. . . . . **NiB $675 Ex $487 Gd $342**
Same as Yellowboy Carbine except w/16.5-inch bbl., 8-round magazine, weighs 6.25 lbs. Disc.

NEW ENGLAND FIREARMS — Gardner, Massachusetts

In 1987, New England Firearms was established as an independent company producing selected H&R models under the NEF logo. In 1991, H&R 1871, Inc. was formed from the residual of the parent company and that took over the New England Firearms facility. H&R 1871 produced firearms under both its logo and the NEF brand name until 1999, when the Marlin Firearms Company acquired the assets of H&R 1871.

HANDI-RIFLE. . . . . **NiB $220 Ex $170 Gd $124**
Single-shot, break-open action w/side-lever release. Calibers: .22 Hornet, .22-250, .223, .243, .270, .30-30, .30-06, .45-70. 22-inch bbl. Weight: 7 lbs. Sights: Ramp front; folding rear. Drilled and tapped for scope mounts. Walnut-finished hardwood or synthetic stock. Blued finish. Made from 1989 to 2008.

NEWTON SPORTING RIFLES — Buffalo, New York Mfd. by Newton Arms Co., Charles Newton Rifles Corp. and Buffalo Newton Rifle Co.

**BUFFALO
SPORTING RIFLE.** . . . . **NiB $2500 Ex $1744 Gd $935**
Same general specifications as Standard Model, Second Type. Made c. 1922 to 1932 by Buffalo Newton Rifle Co.

**MAUSER
SPORTING RIFLE.** . . . . **NiB $2000 Ex $1586 Gd $1084**
Mauser (Oberndorf) action. Caliber: .256 Newton. Five round box magazine, hinged floorplate. Double-set triggers. 24-inch bbl. Open rear sight, ramp front sight. Sporting stock w/checkered pistol-grip. Weight: 7 lbs. Made c. 1914 by Newton Arms Co.

**STANDARD MODEL
SPORTING RIFLE, FIRST TYPE** . . . . **NiB $3500 Ex $1968 Gd $971**
Newton bolt action, interrupted screw-type breech-locking mechanism, double-set triggers. Calibers: .22, .256, .280, .30, ,33, ,35 Newton; ,30-06. 24-inch bbl. Sights: Open rear or cocking-piece peep; ramp front. Checkered pistol-grip stock. Weight: 7 to 8 lbs., depending on caliber. Made c. 1916 to 1918 by Newton Arms Co. Second type was prototype only; never manufactured.

NEWTON SPRINGFIELD. . . . . **NiB $1200 Ex $807 Gd $565**
Kit including a Marlin-built sporting stock with .256 Newton barrel. Springfield 1903 action and sights provided by customer. Original has square-cut barrels marked "Newton Arms Co. Buffalo, NY." Mfg. 1914 to 1917.

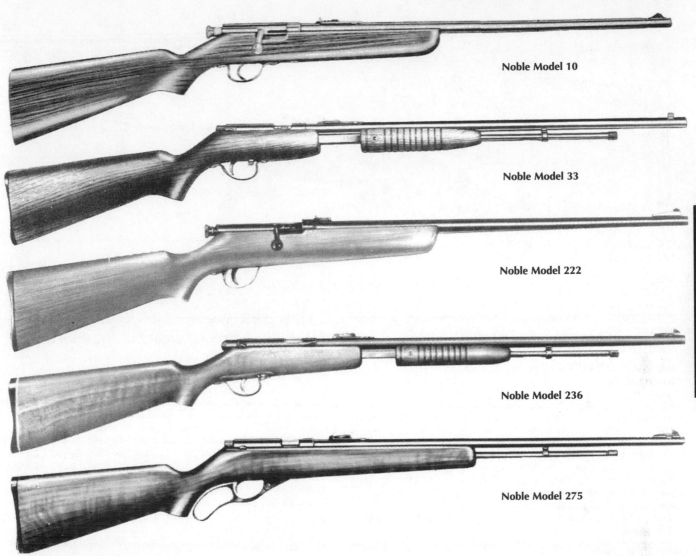

Noble Model 10

Noble Model 33

Noble Model 222

Noble Model 236

Noble Model 275

NIKKO FIREARMS, LTD. — Tochiga, Japan

See listings under Golden Eagle Rifles.

NOBLE MFG. CO. — Haydenville, Massachusetts

MODEL 10 BOLT-ACTION
SINGLE-SHOT RIFLE . . . . **NiB $94 Ex $87 Gd $66**
Caliber: .22 LR. Long, Short. 24-inch bbl. Plain pistol-grip stock.
Sights: Open rear, bead front. Weight: 4 lbs. Made 1955 to 1958.

MODEL 20 BOLT-ACTION
SINGLE-SHOT RIFLE . . . . **NiB $97 Ex $82 Gd $63**
Manually cocked. Caliber: .22 LR. Long, Short. 22-inch bbl. Weight:
5 lbs. Sights: Open rear; bead front. Walnut stock w/pistol grip.
Made from 1958 to 1963.

MODEL 33 SLIDE-ACTION REPEATER . . . . . . **NiB $117 Ex $97 Gd $73**
Hammerless. Caliber: .22 LR. Long, Short. Tubular magazine holds
21 Short, 17 Long, 15 LR. 24-inch bbl. Weight: 6 lbs. Sights: Open
rear; bead front. Tenite stock and slide handle. Made 1949 to 1953.

MODEL 33A . . . . **NiB $104 Ex $87 Gd $66**
Same general specifications as Model 33 except w/wood stock and
slide handle. Made from 1953 to 1955.

MODEL 222 BOLT-ACTION
SINGLE-SHOT RIFLE . . . . **NiB $117 Ex $97 Gd $73**
Manually cocked. Caliber: .22 LR. Long, Short. Barrel integral
w/receiver. Overall length: 38 inches. Weight: 5 lbs. Sights:
Interchangeable V-notch and peep rear; ramp front. Scope mounting
base. Pistol-grip stock. Made from 1958 to 1971.

MODEL 236 SLIDE-ACTION
REPEATING RIFLE . . . . **NiB $129 Ex $110 Gd $93**
Hammerless. Caliber: .22 Short, Long, LR. Tubular magazine holds
21 Short, 17 Long, 15 LR. 24-inch bbl. Weight: 5.5 lbs. Sights:
Open rear; ramp front. Pistol-grip stock, grooved slide handle.
Made from 1951 to 1971.

MODEL 275 LEVER-ACTION RIFLE . . . . **NiB $174 Ex $118 Gd $92**
Hammerless. Caliber: .22 Short, Long, LR. Tubular magazine holds
21 Short, 17 Long, 15 LR. 24-inch bbl. Weight: 5.5 lbs. Sights: Open
rear; ramp front. Stock w/semipistol-grip. Made from 1958 to 1971.

Parker-Hale Model 81 Classic

Parker-Hale Model 87

NORINCO — Mfd. by Northern China Industries Corp., Beijing, China, *Imported by Century International Arms; Interarms; KBI and others.*

MODEL 81S/AK SEMIAUTOMATIC RIFLE
Semiautomatic Kalashnikov style AK-47 action. Caliber: 7.62x39mm. Five, 30- or 40-round magazine. 17.5-inch bbl. 36.75 inches overall. Weight: 8.5 lbs. Hooded post front sight, 500 meters leaf rear sight. Oil-finished hardwood (military style) buttstock, pistol grip, forearm and hand-guard or folding metal stock. Black oxide finish. Imported 1988 to 1989.
Model 81S (w/wood stock) . . . . NiB $1200 Ex $912 Gd $680
Model 81S-1 (w/under-folding metal stock) . . NiB $1222 Ex $991 Gd $676
Model 81S-5/56S-2 (w/side-folding metal stock) . . . . NiB $1289 Ex $984 Gd $722

MODEL 84S/AK SEMIAUTOMATIC RIFLE
Semiautomatic Kalashnikov style AK-47 action. Caliber: .223 (5.56mm). 30-round magazine. 16.25-inch bbl. 35.5 inches overall. Weight: 8.75 lbs. Hooded post front sight, 800 meters leaf rear sight. Oil-finished hardwood (military style) buttstock, pistol grip, forearm and handguard; sporterized composite fiberglass stock or folding metal stock. Black oxide finish. Imported from 1988 to 1989.
Model 84S (w/wood stock) . . . . NiB $1450 Ex $991 Gd $658
Model 84S-1 (w/under-folding metal stock) . . NiB $1655 Ex $912 Gd $631
Model 84S-3 (w/composite stock) . . . . . . NiB $1295 Ex $987 Gd $614
Model 84S-5 (w/side-folding metal stock) . . . . NiB $1613 Ex $981 Gd $687

MODEL AK-47 THUMBHOLE SPORTER
Semiautomatic AK-47 sporterized variant. Calibers: .223 (5.56mm) or 7.62x39mm. Five round magazine. 16.25-inch bbl. or 23.25-inch bbl. 35.5 or 42.5 inches overall. Weight: 8.5 to 10.3 lbs. Adj. post front sight, open adj. rear. Forged receiver w/black oxide finish. Walnut-finished thumbhole stock w/recoil pad. Imported from 1991 to 1993.
Model AK-47 Sporter (5.56mm) . . . . NiB $750 Ex $443 Gd $313
Model AK-47 Sporter (7.62x39mm) . . . . . . NiB $519 Ex $422 Gd $299

MODEL MAK 90/01 SPORT . . . . . . NiB $700 Ex $418 Gd $300
Similar to Model AK-47 Thumbhole Sporter except w/minor modifications implemented to meet importation requirements. Imported from 1994 to 1995.

OLYMPIC ARMS — Olympia, Washington

PCR SERIES
Gas-operated semi-auto action. Calibers: .17 Rem., .223, 7.62x39, 6x45, 6PPC or 9mm, .40 S&W, 4.5ACP (in carbine version only). Ten-round magazine. 16-, 20- or 24-inch bbl. Weight: 7 to 10.2 lbs. Black composite stocks. Post front, rear adj. sights; scope ready flat-top. Barrel fluting. William set trigger. Made from 1994 to date.
PCR-1/Ultra Match . . . . NiB $950 Ex $736 Gd $576
PCR-2/MultiMatch ML-1 . . . . NiB $985 Ex $880 Gd $618
PCR-3/MultiMatch ML-2 . . . . NiB $1042 Ex 936 Gd $627
PCR-4/AR-15 Match . . . . NiB $850 Ex $751 Gd $635
PCR-5/CAR-15 (.223 Rem.) . . . . NiB $950 Ex $782 Gd $499
PCR-5/CAR-15 (9mm, 40S&W, 45ACP) . . . . NiB $872 Ex $774 Gd $511
PCR-5/CAR-15 (.223 Rem.) . . . . NiB $925 Ex $661 Gd $465
PCR-6/A-2 (7.62x39mm) . . . . NiB $895 Ex $692 Gd $486

PARKER-HALE LIMITED — Birmingham, England

MODEL 81 AFRICAN . . . . NiB $875 Ex $769 Gd $511
Same general specifications as Model 81 Classic except in caliber .375 H&H only. Sights: African Express rear; hooded blade front. Barrel-band swivel. All-steel trigger guard. Checkered European walnut stock w/pistol grip and recoil pad. Engraved receiver. Imported from 1986 to 1991.

MODEL 81 CLASSIC
BOLT-ACTION RIFLE . . . . NiB $715 Ex $600 Gd $408
Calibers: .22-250, .243 Win., .270 Win., 6mm Rem., 6.5x55, 7x57, 7x64, .308 Win., .30-06, .300 Win. Mag., 7mm Rem. Mag. Four round magazine. 24-inch bbl. Weight: 7.75 lbs. Sights: Adj. open rear, hooded ramp front. Checkered pistol-grip stock of European walnut. Imported from 1984 to 1991.

MODEL 85 SNIPER RIFLE . . . . . . NiB $2650 Ex $1930 Gd $937
Caliber: .308 Win. Ten or 20-round M-14-type magazine. 24.25-inch bbl. 45 inches overall. Weight: 12.5 lbs. Blade front sight, folding aperture rear. McMillan fiberglass stock w/detachable bipod. Imported from 1989 to 1991.

Parker-Hale Model 1100
Lightweight

Parker-Hale Model 1200
Super Clip

MODEL 87 BOLT-ACTION
REPEATING TARGET RIFLE . . . . . **NiB $1385 Ex $1202 Gd $738**
Calibers: .243 Win., 6.5x55, .308 Win., .30-06 Springfield, .300 Win. Mag. Five-round detachable box magazine. 26-inch bbl. 45 inches overall. Weight: 10 lbs. No sights; grooved for target-style scope mounts. Stippled walnut stock w/adj. buttplate. Sling swivel studs. Parkerized finish. Folding bipod. Imported 1988 to 1991.

MODEL 1000 STANDARD RIFLE . . . . **NiB $400 Ex $321 Gd $237**
Calibers: .22-250, .243 Win., .270 Win., 6mm Rem., .308 Win., .30-06. Four-round magazine. Bolt action. 22-inch or 24-inch (22-250) bbl. 43 inches overall. 7.25 lbs. Checkered walnut Monte Carlo-style stock w/satin finish. Imported from 1984 to 1988.

MODEL 1100 LIGHTWEIGHT
BOLT-ACTION RIFLE . . . . **NiB $495 Ex $400 Gd $316**
Same general specifications as Model 1000 Standard except w/22-inch lightweight profile bbl., hollow bolt handle, alloy trigger guard and floorplate, 6.5 lbs., Schnabel forend. Imported 1984 to 1991.

MODEL 1100M AFRICAN
MAGNUM RIFLE . . . . **NiB $800 Ex $720 Gd $489**
Same as Model 1000 Standard except w/24-inch bbl. in calibers .404 Jeffery, .458 Win. Mag. Weight: 9.5 lbs. Sights: Adj. rear; hooded post front. Imported from 1984 to 1991.

MODEL 1200 SUPER CLIP
BOLT-ACTION RIFLE . . . . **NiB $542 Ex $499 Gd $319**
Same as Model 1200 Super except w/detachable box magazine in calibers .243 Win., 6mm Rem., .270 Win. .30-06 and .308 Win., .300 Win. Mag., 7mm Rem. Mag. Imported from 1984 to 1991.

MODEL 1200 SUPER BOLT-ACTION
SPORTING RIFLE . . . . **NiB $542 Ex $489 Gd $309**
Mauser-type bolt action. Calibers: .22-250, .243 Win., 6mm Rem., .25-06, .270 Win., .30-06, .308 Win. Four round magazine. 24-inch bbl. Weight: 7.25 lbs. Sights: Folding open rear, hooded ramp front. European walnut stock w/rollover Monte Carlo cheekpiece, rosewood forend tip and pistol-grip cap, skip checkering, recoil pad, sling swivels. Imported from 1968 to 1991.

MODEL 1200 SUPER MAGNUM . . . . **NiB $634 Ex $515 Gd $335**
Same general specifications as 1200 Super except calibers 7mm Rem. Mag. and .300 Win. Mag., 3-round magazine. Imported 1988 to 1991.

MODEL 1200P PRESENTATION . . . . **NiB $545 Ex $443 Gd $313**
Same general specifications as 1200 Super except w/scroll-engraved action, trigger guard and floorplate, no sights. QD swivels. Calibers: .243 Win. and .30-06. Imported from 1969 to 1975.

MODEL 1200V VARMINT . . . . **NiB $527 Ex $474 Gd $417**
Same general specifications as 1200 Super, except w/24-inch heavy bbl., no sights, weight: 9.5 lbs. Calibers: .22-250, 6mm Rem., .25-06, .243 Win. Imported from 1969-89.

MODEL 1300C SCOUT . . . . **NiB $695 Ex $660 Gd $531**
Calibers: .243, .308 Win. 10-round magazine. 20-inch bbl. w/muzzle brake. 41 inches overall. Weight: 8.5 lbs. No sights, drilled and tapped for scope. Checkered laminated birch stock w/QD swivels. Imported in 1991.

MODEL 2100 MIDLAND
BOLT-ACTION RIFLE . . . . **NiB $325 Ex $308 Gd $210**
Calibers: .22-250, .243 Win., 6mm Rem., .270 Win., 6.5x55, 7x57, 7x64, .308 Win, .30-06. Four-round box magazine. 22-inch or 24-inch (22-250) bbl. 43-inches overall. Weight: 7 lbs. Sights: Adj. folding rear; hooded ramp front. Checkered European walnut Monte Carlo stock w/pistol-grip. Imported from 1984 to 1991.

MODEL 2700 LIGHTWEIGHT . . . . **NiB $340 Ex $313 Gd $210**
Same general specifications as Model 2100 Midland except w/tapered lightweight bbl. and aluminum trigger guard. Weight: 6.5 lbs. Imported in 1991.

MODEL 2800 MIDLAND . . . . **NiB $349 Ex $287 Gd $234**
Same general specifications as model 2100 except w/laminated birch stock. Imported in 1991.

PEDERSEN CUSTOM GUNS — North Haven, Connecticut, Division of O.F. Mossberg & Sons, Inc.

MODEL 3000 GRADE I
BOLT-ACTION RIFLE . . . . **NiB $990 Ex $777 Gd $515**
Richly engraved w/silver inlays, full-fancy American black walnut stock. Mossberg Model 810 action. Calibers: .270 Win., .30-06, 7mm Rem. Mag., .338 Win. Mag. Three-round magazine, hinged floorplate. 22-inch bbl. in .270 and .30-06, 24-inch in Magnums. Weight: 7 to 8 lbs. Sights: Open rear; hooded ramp front. Monte Carlo stock w/roll-over cheekpiece, wraparound hand checkering on pistol grip and forearm, rosewood pistol-grip cap and forend tip, recoil pad or steel buttplate w/trap, detachable swivels. Imported 1973 to 1975.

MODEL 3000 GRADE II . . . . **NiB $660 Ex $453 Gd $357**
Same as Model 3000 Grade I except less elaborate engraving, no inlays, fancy grade walnut stock w/recoil pad. Imported 1973 to 1975.

MODEL 3000 GRADE III . . . . **NiB $550 Ex $350 Gd $287**
Same as Model 3000 Grade I except no engraving or inlays, select grade walnut stock w/recoil pad. Imported from 1973 to 1974.

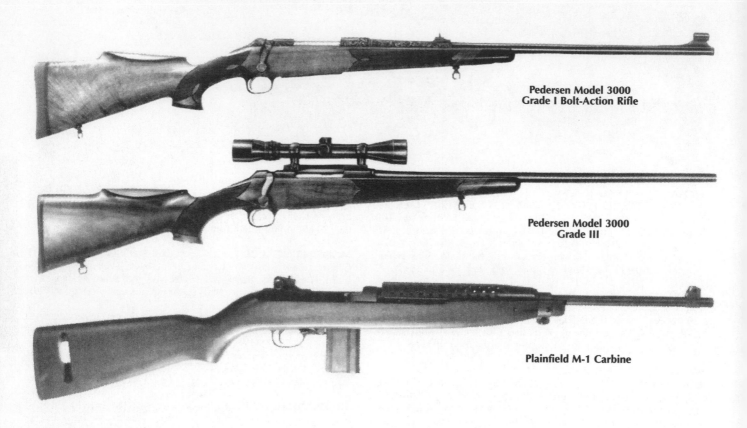

**Pedersen Model 3000
Grade I Bolt-Action Rifle**

**Pedersen Model 3000
Grade III**

Plainfield M-1 Carbine

**MODEL 4700 CUSTOM
DELUXE LEVER-ACTION RIFLE.........NiB $250 Ex $230 Gd $166**
On Mossberg Model .472 action. Calibers: .30-30, 35 Rem. Five-round tubular magazine. 24-inch bbl. Weight: 7.5 lbs. Sights: Open rear, hooded ramp front. Hand-finished black walnut stock and beavertail forearm, barrel band swivels. Imported in 1975.

J.C. PENNEY CO., INC. — Dallas, Texas

Firearms sold under the J.C. Penney label were mfd. by Marlin, High Standard, Stevens, Savage and Springfield.

MODEL 2025 BOLT-ACTION REPEATER......NiB $92 Ex $62 Gd $57
Takedown. Caliber: .22 RF. Eight round detachable box magazine. 24-inch bbl. Weight: 6 lbs. Sights: Open rear; bead front. Plain pistol-grip stock. Manufactured by Marlin.

MODEL 2035 BOLT-ACTION REPEATER......NiB $92 Ex $62 Gd $57
Takedown. Caliber: .22 RF. Eight round detachable box magazine. 24-inch bbl. Weight: 6 lbs. Sights: Open rear; bead front. Plain pistol-grip stock. Manufactured by Marlin.

MODEL 2935 LEVER-ACTION RIFLE.....NiB $201 Ex $166 Gd $115
Same general specifications as Marlin Model 336.

**MODEL 6400 BOLT-ACTION
CENTERFIRE RIFLE.............NiB $186 Ex $150 Gd $105**
Same general specifications as Savage Model 340.

**MODEL 6660
AUTOLOADING RIFLE..................NiB $97 Ex $82 Gd $72**
Caliber: .22 RF. Tubular magazine. 22-inch bbl. Weight: 5.5 lbs. Sights: Open rear; hooded ramp front. Plain pistol-grip stock. Manufactured by Marlin.

PLAINFIELD MACHINE COMPANY — Dunellen, New Jersey

M-1 CARBINE................NiB $202 Ex $157 Gd $121
Same as U.S. Carbine, Cal. .30, M-1 except also available in caliber 5.7mm (.22 caliber w/necked-down .30 Carbine cartridge case). Current production w/ventilated metal handguard and barrel band w/o bayonet lug; earlier models have standard military-type fittings. Made from 1960 to 1977.

**M-1 CARBINE,
COMMANDO MODEL................NiB $208 Ex $177 Gd $131**
Same as M-1 Carbine except w/paratrooper-type stock w/telescoping wire shoulderpiece. Made from 1960 to 1977.

M-1 CARBINE, MILITARY SPORTER......NiB $202 Ex $172 Gd $136
Same as M-1 Carbine except w/unslotted buttstock and wood handguard. Made from 1960 to 1977.

M-1 DELUXE SPORTER..........NiB $208 Ex $177 Gd $131
Same as M-1 Carbine except w/Monte Carlo sporting stock Made from 1960 to 1973.

Polish Model 1929 Mauser

Purdey Double Rifle

Purdey Bolt-Action Rifle

POLISH MILITARY RIFLES — Manufactured by Government Arsenals at Radom and Warsaw, Poland

MODEL 1898 (KARABIN 98, K98)
MAUSER MILITARY CARBINE . . . . **Nib $304 Ex $197 Gd $156**
Same as German Kar. 98A except for minor details. First manufactured during early 1920s.

MODEL 1898 (KARABIN 98, WZ98A)
MAUSER MILITARY RIFLE . . . . **NiB $266 Ex $177 Gd $141**
Same as German Kar. 98 used in WWI except for minor details. Manufacture began c. 1921.

MODEL 1929 (KARABIN 29, WZ29)
MAUSER MILITARY RIFLE . . . . **NiB $304 Ex $207 Gd $156**
Same as Czech Model 24, mfd. 1929 thru WWII except for minor details. A similar model produced during German occupation was designated Gew. 29/40.

WILLIAM POWELL & SON LTD. — Birmingham, England

DOUBLE-BARREL RIFLE . . . . **NiB $31,250 Ex $25,000 Gd $17,000**
Boxlock. Made to order in any caliber during the time that rifle was manufactured. Bbls.: Made to order in any legal length, but 26 inches recommended. Highest grade French walnut buttstock and forearm w/fine checkering. Metal is elaborately engraved. Imported by Stoeger from 1938 to 1951.

BOLT-ACTION RIFLE . . . . **NiB $2790 Ex $2265 Gd $1593**
Mauser-type bolt action. Calibers: 6x54 through .375 H&H Magnum. Three and 4-shot magazine, depending upon chambering. 24-inch bbl. Weight: 7.5 to 8.75 lbs. Sights: Folding leaf rear; hooded ramp front. Cheekpiece stock, checkered forearm and pistol grip, swivels. Imported by Stoeger from 1938 to 1951.

JAMES PURDEY & SONS LTD. — London, England

DOUBLE RIFLE
Sidelock action, hammerless, ejectors. Almost any caliber is available but the following are the most popular: .375 Flanged Magnum Nitro Express, .500/465 Nitro Express .470 Nitro Express, .577 Nitro Express. 25.5-inch bbls. (25-inch in .375). Weight: 9.5 to 12.75 lbs. Sights: Folding leaf rear; ramp front. Cheekpiece stock, checkered forearm and pistol-grip, recoil pad, swivels. Currently manufactured to individual measurements and specifications; same general specifications apply to pre-WWII model.
H&H calibers . . . . **NiB $69,375 Ex $55,500 Gd $37,740**
NE calibers . . . . **NiB $85,000 Ex $55,500 Gd $37,774**

BOLT-ACTION RIFLE . . . . **NiB $22,000 Ex $19,000 Gd $12,000**
Mauser-type bolt action. Calibers: 7x57, .300 H&H Magnum, .375 H&H Magnum, 10.75x73. Three round magazine. 24-inch bbl. Weight: 7.5 to 8.75 lbs. Sights: Folding leaf rear; hooded ramp front. Cheekpiece stock, checkered forearm and pistol-grip, swivels. Currently manufactured; same general specifications apply to pre-WWII model.

RAPTOR ARMS COMPANY, INC. — Newport, New Hampshire

BOLT-ACTION RIFLE
Calibers: .243 Win., .270 Win., .30-06 or .308 Win. Four round magazine. 22-inch sporter or heavy bbl. Weight: 7.3 to 8 lbs. 42.5 inches overall. No sights w/drilled and tapped receiver or optional blade front, adjustable rear. Blue, stainless or "Taloncote" rust-resistant finish. Checkered black synthetic stock w/Monte Carlo cheepiece and vented recoil pad. Imported from 1997 to 1999.
Raptor Sporter model . . . . **NiB $231 Ex $181 Gd $147**
Raptor Deluxe Peregrine model (Disc. 1998) . . . . **NiB $233 Ex $455 Gd $195**
Raptor heavy barrel model . . . . **NiB $267 Ex $212 Gd $188**
Raptor stainless barrel model . . . . **NiB $281 Ex $247 Gd $202**
W/optional sights, add $30

Remington No. 7
Target and Sporting Rifle

REMINGTON ARMS COMPANY — Ilion, New York and Mayfield, KY.

To facilitate locating Remington firearms, models are grouped into four categories: Single-shot rifles, bolt-action repeating rifles, slide-action (pump) rifles, and semiautomatic rifles. For a complete listing, please refer to the index.

SINGLE-SHOT RIFLES

NO. 1 SPORTING RIFLE . . . . . NiB $6000 Ex $3701 Gd $2188
Single-Shot, rolling-block action. Calibers: .40-50, .40-70, .44-77, .50-45, .50-70 Gov't. centerfire and .44 Long, .44 Extra Long, .45-70, .46 Long, .46 Extra Long, .50-70 rimfire. Bbl. lengths: 28- or 30-inch part octagon. Weight: 5 to 7.5 lbs. Sights: Folding leaf rear sight; sporting front, dovetail bases. Plain walnut straight stock; flanged-top, semicarbine buttplate. Plain walnut forend with thin, rounded front end. Made from 1868 to 1902.

NO. 1 1/2 SPORTING RIFLE . . . NiB $4000 Ex $3086 Gd $1755
Single-Shot, rolling-block action. Calibers: .22 Short, Long, or Extra Long. 25 Stevens, .32, and .38 rimfire cartridges. .32-20, .38-40 and .44-40 centerfire. Bbl. lengths: 24-, 26-, 28- or 30-inch part octagon. Remaining features similar to Remington No. 1. Made from 1869 to 1902.

NO. 2 SPORTING RIFLE
Single-shot, rolling-block action. Calibers: .22, .25, .32, .38, .44 rimfire or centerfire. Bbl. lengths: 24, 26, 28 or 30 inches. Weight: 5 to 6 lbs. Sights: Open rear; bead front. Straight-grip sporting stock and knobtip forearm of walnut. Made from 1873 to 1909.
Calibers: .22, .25, .32 . . . . NiB $3500 Ex $1958 Gd $923
Calibers: .38, .44 . . . . NiB $3515 Ex $2084 Gd $1049

NO. 3 CREEDMOOR
AND SCHUETZEN RIFLES . . . . . NiB $16,187 Ex $12,750 Gd $10,510
Produced in a variety of styles and calibers, these are collector's items and bring far higher prices than the sporting types. The Schuetzen Special, which has an under-lever action, is especially rare — perhaps fewer than 100 have been made.

NO. 3 HIGH POWER RIFLE
Single-shot, Hepburn falling-block action w/side lever. Calibers: .30-30, .30-40, .32 Special, .32-40, .38-55, .38-72 (high-power cartridges). Bbl. lengths: 26-, 28-, 30-inch. Weight: About 8 lbs. Open sporting sights. Checkered pistol-grip stock and forearm. Made from 1893 to 1907.
Calibers: .30-30, .30-40,
.32 Special, .32-40 . . . . NiB $9000 Ex $7828 Gd $5057
Calibers: .38-55, .38-72 . . . . NiB $9500 Ex $7981 Gd $6305

NO. 3 SPORTING RIFLE . . . . . . NiB $9000 Ex $7141 Gd $6606
Single-shot, Hepburn falling-block action w/side lever. Calibers: .22

WCF, .22 Extra Long, .25-20 Stevens, .25-21 Stevens, .25-25 Stevens, .32 WCF, .32-40 Ballard & Marlin, .32-40 Rem., .38 WCF, .38-40 Rem., 38-.38-50 Rem., .38-55 Ballard & Marlin, .40-60 Ballard & Marlin, .40-60 WCF, .40-65 Rem. Straight, .40-82 WCF, .45-70 Gov., .45-90 WCF, also was supplied on special order in bottle-necked .40-50, .40-70, .40-90, .44-77, .44-90, .44-105, .50-70 Gov., .50-90 Sharps Straight. Bbl. lengths: 26-inch (22, 25, 32 cal. only), 28-inch, 30-inch; half-octagon or full-octagon. Weight: 8 to 10 lbs. Sights: Open rear; blade front. Checkered pistol-grip stock and forearm. Made from 1880 to c. 1911.

NO. 4 SINGLE-SHOT RIFLE . . . . NiB $1500 Ex $909 Gd $752
Rolling-block action. Solid frame or takedown. Calibers: .22 Short and Long, .22 LR. .25 Stevens R.F., .32 Short and Long R.F. 22.5-inch octagon bbl., 24-inch available in .32 caliber only. Weight: About 4.5 lbs. Sights: Open rear; blade front. Plain walnut stock and forearm. Made from 1890-1933.

NO. 4S MILITARY MODEL 22
SINGLE-SHOT RIFLE . . . . NiB $2500 Ex $1987 Gd $955
Rolling-block action. Calibers: .22 Short only, .22 LR. only. 28-inch bbl. Weight: About 5 lbs. Sights: Military-type rear; blade front. Military-type stock w/handguard, stacking swivel, sling. Has a bayonet stud on the barrel; bayonet and scabbard were regularly supplied. Note: At one time the Military Model was the official rifle of the Boy Scouts of America and was called the Boy Scout Rifle. Made from 1913 to 1933.

NO. 5 SPECIAL SINGLE-SHOT RIFLE
Single-shot, rolling-block action. Calibers: 7mm Mauser, .30-30, .30-40 Krag, .303 British, .32-40, .32 Special, .38-55 (high-power cartridges). Bbl. lengths: 24, 26 and 28 inches. Weight: About 7 lbs. Open sporting sights. Plain straight-grip stock and forearm. Made 1902 to 1918. Note: Models 1897 and 1902 Military Rifles, intended for the export market, are almost identical with the No. 5, except for 30-inch bbl. full military stock and weight (about 8.5 lbs.); a carbine was also supplied. The military rifles were produced in caliber 8mm Lebel for France, 7.62mm Russian for Russia and 7mm Mauser for the Central and South American government trade. Also offered to retail buyers.
Sporting model . . . . NiB $877 Ex $709 Gd $495
Military model . . . . NiB $652 Ex $529 Gd $373

NO. 6 TAKEDOWN RIFLE . . . . NiB $650 Ex $511 Gd $436
Single-shot, rolling-block action. Calibers: .22 Short, .22 Long, .22 LR, .32 Short/Long RF. 20-inch bbl. Weight: Avg. 4 lbs. Sights: Open front and rear; tang peep. Plain straight-grip stock, forearm. Made from 1901 to 1933.

NO. 7 TARGET AND SPORTING RIFLE . . . . NiB $9000 Ex $7089 Gd $6647
Single-shot. Rolling-block Army Pistol frame. Calibers: .22 Short, .22 LR. 25-10 Stevens R.F. (other calibers available on special order). Half-octagon bbls.: 24-, 26-, 28-inch. Weight: About 6 lbs. Sights: Lyman combination rear; Beach combination front. Fancy walnut stock, Swiss buttplate available. Made from 1903 to 1911.

Remington
Model 40X Standard Rimfire

Remington
Model 40-XB Centerfire

Remington
Model 40-XB Rimfire

RIFLES

MODEL 33 BOLT-ACTION
SINGLE-SHOT RIFLE . . . . **NiB $250 Ex $165 Gd $122**
Takedown. Caliber: .22 Short, Long, LR. 24-inch bbl. Weight: About
4.5 lbs. Sights: Open rear, bead front. Plain, pistol-grip stock, forearm with grasping grooves. Made from 1931 to 1936.

MODEL 33 NRA
JUNIOR TARGET RIFLE . . . . **NiB $500 Ex $381 Gd $227**
Same as Model 33 Standard except has Lyman peep rear sight,
Partridge-type front sight, 0.88-inch sling and swivels, weighs about
5 lbs.

MODEL 40X
CENTERFIRE RIFLE . . . . **NiB $2560 Ex $1932 Gd $995**
Specifications same as for Model 40X Rimfire (heavy weight).
Calibers: .222 Rem., .222 Rem. Mag., 7.62mm NATO, .30-06 (oth-
ers were available on special order). Made from 1961 to 1964.
Value shown is for rifle w/o sights.

MODEL 40X HEAVYWEIGHT BOLT-ACTION TARGET RIFLE (RIMFIRE)
Caliber: .22 LR. Single shot. Action similar to Model 722. Click adj.
trigger. 28-inch heavy bbl. Redfield Olympic sights. Scope bases.
High-comb target stock bedding device, adj. swivel, rubber
buttplate. Weight: 12.75 lbs. Made from 1955 to 1964.
With sights. . . . . **NiB $3000 Ex $1985 Gd $949**
Without sights . . . . **NiB $2293 Ex $982 Gd $446**

MODEL 40-X SPORTER . . . . **NiB $3000 Ex $1947 Gd $935**
Same general specifications as Model 700 C Custom (see that listing
in this section) except in caliber .22 LR. Made from 1972 to 1977.

MODEL 40X STANDARD BARREL
Same as Model 40X Heavyweight except has lighter barrel.
Weight: 10.75 lbs.
With sights. . . . . **NiB $550 Ex $396 Gd $299**
Without sights . . . . **NiB $454 Ex $309 Gd $239**

MODEL 40-XB CENTERFIRE MATCH RIFLE . . . **NiB $550 Ex $432 Gd $341**
Bolt-action, single-shot. Calibers: .222 Rem., .222 Rem. Mag.,
.223 Rem., .22-250, 6x47mm, 6mm Rem., .243 Win., .25-06,
7mm Rem. Mag., .30-06, .308 Win. (7.62mm NATO), .30-338,
(7.62mm NATO), .30-338, .300 Win. Mag. 27 25-inch standard or
heavy bbl. Target stock w/adj. front swivel block on guide rail, rubber buttplate. Weight w/o sights: Standard bbl., 9.25 lbs.; heavy
bbl., 11.25 lbs. Value shown is for rifle without sights. Made from
1964 to date.

MODEL 40-XB RANGEMASTER CENTERFIRE
Single-shot target rifle with same basic specifications as Model 40-
XB Centerfire Match. Additional calibers in .220 Swift, 6mm BR
Rem. and 7mm BR Rem., and stainless bbl. only. American walnut
or Kevlar (weighs 1 lb. less) target stock with forend stop.
Discontinued 1994.
Model 40-XB right-hand model . . . . **NiB $779 Ex $573 Gd $412**
Model 40-XB left-hand model . . . . **NiB $779 Ex $573 Gd $412**
For 2-oz. trigger, add **$100**
Model 40-XB KS (Kevlar stock, R.H.) . . . **NiB $2150 Ex $1977 Gd $982**
Model 40-XB KS (Kevlar stock, L.H.) . . . . **NiB $2150 Ex $1977 Gd $982**
For 2-oz. trigger, add **$100**
For Repeater model, add **$100**

MODEL 40-XB RANGEMASTER
RIMFIRE MATCH RIFLE . . . . **NiB $804 Ex $761 Gd $385**
Bolt-action, single-shot. Caliber: .22 LR. 28-inch standard or heavy
bbl. Target stock with adj. front swivel block on guide rail, rubber
buttplate. Weight w/o sights: Standard bbl., 10 lbs.; heavy bbl., 11.25
lbs. Value shown is for rifle without sights. Made from 1964-74.

MODEL 40-XB
VARMINT SPECIAL RIFLE . . . . **NiB $1293 Ex $829 Gd $438**
Same general specifications as Model 40-XB Repeater except has
synthetic stock (Kevlar). Made from 1987-94.

MODEL 40-XBBR BENCH REST RIFLE
Bolt action, single shot. Calibers: .222 Rem., .222 Rem. Mag.,
.223 Rem., 6x47mm, .308 Win. (7.62mm NATO). 20- or 26-inch
unblued stainless-steel bbl. Supplied w/o sights. Weight: With
20-inch bbl., 9.25 lbs., with 26-inch bbl., 12 lbs. (Heavy Varmint
class; 7.25 lbs. w/Kevlar stock (Light Varmint class). Made from
1974 to 2004; reintroduced 2007.
Model 40-XBBR (discontinued) . . . . **NiB $3452 Ex $2763 Gd $1529**

Remington
Model 40-XB Varmint Special

Remington
Model 40-XBR

Remington
Model 40-XC

Remington
Model 40-XR Custom Sporter Grade II

Remington
Model 40-XR Rimfire Position Rifle

MODEL 40-XC NATIONAL MATCH COURSE RIFLE

Bolt-action repeater. Caliber: .308 Win. (7.62mm NATO). Five round magazine, clip slot in receiver. 24-inch bbl. Supplied w/o sights. Weight: 11 lbs. Thumb groove stock w/adj. hand stop and sling swivel, adj. buttplate. Disc 2004, reintroduced 2006.

Mdl. 40-XC (wood stock) (disc.) . . . . . . NiB $3092 Ex $2715 Gd $1484
Mdl. 40-XC KS (Kevlar stk. disc. 1994) . NiB $3084 Ex $2781 Gd $1546

MODEL 40-XR CUSTOM SPORTER RIFLE

Caliber: .22 RF. 24-inch contoured bbl. Supplied w/o sights. Made in four grades of checkering, engraving and other custom features. Made from 1987 to date. High grade model discontinued 1991.

Grade I . . . . NiB $1174 Ex $1004 Gd $772
Grade II . . . . NiB $1995 Ex $1789 Gd $1121
Grade III . . . . NiB $2910 Ex $2027 Gd $1246
Grade IV . . . . NiB $4891 Ex $4001 Gd $2838

MODEL 40-XR RIMFIRE POSITION RIFLE

Bolt action, single shot. Caliber: .22 LR. 24-inch heavy bbl. Supplied w/o sights. Weight: 10 lbs. Position-style stock w/thumb groove, adj. hand stop and sling swivel on guide rail, adj. buttplate. Made from 1974. Discontinued 2004.

Model 40-XR . . . . NiB $1192 Ex $1012 Gd $600
Model 40-XR KS (Kevlar stock) . . . . NiB $1295 Ex $1084 Gd $677

MODEL 41A TARGETMASTER BOLT-ACTION

SINGLE-SHOT RIFLE . . . . NiB $256 Ex $174 Gd $118
Takedown. Caliber: .22 Short, Long, LR. 27-inch bbl. Weight: About 5.5 lbs. Sights: Open rear; bead front. Plain pistol-grip stock. Made 1936 to 1940.

MODEL 41AS . . . . NiB $350 Ex $194 Gd $118
Same as Model 41A except chambered for .22 Remington Special (.22 W.R.F.).

MODEL 41P . . . . NiB $275 Ex $174 Gd $118
Same as Model 41A except has peep rear sight, hooded front sight.

MODEL 41SB . . . . NiB $400 Ex $149 Gd $123
Same as Model 41A except smoothbore for use with shot cartridges.

MODEL 510A TARGETMASTER

BOLT-ACTION SINGLE-SHOT RIFLE . . . . . . NiB $200 Ex $149 Gd $108
Takedown. Caliber: 22 Short, Long, LR. 25-inch bbl. Weight: About 5.5 lbs. Sights: Open rear; bead front. Plain pistol-grip stock. Made from 1939 to 1962.

MODEL 510P . . . . NiB $250 Ex $159 Gd $116
Same as Model 510A except has peep rear sight, Partridge front on ramp.

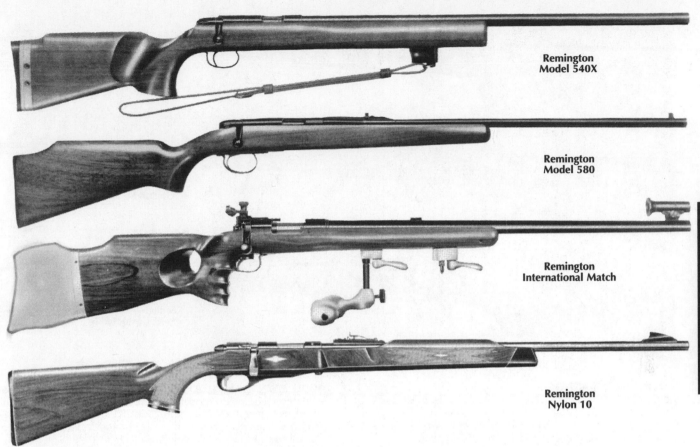

Remington
Model 540X

Remington
Model 580

Remington
International Match

Remington
Nylon 10

MODEL 510-X SB . . . . NiB $352 Ex $229 Gd $177
Same as Model 510A except smoothbore for use with shot cartridges, shotgun bead front sight, no rear sight.

**MODEL 510X BOLT-ACTION
SINGLE-SHOT RIFLE** . . . . NiB $200 Ex $174 Gd $113
Same as Model 510A except improved sights. Made from1964-66.

**MODEL 514 BOLT-ACTION
SINGLE-SHOT** . . . . NiB $163 Ex $149 Gd $113
Takedown. Caliber: .22 Short, Long, LR. 24-inch bbl. Weight:
4.75 lbs. Sights: Open rear; bead front. Plain pistol-grip stock.
Made from1948 to 1971.

MODEL 514BC BOY'S CARBINE . . . . NiB $200 Ex $154 Gd $118
Same as Model 514 except has 21-inch bbl., 1-inch shorter stock.
Made from1961 to 1971.

MODEL 514P . . . . NiB $200 Ex $153 Gd $118
Same as Model 514 except has receiver peep sight.

MODEL 540-X RIMFIRE TARGET RIFLE . . . NiB $425 Ex $288 Gd $134
Bolt-action, single-shot. Caliber: .22 R. 26-inch heavy bbl. Supplied
w/o sights. Weight: About 8 lbs. Target stock w/Monte Carlo cheekpiece and thumb groove, guide rail for hand stop and swivel, adj.
buttplate. Made from 1969 to 1974.

MODEL 540-XR POSITION RIFLE . . . . NiB $425 Ex $314 Gd $184
Bolt-action, single-shot. Caliber: .22 LR. 26-inch medium-weight bbl. Supplied
w/o sights. Weight: 8 lbs., 13 oz. Position-style stock w/thumb groove, guide
rail for hand stop and swivel, adj. buttplate. Made from 1974 to 1984.

MODEL 540-XRJR . . . . NiB $375 Ex $314 Gd $185
Same as Model 540-XR except 1.75-inch shorter stock. Made
from 1974 to 1984.

**MODEL 580 BOLT-ACTION
SINGLE-SHOT** . . . . NiB $184 Ex $144 Gd $104
Caliber: .22 Short, Long, LR. 24-inch bbl. Weight: 4.75 lbs. Sights:
Bead front; U-notch rear. Monte Carlo stock. Made 1967 to 1978.

MODEL 580BR BOY'S RIFLE . . . . . . NiB $185 Ex $154 Gd $111
Same as Model 580 except w/1-inch shorter stock. Made 1971 to 1978.

MODEL 580SB SMOOTH BORE . . . NiB $266 Ex $200 Gd $143
Same as Model 580 except smooth bore for .22 Long Rifle shot cartridges. Made from 1967 to 1978.

INTERNATIONAL FREE RIFLE . . . . NiB $1022 Ex $765 Gd $456
Same as Model 40-XB rimfire and centerfire except has free rifle-
type stock with adj. buttplate and hook, adj. palm rest, movable
front sling swivel, 2-oz. trigger. Weight: About 15 lbs. Made from
1964 to 1974. Value shown is for rifle with professionally finished stock, no sights.

INTERNATIONAL MATCH FREE RIFLE . . . NiB $1081 Ex $952 Gd $540
Calibers: .22 LR, .222 Rem., .222 Rem. Mag., 7.62mm NATO, .30-
06 (others were available on special order). Model 40X-type bolt-
action, single-shot. 2-oz. adj. trigger. 28-inch heavy bbl. Weight:
About 15.5 lbs. Free rifle-style stock with thumbhole (furnished
semifinished by mfr.); interchangeable and adj. rubber buttplate and
hook buttplate, adj. palm rest, sling swivel. Made 1961 to 1964.
Value shown is for rifle with professionally-finished stock, no sights.

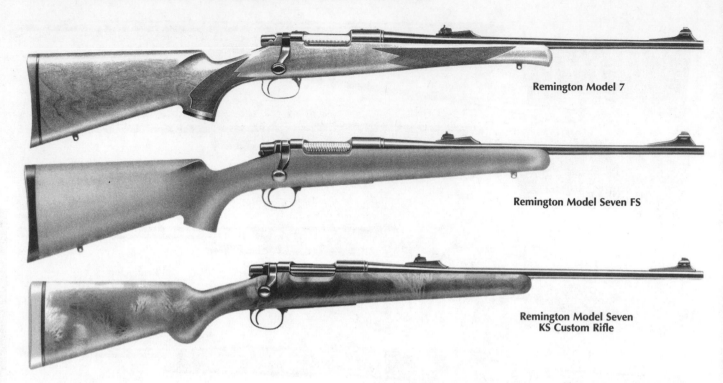

Remington Model 7

Remington Model Seven FS

Remington Model Seven
KS Custom Rifle

NYLON 10 BOLT-ACTION
SINGLE-SHOT RIFLE . . . . **NiB $295 Ex $152 Gd $121**
Caliber: .22 Short, Long, LR. 19.13-inch bbl. Weight: 4.25 lbs. Open rear sight; ramped blade front. Receiver grooved for scope mount. Brown nylon stock. Made from 1962 to 1966.

BOLT-ACTION REPEATING RIFLES

MODEL SEVEN (7) CF BOLT-ACTION RIFLE
Calibers: .17 Rem., .222 Rem., .223 Rem., .243 Win., 6mm Rem., 7mm-08 Rem., .308 Win. Magazine capacity: 5-round in .17 Rem., .222 Rem., .223 Rem., 4-round in other calibers. 18.5-inch bbl. Weight: 6.5 lbs. Walnut stock checkering, and recoil pad. Made from 1983 to 1999. .223 Rem. added in 1984.
Standard calibers except
.17 Rem. & .222 Rem.. . . . . **NiB $475 Ex $416 Gd $287**
Caliber .17 Rem & .222 Rem.. . . . . **NiB $519 Ex $437 Gd $298**

MODEL SEVEN (7)
FS RIFLE. . . . . **NiB $527 Ex $468 Gd $328**
Calibers: .243, 7mm-08 Rem., .308 Win. 18.5-inch bbl. 37.5 inches overall. Weight: 5.25 lbs. Hand layup fiberglass stock, reinforced with DuPont Kevlar at points of bedding and stress. Made 1987 to 1989.

MODEL SEVEN (7) KS RIFLE . . . . . **NiB $2225 Ex $986 Gd $754**
Calibers: .223 Rem., 7mm-08, .308, .35 Rem. and .350 Rem. Mag. 20-inch bbl. Custom-made in Remington's Custom Shop with Kevlar stock. Made from 1987 to date.

MODEL SEVEN (7) LS RIFLE . . . . . . **NiB $595 Ex $468 Gd $288**
Calibers: .223 Rem., .243 Win., .260 Rem., 7mm-08 and 308 Win. 20-inch matte bbl. Laminated hardwood stock w/matte brown finish. Weight: 6.5 lbs. Made from 2000 to 2005.

MODEL SEVEN (7) LSS RIFLE . . . . . **NiB $610 Ex $468 Gd $313**
Similar to Model 7 LS except stainless bbl. w/o sights. Calibers: .22-250 Rem., .243 Win. or 7mm-08. Made from 2000 to 2003.

MODEL SEVEN (7) MS CUSTOM RIFLE . **NiB $2575 Ex $1910 Gd $949**
Similar to the standard Model 7 except fitted with a laminated full Mannlicher-style stock. Weight: 6.75 lbs. Calibers: .222 Rem., .22-250, .243, 6mm Rem.,7mm-08, .308, .350 Rem. Additional calibers available on special order. Made from 1993 to 1999.

MODEL SEVEN (7) SS RIFLE . . . . . . **NiB $650 Ex $445 Gd $316**
Same as Model 7 except 20-inch stainless bbl., receiver and bolt; black synthetic stock. Calibers: .243, 7mm-08 or .308. Made 1994 to 2006.

MODEL SEVEN (7) YOUTH RIFLE. . . . . **NiB $525 Ex $337 Gd $260**
Similar to the standard Model 7 except fitted with hardwood stock with a 12.19-inch pull. Calibers: .243, 6mm, 7mm-08 only. Made 1993 to 2007.

MODEL 30A BOLT-ACTION
EXPRESS RIFLE. . . . . **NiB $608 Ex $493 Gd $347**
Standard Grade. Modified M/1917 Enfield Action. Calibers: .25, .30, .32 and .35 Rem., 7mm Mauser, .30-06. Five round box magazine. 22-inch bbl. Weight: About 7.25 lbs. Sights: Open rear; bead front. Walnut stock w/checkered pistol grip and forearm. Made 1921 to 1940. Note: Early Model 30s had a slender forend with Schnabel tip, military-type double-pull trigger.

MODEL 30R CARBINE . . . . **NiB $625 Ex $524 Gd $401**
Same as Model 30A except has 20-inch bbl., plain stock weight about 7 lbs.

MODEL 30S SPORTING RIFLE . . . . **NiB $750 Ex $610 Gd $431**
Special Grade. Same action as Model 30A. Calibers: .257 Roberts, 7mm Mauser, .30-06. Five round box magazine. 24-inch bbl. Weight: About 8 lbs. Lyman No. 48 Receiver sight, bead front sight. Special high comb stock with long, full forearm, checkered. Made 1930 to 1940.

MODEL 34 BOLT-ACTION REPEATER. . . . . **NiB $178 Ex $152 Gd $117**
Takedown. Caliber: .22 Short, Long, LR. Tubular magazine holds 22 Short, 17 Long or 15 LR. 24-inch bbl. Weight: 5.25 lbs. Sights: Open rear; bead front. Plain, pistol-grip stock, forearm w/grasping grooves. Made from 1932 to 1936.

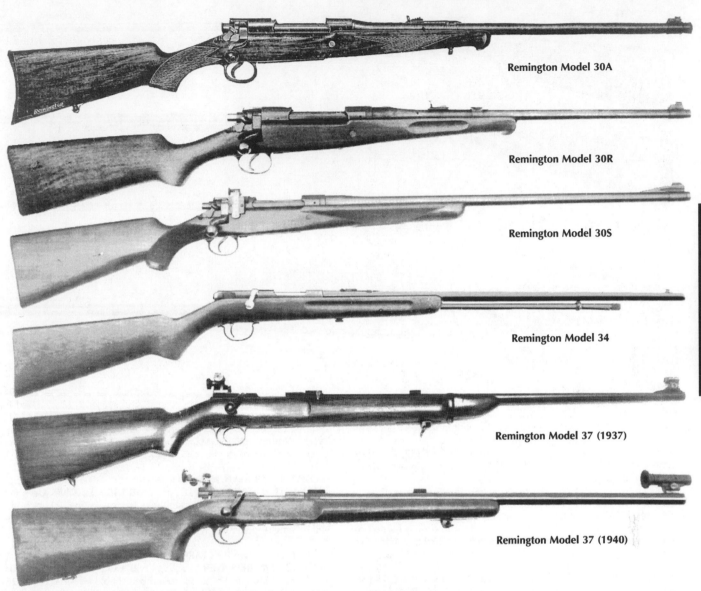

Remington Model 30A

Remington Model 30R

Remington Model 30S

Remington Model 34

Remington Model 37 (1937)

Remington Model 37 (1940)

MODEL 34 NRA TARGET RIFLE. . . . . NiB $500 Ex $370 Gd $241
Same as Model 34 Standard except has Lyman peep rear sight, Partridge-type front sight, .88-inch sling and swivels, weight: About 5.75 lbs.

MODEL 37 RANGEMASTER BOLT-ACTION TARGET RIFLE (I)
Model of 1937. Caliber: .22 LR. Five round box magazine, single shot adapter also supplied as standard equipment. 28-inch heavy bbl. Weight: About 12 lbs. Remington front and rear sights, scope bases. Target stock, swivels, sling. Note: Original 1937 model had a stock with outside bbl. band similar in appearance to that of the old-style Winchester Model 52, forearm design was modified and bbl. band eliminated in 1938. Made from 1937 to 1940.
With factory sights . . . . NiB $1100 Ex $676 Gd $347
Without sights . . . . NiB $953 Ex $550 Gd $295

MODEL 37 RANGEMASTER BOLT-ACTION TARGET RIFLE (II)
Model of 1940. Same as Model of 1937 except has "Miracle" trigger mechanism and Randle-design stock with high comb, full pistol-grip and wide beavertail forend. Made from 1940 to 1954.
With factory sights . . . . NiB $1100 Ex $610 Gd $429
Without sights . . . . NiB $953 Ex $451 Gd $318

MODEL 40-XB
CENTERFIRE REPEATER. . . . . NiB $2140 Ex $925 Gd $650
Same as Model 40-XB Centerfire except 5-round repeater. Calibers: .222 Rem., .222 Rem. Mag., .223 Rem., .22-250, 6x47mm, 6mm Rem., .243 Win., .308 Win. (7.62mm NATO). Heavy bbl. only. Discontinued.

MODEL 788 SPORTSMAN
BOLT-ACTION RIFLE. . . . . NiB $465 Ex $359 Gd $287
Similar to Model 700 ADL except with straight-comb walnut-finished hardwood stock in calibers .223 Rem., .243 Win., .270 Win., .30-06 Springfield and .308 Win. 22-inch bbl. Weight: 7 lbs. Adj. sights. Made from 1967 to 1983.

MODEL 341A SPORTSMASTER
BOLT-ACTION REPEATER . . . . NiB $250 Ex $159 Gd $115
Takedown. Caliber: .22 Short, Long, LR. Tubular magazine holds 22 Short, 17 Long, 15 LR. 27-inch bbl. Weight: About 6 lbs. Sights: Open rear; bead front. Plain pistol-grip stock. Made from 1936 to 1940.

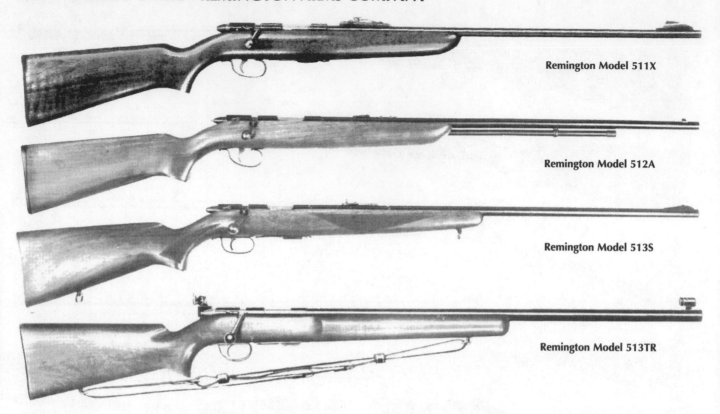

Remington Model 511X

Remington Model 512A

Remington Model 513S

Remington Model 513TR

MODEL 341P . . . . **NiB $325 Ex $185 Gd $133**
Same as Model 341A except has peep rear sight, hooded front sight.

MODEL 341SB . . . . **NiB $500 Ex $257 Gd $179**
Same as Model 341A previously listed except smoothbore for use with shot cartridges.

**MODEL 511A SCOREMASTER BOLT-ACTION
BOX MAGAZINE REPEATER** . . . . **NiB $225 Ex $174 Gd $126**
Takedown. Caliber: 22 Short, Long, LR. Six round detachable box magazine. 25-inch bbl. Weight: About 5.5 lbs. Sights: Open rear; bead front. Plain pistol-grip stock. Made 1939 to 1962.

MODEL 511P . . . . **NiB $250 Ex $179 Gd $130**
Same as Model 511A except has peep rear sight, Partridge-type blade front on ramp.

MODEL 511X BOLT-ACTION REPEATER . . **NiB $225 Ex $185 Gd $133**
Clip type. Same as Model 511A except improved sights. Made from 1964 to 1966.

**MODEL 512A SPORTSMASTER
BOLT-ACTION REPEATER** . . . . **NiB $225 Ex $165 Gd $130**
Takedown. Caliber: .22 Short, Long, LR. Tubular magazine holds 22 Short, 17 Long, 15 LR. 25-inch bbl. Weight: About 5.75 lbs. Sights: Open rear; bead front. Plain pistol-grip stock w/semibeavertail forend. Made from 1940 to 1962.

MODEL 512P . . . . **NiB $251 Ex $205 Gd $148**
Same as Model 512A except has peep rear sight, blade front, on ramp.

MODEL 512X BOLT-ACTION REPEATER . . . **NiB $225 Ex $215 Gd $155**
Tubular magazine type. Same as Model 512A except has improved sights. Made from 1964 to 1966.

MODEL 513S BOLT-ACTION RIFLE . . . . . **NiB $854 Ex $492 Gd $312**
Caliber: .22 LR. Six round detachable box magazine. 27-inch bbl. Weight: About 6.75 lbs. Marble open rear sight, Partridge-type front. Checkered sporter stock. Made from 1941 to 1956.

**MODEL 513TR MATCHMASTER
BOLT-ACTION TARGET RIFLE** . . . . . **NiB $450 Ex $299 Gd $211**
Caliber: .22 LR. Six round detachable box magazine. 27-inch bbl. Weight: About 9 lbs. Sights: Redfield No. 75 rear; globe front. Target stock. Sling and swivels. Made from 1941 to 1969.

**MODEL 521TL JUNIOR TARGET
BOLT-ACTION REPEATER** . . . . **NiB $398 Ex $267 Gd $191**
Takedown. Caliber: .22 LR. Six round detachable box magazine. 25-inch bbl. Weight: About 7 lbs. Sights: Lyman No. 57RS rear; dovetailed blade front. Target stock. Sling and swivels. Made from 1947 to 1969.

MODEL 522 VIPER . . . . **NiB $129 Ex $128 Gd $102**
Calibers: .22 LR. 10-round magazine. 20-inch bbl. 40 inches overall. Weight: 4.63 lbs. Checkered black PET resin stock with beavertail forend. Dupont high-tech synthetic lightweight receiver. Matte black finish on all exposed metal. Made from 1993 to date.

MODEL 541-S CUSTOM SPORTER. . . . . . . **NiB $750 Ex $599 Gd $418**
Bolt-action repeater. Scroll engraving on receiver and trigger guard. Caliber: .22 Short, Long, LR. Five round clip magazine. 24-inch bbl. Weight: 5.5 lbs. Supplied w/o sights. Checkered walnut stock w/rosewood-finished forend tip, pistol-grip cap and buttplate. Made from 1972 to 1984.

MODEL 541-T BOLT-ACTION RIFLE
Caliber: .22 RF. Clip-fed, Five round. 24-inch bbl. Weight: 5.88 lbs. Checkered walnut stock. Made from 1986 to date; heavy bbl. model intro. 1993.
Model 541-T Standard . . . . **NiB $500 Ex $311 Gd $193**
Model 541-T-HB heavy bbl. . . . . **NiB $466 Ex $337 Gd $249**

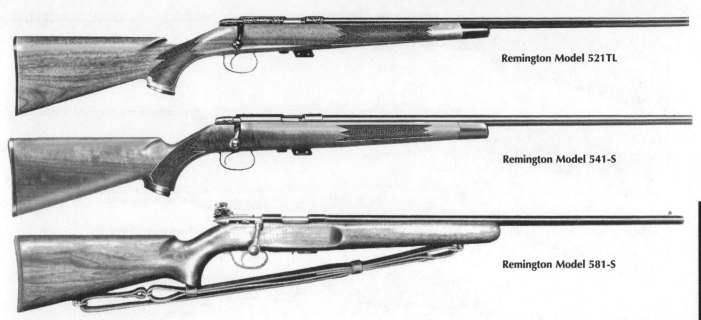

Remington Model 521TL

Remington Model 541-S

Remington Model 581-S

MODEL 581 CLIP REPEATER
Same general specifications as Model 580 except has 5-round clip magazine. Made from 1967 to 1984.
Model 581............................ NiB $225 Ex $155 Gd $114
Model 581 left hand
(made 1969-1984) .... NiB $221 Ex $180 Gd $132

MODEL 581-S BOLT-ACTION RIFLE...... NiB $176 Ex $150 Gd $129
Caliber: .22 RF. Clip-fed, 5-round. 24-inch bbl. Weight: 4.75 lbs. Plain walnut-colored stock. Made from 1987 to 1992.

MODEL 582 TUBULAR REPEATER .... NiB $225 Ex $160 Gd $117
Same general specifications as Model 580 except has tubular magazine holding 20 Short, 15 Long, 14 LR. Weight: About 5 lbs. Made from 1967 to 1984.

MODEL 591 BOLT-ACTION
CLIP REPEATER...................... NiB $277 Ex $227 Gd $163
Caliber: 5mm Rimfire Magnum. Four round clip magazine. 24-inch bbl. Weight: 5 lbs. Sights: Bead front; U-notch rear. Monte Carlo stock. Made from 1970 to 1973.

MODEL 592 TUBULAR REPEATER .... NiB $275 Ex $175 Gd $128
Same as Model 591 except has tubular magazine holding 10 rounds, weight: 5.5 lbs. Made from 1970 to 1973.

MODEL 600 BOLT-ACTION CARBINE
Calibers: .222 Rem., .223 Rem., .243 Win., 6mm Rem., .308 Win., 35 Rem., 5-round magazine (6-round in .222 Rem.) 18.5-inch bbl. with ventilated rib. Weight: 6 lbs. Sights: Open rear; blade ramp front. Monte Carlo stock w/pistol-grip. Made from 1964 to 1967.
.222 Rem. .... NiB $524 Ex $397 Gd $288
.223 Rem..................... NiB $1052 Ex $885 Gd $694
.35 Rem. .... NiB $614 Ex $504 Gd $488
Standard calibers............... NiB $475 Ex $355 Gd $292

MODEL 600 MAGNUM .... NiB $975 Ex $715 Gd $613
Same as Model 600 except calibers 6.5mm Mag. and .350 Rem. Mag., 4-round magazine, special Magnum-type bbl. with bracket for scope back-up, laminated walnut and beech stock w/recoil pad. QD swivels and sling; weight: About 6.5 lbs. Made 1965 to 1967.

MODEL 600 MONTANA
TERRITORIAL CENTENNIAL $900
Same as Model 600 except has commemorative medallion embedded in buttstock. Made in 1964. Value is for rifle in new, unfired condition.

MODEL 660 STP
Calibers: .222 Rem., 6mm Rem., .243 Win., .308 Win., 5-round magazine. (6-round in .222 Rem.) 20-inch bbl. Weight: 6.5 lbs. Sights: Open rear; bead front on ramp. Monte Carlo stock, checkered, black pistol-grip cap and forend tip. Made from 1968 to 1971.
.222 Rem..................... NiB $420 Ex $338 Gd $278
Other calibers .... NiB $528 Ex $401 Gd $323

MODEL 660 MAGNUM .... NiB $925 Ex $733 Gd $604
Same as Model 660 except calibers 6.5mm Rem. Mag. and .350 Rem. Mag., 4-round magazine, laminated walnut-and-beech stock with recoil pad. QD swivels and sling. Made from 1968 to 1971.

MODEL 700 ADL CENTERFIRE RIFLE..... NiB $475 Ex $330 Gd $226
Calibers: .22-250, .222 Rem., .25-06, 6mm Rem., .243 Win., .270 Win., .30-06, .308 Win., 7mm Rem. Mag. Magazine capacity: 6-round in .222 Rem.; 4-round in 7mm Rem. Mag. Five round in other calibers. Bbl. lengths: 24-inch in .22-250, .222 Rem., .25-06, 7mm Rem. Mag.; 22-inch in other calibers. Weight: 7 lbs. standard; 7.5 lbs. in 7mm Rem. Mag. Sights: Ramp front; sliding ramp open rear. Monte Carlo stock w/cheekpiece, skip checkering, recoil pad on Magnum. Laminated stock also avail. Made from 1962 to 2005.

MODEL 700 APR BOLT-ACTION RIFLE   NiB $2384 Ex $1088 Gd $925
Acronym for African Plains Rifle. Calibers: 7mm Rem. Mag., 7mm STW, 300 Win. Mag., 300 Wby. Mag., 300 Rem. Ultra Mag., 338 Win. Mag., 375 H&H. Three round magazine. 26-inch bbl. on a magnum action. 46.5 inches overall. Weight: 7.75 lbs. Matte blue finish. Checkered classic-style laminated wood stock w/black magnum recoil pad. Made 1994 to 2004.

MODEL 700 AS BOLT-ACTION RIFLE
Similar to the Model 700 BDL except with non-reflective matte black metal finish, including the bolt body. Weight: 6.5 lbs. Straight comb synthetic stock made of Arylon, a fiberglass-reinforced thermoplastic resin with non-reflective matte finish. Made from 1988 to 1992.
Standard caliber .... NiB $498 Ex $404 Gd $283
Magnum caliber .... NiB $537 Ex $435 Gd $305

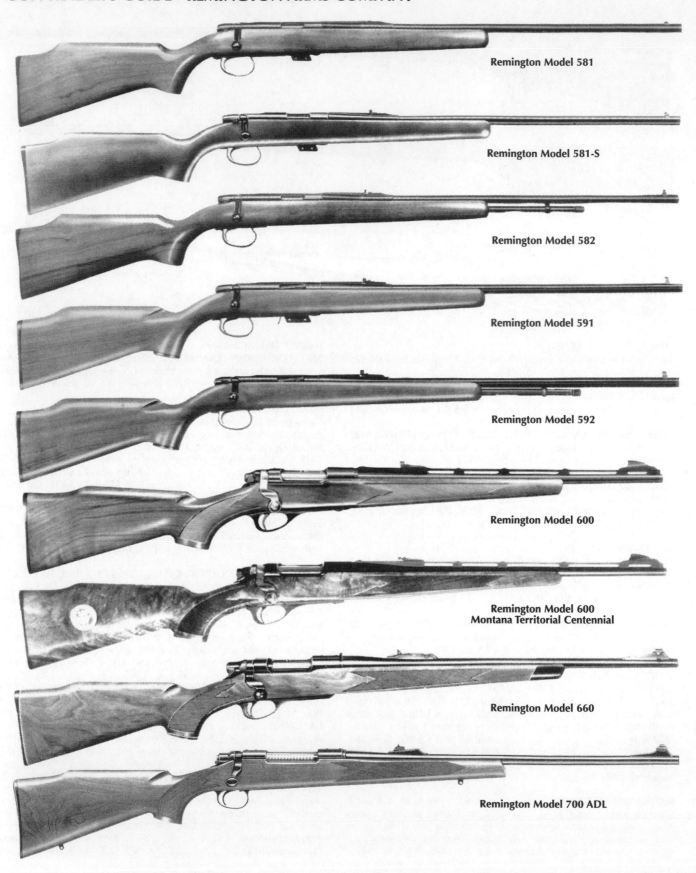

Remington Model 581

Remington Model 581-S

Remington Model 582

Remington Model 591

Remington Model 592

Remington Model 600

Remington Model 600
Montana Territorial Centennial

Remington Model 660

Remington Model 700 ADL

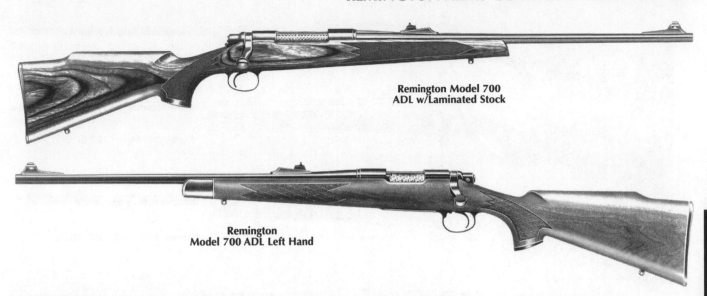

**Remington Model 700
ADL w/Laminated Stock**

**Remington
Model 700 ADL Left Hand**

MODEL 700 AWR
BOLT-ACTION RIFLE . . . . **NiB $1495 Ex $1200 Gd $1045**
Acronym for Alaskan Wilderness Rifle, similar to Model 700 APR except w/24-inch stainless bbl. and black chromed action. Matte gray or black Kevlar stock w/straight comb and raised cheekpiece fitted w/black magnum recoil pad. Made from 1994 to 2004.

MODEL 700 BDL CENTERFIRE RIFLE
Same as Model 700 ADL except has hinged floorplate hooded ramp front sight, stock w/black forend tip and pistol-grip cap, cut checkering, QD swivels and sling. Additional calibers: .17 Rem., .223 Rem., .264 Win. Mag., 7mm-08, .280, .300 Sav., .300 Win. Mag., 8mm Rem. Mag., .338 Win. Mag., .35 Whelen. All have 24-inch bbls. Magnums have 4-round magazine, recoil pad, weighs 7.5 lbs; .17 Rem. has 6-round magazine, weighs 7 lbs. Made 1962 to date. Made from 1973 to 2004.

Standard calibers except .17 Rem.	NiB $775	Ex $434	Gd $307
Magnum calibers and .17 Rem.	NiB $800	Ex $485	Gd $342
Left-hand, .270 Win. and .30-06	NiB $795	Ex $444	Gd $314
Left-hand, 7mm Rem. Mag and .222 Rem.	NiB $753	Ex $526	Gd $449

MODEL 700 BDL EUROPEAN RIFLE
Same general specifications as Model 700 BDL, except has oil-finished walnut stock. Calibers: .243, .270, 7mm-08, 7mm Mag., .280 Rem., .30-06. Made from 1993 to 1995.

Standard calibers	NiB $445	Ex $389	Gd $320
Magnum calibers	NiB $552	Ex $510	Gd $397

MODEL 700 BDL SS BOLT-ACTION RIFLE
Same as Model 700 BDL except w/24-inch stainless bbl., receiver and bolt plus black synthetic stock. Calibers: .223 Rem., .243 Win., 6mm Rem., .25-06 Rem., .270 Win. .280 Rem., 7mm-08, 7mm Rem. Mag., 7mm Wby. Mag., .30-06, .300 Win., .308 Win., .338 Win. Mag. .375 H&H. Made from 1992 to 1994.

Standard calibers	NiB $585	Ex $486	Gd $325
Magnum calibers, add			$80
DM (detachable magazine), add			$40
DM-B (muzzle brake), add			$90

MODEL 700 BDL
VARMINT SPECIAL . . . . **NiB $695 Ex $449 Gd $315**
Same as Model 700 BDL except has 24-inch heavy bbl., no sights, weighs 9 lbs. (8.75 lbs. in 308 Win.). Calibers: .22-250, .222 Rem., .223 Rem., .25-06, 6mm Rem., .243 Win., 308 Win. Made 1967 to 1994.

REMINGTON MODEL 700 CS BOLT-ACTION RIFLE
Similar to Model 700 BDL except with nonreflective matte black metal finish, including the bolt body. Straight comb synthetic stock camouflaged in Mossy Oak Bottomland pattern. Made 1992 to 1994.

Standard calibers	NiB $546	Ex $444	Gd $314
Magnum calibers	NiB $584	Ex $475	Gd $335

MODEL 700 CLASSIC
Same general specifications as Model 700 BDL except has "Classic" stock of high-quality walnut with full-pattern cut-checkering, special satin wood finish; Schnabel forend. Brown rubber buttpad. Hinged floorplate. No sights. Weight: 7 lbs. Also chambered for "Classic" cartridges such as .257 Roberts and .250-3000. Introduced in 1981.

Standard calibers	NiB $852	Ex $397	Gd $294
Magnum calibers	NiB $903	Ex $449	Gd $315

MODEL 700 CUSTOM BOLT-ACTION RIFLE
Same general specifications as Model 700 BDL except custom-built; available in choice of grades, each with higher quality wood, different checkering patterns, engraving, high-gloss blued finish. Introduced in 1965.

Model 700 C Grade I	NiB $1896	Ex $1040	Gd $727
Model 700 C Grade II	NiB $2413	Ex $1777	Gd $1244
Model 700 C Grade III	NiB $2859	Ex $2294	Gd $1596
Model 700 C Grade IV	NiB $4875	Ex $3196	Gd $2895
Model 700 D Peerless	NiB $2742	Ex $1519	Gd $1059
Model 700 F Premier	NiB $3536	Ex $2852	Gd $1976

MODEL 700 FS BOLT-ACTION RIFLE
Similar to Model 700 ADL except with straight comb fiberglass stock reinforced with DuPont Kevlar, finished in gray or gray camo with Old English-style recoil pad. Made from 1987 to 1989.

Standard calibers	NiB $530	Ex $450	Gd $344
Magnum calibers	NiB $653	Ex $550	Gd $395

MODEL 700 KS CUSTOM MOUNTAIN RIFLE
Similar to standard Model 700 MTN Rifle, except with custom Kevlar reinforced resin synthetic stock with standard or wood-grain finish. Calibers: .270 Win., .280 Rem., 7mm Rem Mag., .30-06, .300 Win. Mag., .300 Wby. Mag., 8mm Rem. Mag., .338 Win. Mag., .35 Whelen, .375 H&H. Four round magazine. 24-inch bbl. Weight: 6.75 lbs. Made from 1986 to 2008.

Standard KS stock (disc. 1993)	NiB $1821	Ex $1341	Gd $1030
Wood-grain KS stock	NiB $1044	Ex $813	Gd $574
SS Model Stainless Synthetic (1995-97) .	NiB $1950	Ex $1360	Gd $908
Left-hand model, add			$65

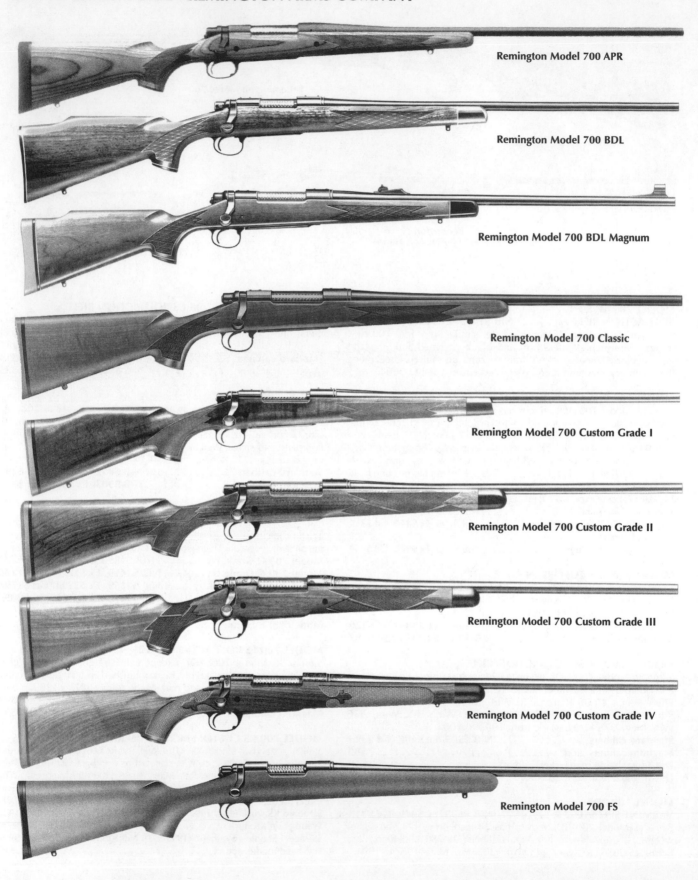

Remington Model 700 APR

Remington Model 700 BDL

Remington Model 700 BDL Magnum

Remington Model 700 Classic

Remington Model 700 Custom Grade I

Remington Model 700 Custom Grade II

Remington Model 700 Custom Grade III

Remington Model 700 Custom Grade IV

Remington Model 700 FS

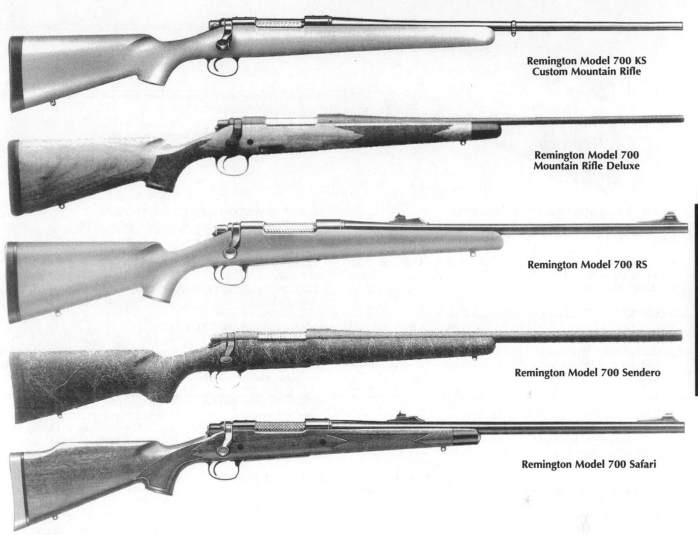

Remington Model 700 KS
Custom Mountain Rifle

Remington Model 700
Mountain Rifle Deluxe

Remington Model 700 RS

Remington Model 700 Sendero

Remington Model 700 Safari

MODEL 700 LS BOLT-ACTION RIFLE

Similar to Model 700 ADL except with checkered Monte Carlo-style laminated wood stock with alternating grain and wood color, impregnated with phenolic resin and finished with a low satin luster. Made from 1988 to 1993.

Standard calibers . . . . NiB $460 Ex $392 Gd $299
Magnum calibers . . . . NiB $622 Ex $503 Gd $365

MODEL 700 LSS BOLT-ACTION RIFLE

Similar to Model 700 BDL except with stainless steel barrel and action. Checkered Monte Carlo-style laminated wood stock with alternating grain and gray tinted color impregnated with phenolic resin and finished with a low satin luster. Made from 1996 to 2004.

Standard calibers . . . . NiB $660 Ex $519 Gd $365
Magnum calibers . . . . NiB $698 Ex $571 Gd $390

MODEL 700 MOUNTAIN RIFLE

Lightweight version of Model 700. Calibers: .243 Win., .25-06, .257 Roberts, .270 Win., 7x57, 7mm-08 Rem., .280 Rem., .30-06 and .308 Win. Four round magazine. 22-inch bbl. Weight: 6.75 lbs. Satin blue or stainless finish. Checkered walnut stock and redesigned pistol grip, straight comb, contoured cheekpiece, Old English-style recoil pad and satin oil finish or black synthetic stock with pressed checkering and blind magazine. Made from 1986 to 1994.

Standard w/blind magazine . . . . NiB $445 Ex $390 Gd $252
Standard w/hinged floorplate (disc. 1994) . NiB $553 Ex $463 Gd $347
DM Model (New 1995) . . . . NiB $685 Ex $443 Gd $339
SS Model stainless synthetic (disc. 1993) . . NiB $450 Ex $390 Gd $287

MODEL 700 RS BOLT-ACTION RIFLE

Similar to the Model 700 BDL except with straight comb DuPont Rynite stock finished in gray or gray camo with Old English style recoil pad. Made from 1987 to 1990.

Standard calibers . . . . NiB $550 Ex $493 Gd $339
Magnum calibers . . . . NiB $622 Ex $493 Gd $365
.280 Rem. calibers (Limited production) . . . NiB $739 Ex $596 Gd $415

MODEL 700 SAFARI GRADE

Big game heavy magnum version of the Model 700 BDL. 8mm Rem. Mag., .375 H&H Mag., .416 Rem. Mag. and .458 Win. Mag. 24-inch heavy bbl. Weight: 9 lbs. Blued or stainless finish. Checkered walnut stock in synthetic/Kevlar stock with standard matte or wood-grain finish with old English style recoil pad. Made from 1962 to 2000.

Safari Classic/Monte Carlo . . . . NiB $1395 Ex $978 Gd $540
Safari KS (Kevlar stock) intro. 1989 . . . . NiB $1288 Ex $1083 Gd $821
Safari KS (Wood-grain) intro. 1992 . . . . . . NiB $1209 Ex $990 Gd $710
Safari KS SS (Stainless) intro. 1993 . . . . . NiB $1495 Ex $1249 Gd $936
Safari left-hand, add $95

Remington Model 721A Deluxe

Remington Model 722A

MODEL 700 SENDERO BOLT-ACTION RIFLE

Same as Model 700 VS except chambered in long action and magnum .25-06 Rem., .270 Win., .280 Rem., 7mm Rem. Mag., .300 Win. Made from 1994 to 2002.

Standard calibers	NiB $635	Ex $539	Gd $368
Magnum calibers, add			$30
SF Model (stainless fluted), add			$115

MODEL 700 VLS (VARMINT LAMINATED STOCK)

BOLT-ACTION RIFLE . . . . NiB $825 Ex $496 Gd $343
Same as Model 700 BDL Varmint Special except with 26-inch polished blue barrel. Laminated wood stock with alternating grain and wood color impregnated with phenolic resin and finished with a satin luster. Calibers: .222 Rem., .223 Rem., .22-250 Rem., .243 Win., 7mm-08 Rem., .308 Win. Weight: 9.4 lbs. Made from 1995 to date.

MODEL 700 VS BOLT-ACTION RIFLE

Same as Model 700 BDL Varmint Special except w/26-inch matte blue or fluted stainless barrel. Textured black or gray synthetic stock reinforced with Kevlar, fiberglass and graphite with full length aluminum bedding block. Calibers: .22-250 Rem., .220 Swift, .223 Rem., .308 Win. Made from 1992 to date.

Model 700 VS	NiB $835	Ex $522	Gd $393
Model 700 VS SF (fluted barrel)	NiB $748	Ex $620	Gd $457
Model 700 VS SF/SF-P (Fluted & ported barrel)	NiB $922	Ex $787	Gd $614

MODEL 720A BOLT-ACTION

HIGH POWER . . . . NiB $1323 Ex $1193 Gd $1038
Modified M/1917 Enfield action. .257 Roberts, .270 Win., .30-06. Five round box magazine. 22-inch bbl. Weight: About 8 lbs. Sights: Open rear; bead front, on ramp. Pistol-grip stock, checkered. Model 720R has 20-inch bbl.; Model 720S has 24-inch bbl. Made in 1941.

MODEL 721 STANDARD GRADE

BOLT-ACTION HIGH-POWER RIFLE . . . . . NiB $450 Ex $388 Gd $327
Calibers: .270 Win., .30-06. Four round box magazine. 24-inch bbl. Weight: About 7.25 lbs. Sights: Open rear; bead front, on ramp. Plain sporting stock. Made from 1948 to 1962.

MODEL 721A MAGNUM

STANDARD GRADE . . . . NiB $594 Ex $466 Gd $388
Caliber: .264 Win. Mag. or .300 H&H Mag. Same as standard model except has 26-inch bbl. Three round magazine and recoil pad. Weight: 8.25 lbs.

MODEL 721ADL/BDL DELUXE

Same as Model 721A Standard or Magnum except has deluxe checkered stock and/or select wood.

Model 721ADL Deluxe Grade	NiB $650	Ex $502	Gd $374
Model 721ADL .300 Magnum Deluxe	NiB $700	Ex $680	Gd $523
Model 721BDL Deluxe Special Grade	NiB $787	Ex $577	Gd $430
Model 721BDL .300 Magnum Deluxe	NiB $760	Ex $644	Gd $495

MODEL 722A STANDARD GRADE SPORTER

Same as Model 721A bolt-action except shorter action. .222 Rem. mag., .243 Win., .257 Roberts, .308 Win., .300 Savage. Four or 5-round magazine. Weight: 7-8 lbs. .222 Rem. introduced 1950; .244 Rem. introduced 1955. Made from 1948 to 1962.

.222 Rem.	NiB $450	Ex $364	Gd $257
.244 Rem.	NiB $409	Ex $333	Gd $237
.222 Rem. Mag. & .243 Win.	NiB $412	Ex $415	Gd $292
Other Calibers	NiB $401	Ex $364	Gd $235

MODEL 722ADL DELUXE GRADE

Same as Model 722A except has deluxe checkered stock.

Standard calibers	NiB $526	Ex $493	Gd $339
.222 Rem. Deluxe Grade	NiB $648	Ex $545	Gd $416
.244 Rem. Deluxe Grade	NiB $764	Ex $677	Gd $419

MODEL 722BDL DELUXE SPECIAL GRADE

Same as Model 722ADL except select wood.

Standard calibers	NiB $796	Ex $545	Gd $442
.222 Rem. Deluxe Special Grade	NiB $796	Ex $545	Gd $442
.224 Rem. Deluxe Special Grade	NiB $711	Ex $543	Gd $419

MODEL 725 KODIAK

MAGNUM RIFLE . . . . NiB $4000 Ex $3358 Gd $2219
Similar to Model 725ADL. Calibers: .375 H&H Mag., .458 Win. Mag. Three round magazine. 26-inch bbl. with recoil reducer built into muzzle. Weight: About 9 lbs. Deluxe, reinforced Monte Carlo stock with recoil pad, black forend tip swivels, sling. Fewer than 100 made in 1961.

MODEL 725ADL BOLT-ACTION REPEATING RIFLE

Calibers: .222, .243, .244, .270, .280, .30-06. Four round box mag. (5-round in 222). 22-inch bbl. (24-inch in .222). Weight: About 7 lbs. Sights: Open rear, hooded ramp front. Monte Carlo comb stock w/pistol-grip, checkered, swivels. Made from 1958 to 1961.

.222 Rem., .243 Win., .244 Rem	NiB $799	Ex $650	Gd $460
.270 Win.	NiB $710	Ex $625	Gd $435
.280 Win.	NiB $920	Ex $760	Gd $475
.30-06	NiB $670	Ex $535	Gd $415

MODEL 788 CENTERFIRE BOLT-ACTION

Calibers: .222 Rem., .22-250, .223 Rem., 6mm Rem., .243 Win., 7mm-08 Rem., .308 Win., .30-30, .44 Rem. Mag. Three round clip magazine (4-round in .222 and .223 Rem.). 24-inch bbl. in .22s, 22-inch in other calibers. Weight: 7.5 lbs. with 24-inch bbl.; 7.25 lbs. with 22-inch bbl. Sights: Blade front on ramp; U-notch rear. Plain Monte Carlo stock. Made 1967 to 1984.

.22-250, .223 Rem., 6mm Rem., .243 Win., .308 Win.	NiB $469	Ex $306	Gd $219
.30-30 Win.	NiB $512	Ex $389	Gd $282
7mm-08 Rem.	NiB $674	Ex $383	Gd $268
.44 Mag.	NiB $598	Ex $420	Gd $293

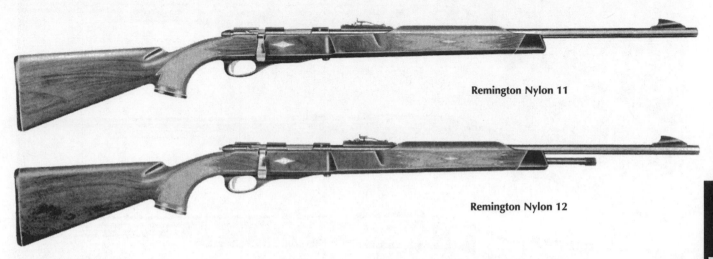

Remington Nylon 11

Remington Nylon 12

RIFLES

NYLON 11 BOLT-ACTION
REPEATER . . . . NiB $450 Ex $284 Gd $173
Clip type. Caliber: .22 Short, Long, LR. Six- or 10-round clip mag. 19.63-inch bbl. Weight: 4.5 lbs. Sights: Open rear; blade front. Nylon stock. Made from 1962 to 1966.

NYLON 12 BOLT-ACTION
REPEATER . . . . NiB $500 Ex $384 Gd $223
Same as Nylon 11 except has tubular magazine holding 22 Short, 17 Long, 15 LR. Made from 1962 to 1966.

SLIDE- AND LEVER-ACTION RIFLES

MODEL SIX (6) SLIDE-ACTION
REPEATER . . . . NiB $650 Ex $365 Gd $258
Hammerless. Calibers: 6mm Rem., .243 Win., .270 Win. 7mm Express Rem., .30-06, .308 Win. 22-inch bbl. Weight: 7.5 lbs. Checkered Monte Carlo stock and forearm. Made 1981 to 1988.

MODEL SIX (6) SLIDE-ACTION
REPEATER, PEERLESS GRADE . . . . NiB $1864 Ex $1607 Gd $989
Same as Model Six Standard except has engraved receiver. Three versions made from 1981 to 1988.

MODEL SIX (6) SLIDE-ACTION REPEATER, PREMIUM GRADES
Same as Model Six Standard except has engraved receiver with gold inlay. Made from 1981 to 1988.
Peerless D Grade . . . . NiB $1879 Ex $1673 Gd $1030
Premier F Grade . . . . NiB $4330 Ex $3492 Gd $2421
Premier Gold F Grade . . . . NiB $6096 Ex $4893 Gd $3399

MODEL 12A, 12B, 12C, 12CS SLIDE-ACTION REPEATERS
Standard Grade. Hammerless. Takedown. Caliber: .22 Short, Long or LR. Tubular magazine holds 15 Short, 12 Long or 10 LR cartridges. 22- or 24-inch round or octagonal bbl. Open rear sight, bead front. Plain, half-pistol-grip stock and grooved slide handle of walnut. Made from 1909 to 1936.
Model 12A . . . . NiB $545 Ex $339 Gd $236
Model 12B
(22 Short only w/octagon bbl.) . . . . NiB $674 Ex $519 Gd $339
Model 12C
(w/24-inch octagon bbl.) . . . . NiB $571 Ex $493 Gd $313
Model 12CS
(22 WRF w/24-inch octagon bbl.) . . . . NiB $545 Ex $416 Gd $287

MODEL 14A HIGH POWER
SLIDE-ACTION REPEATING RIFLE . . . . . . NiB $1000 Ex $742 Gd $590
Standard grade. Hammerless. Takedown. Calibers: .25, .30, .32 and .35 Rem. Five round tubular magazine. 22-inch bbl. Weight: About 6.75 lbs. Sights: Open rear; bead front. Plain half-pistol-grip stock and grooved slide handle of walnut. Made from 1912 to 1935.

MODEL 14R CARBINE . . . . NiB $1200 Ex $940 Gd $457
Same as Model 14R except has 18.5-inch bbl., straight-grip stock, weight: About 6 lbs.

MODEL 14 1/2 CARBINE . . . . NiB $1200 Ex $914 Gd $531
Same as Model 14A Rifle previously listed, except has 9-round magazine, 18.5-inch bbl.

MODEL 14 1/2 RIFLE . . . . NiB $1600 Ex $946 Gd $514
Similar to Model 14A except calibers: .38-40 and .44-40, 11-round full magazine, 22.5-inch bbl. Made from 1912 to early 1920's.

MODEL 25A SLIDE-ACTION
REPEATER . . . . NiB $1000 Ex $664 Gd $435
Standard Grade. Hammerless. Takedown. Calibers: .25-20, .32-20. 10-round tubular magazine. 24-inch bbl. Weight: About 5.5 lbs. Sights: Open rear; bead front. Plain, pistol-grip stock, grooved slide handle. Made from 1923 to 1936.

MODEL 25R CARBINE . . . . NiB $1100 Ex $690 Gd $461
Same as Model 25A except has 18-inch bbl. Six round magazine, straight-grip stock, weight: About 4.5 lbs.

MODEL 121A
FIELDMASTER
SLIDE-ACTION REPEATER . . . . NiB $596 Ex $442 Gd $287
Standard Grade. Hammerless. Takedown. Caliber: .22 Short, Long, LR. Tubular magazine holds 20 Short, 15 Long or 14 LR cartridges. 24-inch round bbl. Weight: 6 lbs. Plain, pistol-grip stock and grooved semi-beavertail slide handle. Made from 1936 to 1954.

MODEL 121S. . . . . NiB $577 Ex $468 Gd $328
Same as Model 121A except chambered for .22 Remington Special (.22 W.R.F.). Magazine holds 12 rounds. Disc.

MODEL 121SB . . . . NiB $668 Ex $540 Gd $377
Same as Model 121A except smoothbore. Disc.

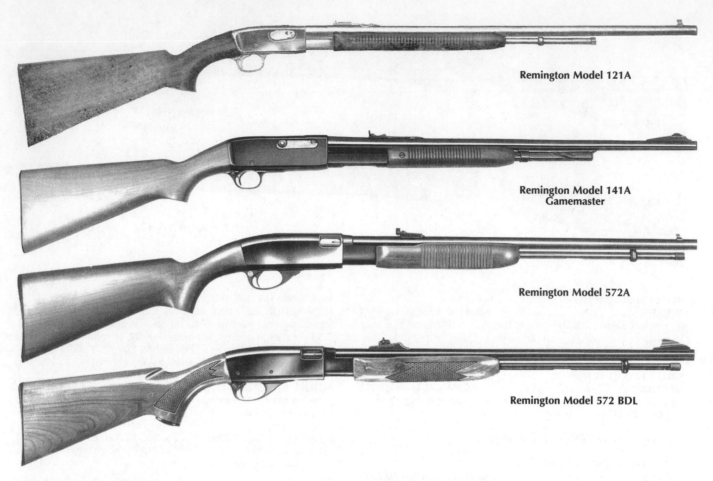

Remington Model 121A

Remington Model 141A Gamemaster

Remington Model 572A

Remington Model 572 BDL

MODEL 141A GAMEMASTER
SLIDE-ACTION REPEATER........ NiB $465 Ex $313 Gd $226
Standard Grade. Hammerless. Takedown. Calibers: .30, .32 and .35 Rem. Five round tubular magazine. 24-inch bbl. Weight: About 7.75 lbs. Sights: Open rear; bead front, on ramp. Plain, pistol-grip stock, semibeavertail forend (slide-handle). Made from 1936 to 1950.

MODEL 572A FIELDMASTER
SLIDE-ACTION REPEATER....... NiB $225 Ex $155 Gd $119
Hammerless. Caliber: .22 Short, Long, LR. Tubular magazine holds 20 Short, 17 Long, 15 LR. 23-inch bbl. Weight: About 5.5 lbs. Sights: Open rear; ramp front. Pistol-grip stock, grooved forearm. Made 1955 to 1988.

MODEL 572BDL DELUXE........ NiB $475 Ex $332 Gd $229
Same as Model 572A except has blade ramp front sight, sliding ramp rear; checkered stock and forearm. Made from 1966 to date.

MODEL 572SB SMOOTH BORE... NiB $500 Ex $383 Gd $261
Same as Model 572A except smoothbore for .22 LR shot cartridges. Made from 1961 to date.

MODEL 760 BICENTENNIAL
COMMEMORATIVE............ NiB $495 Ex $352 Gd $223
Same as Model 760 except has commemorative inscription on receiver. Made in 1976.

MODEL 760 CARBINE .... NiB $450 Ex $381 Gd $239
Same as Model 760 Rifle except made in calibers .270 Win., .280 Rem., .30-06 and .308 Win. only, has 18.5-inch bbl., weight: 7.25 lbs. Made 1961 to 1980.

MODEL 760 GAMEMASTER
STANDARD GRADE SLIDE-ACTION REPEATING RIFLE
Hammerless. Calibers: .223 Rem., 6mm Rem., .243 Win., .257 Roberts, .270 Win. .280 Rem., .30-06, .300 Sav., .308 Win., .35 Rem. 22-inch bbl. Weight: About 7.5 lbs. Sights: Open rear; bead front, on ramp. Plain pistol-grip stock, grooved slide handle on early models; current production has checkered stock and slide handle. Made from 1952 to 1980.

.222 Rem.	NiB $1156	Ex $993	Gd $632
.223 Rem.	NiB $1360	Ex $1089	Gd $688
.257 Roberts	NiB $850	Ex $745	Gd $462
Other calibers	NiB $425	Ex $371	Gd $382

MODEL 760ADL
DELUXE GRADE..................... NiB $451 Ex $359 Gd $330
Same as Model 760 except has deluxe checkered stock, standard or high comb, grip cap, sling swivels. Made from 1953 to 1963.

MODEL 760BDL
CUSTOM DELUXE .... NiB $598 Ex $404 Gd $272
Same as Model 760 Rifle except made in calibers .270, .30-06 and .308 only, has Monte Carlo cheekpiece stock forearm with black tip, basket-weave checkering. Available also in left-hand model. Made from 1953 to 1980.

MODEL 760D
PEERLESS GRADE .... NiB $2495 Ex $1085 Gd $832
Same as Model 760 except scroll engraved, fancy wood. Made from 1953 to 1980.

**Remington Model 760
Bicentennial Commemorative**

**Remington Model 760
Gamemaster**

Remington Model 7600 Carbine

Remington Model 7600 Rifle

Remington Nylon 76 Lever-Action

Remington Sportsman 76

RIFLES

MODEL 760F PREMIER GRADE
Same as Model 760 except extensively engraved with game scenes and scroll, finest grade wood. Also available with receiver inlaid with gold; adds 50 percent to value. Made from 1953 to 1980.
Premier F Grade . . . . NiB $5000 Ex $3126 Gd $2484
Premier Gold F Grade . . . . NiB $7094 Ex $5908 Gd $4394

MODEL 7600 SLIDE-ACTION
CARBINE . . . . NiB $645 Ex $365 Gd $262
Same general specifications as Model 7600 Rifle except has 18.5-inch bbl. and weighs 7.25 lbs. Made from 1987 to date.

MODEL 7600 SLIDE-ACTION RIFLE . . . . . . NiB $649 Ex $421 Gd $257
Similar to Model Six except has lower grade finishes. Made from 1981 to date.

MODEL 7600 SPECIAL PURPOSE . . . . NiB $420 Ex $390 Gd $236
Same general specification as the Model 7600, except chambered only in .270 or .30-06. Special Purpose matte black finish on all exposed metal. American walnut stock with SP non-glare finish.

NYLON 76 LEVER-ACTION REPEATER . . . . NiB $800 Ex $585 Gd $382
Short-throw lever action. Caliber: .22 LR. 14-round buttstock tubular magazine. Weight: 4 lbs. Black (add $700) or brown nylon stock and forend. Made 1962-64. Remington's only lever-action rifle.

SPORTSMAN 76 SLIDE-ACTION RIFLE . . . NiB $300 Ex $260 Gd $182
Caliber: .30-06, 4-round magazine. 22-inch bbl. Weight: 7.5 lbs. Open rear sight; front blade mounted on ramp. Uncheckered hardwood stock and forend. Made from 1985 to 1987.

GRADING: **NiB** = New in Box   **Ex** = Excellent or NRA 95%   **Gd** = Good or NRA 68%

SEMIAUTOMATIC RIFLES

MODEL FOUR (4) AUTOLOADING RIFLE
Hammerless. Calibers: 6mm Rem., .243 Win., .270 Win. 7mm Express Rem., .30-06, .308 Win. 22-inch bbl. Weight: 7.5 lbs. Sights: Open rear; bead front, on ramp. Monte Carlo checkered stock and forearm. Made from 1981 to 1988.

Standard . . . . NiB $654 Ex $425 Gd $290
Peerless Grade (Engr. receiver) . . . . NiB $2143 Ex $1237 Gd $855
Premier Grade (Engr. receiver) . . . . NiB $3900 Ex $3129 Gd $2167
Prem. Gr. (Engr. rec., gold inlay) . . . . . . NiB $6424 Ex $5170 Gd $3472

MODEL FOUR DIAMOND
ANNIVERSARY LTD. EDITION Nib $1300 . . . . . . Ex $1000 . . . . Gd $895
Same as Model Four Standard except has engraved receiver w/inscription, checkered high-grade walnut stock and forend. Only 1,500 produced. Made in 1981 only. (Value for new condition.)

MODEL 8A AUTOLOADING RIFLE . . . . . . NiB $700 Ex $610 Gd $405
Standard Grade. Takedown. Calibers: .25, .30, .32 and .35 Rem. Five-round, clip-loaded magazine. 22-inch bbl. Weight: 7.75 lbs. Sights: Adj. and dovetailed open rear; dovetailed bead front. Half-moon metal buttplate on plain straight-grip walnut stock; plain walnut forearm with thin curved end. Made from 1906 to 1936.

MODEL 16 AUTOLOADING RIFLE. . . . . . . NiB $700 Ex $439 Gd $310
Takedown. Closely resembles the Winchester Model 03 semiautomatic rifle. Calibers: .22 Short, .22 LR, 22 Rem. Auto. 15-round tubular magazine in buttstock. 22-inch bbl. Weight: 5.75 lbs. Sights: Open rear; dovetailed bead front. Plain straight-grip stock and forearm. Made from 1914 to 1928. Note: In 1918 this model was discontinued in all calibers except .22 Rem. Auto; specifications are for that model.

MODEL 24A AUTOLOADING RIFLE . . . . . NiB $450 Ex $313 Gd $210
Standard Grade. Takedown. Calibers: .22 Short only, .22 LR. only. Tubular magazine in buttstock, holds 15 Short or 10 LR. 21-inch bbl. Weight: About 5 lbs. Sights: Dovetailed adj. open rear; dovetailed bead front. Plain walnut straight-grip buttstock; plain walnut forearm. Made 1922 to 1935.

MODEL 81A WOODSMASTER
AUTOLOADER . . . . NiB $571 Ex $442 Gd $262
Standard Grade. Takedown. Calibers: .30, .32 and .35 Rem., .300 Sav. Five round box magazine (not detachable). 22-inch bbl. Weight: 8.25 lbs. Sights: Open rear; bead front. Plain walnut pistol-grip stock, forearm. Made from 1936 to 1950.

MODEL 141A SPEEDMASTER
AUTOLOADER . . . . NiB $465 Ex $283 Gd $180
Standard Grade. Takedown. Calibers: .22 Short only, .22 LR. only. Tubular magazine in buttstock, holds 15 Short or 10 LR. 24-inch bbl. Weight: About 6 lbs. Sights: Open rear, bead front. Plain walnut stock and forearm. Made from 1935 to 1951.

MODEL 550A AUTOLOADER . . . . . NiB $275 Ex $180 Gd $105
Has "Power Piston" or floating chamber, which permits interchangeable use of 22 Short, Long or LR cartridges. Tubular magazine holds 22 Short, 17 Long, 15 LR. 24-inch bbl. Weight: About 6.25 lbs. Sights: Open rear; bead front. Plain, one-piece pistol-grip stock. Made from 1941 to 1971.

MODEL 550P . . . . NiB $299 Ex $180 Gd $105
Same as Model 550A except has peep rear sight, blade front, on ramp.

MODEL 550-2G . . . . NiB $355 Ex $258 Gd $155
"Gallery Special." Same as Model 550A except has 22-inch bbl., screw eye for counter chain and fired shell deflector.

**Remington Sportsman 742
Canadian Centennial**

MODEL 552A SPEEDMASTER
AUTOLOADER . . . . NiB $275 Ex $184 Gd $107
Caliber: .22 Short, Long, LR. Tubular magazine holds 20 Short, 17 Long, 15 LR. 25-inch bbl. Weight: About 5.5 lbs. Sights: Open rear; bead front. Pistol-grip stock, semi-beavertail forearm. Made from 1957 to 1988.

MODEL 552BDL DELUXE . . . . NiB $475 Ex $326 Gd $259
Same as Model 552A except has checkered walnut stock and forearm. Made from 1966 to date.

MODEL 552C CARBINE . . . . NiB $277 Ex $184 Gd $132
Same as Model 552A except has 21-inch bbl. Made 1961 to 1977.

MODEL 552GS GALLERY SPECIAL . . . . . . NiB $350 Ex $226 Gd $159
Same as Model 552A except chambered for .22 Short only. Made from 1957 to 1977.

MODEL 740A WOODSMASTER AUTOLOADER
Standard Grade. Gas-operated. Calibers: .30-06 or .308. Four round detachable box magazine. 22-inch bbl. Weight: About 7.5 lbs. Plain pistol-grip stock, semibeavertail forend with finger grooves. Sights: Open rear; ramp front. Made from 1955 to 1959.
Rifle model . . . . NiB $325 Ex $245 Gd $182
Carbine model . . . . NiB $424 Ex $396 Gd $268

MODEL 740ADL/BDL DELUXE
Same as Model 740A except has deluxe checkered stock, standard or high comb, grip cap, sling swivels. Model 740 BDL also has select wood. Made from 1955 to 1960.
Model 740 ADL Deluxe Grade . . . . NiB $400 Ex $510 Gd $379
Model 740 BDL Deluxe Special Grade . . . NiB $400 Ex $510 Gd $379

MODEL 742 BICENTENNIAL
COMMEMORATIVE. . . . . Nib $472 Ex $359 Gd $295
Same as Model 742 Woodsmaster rifle except has commemorative inscription on receiver. Made in 1976. (Value for new condition.)

MODEL 742 CARBINE . . . . NiB $450 Ex $310 Gd $243
Same as Model 742 Woodsmaster Rifle except made in calibers .30-06 and .308 only, has 18.5-inch bbl., weight 6.75 lbs. Made from 1961 to 1980.

MODEL 742 WOODSMASTER
AUTOMATIC BIG GAME RIFLE . . . . NiB $655 Ex $459 Gd $248
Gas-operated semiautomatic. Calibers: 6mm Rem., .243 Win., .280 Rem., .30-06, .308 Win. Four round clip magazine. 22-inch bbl. Weight: 7.5 lbs. Sights: Open rear; bead front, on ramp. Checkered pistol-grip stock and forearm. Made from 1960 to 1980.

Remington Model 7400

Remington Model 7400 Carbine

Remington Nylon 66
Bicentennial Commemorative

Remington Nylon 66 Mohawk

Remington Sportsman 74

MODEL 742BDL CUSTOM DELUXE...... NiB $475 Ex $393 Gd $262
Same as Model 742 Rifle except made in calibers .30-06 and .308 only, Monte Carlo cheekpiece stock, forearm with black tip, basket-weave checkering. Available in left-hand model. Made from 1966 to 1980.

MODEL 742D PEERLESS GRADE......... NiB $2500 Ex $1937 Gd $996
Same as Model 742 except scroll engraved, fancy wood. Made from 1961 to 1980.

MODEL 742F PREMIER GRADE
Same as Model 742 except extensively engraved with game scenes and scroll, finest grade wood. Also available with receiver inlaid with gold; adds 50 percent to value. Made from 1961 to 1980.
Premier F Grade .... NiB $5000 Ex $3170 Gd $2198
Premier Gold F Grade .... NiB $7000 Ex $4902 Gd $3388

MODEL 7400 AUTOLOADER
Similar to Model Four w/lower grade finishes. Made from 1981 to date.
Model 7400 Standard .... NiB $515 Ex $393 Gd $275
Model 7400 HG
(High gloss finish) .... NiB $515 Ex $393 Gd $275

MODEL 7400 CARBINE .... NiB $515 Ex $342 Gd $265
Caliber: .30-06 only. Similar to the Model 7400 rifle except has 18.5-inch bbl. and weight: 7.25 lbs. Made from 1988 to date.

MODEL 7400 SPECIAL PURPOSE........ NiB $435 Ex $365 Gd $236
Same general specification as the Model 7400 except chambered only in .270 or .30-06. Special Purpose matte black finish on metal. American walnut stock with SP nonglare finish. Made 1993 to 1995.

NYLON 66 APACHE BLACK ...... NiB $230 Ex $153 Gd $117
Same as Nylon 66 Mohawk Brown listed below except bbl. and receiver cover chrome-plated, black stock. Made 1962 to 1984.

**NYLON 66 BICENTENNIAL
COMMEMORATIVE** .... NiB $550 Ex $378 Gd $227
Same as Nylon 66 Mohawk Brown listed below except has commemorative inscription on receiver. Made 1976 only.

NYLON 66MB AUTOLOADING RIFLE.... NiB $450 Ex $253 Gd $197
Similar to the early production Nylon 66 Black Apache except with blued bbl. and receiver cover. Made from 1978 to 1987.

**NYLON 66 MOHAWK
BROWN AUTOLOADER** .... NiB $400 Ex $226 Gd $181
Caliber: .22 LR. Tubular magazine in buttstock holds 14 rounds. 19.5-inch bbl. Weight: About 4 lbs. Sights: Open rear; blade front. Brown nylon stock and forearm. Made from 1959 to 1987.

NYLON 77 CLIP REPEATER....... NiB $350 Ex $242 Gd $196
Same as Nylon 66 except has 5-round clip magazine. Made 1970 to 1971.

GRADING: **NiB** = New in Box   **Ex** = Excellent or NRA 95%   **Gd** = Good or NRA 68%

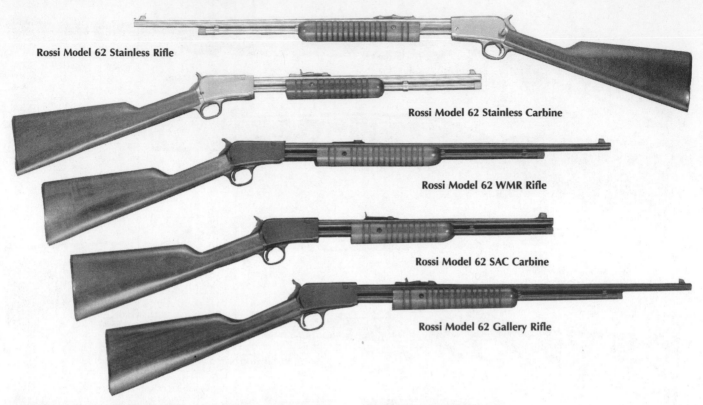

Rossi Model 62 Stainless Rifle

Rossi Model 62 Stainless Carbine

Rossi Model 62 WMR Rifle

Rossi Model 62 SAC Carbine

Rossi Model 62 Gallery Rifle

SPORTSMAN 74 AUTOLOADING RIFLE . . . . . NiB $350 Ex $262 Gd $179
Caliber: .30-06, 4-round magazine. 22-inch bbl. Uncheckered buttstock and forend. Open rear sight; ramped blade front sight. Made 1985 to 1988.

JOHN RIGBY & CO. — Paso Robles, CA

MODEL 275 MAGAZINE SPORTING RIFLE   NiB $6320 Ex $5070 Gd $3470
Mauser action. Caliber: .275 High Velocity or 7x57mm; 5-round box magazine. 25-inch bbl. Weight: about 7.5 lbs. Sights: Folding leaf rear; bead front. Sporting stock w/half-pistol-grip, checkered. Specifications given are those of current model; however, in general, they apply also to prewar model.

**MODEL 275 LIGHTWEIGHT
MAGAZINE RIFLE . . . . NiB $5055 Ex $4055 Gd $2775**
Same as standard .275 rifle except has 21-inch bbl. Weight: 6.75 lbs.

**MODEL 350 MAGNUM
MAGAZINE SPORTING RIFLE . . . . NiB $3995 Ex $3548 Gd $2425**
Mauser action. Caliber: .350 Magnum. Five round box magazine. 24-inch bbl. Weight: About 7.75 lbs. Sights: Folding leaf rear; bead front. Sporting stock with full pistol-grip, checkered. Currently mfd.

**MODEL 416 BIG GAME
MAGAZINE SPORTING RIFLE . . . . NiB $7580 Ex $6080 Gd $4160**
Mauser action. Caliber: .416 Big Game. Four round box magazine. 24-inch bbl. Weight: 9 to 9.25 lbs. Sights: Folding leaf rear; bead front. Sporting stock with full pistol-grip, checkered. Currently mfd.

**BEST QUALITY HAMMERLESS
EJECTOR DOUBLE RIFLE . . . . NiB $72,500 Ex $59,000 Gd $36,520**
Sidelocks. Calibers: .275 Magnum, .350 Magnum, .470 Nitro Express. 24- to 28-inch bbls. Weight: 7.5 to 10.5 lbs. Sights: Folding leaf rear; bead front. Checkered pistol-grip stock and forearm.

**SECOND QUALITY HAMMERLESS
EJECTOR DOUBLE RIFLE . . . . NiB $12,875 Ex $10,500 Gd $9900**
Same general specifications as Best Quality double rifle except boxlock.

**THIRD QUALITY HAMMERLESS
EJECTOR DOUBLE RIFLE . . . . NiB $10,375 Ex $9100 Gd $6732**
Same as Second Quality double rifle except plainer finish and not of as high quality.

ROSS RIFLE CO. — Quebec, Canada

**MODEL 1910 BOLT-ACTION
SPORTING RIFLE . . . . NiB $662 Ex $245 Gd $224**
Straight-pull bolt-action with interrupted screw-type lugs. Calibers: .280 Ross, .303 British. Four round or 5-round magazine. Bbl. lengths: 22, 24, 26 inches. Sights: Two-leaf open rear; bead front. Checkered sporting stock. Weight: About 7 lbs. Made c. 1910 to end of World War I. Note: Most firearm authorities agree that this and other Ross models with interrupted screw-type lugs are unsafe to fire.

ROSSI RIFLES — Sao Leopoldo, Brazil
Manufactured by Amadeo Rossi, S.A.

62 GALLERY MODEL SAC CARBINE
Same as standard Gallery Model except in .22 LR only with 16.25-inch bbl.; weight 5.5 lbs. Imported 1975 to 1998.
Blued finish . . . . NiB $185 Ex $140 Gd $119
Nickel finish . . . . NiB $195 Ex $150 Gd $130
Stainless . . . . NiB $195 Ex $150 Gd $1350

62 GALLERY MODEL MAGNUM . . . . NiB $220 Ex $191 Gd $129
Same as standard Gallery Model except chambered for .22 WMR, 10-shot magazine. Imported from 1975 to 1998.

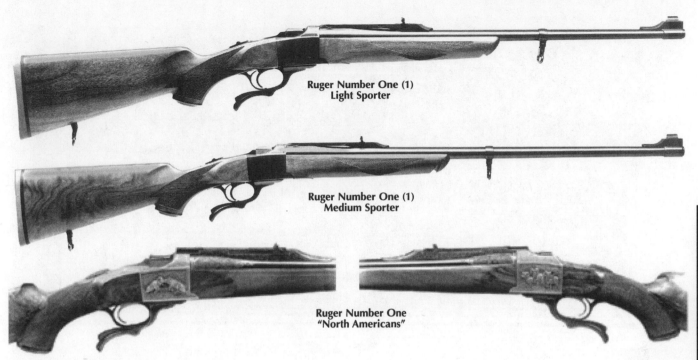

Ruger Number One (1)
Light Sporter

Ruger Number One (1)
Medium Sporter

Ruger Number One
"North Americans"

62 GALLERY MODEL SLIDE-ACTION REPEATER
Similar to Winchester Model 62. Calibers: .22 LR. Long, Short or .22 WMR. Tubular magazine holds 13 LR, 16 Long, 20 Short. 23-inch bbl. 39.25 inches overall. Weight: 5.75 lbs. Sights: Open rear; bead front. Straight-grip stock, grooved slide handle. Blued, nickel or stainless finish. Imported 1970 to 1998. Values same as SAC Model.

LEVER-ACTION 65/92 CARBINE
Similar to Winchester Model 92. Caliber: .38 Special/.357 Mag., .44 Mag., .44-40, .45 LC. 8- or 10-round magazine. 16-, 20- or 24-inch round or half-octagonal bbl. Weight: 5.5 to 6 lbs. 33.5- to 41.5-inches overall. Satin blue, chrome or stainless finish. Brazilian hardwood buttstock and forearm. Made from 1978 to 1998.

Model M92 SRC .45LC	NiB $285	Ex $225	Gd $184
Model M92 SRC .38/357, .44 Mag	NiB $285	Ex $225	Gd $184
Model M92 w/octagon bbl	NiB $355	Ex $295	Gd $259
Model M92 LL Lever	NiB $465	Ex $360	Gd $258
Engraved, add			$75
Chrome, add			$25
Stainless, add			$40

RUGER RIFLES — Southport, Connecticut Manufactured by Sturm, Ruger & Co.

NUMBER ONE (1) LIGHT SPORTER...... NiB $925 Ex $579 Gd $395
Same as No.1 Standard except has 22-inch bbl., folding leaf rear sight on quarter-rib and ramp front sight, Henry pattern forearm. Made from 1966 to date.

NUMBER ONE (1) MEDIUM SPORTER ... NiB $925 Ex $529 Gd $395
Same as No. 1 Light Sporter except has 26-inch bbl. 22-inch in 45-70); weight: 8 lbs (7.25 lbs. in .45-70). Calibers: 7mm Rem. Mag., .300 Win. Mag., .45-70. Made from 1966 to date.

NUMBER ONE (1) "NORTH AMERICANS"
PRESENTATION RIFLE .... NiB $52,570
Same general specifications as the Ruger No. 1 Standard except highly customized with elaborate engravings, carvings, fine-line checkering and gold inlays. This was a series of 21 rifles depicting a North American big-game animal, chambered in the caliber appropriate to the game. Stock is of Northern California English walnut. Comes in trunk-style Huey case with Leupold scope and other accessories.

NUMBER ONE (1) RSI INTERNATIONAL
SINGLE-SHOT RIFLE.................. NiB $975 Ex $601 Gd $537
Similar to the No. 1 Light Sporter except with lightweight 20-inch bbl. and full Mannlicher-style forend, in calibers .243 Win., .270 Win., 7x57mm, .30-06. Weight: 7.25 lbs.

NUMBER ONE (1)
SPECIAL VARMINTER .... NiB $925 Ex $601 Gd $437
Same as No. 1 Standard except has heavy 24-inch bbl. with target scope bases, no quarter-rib. Weight: 9 lbs. Calibers: .22-250, .25-06, 7mm Rem. Mag., .300 Win. Mag. Made from 1966 to date.

NUMBER ONE (1)
STANDARD RIFLE..................... NiB $925 Ex $600 Gd $435
Falling-block single-shot action with Farquharson-type lever. Calibers: .22-250, .243 Win., 6mm Rem., .25-06, .270 Win., .30-06, 7mm Rem. Mag., .300 Win. Mag. 26-inch bbl. Weight: 8 lbs. No sights, has quarter-rib for scope mounting. Checkered pistol-grip buttstock and semibeavertail forearm, QD swivels, rubber buttplate. Made from 1966 to date.

NUMBER ONE (1) TROPICAL RIFLE...... NiB $925 Ex $600 Gd $435
Same as No. 1 Light Sporter except has heavy 24-inch bbl.; calibers are .375 H&H .404 Jeffery, .416 Rigby, and .458 Win. Mag. Weight: 8.25 to 9 lbs. Made from 1966 to date.

NUMBER THREE (3) SINGLE-SHOT
CARBINE...................... NiB $750 Ex $450 Gd $270
Falling-block action with American-style lever. Calibers: .22 Hornet .223 Rem., .30-40 Krag, .357 Win., .44 Mag., .45-70. 22-inch bbl. Weight: 6 lbs. Sights: Folding leaf rear; gold bead front. Carbine-style stock w/curved buttplate, forearm with bbl. band. Made 1972 to 1987.

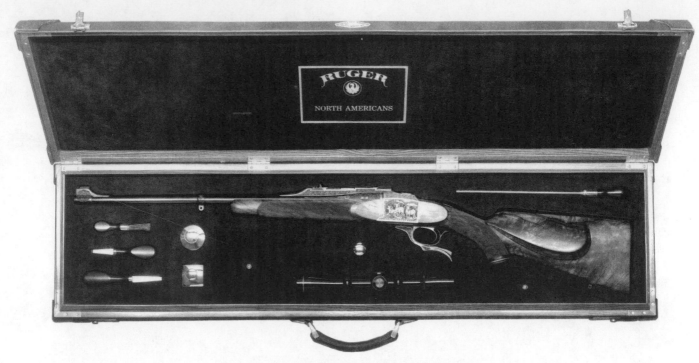

Ruger Number One "North Americans" Presentation Set

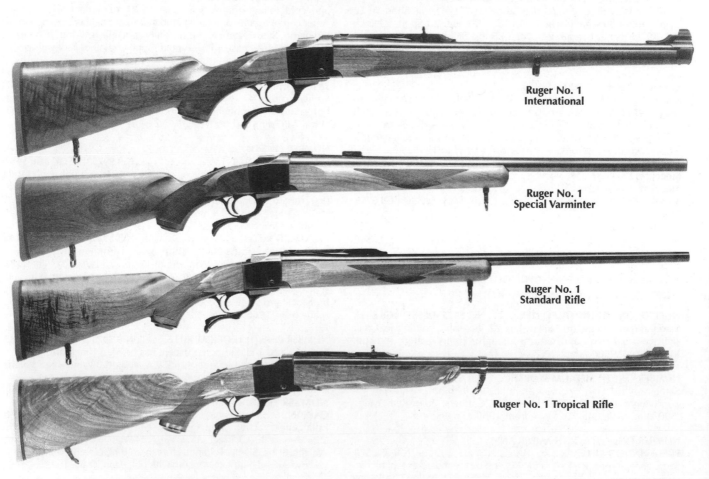

Ruger No. 1
International

Ruger No. 1
Special Varminter

Ruger No. 1
Standard Rifle

Ruger No. 1 Tropical Rifle

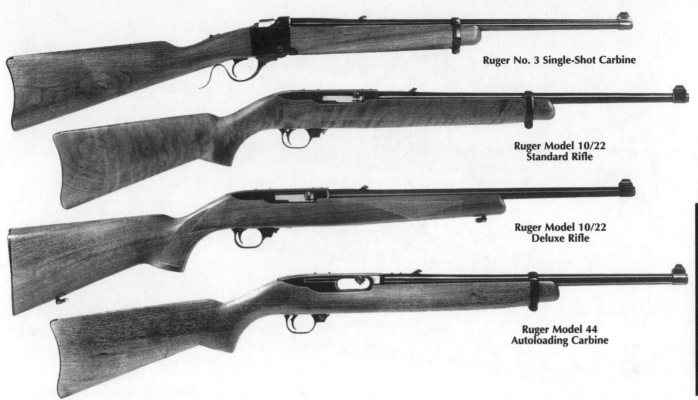

Ruger No. 3 Single-Shot Carbine

Ruger Model 10/22 Standard Rifle

Ruger Model 10/22 Deluxe Rifle

Ruger Model 44 Autoloading Carbine

RIFLES

MODEL 10/22 AUTOLOADING CARBINE

Caliber: .22 LR. Detachable 10-round rotary magazine. 18.5-inch bbl. Weight: 5 lbs. Sights: Folding leaf rear; bead front. Carbine-style stock with bbl. band and curved buttplate (walnut stock discontinued 1980). Made from 1964 to date. International and Sporter versions discontinued 1971.

10/22 Standard Carbine (Walnut stock)	NiB $220	Ex $179	Gd $136
10/22 Int'l. (w/Mannlicher style stock, swivels) Disc.1971	NiB $650	Ex $447	Gd $344
10/22 RB (Birch stock, blued)	NiB $220	Ex $162	Gd $126
K10/22 RB (Birch stock, stainless)	NiB $220	Ex $187	Gd $136
10/22 Sporter (MC stock, flat buttplate, swivels) Disc.1971	NiB $220	Ex $187	Gd $136
10/22 SP Deluxe Sporter (made since 1966)	NiB $220	Ex $187	Gd $136
10/22 RBI Int'l. (blued); made since 1994	NiB $650	Ex $445	Gd $344
10/22 RBI Int'l. (stainless); made since 1995	NiB $650	Ex $445	Gd $344

MODEL 44 AUTOLOADING CARBINE

Gas-operated. Caliber: .44 Magnum. Four round tubular magazine (with magazine release button since 1967). 18.5-inch bbl. Weight: 5.75 lbs. Sights: Folding leaf rear; gold bead front. Carbine-style stock w/bbl. band and curved buttplate. Made from 1961 to 1986. International and Sporter versions discontinued 1971.

Model 44 Standard autoloading carbine	NiB $550	Ex $405	Gd $292
Model 44 Int'l (w/Mannlicher-style stock, swivels)	NiB $825	Ex $560	Gd $457
Mdl. 44 Sporter (MC stk. w/fingergroove)	NiB $663	Ex $714	Gd $508
Model 44RS Carbine (w/rear peep sight, disc. 1978)	NiB $650	Ex $457	Gd $349

MODEL 77 BOLT-ACTION RIFLE

Receiver with integral scope mount base or with round top. Short stroke or magnum length action (depending on caliber) in the former type receiver, magnum only in the latter. .22-250, .220 Swift, 6mm Rem., .243 Win., .250-3000, .25-06, .257 Roberts, 6.5 Rem. Mag., .270 Win., 7x57mm, 7mm-08 7mm Rem. Mag., .280 Rem., .284 Win., .308 Win., .30-06, .300 Win. Mag. .338 Win. Mag., .350 Rem. Mag., .458 Win. Mag. Five round magazine standard, 4-round in .220 Swift, 3-round in magnum calibers. 22 24- or 26-inch bbl. (depending on caliber). Weight: About 7 lbs.; .458 Mag. model, 8.75 lbs. Round-top model furnished w/folding leaf rear sight and ramp front; integral base model furnished w/scope rings, with or w/o open sights. Stock w/checkered pistol grip and forearm, pistol-grip cap, rubber recoil pad, QD swivel studs. Made from 1968 to 1992.

Model 77, integral base, no sights	NiB $450	Ex $382	Gd $247
6.5 Rem. Mag., add			$75
.284 Win., add			$30
.338 Win. Mag., add			$50
.350 Rem. Mag., 6.5 Rem. Mag., add			$75
Model 77RL Ultra Light, no sights,	NiB $500	Ex $393	Gd $265
Model 77RL Ultra Light, open sights,	NiB $525	Ex $424	Gd $300
Model 77RS, integral base, open sights	NiB $525	Ex $418	Gd $298
.338 Win. Mag., .458 Win. Mag., with standard stock, add			$75
Model 77RSC, .458 Win. Mag. with fancy Circassian walnut stock, add			$525
Model 77RSI International, Mannlicher stock, short action, 18.5-inch bbl., 7 lbs.	NiB $575	Ex $403	Gd $275
Model 77ST, round top, open sights	NiB $550	Ex $414	Gd $331
.338 Win. Mag., add			$50
Model 77V, Varmint, integral base, no sights	NiB $500	Ex $434	Gd $249
Model 77NV, Varmint, integral base, no sights, stainless steel barrel, laminated wood stock	NiB $525	Ex $445	Gd $300

MODEL 77 MARK II ALL-WEATHER RIFLE	NiB $480	Ex $395	Gd $275

Revised Model 77 action. Same general specifications as Model M-77 Mark II except with stainless bbl. and action. Zytel injection-molded stock. Calibers: .223, .243, .270, .308, .30-06, 7mm Mag., .300 Win. Mag., .338 Win. Mag. Made from 1999 to 2008.

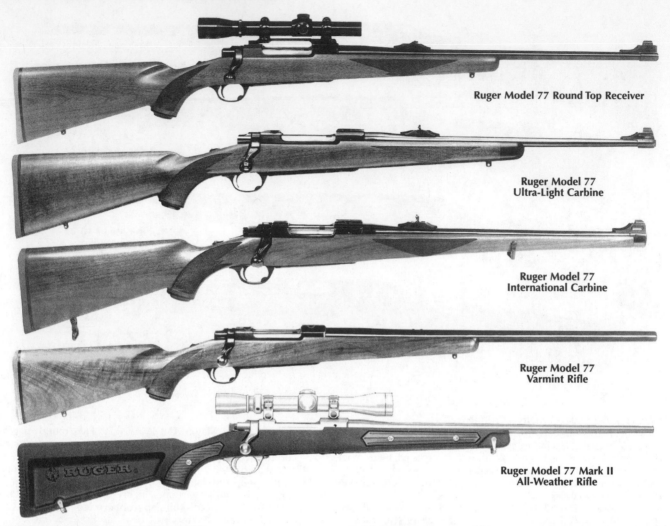

Ruger Model 77 Round Top Receiver

Ruger Model 77 Ultra-Light Carbine

Ruger Model 77 International Carbine

Ruger Model 77 Varmint Rifle

Ruger Model 77 Mark II All-Weather Rifle

MODEL 77 MARK II BOLT-ACTION RIFLE

Revised Model 77 action. Same general specifications as Model M-77 except with new 3-position safety and fixed blade ejector system. Calibers .22 PPC, .223 Rem., 6mm PPC, 6.5x55 Swedish, .375 H&H, .404 Jeffery and .416 Rigby also available. Weight: 6 to 10.25 lbs. Made from 1989 to date.

Model 77 MKIIR, integral base, no sights . . NiB $480 Ex $407 Gd $286
Left-hand Model 77LR MKII, add $25
Model 77RL MKII, Ultra Light, no sights. . . NiB $480 Ex $407 Gd $286
Model 77RLS MKII, Ultra
Light, open sights . . . . NiB $480 Ex $407 Gd $286
Model 77RS MKII, integral base, open sights . . . NiB $480 Ex $407 Gd $286
Model 77RS MKII, Express, with fancy French
walnut stock, integral base, open sights NiB $1250 Ex $1050 Gd $727
Model 77RSI MKII,
International, Mannlicher . . . . NiB $740 Ex $438 Gd $308
Model 77RSM MKII magnum, with fancy Circassian
walnut stock, integral base, open sights. . . . . . NiB $1377 Ex $1068 Gd $759
Model 77VT (VBZ or VTM)
MKII Varmint/Target stainless steel action,
laminated wood stock. . . . . NiB $480 Ex $403 Gd $288

MODEL 77/.22 HORNET BOLT-ACTION RIFLE

Mini-Sporter built on the 77/.22 action in caliber .22 Hornet. Six round rotary magazine. 20- inch bbl. 40 inches overall. Weight: 6 lbs. Receiver machined for Ruger rings (included). Beaded front sight and open adj. rear, or no sights. Blued or stainless finish. Checkered American walnut stock. Made from 1994 to date.

Model 77/.22RH (rings, no sights) . . . . NiB $580 Ex $343 Gd $240
Model 77/.22RSH (rings & sights) . . . . NiB $580 Ex $343 Gd $240
Model 77/.22VHZ (S/S w/
laminated wood stock) . . . . NiB $685 Ex $494 Gd $366

MODEL 77/.22 RIMFIRE BOLT-ACTION RIFLE

Calibers: .22 LR. or .22 WMR. 10-shot (.22 LR) or 9-shot (.22 WMR) rotary magazine. 20-inch bbl. 39.75 inches overall. Weight: 5.75 lbs. Integral scope bases; with or w/o sights. Checkered American walnut or Zytel injection-molded stock. Stainless or blued finish. Made 1983 to date. (Blued); stainless. Introduced 1989.

77/.22 R, rings, no sights, walnut stock . . . . . . NiB $580 Ex $347 Gd $227
77/.22 RS, rings, sights, walnut. . . . . NiB $580 Ex $317 Gd $227
77/.22 RP, rings, no sights, synthetic stock . . . . NiB $580 Ex $347 Gd $227
77/.22 RSP, rings, sights, synthetic stock . . . . . NiB $580 Ex $347 Gd $227
K77/.22 RP, S/S rings, no sights, synthetic . . . . NiB $580 Ex $347 Gd $227
K77/.22 RSP, S/S, rings, sights, synthetic . . . . . NiB $580 Ex $347 Gd $227
77/.22 RM, .22 WMR,
rings, no sights, walnut . . . . NiB $580 Ex $317 Gd $230
77/.22 RSM, .22 WMR, rings, sights, walnut . . . NiB $580 Ex $333 Gd $227
K77/.22 RSMP, .22 WMR, S/S, rings,
sights, synthetic. . . . . NiB $685 Ex $438 Gd $341
K77/.22 RMP, .22 WMR,
S/S, no sights, synthetic . . . . NiB $580 Ex $347 Gd $227
K77/.22 VBZ, .22 WMR,
no sights, laminated. (1993) . . . . NiB $685 Ex $438 Gd $341

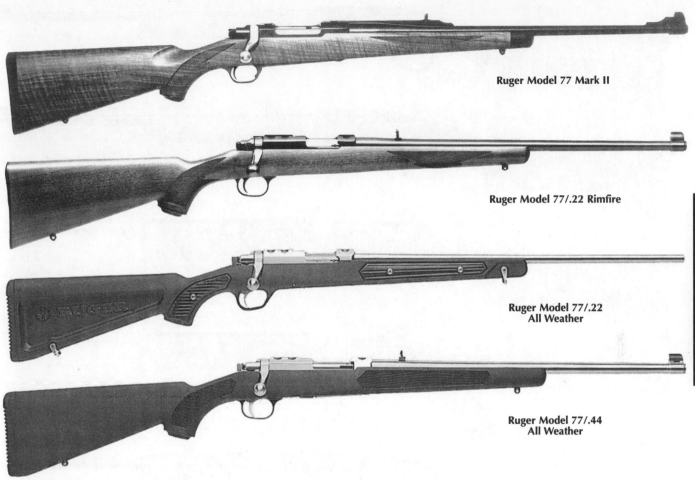

Ruger Model 77 Mark II

Ruger Model 77/.22 Rimfire

Ruger Model 77/.22
All Weather

Ruger Model 77/.44
All Weather

MODEL 77/.44 BOLT-ACTION
Short-action, carbine-style M77 similar to the 77/.22RH. Chambered .44 Rem. Mag. Four round rotary magazine. 18.5-inch bbl. 38.25 inches overall. Weight: 6 lbs. Gold bead front sight, folding adjustable rear w/integral scope base and Ruger rings. Blue or stainless finish. Synthetic or checkered American walnut stock w/rubber buttpad and swivels. Made from 1997 to 2004.

Model 77/.44 blued . . . . NiB $580 Ex $317 Gd $247
Model 77/.44 stainless . . . . NiB $510 Ex $306 Gd $222

MODEL 96 LEVER ACTION CARBINE
Caliber: .22 LR. .22 Mag., .44 Mag. Detachable 10-, 9- or 4-round magazine. 18.5-inch bbl. Weight: 5.25 lbs. Front gold bead sights. Drilled and tapped for scope. American hardwood stock. Made from 1996 to 2008.

.22 Long Rifle . . . . NiB $345 Ex $232 Gd $160
.22 Magnum . . . . NiB $355 Ex $242 Gd $170
.44 Magnum . . . . NiB $355 Ex $242 Gd $170

MINI-14 SEMIAUTOMATIC RIFLE
Gas-operated. Caliber: .223 Rem. (5.56mm). 5-, 10- or 20-round box magazine. 18.5-inch bbl. Weight: About 6.5 lbs. Sights: Peep rear; blade front mounted on removable barrel band. Pistol-grip stock w/curved buttplate, handguard. Made from 1974 to 2004.

Mini-14/5 blued . . . . NiB $675 Ex $540 Gd $344

K-Mini-14/5 stainless steel . . . . NiB $775 Ex $550 Gd $395

Mini-14/5F blued, folding stock . . . . NiB $1075 Ex $955 Gd $759
K-Mini-14/5F stainless, folding stock . . . . NiB $794 Ex $665 Gd $485
Mini-14 Ranch Rifle,
scope model, 6.25 lbs. . . . . NiB $613 Ex $562 Gd $356
K-Mini-1H Ranch Rifle,
scope model, stainless . . . . NiB $1098 Ex $588 Gd $381

MINI-THIRTY (30) AUTOLOADER
Caliber: 7.62 x 39mm. 5-round detachable magazine. 18.5-inch bbl. 37.25 inches overall. Weight: 7 lbs. 3 oz. Designed for use with telescopic sights. Walnut stained stock. Sights: Peep rear; blade front mounted on bbl. band. Blued or stainless finish. Made from 1987 to 2004.

Blued . . . . NiB $540 Ex $551 Gd $335
Stainless . . . . NiB $765 Ex $602 Gd $345

PC SERIES SEMIAUTOMATIC CARBINES
Calibers: 9mm Parabellum or .40 S&W. 10-round magazine. 15.25-inch bbl. Weight: 6.25 lbs. Integral Ruger scope mounts with or without sights. Optional blade front sight, adjustable open rear. Matte black oxide finish. Matte black Zytel stock w/checkered pistol-grip and forearm. Made from 1997 to date.

Model PC9 (w/o sights) . . . . NiB $470 Ex $419 Gd $265
Model PC4 (w/o sights) . . . . NiB $496 Ex $445 Gd $290
W/adjustable sights, add $40

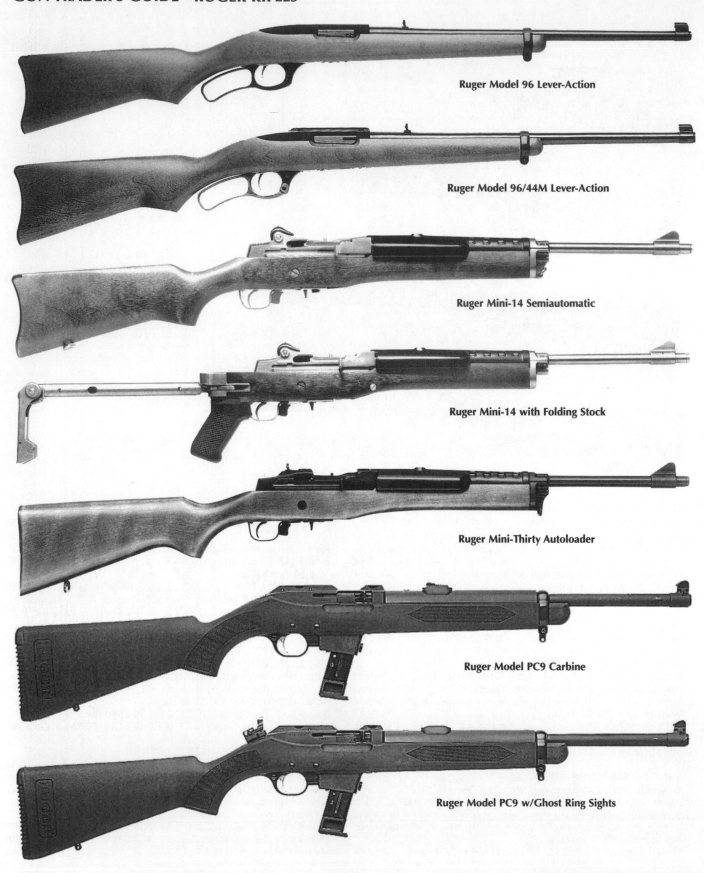

Ruger Model 96 Lever-Action

Ruger Model 96/44M Lever-Action

Ruger Mini-14 Semiautomatic

Ruger Mini-14 with Folding Stock

Ruger Mini-Thirty Autoloader

Ruger Model PC9 Carbine

Ruger Model PC9 w/Ghost Ring Sights

RUSSIAN MILITARY RIFLES — Principal U.S.S.R. Arms Plant, Tula

MODEL 1891
MOSIN MILITARY RIFLE . . . . **NiB $440 Ex $131 Gd $85**
Nagant system bolt action. Caliber: 7.62mm Russian. Five round box magazine. 31.5-inch bbl. Weight: About 9 lbs. Sights: Open rear; blade front. Full stock w/straight grip. Specifications given are for WWII version; earlier types differ slightly. Note: In 1916, Remington Arms Co. and New England Westinghouse Co. produced 250,000 of these rifles on a contract from the Imperial Russian Government. Few were delivered to Russia and the balance bought by the U.S. Government for training in 1918. Eventually, many of these rifles were sold to N.R.A. members for about $3 each by the Director of Civilian Marksmanship.

TOKAREV MODEL 40 SEMIAUTOMATIC
MILITARY RIFLE . . . . **NiB $813 Ex $403 Gd $249**
Gas-operated. Caliber: 7.62mm Russian. 10-round detachable box magazine. 24.5-inch bbl. Muzzle brake. Weight: About 9 lbs. Sights: Leaf rear, hooded post front. Full stock w/pistol grip. Differences among Models 1938, 1940 and 1941 are minor.

SAKO RIFLES — Riihimaki, Finland Manufactured by Sako L.T.D.

Formerly imported by Stoeger Industries, Wayne NJ (formerly by Garcia Corp.) until 2000. Imported by Beretta USA 2001 to date.

MODEL 72 . . . . **NiB $1032 Ex $826 Gd $620**
Single model designation replacing Vixen Sporter, Vixen Carbine, Vixen Heavy Barrel, Forester Sporter, Forester Carbine, Forester Heavy Barrel, Finnbear Sporter, and Finnbear Carbine, with same specifications, except all but heavy barrel models fitted with open rear sight. Values same as for corresponding earlier models. Imported from 1972 to 1974.

MODEL 73 LEVER-ACTION RIFLE . . . . . . **NiB $1584 Ex $929 Gd $620**
Same as Finnwolf except has 3-round clip magazine, flush floorplate; stock has no cheekpiece. Imported from 1973 to 1975.

MODEL 74 CARBINE . . . . **NiB $1035 Ex $698 Gd $559**
Long Mauser-type bolt action. Caliber: .30-06. Five round magazine. 20-inch bbl. Weight: 7.5 lbs. No sights. Checkered Mannlicher-type full stock of European walnut, Monte Carlo cheekpiece. Imported from 1974 to 1978.

MODEL 74 HEAVY BARREL RIFLE,
LONG ACTION . . . . **NiB $1032 Ex $698 Gd $466**
Same specifications as short action except w/24-inch heavy bbl., weighs 8.75 lbs.; magnum w/4-round magazine. Calibers: .25-06, 7mm Rem. Mag. Imported from 1974 to 1978.

MODEL 74 HEAVY BARREL RIFLE,
MEDIUM ACTION . . . . **NiB $1032 Ex $694 Gd $466**
Same specifications as short action except w/23-inch heavy bbl., weighs 8.5 lbs. Calibers: .220 Swift, .22-250, .243 Win., .308 Win. Imported from 1974 to 1978.

MODEL 74 HEAVY BARREL RIFLE,
SHORT ACTION . . . . **NiB $1084 Ex $878 Gd $517**
Mauser-type bolt action. Calibers: .222 Rem., .223 Rem. Five round magazine. 23.5-inch heavy bbl. Weight: 8.25 lbs. No sights. Target-style checkered European walnut stock w/beavertail forearm. Imported from 1974 to 1978.

MODEL 74 SUPER SPORTER,
LONG ACTION . . . . **NiB $1032 Ex $732 Gd $466**
Same specifications as short action except w/24-inch bbl., weight: 8 lbs.; magnums have 4-round magazine, recoil pad. Calibers: .25-06, .270 Win. 7mm Rem. Mag., .30-06, .300 Win. Mag., .338 Win. Mag., .375 H&H Mag. Imported from 1974-78.

MODEL 74 SUPER SPORTER,
MEDIUM ACTION . . . . **NiB $1058 Ex $758 Gd $492**
Same specifications as short action except weight: 7.25 lbs. Calibers: .220 Swift, .22-250, .243 Win. Imported from 1974-78.

MODEL 74 SUPER SPORTER,
SHORT ACTION . . . . **NiB $1058 Ex $723 Gd $466**
Mauser-type bolt action. Calibers: .222 Rem., .223 Rem. Five round magazine. 23.5-inch bbl. Weight: 6.5 lbs. No sights. Checkered European walnut stock w/Monte Carlo cheekpiece, QD swivel studs. Imported 1974. Disc.

MODEL 75 DELUXE . . . . **NiB $1339 Ex 1083 Gd $755**
Same specifications as Sako 75 Hunter Model except w/hinged floor plate, deluxe high gloss checkered walnut stock w/rosewood forend cap and grip cap w/silver inlay. Imported from 1998-2006. Disc.

MODEL 75 HUNTER . . . . **NiB $1125 Ex $789 Gd $567**
New bolt action design available in four action lengths fitted with a new bolt featuring three front locking lugs with an external extractor positioned under the bolt. Calibers: .17 Rem., .222 Rem., .223 Rem., (I); .22-250 Rem., .243 Win., 7mm-08 Rem., .308 Win., (III); .25-06 Rem., .270 Win., .280 Rem., .30-06, (IV); 7mm Rem Mag., .300 Win. Mag., .300 Wby. Mag., .338 Win. Mag. 7mm STW, .300 Wby. Mag., .340 Wby. Mag., .375 H&H Mag. and .416 Rem. Mag.,(V). 4-, 5- or 6-round magazine w/detachable magazine. 22-, 24-, and 26-inch bbls. 41.75 to 45.6 inches over all. Weight: 6.3 to 9 lbs. Sako dovetail scope base integral with receiver with no sights. Checkered high-grade walnut stock w/recoil pad and sling swivels. Made from 1997 to 2006.

MODEL 75 STAINLESS SYNTHETIC . . . . . **NiB $1150 Ex $902 Gd $630**
Similar to Model 75 Hunter except chambered for .22-250 Rem., .243 Win., .25-06 Rem., .270 Win., 7mm-08 Rem., 7mm STW, .30-06, .308 Win., 7mm Rem Mag., .300 Win. Mag., .338 Win. Mag. or .375 H&H Mag. 22-, 24-, and 26-inch bbls. Black composite stock w/soft rubber grips inserts. Matte stainless steel finish. Made from 1997 to 2006.

MODEL 75 VARMINT RIFLE . . . . . **NiB $1400 Ex $804 Gd $624**
Similar to Model 75 Hunter except chambered .17 Rem., .222 Rem., .223 Rem. and .22-250 Rem. 24-inch bbl. Matte lacquered walnut stock w/beavertail forearm. Made from 1998 to 2006.

MODEL 78 SUPER HORNET SPORTER . . . . **NiB $599 Ex $471 Gd $316**
Same specifications as Model 78 Rimfire except chambered for .22 Hornet, 4-round magazine. Imported from 1977 to 1987.

MODEL 78 SUPER RIMFIRE SPORTER . . . . **NiB $548 Ex $445 Gd $265**
Bolt action. Caliber: .22 LR. Five round magazine. 22.5-inch bbl. Weight, 6.75 lbs. No sights. Checkered European walnut stock, Monte Carlo cheekpiece. Imported from 1977 to 1986.

MODEL 85 CLASSIC BOLT-ACTION RIFLE
Calibers: .25-06 Rem., .270 Win., .30-06, .308 Win., .300 Win. Mga., .338 Win. Mag., .370 Sako Mag., .375 H&H Mag.., .270 WSM., .300 WSM., 7mm Mag. detachable mag., single stage trigger, pistol grip, checkered walnut stock. Weight: 7 lbs. New 2009.
Standard calibers . . . . **NiB $1875 Ex $1137 Gd $915**
Magnum caliber . . . . **Add $110**

RIFLES

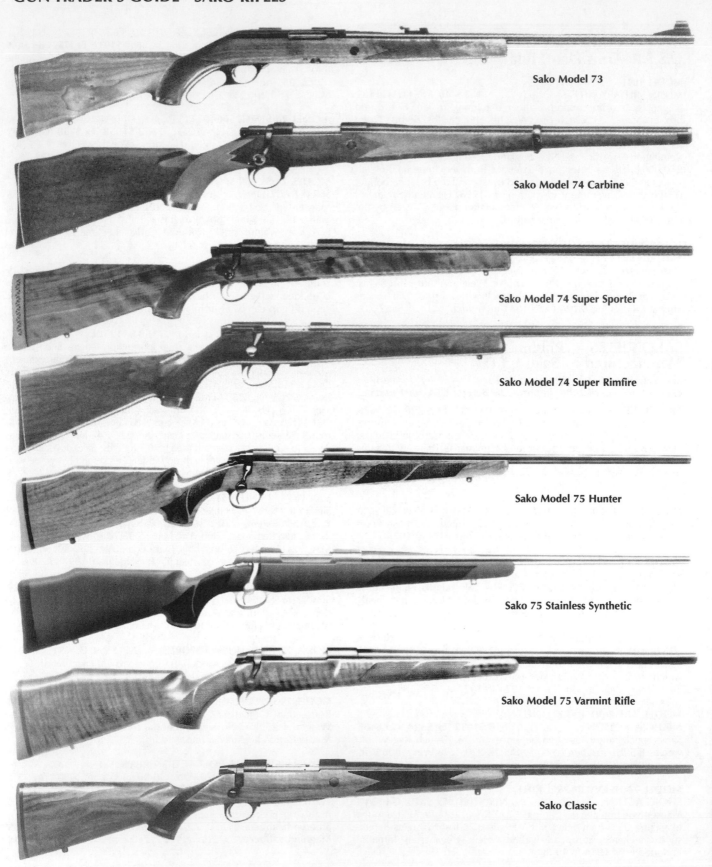

Sako Model 73

Sako Model 74 Carbine

Sako Model 74 Super Sporter

Sako Model 74 Super Rimfire

Sako Model 75 Hunter

Sako 75 Stainless Synthetic

Sako Model 75 Varmint Rifle

Sako Classic

Sako Deluxe Lightweight

Sako Fiberglass

Sako Finnfire

Sako Finnfire Heavy Barrel

Sako Finnwolf

DELUXE GRADE AI . . . . NiB $1185 Ex $828 Gd $597
Same specifications as Standard Grade except w/22 lines to the inch French checkering, rosewood grip cap and forend tip, semibeavertail forend. Disc.

DELUXE GRADE AII . . . . NiB $1063 Ex $754 Gd $522
Same specifications as Standard Grade except w/22 lines per inch French checkering, rosewood grip cap and forend tip, semi beavertail forend. Disc.

DELUXE GRADE AIII . . . . NiB $1376 Ex $1072 Gd $681
Same specifications as w/standard except w/French checkering, rosewood grip cap and forend tip, semibeavertail forend. Disc.

**DELUXE LIGHTWEIGHT
BOLT-ACTION RIFLE** . . . . NiB $1151 Ex $933 Gd $655
Same general specifications as Hunter Lightweight except w/beautifully grained French walnut stock; superb high-gloss finish, fine hand-cut checkering, rosewood forend tip and grip cap. Imported from 1985-97.

**FIBERCLASS BOLT-ACTION
RIFLE** . . . . NiB $1093 Ex $990 Gd $604
All-weather fiberglass stock version of Sako barreled long action. Calibers: .25-06, .270, .30-06, 7mm Rem. Mag., .300 Win. Mag., .338 Win. Mag., .375 H&H Mag. Bbl. length: 22.5 inches. Overall length: 44.25 inches. Weight: 7.25 lbs. Imported 1984 to 1996.

FINNBEAR CARBINE . . . . NiB $1100 Ex $885 Gd $540
Same as Finnbear Sporter except w/20-inch bbl., Mannlicher-type full stock. Imported 1971. Disc.

FINNBEAR SPORTER . . . . NiB $1100 Ex $905 Gd $550
Long Mauser-type bolt action. Calibers: .25-06, .264 Mag. .270, .30-06, .300 Win. Mag., .338 Mag., 7mm Mag., .375 H&H Mag. Magazine holds 5 standard or 4 magnum cartridges. 24-inch bbl. Weight: 7 lbs. Hooded ramp front sight. Sporter stock w/Monte Carlo cheekpiece, checkered pistol-grip and forearm, recoil pad, swivels. Imported from 1961 to 1971.

FINNFIRE BOLT-ACTION RIFLE
Mini-Sporter built for rimfires on a scaled-down Sako design. Caliber: .22 LR. 5- or 10-round magazine. 22-inch bbl. 39.5 inches overall. Weight: 5.25 lbs. Receiver machined for 11mm dovetail scope rings. Beaded blade front sight, open adj. rear. Blued finish. Checkered European walnut stock. Imported from 1994 to 2005.
Hunter model . . . . NiB $850 Ex $649 Gd $479
Varmint model . . . . NiB $895 Ex $659 Gd $504
Sporter model . . . . NiB $975 Ex $788 Gd $549

FINNWOLF LEVER-ACTION RIFLE . . . . NiB $895 Ex $648 Gd $583
Hammerless. Calibers: .243 Win., .308 Win. Four round clip magazine. 23-inch bbl. Weight: 6.75 lbs. Hooded ramp front sight. Sporter stock w/Monte Carlo cheekpiece, checkered pistol-grip and forearm, swivels (available w/right- or left-hand stock). Imported 1963 to 1972.

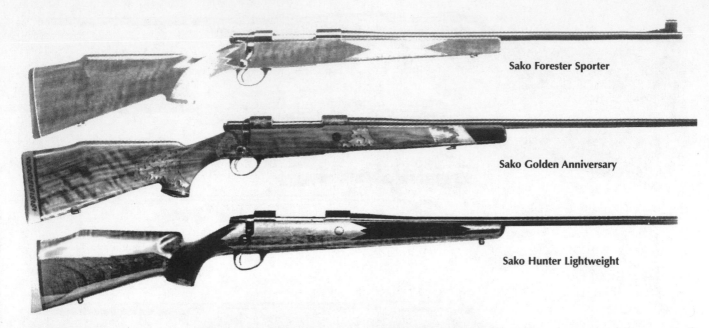

Sako Forester Sporter

Sako Golden Anniversary

Sako Hunter Lightweight

FINNSPORT 2700 . . . . NiB $750 Ex $568 Gd $410
Bolt-action centerfire rifle. Calibers: .270, .30-06, 7mm Rem. Mag., .300 Win. Mag. Bbl. length: 24 inches. Weight: 8 lbs. Imported 1984 to 1986.

FORESTER CARBINE . . . . NiB $1050 Ex $902 Gd $538
Same as Forester Sporter except w/20-inch bbl., Mannlicher-type full stock. Imported from 1958 to 1971.

FORESTER HEAVY BARREL . . . . . . NiB $1375 Ex $972 Gd $683
Same as Forester Sporter except w/24-inch heavy bbl. Weight 7.5 lbs. Imported from 1958 to 1971.

FORESTER SPORTER . . . . NiB $1050 Ex $998 Gd $508
Medium-length Mauser-type bolt action. Calibers: .22-250, .243 Win., .308 Win. Five round magazine. 23-inch bbl. Weight: 6.5 lbs. Hooded ramp front sight. Sporter stock w/Monte Carlo cheekpiece, checkered pistol grip and forearm, swivels. Imported 1957 to 1971.

GOLDEN ANNIVERSARY MODEL . . . . NiB $2750 Ex $2125 Gd $1440
Special presentation-grade rifle issued in 1973 to commemorate Sako's 50th anniversary. 1,000 (numbered 1 to 1,000) made. Same specifications as Deluxe Sporter: Long action, 7mm Rem. Mag. receiver, trigger guard and floorplate decorated w/gold oak leaf and acorn motif. Stock of select European walnut, checkering bordered w/hand-carved oak leaf pattern.

HIGH-POWER MAUSER SPORTING RIFLE . . . . . . NiB $1097 Ex $994 Gd $788
FN Mauser action. Calibers: .270, .30-06. Five round magazine. 24-inch bbl. Sights: Open rear leaf; Partridge front; hooded ramp. Checkered stock w/Monte Carlo comb and cheekpiece. Weight: 7.5 lbs. Imported from 1950 to 1957.

HUNTER LIGHTWEIGHT BOLT-ACTION RIFLE
5- or 6-round magazine. Bbl. length: 21.5 inches, AI; 22 inches, AII; 22.5 inches, AIII. Overall length: 42.25-44.5 inches. Weight: 5.75 lbs., AI; 6.75 lbs. AII; 7.25 lbs., AIII. Monte Carlo-style European walnut stock, oil finished. Hand-checkered pistol-grip and forend. Imported from 1985-97. Left-hand version intro. 1987.
AI (Short Action) .17 Rem. . . . . NiB $1400 Ex $1174 Gd $967
.222 Rem., .223 Rem. . . . . NiB $1030 Ex $799 Gd $567
AII (medium action)
.22-250 Rem., .243 Win., .308 Win. . . . . . . NiB $920 Ex $766 Gd $508

AII (long action) .25-06 Rem.,
.270 Win., .30-06 . . . . NiB $978 Ex $792 Gd $553
.338 Win. Mag. . . . . NiB $1115 Ex $915 Gd $660
.375 H&H Mag. . . . . NiB $1216 Ex $997 Gd $716
Left-hand model (standard cal.) . . . . NiB $1244 Ex $1007 Gd $700
Magnum calibers. . . . . NiB $1509 Ex $1233 Gd $881

**LAMINATED STOCK
BOLT-ACTION RIFLES**
Similar in style and specifications to Hunter Grade except w/stock of resin-bonded hardwood veneers. Available 18 calibers in AI (Short), AII (Medium) or AV action, left-hand version in 10 calibers, AV only. Imported from 1987 to 1995.
Short or medium action . . . . NiB $985 Ex $843 Gd $560
Long action/Magnum . . . . NiB $1049 Ex $869 Gd $586

MAGNUM MAUSER . . . . NiB $1506 Ex $1197 Gd $862
Similar specifications as Standard Model except w/recoil pad and redesigned longer AIII action to handle longer magnum cartridges. Calibers: .300 H&H Magnum, .375 H&H Magnum, standard at time of introduction. Disc.

MANNLICHER-STYLE CARBINE
Similar to Hunter Model except w/full Mannlicher-style stock and 18.5-inch bbl. Weighs 7.5 lbs. Chambered in .243, .25-06, .270, .308, .30-06, 7mm Rem. Mag., .300 Win. Mag., .338 Win. Mag., .375 H&H. Intro. in 1977. Disc.
Standard calibers . . . . NiB $1249 Ex $963 Gd $628
Magnum calibers (except .375) . . . . NiB $1272 Ex $989 Gd $670
.375 H&H . . . . NiB $1288 Ex $1015 Gd $706

SAFARI GRADE . . . . NiB $2487 Ex $1925 Gd $1096
Classic bolt-action. Calibers: .300 Win. Mag., .338 Win. Mag., .375 H&H. Oil-finished European walnut stock w/hand-checkering. Barrel band swivel, express-type sight rib; satin or matte blue finish. Imported from 1980 to 1996.

SPORTER DELUXE . . . . NiB $1242 Ex $959 Gd $624
Same as Vixen, Forester, Finnbear and Model 74 except w/fancy French walnut stock w/skip checkering, rosewood forend tip and pistol-grip cap, recoil pad, inlaid trigger guard and floorplate. Disc.

Sako Mannlicher-Style Carbine

Sako Sporter Deluxe

Sako TRG-21 Target Rifle

STANDARD GRADE AI . . . . **NiB $1028 Ex $745 Gd $410**
Short bolt-action. Calibers: .17 Rem., .222 Rem., .223 Rem. Five round magazine. 23.5-inch bbl. Weight: 6.5 lbs. No sights. Checkered European walnut stock w/Monte Carlo cheekpiece, QD swivel studs. Imported 1978 to 1985.

STANDARD GRADE AII . . . . **NiB $1039 Ex $761 Gd $436**
Medium bolt-action. Calibers: .22-250 Rem., .243 Win., .308 Win. 23.5-inch bbl. in .22-250; 23-inch bbl. in other calibers. Five round magazine. Weight: 7.25 lbs. Checkered European walnut stock w/Monte Carlo cheekpiece, QD swivel studs. Imported from 1978 to 1985.

STANDARD GRADE AIII . . . . **NiB $1075 Ex $797 Gd $488**
Long bolt action. Calibers: .25-06 Rem., .270 Win., .30-06, 7mm Rem. Mag., .300 Win. Mag., .338 Win. Mag., .375 H&H. 24-inch bbl. 4-round magazine. Weight: 8 lbs. Imported from 1978 to 1984.

SUPER DELUXE RIFLE . . . . **NiB $2400 Ex $2116 Gd $1266**
Available in AI, AII, AIII calibers. Select European walnut stock, hand-checkered, deep oak leaf hand-engraved design. Disc.

TRG-BOLT-ACTION TARGET RIFLE
Caliber: .308 Win., .330 Win. or .338 Lapua Mag. Detachable 10-round magazine. 25.75- or 27.2-inch bbl. Weight: 10.5 to 11 lbs. Blued action w/stainless barrel. Adjustable two-stage trigger. modular reinforced polyurethane target stock w/adj. cheekpiece and buttplate. Options: Muzzle break; detachable bipod; QD sling swivels and scope mounts w/1-inch or 30mm rings. Imported from 1993 to 2004.

TRG-21 .308 Win . . . . **NiB $2300 Ex $2049 Gd $1489**
TRG-22 .308 Win. . . . . **NiB $2375 Ex $2210 Gd $1545**
TRG-41 .338 Lapua. . . . . **NiB $2700 Ex $2586 Gd $1797**
TRG-42 .300 Win. or .338 Lapua . . . . . **NiB $3154 Ex $2651 Gd $1835**

TRG-S BOLT-ACTION RIFLE
Calibers: .243, 7mm-08, .270, .30-06, 7mm Rem. Mag., .300 Win. Mag., .338 Win. Mag. Five shot magazine (standard calibers), 4-shot (magnum), 22- or 24-inch bbl. 45.5 inches overall. Weight: 7.75 lbs. No sights. Reinforced polyurethane stock w/Monte Carlo. Introduced in 1993.
Standard calibers . . . . **NiB $775 Ex $687 Gd $429**
Magnum calibers . . . . **NiB $850 Ex $785 Gd $515**

VIXEN CARBINE . . . . **NiB $1002 Ex $905 Gd $815**
Same as Vixen Sporter except w/20-inch bbl., Mannlicher-type full stock. Imported from 1947 to 1971.

VIXEN HEAVY BARREL . . . . **NiB $1054 Ex $878 Gd $502**
Same as Vixen Sporter except calibers .222 Rem., .222 Rem. Mag., .223 Rem., heavy bbl., target-style stock w/beavertail forearm. Weight: 7.5 lbs. Imported from 1947-71.

VIXEN SPORTER . . . . **NiB $1055 Ex $932 Gd $517**
Short Mauser-type bolt-action. Cals.: .218 Bee, .22 Hornet, .222 Rem., .222 Rem. Mag., .223 Rem. Five round magazine. 23.5-inch bbl. Weight: 6.5 lbs. Hooded ramp front sight. Sporter stock w/Monte Carlo cheekpiece, checkered pistol-grip and forearm, swivels. Imported from 1946 to 1971.

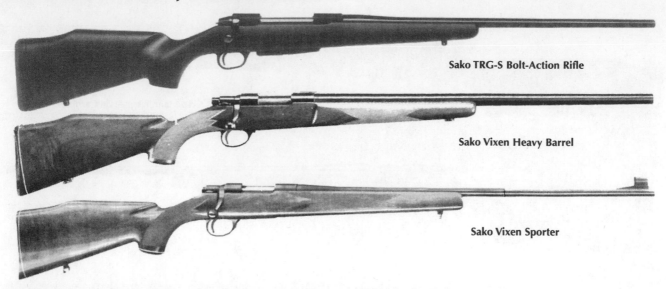

Sako TRG-S Bolt-Action Rifle

Sako Vixen Heavy Barrel

Sako Vixen Sporter

J. P. SAUER & SOHN — Eckernforde, Germany, (Formerly Suhl, Germany), Imported by Sigarms Exeter, NH , (Previously by Paul Company Inc. and G.U. Inc.)

MAUSER BOLT-ACTION
SPORTING RIFLE . . . . NiB $1395 Ex $1054 Gd $729
Calibers: 7x57 and 8x57mm most common, but these rifles were produced in a variety of calibers including most of the popular Continental calibers as well as our .30-06. Five round box magazine. 22- or 24-inch Krupp steel bbl., half-octagon w/raised matted rib. Double-set trigger. Weight: 7.5 lbs. Sights: Three-leaf open rear; ramp front. Sporting stock w/cheekpiece, checkered pistol grip, raised side-panels, Schnabel tip, swivels. Also made w/20-inch bbl. and full-length stock. Mfd. before WWII.

MODEL S-90 BOLT-ACTION RIFLES
Calibers: .243 Win., .308 Win. (Short action); .25-06, .270 Win., .30-06 (Medium action); 7mm Rem. Mag., .300 Win. Mag., .300 Wby., .338 Win., .375 H&H (Magnum action). Four round (standard) or 3-round magazine (magnum). Bbl. length: 20-inch (Stutzen), 24-inch. Weight: 7.6 to 10.75 lbs. Adjustable (Supreme) checkered Monte Carlo style stock. contrasting forend and pistol grip cap w/high-gloss finish or European (Lux) checkered Classic-style European walnut stock w/satin oil finish. Imported from 1983 to 1989.
S-90 Standard . . . . NiB $1089 Ex $960 Gd $548
S-90 Lux . . . . NiB $1305 Ex $1037 Gd $574
S-90 Safari. . . . . NiB $1279 Ex $1012 Gd $574
S-90 Stutzen . . . . NiB $1099 Ex $960 Gd $548
S-90 Supreme . . . . NiB $1412 Ex $1144 Gd $784
Grade I engraving, add $600
Grade II engraving, add $800
Grade III engraving add $1000
Grade IV engraving, add $1500

MODEL 200 BOLT-ACTION RIFLES
Calibers: .243 Win., .25-06, .270 Win., 7mm Rem Mag., .30-06, .308 Win., .300 Win. Mag., Detachable box magazine. 24-inch (American) or 26-inch (European) interchangeable bbl. Standard (steel) or lightweight (alloy) action. Weight: 6.6 to 7.75 lbs. 44 inches overall. Stock options: American Model w/checkered Monte Carlo style 2-piece stock contrasting forend and pistol grip cap w/high gloss finish and no sights. European walnut stock w/Schnabel forend, satin oil finish and iron sights. Contemporary Model w/synthetic carbon fiber stock. Imported from 1986 to 1993.
Standard model. . . . . NiB $1225 Ex $1015 Gd $655

Lightweight model . . . . NiB $1225 Ex $963 Gd $551
Contemporary model . . . . NiB $1219 Ex $1019 Gd $607
American model . . . . NiB $1395 Ex $1044 Gd $607
European model . . . . NiB $1395 Ex $1070 Gd $532
Left-hand model, add $150
Magnum calibers, add. $115
Interchangeable barrel assembly, add $295

MODEL 202 BOLT-ACTION RIFLES
Calibers: .243 Win., 6.5x55, 6.5x57, 6.6x68, .25-06, .270 Win., .280 7x64, .308, .30-06, Springfield, 7mm Rem. Mag., .300 Win. Mag., .300 Wby. Mag., 8x68S, .338 Win. Mag., .375 H&H Mag. Removable 3-round box magazine. 23.6- and 26-inch interchangable bbl. 44.3 and 46 inches overall. Modular receiver drilled and tapped for scope bases. Adjustable two-stage trigger w/dual release safety. Weight: 7.7 to 8.4 lbs. Stock options: Checkered Monte Carlo-style select American walnut two-piece stock; Euro-classic French walnut two-piece stock w/semi Schnabel forend and satin oil finish; Super Grade Claro walnut two-piece stock fitted w/rosewood forend and grip cap w/high-gloss epoxy finish. Imported from 1994 to 2004.
Standard model. . . . . NiB $2595 Ex $1813 Gd $955
Euro-Classic model . . . . NiB $1295 Ex $838 Gd $555
Super Grade model . . . . NiB $1020 Ex $864 Gd $579
Left-hand model, add $150
Magnum calibers, add. $125
Interchangeable barrel assembly, add $295

SAVAGE INDUSTRIES — Westfield, Massachusetts, (Formerly Chicopee Falls, MA and Utica, NY)

MODEL 3 BOLT-ACTION
SINGLE-SHOT RIFLE . . . . NiB $88 Ex $53 Gd $45
Takedown. Caliber: .22 Short, Long, L.R. 26-inch bbl. on prewar rifles, postwar production w/24-inch bbl. Weight: 5 lbs. Sights: Open rear; bead front. Plain pistol-grip stock. Made 1933 to 1952.

MODEL 3S. . . . . NiB $100 Ex $78 Gd $47
Same as Model 3 except w/peep rear sight, hooded front. Made 1933 to 1942.

MODEL 3ST. . . . . NiB $110 Ex $74 Gd $42
Same as Model 3S except fitted w/swivels and sling. Made from 1933 to 1942.

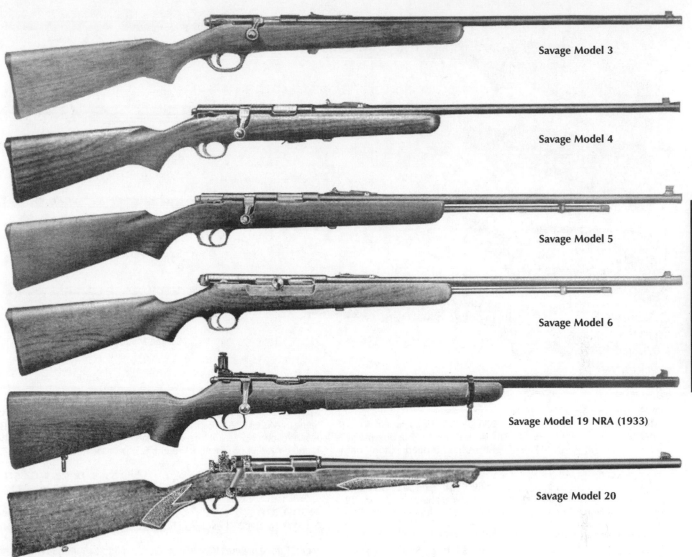

Savage Model 3

Savage Model 4

Savage Model 5

Savage Model 6

Savage Model 19 NRA (1933)

Savage Model 20

MODEL 4 BOLT-ACTION REPEATER. . . . . **NiB $125 Ex $83 Gd $42**
Takedown. Caliber: .22 Short, Long, LR. Five round detachable box magazine. 24-inch bbl. Weight: 5.5 lbs. Sights: Open rear; bead front. Checkered pistol-grip stock on prewar models, early production had grooved forearm; postwar rifles have plain stocks. Made from 193 to 1965.

MODEL 4M . . . . **NiB $110 Ex $82 Gd $56**
Same as Model 4 except chambered for .22 Rimfire Magnum. Made from 1961 to 1965.

MODEL 4S. . . . . **NiB $120 Ex $72 Gd $41**
Same as Model 4 except w/peep rear sight, hooded front. Made from 1933 to 1942.

MODEL 5 BOLT-ACTION
REPEATER . . . . **NiB $114 Ex $72 Gd $51**
Same as Model 4 except w/tubular magazine (holds 21 Short, 17 Long, 15 LR), weight: 6 lbs. Made from 1936 to 1961.

MODEL 5S. . . . . **NiB $120 Ex $68 Gd $42**
Same as Model 5 except w/peep rear sight, hooded front. Made 1936 to 1942.

MODEL 6 AUTOLOADING RIFLE. . . . . **NiB $154 Ex $88 Gd $47**
Takedown. Caliber: .22 Short, Long, LR. Tubular magazine holds 21 Short, 17 Long, 15 LR. 24-inch bbl. Weight: 6 lbs. Sights: Open rear; bead front. Checkered pistol-grip stock on prewar models, postwar rifles have plain stocks. Made from 1938 to 1968.

MODEL 6S. . . . . **NiB $150 Ex $89 Gd $42**
Same as Model 6 except w/peep rear sight, bead front. Made 1938 to 1942.

MODEL 7 AUTOLOADING RIFLE. . . . . **NiB $150 Ex $84 Gd $47**
Same general specifications as Model 6 except w/5-round detachable box magazine. Made from 1939 to 1951.

MODEL 7S. . . . . **NiB $150 Ex $98 Gd $57**
Same as Model 7 except w/peep rear sight, hooded front. Made from 1938 to 1942.

MODEL 19 BOLT-ACTION TARGET RIFLE. . . . . **NiB $300 Ex $245 Gd $182**
Model of 1933. Speed lock. Caliber: .22-LR. Five round detachable box magazine. 25-inch bbl. Weight: 8 lbs. Adj. rear peep sight, blade front on early models, later production equipped w/extension rear sight, hooded front. Target stock w/full pistol-grip and beavertail forearm. Made 1933 to 1946.

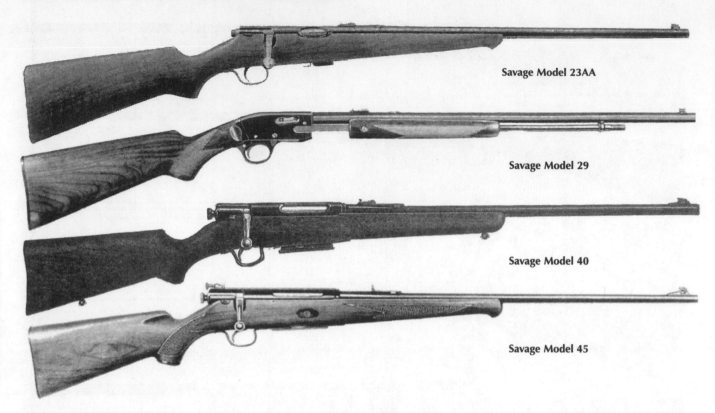

Savage Model 23AA

Savage Model 29

Savage Model 40

Savage Model 45

MODEL 19 NRA BOLT-ACTION
MATCH RIFLE . . . . **NiB $275 Ex $196 Gd $115**
Model of 1919. Caliber: .22 LR. Five round detachable box magazine. 25-inch bbl. Weight: 7 lbs. Sights: Adj. rear peep; blade front. Full military stock w/pistol-grip. Made from 1919 to 1933.

MODEL 19H . . . . **NiB $550 Ex $322 Gd $242**
Same as standard Model 19 (1933) except chambered for .22 Hornet, w/Model 23D-type bolt mechanism, loading port and magazine. Made from 1933 to 1942.

MODEL 19L. . . . . **NiB $330 Ex $285 Gd $182**
Same as standard Model 19 (1933) except equipped w/Lyman No. 48Y receiver sight, 17A front sight. Made from 1933 to 1942.

MODEL 19M. . . . . **NiB $330 Ex $445 Gd $213**
Same as standard Model 19 (1933) except w/heavy 28-inch bbl. w/scope bases, weight: 9.25 lbs. Made from 1933 to 1942.

MODEL 20-1926
HI-POWER . . . . **NiB $900 Ex $693 Gd $390**
Same as Model 1920, listed on page 354, except w/24-inch medium weight bbl., improved stock, Lyman 54 rear peep sight, weight: 7 lbs. Made from 1926 to 1929.

MODEL 23A BOLT-ACTION
SPORTING RIFLE. . . . . **NiB $253 Ex $196 Gd $160**
Caliber: 22 LR. Five round detachable box magazine. 23-inch bbl. Weight: 6 lbs. Sights: Open rear, blade or bead front. Plain pistol-grip stock w/slender forearm and Schnabel tip. Made 1923 to 1933.

MODEL 23AA . . . . **NiB $300 Ex $283 Gd $191**
Model of 1933. Improved version of Model 23A w/same general specifications except w/speed lock, improved stock, weighs 6.5 lbs. Made from 1933-42.

MODEL 23B . . . . **NiB $305 Ex $206 Gd $155**
Same as Model 23A except caliber .25-20, 25-inch bbl. Model of 1933 w/improved stock w/full forearm instead of slender forearm w/Schnabel found on earlier production. Weight: 6.5 lbs. Made from 1923 to 1942.

MODEL 23C . . . . **NiB $355 Ex $253 Gd $160**
Same as Model 23B except caliber .32-20. Made 1923 to 1942.

MODEL 23D . . . . **NiB $375 Ex $283 Gd $206**
Same as Model 23B except caliber .22 Hornet. Made 1933 to 1947.

MODEL 25 SLIDE-ACTION REPEATER . . . . **NiB $346 Ex $391 Gd $237**
Takedown. Hammerless. Caliber: .22 Short, Long, LR. Tubular magazine holds 20 Short, 17 Long, 15 LR. 24-inch octagon bbl. Weight: 5.75 lbs. Sights: Open rear; blade front. Plain pistol-grip stock, grooved slide handle. Made from 1925 to 1929.

MODEL 29 SLIDE-ACTION
REPEATER . . . . **NiB $473 Ex $343 Gd $241**
Takedown. Hammerless. Caliber: .22 Short, Long, LR. Tubular magazine holds 20 Short, 17 Long, 15 LR. 24-inch bbl., octagon on prewar, round on postwar production. Weight: 5.5 lbs. Sights: Open rear; bead front. Stock w/checkered pistol grip and slide handle on prewar, plain stock and grooved forearm on postwar production. Made from 1929 to 1967.

MODEL 40 BOLT-ACTION
SPORTING RIFLE. . . . . **NiB $354 Ex $260 Gd $213**
Standard Grade. Calibers: .250-3000, .300 Sav., .30-30, .30-06. Four round detachable box magazine. 22-inch bbl. in calibers .250-3000 and .30-30; 24-inch in .300 Sav. and .30-06. Weight: 7.5 lbs. Sights: Open rear; bead front, on ramp. Plain pistol-grip stock w/tapered forearm and Schnabel tip. Made 1928 to 1940.

MODEL 45 SUPER SPORTER. . . . . . . **NiB $386 Ex $242 Gd $192**
Special Grade. Same as Model 40 except w/checkered pistol-grip and forearm, Lyman No. 40 receiver sight. Made 1928 to 1940.

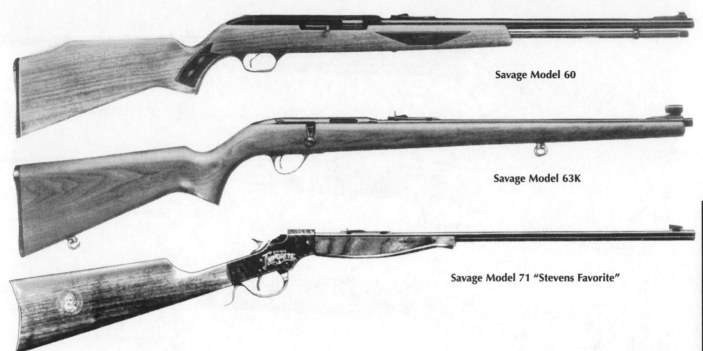

Savage Model 60

Savage Model 63K

Savage Model 71 "Stevens Favorite"

MODEL 60 AUTOLOADING RIFLE. . . . . **NiB $99 Ex $76 Gd $43**
Caliber: .22 LR. 15-round tubular magazine. 20-inch bbl. Weight: 6 lbs. Sights: Open rear, ramp front. Monte Carlo stock of walnut w/checkered pistol-grip and forearm. Made from 1969 to 1972.

MODEL 63K KEY LOCK BOLT-ACTION
SINGLE-SHOT RIFLE . . . . **NiB $106 Ex $85 Gd $54**
Trigger locked w/key. Caliber: .22 Short, Long, LR. 18-inch bbl. Weight: 4 lbs. Sights: Open rear; hooded ramp front. Full-length stock w/pistol grip, swivels. Made from 1970 to 1972.

MODEL 63KM . . . . **NiB $115 Ex $90 Gd $56**
Same as Model 63K except chambered for .22 WMR. Made 1970 to 1972.

MODEL 64F AUTOLOADING RIFLE. . . . . . . **NiB $176 Ex $110 Gd $85**
Same general specifications as Model 64G except w/black graphite/polymer stock. Weight: 5 lbs. Made from 1997 to date.

MODEL 64G AUTOLOADING RIFLE . . . . . . **NiB $156 Ex $116 Gd $95**
Caliber: 22 LR. 10-round magazine. 20-inch bbl. Weight: 5.5 lbs. 40 inches overall. Sights: Adj. open rear; bead front. Grooved receiver for scope mounts. Stamped checkering on walnut-finished hardwood stock w/Monte Carlo cheekpiece. Made from 1996 to date.

MODEL 71 "STEVENS FAVORITE"
SINGLE-SHOT LEVER-ACTION RIFLE . . . . . . **NiB $200 Ex $103 Gd $90**
Replica of original Stevens Favorite issued as a tribute to Joshua Stevens, "Father of .22 Hunting." Caliber: .22 LR. 22-inch full-octagon bbl. Brass-plated hammer and lever. Sights: Open rear; brass blade front. Weight: 4.5 lbs. Plain straight-grip buttstock and Schnabel forend; brass commemorative medallion inlaid in buttstock, brass crescent-shaped buttplate. 10,000 produced. Made in 1971 only. Top value is for new, unfired gun.

MODEL 90 AUTO-LOADING
CARBINE. . . . . **NiB $177 Ex $147 Gd $107**
Similar to Model 60 except w/16.5-inch bbl. w/folding leaf rear sight, bead front. 10-round tubular magazine. Uncheckered, carbine-

style walnut stock w/bbl. Band and sling swivels. Weight: 5.75 lbs. Made from 1969 to 1972.

MODEL 93G BOLT-ACTION RIFLE . . . . . . **NiB $210 Ex $152 Gd $116**
Caliber: .22 Win Mag. 5-round magazine. 20.75-inch bbl. 39.5 inches overall. Weight: 5.75 lbs. Sights: Adj. open rear; bead front. Grooved receiver for scope mounts. Stamped checkering on walnut-finished hardwood stock w/Monte Carlo cheekpiece. Made from 1996 to date.

MODEL 93F BOLT-ACTION RIFLE . . . . **NiB $252 Ex $105 Gd $100**
Same general specifications as Model 93G except w/black graphite/polymer stock. Weight: 5.2 lbs. Made from 1997 to date.

NOTE: MODEL 99 LEVER-ACTION REPEATER
Introduced in 1899, this model has been produced in a variety of styles and calibers. Original designation "Model 1899" was changed to "Model 99" c.1920. Earlier rifles and carbines — similar to Models 99A, 99B and 99H — were supplied in calibers .25-35, .30-30, .303 Sav., .32-40 and .38-55. Post-WWII Models 99A, 99C, 99CD, 99DE, 99DL, 99F and 99PE have top tang safety other 99s have slide safety on right side of trigger guard. Models 99C and 99CD have detachable box magazine instead of traditional Model 99 rotary magazine.

MODEL 99A (I) . . . . **NiB $975 Ex $714 Gd $528**
Hammerless. Solid frame. Calibers: .30-30, .300 Sav., .303 Sav. Five-round rotary magazine. 24-inch bbl. Weight: 7.25 lbs. Sights: Open rear; bead front, on ramp. Plain straight-grip stock, tapered forearm. Made from 1920 to 1936.

MODEL 99A (II) . . . . **NiB $875 Ex $614 Gd $308**
Current model. Similar to original Model 99A except w/top tang safety, 22-inch bbl., folding leaf rear sight, no crescent buttplate. Calibers: .243 Win., .250 Sav., .300 Sav., .308 Win. Made from 1971 to 1982.

MODEL 99B . . . . **NiB $1200 Ex $864 Gd $534**
Takedown. Otherwise same as Model 99A except weight: 7.5 lbs.

Savage Model 90

Savage Model 99A 1971 Issue

Savage Model 99C

Savage Model 99CD

Savage Model 99DE

MODEL 99C . . . . **NiB $535 Ex $445 Gd $385**
Current model. Same as Model 99F except w/clip magazine instead
of rotary. Calibers: .243 Win., .284 Win., .308 Win. Four round
detachable magazine holds one round less in .284. Weight: 6.75
lbs. Made from 1965-98.

MODEL 99CD . . . . **NiB $661 Ex $584 Gd $352**
Deluxe version of Model 99C. Calibers: .243 Win., .250 Sav., .308
Win. Hooded ramp front sight. Weight: 8.25 lbs. Stock w/Monte
Carlo comb and cheekpiece, checkered pistol-grip, grooved fore-
arm, swivels and sling. Made from 1975 to 81.

MODEL 99DE CITATION GRADE. . . . . **NiB $921 Ex $638 Gd $458**
Same as Model 99PE except w/less elaborate engraving. Made from
1968-70.

MODEL 99DL DELUXE . . . . **NiB $705 Ex $542 Gd $339**
Postwar model. Calibers: .243 Win., .308 Win. Same as Model 99F,
except w/high comb Monte Carlo stock, sling swivels. Weight: 6.75
lbs. Made from 1960-73.

MODEL 99E CARBINE (I) . . . . **NiB $604 Ex $450 Gd $367**
Pre-WWII type. Solid frame. Calibers: .22 Hi-Power, .250/3000,
.30/30, .300 Sav., .303 Sav. w/22-inch bbl.; .300 Sav. 24-inch.
Weight: 7 lbs. Other specifications same as Model 99A. Made
from 1920-36.

MODEL 99E CARBINE (II) . . . . **NiB $655 Ex $475 Gd $387**
Current model. Solid frame. Calibers: .250 Sav., .243 Win., .300
Sav., .308 Win. 20- or 22-inch bbl. Checkered pistol-grip stock and
forearm. Made from 1960-89.

Savage Model 99E 1969 Issue

Savage Model 99EG (Post WWII)

Savage Model 99F

Savage Model 99G

Savage Model 99PE Early Issue

Savage Model 99PE Late Issue

MODEL 99EG (I) . . . . **NiB $795 Ex $619 Gd $436**
Pre-WWII type. Solid frame. Plain pistol-grip stock and forearm. Otherwise same as Model G. Made from 1936 to 1941.

MODEL 99EG (II) . . . . **NiB $968 Ex $762 Gd $559**
Post-WWII type. Same as prewar model except w/checkered stock and forearm. Calibers: .250 Sav., .300 Sav., .308 Win. (intro. 1955), .243 Win., and .358 Win. Made from 1946 to 1960.

MODEL 99F
FEATHERWEIGHT (I) . . . . **NiB $755 Ex $668 Gd $477**
Pre-WWII type. Takedown. Specifications same as Model 99E, except weight: 6.5 lbs. Made 1920 to 1942. Some marked 99M.

MODEL 99F
FEATHERWEIGHT (II) . . . . **NiB $854 Ex $698 Gd $544**
Postwar model. Solid frame. Calibers: .243 Win., .300 Sav., .308 Win. 22-inch bbl. Checkered pistol-grip stock and forearm. Weight: 6.5 lbs. Made from 195 to 1973.

MODEL 99G . . . . **NiB $1250 Ex $868 Gd $677**
Takedown. Checkered pistol-grip stock and forearm. Weight: 7.25 lbs. Other specifications same as Model 99E. Made 1920 to 1942.

MODEL 99H CARBINE . . . . **NiB $864 Ex $555 Gd $400**
Solid frame. Calibers: .250/3000, .30/30, .303 Sav. 20-inch special weight bbl. Walnut carbine stock w/metal buttplate; walnut forearm w/bbl. band. Weight: 6.5 lbs. Open rear sights; ramped blade front sight. Other specifications same as Model 99A. Made 1931 to 1942.

MODEL 99K . . . . **NiB $3756 Ex $2531 Gd $1920**
Deluxe version of Model G w/similar specifications except w/fancy stock and engraving on receiver and bbl. Lyman peep rear sight and folding middle. Made from 1931 to 1942.

MODEL 99PE PRESENTATION GRADE . . . **NiB $1920 Ex $1662 Gd $786**
Same as Model 99DL except w/engraved receiver (game scenes on sides), tang and lever, fancy walnut Monte Carlo stock and forearm w/hand checkering, QD swivels. Calibers: .243, .284, .308. Made 1968 to 1970.

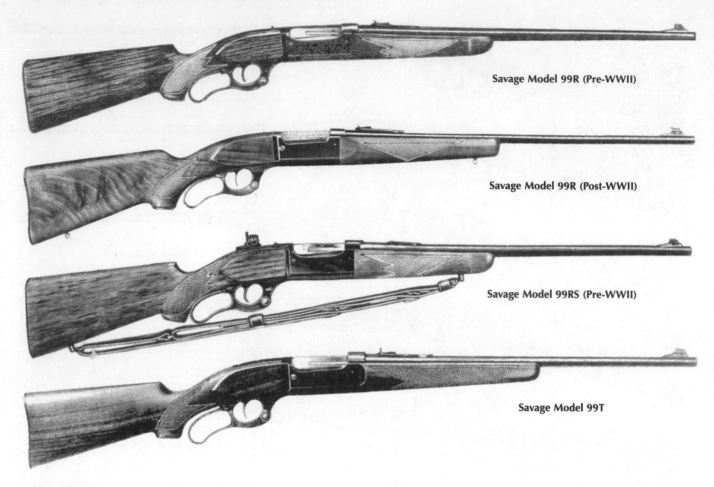

Savage Model 99R (Pre-WWII)

Savage Model 99R (Post-WWII)

Savage Model 99RS (Pre-WWII)

Savage Model 99T

MODEL 99R (I) . . . . NiB $690 Ex $563 Gd $483
Pre-WWII type. Solid frame. Calibers: .250-3000 (22-inch bbl.), .300 Sav. (24-inch bbl.). Weight: 7.5 lbs. Special large pistol-grip stock and forearm, checkered. General specifications same as other Model 99 rifles. Made from 1936 to 1942.

MODEL 99R (II) . . . . NiB $648 Ex $457 Gd $328
Post-WWII type. Same as prewar mod except w/24-inch bbl. only, w/screw eyes for sling swivels. Calibers: .250 Sav., .300 Sav., .308 Win., .243 Win. and .358 Win. Made from 1946 to 1960.

MODEL 99RS (I) . . . . NiB $853 Ex $586 Gd $457
Pre-WWII type. Same as prewar Model 99R except equipped w/Lyman rear peep sight and folding middle sight, quick detachable swivels and sling. Made from 1932 to 1942.

MODEL 99RS (II) . . . . NiB $700 Ex $560 Gd $431
Post-WWII type. Same as postwar Model 99RS except equipped w/Redfield 70LH receiver sight, blank in middle sight slot. Made from 1946 to 1960.

MODEL 99T . . . . NiB $1608 Ex $983 Gd $669
Featherweight. Solid frame. Calibers: .22 Hi-Power, .30/30, .303 Sav. w/20-inch bbl.; .300 Sav. w/22-inch bbl. Checkered pistol-grip stock and beavertail forearm. Weight: 7 lbs. General specifications same as other Model 99 rifles. Made from 1936 to 1942.

MODEL 99-358 . . . . NiB $1100 Ex $845 Gd $642
Similar to current Model 99A except caliber .358 Win. has grooved forearm, recoil pad, swivel studs. Made from 1977 to 1980.

MODEL 110 SPORTER
BOLT-ACTION RIFLE . . . . NiB $375 Ex $280 Gd $129
Calibers: .243, .270, .308, .30-06. Four round box magazine. 22-inch bbl. Weight: About 6.75 lbs. Sights: Open rear; ramp front. Standard sporter stock with checkered pistol-grip. Made 1958 to 1963.

MODEL 110B BOLT-ACTION RIFLE
Same as Model 110E except with checkered select walnut Monte Carlo-style stock (early models) or brown laminated stock (late models). Calibers: .243 Win., .270 Win. .30-06, 7mm Rem. Mag., .338 Win. Mag. Made from 1976 to 1991.
Early model . . . . NiB $398 Ex $283 Gd $201
Laminated stock model . . . . NiB $367 Ex $299 Gd $211

MODEL 110BL . . . . NiB $406 Ex $330 Gd $232
Same as Model 110B except has left-hand action.

MODEL 110C
Calibers: .22-250, .243, .25-06, .270, .308, .30-06, 7mm Rem. Mag., .300 Win. Mag. Four round detachable clip magazine (3-round in Magnum calibers). 22-inch bbl. (24-inch in .22-250 Magnum calibers). Weight: 6.75 lbs., Magnum, 7.75 to 8 lbs. Sights: Open rear; ramp front. Checkered Monte Carlo-style walnut stock (Magnum has recoil pad). Made from 1966 to 1988.
Standard calibers . . . . NiB $435 Ex $379 Gd $219
Magnum calibers . . . . NiB $583 Ex $425 Gd $245

Savage Model 110

Savage Model 110B

Savage Model 110BL

Savage Model 110C

Savage Model 110E

Savage Model 110 MCL

MODEL 110CL
Same as Model 110C except has left-hand action. (Available only in .243 Win., .30-06, .270 Win. and 7mm Mag.) Made 1963 to 1966.
Standard calibers . . . . NiB $425 Ex $310 Gd $223
Magnum calibers . . . . NiB $408 Ex $310 Gd $228

MODEL 110CY
YOUTH/LADIES RIFLE . . . . NiB $425 Ex $336 Gd $207
Same as Model 110G except with walnut-finished hardwood stock with 12.5-inch pull. Calibers: .243 Win. and .300 Savage. Made from 1991 to 2009.

MODEL 110D
Similar to Model 110C except has internal magazine with hinged floorplate. Calibers: .243 Win., .270 Win., .30-06, 7mm Rem. Mag., .300 Win. Mag. Made from 1972 to 1988.
Standard calibers . . . . NiB $350 Ex $319 Gd $229
Magnum calibers . . . . NiB $395 Ex $340 Gd $243

MODEL 110DL
Same as Model 110D except has left-hand action. Discontinued.
Standard calibers . . . . NiB $454 Ex $371 Gd $264
Magnum calibers . . . . NiB $487 Ex $396 Gd $281

Savage Model 110P

Savage Model 110PE

MODEL 110E . . . . NiB $355 Ex $234 Gd $182
Calibers: .22-250, .223 Rem., .243 Win., .270 Win., .308, 7mm Rem.
Mag., .30-06. Four round box magazine (3-round in Magnum). 20- or
22-inch bbl. (24-inch stainless steel in Magnum). Weight: 6.75 lbs.;
Magnum, 7.75 lbs. Sights: Open rear; ramp front. Plain Monte Carlo
stock on early production; current models have checkered stocks of walnut-finished hardwood (Magnum has recoil pad). Made 1963 to 1989.

MODEL 110EL . . . . NiB $343 Ex $280 Gd $200
Same as Model 110E except has left-hand action made in .30-06
and 7mm Rem. Mag. only. Made from 1969 to 1973.

MODEL 110F/110K BOLT-ACTION RIFLE
Same as Model 110E except Model 110F has black Rynite synthet-
ic stock, swivel studs; made 1988 to 1993. Model 110K has lami-
nated camouflage stock; made from 1986 to 1988.
Model 110F, adj. sights . . . . NiB $720 Ex $411 Gd $321
Model 110FNS, no sights . . . . NiB $700 Ex $322 Gd $228
Model 110K, standard calibers . . . . NiB $325 Ex $302 Gd $235
Model 110K, magnum calibers . . . . NiB $460 Ex $373 Gd $263

MODEL 110FM SIERRA ULTRA LIGHT . . . . NiB $338 Ex $311 Gd $213
Calibers: .243 Win., .270 Win., .30-06, .308 Win. Five round magazine. 20-inch bbl. 41.5 inches overall. Weight: 6.25 lbs. No sights
w/drilled and tapped receiver. Black graphite/fiberglass composition
stock. Non-glare matte blue finish. Made 1996 to date.

MODEL 110FP POLICE RIFLE . . . . . NiB $575 Ex $330 Gd $227
Calibers: .223, .308 Win. Four round magazine. 24-inch bbl. 45.5
inches overall. Weight: 9 lbs. Black Rynite composite stock. Matte
blue finish. Made from 1990 to date.

MODEL 110G BOLT-ACTION RIFLE
Calibers: .223, .22-250, .243 Win., .270, 7mm Rem. Mag., .308 Win.,
.30-06, .300 Win. Mag. Five round (standard) or 4-round magazine
(magnum). 22- or 24-inch bbl. 42.38 overall (standard). Weight: 6.75 to
7.5 lbs. Ramp front sight, adj. rear. Checkered walnut-finished hardwood stock with rubber recoil pad. Made from 1989 to 1993.
Model 110G, standard calibers . . . . NiB $388 Ex $285 Gd $182
Model 110G, magnum calibers . . . . NiB $414 Ex $311 Gd $224
Model 110GLNS, left-hand, no sights . . . . . NiB $420 Ex $342 Gd $241

MODEL 110GV VARMINT RIFLE . . . . NiB $325 Ex $301 Gd $208
Similar to the Model 110G except fitted with medium-weight
varmint bbl. with no sights. Receiver drilled and tapped for scope
mounts. Calibers .22-250 and .223 only. Made from 1989-93.

MODEL 110M MAGNUM
Same as Model 110MC except calibers: 7mm Rem. Mag. .264, .300
and .338 Win. 24-inch bbl. Stock with recoil pad. Weight: 7.75 to
8 lbs. Made from 1963 to 1969.
Model 110M Magnum . . . . NiB $395 Ex $324 Gd $244

MODEL 110MC
Same as Model 110 except has Monte Carlo-style stock. Calibers:
.22-250, .243 Win., .270, .308, .30-06. 24-inch bbl. in .22-250.
Made from 1959 to 1969.
Model 110MC . . . . NiB $385 Ex $206 Gd $139
Model 110MCL . . . . NiB $364 Ex $217 Gd $156

MODEL 110P PREMIER GRADE
Calibers: .243 Win., 7mm Rem. Mag., .30-06. Four round magazine
(3-round in Magnum). 22-inch bbl. (24-inch stainless steel in
Magnum). Weight: 7 lbs.; Magnum, 7.75 lbs. Sights: Open rear folding leaf; ramp front. French walnut stock w/Monte Carlo comb and
cheekpiece, rosewood forend tip and pistol-grip cap, skip checkering, sling swivels (Magnum has recoil pad). Made 1964 to 1970.
Calibers .243 Win. and .30-06 . . . . . NiB $491 Ex $363 Gd $260
Caliber 7mm Rem. Mag. . . . . NiB $507 Ex $388 Gd $285

MODEL 110PE PRESENTATION GRADE
Same as Model 110P except has engraved receiver, floorplate and trig-
ger guard, stock of choice grade French walnut. Made from 1968 to 1970.
Calibers .243 Win. and .30-06 . . . . . NiB $750 Ex $607 Gd $426
Caliber 7mm Rem. Mag. . . . . NiB $807 Ex $654 Gd $458

MODEL 110PEL PRESENTATION GRADE
Same as Model 110PE except has left-hand action.
Calibers .243 Win. and .30-06 . . . . . NiB $807 Ex $654 Gd $458
Caliber 7mm Rem. Mag. . . . . NiB $879 Ex $710 Gd $496

MODEL 110PL PREMIER GRADE
Same as Model 110P except has left-hand action.
Calibers .243 Win. and .30-06 . . . . . NiB $528 Ex $401 Gd $271
Caliber 7mm Rem. Mag. . . . . NiB $549 Ex $401 Gd $293

MODEL 110S/110V
Same as Model 110E except Model 110S in .308 Win. only; dis-
continued 1985. Model 110V in .22-250 and .223 Rem. w/heavy 2-
inch barrel, 47 inches overall, weight: 9 lbs. Discontinued. 1989.
Model 110S . . . . NiB $340 Ex $300 Gd $229
Model 110V . . . . NiB $370 Ex $317 Gd $243

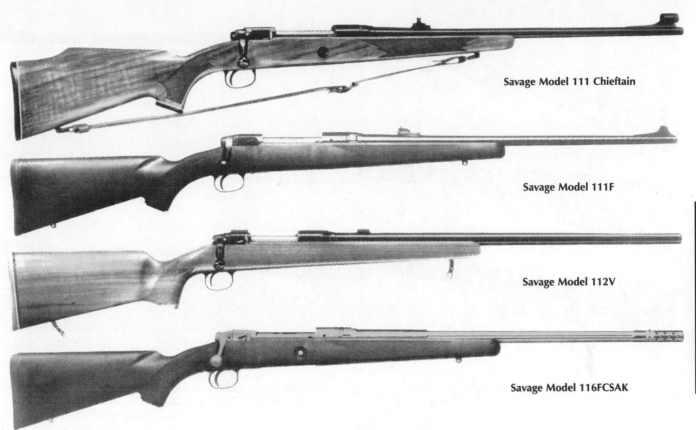

Savage Model 111 Chieftain

Savage Model 111F

Savage Model 112V

Savage Model 116FCSAK

MODEL 111 CHIEFTAIN BOLT-ACTION RIFLE

Calibers: .243 Win., .270 Win., 7x57mm, 7mm Rem. Mag. .30-06. 4-round clip magazine (3-round in Magnum). 22-inch bbl. (24-inch in Magnum). Weight: 7.5 lbs., 8.25 lbs. Magnum. Sights: Leaf rear; hooded ramp front. Select walnut stock w/Monte Carlo comb and cheekpiece, checkered, pistol-grip cap, QD swivels and sling. Made from 1974 to 1979.

Standard calibers . . . . **NiB $375 Ex $368 Gd $239**
Magnum calibers . . . . **NiB $395 Ex $388 Gd $259**

MODELS 111F, 111FC, 111FNS CLASSIC HUNTERS

Similar to the Model 111G except with graphite/fiberglass composite stock. Weight: 6.25 lbs. Made from 1994 to date.

Model 111F (Box mag., right/left hand) . . . **NiB $465 Ex $365 Gd $213**
Model 111FC (Detachable magazine) . . . . . **NiB $400 Ex $302 Gd $239**
**Model 111FNS (Box mag.,
no sights, R/L hand)** . . . . **NiB $525 Ex $401 Gd $276**

MODELS 111G, 111GC, 111GNS CLASSIC HUNTERS

Calibers: .22-250 Rem., .223 Rem., .243 Win., .25-06 Rem. .250 Sav., .270 Win., 7mm-08 Rem., 7mm Rem. Mag., .30-06, .300 Sav., .300 Win. Mag., .308 Win., .338 Win. 22- or 24-inch bbl. Weight: 7 lbs. Ramp front sight, adj. open rear. Walnut-finished hardwood stock. Blued finish. Made from 1994 to date.

Model 111G (Box mag., right/left hand) . . . **NiB $330 Ex $286 Gd $187**
**Model 111GC (Detachable
mag., R/L hand)** . . . . **NiB $430 Ex $321 Gd $198**
Model 111GNS (Box mag., no sights) . . . . . **NiB $325 Ex $270 Gd $162**

MODEL 112BV,112BVSS HEAVY VARMINT RIFLES

Similar to the Model 110G except fitted with 26-inch heavy bbl. Laminated wood stock with high comb. .22-250 and .223 only.

Model 112BV (Made 1993-94) . . . . **NiB $475 Ex $355 Gd $242**
**Model 112BVSS (Fluted stainless
bbl.; made since 1994)** . . . . **NiB $495 Ex $381 Gd $278**

MODEL 112FV,112FVS,112FVSS
VARMINT RIFLES

Similar to the Model 110G except fitted with 26-inch heavy bbl. and Dupont Rynite stock. Calibers: .22-250, .223 and .220 Swift (112FVS only). Blued or stainless finish. Made from 1991 to date.

Model 112FV (blued) . . . . **NiB $375 Ex $324 Gd $231**
**Model 112FV-S (blued, single
shot), disc. 1993** . . . . **NiB $489 Ex $403 Gd $259**
Model 112FVSS (stainless) . . . . **NiB $589 Ex $503 Gd $359**
Model 112 FVSS-S (stainless, single shot) . . **NiB $589 Ex $503 Gd $359**

MODEL 112V VARMINT RIFLE . . . . **NiB $350 Ex $267 Gd $183**

Bolt action, single shot. Caliber: .220 Swift, .222 Rem., .223 Rem., .22-250, .243 Win., .25-06. 26-inch heavy bbl. with scope bases. Supplied w/o sights. Weight: 9.25 lbs. Select walnut stock in varmint style w/checkered pistol-grip, high comb, QD sling swivels. Made from 1975 to 1979.

MODEL 114C, 114CE, 114CU RIFLES

Calibers: .270 Win., 7mm Rem. Mag., .30-06, .300 Win. Mag. 22- or 24-inch bbl. Weight: 7 lbs. Detachable 3- or 4-round magazine. Ramp front sight; adjustable, open rear; (114CU has no sights). Checkered select walnut stock w/oil finish, red butt pad. Schnabel forend and skip-line checkering (114CE). High-luster blued finish. Made from 1991 to date.

Model 114C (Classic) . . . . **NiB $675 Ex $455 Gd $280**
Model 114CE (Classic European) . . . . **NiB $480 Ex $355 Gd $285**
Model 114CU (Classic Ultra) . . . . **NiB $485 Ex $329 Gd $2400**

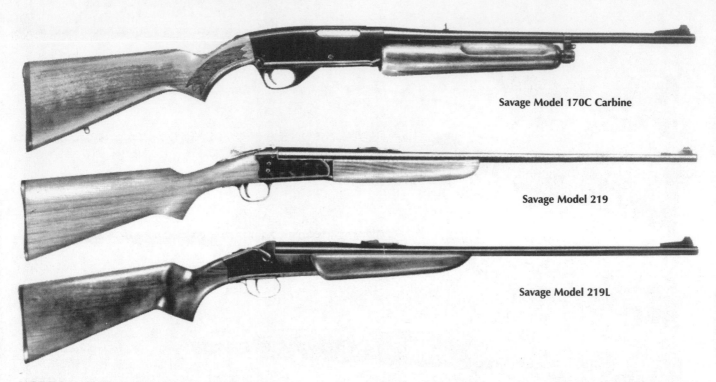

Savage Model 170C Carbine

Savage Model 219

Savage Model 219L

MODELS 116FSAK, 116FCSAK BOLT-ACTION RIFLES
Similar to the Model 116FSK except in calibers .270 Win., .30-06, 7mm Mag., .300 Win. Mag., .338 Win. Mag. Fluted 22-inch stainless bbl. w/adj. muzzle brake. Weight: 6.5 lbs. Made from 1994 to date.
Model 116FSAK .... NiB $560 Ex $401 Gd $318
Model 116FCSAK (detachable mag.)...... NiB $604 Ex $507 Gd $347

MODELS 116FSC, 116FSS BOLT-ACTION RIFLES
Improved Model 110 with satin stainless action and bbl. Calibers: .223, .243, .270, .30-06, 7mm Rem. Mag., .300 Win. Mag., .338 Win. Mag. 22- or 24-inch bbl. Four or 5-round capacity. Weight: About 7.5 lbs. Black Rynite stock w/recoil pad and swivel studs. Receiver drilled and tapped for scope mounts, no sights. Made from 1991 to date.
Model 116FSS......................... NiB $635 Ex $511 Gd $321
Model 116FSC, detachable magazine ..... NiB $655 Ex $524 Gd $348

MODEL 116FSK KODIAK RIFLE .... NiB $495 Ex $350 Gd $247
Similar to the Model 116FSS except with 22-inch bbl. chambered for 338 Win. Mag. only. "Shock Suppressor" recoil reducer. Made from 1994 to 2000.

MODEL 116-SE, 116-US RIFLES
Calibers: .270 Win., 7mm Rem Mag., .30-06, .300 Win. Mag. (116US); .300 Win. Mag., .338 Win. mag., .425 Express, .458 Win. Mag. (116SE). 24-inch stainless barrel (with muzzle brake 116SE only). 45.5 inches overall. Weight: 7.2 to 8.5 lbs. Three round magazine. 3-leaf Express sights 116SE only. Checkered Classic style select walnut stock with ebony forend tip. Stainless finish. Made from 1994 to 2004.
Model 116SE (Safari Express) ..... NiB $895 Ex $742 Gd $510
Model 116US (Ultra Stainless) .... NiB $625 Ex $462 Gd $382

MODEL 170 PUMP-ACTION
CENTERFIRE RIFLE .... NiB $225 Ex $172 Gd $95
Calibers: .30-30, .35 Rem. Three round tubular magazine. 22-inch bbl. Weight: 6.75 lbs. Sights: Folding leaf rear; ramp front. Select walnut stock w/checkered pistol-grip Monte Carlo comb, grooved slide handle. Made from 1970 to 1981.

MODEL 170C CARBINE .... NiB $250 Ex $297 Gd $155
Same as Model 170 Rifle except has 18.5-inch bbl., straight comb stock, weight: 6 lbs.; caliber .30-30 only. Made from 1974 to 1981.

MODEL 219 SINGLE-SHOT RIFLE
Hammerless. Takedown. Shotgun-type action with top lever. Calibers: .22 Hornet, .25-20, .32-20, .30-30. 26-inch bbl. Weight: about 6 lbs. Sights: Open rear; bead front. Plain pistol-grip stock and forearm. Made from 1938 to 1965.
Model 219............................ NiB $195 Ex $96 Gd $50
Model 219L (w/side lever, made 1965-67)... NiB $135 Ex $85 Gd $69

MODEL 221-229 UTILITY GUNS
Same as Model 219 except in various calibers, supplied in combination with an interchangeable shotgun bbl. All versions discontinued.
Model 221 (.30-30,12-ga. 30-inch bbl.)..... NiB $130 Ex $70 Gd $44
Model 222 (.30-30,16-ga. 28-inch bbl.) ..... NiB $130 Ex $70 Gd $44
Model 223 (.30-30, 20-ga. 28-inch bbl.) ..... NiB $130 Ex $70 Gd $44
Model 227 (.22 Hornet, 12-ga. 30-inch bbl.) ..... NiB $130 Ex $70 Gd $44
Model 228 (.22 Hornet, 16-ga. 28-inch bbl.).... NiB $130 Ex $70 Gd $44
Model 229 (.22 Hornet, 20-ga. 28-inch bbl.) ... NiB $130 Ex $70 Gd $44

MODEL 340 BOLT-ACTION REPEATER
Calibers: .22 Hornet, .222 Rem., .223 Rem., .225 Win., .30-30. Clip magazine; 4-round capacity (3-round in 30-30). Bbl. lengths: Originally 20-inch in .30-30, 22-inch in .22 Hornet; later 22-inch in .30-30, 24-inch in other calibers. Weight: 6.5 to 7.5 lbs. depending on caliber and vintage. Sights: Open rear (folding leaf on recent production); ramp front. Early models had plain pistol-grip stock, checkered since 1965. Made from 1950-85. (Note: Those rifles produced between 1947-1950 were .22 Hornet Stevens Model .322 and .30-30 Model .325. The Savage model, however, was designated Model .340 for all calibers.)
Pre-1965 with plain stock .... NiB $225 Ex $172 Gd $85
Savage Model 340C Carbine .... NiB $235 Ex $182 Gd $95

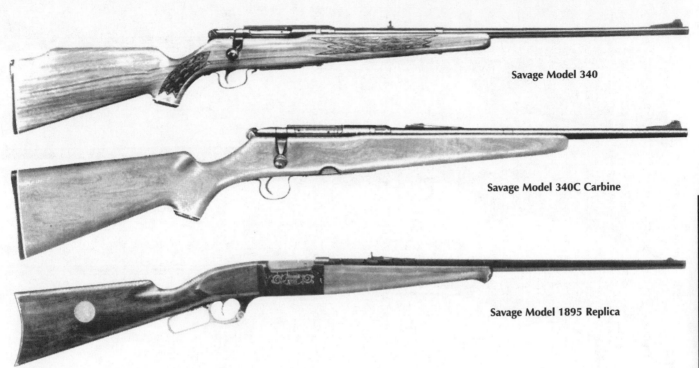

Savage Model 340

Savage Model 340C Carbine

Savage Model 1895 Replica

MODEL 340S DELUXE . . . . NiB $300 Ex $252 Gd $175
Same as Model 340 except has checkered stock, screw eyes for sling, peep rear sight, hooded front. Made from 1955 to 1960.

MODEL 342 . . . . NiB $300 Ex $254 Gd $181
Designation, 1950 to 1955, of Model 340 .22 Hornet.

MODEL 342S DELUXE . . . . NiB $300 Ex $254 Gd $181
Designation, 1950 to 1955, of Model 340S .22 Hornet.

**ANNIVERSARY MODEL
1895 LEVER-ACTION** . . . . NiB $6000 Ex $4495 Gd $2086
Replica of Savage Model 1895 Hammerless Lever-Action Rifle issued to commemorate the 75th anniversary (1895-1970) of Savage Arms. Caliber: .308 Win. Five round rotary magazine. 24-inch full-octagon bbl. Engraved receiver. Brass-plated lever. Sights: Open rear; brass blade front. Plain straight-grip buttstock, Schnabel-type forend; brass medallion inlaid in buttstock, brass crescent-shaped buttplate. 9,999 produced. Made in 1970 only. Top value is for new, unfired specimen.

**MODEL 1903 SLIDE-ACTION
REPEATER** . . . . NiB $675 Ex $484 Gd $323
Hammerless. Takedown. Caliber: .22 Short, Long, LR. Detachable box magazine. 24-inch octagon bbl. Weight: About 5 lbs. Sights: Open rear; bead front. Pistol-grip stock, grooved slide handle. Made 1903 to 1921.

**MODEL 1904 BOLT-ACTION
SINGLE-SHOT RIFLE** . . . . NiB $181 Ex $130 Gd $78
Takedown. .22 Short, Long, LR. 18-inch bbl. Weight: About 3 lbs. Sights: Open rear; bead front. Plain, straight-grip, one-piece stock. Made from 1904 to 1917.

**MODEL 1905 BOLT-ACTION
SINGLE-SHOT RIFLE** . . . . NiB $175 Ex $130 Gd $78
Takedown. .22 Short, Long, LR. 22-inch bbl. Weight: About 5 lbs. Sights: Open rear; bead front. Plain, straight-grip one-piece stock. Made from 1905 to 1919.

**MODEL 1909 SLIDE-ACTION
REPEATER** . . . . NiB $750 Ex $486 Gd $309
Hammerless. Takedown. Similar to Model 1903 except has 20-inch round bbl., plain stock and forearm, weight: Approximately 4.75 lbs. Made from 1909 to 1915.

**MODEL 1912
AUTOLOADING RIFLE** . . . . NiB $750 Ex $534 Gd $299
Takedown. Caliber: 22 LR. only. Seven round detachable box magazine. 20-inch bbl., plain stock and forearm. Made 1912 to 1916.

**MODEL 1914 SLIDE-ACTION
REPEATER** . . . . NiB $450 Ex $286 Gd $209
Hammerless. Takedown. Caliber: .22 Short, Long, LR, Tubular magazine holds 20 Short, 17 Long, 15 LR. 24-inch octagon bbl. Weight: About 5.75 lbs. Sights: Open rear; bead front. Plain pistol-grip stock, grooved slide handle. Made from 1914 to 1924.

MODEL 1920 HI-POWER BOLT-ACTION RIFLE
Short Mauser-type action. Calibers: .250/3000, .300 Sav. Five round box magazine. 22-inch bbl. in .250 cal.; 24-inch in .300 cal. Weight: About 6 lbs. Sights: Open rear; bead front. Checkered pistol-grip stock w/slender forearm and Schnabel tip. Made from 1920 to 1926.
**Model 1920
Hi-Power
(.250-3000 Sav.)** . . . . NiB $990 Ex $799 Gd $655
**Model 1920
Hi-Power
(.300 Sav.)** . . . . NiB $900 Ex $725 Gd $549

NOTE: *In 1965, Savage began the importation of rifles manufactured by J. G. Anschutz GmbH, Ulm, West Germany. Models designated "Savage/Anschutz" are listed in this section, those marketed in the U.S. under the "Anschutz" name are included in that firm's listings. Anschutz rifles are now distributed in the U.S. by Precision Sales Int'l., Westfield, Mass. See "Anschutz" for detailed specifications.*

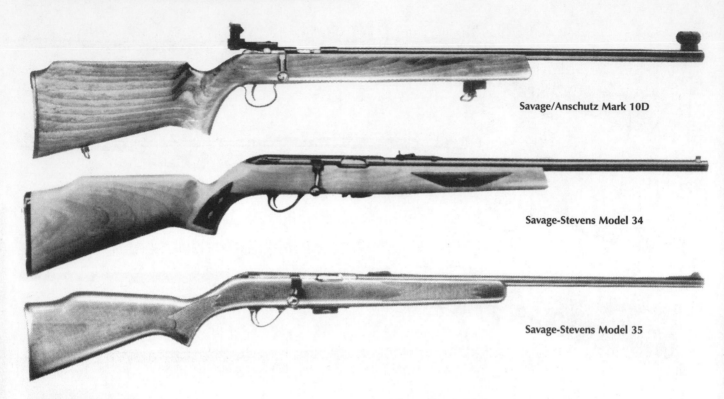

Savage/Anschutz Mark 10D

Savage-Stevens Model 34

Savage-Stevens Model 35

MARK 10 BOLT-ACTION
TARGET RIFLE . . . . **NiB $493   Ex $334   Gd $236**
Single shot. Caliber: .22 LR. 26-inch bbl. Weight: 8.5 lbs. Sights: Anschutz micrometer rear; globe front. Target stock w/full pistol-grip and cheekpiece, adj. hand stop and swivel. Made 1967 to 1972.

MARK 10D . . . . **NiB $519   Ex $339   Gd $236**
Same as Mark 10 except has redesigned stock with Monte Carlo comb, different rear sight. Weight: 7.75 lbs. Made in 1972.

MODEL 54
CUSTOM SPORTER . . . . **NiB $735   Ex $606   Gd $349**
Same as Anschutz Model 1422D.

MODEL 54M . . . . **NiB $900   Ex $642   Gd $410**
Same as Anschutz Model 1522D.

MODEL 64 BOLT-ACTION
TARGET RIFLE . . . . **NiB $606   Ex $452   Gd $297**
Same as Anschutz Model 1403.

MODEL 153 BOLT-ACTION
SPORTER . . . . **NiB $658   Ex $452   Gd $323**
Caliber: .222 Rem. Three round clip magazine. 24-inch bbl. Sights: Folding leaf open rear; hooded ramp front. Weight: 6.75 lbs. French walnut stock w/cheekpiece, skip checkering, rosewood forend tip and grip cap, swivels. Made from 1964 to 1967.

MODEL 153S . . . . **NiB $735   Ex $529   Gd $349**
Same as Model 153 except has double-set trigger. Made 1965 to 1967.

MODEL 164 CUSTOM SPORTER . . . . **NiB $555   Ex $400   Gd $246**
Same as Anschutz Model 1416.

MODEL 164M . . . . **NiB $632   Ex $426   Gd $272**
Same as Anschutz Model 1516.

MODEL 184 SPORTER . . . . **NiB $606   Ex $452   Gd $246**
Same as Anschutz Model 1441.

NOTE: *Since J. Stevens Arms (see also separate listing) is a division of Savage Industries, certain Savage models carry the "Stevens" name.*

MODEL 34 BOLT-ACTION
REPEATER . . . . **NiB $170   Ex $114   Gd $72**
Caliber: .22 Short, Long, LR. 20-inch bbl. Weight: 4.75 lbs. Sights: Open rear; bead front. Plain pistol-grip stock. Made 1965 to 1980.

MODEL 34M . . . . **NiB $155   Ex $119   Gd $88**
Same as Model 34 except chambered for 22 WMR. Made 1969 to 1973.

MODEL 35 . . . . **NiB $155   Ex $119   Gd $88**
Bolt-action repeater. Caliber: 22 LR. Six round clip magazine. 22-inch bbl. Weight: About 5 lbs. Sights: Open rear; ramp front. Monte Carlo stock w/checkered pistol grip and forearm. Made from 1982 to 1985.

MODEL 35M . . . . **NiB $180   Ex $129   Gd $93**
Same as Model 35 except chambered for 22 WMR. Made from 1982 to 1985.

MODEL 46 BOLT-ACTION
RIFLE . . . . **NiB $165   Ex $119   Gd $88**
Caliber: .22 Short, Long, LR. Tubular magazine holds 22 Short, 17 Long, 15 LR. 20-inch bbl. Weight: 5 lbs. Plain pistol-grip stock on early production; later models have Monte Carlo stock w/checkering. Made from 1969 to 1073.

MODEL 65
BOLT-ACTION RIFLE . . . . **NiB $180   Ex $129   Gd $88**
Caliber: .22 Short, Long, LR. Five round clip magazine. 20-inch bbl. Weight: 5 lbs. Sights: Open rear; ramp front. Monte Carlo stock w/checkered pistol grip and forearm. Made from 1969 to 1973.

Savage-Stevens Model 46

Savage-Stevens Model 65

Savage-Stevens Model 72 — Crackshot

Savage-Stevens Model 73

Savage-Stevens Model 80

MODEL 65M . . . . **NiB $150 Ex $109 Gd $78**
Same as Model 65 except chambered for .22 WMR, has 22-inch bbl., weighs 5.25 lbs. Made from 1969 to 1981.

NOTE: *The Model 72 is a "Favorite"-type single-shot unlike the smaller, original "Crackshot" made by Stevens from 1913 to 1939.*

MODEL 72 CRACKSHOT SINGLE-SHOT
LEVER-ACTION RIFLE. . . . . **NiB $145 Ex $97 Gd $56**
Falling-block action. Casehardened frame. Caliber: .22 Short, Long, LR. 22-inch octagon bbl. Weight: 4.5lbs. Sights: Open rear; bead front. Plain straight-grip stock and forend of walnut. Made 1972 to 1989.

MODEL 73 BOLT-ACTION SINGLE-SHOT . . **NiB $125 Ex $109 Gd $88**
Caliber: .22 Short, Long, LR. 20-inch bbl. Weight: 4.75 lbs. Sights: Open rear; bead front. Plain pistol-grip stock. Made 1965 to 1980.

MODEL 73Y YOUTH MODEL . . . . . . **NiB $134 Ex $104 Gd $88**
Same as Model 73 except has 18-inch bbl., 1.5-inch shorter buttstock, weight: 4.5 lbs. Made from 1965 to 1980.

MODEL 74
LITTLE FAVORITE . . . . **NiB $140 Ex $109 Gd $89**
Same as Model 72 Crackshot except has black-finished frame, 22-inch round bbl., walnut-finished hardwood stock. Weight: 4.75 lbs. Made from 1972 to 1974.

MODEL 80
AUTOLOADING RIFLE. . . . . **NiB $180 Ex $150 Gd $110**
Caliber: 22 LR. 15-round tubular magazine. 20-inch bbl. Weight: 6 lbs. Sights: Open rear, bead front. Monte Carlo stock of walnut w/checkered pistol-grip and forearm. Made from 1976 to date. (Note: This rifle is essentially the same as the Model 60 of 1969 to 1972 except for a different style of checkering, side instead of top safety and plain bead instead of ramp front sight.)

MODEL 88
AUTOLOADING RIFLE. . . . . **NiB $155 Ex $94 Gd $53**
Similar to Model 60 except has walnut-finished hardwood stock, plain bead front sight. Weight: 5.75 lbs. Made from 1969 to 1972.

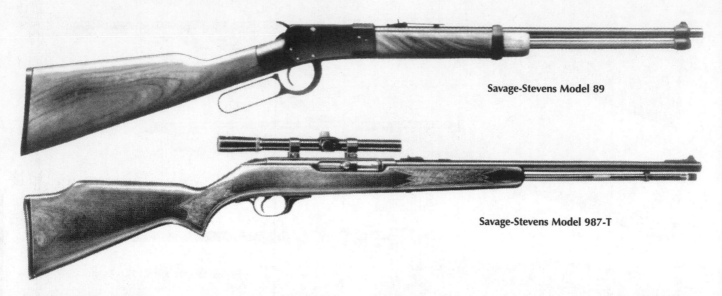

Savage-Stevens Model 89

Savage-Stevens Model 987-T

MODEL 89 SINGLE-SHOT
LEVER-ACTION CARBINE . . . . NiB $89 Ex $73 Gd $47
Martini-type action. Caliber: .22 Short, Long, LR. 18.5-inch bbl.
Weight: 5 lbs. Sights: Open rear; bead front. Western-style carbine
stock w/straight grip, forearm with bbl. band. Made 1976 to 1989.

MODEL 987-T
AUTOLOADING RIFLE . . . . NiB $180 Ex $150 Gd $110
Caliber: .22 LR. 15-round tubular magazine. 20-inch bbl. Weight: 6
lbs. Sights: Open rear; ramp front. Monte Carlo stock w/checkered
pistol grip and forearm. Made from 1981 to 1989.

"STEVENS FAVORITE"
See Savage Model 71.

V.C. SCHILLING — Suhl, Germany

MAUSER-MANNLICHER
BOLT ACTION SPORTING RIFLE . . NiB $889 Ex $721 Gd $507
Same general specifications as given for the Haenel Mauser-
Mannlicher Sporter. See separate listing.

'88 MAUSER SPORTER . . . . NiB $856 Ex $696 Gd $490
Same general specifications as Haenel '88 Mauser Sporter. See
separate listing.

SCHULTZ & LARSEN GEVAERFABRIK — Otterup, Denmark

MATCH RIFLE NO. 47 . . . . NiB $665 Ex $519 Gd $339
Caliber: .22 LR. Bolt-action, single-shot, set trigger. 28.5-inch heavy
bbl. Weight: 14 lbs. Sights: Micrometer receiver, globe front. Free-
rifle stock w/cheekpiece, thumbhole, adj. Schuetzen-type buttplate,
swivels, palmrest.

FREE RIFLE MODEL 54 . . . . NiB $832 Ex $752 Gd $569
Calibers: 6.5x55mm or any standard American centerfire caliber.
Schultz & Larsen M54 bolt-action, single-shot, set trigger. 27.5-inch
heavy bbl. Weight: 15.5 lbs. Sights: Micrometer receiver; globe
front. Free-rifle stock w/cheekpiece, thumbhole, adj. Schuetzen-
type buttplate, swivels, palm rest.

MODEL 54J
SPORTING RIFLE . . . . NiB $650 Ex $504 Gd $398
Calibers: .270 Win., .30-06, 7x61 Sharpe & Hart. Schultz & Larsen
bolt action. Three-round magazine. 24-inch bbl. in .270 and .30-06,
26-inch in 7x61 S&H. Checkered stock w/Monte Carlo comb and
cheekpiece. Value shown is for rifle less sights.

SEARS, ROEBUCK & COMPANY — Chicago, Illinois

*The most encountered brands or model designations used by Sears
are J. C. Higgins and Ted Williams. Firearms sold under these designations have been mfd. by various firms including Winchester,
Marlin, Savage, Mossberg, etc.*

MODEL 2C
BOLT-ACTION RIFLE . . . . NiB $126 Ex $106 Gd $88
Caliber: .22RF. Seven round clip mag. 21-inch bbl. Weight: 5 lbs.
Sights: Open rear; ramp front. Plain Monte Carlo stock. Mfd. by Win.

MODEL 42
BOLT-ACTION REPEATER . . . . NiB $126 Ex $106 Gd $79
Takedown. Caliber: .22RF. Eight round detachable box magazine.
24-inch bbl. Weight: 6 lbs. Sights: Open rear; bead front. Plain pistol-grip stock. Mfd. by Marlin.

MODEL 42DL
BOLT-ACTION REPEATER . . . . NiB $126 Ex $106 Gd $85
Same general specifications as Model 42 except fancier grade
w/peep sight, hooded front sight and swivels.

MODEL 44DL
LEVER-ACTION RIFLE . . . . NiB $203 Ex $162 Gd $116
Caliber: .22RF. Tubular magazine holds 19 LR cartridges. 22-inch
bbl. Weight: 6.25 lbs. Sights: Open rear; hooded ramp front. Monte
Carlo-style stock w/pistol grip. Mfd. by Marlin.

MODEL 53
BOLT-ACTION RIFLE . . . . NiB $253 Ex $177 Gd $136
Calibers: .243, .270, .308, .30-06. Four-round magazine. 22-inch
bbl. Weight: 6.75 lbs. Sights: Open rear; ramp front. Standard
sporter stock w/pistol-grip, checkered. Mfd. by Savage.

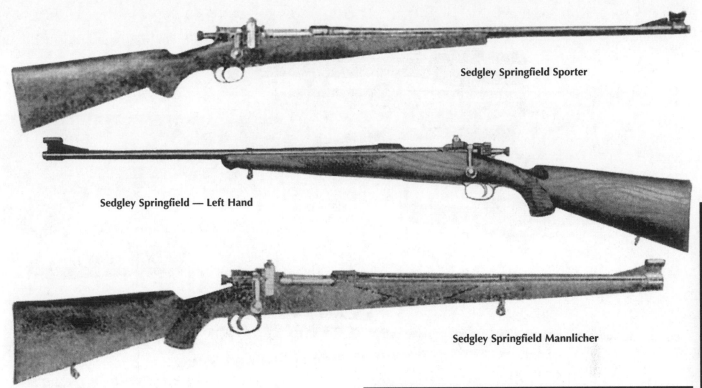

Sedgley Springfield Sporter

Sedgley Springfield — Left Hand

Sedgley Springfield Mannlicher

**MODEL 54 LEVER-ACTION
RIFLE**. . . . . **NiB $204 Ex $179 Gd $128**
Similar general specifications as Winchester Model 94 carbine.
Made in .30-30 caliber only. Mfd. by Winchester.

**MODEL 103 SERIES
BOLT-ACTION REPEATER**. . . . . **NiB $210 Ex $102 Gd $82**
Same general specifications as Model 103.2 w/minor changes. Mfd.
by Marlin.

**MODEL 103.2 BOLT-ACTION
REPEATER** . . . . **NiB $128 Ex $103 Gd $81**
Takedown. Caliber: .22RF. Eight-round detachable box magazine.
24-inch bbl. Weight: 6 lbs. Sights: Open rear; bead front. Plain pistol-grip stock. Mfd. by Marlin.

R. F. SEDGLEY, INC. —
Philadelphia, Pennsylvania

SPRINGFIELD SPORTER . . . . **NiB $1250 Ex $1107 Gd $592**
Springfield '03 bolt action. Calibers: .220 Swift, .218 Bee, .22-3000,
R, .22-4000, .22 Hornet, .25-35, .250-3000, .257 Roberts, .270
Win., 7mm, .30-06. 24-inch bbl. Weight: 7.5 lbs. Sights: Lyman No.
48 receiver; bead front on matted ramp. Checkered walnut stock,
grip cap, sling swivels. Disc. 1941.

SPRINGFIELD LEFT-HAND SPORTER . . . **NiB $1575 Ex $1308 Gd $880**
Bolt-action reversed for left-handed shooter; otherwise the same as
standard Sedgley Springfield Sporter. Disc. 1941.

**SEDGLEY SPRINGFIELD
MANNLICHER-TYPE SPORTER** . . . . **NiB $1459 Ex $1396 Gd $1010**
Same as standard Sedgley Springfield Sporter except w/20-
inch bbl., Mannlicher-type full stock w/cheekpiece, weight:
7.75 lbs. Disc. 1941.

SHILEN RIFLES, INC. — Enis, Texas

DGA BENCHREST RIFLE . . . . **NiB $1469 Ex $1186 Gd $903**
DGA single-shot bolt-action. Calibers as listed for Sporter. 26-inch medium-
heavy or heavy bbl. Weight: From 10.5 lbs. No sights. Fiberglass or walnut
stock, classic or thumbhole pattern. Currently manufactured.

DGA SPORTER . . . . **NiB $1476 Ex $1110 Gd $796**
DGA bolt action. Calibers: .17 Rem., .222 Rem., .223 Rem. .22-250,
.220 Swift, 6mm Rem., .243 Win., .250 Sav., .257 Roberts, .284 Win.,
.308 Win., .358 Win. Three round blind magazine. 24-inch bbl.
Average weight: 7.5 lbs. No sights. Select Claro walnut stock
w/cheekpiece, pistol grip, sling swivel studs. Currently manufactured.

DGA VARMINTER . . . . **NiB $1395 Ex $1162 Gd $813**
Same as Sporter except w/25-inch medium-heavy bbl. Weight: 9 lbs.

SHILOH RIFLE MFG. CO. — Big Timber, MT

SHARPS MODEL 1874 BUSINESS RIFLE NiB $1149 Ex $1072 Gd $698

Replica of 1874 Sharps similar to No. 3 Sporting Rifle. .32-40, .38-
55, .40-50 BN, .40-70 BN, .40-90 BN, .45-70 ST, .45-90 ST, .50-
70 ST, .50-100 ST. 28-inch round heavy bbl. Blade front sight,
buckhorn rear. Double-set triggers. Straight-grip walnut stock
w/steel crescent buttplate. Made from 1986 to date.

**SHARPS MODEL 1874 LONG
RANGE EXPRESS RIFLE** . . . . **NiB $1723 Ex $1671 Gd $1100**
Replica of 1874 Sharps w/single-shot falling breech action. .32-40, .38-
55, .40-50 BN, .40-70 BN, .40-90 BN, .45-70 ST, .45-90 ST, .45-110 ST,
.50-70 ST, .50-90 ST, .50-110 ST. 34-inch tapered octagon bbl. 51 inches overall. Weight: 10.75 lbs. Globe front sight, sporting tang peep rear.
Walnut buttstock w/pistol-grip and Schnabel-style forend. Color casehardened action w/double-set triggers Made from 1986 to date.

Shilen DGA
Benchrest Rifle

Shilen DGA Sporter

Shilen DGA Varminter

SHARPS MODEL 1874 SADDLE RIFLE . . NiB $1198 Ex $1090 Gd $683
Similar to 1874 Express Rifle except w/30-inch bbl., blade front sight and buckhorn rear. Made from 1986 to date.

**SHARPS MODEL 1874
SPORTING RIFLE NO. 1 . . . . NiB $1291 Ex $1090 Gd $691**
Similar to 1874 Express Rifle except w/30-inch bbl., blade front sight and buckhorn rear. Made from 1986 to date.

**SHARPS MODEL 1874
SPORTING RIFLE NO. 3 . . . . NiB $1095 Ex $966 Gd $657**
Similar to 1874 Sporting Rifle No. 1 except w/straight-grip stock w/steel crescent buttplate. Made from 1986 to date.

SHARPS MODEL 1874 MONTANA ROUGHRIDER
Similar to 1874 Sporting Rifle No. 1 except w/24- to 34-inch half-octagon or full-octagon bbl. Standard or deluxe walnut stock w/pistol-grip or military-style buttstock. Made from 1989 to date.
Standard model . . . . NiB $1090 Ex $683 Gd $606
Deluxe model . . . . NiB $1224 Ex $940 Gd $580

SIG SWISS INDUSTRIAL COMPANY —
Neuhausen-Rhine Falls, Switzerland

AMT SEMIAUTOMATIC RIFLE . . . . NiB $4750 Ex $3141 Gd $2628
.308 Win.(7.62 NATO). Five, 10, or 20-round magazine. 18.5-inch bbl. w/flash suppressor. Weight: 9.5 lbs. Sights: Adj. aperture rear, post front. Walnut buttstock and forend w/synthetic pistol grip. Imported 1980 to 1988.

AMT SPORTING RIFLE . . . . NiB $4750 Ex $2970 Gd $2193
Semiautomatic version of SG510-4 automatic assault rifle based on Swiss Army SIGW57. Roller-delayed blowback action. Caliber: 7.62x51mm NATO (.308 Win.). Five, 10- and 20-round magazines. 19-inch bbl. Weight: 10 lbs. Sights, aperture rear, post front. Wood buttstock and forearm, folding bipod. Imported from 1960 to 1988.

PE-57 SEMIAUTOMATIC RIFLE. . . . . . . NiB $6500 Ex $4289 Gd $2973
Caliber: 7.5 Swiss. 24-round magazine. 23.75-inch bbl. Weight: 12.5 lbs. Sights: Adj. aperture rear; post front. High-impact synthetic stock. Imported from Switzerland during the 1980s.

Smith & Wesson
Model 1500DL

Smith & Wesson
Model 1700 LS Classic Hunter

Springfield Armory
BM-59

SMITH & WESSON — Springfield, Massachusetts, Mfd. by Husqvarna, Vapenfabrik A.B., Huskvarna, Sweden & Howa Machinery LTD., Shinkawa-Chonear, Nagota 452, Japan

MODEL 1500 . . . . **NiB $350 Ex $300 Gd $213**
Bolt-action. .243 Win., .270 Win., .30-06, 7mm Rem. Mag. 22-inch bbl. (24-inch in 7mm Rem. Mag.). Weight: 7.5 lbs. American walnut stock w/Monte Carlo comb and cheekpiece, cut checkering. Sights: Open rear, hooded ramp, gold bead-front. This model was also imported by Mossberg (see separate listings); Imported from 1979 to 1984.

MODEL 1500DL DELUXE . . . . **NiB $350 Ex $300 Gd $213**
Same as standard model, except w/o sights; w/engine-turned bolt, decorative scroll on floorplate, French checkering. Imported from 1983 to 1984.

MODEL 1700 LS "CLASSIC HUNTER" . . . . **NiB $400 Ex $348 Gd $234**
Bolt action. Calibers: .243 Win., .270 Win., .30-06, 5-round magazine. 22-inch bbl. Weight: 7.5 lbs. Solid recoil pad, no sights, Schnabel forend, checkered walnut stock. Imported 1983 to 1984.

MODEL A BOLT-ACTION RIFLE . . . . **NiB $385 Ex $300 Gd $275**
Similar to Husqvarna Model 9000 Crown Grade. Mauser-type bolt action. Calibers: .22-250, .243 Win., .270 Win., .308 Win., .30-06, 7mm Rem. Mag., .300 Win. Mag. Five round magazine except 3-round capacity in latter two calibers. 23.75-inch bbl. Weight: 7 lbs. Sights: Folding leaf rear; hooded ramp front. Checkered walnut stock w/Monte Carlo cheekpiece, rosewood forend tip and pistol-grip cap, swivels. Made from 1969 to 1972.

MODEL B . . . . **NiB $425 Ex $342 Gd $208**
Same as Model A except w/20.25-inch extra-light bbl., Monte Carlo cheekpiece w/Schnabel-style forearm, weight: 6 lbs., 10 oz. Calibers: .243 Win., .30-06.

MODEL C . . . . **NiB $425 Ex $347 Gd $208**
Same as Model B except w/cheekpiece stock w/straight comb.

MODEL D . . . . **NiB $550 Ex $440 Gd $311**
Same as Model C except w/full-length Mannlicher-style forearm.

MODEL E. . . . . **NiB $550 Ex $440 Gd $311**
Same as Model B except w/full-length Mannlicher-style forearm.

SPRINGFIELD, INC. — Colona, Illinois (Formerly Springfield Armory of Geneseo, Ill.)

This is a private firm not to be confused with the former U.S. Government facility in Springfield, Mass.

BM-59 SEMIAUTOMATIC RIFLE
Gas-operated. Caliber: .308 Win. (7.62mm NATO). 20-round detachable box magazine. 19.3-inch bbl. w/flash suppressor. About 43 inches overall. Weight: 9.25 lbs. Adj. military aperture rear sight, square post front; direct and indirect grenade launcher sights. European walnut stock w/handguard or folding buttstock (Alpine Paratrooper). Made from 1981 to 1990.
**Standard
model** . . . . **NiB $1745 Ex $1236 Gd $811**
**Paratrooper
model** . . . . **NiB $2025 Ex $1667 Gd $1406**

**Springfield Armory
SAR-8 Sporter Rifle**

M-1 GARAND SEMIAUTOMATIC RIFLE
Gas-operated. Calibers: .308 Win. (7.62 NATO), .30-06. Eight round stripper clip. 24-inch bbl. 43.5 inches overall. Weight: 9.5 lbs. Adj. aperture rear sight, military square blade front. Standard "Issue-grade" walnut stock or folding buttstock. Made from 1979 to 1990.

Standard model	NiB $725	Ex $545	Gd $313
National match	NiB $850	Ex $771	Gd $465
Ultra match	NiB $950	Ex $731	Gd $522
Sniper model	NiB $1100	Ex $799	Gd $622
Tanker model	NiB $850	Ex $619	Gd $436
Paratrooper w/folding stock	NiB $1375	Ex $1022	Gd $991

MATCH M1A
Same as Standard M1A except w/National Match-grade bbl. w/modified flash suppressor, National Match sights, turned trigger pull, gas system assembly in one unit, modified mainspring guide glass-bedded walnut stock. Super Match M1A w/premium-grade heavy bbl. (weight: 10 lbs).

Match M1A	NiB $2000	Ex $1799	Gd $1194
Super Match M1A	NiB $2550	Ex $1811	Gd $1624

STANDARD M1A SEMIAUTOMATIC
Gas-operated. Similar to U.S. M14 service rifle except w/o provision for automatic firing. Caliber: 7.65mm NATO (.308 Win.). Five, 10- or 20-round detachable box magazine. 25.13-inch bbl w/flash suppressor. Weight: 9 lbs. Sights: Adj. aperture rear; blade front. Fiberglass, birch or walnut stock, fiberglass handguard, sling swivels. Made from 1996 to 2000.

W/fiberglass or birch stock	NiB $1109	Ex $856	Gd $573
W/walnut stock	NiB $1258	Ex $1045	Gd $774

M-6 SCOUT RIFLE/SHOTGUN COMBO
Similar to (14-inch) short-barrel Survival Gun provided as backup weapon to U.S. combat pilots. Calibers: .22 LR/.410 and .22 Hornet/.410. 18.5-inch bbl. 32 inches overall. Weight: 4 lbs. Parkerized or stainless steel finish. Folding detachable stock w/storage for fifteen .22 LR cartridges and four .410 shells. Drilled and tapped for scope mounts. Intro. 1982 and imported from Czech Republic 1995 to 2004.

First Issue (no trigger guard)	NiB $1650	Ex $1382	Gd $1008
Second Issue (w/trigger guard)	NiB $1724	Ex $1364	Gd $1004

SAR-8 SPORTER RIFLE
Similar to H&K 911 semiautomatic rifle. Calibers: .308 Win., (7.62x51) NATO. Detachable 5- 10- or 20-round magazine. 18- or 20-inch bbl. 38.25 or 45.3 inches overall. Weight: 8.7 to 9.5 lbs. Protected front post and rotary adj. rear sight. Delayed roller-locked blow-back action w/fluted chamber. Kevlar-reinforced fiberglass thumb-hole style wood stock. Imported from 1990 to 1998.

SAR-8 w/wood stock (disc. 1994)	NiB $1015	Ex $846	Gd $634
SAR-8 w/thumb-hole stock	NiB $1080	Ex $936	Gd $653

SAR-48, SAR-4800
Similar to Browning FN FAL/LAR semiautomatic rifle. Calibers: .233 Rem. (5.56x45) and 3.08 Win. (7.62x51) NATO. Detachable 5- 10- or 20-round magazine. 18- or 21-inch chrome-lined bbl. 38.25 or 45.3 inches overall. Weight: 9.5 to 13.25 lbs. Protected post front and adj. rear sight. Forged receiver and bolt w/adj. gas system. Pistol-grip or thumb-hole style; synthetic or wood stock. Imported 1985; reintroduced 1995.

SAR-48 w/pistol-grip stock (disc. 1989)	NiB $1675	Ex $1162	Gd $950
SAR-48 w/wood stock (disc. 1989)	NiB $2454	Ex $1986	Gd $1426
SAR-48 w/folding stock (disc. 1989)	NiB $2753	Ex $2220	Gd $1582
SAR-48 w/thumb-hole stock	NiB $1269	Ex $1031	Gd $726

SQUIRES BINGHAM CO., INC. —
Makati, Rizal, Philippines

**MODEL 14D DELUXE BOLT-ACTION
REPEATING RIFLE** . . . . NiB $128 Ex $103 Gd $77
Caliber: .22 LR. Five round box magazine. 24-inch bbl. Sights: V-notch rear; hooded ramp front. Receiver grooved for scope mounting. Pulong Dalaga stock w/contrasting forend tip and grip cap, checkered forearm and pistol-grip. Weight: 6 lbs. Disc.

MODEL 15 . . . . NiB $153 Ex $108 Gd $102
Same as Model 14D except chambered for .22 WMR. Importation. Disc.

MODEL M16 SEMIAUTOMATIC RIFLE . . . . NiB $148 Ex $153 Gd $118
Styled after U.S. M16 military rifle. Caliber: .22 LR. 15-round box magazine. 19.5-inch bbl. w/muzzle brake/flash hider. Rear sight in carrying handle, post front on high ramp. Black-painted mahogany buttstock and forearm. Weight: 6.5 lbs. Importation disc.

MODEL M20D DELUXE . . . . NiB $230 Ex $204 Gd $123
Caliber: .22 LR. 15-round box magazine. 19.5-inch bbl. w/muzzle brake/flash hider. Sights: V-notch rear; blade front. Receiver grooved for scope mounting. Pulong Dalaga stock w/contrasting forend tip and grip cap, checkered forearm/pistol-grip. Weight: 6 lbs. Importation disc.

STANDARD ARMS COMPANY —
Wilmington, Delaware

MODEL G AUTOMATIC RIFLE . . . . . NiB $775 Ex $549 Gd $341
Gas-operated. Autoloading. Hammerless. Takedown. .25-35, .30-30, .25 Rem., .30 Rem., .35 Rem. Magazine capacity: 4 rounds in .35 Rem., 5 rounds in other calibers. 22.38-inch bbl. Weight: 7.75 lbs. Sights: Open sporting rear; ivory bead front. Shotgun-type stock. Made c. 1910. Note: This was the first gas-operated rifle manufactured in the U.S. While essentially an autoloader, the gas port can be closed and the rifle may be operated as a slide-action repeater.

**Star
Rolling Block Carbine**

MODEL M HAND-OPERATED RIFLE . . . . . NiB $700 Ex $511 Gd $382
Slide-action repeater w/same general specifications as Model G except lacks autoloading feature. Weight: 7 lbs.

STAR — Eibar, Spain
Mfd. by Bonifacio Echeverria, S.A.

ROLLING BLOCK CARBINE . . . . . . NiB $450 Ex $292 Gd $140
Single-shot, similar to Remington Rolling Block. .30-30, .357 Mag., .44 Mag. 20-inch bbl. Weight: 6 lbs. Sights: Folding leaf rear; ramp front. Walnut straight-grip stock w/crescent buttplate, forearm w/bbl. band. Imported 1934 to 1975.

STERLING — Imported by Lanchester U.S.A., Inc., Dallas, Texas

MARK 6 SEMIAUTOMATIC CARBINE . . NiB $1750 Ex $1135 Gd $950
Caliber: 9mm Para 34-round magazine. Bbl.: 16.1 inches. Weight: 7.5 lbs. Flip-type rear peep sight, ramp front. Folding metal skeleton stock. Made from 1983 to 1994.

J. STEVENS ARMS CO. — Chicopee Falls, Massachusetts, Div. of Savage Industries, Westfield, Mass.

J. Stevens Arms eventually became a division of Savage Industries. Consequently, the "Stevens" brand name is used for some rifles by Savage; see separate Savage-Stevens listings under Savage.

NO. 12 MARKSMAN SINGLE-SHOT RIFLE. NiB $425 Ex $285 Gd $154
Lever-action, tip-up. Takedown. Calibers: .22 LR, .25 R.F., .32 R.F. 22-inch bbl. Plain straight-grip stock, small tapered forearm.

**NO. 14 LITTLE SCOUT
SINGLE-SHOT RIFLE . . . . NiB $425 Ex $285 Gd $154**
Caliber: .22 RF. 18-inch bbl. One-piece slab stock readily distinguishes it from the No. 14X that follows. Made from 1906 to 1910.

**NO. 14 1/2 LITTLE SCOUT
SINGLE-SHOT RIFLE . . . . NiB $425 Ex $275 Gd $174**
Rolling block. Takedown. Caliber: .22 LR. 18- or 20-inch bbl. Weight: 2.75 lbs. Sights: open rear; blade front. Plain straight-grip stock, small tapered forearm.

MODEL 15 . . . . NiB $200 Ex $130 Gd $120
Same as Stevens-Springfield Model 15 except w/24-inch bbl., weight: 5 lbs., w/redesigned stock. Made from 1948 to 1965.

MODEL 15Y YOUTH'S RIFLE . . . . . NiB $181 Ex $125 Gd $110
Same as Model 15 except w/21-inch bbl., short buttstock, weight: 4.75 lbs. Made from 1958 to 1965.

**NO. 44 IDEAL
SINGLE-SHOT RIFLE . . . . NiB $650 Ex $442 Gd $348**
Rolling block. Lever-action. Takedown. Calibers: .22 LR. .25 R.F., .32 R.F., .25-20 S.S., .32-20, .32-40, .38-40, .38-55, .44-40. Bbl. lengths: 24-inch, 26-inch (round, half-octagon, full-octagon). Weight: 7 lbs w/26-inch round bbl. Sights: Open rear; Rocky Mountain front. Plain straight-grip stock and forearm. Made from 1894 to 1932.

NO. 44 1/2 IDEAL SINGLE-SHOT RIFLE . . NiB $950 Ex $807 Gd $562
Falling-block. Lever-action rifle. Aside from the new design action intro. 1903, specifications of this model are the same as those of Model 44. Model 44X disc. 1916.

NOS. 45 TO 54 IDEAL SINGLE-SHOT RIFLES
These are higher-grade models, differing from the standard No. 44 and 44.5 chiefly in finish, engraving, set triggers, levers, bbls., stock, etc. The Schuetzen types (including the Stevens-Pope models) are in this series. Model Nos. 45 to 54 were intro. 1896 and originally had the No. 44-type rolling-block action, which was superseded in 1903 by the No. 44.5-type falling-block action. These models were all disc. about 1916. Generally speaking, the 45-54 series rifles, particularly the Stevens Pope and higher grade Schuetzen models are collector's items, bringing much higher prices than the ordinary No. 44 and 44.5.

**MODEL 66 BOLT-ACTION
REPEATING RIFLE . . . . NiB $209 Ex $128 Gd $110**
Takedown. Caliber: .22 Short, Long, LR. Tubular magazine holds 13 LR, 15 Long, 19 Short. 24-inch bbl. Weight: 5 lbs. Sights: Open rear, bead front. Plain pistol-grip stock w/grooved forearm. Made from 1931 to 1935.

**NO. 70 VISIBLE LOADING
SLIDE-ACTION . . . . NiB $550 Ex $381 Gd $228**
Exposed hammer. Caliber: .22 LR., Long, Short. Tubular magazine holds 11 LR., 13 Long, 15 Short. 22-inch bbl. Weight: 4.5 lbs. Sights: Open rear; bead front. Plain straight-grip stock, grooved slide handle. Made 1907-34. Note: Nos. 702, 71, 712, 72, 722 essentially the same as No. 70, differing chiefly in bbl. length or sight tooling.

MODEL 87 AUTOLOADING RIFLE. . . . . . . NiB $150 Ex $103 Gd $88
Takedown. Caliber: .22 LR. 15-round tubular magazine. 24-inch bbl. (20-inch on current model). Weight: 6 lbs. Sights: Open rear, bead front. Pistol-grip stock. Made 1938 to date. Note: This model originally bore the "Springfield" brand name, disc. in 1948.

**MODEL 322 HI-POWER
BOLT-ACTION CARBINE . . . . NiB $450 Ex $29
1 Gd $183**
Caliber: .22 Hornet. 4-round detachable magazine. 21-inch bbl. Weight: 6.75 lbs. Sights: Open rear; ramp front. Pistol-grip stock.

Stevens No. 14 Little Scout

Stevens No. 14.5 Little Scout

Stevens No. 44 Ideal

Stevens Ideal Schuetzen Rifle

Stevens Model 87

MODEL 322-S . . . . **NiB $450 Ex $315 Gd $188**
Same as Model 325 except w/peep rear sight. (See Savage models 340S, 342S.)

MODEL 325 HI-POWER
BOLT-ACTION CARBINE . . . . **NiB $450 Ex $3290 Gd $262**
Caliber: .30-30. Three round detachable box magazine. 21-inch bbl. Weight: 6.75 lbs. Sights: Open rear; bead front. Plain pistol-grip stock. Made from 1947 to 1950. (See Savage Model 340.)

MODEL 325-S . . . . **NiB $450 Ex $320 Gd $193**
Same as Model 325 except w/peep rear sight. (See Savage Model 340S.)

NO. 414 ARMORY MODEL
SINGLE-SHOT RIFLE . . . . **NiB $450 Ex $373 Gd $290**
No. 44-type lever-action. Calibers: .22 LR only, .22 Short only. 26-inch bbl. Weight: 8 lbs. Sights: Lyman receiver peep; blade front. Plain straight-grip stock, military-type forearm, swivels. Made from 1912 to 1932.

MODEL 416 BOLT-ACTION
TARGET RIFLE . . . . **NiB $140 Ex $97 Gd $52**
Caliber: .22 LR. Five round detachable box magazine. 26-inch heavy bbl. Weight: 9.5 lbs. Sights: Receiver peep; hooded front. Target stock, swivels, sling. Made from 1937 to 1949.

NO. 419 JUNIOR TARGET MODEL
BOLT-ACTION SINGLE-SHOT RIFLE . . . . . . **NiB $385 Ex $283 Gd $206**
Takedown. Caliber: .22 LR. 26-inch bbl. Weight: 5.5 lbs. Sights: Lyman No. 55 rear peep; blade front. Plain junior target stock w/pistol grip and grooved forearm, swivels, sling. Made 1932 to 1936.

BUCKHORN MODEL 053 BOLT-ACTION
SINGLE-SHOT RIFLE . . . . **NiB $165 Ex $136 Gd $100**
Takedown. Calibers: .22 Short, Long, LR., .22 WRF. .25 Stevens R.F. 24-inch bbl. Weight: 5.5 lbs. Sights: Receiver peep; open middle; hooded front. Sporting stock w/pistol-grip and black forend tip. Made 1935 to 1948.

BUCKHORN MODEL 53 . . . . **NiB $208 Ex $177 Gd $116**
Same as Buckhorn Model 053 except w/open rear sight and plain bead front sight.

Stevens No. 414 Armory

Stevens Model 416

Stevens Buckhorn Model 53

Stevens Buckhorn Model 055

Stevens Buckhorn Model 56

BUCKHORN 055 . . . . NiB $210 Ex $179 Gd $118
Takedown. Same as Model 056 except in single-shot configuration. Weight: 5.5 lbs. Caliber: .22 LR., Long, Short. 24-inch bbl. Weight: 6 lbs. Sights: Receiver peep, open middle, hooded front. Made from 1935 to 1948.

**BUCKHORN MODEL 056
BOLT-ACTION . . . . NiB $215 Ex $179 Gd $123**
Takedown. Caliber: .22 LR., Long, Short. Five round detachable box magazine. 24-inch bbl. Weight: 6 lbs. Sights: Receiver peep, open middle, hooded front. Sporting stock w/pistol grip and black forend tip. Made from 1935 to 1948.

**BUCKHORN
MODEL 56 . . . . NiB $204 Ex $153 Gd $118**
Same as Buckhorn Model 056 except w/open rear sight and plain bead front sight.

BUCKHORN NO. 057 . . . . NiB $191 Ex $128 Gd $103
Same as Buckhorn Model 076 except w/5-round detachable box magazine. Made from 1939 to 1948.

BUCKHORN NO. 57 . . . . NiB $189 Ex $128 Gd $102
Same as Buckhorn Model 76 except w/5-round detachable box magazine. Made from 1939 to 1948.

**BUCKHORN MODEL 066
BOLT-ACTION REPEATING RIFLE . . . . NiB $257 Ex $206 Gd $112**
Takedown. Caliber: .22 LR, Long, Short. Tubular magazine holds 21 Short, 17 Long, 15 LR. 24-inch bbl. Weight: 6 lbs. Sights: Receiver peep; open middle; hooded front. Sporting stock w/pistol grip and black forend tip. Made from 1935 to 1948.

BUCKHORN MODEL 66 . . . . NiB $189 Ex $128 Gd $202
Same as Buckhorn Model 066 except w/open rear sight, plain bead front sight.

**BUCKHORN NO. 076
AUTOLOADING RIFLE . . . . NiB $204 Ex $179 Gd $123**
Takedown. Caliber: .22 LR. 15-round tubular magazine. 24-inch bbl. Weight: 6 lbs. Sights: Receiver peep; open middle; hooded front. Sporting stock w/pistol grip, black forend tip. Made 1938 to 1948.

BUCKHORN NO. 76 . . . . NiB $204 Ex $179 Gd $118
Same as Buckhorn No. 076 except w/open rear sight, plain bead front sight.

**CRACKSHOT NO. 26
SINGLE-SHOT RIFLE . . . . NiB $295 Ex $207 Gd $155**
Lever-action. Takedown. Calibers: .22 LR, .32 R.F. 18-inch or 22-inch bbl. Weight: 3.25 lbs. Sights: Open rear; blade front. Plain straight-grip stock, small tapered forearm. Made from 1913 to 1939.

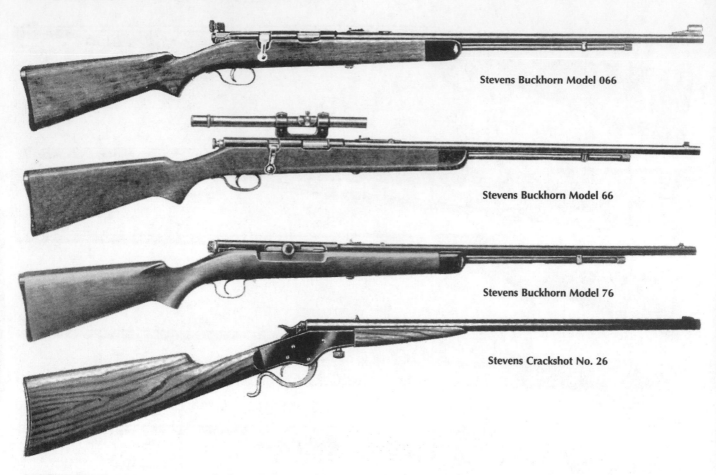

Stevens Buckhorn Model 066

Stevens Buckhorn Model 66

Stevens Buckhorn Model 76

Stevens Crackshot No. 26

CRACKSHOT NO. 26.5 . . . . **NiB $295 Ex $206 Gd $181**
Same as Crackshot No. 26 on previous page except w/smoothbore bbl. for shot cartridges.

FAVORITE NO. 17
SINGLE-SHOT RIFLE . . . . **NiB $308 Ex $206 Gd $155**
Lever-action. Takedown. Calibers: .22 LR, .25 R.F., .32 R.F. 24-inch round bbl; other lengths were available. Weight: 4.5 lbs. Sights: Open rear; Rocky Mountain front. Plain straight-grip stock, small tapered forearm. Made from 1894 to 1935.

FAVORITE NO. 18. . . . . **NiB $385 Ex $283 Gd $155**
Same as Favorite No. 17 except w/Vernier peep rear sight, leaf middle sight, Beach combination front sight.

FAVORITE NO. 19. . . . . **NiB $410 Ex $308 Gd $181**
Same as Favorite No. 17 except w/Lyman combination rear sight, leaf middle sight, Lyman front sight.

FAVORITE NO. 20. . . . . **NiB $385 Ex $308 Gd $206**
Same as Favorite No. 17 except w/smoothbore barrel.

FAVORITE NO. 27. . . . . **NiB $410 Ex $308 Gd $222**
Same as Favorite No. 17 except w/octagon bbl.

FAVORITE NO. 28. . . . . **NiB $385 Ex $283 Gd $206**
Same as Favorite No. 18 except w/octagon bbl.

FAVORITE NO. 29. . . . . **NiB $410 Ex $283 Gd $206**
Same as Favorite No. 19 except w/octagon bbl.

WALNUT HILL NO. 417-0
SINGLE-SHOT TARGET RIFLE . . . . **NiB $875 Ex $738 Gd $485**
Lever-action. Calibers: .22 LR only, .22 Short only, .22 Hornet. 28-inch heavy bbl. (extra heavy 29-inch bbl. also available). Weight: 10.5 lbs. Sights: Lyman No. 52L extension rear; 17A front, scope bases mounted on bbl. Target stock w/full pistol-grip, beavertail forearm, bbl. band, swivels, sling. Made from 1932 to 1947.

WALNUT HILL NO. 417-1 . . . . **NiB $875 Ex $738 Gd $485**
Same as No. 417-0 except w/Lyman No. 48L receiver sight.

WALNUT HILL NO. 417-2 . . . . **NiB $875 Ex $738 Gd $485**
Same as No. 417-0 except w/Lyman No. 144 tang sight.

WALNUT HILL NO. 417-3 . . . . **NiB $875 Ex $738 Gd $485**
Same as No. 417-0 except w/o sights.

WALNUT HILL NO. 417.5
SINGLE-SHOT RIFLE . . . . **NiB $875 Ex $738 Gd $485**
Lever-action. Calibers: .22 LR, .22 WMR, .25 R.F., .22 Hornet. 28-inch bbl. Weight: 8.5 lbs. Sights: Lyman No. 144 tang peep, folding middle; bead front. Sporting stock w/pistol-grip, semi-beavertail forearm, swivels, sling. Made from 1932 to 1940.

WALNUT HILL NO. 418
SINGLE-SHOT RIFLE . . . . **NiB $950 Ex $739 Gd $562**
Lever-action. Takedown. Calibers: .22 LR only, .22 Short only. 26-inch bbl. Weight: 6.5 lbs. Sights: Lyman No. 144 tang peep; blade front. Pistol-grip stock, semi-beavertail forearm, swivels, sling. Made from 1932 to 1940.

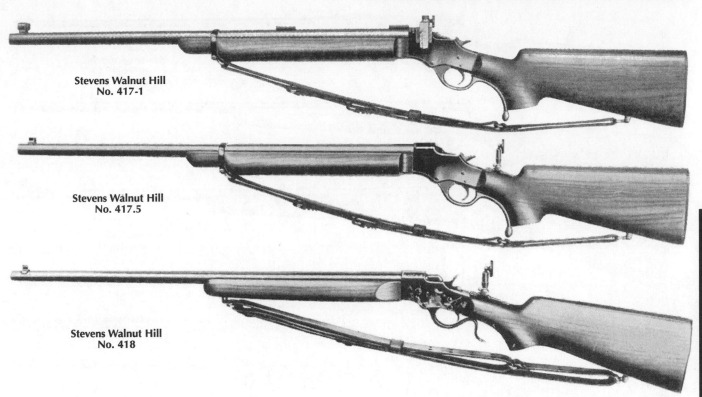

Stevens Walnut Hill
No. 417-1

Stevens Walnut Hill
No. 417.5

Stevens Walnut Hill
No. 418

WALNUT HILL NO. 418.5 . . . . **NiB $950 Ex $594 Gd $431**
Same as No. 418 except also available in calibers .22 WRF and .25
Stevens R.F., w/Lyman No. 2A tang peep sight, bead front sight.

MODEL 15 SINGLE-SHOT
BOLT-ACTION RIFLE . . . . **NiB $177 Ex $126 Gd $100**
Takedown. Caliber: .22 LR, Long, Short. 22-inch bbl. Weight: 4 lbs.
Sights: Open rear, bead front. Plain pistol-grip stock. Made 1937 to 1948.

MODEL 82 BOLT-ACTION
SINGLE-SHOT RIFLE . . . . **NiB $148 Ex $131 Gd $100**
Takedown. Caliber: .22 LR, Long, Short. 22-inch bbl. Weight: 4 lbs.
Sights: Open rear; gold bead front. Plain pistol-grip stock w/grooved
forearm. Made from 1935 to 1939.

MODEL 83 BOLT-ACTION
SINGLE-SHOT RIFLE . . . . **NiB $175 Ex $116 Gd $95**
Takedown. Calibers: .22 LR, Long, Short; .22 WRF, .25 Stevens R.F.
24-inch bbl. Weight: 4.5 lbs. Sights: Peep rear; open middle; hooded
front. Plain pistol-grip stock w/grooved forearm. Made 1935 to 1939.

MODEL 84 . . . . **NiB $200 Ex $177 Gd $118**
Same as Model 86 except w/5-round detachable box magazine.
Pre-1948 rifles of this model were designated Springfield Model 84,
later known as Stevens Model 84. Made from 1940 to 1965.

MODEL 84-S (084) . . . . **NiB $200 Ex $177 Gd $121**
Same as Model 84 except w/peep rear sight and hooded front sight.
Pre-1948 rifles of this model were designated Springfield Model
084, later known as Stevens Model 84-S. Disc.

MODEL 85 . . . . **NiB $218 Ex $136 Gd $106**
Same as Stevens Model 87 except w/5-round detachable box magazine. Made
1939 to date. Pre-1948 rifles of this model were designated Springfield Model 85,
currently known as Stevens Model 85. Earlier models command slight premiums.

MODEL 85-S (085) . . . . **NiB $202 Ex $151 Gd $116**
Same as Model 85 except w/peep rear sight and hooded front sight.
Pre-1948 models were designated Springfield Model 085; also
known as Stevens Model 85-S.

MODEL 86
BOLT-ACTION . . . . **NiB $202 Ex $156 Gd $116**
Takedown. Caliber: .22 LR, Long, Short. Tubular magazine holds 15
LR, 17 Long, 21 Short. 24-inch bbl. Weight: 6 lbs. Sights: Open
rear, gold bead front. Pistol-grip stock, black forend tip on later production. Made 1935 to 1965. Note: The Springfield brand name
was disc. in 1948.

MODEL 86-S (086) . . . . **NiB $210 Ex $177 Gd $126**
Same as Model 86 except w/peep rear sight and hooded front sight.
Pre-1948 rifles of this model were designated as Springfield Model
086, later known as Stevens Model 86-S. Disc.

MODEL 87-S (087) . . . . **NiB $218 Ex $202 Gd $131**
Same as Stevens Model 87 except w/peep rear sight and
hooded front sight. Pre-1948 rifles of this model were designated as Springfield Model 087, later known as Stevens Model
87-S. Disc.

STEYR DAIMLER PUCH A.G. — Steyr, Austria
See also listings under Mannlicher.

AUG-SA
SEMIAUTOMATIC RIFLE . . . . **NiB $3996 Ex $3225 Gd $2248**
Gas-operated. Caliber: .223 Rem. (5.56mm). Thirty or 40-round
magazine. 20-inch bbl. standard; optional 16-inch or 24-inch heavy
bbl. w/folding bipod. 31 inches overall. Weight: 8.5 lbs. Sights:
Integral 1.5x scope and mount. Green high-impact synthetic stock
w/folding vertical grip.

Stevens-Springfield
Model 15

Stevens-Springfield
Model 82

Stevens-Springfield
Model 83

Stevens-Springfield
Model 84

Stevens-Springfield
Model 85

Stevens-Springfield
Model 86-S

SMALL BORE CARBINE. . . . . **NiB $395 Ex $275 Gd $125**
Bolt-action repeater. Caliber: .22 LR. Five round detachable box
magazine. 19.5-inch bbl. Sights: Leaf rear; hooded bead front.
Mannlicher-type stock, checkered, swivels. Made 1953 to 1967.

STOEGER RIFLE — Mfd. by Franz Jaeger & Co., Suhl, Germany; dist. in the U.S. by A. F. Stoeger, Inc., New York, N.Y.

HORNET RIFLE . . . . **NiB $1352 Ex $966 Gd $631**
Same specifications as Herold Rifle, designed and built on a
Miniature Mauser-type action. See listing under Herold Bolt-
Action Repeating Sporting Rifle for additional specifications.
Imported during the 1930s.

SURVIVAL ARMS — Orange, CT

AR-7 EXPLORER . . . . **NiB $150 Ex $128 Gd $87**
Caliber: .22 LR. Eight round magazine. Weight: 3 lbs. Polymer
stocks. Drift adj. sights. Disassembles into five separate elements,

allowing barrel, action and magazine to fit into buttstock; assem-
bles quickly w/o tools. Choice of camo, silvertone or black matte
finishes. Made from 1992 to 1995.

THOMPSON/CENTER ARMS — (Div. of Smith & Wesson, Springfield, MA; formerly Rochester, NH)

CONTENDER CARBINE
Calibers: .22 LR, .22 Hornet, .222 Rem., .223 Rem., 7mm T.C.U.,
7x30 Waters, .30-30 Win., .35 Rem., .44 Mag., .357 Rem. Max. and
.410 bore. 21-inch interchangeable bbls. 35 inches overall. Adj.
iron sights. Checkered American walnut or Rynite stock and forend.
Made from 1986 to 2000.
Standard model (rifle calibers) . . . . **NiB $415 Ex $248 Gd $171**
Standard model (.410 bore). . . . . . . **NiB $435 Ex $260 Gd $195**
Rynite stock model
(rifle calibers) . . . . **NiB $335 Ex $270 Gd $212**
Rynite stock model (.410 bore) . . . . **NiB $370 Ex $295 Gd $240**
Extra bbls. (rifle calibers) . . . . **NiB $Add $10**
Extra bbls. (.410 bore) . . . . **Add $25**
Youth model (all calibers
and .410 bore). . . . . **NiB $450 Ex $280 Gd $200**

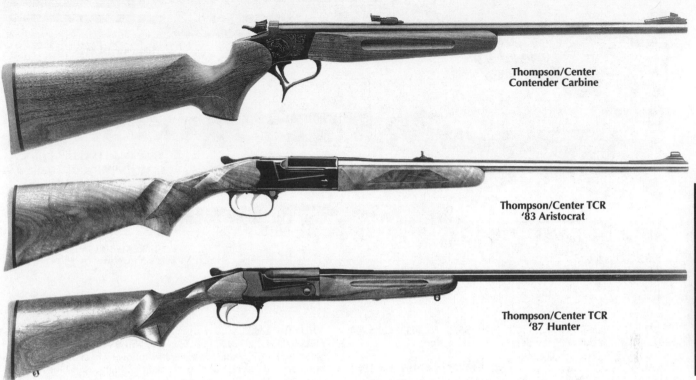

Thompson/Center Contender Carbine

Thompson/Center TCR '83 Aristocrat

Thompson/Center TCR '87 Hunter

CONTENDER CARBINE
SURVIVAL SYSTEM . . . . NiB $615 Ex $445 Gd $342
Similar to standard Contender Carbine w/Rynite stock and forend. Comes w/two 16.25-inch bbls. chambered in .223 and .45/.410 bore. Camo Cordura case.

STAINLESS CONTENDER CARBINE
Same as standard Contender Carbine Model, except stainless steel w/blued sights. Calibers: .22 LR, .22 Hornet, .223 Rem., 7-30 Waters, .30-30 Win., .410. Walnut or Rynite stock and forend. Made from 1993 to 2000.
Walnut stock model . . . . NiB $415 Ex $376 Gd $287
Rynite stock model . . . . NiB $468 Ex $390 Gd $277
Youth stock model . . . . NiB $442 Ex $365 Gd $262
Extra bbls. (rifle calibers) . . . . NiB $Add $11

TCR '83 ARISTOCRAT MODEL
Break frame, overlever action. Calibers: .223 Rem., .22/250 Rem., .243 Win., 7mm Rem. Mag., .30-06 Springfield. Interchangeable bbls.: 23 inches in length. Weight: 6 lbs., 14 oz. American walnut stock and forearm, checkered, black rubber recoil pad, cheekpiece. Made from 1983 to 1987.
TCR '83 Standard model . . . . NiB $468 Ex $416 Gd $236
TCR '83 Aristocrat . . . . NiB $540 Ex $390 Gd $262
Extra bbls. (rifle calibers) . . . . NiB $256 Ex $210 Gd $153

TCR '87 HUNTER RIFLE
Similar to TCR '83 except in calibers .22 Hornet, ..222 Rem., 223 Rem., .22-250 Rem., .243 Win., .270 Win., 7mm-08, .308 Win., .30-06, .32-40 Win. Also 12-ga. slug and 10- and 12-ga. field bbls. 23-inch standard or 25.88-inch heavy bbl. interchangeable. 39.5 to 43.38 inches overall. Weight: 6 lbs., 14 oz. to 7.5 lbs. Iron sights optional. Checkered American black walnut buttstock w/fluted end. Disc. 1992.

Standard model . . . . NiB $500 Ex $342 Gd $262
Extra bbl. (rifle calibers and
10- or 12-ga. Field) . . . . NiB $275 Ex $226 Gd $163
Extra bbl. (12-ga. slug) . . . . NiB $319 Ex $262 Gd $188

TIKKA RIFLES — Mfg. by Sako, Ltd. of Riihimaki, Finland & Armi Marocchi in Italy

Imported by Beretta USA

NOTE: *Tikka New Generation, Battue and Continental series bolt action rifles are being manufactured by Sako, Ltd., in Finland. Tikka O/U rifles (previously Valmet) are being manufactured in Italy by Armi Marocchi. For earlier importation see additional listings under Ithaca LSA and Valmet 412S models.*

T3 HUNTER. . . . . NiB $600 Ex $488 Gd $363
Calibers:..223, .22-250, .243Win., .308 Win., .25-06, .270 Win., 6.5x55, 270 WSM, 7mm Rem. Mag., .30-06, 300 WSM, .300 Win. Mag., .338 Win. Mag., Bbl: 22 7/16 inches (24 3/8 in magnum calibers. Weight: 6 3/4 pounds. No sights. Walnut stock with rubber butt pad. Introduced 2003.

T3 LAMINATED
STAINLESS. . . . . NiB $725 Ex $635 Gd $555
Same as T3 Hunter but with stainless barrel and action; laminated stock.

T3 LITE . . . . NiB $515 Ex $453 Gd $388
Similar to T3 Hunter but with synthetic stock; weight: 6 pounds, 3 ounces. Introduced 2003.

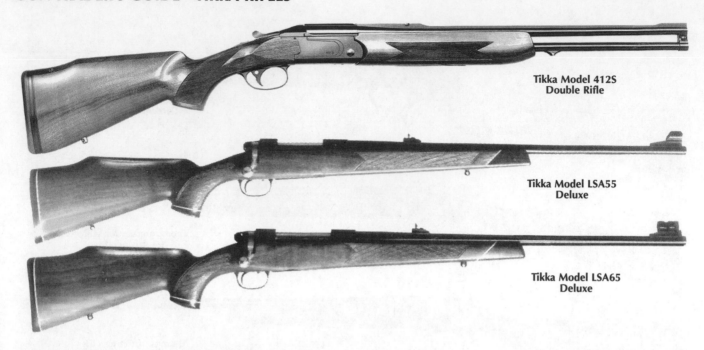

Tikka Model 412S
Double Rifle

Tikka Model LSA55
Deluxe

Tikka Model LSA65
Deluxe

T3 LITE STAINLESS . . . . **NiB $560 Ex $453 Gd $348**
Same as T3 Lite but with stainless barrel and action.

T3 TACTICAL . . . . **NiB $1427 Ex $1162 Gd $962**
Calibers: .223, .308 Win. Similar to T3 Hunter but designed for law enforcement. Bbl.: 20 inches. Black phosphate finish, synthetic stock with adjustable comb. Five round detachable magazine. Picatinny rail on action, fitted for muzzle brake and bipod use.

T3 VARMINT . . . . **NiB $795 Ex $678 Gd $533**
Calibers: .223, .22-250, .308 Win. Similar to T3 Hunter but with heavy bull barrel, synthetic stock, adjustable trigger. Five round detachable magazine.

**T3 VARMINT
STAINLESS** . . . . **NiB $795 Ex $633 Gd $558**
Similar to T3 Varmint but with stainless barrel and action.

**MODEL 412S
DOUBLE RIFLE**
Calibers: .308 Win., .30-06, 9.3x74R. 24-inch bbl. w/quarter rib machined for scope mounts; automatic ejectors (9.3x74R only). 40 inches overall. Weight: 8.5 lbs. Ramp front and folding adj. rear sight. Barrel selector on trigger. European walnut buttstock and forearm. Model 412S was replaced by the 512S version in 1994. Imported from 1989 to 1993.

**Model 412S
(disc. 1993)** . . . . **NiB $1050 Ex $897 Gd $639**
**Extra barrel assembly
(O/U shotgun), add.** **$650**
**Extra barrel assembly
(O/U Combo), add** **$775**
**Extra barrel assembly
(O/U rifle), add.** **$995**
MODEL 512S DOUBLE RIFLE
Formerly Valmet 412S. In 1994, following the joint venture of 1989, the model designation was changed to 512S. Imported from 1994 to 1997.
Model 512S. . . . . **NiB $1525 Ex $1386 Gd $1026**
Extra barrel assembly

(O/U rifle), add. **$755**
LSA55 DELUXE . . . . **NiB $548 Ex $496 Gd $419**
Same as LSA55 Standard except w/rollover cheekpiece, rosewood grip cap and forend tip, skip checkering, high-luster blue. Imported from 1965 to 1988.

LSA55 SPORTER . . . . **NiB $541 Ex $440 Gd $310**
Same as LSA55 except has 22.8-inch heavy bbl. w/o sights, special stock w/beavertail forearm, not available in 6mm Rem. Weighs 9 lbs. Imported from 1965 to 1988.

**LSA55 STANDARD
BOLT-ACTION REPEATER** . . . . **NiB $496 Ex $368 Gd $239**
Mauser-type action. Calibers: .222 Rem., .22-250, 6mm Rem. Mag., .243 Win., .308 Win. Three round clip magazine. 22.8-inch bbl. Weight: 6.8 lbs. Sights: Folding leaf rear; hooded ramp front. Checkered walnut stock w/Monte Carlo cheekpiece, swivels. Made from 1965-88.
LSA65 DELUXE . . . . **NiB $572 Ex $496 Gd $342**
Same as LSA65 Standard except w/special features of LSA55 Deluxe. Imported from 1970 to 1988.

LSA65 STANDARD . . . . **NiB $461 Ex $368 Gd $239**
Same as LSA55 Standard except calibers: .25-06, 6.5x55 .270 Win., .30-06. Five round magazine, 22-inch bbl., weight: 7.5 lbs. Imported 1970 to 1988.
MODEL M 55
Bolt action. Calibers: .222 Rem., .22-250 Rem., .223 Rem. .243 Win., .308 Win. (6mm Rem. and 17 Rem. available in Standard and Deluxe models only). 23.2-inch bbl. (24.8-inch in Sporter and Heavy Barrel models). 42.8 inches overall (44 inches in Sporter and Heavy Barrel models). Weight: 7.25 to 9 lbs. Monte Carlo-style stock w/pistol-grip. Sling swivels. Imported 1965 to 1988.
Continental . . . . **NiB $709 Ex $529 Gd $380**
Deluxe model . . . . **NiB $751 Ex $534 Gd $400**
Sporter. . . . . **NiB $684 Ex $555 Gd $375**
Sporter w/sights . . . . **NiB $709 Ex $532 Gd $379**
Standard . . . . **NiB $632 Ex $503 Gd $349**
Super Sporter . . . . **NiB $789 Ex $650 Gd $402**
Super Sporter w/sights . . . . **NiB $858 Ex $430 Gd $486**
Trapper . . . . **NiB $724 Ex $517 Gd $399**

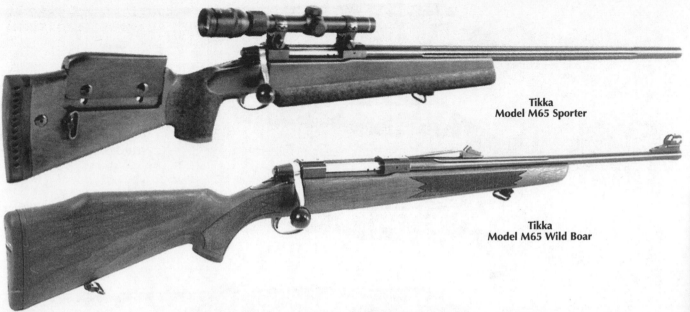

**Tikka
Model M65 Sporter**

**Tikka
Model M65 Wild Boar**

MODEL M65

Bolt action. Calibers: .25-06, .270 Win., .308 Win., .30-06, 7mm Rem. Mag., .300 Win. Mag. (Sporter and Heavy Bbl. models in .270 Win., .308 Win. and .30-06 only). 22.4-inch bbl. (24.8-inch in Sporter and Heavy Bbl. models). 43.2 inches overall (44 inches in Sporter, 44.8 inches in Heavy Bbl.). Weight: 7.5 to 9.9 lbs. Monte Carlo-style stock w/pistol-grip. Disc. 1989.

Continental	NiB $711	Ex $531	Gd $392
Deluxe Magnum	NiB $789	Ex $650	Gd $449
Deluxe model	NiB $737	Ex $531	Gd $377
Magnum	NiB $686	Ex $480	Gd $402
Sporter	NiB $557	Ex $505	Gd $351
Sporter w/sights	NiB $742	Ex $608	Gd $402
Standard	NiB $634	Ex $505	Gd $351
Super Sporter	NiB $863	Ex $662	Gd $456
Super Sporter w/sights	NiB $868	Ex $658	Gd $507
Super Sporter Master	NiB $1097	Ex $897	Gd $582

MODEL M65 WILD BOAR . . . . NiB $735 Ex $606 Gd $442
Same general specifications as Model M 65 except 20.8-inch bbl., overall length of 41.6 inches, weight: of 7.5 lbs. Disc. 1989.

NEW GENERATION RIFLES

Short-throw bolt available in three action lengths. Calibers: .22-250 Rem., .223 Rem., .243 Win., .308 Win., (medium action) .25-06 Rem., .270 Win., .30.06, (Long Action) 7mm Rem. Mag., .300 Win. Mag., .338 Win. Mag., (Magnum Action). 22- to 26-inch bbl. 42.25 to 46 inches overall. Weight: 7.2 to 8.5 lbs. Available w/o sights or w/hooded front and open rear sight on quarter rib. Quick-release 3- or 5-round detachable magazine w/recessed side release. Barrel selector on trigger and cocking indicators in tang. European walnut buttstock and forearm matte lacquer finish. Imported 1989 to 1994.
Standard calibers . . . . NiB $726 Ex $652 Gd $440
Magnum calibers . . . . Add $25

PREMIUM GRADE RIFLE

Similar to New Generation rifles except w/hand-checkered deluxe wood stock w/roll-over check-piece and rosewood grip cap and forend tip. High polished blued finish. Imported from 1989 to 1994.
Standard calibers . . . . NiB $860 Ex $711 Gd $456
Magnum calibers . . . . Add $40

WHITETAIL BOLT-ACTION RIFLE SERIES

New Generation design in multiple model configurations and three action lengths chambered .22-250 to .338 Win. Mag.

BATTUE MODEL

Similar to Hunter Model except designed for snapshooting w/hooded front and open rear sights on quarter rib. Blued finish. Checkered select walnut stock w/matt lacquered finish. Imported 1991 to 1997.
Battue model (standard w/sights) . . NiB $525 Ex $451 Gd $347
Magnum calibers, add $30

CONTINENTAL MODEL

Similar to Hunter Model except w/prone-style stock w/wider forearm and 26-inch heavy bbl. chambered for 17 Rem., .22-250 Rem., .223 Rem., .308 Win. (Varmint); .25-06 Rem., .270 Win., 7mm Rem. Mag., .300 Win. Mag. (Long Range). Weight: 8.6 lbs. Imported from 1991 to 2003.
Continental Long-Range model . . . . NiB $640 Ex $527 Gd $378
Continental Varmint model . . . . NiB $615 Ex $527 Gd $373
Magnum calibers, add $40

SPORTER MODEL . . . . NiB $845 Ex $735 Gd $581
Similar to Hunter Model except 23.5-inch bbl. Five round detachable mazigine. Chambered .22-250 Rem., .223 Rem., .308 Win. Weight: 8.6 lbs. Adjustable buttplate and cheekpiece w/stippled pistol grip and forend. Imported from 1998 to 2003.

WHITETAIL HUNTER MODEL

Calibers: .22-250 Rem., .223 Rem., .243 Win., .25-06 Rem., .270 Win., 7mm Rem. Mag., .308 Win .30.06, .300 Win. Mag., .338 Win. Mag. Three or 5-round detachable box magazine. 20.5- to 24.5-inch bbl. with no sights. 42 to 44.5 inches overall. Weight: 7 to 7.5 lbs. Adj. single-stage or single-set trigger. Blued or stainless finish. All-Weather synthetic or checkered select walnut stock w/matt lacquered finish. Imported from 1991 to 2002.
Standard model	NiB $590	Ex $504	Gd $374
Deluxe model	NiB $650	Ex $504	Gd $424
Synthetic model	NiB $650	Ex $504	Gd $424
Stainless model	NiB $650	Ex $504	Gd $424

Magnum calibers, add $30
Left-hand model, add $70

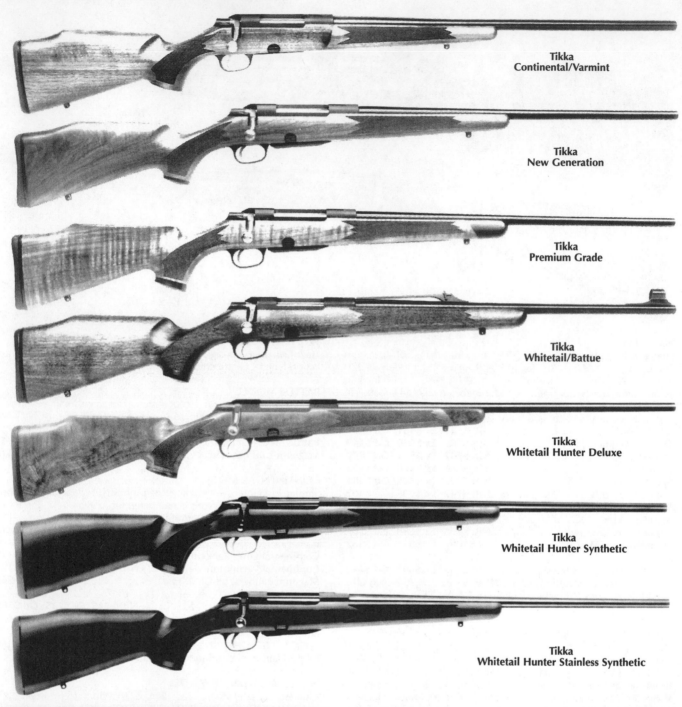

Tikka
Continental/Varmint

Tikka
New Generation

Tikka
Premium Grade

Tikka
Whitetail/Battue

Tikka
Whitetail Hunter Deluxe

Tikka
Whitetail Hunter Synthetic

Tikka
Whitetail Hunter Stainless Synthetic

UBERTI RIFLES — Lakeville, Connecticut
Mfd. By Aldo Uberti, Ponte Zanano, Italy
Imported by Stoeger Industries, Accokeek, MD

MODEL 1866 SPORTING RIFLE
Replica of Winchester Model 1866 lever-action repeater. Calibers: .22 LR, .22 WMR, .38 Spec., .44-40, .45 LC. 24.25-inch octagonal bbl. 43.25 inches overall. Weight: 8.25 lbs. Blade front sight, rear elevation leaf. Brass frame and buttplate. Bbl., magazine tube, other metal parts blued. Walnut buttstock and forearm.

Model 1866 Rifle. . . . . NiB $925 Ex $639 Gd $356
Model 1866 Carbine
(19-inch round bbl.) . . . . NiB $900 Ex $588 Gd $382
Model 1866 Trapper
(16-inch bbl.)
Disc. 1989. . . . . NiB $1100 Ex $803 Gd $577
Model 1866
Rimfire
(Indian Rifle) . . . . NiB $700 Ex $485 Gd $356
Model 1866 Rimfire
(Indian Carbine) . . . . NiB $700 Ex $485 Gd $356

Uberti Model
1873 Carbine

MODEL 1873
SPORTING RIFLE

Replica of Winchester Model 1873 lever-action repeater. Calibers: .22 LR, .22 WMR, .38 Spec., .357 Mag., .44-40, .45 LC. 24.25- or 30-inch octagonal bbl. 43.25 inches overall. Weight: 8 lbs. Blade front sight; adj. open rear. Color case-hardened frame. Bbl., magazine tube, hammer, lever and buttplate blued. Walnut buttstock and forearm.

Model 1873 Rifle . . . . NiB $1000 Ex $753 Gd $505
Model 1873 Carbine
(19-inch round bbl.) . . . . NiB $750 Ex $622 Gd $395
Model 1873 Trapper
(16-inch bbl.)
Disc. 1990 . . . . NiB $1000 Ex $660 Gd $480

HENRY RIFLE

Replica of Henry lever-action repeating rifle. Calibers: .44-40, .45 LC. 24.5-inch half-octagon bbl. 43.75 inches overall. Weight: 9.25 lbs. Blade front sight; rear sight adj. for elevation. Brass frame, buttplate and magazine follower. Bbl., magazine tube and remaining parts blued. Walnut buttstock.

Henry Rifle . . . . NiB $1100 Ex $711 Gd $531
Henry Carbine
(22.5-inch bbl.) . . . . NiB $1100 Ex $711 Gd $531
Henry Trapper
(16- or 18-inch bbl.) . . . . NiB $1100 Ex $711 Gd $531
Steel frame, add. $90

MODEL 1875
ARMY TARGET . . . . NiB $423 Ex $348 Gd $273

Calibers: .357 Mag., .44-40 Colt. Six-round cylinder. Bbl.: 18 inches. Overall length: 37 inches. Weight: 4 1/2 pounds. Carbine version of Model 1875 single-action revolver. Sights: Adjustable rear, ramp front. Plain walnut stock, polished brass butt plate and trigger guard. Case-hardened frame. Blued or nickel-plated cylinder and barrel. Made in Italy. Introduced in 1987, discontinued 1989.
Nickel finish, add. $25

ROLLING BLOCK
BABY CARBINE . . . . NiB $400 Ex $325 Gd $285

Calibers: .22 LR, .22WMR, .22 Hornet, .357 Mag. Bbl.: 22 inches. Overall length: 35 1/2 inches. Weight: 4 3/4 pounds. Copy of Remington New Model No. 4 carbine featuring brass butt plate and trigger guard; blued barrel; color case-hardened frame. Introduced in 1986.

ULTRA-HI PRODUCTS COMPANY —
Hawthorne, New Jersey

MODEL 2200 SINGLE-SHOT
BOLT-ACTION RIFLE . . . . NiB $180 Ex $139 Gd $103

Caliber: .22 LR, Long, Short. .23-inch bbl. Weight: 5 lbs. Sights: Open rear; blade front. Monte Carlo stock w/pistol grip. Made in Japan. Intro. 1977; Disc.

ULTRA LIGHT ARMS COMPANY — Granville, West Virginia

MODEL 20 BOLT-ACTION RIFLE

Calibers: .22-250 Rem., .243 Win., 6mm Rem., .250-3000 Savage, .257 Roberts, .257 Ack., 7mm Mauser, 7mm Ack., 7mm-08 Rem., .284 Win., .300 Savage, .308 Win., .358 Win. Box magazine. 22-inch ultra light bbl. Weight: 4.75 lbs. No sights. Synthetic stock of Kevlar or graphite finished, seven different colors. Nonglare matte or bright metal finish. Medium-length action available L.H. models. Made from 1985 to 1999.
Standard model . . . . NiB $2225 Ex $1996 Gd $1116
Left-hand model . . . . Add $100

MODEL 20S BOLT-ACTION RIFLE

Same general specifications as Model 20 except w/short action in calibers 17 Rem., .222 Rem., .223 Rem., .22 Hornet only.
Standard model . . . . NiB $2398 Ex $2022 Gd $1121
Left-hand model . . . . Add $100

MODEL 24 BOLT-ACTION RIFLE

Same general specifications as Model 20 except w/long action in calibers .25-06, .270 Win., .30-06 and 7mm Express only.
Standard model . . . . NiB $2225 Ex $2038 Gd $1116
Left-hand model . . . . Add$100

MODEL 28 BOLT-ACTION RIFLE . . . . . NiB $2622 Ex $1951 Gd $1240

Same general specifications as Model 20 except w/long magnum action in calibers .264 Win. Mag., 7mm Rem. Mag., .300 Win. Mag., .338 Win. Mag. only. Offered w/recoil arrester. Left-hand model available.

MODEL 40 BOLT-ACTION RIFLE

Similar to Model 28 except in calibers .300 Wby. and .416 Rigby. Weight: 5.5 lbs. Made from 1994 to 1999.
Standard model . . . . NiB $2625 Ex $1951 Gd $1240
Left-hand, model . . . . Add $100

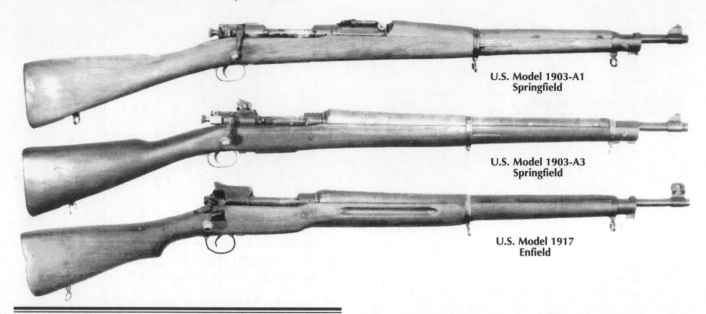

U.S. Model 1903-A1
Springfield

U.S. Model 1903-A3
Springfield

U.S. Model 1917
Enfield

UNIQUE RIFLE — Hendaye, France
Mfd. by Manufacture d'Armes des Pyrénées Francaises

T66 MATCH RIFLE. . . . . **NiB $425 Ex $342 Gd $243**
Single-shot bolt-action rifle. Caliber: .22 LR. 25.5-inch bbl. Weight: 10.5 lbs. Sights: Micrometer aperture rear; globe front. French walnut target stock w/Monte Carlo comb, bull pistol-grip, wide and deep forearm, stippled grip surfaces, adj. swivel on accessory track, adj. rubber buttplate. Made in 1966. Disc.

U.S. MILITARY RIFLES — Mfd. by Springfield Armory, Remington Arms Co., Winchester Repeating Arms Co., Inland Mfg. Div. of G.M.C., and other contractors. See notes.

Unless otherwise indicated, the following U.S. military rifles were mfg. at Springfield Armory, Springfield, Mass.

MODEL 1898
KRAG-JORGENSEN CARBINE . . **NiB $2017 Ex $1811 Gd $1054**
Same general specifications as Model 1898 Rifle except w/22-inch bbl., weight: 8 lbs., carbine-type stock. Note: The foregoing specifications apply, in general, to Carbine models 1896 and 1899, which differed from Model 1898 only in minor details.

MODEL 1898
KRAG-JORGENSEN MILITARY RIFLE . . **NiB $2017 Ex $1711 Gd $1064**
Bolt action. Caliber: .30-40 Krag. Five round hinged box magazine. 30-inch bbl. Weight: 9 lbs. Sights: Adj. rear; blade front. Military-type stock, straight grip. Note: The foregoing specifications apply, in general, to Rifle models 1892 and 1896, which differed from Model 1898.

MODEL 1903 MARK I SPRINGFIELD . . . **NiB $1991 Ex $1785 Gd $884**
Same as Standard Model 1903 except altered to permit use of the Pedersen Device. This device, officially designated "U.S. Automatic Pistol Model 1918," converted the M/1903 to a semiautomatic weapon firing a .30 caliber cartridge similar to .32 automatic pistol ammunition. Mark I rifles have a slot milled in the left side of the receiver to serve as an ejection port when the Pedersen Device was in use; these rifles were also fitted w/a special sear and cut-off. Some 65,000 of these devices were manufactured and, presumably, a like number of M/1903 rifles were converted to handle them. During the early 1930s, all Pedersen Devices were ordered destroyed and the Mark I rifles were reconverted by replacement of the special sear and cut-off w/standard components. Some 20-odd specimens are known to have escaped destruction and are in government museums and private collections. Probably more are extant. Rarely is a Pedersen Device offered for sale, so a current value cannot be assigned. However, many of the altered rifles were bought by members of the National Rifle Association through the Director of Civilian Marksmanship. Value shown is for the Mark I rifle w/o the Pedersen Device.

MODEL 1903 NATIONAL
MATCH SPRINGFIELD . . . . **NiB $1685 Ex $1502 Gd $904**
Same general specifications as Standard Model 1903 except specially selected w/star-gauged bbl., Type C pistol-grip U.S. Model 1903 National Match Springfield (Con't) stock, polished bolt assembly; early types have headless firing pin assembly and reversed safety lock. Produced especially for target shooting.

MODEL 1903 SPRINGFIELD MILITARY RIFLE
Modified Mauser-type bolt action. Caliber: .30-06. Five round box magazine. 23.79-inch bbl. Weight: 8.75 lbs. Sights: Adj. rear; blade front. Military-type stock straight grip. Note: M/1903 rifles of Springfield manufacture w/serial numbers under 800,000 (1903 to 1918) have case-hardened receivers; those between 800,000 and 1,275,767 (1918 to 1927) were double heat-treated; rifles numbered over 1,275,767 have nickle steel bolts and receivers. Rock Island production from No. 1 to 285,507 have case-hardened receivers. Improved heat treatment was adopted in May 1918 with No. 285,207; about three months later, with No. 319,921, the use of nickel steel was begun, but the production of some double-heat-treated carbon-steel receivers and bolts continued. Made 1903 to 1930 at Springfield Armory during WWI, M/1903 rifles were also made at Rock Island Arsenal, Rock Island, Ill.
W/case-hardened receiver. . . . . **NiB $5410 Ex $4637 Gd $2165**
W/double heat-treated receiver . . . **NiB $4305 Ex $3584 Gd $1586**
W/nickel steel receiver . . . . **NiB $1642 Ex $1436 Gd $921**

MODEL 1903 SPRINGFIELD SPORTER. . **NiB $1361 Ex $1885 Gd $778**
Same general specifications as National Match except w/sporting design stock, Lyman No. 48 receiver sight.

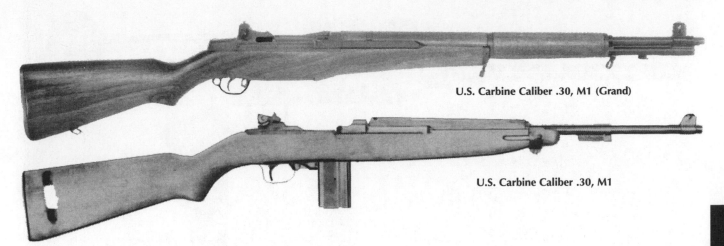

U.S. Carbine Caliber .30, M1 (Grand)

U.S. Carbine Caliber .30, M1

MODEL 1903 STYLE T
SPRINGFIELD MATCH RIFLE . . . . NiB $1550 Ex $1253 Gd $874
Same specifications as Springfield Sporter except w/heavy bbl. (26-, 28- or 30-inch), scope bases, globe front sight, weight: 12.5 lbs. w/26-inch bbl.

MODEL 1903 TYPE A
SPRINGFIELD FREE RIFLE . . . . . NiB $1840 Ex $1485 Gd $1032
Same as Style T except made w/28-inch bbl. only, w/Swiss buttplate, weight: 13.25 lbs.

MODEL 1903 TYPE B
SPRINGFIELD FREE RIFLE . . . . . NiB $2440 Ex $1973 Gd $1369
Same as Type A, except w/cheekpiece stock, palm rest, Woodie double-set triggers, Garand fast firing pin, weight: 14.75 lbs.

MODEL 1903-A1 SPRINGFIELD
Same general specifications as Model 1903 except may have Type C pistol-grip stock adopted in 1930. The last Springfields produced at the Springfield Armory were of this type; final serial number was 1,532,878, made in 1939. Note: Late in 1941, Remington Arms Co., Ilion, N.Y., began production, under government contract, of Springfield rifles of this type w/a few minor modifications. These rifles are numbered 3,000,001-3,348,085 and were manufactured before the adoption of Model 1903-A3.
Springfield manufacture . . . . NiB $1335 Ex $1191 Gd $676
Remington manufacture . . . . NiB $895 Ex $755 Gd $513

MODEL 1903-A3 SPRINGFIELD . . . . . . NiB $1598 Ex $1402 Gd $398
Same general specifications as Model 1903-A1, except modified to permit increased production and lower cost; may have either straight-grip or pistol-grip stock, bolt is not interchangeable w/earlier types, w/receiver peep sight, many parts are stamped sheet steel, including the trigger guard and magazine assembly. Quality of these rifles, lower than that of other 1903 Springfields, reflects the emergency conditions under which they were produced. Mfd. during WWII by Remington Arms Co. and L. C. Smith Corona Typewriters, Inc.

MODEL 1922-M1 22
SPRINGFIELD TARGET RIFLE . . . . NiB $1190 Ex $964 Gd $676
Modified Model 1903. Caliber: .22 LR. Five round detachable box magazine. 24.5-inch bbl. Weight: 9 lbs. Sights: Lyman No. 48C receiver, blade front. Sporting-type stock similar to that of Model 1903 Springfield Sporter. Issued 1927. Note: The earlier Model 1922, which is seldom encountered, differs from the foregoing chiefly in the bolt mechanism and magazine.

M2 22 SPRINGFIELD TARGET RIFLE . . . NiB $1285 Ex $1007 Gd $569
Same general specifications as Model 1922-M1 except w/speed-lock, improved bolt assembly adj. for headspace. Note: These improvements were later incorporated in many rifles of the preceding models (M1922, M1922MI) and arms so converted were marked "M1922M2" or "M1922MII."

NOTE: *The WWII-vintage .30-caliber U.S. Carbine was mfd. by Inland Mfg. Div. of G.M.C., Dayton, OH; Winchester Repeating Arms Co., New Haven, CT, and other contractors: International Business Machines Corp., Poughkeepsie, NY; National Postal Meter Co., Rochester, NY; Quality Hardware & Machine Co., and Rock-Ola Co., Chicago, IL; Saginaw Steering Gear Div. of G.M.C., Saginaw, M1; Standard Products Co., Port Clinton, OH; Underwood-Elliott-Fisher Co., Hartford, CT.*

CALIBER .30, M1
(GARAND) MIL. RIFLE . . . . NiB $1343 Ex $1137 Gd $1060
Clip-fed, gas-operated, air-cooled semiautomatic. Uses a clip containing 8 rounds. 24-inch bbl. Weight: W/o bayonet, 9.5 lbs. Sights: Adj. peep rear; blade front w/guards. Pistol-grip stock, handguards. Made 1937-57. Note: Garand rifles have also been produced by Winchester Repeating Arms Co., Harrington & Richardson Arms Co. and International Harvester Co. Deduct 25% for arsenal-assembled mismatches.

CALIBER .30, M1,
NATIONAL MATCH . . . . NiB $2238 Ex $1671 Gd $693
Accurized target version of the Garand. Glass-bedded stock; match grade bbl., sights, gas cylinder. "NM" stamped on bbl. forward of handguard.

MODEL 1917 ENFIELD MILITARY RIFLE . . NiB $857 Ex $741 Gd $295
Modified Mauser-type bolt action. Caliber: .30-06. Five round box magazine. 26-inch bbl. Weight: 9.25 lbs. Sights: Adj. rear; blade front w/guards. Military-type stock w/semi-pistol-grip. This design originated in Great Britain as the, "Pattern 14" and was mfd. in caliber .303 for the British Government in three U.S. plants. In 1917, the U.S. Government contracted w/these firms to produce the same rifle in caliber .30-06; over two million of these Model 1917 Enfields were mfd. While no more were produced after WWI, the U.S. supplied over a million of them to Great Britain during WWII.

NOTE: *The U.S. Model 1917 Enfield was mfd. 1917 to 1918 by Remington Arms Co. of Delaware (later Midvale Steel & Ordnance Co., Eddystone, PA); Remington Arms Co., Ilion, NY; Winchester Repeating Arms Co., New Haven, CT.*

Uzi Semiautomatic
Model B Carbine

Valmet M-62S

Valmet Hunter

**CARBINE,
CALIBER 30, M1** . . . . **NiB $786 Ex $638 Gd $449**
Gas-operated (short-stroke piston), semiautomatic. 15- or 30-round detachable box magazine. 18-inch bbl. Weight: 5.5 lbs. Sights: adj. rear; blade front sight w/guards. Pistol-grip stock w/handguard, side-mounted web sling. Made 1942 to 1945. In 1963, 150,000 surplus M1 Carbines were sold at $20 each to members of the National Rifle Assn. by the Dept. of the Army. Note: For Winchester and Rock-Ola, add 30%; for Irwin Pedersen, add 80%. Quality Hardware did not complete its production run. Guns produced by other manufacturers were marked "Unquality" & command premium prices.

U.S. REPEATING ARMS CO.

See Winchester Rifle listings.

UNIVERSAL FIREARMS, INC. — Miami, FL

DELUXE CARBINE. . . . . **NiB $425 Ex $313 Gd $186**
Same as standard model except also available in caliber .256, w/deluxe walnut Monte Carlo stock and handguard. Made fro 1965 to 1987.

STANDARD M-1 CARBINE . . . . **NiB $375 Ex $246 Gd $175**
Same as U.S. Carbine, Cal. .30, M1 except may have either wood or metal handguard, bbl. band w/ or w/o bayonet lug; 5-round magazine standard. Made from 1964 to 1987.

UZI CARBINE — Mfd. by Israel Military Industries, Israel

SEMIAUTOMATIC MODEL B CARBINE
Calibers: 9mm Parabellum, .41 Action Express, .45 ACP. 20- to 50-round magazine. 16.1-inch bbl. Weight: 8.4 lbs. Metal folding stock. Front post-type sight, open rear, both adj. Imported by Action Arms 1983 to 1989. NFA (Selective Fire) models imported by UZI America, INC., 1983 to 1994.
Model B Carbine (9mm or .45 ACP) . . . . NiB $1500 Ex $1149 Gd $963
Model B Carbine (.41 AE) . . . . NiB $1500 Ex $1149 Gd $963
Centerfire conversion unit, add $215
Rimfire conversion unit, add. $150

SEMIAUTOMATIC
MINI CARBINE . . . . **NiB $2375 Ex $2153 Gd $1535**
Similar to Uzi Model B except with 19.75-inch bbl. and chambered 9mm Parabellum only. 20-round magazine. Weight: 7.2 lbs. Imported in 1989.

**Vickers Jubilee
Single-Shot Target Rifle**

VALMET — Jyväskylä, Finland

M-62S SEMIAUTOMATIC RIFLE ...... **NiB $2500 Ex $1941 Gd $1571**
Semiautomatic version of Finnish M-62 automatic assault rifle based on Russian AK-47. Gas-operated rotating bolt action. Caliber: 7.62mmX39 Russian. 15- and 30-round magazines. 16.63-inch bbl. Weight: 8 lbs. w/metal stock. Sights: Tangent aperture rear; hooded blade front w/luminous flip-up post for low-light use. Tubular steel or wood stock. Intro. 1962. Disc.

M-71S .... **NiB $1914 Ex $1695 Gd $974**
Same specifications as M-62S except caliber 5.56mmx45 (.223 Rem.), w/open rear sight, reinforced resin or wood stock, weight: 7.75 lbs. w/former. Made from 1971 to 1989.

M-76 SEMIAUTOMATIC RIFLE
Semiautomatic assault rifle. Gas-operated, rotating bolt action. Caliber: 223 Rem. 15- and 30-round magazines. Made 1984 to 1989.
Wood stock .... **NiB $1700 Ex $1304 Gd $956**
Folding stock .... **NiB $1870 Ex $1440 Gd $1060**

M-78 SEMIAUTOMATIC RIFLE .... **NiB $1750 Ex $1443 Gd $1204**
Caliber: 7.62x51 (NATO). 24.13-inch bbl. Overall length: 43.25 inches. Weight: 10.5 lbs.

M-82 SEMIAUTOMATIC CARBINE .... **NiB $1676 Ex $1309 Gd $1105**
Caliber: .223 Rem. 15- or 30-round magazine. 17-inch bbl. 27 inches overall. Weight: 7.75 lbs.

MODEL 412 S DOUBLE RIFLE .... **NiB $1025 Ex $963 Gd $807**
Boxlock. Manual or automatic extraction. Calibers: .243, .308, .30-06, .375 Win., 9.3x74R. Bbls.: 24-inch over/under. Weight: 8.63 lbs. American walnut checkered stock and forend.

HUNTER SEMIAUTOMATIC RIFLE .... **NiB $895 Ex $725 Gd $568**
Similar to M-78 except in calibers .223 Rem. (5.56mm), .243 Win., .308 Win. (7.62 NATO) and .30-06. Five , 9- or 15-round magazine. 20.5-inch plain bbl. 42 inches overall. Weight: 8 lbs. Sights: Adj. combination scope mount/rear; blade front, mounted on gas tube. Checkered European walnut buttstock and extended checkered forend and handguard. Imported from 1986 to 1989.

VICKERS LTD. — Crayford, Kent, England

**JUBILEE MODEL SINGLE-SHOT-
TARGET RIFLE** .... **NiB $466 Ex $363 Gd $234**
Round-receiver Martini-type action. Caliber: .22 LR. 28-inch heavy bbl. Weight: 9.5 lbs. Sights: Parker-Hale No. 2 front; Perfection rear peep. One-piece target stock w/full forearm and pistol-grip. Made before WWII.

EMPIRE MODEL .... **NiB $517 Ex $388 Gd $260**
Similar to Jubilee Model except w/27- or 30-inch bbl., straight-grip stock, weight: 9.25 lbs. w/30-inch bbl. Made before WWII.

VOERE — Manufactured in Vohrenvach, Ger.

**VEC-91 LIGHTNING
BOLT-ACTION RIFLE** .... **NiB $2602 Ex $2099 Gd $1457**
Features unique electronic ignition system to activate or fire caseless ammunition. Calibers: .5.56 UCC (.222 Cal.), 6mm UCC caseless. Five round magazine. 20-inch bbl. 39 inches overall. Weight: 6 lbs. Open adj. rear sight. Drilled and tapped for scope mounts. European walnut stock w/cheekpiece. Twin forward locking lugs. Imported from 1992 to date.

VOERE, VOELTER & COMPANY — Vaehrenbach, Germany

Mauser-Werke acquired Voere in 1987 and all models are now marketed under new designations.

MODEL 1007 BIATHLON REPEATER ..... **NiB $391 Ex $314 Gd $211**
Caliber: 22 LR. Five round magazine. 19.5-inch bbl. 39 inches overall. Weight: 5.5 lb. Sights: Adj. rear, blade front. Plain beechwood stock. Imported from 1984 to 1986.

MODEL 1013 BOLT-ACTION REPEATER ..... **NiB $710 Ex $504 Gd $350**
Same as Model 1007 except w/military-style stock in 22 WMR caliber. Double-set triggers optional. Imported 1984 to 1986 by KDF, Inc.

MODEL 2107 BOLT-ACTION REPEATER
Caliber: 22 LR. Five or 8-round magazine. 19.5-inch bbl. 41 inches overall. Weight: 6 lbs. Sights: Adj. rear sight, hooded front. European hardwood Monte Carlo-style stock. Imported 1986 by KDF, Inc.
Standard model .... **NiB $388 Ex $260 Gd $182**
Deluxe model .... **NiB $440 Ex $311 Gd $234**

WALTHER RIFLES — Mfd. by the German firms of Waffenfabrik Walther and Carl Walther Sportwaffenfabrik

The following Walther rifles were mfd. before WWII by Waffenfabrik Walther, Zella-Mehlis (Thür.), Germany.

**MODEL 1 AUTOLOADING
RIFLE (LIGHT)** .... **NiB $895 Ex $666 Gd $408**
Similar to Standard Model 2 but w/20-inch bbl., lighter stock, weight: 4.5 lbs.

MODEL 2 AUTOLOADING RIFLE .... **NiB $995 Ex $614 Gd $483**
Bolt-action, may be used as autoloader, manually operated repeater or single-shot. Caliber: .22 LR. Five or 9-round detachable box magazine. 24.5-inch bbl. Weight: 7 lbs. Sights: Tangent-curve rear; ramp front. Sporting stock w/checkered pistol grip, grooved forearm, swivels. Disc.

RIFLES

Walther Model 1

Walther Model 2

Walther Model GX-1

Walther Model KKM-S

Walther Model U.I.T.
Super Match

OLYMPIC BOLT-ACTION
MATCH RIFLE . . . . **NiB $1261 Ex $1019 Gd $715**
Single-shot. Caliber: .22 LR. 26-inch heavy bbl. Weight: 13 lbs.
Sights: Micrometer extension rear; interchangeable front. Target
stock w/checkered pistol-grip, thumbhole, full beavertail forearm
covered w/corrugated rubber, palm rest, adj. Swiss-type buttplate,
swivels. Disc.

MODEL V BOLT-ACTION
SINGLE-SHOT RIFLE . . . . **NiB $597 Ex $433 Gd $314**
Caliber: .22 LR. 26-inch bbl. Weight: 7 lbs. Sights: Open rear; ramp
front. Plain pistol-grip stock w/grooved forearm. Disc.

MODEL V MEISTERBÜCHSE
(CHAMPION) . . . . **NiB $675 Ex $494 Gd $335**
Same as standard Model V except w/micrometer open rear sight and
checkered pistol-grip. Disc.

POST WWII MODELS
*The Walther rifles listed below have been manufactured since WWII
by Carl Walther Sportwaffenfabrik, Ulm (Donau), Germany.*

MODEL GX-1 FREE RIFLE . . . . . . **NiB $1895 Ex $1487 Gd $869**
Bolt-action, single-shot. Caliber: .22 LR. 25.5-inch heavy bbl.
Weight: 15.9 lbs. Sights: Micrometer aperture rear; globe front.
Thumbhole stock w/adj. cheekpiece and buttplate w/removable
hook, accessory rail. Left-hand stock available. Accessories furnished include hand stop and sling swivel, palm rest, counterweight assembly.

MODEL KKJ SPORTER . . . . **NiB $1250 Ex $1064 Gd $570**
Bolt action. Caliber: .22 LR. Five round box magazine. 22.5-
inch bbl. Weight: 5.5 lbs. Sights: Open rear; hooded ramp front.
Stock w/cheekpiece, checkered pistol-grip and forearm, sling
swivels. Disc.

MODEL KKJ-HO . . . . **NiB $1454 Ex $1348 Gd $1014**
Same as Model KKJ except chambered for .22 Hornet. Disc.

MODEL KKJ-MA . . . . **NiB $1250 Ex $1194 Gd $566**
Same as Model KKJ except chambered for .22 WMR. Disc.

MODEL KKM INTERNATIONAL
MATCH RIFLE . . . . **NiB $880 Ex $617 Gd $570**
Bolt-action, single-shot. Caliber: .22 LR. 28-inch heavy bbl. Weight: 15.5 lbs. Sights: Micrometer aperture rear; globe front. Thumbhole stock w/high comb, adj. hook buttplate, accessory rail. Left-hand stock available. Disc.

MODEL KKM-S . . . . **NiB $935 Ex $829 Gd $596**
Same specifications as Model KKM, except w/adj. cheekpiece. Disc.

MOVING TARGET MATCH RIFLE . . . . **NiB $1005 Ex $747 Gd $495**
Bolt-action, single-shot. Caliber: .22 LR. 23.6-inch bbl. w/weight. Weight: 8.6 lbs. Supplied w/o sights. Thumbhole stock w/adj. cheekpiece and buttplate. Left-hand stock available.

PRONE 400 TARGET RIFLE . . . . **NiB $750 Ex $691 Gd $459**
Bolt-action, single-shot. Caliber: .22 LR. 25.5-inch heavy bbl. Weight: 10.25 lbs. Supplied w/o sights. Prone stock w/adj. cheekpiece and buttplate, accessory rail. Left-hand stock available. Disc.

MODEL SSV VARMINT RIFLE . . . . . **NiB $700 Ex $663 Gd $457**
Bolt-action, single-shot. Calibers: .22 LR, .22 Hornet. 25.5-inch bbl. Weight: 6.75 lbs. Supplied w/o sights. Monte Carlo stock w/high cheekpiece, full pistol grip and forearm. Disc.

MODEL U.I.T. SPECIAL MATCH RIFLE . . . . . **NiB $1125 Ex $1011 Gd $727**
Bolt-action, single-shot. Caliber: .22 LR. 25.5-inch bbl. Weight: 10.2 lbs. Sights: Micrometer aperture rear; globe front. Target stock w/high comb, adj. buttplate, accessory rail. Left-hand stock avail. Disc. 1993.

MODEL U.I.T. SUPER MATCH RIFLE . . . . . . **NiB $1125 Ex $1036 Gd $753**
Bolt-action, single-shot. Caliber: .22 LR. 25.5-inch heavy bbl. Weight: 10.2 lbs. Micrometer aperture rear; globe front. Target stock w/support for off-hand shooting, high comb, adj. buttplate and swivel. Left-hand stock available. Disc. 1993.

MONTGOMERY WARD — Chicago, Illinois
Western Field and Hercules Models

Firearms under the "private label" names of Western Field and Hercules are manufactured by such firms as Mossberg, Stevens, Marlin, and Savage for distribution and sale by Montgomery Ward.

MODEL 14M-497B WESTERN FIELD
BOLT-ACTION RIFLE . . . . **NiB $126 Ex $106 Gd $79**
Caliber: .22 RF. Seven round detachable box magazine. 24-inch bbl. Weight: 5 lbs. Sights: Receiver peep; open rear; hooded ramp front. Pistol-grip stock. Mfg. by Mossberg.

MODEL M771 WESTERN FIELD
LEVER-ACTION RIFLE . . . . **NiB $177 Ex $151 Gd $121**
Calibers: .30-30, .35 Rem. Six round tubular magazine. 20-inch bbl. Weight: 6.75 lbs. Sights: Open rear; ramp front. Pistol-grip or straight stock, forearm w/barrel band. Mfg. by Mossberg.

MODEL M772 WESTERN FIELD
LEVER-ACTION RIFLE . . . . **NiB $202 Ex $177 Gd $126**
Calibers: .30-30, .35 Rem. Six round tubular magazine. 20-inch bbl. Weight: 6.75 lbs. Sights: Open rear; ramp front. Pistol-grip or straight stock, forearm w/bbl. band. Mfg. by Mossberg.

MODEL M775
BOLT-ACTION RIFLE . . . . **NiB $136 Ex $121 Gd $95**
Calibers: .222 Rem., .22-250, .243 Win., .308 Win. Four round magazine. Weight: 7.5 lbs. Sights: Folding leaf rear; ramp front. Monte Carlo stock w/cheekpiece, pistol-grip. Mfg by Mossberg.

MODEL M776
BOLT-ACTION RIFLE . . . . **NiB $228 Ex $202 Gd $144**
Calibers: .222 Rem., .22-250, .243 Win., .308 Win. Four round magazine. Weight: 7.5 lbs. Sights: Folding leaf rear; ramp front. Monte Carlo stock w/cheekpiece, pistol-grip. Mfg. by Mossberg.

MODEL M778
LEVER-ACTION . . . . **NiB $223 Ex $177 Gd $126**
Calibers: .30-30, .35 Rem. Six round tubular magazine. 20-inch bbl. Weight: 6.75 lbs. Sights: Open rear; ramp front. Pistol-grip or straight stock, forearm w/bbl. band. Mfg. by Mossberg.

MODEL M780
BOLT-ACTION RIFLE . . . . **NiB $228 Ex $202 Gd $151**
Calibers: .222 Rem., .22-250, .243 Win., .308 Win. Four round magazine. Weight: 7.5 lbs. Sights: Folding leaf rear; ramp front. Monte Carlo stock w/cheekpiece, pistol grip. Mfg. by Mossberg.

MODEL M782
BOLT-ACTION RIFLE . . . . **NiB $228 Ex $202 Gd $151**
Same general specifications as Model M780.

MODEL M808 . . . . **NiB $128 Ex $111 Gd $84**
Takedown. Caliber: .22RF. Fifteen round tubular magazine. Bbls.: 20- and 24-inch. Weight: 6 lbs. Sights: Open rear; bead front. Pistol-grip stock. Mfg. by Stevens.

MODEL M832 BOLT-ACTION RIFLE . . . . . . **NiB $136 Ex $116 Gd $85**
Caliber: .22 RF. Seven round clip magazine. 24-inch bbl. Weight: 6.5 lbs. Sights: Open rear; ramp front. Mfg. by Mossberg.

MODEL M836 . . . . **NiB $141 Ex $116 Gd $95**
Takedown. Caliber: .22RF. Fifteen round tubular magazine. Bbls.: 20- and 24-inch. Weight: 6 lbs. Sights: Open rear; bead front. Pistol-grip stock. Mfg. by Stevens.

MODEL M865 LEVER-ACTION CARBINE . . **NiB $167 Ex $126 Gd $111**
Hammerless. Caliber: .22RF. Tubular magazine. Made w/both 18.5-inch and 20-inch bbls., forearm w/bbl. band, swivels. Weight: 5 lbs. Mfg. by Mossberg.

MODEL M894
AUTO-LOADING CARBINE . . . . . . **NiB $151 Ex $126 Gd $100**
Caliber: .22 RF. Fifteen round tubular magazine. 20-inch bbl. Weight: 6 lbs. Sights: Open rear; ramp front. Monte Carlo stock w/pistol-grip. Mfg. by Mossberg.

MODEL M-SD57 . . . . **NiB $136 Ex $116 Gd $85**
Takedown. Caliber: .22RF. 15-round tubular magazine. Bbls.: 20- and 24-inch. Weight: 6 lbs. Sights: Open rear; bead front. Pistol-grip stock. Mfg. by Stevens.

WEATHERBY, INC. — Atascadero, CA
(Formerly South Gate, CA)

CROWN CUSTOM RIFLE . . . . . **NiB $8250 Ex $6200 Gd $4243**
Calibers: .240, .30-06, .257, .270, 7mm, .300, and .340. Bbl.: Made to order. Super fancy walnut stock. Also available w/engraved barreled action including gold animal overlay.

RIFLES

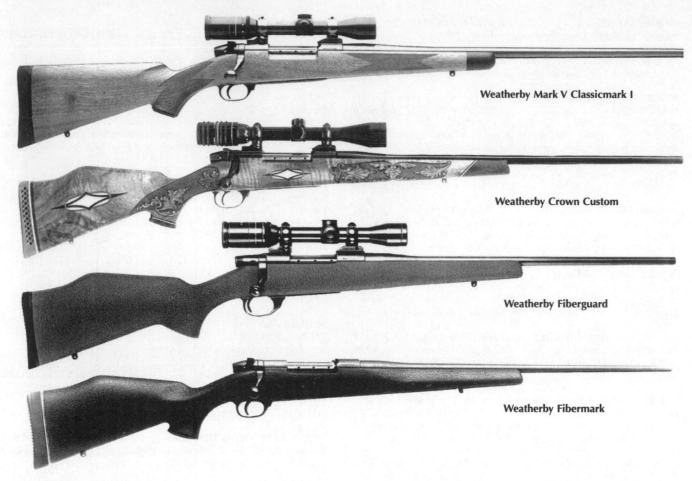

Weatherby Mark V Classicmark I

Weatherby Crown Custom

Weatherby Fiberguard

Weatherby Fibermark

DELUXE .378 MAGNUM RIFLE ...... NiB $2175 Ex $2085 Gd $1451
Same general specifications as Deluxe Magnum in other calibers
except caliber .378 W. M. Schultz & Larsen action; 26-inch bbl.
Disc. 1958.

DELUXE MAGNUM RIFLE..... NiB $1775 Ex $1540 Gd $1122
Calibers: .220 Rocket, .257 Weatherby Mag., .270 W.M. 7mm
W.M., .300 W.M., .375 W.M. Specially processed FN Mauser
action. 24-inch bbl. (26-inch in .375 cal.). Monte Carlo-style stock
w/cheekpiece, black forend tip, grip cap, checkered pistol-grip and
forearm, quick-detachable sling swivels. Value shown is for rifle w/o
sights. Disc. 1958.

DELUXE RIFLE.............. NiB $1775 Ex $1141 Gd $832
Same general specifications as Deluxe Magnum except chambered
for standard calibers such as .270, .30-06, etc. Disc. 1958.

FIBERGUARD RIFLE .... NiB $763 Ex $634 Gd $454
Same general specifications as Vanguard except for fiberglass stock
and matte metal finish. Disc. 1988.

FIBERMARK RIFLE............. NiB $1310 Ex $980 Gd $671
Same general specifications as Mark V except w/molded fiberglass
stock, finished in a nonglare black wrinkle finish. The metal is finished in a non-glare matte finish. Disc. 1993.

MARK V ACCUMARK BOLT-ACTION REPEATING
Weatherby Mark V magnum action. Calibers: .257 Wby., .270 Wby.,
7mm Rem. Mag., 7mm Wby., 7mm STW, .300 Win. Mag., .300 Wby.
Mag., .30-338 Wby., .30-378 Wby. and .340 Wby. 26- or 28-inch

stainless bbl. w/black oxide flutes. 46.5 or 48.5 inches overall.
Weight: 8 to 8.5 lbs. No sights, drilled and tapped for scope.
Stainless finish w/blued receiver. H-S Precision black synthetic stock
w/aluminum bedding plate, recoil pad and sling swivels. Imported
from 1996 to date.
Mark V Accumark (.30-338
& .30-378 Wby. Mag.)............... NiB $1575 Ex $1150 Gd $804
Mark V Accumark (All other calibers).... NiB $1550 Ex $991 Gd $696
Mark V Left-Action, add $75

MARK V ACCUMARK
LIGHT WEIGHT RIFLE........ NiB $1300 Ex $1105 Gd $667
Similar to the Mark V Accumark except w/LightWeight Mark V
action designed for standard calibers w/sixlocking lugs rather than
nine. 24-inch stainless bbl. Weight: 5.75 lbs. Gray or black Monte
Carlo-style composite Kevlar/fiberglass stock w/Pachmayr
"Decelerator" pad. No sights. Imported from 1997 to 2004.

MARK V
CLASSICMARK I RIFLE
Same general specifications as Mark V except w/checkered select
American Claro walnut stock w/oil finish and presentation recoil
pad. Satin metal finish. Imported from 1992 to 1993.
Calibers .240 to .300 Wby. .... NiB $1095 Ex $854 Gd $535
Caliber .340 Wby. .... NiB $1095 Ex $860 Gd $535
Caliber .378 Wby. .... NiB $1125 Ex $870 Gd $535
Caliber .416 Wby. .... NiB $1150 Ex $922 Gd $535
Caliber .460 Wby. .... NiB $1250 Ex $999 Gd $561

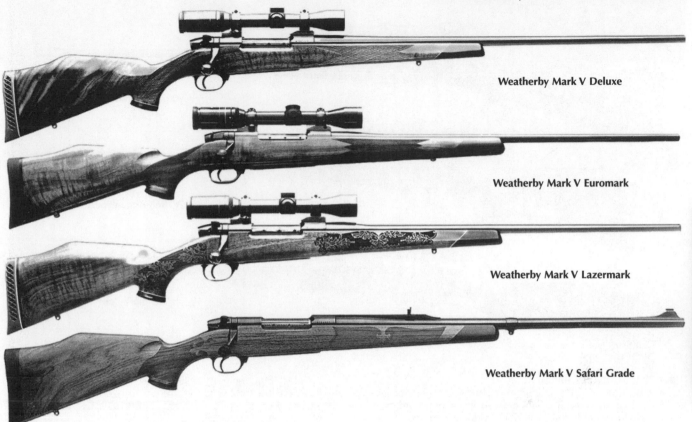

Weatherby Mark V Deluxe

Weatherby Mark V Euromark

Weatherby Mark V Lazermark

Weatherby Mark V Safari Grade

MARK V CLASSICMARK LL RIFLE

Same general specifications as Classicmark I except w/checkered select American walnut stock w/oil finish steel grip cap and Old English recoil pad. Satin metal finish. Right-hand only. Imported from 1992 to 1993.

Calibers .240 to .340 Wby.
(26-inch bbl.). . . . . NiB $1525 Ex $952 Gd $792
Caliber .378 Wby. . . . . NiB $1125 Ex $978 Gd $843
Caliber .416 Wby. . . . . NiB $1150 Ex $1005 Gd $991
Caliber .460 Wby. . . . . NiB $1250 Ex $1136 Gd $1024

MARK V DELUXE RIFLE. . . . . . . NiB $2575 Ex $1793 Gd $1555

Similar to Mark V Sporter except w/Lightweight Mark V action designed for standard calibers w/sixlocking lugs rather than nine, 4- or 5-round magazine. 24-inch bbl. 44 inches overall. Weight: 6.75 lbs. Checkered Monte Carlo American walnut stock w/rosewood forend and pistol grip and diamond inlay. Imported from 1957 to date.

WEATHERBY MARK V DELUXE BOLT-ACTION SPORTING RIFLE

Mark V action, right or left hand. Calibers: .22-250, .30-06- .224 Weatherby Varmintmaster; .240, .257, .270, 7mm, .300, .340, .375, .378, .416, .460 Weatherby Magnums. Box magazine holds 2 to 5 cartridges depending on caliber. 24- or 26-inch bbl. Weight: 6.5 to 10.5 lbs. Monte Carlo-style stock w/cheekpiece, skip checkering, forend tip, pistol-grip cap, recoil pad, QD swivels. Values shown are for rifles w/o sights. Made in Germany 1958 to 1969; in Japan 1970 to 1994. Values shown for Japanese production.

Calibers .22-250, .224 . . . . NiB $1750 Ex $1373 Gd $921
Caliber .375 H&H Magnum . . . . NiB $1775 Ex $1018 Gd $709
Caliber .378 Weatherby Magnum . . . . . . NiB $2175 Ex $1097 Gd $865
Caliber .416 Weatherby Magnum . . . . . . NiB $2175 Ex $1148 Gd $786
Caliber .460 Weatherby Magnum . . . . . NiB $2575 Ex $1377 Gd $1047

MARK V EUROMARK BOLT-ACTION RIFLE

Same general specifications as other Mark V rifles except w/hand-rubbed, satin oil finish Claro walnut stock and nonglare special process blue matte barreled action. Left-hand models available. Imported from 1986 to 1993. Reintroduced in 1995.

Caliber .378 Wby. Mag.. . . . . NiB $1785 Ex $1144 Gd $884
Caliber .416 Wby. Mag.. . . . . NiB $1785 Ex $1144 Gd $884
Caliber .460 Wby Mag. . . . . NiB $1847 Ex $1435 Gd $1048
Other calibers . . . . NiB $1553 Ex $783 Gd $530

MARK V LAZERMARK RIFLE

Same general specifications as Mark V except w/laser-carved stock.
Caliber .378 Wby. Mag.. . . . . NiB $1953 Ex $1541 Gd $892
Caliber .416 Wby. Mag.. . . . . NiB $1953 Ex $1541 Gd $892
Caliber .460 Wby. Mag.. . . . . NiB $1450 Ex $1145 Gd $904
Other calibers . . . . NiB $1403 Ex $1094 Gd $713

MARK V SAFARI GRADE RIFLE. . . . . . . NiB $2300 Ex $1841 Gd $1283

Same general specifications as Mark V except extra capacity magazine, bbl. sling swivel, and express rear sight typical "Safari" style.

MARK V SPORTER RIFLE

Sporter version of Mark V Magnum w/low-luster metal finish. Checkered Carlo walnut stock w/o grip cap or forend tip. No sights. Imported from 1993 to date.

Calibers .257 to .300 Wby.. . . . . . NiB $1425 Ex $860 Gd $674
.340 Weatherby . . . . NiB $1587 Ex $890 Gd $500
.375 H&H . . . . NiB $1518 Ex $890 Gd $500

MARK V LIGHTWEIGHT SPORTER RIFLE   NiB $983 Ex $803 Gd $468

Similar to Mark V Sporter except w/Lightweight Mark V action designed for standard calibers w/six locking lugs rather than nine. Imported from 1998 to date.

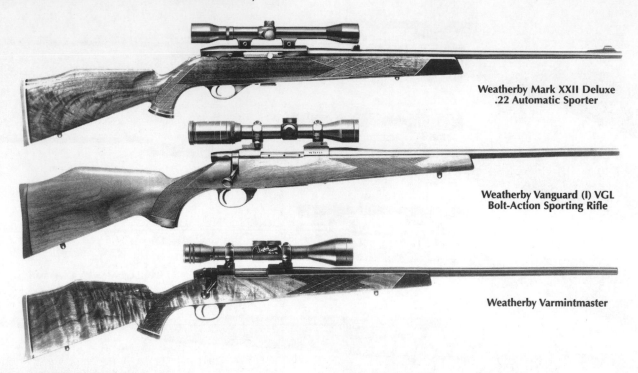

Weatherby Mark XXII Deluxe
.22 Automatic Sporter

Weatherby Vanguard (I) VGL
Bolt-Action Sporting Rifle

Weatherby Varmintmaster

MARK V STAINLESS RIFLE
Similar to the Mark V Magnum except in 400-series stainless steel w/bead-blasted matte finish. Weight: 8 lbs. Monte Carlo synthetic stock w/aluminum bedding block. Imported from 1997 to 2002.
Mark V Stainless (.30-.378 Wby.).. NiB $1420 Ex $903 Gd $550
Mark V Stainless (.375 H&H.) . . . NiB $1390 Ex $1003 Gd $550
All other calibers. . . . . NiB $1075 Ex $778 Gd $550
W/fluted bbl., add. $100

MARK V (LW) STAINLESS RIFLE . . . . NiB $1075 Ex $778 Gd $447
Similar to the Mark V (standard calibers) except in 400-series stainless steel w/bead-blasted matte finish. Five round magazine. 24-inch bbl. 44 inches overall. Weight: 6.5 lbs. Monte Carlo synthetic stock w/aluminum bedding block. Imported from 1997 to 2002.

MARK V SLS RIFLE
Acronym for Stainless Laminated Sporter. Similar to the Mark V Magnum Sporter, except w/stainless 400-series action and 24- or 26-inch stainless bbl. Laminated wood stock. Weight: 8.5 lbs. Black oxide bead-blasted matte blue finish. Imported from 1997 to date.
Mark V SLS (.340 Wby.). . . . . NiB $1124 Ex $1017 Gd $756
All other calibers. . . . . NiB $1200 Ex $981 Gd $644

MARK V SYNTHETIC RIFLE
Similar to the Mark V Magnum except w/Monte Carlo synthetic stock w/aluminum bedding block. 24- or 26-inch standard tapper or fluted bbl. Weight: 7.75 to 8 lbs. Matte blue finish. Imported from 1995 to date.
Mark V Synthetic (.340 Wby.) . . . . NiB $1045 Ex $775 Gd $518
Mark V Synthetic (.30-378 Wby.) . . . . NiB $1084 Ex $754 Gd $518
All other calibers . . . . NiB $789 Ex $608 Gd $428
W/fluted bbl., add. $100

MARK V ULTRA LIGHT WEIGHT RIFLE
Similar to the Mark V Magnum except w/skeletonized bolt handle. 24- or 26-inch fluted stainless bbl. chambered .257 Wby., .270 Wby., 7mm Rem. Mag., 7mm Wby., .300 Win. Mag., .300 Wby. Monte Carlo synthetic stock w/aluminum bedding block. Weight:

6.75 lbs. Imported from 1998 to date.
Mark V Ultra Lightweight
(standard calibers). . . . . NiB $1559 Ex $1321 Gd $826
Mark V Ultra Lightweight
(Weatherby calibers) . . . . NiB $1784 Ex $1472 Gd $1012
Mark V Ultra Lightweight
(Left-hand action), add $170

MARK XXII DELUXE .22 AUTOMATIC
SPORTER, CLIP-FED MODEL . . . . NiB $795 Ex $492 Gd $365
Semiautomatic w/single-shot selector. Caliber: .22 LR. Five and 10-round clip magazines. 24-inch bbl. Weight: 6 lbs. Sights: Folding leaf open rear; ramp front. Monte Carlo-type stock w/cheekpiece, pistol-grip, forend tip, grip cap, skip checkering, QD swivels. Intro. 1964. Made in Italy from 1964 to 1969; in Japan, from 1970 to 191981; in the U.S., from 1982 to 1990.

MARK XXII, TUBULAR
MAGAZINE MODEL . . . . NiB $795 Ex $492 Gd $365
Same as Mark XXII, clip-fed model except w/15-round tubular magazine. Made in Japan from 1973-81; in the U.S., from 1982-90.

VANGUARD (I) BOLT-ACTION SPORTING RIFLE
Mauser-type action. Calibers: .243 Win., .25-06, .270 Win., 7mm Rem. Mag., .30-06, .300 Win. Mag. Five round magazine; (3-round in Magnum calibers). 24-inch bbl. Weight: 7 lbs. 14 oz. No sights. Monte Carlo-type stock w/cheekpiece, rosewood forend tip and pistol-grip cap, checkering, rubber buttpad, QD swivels. Imported from 1970 to 1984.
Vanguard Standard. . . . . NiB $435 Ex $396 Gd $262
Vanguard VGL (w/shorter
20-inch bbl., plain checkered
stock matte finish, 6.5 lbs . . . . NiB $595 Ex $490 Gd $367
Vanguard VGS (w/24-inch
bbl., plain checkered stock,
matte finish. . . . . NiB $419 Ex $369 Gd $287
Vanguard VGX
(w/higher grade finish) . . . . NiB $625 Ex $468 Gd $313

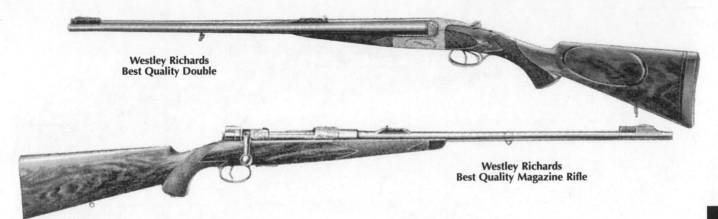

Westley Richards
Best Quality Double

Westley Richards
Best Quality Magazine Rifle

VANGUARD CLASSIC I RIFLE.... **NiB $480 Ex $391 Gd $293**
Same general specifications as Vanguard VGX Deluxe except w/hand-checkered classic-style stock, black buttpad and satin finish. Calibers .223 Rem., .243 Win. .270 Win., 7mm-08, 7mm Rem. Mag., .30-06 and .308 Win. Imported 1989 to 1994.

VANGUARD CLASSIC II RIFLE .... **NiB $675 Ex $562 Gd $416**
Same general specifications as Vanguard VGX Deluxe except custom checkered classic-style American walnut stock w/black forend tip, grip cap and solid black recoil pad, satin finish. Imported 1989 to 1994.

VANGUARD VGX DELUXE .... **NiB $625 Ex $540 Gd $390**
Calibers: .22-250 Rem., .243 Rem., .270 Wby. Mag., .270 Win., 7mm Rem. Mag., .30-06, .300 Win. Mag., .300 Wby. Mag., .338 Win. Mag. Three or 5-round capacity. 24-inch bbl. About 44 inches overall. Weight: 7 to 8.5 lbs. Custom checkered American walnut stock w/Monte Carlo and recoil pad. Rosewood forend tip and pistol-grip cap. High-luster finish. Disc. 1994.

VARMINT SPECIAL BOLT-ACTION RIFLE ... **NiB $595 Ex $409 Gd $840**
Calibers: .224 Wby., .22-250, 4-round magazine. 26-inch bbl. 45 inches overall. Weight: 7.75 lbs. Checkered walnut stock. No sights. Disc.

WEATHERMARK RIFLE
Same gen. specs. as Classicmark except w/checkered blk. Weathermark composite stock. Mark V bolt act. Cal: .240, .257, .270, .300, .340, .378, .416 and .460 Weatherby Mag.; plus .270 Win., 7mm Rem. Mag., .30-06 and .375 H&H Mag. Wt: 8 to 10 lbs. Right-hand only. Imp. 1992 to 1994.
Calibers .257 to .300 Wby........ **NiB $758 Ex $583 Gd $402**
Caliber .340 Weatherby.......... **NiB $789 Ex $608 Gd $413**
Caliber .375 H&H .... **NiB $1035 Ex $716 Gd $510**
Other non-Wby. calibers .... **NiB $755 Ex $550 Gd $400**
WEATHERMARK ALASKAN RIFLE........ **NiB $625 Ex $484 Gd $378**
Same general specifications as Weathermark except w/nonglare electroless nickel finish. Right-hand only. Imported from 1992 to 1994.

WEIHRAUCH — Melrichstadt, West Germany
Imported by European American Armory, Sharpes, FL.

MODEL HW 60 TARGET RIFLE .... **NiB $625 Ex $523 Gd $394**
Single-shot. Caliber: .22 LR. 26.75-inch bbl. Walnut stock. Adj. buttplate and trigger. Hooded ramp front sight. Push button safety. Imported 1995 to 1997.

MODEL HW 66 BOLT-ACTION RIFLE .... **NiB $575 Ex $442 Gd $296**
Caliber: .22 Hornet. 22.75-inch bbl. 41.75 inches overall. Weight: 6.5 lbs. Walnut stock w/cheekpiece. Hooded blade ramp front sight.

Checkered pistol grip and forend. Imported from1989 to 1990.
MODEL HW 660 MATCH
BOLT-ACTION RIFLE........... **NiB $850 Ex $705 Gd $450**
Caliber: .22 LR. 26-inch bbl. 45.33 inches overall. Weight: 10.75 lbs. Walnut or laminated stock w/adj. cheekpiece and buttplate. Checkered pistol grip and forend. Adj. trigger. Imported 1991 to 2005.

WESTERN FIELD RIFLES

See listings under "W" for Montgomery Ward.

WESTLEY RICHARDS & CO., LTD. — London, England

BEST QUALITY
DOUBLE RIFLE........ **NiB $34,375 Ex $27,500 Gd $18,700**
Boxlock, hammerless, ejector. Hand-detachable locks. Calibers: .30-06, .318 Accelerated Express, .375 Mag., .425 Mag. Express, .465 Nitro Express, .470 Nitro Express. 25-inch bbls. Weight: 8.5 to 11 lbs. Sights: leaf rear; hooded front. French walnut stock w/cheekpiece, checkered pistol grip and forend.

BEST QUALITY MAGAZINE RIFLE
Mauser or Magnum Mauser action. Calibers: 7mm High Velocity, .30-06, .318 Accelerated Express, .375 Mag., .404 Nitro Express, .425 Mag. Bbl. lengths: 24-inch; 7mm, 22-inch; .425 caliber, 25-inch. Weight 7.25 to 9.25 lbs. Sights: Leaf rear; hooded front.
Standard action .... **NiB $11,000 Ex $7000 Gd $5000**
Magnum action .... **NiB $12,953 Ex $10,390 Gd $7110**

WICHITA ARMS — Wichita, Kansas

MODEL WCR CLASSIC BOLT-ACTION RIFLE
Single-shot. Calibers: .17 Rem through .308 Win. 21-inch octagon bbl. Hand-checkered walnut stock. Drilled and tapped for scope w/no sights. Right or left-hand action w/Canjar trigger. Non-glare blued finish. Made from 1978 to date.
Right-hand model .... **NiB $2506 Ex $1934 Gd $1707**
Left-hand model .... **NiB $3423 Ex $2806 Gd $2017**

MODEL WSR SILHOUETTE BOLT-ACTION RIFLE
Single-shot, bolt action, chambered in most standard calibers. Right or left-hand action w/fluted bolt. Drilled and tapped for scope mount with no sights. 24-inch bbl. Canjar trigger. Metallic gray Fiberthane stock w/vented rubber recoil pad. Made 1983 to 1995.
Right-hand model .... **NiB $2479 Ex $1964 Gd $1372**
Left-hand model .... **NiB $2602 Ex $2144 Gd $1559**

RIFLES

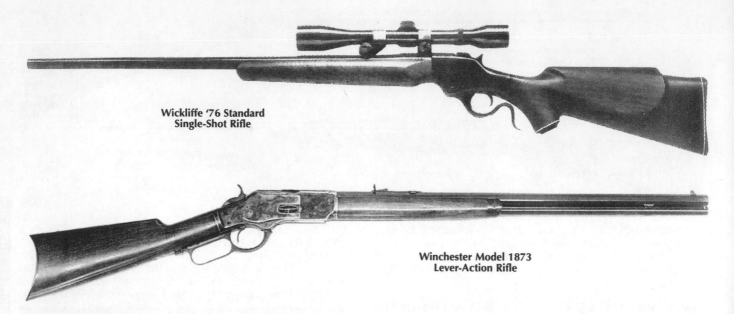

Wickliffe '76 Standard
Single-Shot Rifle

Winchester Model 1873
Lever-Action Rifle

**MODEL WMR STAINLESS
MAGNUM BOLT-ACTION RIFLE** . . . . **NiB $2147 Ex $1833 Gd $1112**
Single-shot or w/blind magazine action chambered .270 Win.
through .458 Win. Mag. Drilled and tapped for scope with no
sights. Fully adj. trigger. 22- or 24-inch bbl. Hand-checkered select
walnut stock. Made from 1980 to 1984.

MODEL WVR VARMINT RIFLE
Calibers: .17 Rem through .308 Win. Three round magazine. Right
or left-hand action w/jeweled bolt. 21-inch bbl. w/o sights. Drilled
and tapped for scope. Hand-checkered American walnut pistol-grip
stock. Made from 1978 to 1997.
Right-hand model . . . . **NiB $2500 Ex $1953 Gd $1242**
Left-hand model . . . . **NiB $2675 Ex $2159 Gd $1567**

WICKLIFFE RIFLES — Wickliffe, Ohio
Mfd. by Triple S Development Co., Inc.

**'76 COMMEMORATIVE
MODEL** . . . . **NiB $1100 Ex $979 Gd $870**
Limited edition of 100. Same as Deluxe Model except w/filled etch-
ing on receiver sidewalls, U.S. silver dollar inlaid in stock, 26-inch
bbl. only, comes in presentation case. Made in 1976 only.

'76 DELUXE MODEL . . . . **NiB $460 Ex $379 Gd $299**
Same as Standard Model except w/22-inch bbl. in .30-06 only;
high-luster blued finish, fancy-grade figured American walnut stock
w/nickel silver grip cap.

**'76 STANDARD MODEL
SINGLE-SHOT RIFLE** . . . . **NiB $395 Ex $257 Gd $197**
Falling-block action. Calibers: .22 Hornet, .223 Rem., .22-250, .243
Win., .25-06, .308 Win., .30-06, .45-70. 22-inch lightweight bbl.
(.243 and .308 only) or 26-inch heavy sporter bbl. Weight: 6.75 or
8.5 lbs., depending on bbl. No sights. Select American walnut
Monte Carlo stock w/right or left cheekpiece and pistol-grip, semi-
beavertail forearm. Intro. 1976. Disc.

STINGER MODEL . . . . **NiB $395 Ex $290 Gd $185**
Falling block, single-shot. Calibers: .22 Hornet and .223 Rem. .22-

inch bbl. w/no sights. American walnut Monte Carlo stock w/conti-
nental-type forend. Made from 1979-80.

TRADITIONALIST MODEL . . . . **NiB $395 Ex $280 Gd $172**
Falling block single-shot. Calibers: .30-06, .45-70. 24-inch bbl.
w/open sights. Hand-checkered. American walnut classic-style buttstock and forearm. Made from 1979 to 1980.

WILKINSON ARMS CO. — Covina, California

TERRY CARBINE . . . . **NiB $475 Ex $346 Gd $287**
Caliber: 9mm Para. Semiautomatic. Thirty round magazine. 16-inch
bbl. 30 inches overall. Weight: 6 lbs. Dovetailed receiver for scope
mounting. Bolt-type safety. Ejection port w/automatic trap door.
Blowback action. Fires from closed bolt. Made from 1975. Disc.

TED WILLIAMS RIFLES

See Sears, Roebuck and Company.

WINCHESTER RIFLES — Winchester
Repeating Arms Company, New Haven, CT

*Formerly Winchester Repeating Arms Co., and then mfd. by
Winchester-Western Div., Olin Corp., later by U.S. Repeating Arms
Company. In 1999, production rights were acquired by Browning
Arms Company.*

EARLY MODELS 1873 – 1918

NOTE: *Most Winchester rifles manufactured prior to 1918 used the
date of approximate manufacture as the model number. For example, the Model 1894 repeating rifle was manufactured from 1894 to
1937. When Winchester started using two-digit model numbers
after 1918, the "18" was dropped and the rifle was then called the
Model 94. The Model 1892 was called the Model 92, etc. In light of
the recent shut-down, Winchester is no longer made at New Haven.*

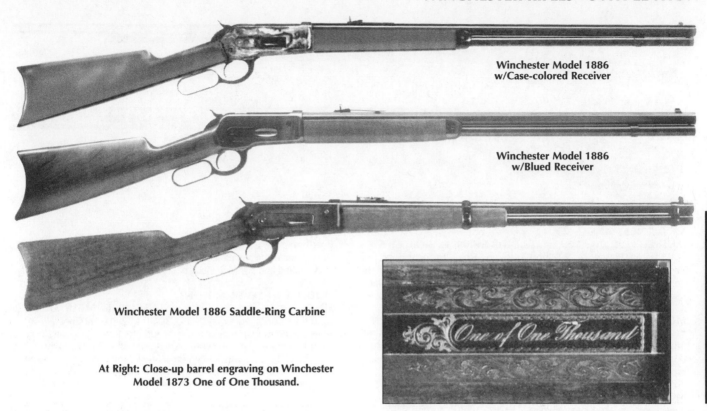

Winchester Model 1886
w/Case-colored Receiver

Winchester Model 1886
w/Blued Receiver

Winchester Model 1886 Saddle-Ring Carbine

At Right: Close-up barrel engraving on Winchester
Model 1873 One of One Thousand.

MODEL 1873 LEVER-ACTION
CARBINE . . . . NiB $4650 Ex $3877 Gd $2422
Same as Standard Model 1873 Rifle except w/20-inch bbl., 12-round magazine, weight: 7.25 lbs.

MODEL 1873 LEVER-ACTION
RIFLE . . . . NiB $4947 Ex $3356 Gd $2056
Calibers: .32-20, .38-40, .44-40; a few were chambered for .22 rimfire. Fifteen round magazine, also made w/6-round half magazine. 24-inch bbl. (round, half-octagon, octagon). Weight: 8.5 lbs. Sights: Open rear; bead or blade front. Plain straight-grip stock and forearm. Made 1873 to 1924. 720,610 rifles of this model were mfd.

MODEL 1873 —
ONE OF ONE THOUSAND . . . . NiB $195,700+ Ex $82,400+ Gd $51,500+
During the late 1870s, Winchester offered Model 1873 rifles of superior accuracy and extra finish, designated "One of One Thousand" grade, at $100. These rifles are marked "1 of 1000" or "One of One Thousand." Only 136 of this model are known to have been manufactured. This is one of the rarest of shoulder arms and, because so few have been sold in recent years, it is extremely difficult to assign a value, however, an "excellent" specimen would probably bring a price upward of $200,000.

MODEL 1873 SPECIAL
SPORTING RIFLE . . . . NiB $10,625 Ex $9090 Gd $5475
Same as Standard Model 1873 Rifle except this type has receiver case-hardened in colors, pistol-grip stock of select walnut, octagon bbl. only.

MODEL 1885 SINGLE-SHOT RIFLE
Designed by John M. Browning, this falling-block, lever-action rifle was manufactured from 1885 to 1920 in a variety of models and chambered for most of the popular cartridges of the period — both rimfire and centerfire — from .22 to .50 caliber. There are two basic styles of frames, low-wall and high-wall. The low-wall was cham-

bered only for the lower-powered cartridges, while the high-wall was supplied in all calibers and made in three basic types. The standard model for No. 3 and heavier barrels is the type commonly encountered; the thin-walled version was supplied with No. 1 and No. 2 light barrels and the thick-walled action in the heavier calibers. Made in both solid frame and takedown versions. Barrels were available in five weights ranging from the lightweight No. 1 to the extra-heavy No. 5 in round, half-octagon and full-octagon styles. Many other variations were also offered.

MODEL 1885 HIGH-WALL
SPORTING RIFLE. . . . . NiB $4895 Ex $2907 Gd $1995
Solid frame or takedown. No. 3, 30-inch bbl., standard. Weight: 9.5 lbs. Standard trigger and lever. Open rear sights; blade front sight. Plain stock and forend.

MODEL 1885 LOW-WALL
SPORTING RIFLE. . . . . NiB $1430 Ex $1316 Gd $989
Solid frame. No. 1, 28-inch round or octagon bbl. Weight: 7 lbs. Open rear sight; blade front sight. Plain stock and forend.

MODEL 1885
SCHUETZEN RIFLE . . . . NiB $9000 Ex $6748 Gd $5264
Solid frame or takedown. High-wall action. Schuetzen double-set trigger. Spur finger lever. No. 3, 30-inch octagon bbl. Weight: 12 lbs. Vernier rear peep sight; wind-gauge front sight. Fancy walnut Schuetzen stock with checkered pistol-grip and forend. Schuetzen buttplate; adj. palm rest.

MODEL 1885
SPECIAL SPORTING RIFLE . . . . NiB $7000 Ex $5373 Gd $4555
Same general specifications as the standard high-wall model except with checkered fancy walnut stock and forend.

Winchester Model 1890

Winchester Model 1892

MODEL 1885 SINGLE-SHOT
MUSKET . . . . **NiB $1500 Ex $890 Gd $762**
Solid frame. Low-wall. .22 Short and Long Rifle. 28-inch round bbl. Weight: 8.6 lbs. Lyman rear peep sight; blade front sight. Military-type stock and forend. Note: The U.S. Government purchased a large quantity of these muskets during World War I for training purposes.

MODEL 1885 SINGLE-SHOT
"WINDER" MUSKET . . . . **NiB $1430 Ex $1166 Gd $967**
Solid frame or takedown. High-wall. Plain trigger. 28-inch round bbl. Weight: 8.5 lbs. Musket rear sight; blade front sight. Military-type stock and forend w/bbl. band and sling stud/rings.

MODEL 1886 LEVER-ACTION RIFLE
Solid frame or takedown. .33 Win., .38-56, .38-70, .40-65, .40-70, .40-82, .45-70, .45-90, .50-100, .50-110. The .33 Win. and .45-70 were the last calibers in which this model was supplied. Eight round tubular magaine; also 4-round half-magazine. 26-inch bbl. (round, half-octagon, octagon). Weight: 7.5 lbs. Sights: Open rear; bead or blade front. Plain straight-grip stock and forend or standard models. Made from 1886 to 1935.
Standard model . . . . **NiB $7150 Ex $4278 Gd $2977**
Takedown model . . . . **NiB $9513 Ex $7252 Gd $5639**
**Deluxe model (pistol-grip and
high-quality walnut)** . . . . **NiB $16,525 Ex $11,000 Gd $8405**

MODEL 1886 SADDLE-RING
CARBINE . . . . **NiB $17,250 Ex $14,139 Gd $11,959**
Same as standard rifle except with 22-inch bbl., carbine buttstock and forend. Carbine rear sight. Saddle ring on left side of receiver.

MODEL 1890 SLIDE-ACTION RIFLE
Visible hammer. Calibers: .22 Short, Long, LR; .22 WRF (not interchangeable). Tubular magazine holds 15 Short, 12 Long, 11 LR; 12 WRF. 24-inch octagon bbl. Weight: 5.75 lbs. Sights: Open rear; bead front. Plain straight-grip stock, grooved slide handle. Originally solid frame; after No. 15,499, all rifles of this model were takedown-type. Fancy checkered pistol-grip stock, nickel-steel bbl. supplied at extra cost, which can also increase the value by 100% or more. Made from 1890 to 1932.
Blue WRF . . . . **NiB $2038 Ex $1668 Gd $1101**
Blue (.22 LR) . . . . **NiB $2095 Ex $2033 Gd $1132**
Color casehardened receiver . . . . **NiB $6538 Ex $5277 Gd $3664**

MODEL 1892 LEVER-ACTION
RIFLE . . . . **NiB $3300 Ex $2130 Gd $1506**
Solid frame or takedown. Calibers: .25-20, .32-20, .38-40, .44-40. Thirteen round tubular magazine; also 7-round half-magazine. 24-inch bbl. (round, octagon, half-octagon). Weight: from 6.75 lbs. up. Sights: Open rear; bead front. Plain straight-grip stock and forend. Pistol-grip fancy walnut stocks were available at extra cost and also doubles the value of the current value for standard models.

MODEL 1892 SADDLE-RING
CARBINE . . . . **NiB $5242 Ex $2433 Gd $1215**
Same general specifications as the Model 1892 rifle except carbine buttstock, forend and sights. 20-inch bbl. Saddle ring on left side of receiver.

MODEL 1894 LEVER-ACTION
RIFLE . . . . **NiB $6400 Ex $4616 Gd $3124**
Solid frame or takedown. .25-35, .30-30, .32-40, .32 Special, .38-55. Seven round tubular magazine or 4-round half-magazine. 26-inch bbl. (round, octagon, half-octagon). Weight: about 7.35 lbs. Sights: Open rear; bead front. Plain straight-grip stock and forearm on standard model; crescent-shaped or shotgun-style buttplate. Made from 1894-1937. See also Winchester Model 94 for later variations of this model.

MODEL 1894 LA DELUXE
. . . . NiB $12,507 Ex $10,230 Gd $8351
Same general specifications as the standard rifle except checkered pistol-grip buttstock and forend using high-grade walnut. Engraved versions are considerably higher in value.

MODEL 1894 SADDLE-RING
CARBINE . . . . **NiB $2800 Ex $1710 Gd $1055**
Same general specifications as the Model 1894 standard rifle except 20-inch bbl., carbine buttstock, forend, and sights. Saddle ring on left side of receiver. Weight: about 6.5 lbs.

MODEL 1894 STANDARD CARBINE . . **NiB $6450 Ex $4794 Gd $3766**
Same general specifications as Saddle-Ringle Carbine except shotgun type buttstock and plate, no saddle ring, standard open rear sight. Sometimes called "Eastern Carbine." See also Winchester Model 94 carbine.

1895 LEVER-ACTION
CARBINE . . . . **NiB $4202 Ex $2947 Gd $1939**
Same as Model 95 Standard Rifle except has 22-inch bbl., carbine-style buttstock and forend, weight: About 8 lbs., calibers .30-40 Krag, .30-03, .30-06 and .303, solid frame only.

1895 LEVER-ACTION RIFLE . . . . **NiB $3225 Ex $2040 Gd $1175**
Calibers: .30-40 Krag, .30-03, .30-60, .303 British, 7.62mm Russian, .35 Win., .38-72, .40-72, .405 Win. Four round box magazine except .30-40 and .303, which have 5-round magazines. Bbl. lengths: 24-, 26-, 28-inches (round, half-octagon, octagon). Weight: About 8.5 lbs. Sights: Open rear; bead or blade front. Plain straight-grip stock and forend (standard). Both solid frame and takedown models were made from1897 to 1931.

MODEL (1897) LEE BOLT-ACTION RIFLE
Straight-pull bolt-action. .236 U.S. Navy, 5-round box magazine, clip loaded. 24- and 28-inch bbl. Weight: 7.5 to 8.5 lbs. Sights: Folding leaf rear sight on musket; open sporting sight on sporting rifle.
Musket model . . . . **NiB $1884 Ex $1730 Gd $1086**
Sporting rifle . . . . **NiB $1987 Ex $1781 Gd $1086**

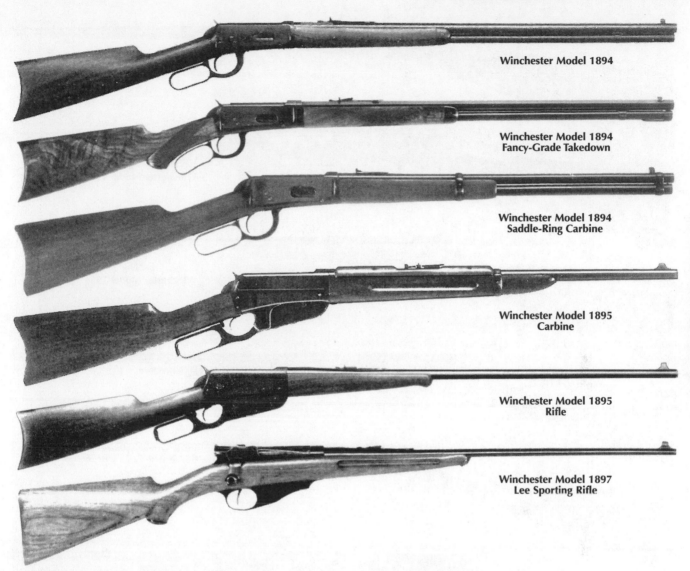

Winchester Model 1894

Winchester Model 1894
Fancy-Grade Takedown

Winchester Model 1894
Saddle-Ring Carbine

Winchester Model 1895
Carbine

Winchester Model 1895
Rifle

Winchester Model 1897
Lee Sporting Rifle

MODEL 1900 BOLT-ACTION
SINGLE-SHOT RIFLE . . . . NiB $580 Ex $471 Gd $331
Takedown. Caliber: .22 Short and Long. 18-inch bbl. Weight: 2.75 lbs. Open rear sight; blade front sight. One-piece, straight-grip stock. Made from 1899 to 1902.

MODEL 1902
BOLT-ACTION
SINGLE-SHOT RIFLE . . . . NiB $445 Ex $341 Gd $239
Takedown. Basically the same as Model 1900 with minor improvements. Calibers: .22 Short and Long, .22 Extra Long, .22 LR. Weight: 3 lbs. Made from 1902 to 1931.

MODEL 1903
SELF-LOADING RIFLE . . . . NiB $1066 Ex $824 Gd $541
Takedown. Caliber: .22 WRA. Ten round tubular magazine in buttstock. 20-inch bbl. Weight: 5.75 lbs. Sights: Open rear; bead front. Plain straight-grip stock and forearm (fancy grade illustrated). Made from 1903 to 1936.

MODEL (1904) 99 THUMB-TRIGGER BOLT-ACTION
SINGLE-SHOT RIFLE . . . . NiB $802 Ex $649 Gd $453

Takedown. Same as Model 1902 except fired by pressing a button behind the cocking piece. Made from 1904 to 1923.

MODEL 1904
BOLT-ACTION
SINGLE-SHOT RIFLE . . . . NiB $442 Ex $339 Gd $236
Similar to Model 1902. Takedown. Caliber: 22 Short, Long Extra Long, LR. 21-inch bbl. Weight: 4 lbs. Made from 1904 to 1931.

MODEL 1905
SELF-LOADING RIFLE . . . . NiB $725 Ex $550 Gd $473
Takedown. Calibers: .32 Win. S. and L., .35 Win. S. and L. Five or 10-round detachable box magazine. 22-inch bbl. Weight: 7.5 lbs. Sights: Open rear; bead front. Plain pistol-grip stock and forearm. Made from 1905 to 1920.

MODEL 1906
SLIDE-ACTION REPEATER . . . . NiB $1500 Ex $914 Gd $557
Takedown. Visible hammer. Caliber: .22 Short, Long, LR. Tubular magazine holds 20 Short, 16 Long or 14 LR. 20-inch bbl. Weight: 5 lbs. Sights: Open rear; bead front. Straight-grip stock and grooved forearm. Made from 1906 to 1932.

GRADING: **NiB** = New in Box   **Ex** = Excellent or NRA 95%   **Gd** = Good or NRA 68%

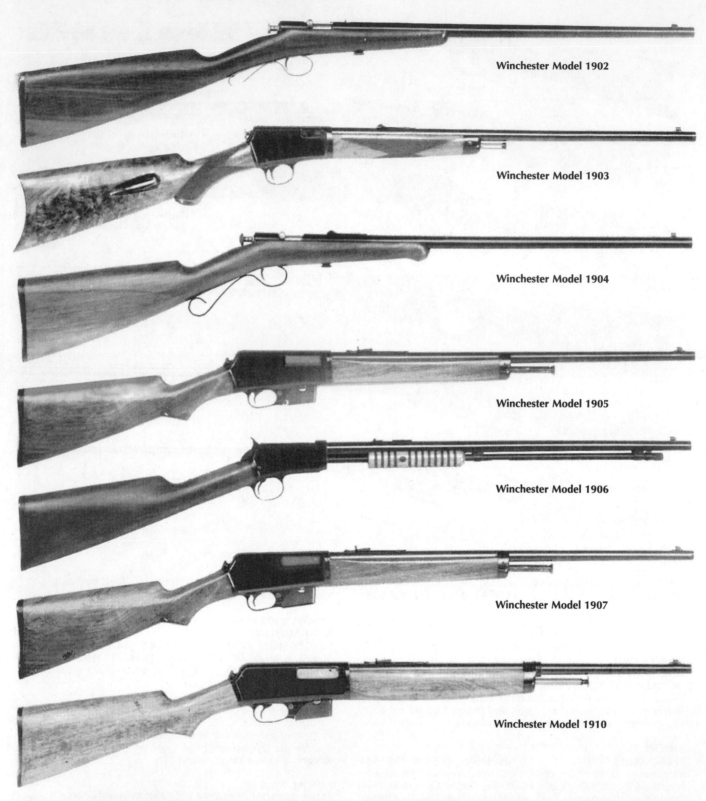

Winchester Model 1902

Winchester Model 1903

Winchester Model 1904

Winchester Model 1905

Winchester Model 1906

Winchester Model 1907

Winchester Model 1910

MODEL 1907 SELF-LOADING RIFLE . . . . . NiB $675 Ex $550 Gd $387
Takedown. Caliber: .351 Win. S. and L. Five or 10-round detachable box magazine. 20-inch bbl. Weight: 7.75 lbs. Sights: Open rear; bead front. Plain pistol-grip stock and forearm. Made 1907 to 1957.

MODEL 1910 SELF-LOADING RIFLE . . . . . NiB $850 Ex $660 Gd $464
Takedown. Caliber: .401 Win. S. and L. Four round detachable box magazine. 20-inch bbl. Weight: 8.5 lbs. Sights: Open rear; bead front. Plain pistol-grip stock and forearm. Made from 1910 to 1936.

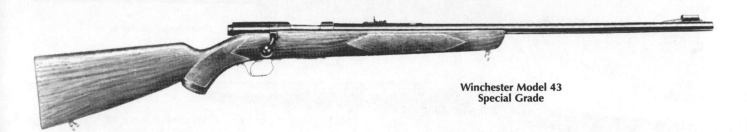

**Winchester Model 43
Special Grade**

MODEL 43 BOLT-ACTION
SPORTING RIFLE . . . . **NiB $800 Ex $658 Gd $452**
Standard Grade. Calibers: .218 Bee, .22 Hornet, .25-20, .32-20 (latter two discontinued 1950). Three round detachable box magazine. 24-inch bbl. Weight: 6 lbs. Sights: Open rear, bead front on hooded ramp. Plain pistol-grip stock with swivels. Made from 1949 to 1957.

MODEL 43 SPECIAL GRADE . . . . . . **NiB $800 Ex $722 Gd $560**
Same as Standard Model 43 except has checkered pistol-grip and forearm, grip cap.

MODEL 47 BOLT-ACTION
SINGLE-SHOT RIFLE . . . . **NiB $388 Ex $311 Gd $208**
Caliber: .22 Short, Long, I.R. 25-inch bbl. Weight: 5.5 lbs. Sights: Peep or open rear; bead front. Plain pistol-grip stock. Made from 1949 to 1954.

MODEL 52 BOLT-ACTION TARGET RIFLE
Standard bbl. First type. .22 LR. Five round box magazine. 28-inch bbl. Weight: 8.75 lbs. Sights: Folding leaf peep rear; blade front sight; standard sights various other combinations available. Scope bases. Semi-military-type target stock w/pistol grip; original model has grasping grooves in forearm; higher comb and semi-beavertail forearm on later models. Numerous changes were made in this model; the most important was the adoption of the speed lock in 1929. Model 52 rifles produced before this change are generally referred to as "slow lock" models. Last arms of this type bore serial numbers followed by the letter "A." Made 1919 to 1937.
Slow Lock model . . . . **NiB $825 Ex $577 Gd $336**
Speed Lock model . . . . **NiB $700 Ex $430 Gd $341**

MODEL 52 HEAVY BARREL . . . . . **NiB $1325 Ex $990 Gd $784**
First type speed lock. Same general specifications as Standard Model 52 of this type except has heavier bbl., Lyman No. 17G front sight, weight: 10 lbs.

MODEL 52 INTERNATIONAL MATCH RIFLE
Similar to Model 52-D Heavy Barrel except has special lead-lapped bbl., laminated "free rifle"-style stock with high comb, thumbhole, hook buttplate, accessory rail, handstop/swivel assembly, palm rest. Weight: 13.5 lbs. Made from 1969 to 1978.
With standard trigger . . . . **NiB $1504 Ex $1032 Gd $852**
With Kenyon or I.S.U. trigger . . . . **Add $300**

MODEL 52 INTERNATIONAL PRONE . . **NiB $1410 Ex $1079 Gd $857**
Similar to Model 52-D Heavy Barrel except has special lead-lapped bbl., prone stock with full pistol-grip, rollover cheekpiece removable for bore-cleaning. Weight 11.5 lbs. Made from 1975 to 1980.

MODEL 52 SPORTING RIFLE
First type. Same as Standard Model 52 of this type except has lightweight 24-inch bbl., Lyman No. 48 receiver sight and gold bead front sight on hooded ramp, deluxe checkered sporting stock with cheekpiece, black forend tip, etc. Weight: 7.75 lbs. Made 1934 to 1958. Reintroduced 1993.

Model 52 Sporter	NiB $4500	Ex $2932	Gd $1490
Model 52A Sporter	NiB $4245	Ex $2615	Gd $1194
Model 52B Sporter	NiB $4500	Ex $2391	Gd $1667
Model 52C Sporter	NiB $5000	Ex $3962	Gd $2566

Model 52 C Sporter
(1993 BAC re-issue) . . . . **NiB $600 Ex $460 Gd $390**

MODEL 52-B BOLT-ACTION RIFLE
Standard bbl. Extensively redesigned action. Supplied with choice of "Target" stock, an improved version of the previous Model 52 stock, or "Marksman" stock with high comb, full pistol grip and beavertail forearm. Weight: 9 lbs. Offered with a wide choice of target sight combinations (Lyman, Marble-Goss, Redfield, Vaver, Winchester), value shown is for rifle less sight equipment. Other specifications as shown for first type. Made from 1935 to 1947. Reintroduced 1997.
Target model . . . . **NiB $1225 Ex $919 Gd $703**
BAC model
(1997 BAC re-issue) . . . . **NiB $1225 Ex $919 Gd $703**
USRAC Sporting model . . . . **NiB $719 Ex $561 Gd $410**

MODEL 52-B BULL GUN
HEAVY BARREL . . . . **NiB $1800 Ex $947 Gd $525**
Same specifications as Standard Model 52-B except Bull Gun has extra heavy bbl., Marksman stock only, weight: 12 lbs. Heavy Bbl. model weight: 11 lbs. Made 1940 to 1947.

MODEL 52-C BOLT-ACTION RIFLE
Improved action with "Micro-Motion" trigger mechanism and new-type "Marksman" stock. General specifications same as shown for previous models. Made from 1947 to 1961, Bull Gun from 1952. Value shown is for rifle less sights.
Bull Gun (extra heavy barrel,
Wt. 12 lbs.) . . . . **NiB $1795 Ex $889 Gd $621**
Standard barrel
(Wt. 9.75 lbs.) . . . . **NiB $1376 Ex $721 Gd $608**
Target model
(heavy barrel) . . . . **NiB $1329 Ex $829 Gd $620**

NOTE: *Following WWI, Winchester had financial difficulties and, like many other firearm firms of the day, failed. However, Winchester continued to operate in the hands of receivers. Then, in 1931, The Western Cartridge Co.—under the leadership of John Olin—purchased all assets of the firm. After that, Winchester leaped ahead of all other firms of the day in firearm and ammunition development.*
The first sporting firearm to come out of the Winchester plant after WWI was the Model 20 shotgun, but this was quickly followed by the famous Model 52 bolt-action rifle. This was also a time when Winchester dropped the four-digit model numbers and began using two-digit numbers instead. This model-numbering procedure, with one exception (Model 677), continued for the next several years.

RIFLES

Winchester Model 47

Winchester Model 52
Standard Barrel

Winchester Model 52
International Match

Winchester Model 52
International Prone Target

MODEL 52-D BOLT-ACTION
TARGET RIFLE . . . . **NiB $1300   Ex $916   Gd $453**
Redesigned Model 52 action, Single-Shot. Caliber: .22 LR. 28-inch standard or heavy bbl., free-floating, with blocks for standard target scopes. Weight: With standard bbl., 9.75 lbs., with heavy barrel, 11 lbs. Restyled Marksman stock with accessory channel and forend stop, rubber buttplate. Made 1961 to 1978. Value shown is for rifle without sights.

MODEL 53 LEVER-ACTION
REPEATER . . . . **NiB $2269   Ex $1832   Gd $1274**
Modification of Model 92. Solid frame or takedown. Calibers: .25-20, .32-20, .44-40. Six round tubular half-magazine in solid frame model. Seven round in takedown. 22-inch nickel steel bbl. Weight: 5.5 to 6.5 lbs. Sights: Open rear; bead front. Redesigned straight-grip stock and forearm. Made from 1924 to 1932.

MODEL 54 BOLT-ACTION
HIGH POWER SPORTING RIFLE (I) . . . . . **NiB $1500   Ex $869   Gd $611**
First type. Calibers: .270 Win., 7x57mm, .30-30, .30-06, 7.65x53mm, 9x57mm. Five round box magazine. 24-inch bbl. Weight: 7.75 lbs. Sights: Open rear; bead front. Checkered stock w/pistol grip, tapered forearm w/Schnabel tip. This type has two-piece firing pin. Made from 1925 to 1930.

MODEL 54 BOLT-ACTION
HIGH POWER SPORTING RIFLE (II) . . . . **NiB $1150   Ex $895   Gd $560**
Standard Grade. Improved type with speed lock and one-piece firing pin. Calibers: .22 Hornet, .220 Swift, .250/3000, .257 Roberts, .270 Win., 7x57mm, .30-06. Five round box magazine. 24-inch bbl., 26-inch in cal. .220 Swift. Weight: About 8 lbs. Sights: Open rear, bead front on ramp. NRA-type stock w/checkered pistol-grip and forearm. Made 1930 to 1936. Add $200 for .22 Hornet caliber.

MODEL 54 CARBINE (I) . . . . **NiB $1495   Ex $884   Gd $601**
First type. Same as Model 54 rifle except has 20-inch bbl., plain lightweight stock with grasping grooves in forearm. Weight: 7.25 lbs.

MODEL 54 CARBINE (II). . . . . **NiB $1750   Ex $935   Gd $626**
Improved type. Same as Model 54 Standard Grade Sporting Rifle of this type except has 20-inch bbl. Weight: About 7.5 lbs. This model may have either NRA-type stock or the lightweight stock found on the first-type Model 54 Carbine.

MODEL 54 NATIONAL
MATCH RIFLE . . . . **NiB $1652   Ex $910   Gd $638**
Same as Standard Model 54 except has Lyman sights, scope bases, Marksman-type target stock, weighs 9.5 lbs. Same calibers as Standard Model.

MODEL 54 SNIPER'S
MATCH RIFLE . . . . **NiB $2405   Ex $1353   Gd $581**
Similar to the earlier Model 54 Sniper's Rifle except has Marksman-type target stock, scope bases, weight: 12.5 lbs. Available in same calibers as Model 54 Standard Grade.

MODEL 54 SNIPER'S RIFLE. . . . . **NiB $2495   Ex $1487   Gd $698**
Same as Standard Model 54 except has heavy 26-inch bbl., Lyman No. 48 rear peep sight and blade front sight semi-military stock, weight: 11.75 pounds, cal. .30-06 only.

MODEL 54 SUPER GRADE . . . . **NiB $3000   Ex $1953   Gd $1090**
Same as Standard Model 54 Sporter except has deluxe stock with cheekpiece, black forend tip, pistol-grip cap, quick detachable swivels, 1-inch sling strap.

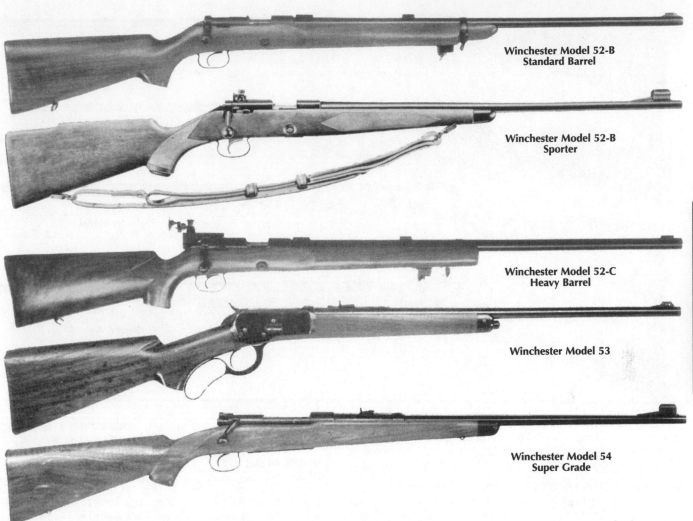

Winchester Model 52-B
Standard Barrel

Winchester Model 52-B
Sporter

Winchester Model 52-C
Heavy Barrel

Winchester Model 53

Winchester Model 54
Super Grade

RIFLES

MODEL 54 TARGET RIFLE . . . . **NiB $775 Ex $523 Gd $351**
Same as Standard Model 54 except has 24-inch medium-weight bbl. (26-inch in cal. .220 Swift), Lyman sights, scope bases, Marksman-type target stock, weight: 10.5 lbs., same calibers as Standard Model.

MODEL 55 "AUTOMATIC"
SINGLE-SHOT . . . . **NiB $349 Ex $272 Gd $194**
Caliber: .22 Short, Long, LR. 22-inch bbl. Sights: Open rear, bead front. One-piece walnut stock. Weight: About 5.5 lbs. Made from 1958 to 1960.

MODEL 55 LEVER-ACTION REPEATER
Modification of Model 94. Solid frame or takedown. Calibers: .25-35, .30-30, .32 Win. Special. Three round tubular half magazine. 24-inch nickel steel bbl. Weight: About 7 lbs. Sights: Open rear; bead front. Made from 1924 to 1932.
Standard model (straight grip) . . . . **NiB $2000 Ex $1542 Gd $929**
Deluxe model (pistol grip) . . . . **NiB $2223 Ex $1680 Gd $1058**

MODEL 56 BOLT-ACTION
SPORTING RIFLE. . . . . **NiB $1130 Ex $1096 Gd $663**
Solid frame. Caliber: .22 LR., .22 Short. Five or 10-round detachable box magazine. 22-inch bbl. Weight: 4.75 lbs. Sights: Open rear; bead front. Plain pistol-grip with Schnabel forend. Made from 1926 to 1929.

MODEL 57 BOLT-ACTION RIFLE
Solid frame. Same as Model 56 except available (until 1929) in .22 Short as well as LR with 5- or 10-round magazine. Has semi-military style target stock, bbl. band on forend, swivels and web sling, Lyman peep rear sight, weight: 5 lbs. Made from 1926 to 1936.
Sporter model . . . . **NiB $745 Ex $616 Gd $462**
Target model . . . . **NiB $694 Ex $642 Gd $488**

MODEL 58 BOLT-ACTION
SINGLE-SHOT. . . . . **NiB $1000 Ex $777 Gd $570**
Similar to Model 52. Takedown. Caliber: .22 Short, Long LR. 18-inch bbl. Weight: 3 lbs. Sights, Open rear; blade front. Plain, flat, straight-grip hardwood stock. Not serial numbered. Made 1928 to 1931.

MODEL 59 BOLT-ACTION
SINGLE-SHOT. . . . . **NiB $1200 Ex $954 Gd $725**
Improved version of Model 58, has 23-inch bbl., redesigned stock w/pistol grip, weight: 4.5 lbs. Made in 1930.

MODEL 60, 60A BOLT-ACTION SINGLE-SHOT
Redesign of Model 59. Caliber: .22 Short, Long, LR. 23-inch bbl. (27-inch after 1933). Weight: 4.25 lbs. Sights: Open rear, blade front. Plain pistol-grip stock. Made 1930 to 1934 (60), 1932 to 1939 (60A).
Model 60. . . . . **NiB $385 Ex $248 Gd $186**
Model 60A. . . . . **NiB $500 Ex $358 Gd $296**

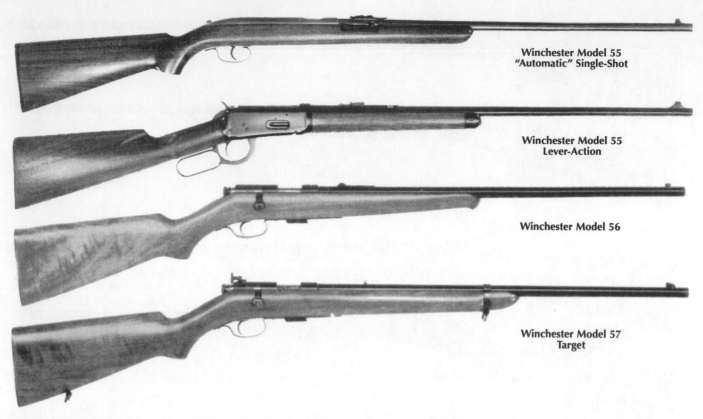

Winchester Model 55 "Automatic" Single-Shot

Winchester Model 55 Lever-Action

Winchester Model 56

Winchester Model 57 Target

MODEL 60A TARGET RIFLE . . . . . . NiB $600 Ex $414 Gd $285
Essentially the same as Model 60 except has Lyman peep rear sight and square top front sight, semi-military target stock and web sling, weight: 5.5 lbs. Made from 1932 to 1939.

MODEL 61 HAMMERLESS SLIDE-ACTION REPEATER
Takedown. Caliber: .22 Short, Long, LR. Tubular magazine holds 20 Short, 16 Long, 14 LR. 24-inch round bbl. Weight: 5.5 lbs. Sights: Open rear; bead front. Plain pistol-grip stock, grooved semi-beavertail slide handle. Also available with 24-inch full-octagon bbl. and only calibers .22 Short, .22 LR or .22 WRF. Note: Octagon barrel model discontinued 1943 to 1944; assembled 1948.
Model 61 (round barrel) . . . . NiB $1150 Ex $951 Gd $455
Model 61 (grooved receiver) . . . . NiB $1219 Ex $1125 Gd $778
Model 61 (octagon barrel) . . . . . NiB $1731 Ex $1397 Gd $970

MODEL 61 MAGNUM . . . . NiB $2375 Ex $1817 Gd $934
Same as Standard Model 61 except chambered for .22 WMR; magazine holds 12 rounds. Made from 1960 to 1963.

MODEL 62 VISIBLE HAMMER. . . NiB $1500 Ex $1250 Gd $995
Modernized version of Model 1890. Caliber: .22 Short, Long, LR. 23-inch bbl. Weight: 5.5 lbs. Plain straight-grip stock, grooved semi-beavertail slide handle. Also available in Gallery Model chambered for .22 Short only. Made from 1932 to 1959. Note: Pre-WWII model (small forearm) commands 25% higher price.

MODEL 63 SELF-LOADING RIFLE
Takedown. Caliber: .22 LR High Speed only. Ten round tubular magazine in buttstock. 23-inch bbl. Weight: 5.5 lbs. Sights: Open rear, bead front. Plain pistol-grip stock and forearm. Originally available with 20-inch bbl. as well as 23-inch. Made from 1933 to 1959. Reintroduced in 1997.
Model 63 w/23-inch bbl. . . . . NiB $1100 Ex $967 Gd $538
Model 63 w/20-inch bbl. . . . . NiB $2653 Ex $1832 Gd $1086
Model 63 grooved receiver) . . . . NiB $2656 Ex $1855 Gd $937

Model 63 Grade I (1997 BAC reissue) . . . . NiB $674 Ex $540 Gd $453
Model 63 High Grade (1997 BAC reissue). . . . . NiB $675 Ex $484 Gd $328

MODEL 64 DELUXE
DEER RIFLE . . . . NiB $1340 Ex $1084 Gd $756
Same as Standard Model 64 calibers .30-30 and .32 Win. Special, except has checkered pistol-grip and semi-beavertail forearm, swivels and sling, weighs 7.75 lbs. Made from 1933 to 1956.

MODEL 64 LEVER-ACTION REPEATER
Standard Grade. Improved version of Models 94 and 55. Solid frame. Calibers: .25-35, .30-30, .32 Win. Special. Five round tubular two-thirds magazine. 20- or 24-inch bbl. Weight: About 7 lbs. Sights: Open rear; bead front on ramp w/sight cover. Plain pistol-grip stock and forearm. Made from 1933 to 1956. Production resumed in 1972 (caliber .30-30, 24-inch bbl.). Discontinued in 1974.
Original model . . . . NiB $1000 Ex $865 Gd $585
1972-74 model . . . . NiB $450 Ex $265 Gd $184

MODEL 64 .219 ZIPPER . . . . . . NiB $4000 Ex $2957 Gd $1933
Same as Standard Grade Model 64 except has 26-inch bbl., peep rear sight. Made from 1937 to 1947.

MODEL 65 LEVER-ACTION
REPEATER . . . . NiB $4947 Ex $3163 Gd $2506
Improved version of Model 53. Solid frame. Calibers: .25-20 and .32-20. Six round tubular half-magazine. 22-inch bbl. Weight: 6.5 lbs. Sights: Open rear, bead front on ramp base. Plain pistol-grip stock and forearm. Made from 1933 to 1947.

MODEL 65 .218 BEE . . . . NiB $4952 Ex $2827 Gd $1919
Same as Standard Model 65 except has 24-inch bbl., peep rear sight. Made from 1938 ti 1947.

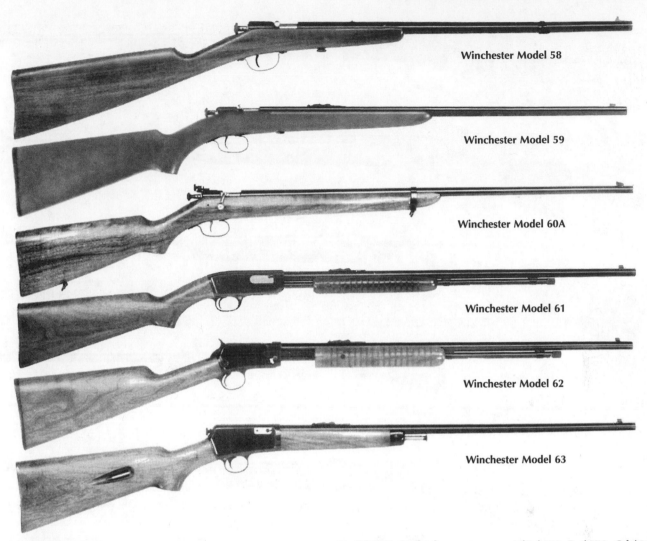

Winchester Model 58

Winchester Model 59

Winchester Model 60A

Winchester Model 61

Winchester Model 62

Winchester Model 63

MODEL 67 BOLT-ACTION
SINGLE-SHOT RIFLE . . . . **NiB $300 Ex $226 Gd $169**
Takedown. Calibers: .22 Short, Long, LR, .22 LR round (smooth-bore), .22 WRF. 27-inch bbl. Weight: 5 lbs. Sights: Open rear, bead front. Plain pistol-grip stock (original model had grasping grooves in forearm). Made from 1934 to 1963.

MODEL 67 BOY'S RIFLE . . . . **NiB $300 Ex $226 Gd $169**
Same as Standard Model 67 except has shorter stock, 20-inch bbl., weighs 4.25 lbs.

MODEL 68 BOLT-ACTION
SINGLE-SHOT . . . . **NiB $300 Ex $226 Gd $169**
Same as Model 67 except has rear peep sight. Made 1934 to 1946.

MODEL 69 BOLT-ACTION RIFLE . . **NiB $400 Ex $313 Gd $184**
Takedown. Caliber: .22 S, L, LR. Five or 10-round box magazine. 25-inch bbl. Weight: 5.5 lbs. Peep or open rear sight. Plain pistol-grip stock. Rifle cocks on closing motion of the bolt. Made from 1935 to 1937.

MODEL 69A BOLT-ACTION RIFLE
Same as the Model 69 except cocking mechanism was changed to cock the rifle by the opening motion of the bolt. Made from 1937 to 1963. Note: Models with grooved receivers command 20% higher prices.

Model 69A standard. . . . . NiB $453 Ex $370 Gd $263
Match Mdl. w/Lyman No. 57E
W receiver sight . . . . NiB $546 Ex $444 Gd $314
(Target Model w/Winchester
peep rear sight, swivels, sling. . . . . NiB $653 Ex $530 Gd $374

MODEL 70
Introduced in 1937, the Model 70 Bolt-Action Repeating Rifle was offered in several styles and calibers. Only minor design changes were made over a period of 27 years and more than 500,000 of these rifles were sold. The original model was dubbed "The Rifleman's Rifle." In 1964, the original Model 70 was superseded by a revised version with redesigned action, improved bolt, swaged (free-floating) barrel, restyled stock. This model again underwent major changes in 1972. Most visible: New stock with contrasting forend tip and grip cap, cut checkering (instead of impressed as in predecessor) knurled bolt handle. The action was machined from a solid block of steel with barrels made from chrome molybdenum steel. Other changes in the design and style of the Model 70 continued. The XTR models were added in 1978 along with the Model 70A, the latter omitting the white liners, forend caps and floor plates. In 1981, an XTR Featherweight Model was added to the line, beginning with serial number G1,440,000. This version featured lighter barrels, fancy-checkered stocks with Schnabel forend. After U.S. Repeating Arms took over the Winchester plant, the Model 70 went through even more changes as described under that section of Winchester rifles.

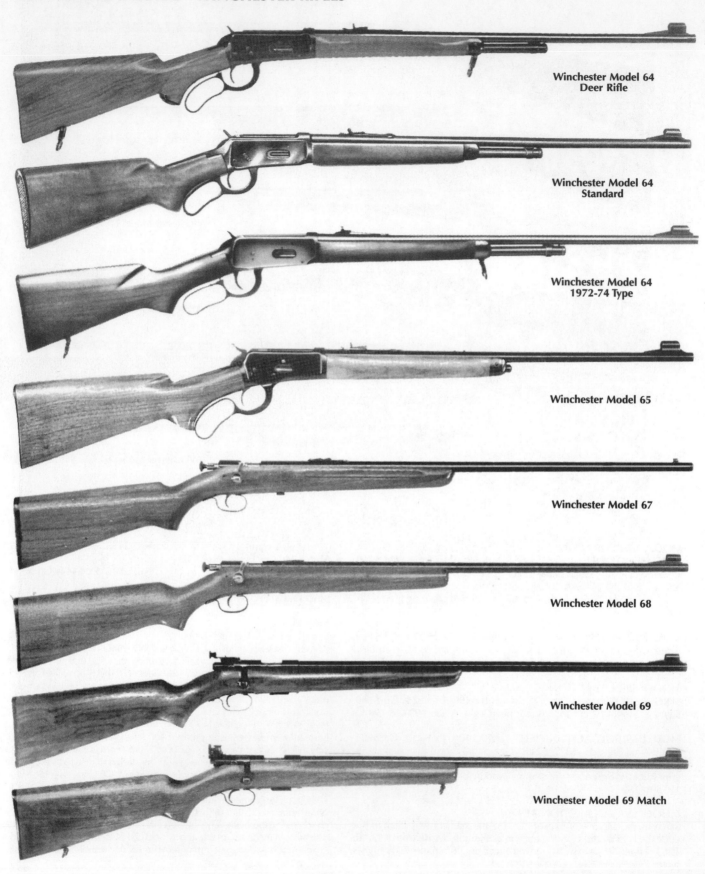

Winchester Model 64
Deer Rifle

Winchester Model 64
Standard

Winchester Model 64
1972-74 Type

Winchester Model 65

Winchester Model 67

Winchester Model 68

Winchester Model 69

Winchester Model 69 Match

Winchester Model 70
Basic Post-WWII Model

Winchester Model 70
Standard Model

Winchester Model 70
Super Grade

Winchester Model 70
African (1964)

Winchester Model 70
Deluxe (1964)

RIFLES

PRE-1964 MODEL 70

MODEL 70
AFRICAN RIFLE . . . . **NiB $7500 Ex $4786 Gd $2778**
Same general specifications as Super Grade Model 70 except w/25-inch bbl., 3-round magazine, Monte Carlo stock w/recoil pad. Weight: 9.5 lbs. Caliber: .458 Winchester Magnum. Made from 1956 to 1963.

MODEL 70 ALASKAN
Same as Standard Model 70 except calibers .338 Win. Mag., .375 H&H Mag.; 3-round magazine in .338, 4-round in .375 caliber; 25-inch bbl.; stock w/recoil pad. Weight: 8 lbs. in .338; 8.75 lbs. in .375 caliber. Made from 1960 to 1963.
.338 Win.
Magnum . . . . **NiB $3500 Ex $1510 Gd $1050**
.375 H&H . . . . **NiB $3770 Ex $1929 Gd $1338**

MODEL 70 BULL GUN . . . . **NiB $4258 Ex $3793 Gd $2248**
Same as Standard Model 70 except w/heavy 28-inch bbl., scope bases, Marksman stock, weighs 13.25 lbs., caliber .300 H&H Magnum and .30-06 only. Disc. in 1963.

MODEL 70
FEATHERWEIGHT SPORTER
Same as Standard Model 70 except w/redesigned stock and 22-inch bbl., aluminum trigger guard, floorplate and buttplate. Calibers: .243 Win., .264 Win. Mag., .270 Win., .308 Win., .30-06, .358 Win. Weight: 6.5 lbs. Made from 1952 to 1963.
.243 Win. . . . . **NiB $1650 Ex $914 Gd $653**
.264 Win. Mag. . . . . **NiB $2050 Ex $1329 Gd $935**
.270 Win. . . . . **NiB $1777 Ex $1124 Gd $793**
.30-06 Springfield . . . . **NiB $975 Ex $758 Gd $511**
.308 Win. . . . . **NiB $1100 Ex $796 Gd $567**
.358 Win. . . . . **NiB $4350 Ex $2871 Gd $1913**

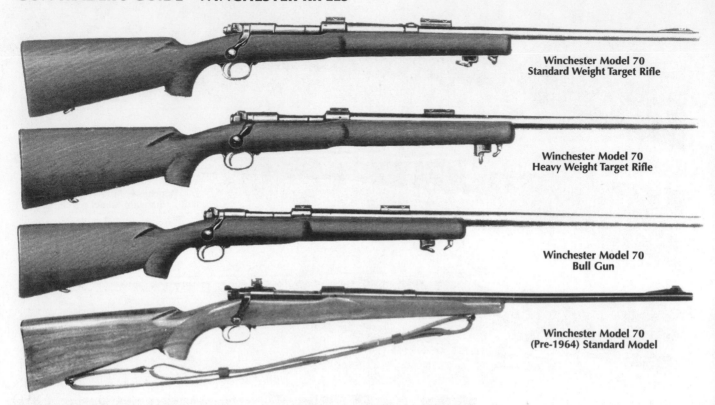

Winchester Model 70
Standard Weight Target Rifle

Winchester Model 70
Heavy Weight Target Rifle

Winchester Model 70
Bull Gun

Winchester Model 70
(Pre-1964) Standard Model

MODEL 70 NATIONAL
MATCH RIFLE . . . . **NiB $3200   Ex $1814   Gd $1531**
Same as Standard Model 70 except w/scope bases, Marksman-type
target stock, weight: 9.5 lbs. caliber .30-06 only. Disc. 1960.

MODEL 70 STANDARD GRADE
Calibers: .22 Hornet, .220 Swift, .243 Win., .250-3000, .257 Roberts, .270
Win., 7x57mm, .30-06, .308 Win., .300 H&H Mag., .375 H&H Mag. Five
round box magazine (4-round in Magnum calibers). 24-inch bbl. standard;
26-inch in .220 Swift and .300 Mag.; 25-inch in .375 Mag.; at one time a 20-
inch bbl. was available. Sights: Open rear; hooded ramp front. Checkered
walnut stock; Monte Carlo comb standard on later production. Weight: From
7.75 lbs. depending on caliber and bbl. length. Made from 1937 to 1963.

.22 Hornet (1937-58) . . . . NiB $3350 Ex $1991 Gd $1181
.220 Swift (1937-63) . . . . NiB $2350 Ex $1194 Gd $833
.243 Win. (1955-63) . . . . NiB $1916 Ex $985 Gd $730
.250-3000 Sav. (1937-49) . . . . NiB $5250 Ex $2160 Gd $1503
.257 Roberts (1937-59) . . . . NiB $3600 Ex $1908 Gd $1048
.264 Win. Mag. (1959-63) limited . . . . . . NiB $1900 Ex $1090 Gd $762
.270 Win. (1937-63) . . . . NiB $2440 Ex $1883 Gd $922
7x57mm Mauser (1937-49) . . . . NiB $6000 Ex $4363 Gd $3650
7.65 Argentine (1937 only) limited . . . . Very Rare
.30-06 Springfield (1937-63) . . . . NiB $3000 Ex $1724 Gd $910
.308 Win. (1952-63) special order . . . . Very Rare
.300 H&H (1937-63) . . . . NiB $3000 Ex $1947 Gd $867
.300 Sav. (1944-50) limited . . . . Rare
.300 Win. Mag. (1962-63) . . . . NiB $1900 Ex $1612 Gd $1120
.338 Win. Mag. (1959-63)
special order only . . . . NiB $1900 Ex $1539 Gd $1069
.35 Rem. (1941-47) limited . . . . Very Rare
.358 Win. (1955-58) . . . . Very Rare
.375 H&H (1937-63) . . . . NiB $4300 Ex $2951 Gd $1960
.458 Win. Mag. (1956-63)
Super Grade only . . . . NiB $3814 Ex $2888 Gd $1903
9x57 Mauser (1937 only) limited . . . . Very Rare

MODEL 70 SUPER GRADE
Same as Standard Grade Model 70 except w/deluxe stock w/cheek-
piece, black forend tip, pistol-grip cap, quick detachable swivels,
sling. Disc. 1960. Prices for Super Grade models also reflect rarity
in both production and caliber. Values are generally twice that of
standard models of similar configuration.

MODEL 70 SUPER GRADE FEATHERWEIGHT
Same as Standard Grade Featherweight except w/deluxe stock
w/cheekpiece, black forend tip, pistol-grip cap, quick detachable
swivels, sling. Disc. 1960. Note: SG-FWs are very rare, but unless
properly documented will not command premium prices. Prices
for authenticated Super Grades Featherweight models are generally 4 to 5 times that of a standard production Featherweight model
w/similar chambering.

MODEL 70 TARGET RIFLE
Same as Standard Model 70 except w/24-inch medium-weight bbl.,
scope bases, Marksman stock, weight 10.5 lbs. Originally offered in
all of the Model 70 calibers, this rifle was available later in calibers
.243 Win. and .30-06. Disc. 1963. Values are generally twice that
of standard models of similar configuration.

MODEL 70 TARGET
HEAVY WEIGHT . . . . **NiB $2835   Ex $1954   Gd $1337**
Same general specifications as Standard Model 70 except w/either
24- or 26-inch heavy weight bbl. weight: 10.5 lbs. No checkering.
.243 and .30-06 calibers.

MODEL 70 TARGET
BULL BARREL . . . . **NiB $4281   Ex $2427   Gd $1824**
Same general specifications as Standard Model 70 except 28-inch
heavy weight bbl. and chambered for either .30-06 or .300 H&H
Mag. Drilled and tapped for front sight base. Receiver slotted for
clip loading. Weight: 13.25 lbs.

Winchester Model 70
International Army Match (1964)

Winchester Model 70
Mannlicher (1964)

Winchester Model 70
Standard (1964)

Winchester Model 70
Target (1964)

MODEL 70
VARMINT RIFLE . . . . NiB $1995 Ex $1228 Gd $1073
Same general specifications as Standard Model 70 except w/26-inch heavy bbl., scope bases, special varminter stock. Calibers: .220 Swift, .243 Win. Made from 1956 to 1963.

MODEL 70
WESTERNER . . . . NiB $653 Ex $494 Gd $270
Same as Standard Model 70 except calibers .264 Win. Mag., .300 Win. Mag.; 3-round magazine; 26-inch bbl. in former caliber, 24-inch in latter. Weight: 8.25 lbs. Made from 1960 to 1963.

1964-TYPE MODEL 70

MODEL 70 AFRICAN . . . . NiB $475 Ex $364 Gd $279
Caliber: .458 Win. Mag. Three round magazine. 22-inch bbl. Weight: 8.5 lbs. Special "African" sights. Monte Carlo stock w/ebony forend tip, hand-checkering, twin stock-reinforcing bolts, recoil pad, QD swivels. Made from 1964 to 1971.

MODEL 70 DELUXE . . . . NiB $700 Ex $507 Gd $398
Calibers: .243, .270 Win., .30-06, .300 Win. Mag. Five round box magazine (3-round in Magnum). 22-inch bbl. (24-inch in Magnum). Weight: 7.5 lbs. Sights: Open rear; hooded ramp front. Monte Carlo stock w/ebony forend tip, hand-checkering, QD swivels, recoil pad on Magnum. Made from 1964 to 1971.

MODEL 70 INTERNATIONAL
ARMY MATCH RIFLE. . . . . NiB $1030 Ex $866 Gd $644
Caliber: .308 Win. (7.62 NATO). Five round box magazine. 24-inch heavy barrel. Externally adj. trigger. Weight: 11 lbs. ISU stock w/military oil finish, forearm rail for standard accessories, vertically adj. buttplate. Made in 1971. Value shown is for rifle w/o sights.

MODEL 70 MAGNUM
Calibers: 7mm Rem. Mag.; .264, .300, .338 Win. Mag.; .375 H&H Mag. Three round magazine. 24-inch bbl. Weight: 7.75 to 8.5 lbs. Sights: Open rear; hooded ramp front. Monte Carlo stock w/cheekpiece, checkering, twin stock-reinforcing bolts, recoil pad, swivels. Made from 1964 to 1971.
Caliber .375 H&H Mag. . . . . NiB $858 Ex $616 Gd $435
Other calibers . . . . NiB $650 Ex $426 Gd $303

MODEL 70 MANNLICHER . . . . NiB $925 Ex $664 Gd $571
Calibers: .243, .270, .308 Win., .30-06. Five round box magazine. 19-inch bbl. Sights: open rear; hooded ramp front. Weight: 7.5 lbs. Mannlicher-style stock w/Monte Carlo comb and cheekpiece, checkering, steel forend cap, QD sling swivels. Made from 1969 to 1971.

MODEL 70 STANDARD. . . . . NiB $600 Ex $390 Gd $267
Calibers: .22-250, .222 Rem., .225, .243, .270, .308 Win., .30-06. Five round box magazine. 22-inch bbl. Weight: 7.5 lbs. Sights: Open rear; hooded ramp front. Monte Carlo stock w/cheekpiece, checkering, swivels. Made from 1964 to 1971.

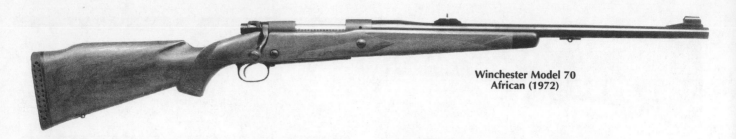

**Winchester Model 70
African (1972)**

MODEL 70 TARGET. . . . . **NiB $4000 Ex $2579 Gd $1406**
Calibers: .308 Win. (7.62 NATO) and .30-06. Five round box magazine. 24-inch heavy bbl. Blocks for target scope. No factory sights installed, but drilled and tapped for front and rear sights. Weight: 10.25 lbs. High-comb Marksman-style stock, aluminum hand stop, swivels. Straight-grain, one-piece stock w/sling swivels, but no checkering. Made from 1964 to 1971.

MODEL 70 VARMINT . . . . **NiB $1995 Ex $1417 Gd $919**
Same as Model 70 Standard except w/24-inch target weight bbl., blocks for target scope. No factory sights installed, but drilled and tapped for front and rear sights. Available in calibers .22-250, .222 Rem., and .243 Win. only. Weight: 9.75 lbs. Made 1964 to 1971.

1972-TYPE MODEL 70

MODEL 70 AFRICAN . . . . **NiB $811 Ex $658 Gd $462**
Similar to Model 70 Magnum except w/22-inch bbl. caliber .458 Win. Mag. w/special African open rear sight, reinforced stock w/ebony forend tip, detachable swivels and sling; front sling swivel stud attached to bbl. Weight: 8.5 lbs. Made from 1972 to 1992.

MODEL 70 CLASSIC SM
Similar to Model 70 Classic Sporter except w/checkered black composite stock and matte metal finish. Made from 1994 to 1996.
Model 70 Classic SM . . . . **NiB $700 Ex $540 Gd $290**
Caliber .375 H&H . . . . **NiB $800 Ex $698 Gd $444**
W/BOSS, add. **$100**
W/open sights, add **$40**

MODEL 70 CLASSIC SPORTER
Similar to Model 70 Sporter except w/pre-64-style action w/controlled round feeding, classic-style stock. Optional open sights. Made from 1994 to 2006.
Standard model . . . . **NiB $700 Ex $502 Gd $346**
W/BOSS, add. **$100**
W/open sights, add **$40**

MODEL 70 CLASSIC SPORTER STAINLESS
Similar to Model 70 Classic Sporter except w/matte stainless steel finish. Weight: 7.5 lbs. No sights. Made from 1994 to 2006.
Standard model . . . . **NiB $775 Ex $576 Gd $288**
Magnum model . . . . **NiB $793 Ex $604 Gd $373**
W/BOSS, add. **$100**

MODEL 70 CUSTOM SHARPSHOOTER
Calibers: .22-250, .223, .308 Win., .300 Win. Mag. 24- or 26-inch bbl. 44.5 inches overall (24-inch bbl.). Weight: 11 lbs. Custom-fitted, hand-honed action. McMillan A-2 target-style stock. Matte blue or stainless finish. Made from 1992 to 1996.
**Model 70 Custom
Sharpshooter (blued)** . . . . **NiB $1956 Ex $1468 Gd $979**
**Model 70 Custom
Sharpshooter (stainless)** . . . . **NiB $1984 Ex $1462 Gd $1033**

MODEL 70 CUSTOM SPORTING SHARPSHOOTER
Similar to Custom Sharpshooter Model except w/sporter-style gray composite stock. Stainless 24- or 26-inch bbl. w/blued receiver. Calibers: .270, 7mm STW, .300 Win. Mag. Made 1993 to 2006.
**Model 70 Custom Sharpshooter
blued (disc. 1995)** . . . . **NiB $1911 Ex $1473 Gd $984**
Model 70 Custom Sharpshooter, stainless NiB $1991 Ex $1528 Gd $1039

**MODEL 70 GOLDEN 50TH ANNIVERSARY EDITION
BOLT-ACTION RIFLE** . . . **Nib $1600** . . . . **Ex $1200** . . . **Gd $995**
Caliber: .300 Win. Three round magazine. 24-inch bbl. 44.5 inches overall. Weight: 7.75 lbs. Checkered American walnut stock. Hand-engraved American scroll pattern on bbl., receiver, magazine cover, trigger guard and pistol-grip cap. Sights: Adj. rear; hooded front ramp. Inscription on bbl. reads "The Rifleman's Rifle 1937 to 1987." Only 500 made 1986 to 1987. (Value for guns in new condition.)

MODEL 70 FEATHERWEIGHT CLASSIC. . . . . . **NiB $675 Ex $473 Gd $333**
Similar to Model 70 XTR Featherweight except w/controlled-round feeding system. Calibers: .270, .280 and .30-06. Made 1992 to 2006.

**MODEL 70 INTERNATIONAL
ARMY MATCH** . . . . **NiB $976 Ex $847 Gd $564**
Caliber: .308 Win. (7.62mm NATO). Five round magazine, clip slot in receiver bridge. 24-inch heavy barrel. Weight: 11 lbs. No sights, but drilled and tapped for front and rear iron sights, and/or scope mounts. ISU target stock. Intro. 1973; disc.

MODEL 70 LIGHTWEIGHT. . . . . . . **NiB $550 Ex $398 Gd $182**
Calibers: .22-250 and .223 Rem.; .243, .270 and .308 Win.; .30-06 Springfield. Five round mag. capacity (6-round .223 Rem.). 22-inch barrel. 42 to 42.5 inches overall. Weight: 6 to 6.25 lbs. Checkered classic straight stock. Sling swivel studs. Made from 1986 to 1995.

MODEL 70 MAGNUM
Same as Model 70 except w/3-round magazine, 24-inch bbl., reinforced stock w/recoil pad. Weight: 7.75 lbs. (except 8.5 lbs. in .375 H&H Mag.). Calibers: .264 Win. Mag., 7mm Rem. Mag., .300 Win. Mag., .338 Win. Mag., .375 H&H Mag. Made from 197 to 1980.
.375 H&H Magnum . . . . **NiB $550 Ex $440 Gd $340**
Other magnum calibers . . . . **NiB $475 Ex $385 Gd $335**

MODEL 70 STANDARD. . . . . **NiB $600 Ex $373 Gd $266**
Same as Model 70A except w/5-round magazine, Monte Carlo stock w/cheekpiece, black forend tip and pistol-grip cap w/white spacers, checkered pistol grip and forearm, detachable sling swivels. Same calibers plus .225 Win. Made from 1972 to 1980.

MODEL 70 STANDARD CARBINE . . . . **NiB $563 Ex $378 Gd $268**
Same general specifications as Standard Model 70 except 19-inch bbl. and weight: 7.25 lbs. Shallow recoil pad. Walnut stock and forend w/traditional Model 70 checkering. Swivel studs. No sights, but drilled and tapped for scope mount.

Winchester Model 70
Featherweight

Winchester Model 70
Golden 50th Anniversary

Winchester Model 70
Featherweight Classic

Winchester Model 70
Lightweight

Winchester Model 70
Magnum

Winchester Model 70
Carbine

RIFLES

MODEL 70 SPORTER DBM
Same general specifications as Model 70 Sporter SSM except w/detachable box magazine. Calibers: .22-250 (disc. 1994), .223 (disc. 1994), .243 (disc. 1994), .270, 7mm Rem. Mag., .308 (disc. 1994), .30-06, .300 Win. Mag. Made from 1992 to 1994.
Model 70 DBM . . . . NiB $650 Ex $480 Gd $285
Model 70 DBM-S (w/iron sights) . . . . NiB $537 Ex $435 Gd $305

MODEL 70 STAINLESS
SPORTER SSM . . . . NiB $600 Ex $435 Gd $305
Same general specifications as Model 70 XTR Sporter except w/checkered black composite stock and matte finished receiver, bbl. and other metal parts. Calibers: .270, 7mm Rem. Mag., .30-06, .300 Win. Mag., .338 Win. Mag. Weight: 7.75 lbs. Made 1992 to 1994.

MODEL 70 CLASSIC SUPER GRADE . . . . . NiB $869 Ex $792 Gd $452

Calibers: .270, 7mm Rem. Mag., .30-06, .300 Win. Mag., .338 Win. Mag. Five round magazine (standard), 3-round (magnum). 24-inch bbl. 44.5 inches overall. Weight: 7.75 lbs. Checkered walnut stock w/sculptured cheekpiece and tapered forend. Scope bases and rings, no sights. Controlled-round feeding system. Made from 1990 to 1995. Improved in 1999. Disc. 2006.

MODEL 70 TARGET. . . . . NiB $893 Ex $816 Gd $455
Calibers: .30-06 and .308 Win. (7.62mm NATO). Five round magazine. 26-inch heavy bbl. Weight: 10.5 lbs. No sights, but drilled and tapped for scope mount and open sights. High-comb Marksman-style target stock, aluminum hand stop and swivels. Intro. 1972. Disc.

MODEL 70 ULTRA MATCH. . . . . . . NiB $921 Ex $844 Gd $484
Similar to Model 70 Target but custom grade w/26-inch heavy bbl. w/deep counterbore, glass bedding, externally adj. trigger. Intro.

GRADING: **NiB** = New in Box   **Ex** = Excellent or NRA 95%   **Gd** = Good or NRA 68%

Winchester Model 70
XTR Sporter

Winchester Model 70A

MODEL 70 VARMINT (HEAVY BARREL)

Same as Model 70 Standard except w/medium-heavy, counter-bored 26-inch bbl., no sights, stock w/less drop. Weight: 9 lbs. Calibers: .22-250 Rem., .223 Rem., .243 Win., .308 Win. Made 1972-93. Model 70 SHB, in .308 Win. only w/black synthetic stock and matte blue receiver/bbl. Made from 1992 to 1993.

Model 70 Varmint . . . . NiB $625 Ex $588 Gd $335
Model 70 SHB (synthetic heavy barrel) . . . NiB $650 Ex $590 Gd $335

MODEL 70 WIN-CAM RIFLE . . . . . . NiB $500 Ex $394 Gd $240

Caliber: .270 Win. and .30-06 Springfield. 24-inch barrel. Camouflage one-piece laminated stock. Recoil pad. Drilled and tapped for scope. Made from 1986 to 1987.

MODEL 70 WINLITE BOLT-ACTION RIFLE . . . . . NiB $750 Ex $505 Gd $382

Calibers: .270 Win., .280 Rem., .30-06 Springfield, 7mm Rem., .300 Win. Mag., and .338 Win. Mag. Five round magazine; 3-round for Magnum calibers. 22-inch bbl.; 24-inch for Magnum calibers. 42.5 inches overall; 44.5, Magnum calibers. Weight: 6.25 to 7 lbs. Fiberglass stock w/rubber recoil pad, sling swivel studs. Made from 1986 to 1990.

MODEL 70 WIN-TUFF BOLT-ACTION RIFLE

Calibers: .22-250, .223, .243, .270, .308 and .30-06 Springfield. 22-inch bbl. Weight: 6.25–7 lbs. Laminated dye-shaded brown wood stock w/recoil pad. Barrel drilled and tapped for scope. Swivel studs. FWT Model made from 1986 to 1994. LW Model intro. 1992.

Featherweight model . . . . NiB $500 Ex $428 Gd $310
Lightweight model (Made 1992–93) . . . . . . NiB $500 Ex $428 Gd $310

MODEL 70 XTR FEATHERWEIGHT . . . . NiB $500 Ex $420 Gd $297

Similar to Standard Win. Model 70 except lightweight American walnut stock w/classic Schnabel forend, checkered. 22-inch bbl., hooded blade front sight, folding leaf rear sight. Stainless-steel magazine follower. Weight: 6.75 lbs. Made from 1984 to 1994.

MODEL 70 XTR SPORTER RIFLE . . . . NiB $650 Ex $423 Gd $294

Calibers: .264 Win. Mag., 7mm Rem. Mag., .300 Win. Mag., .200 Weatherby Mag., and .338 Win. Mag. Three round magazine. 24-inch barrel. 44.5 inches overall. Weight: 7.75 lbs. Walnut Monte Carlo stock. Rubber buttpad. Receiver tapped and drilled for scope mounting. Made from 1986 to 1994.

MODEL 70 XTR SPORTER MAGNUM . . . . NiB $552 Ex $423 Gd $294

Calibers: .264 Win. Mag., 7mm Rem. Mag., .300 Win. Mag., .338 Win. Mag. Three round magazine. 24-inch bbl. 44.5 inches overall. Weight: 7.75 lbs. No sights furnished, optional adj. folding leaf rear; hooded ramp. Receiver drilled and tapped for scope. Checkered American walnut Monte Carlo-style stock w/satin finish. Made from 1986 to 1994.

MODEL 70 XTR
SPORTER VARMINT . . . . NiB $700 Ex $420 Gd $268

Same general specifications as Model 70 XTR Sporter, except in calibers .223, .22-250, .243 only. Checkered American walnut Monte Carlo-style stock w/cheekpiece. Made from 1986 to 1994.

MODEL 70A . . . . NiB $450 Ex $313 Gd $231

Calibers: .222 Rem., .22-250, .243 Win., .25-06, .270 Win., .30-06, .308 Win. Four round magazine. 22-inch bbl. (except 24- or 26-inch in 25-06). Weight: 7.5 lbs. Sights: Open rear; hooded ramp front. Monte Carlo stock w/checkered pistol grip and forearm, sling swivels. Made from 1972 to 1978.

MODEL 70A MAGNUM . . . . NiB $476 Ex $313 Gd $236

Same as Model 70A except w/3-round magazine, 24-inch bbl., recoil pad. Weight: 7.75 lbs. Calibers: .264 Win. Mag., 7mm Rem. Mag., .300 Win. Mag. Made from 1972 to 1978

MODEL 70 ULTIMATE CLASSIC BOLT-ACTION RIFLE

Calibers: .25-06 Rem., .264 Win., .270 Win., .270 Wby. Mag., .280 Rem., 7mm Rem. Mag., 7mm STW, .30-06, Mag., .300 Win. Mag., .300 Wby. Mag., .300 H&H Mag., .338 Win. Mag., .340 Wby. Mag., .35 Whelen, .375 H&H Mag., .416 Rem. Mag. and .458 Win. Mag. Three, 4- or 5-round magazine. 22- 24- 26-inch stainless bbl. in various configurations including: full-fluted tapered round, half round and half octagonal or tapered full octagonal. Weight: 7.75 to 9.25 lbs. Checkered fancy walnut stock. Made in 1995.

Model 70
Ultimate Classic . . . . NiB $2153 Ex $1999 Gd $1098
For Mag. calibers (.375 H&H,
.416 and .458), add. $250

MODEL 70 LAMINATED STAINLESS
BOLT-ACTION RIFLE . . . . NiB $2150 Ex $1792 Gd $952

Calibers: .270 Win., .30-06 Spfld., 7mm Rem. Mag., .300 Win. Mag., and .338 Win. Mag. Five round magazine. 24-inch bbl. 44.75 inches overall. Weight: 8 to 8.525 lbs. Gray/Black laminated stock. Made from 1998 to 1999.

MODEL 70 CHARACTERISTICS

MODEL 70 FIRST MODEL (SERIAL NUMBERS 1 – 80,000)

First manufactured in 1936; first sold in 1937. Receiver drilled for Lyman No. 57W or No. 48WJS receiver peep sights. Also drilled and tapped for Lyman or Fecker scope sight block. Weight w/24-inch bbl. in all calibers except .375 H&H Mag.: 8.25 lbs. 9 lbs. in H&H Mag. Early type safety located on bolt top. Production of this model ended in 1942 near serial number 80,000 due to World War II.

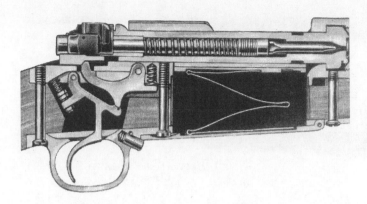

Cross-sectional view of the pre-1964 Winchester Model 70's speed lock action. This action cocks on the opening movement of the bolt with polished, smooth-functioning cams and guide lug, insuring fast and smooth operation.

MODEL 70 SECOND MODEL (SERIAL NUMBERS 80,000 – 350,000)

All civilian production of Winchester Model 70 rifles halted during World War II. Production resumed in 1947 w/improved safety and integral front-sight ramp. Serial numbers started at around 80,000. This model type was produced until 1954, ending around serial number 350,000.

MODEL 70 THIRD MODEL (SERIAL NUMBERS 350,000 – 400,000)

This variety was manufactured from 1954 to 1960 and retained many features of the Second Model except that a folding rear sight replaced the earlier type and front-sight ramps were brazed onto the bbl. rather than being an integral part of the bbl. The Model 70 Featherweight Rifle was intro. in 1954 in .308 WCF caliber. It was fitted w/light 22-inch bbl. and was also available w/either a Monte Carlo or Standard stock. The .243 Win. cartridge was added in 1955 in all grades of the Winchester Model 70 except the National Match and Bull Gun models. The .358 Win. cartridge was also intro. in 1955, along w/new Varmint Model chambered in .243 caliber only.

MODEL 70 FOURTH MODEL (SERIAL NUMBERS 400,000 – 500,000)

Different markings were inscribed on the barrels of these models and new magnum calibers were added; that is, .264 Win Mag., .338 Win. Mag, and .458 Win. Mag. All bbls. of this variation were about 0.13 inch shorter than previous ones. The .22 Hornet and .257 Roberts were disc. in 1962; the .358 Win. caliber in 1963.

MODEL 70 FIFTH MODEL (SERIAL NUMBERS 500,000 TO ABOUT 570,000)

These rifles may be recognized by slightly smaller checkering patterns and slightly smaller lightweight stocks. Featherweight bbls. were marked "Featherweight." Webbed recoil pads were furnished on magnum calibers.

POST-1964 MODEL 70 RIFLES

In 1964, the Winchester-Western Division of Olin Industries claimed that they were losing money on every Model 70 they produced. Both labor and material costs had increased to a level that could no longer be ignored. Other models followed suit. Consequently, sweeping changes were made to the entire Winchester line. Many of the older, less popular models were discontinued. Models that were to remain in production were modified for lower production costs.

1964 WINCHESTER MODEL 70 RIFLES
SERIAL NUMBERS 570,000 TO ABOUT 700,000)

The first version of the "New Model 70s" utilized a free-floating barrel, swaged rifle bore, new stock and sights, new type of bolt and receiver, and a different finish throughout on both the wood and metal parts. The featherweight grade was dropped, but six other grades were available in this new line:

Standard
Deluxe (Replaced Previous Super Grade)
Magnum
Varmint
Target
African

1966 MODEL 70 RIFLES
(SERIAL NUMBERS 700,000-G TO ABOUT 1,005,000)

In general, this group of Model 70s had fancier wood checkering, cross-bolt stock reinforcement, improved wood finish and improved action. One cross-bolt reinforcement was used on standard guns. Magnum calibers, however, used an additional forward cross-bolt and red recoil pad. The free-floating barrel clearance forward of the breech taper was reduced in thickness. Impressed checkering was used on the Deluxe models until 1968. Hand checkering was once again used on Deluxe and Carbine models in 1969; the big, red "W" was removed from all grip caps. A new, red safety-indicator and undercut cheekpiece was introduced in 1971.

1972 MODEL 70 RIFLES
(SERIAL NUMBERS G1,005,000 TO ABOUT G1,360,000)

Both the barrels and receivers for this variety of Model 70s were made from chrome molybdenum (C-M) steel. The barrels were tapered w/spiral rifling, ranging in length from 22 to 24 inches. Calibers .222 Rem., .225 Win. .22-250, .243 Win., .25-06, .270, .308 Win., .30-06 and .458 WM used the 22-inch length, while the following calibers used the 24-inch length: .222 Rem., .22-250, .243 Win., .264 Win. Mag., 7mm Mag., .300 and .375 H&H Mag. The .225 Win caliber was dropped in 1973; Mannlicher stocks were also disc. in 1973. The receiver for this variety of Model 70s was machined from a block of C-M steel. A new improved anti-bind bolt was introduced along with a new type of ejector. Other improvements included hand-cut checkering, pistol-grip stocks with pistol-grip and dark forend caps. An improved satin wood finish was also utilized.

1978 MODEL 70 RIFLES
(SERIAL NUMBERS BEGAN AROUND G1,360,000)

This variety of Model 70 was similar to the 1972 version except that a new XTR style was added which featured high-luster wood and metal finishes, fine-cut checkering, and similar embellishments. All Model 70 rifles made during this period used the XTR style; no standard models were available. In 1981, beginning with serial number G1,440,000 (approximately), a Featherweight version of the Model 70 XTR was introduced. The receiver was identical to the 1978 XTR, but lighter barrels were fitted. Stocks were changed to a lighter design with larger scroll checkering patterns and a Schnabel forend with no Monte Carlo comb. A satin sheen stock finish on the featherweight version replaced the high-luster finish used on the other XTR models. A new-style red buttplate with thick, black rubber liner was used on the Featherweight models. The grip cap was also redesigned for this model.

RIFLES

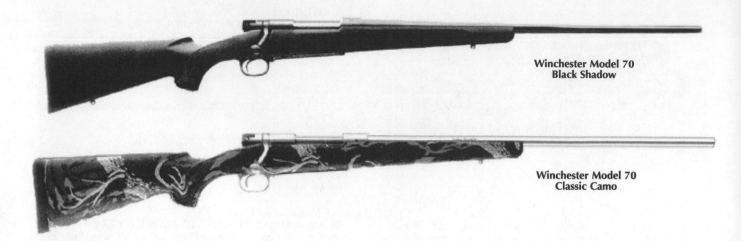

**Winchester Model 70
Black Shadow**

**Winchester Model 70
Classic Camo**

U.S. REPEATING ARMS MODEL 70 — 2006

In the early 1980s, negotiations began between Olin Industries and an employee-based corporation. The result of these negotiations ended with Olin selling all tools, machinery, supplies, etc. at the New Haven plant to the newly-formed corporation which was eventually named U.S. Repeating Arms Company. Furthermore, U.S. Repeating Arms Company purchased the right to use the Winchester name and logo. Winchester Model 70s went through very few changes the first two years after the transition. However, in 1984, the Featherweight Model 70 XTR rifles were offered in a new short action for .22-250 Rem., .223 Rem., .243 Win. and .308 Win. calibers, in addition to their standard action which was used for the longer cartridges. A new Model 70 lightweight carbine was also introduced this same year. Two additional models were introduced in 1985 — the Model 70 Lightweight Mini-Carbine Short Action and the Model 70 XTR Sporter Varmint. The Model 70 Winlite appeared in the 1986 "Winchester" catalog, along with two economy versions of the Model 70 — the Winchester Ranger and the Ranger Youth Carbine. Five or six different versions of the Winchester Model 70 had been sufficient for 28 years (1937 to 1964). Now, changes in design and the addition of new models each year seemed to be necessary to keep the rifle alive. New models were added, old models dropped, changed in design, etc., on a regular basis. Still, the Winchester Model 70 Bolt-Action Repeating Rifle — in any of its variations — is the most popular bolt-action rifle ever built.

MODEL 70 BLACK SHADOW . . . . . NiB $475 Ex $339 Gd $262
Calibers: .243 Win., .270 Win., .300 Win. Mag., .308 Win., .338 Win. Mag., .30-06 Spfld., 7mm STW., 7mm Rem. Mag. and 7mm-08 Rem. Three, 4- or 5-round magazine. 20- 24- 25- or 26-inch bbls. 39.5 to 46.75 inches overall.Weight: 6.5 to 8.25 lbs. Composite, Walnut or Gray/Black laminated stocks. Made from 1998 to 2006.

MODEL 70 CLASSIC
CAMO BOLT-ACTION RIFLE . . . . . . NiB $903 Ex $825 Gd $465
Calibers: .270 Win., 30-06 Spfld., 7mm Rem. Mag., .300 Win. Mag. Three or 5-round magazine. 24- or 26-inch bbl. 44.75 to 46.75 inches overall. Weight; 7.25 to 7.5 lbs. Mossy Oak finish and composite stock. Made from 1998 to 2006.

MODEL 70 CLASSIC
COMPACT BOLT-ACTION RIFLE NiB $2999 Ex $2147 Gd $1917
Calibers: .243 Win., .308 Win., and 7mm-08 Rem. Three round magazine. 20-inch bbl., 39.5 inches overall. Weight: 6.5 lbs. Walnut stock. Made from 1998 to 2006.

MODEL 70 CLASSIC LAREDO RANGE HUNTER
BOLT-ACTION RIFLE
Calibers: 7mm STW, 7mm Rem. mag., .300 Win. Mag. Three round magazine. 26-inch bbl. 46.75 inches overall. Weight: 9.5 lbs. Composite stock. Made from 1996 to 1999.
Classic Laredo . . . . NiB $721 Ex $593 Gd $459
Classic Laredo Fluted
(Made 1998 to date) . . . . NiB $747 Ex $618 Gd $438
Bossâ Classic Laredo . . . . NiB $728 Ex $593 Gd $420

MODEL 70 COYOTE . . . . NiB $875 Ex $612 Gd $432
Calibers: .22-250 Rem., .223 Rem., and .243 Win. Five or 6-round magazine. 24- inch bbl., 44 inches overall. Weight: 9 lbs. Medium-heavy stainless steel barrel w/laminated stock. Reverse taper forend. Made from 1999. Disc.

MODEL 70 RANGER
COMPACT RIFLE. . . . . NiB $475 Ex $324 Gd $210
Calibers: .22-250 Rem., .223 Rem., .243 Win., 7mm-08 Rem., Mag., and .308 Win. Five or 6-round magazine. 20- or 22-inch bbl. 41 inches overall. Weight: 6.5 lbs. Adjustable TRUGLO front and rear fiber optic sights. Push-feed action. Made from 1999 to 2000.

MODEL 70
STEALTH RIFLE . . . . NiB $846 Ex $654 Gd $384
Varminter style bolt-action rifle. Calibers: .22-250 Rem., .223 Rem., and .308 Win. Five or 6-round magazine. 26- inch bbl. 46 inches overall. Weight: 10.75 lbs. Black synthetic stock w/Pillar Plus Accu Block and full-length aluminum bedding block. Matte blue finish. Made from 1999. Disc.

MODEL 71 LEVER-ACTION REPEATER
Solid frame. Caliber: .348 Win. Four round tubular magazine. 20- or 24-inch bbl. Weight: 8 lbs. Sights: Open or peep rear; bead front on ramp w/hood. Walnut stock. Made from 1935 to 1957.
Special Grade (checkered pistol-grip
and forearm, grip cap, quick-detachable
swivels and sling . . . . NiB $2004 Ex $1618 Gd $1077
Special Grade Carbine
(20-inch bbl.; disc. 1940) . . . . NiB $2539 Ex $2051 Gd $1427
Standard Grade
(lacks checkering,
grip cap, sling and swivels) . . . . NiB $1206 Ex $1051 Gd $614
Standard Grade
Carbine (20-inch
bbl.; disc. 1940) . . . . NiB $2152 Ex $1740 Gd $1117

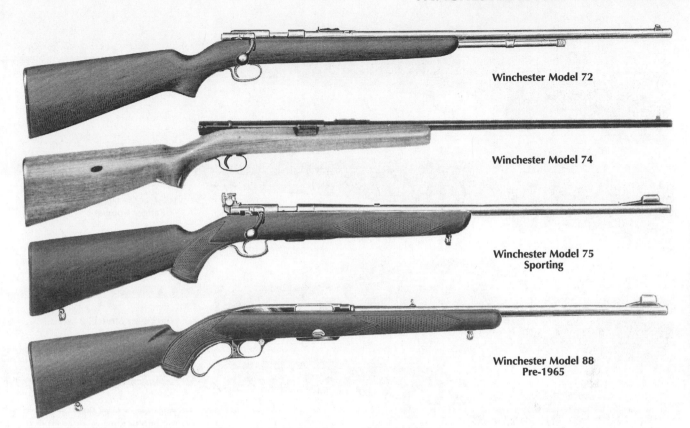

Winchester Model 72

Winchester Model 74

Winchester Model 75
Sporting

Winchester Model 88
Pre-1965

RIFLES

MODEL 72 BOLT-ACTION REPEATER. . . . . NiB $455 Ex $367 Gd $238
Tubular magazine. Takedown. Caliber: .22 Short, Long, LR. Magazine holds 20 Short, 16 Long or 15 LR. 25-inch bbl. Weight: 5.75 lbs. Sights: Peep or open rear; bead front. Plain pistol-grip stock. Made from 1938 to 1959.

MODEL 73 LEVER-ACTION REPEATER
See Model 1873 rifles, carbines, "One of One Thousand" and other variations of this model at the beginning of Winchester Rifle Section. Note: The Winchester Model 1873 was the first lever-action repeating rifle bearing the Winchester name.

MODEL 74 SELF-LOADING RIFLE . . . . NiB $312 Ex $261 Gd $183
Takedown. Calibers: .22 Short only, .22 LR only. Tubular magazine in buttstock holds 20 Short, 14 LR. 24-inch bbl. Weight: 6.25 lbs. Sights: Open rear; bead front. Plain pistol-grip stock, one-piece. Made from 1939 to 1955.

MODEL 75 SPORTING RIFLE . . . . . NiB $550 Ex $266 Gd $185
Same as Model 75 Target except has 24-inch bbl., checkered sporter stock, open rear sight; bead front on hooded ramp, weight: 5.5 lbs.

MODEL 75 TARGET RIFLE. . . . . . . NiB $550 Ex $266 Gd $185
Caliber: .22 LR. 5- or 10-round box magazine. 28-inch bbl. Weight: 8.75 lbs. Target sights (Lyman, Redfield or Winchester). Target stock w/pistol grip and semi-beavertail forearm, swivels and sling. Made from 1938 to 1959.

MODEL 77 SEMIAUTOMATIC RIFLE,
CLIP TYPE. NiB $250 Ex $161 Gd $103
Solid frame. Caliber: .22 LR. Eight round clip magazine. 22-inch bbl. Weight: About 5.5 lbs. Sights: Open rear; bead front. Plain, one-piece pistol-grip stock. Made from 1955 to 1963.

MODEL 77,
TUBULAR MAGAZINE . . . . NiB $302 Ex $211 Gd $153
Same as Model 77. Clip type except has tubular magazine holding 15 rounds. Made from 1955 to 1963.

MODEL 86 CARBINE AND RIFLE
See Model 1886 at beginning of Winchester Rifle section.

MODEL 88 CARBINE
Same as Model 88 Rifle except has 19-inch bbl., plain carbine-style stock and forearm with bbl. band. Weight: 7 lbs. Made 1968 to 1973.
88 Carbine. . . . . NiB $1222 Ex $948 Gd $773
.284 Win.. . . . . NiB $2000 Ex $1701 Gd $992

MODEL 88 LEVER-ACTION RIFLE
Hammerless. Calibers: .243 Win., .284 Win., .308 Win., .358 Win. Four round box magazine. Three round in pre-1963 models and in .284. 22-inch bbl. Weight: About 7.25 lbs. One-piece walnut stock with pistol-grip, swivels (1965 and later models have basket-weave ornamentation instead of checkering). Made from 1955 to 1973. Note: .243 and .358 introduced 1956, later discontinued 1964; .284 introduced 1963.
Model 88 (checkered stock) . . . . NiB $925 Ex $660 Gd $390
Model 88 (basketweave stock) . . . . NiB $925 Ex $660 Gd $390
.284 Win. . . . . NiB $1224 Ex $944 Gd $664
.284 Win. . . . . NiB $3000 Ex $1996 Gd $968

MODEL 1892 GRADE 1 LEVER-ACTION RIFLE
Similar to the original Model 1892. Calibers: .357 Mag., .44-40, .44 Mag., .45 LC. Ten round magazine. 24-inch round bbl. Weight: 6.25 lbs. 41.25 inches overall. Bead front sight, adjustable buckhorn rear. Etched receiver and gold trigger. Blue finish. Smooth straight-grip walnut stock and forewarn w/ metal grip cap. Made from 1997 to 1999.
Standard Rifle . . . . NiB $615 Ex $498 Gd $350
Short Rifle w/20-inch bbl. (.44 Mag. only) . . . NiB $595 Ex $483 Gd $340

Winchester Model 70
Coyote

Winchester Model 70
Ranger Compact

Winchester Model 70
Stealth

Winchester Model 94
Traditional

MODEL 94
ANTIQUE CARBINE . . . . NiB $459 Ex $373 Gd $246
Same as standard Post-64 Model 94 Carbine except has decorative scrollwork and casehardened receiver, brass-plated loading gate, saddle ring; caliber .30-30 only. Made from 1964 to 1984.

MODEL 94 CARBINE
Same as Model 1894 Rifle except 20-inch round bbl., 6-round full-length magazine. Weight: About 6.5 lbs. Originally made in calibers .25-35, .30-30, .32 Special and .38-55. Original version discontinued 1964.
Pre WWII (under No. 1,300,000). . . . . NiB $6450 Ex $5094 Gd $3766
Postwar, pre-1964
(under No. 2,700,000) . . . . NiB $748 Ex $606 Gd $425

MODEL 94
CLASSIC CARBINE . . . . NiB $590 Ex $416 Gd $325
Same as Canadian Centennial '67 Commemorative Carbine except without commemorative details; has scroll-engraved receiver, gold-plated loading gate. Made from 1967 to 1970.

MODEL 94
CLASSIC RIFLE . . . . NiB $6400 Ex $5285 Gd $4260
Same as Model 67 Rifle except without commemorative details; has scroll-engraved receiver, gold-plated loading gate. Made from 1968 to 1970.
MODEL 94
DELUXE CARBINE. . . . . NiB $775 Ex $525 Gd $329

Caliber: .30-30 Win. Six round magazine. 20-inch bbl. 37.75 inches overall. Weight: 6.5 lbs. Semi-fancy American walnut stock with rubber buttpad, long forearm and specially cut checkering. Engraved with "Deluxe" script. Made from 1987 to 2006.

MODEL 94 LONG BARREL RIFLE. . . . . . . NiB $563 Ex $391 Gd $272
Caliber: .30-30 Win. Seven round magazine. 24-inch bbl. 41.75 inches overall. Weight: 7 lbs. American walnut stock. Blade front sight. Made from 1987 to 2006.

MODEL 94 TRAPPER. . . . . NiB $685 Ex $475 Gd $359
Same as Winchester Model 94 Carbine except 16-inch bbl. and weight: 6 lbs., 2 oz. Made from 1980 to 2006.

MODEL 94 WIN-TUFF RIFLE . . . . . NiB $487 Ex $360 Gd $243
Caliber: .30-30 Win. Six round magazine. 20-inch bbl. 37.75 inches overall. Weight: 6.5 lbs. Brown laminated wood stock. Made from 198 to -2006.

MODEL 94 WRANGLER CARBINE
Same as standard Model 94 Carbine except has 16-inch bbl., engraved receiver and chambered for .32 Special & .38-55 Win.
**Wrangler, Top
Eject (disc.1984)** . . . . NiB $550 Ex $385 Gd $278
**Wrangler II,
Angle Eject (disc. 1985)** . . . . NiB $445 Ex $274 Gd $192

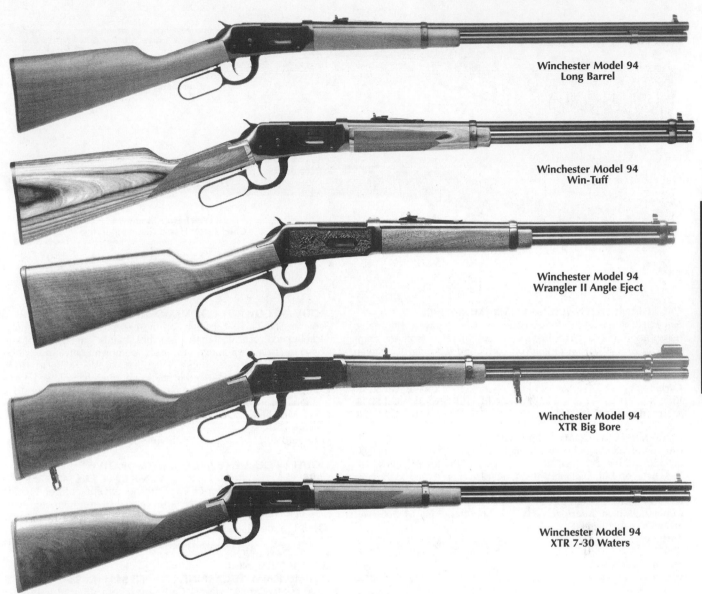

Winchester Model 94
Long Barrel

Winchester Model 94
Win-Tuff

Winchester Model 94
Wrangler II Angle Eject

Winchester Model 94
XTR Big Bore

Winchester Model 94
XTR 7-30 Waters

MODEL 94 XTR BIG BORE . . . . **NiB $650 Ex $491 Gd $393**
Modified Model 94 action for added strength. Caliber: .375 Win. 20-inch bbl. Rubber buttpad. Checkered stock and forearm. Weight: 6.5 lbs. Made from 1978 to 2006.

**MODEL 94 XTR
LEVER-ACTION RIFLE** . . . . **NiB $650 Ex $495 Gd $392**
Same general specifications as standard Angle Eject M94 except chambered .30-30 and 7-30 Waters and has 20- or 24-inch bbl. Weight: 7 lbs. Made 1985 to 1988 by U.S. Repeating Arms.

MODEL 94 COMMEMORATIVES

MODEL 94 ANTLERED GAME . . . . . **NiB $716 Ex $581 Gd $408**
Standard Model 94 action. Gold-colored medallion inlaid in stock. Antique gold-plated receiver, lever tang and bbl. bands. Medallion and receiver engraved with elk, moose, deer and caribou. 20.5-inch bbl. Curved steel buttplate. In .30-30 caliber. 19,999 made in 1978.

**MODEL 94 BICENTENNIAL
'76 CARBINE** . . . . **NiB $872 Ex $743 Gd $553**
Same as Standard Model 94 Carbine except caliber .30-30 Win. only; antique silver-finished, engraved receiver; stock and forearm of fancy walnut, checkered, Bicentennial medallion embedded in buttstock, curved buttplate. 20,000 made in 1976.

MODEL 94 BUFFALO BILL COMMEMORATIVE
Same as Centennial '66 Rifle except receiver is black-chromed, scroll-engraved and bears name "Buffalo Bill"; hammer, trigger, loading gate, saddle ring, forearm cap, and buttplate are nickel-plated; Buffalo Bill Memorial Assn. commemorative medallion embedded in buttstock; "Buffalo Bill Commemorative" inscribed on bbl., facsimile signature "W.F. Cody, Chief of Scouts" on tang. Carbine has 20-inch bbl., 6-round magazine, 7-lb. weight. 112,923 made in 1968.
Carbine . . . . **NiB $623 Ex $506 Gd $358**
Rifle . . . . **NiB $655 Ex $532 Gd $376**
Matched carbine rifle set . . . . **NiB $1487 Ex $1210 Gd $849**

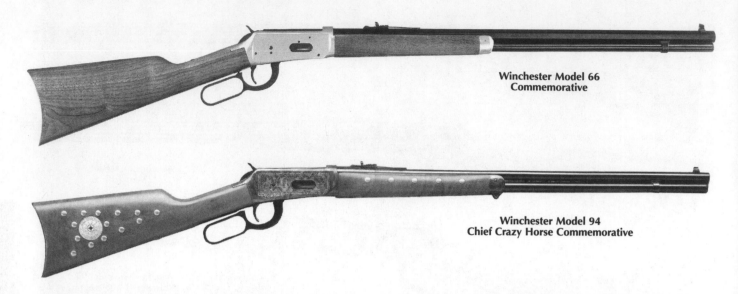

Winchester Model 66 Commemorative

Winchester Model 94 Chief Crazy Horse Commemorative

CANADIAN CENTENNIAL '67 COMMEMORATIVE

Same as Centennial '66 Rifle except receiver engraved with maple leaves and forearm cap is black-chromed, buttplate is blued, commemorative inscription in gold on barrel and top tang: "Canadian Centennial 1867–1967." Carbine has 20-inch bbl., 6-round magazine, weight: 7 lb., 90,398 made in 1967.

Carbine	NiB $595	Ex $306	Gd $258
Rifle	NiB $595	Ex $306	Gd $258
Matched carbine/rifle set	NiB $657	Ex $466	Gd $320

CENTENNIAL '66 COMMEMORATIVE

Commemorates Winchester's 100th anniversary. Standard Model 94 action. Caliber: .30-30. Full-length magazine holds 8 rounds. 26-inch octagon bbl. Weight: 8 lbs. Gold-plated receiver and forearm cap. Sights: Open rear; post front. Saddle ring. Walnut buttstock and forearm with high-gloss finish, solid brass buttplate. Commemorative inscription on bbl. and top tang of receiver. 100,478 made in 1966.

Carbine	NiB $655	Ex $508	Gd $360
Rifle	NiB $655	Ex $508	Gd $360
Matched carbine/ rifle set	NiB $1499	Ex $1217	Gd $856

MODEL 94 CHEYENNE

COMMEMORATIVE . . . . NiB $895 Ex $627 Gd $571
Available in Canada only. Same as Standard Model 94 Carbine except chambered for .44-40. 11,225 made in 1977.

MODEL 94
CHIEF CRAZY HORSE

COMMEMORATIVE. . . . . NiB $794 Ex $611 Gd $430
Cailber: .38-55, 7-round tubular magazine. 24-inch bbl., 41.75 inches overall. Walnut stock with medallion of the United Sioux Tribes; buttstock and forend also decorated with brass tacks. Engraved receiver. Open rear sights; bead front sight. 19,999 made in 1983.

MODEL 94 COLT COMMEMORATIVE

CARBINE SET. . . . . NiB $2525 Ex $1944 Gd $1267
Standard Model 94 action. Caliber: .44-40 Win. 20-inch bbl. Weight: 6.25 lbs. Features the horse-and-rider trademark and distinctive WC monogram in gold etching on left side of receiver. Sold in set with Colt Single Action Revolver chambered for same caliber.

MODEL 94 COWBOY COMMEMORATIVE CARBINE

Same as Standard Model 94 Carbine except caliber .30-30 only; nickel-plated receiver, tangs, lever, bbl. bands; engraved receiver, "Cowboy Commemorative" on bbl., commemorative medallion embedded in buttstock; curved buttplate. 20,915 made in 1970. Nickel-silver medallion inlaid in stock. Antique silver-plated receiver engraved with scenes of the old frontier. Checkered walnut stock and forearm. 19,999 made in 1970.

Cowboy carbine	NiB $653	Ex $506	Gd $358
Cowboy carbine (1 of 300)	NiB $3000	Ex $3135	Gd $2181

MODEL 94 GOLDEN SPIKE COMMEMORATIVE

CARBINE. . . . . NiB $744 Ex $542 Gd $412
Same as Standard Model 94 Carbine except caliber .30-30 only; gold-plated receiver, tangs and bbl. bands; engraved receiver, commemorative medallion embedded in stock. 64,758 made in 1969.

MODEL 94 ILLINOIS
SESQUICENTENNIAL

COMMEMORATIVE CARBINE. . . . . NiB $494 Ex $342 Gd $212
Same as Standard Model 94 Carbine except caliber .30-30 only; gold-plated buttplate, trigger, loading gate, and saddle ring; receiver engraved with profile of Lincoln, commemorative inscription on receiver, bbl.; souvenir medallion embedded in stock. 31,124 made in 1968.

MODEL 94 LEGENDARY
FRONTIERSMEN

COMMEMORATIVE. . . . . NiB $695 Ex $584 Gd $411
Standard Model 94 action. Caliber: .39-55. 24-inch round bbl. Nickel-silver medallion inlaid in stock. Antique silver-plated receiver engraved with scenes of the old frontier. Checkered walnut stock and forearm. 19,999 made in 1979.

MODEL 94
LEGENDARY LAWMEN

COMMEMORATIVE. . . . . NiB $695 Ex $584 Gd $411
Same as Standard Model 94 Carbine except .30-30 Win. only; antique silver-plated receiver engraved with action law-enforcement scenes. 16-inch Trapper bbl., antique silver-plated bbl. bands. 19,999 made in 1978.

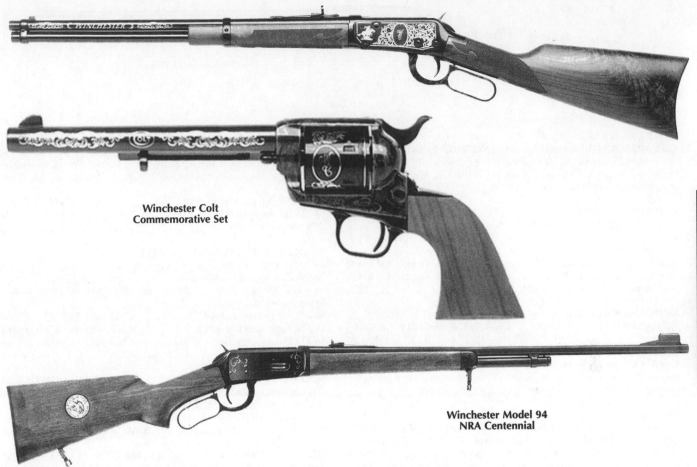

**Winchester Colt
Commemorative Set**

**Winchester Model 94
NRA Centennial**

MODEL 94 LONE STAR COMMEMORATIVE
Same as Theodore Roosevelt Rifle except yellow-gold plating; "Lone Star" engraving on receiver and bbl., commemorative medallion embedded in buttstock. 30,669 made in 1970.
Rifle or carbine . . . . **NiB $653 Ex $506 Gd $358**
Matched carbine/rifle set . . . . . . **NiB $1378 Ex $1196 Gd $836**

MODEL 94 NRA
CENTENNIAL MUSKET . . . . **NiB $598 Ex $479 Gd $339**
Commemorates 100th anniversary of National Rifle Association of America. Standard Model 94 action. Caliber: .30-30. Seven round magazine. 26-inch bbl. Sights: Military folding rear; blade front. Black chrome-finished receiver engraved "NRA 1871–1971" plus scrollwork. Barrel inscribed "NRA Centennial Musket." Musket-style buttstock and full-length forearm; commemorative medallion embedded in buttstock. Weight: 7.13 lbs. Made in 1971.

MODEL 94 NRA
CENTENNIAL RIFLE . . . . **NiB $595 Ex $501 Gd $353**
Same as Model 94 Rifle except has commemorative details as in NRA Centennial Musket (barrel inscribed "NRA Centennial Rifle"); caliber .30-30, 24-inch bbl., QD sling swivels. Made in 1971.

MODEL 94 NRA
CENTENNIAL MATCHED SET . . . **NiB $1293 Ex $1047 Gd $734**
Rifle and musket were offered in sets with consecutive serial numbers. Note: Production figures not available. These rifles offered in Winchester's 1972 catalog.

MODEL 94
NEBRASKA CENTENNIAL
COMMEMORATIVE CARBINE . . . . **NiB $1000 Ex $843 Gd $524**
Same as Standard Model 94 Carbine except caliber .30-30 only; gold-plated hammer, loading gate, bbl. band, and buttplate; souvenir medallion embedded in stock, commemorative inscription on bbl. 2,500 made in 1966.

MODEL 94 THEODORE ROOSEVELT
COMMEMORATIVE RIFLE/CARBINE
Standard Model 94 action. Caliber: .30-30. Rifle has 6-round half-magazine, 26-inch octagon bbl., weight: 7.5-lb. Carbine has 6-round full magazine, 20-inch bbl., weight: 7-lb. White gold-plated receiver, upper tang, and forend cap; receiver engraved with American Eagle, "26th President 1901–1909," and Roosevelt's signature. Commemorative medallion embedded in buttstock. Saddle ring. Half pistol-grip, contoured lever. 49,505 made in 1969.
Carbine . . . . **NiB $655 Ex $476 Gd $336**
Rifle . . . . **NiB $655 Ex $476 Gd $336**
Matched set . . . . **NiB $1415 Ex $1153 Gd $797**

MODEL 94
TEXAS RANGER
ASSOCIATION CARBINE . . . . **NiB $695 Ex $550 Gd $447**
Same as Texas Ranger Commemorative Model 94 except special edition of 150 carbines, numbered 1 through 150, with hand-checkered full-fancy walnut stock and forearm. Sold only through Texas Ranger Association. Made in 1973.

Winchester Model 100

MODEL 94 TEXAS RANGER
COMMEMORATIVE CARBINE . . . . . . NiB $595 Ex $415 Gd $370
Same as Standard Model 94 Carbine except caliber .30-30 Win. only, stock and forearm of semi-fancy walnut, replica of Texas Ranger star embedded in buttstock, curved buttplate. 5,000 made in 1973.

MODEL 94 TRAPPER
Same as Winchester Model 94 Carbine except w/16-inch bbl. and weighs 6 lbs. 2 oz. Angle Eject introduced in 1985 also chambered for .357 Mag., .44 Mag. and .45 LC. Made from 1980 to 2006.
94 Trapper, Top Eject (disc. 1984) . . . . NiB $675 Ex $487 Gd $310
94 Trapper, Angle Eject (.30-30) . . . . NiB $339 Ex $231 Gd $159
.357 Mag., .44 Mag. or .45 LC, add. $25

MODEL 94 JOHN WAYNE
COMMEMORATIVE CARBINE . . . . . NiB $1450 Ex $1043 Gd $730
Standard Model 94 action. Caliber: .32-40. 18.5-inch bbl. Receiver is pewter-plated with engraving of Indian attack and cattle drive scenes. Oversized bow on lever. Nickel-silver medallion in buttstock bears a bas-relief portrait of Wayne. Selected American walnut stock with deep-cut checkering. Introduced by U.S. Repeating Arms in 1981.

MODEL 94 WELLS FARGO & CO.
COMMEMORATIVE CARBINE . . . . . . NiB $650 Ex $486 Gd $313
Same as Standard Model 94 Carbine except .30-30 Win. only; antique silver-finished, engraved receiver; stock and forearm of fancy walnut, checkered, curved buttplate. Nickel-silver stagecoach medallion (inscribed "Wells Fargo & Co. —1852–1977—125 Years") embedded in buttstock. 20,000 made in 1977.

MODEL 94 O. F. WINCHESTER
COMMEMORATIVE RIFLE . . . . NiB $753 Ex $597 Gd $557
Standard Model 94 action. Caliber: .38-55. 24-inch octagonal bbl. Receiver is satin gold-plated with distinctive engravings. Stock and forearm semi-fancy American walnut with high grade checkering.

MODEL 94 WRANGLER CARBINE
Same as standard Model 94 Carbine except w/16-inch bbl., engraved receiver and chambered for .32 Special and .38-55 Win. Angle Eject introduced in 1985 as Wrangler II, also chambered for .30-30 Win., .44 Mag. and .45 LC. Made 1980 to 1986. Re-introduced in 1992.
94 Wrangler, Top Eject (disc. 1984) . . . . NiB $315 Ex $260 Gd $182
94 Wrangler II, Angle Eject (.30-30) . . . . NiB $311 Ex $234 Gd $172
.44 Mag. or .45 LC., add. $25

MODEL 94 WYOMING DIAMOND JUBILEE
COMMEMORATIVE CARBINE . . . . NiB $1994 Ex $1612 Gd $1120
Same as Standard Model 94 Carbine except caliber .30-30 Win. only, receiver engraved and casehardened in colors, brass saddle ring and loading gate, souvenir medallion embedded in buttstock, commemorative inscription on bbl. 1,500 made in 1964.

MODEL 94 ALASKAN PURCHASE CENTENNIAL
COMMEMORATIVE CARBINE . . . . NiB $2134 Ex $1723 Gd $1198
Same as Wyoming issue except different medallion and inscription. 1,501 made in 1967.

MODEL 94 XTR BIG BORE
Modified Model 94 action for added strength. Calibers: .307 Win., .356 Win., .375 Win. or .444 Marlin. 20-inch bbl. Six round magazine. Rubber buttpad. Checkered stock and forearm. Weight: 6.5 lbs. Made from 1978 to date.
94 XTR BB, Top Eject (disc. 1984) . . . . NiB $650 Ex $487 Gd $384
94 XTR BB, Angle Eject (intro. 1985) . . . . NiB $313 Ex $231 Gd $184
.356 Win. or .375 Win., add $150

MODEL 94 XTR LEVER-ACTION RIFLE
Same general specifications as standard M94 and Angle Eject M94 except chambered for .30-30 Win. and 7-30 Waters and has 20- or 24-inch bbl. Weight: 6.5 to 7 lbs. Made from 1978 to 1988 by U.S. Repeating Arms.
94 XTR Top Eject (disc. 1984) . . . . NiB $655 Ex $472 Gd $384
94 XTR Angle Eject (.30-30) . . . . NiB $655 Ex $472 Gd $384
94 XTR Deluxe Angle Eject (.30-30) . . . . NiB $655 Ex $472 Gd $384
7-30 Waters, add $80

MODEL 100 AUTOLOADING RIFLE . . . . NiB $550 Ex $476 Gd $403
Gas-operated semiautomatic. Calibers: .243, .284, .308 Win. Four round clip magazine (3-round in .284). 22-inch bbl. Weight: 7.25 lbs. Sights: Open rear; hooded ramp front. One-piece stock w/pistol grip, basket-weave checkering, grip cap, sling swivels. Made from 1961 to 1973.

MODEL 100 CARBINE . . . . NiB $725 Ex $534 Gd $354
Same as Model 100 Rifle except has 19-inch bbl., plain carbine-style stock and forearm with bbl. band. Weight: 7 lbs. Made 1967 to 1973.

MODEL 121 DELUXE . . . . NiB $127 Ex $95 Gd $74
Same as Model 121 Standard except has ramp front sight, stock with fluted comb and sling swivels. Made from 1967 to 1973.

MODEL 121 STANDARD
BOLT-ACTION SINGLE SHOT . . . . NiB $115 Ex $90 Gd $70
Caliber: .22 Short, Long, LR. 20.75-inch bbl. Weight: 5 lbs. Sights: Open rear; bead front. Monte Carlo-style stock. Made 1967 to 1973.

MODEL 121 YOUTH . . . . NiB $115 Ex $90 Gd $79
Same as Model 121 Standard except has 1.25-inch shorter stock. Made from 1967 to 1973.

MODEL 131 BOLT-ACTION REPEATER . . . . . . NiB $230 Ex $165 Gd $121
Caliber: .22 Short, Long or LR. Seven round clip magazine. 20.75-inch bbl. Weight: 5 lbs. Sights: Open rear; ramp front. Plain Monte Carlo stock. Made from 1967 to 1973.

MODEL 135 . . . . NiB $187 Ex $155 Gd $114
Same as Model 131 except chambered for .22 WMR cartridge. Magazine holds 5 rounds. Made in 1967.

MODEL 141
BOLT-ACTION
TUBULAR REPEATER . . . . NiB $222 Ex $180 Gd $124
Same as Model 131 except has tubular magazine in buttstock; holds 19 Short, 15 Long, 13 LR. Made from 1967 to 1973.

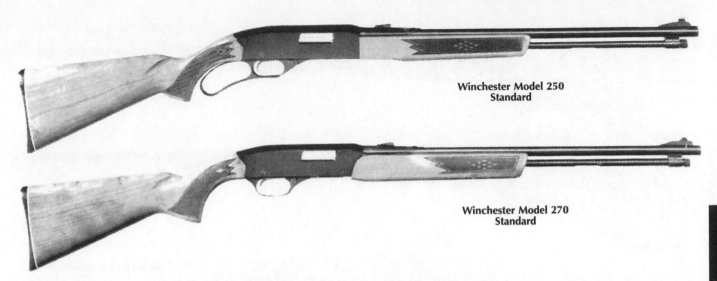

Winchester Model 250
Standard

Winchester Model 270
Standard

MODEL 145 . . . . **NiB $211 Ex $180 Gd $124**
Same as Model 141 except chambered for .22 WMR; magazine holds 9 rounds. Made in 1967.

MODEL 150 LEVER-ACTION CARBINE . . . . . . **NiB $180 Ex $155 Gd $103**
Same as Model 250 except has straight loop lever, plain carbine-style straight-grip stock and forearm with bbl. band. Made from 1967 to 1973.

MODEL 190 CARBINE . . . . **NiB $180 Ex $155 Gd $103**
Same as Model 190 rifle except has carbine style forearm with bbl. band. Made from 1967 to 1973.

MODEL 190 SEMIAUTOMATIC RIFLE . . . . **NiB $190 Ex $129 Gd $93**
Same as current Model 290 except has plain stock and forearm. Made from 1966 to 1978.

MODEL 250 DELUXE RIFLE . . . . . . **NiB $258 Ex $206 Gd $129**
Same as Model 250 Standard Rifle except has fancy walnut Monte Carlo stock and forearm, sling swivels. Made from 1965 to 1971.

**MODEL 250 STANDARD
LEVER-ACTION RIFLE** . . . . **NiB $180 Ex $150 Gd $110**
Hammerless. Caliber: .22 Short, Long or LR. Tubular magazine holds 21 Short, 17 Long, 15 LR. 20.5-inch bbl. Sights: Open rear; ramp front. Weight: About 5 lbs. Plain stock and forearm on early production; later model has checkering. Made from 1963 to 1973.

MODEL 255 DELUXE RIFLE . . . . . . **NiB $258 Ex $222 Gd $108**
Same as Model 250 Deluxe Rifle except chambered for .22 WMR cartridge. Magazine holds 11 rounds. Made 1965 to 1973.

MODEL 255 STANDARD RIFLE. . . . . **NiB $220 Ex $171 Gd $131**
Same as Model 250 Standard Rifle except chambered for .22 WMR cartridge. Magazine holds 11 rounds. Made from 1964 to 1970.

MODEL 270 DELUXE RIFLE . . . . . . **NiB $226 Ex $180 Gd $119**
Same as Model 270 Standard Rifle except has fancy walnut Monte Carlo stock and forearm. Made from 1965 to 1973.

**MODEL 270 STANDARD
SLIDE-ACTION RIFLE** . . . . **NiB $159 Ex $129 Gd $98**
Hammerless. Caliber: .22 Short, Long or LR. Tubular magazine holds 21 Short, 17 Long, 15 LR. 20.5-inch bbl. Sights: Open rear; ramp front. Weight: About 5 lbs. Early production had plain walnut stock and forearm (slide handle); latter also furnished in plastic (Cycolac); last model has checkering. Made from 1963 to 1973.

MODEL 275 DELUXE RIFLE . . . . . . **NiB $258 Ex $206 Gd $129**
Same as Model 270 Deluxe Rifle except chambered for .22 WMR cartridge. Tubular magazine holds 11 rounds. Made 1965–70.

**MODEL 275
STANDARD RIFLE** . . . . **NiB $191 Ex $155 Gd $119**
Same as Model 270 Standard Rifle except chambered for .22 WMR cartridge. Magazine holds 11 rounds. Made from 1964–70.

MODEL 290 DELUXE RIFLE . . . . . . **NiB $225 Ex $172 Gd $108**
Same as Model 290 Standard Rifle except has fancy walnut Monte Carlo stock and forearm. Made from 1965 to 1973.

MODEL 290 STANDARD SEMIAUTOMATIC RIFLE
Caliber: .22 Long or LR. Tubular magazine holds 17 Long, 15 LR. 20.5-inch bbl. Sights: Open rear; ramp front. Weight: About 5 lbs. Plain stock and forearm on early production; current model has checkering. Made from 1963 to 1977.
W/plain stock/forearm . . . . **NiB $228 Ex $202 Gd $108**
W/checkered
stock/forearm . . . . **NiB $253 Ex $202 Gd $108**

**MODEL 310 BOLT-ACTION
SINGLE SHOT** . . . . **NiB $200 Ex $177 Gd $145**
Caliber: .22 Short, Long, LR. 22-inch bbl. Weight: 5.63 lbs. Sights: Open rear; ramp front. Monte Carlo stock w/checkered pistol-grip and forearm, sling swivels. Made from 1972 to 1975.

**MODEL 320 BOLT-ACTION
REPEATER** . . . . **NiB $330 Ex $288 Gd $185**
Same as Model 310 except has 5-round clip magazine. Made from 1972 to 1974.

**MODEL 490
SEMIAUTOMATIC RIFLE** . . . . **NiB $330 Ex $263 Gd $185**
Caliber: .22 LR. Five round clip magazine. 22-inch bbl. Weight: 6 lbs. Sights: Folding leaf rear; hooded ramp front. One-piece walnut stock w/checkered pistol grip and forearm. Made 1975 to 1977.

**MODEL 670 BOLT-ACTION
SPORTING RIFLE.** . . . . **NiB $300 Ex $288 Gd $216**
Calibers: .225 Win., .243 Win., .270 Win., .30-06, .308 Win. Four round magazine. 22-inch bbl. Weight: 7 lbs. Sights: Open rear; ramp front. Monte Carlo stock w/checkered pistol-grip and forearm. Made from 1967 to 1973.

Winchester Model 310

Winchester Model 320

Winchester Model 490 Rifle

Winchester Model 670 Bolt-Action Rifle

Winchester Model 670 Magnum

Winchester Model 770

MODEL 670 CARBINE . . . . NiB $300 Ex $276 Gd $209
Same as Model 670 Rifle except has 19-inch bbl. Weight: 6.75 lbs. Calibers: .243 Win., .270 Win., .30-06. Made from 1967 to 1970.

MODEL 670 MAGNUM . . . . NiB $330 Ex $271 Gd $209
Same as Model 670 Rifle except has 24-inch bbl., reinforced stock with recoil pad with slightly different checkering pattern. Weight: 7.25 lbs. Calibers: .264 Win. Mag., 7mm Rem. Mag., .300 Win. Mag. Open rear sight; ramp front sight with hood. Made from 1967 to 1970.

**MODEL 770 BOLT-ACTION
SPORTING RIFLE.** . . . . NiB $375 Ex $291 Gd $231
Model 70-type action. Calibers: .22-250, .222 Rem., .243, .270 Win., .30-06. Four round box magazine. 22-inch bbl. Sights: Open rear; hooded ramp front. Weight: 7.13 lbs. Monte Carlo stock, checkered pistol-grip and forend; sling swivels. Made from 1969 to 1971.

MODEL 770 MAGNUM . . . . NiB $395 Ex $263 Gd $185
Same as Standard Model 770 except 24-inch bbl., weight: 7.25 lbs., recoil pad. Calibers: 7mm Rem. Mag., .264 and .300 Win. Mag. Made from 1969 to 1971.

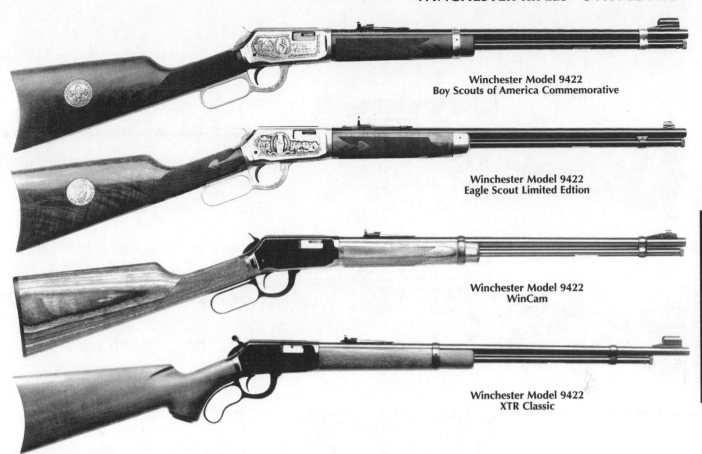

Winchester Model 9422
Boy Scouts of America Commemorative

Winchester Model 9422
Eagle Scout Limited Edtion

Winchester Model 9422
WinCam

Winchester Model 9422
XTR Classic

MODEL 9422 LEVER-ACTION RIMFIRE RIFLES

Similar to the standard Model 94 except chambered for .22 Rimfire. Calibers: .22 Short, Long, LR. (9422) or .22 WMR (9422M). Tubular magazine holds 21 or 15 Short.17 or 12 Long, 15 or 11 LR (9422 or Trapper) or 11 or 8 WRM (9422M or Trapper M). 16.5- or 20.5 inch bbl. 33.125- to 37.125 inches overall. Weight: 5.75 to 6.25 lbs. Open rear sight; hooded ramp front. Carbine-style stock and barrel-band forearm. Stock options: Walnut (Standard), laminated brown (WinTuff), laminated green (WinCam). Made from 1972. Disc.

Walnut (Standard)	NiB $575	Ex $311	Gd $208
WinCam	NiB $625	Ex $316	Gd $213
WinTuff.	NiB $475	Ex $270	Gd $193
Legacy	NiB $750	Ex $463	Gd $208
Trapper (16.5-inch bbl.)	NiB $700	Ex $396	Gd $208
XTR Classic	NiB $725	Ex $491	Gd $337
High Grade Series I	NiB $1275	Ex $988	Gd $655
High Grade Series II	NiB $1275	Ex $988	Gd $655
25th Anniversary Edition Grade I(1of 2500)	NiB $725	Ex $498	Gd $395
25th Anniversary Edition High Grade (1of 250)	NiB $1550	Ex $1064	Gd $755
Boy Scout Commemorative (1of 15,000)	NiB $759	Ex $597	Gd $401
Eagle Scout Commemorative (1of 1000)	NiB $1325	Ex $908	Gd $721
22 WRM, add 10%			

DOUBLE XPRESS RIFLE. . . . . . . NiB $3535 Ex $2770 Gd $1647
Over/under double rifle. Caliber: .30-06. 23.5-inch bbl. Weight: 8.5 lbs. Made for Olin Corp. by Olin-Kodensha in Japan. Introduced 1982.

RANGER YOUTH

BOLT-ACTION CARBINE . . . . NiB $395 Ex $287 Gd $184
Calibers: .223 (discontinued 1989), .243 Win., and .308 Win. Four and 5-round magazine. Bbl.: 20-inch. Weight: 5.75 lbs. American hardwood stock. Open rear sight. Made 1985 to 2006 by U.S. Repeating Arms.

RANGER LEVER-ACTION CARBINE . . . . . . NiB $525 Ex $328 Gd $265
Caliber: .30-30. Five round tubular magazine. Bbl.: 20-inch round. Weight: 6.5 lbs. American hardwood stock. Economy version of Model 94. Made from 1985 to 2006 by U.S. Repeating Arms.

RANGER BOLT-ACTION CARBINE . . . . NiB $365 Ex $298 Gd $212
Calibers: .223 Rem., .243 Win., .270, .30-06, 7mm Rem. (discontinued 1985), Mag. Three and 4-round magazine. Bbl.: 24-inch in 7mm; 22-inch in .270 and .30-06. Open sights. American hardwood stock. Made from 1985 to 1999 by U.S. Repeating Arms.

MODEL 1892 GRADE I LEVER-ACTION RIFLE

Similar to the original Model 1892. Calibers: .357 Mag., .44-40, .44 Mag., .45 LC. 10-round magazine. 24-inch round bbl. Weight: 6.25 lbs. 41.25 inches overall. Bead front sight, adjustable buckhorn rear. Etched receiver and gold trigger. Blue finish. Smooth straight-grip walnut stock and forearm w/ metal grip cap. Made from 1997. Disc.

Standard Rifle . . . . NiB $725 Ex $644 Gd $382
Short Rifle w/20-inch bbl.
(.44 Mag. only) . . . . NiB $750 Ex $495 Gd $352

MODEL 1892 GRADE

II LEVER-ACTION RIFLE . . . . NiB $1250 Ex $1074 Gd $683
Similar to the Grade I Model 1892 except w/gold appointments and receiver game scene. Chambered .45 LC only. Limited production of 1,000 in 1997.

Winslow Commander Grade

Winslow Crown Grade

Winslow Regent Grade
Bushmaster Stock

Commander Grade	NiB $1755	Ex $1229	Gd $1085
Regal Grade	NiB $1875	Ex $1448	Gd $1252
Regent Grade	NiB $1995	Ex $1714	Gd $1329
Regimental Grade	NiB $2750	Ex $2302	Gd $1673
Crown Grade	NiB $3000	Ex $2309	Gd $1851
Royal Grade	NiB $3450	Ex $2515	Gd $1954
Imperial Grade	NiB $3850	Ex $2928	Gd $2404
Emperor Grade	NiB $6205	Ex $5011	Gd $4355

WINSLOW ARMS COMPANY — Camden, South Carolina

BOLT-ACTION SPORTING RIFLE
Action: FN Supreme Mauser, Mark X Mauser, Remington 700 and 788, Sako, Winchester 70. Standard calibers: .17-222, .17-223, .222 Rem., .22-250, .243 Win., 6mm Rem., .25-06, .257 Roberts, .270 Win., 7x57, .280 Rem., .284 Win., .308 Win., .30-06, .358 Win. Magnum calibers: .17-222 Mag., .257 Wby., .264 Win., .270 Wby., 7mm Rem., 7mm Wby., .300 H&H, .300 Wby., .300 Win., .308 Norma, 8mm Rem., .338 Win., .358 Norma, .375 H&H, .375 Wby., .458 Win. Three-round magazine in standard calibers, 2-round in magnum. 24-inch barrel in standard calibers, 26-inch in magnum. Weight: With 24-inch bbl., 7 to 7.5 lbs.; with 26-inch bbl., 8 to 9 lbs. No sights. Stocks: "Bushmaster" with slender pistol-grip and beavertail forearm, "Plainsmaster" with full curl pistol-grip and flat forearm; both styles have Monte Carlo cheekpiece. Values shown are for basic rifle in each grade; extras such as special fancy wood, more elaborate carving, inlays and engraving can increase these figures considerably. Made from 1962 to 1989.

ZEPHYR DOUBLE RIFLES Manufactured by Victor Sarasqueta Company — Eibar, Spain

DOUBLE RIFLE . . . . NiB $21,025 Ex $16,900 Gd $11,625
Boxlock. Calibers: Available in practically every caliber from .22 Hornet to .505 Gibbs. Bbls.: 22 to 28 inches standard, but any lengths were available on special order. Weight: 7 lbs. for the smaller calibers up to 12 or more lbs. for the larger calibers. Imported by Stoeger from about 1938 to 1951.

34th Edition
GUN TRADER'S GUIDE

Shotguns

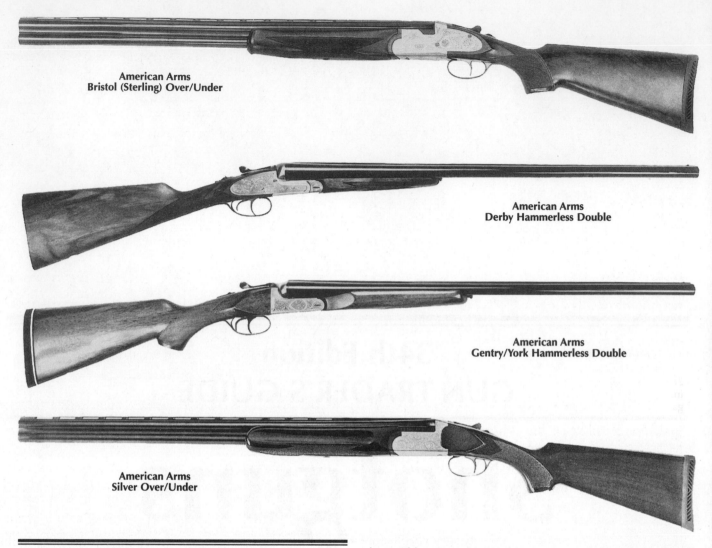

American Arms
Bristol (Sterling) Over/Under

American Arms
Derby Hammerless Double

American Arms
Gentry/York Hammerless Double

American Arms
Silver Over/Under

ALDENS SHOTGUN — Chicago, Illinois

MODEL 670 CHIEFTAIN SLIDE ACTION . . NiB $263 Ex $219 Gd $174
Hammerless. Gauges: 12, 20 and others. Three round tubular magazine. Bbl.: 26- to 30-inch; various chokes. Weight: 6.25 to 7.5 lbs. depending on bbl. length and ga. Walnut-finished hardwood stock.

AMERICAN ARMS — N. Kansas City, Missouri

See also Franchi Shotguns.

BRISTOL (STERLING) O/U . . . . NiB $790 Ex $583 Gd $449
Boxlock w/Greener crossbolt and engraved sideplates. Single selective trigger. Selective automatic ejectors. Gauges: 12, 20; 3-inch chambers. 26-, 28-, 30-, or 32-inch vent-rib bbls. w/screw-in choke tubes (Improved Cylinder/Modified/Full). Weight: 7 lbs. Antique-silver receiver w/game scene or scroll engraving. Checkered full pistol-grip-style buttstock and forearm w/high-gloss finish. Imported 1986-88 designated Bristol; redesignated Sterling 1989 to 1990.

BRITTANY HAMMERLESS DOUBLE . . . . . . NiB $780 Ex $637 Gd $449
Boxlock w/engraved case-colored receiver. Single selective trigger. Selective automatic ejectors. Gauges: 12, 20. 3-inch chambers. Bbls.: 25- or 27-inch w/screw-in choke tubes (IC/M/F). Weight: 6.5 lbs. (20 ga.). Checkered English-style walnut stock w/semi-beavertail forearm or pistol-grip stock w/high-gloss finish. Imported 1989 to 2000.

CAMPER SPECIAL . . . . NiB $153 Ex $112 Gd $84
Similar to the Single Barrel except takedown model w/21-inch bbl., M choke and pistol-grip stock. Made in 1989.

COMBO . . . . NiB $243 Ex $183 Gd $138
Similar to the Single-Barrel model except available w/interchangeable rifle and shotgun bbls. .22 LR/20-ga. shotgun or .22 Hornet/12-ga. shotgun. Rifle bbl. has adj. rear sights; blade-type front sight. Made in 1989.

DERBY HAMMERLESS DOUBLE
Sidelock w/engraved sideplates. Single non-selective or double triggers. Selective automatic ejectors. Gauges: 12, 20, 28 and .410. 3 inch chambers. Bbls.: 26-inch (IC/M) or 28-inch (M/F). Weight: 6 lbs. (20 ga.). Checkered English-style walnut stock and splinter forearm w/hand-rubbed oil finish. Engraved frame/sideplates w/antique silver finish. Imported 1986 to 1994.
12 or 20 ga.. . . . . NiB $1185 Ex $743 Gd $537
28 or .410 ga. (disc. 1991) . . . . . . NiB $1239 Ex $887 Gd $715

American Arms
WS/SS Hammerless Double

F.S. SERIES O/U
Greener crossbolt in Trap and Skeet configuration. Single selective trigger. Selective automatic ejectors. 12 gauge only. 26-, 28-, 30-, or 32-inch separated bbls. Weight: 6.5 to 7.25 lbs. Black or chrome receiver. Checkered walnut buttstock and forearm. Imported 1986 to 1987.

Model F.S. 200 Boxlock. . . . . **NiB $799 Ex $630 Gd $450**
Model F.S. 300 Boxlock. . . . . **NiB $959 Ex $756 Gd $552**
Model F.S. 400 Sidelock . . . . **NiB $1291 Ex $1100 Gd $771**
Model F.S. 500 Sidelock . . . . **NiB $1291 Ex $1100 Gd $771**

GENTRY/YORK HAMMERLESS DOUBLE
Chrome, coin-silver or color casehardened boxlock receiver w/scroll engraving. Double triggers. Extractors. Gauges: 12, 16, 20, 28, .410. 3-inch chambers (16 and 28 have 2.75-inch). Bbls.: 26-inch (IC/M) or 28-inch (M/F, 12, 16 and 20). Weight: 6.75 lbs. (12 ga.). Checkered walnut buttstock w/pistol-grip and beavertail forearm; both w/semi-gloss oil finish. Imported as York from 1986 to 1988, redesignated Gentry 1989 to 2000.

Gentry 12, or 16 or 20 ga. . . . .**NiB $625 Ex $535 Gd $377**
Gentry 28 or .410 ga. . . . .**NiB $670 Ex $552 Gd $469**
York 12, 16 or 20 ga. (disc. 1988) . . . .**NiB $625 Ex $535 Gd $377**
York 28 or .410 ga. (disc. 1988) . . . .**NiB $625 Ex $552 Gd $377**

GRULLA #2 HAMMERLESS DOUBLE
True sidelock w/engraved detachable sideplates. Double triggers. Extractors and cocking indicators. Gauges: 12, 20, .410 w/3-inch chambers; 28 w/2.75-inch. 26-inch bbl. Imported 1989 to 2000.

Standard model. . . . . **NiB $3596 Ex $2790 Gd $1996**
Two-bbl. set (disc. 1995) . . . . . . **NiB $3600 Ex $3595 Gd $2494**

SILVER I O/U
Boxlock. Single selective trigger. Extractors. Gauges: 12, 20 and .410 w/3-inch chambers; 28 w/2.75 inch. Bbls.: 26-inch (IC/M), 28-inch (M/F, 12 and 20 ga. only). Weight: 6.75 lbs. (12 ga.). Checkered walnut stock and forearm. Antique-silver receiver w/scroll engraving. Imported 1987 to 2000.

12 or 20 ga.. . . . .**NiB $536 Ex $493 Gd $341**
28 or .410 ga. . . . .**NiB $565 Ex $499 Gd $372**

SILVER II O/U
Similar to Model Silver I except w/selective automatic ejectors and 26-inch bbls. w/screw-in tubes (12 and 20 ga.). Fixed chokes (28 and .410). Made 1987 to 2000.

12 or 20 ga . . . .**NiB $670 Ex $541 Gd $429**
28 or .410 ga. . . . .**NiB $730 Ex $652 Gd $464**
Upland Lite II . . . .**NiB $1110 Ex $741 Gd $5214**
Two-bbl. set. . . . .**NiB $1173 Ex $973 Gd $753**

SILVER LITE O/U
Similar to Model Silver II except w/blued, engraved alloy receiver. Available in 12 and 20 ga. only. Imported from 1990 to 1992.

Standard Model. . . . . **NiB $800 Ex $546 Gd $393**

Two-bbl. Set . . . . **NiB $1096 Ex $845 Gd $668**
SILVER SKEET/TRAP. . . . . **NiB $790 Ex $550 Gd $319**
Similar to the Silver II Model except has 28-inch (Skeet) or 30-inch (Trap) ported bbls. w/target-style rib and mid-bead sight. Imported 1992 to 1994.

SILVER SPORTING O/U . . . . **NiB $835 Ex $780 Gd $548**
Boxlock. Single selective trigger. Selective automatic ejectors. Gauges: 12, 2.75-inch chambers. 28-inch bbls.w/Franchoke tubes (SK, IC, M and F). Weight: 7.5 lbs. Checkered walnut stock and forearm. Special broadway rib and vented side ribs. Engraved receiver w/chrome-nickel finish. Imported from 1990 to 2000.

SINGLE-SHOT SHOTGUN
Break-open action. Gauges: 10 (3.5), 12, 20, .410, 3-inch chamber. Weight: about 6.5 lbs. Bead front sight. Walnut-finished hardwood stock w/checkered grip and forend. Made from 1988 to 1990.

10 ga. (3.5-inch) . . . . **NiB $110 Ex $73 Gd $60**
12, 20 or .410 ga. . . . . **NiB $105 Ex $78 Gd $60**
Multi-choke bbl., add **$30**

SLUGGER SINGLE-SHOT SHOTGUN . . . . **NiB $100 Ex $88 Gd $67**
Similar to the Single-Shot model except in 12 and 20 ga. only w/24-inch slug bbl. Rifle-type sights and recoil pad. Made 1989 to 1990.

TS/OU 12 SHOTGUN. . . . . **NiB $660 Ex $477 Gd $358**
Turkey Special. Boxlock. Single selective trigger. Selective automatic ejectors. Gauge: 12, 3.5-inch chambers. Bbls.: 24-inch O/U w/screw-in choke tubes (IC, M, F). Weight: 6 lbs. 15 oz. Checkered European walnut stock and beavertail forearm. Matte blue metal finish. Imported 1987 to 2000.

TS/SS 10 HAMMERLESS DOUBLE . . . . **NiB $560 Ex $396 Gd $265**
Turkey Special. Same general specifications as Model WS/ SS 10, except w/26-inch side-by-side bbls., screw-in choke tubes (F/F) and chambered for 10-ga. 3.5-inch shells. Weight: 10 lbs., 13 oz. Imported 1987 to 1993.

TS/SS 12 HAMMERLESS DOUBLE . . . . **NiB $675 Ex $468 Gd $390**
Same general specifications as Model WS/SS 10 except in 12 ga. w/26-inch side-by-side bbls. and 3 screw-in choke tubes (IC/M/F). Weight: 7 lbs., 6 oz. Imported 1987 to 2000.

WS/OU 12 SHOTGUN . . . . **NiB $560 Ex $448 Gd $300**
Waterfowl Special. Boxlock. Single selective trigger. Selective automatic ejectors. Gauge: 12; 3.5-inch chambers. Bbls.: 28-inch O/U w/screw-in tubes (IC/M/F). Weight: 7 lbs. Checkered European walnut stock and beavertail forearm. Matte blue metal finish. Imported 1987-2000.

WS/SS 10 HAMMERLESS DOUBLE. . . . . . . **NiB $785 Ex $547 Gd $348**
Waterfowl Special. Boxlock. Double triggers. Extractors. Gauge: 10; 3.5-inch chambers. Bbls.: 32-inch side/side choked F/F. Weight: About 11 lbs. Checkered walnut stock and beavertail forearm w/satin finish. Parkerized metal finish. Imported from 1987 to 1995.

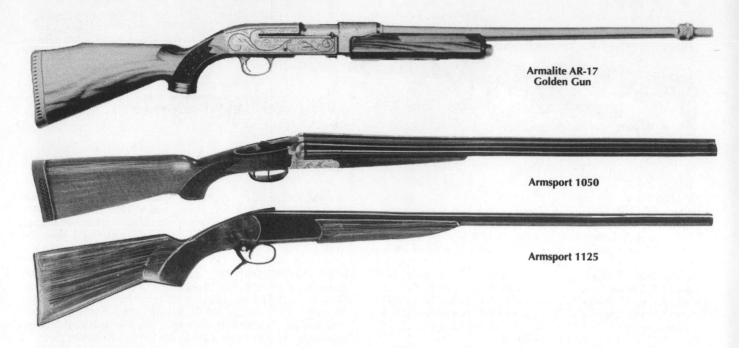

Armalite AR-17 Golden Gun

Armsport 1050

Armsport 1125

WT/OU 10 Shotgun . . . . **NiB $775 Ex $612 Gd $472**
Same general specifications as Model WS/OU 12 except chambered
for 10-ga. 3.5-inch shells. Extractors. Satin wood finish and matte
blue metal. Imported 1987 to 2000.

ARMALITE, INC. — Costa Mesa, California

AR-17 GOLDEN GUN . . . . **NiB $795 Ex $570 Gd $448**
Recoil-operated semiautomatic. High-test aluminum bbl. and
receiver housing. 12 ga. only. Two round capacity. 24-inch bbl.
w/interchangeable choke tubes: IC/M/F. Weight: 5.6 lbs.
Polycarbonate stock and forearm recoil pad. Gold-anodized
finish standard, also made w/black finish. Made 1964 to 1965.
Fewer than 2,000 produced.

ARMSCOR (Arms Corp.) — Manila, Philippines, *Imported until 1991 by Armscor Precision, San Mateo, CA; 1991-95 by Ruko Products, Inc., Buffalo NY*

MODEL M-30 FIELD PUMP SHOTGUN
Double slide-action bars w/damascened bolt. Gauge: 12 only w/3-
inch chamber. Bbl.: 28-inch w/fixed chokes or choke tubes. Weight:
7.6 lbs. Walnut or walnut finished hardwood stock.
Model M30-F (w/hard-
wood stock and fixed chokes) . . . . . NiB $225 Ex $191 Gd $124
Model M-30F (w/hard-
wood stock and choke tubes) . . . . . NiB $225 Ex $191 Gd $124
Model M-30F/IC (w/walnut
stock and choke tubes) . . . . NiB $180 Ex $121 Gd $94

MODEL M-30 RIOT PUMP
Double-action slide bar w/damascened bolt. Gauge: 12 only w/3-
inch chamber. Bbls: 18.5 and 20-inch w/IC bore. Five- or 7-round
magazine. Weight: 7 lbs, 2 ozs. Walnut finished hardwood stock.
Model M-30R6 (5-round magazine) . . . . NiB $155 Ex $108 Gd $69
Model M-30R8 (7-round magazine) . . . . NiB $165 Ex $98 Gd $57

MODEL M-30 SPECIAL COMBO
Simlar to Special Purpose Model except has detachable synthetic
stock that removes to convert to pistol-grip configuration.
Model M-30C (disc. 1995) . . . . NiB $212 Ex $177 Gd $130
Model M-30RP (disc. 1995) . . . . . NiB $212 Ex $177 Gd $130

MODEL M-30 SPECIAL PURPOSE
Double-action slide bar w/damascened bolt. Seven round maga-
zine.   Gauge: 12 only w/3-inch chamber. 20-inch bbl. w/cylinder
choke. Iron sights (DG Model) or venter handguard (SAS Model).
Weight: 7.5 lbs. Walnut finished hardwood stock.
Model M-30DG (Deer Gun) . . . . NiB $218 Ex $188 Gd $124
Model M-30SAS (Special Air Services) . . . . NiB $235 Ex $199 Gd $99

ARMSPORT, INC. — Miami, Florida
1000 SERIES HAMMERLESS DOUBLES
Side-by-side w/engraved receiver, double triggers and extractors.
Gauges: 10 (3.5), 12, 20, .410- 3-inch chambers. Model 1033:
10 ga., 32-inch bbl. Model 1050/51: 12 ga., 28-inch bbl., M/F
choke. Model 1052/53: 20 ga., 26-inch bbl., I/M choke. Model
1054/57: .410 ga., 26-inch bbl., I/M. Model 1055: 28 ga.,
Weight: 5.75 to 7.25 lbs. European walnut buttstock and forend.
Made in Italy. Importation disc. 1993.
Model 1033 (10 ga. disc. 1989) . . . . . . NiB $789 Ex $644 Gd $453
Model 1050 (12 ga. disc. 1993) . . . . . NiB $702 Ex $656 Gd $435
Model 1051 (12 ga. disc. 1985) . . . . . NiB $465 Ex $382 Gd $277
Model 1052 (20 ga. disc. 1985) . . . . . NiB $437 Ex $360 Gd $261
Model 1053 (20 ga. disc. 1993) . . . . . NiB $748 Ex $610 Gd $431
Model 1054 (.410 disc. 1992) . . . . NiB $825 Ex $671 Gd $473
Model 1055 (28 ga. disc. 1992) . . . . . . NiB $507 Ex $416 Gd $300
Model 1057 (.410 disc. 1985) . . . . NiB $543 Ex $445 Gd $318

MODEL 1125 SINGLE-SHOT SHOTGUN . . . . . NiB $115 Ex $100 Gd $74
Bottom-opening lever. Gauges: 12, 20. 3-inch chambers. Bead front
sight. Plain stock and forend. Imported 1987-89.

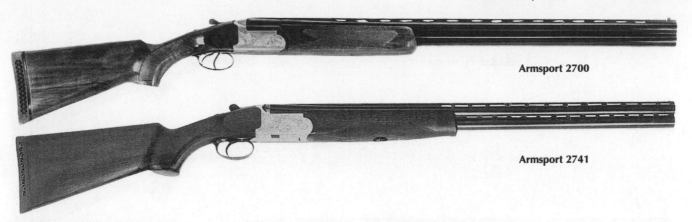

Armsport 2700

Armsport 2741

MODEL 2700 GOOSE GUN

Similar to the 2700 Standard Model except 10 ga. w/3.5-inch chambers. Double triggers w/28-inch bbl. choked IC/M or 32-inch bbl., F/F. 12mm wide vent rib. Weight: 9.5 lbs. Canada geese engraved on receiver. Antiqued silver-finished action. Checkered European walnut stock w/rubber recoil pad. Imported from Italy 1986 to 1993.

W/fixed chokes	NiB $1075	Ex $858	Gd $593
W/choke tubes	NiB $1364	Ex $934	Gd $654

MODEL 2700 OVER/UNDER SERIES

Hammerless, takedown shotgun w/engraved receiver. Selective single or double triggers. Gauges: 10, 12, 20, 28 and .410. Bbl.: 26-or 28-inch w/fixed chokes or choke tubes. Weight: 8 lbs. Checkered European walnut buttstock and forend. Made in Italy. Importation disc. 1993.

Model 2701 12 ga. (disc. 1985)	NiB $554	Ex $453	Gd $324
Model 2702 12 ga.	NiB $592	Ex $484	Gd $345
Model 2703 20 ga. (disc. 1985)	NiB $579	Ex $473	Gd $338
Model 2704 20 ga.	NiB $624	Ex $509	Gd $362
Model 2705 (.410, DT, fixed chokes)	NiB $724	Ex $591	Gd $419
Model 2730/31 (Boss-style action, SST Choke tubes)	NiB $814	Ex $665	Gd $468
Model 2733/35 (Boss-style action, extractors)	NiB $757	Ex $616	Gd $436
Model 2741 (Boss-style action, ejectors)	NiB $641	Ex $540	Gd $384
Model 2742 Sporting Clays (12 ga./choke tubes)	NiB $788	Ex $642	Gd $454
Model 2744 Sporting Clays (20 ga./choke tubes)	NiB $801	Ex $642	Gd $461
Model 2750 Sporting Clays (12 ga./sideplates)	NiB $856	Ex $697	Gd $493
Model 2751 Sporting Clays (20 ga./sideplates)	NiB $888	Ex $722	Gd $501

MODEL 2755 SLIDE-ACTION SHOTGUN

Gauge: 12 w/3-inch chamber. Tubular magazine. Bbls.: 28- or 30-inch w/fixed choke or choke tubes. Weight: 7 lbs. European walnut stock. Made in Italy 1986 to 1987.

Standard model, fixed choke	NiB $374	Ex $323	Gd $215
Standard model, choke tubes	NiB $552	Ex $440	Gd $317
Police model, 20-inch bbl.	NiB $343	Ex $297	Gd $205

MODEL 2900 TRI-BARREL (TRILLING) SHOTGUN

Boxlock. Double triggers w/top-tang bbl. selector. Extractors. Gauge: 12; 3-inch chambers. Bbls.: 28-inch (IC, M and F). Weight: 7.75 lbs. Checkered European walnut stock and forearm. Engraved silver receiver. Imported 1986 to 1987 and 1990 to 1993.

Model 2900 (fixed chokes)	NiB $2210	Ex $1797	Gd $1266
Model 2900 (choke tubes)	NiB $2945	Ex $2385	Gd $1669
Deluxe grades, add			$500

ARRIETA, S.L. — Elgoibar, Spain
Imported by New England Arms Corp., Wingshooting Adventures Quality Arms, Griffin & Howe and Orvis.

Custom double-barreled shotguns with frames scaled to individual gauges. Standard gauges are 12 and 16. Add: 5% for small gauges (20, 24, 28, 32 and .410 bore) on currently manufactured models; $900 for single trigger (most actions); 5% for matched pairs; 10% for rounded action on standard models; extra bbls., add $1375 to $2000 per set.

MODEL 557 STANDARD . . . . . . .NiB $4170 Ex $2685 Gd $1935
Gauges: 12, 16 or 20. Demi-Bloc steel barrels, detachable engraved sidelocks, double triggers, ejectors.

MODEL 570 LIEJA . . . . NiB $4775 Ex $3210 Gd $2480
Gauges: 12, 16 or 20. Non-detachable sidelocks.

MODEL 578 VICTORIA . . . . NiB $5510 Ex $3270 Gd $2185
Gauges: 12, 16 or 20. Similar to Model 570 but with fine English scrollwork.

LIGERA MODEL . . . . NiB $5525 Ex $4150 Gd $3100
Available in all gauges. Lightweight 12 ga. has 2-inch chambers, lightweight or standard action. Includes unique frame engraving and Turkish wood upgrade. Wt. appox. 6 pounds.

MODEL 590 REGINA . . . . NiB $3425 Ex $3050 Gd $2125
Gauges: 12, 16 or 20. Similar to Model 570 but has more elaborate engraving.

MODEL 595 PRINCIPE . . . . NiB $5475 Ex $4235 Gd $3325
Available in all gauges, sidelock, engraved hunting scenes, ejectors,double triggers.

MODEL 600 IMPERIAL . . . . NiB $8960 Ex $5785 Gd $3460
Gauges: 12, 16 or 20. Self-opening action, very ornate engraving throughout.

MODEL 601 IMPERIAL TYRO . . . NiB $9100 Ex $5895 Gd $4130
Available in all gauges, sidelock, nickel plating, ejectors,single selective trigger, border engraving.

MODEL 801 . . . . NiB $12,355 Ex $10,905 Gd $9630
All gauges, detachable sidelocks, ejectors,coin-wash finish, Churchill-style engraving.

SHOTGUNS

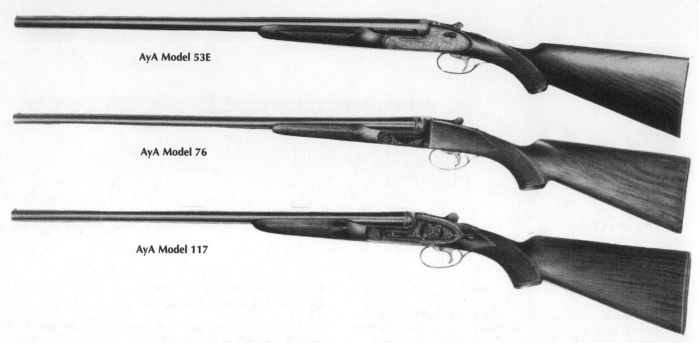

AyA Model 53E

AyA Model 76

AyA Model 117

MODEL 802 . . . . NiB $12,755 Ex $10,150 Gd $7590
Gauges: 12, 16 or 20. Similar to Model 801 except with non-detachable sidelocks, finest Holland-style engraving.

BOSS ROUND BODY . . . . NiB $8255 Ex $7640 Gd $6395
Available in all gauges, Boss pattern best quality engraving, wood upgrade.

MODEL 803 . . . . NiB $10,255 Ex $8185 Gd $5885
Available in all gauges. Similar to Model 801 except finest Purdey-style engraving.

MODEL 871 . . . . NiB $6650 Ex $4072 Gd $2522
Available in all gauges. Rounded frame sidelock action with Demi-Bloc barrels, scroll engraving, ejectors,double trigger.

MODEL 871 EXTRA FINISH . . . . NiB $6990 Ex $4655 Gd $3855
Similar to Model 871 except with standard game scene engraving with woodcock and ruffed grouse.

MODEL 872 . . . . NiB $16,000 Ex $12,625 Gd $9300
Available in all gauges, rounded frame sidelock action, Demi-Bloc barrels, elaborate scroll engraving with third lever fastener.

MODEL 873 . . . . NiB $16,750 Ex $13,000 Gd $10,680
Available in all gauges. Sidelock, gold line engraved action, ejectors, single selective trigger.

MODEL 874 . . . . NiB $18,675 Ex $14,210 Gd $12,985
Available in all gauges. Sidelock, gold line engraved action, Demi-Bloc barrels.

MODEL 875 . . . . NiB $14,000 Ex $11,975 Gd $9600
Available in all gauges. Custom model built to individual specifications only, elaborate engraving, gold inlays

MODEL 931 . . . . NiB $25,995 Ex $18,595 Gd $14,650
Available in all gauges. Self-opening action, elaborate engraving, H&H selective ejectors.

ASTRA SHOTGUNS — Guernica, Spain
Manufactured by Unceta y Compania

MODEL 650 O/U SHOTGUN
Hammerless, takedown w/double triggers. 12 ga. w/.75-inch chambers. Bbls.: 28-inch (M/F or SK/SK); 30-inch (M/F). Weight: 6.75 lbs. Checkered European walnut buttstock and forend. Disc. 1987.
W/extractors . . . . NiB $652 Ex $517 Gd $379
W/ejectors . . . . NiB $772 Ex $624 Gd $430

MODEL 750 O/U SHOTGUN
Similar to the Model 650 except w/selective single trigger and ejectors. Made in field, skeet and trap configurations from 1980. Disc. 1987.
Field model w/extractors. . . . . NiB $723 Ex $587 Gd $424
Field model w/ejectors . . . . NiB $844 Ex $672 Gd $478
Trap or Skeet . . . . NiB $989 Ex $792 Gd $559

AYA (Aguirre Y Aranzabal) — Eibar, Spain
(Previously Mfd. by Diarm), *Imported by*
Armes De Chasse, Hertford, NC

MODEL 1
HAMMERLESS DOUBLE
A Holland & Holland sidelock similar to the Model 2 except in 12 and 20 ga. only, w/special engraving and exhibition-grade wood. Weight: 5-8 lbs., depending on ga. Imported by Diarm until 1987, since 1992 by Armes de Chasse.
Model 1 Standard . . . . NiB $8555 Ex $5347 Gd $3115
Model 1 Deluxe . . . . NiB $11,745 Ex $9887 Gd $7327
Extra set of bbls., add $2550

AyA Matador II

AyA Model XXV Boxlock

MODEL 2 HAMMERLESS DOUBLE
Sidelock action w/selective single or double triggers automatic ejectors and safety. Gauges: 12, 20, 28, (2.75-inch chambers); .410 (3-inch chambers). Bbls.: 26- or 28-inch w/various fixed choke combinations. Weight: 7 lbs. (12 ga.). English-style straight walnut buttstock and splinter forend. Imported by Diarm until 1987, since 1992 by Armes de Chasse.

12 or 20 ga. w/double triggers . NiB $4427 Ex $2790 Gd $1650
12 or 20 ga. w/single trigger . . . NiB $4427 Ex $2790 Gd $1650
28 or .410 ga. w/double triggers NiB $4427 Ex $2790 Gd $1650
28 or .410 ga. w/single trigger NiB $3316 Ex $2790 Gd $1650
Extra set of bbls., add $1350

MODEL 4
HAMMERLESS DOUBLE
Lightweight Anson & Deely boxlock, scalloped frame. Gauges: 12, 16, 20, 28, and .410. Bbls.: 25- to 28-inch w/concave rib. Importation disc. 1987 and resumed in 1992 by Armes de Chasse.

12 ga. . . . . NiB $2010 Ex $1295 Gd $971
16 ga. (early importation) . . . . . . NiB $2010 Ex $1295 Gd $971
20 ga. . . . . NiB $2010 Ex $1295 Gd $971
28 ga. . . . . NiB $2010 Ex $1295 Gd $971
.410 ga. . . . . NiB $2010 Ex $1295 Gd $971
Deluxe grades, add $650

MODEL 37 SUPER
O/U SHOTGUN . . . . NiB $3071 Ex $2196 Gd $1913
Sidelock. automatic ejectors. Selective single trigger. Made in all gauges, bbl. lengths and chokes. Vent rib bbls. Elaborately engraved. Checkered stock (w/straight or pistol grip) and forend. Disc. 1995.

MODEL 37 SUPER A
O/U SHOTGUN . . . . NiB $14,211 Ex $12,017 Gd $10,488
Similar to the Standard Model 37 Super except has nickel steel frame and is fitted w/detachable sidelocks engraved w/game scenes. Importation disc. 1987 and resumed 1992 by Armes de Chasse. Disc.

MODEL 53E
. . . . NiB $2481 Ex $2014 Gd $1407
Same general specifications as Model 117 except more elaborate engraving and select figured wood. Importation disc. 1987 and resumed in 1992 by Armes de Chasse.

MODEL 56 HAMMERLESS DOUBLE
Pigeon weight Holland & Holland sidelock w/Purdey-style third lug and sideclips. Gauges: 12, 16, 20. Receiver has fine-line scroll and rosette engraving; gold-plated locks. Importation disc. 1987 and resumed 1992 by Armes de Chasse.
12 ga. . . . . NiB $5354 Ex $3754 Gd $2875

16 ga. (early importation) . . . . . NiB $5354 Ex $3754 Gd $2875
20 ga. (early importation). . . . . NiB $5354 Ex $3754 Gd $2875

MODEL 76 HAMMERLESS DOUBLE . . NiB $896 Ex $742 Gd $459
Anson & Deeley boxlock. Auto ejectors. Selective single trigger. Gauges: 12, 20 (3-inch). Bbls.: 26-, 28-, 30-inch (latter in 12 ga. only), any standard choke combination. Checkered pistol-grip stock/beavertail forend. Disc.

MODEL 76—.410 GA. . . . . NiB $925 Ex $754 Gd $528
Same general specifications as 12 and 20 ga. Model 76 except chambered for 3-inch shells in .410, has extractors, double triggers, 26-inch bbls. only, English-style stock w/straight grip and small forend. Disc.

MODEL 117 HAMMERLESS DOUBLE NiB $1747 Ex $939 Gd $718
Holland & Holland-type sidelocks, hand-detachable. Engraved action. Automatic ejectors. Selective single trigger. Gauges: 12, 20 (3-inch). Bbls.: 26-, 27-, 28-, 30-inch; 27- and 30-inch in 12 ga. only; any standard choke combination. Checkered pistol-grip stock and beavertail forend of select walnut. Manufactured in 1985.

BOLERO . . . . NiB $478 Ex $359 Gd $290
Same general specifications as Matador except non-selective single trigger and extractors. Gauges: 12 16, 20, 20 Magnum (3-inch), .410 (3-inch). Note: This model, prior to 1956, was designated F. I. Model 400 by the importer. Made from 1955 to 63.

CONTENTO OVER/UNDER SHOTGUN
Boxlock w/Woodward side lugs and double internal bolts. Gauge: 12 (2.75-inch chambers). Bbls.: 26-, 28-inch field; 30-, 32-inch trap; fixed chokes as required or screw-in choke tubes. Hand-checkered European walnut stock and forend. Single selective trigger and automatic ejectors.
M.K.2. . . . . NiB $1045 Ex $832 Gd $591
M.K.3. . . . . NiB $1752 Ex $1434 Gd $1005
W/Interchangeable single bbl., add. $400

MATADOR
HAMMERLESS DOUBLE . . . . NiB $548 Ex $420 Gd $295
Anson & Deeley boxlock. Selective automatic ejectors. Selective single trigger. Gauges: 12, 16, 20, 20 Magnum (3-inch). Bbls: 26-, 28-, 30-inches; any standard choke combination. Weight: 6.5 to 7.5 lbs., depending on ga. and bbl. length. Checkered pistol-grip stock and beavertail forend. Note: This model, prior to 1956, was designated F. I. Model 400E by the U. S. importer, Firearms Int'l. Corp. of Washington, D.C. Made from 1955 to 1963.

SHOTGUNS

MATADOR II . . . . **NiB $675 Ex $522 Gd $371**
Improved version of Matador w/same general specifications except has vent-rib bbls. Made 1964 to 1969.

MATADOR III . . . . **NiB $796 Ex $696 Gd $508**
Same general specifications as AyA Matador II. Made 1970 to 1985.

MODEL XXV BOXLOCK
Anson & Deeley boxlock w/double locking lugs. Gauges: 12 and 20. 25-inch chopper lump, satin blued bbls. w/Churchill rib. Weight: 5 to 7 lbs. Double triggers. Automatic safety and ejectors. Color-case-hardened receiver w/Continental-style scroll and floral engraving. European walnut stock. Imported 1979 to 1986 and 1991.
12 or 20 ga. . . . . **NiB $3105 Ex $2615 Gd $1983**
Extra set of bbls., add **$1050**

MODEL XXV SIDELOCK
Holland & Holland-type sidelock. Gauges: 12, 20, 28 and .410; 25-, 26-, 27- 28-, 29-, and 32-inch bbls. Chopper lump, satin blued bbls. w/Churchill rib. Weight: 5 to 7 lbs. Double triggers standard or selective or non-selective single trigger optional. Automatic safety and ejectors. Cocking indicators. Color-casehardened or coin-silver-finished receiver w/Continental-style scroll and floral engraving. Select European walnut stock w/hand-cut checkering and oil finish. Imported 1979 to 1986 and 1991.
12 or 20 ga. . . . . **NiB $5800 Ex $3995 Gd $2931**
28 ga. (disc. 1997) . . . . **NiB $6000 Ex $4984 Gd $3421**
.410 ga. (disc. 1997) . . . . **NiB $6000 Ex $4984 Gd $3421**
Single trigger, add **$75**
Single selective trigger, add **$120**
Extra set of bbls., add **$2000**

BAIKAL SHOTGUNS — Izhevsk and Tula, Russia

MODEL IZH-18M SINGLE SHOT . . . . . **NiB $91 Ex $78 Gd $60**
Hammerless w/cocking indicator. Automatic ejector. Manual safety. Gauges: 12 , 20, 16 w/2.75-inch chamber or .410 w/3-inch chamber. Bbls.: 26-, 28-inch w/fixed chokes (IC, M, F). Weight: 5.5 to 6 lbs. Made in Russia.

MODEL IZH-27 FIELD O/U . . . . . . **NiB $400 Ex $341 Gd $244**
Boxlock. Double triggers w/extractors. 12 ga.; 2.75-inch chambers. Bbls.: 26-inch, IC/M; 28-inch, M/F w/fixed chokes. Weight: 6.75 lbs. Made in Russia.

MODEL IZH-43 FIELD SIDE-BY-SIDE
Side-by-side; boxlock. Double triggers; extractors. 12 or 20 ga. w/2.75-inch chambers. Bbls: 20-inch cylinder bbl and 26-or 28-inch modified full bbl. Weight: 6.75 to 7 lbs. Checkered walnut stock, forend. Blued, engraved receiver. Imported 1994 to 1996.
Model IJ-43 Field w/20-inch bbls. . . . . **NiB $339 Ex $222 Gd $163**
**Model IJ-43 Field
w/26- or 28-inch bbls** . . . . **NiB $339 Ex $222 Gd $163**

IZH-43 SERIES SIDE-BY-SIDE
Boxlock. Gauges: 12, 16, 20 or .410 w/2.75- or 3-inch chambers. Bbls.: 20-, 24-, 26- or 28-inch w/fixed chokes or choke tubes. Single selective or double triggers. Weight: 6.75 lbs. Checkered hardwood (standard on Hunter II Model) or walnut stock and forend (standard on Hunter Model). Blued, engraved receiver. Imported 1994 to 1996.
**Model IZH-43Hunter
(12 ga. w/walnut stock)** . . . . **NiB $345 Ex $289 Gd $171**
Model IZH-43 Hunter

(20, 16 or .410 ga.) . . . . **NiB $375 Ex $328 Gd $202**
**Model IZH-43 Hunter II
(12 ga. w/external hammers)** . . . . . . **NiB $389 Ex $275 Gd $221**
**Model IZH-43 Hunter II
(12 ga. hammerless)** . . . . **NiB $389 Ex $275 Gd $221**
Model IZH-43 Hunter II (20, 16 or .410 ga.) . . . . **NiB $389
Ex $275 Gd $221**
Hunter II w/walnut stock, add **$35**
Hunter II w/single selective trigger, add **$45**

MODEL IZH-27 O/U
Boxlock. Single selective trigger w/automatic ejectors or double triggers w/extractors. Gauges: 12 or 20 w/2.75-inch chambers. Bbls.: 26-inch or 28-inch w/fixed chokes. Weight: 7 lbs. Checkered European hardwood stock and forearm. Made in Russia.
**Model IJ-27 (w/double
triggers and extractors.)** . . . . **NiB $400 Ex $334 Gd $171**
**Model IJ-27
(single selective
trigger and ejectors)** . . . . **NiB $400 Ex $334 Gd $171**

BAKER SHOTGUNS — Batavia, New York Made 1903-1933 by Baker Gun Company

BATAVIA LEADER HAMMERLESS DOUBLE
Sidelock. Plain extractors or automatic ejectors. Double triggers. Gauges: 12, 16, 20. Bbls.: 26- to 32-inch; any standard boring. Weight: About 7.75 lbs. (12 ga. w/30-inch bbls.). Checkered pistol-grip stock and forearm.
W/plain extractors . . . . **NiB $995 Ex $629 Gd $436**
W/automatic ejectors . . . . **NiB $938 Ex $506 Gd $333**

BATAVIA EJECTOR . . . . **NiB $1191 Ex $1218 Gd $655**
Same general specifications as the Batavia Leader except higher quality and finer finish throughout; has Damascus or homotensile steel bbls., checkered pistol-grip stock and forearm of select walnut; automatic ejectors standard; 12 and 16 ga. only. Deduct 60% for Damascus bbls.

BATAVIA SPECIAL . . . . **NiB $800 Ex $655 Gd $444**
Same general specifications as the Batavia Leader except 12 and 16 ga. only; extractors, Homotensile steel bbls.

BLACK BEAUTY
Same general specifications as the Batavia Leader except higher quality and finer finish throughout; has line engraving, special steel bbls., select walnut stock w/straight, full or half-pistol-grip.
Black Beauty w/plain extractors . . . **NiB $800 Ex $572 Gd $396**
**Black Beauty Special
w/plain extractors** . . . . **NiB $1097 Ex $706 Gd $474**
**Black Beauty Special
w/automatic ejectors** . . . . **NiB $1045 Ex $735 Gd $477**

GRADE R . . . . **NiB $2400 Ex $1584 Gd $945**
High-grade gun w/same general specifications as the Batavia Leader except has fine Damascus or Krupp fluid steel bbls., engraving in line, scroll and game scene designs, checkered stock and forearm of fancy European walnut; 12 and 16 ga. only. Deduct 60% for Damascus bbls.

GRADE S
Same general specifications as the Batavia Leader except higher quality and finer finish throughout; has Flui-tempered steel bbls., line and scroll engraving, checkered stock w/half-pistol-grip and forearm of semi-fancy imported walnut; 10, 12 and 16 ga.
Non-ejector . . . . **NiB $1800 Ex $1154 Gd $993**
W/automatic ejectors . . . . **NiB $2100 Ex $1450 Gd $1295**

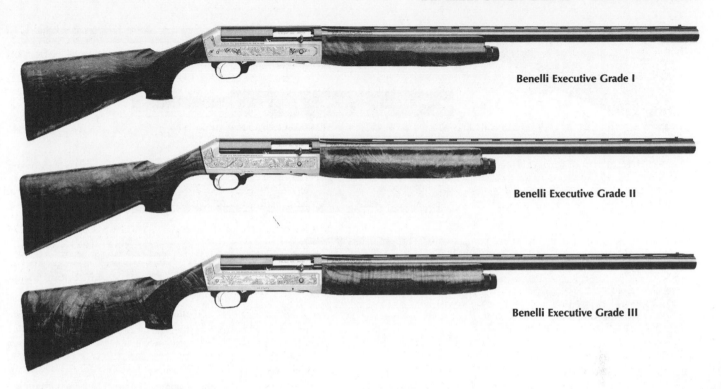

Benelli Executive Grade I

Benelli Executive Grade II

Benelli Executive Grade III

PARAGON, EXPERT AND DELUXE GRADES

Made to order only, these are the higher grades of Baker hammerless sidelock double-bbl. shotguns. After 1909, the Paragon Grade, as well as the Expert and Deluxe intro. that year, had a crossbolt in addition to the regular Baker system taper wedge fastening. There are early Paragon guns w/Damascus bbls. and some are non-ejector, but this grade was also produced w/automatic ejectors and w/the finest fluid steel bbls., in lengths to 34 inches, standard on Expert and Deluxe guns. Differences among the three models are in overall quality, finish, engraving and grade of fancy figured walnut in the stock and forearm; Expert and Deluxe wood may be carved as well as checkered. Choice of straight, full or half-pistol grip was offered. A single trigger was available in the two higher grades. The Paragon was available in 10 ga (Damascus bbls. only), and the other two models were regularly produced in 12, 16 and 20 ga.

Paragon grade, non-ejector . . . . NiB $4010 Ex $2571 Gd $1971
Paragon grade, Auto ejectors. . . NiB $4300 Ex $2895 Gd $2185
Expert grade . . . . NiB $6010 Ex $4492 Gd $2735
Deluxe grade . . . . NiB $10,338 Ex $8521 Gd $6429
For ejectors, add $300

BELKNAP SHOTGUNS — Louisville, Kentucky

MODEL B-68 SINGLE-SHOT SHOTGUN NiB $169 Ex $124 Gd $93
Takedown. Visible hammer. Automatic ejector. Gauges: 12, 16, 20 and .410. Bbls.: 26-inch to 36-inch; F choke. Weight: 6 lbs. Plain pistol-grip stock and forearm.

MODEL B-63 SINGLE-SHOT SHOTGUN . . . NiB $175 Ex $119 Gd $90
Takedown. Visible hammer. Automatic ejector. Gauges: 12, 20 and .410. Bbls.: 26- to 36-inch, F choke. Weight: Average 6 lbs. Plain pistol-grip stock and forearm.

MODEL B-63E SINGLE-SHOT SHOTGUN . . . NiB $165 Ex $114 Gd $86
Same general specifications as Model B-68 except has side lever opening instead of top lever.

MODEL B-64

SLIDE-ACTION SHOTGUN. . . . . NiB $297 Ex $217 Gd $154
Hammerless. Gauges: 12, 16, 20 and .410. Three round tubular magazine. Various bbl. lengths and chokes from 26-inch to 30-inch. Weight: 6.25 to 7.5 lbs. Walnut-finished hardwood stock.

MODEL B-65C

AUTOLOADING SHOTGUN . . . . . . NiB $445 Ex $337 Gd $241
Browning-type lightweight alloy receiver. 12 ga. only. Four round tubular magazine. Bbl.: plain, 28-inch. Weight: About 8.25 lbs. Disc. 1949.

BENELLI SHOTGUNS — Urbino, Italy
Imported by Benelli USA, Accokeek, MD

MODEL 121 M1 MILITARY/POLICE

AUTOLOADING SHOTGUN . . . . NiB $546 Ex $458 Gd $318
Gauge: 12. Seven round magazine. 19.75-inch bbl. 39.75 inches overall. Cylinder choke, 2.75-inch chamber. Weight: 7.4 lbs. Matte black finish and European hardwood stock. Post front sight, fixed buckhorn rear sight. Imported in 1985. Disc.

BLACK EAGLE
AUTOLOADING SHOTGUN

Two-piece aluminum and steel receiver. Ga: 12; 3-inch chamber. Four round magazine. Screw-in choke tubes (SK, IC, M, IM, F). Bbls.: Ventilated rib; 21, 24, 26 or 28 inches w/bead front sight; 24-inch rifled slug. 42.5 to 49.5 inches overall. Weight: 7.25 lbs. (28-inch bbl.). Matte black lower receiver w/blued upper receiver and bbl. Checkered walnut stock w/high-gloss finish and drop adjustment. Imported from 1989 to 1990 and 1997 to 1998.

Limited edition. . . . . NiB $1500 Ex $1034 Gd $912
Competition model . . . . NiB $876 Ex $692 Gd $438
Slug model (disc. 1992) . . . . NiB $735 Ex $570 Gd $414
Standard model (disc. 1990) . . . . NiB $800 Ex $628 Gd $458

SHOTGUNS

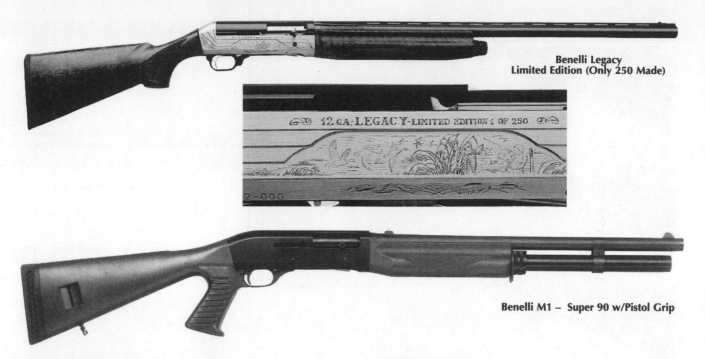

**Benelli Legacy
Limited Edition (Only 250 Made)**

Benelli M1 – Super 90 w/Pistol Grip

BLACK EAGLE EXECUTIVE
Custom Black Eagle Series. Montefeltro-style rotating bolt w/three locking lugs. All-steel lower receiver engraved, gold inlay by Bottega Incisione di Cesare Giovanelli. 12 ga. only. 21-, 24-, 26-, or 28-inch vent-rib bbl. w/5 screw-in choke tubes (Type I) or fixed chokes. Custom deluxe walnut stock and forend. Built to customer specifications on special order.

Executive Grade I	NiB $4120	Ex $3225	Gd $2223
Executive Grade II	NiB $4341	Ex $3485	Gd $2403
Executive Grade III	NiB $5473	Ex $4088	Gd $2815

LEGACY AUTOLOADING SHOTGUN
Gauges: 12 and 20 ga. w/3-inch chambers. 24- 26- or 28-inch bbl. 47.63 to 49.62 inches overall. Weight: 5.8 to 7.5 lbs. Four round magazine. Five screw-in choke tubes. Lower alloy receiver and upper steel reciever cover. Features Benelli's inertia recoil operating system. Imported 1998 to date.

Legacy model	NiB $1248	Ex $987	Gd $832
Legacy model Limited Edition	NiB $1848	Ex $1534	Gd $936

M1 FIELD AUTO SHOTGUN . . . . . . NiB $822 Ex $725 Gd $620
Gauge: 20. Chambers: 2.75 or 3 inches. Bbl. 24 or 26 inches, stepped ventilated rib and red bar sights. Stock: Synthetic, black or camo. Weight: 5.7 to 5.8 lbs. Includes set of five choke tubes. Imported from Italy.

M1 SUPER 90
AUTO-LOADING SHOTGUN . . . . . NiB $890 Ex $760 Gd $470
Gauge: 12. Seven round magazine. Cylinder choke. 19.75-inch bbl. 39.75 inches overall. Weight: 7 lbs., 4 oz. to 7 lbs., 10 oz. Matte black finish. Stock and forend made of fiberglass-reinforced polymer. Sights: Post front, fixed buckhorn rear, drift adj. Introduced 1985; when the model line expanded in 1989, this configuration was discontinued.

M1 SUPER 90
DEFENSE AUTOLOADER . . . . NiB $1033 Ex $824 Gd $450
Same general specifications as Model Super 90 except w/pistol-grip stock. Available w/Ghost-Ring sight option. Imported 1986 to 1998.

M1 SUPER 90 FIELD
Inertia-recoil semiautomatic shotgun. Gauge: 12; 3-inch chamber. Three round magazine. Bbl.: 21, 24, 26 or 28 inches. 42.5 to 49.5 inches overall. Choke: SK, IC, M, IM, F. Matte receiver. Standard polymer stock or satin walnut (26- or 28-inch bbl. only). Bead front sight. Imported from 1990 to 2006.

W/Realtree camo	NiB $915	Ex $649	Gd $415
W/polymer stock	NiB $685	Ex $491	Gd $363
W/walnut stock	NiB $940	Ex $519	Gd $389

M1 SUPER 90 SLUG AUTOLOADER
Same general specifications as M1 Super 90 Field except w/5-round magazine. 18.5-inch bbl. Cylinder bore. 39.75 inches overall. Weight: 6.5 lbs. Polymer standard stock. Rifle or Ghost-Ring sights. Imported 1986 to 1998.

W/rifle sights	NiB $895	Ex $571	Gd $467
W/ghost-ring sights	NiB $1000	Ex $697	Gd $467
W/Realtree camo finish, add			$105

M1 SUPER 90 SPORTING
SPECIAL AUTOLOADER . . . . NiB $750 Ex $542 Gd $446
Same general specifications as M1 Super 90 Field except w/18.5-inch bbl. 39.75 inches overall. Weight: 6.5 lbs. Ghost-ring sights. Polymer stock. Imported from 1994 to 1998.

M3 SUPER 90 PUMP/AUTOLOADER
Inertia-recoil semiautomatic and/or pump action. Gauge: 12. Seven round magazine. Cylinder choke. 19.75-inch bbl. 41 inches overall (31 inches folded). Weight: 7 to 7.5 lbs. Matte black finish. Stock: standard synthetic, pistol-grip or folding tubular steel. Standard rifle or Ghost-Ring sights. Imported 1989 to date. Caution: Increasing the magazine capacity to more than 5 rounds in M3 shotguns w/pistol-grip stocks violates provisions of the 1994 Crime Bill. This model may be used legally only by the military and law-enforcement agencies.

Standard model	NiB $1350	Ex $971	Gd $675
Pistol-grip model	NiB $1544	Ex $1098	Gd $898
W/folding stock	NiB $1110	Ex $899	Gd $629
W/laser sight	NiB $1690	Ex $1237	Gd $996
For ghost ring sights, add			$50

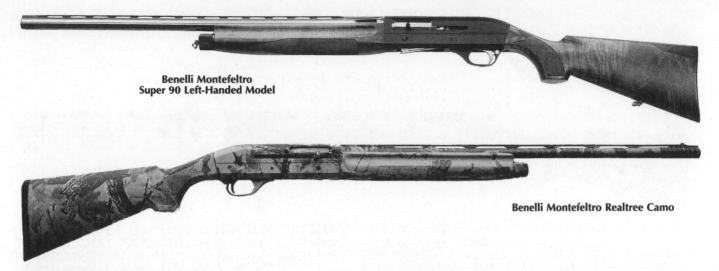

Benelli Montefeltro
Super 90 Left-Handed Model

Benelli Montefeltro Realtree Camo

MONTEFELTRO/SUPER 90
SEMIAUTOMATIC

Gauges: 12 or 20 gauge w/3-inch chamber. 21- 24- 26- or 28-inch bbl. 43.7 to 49.5 inches overall. Weight: 5.3 to 7.5 lbs. Four round magazine. Five screw-in choke tubes (C, IC, M, IM, F). High gloss or satin walnut or Realtree Camo stock. Blued metal finish. Imported 1987 to 1992.

Standard Hunter model	NiB $1085	Ex $765	Gd $463
Slug model (disc. 1992)	NiB $648	Ex $579	Gd $364
Turkey model	NiB $648	Ex $579	Gd $364
Uplander model	NiB $648	Ex $572	Gd $364
Limited Edition (1995-96)	NiB $1960	Ex $1580	Gd $1098
20 ga. w/Realtree camo	NiB $1175	Ex $861	Gd $563
20 ga. Youth Model w/short stock, add			$40
Left-hand model, add			$25

NOVA PUMP SHOTGUN . . . . NiB $365 Ex $244 Gd $198

Gauge: 12 or 20. Chambers: 2.75 or 3 inches; 3.5 inch chambers in 12 gauge only Four-round magazine. Bbl. 24, 26 or 28 inches; red bar sights. Stock: Synthetic,(Xtra Brown in 12 gauge or Timber HD in 20 gauge). Montefeltro rotating bolt, magazine cutoff, synthetic trigger assembly. Introduced 1999. Imported from Italy.

SL 121V SEMIAUTO
(SL-80 SERIES) . . . . NiB $397 Ex $309 Gd $239

Recoil-operated semiautomaticw/split receiver design. Gauge: 12. Five round capacity. 26-, 28- or 30-inch ventilated rib bbl. (26-inch choked M, IM, IC, 28-inch, F, M, IM; 30-inch, F choke - Mag.). Straight walnut stock w/hand-checkered pistol grip and forend. Importation disc. in 1985.

SL 121V SLUG SHOTGUN
(SL-80 SERIES) . . . . NiB $395 Ex $319 Gd $261

Same general specifications as Benelli SL 121V except designed for rifled slugs and equipped w/rifle sights. Disc. in 1985.

SL 123V SEMIAUTO
(SL-80 SERIES) . . . . NiB $429 Ex $315 Gd $206

Gauge: 12. 26- and 28-inch bbls. 26-inch choked IM, M, IC; 28-inch choked F, IM, M. Disc. in 1985.

SL 201 SEMIAUTOMATIC
(SL-80 SERIES) . . . . NiB $399 Ex $334 Gd $268

Gauge: 20. 26-inch bbl. Mod. choke. Weight: 5 lbs., 10 oz. Ventilated rib. Disc. in 1985.

SPORT AUTOLOADING
SHOTGUN . . . . NiB $1125 Ex $845 Gd $595

Similar to the Black Eagle Competition model except has one-piece matte- finished alloy receiver w/inscribed red Benelli logo. 26 or 28 inches bbl. w/2 inchangable carbon fiber vent ribs. Oil-finished checkered walnut stock w/adjustable buttpad and buttstock. Imported 1997 to 2002.

SUPER BLACK EAGLE
AUTOLOADING SHOTGUN

Same general specifications as Black Eagle except w/3.5-inch chamber that accepts 2.75-, 3- and 3.5-inch shells. Two round magazine (3.5-inch), 3-round magazine (2.75- or 3-inch). High-gloss, satin finish or camo stock. Realtree camo, matte black or blued metal finish. Imported 1991 to 2005.

Standard model	NiB $1077	Ex $886	Gd $636
Realtree camo	NiB $1169	Ex $1006	Gd $708
Custom slug model	NiB $1110	Ex $853	Gd $603
Limited edition	NiB $1828	Ex $1568	Gd $1094
W/wood stock, add			$10
Left-hand model, add			$75

BERETTA USA CORP. — Accokeek, Maryland
Mfd. by Fabbrica D'Armi Pietro Beretta S.p.A.
in Gardone Val Trompia (Brescia), Italy
Imported by Beretta USA (Previously by Garcia Corp.)

MODEL 409PB
HAMMERLESS DOUBLE . . . . NiB $855 Ex $646 Gd $481

Boxlock. Double triggers. Plain extractors. Gauges: 12, 16, 20, 28. Bbls.: 27.5-, 28.5- and 30-inch, IC/M choke or M/F choke. Weight: from 5.5 to 7.75 lbs., depending on ga. and bbl. length. Straight or pistol-grip stock and beavertail forearm, checkered. Imported 1934 to 1964.

MODEL 410E

Same general specifications as Model 409PB except has automatic ejectors and is of higher quality throughout. Imported 1934 to 1964.

Model 410E (12 ga.)	NiB $1275	Ex $1031	Gd $813
Model 410E (20 ga.)	NiB $2750	Ex $1918	Gd $12060
Model 410E (28 ga.)	NiB $3775	Ex $2965	Gd $2400

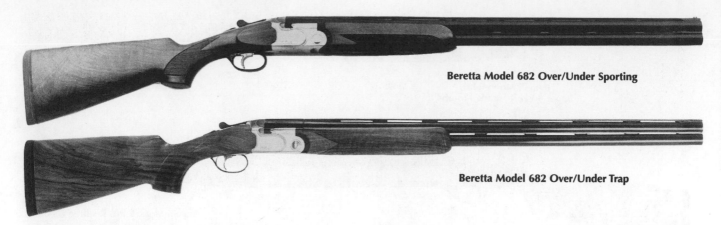

Beretta Model 682 Over/Under Sporting

Beretta Model 682 Over/Under Trap

MODEL 410 10-GA. MAGNUM . . . NiB $1200 Ex $864 Gd $648
Same as Model 410E except heavier construction. Plain extractors. Double triggers. 10-ga. Magnum, 3.5-inch chambers. 32-inch bbls., both F choke. Weight: about 10 lbs. Checkered pistol-grip stock and forearm, recoil pad. Imported 1934 to 1984.

MODEL 411E
Same general specifications as Model 409PB except has sideplates, automatic ejectors and is of higher quality throughout. Imported 1934 to 1964.
Model 411E (12 ga.) . . . . NiB $2000 Ex $1629 Gd $1132
Model 411E (20 ga.) . . . . NiB $2750 Ex $2123 Gd $1478
Model 411E (28 ga.) . . . . NiB $4250 Ex $3880 Gd $2684

MODEL 424 HAMMERLESS
DOUBLE . . . . NiB $1194 Ex $1198 Gd $835
Boxlock. Light border engraving. Plain extractors. Gauges: 12, 20; chambers 2.75-inch in former, 3-inch in latter. Bbls.: 28-inch M/F choke, 26-inch IC/M choke. Weight: 5 lbs. 14 oz. to 6 lbs. 10 oz., depending on ga. and bbl. length. English-style straight-grip stock and forearm, checkered. Imported 1977 to 1984.

MODEL 426E. . . . . NiB $1495 Ex $1170 Gd $988
Same as Model 424 except action body is finely engraved, silver pigeon inlaid in top lever; has selective automatic ejectors and selective single trigger, stock and forearm of select European walnut. Imported 1977-84.

MODEL 450 SERIES HAMMERLESS DOUBLES
Custom English-style sidelock. Single, non-selective trigger or double triggers. Manual safety. Selective automatic ejectors. Gauge: 12; 2.75- or 3-inch chambers. Bbls.: 26, 28 or 30 inches choked to customers' specifications. Weight: 6.75 lbs. Checkered high-grade walnut stock. Receiver w/coin-silver finish. Imported 1948. Disc.
Model 450 EL (disc. 1982). . . . . NiB $8000 Ex $6316 Gd $4354
Model 450 EELL (disc. 1982). . . NiB $9995 Ex $6685 Gd $4595
Model 451 (disc. 1987). . . . . . . NiB $6249 Ex $5484 Gd $3789
Model 451 E (disc. 1989) . . . . . NiB $6750 Ex $6004 Gd $4142
Model 451 EL (disc. 1985) . . . NiB $16,750 Ex $13,348 Gd $10,037
Model 451 EELL (disc. 1990) . . . NiB $14,202 Ex $11,362 Gd $9726
Model 452 (Intro. 1990) . . . . . NiB $28,750 Ex $20,200 Gd $17,376
Model 452 EELL (intro. 1992) . . NiB $39,000 Ex $34,180 Gd $26,442
Extra set of bbls., add 30%

MODEL 470 SERIES HAMMERLESS DOUBLE
Gauge: 12 and 20 ga. w/3-inch chambers. 26- or 28-inch bbl. Weight: 5.9 to 6.5 lbs. Low profile, improved box lock action w/single selective trigger. Selected walnut, checkered stock and forend. Metal front bead sight. Scroll-engraved receiver w/gold inlay and silver chrome finish. Imported 1999 to date.

Model 470 Silver Hawk 12 ga. . . . . . . NiB $8250 Ex $6708 Gd $5387
Model 470 Silver Hawk 20 ga. . . . . . . NiB $8682 Ex $6153 Gd $5499
Model 470 EL Silver Hawk 12 ga. . . . NiB $8130 Ex $6921 Gd $5315
Model 470 EL Silver Hawk 20 ga. . . . NiB $8298 Ex $6046 Gd $5387
Model 470 EELL (Jubilee II) 12 ga. . . . NiB $8149 Ex $6140 Gd $4526
Model 470 EELL (Jubilee II) 20 ga. . . . NiB $8611 Ex $6923 Gd $4776
Extra set of bbls., add. 30%

MODEL 625 S/S HAMMERLESS DOUBLE
Boxlock. Gauges: 12 or 20. Bbls.: 26-, 28- or 30-inch w/fixed choke combinations. Single selective or double triggers w/extractors. Checkered English-style buttstock and forend. Imported 1984 to 1987.
W/double triggers . . . . NiB $1535 Ex $837 Gd $596
W/single selective trigger . . . . NiB $1792 Ex $970 Gd $687
20 ga., add. $150

MODEL 626 S/S HAMMERLESS DOUBLE
Field Grade side-by-side. Boxlock action w/single selective trigger, extractors and automatic safety. Gauges: 12 (2.75-inch chambers); 20 (3-inch chambers). Bbls.: 26- or 28-inch w/Mobilchoke or various fixed-choke combinations. Weight: 6.75 lbs. (12 ga.). Bright chrome finish. Checkered European walnut buttstock and forend in straight English style. Imported 1985 to 1994.
Model 626 Field (disc. 1988). . . . NiB $1292 Ex $1074 Gd $580
Model 626 Onyx . . . . NiB $1656 Ex $1156 Gd $864
Model 626 Onyx (3.5-inch
Magnum, disc. 1993). . . . . NiB $1654 Ex $1229 Gd $865
20 ga., add. 50%

MODEL 627 S/S HAMMERLESS DOUBLE
Same as Model 626 S/S except w/engraved sideplates and pistol-grip or straight English-style stock. Imported 1985 to 1994.
Model 627 EL Field . . . . NiB $2250 Ex $2015 Gd $1485
Model 627 EL Sport. . . . . NiB $2500 Ex $2072 Gd $1523
Model 627 EELL. . . . . NiB $4305 Ex $3727 Gd $2599

MODEL 682 O/U SHOTGUN
Hammerless takedown w/single selective trigger. Gauges: 12, 20, 28, .410. Bbls.: 26- to 34-inch w/fixed chokes or Mobilchoke tubes. Checkered European walnut buttstock/forend in various grades and configurations. Imported 1984 to 2000.
Model 682 Comp Skeet . . . . . . NiB $1435 Ex $1046 Gd $9 49
Model 682 Comp Skeet Deluxe. . . . . NiB $1652 Ex $1381 Gd $1071
Mdl. 682 Comp Super Skeet . . . . NiB $2430 Ex $1963 Gd $1366
Mdl. 682 Comp Skeet 2-bbl.
set (disc. 1989) . . . . NiB $4981 Ex $4000 Gd $2771
Mdl. 682 Comp Skeet
4 bbl. Set (disc. 1996) . . . . NiB $5695 Ex $4589 Gd $3175
Mdl. 682 Sporting Continental. . . . . . NiB $1451 Ex $1042 Gd $945
Mdl. 682 Sporting Combo . . . . NiB $1679 Ex $1447 Gd $1065

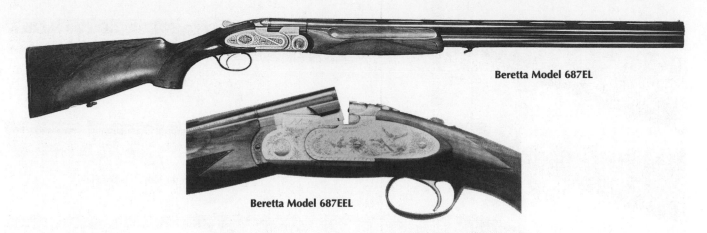

Beretta Model 687EL

Beretta Model 687EEL

Mdl. 682 Gold Sporting	NiB $1670	Ex $1140	Gd $976
Mdl. 682 Super Sporting	NiB $1491	Ex $1275	Gd $1167
Mdl. 682 Comp Trap Gold X	NiB $2135	Ex $1646	Gd $1149
Mdl. 682 Comp Trap Top Sgle. (1986-95)	NiB $1997	Ex $1599	Gd $1085
Mdl. 682 Comp Trap Live Pig. (1990-98)	NiB $2642	Ex $2121	Gd $1480
Mdl. 682 Comp Mono/ComboTrp. Gld. X	NiB $2845	Ex $2355	Gd $1629
Mdl. 682 Comp Mono Trap (1985-88)	NiB $1773	Ex $1436	Gd $1005
Mdl. 682 Super Trap Gold X (1991-95)	NiB $2124	Ex $1710	Gd $1184
Mdl. 682 Sup. Trap Combo Gld. X (1991-97)	NiB $2969	Ex $2398	Gd $1668
Mdl. 682 Super Trap Top Sgle. Gld. X (1991-95)	NiB $2194	Ex $1769	Gd $1238
Mdl. 682 Sup. Trap Unsingle (1992-94)	NiB $2149	Ex $1660	Gd $1165

MODEL 686 O/U SHOTGUN

Low-profile improved boxlock action. Single selective trigger. Selective automatic ejectors. Gauges: 12, 20, 28 w/3.5- 3- or 2.75-inch chambers, depending upon ga. Bbls.: 26-, 28-, 30-inch w/fixed chokes or Mobilchoke tubes. Weight: 5.75 to 7.5 lbs. Checkered American walnut stock and forearm of various qualities, depending upon model. Receiver finishes also vary, but all have blued bbls. Sideplates to simulate sidelock action on EL models. Imported 1988 to 1995.

Model 686 Field Onyx	NiB $1200	Ex $1061	Gd $620
Mdl. 686 (3.5-inch Mag., disc. 1993 & reintro.1996)	NiB $4100	Ex $2772	Gd $2024
Model 686 EL Gold Perdiz (1992-97)	NiB $1925	Ex $1405	Gd $964
Model 686 Essential (1994-96)	NiB $969	Ex $774	Gd $535
Model 686 Silver Essential (1997-98)	NiB $1076	Ex $869	Gd $594
Model 686 Sil. Pig. Onyx (intro. 1996)	NiB $1419	Ex $1127	Gd $787
Mdl. 686 Sil. Perdiz Onyx (disc. 1996)	NiB $1382	Ex $1094	Gd $769
Model 686 Sil. Pig./Perdiz Onyx Combo	NiB $958	Ex $759	Gd $577
Model 686 L Silver Perdiz (disc. 1994)	NiB $1158	Ex $894	Gd $629
Model 686 Skeet Silver Pigeon (1996-98)	NiB $1183	Ex $945	Gd $665
Model 686 Skeet Silver Perdiz (1994-96)	NiB $1459	Ex $1128	Gd $789
Model 686 Skeet Sil. Pig./Perdiz Combo	NiB $1459	Ex $1158	Gd $789
Model 686 Sporting Special (1987-93)	NiB $1659	Ex $1296	Gd $906
Model 686 Sporting English (1991-92)	NiB $1698	Ex $1370	Gd $958
Model 686 Sporting Onyx w/fixed chokes (1991-92)	NiB $1649	Ex $1304	Gd $906
Model 686 Sporting Onyx w/tubes (intro. 1992)	NiB $1239	Ex $993	Gd $695
Mdl. 686 Sporting Onyx Gld. (disc. 1993)	NiB $1767	Ex $1425	Gd $988
Mdl. 686 Sporting Sil. Pig. (intro. 1996)	NiB $1477	Ex $1189	Gd $812
Model 686 Sporting Sil. Perdiz (1993-96)	NiB $1422	Ex $1141	Gd $793
Mdl. 686 Sporting Coll. Sport (1996-97)	NiB $1072	Ex $875	Gd $610
Model 686 Sporting Combo	NiB $2529	Ex $2025	Gd $1405
Model 686 Trap International (1994-95)	NiB $1074	Ex $856	Gd $602
Model 686 Trap Silver Pigeon (intro. 1997)	NiB $1149	Ex $919	Gd $644
Model 686 Trap Top Mono (intro. 1998)	NiB $1193	Ex $963	Gd $669

Model 686 Ultralight Onyx (intro. 1992)	NiB $1499	Ex $1207	Gd $841
Mdl. 686 Ultralight Del. Onyx (intro. 1998)	NiB $1909	Ex $1501	Gd $1043

MODEL 687 O/U SHOTGUN

Same as Model 686 except w/decorative sideplates and varying grades of engraving and game-scene motifs.

Model 687 L Onyx (disc. 1991)	NiB $1398	Ex $1144	Gd $795
Model 687 L Onyx Gold Field (1988-89)	NiB $1598	Ex $1277	Gd $892
Model 687 L Onyx Silver Pigeon	NiB $1219	Ex $1623	Gd $1128
Model 687 EL Onyx (disc. 1990)	NiB $2756	Ex $2214	Gd $1547
Model 687 EL Gold Pigeon	NiB $3143	Ex $2531	Gd $1768
Model 687 EL Gold Pigeon Sm. Fr.	NiB $2918	Ex $2360	Gd $1646
Mdl. 687 EL Gld. Pig. Sporting (Int. 1993)	NiB $4292	Ex $3464	Gd $2405
Model 687 EELL Diamond Pigeon	NiB $4292	Ex $3464	Gd $2405
Mdl. 687 EELL Diamond Pig. Skeet	NiB $4160	Ex $3450	Gd $2328
Mdl. 687 EELL Diam. Pig. Sporting	NiB $4381	Ex $3528	Gd $2447
Mdl. 687 EELL Diam. Pig. X Trap	NiB $3845	Ex $3098	Gd $2156
Mdl. 687 EELL Diam. Pig. Mono Trap	NiB $3923	Ex $3185	Gd $2214
Mdl. 687 EELL Diam. Pig. Trap Combo	NiB $5344	Ex $4305	Gd $2990
Model 687 EELL Field Combo	NiB $4460	Ex $3603	Gd $2507
Model 687 EELL Skeet 4-bbl. set	NiB $7321	Ex $5895	Gd $3483
Model 687 EELL Gallery Special	NiB $6798	Ex $5473	Gd $3688
Model 687 EELL Gallery Special Combo	NiB $8098	Ex $6511	Gd $4469
Model 687 EELL Gallery Special pairs	NiB $15,820	Ex $12,674	Gd $8557
Model 687 Sporting English (1991-92)	NiB $2196	Ex $1771	Gd $1239
Mdl. 687 Sporting Sil. Pig. (intro. 1996)	NiB $1968	Ex $1588	Gd $1115
Mdl. 687 Sporting Sil. Perdiz (1993-96)	NiB $2047	Ex $1651	Gd $1250

MODEL 1200 SERIES SEMIAUTOLOADING SHOTGUN

Short recoil action. Gauge: 12; 2.75- or 3-inch chamber. Six round magazine. 24-, 26- or 28-inch vent-rib bbl. w/fixed chokes or Mobilchoke tubes. Weight: 7.25 lbs. Matte black finish. Adj. technopolymer stock and forend. Imported 1988 to 1990.

Model 1200 w/fixed choke (disc. 1989)	NiB $390	Ex $293	Gd $142
Model 1200 Riot (disc. 1989)	NiB $410	Ex $310	Gd $251
Model 1201 w/Mobilchoke (disc. 1994)	NiB $672	Ex $536	Gd $359
Model 1201 Riot	NiB $734	Ex $541	Gd $382
W/Pistol-grip stock, add			$45
W/Tritium sights, add			$80

MODEL A-301

AUTOLOADING SHOTGUN. . . . . . . NiB $588 Ex $414 Gd $298
Field Gun. Gas-operated. Scroll-decorated receiver. Gauge: 12 or 20; 2.75-inch chamber in former, 3-inch in latter. Three round magazine. Bbl.: Ventilated rib; 28-inch F or M choke, 26-inch IC. Weight: 6 lbs., 5 oz. – 6 lbs., 14 oz., depending on gauge and bbl. length. Checkered pistol-grip stock/forearm. Imported 1977 to 1982.

SHOTGUNS

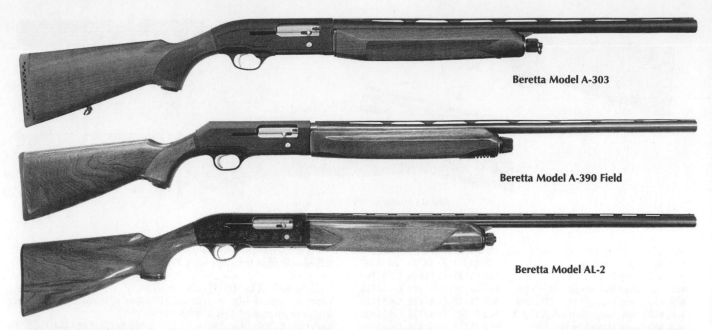

Beretta Model A-303

Beretta Model A-390 Field

Beretta Model AL-2

MODEL A-301 MAGNUM . . . . NiB $395 Ex $248 Gd $190
Same as Model A-301 Field Gun except chambered for 12 ga. Three inch Magnum shells, 30-inch F choke bbl. only, stock w/recoil pad. Weight: 7.25 lbs.

MODEL A-301 SKEET GUN . . . . NiB $395 Ex $248 Gd $190
Same as Model A-301 Field Gun except 26-inch bbl. SK choke only, skeet-style stock, gold-plated trigger.

MODEL A-301 SLUG GUN . . . . NiB $395 Ex $248 Gd $190
Same as Model A-301 Field Gun except has plain 22-inch bbl., slug choke, w/rifle sights. Weight: 6 lbs., 14 oz.

MODEL A-301 TRAP GUN . . . . NiB $385 Ex $250 Gd $200
Same as Model A-301 Field Gun except has 30-inch bbl. in F choke only, checkered Monte Carlo stock w/recoil pad, gold-plated trigger. Blued bbl. and receiver. Weight: 7 lbs., 10 oz. Imported 1978 to 1982.

MODEL A-302 SEMIAUTOLOADING SHOTGUN
Similar to gas-operated Model 301. Hammerless, takedown shotgun w/tubular magazine and Mag-Action that handles both 2.75- and 3-inch Magnum shells. Gauge: 12 or 20; 2.75- or 3-inch Mag. chambers. Bbl.: Vent or plain; 22-inch/Slug (12 ga.); 26-inch/IC (12 or 20) 28-inch/M (20 ga.), 28-inch/Multi-choke (12 or 20 ga.) 30-inch/F (12 ga.). Weight: 6.5 lbs., 20 ga.; 7.25.lbs., 12 ga. Blued/ black finish. Checkered European walnut, pistol-grip stock and forend. Imported from 1983 to c. 1987.
Standard model w/fixed choke . . . . NiB $395 Ex $248 Gd $190
Standard model w/multi-choke . . . . NiB $430 Ex $278 Gd $220

MODEL A-302 SUPER LUSSO . . NiB $1723 Ex $1389 Gd $1087
A custom A-302 in presentation grade w/hand-engraved receiver and custom select walnut stock.

MODEL A-303 SEMIAUTOLOADER
Similar to Model 302, except w/target specifications in Trap, Skeet and Youth configurations, and weighs 6.5 to 8 lbs. Imported from 1983 to 1996.
Field and Upland models. . . . . NiB $450 Ex $361 Gd $222
Skeet and Trap (disc. 1994) . . . . . . NiB $400 Ex $287 Gd $214
Slug model (disc. 1992) . . . . NiB $397 Ex $361 Gd $222

Sporting Clays . . . . NiB $495 Ex $367 Gd $269
Super Skeet . . . . NiB $425 Ex $367 Gd $279
Super Trap . . . . NiB $550 Ex $422 Gd $355
Waterfowl/Turkey (disc. 1992) . . . . NiB $450 Ex $315 Gd $245
Mobil choke, add. $40

MODEL A-303 YOUTH GUN . . . . . NiB $400 Ex $318 Gd $210
Locked-breech, gas-operated action. Ga: 12 and 20; 2-round magazine. Bbls.: 24, 26, 28, 30 or 32-inches, vent rib. Weight: 7 lbs. (12 ga.), 6 lbs. (20 ga.). Crossbolt safety. Length of pull shortened to 12.5 inches. Imported 1988-96.

MODEL AL-390
SEMIAUTOMATIC SHOTGUN
Gas-operated, self-regulating action designed to handle any size load. Gauges: 12 or 20 w/ 3-inch chamber. Three round magazine. Bbl.: 24, 26, 28 or 30 inches w/vent rib and Mobilchoke tubes. Weight: 7.5 lbs. Select walnut stock w/adj. comb. Blued or matte black finish. Imported 1992-96. Superseded by AL-390 series.
Standard model/Slug model . . . . . . NiB $450 Ex $311 Gd $265
Field model/Silver Mallard . . . . NiB $450 Ex $311 Gd $265
Deluxe model/Gold Mallard . . . . . . NiB $395 Ex $254 Gd $193
Turkey/Waterfowl model
(matte finish) . . . . NiB $525 Ex $323 Gd $265
For 20 ga., add $30

MODEL AL-390 TARGET
Similar to the Model 390 Field except w/2.75-inch chamber. Skeet: 28-inch ported bbl. w/wide vent rib and fixed choke (SK). Trap: 30- or 32-inch w/Mobilchoke tubes. Weight: 7.5 lbs. Fully adj. buttstock. Imported from 1993 to 1996.
Sport Trap model . . . . NiB $495 Ex $313 Gd $265
Sport Skeet model . . . . NiB $425 Ex $302 Gd $258
Sporting Clays model (unported). . . NiB $642 Ex $524 Gd $374
Super Trap model (ported). . . . . NiB $495 Ex $313 Gd $265
Super Skeet model (ported) . . . . NiB $495 Ex $313 Gd $265
W/ported bbl., add $85
20 ga., add. $35

MODEL AL-1 FIELD GUN . . . . NiB $495 Ex $313 Gd $265
Same as Model AL-2 gas-operated Field Gun except has bbl. w/o rib, no engraving on receiver. Imported from 1971 to 1973.

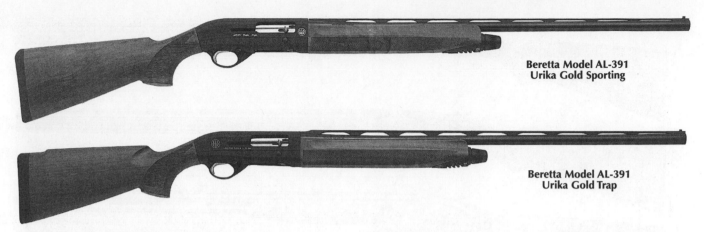

**Beretta Model AL-391
Urika Gold Sporting**

**Beretta Model AL-391
Urika Gold Trap**

MODEL AL-2 AUTOLOADING SHOTGUN
Field Gun. Gas-operated. Engraved receiver (1968 version, 12 ga. only, had no engraving). Gauge: 12 or 20. 2.75-inch chamber. Three round magazine. Bbls.: Vent rib; 30-inch F choke, 28-inch F or M choke, 26-inch IC. Weight: 6.5 to 7.25 lbs, depending on ga. and bbl. length. Checkered pistol-grip stock and forearm. Imported from 1968 to 1975.
W/Plain receiver . . . . **NiB $350 Ex $273 Gd $187**
W/Engraved receiver . . . . **NiB $569 Ex $466 Gd $335**

MODEL AL-2 MAGNUM . . . . **NiB $425 Ex $324 Gd $206**
Same as Model AL-2 Field Gun except chambered for 12 ga. 3-inch Magnum shells; 30-inch F or 28-inch M choke bbl. only. Weight: About 8 lbs. Imported from 1973 to 1975.

MODEL AL-2 SKEET GUN . . . . **NiB $399 Ex $263 Gd $192**
Same as Model AL-2 Field Gun except has wide rib, 26-inch bbl. in SK choke only, checkered pistol-grip stock and beavertail forearm. Imported 1973 to 1975.

MODEL AL-2 TRAP GUN . . . . **NiB $377 Ex $293 Gd $185**
Same as Model AL-2 Field Gun except has wide rib, 30 inch bbl. in F choke only, beavertail forearm. Monte Carlo stock w/recoil pad. Weight: About 7.75 lbs. Imported from 1973 to 1975.

MODEL AL-3
Similar to corresponding AL-2 models in design and general specifications. Imported from 1975 to 1976.
Field model . . . . **NiB $399 Ex $260 Gd $192**
Magnum model . . . . **NiB $399 Ex $260 Gd $192**
Skeet model . . . . **NiB $420 Ex $319 Gd $263**
Trap model . . . . **NiB $385 Ex $250 Gd $180**

MODEL AL-3 DELUXE TRAP GUN . . . . **NiB $620 Ex $484 Gd $252**
Same as standard Model AL-3 Trap Gun except has fully-engraved receiver, gold-plated trigger and safety, stock and forearm of premium-grade European walnut, gold monogram escutcheon inlaid in buttstock. Imported 1975 to 1976.

AL390 FIELD SHOTGUN
Lightweight version of A-390 series. Gauges: 12 or 20 ga. 22- 24-, 26-, 28-, or 30-inch bbl., 41.7 to 47.6 inches overall. Weight: 6.4 to 7.5 lbs. Imported 1992 to 1999.
Mdl. AL390 Field/Sil. Mallard (12 or 20 ga.) . . . **NiB $595 Ex $409 Gd $235**
Mdl. AL390 Field/Sil. Mallard Yth. (20 ga.) . . . . **NiB $452 Ex $315 Gd $238**
Model AL390 Field/Slug (12 ga. only) . . . . **NiB $470 Ex $396 Gd $226**
Model AL390 Silver Mallard camouflage . . **NiB $459 Ex $329 Gd $266**
Model AL390 Silver Mallard synthetic . . . . **NiB $470 Ex $396 Gd $226**
Model AL390 Gold Mallard (12 or 20 ga.) **NiB $724 Ex $594 Gd $396**
Model AL390 NWTF Spec. camouflage . . . **NiB $525 Ex $318 Gd $281**
Model AL390 NWTF Spec. synthetic . . . . . **NiB $493 Ex $369 Gd $270**

Mdl. AL390 NWTF Spec. Yth. . . . . **NiB $525 Ex $318 Gd $257**

AL390 SPORT SPORTING SHOTGUN
Similar to Model AL-390 Sport Skeet. Gauges: 12 or 20 ga., 28- or 30-inch bbls. Weight: 6.8 to 8 lbs. Imported from 1995-1999.
Model AL390 Sport Sporting . . . . **NiB $499 Ex $313 Gd $236**
Model AL390 Sport Sporting Collection . . . . . . **NiB $525 Ex $341 Gd $260**
**Mdl. AL390 Sport Sporting
Yth. (20 ga. only)** . . . . **NiB $530 Ex $388 Gd $268**
Model AL390 Sport Gold Sporting . . . . **NiB $726 Ex $509 Gd $373**
**Mdl. AL390 EELL Sport
Diamond Sporting.** . . . . **NiB $2000 Ex $1378 Gd $992**
W/Ported bbl., add **$75**

AL390 SPORT SKEET SHOTGUN
Gauges: 12 ga. only. 26- or 28-inch bbl. w/3-round magazine. Weight: 7.6 to 8 lbs. Matte finish wood and metal. Imported 1995 to 1999.
Model AL390 Sport Skeet . . . . **NiB $425 Ex $319 Gd $239**
Mdl. AL390 Sport Super Skeet (Semi-Auto) . . . . **NiB $495 Ex $329 Gd $282**
W/ported bbl., add **$100**

BERETTA AL390 SPORT TRAP SHOTGUN
Gauges: 12 ga. only. 30- or 32-inch bbl. w/3-round chamber. Weight: 7.8 to 8.25 lbs. Matte finish wood and metal. Black recoil rubber pad. Imported from 1995 to 1999.
Model AL390 Sport Trap . . . . **NiB $495 Ex $319 Gd $239**
Model AL390 Sport Super Trap . . . . **NiB $620 Ex $462 Gd $302**
Multi-choke bbl. (30" only), add **$40**
Ported bbl., add **$95**

AL391 URIKA AUTOLOADING SHOTGUN
Gauge: 12 and 20 ga. w/3-inch chambers. 28- 30- or 32-inch bbl. Weight: 6.6 to 7.7 lbs. Self-compensating gas valve. Adjustable synthetic and walnut stocks w/ five interchangeable chokes. Imported from 2001 to 2006.
Model AL391 Urika. . . . . **NiB $850 Ex $719 Gd $520**
Model AL391 Urika synthetic . . . . **NiB $775 Ex $724 Gd $510**
**Model AL391 Urika camo
w/Realtree Hardwoods** . . . . **NiB $895 Ex $793 Gd $577**
**Model AL391 Urika
Gold w/black receiver** . . . . **NiB $795 Ex $536 Gd $388**
**Model AL391 Urika Gold
w/silver receiver, lightweight** . . . . **NiB $1108 Ex $899 Gd $632**
Model AL391 Urika Youth. . . . . **NiB $800 Ex $706 Gd $496**
Model AL391 Urika Sporting . . . . **NiB $1025 Ex $828 Gd $568**
**Model AL391 Urika Gold
Sporting w/black receiver** . . . . **NiB $795 Ex $571 Gd $412**
**Model AL391 Urika
Gold Sporting w/silver receiver** . . . . . **NiB $1144 Ex $927 Gd $651**
Model AL391 Urika Trap. . . . . **NiB $950 Ex $717 Gd $574**
Model AL391 Gold Trap . . . . **NiB $995 Ex $800 Gd $632**
Model AL391 Parallel Target . . . . **NiB $995 Ex $794 Gd $559**

SHOTGUNS

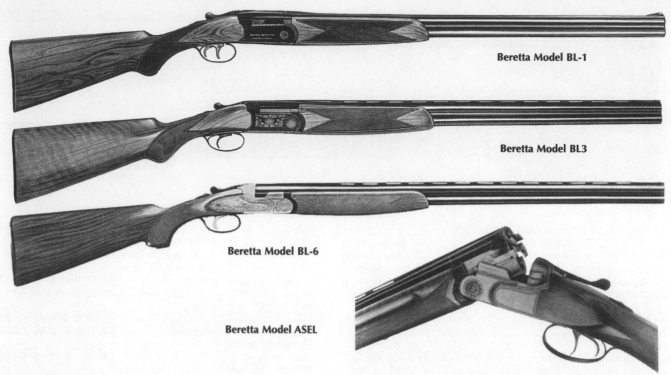

Beretta Model BL-1

Beretta Model BL3

Beretta Model BL-6

Beretta Model ASEL

MODEL ASE 90 O/U SHOTGUN

Competition-style receiver w/coin-silver finish and gold inlay featuring drop-out trigger group. Gauge: 12; 2.75-inch chamber. Bbls.: 28- or 30-inch w/fixed or Mobilchoke tubes; vent rib. Weight: 8.5 lbs. (30-inch bbl.). Checkered high-grade walnut stock. Imported 1992 to 1994.

Pigeon, Skeet, Trap models	NiB $3600	Ex $2318	Gd $1866
Sporting Clays model	NiB $8023	Ex $6464	Gd $4469
Trap Combo model	NiB $12,240	Ex $9874	Gd $6756
Deluxe (introduced 1996)	NiB $15,380	Ex $11,544	Gd $8006

MODEL ASE SERIES O/U SHOTGUN

Boxlock. Single non-selective trigger. Selective automatic ejectors. gauges: 12 and 20. Bbls. 26-, 28-, 30-inch; IC and M choke or M and F choke. Weight: about 5.75-7 lbs. Checkered pistol-grip stock and forearm. Receiver w/various grades of engraving. Imported 1947 to 1964.

Model ASE (light scroll engraving)	NiB $2253	Ex $1826	Gd $1279
Model ASEL (half coverage engraving)	NiB $3195	Ex $2581	Gd $1789
Model ASEELL (full coverage engraving)	NiB $4879	Ex $3937	Gd $2732
For 20 ga. models, add			95%

MODEL BL-1/BL-2 O/U

Boxlock. Plain extractors. Double triggers.12 gauge, 2.75-inch chambers only. Bbls.: 30-and 28-inch M/F choke, 26-inch IC/M choke. Weight: 6.75-7 lbs., depending on bbl. length. Checkered pistol-grip stock and forearm. Imported 1968 to 1973.

Model BL-1	NiB $395	Ex $258	Gd $158
Model BL-2 (single selective trigger)	NiB $534	Ex $436	Gd $311

MODEL BL-2/S . . . . **NiB $475 Ex $390 Gd $262**
Similar to Model BL-1, except has selective "Speed-Trigger," vent-rib bbls., 2.75- or 3-inch chambers. Weight: 7-7.5 lbs. Imported 1974 to 1976.

MODEL BL-3 . . . . **NiB $600 Ex $527 Gd $442**
Same as Model BL-1, except has deluxe engraved receiver, selective single trigger, vent-rib bbls., 12 or 20 ga., 2.75-inch or 3-inch

chambers in former, 3-inch in latter. Weight: 6-7.5 lbs. depending on ga. and bbl. length. Imported 1968 to 1976.

MODELS BL-4, BL-5 AND BL-6

Higher grade versions of Model BL-3 w/more elaborate engraving and fancier wood; Model BL-6 has sideplates. Selective automatic ejectors standard. Imported 1968-76.

Model BL-4	NiB $857	Ex $729	Gd $546
Model BL-5	NiB $900	Ex $708	Gd $558
Model BL-6 (1973-76)	NiB $1177	Ex $1045	Gd $891

SERIES BL SKEET GUNS

Models BL-3, BL-4, BL-5 and BL-6 w/standard features of their respective grades plus wider rib and skeet-style stock, 26-inch bbls. SK choked. Weight: 6-7.25 lbs. depending on ga.

Model BL-3 skeet gun	NiB $1000	Ex $787	Gd $476
Model BL-4 skeet gun	NiB $700	Ex $588	Gd $357
Model BL-5 skeet gun	NiB $875	Ex $635	Gd $447
Model BL-6 skeet gun	NiB $1009	Ex $982	Gd $664

SERIES BL TRAP GUNS

Models BL-3, BL-4, BL-5 and BL-6 w/standard features of their respective grades plus wider rib and Monte Carlo stock w/recoil pad; 30-inch bbls., improved M/F or both F choke. Weight: About 7.5 lbs.

Model BL-3 trap gun	NiB $559	Ex $319	Gd $242
Model BL-4 trap gun	NiB $600	Ex $482	Gd $284
Model BL-5 trap gun	NiB $875	Ex $640	Gd $432
Model BL-6 trap gun	NiB $1000	Ex $718	Gd $521

MODEL FS-1

FOLDING SINGLE . . . . **NiB $175 Ex $95 Gd $78**
Formerly "Companion." Folds to length of bbl. Hammerless. Underlever. Gauge: 12, 16, 20, 28 or .410. Bbl.: 30-inch in 12 ga., 28-inch in 16 and 20 ga.; 26-inch in 28 and .410 ga.; all F choke. Checkered semipistol-grip stock/forearm. Weight: 4.5-5.5 lbs. depending on ga. Disc. 1971.

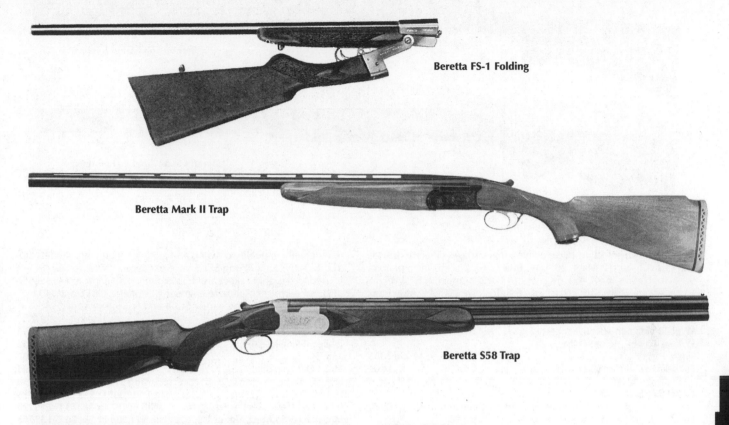

Beretta FS-1 Folding

Beretta Mark II Trap

Beretta S58 Trap

MODEL GR-2 HAMMERLESS DOUBLE ... NiB $900 Ex $739 Gd $572
Boxlock. Plain extractors. Double triggers. Gauges: 12, 20; 2.75-inch chambers in former, 3-inch in latter. Bbls.: Vent rib; 30-inch M/F choke (12 ga. only); 28-inch M/F choke, 26-inch IC/M choke. Weight: 6.5 to 7.5 lbs. depending on ga. and bbl. length. Checkered pistol-grip stock and forearm. Imported 1968 to 1976.

MODEL GR-3 .... NiB $1097 Ex $947 Gd $666
Same as Model GR-2 except has selective single trigger chambered for 12-ga. Three inch or 2.75-inch shells. Magnum model has 30-inch M/F choke bbl., recoil pad. Weight: about 8 lbs. Imported 1968 to 1976.

MODEL GR-4 .... NiB $1275 Ex $1074 Gd $889
Same as Model GR-2 except has automatic ejectors and selective single trigger, higher grade engraving and wood. 12 ga., 2.75-inch chambers only. Imported 1968 to 1976.

GRADE 100 O/U
SHOTGUN .... NiB $2045 Ex $1636 Gd $1139
Sidelock. Double triggers. Automatic ejectors. 12 ga. only. Bbls.: 26-, 28-, 30-inch, any standard boring. Weight: About 7.5 lbs. Checkered stock and forend, straight or pistol grip. Disc.

GRADE 200 .... NiB $2667 Ex $2150 Gd $1501
Same general specifications as Grade 00 except higher quality; bores and action parts hard chrome plated. Disc.

MARK II SINGLE-BARREL TRAP GUN .... NiB $674 Ex $516 Gd $366
Boxlock action similar to that of Series "BL" over-and-unders. Engraved receiver. Automatic ejector. 12 ga. only. 32- or 34-inch bbl. w/wide vent rib. Weight: About 8.5 lbs. Monte Carlo stock w/pistol grip and recoil pad, beavertail forearm. Imported 1972 to 1976.

MODEL S55B O/U
SHOTGUN .... NiB $559 Ex $429 Gd $290
Boxlock. Plain extractors. Selective single trigger. Gauges: 12, 20; 2.75- or 3-inch chambers in former, 3-inch in latter. Bbls. vent rib; 30-inch M/F choke or both F choke in 12-ga. Three inch Magnum only; 28-inch M/F choke; 26 inch IC/M choke. Weight: 6.5 to 7.5 lbs. depending on ga. and bbl. length. Checkered pistol-grip stock and forearm. Introduced in 1977. Disc.

MODEL S56E.................. NiB $746 Ex $476 Gd $268
Same as Model S55B except has scroll-engraved receiver selective automatic ejectors. Introduced in 1977. Disc.

MODEL S58 SKEET GUN .... NiB $774 Ex $534 Gd $368
Same as Model S56E except has 26-inch bbls. of Boehler Antinit Anticorro steel, SK choked, w/wide vent rib; skeet-style stock and forearm. Weight: 7.5 lbs. Introduced in 1977.

MODEL S58 TRAP GUN .... NiB $620 Ex $494 Gd $368
Same as Model S58 Skeet Gun except has 30-inch bbls. bored IM/F Trap, Monte Carlo stock w/recoil pad. Weight: 7 lbs. 10 oz. Introduced in 1977. Disc.

SILVER HAWK FEATHERWEIGHT
HAMMERLESS DOUBLE-BARREL SHOTGUN
Boxlock. Double triggers or non-selective single trigger. Plain extractor. Gauges: 12, 16, 20, 28, 12 Mag. Bbls.: 26- to 32-inch w/high matted rib, all standard choke combinations. Weight: 7 lbs. (12 ga. w/26-inch bbls.). Checkered walnut stock w/beavertail forearm. Disc. 1967.
W/double triggers .... NiB $1010 Ex $742 Gd $360
For non-selective single trigger, add $150

SHOTGUNS

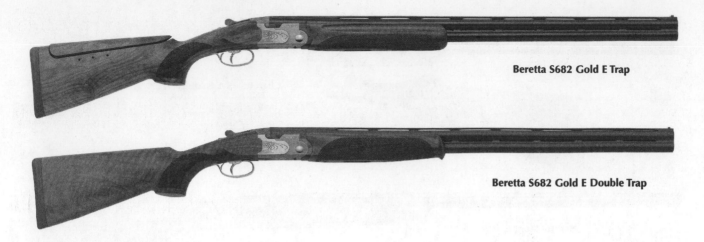

Beretta S682 Gold E Trap

Beretta S682 Gold E Double Trap

SILVER SNIPE O/U SHOTGUN
Boxlock. Non-selective or selective single trigger. Plain extractor. Gauges: 12, 20, 12 Mag., 20 Mag. Bbls.: 26-, 28-, 30-inch; plain or vent rib; chokes IC/M, M/F, SK number 1 and number 2, F/F. Weight: From about 6 lbs. in 20 ga. to 8.5 lbs. in 12 ga. (Trap gun). Checkered walnut pistol-grip stock, forearm. Imported 1955 to 1967.

W/plain bbl., non-selective trigger........ NiB $700 Ex $544 Gd $386
W/vent rib bbl., non-selective
single trigger.......................... NiB $700 Ex $544 Gd $386
For selective single trigger, add $65

GOLDEN SNIPE O/U
Same as Silver Snipe (see page 430) except has automatic ejectors, vent rib is standard feature. Imported 1959 to 1967.
W/non-selective single trigger .... NiB $1145 Ex $940 Gd $528

MODEL 57E O/U
Same general specifications as Golden Snipe, but higher quality throughout. Imported 1955 to 1967.
W/non-selective single trigger .... NiB $900 Ex $695 Gd $469
W/selective single trigger .... NiB $1077 Ex $953 Gd $658

MODEL SL-2 PIGEON SERIES PUMP GUN
Hammerless. Takedown.12 ga. only. Three round magazine. Bbls.: Vent rib; 30-inch F choke, 28-inch M, 26-inch IC. Weight: 7-7.25 lbs., depending on bbl. length. Receiver w/various grades of engraving. Checkered pistol-grip stock and forearm. Imported 1968 to 1971.
Model SL-2 .... NiB $490 Ex $398 Gd $273
Silver Pigeon .... NiB $395 Ex $317 Gd $231
Gold Pigeon.................... NiB $592 Ex $467 Gd $333
Ruby Pigeon.................... NiB $752 Ex $587 Gd $414

"SO" SERIES SHOTGUNS
Jubilee Series introduced in 1998. The Beretta Boxlock is made with mechanical works from a single block of hot forged, high-resistance steel. The gun is richly engraved in scroll and game scenes. All engraving is signed by master engravers. High-quality finishing on the inside with high polishing of all internal points. Sidelock. Selective automatic ejectors. Selective single trigger or double triggers. 12 ga. only, 2.75- or 3-inch chambers. Bbls.: Vent rib (wide type on skeet and trap guns); 26-, 27-, 29-, 30-inch; any combination of standard chokes. Weight: 7 to 7.75 lbs., depending on bbl. length, style of stock and density of wood. Stock and forearm of select walnut, finely checkered; straight or pistol-grip, field, skeet and trap guns have appropriate styles of stock and forearm. Models

differ chiefly in quality of wood and grade of engraving. Models SO-3EL, SO-3EELL, SO4 and SO-5 have hand-detachable locks. "SO-4" is used to designate skeet and trap models derived from Model SO-3EL, but with less elaborate engraving. Models SO3EL and SO-3EELL are similar to the earlier SO-4 and SO-5, respectively. Imported 1933 to date.
Jubilee O/U 410-28-20-12 .... NiB $17,933 Ex $14,347 Gd $9756
Jubilee II Side-by-side .... NiB $19,441 Ex $14,637 Gd $9953
Mdl. SO-2 .... NiB $8573 Ex $4570 Gd $3107
Mdl. SO-3 .... NiB $7143 Ex $6629 Gd $4508
Mdl. SO-3EL........................ NiB $9145 Ex $7773 Gd $5286
Mdl. SO-3EELL...................... NiB $10,861 Ex $11,434 Gd $7775
Mdl. SO-4 Field, Skeet or Trap gun ..... NiB $9197 Ex $8313 Gd $6220
Model SO-5 Sporting, Skt. or Trp. ..... NiB $11,830 Ex $9880 Gd $7768
W/extra bbl. set, add..................................... 25%

MODELS SO-6 AND SO-9
PREMIUM GRADE SHOTGUNS
High-grade over/unders in the SO series. Gauges: 12 ga. only (SO-6); 12, 20, 28 and .410 (SO-9). Fixed or Mobilchoke (12 ga. only). Sidelock action. Silver or casehardened receiver (SO-6); English custom hand-engraved scroll or game scenes (SO-9). Supplied w/leather case and accessories. Imported 1990 to date.
SO-6 O/U .... NiB $8056 Ex $6872 Gd $4692
SO-6 EELL O/U .... NiB $7474 Ex $6790 Gd $5997
SO-9 O/U $48,727
SO-9 EELL custom engraving $100,000
W/extra bbl. set, add................................... 25%

MODEL SO6/SO-7 S/S DOUBLES
Side-by-side shotgun w/same general specifications as SO Series over/unders except higher grade w/more elaborate engraving, fancier wood.
SO-6 SxS (imported 1948-82) ..NiB $6987 Ex $5900 Gd $4850
SO-7 SxS (imported 1948-90) ..NiB $8856 Ex $7100 Gd $5975

MODEL TR-1 SINGLE-SHOT
TRAP GUN...................... NiB $275 Ex $163 Gd $93
Hammerless. Underlever action. Engraved frame.12 ga. only. 32-inch bbl. w/vent rib. Weight: About 8.25 lbs. Monte Carlo stock w/pistol grip and recoil pad, beavertail forearm. Imported 1968 to 1971.

MODEL TR-2 .... NiB $296 Ex $187 Gd $126
Same as Model TR-1 except has extended ventilated rib. Imported 1969-73.

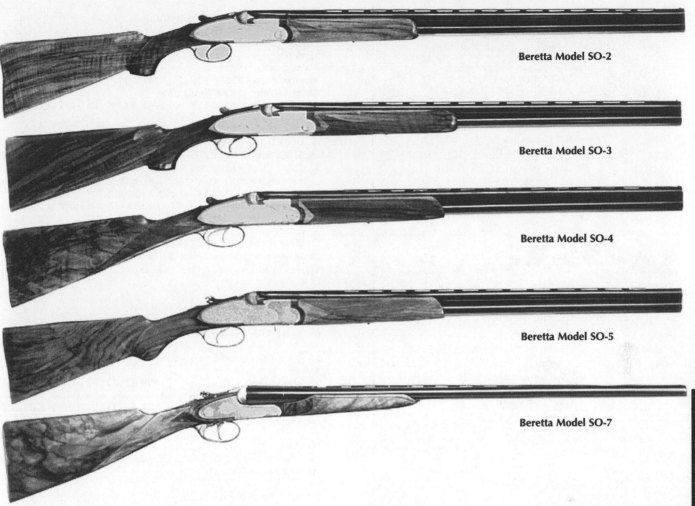

Beretta Model SO-2

Beretta Model SO-3

Beretta Model SO-4

Beretta Model SO-5

Beretta Model SO-7

VICTORIA PINTAIL (ES100) SEMIAUTOLOADER
Short Montefeltro-type recoil action. Gauge: 12 w/3-inch chamber. Bbl.: 24-inch slug, 24-, 26- or 28-inch vent rib w/Mobilchoke tubes. Weight: 7 lbs. to 7 lbs., 5 oz. Checkered synthetic or walnut buttstock and forend. Matte finish on both metal and stock. Imported 1993 and 2005.
Field model w/synthetic
stock (intro. 1998) . . . . NiB $435 Ex $263 Gd $197
Field model w/walnut stock (disc. 1998). . . . . . NiB $672 Ex $518 Gd $374
Rifled slug model w/synthetic
stock (intro. 1998) . . . . NiB $495 Ex $327 Gd $275
Standard slug model
w/walnut stock (disc. 1998). . . . . NiB $495 Ex $296 Gd $158
Wetland Camo model (intro. 2000) . . . . . . NiB $620 Ex $423 Gd $252

VINCENZO BERNARDELLI —
Gardone V.T. (Brescia), Italy
Previously imported by Armsport, Miami, FL (formerly by Magnum Research, Inc., Quality Arms, Stoeger Industries, Inc. & Action Arms, LTD).

115 SERIES O/U SHOTGUNS
Boxlock w/single trigger and ejectors. 12 ga. only. 25.5-, 26.75-, and 29.5-inch bbls. Concave top and vented middle rib. Anatomical grip stock. Blued or coin-silver finish w/various grades of engraving. Imported 1985 to 1997.

Standard Model . . . . NiB 1770 Ex $1464 Gd $1091
Hunting Model 115E (disc. 1990). . . . . NiB $2154 Ex $1939 Gd $1553
Hunting Model 115L (disc. 1990). . . . . NiB $2600 Ex $2203 Gd $1995
Hunting Model 115S (disc. 1990). . . . . NiB $3516 Ex $2996 Gd $2026
Target Model 115 (disc. 1992). . . . . NiB $1878 Ex $1563 Gd $1331
Target Model 115E (disc. 1992) . . . . . . NiB $5990 Ex $5240 Gd $3633
Target Model 115L (disc. 1992) . . . . . . NiB $3700 Ex $3254 Gd $2256
Target Model 115S (disc. 1992) . . . . . . NiB $5905 Ex $4045 Gd $3630
Trap/Skeet Model 115S
(imported 1996-97) . . . . NiB $3252 Ex $2421 Gd $1691
Sporting Clays Model 115S
(imported 1995-97) . . . . NiB $3850 Ex $3137 Gd $2456

BRESCIA
HAMMER DOUBLE. . . . . NiB $1499 Ex $956 Gd $706
Back-action sidelock. Plain extractors. Double triggers. Gauges: 12, 20. Bbls.: 27.5 or 29.5-inch M/F choke in 12 ga. 25.5-inch IC/M choke in 20 ga.. Weight: From 5.75 to 7 lbs., depending on ga. and bbl. length. English-style stock and forearm, checkered. No longer imported.

ELIO . . . . NiB $1145 Ex $927 Gd $709
Lightweight game gun, 12 ga. only, w/same general specifications as Standard Gamecock (S. Uberto 1) except weight: About 6 to 6.25 lbs.; has automatic ejectors, fine English-pattern scroll engraving. No longer imported.

Bernardelli Gamecock

Bernardelli Standard Gamecock

Bernardelli Gardone

Bernardelli Italia

Bernardelli Roma 6

GAMECOCK, PREMIER (ROME 3)
Same general specifications as Standard Gamecock (S. Uberto 1) except has sideplates, auto ejectors, single trigger. No longer imported.
Roma 3 (disc. 1989,
Reintroduced 1993-97) . . . . NiB $1719 Ex $1373 Gd $957
Roma 3E (disc. 1950) Roma 3M
w/single trigger (disc. 1997) . . . NiB $1897 Ex $1524 Gd $1060

GAMECOCK, STANDARD
(S. UBERTO 1) HAMMERLESS
DOUBLE-BARREL SHOTGUN . . . . . NiB $853 Ex $668 Gd $480
Boxlock. Plain extractors. Double triggers. Gauges: 12, 16, 20; 2.75-inch chambers in 12 and 16, 3-inch in 20 ga. Bbls. 25.5-inch IC/M choke; 27.5-inch M/F choke. Weight: 5.75-6.5 lbs., depending on ga. and bbl. length. English-style straight-grip stock and forearm, checkered. No longer imported.

GARDONE HAMMER DOUBLE . . . NiB $2693 Ex $2168 Gd $1541
Same general specifications as Brescia except for higher grade engraving and wood, but not as high as the Italia. Half-cock safety. Disc. 1956.

HEMINGWAY HAMMERLESS DOUBLE
Boxlock. Single or double triggers w/hinged front. Selective automatic ejectors. Gauges: 12 and 20 w/2.75- or 3-inch chambers, 16 and 28 w/2.75-inch. Bbls.: 23.5- to 28-inch w/fixed chokes. Weight: 6.25 lbs. Checkered English-style European walnut stock. Silvered and engraved receiver.
Standard model . . . . NiB $2182 Ex $1757 Gd $1240
Deluxe model
w/sideplates (disc. 1993) . . . . . . NiB $2521 Ex $2034 Gd $1430
For single trigger, add $100

ITALIA . . . . NiB $1750 Ex $937 Gd $760
Same general specifications as Brescia except higher grade engraving and wood. Disc. 1986.

ROMA 4 AND ROMA 6
Same as Premier Gamecock (Rome 3) except higher grade engraving and wood, double triggers. Disc. 1997.
Roma 4 (disc. 1989) . . . . NiB $1778 Ex $1329 Gd $998
Roma 4E (disc. 1997) . . . . NiB $1740 Ex $1394 Gd $978
Roma 6 (disc. 1989) . . . . NiB $1396 Ex $1160 Gd $819
Roma 6E (disc. 1997) . . . . NiB $2427 Ex $1917 Gd $1205

ROMA 7, 8, AND 9
Side-by-side. Anson & Deeley boxlock; hammerless. Ejectors; double triggers. 12 ga. Barrels: 27.5-or 29.5-inch. M/F chokes. Fancy hand-checkered European walnut straight or pistol-grip stock, forearm. Elaborately engraved, silver-finished sideplates. Imported 1994 to 1997.
Roma 7 . . . . NiB $3200 Ex $2052 Gd $1436
Roma 8 . . . . NiB $3700 Ex $2478 Gd $1779
Roma 9 . . . . NiB $4550 Ex $3645 Gd $2815

S. UBERTO 2 . . . . NiB $1375 Ex $1215 Gd $844
Same as Standard Gamecock (S. Uberto 1) except higher grade engraving and wood. Currently imported.

S. UBERTO F.S.
Same as Standard Gamecock except w/higher grade engraving, wood and has auto-ejectors. Disc. 1989, reintro. 1993 to 1997.
Model FS . . . . NiB $1698 Ex $1490 Gd $1032
Model V.B. Incisio . . . . NiB $2105 Ex $1698 Gd $1176
W/single trigger, add $65

HOLLAND V.B. SERIES SHOTGUNS
Holland & Holland-type sidelock action. Auto-ejectors. Double triggers. 12 ga. only. Bbl. length or choke to custom specification. Silver-finish receiver (Liscio) or engraved coin finish receiver (Incisio). Extra-select wood and game scene engraving (Lusso). Checkered stock (straight or pistol-grip). Imported 1992 to 1997.

Model V.B. Liscio . . . . NiB $10,359 Ex $9092 Gd $6496
Model V.B. Incisio . . . . NiB $10,7001 Ex $8323 Gd $6343
Model V.B. Lusso. . . . . NiB $8798 Ex $7545 Gd $5183
Model V.B. Extra. . . . . NiB $13,256 Ex $9580 Gd $7834
Model V.B. Gold. . . . . NiB $47,636 Ex $34,108 Gd $27,473
Engraving Pattern
No. 4, add. $1040
Engraving Pattern
No. 12, add. $4550
Engraving Pattern No. 20, add $8950
Single trigger, add. $625

BOSS & COMPANY — London, England

HAMMERLESS DOUBLE-BARREL
SHOTGUN . . . . NiB $62,676 Ex $50,000 Gd $32,800
Sidelock. Automatic ejectors. Double triggers, non-selective or selective single trigger. Made in all gauges, bbl. lengths and chokes. Checkered stock and forend, straight or pistol-grip.

HAMMERLESS O/U
SHOTGUN . . . . NiB $110,663 Ex $80,500 Gd $40,000
Sidelock. Automatic ejectors. Selective single trigger. Made in all gauges, bbl. lengths and chokes. Checkered stock and forend, straight or pistol-grip. Disc.

BREDA MECCANICA BRESCIANA — Brescia, Italy, *formerly ERNESTO BREDA, Milan, Italy*

Previously imported by Tristar (Kansas City, MO), Gryphon International (Kansas City, MO) and Diana Imports Co., (San Francisco, CA).

VEGA SPECIAL O/U SHOTGUN. . . NiB $595 Ex $470 Gd $345
12 or 20 gauge. Box lock action. Bbl. 26 or 28 inches; single trigger; ejectors. Blue only.

VEGA SPECIAL TRAP. . . . . NiB $895 Ex $617 Gd $497
12 or 20 gauge. Box lock action. Competition triggers and lock. Bbl. 30 or 32 inches; single trigger; ejectors. Blue only.

VEGA LUSSO . . . . NiB $1695 Ex $1215 Gd $990
12 gauge only, 3-inch chambers. Scalloped box lock action, single selective trigger, ejectors. Bbl. 26 or 28 inches, ventilated rib. Coin finished receiver with light engraving. Deluxe checkered Circassian walnut stock and forearm. Imported 2001 to 2002.

SIRIO STANDARD. . . . . NiB $2090 Ex $1692 Gd $1237
12 or 20 gauge. Engraved box lock action. Bbl. 26 or 28 inches; single trigger; ejectors. Blue only. Also available in skeet model.

ANDROMEDA SPECIAL . . . . NiB $655 Ex $570 Gd $415
Side-by-side.12 gauge, single trigger; ejectors, select checkered walnut stock; satin finish on receiver with elaborate engraving.

GOLD SERIES SEMIAUTOMATIC SHOTGUN
12 or (lightweight) 20 gauge, 2.75-inch chamber. Bbl. 25 or 27 inches; ventilated rib standard. Recoil operated
Antares Standard Model . . . . NiB $455 Ex $315 Gd $295

**Boss Hammerless
Double-Barrel**

Argus Model . . . . NiB $465 Ex $325 Gd $215
Aries Model. NiB $465 Ex $345 Gd $235

STANDARD GRADE GOLD SERIES   NiB $310 Ex $245 Gd $210
12 gauge, 2-3/4-inch chamber. Recoil operated. Bbl. 25 or 27 inches. Light engraving. Disc.

GRADE 1 . . . . NiB $575 Ex $405 Gd $295
Similar to Standard model but with fancier wood and engraving.

GRADE 2 . . . . NiB $695 Ex $545 Gd $420
Similar to Grade 1 but with more engraving, etc.

GRADE 3 . . . . NiB $852 Ex $707 Gd $582
Same as Grade 1 but with custom-quality embellishments.

MAGNUM MODEL . . . . NiB $485 Ex $320 Gd $215
Similar to Standard Grade but with 3-inch chambers.

ALTAIR SPECIAL . . . . NiB $455 Ex $340 Gd $280
12 gauge, 2.75-inch chamber. Gas-operated. Bbl. 25 or 27 inches, ventilated rib standard. Alloy construction, blue or chrome receiver.

ASTRO. . . . . NiB $1051 Ex $781 Gd $556
12 gauge (disc. 2002) or 20 gauge, 3-inch chamber. Inertia action. Bbl. 22 (slug), 24, 26, 28 or 30 inches; ventilated rib. Black synthetic, Advantage camo, or Circassian walnut stock and forearm. Imported 2001.
Advantage camo model, add. $100

ASTROLUX . . . . NiB $1473 Ex $1288 Gd $963
Similar to Astro model except has two-tone receiver with engraving and deluxe checkered Circassian walnut stock and forearm. Imported 2001 to 2002.

ERMES SERIES . . . . NiB $947 Ex $717 Gd $572
12 gauge, 3-inch chamber. Semiautomatic. Inertia recoil operating system, aluminum alloy receiver, nickeel plated or blue finish on lower receiver. Bbl. 24, 26, or 28 inches. Deluxe checkered Circassian walnut stock and forearm. Imported 2001.
Ermes Silver. . . . . NiB $1200 Ex $1039 Gd $839
Ermes Gold. . . . . NiB $1325 Ex $1021 Gd $941

MIRA. . . . . NiB $710 Ex $555 Gd $425
12 gauge, 3-inch chamber. Semiautomatic, gas-operated. Aluminum alloy receiver; black or Advantage camo finish. Bbl. 22 (slug), 24, 26, 28 or 30 inches, ventilated rib. Circassian walnut or black synthetic stock and forearm. Imported 2001.
Black synthetic stock and forearm, deduct 10%
Sporting Clays model, add $25

SHOTGUNS

ARIES 2 . . . . **NiB $815 Ex $770 Gd $615**
12 gauge, 2-3/4-inch chamber. Semiautomatic, gas-operated. Engraved two-tone receiver. Bbl. 20 or 30 inches, ventilated rib. Deluxe checkered Circassian walnut or black synthetic stock and forearm. Imported 2001 only.

BRETTON SHOTGUNS — St. Etienne (Cedex1), France

BABY STANDARD SPRINT O/U . . . . **NiB $995 Ex $793 Gd $543**
Inline sliding breech action. 12 or 20 gauge w/2.75-inch chambers. 27.5-inch separated bbls. w/vent rib and choke tubes. Weight: 4.8 to 5 lbs. Engraved alloy receiver. Checkered walnut buttstock and forearm w/satin oil finish. Limited import.

SPRINT DELUXE O/U. . . . . **NiB $900 Ex 766 Gd $578**
Similar to the Standard Model except w/engraved coin-finished receiver and chambered 12, 16 and 20 ga. Limited import.

FAIR PLAY O/U . . . . **NiB $972 Ex $803 Gd $563**
Lightweight action similar to the Sprint Model except w/hinged action that pivots open and is chambered 12 or 20 gauge only. Limited import.

BRNO SHOTGUNS — Brno and Uherski Brod, Czech Republic, (formerly Czechoslovakia)

500 O/U SHOTGUN . . . . **NiB $843 Ex $715 Gd $506**
Hammerless boxlock w/double triggers and ejectors.12 ga. w/2.75-inch chambers. 27.5-inch bbls.. choked M/F. 44 inches overall. Weight: 7 lbs. Etched receiver. Checkered walnut stock w/classic style cheekpiece. Imported from 1987 to 1991.

500 SERIES O/U COMBINATION GUNS
Similar to the 500 Series over/under shotgun above, except w/lower bbl. chambered in rifle calibers and set trigger option. Imported from 1987 to 1995.
Model 502 12/222, 12/243 (disc. 1991). . . . **NiB $1962 Ex $1140 Gd $965**
Model 502 12/308, 12/30.06 (disc. 1991) . . . **NiB $1062 Ex $940 Gd $665**
Model 571 12/6x65R (disc. 1993) . . . . **NiB $800 Ex $656 Gd $506**
Model 572 12/7x65R (imported since 1992) . . . . . . **NiB $823 Ex $615 Gd $447**
Model 584 12/7x57R (imported since 1992) . . . . . **NiB $1156 Ex $940 Gd $665**
Sport Series 4-bbl. set (disc. 1991) . . . . **NiB $3008 Ex $2436 Gd $1704**

CZ 581 SOLO O/U SHOTGUN. . . . . **NiB $864 Ex $701 Gd $493**
Hammerless boxlock w/double triggers, ejectors and automatic safety. 12 ga. w/2.75- or 3-inch chambers. 28-inch bbls. choked M/F. Weight: 7.5 lbs. Checkered walnut stock. Disc. 1996.

SUPER SERIES O/U SHOTGUN
Hammerless sidelock w/selective single or double triggers and ejectors. 12 ga. w/2.75- or 3-inch chambers. 27.5-inch bbls. choked M/F. 44.5 inches overall. Weight: 7.25 lbs. Etched or engraved side plates. Checkered European walnut stock w/classic-style cheekpiece. Imported from 1987 to 1991.
Super Series Shotgun (disc. 1992). . . . . **NiB $794 Ex $679 Gd $516**
Super Series Combo (disc. 1992) . . . . **NiB $1966 Ex $1125 Gd $896**
Super Ser. 3-bbl. set (disc. 1990). . . . . **NiB $1925 Ex $1519 Gd $1205**
Super Series engraving, add **$1250**

ZH 300 SERIES O/U SHOTGUNS
Hammerless boxlock w/double triggers. Gauge: 12 or 16 w/2.75- or 3-inch chambers. Bbls.: 26, 27.5 or 30 inches; choked M/F. Weight: 7 lbs. Skip-line checkered walnut stock w/classic-style cheekpiece.

Imported from 1986-93.
Model 300 (disc. 1993) . . . . **NiB $695 Ex $508 Gd $357**
Model 301 Field (disc. 1991) . . . . **NiB $600 Ex $519 Gd $365**
Model 302 Skeet (disc. 1992) . . . . **NiB $650 Ex $506 Gd $404**
Model 303 Trap (disc. 1992) . . . . **NiB $648 Ex $508 Gd $419**

ZH 300 SERIES O/U
COMBINATION GUNS
Similar to the 300 Series over/under shotgun except lower bbl. chambered in rifle calibers.
Model 300 Combo
8-bbl. Set (disc. 1991) . . . . **NiB $695 Ex $473 Gd $308**
Model 304 12 ga./7x57R (disc. 1995) . . . . **NiB $738 Ex $603 Gd $430**
Model 305 12 ga./5.6x52R (disc. 1993) . . . . . . **NiB $828 Ex $675 Gd $479**
Model 306 12 ga./5.6x50R (disc. 1993) . . . . . . **NiB $866 Ex $706 Gd $500**
Model 307 12 ga./.22 Hornet
(Imported since 1995) . . . . **NiB $771 Ex $629 Gd $447**
Model 324 16 ga./7x57R (disc. 1987 . . . . **NiB $803 Ex $654 Gd $465**

ZP 149 HAMMERLESS DOUBLE
Sidelock action w/double triggers, automatic ejectors and automatic safety.12 ga. w/2.75- or 3-inch chambers. 28.5-inch bbls. choked M/F. Weight: 7.25 lbs. Checkered walnut buttstock with cheekpiece.
Standard model . . . . **NiB $574 Ex $351 Gd $295**
Engraved model . . . . **NiB $594 Ex $371 Gd $315**

BROLIN ARMS, INC. — Pomona, California

FIELD SERIES PUMP SHOTGUN
Slide-action. Gauge: 12 ga. w/3-inch chamber. 24-, 26-, 28- or 30-inch bbl. 44 and 50 inches overall. Weight: 7.3 to 7.6 lbs. Cross-bolt safety. Vent rib bbl. w/screw-in choke tube and bead sights. Non-reflective metal finish. Synthetic or oil-finished wood stock w/swivel studs. Made from 1997 to 1998.
Synthetic stock model . . . . **NiB $197 Ex $117 Gd $85**
Wood stock model. . . . . **NiB $154 Ex $92 Gd $77**

COMBO MODEL PUMP SHOTGUN
Similar to the Field Model except w/extra 18.5- or 22-inch bbl. w/bead or rifle sight. Made from 1997 to 1998.
Synthetic stock model . . . . **NiB $230 Ex $169 Gd $116**
Wood stock model. . . . . **NiB $276 Ex $218 Gd $154**

LAWMAN MODEL
PUMP SHOTGUN
Similar to the Field Model except has 18.5-inch bbl. w/cylinder bore fixed choke. Weight: 7 lbs. Dual operating bars. Bead, rifle or ghost ring sights. Black synthetic or wood stock. Matte chrome or satin nickel finish. Made from 1997 to 1999.
Synthetic stock model . . . . **NiB $165 Ex $108 Gd $74**
Wood stock model . . . . **NiB $165 Ex $108 Gd $74**
Rifle sights, add. **$20**
Ghost ring sights, add **$35**
Satin nickel finish (disc. 1997), add **$25**

SLUG MODEL PUMP SHOTGUN
Similar to the Field Model except has 18.5- or 22-inch bbl. w/IC fixed choke or 4-inch extended rifled choke. Rifle or ghost ring sights or optional cantilevered scope mount. Black synthetic or wood stock. Matte blued finish. Made from 1998 to 1999.
Synthetic stock model . . . . **NiB $230 Ex $198 Gd $144**
Wood stock model . . . . **NiB $248 Ex $188 Gd $137**
W/rifled bbl., add. **$10**
W/cantilevered scope mount, add **$20**

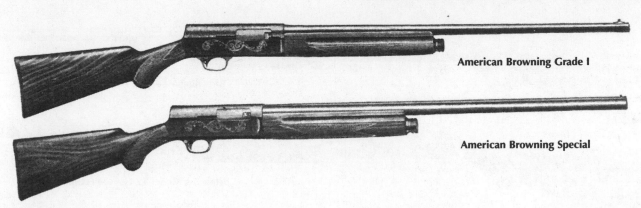

American Browning Grade I

American Browning Special

TURKEY SPECIAL PUMP SHOTGUN
Similar to the Field Model except has 22-inch vent-rib bbl. w/extended extra-full choke. Rifle or ghost ring sights or optional cantilevered scope mount. Black synthetic or wood stock. Matte blued finish. Made from 1998 to 1999.

Synthetic stock model	NiB $232	Ex $171	Gd $109
Wood stock model	NiB $230	Ex $181	Gd $132

W/cantilevered
scope mount, add $25

BROWNING SHOTGUNS —
Morgan (formerly Ogden), Utah

AMERICAN BROWNING SHOTGUNS

Designated "American" Browning because they were produced in Ilion, New York, the following Remington-made Brownings are almost identical to the Remington Model 11A and Sportsman and the Browning Auto-5. They are the only Browning shotguns manufactured in the U.S. during the 20th century and were made for Browning Arms when production was suspended in Belgium because of WW II.

NOTE: *Fabrique Nationale Herstal (formerly Fabrique Nationale d'Armes de Guerre) of Herstal, Belgium, is the longtime manufacturer of Browning shotguns dating back to 1900. Miroku Firearms Mfg. Co. of Tokyo, Japan, bought into the Browning company and has, since the early 1970s, undertaken some of the production. The following shotguns were manufactured for Browning by these two firms.*

GRADE I AUTOLOADER (AUTO-5)
Recoil-operated autoloader. Similar to the Remington Model 11A except w/different style engraving and identified w/the Browning logo. Gauges: 12, 16 or 20. Plain 26- to 32-inch bbl. w/any standard boring. Two or four shell tubular magazine w/magazine cut-off. Weight: About 6.88 lbs. (20 ga.) to 8 lbs. (12 ga.). Checkered pistol-grip stock and forearm. Made from 1940 to 1949.

American Browning Grade I

Auto-5, 12 or 16 ga. .... NiB $725 Ex $640 Gd $306
20 ga., add. 20%

SPECIAL 441
Same general specifications as Grade I except supplied w/raised matted rib or vent rib. Disc. 1949.

W/raised matted rib .... NiB $843 Ex $720 Gd $385
W/vent rib .... NiB $858 Ex $745 Gd $395
20 ga., add. 20%

SPECIAL SKEET MODEL .... NiB $744 Ex $589 Gd $416
Same general specifications as Grade I except has 26-inch bbl. w/vent rib and Cutts Compensator. Disc. 1949.

UTILITY FIELD GUN .... NiB $573 Ex $357 Gd $254
Same general specifications as Grade I except has 28-inch plain bbl. w/Poly Choke. Disc. 1949.

MODEL 12 PUMP SHOTGUN
Special limited edition Winchester Model 12. Gauge: 20 or 28. Five-round tubular magazine. 26-inch bbl., M choke. 45 inches overall. Weight: about 7 lbs. Grade I has blued receiver, checkered walnut stock w/matte finish. Grade V has engraved receiver, checkered deluxe walnut stock w/high-gloss finish. Made from 1988 to 1992. See illustration next page.

Grade I, 20 ga. (8600)	NiB $775	Ex $512	Gd $363
Grade I, 28 ga.	NiB $1050	Ex $837	Gd $681
Grade V, 20 ga (4000)	NiB $1353	Ex $1088	Gd $725
Grade V, 28 ga	NiB $1678	Ex $1258	Gd $903

MODEL 42 LIMITED EDITION SHOTGUN
Special limited edition Winchester Model 42 pump shotgun. Same general specifications as Model 12 except w/smaller frame in .410 ga. and 3-inch chamber. Made from 1991 to 1993.

Grade I
(6000 produced) .... NiB $898 Ex $660 Gd $397
Grade V
(6000 produced) .... NiB $1491 Ex $1076 Gd $724

2000 BUCK SPECIAL .... NiB $461 Ex $369 Gd $265
Same as Field Model except has 24-inch plain bbl. Bored for rifled slug and buckshot, fitted w/rifle sights (open rear, ramp front). 12 ga., 2.75-inch or 3-inch chamber; 20 ga., 2.75-inch chamber. Weight: 12 ga., 7 lbs., 8 oz.; 20 ga., 6 lbs., 10 oz. Made from 1974 to 1981 by FN.

2000 GAS AUTOMATIC SHOTGUN, FIELD MODEL
Gas-operated. Gauge: 12 or 20. 2.75-inch chamber. Four-round magazine. Bbl.: 26-, 28-, 30-inch, any standard choke plain matted bbl. (12 ga. only) or vent rib. Weight: 6 lbs. 11 oz.-7 lbs. 12 oz. depending on ga. and bbl. length. Checkered pistol-grip stock/forearm. Made from 1974 to 1981 by FN; assembled in Portugal.

W/plain matted bbl. .... NiB $495 Ex $386 Gd $283

2000 MAGNUM MODEL .... NiB $495 Ex $312 Gd $228
Same as Field Model except chambered for 3-inch shells, three-round magazine. Bbl.: 26- (20 ga. only), 28-, 30- or 32-inch (latter two 12 ga. only); any standard choke; vent rib. Weight: 6 lbs., 11 oz.-7 lbs., 13 oz. depending on ga. and bbl. Made from 1974 to 1983 by FN.

SHOTGUNS

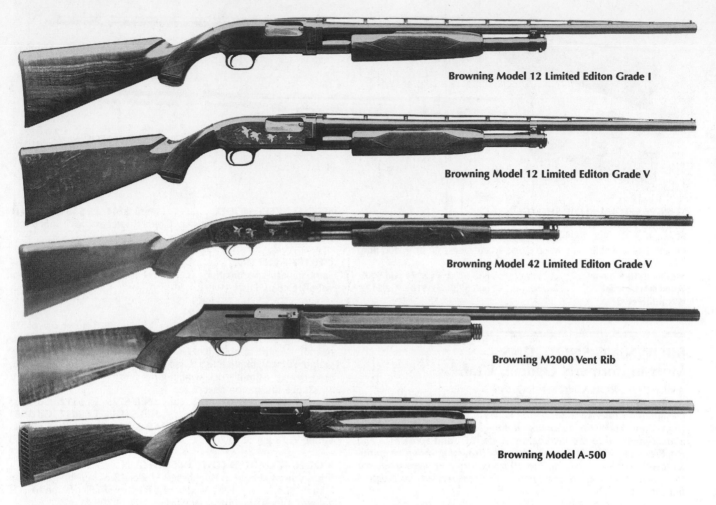

Browning Model 12 Limited Editon Grade I

Browning Model 12 Limited Editon Grade V

Browning Model 42 Limited Editon Grade V

Browning M2000 Vent Rib

Browning Model A-500

2000 SKEET MODEL . . . . **NiB $450 Ex $375 Gd $282**
Same as Field Model except has skeet-style stock w/recoil pad, 26-inch vent-rib bbl., SK choke. 12 or 20 ga., 2.75-inch chamber. Weight: 8 lbs., 1 oz. (12 ga.); 6 lbs., 12 oz. (20 ga.) Made 1974 to 1981 by FN.

2000 TRAP MODEL . . . . **NiB $450 Ex $375 Gd $282**
Same as Field Model except has Monte Carlo stock w/recoil pad, 30- or 32-inch bbl. w/high-post vent rib and receiver extension, M/I/F chokes. 12 ga., 2.75-inch chamber. Weight: About 8 lbs., 5 oz. Made 1974 to 1981 by FN.

A-500G GAS-OPERATED SEMIAUTOMATIC
Same general specifications as Browning Model A-500R except gas-operated. Made 1990 to 1993.
Buck Special . . . . **NiB $525 Ex $413 Gd $263**
Hunting model . . . . **NiB $575 Ex $414 Gd $320**

A-500G SPORTING CLAYS . . . . **NiB $575 Ex $414 Gd $320**
Same general specifications as Model A-500G except has matte blued receiver w/"Sporting Clays" logo. 28- or 30-inch bbl. w/Invector choke tubes. Made 1992 to 1993.

A-500R SEMIAUTOMATIC
Recoil-operated. Gauge: 12. 26- to 30-inch vent-rib bbls. 24-inch Buck Special. Invector choke tube system. 2.75- or 3-inch Magnum cartridges. Weight: 7 lbs., 3 oz.-8 lbs., 2 oz. Cross-bolt safety. Gold-plated trigger. Scroll-engraved receiver. Gloss-finished walnut stock

and forend. Made by FN from 1987 to 1993.
Hunting model . . . . **NiB $525 Ex $413 Gd $263**
Buck Special . . . . **NiB $558 Ex $46 Gd $296**

A-BOLT SERIES SHOTGUN
Bolt-action repeating single-barrel shotgun. 12 ga. only w/3-inch chambers, 2-round magazine. 22- or 23-inch rifled bbl., w/or w/o a rifled invector tube. Receiver drilled and tapped for scope mounts. Bbl. w/ or w/o open sights. Checkered walnut or graphite/fiberglass composite stock. Matte black metal finish. Imported 1995 to 1998.
Stalker model w/
composite stock . . . . **NiB $1250 Ex $964 Gd $760**
Hunter model w/walnut stock . . . . **NiB $1250 Ex $964 Gd $760**
W/rifled bbl., add **$150**
W/open sights, add **$45**

AUTOLOADING SHOTGUNS,
GRADES II, III AND IV
These higher grade models differ from the Standard or Grade I in general quality, grade of wood, checkering, engraving, etc., otherwise specifications are the same. Grade IV guns, sometimes called Midas Grade, are inlaid w/yellow and green gold. Disc. in 1940.
Grade II, plan bbl. . . . . **NiB $1592 Ex $1280 Gd $897**
Grade III, plain bbl. . . . . **NiB $1425 Ex $1085 Gd $897**
Grade IV, plain bbl. . . . . **NiB $4250 Ex $3657 Gd $2767**
For raised matte rib bbl., add **15%**
For vent rib bbl., add **30%**

Browning Model A-Bolt Hunter

Browning Model A-Bolt Stalker

Browning Automatic-5 Gold Classic

Browning Automatic-5 Buck Special

Browning Automatic-5 Classic

AUTOMATIC-5, LIGHT 20
Same general specifications as Standard Model except lightweight and 20 ga. Bbl.: 26- or 28-inch; plain or vent rib. Weight: About 6.25-6.5 lbs. depending on bbl. Made 1958 to 1976 by FN, since then by Miroku.

FN manuf., plain bbl. . . . . **NiB $785 Ex $547 Gd $362**
FN manuf., vent-rib bbl. . . . . **NiB $1153 Ex $865 Gd $550**
Miroku manuf., vent rib,fixed choke . . **NiB $865 Ex $680 Gd $376**
Miroku manuf., vent rib, invectors . . . **NiB $955 Ex $757 Gd $457**

AUTOMATIC-5, BUCK SPECIAL MODELS
Same as Light 12, Magnum 12, Light 20, Magnum 20, in respective gauges, except 24-inch plain bbl. bored for rifled slug and buckshot, fitted w/rifle sights (open rear, ramp front). Weight: 6.13-8.25 lbs. depending on ga. Made 1964 to 1976 by FN, since then by Miroku.

FN manuf., w/plain bbl. . . . . **NiB $1199 Ex $789 Gd $417**
Miroku manuf., ... **NiB $825 Ex $693 Gd $422**
W/3-inch mag. rec., add **10%**

AUTOMATIC-5 CLASSIC . . . . **NiB $9755 Ex $959 Gd $856**
Gauge: 12. 5-round capacity. 28-inch vent rib bbl./M choke. 2.75-

inch chamber. Engraved silver-gray receiver. Gold-plated trigger. Crossbolt safety. High-grade, hand-checkered select American walnut stock w/rounded pistol grip. 5,000 issued; made in Japan in 1984, engraved in Belgium.

AUTOMATIC-5 GOLD CLASSIC . . . . . . **NiB $9770 Ex $6469 Gd $4594**
Same general specifications as Automatic-5 Classic except engraved receiver inlaid w/gold. Pearl border on stock and forend plus fine-line hand-checkering. Each gun numbered "One of Five Hundred," etc. 500 issued in 1984; made in Belgium.

AUTOMATIC-5, LIGHT 12
12 ga. only. Same general specifications as Standard Model except lightweight (about 7.25 lbs.), has gold-plated trigger. Guns w/rib have striped matting on top of bbl. Fixed chokes or Invector tubes. Made 1948 to 1976 by FN, since then by Miroku.

FN manuf., plain bbl. . . . . **NiB $759 Ex $542 Gd $394**
FN manuf., raised matte rib . . . . . . **NiB $825 Ex $645 Gd $527**
FN manuf., ventilated rib . . . . **NiB $950 Ex $848 Gd $544**
Miroku manuf., vent rib, fixed choke . . **NiB $759 Ex $542 Gd $394**
Miroku manuf., vent rib, invectors . . . **NiB $950 Ex $692 Gd $439**

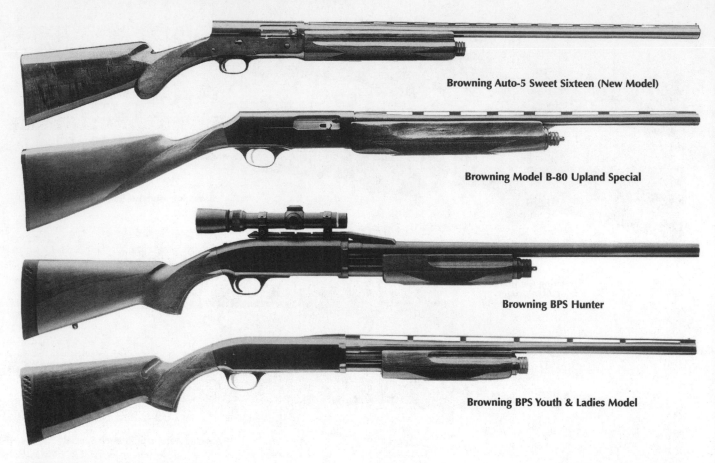

Browning Auto-5 Sweet Sixteen (New Model)

Browning Model B-80 Upland Special

Browning BPS Hunter

Browning BPS Youth & Ladies Model

AUTOMATIC-5, MAGNUM 12 GAUGE
Same general specifications as Standard Model. Chambered for 3-inch Magnum 12-ga. shells. Bbl.: 28-inch M/F, 30- or 32-inch F/F, plain or vent rib. Weight: 8.5-9 lbs. depending on bbl. Buttstock has recoil pad. Made 1958 to 1976 by FN, since then by Miroku. Fixed chokes or Invector tubes.

FN manuf., plain bbl.	NiB $875	Ex $697	Gd $495
FN manuf., vent rib bbl.	NiB $1150	Ex $857	Gd $637
Miroku manuf., vent rib, fixed chokes	NiB $750	Ex $583	Gd $414
Miroku manuf., vent rib, invectors	NiB $925	Ex $650	Gd $463

AUTOMATIC-5, MAGNUM 20 GAUGE
Same general specifications as Standard Model except chambered for 3-inch Magnum 20-ga. shell. Bbl.: 26- or 28-inch, plain or vent rib. Weight: 7 lbs., 5 oz.-7 lbs., 7 oz. depending on bbl. Made 1967 to 1976 by FN, since then by Miroku.

FN manuf., plain bbl.	NiB $875	Ex $698	Gd $497
FN manuf., vent rib bbl.	NiB $1150	Ex $919	Gd $720
Miroku manuf., vent rib, invectors	NiB $925	Ex $683	Gd $516

AUTOMATIC-5, SKEET MODEL
12 ga. only. Same general specifications as Light 12. Bbl.: 26-or 28-inch, plain or vent rib, SK choke. Weight: 7 lbs., 5 oz.-7 lbs., 10 oz. depending on bbl. Made by FN prior to 1976, since then by Miroku.

FN manuf., plain bbl.	NiB $1075	Ex $854	Gd $567
FN manuf., vent rib bbl.	NiB $1655	Ex $1089	Gd $890
Miroku manuf., vent rib bbl.	NiB $895	Ex $632	Gd $438

AUTOMATIC-5 STALKER
Same general specifications as Automatic-5 Light and Magnum models except w/matte blue finish and black graphite fiberglass stock and forearm. Made from 1992 to 1997.

Light model	NiB $850	Ex $747	Gd $514
Magnum model	NiB $955	Ex $846	Gd $615

AUTOMATIC-5, STANDARD (GRADE I)
Recoil-operated. Gauge: 12 or 16 (16-gauge guns made prior to WW II were chambered for 2-inch shells; standard 16 disc. 1964). Four shell magazine in 5-round model, prewar guns were also available in 3-round model. Bbls.: 26- to 32-inch; plain, raised matted or vent rib; choice of standard chokes. Weight: About 8 lbs., in 12 ga., 7.5 lbs., in 16 ga. Checkered pistol-grip stock and forearm. (Note: Browning Special, disc. about 1940.) Made from 1900 to 1973 by FN.

Grade I, plain bbl.	NiB $725	Ex $570	Gd $408
Grade I or Browning Special, Raised matted rib	NiB $875	Ex $723	Gd $514
Grade I or Browning Special, vent rib	NiB $875	Ex $743	Gd $528

AUTOMATIC-5, SWEET 16
16 ga. Same general specifications as Standard Model except lightweight (about 6.75 lbs.), has gold plated trigger. Guns w/rib have striped matting on top of bbl. Made 1937 to 1976 by FN.

W/plain bbl.	NiB $1075	Ex $652	Gd $466
W/raised matted or ventilated rib	NiB $1650	Ex $910	Gd $617

AUTO-5,
SWEET SIXTEEN NEW MODEL . . . NiB $1295 Ex $987 Gd $658
Reissue of popular 16-gauge Hunting Model w/5-round capacity, 2.75-inch chamber, scroll-engraved blued receiver, high-gloss French walnut stock w/rounded pistol grip. 26- or 28-inch vent-rib bbl. F choke tube. Weight: 7 lbs., 5 oz. Reintro. 1987 to 1993.

Browning BPS
Waterfowl – Mossy Oak Shadow Grass

Browning BPS Stalker

AUTOMATIC-5, TRAP MODEL . . . NiB $1164 Ex $837 Gd $680
12 ga. only. Same general specifications as Standard Model except has trap-style stock, 30-inch vent-rib bbl. F choke. Weight: 8.5 lbs. Disc. 1971.

MODEL B-80 GAS-OPERATED
AUTOMATIC . . . . NiB $590 Ex $468 Gd $333
Gauge: 12 or 20; 2.75-inch chamber. Four round magazine. Bbl.: 26-, 28- or 30-inch, any standard choke, vent-rib bbl. w/fixed chokes or Invector tubes. Weight: 6 lbs., 12 oz.-8 lbs., 1 oz. depending on ga. and bbl. Checkered pistol-grip stock and forearm. Made 1981 to 1988.

MODEL B-80 PLUS . . . . NiB $675 Ex $504 Gd $361
Same general specifications as Browning Model B-80 except chambered for 3-inch shotshells. Made in 1988.

MODEL B-80 SUPERLIGHT . . . . NiB $585 Ex $463 Gd $333
Same as Standard Model except weighs 1 lb. less.

MODEL B-80 UPLAND SPECIAL . . . NiB $587 Ex $473 Gd $339
Gauge: 12 or 20. 22-inch vent-rib bbl. Invector choke tube system. 2.75-inch chambers. 42 inches overall. Weight: 5 lbs., 7 oz. (20 ga.); 6 lbs., 10 oz. (12 ga.). German nickel silver sight bead. Crossbolt safety. Checkered walnut straight-grip stock and forend. Disc. 1988.

BPS DEER HUNTER SPECIAL . . . . . NiB $625 Ex $416 Gd $305
Same general specifications as Standard BPS model except has 20.5-inch bbl. w/adj. rifle-style sights. Solid scope mounting system. Checkered walnut stock w/sling swivel studs. Made from 1992 to date.

BPS GAME GUN TURKEY SPECIAL . . . . . . NiB $410 Ex $327 Gd $288
Same general specifications as Standard BPS model except w/matte blue metal finish and satin-finished stock. Chambered for 12 ga. 3-inch only. 20.5-inch bbl. w/extra full invector choke system. Receiver drilled and tapped for scope. Made from 1992 to 2001.

BPS PIGEON GRADE . . . . NiB $550 Ex $349 Gd $283
Same general specifications as Standard BPS model except w/select grade walnut stock and gold-trimmed receiver. Available in 12 ga. from only w/26- or 28-inch vent-rib bbl. Made 1992 to 1998.

BPS PUMP INVECTOR STALKER
Same general specifications as BPS Pump Shotgun except in 10 and 12 ga. w/Invector choke system, 22-, 26-, 28- or 30-inch bbls.; matte blue metal finish w/matte black stock. Made from 1987 to date.
12 ga. model (3-inch) . . . . NiB $485 Ex $293 Gd $200
10- & 12 ga. model (3.5-inch) . . . . NiB $676 Ex $547 Gd $383

BPS PUMP SHOTGUN
Takedown. Gauges: 10, 12 (3.5-inch chamber); 12, 20 and .410 (3-inch) and 28 ga. chambered 2.75-inch. Bbls.: 22-, 24-, 26-, 28-, 30-, or 32-inch; fixed choke or Invector tubes. Weight: 7.5 lbs. (w/28-inch bbl.). Checkered select walnut pistol-grip stock and semi-beavertail forearm, recoil pad. Introduced in 1977 by Miroku.
Model BPS Magnum Hunter . . . . NiB $600 Ex $539 Gd $398
Model BPS Magnum Stalker . . . . NiB $600 Ex $524 Gd $387
Model BPS Magnum Camo . . . . NiB $725 Ex $588 Gd $432
Model BPS Hunter . . . . NiB $600 Ex $457 Gd $342
Model BPS Upland . . . . NiB $525 Ex $457 Gd $342
Model BPS Stalker (26- 28- or 30-inch bbl.) . . NiB $485 Ex $441 Gd $331
Model BPS Stalker 24-inch bbl . . . . NiB $485 Ex $392 Gd $275
Model BPS Game Gun—Turkey Special . . . . . . NiB $400 Ex $288 Gd $193
Model BPS Game Gun—fully rifled bbl. . . . . . . NiB $625 Ex $544 Gd $405
Model BPS Hunter 20 ga. . . . . NiB $525 Ex $457 Gd $342
Model BPS Upland 20 ga. . . . . NiB $525 Ex $457 Gd $342
Model BPS Micro . . . . NiB $385 Ex $357 Gd $242
Model BPS Hunter 28 ga. . . . . NiB $525 Ex $443 Gd $360
Model BPS Bore Hunter .410 . . . . NiB $565 Ex $483 Gd $360
Model BPS Buck Spec. (10 or 12 ga., 3.5-inch) . NiB $625 Ex $529 Gd $380
Model BPS Buck Spec. (12 or 20 ga.) . . . . NiB $335 Ex $289 Gd $195
Model BPS Waterfowl
(10 or 12 ga., 3.5-inch) . . . . NiB $615 Ex $507 Gd $414
W/fixed choke, deduct $50

BPS YOUTH AND LADIES' MODEL
Lightweight (6 lbs., 11 oz.) version of BPS Pump Shotgun in 20 ga. w/22-inch bbl. and floating vent rib, F choke (invector) tube. Made 1986 to 2002.
Standard Invector model (disc. 1994) . . . . NiB $325 Ex $227 Gd $155
Invector Plus model . . . . NiB $385 Ex $257 Gd $190

BSA 10 SEMIAUTOMATIC SHOTGUN
Gas-operated short-stroke action. 10 ga.; 3.5-inch chamber. Five round magazine. Bbls.: 26-, 28-or 30-inches w/Invector tubes and vent rib. Weight: 10.5 lbs. Checkered select walnut buttstock and forend. Blued finish. Made 1993 to date. Note: Although intro. as the BSA 10, this model is now marketed as the Gold Series. See separate listing for pricing.

B-SS SIDE-BY-SIDE
Boxlock. Automatic ejectors. Non-selective single trigger (early production) or selective-single trigger (late production). Gauges: 12 or 20 w/3-inch chambers. Bbls.: 26-, 28-, or 30-inches; IC/M, M/F, or F/F chokes; matte solid rib. Weight: 7 to 7.5 lbs. Checkered straight-grip stock and beavertail forearm. Made from 1972 to 1988 by Miroku.
Standard model (early/NSST) . . . . NiB $1175 Ex $891 Gd $751
Standard model (late/SST) . . . . NiB $1175 Ex $891 Gd $751
Grade II (antique silver receiver) . . . . NiB $3250 Ex $2843 Gd $1962
20 ga. models, add $500

SHOTGUNS

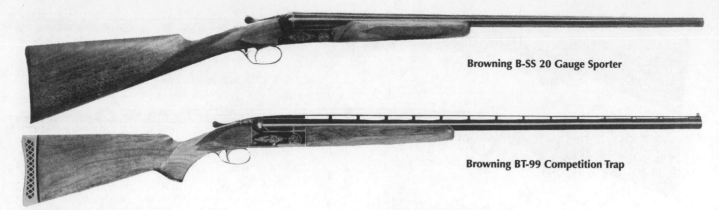

Browning B-SS 20 Gauge Sporter

Browning BT-99 Competition Trap

B-SS SIDE-BY-SIDE SIDELOCK
Same general specifications as B-SS boxlock models except sidelock version available in 26- or 28-inch bbl. lengths. 26-inch choked IC/M; 28-inch, M/F. Double triggers. Satin-grayed receiver engraved w/rosettes and scrolls. German nickel-silver sight bead. Weight: 6.25 lbs. to 6 lbs., 11 oz. 12 ga. made in 1983; 20 ga. Made in 1984. Disc. 1988.

12 ga. model	NiB $3750	Ex $2963	Gd $1947
20 ga. model	NiB $4993	Ex $3290	Gd $2760

B-SS S/S 20 GAUGE SPORTER . NiB $3150 Ex $2654 Gd $1464
Same as standard B-SS 20 ga. except has selective single trigger, straight-grip stock. Introduced 1977. Disc. 1987.

BT-99 GRADE I SINGLE BBL. TRAP ...... NiB $995 Ex $700 Gd $495
Boxlock. Automatic ejector. 12 ga. only. 32- or 34-inch vent rib bbl., M, IM or F choke. Weight: About 8 lbs. Checkered pistol-grip stock and beavertail forearm, recoil pad. Made 1971 to 1976 by Miroku.

BT-99 MAX
Boxlock. 12 ga. only w/ejector selector and no safety. 32- or 34-inch ported bbl. w/high post vent rib. Checkered select walnut buttstock and finger-grooved forend w/high luster finish. Engraved receiver w/blued or stainless metal finish. Made 1995 to 1996.

Blued	NiB $1300	Ex $1014	Gd $714
Stainless	NiB $1880	Ex $1496	Gd $1043

BT-99 PLUS
Similar to the BT-99 Competition except w/Browning Recoil Reduction System. Made 1989 to 1995.

Grade I	NiB $1775	Ex $1197	Gd $974
Pigeon grade	NiB $1875	Ex $1131	Gd $783
Signature grade	NiB $1756	Ex $1100	Gd $772
Stainless model	NiB $1955	Ex $1201	Gd $842
Golden Clays	NiB $2700	Ex $2385	Gd $2127

BT-99 PLUS MICRO. .... NiB $1125 Ex $977 Gd $722
Same general specifications as BT-99 Plus except scaled down for smaller shooters. 30-inch bbl. w/adj. rib and Browning's recoil reducer system. Made 1991 to 1996.

BT-100 COMPETITION TRAP SPECIAL
Same as BT-99 except has super-high wide rib and standard Monte Carlo or fully adj. stock. Available w/adj. choke or Invector Plus tubes w/optional porting. Made 1976 to 2000.

Grade I w/fixed choke (disc. 1992).	NiB $1700	Ex $986	Gd $740
Grade I w/Invectors	NiB $1900	Ex $1086	Gd $940
Grade I stainless (disc. 1994)	NiB $2210	Ex $1888	Gd $993
Grade I Pigeon Grade (disc. 1994)	NiB $1400	Ex $1116	Gd $944

BT-100 SINGLE-SHOT TRAP
Similar to the BT-99 Max, except w/additional stock options and removable trigger group. Made 1995 to 2002.

Model BT-100 Grade I blued	NiB $1900	Ex $1227	Gd $834
Model BT-100 stainless	NiB $2210	Ex $1887	Gd $1167
Model BT-100 satin	NiB $1393	Ex $1125	Gd $789
Model BT-100 w/adj. comb, add			$100
Thumbhole stock, add			$295
Replacement trigger assembly, add			$495
Fixed choke, deduct			$65

CITORI HUNTING O/U MODELS
Boxlock. Gauges: 12, 16 (disc. 1989), 20, 28 (disc. 1992) and .410 bore (disc. 1989). Bbl. lengths: 24-, 26-, 28-, or 30-inch w/vent rib. Chambered 2.75-, 3- or 3.5-inch mag. Chokes: IC/M, M/F (Fixed Chokes); Standard Invector, or Invector plus choke systems. Overall length ranges from 41-47 inches. 2.75-, 3- or 3-inch Mag. loads, depending on ga. Weight: 5.75 lbs. to 7 lbs. 13 oz. Single selective, gold-plated trigger. Medium raised German nickel-silver sight bead. Checkered, rounded pistol-grip walnut stock w/beavertail forend. Invector Chokes and Invector Plus became standard in 1988 and 1995, respectively. Made from 1973 to date by Miroku.

Grade I (disc. 1994)	NiB $950	Ex $694	Gd $488
Grade I - 3.5-inch Mag.(1989 to date)	NiB $950	Ex $726	Gd $548
Grade II (disc. 1983)	NiB $1200	Ex $954	Gd $599
Grade III (1985-95)	NiB $1900	Ex $1178	Gd $983
Grade V (disc. 1984)	NiB $2750	Ex $1958	Gd $1146
Grade VI (1985-95)	NiB $2750	Ex $2107	Gd $1947
Model Sporting Hunter (12 and 20 ga.; 1998 to date)	NiB $1250	Ex $823	Gd $575
Model Satin Hunter (12 ga. only; 1998 to date)	NiB $1150	Ex $945	Gd $623
Mdls. w/o Inv. choke syst., deduct			$120
For 3.5-inch Mag., add			$90
For disc. ga 16, 28 and .410, add			15%

CITORI LIGHTNING O/U MODELS
Same general specifications as the Citori Hunting models except w/classic Browning rounded pistol-grip stock. Made from 1988 to date by Miroku.

Grade I	NiB $992	Ex $717	Gd $506
Grade III	NiB $1866	Ex $1068	Gd $732
Grade VI	NiB $3094	Ex $1915	Gd $1055
Gran Lightning model	NiB $1849	Ex $1126	Gd $785
Feather Model (alloy receiver)	NiB $1400	Ex $1068	Gd $913
Feather Combo model (2-bbl. set)	NiB $3200	Ex $2620	Gd $1910
Privilege Mdl. (engraved w/sideplates)	NiB $4779	Ex $3853	Gd $2668
Micro model, add			10%
Models w/o Invector choke system, deduct			$200
28 and .410 ga., add			15%

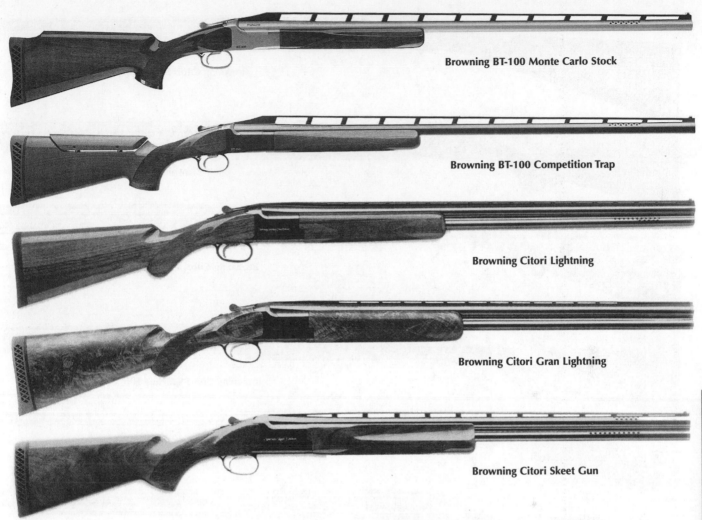

Browning BT-100 Monte Carlo Stock

Browning BT-100 Competition Trap

Browning Citori Lightning

Browning Citori Gran Lightning

Browning Citori Skeet Gun

SHOTGUNS

CITORI SKEET GUN

Same as Hunting model except has skeet-style stock and forearm, 26- or 28-inch bbls., both bored SK choke. Available w/either standard vent rib or special target-type, high-post, wide vent rib. Weight (w/26-inch bbls.): 12 ga., 8 lbs., 20 ga., 7 lbs. Made 1974 to date by Miroku.

Grade I	NiB $1294	Ex $1055	Gd $643
Grade II	NiB $1600	Ex $1253	Gd $972
Grade III	NiB $1678	Ex $1102	Gd $774
Grade VI (disc. 1995)	NiB $2200	Ex $1628	Gd $1136
Golden Clays	NiB $2725	Ex $1797	Gd $123
28 and .410 ga., add			15%
3-bbl. Set, Grade I (disc. 1996)	NiB $2256	Ex $1975	Gd $1401
3-bbl. Set, Grade III (disc. 1996)	NiB $3442	Ex $2123	Gd $1490
3-bbl. Set, Grade VI (disc. 1994)	NiB $3649	Ex $2394	Gd $1686
3-bbl. Set, Golden Clays (disc. 1995)	NiB $4250	Ex $2982	Gd $2161
4-bbl. Set, Grade I	NiB $3498	Ex $2849	Gd $1995
4-bbl. Set, Grade III	NiB $4250	Ex $3145	Gd $2206
4-bbl. Set, Grade VI (disc. 1994)	NiB $4609	Ex $3295	Gd $2349
4-bbl. Set, Golden Clays (disc. 1995)	NiB $5656	Ex $3892	Gd $2721

CITORI SPORTING CLAYS

Similar to the standard Citori Lightning model except Classic-style stock with rounded pistol-grip. 30-inch back-bored bbls. with Invector Plus tubes. Receiver with "Lightning Sporting Clays Edition" logo. Made from 1989 to date.

GTI model (disc. 1995)	NiB $1089	Ex $996	Gd $658
GTI Golden Clays model (1993-94)	NiB $2378	Ex $1663	Gd $1171
Lightning model (intro. 1989)	NiB $1304	Ex $1002	Gd $717
Lightning Golden Clays (1993-98)	NiB $2602	Ex $1742	Gd $1212
Lightning Pigeon Grade (1993-94)	NiB $1503	Ex $1065	Gd $760
Micro Citori Lightning model (w/low rib)	NiB $1475	Ex $994	Gd $674
Special Sporting model (intro. 1989)	NiB $1477	Ex $1019	Gd $696
Special Sporting Golden Clays (1993-98)	NiB $3150	Ex $2977	Gd $1992
Special Sporting Pigeon Gr. (1993-94)	NiB $1375	Ex $1090	Gd $776
Ultra mdl. (intro. 1995-previously GTI)	NiB $1507	Ex $1175	Gd $794
Ultra Golden Clays (intro. 1995)	NiB $1900	Ex $1695	Gd $1404
Model 325 (1993-94)	NiB $1194	Ex $1076	Gd $771
Model 325 Golden Clays (1993-94)	NiB $2451	Ex $1709	Gd $1216
Model 425 Grade I (intro. 1995)	NiB $1625	Ex $1145	Gd $817
Model 425 Golden Clays (intro. 1995)	NiB $2450	Ex $1982	Gd $1401
Model 425 WSSF (intro. 1995)	NiB $175 4	Ex $1099	Gd $785
Model 802 Sporter (ES) Extended Swing (intro. 1996	NiB $1393	Ex $1193	Gd $836
For 2 bbl. set, add			$850
For adjustable stock, add			$200
For high rib, add			$85
For ported barrels, add			$75

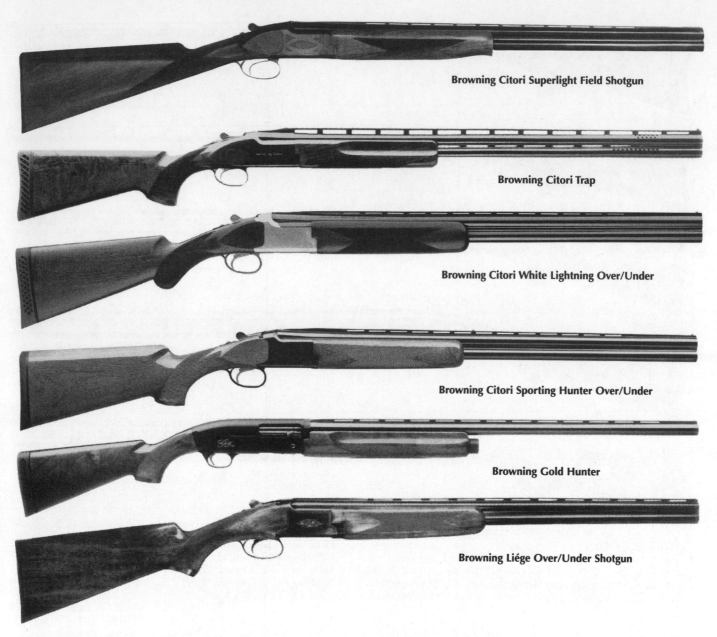

Browning Citori Superlight Field Shotgun

Browning Citori Trap

Browning Citori White Lightning Over/Under

Browning Citori Sporting Hunter Over/Under

Browning Gold Hunter

Browning Liége Over/Under Shotgun

CITORI SUPERLIGHT O/U FIELD SHOTGUNS
Similar to the Citori Hunting model except w/straight-grip stock and Schnabel forend tip. Made by Miroku 1982 to date.

Grade I . . . . NiB $995 Ex $776 Gd $555
Grade III . . . . NiB $1900 Ex $1504 Gd $983
Grade V (disc. 1985) . . . . NiB $2951 Ex $2297 Gd $1974
Grade VI . . . . NiB $2756 Ex $2185 Gd $1488
Models w/o Invector choke system, deduct $275
28 and .410 ga., add 10%

CITORI TRAP GUN
Same as Hunting model except 12 ga. only, has Monte Carlo or fully adjustable stock and beavertail forend, trap-style recoil pad; 20- or 32-inch bbls.; M/F, IM/F, or F/F. Available with either standard vent rib or special target-type, high-post, wide vent rib. Weight: 8 lbs. Made from 1974 to 2001 by Miroku.

Grade I Trap . . . . NiB $900 Ex $750 Gd $551
Grade I Trap Pigeon grade
(disc. 1994) . . . . NiB $1716 Ex $1432 Gd $1065
Grade I Trap Signature grade (disc. 1994) . . . NiB $1592 Ex $1205 Gd $987
Grade I Plus Trap (disc. 1994) . . NiB $2775 Ex $2182 Gd $1933
Grade I Plus Trap
w/ported bbls. (disc. 1994) . . . . . NiB $1895 Ex $1365 Gd $997
Grade I Plus Trap
Combo (disc. 1994) . . . . NiB $2773 Ex $2078 Gd $1760
Grade I Plus Trap
Golden Clays (disc. 1994) . . . . NiB $3000 Ex $2476 Gd $1937
Grade II w/HP rib (disc. 1984) . . NiB $1892 Ex $1302 Gd $919
Grade III Trap . . . . NiB $1896 Ex $1575 Gd $1116
Grade V Trap (disc. 1984) . . . . . NiB $1754 Ex $1734 Gd $1222
Grade VI Trap (disc. 1994). . . . . NiB $1995 Ex $1786 Gd $1399
Grade VI Trap
Golden Clays (disc. 1994) . . . . NiB $2756 Ex $2408 Gd $1682

CITORI UPLAND SPECIAL O/U SHOTGUN
A shortened version of the Hunting model fitted with 24-inch bbls. and straight-grip stock.
Upland Special 12, 20 ga. models...... NiB $1196 Ex $975 Gd $686
Upland Spec. 16 ga. (disc. 1989) ...... NiB $1333 Ex $1136 Gd $796
Models w/o Inv. choke sys., deduct $120

CITORI WHITE LIGHTNING O/U SHOTGUN
Similar to the standard Citori Lightning model except w/silver nitride receiver w/scroll and rosette engraving. Satin wood finish w/round pistol grip. Made 1998 to 2001.
12, 20 ga. models................. NiB $1675 Ex $1140 Gd $800
28, .410 ga. models (Intro. 2000)..... NiB $1753 Ex $1274 Gd $1063

CITORI WHITE UPLAND SPECIAL...... NiB $1252 Ex $998 Gd $700
Similar to the standard Citori Upland model except w/silver nitride receiver w/scroll and rosette engraving. Satin wood finish w/round pistol grip. Made 2000 to 2001.

DOUBLE AUTOMATIC (STEEL RECEIVER)
Short recoil system. Takedown. 12 ga. only. Two round capacity. Bbls.: 26-, 28-, 30-inches; any standard choke. Checkered pistol-grip stock and forend. Weight: About 7.75 lbs. Made 1955 to 1961.
With plain bbl. .... NiB $823 Ex $534 Gd $380
With recessed-rib bbl. .... NiB $955 Ex $663 Gd $468

GOLD DEER HUNTER AUTOLOADING SHOTGUN
Similar to the Standard Gold Hunter model except chambered 12 ga. only. 22-inch bbl. W/rifled bore or smooth bore w/5-inch rifled invector tube. Cantilevered scope mount. Made 1997 to 2005.
Gold Deer Hunter (w/standard finish) .... NiB $910 Ex $666 Gd $481
Field model (w/Mossy Oak finish) .... NiB $956 Ex $619 Gd $495

GOLD HUNTER SERIES
Self-cleaning, gas-operated, short-stroke action. Gauges: 10 or 12 (3.5-inch chamber); 12 or 20 (3-inch chamber). 26-, 28-, or 30-inch bbl. w/Invector or Invector Plus choke tubes. Checkered walnut stock. Polished or matte black metal finish. Made 1990 to date.
Gold Hunter (Light 10 ga. 3.5-inch w/wal. St.) . NiB $1324 Ex $1143 Gd $924
Gold Hunter (12 ga. 3.5-inch).......... NiB $872 Ex $702 Gd $468
Gold Hunter (12 or 20 ga. 3-inch)...... NiB $986 Ex $767 Gd $533
Gld. Hunter Clas. Mdl. (12 or 20 Ga. 3-inch) ..... NiB $800 Ex $693 Gd $553
Gld. Hunter High Gr.
Classic (12 or 20 ga. 3-inch).......... NiB $1575 Ex $1174 Gd $986
Gold Deer Hunter
(12 ga. w/22-inch bbl.) .... NiB $910 Ex $725 Gd $576
Gold Turkey Hunter Camo
(12 ga. w/24-inch bbl.) .... NiB $875 Ex $588 Gd $451
Gold Waterfowl Hunter
Camo (12 ga. w/24-inch bbl.).......... NiB $875 Ex $588 Gd $541

GOLD STALKER SERIES
Self-cleaning, gas-operated, short-stroke action. Gauges: 10 or 12 (3.5-inch chamber); 12 or 20 (3-inch chamber). 26-, 28-, or 30-inch bbl. w/Invector or Invector Plus choke tubes. Graphite/fiberglass composite stock. Polished or matte black finish. Made 1998 to 2007.
Gold Stalker (Light 10 ga.
3.5-inch w/composite stock).......... NiB $1329 Ex $1141 Gd $927
Gold Stalker (12 ga. 3.5-inch).......... NiB $988 Ex $785 Gd $589
Gold Stalker (12 or 20 ga. 3-inch) .... NiB $800 Ex $572 Gd $342
Gold Stalker Classic
Model (12 or 20 ga. 3-inch).......... NiB $1580 Ex $1177 Gd $945
Gold Deer Stalker
(12 ga. w/22-inch bbl.) .... NiB $855 Ex $529 Gd $380
Gold Turkey Stalker Camo
(12 ga. w/24-inch bbl.) .... NiB $799 Ex $482 Gd $355

Browning Over/Under Gold Classic

Gold Waterfowl Stalker
Camo (12 Ga. w/24-inch bbl.) .... NiB $828 Ex $571 Gd $479

GOLD SPORTING CLAYS SERIES
Similar to Gold Hunter Series except w/2.75-inch chamber and 28- or 30-inch ported bbl. w/Invector Plus chokes. Made 1996 to 2008.
Gold Sporting Clays (standard) .... NiB $1000 Ex $737 Gd $588
Gold Sporting Clays (youth or ladies)... NiB $1575 Ex $1152 Gd $995
Gold Sporting Clays w/Eng. nick. rec.... NiB $1650 Ex $1107 Gd $945

LIÈGE O/U SHOTGUN (B26/27)
Boxlock. Automatic ejectors. Non-selective single trigger. 12 ga. only. Bbls.: 26.5-, 28-, or 30-inch; 2.75-inch chambers in 26.5- and 28-inch, 3-inch in 30-inch, IC/M, M/F, or F/F chokes; vent rib. Weight: 7 lbs., 4 oz.to 7 lbs., 14 oz., depending on bbls. Checkered pistol-grip stock and forearm. Made 1973 to 1975 by FN.
Liège (B-26 BAC production) .... NiB $1325 Ex $965 Gd $750
Liège (B-27 FN prod.) Stand. Game Mdl. . NiB $1325 Ex $965 Gd $750
Deluxe Game model................. NiB $1432 Ex $1129 Gd $883
Grand Delux Game model .... NiB $1575 Ex $1207 Gd $997
Deluxe Skeet model .... NiB $1325 Ex $1065 Gd $909
Deluxe Trap model .... NiB $1325 Ex $1065 Gd $909
COL Commemorative model .... NiB $1750 Ex $1399 Gd $1138

LIGHT SPORTING 802ES ...... NiB $1396 Ex $1102 Gd $774
Over/under. Invector-plus choke tubes. 12 ga. only with 28-inch bbl. Weight: 7 lbs., 5 oz.

LIGHTNING SPORTING CLAYS
Similar to the standard Citori Lightning model except Classic-style stock with rounded pistol grip. 30-inch back-bored bbls. with Invector Plus tubes. Receiver with "Lightning Sporting Clays Edition" logo. Made 1989 to 1994.
Standard model .... NiB $1295 Ex $942 Gd $656
Pigeon grade .... NiB $1267 Ex $1019 Gd $714

O/U CLASSIC .... NiB $2255 Ex $1810 Gd $1266
Gauge: 20, 2.75-inch chambers. 26-inch blued bbls. choked IC/M. Gold-plated, single selective trigger. Manual, top-tang-mounted safety. Engraved receiver. High grade, select American walnut straight-grip stock with Schnabel forend. Fine-line checkering with pearl borders. High-gloss finish. 5,000 issued in 1986; made in Japan, engraved in Belgium.

O/U GOLD CLASSIC.............. NiB $5499 Ex $4520 Gd $3024
Same general specifications as Over/Under Classic except more elaborate engravings, enhanced in gold, including profile of John M. Browning. Fine oil finish. 500 issued; made in 1986 in Belgium.

RECOILLESS TRAP SHOTGUN
The action and bbl. are driven forward when firing to achieve 72 percent less recoil. 12 ga, 2.75-inch chamber. 30-inch bbl. with Invector Plus tubes; adjustable vent rib. 51.63 inches overall. Weight: 9 lbs. Adj. checkered walnut buttstock and forend. Blued finish. Made from 1993 to 1996.

SHOTGUNS

Browning Superposed Broadway 12 Trap

Browning Superposed Grade I Lightning

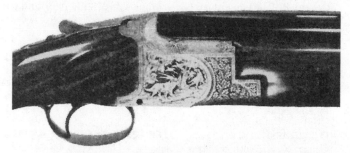

Left Side

Right Side

Browning Superposed Bicentennial

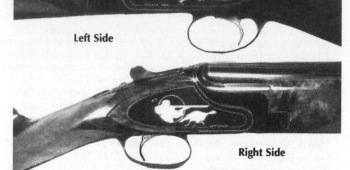

Browning Superposed Grade IV Diana (Postwar)

Browning Superposed Grade V Midas (Postwar)

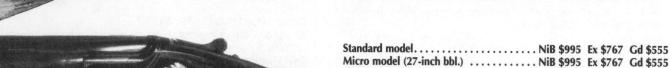

Standard model . . . . NiB $995 Ex $767 Gd $555
Micro model (27-inch bbl.) . . . . NiB $995 Ex $767 Gd $555
Signature model (27-inch bbl.) . . . . NiB $995 Ex $767 Gd $555

**SUPERPOSED BICENTENNIAL
COMMEMORATIVE** . . . . NiB $12,000 Ex $10,708 Gd $7330
Special limited edition issued to commemorate U.S. Bicentennial. 51 guns, one for each state in the Union plus one for Washington, D.C. Receiver with sideplates has engraved and gold-inlaid hunter and wild turkey on right side, U.S. flag and bald eagle on left side, together with state markings inlaid in gold, on blued background. Checkered straight-grip stock and Schnabel-style forearm of highly-figured American walnut. Velvet-lined wood presentation case. Made in 1976 by FN. Value shown is for gun in new, unfired condition. See illustration next page.

**SUPERPOSED
BROADWAY 12 TRAP** . . . . NiB $19506 Ex $1684 Gd $1170
Same as Standard Trap Gun except has 30- or 32-inch bbls. with wider Broadway rib. Disc. 1976.

SUPERPOSED SHOTGUNS, HUNTING MODELS
Over/under boxlock. Selective automatic ejectors. Selective single trigger; earlier models (worth 25% less) supplied w/double triggers, twin selective triggers or non-selective single trigger. Gauges: 12, 20 (intro. 1949, 3-inch chambers in later production), 28, .410 (latter two ga. intro. 1960). Bbls.: 26.5-, 28-, 30-, 32-inch, raised matted or vent rib, prewar Lightning Model made w/ribbed bbl., postwar version supplied only w/vent rib; any combination of standard chokes. Weight (w/26.5-inch vent-rib bbls.): Standard 12, 7 lbs., 11 oz., Lightning 12, 7 lbs., 6 oz.; Standard 20, 6 lbs., 8 oz.; Lightning 20, 6 lbs., 4 oz.; Lightning 28, 6 lbs., 7 oz.; Lightning .410, 6 lbs., 10 oz. Checkered pistol-grip stock/forearm.
Higher grades (Pigeon, Pointer, Diana, Midas, Grade VI) differ from standard Grade I models in overall quality, engraving, wood and checkering; otherwise, specifications are the same. Midas Grade and Grade VI guns are richly gold inlaid. Made by FN 1928-1976. Prewar models may be considered as disc. in 1940 when Belgium was occupied by Germany. Grade VI offered 1955-1960. Pointer Grade disc. in 1966, Grade I Standard in 1973, Pigeon Grade in 1974. Lightning Grade I, Diana and Midas Grades were not offered after 1976.
Grade I standard weight . . . . . . NiB $2250 Ex $1857 Gd $1625
Grade I Lightning . . . . NiB $2178 Ex $1757 Gd $1241
Grade I Lightning, prewar,
matted bbl., no rib . . . . NiB $1871 Ex $1548 Gd $1189
Grade II—Pigeon . . . . NiB $4200 Ex $2668 Gd $1873

**Browning Superposed Ltd.
Pintail Duck Issue**

Grade III—Pointer. . . . . NiB $4800   Ex $3590   Gd $2826
Grade IV—Diana. . . . . NiB $8000   Ex $6152   Gd $4198
Grade V—Midas . . . . NiB $7000   Ex $4753   Gd $3353
Grade VI. . . . . NiB $10,000   Ex $8292   Gd $6659
Add for 20 ga. 20%
Add for 28 ga. 75%
Add for .410. . . . . 45%
Values shown are for models w/ventilated rib.
If gun has raised matted rib, deduct 10%

SUPERPOSED LIGHTNING AND SUPERLIGHT MODELS
(REISSUE B-25)
Reissue of popular 12-and 20-ga. Superposed shotguns. Lightning models available in 26.5- and 28-inch bbl. lengths w/2.75- or 3-inch chambering, full pistol grip. Superlight models available in 26.5-inch bbl. lengths w/2.75-inch chambering only, and straight-grip stock w/Schnabel forend. Both have hand-engraved receivers, fine-line checkering, gold-plated single selective trigger, automatic selective ejectors, manual safety. Weight: 6 to 7.5 lbs. Reintroduced 1985.
Grade I, Standard . . . . NiB $2250   Ex $1725   Gd $1288
Grade II, Pigeon . . . . NiB $5564   Ex $3617   Gd $2148
Grade III, Pointer . . . . NiB $8750   Ex $5260   Gd $3273
Grade IV, Diana. . . . . NiB $7750   Ex $5585   Gd $3509
Grade V, Midas . . . . NiB $12,500   Ex $10,663   Gd $9347
W/extra bbls., add 45%

SUPERPOSED MAGNUM . . . . . . NiB $1850   Ex $1384   Gd $972
Same as Grade I except chambered for 12-ga. 3-inch shells, 30-inch vent-rib bbls., stock w/recoil pad. Weight: About 8.25 lbs. Disc. 1976.

SUPERPOSED LTD.
BLACK DUCK ISSUE . . . . NiB $9500   Ex $6064   Gd $4310
Gauge: 12. Superposed Lightning action. 28-inch vent-rib bbls. Choked M/F. 2.75-inch chambers. Weight: 7 lbs., 6 oz. Gold-inlaid receiver and trigger guard engraved w/black duck scenes. Gold-plated, single selective trigger. Top-tang mounted manual safety. Automatic, selective ejectors. Front and center ivory sights. High-grade, hand-checkered, hand-oiled select walnut stock and forend. 500 issued in 1983.

SUPERPOSED LTD.
MALLARD DUCK ISSUE . . . . . . NiB $9500   Ex $6204   Gd $4310
Same general specifications as Ltd. Black Duck issue except mallard duck scenes engraved on receiver and trigger guard, dark French walnut stock w/rounded pistol-grip. 500 issued in 1981.

SUPERPOSED LTD.
PINTAIL DUCK ISSUE . . . . NiB $9500   Ex $6064   Gd $4310
Same general specifications as Ltd. Black Duck issue except pintail duck scenes engraved on receiver and trigger guard. Stock is of dark French walnut w/rounded pistol-grip. 500 issued in 1982.

SUPERPOSED, PRESENTATION GRADES
Custom versions of Super-Light, Lightning Hunting, Trap and Skeet Models, w/same general specifications as those of standard guns, but of higher overall quality. The four Presentation grades differ in receiver finish (grayed or blued), engraving gold inlays, wood and checkering. Presentation 4 has sideplates. Made by FN, these models were Intro. in 1977.
Presentation 1 . . . . NiB $3350   Ex $2633   Gd $1834
Presentation 1, gold-inlaid. . . . . NiB $4750   Ex $2988   Gd $2102
Presentation 2 . . . . NiB $4800   Ex $3358   Gd $2358
Presentation 2, gold-inlaid. . . . . NiB $7000   Ex $4939   Gd $3739
Presentation 3, gold-inlaid. . . . . NiB $9000   Ex $7108   Gd $5550
Presentation 4 . . . . NiB $8000   Ex $5700   Gd $3955
Presentation 4, gold-inlaid. . NiB $12,000   Ex $10,372   Gd $9814

SUPERPOSED SKEET GUNS, GRADE I
Same as standard Lightning 12, 20, 28 and .410 Hunting models, except has skeet-style stock and forearm, 26.5- or 28-inch vent-rib bbls. w/SK choke. Available also in All Gauge Skeet Set: Lightning 12 w/one removable forearm and three extra sets of bbls. in 20, 28 and .410 ga. in fitted luggage case. Disc. 1976. (For higher grades see listings for comparable Hunting models)
12 or 20 ga. . . . . NiB $1958   Ex $1585   Gd $1097
28 or .410 ga. . . . . NiB $2427   Ex $1957   Gd $1366
All ga. skeet set . . . . NiB $6160   Ex $4976   Gd $3407

SUPERPOSED SUPER
LIGHT MODEL . . . . NiB $6510   Ex $4560   Gd $3480
Ultralight field gun version of Standard Lightning Model has classic straight-grip stock and slimmer forearm. Available only in 12 and 20 gauges (2.75-inch chambers), w/26.5-inch vent-rib bbls. Weight: 6.5 lbs., (12 ga.); 6 lbs., (20 ga.). Made 1967 to 1976.

SUPERPOSED TRAP GUN . . . . . NiB $4955   Ex $3123   Gd $1917
Same as Grade I except has trap-style stock, beavertail forearm, 30-inch vent-rib bbls., 12 ga. only. Disc. 1976. (For higher grades see listings for comparable hunting models)

TWELVETTE DOUBLE AUTOMATIC
Lightweight version of Double Automatic w/same general specifications except aluminum receiver. Bbl. w/plain matted top or vent rib. Weight: 6.75 to 7 lbs., depending on bbl. Receiver is finished in black w/gold engraving; 1956-1961 receivers were also anodized in gray, brown and green w/silver engraving. Made 1955 to 1971
W/plain bbl. . . . . NiB $599   Ex $484   Gd $344
W/vent rib bbl. . . . . NiB $722   Ex $587   Gd $415

CENTURY INTERNATIONAL ARMS, INC. — St. Albans, VT and Boca Raton, FL.

ARTHEMIS. . . . . NiB $425   Ex $321   Gd $225
O/U boxlock action with double triggers and extractors. 12, 20, 28 ga. or .410 bore. 3-inch chambers. 28-inch bbls. Single set trigger, extractors. Checkered wood stock and forearm. Weight: 5.3 to 7.4 lbs. Mfg. in Turkey by Khan. Disc.

SHOTGUNS

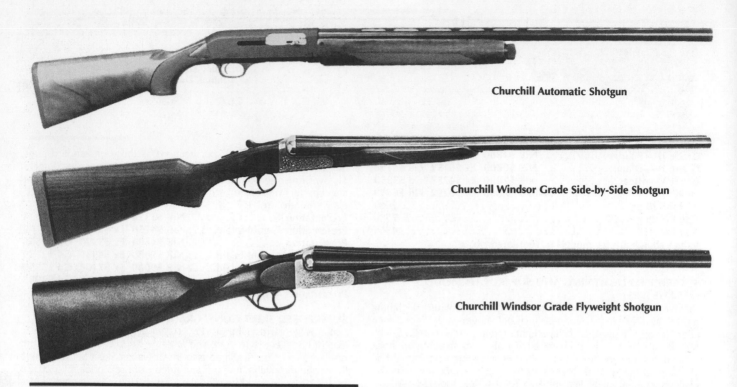

Churchill Automatic Shotgun

Churchill Windsor Grade Side-by-Side Shotgun

Churchill Windsor Grade Flyweight Shotgun

CHURCHILL SHOTGUNS — Italy and Spain
Imported by Ellett Brothers, Inc., Chapin, SC; previously by Kassnar Imports, Inc., Harrisburg, PA

AUTOMATIC SHOTGUN
Gas-operated. Gauge: 12, 2.75- or 3-inch chambers. Five round magazine w/cutoff. Bbl.: 24-, 25-, 26-, 28-inch w/ICT choke tubes. Checkered walnut stock w/satin finish. Imported from 1990 to 1994.
Standard model . . . . NiB $574 Ex $481 Gd $350
Turkey model . . . . NiB $590 Ex $492 Gd $353

MONARCH O/U SHOTGUN
Hammerless, takedown w/engraved receiver. Selective single or double triggers. Gauges: 12, 20, 28, .410; 3-inch chambers. Bbls.: 25- or 26-inch (IC/M); 28-inch (M/F). Weight: 6.5-7.5 lbs. Checkered European walnut buttstock and forend. Made in Italy from 1986 to 1993.
W/double triggers . . . . NiB $405 Ex $332 Gd $200
W/single trigger . . . . NiB $465 Ex $378 Gd $241

REGENT O/U SHOTGUNS
Gauges: 12 or 20; 2.75-inch chambers. 27-inch bbls. w/interchangeable choke tubes and wide vent rib. Single selective trigger, selective automatic ejectors. Checkered pistol-grip stock in fancy walnut. Imported from Italy 1984 to 1988 and 1990 to 1994.
Regent V(disc. 1988) . . . . NiB $896 Ex $660 Gd $520
Regent VII w/
sideplates (disc. 1994) . . . . NiB $799 Ex $667 Gd $484

REGENT SKEET
. . . . NiB $799 Ex $627 Gd $499
12 or 20 ga. w/2.75-inch chambers. Selective automatic ejectors, single-selective trigger. 26-inch over/under bbls. w/vent rib. Weight: 7 lbs. Made in Italy from 1984 to 1988.

REGENT TRAP
. . . . NiB $795 Ex $517 Gd $397
12-ga. competition shotgun w/2.75-inch chambers. 30-inch over/under bbls. choked IM/F, vent side ribs. Weight: 8 lbs. Selective automatic ejectors, single selective trigger. Checkered Monte Carlo stock w/Supercushion recoil pad. Made in Italy 1984 to 1988.

SPORTING CLAYS O/U
. . . . NiB $800 Ex $657 Gd $435
Same general specifications as Windsor IV except in 12 ga. only w/28-inch ported bbls. and choke tubes. Selective automatic ejectors. Weight: 7.5 lbs. Made from 1992 to 1994.

WINDSOR O/U SHOTGUNS
Hammerless, boxlock w/engraved receiver, selective single trigger. Extractors or ejectors. Gauges: 12, 20, 28 or .410; 3-inch chambers. Bbls.: 24 to 30 inches w/fixed chokes or choke tubes. Weight: 6 lbs., 3 oz. (Flyweight) to 7 lbs., 10 oz. (12 ga.). Checkered straight (Flyweight) or pistol-grip stock and forend of European walnut. Imported from Italy 1984 to 1993.
Windsor III w/fixed chokes . . . . NiB $550 Ex $371 Gd $295
Windsor III w/choke tubes . . . . NiB $695 Ex $702 Gd $495
Windsor IV w/fixed chokes (disc. 1993) . . . NiB $625 Ex $585 Gd $388
Windsor IV w/choke tubes . . . . NiB $725 Ex $685 Gd $488

WINDSOR SIDE-BY-SIDE SHOTGUNS
Boxlock action w/double triggers, ejectors or extractors and automatic safety. Gauges: 10, (3.5-inch chambers); 12, 20, 28, .410 (3-inch chambers), 16 (2.75-inch chambers). Bbls.: 23 to 32 inches w/various fixed choke or choke tube combinations. Weight: 5 lbs., 12 oz. (Flyweight) to 11.5 lbs. (10 ga.). European walnut buttstock and forend. Imported from Spain 1984 to 1990.
Windsor I 10 ga. . . . . NiB $497 Ex $341 Gd $255
Windsor I 12 thru .410 ga. . . . . NiB $497 Ex $341 Gd $255
Windsor II 12 or 20 ga. . . . . NiB $497 Ex $341 Gd $255
Windsor VI 12 or 20 ga. . . . . NiB $497 Ex $341 Gd $255

E.J. CHURCHILL, LTD. —
Surrey (previously London), England

The E.J. Churchill shotguns listed below are no longer imported.

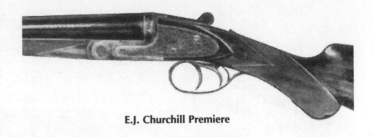

E.J. Churchill Premiere

PREMIERE QUALITY HAMMERLESS DOUBLE
Sidelock. Automatic ejectors. Double triggers or selective single trigger. Gauges: 12, 16, 20, 28. Bbls.: 25-, 28- 30-, 32-inch; any degree of boring. Weight: 5-8 lbs. depending on ga. and bbl. length. Checkered stock and forend, straight or pistol-grip.
W/double triggers . . . . NiB $44,148 Ex $34,758 Gd $28,650
W/selective single trigger, add 10%

FIELD MODEL HAMMERLESS DOUBLE
Sidelock Hammerless ejector gun w/same general specifications as Premiere Model but of lower quality.
W/double triggers . . . . NiB $9,240 Ex $8160 Gd $7120
W/selective single trigger, add 10%

PREMIERE QUALITY O/U SHOTGUN
Sidelock. Automatic ejectors. Double triggers or selective single trigger. Gauges: 12, 16, 20, 28. Bbls.: 25-, 28-, 30-, 32-inch, any degree of boring. Weight: 5-8 lbs. depending on ga. and bbl. length. Checkered stock and forend, straight or pistol-grip.
W/double triggers . . . . NiB $52,450 Ex $36,420 Gd $21,261
W/selective single trigger, add 10%
Raised vent rib, add 15%

UTILITY MODEL HAMMERLESS DOUBLE-BARREL
Anson & Deeley boxlock action. Double triggers or single trigger. Gauges: 12, 16, 20, 28, .410. Bbls.: 25-, 28-, 30-, 32-inch, any degree of boring. Weight: 4.5-8 lbs. depending on ga. and bbl. length. Checkered stock and forend, straight or pistol-grip.
W/double triggers . . . . NiB $6250 Ex $5030 Gd $3730
W/selective single trigger, add 10%

XXV PREMIERE
HAMMERLESS DOUBLE. NiB $44576 Ex $34,030 Gd $29,620
Sidelock. Assisted opening. Automatic ejectors. Double triggers. Gauges: 12, 20. 25-inch bbls. w/narrow, quick-sighting rib; any standard choke combination. English-style straight-grip stock and forearm, checkered.

XXV IMPERIAL. . . . . NiB $13,532 Ex $11,666 Gd $7997
Similar to XXV Premiere but no assisted opening feature.

XXV HERCULES . . . . NiB $9,149 Ex $8047 Gd $5587
Boxlock, otherwise specifications same as for XXV Premiere.

XXV REGAL . . . . NiB $6010 Ex $4625 Gd $3211
Similar to XXV Hercules but w/o assisted opening feature. Gauges: 12, 20, 28, .410.

CLASSIC DOUBLES — Tochigi, Japan

Imported by Classic Doubles International, St. Louis, MO, and previously by Olin as Winchester Models 101 and 23.

MODEL 101 O/U SHOTGUN
Boxlock. Engraved receiver w/single selective trigger, auto ejectors and combination bbl. selector and safety. Gauges: 12, 20, 28 or .410, 2.75- 3-inch chambers, 25.5- 28- or 30-inch vent-rib bbls. Weight: 6.25 – 7.75 lbs. Checkered French walnut stock. Imported from 1987 to 1990.

Classic I Field	NiB $1477	Ex $1355	Gd $969
Classic II Field	NiB $1779	Ex $1527	Gd $1078
Classic Sporter	NiB $1995	Ex $1634	Gd $1151
Classic Sporter combo	NiB $3242	Ex $2630	Gd $1848
Classic Trap	NiB $1251	Ex $1045	Gd $854
Classic Trap Single	NiB $1300	Ex $1066	Gd $969
Classic Trap combo.	NiB $2400	Ex $1980	Gd $1397
Classic Skeet.	NiB $1695	Ex $1524	Gd $1108
Classic Skeet 2-bbl. set	NiB $2695	Ex $2139	Gd $1509
Classic Skeet 4-bbl. set	NiB $4283	Ex $3607	Gd $2545
ClassicWaterfowler.	NiB $1332	Ex $1153	Gd $822
For Grade II (28 ga.), add			$750
For Grade II (.410 ga.), add			$250

MODEL 201 SIDE-BY-SIDE SHOTGUN
Boxlock. Single selective trigger, automatic safety, selective ejectors. Gauges: 12 or 20; 3-inch chambers. 26- or 28-inch vent-rib bbl., fixed chokes or internal tubes. Weight: 6 to 7 lbs. Checkered French walnut stock and forearm. Imported 1987 to 1990.
Field model . . . . NiB $2553 Ex $1370 Gd $1160
Skeet model . . . . NiB $2553 Ex $1370 Gd $1160
With internal choke tubes, add $100

MODEL 201
SMALL BORE SET . . . . NiB $4259 Ex $3113 Gd $2818
Same general specifications as the Classic Model 201 except w/smaller frame, in 28 ga. (IC/M) and .410 (F/M). Weight: 6-6.5 lbs. Imported from 1987 to 1990.

COGSWELL & HARRISON, LTD. —
London, England

AMBASSADOR HAMMERLESS
DOUBLE-BARREL SHOTGUN . . . . . . NiB $5586 Ex $4388 Gd $3580
Boxlock. Sideplates w/game scene or rose scroll engraving. Automatic ejectors. Double triggers. Gauges: 12, 16, 20. Bbls.: 26-28-, 30-inch; any choke combination. Checkered straight-grip stock and forearm. Disc.

AVANT TOUT SERIES HAMMERLESS
DOUBLE-BARREL SHOTGUNS NiB $2550 Ex $1911 Gd $1690
Boxlock. Sideplates (except Avant Tout III Grade). Automatic ejectors. Double triggers or single trigger (selective or non-selective). Gauges: 12, 16, 20. Bbls.: 25-, 27.5-, 30-inch, any choke combination. Checkered stock and forend, straight grip standard. Made in three models (Avant Tout I or Konor, Avant Tout II or Sandhurst.

SHOTGUNS

Colt Auto Shotgun
Ultra Light Standard

Colt Custom
Hammerless Double

Colt Standard Pump

Cogswell & Harrison
Best Quality
Hammerless Sidelock

Colt-Sauer
Drilling

Avant Tout III or Rex) which differ chiefly in overall quality of engraving, grade of wood, checkering, etc. General specifications are the same. Disc.

Avant Tout I . . . . NiB $3279	Ex $2998	Gd $2121
Avant Tout II. . . . . NiB $2801	Ex $2659	Gd $1877
Avant Tout III . . . . NiB $2151	Ex $2054	Gd $1457
Single trigger, non-selective, add. $225
Single trigger, selective, add $395

BEST QUALITY HAMMERLESS
SIDELOCK DOUBLE-BARREL SHOTGUN
Hand-detachable locks. Automatic ejectors. Double triggers or single trigger (selective or non-selective). Gauges: 12, 16, 20. Bbls.: 25-, 26-, 28-, 30-inch, any choke combination. Checkered stock and forend, straight grip standard.

Victor model . . . . NiB $6233	Ex $5251	Gd $3112
Primic model (disc.). . . . . NiB $6276	Ex $5075	Gd $4049
Single trigger, non-selective, add $225
Single trigger, selective, add $395

HUNTIC MODEL HAMMERLESS DOUBLE
Sidelock. Automatic ejectors. Double triggers or single trigger (selective or non-selective). Gauges: 12, 16, 20. Bbls.: 25-, 27.5-, 30-inch; any choke combination. Checkered stock and forend, straight grip standard. Disc.

W/double triggers . . . . NiB $3902	Ex $2710	Gd $1638
Single trigger, non-selective, add. $225
Single trigger, selective, add $350

MARKOR HAMMERLESS DOUBLE
Boxlock. Non-ejector or ejector. Double triggers. Gauges: 12, 16, 20. Bbls.: 27.5 or 30-inch; any choke combination. Checkered stock and forend, straight grip standard. Disc.

Non-ejector . . . . NiB $1676	Ex $1454	Gd $1085
Ejector model . . . . Add 20%

REGENCY HAMMERLESS DOUBLE. . . NiB $4274 Ex $3570 Gd $2 805
Anson & Deeley boxlock action. Automatic ejectors. Double triggers. Gauges: 12, 16, 20. Bbls.: 26-, 28-, 30-inch, any choke combination. Checkered straight-grip stock and forearm. Introduced in 1970 to commemorate the firm's bicentennial, this model has deep scroll engraving and the name "Regency" inlaid in gold on the rib. Disc.

COLT INDUSTRIES — Hartford, Connecticut
Auto Shotguns were made by Franchi and are similar to corresponding models of that manufacturer.

AUTO SHOTGUN — ULTRA LIGHT STANDARD
Recoil-operated. Takedown. Alloy receiver. Gauges: 12, 20. Mag. holds 4 rounds. Bbls.: plain, solid or vent rib, chrome-lined; 26-inch IC or M choke, 28-inch M or F choke, 30-inch F choke, 32-inch F choke. Weight: 12 ga., about 6.25 lbs. Checkered pistol-grip stock and forearm. Made 1964 to 1966.

W/plain bbl. . . . . NiB $375	Ex $237	Gd $192
W/solid rib bbl. . . . . NiB $425	Ex $287	Gd $232
W/vent rib bbl. . . . . NiB $425	Ex $287	Gd $232

AUTO SHOTGUN — MAGNUM CUSTOM
Same as Magnum except has engraved receiver, select walnut stock and forearm. Made 1964 to 66.
W/Solid-rib bbl. . . . . NiB $485 Ex $382 Gd $251
W/ventilated rib bbl. . . . . NiB $525 Ex $422 Gd $301

AUTO SHOTGUN — ULTRA LIGHT CUSTOM
Same as Standard Auto except has engraved receiver, select walnut stock and forearm. Made 1964 to 1966.
W/solid-rib bbl. . . . . NiB $475 Ex $414 Gd $298
W/ventilated-rib bbl. . . . . NiB $525 Ex $440 Gd $315

AUTO SHOTGUN — MAGNUM
Same as Standard Auto except steel receiver, chambered for 3-inch Magnum shells, 30- and 32-inch bbls. in 12 ga., 28-inch in 20 ga. Weight: 12 ga., about 8.25 lbs. Made 1964 to 1966.
W/plain bbl. . . . . NiB $496 Ex $398 Gd $287
W/solid-rib bbl. . . . . NiB $558 Ex $440 Gd $315
W/ventilated rib bbl. . . . . NiB $574 Ex $461 Gd $330

CUSTOM HAMMERLESS DOUBLE . . . . NiB $685 Ex $472 Gd $379
Boxlock. Double triggers. Auto ejectors. Gauges: 12 Mag., 16. Bbls.: 26-inch IC/M; 28-inch M/F; 30-inch F/F. Weight: 12 ga., about 7.5 lbs. Checkered pistol-grip stock and beavertail forearm. Made in 1961.

COLTSMAN PUMP
SHOTGUN . . . . NiB $427 Ex $311 Gd $229
Takedown. Gauges: 12, 16, 20. Magazine holds 4 rounds. Bbls.: 26-inch IC; 28-inch M or F choke; 30-inch F choke. Weight: About 6 lbs. Plain pistol-grip stock and forearm. Made 1961 to 1965 by Manufrance.

CUSTOM PUMP . . . . NiB $442 Ex $346 Gd $248
Same as Standard Pump shotgun except has checkered stock, vent-rib bbl. Weight: About 6.5 lbs. Made 1961 to 1963 by Manufrance.

SAUER DRILLING . . . . NiB $4329 Ex $3621 Gd $2235
Three-bbl. combination gun. Boxlock. Set rifle trigger. Tang bbl. selector, automatic rear sight positioner. 12 ga. over .30-06 or .243 rifle bbl. 25-inch bbls., F and M choke. Weight: About 8 lbs. Folding leaf rear sight, blade front w/brass bead. Checkered pistol-grip stock and beavertail forearm, recoil pad. Made 1974 to 1985 by J. P. Sauer & Sohn, Eckernförde, Germany.

CONNECTICUT VALLEY CLASSICS — Westport, Connecticut

SPORTER 101 O/U
Gauge: 12; 3-inch chamber. Bbls.: 28-, 30- or 32-inch w/ screw-in tubes. Weight: 7.75 lbs. Engraved stainless or nitrided receiver; blued bbls. Checkered American black walnut buttstock and forend w/low-luster satin finish. Made from 1993 to 1998.
Classic Sporter . . . . NiB $1879 Ex $1529 Gd $1290
Stainless Classic Sporter . . . . . . NiB $2696 Ex $2133 Gd $1503

FIELD O/U
Similar to the standard Classic Sporter over/under model except w/30-inch bbls. only and non-reflective matte blued finish on both bbls. and receiver for Waterfowler; other grades w/different degrees of embellishment; Grade I the lowest and Grade III the highest. Made 1993 to 1998.
Grade I . . . . NiB $2699 Ex $2192 Gd $1559
Grade II . . . . NiB $3027 Ex $2335 Gd $1642
Grade III . . . . NiB $3577 Ex $2633 Gd $1845
Waterfowler . . . . NiB $2491 Ex $2177 Gd $1487

CONNENTO/VENTUR — Formerly imported by Ventura, Seal Beach, California

Model 51 . . . . NiB $395 Ex $305 Gd $280
Gauge: 12, 16, 20, 28 and .410. Double-barrel, box-lock action. Barrels: 26, 28, 30 and 32 inches; various chokes; extractors; and double triggers. Checkered walnut stock. Introduced in 1980, discontinued 1985.

Model 52 . . . . NiB $545 Ex $380 Gd $280
Same as Model 51 except in 10 gauge.

Model 53 . . . . NiB $470 Ex $385 Gd $285
Same as Model 51 except with scalloped receiver, automatic ejectors and optional single selective trigger. Discontinued in 1985.

W/single trigger, add 25%

Model 62 . . . . NiB $1017 Ex $807 Gd $632
Holland & Holland-design sidelock shotgun with various barrel lengths and chokes; automatic ejectors; cocking indicators. Floral engraved receiver, checkered walnut stock. Discontinued in 1982.

Model 64 . . . . NiB $1266 Ex $941 Gd $771
Same as Model 62 except deluxe finish. Discontinued.

Grade I . . . . NiB $1192 Ex $867 Gd $742
Gauge: 12. Over/under shotgun. Barrels: 32 inches; screw-in choke tubes; high ventilated rib; automatic ejectors; single selective trigger standard. Checkered Monte Carlo walnut stock.

Mark II . . . . NiB $1476 Ex $1141 Gd $971
Same as Mark I model but with an extra single barrel and fitted leather case.

Mark III . . . . NiB $1656 Ex $1346 Gd $971
Same as Mark I model but with finely figured walnut stock and engraved metal.

Mark III Combo . . . . NiB $2748 Ex $2138 Gd $1903
Same as Mark III model above but with extra single barrel and fitted leather case.

CHARLES DALY, INC. — New York, New York

The pre-WWII Charles Daly shotguns, w/the exception of the Commander, were manufactured by various firms in Suhl, Germany. The postwar guns, except for the Novamatic series, were produced by Miroku Firearms Mfg. Co., Tokyo. Miroku ceased production in 1976 and the Daly trademark was acquired by Outdoor Sports Headquarters, in Dayton, Ohio. OSHI continued to market O/U shotguns from both Italy and Spain under the Daly logo. Automatic models were produced in Japan for distribution in the USA. In 1996, KBI, Inc. in Harrisburg, PA acquired the Daly trademark and currently imports firearms under that logo.

COMMANDER O/U SHOTGUN
Daly-pattern Anson & Deeley system boxlock action. Automatic ejectors. Double triggers or Miller selective·single trigger. Gauges: 12, 16, 20, 28, & .410. Bbls.: 26- to 30-inch, IC/M or M/F choke. Weight: 5.25 to 7.25 lbs. depending on ga. and bbl. length. Checkered stock and forend, straight or pistol grip. The two models, 100 and 200, differ in general quality, grade of wood, checkering, engraving, etc., otherwise specs are the same. Made in Belgium c. 1939.

SHOTGUNS

Charles Daly Over/Under
Field Grade (Postwar)

Model 100 .... NiB $582 Ex $468 Gd $343
Model 200 .... NiB $759 Ex $603 Gd $428
Miller single trigger, add $100

HAMMERLESS DOUBLE-BARREL SHOTGUN
Daly-pattern Anson & Deeley system boxlock action. Automatic ejectors except "Superior Quality" is non-ejector. Double triggers. Gauges: 10, 12, 16, 20, 28, .410. Bbls.: 26- to 32-inch, any combination of chokes. Weight: from 4 to 8.5 lbs. depending on ga. and bbl. length. Checkered pistol-grip stock and forend. The four grades—Regent Diamond, Diamond, Empire, Superior—differ in general quality, grade of wood, checkering, engraving, etc.; otherwise specifications are the same. Disc. about 1933.
Diamond quality .... NiB $11,526 Ex $9250 Gd $6338
Empire quality .... NiB $5596 Ex $4490 Gd $3076
Regent Diamond quality .... NiB $13,875 Ex $11,145 Gd $7651
Superior quality .... NiB $1323 Ex $1105 Gd $752

HAMMERLESS DRILLING
Daly pattern Anson & Deeley system boxlock action. Plain extractors. Double triggers, front single set for rifle bbl. Gauges: 12, 16, 20, .25-20, .25-35, .30-30 rifle bbl. Supplied in various bbl. lengths and weights. Checkered pistol-grip stock and forend. Auto rear sight operated by rifle bbl. selector. The three grades — Regent Diamond, Diamond, Superior—differ in general quality, grade of wood, checkering, engraving, etc.; otherwise, specifications are the same. Disc. 1933.
Diamond quality .... NiB $6486 Ex $5240 Gd $3609
Regent Diamond quality ... NiB $13,506 Ex $10,841 Gd $7429
Superior quality .... NiB $3549 Ex $2854 Gd $1991

HAMMERLESS DOUBLE
EMPIRE GRADE .... NiB $1747 Ex $1022 Gd $913
Boxlock. Plain extractors. Non-selective single trigger. Gauges: 12, 16, 20; 3-inch chambers in 12 and 20, 2.75-inch in 16 ga. Bbls.: vent rib; 26-, 28-, 30-inch (latter in 12 ga. only); IC/M, M/F, F/F. Weight: 6 to 7.75 lbs., depending on ga. and bbls. Checkered pistol-grip stock and beavertail forearm. Made 1968 to 1971.

1974 WILDLIFE COMMEMORATIVE .... NiB $2387 Ex $1946 Gd $1382
Limited issue of 500 guns. Similar to Diamond Grade over/under. 12-ga. trap and skeet models only. Duck scene engraved on right side of receiver, fine scroll on left side. Made in 1974.

NOVAMATIC LIGHTWEIGHT AUTOLOADER
Same as Breda. Recoil-operated. Takedown.12 ga., 2.75-inch chamber. Four-round tubular magazine. Bbls.: Plain vent rib; 26-inch IC or Quick-Choke w/three interchangeable tubes, 28-inch M or F choke. Weight (w/26-inch vent-rib bbl.): 7 lbs., 6 oz. Checkered pistol-grip stock and forearm. Made 1968 by Ernesto Breda, Milan, Italy.
W/plain bbl. .... NiB $309 Ex $215 Gd $157
W/vent rib bbl. .... NiB $340 Ex $145 Gd $195
W/Quick-Choke, add $20

NOVAMATIC SUPER LIGHTWEIGHT
Lighter version of Novamatic Lightweight. Gauges: 12, 20. Weight (w/26-inch vent-rib bbl.): 12 ga., 6 lbs., 10 oz.; 20 ga., 6 lbs. SK

choke available in 26-inch vent-rib bbl. 28-inch bbls. in 12 ga. only. Quick-Choke in 20 ga. w/plain bbl. Made 1968 by Ernesto Breda, Milan, Italy.
12 ga., plain bbl. .... NiB $330 Ex $254 Gd $156
12 ga., vent rib bbl. .... NiB $330 Ex $254 Gd $156
20 ga., plain bbl. .... NiB $447 Ex $359 Gd $259
20 ga., plain bbl. w/Quick-Choke .... NiB $342 Ex $285 Gd $177
20 ga., vent rib bbl. .... NiB $370 Ex $246 Gd $192

NOVAMATIC SUPER LIGHTWEIGHT
20 GA. MAGNUM...................... NiB $330 Ex $254 Gd $191
Same as Novamatic Super Lightweight 2, except 3-inch chamber, has 3-round magazine, 28-inch vent-rib bbl., F choke.

NOVAMATIC
12 GA. MAGNUM....................... NiB $330 Ex $231 Gd $195
Same as Novamatic Lightweight, except chambered for 12-ga. Magnum 3-inch shell. Has 3-round magazine, 30-inch vent rib bbl., F choke, and stock w/recoil pad. Weight: 7.75 lbs.

Post-War Charles Daly shotguns were imported by Sloan's Sporting Goods trading as Charles Daly in New York. In 1976, Outdoor Sports Headquarters acquired the Daly trademark and continued to import European-made shotguns under that logo. In 1996, KBI, Inc., in Harrisburg, PA, acquired the Daly trademark and currently imports firearms under that logo.

NOVAMATIC TRAP GUN .... NiB $552 Ex $444 Gd $319
Same as Novamatic Lightweight except has 30-inch vent rib bbl., F choke and Monte Carlo stock w/recoil pad. Weight: 7.75 lbs.

O/U SHOTGUNS (PREWAR)
Daly-pattern Anson & Deeley-system boxlock action. Sideplates. Auto ejectors. Double triggers. Gauges: 12, 16, 20. Supplied in various bbl. lengths and weights. Checkered pistol-grip stock and forend. The two grades — Diamond and Empire — differ in general quality, grade of wood, checkering, engraving, etc.; otherwise specifications are the same. Disc. about 1933.
Diamond Quality............. NiB $5954 Ex $4811 Gd $3349
Empire Quality .... NiB $4581 Ex $3719 Gd $2594

O/U SHOTGUNS (POSTWAR)
Boxlock. Auto ejectors or selective auto/manual ejection. Selective single trigger. Gauges: 12, 12 Magnum (3-inch chambers), 20 (3-inch chambers), 28, .410. Bbls.: Vent rib; 26-, 28-, 30-inch; standard choke combinations. Weight: 6 to 8 lbs. depending on ga. and bbls. Select walnut stock w/pistol grip, fluted forearm checkered; Monte Carlo comb on trap guns; recoil pad on 12-ga. mag. and trap models. The various grades differ in quality of engraving and wood. Made from 1963 to 1976.
Diamond grade .... NiB $1460 Ex $1181 Gd $850
Field grade .... NiB $868 Ex $704 Gd $521
Superior grade................. NiB $1084 Ex $886 Gd $645
Venture grade .... NiB $834 Ex $678 Gd $493

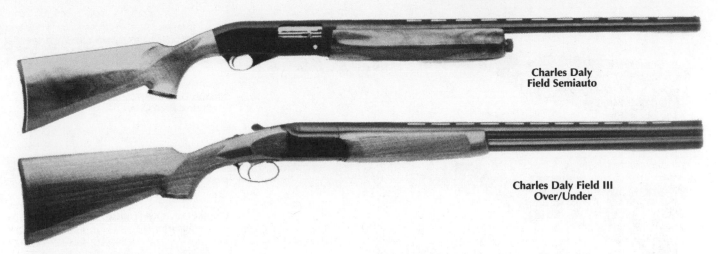

**Charles Daly
Field Semiauto**

**Charles Daly Field III
Over/Under**

SEXTUPLE MODEL SINGLE-BARREL TRAP GUN

Daly-pattern Anson & Deeley system boxlock action. Six locking bolts. Auto ejector. 12 ga. only. Bbls.: 30-, 32-, 34-inch, vent rib. Weight: 7.5 to 8.25 lbs. Checkered pistol-grip stock and forend. The two models made Empire and Regent Diamond differ in general quality, grade of wood, checkering, engraving, etc., otherwise specifications are the same. Disc. about 1933.

Regent Diamond quality (Linder)	NiB $2657	Ex $1527	Gd $986
Empire quality (Linder)	NiB $5184	Ex $4197	Gd $2934
Regent Diamond quality (Sauer)	NiB $3707	Ex $3006	Gd $2109
Empire quality (Sauer)	NiB $2773	Ex $2254	Gd $1590

SINGLE-SHOT TRAP GUN

Daly-pattern Anson & Deeley system boxlock action. Auto ejector. 12 ga. only. Bbls.: 30-, 32-, 34-inch, vent rib. Weight: 7.5 to 8.25 lbs. Checkered pistol-grip stock and forend. This model was made in Empire Quality only. Disc. about 1933.

Empire grade (Linder)	NiB $4586	Ex $3714	Gd $2599
Empire grade (Sauer)	NiB $2326	Ex $1896	Gd $1347

SUPERIOR GRADE SINGLE-SHOT TRAP .. NiB $896 Ex $741 Gd $533

Boxlock. Automatic ejector. 12 ga. only. 32- or 34-inch vent-rib bbl., F choke. Weight: About 8 lbs. Monte Carlo stock w/pistol grip and recoil pad, beavertail forearm, checkered. Made 1968 to 1976.

DIAMOND GRADE O/U

Boxlock. Single selective trigger. Selective automatic ejectors. Gauges: 12 and 20, 3-inch chambers (2.75 target grade). Bbls.: 26, 27- or 30-inch w/fixed chokes or screw-in tubes. Weight: 7 lbs. Checkered European walnut stock and forearm w/oil finish. Engraved antique silver receiver and blued bbls. Made from 1984 to 1990.

Standard model	NiB $959	Ex $757	Gd $550
Skeet model	NiB $1025	Ex $819	Gd $593
Trap model	NiB $1070	Ex $870	Gd $628

DIAMOND GTX DL HUNTER O/U SERIES

Sidelock. Single selective trigger and selective auto ejectors. Gauges: 12, 20, 28 ga. or .410 bore. 26-, 28- and 30-inch bbls w/3-inch chambers (2.75-inch 28 ga.). Choke tubes (12 and 20 ga.), Fixed chokes (28 and 410). Weight: 5-8 lbs. Checkered European walnut stock w/hand-rubbed oil finish and recoil pad. Made from 1997 to 2001.

Diamond GTX DL Hunter	NiB $10,056	Ex $8092	Gd $5579
Diamond GTX EDL Hunter	NiB $12,262	Ex $9838	Gd $6735
Diamond GTX Sporting (12 or 20 ga.)	NiB $5744	Ex $4553	Gd $3157
Diamond GTX Skeet (12 or 20 ga.)	NiB $5354	Ex $4247	Gd $2945
Diamond GTX Trap (12 ga. only)	NiB $5975	Ex $4402	Gd $3090

EMPIRE DL HUNTER O/U ..... NiB $1308 Ex $1126 Gd $736

Boxlock. Ejectors. Single selective trigger. Gauges:12, 20, 28 ga. and .410 bore. 26- or 28- inch bbls. w/3-inch chambers (2.75-inch 28 ga.). Choke tubes (12 and 20 ga.), Fixed chokes (28 and .410). Engraved coin-silver receiver w/game scene. Imported from 1997 to 1998.

EMPIRE EDL HUNTER SERIES

Similar to Empire DL Hunter except engraved sideplates. Made 1998 to date.

Empire EDL Hunter	NiB $1337	Ex $1077	Gd $769
Empire Sporting	NiB $1295	Ex $1051	Gd $751
Empire Skeet	NiB $1263	Ex $1025	Gd $734
Empire Trap	NiB $1327	Ex $1077	Gd $769
28 ga., add.			$95
.410 ga, add.			$120
Multi-chokes w/Monte Carlo stock, add			$125

DSS HAMMERLESS DOUBLE ..... NiB $786 Ex $620 Gd $445

Boxlock. Single selective trigger. Selective automatic ejectors. Gauges: 12 and 20; 3-inch chambers. 26-inch bbls. w/screw-in choke tubes. Weight: 6.75 lbs. Checkered walnut pistol-grip stock and semi-beavertail forearm w/recoil pad. Engraved antique silver receiver and blued bbls. Made from 1990. Disc.

FIELD GRADE O/U .... NiB $599 Ex $470 Gd $342

Boxlock. Single selective trigger. Extractors. Gauges: 12 and 20; 3-inch chambers. Bbls.: 26-inch, IC/M; 28-inch, M/F. Weight: 6.75 lbs. (12 ga.). Checkered walnut stock and forearm w/semi-gloss finish and recoil pad. Engraved color-casehardened receiver and blued bbls. Made from 1989. Disc.

FIELD SEMIAUTO SHOTGUN..... NiB $467 Ex $375 Gd $277

Recoil-operated. Takedown. 12-ga. and 12-ga. Magnum. Bbls.: 27- and 30-inch; vent rib. Made from 1982 to 1988.

FIELD III O/U SHOTGUN .... NiB $592 Ex $479 Gd $348

Boxlock. Plain extractors. Non-selective single trigger. Gauges: 12 or 20. Bbls.: vent rib; 26- and 28-inch; IC/M, M/F. Weight: 6 to 7.75 lbs. depending on ga. and bbls. Chrome-molybdenum steel bbls. Checkered pistol-grip stock and forearm. Made from 1982. Disc.

LUXIE O/U .... NiB $861 Ex $681 Gd $490

Similar to the Field Grade except w/selective automatic ejectors and choke tubes. Gauges: 12, 20, 28 and .410. Receiver w/antique silver finish and blued bbls. Made from 1989 to 1994.

SHOTGUNS

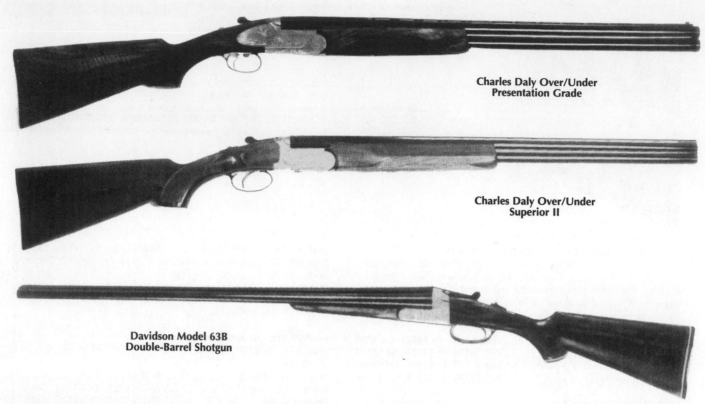

Charles Daly Over/Under Presentation Grade

Charles Daly Over/Under Superior II

Davidson Model 63B Double-Barrel Shotgun

MULTI-XII SELF-LOADING SHOTGUN . . . . . . NiB $591 Ex $468 Gd $327
Similar to the gas-operated field semiauto except w/new Multi-Action gas system designed to shoot all loads w/o adjustment. 12 ga. w/3-inch chamber. 27-inch bbl. w/Invector choke tubes, vent rib. Made in Japan from 1987 to 1988.

O/U
PRESENTATION GRADE . . . . .NiB $1181 Ex $942 Gd $658
Purdey boxlock w/double cross-bolt. Gauges: 12 or 20. Engraved receiver w/single selective trigger and auto-ejectors. 27-inch chrome-molybdenum steel, rectified, honed and internally chromed, vent-rib bbls. Hand-checkered deluxe European walnut stock. Made from 1982 to 1986.

O/U
Superior II Shotgun . . . . NiB $993 Ex $806 Gd $567
Boxlock. Plain extractors. Non-selective single trigger. Gauges: 12 or 20. Bbls.: chrome-molybdenum vent rib 26-, 28-, 30-inch, latter in magnum only, assorted chokes. Silver engraved receiver. Checkered pistol-grip stock and forearm. Made from 1982 to 1988.

SPORTING CLAYS O/U . . . . NiB $772 Ex $609 Gd $501
Similar to the Field Grade except in 12 ga. only w/ported bbls. and internal choke tubes. Made from 1990 to 1996.

DAKOTA ARMS, INC. — Sturgis, South Dakota

CLASSIC FIELD GRADE
S/S SHOTGUN . . . . NiB $7453 Ex $6476 Gd $4381
Boxlock. Gauge: 20 ga. 27-inch bbl. w/fixed chokes. Double triggers. Selective ejectors. Color-casehardened receiver. Weight: 6 lbs. Checkered English walnut stock and splinter forearm w/hand-rubbed oil finish. Made from 1996 to 1998.

PREMIER GRADE
S/S SHOTGUN . . . . NiB $13,956 Ex $10,758 Gd $7910
Similar to Classic Field Grade model except w/50% engraving coverage. Exhibition grade English walnut stock. Made from 1996 to date.

AMERICAN LEGEND
S/S SHOTGUN . . . . NiB $16,000 Ex $14,250 Gd $10,900
Limited edition built to customer's specifications. Gauge: 20 ga. 27-inch bbl. Double triggers. Selective ejectors. Fully engraved, coin-silver finished receiver w/gold inlays. Weight: 6 lbs. Hand checkered special-selection English walnut stock and forearm. Made from 1996 to 2005.

DARNE S.A. — Saint-Etienne, France

HAMMERLESS DOUBLE-BARREL SHOTGUNS
Sliding-breech action w/fixed bbls. Auto ejectors. Double triggers. Gauges: 12, 16, 20, 28; also 12 and 20 Magnum w/3-inch chambers. Bbls.: 27.5-inch standard, 25.5- to 31.5-inch lengths available; any standard choke combination. Weight: 5.5 to 7 lbs. depending on ga. and bbl. length. Checkered straight-grip or pistol-grip stock and forearm. The various models differ in grade of engraving and wood. Manufactured from 1881 to 1979.
Model R11
(Bird Hunter) . . . . NiB $6800 Ex $4541 Gd $2555
Model R15
(Pheasant Hunter) . . . . NiB $14,320 Ex $12,011 Gd $9353
Model R16 (Magnum) . . . . NiB $3456 Ex $2552 Gd $1908
Model V19
(Quail Hunter) . . . . NiB $20,885 Ex $15,445 Gd $13,925
Model V22 . . . . NiB $29,986 Ex $24,740 Gd $21,722
Model V Hors Série No. 1 . . . . . . NiB $75,030 Ex $56,090 Gd $44,925

DAVIDSON GUNS — Mfd. by Fabrica de Armas ILJA, Eibar, Spain; distributed by Davidson Firearms Co., Greensboro, North Carolina

MODEL 63B DOUBLE-BARREL
SHOTGUN.............**NiB $352 Ex $229 Gd $155**
Anson & Deeley boxlock action. Frame engraved and nickel plated. Plain extractors. Auto safety. Double triggers. Gauges: 12, 16, 20, 28, .410. Bbl. lengths: 25 (.410 only), 26, 28, 30 inches (latter 12 ga. only). Chokes: IC/ M, M/F, F/F. Weight: 5 lbs., 11 oz. (.410) to 7 lbs. (12 ga.). Checkered pistol-grip stock and forearm of European walnut. Made in 1963. Disc.

MODEL 63B MAGNUM
Similar to standard Model 63B except chambered for 10 ga. 3.5-inch, 12 and 20 ga. 3-inch Magnum shells; 10 ga. has 32-inch bbls., choked F/F. Weight: 10 lb., 10 oz. Made from 1963. Disc.
12-and 20 ga. magnum ....**NiB $397 Ex $252 Gd $173**
10 ga. magnum...............**NiB $424 Ex $353 Gd $214**

MODEL 69SL DOUBLE-BARREL
SHOTGUN ....**NiB $415 Ex $370 Gd $235**
Sidelock action w/detachable sideplates, engraved and nickel plated. Plain extractors. Auto safety. Double triggers. 12 and 20 ga. Bbls.: 26-inch IC/M, 28-inch M/F. Weight: 12 ga., 7 lbs., 20 ga., 6.5 lbs. Pistol-grip stock and forearm of European walnut, checkered. Made from 1963 to 1976.

MODEL 73 STAGECOACH
HAMMER DOUBLE ....**NiB $283 Ex $205 Gd $119**
Sidelock action w/detachable sideplates and exposed hammers. Plain extractors. Double triggers. Gauges: 12, 20, 3-inch chambers. 20-inch bbls, M/F chokes. Weight: 7 lbs., 12 ga.; 6.5 lbs., 20 ga. Checkered pistol-grip stock and forearm. Made from 1976. Disc.

DIAMOND

Currently imported by ADCO Sales, Inc, Woburn, MA. Company established circa 1981, all guns manufactured in Turkey.

GOLD SERIES (SEMIAUTOMATIC). NiB $315 Ex $240 Gd $145
12 gauge, 3-inch chamber. Gas operated. Bbl. 24 (slug) or 28 inches. Ventilated rib with three choke tubes. Semi-humpback design, anodized alloy frame, gold etching. Rotary bolt. Black synthetic or checkered Turkish walnut forearm and stock with recoil pad. Value $50 less for slug version.

IMPERIAL SERIES.............**NiB $435 Ex $300 Gd $225**
12 (3.5-inch) or 20 (3-inch); bbl. 24 (12 gauge slug), 26 (20 gauge) or 28 inches; ventilated rib, rotary bi-lateral bolt; deluxe checkered stock and forearm. Imported 2003.

ELITE SERIES ....**NiB $375 Ex $290 Gd $165**
12 gauge, 3-inch chamber. Bbl. 22 (slug), 24, 26 or 28 inches; ventilated rib, deluxe checkered walnut stock and forearm. Imported 2001. Value $20 less for slug version.

PANTHER SERIES.............**NiB $355 Ex $295 Gd $1750**
12 gauge, 3-inch chamber. Gas-operated. Black synthetic stock and forearm. Bbl. 20 (slug or regular) or 28 inches. Imported 2002.

Walnut stock and forearm, add **$50**
Slug version ....**deduct $25**

MARINER ....**NiB $275 Ex $140 Gd $95**
12 gauge, 3-inch chamber. Gas-operated. Bbl. 20 (slug), or 22 inches; ventilated rib. Anodized alloy frame receiver, satin silver metal finish; checkered walnut stock and forearm. Imported 2002. Value $20 less for slug version.

GOLD ELITE SERIES (Slide-Action).. NiB $300 Ex $233 Gd $188
12 gauge, 3-inch chamber. Bbl. 24 (slug with open sights), or 28 inches; ventilated rib. Semi-humpback design. Anodized alloy frame, synthetic black or Turkish walnut stock and forearm. Weight: 7 lbs. Imported 2001. Value $40 less for synthetic stock.

IMPERIAL SERIES ....**NiB $335 Ex $238 Gd $178**
12 gauge, 3.5-inch chamber; slide-action. Bbl. 28 inches; ventilated rib, deluxe checkered wood stock and forearm. Imported 2003.

ELITE SERIES ....**NiB $310 Ex $258 Gd $183**
12 gauge, 3-inch chamber. Similar to Gold Elite Series except has engraved receiver. Bbl. 20 (slug or regular), 24, or 28 inches; ventilated rib, deluxe checkered walnut stock and forearm. Imported 2001. Value $25 less for slug version.

PANTHER SERIES ....**NiB $225 Ex $143 Gd $108**
12 gauge, 3-inch chamber. Similar to Elite Series except with black synthetic stock and forearm. Bbl. 18.5 (slug) 20, 22 (slug) or 28 inches. Imported 2001.

MARINER MODEL ....**NiB $250 Ex $123 Gd $98**
12 gauge, 3-inch chamber. Bbl. 18.5-inch plain or 22 inches; ventilated rib. Five shell magazine. Black synthetic stock and forearm. Imported 2003. Value $20 less for 18.5 plain barrel version.

EXCEL ARMS OF AMERICA — Gardner, Massachusetts

SERIES 100 O/U SHOTGUN
Gauge: 12. Single selective trigger. Selective auto ejectors. Hand-checkered European walnut stock w/full pistol grip, tulip forend. Black metal finish. Chambered for 2.75-inch shells (Model 103 for 3-inch). Weight: 6. 88 to 7.88 lbs. Disc 1988.
Model 101, 26-inch bbl., IC/M ....**NiB $400 Ex $327 Gd $234**
Model 102, 28-inch bbl., IC/M ....**NiB $400 Ex $327 Gd $234**
Model 103, 30-inch bbl., M/F ....**NiB $400 Ex $327 Gd $234**
Model 104, 28-inch bbl., IC/IM ....**NiB $400 Ex $327 Gd $234**
Model 105, 28-inch bbl., 5 choke tubes ..NiB $560 Ex $419 Gd $337
Model 106, 28-inch bbl., 5 choke tubes ..NiB $725 Ex $631 Gd $517
Model 107 Trap, 30-inch bbl., Full or 5 tubes . NiB $725 Ex $631 Gd $517

SERIES 200 SIDE-BY-SIDE
SHOTGUN....................**NiB $575 Ex $453 Gd $324**
Gauges: 12, 20, 28 and .410. Bbls.: 26-, 27- and 28-inch; various choke combinations. Weight: 7 lbs. average. American or European-style stock and forend. Made from 1985 to 1987.

SERIES 300 O/U
SHOTGUN.................**NiB $1255 Ex $1029 Gd $982**
Gauge: 12. Bbls.: 26-, 28- and 29-inch. Non-glare black-chrome matte finish. Weight: 7 lbs. average. Selective auto ejectors, engraved receiver. Hand-checkered European walnut stock and forend. Made from 1985 to 1986.

SHOTGUNS

Fox Model B

FABARM SHOTGUNS — Brescia, Italy

Currently imported by Heckler & Koch, Inc., of Sterling, VA (previously by Ithaca Acquisition Corp., St. Lawrence Sales, Inc. and Beeman Precision Arms, Inc.)

See Current listings under "Heckler & Koch."

FIAS — Fabrica Italiana Armi Sabatti Gardone Val Trompia, Italy

GRADE I O/U
Boxlock. Single selective trigger. Gauges: 12, 20, 28, .410; 3-inch chambers. Bbls.: 26-inch IC/M; 28-inch M/F; screw-in choke tubes. Weight: 6.5 to 7.5 lbs. Checkered European walnut stock and forearm. Engraved receiver and blued finish.
12 ga. model . . . . NiB $538 Ex $432 Gd $310
20 ga. model . . . . NiB $592 Ex $483 Gd $345
28 and .410 ga. models . . . . NiB $752 Ex $611 Gd $432

FOX SHOTGUNS — Made by A. H. Fox Gun Co., Philadelphia, PA, 1903 to 1930, and since then by Savage Arms, originally of Utica, NY, now of Westfield, MA. In 1993, Connecticut Manufacturing Co. of New Britain, CT, reintroduced selected models.

Values shown are for 12 and 16 ga. doubles made by A. H. Fox. Twenty gauge guns often are valued up to 75% higher. Savage-made Fox models generally bring prices 25% lower. With the exception of Model B, production of Fox shotguns was discontinued about 1942.

MODEL B HAMMERLESS DOUBLE . . . . . . NiB $450 Ex $291 Gd $204
Boxlock. Double triggers. Plain extractor. Gauges: 12, 16, 20, .410. 24- to 30-inch bbls., vent rib on current production; chokes: M/F, C/M, F/F (.410 only). Weight: About 7.5 lbs., 12 ga. Checkered pistol-grip stock and forend. Made about 1940 to 1985.

MODEL B-ST . . . . NiB $576 Ex $430 Gd $308
Same as Model B except has non-selective single trigger. Made from 1955-66.

MODEL B-DE . . . . NiB $575 Ex $454 Gd $324
Same as Model B-ST except frame finished in satin chrome, select walnut buttstock w/checkered pistol grip and beavertail forearm. Made from 1965 to 1966.

MODEL B-DL . . . . NiB $600 Ex $492 Gd $358
Same as Model B-ST except frame finished in satin chrome, select walnut buttstock w/checkered pistol grip side panels, beavertail forearm. Made from 1962 to 1966.

MODEL B-SE . . . . NiB $850 Ex $656 Gd $463
Same as Model B except has selective ejectors and single trigger. Made from 1966 to 1989.

HAMMERLESS DOUBLE-BARREL SHOTGUNS
The higher grades have the same general specifications as the standard Sterlingworth model, w/differences chiefly in workmanship and materials. Higher grade models are stocked in fine select walnut; quantity and quality of engraving increases w/grade and price. Except for Grade A, all other grades have auto ejectors.
Grade A . . . . NiB $3074 Ex $2472 Gd $1740
Grade AE . . . . NiB $3483 Ex $2842 Gd $1986
Grade BE . . . . NiB $4850 Ex $3864 Gd $2710
Grade CE . . . . NiB $6070 Ex $4906 Gd $3416
Grade DE . . . . NiB $11,544 Ex $10,578 Gd $10,953
Grade FE . . . . NiB $21,657 Ex $17,385 Gd $11,918
Grade XE . . . . NiB $7662 Ex $6176 Gd $4000
Kautzky selective single trigger, add $350
Ventilated rib, add $450
Beavertail forearm, add. $275
20 ga., add. 60%

SINGLE-BARREL TRAP GUNS
Boxlock. Auto ejector. 12 ga. only. 30- or 32-inch vent-rib bbl. Weight: 7.5 to 8 lbs. Trap-style stock and forearm of select walnut, checkered, recoil pad optional. The four grades differ chiefly in quality of wood and engraving; Grade M guns, built to order, have finest Circassian walnut. Stock and receiver are elaborately engraved and inlaid w/gold. Disc. 1942. Note: In 1932, the Fox Trap Gun was redesigned and those manufactured after that date have a stock w/full pistol grip and Monte Carlo comb; at the same time frame was changed to permit the rib line to extend across it to the rear.
Grade JE . . . . NiB $3852 Ex $2263 Gd $1973
Grade KE . . . . NiB $5200 Ex $4819 Gd $3350
Grade LE . . . . NiB $6528 Ex $4649 Gd $3614
Grade ME . . . . NiB $14,736 Ex $11,814 Gd $8073

"SKEETER" DOUBLE-BARREL SHOTGUN
. . . . NiB $4864 Ex $3947 Gd $2774
Boxlock. Gauge: 12 or 20. Bbls.: 28 inches w/full-length vent rib. Weight: Approx. 7 lbs. Buttstock and beavertail forend of select American walnut, finely checkered. Soft rubber recoil pad and ivory bead sights. Made in early 1930s.

STERLINGWORTH DELUXE
Same general specifications as Sterlingworth except 32-inch bbl. also available, recoil pad, ivory bead sights.
W/plain extractors. . . . . NiB $2096 Ex $1466 Gd $1044
W/automatic ejectors . . . . NiB $2285 Ex $1849 Gd $1338
20 ga., add. 45%

STERLINGWORTH HAMMERLESS DOUBLE
Boxlock. Double triggers (Fox-Kautzky selective single trigger extra). Plain extractors (auto ejectors extra). Gauges: 12,16, 20. Bbl. lengths: 26-, 28-, 30-inch; chokes F/F, M/F, C/M (any combination of C to F choke borings was available at no extra cost). Weight: 12 ga., 6.88 to 8.25 lbs.; 16 ga., 6 to 7 lbs.; 20 ga., 5.75 to 6.75 lbs. Checkered pistol-grip stock and forearm.
W/plain extractors . . . . NiB $1644 Ex $1319 Gd $929
W/automatic ejectors . . . . NiB $2059 Ex $1660 Gd $1161
Selective single trigger, add 25%

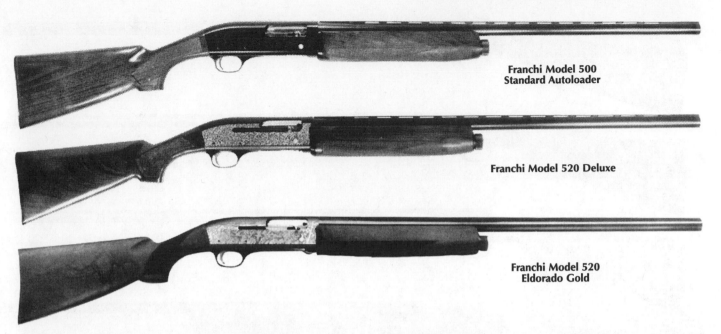

Franchi Model 500
Standard Autoloader

Franchi Model 520 Deluxe

Franchi Model 520
Eldorado Gold

STERLINGWORTH SKEET AND UPLAND GAME GUN
Same general specifications as the standard Sterlingworth except has 26- or 28-inch bbls. w/skeet boring only, straight-grip stock. Weight: 7 lbs. (12 ga.).

W/plain extractors. . . . . **NiB $2458 Ex $1982 Gd $1398**
W/automatic ejectors . . . . **NiB $2899 Ex $2342 Gd $1651**
20 ga., add. **45%**

SUPER HE GRADE. . . . . **NiB $5623 Ex $4538 Gd $3177**
Long-range gun made in 12 ga. only (chambered for 3-inch shells on order), 30- or 32-inch full choke bbls., auto ejectors standard. Weight: 8.75 to 9.75 lbs. General specifications same as standard Sterlingworth.

HAMMERLESS DOUBLE-BARREL SHOTGUNS
High-grade doubles similar to the original Fox models. 20 ga. only. 26- 28- or 30-inch bbls. Double triggers automatic safety and ejectors. Weight: 5.5 to 7 lbs. Custom Circassian walnut stock w/hand-rubbed oil finish. Custom stock configuration: straight, semi- or full pistol-grip stock w/traditional pad, hard rubber plate checkered or skeleton butt; Schnabel, splinter or beavertail forend. Made 1993 to date.
CE grade . . . . **NiB $8269 Ex $6670 Gd $4624**
XE grade . . . . **NiB $8733 Ex $7045 Gd $4885**
DE grade . . . . **NiB $12,4694 Ex $10,000 Gd $6840**
FE grade . . . . **NiB $16,733 Ex $13,420 Gd $9180**
Exhibition grade . . . . **NiB $24,014 Ex $19,265 Gd $13,187**

LUIGI FRANCHI S.P.A. — Brescia, Italy

MODEL 48/AL ULTRA LIGHT SHOTGUN
Recoil-operated, takedown, hammerless shotgun w/tubular magazine. Gauges: 12 or 20 (2.75-inch); 12-ga. Magnum (3-inch chamber). Bbls.: 24- to 32-inch w/various choke combinations. Weight: 5 lbs., 2 oz. (20 ga.) to 6.25 lbs. (12 ga.). Checkered pistol-grip walnut stock and forend w/high-gloss finish.
Standard model . . . . **NiB $696 Ex $493 Gd $374**
Hunter or magnum models . . . . . **NiB $850 Ex $523 Gd $395**

MODEL 500 STANDARD AUTOLOADER . . . . **NiB $332 Ex $251 Gd $168**
Gas-operated. 12 gauge. Four round magazine. Bbls.: 26-, 28-inch; vent rib; IC, M, IM, F chokes. Weight: About 7 lbs. Checkered pistol-grip stock and forearm. Made from 1976 to 1980.

MODEL 520 DELUXE . . . . **NiB $395 Ex $257 Gd $243**
Same as Model 500 except higher grade w/engraved receiver. Made from 1975 to 1979.

MODEL 520 ELDORADO GOLD . . . . **NiB $990 Ex $805 Gd $620**
Same as Model 520 except custom grade w/engraved and gold-inlaid receiver, finer quality wood. Intro. 1977.

MODEL 610VS SEMIAUTOMATIC SHOTGUN
Gas-operated Variopress system adjustable to function w/2.75- or 3-inch shells. 12 gauge. Four round magazine. 26- or 28-inch vent rib bbls. w/Franchoke tubes. Weight: 7 lbs., 2 oz. 47.5 inches overall. Alloy receiver w/four-lug rotating bolt and loaded chamber indicator. Checkered European walnut buttstock and forearm w/satin finish. Imported from 1997.
Standard SV model . . . . **NiB $650 Ex $554 Gd $407**
Engraved SVL model . . . . **NiB $696 Ex $610 Gd $459**

MODEL 612 VARIOPRESS AUTOLOADING SHOTGUN
Gauge: 12 ga. Only. 24- to 28-inch bbl. 45 to 49-inches overall. Weight: 6.8 to 7 lbs. Five round magazine. Bead type sights with C, IC, M chokes. Blued, matte or Advantage camo finish. Imported from 1999 to 2004.
Model 612 satin walnut
stock w/blued finish. . . . . **NiB $554 Ex $424 Gd $310**
Model 612 synthetic
stock w/matte finish. . . . . **NiB $570 Ex $449 Gd $327**
Model 612 Advantage stock and finish . . . . **NiB $659 Ex $500 Gd $362**
Model 612 Defense . . . . **NiB $525 Ex $398 Gd $292**
Model 612 Sporting . . . . **NiB $825 Ex $651 Gd $494**

MODEL 620 VARIOPRESS AUTOLOADING SHOTGUN
Gauge: 20 ga. Only. 24- 26- or 28-inch bbl. 45 to 49-inches overall. Weight: 5.9 to 6.1 lbs. Five round magazine. Bead type sights with C, IC, M chokes. Satin walnut or Advantage camo stock. Imported from 1999 to 2004.
Model 620 satin walnut
stock w/matte finish. . . . . **NiB $570 Ex $432 Gd $318**
Model 620 Advantage
camo stock and finish . . . . **NiB $660 Ex $488 Gd $360**
Model 620 Youth (short stock). . . . . **NiB $565 Ex $447 Gd $333**

Franchi 612 Variopress Advantage

Franchi 612 Variopress Sporting

Franchi 612 Variopress

Franchi 620 Variopress Advantage

Franchi 620 Variopress

**Franchi Model 2004
Trap Single Barrel**

MODEL 2003 TRAP O/U . . . . **NiB $1205 Ex $1046 Gd $935**
Boxlock. Auto ejectors. Selective single trigger. 12 ga. Bbls.: 30-, 32-inch
IM/F, F/F, high-vent rib. Weight (w/30-inch bbl.): 8.25 lbs. Checkered walnut beavertail forearm and stock w/straight or Monte Carlo comb, recoil
pad. Luggage-type carrying case. Introduced 1976. Disc.

MODEL 2004 TRAP SINGLE BARREL . . . **NiB $1205 Ex $1135 Gd $803**
Same as Model 2003 except single bbl., 32- or 34-inch. Full choke.
Weight (w/32-inch bbl.): 8.25 lbs. Introduced 1976. Disc.

MODEL 2005 COMBINATION TRAP . . **NiB $1818 Ex $1596 Gd $1137**
Model 2004/2005 type gun w/two sets of bbls., single and
over/under. Introduced 1976. Disc.

MODEL 2005/3 COMBINATION TRAP . . . . . **NiB $2430 Ex $2041 Gd $1590**
Model 2004/2005 type gun w/three sets of bbls., any combination
of single and over/under. Introduced 1976. Disc.

MODEL 3000/2 COMBINATION TRAP . . . . . **NiB $2752 Ex $2529 Gd $1797**
Boxlock. Automatic ejectors. Selective single trigger. 12 ga. only.
Bbls.: 32-inch over/under choked F/IM, 34-inch underbarrel M
choke; high vent rib. Weight (w/32-inch bbls.): 8 lbs., 6 oz. Choice
of six different castoff buttstocks. Introduced 1979. Disc.

ALCIONE HAMMERLESS DOUBLE . . . . . . **NiB $675 Ex $560 Gd $455**
Boxlock. Anson & Deeley system action. Auto ejectors. Double triggers. 12 ga. Various bbl. lengths, chokes, weights. Checkered
straight-grip stock and forearm. Made from 1940-50.

ALCIONE O/U SHOTGUN
Hammerless, takedown shotgun w/engraved receiver. Selective sin-
gle trigger and ejectors. 12 ga. w/3-inch chambers. Bbls.: 26-inch
(IC/M, 28-inch (M/F). Weight: 6.75 lbs. Checkered French walnut
buttstock and forend. Imported from Italy. 1982 to 1989.
Standard model . . . . **NiB $677 Ex $593 Gd $421**
SL model
(disc. 1986) . . . . **NiB $1145 Ex $997 Gd $705**

ALCIONE FIELD (97-12 IBS) O/U
Similar to the Standard Alcione model except w/nickel-finished
receiver. 26- or 28-inch bbls. w/Franchoke tubes. Imported from
1998 to 2005.
Standard Field model . . . . **NiB $1125 Ex $760 Gd $540**
SL Field model (w/sideplates, disc.) . . . . . **NiB $1150 Ex $922 Gd $653**

ALCIONE SPORT (SL IBS) O/U . . . . . NiB $1435 Ex $1229 Gd $1060
Similar to the Alcione Field model except chambered for 2.75 or 3-inch shells. Ported 29-inch bbls. w/target vent rib and Franchoke tubes.

ALCIONE 2000 SX O/U SHOTGUN . . . . NiB $1672 Ex $1294 Gd $934
Similar to the Standard Alcione model except w/silver finished receiver and gold inlays. 28-inch bbls. w/Franchoke tubes. Weight: 7.25 lbs. Imported from 1996 to 1997.

**ARISTOCRAT FIELD
MODEL O/U** . . . . NiB $671 Ex $542 Gd $390
Boxlock. Selective auto ejectors. Selective single trigger. 12 ga. Bbls.: 26-inch IC/M; 28- and 30-inch M/F choke, vent rib. Weight (w/26-inch bbls.): 7 lbs. Checkered pistol-grip stock and forearm. Made from 1960 to 1969.

ARISTOCRAT DELUXE AND SUPREME GRADES
Available in Field, Skeet and Trap models w/the same specifications as standard guns of these types. Deluxe and Supreme Grades are of higher quality, w/stock and forearm of select walnut, elaborate relief engraving on receiver, trigger guard, tang and top lever. Supreme game birds inlaid in gold. Made from 1960 to 1966.
Deluxe grade . . . . NiB $990 Ex $748 Gd $586
Supreme grade . . . . NiB $1434 Ex $1239 Gd $949

ARISTOCRAT IMPERIAL AND MONTE CARLO GRADES
Custom guns made in Field, Skeet and Trap models w/the same general specifications as standard for these types. Imperial and Monte Carlo grades are of highest quality w/stock and forearm of select walnut, fine engraving — elaborate on latter grade. Made 1967 to 1969.
Imperial grade . . . . NiB $3955 Ex $2351 Gd $1905
Monte Carlo grade . . . . NiB $3525 Ex $2785 Gd $1975

ARISTOCRAT MAGNUM MODEL . . . . NiB $670 Ex $507 Gd $427
Same as Field Model except chambered for 3-inch shells, has 32-inch bbls. choked F/F; stock has recoil pad. Weight: About 8 lbs. Made from 1962 to 1965.

ARISTOCRAT SILVER KING . . . . NiB $760 Ex $610 Gd $483
Available in Field, Magnum, Meet and Trap models w/the same general specifications as standard guns of these types. Silver King has stock and forearm of select walnut more elaborately engraved silver-finished receiver. Made 1962 to 1969.

ARISTOCRAT SKEET MODEL . . . . . NiB $745 Ex $628 Gd $472
Same general specifications as Field Model except made only w/26-inch vent-rib bbls. w/SK chokes No. 1 and No. 2, skeet-style stock and forearm. Weight: About 7.5 lbs. Later production had wider (10mm) rib. Made from 1960 to 1969.

ARISTOCRAT TRAP MODEL . . . . . . NiB $745 Ex $663 Gd $465
Same general specifications as Field Model except made only w/30-inch vent-rib bbls., M/F choke, trap-style stock w/recoil pad, beaver-tail forearm. Later production had Monte Carlo comb, 10mm rib. Made from 1960 to 1969.

ASTORE HAMMERLESS DOUBLE . . . . NiB $995 Ex $791 Gd $642
Boxlock. Anson & Deeley system action. Plain extractors. Double triggers. 12 ga. Various bbl. lengths, chokes, weights. Checkered straight-grip stock and forearm. Made 1937 to 1960.

ASTORE II . . . . NiB $1210 Ex $1012 Gd $788
Similar to Astore S but not as high grade. Furnished w/either plain extractors or auto ejectors, double triggers, pistol-grip stock. Bbls.: 27-inch IC/IM; 28-inch M/F chokes. Currently manufactured for Franchi in Spain.

Franchi Astore 5

ASTORE 5 . . . . NiB $2200 Ex $1877 Gd $1340
Same as Astore except has higher grade wood, fine engraving. automatic ejectors, single trigger, 28-inch bbl. M/F or IM/F chokes are standard on current production. Disc.

STANDARD MODEL AUTOLOADER
Recoil operated. Light alloy receiver. Gauges: 12, 20. Four round magazine. Bbls.: 26-, 28-, 30-inch; plain, solid or vent rib, IC/ M, F chokes. Weight: 12 ga., about 6.25 lbs. 20 ga., 5.13 lbs. Checkered pistol-grip stock and forearm. Made from 1950. Disc.
W/plain bbl. . . . . NiB $415 Ex $306 Gd $236
W/solid rib . . . . NiB $492 Ex $449 Gd $298
W/vent rib . . . . NiB $524 Ex $452 Gd $335

CROWN, DIAMOND AND IMPERIAL GRADE
Same general specifications as Standard Model except these are custom guns of the highest quality. Crown Grade has hunting scene engraving, Diamond Grade has silver-inlaid scroll engraving; Imperial Grade has elaborately engraved hunting scenes w/figures inlaid in gold. Stock and forearm of fancy walnut. Made from 1954 to 1975.
Crown grade . . . . NiB $1549 Ex $1439 Gd $1007
Diamond grade . . . . NiB $1986 Ex $1564 Gd $1111
Imperial grade . . . . NiB $2420 Ex $2011 Gd $1609

STANDARD MODEL MAGNUM
Same general specifications as Standard model except has 3-inch chamber, 32-inch (12 ga.) or 28-inch (20 ga.) F choke bbl., recoil pad. Weight: 12 ga., 8.25 lbs.; 20 ga., 6 lbs. Formerly designated "Superange Model." Made from 1954 to 1988.
W/plain bbl. . . . . NiB $435 Ex $354 Gd $243
W/vent rib . . . . NiB $535 Ex $454 Gd $343

DYNAMIC-12
Same general specifications and appearance as Standard Model, except 12 ga. only, has heavier steel receiver. Weight: About 7.25 lbs. Made from 1965 to 1972.
W/plain bbl. . . . . NiB $455 Ex $366 Gd $290
W/vent rib . . . . NiB $489 Ex $396 Gd $290

DYNAMIC-12 SLUG GUN . . . . NiB $499 Ex $427 Gd $297
Same as standard gun except 12 ga. only, has heavier steel receiver. Made 1965 to 1972.

DYNAMIC-12 SKEET GUN . . . . NiB $593 Ex $497 Gd $363
Same general specifications and appearance as Standard model except has heavier steel receiver, made only in 12 ga. w/26-inch vent-rib bbl., SK choke, stock and forearm of extra fancy walnut. Made from 1965 to 1972.

ELDORADO MODEL . . . . NiB $460 Ex $335 Gd $263
Same general specifications as Standard model except highest grade w/gold-filled engraving, stock and forearm of select walnut, vent-rib bbl. only. Made from 1954 to 1975.

SHOTGUNS

Franchi Falconet Over/Under Buckskin

Franchi Crown Grade

Franchi Diamond Grade

Franchi Eldorado

FALCONET INTERNATIONAL SKEET MODEL... NiB $1045 Ex $901 Gd $714
Similar to Standard Skeet model but higher grade. Made 1970 to 1974.

**FALCONET INTERNATIONAL
TRAP MODEL . . . . NiB $1048 Ex $920 Gd $727**
Similar to Standard model but higher grade; w/straight or Monte Carlo comb stock. Made from 1970 to 1974.

FALCONET O/U FIELD MODELS
Boxlock. Auto ejectors. Selective single trigger. Gauges: 12, 16, 20, 28, .410. Bbls.: 24-, 26-, 28-, 30-inch; vent rib. Chokes: C/IC, IC/M, M/F. Weight: from about 6 lbs. Engraved lightweight alloy receiver, light-colored in Buckskin model, blued in Ebony model, pickled silver in Silver model. Checkered walnut stock and forearm. Made from 1968 to 1975.
Buckskin or Ebony model . . . . NiB $550 Ex $428 Gd $350
Silver model . . . . NiB $550 Ex $428 Gd $350

FALCONET STANDARD SKEET MODEL . . . . . NiB $939 Ex $765 Gd $607
Same general specifications as Field models except made only w/26-inch bbls. w/SK chokes No. 1 and No. 2, wide vent rib, color-casehardened receiver skeet-style stock and forearm. Weight: 12 ga., about 7.75 lbs. Made from 1970 to 1974.

FALCONET STANDARD TRAP MODEL . . . . . NiB $1200 Ex $868 Gd $623
Same general specifications as Field models except made only in 12 ga. w/30-inch bbls., choked M/F, wide vent rib, color-casehardened receiver, Monte Carlo trap style stock and forearm, recoil pad. Weight: About 8 lbs. Made from 1970 to 1974.

GAS-OPERATED SEMIAUTOMATIC SHOTGUN
Gas-operated, takedown, hammerless shotgun w/tubular magazine. 12 ga. w/2.75-inch chamber. Five round magazine. Bbls.: 24 to 30 inches w/vent rib. Weight: 7.5 lbs. Gold-plated trigger. Checkered pistol-grip stock and forend of European walnut. Imported from Italy 1985 to 1990.
Prestige model . . . . NiB $575 Ex $411 Gd $325
Elite model . . . . NiB $599 Ex $464 Gd $322

HAMMERLESS SIDELOCK DOUBLES
Hand-detachable locks. Self-opening action. Auto ejectors. Double triggers or single trigger. Gauges: 12,16, 20. Bbl. lengths, chokes, weights according to customer's specifications. Checkered stock and forend, straight or pistol grip. Made in six grades — Condor, Imperiale, Imperiale S, Imperiale Montecarlo No. 5, Imperiale Montecarlo No.11, Imperiale Montecarlo Extra — which differ chiefly in overall quality, engraving, grade of wood, checkering, etc.; general specifications are the same. Only the Imperial Montecarlo Extra Grade is currently manufactured.
Condor grade . . . . NiB $7700 Ex $6053 Gd $4797
Imperial, Imperiales grades . . . . NiB $10,450 Ex $9705 Gd $6638
**Imperial Monte Carlo
grades No. 5, 11 . . . . NiB $30,032 Ex $23,659 Gd $19,343**
Imperial Monte Carlo Extra grade . . . . Custom only. Prices start at $110,000

HUNTER MODEL
Same general specifications as Standard Model except higher grade w/engraved receiver; w/ribbed bbl. only. Made from 1950 to 1990.
W/solid rib . . . . NiB $419 Ex $352 Gd $291
W/vent rib . . . . NiB $522 Ex $438 Gd $298

HUNTER MODEL MAGNUM . . . . NiB $435 Ex $371 Gd $237
Same as Standard Model Magnum except higher grade w/engraved receiver, vent rib bbl. only. Formerly designated "Wildfowler Model." Made from 1954 to 1973.

PEREGRINE MODEL 400 . . . . NiB $605 Ex $451 Gd $267
Same general specifications as Model 451 except has steel receiver. Weight (w/26.5-inch bbl.): 6 lbs., 15 oz. Made from 1975 to 1978.

PEREGRINE MODEL 451 O/U . . . . NiB $605 Ex $451 Gd $267
Boxlock. Lightweight alloy receiver. Automatic ejectors. Selective single trigger. 12 ga. Bbls.: 26.5-, 28-inch; choked C/IC, M/F; vent rib. Weight (w/26.5-inch bbls.): 6 lbs., 1 oz. Checkered pistol-grip stock and forearm. Made from 1975 to 1978.

SKEET GUN . . . . NiB $390 Ex $265 Gd $163
Same general specifications and appearance as Standard Model except made only w/26-inch vent-rib bbl., SK choke. Stock and forearm of extra fancy walnut. Made from 1972 to 1974.

SLUG GUN . . . . NiB $360 Ex $238 Gd $137
Same as Standard Model except has 22-inch plain bbl., Cyl. bore, folding leaf open rear sight, gold bead front sight. Made 1960 to 1990. Disc.

Franchi Hunter Model w/Ventilated Rib

Franchi Black Magic 48/AL Semiautomatic

Franchi LAW-12

Franchi SPAS-12

Franchi Sporting 2000

TURKEY GUN . . . . **NiB $424 Ex $328 Gd $266**
Same as Standard Model Magnum except higher grade w/turkey scene engraved receiver, 12 ga. only, 36-inch matted-rib bbl., Extra Full choke. Made from 1963 to 1965.

BLACK MAGIC 48/AL SEMIAUTOMATIC
Similar to the Franchi Model 48/AL except w/Franchoke screw-in tubes and matte black receiver w/Black Magic logo. Gauge: 12 or 20, 2.75-inch chamber. Bbls.: 24-, 26-, 28-inch w/vent rib; 24-inch rifled slug w/sights. Weight: 5.2 lbs. (20 ga.). Checkered walnut buttstock and forend. Blued finish.
Standard model . . . . **NiB $550 Ex $422 Gd $350**
Trap model . . . . **NiB $615 Ex $472 Gd $415**

FALCONET 2000 O/U . . . . **NiB $1250 Ex $1012 Gd $869**
Boxlock. Single selective trigger. Selective automatic ejectors. Gauge: 12, 2.75-inch chambers. Bbls.: 26-inch w/Franchoke tubes; IC/M/F. Weight: 6 lbs. Checkered walnut stock and forearm. Engraved silver receiver w/gold-plated game scene. Imported from 1992 to 1993.

LAW-12 SHOTGUN. . . . . **NiB $581 Ex $326 Gd $238**
Similar to the SPAS-12 Model except gas-operated semiautomatic action only, ambidextrous safety, decocking lever and adj. sights. Made from 1983 to 1994.

SPAS-12 SHOTGUN
Selective operating system functions as a gas-operated semi-automatic or pump action. Gauge: 12, 2.75-inch chamber. Seven round magazine. Bbl.: 21.5 inches w/cylinder bore and muzzle protector or optional screw-in choke tubes, matte finish. 41 inches overall w/fixed stock. Weight: 8.75 lbs. Blade front sight, aperture rear sight. Folding or black nylon buttstock w/pistol grip and forend, non-reflective anodized finish. Made from 1983 to 1994.
Fixed stock model . . . . **NiB $675 Ex $474 Gd $347**
Folding stock model . . . . **NiB $675 Ex $474 Gd $347**
Optional choke tubes, add $125

SPORTING 2000 O/U . . . . **NiB $1255 Ex $1010 Gd $880**
Similar to the Franchi Falconet 2000. Boxlock. Single selective trigger. Selective automatic ejectors. Gauge: 12; 2.75-inch chambers. Ported (1992-93) or unported 28-inch bbls., w/vent rib. Weight: 7.75 lbs. Blued receiver. Bead front sight. Checkered walnut stock and forearm; plastic composition buttplate. Imported from 1992-93 and 1997 to 1998.

Francotte Model 8446

Francotte Model 6886

Francotte Model
10/18E628

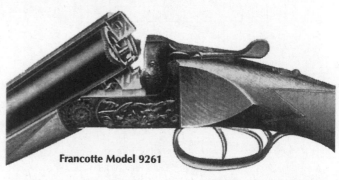

Francotte Model 9261

AUGUSTE FRANCOTTE & CIE., S.A. — Liège, Belgium

Francotte shotguns for many years were distributed in the U.S. by Abercrombie & Fitch of New York City. This firm has used a series of model designations for Francotte guns which do not correspond to those of the manufacturer. Because so many Francotte owners refer to their guns by the A & F model names and numbers, the A & F series is included in a listing separate from that of the standard Francotte numbers.

BOXLOCK HAMMERLESS DOUBLES

Anson & Deeley system. Side clips. Greener crossbolt on models 6886, 8446, 4996 and 9261; square crossbolt on Model 6930, Greener-Scott crossbolt on Model 8457, Purdey bolt on Models 11/18E and 10/18E/628. Auto ejectors. Double triggers. Made in all standard gauges, barrel lengths, chokes, weights. Checkered stock and forend, straight or pistol-grip. The eight models listed vary chiefly in fastenings as described above, finish and engraving, etc.; custom options increase value. Disc.

Model 6886 . . . . NiB $13,650 Ex $12,994 Gd $10,089
Model 8446 (Francotte Special),
6930, 4996. . . . . NiB $14,090 Ex $13,316 Gd $12,239
Model 8457,
9261 (Francotte Original), 11/18E NiB $15,249 Ex $14,270 Gd $12,990
Model 10/18E/628 . . . . NiB $16,598 Ex $15,360 Gd $13,753

BOXLOCK HAMMERLESS DOUBLES — A & F SERIES

Boxlock, Anson & Deeley type. Crossbolt. Sideplate on all except Knockabout Model. Side clips. Auto ejectors. Double triggers. Gauges: 12, 16, 20, 28, .410. Bbls.: 26- to 32-inch in 12 ga., 26- and 28-inch in other ga.; any boring. Weight: 4.75 to 8 lbs. depending on gauge and barrel length. Checkered stock and forend; straight, half or full pistol grip. The seven grades (No. 45 Eagle Grade, No. 30, No. 25, No. 20, No. 14, Jubilee Model, Knockabout Model) differ chiefly in overall quality, engraving, grade of wood, checkering, etc.; general specifications are the same. Disc.

Jubilee model
No. 14 . . . . NiB $2753 Ex $1915 Gd $1379
Jubilee model
No. 18. . . . . NiB $3830 Ex $2450 Gd $1747
Jubilee model
No. 20 . . . . NiB $4503 Ex $3081 Gd $2183
Jubilee model
No. 25 . . . . NiB $5000 Ex $3006 Gd $2038
Jubilee model
No. 30 . . . . NiB $6499 Ex $4947 Gd $3474
Eagle grade
No. 45 . . . . NiB $9223 Ex $6828 Gd $4774
Knockabout
model . . . . NiB $2750 Ex $2231 Gd $1603

BOXLOCK HAMMERLESS DOUBLES (SIDEPLATES)

Anson & Deeley system. Reinforced frame w/side clips. Purdey-type bolt except on Model 8455, which has Greener crossbolt. Auto ejectors. Double triggers. Made in all standard gauges, bbl. lengths, chokes, weights. Checkered stock and forend, straight or pistol grip. Models 10594, 8455 and 6982 are of equal quality, differing chiefly in style of engraving; Model 9/40E/38321 is a higher grade gun in all details and has fine English-style engraving. Built to customer specifications.

Models 10594, 8455, 6982 . . . . NiB $5291 Ex $4298 Gd $3067
Model 9/40E/38321 . . . . NiB $6495 Ex $5185 Gd $3639

Galef Silver Snipe Over/Under Shotgun

Galef Companion Folding Single-Barrel Shotgun

Galef Zabala Hammerless Double-Barrel Shotgun

FINE O/U SHOTGUN **$9461**
Model 9/40.SE. Boxlock, Anson & Deeley system. Auto ejectors. Double triggers. Made in all standard gauges; bbl. length, boring to order. Weight: About 6.75 lbs. 12 ga. Checkered stock and forend, straight or pistol grip. Manufactured to customer specifications. Disc 1990.

FINE SIDELOCK
HAMMERLESS DOUBLE . . . . **NiB $24,819 Ex $19,910 Gd $13,627**
Model 120.HE/328. Automatic ejectors. Double triggers. Made in all standard ga.; bbl. length, boring, weight to order. Checkered stock and forend, straight or pistol-grip. Manufactured to customer specifications. Disc. 1990.

HALF-FINE O/U SHOTGUN . . . . **NiB $10,244 Ex $8223 Gd $5587**
Model SOB.E/11082. Boxlock, Anson & Deeley system. Auto ejectors. Double triggers. Made in all standard gauges; barrel length, boring to order. Checkered stock and forend, straight or pistol grip. Note: This model is similar to No. 9/40.SE except general quality lower. Disc. 1990.

GALEF SHOTGUNS — Manufactured for J. L. Galef & Son, Inc., New York, New York, by M. A. V. I., Gardone F. T., Italy, by Zabala Hermanos, Eiquetta, Spain, and by Antonio Zoli, Gardone V. T., Italy

SILVER SNIPE OVER/UNDER SHOTGUN . . . . **NiB $555 Ex $454 Gd $336**
Boxlock. Plain extractors. Single trigger. Gauges: 12, 20; 3-inch chambers. Bbls: 26-, 28-, 30-inch (latter in 12 ga. only); IC/M, M/F chokes; vent rib. Weight: 12 ga. w/28-inch bbls., 6.5 lbs. Checkered walnut pistol-grip stock and forearm. Introduced by Antonio Zoli in 1968. Disc. See illustration previous page.

GOLDEN SNIPE . . . . **NiB $599 Ex $503 Gd $381**
Same as Silver Snipe, except has selective automatic ejectors. Made by Antonio Zoli 1968 to date.

MONTE CARLO TRAP
SINGLE-BARREL SHOTGUN . . . . **NiB $245 Ex $179 Gd $145**
Hammerless. Underlever. Plain extractor. 12 ga. 32-inch bbl., F choke, vent rib. Weight: About 8.25 lbs. Checkered pistol-grip stock w/Monte Carlo comb and

recoil pad, beavertail forearm. Introduced by M. A. V. I. in 1968. Disc.

SILVER HAWK HAMMERLESS DOUBLE . . . . . . **NiB $483 Ex $342 Gd $223**
Boxlock. Plain extractors. Double triggers. Gauges: 12, 20; 3-inch chambers. Bbls.: 26-, 28-, 30-inch (latter in 12 ga. only); IC/M, M/F chokes. Weight: 12 ga. w/26-inch bbls., 6 lbs. 6 oz. Checkered walnut pistol-grip stock and beavertail forearm. Made by Angelo Zoli 1968 to 1972.

COMPANION FOLDING SINGLE-BARREL SHOTGUN
Hammerless. Underlever. Gauges: 12 Mag., 16, 20 Mag., 28, .410. Bbls.: 26-inch (.410 only), 28-inch (12, 16, 20, 28) 30-inch (12-ga. only); F choke; plain or vent rib. Weight: 4.5 lbs. for .410 to 5 lbs., 9 oz. for 12 ga. Checkered pistol-grip stock and forearm. Made by M. A. V. I. from 1968-83.
W/plain bbl. . . . . **NiB $170 Ex $106 Gd $79**
W/ventilated rib . . . . **NiB $215 Ex $159 Gd $116**

ZABALA HAMMERLESS DOUBLE-BARREL SHOTGUN
Boxlock. Plain extractors. Double triggers. Gauges: 10 Mag., 12 Mag., 16, 20 Mag., 28, .410. Bbls.: 22-, 26-, 28-, 30-, 32-inch; IC/IC, IC/M, M/F chokes. Weight: 12 ga. w/28-inch bbls., 7.75 lbs. Checkered walnut pistol-grip stock and beavertail forearm, recoil pad. Made by Zabala from 1972-83.
10 ga. . . . . **NiB $270 Ex $176 Gd $103**
Other ga. . . . . **NiB $200 Ex $145 Gd $101**

GAMBA — Gardone V. T. (Brescia), Italy

DAYTONA COMPETITION O/U
Boxlock w/Boss-style locking system. Anatomical single trigger; optional adj., single-selective release trigger. Selective automatic ejectors. Gauge: 12 or 20; 2.75- or 3-inch chambers. Bbls.: 26.75-, 28-, 30- or 32-inch choked SK/SK, IM/F or M/F. Weight: 7.5 to 8.5 lbs. Black or chrome receiver w/blued bbls. Checkered select walnut stock and forearm w/oil finish. Imported by Heckler & Koch until 1992.
American Trap model . . . . **NiB $2190 Ex $1596 Gd $909**
Pigeon, Skeet, Trap models . . . . **NiB $1210 Ex $969 Gd $772**

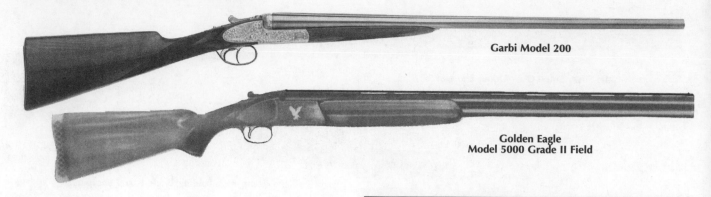

Garbi Model 200

Golden Eagle
Model 5000 Grade II Field

Sporting model . . . . NiB $5454 Ex $4320 Gd $2998
Sideplate model . . . . NiB $10,724 Ex $8601 Gd $5884
Engraved models . . . . NiB $12,895 Ex $9,345 Gd $6081
Sidelock model . . . . NiB $27,762 Ex $22,280 Gd $15,262

GARBI SHOTGUNS — Eibar, Spain

MODEL 100
SIDELOCK SHOTGUN . . . . NiB $5500 Ex $3293 Gd $2319
Gauges: 12, 16, 20 and 28. Bbls.: 25-, 28-, 30-inch. Action: Holland &
Holland pattern sidelock; automatic ejectors and double trigger. Weight:
5 lbs., 6 oz. to 7 lbs. 7 oz. English-style straight grip stock w/fine-line
hand-checkered butt; classic forend. Made from 1985 to date.

MODEL 101
SIDELOCK SHOTGUN . . . . NiB $6505 Ex $4137 Gd $2898
Same general specifications as Model 100 above, except the sidelocks are handcrafted w/hand-engraved receiver; select walnut
straight-grip stock.

MODEL 102
SIDELOCK SHOTGUN . . . . NiB $7000 Ex $4415 Gd $3089
Similar to the Model 101 except w/large scroll engraving. Made
from 1985 to 1993.

MODEL 103
HAMMERLESS DOUBLE
Similar to Model 100 except w/Purdey-type, higher grade engraving.
Model 103A Standard . . . . . NiB $13,000 Ex $10,477 Gd $9131
Model 103A Royal Deluxe . . . NiB $10,115 Ex $8133 Gd $5642
Model 103B . . . . NiB $20,500 Ex $16,000 Gd $14,650
Model 103B Royal Deluxe . . . NiB $24,173 Ex $21,369 Gd $17,780

MODEL 200
HAMMERLESS DOUBLE. . NiB $16,252 Ex $13,591 Gd $10,584
Similar to Model 100 except w/double heavy-duty locks. Continental-style
floral and scroll engraving. Checkered deluxe walnut stock and forearm.

GARCIA CORPORATION —
Teaneck, New Jersey

BRONCO 22/.410 O/U COMBO . . . NiB $248 Ex $124 Gd $93
Swing-out action. Takedown. 18.5-inch bbls.; .22 LR over, .410 ga.
under. Weight: 4.5 lbs. One-piece stock and receiver, crackle finish.
Intro. In 1976. Disc.

BRONCO .410 SINGLE SHOT. . . . . . NiB $195 Ex $103 Gd $79
Swing-out action. Takedown. .410 ga. 18.5-inch bbl. Weight: 3.5 lbs.
One-piece stock and receiver, crackle finish. Intro. In 1967. Disc.

GOLDEN EAGLE FIREARMS INC. —

Houston, Texas, Mfd. By Nikko Firearms Ltd., Tochigi, Japan

EAGLE MODEL 5000
GRADE I FIELD O/U . . . . NiB $856 Ex $760 Gd $599
Receiver engraved and inlaid w/gold eagle head. Boxlock. Auto
ejectors. Selective single trigger. 12, 20 ga.; 2.75- or 3-inch chambers, 12 ga., 3-inch, 20 ga. Bbls.: 26-, 28-, 30-inch (latter only in 12-
ga. 3-inch Mag.); IC/M, M/F chokes; vent rib. Weight: 6.25 lbs., 20
ga.; 7.25 lbs., 12 ga.; 8 lbs., 12-ga. Mag. Checkered pistol-grip stock
and semi-beavertail forearm. Imported 1975-82. Note: Guns marketed 1975 to 1976 under the Nikko brand name have white
receivers; guns made since 1976 are blued.

EAGLE MODEL 5000
GRADE I SKEET . . . . NiB $875 Ex $639 Gd $494
Same as Field model except has 26- or 28-inch bbls. w/wide (11
mm) vent rib, SK choked. Imported from 1975 to 1982.

EAGLE MODEL 5000
GRADE I TRAP . . . . NiB $875 Ex $635 Gd $491
Same as Field model except has 30-, or 32-inch bbls. w/wide (11
mm) vent rib (M/F, IM/F, F/F chokes), trap-style stock w/recoil pad.
Imported from 1975 to 1982.

EAGLE MODEL 5000
GRADE II FIELD . . . . NiB $955 Ex $775 Gd $619
Same as Grade I Field model except higher grade w/fancier wood,
more elaborate engraving and "screaming eagle" inlaid in gold.
Imported from 1975 to 1982.

EAGLE MODEL 5000
GRADE II SKEET . . . . NiB $975 Ex $800 Gd $650
Same as Grade I Skeet model except higher grade w/fancier wood,
more elaborate engraving and "screaming eagle" inlaid in gold;
inertia trigger, vent side ribs. Imported from 1975-82.

EAGLE MODEL 5000
GRADE II TRAP . . . . NiB $975 Ex $800 Gd $650
Same as Grade I Trap model except higher grade w/fancier wood,
more elaborate engraving and "screaming eagle" inlaid in gold;
inertia trigger, vent side ribs. Imported from 1975 to 1982.

EAGLE MODEL 5000
GRADE III GRANDEE . . . . NiB $2505 Ex $2086 Gd $1684
Best grade, available in Field, Skeet and Trap models w/same general
specifications as lower grades. Has sideplates w/game scene engraving, scroll on frame and bbls., fancy wood (Monte Carlo comb, full
pistol-grip and recoil pad on Trap model). Made from 1976 to 1982.

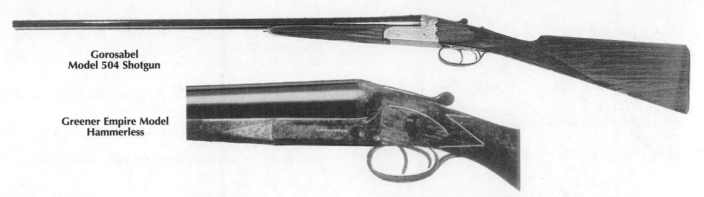

Gorosabel
Model 504 Shotgun

Greener Empire Model
Hammerless

Greener
Far-Killer

GOROSABEL SHOTGUNS — Spain

MODEL 503 SHOTGUN . . . . **NiB $965 Ex $788 Gd $561**
Gauges: 12, 16, 20 and .410. Action: Anson & Deely-style boxlock. Bbls.: 26-, 27-, and 28-inch. Select European walnut, English or pistol grip, sliver or beavertail forend, hand-checkering. Scalloped frame and scroll engraving. Intro. 1985; disc.

MODEL 504 SHOTGUN . . . . **NiB $1036 Ex $844 Gd $599**
Gauge: 12 or 20. Action: Holland & Holland-style sidelock. Bbl.: 26-, 27-, or 28-inch. Select European walnut, English or pistol grip, sliver or beavertail forend, hand-checkering. Holland-style large scroll engraving. Inro. 1985; disc.

MODEL 505 SHOTGUN . . . . **NiB $1446 Ex $1149 Gd $807**
Gauge: 12 or 20. Action: Holland & Holland-style sidelock. Bbls.: 26-, 27-, or 28-inch. Select European walnut, English or pistol grip, silver or beavertail forend, hand-checkering. Purdey-style fine scroll and rose engraving. Intro. 1985; disc.

STEPHEN GRANT — Hertfordshire, England

BEST QUALITY SELF-OPENER DOUBLE-BARREL

SHOTGUN . . . . **NiB $18,468 Ex $15,405 Gd $11,485**
Sidelock, self-opener. Gauges: 12, 16 and 20. Bbls.: 25 to 30 inches standard. Highest-grade English or European walnut straight-grip buttstock and forearm w/Greener type lever. Imported by Stoeger in the 1950s.

BEST QUALITY SIDE-LEVER DOUBLE-BARREL

SHOTGUN . . . . **NiB $12,000 Ex $10,628 Gd $7268**
Sidelock, self-lever. Gauges: 12, 16 and 20. Bbls.: 25 to 30 inches standard. Highest-grade English or European walnut straight-grip buttstock and forearm w/Greener type lever. Imported by Stoeger in the 1950s.

W. W. GREENER, LTD. — Birmingham, England

EMPIRE MODEL HAMMERLESS DOUBLES

Boxlock. Non-ejector or w/automatic ejectors. Double triggers. 12 ga. only (2.75-inch or 3-inch chamber). Bbls.: 28- to 32-inch; any choke combination. Weight: from 7.25 to 7.75 lbs. depending on bbl. length. Checkered stock and forend, straight- or half-pistol grip. Also furnished in "Empire Deluxe Grade," this model has same general specs, but deluxe finish.
Empire model, non-ejector . . . . **NiB $1761 Ex $1591 Gd $1281**
Empire model, ejector . . . . **NiB $1808 Ex $1641 Gd $1383**
Empire Deluxe model, non-ejector . . . **NiB $1980 Ex $1800 Gd $1298**
Empire Deluxe model, ejector . . . . **NiB $2513 Ex $2051 Gd $1468**

FARKILLER MODEL GRADE F35
HAMMERLESS DOUBLE-BARREL SHOTGUN

Boxlock. Non-ejector or w/automatic ejectors. Double triggers. Gauges: 12 (2.75-inch or 3-inch), 10, 8. Bbls.: 28- 30- or 32-inch. Weight: 7.5 to 9 lbs. in 12 ga. Checkered stock, forend; straight or half-pistol grip.
Non-ejector, 12 ga. . . . . **NiB $1434 Ex $1039 Gd $836**
Ejector, 12 ga. . . . . **NiB $3742 Ex $3038 Gd $2162**
Non-ejector, 10 or 8 ga. . . . . . . **NiB $2784 Ex $2015 Gd $1876**
Ejector, 10 or 8 ga. . . . . **NiB $5256 Ex $4082 Gd $2994**

G. P. (GENERAL PURPOSE)
SINGLE BARREL . . . . **NiB $350 Ex $241 Gd $160**
Greener Improved Martini Lever Action. Takedown. Ejector. 12 ga. only. Bbl. lengths: 26-, 30-, 32-inch. M or F choke. Weight: 6.25 to 6.75 lbs. depending on bbl. length. Checkered straight-grip stock and forearm.

HAMMERLESS EJECTOR
DOUBLE-BARREL SHOTGUNS

Boxlock. Auto ejectors. Double triggers, non-selective or selective single trigger. Gauges: 12, 16, 20, 28, .410 (two latter gauges not supplied in Grades DH40 and DH35). Bbls.: 26-, 28-, 30-inch; any choke combination. Weight: From 4.75 to 8 lbs. Depending on ga. and bbl. length. Checkered stock and forend, straight- or half-pistol grip. The Royal, Crown, Sovereign and Jubilee models differ in quality, engraving, grade of wood, checkering, etc. General specifications are the same.
Royal Model Grade DH75 . . . . . **NiB $4043 Ex $2917 Gd $2032**
Crown Model Grade DH55 . . . . **NiB $5028 Ex $3044 Gd $2168**
Sovereign Model Grade DH40 . . . . **NiB $5000 Ex $2914 Gd $1945**
Jubilee Model Grade DH35 . . . . **NiB $4000 Ex $2971 Gd $1932**
W/selective single trigger, add $330
W/non-selective single trigger, add $250
W/ventilated rib, add $395
W/single trigger, add $425

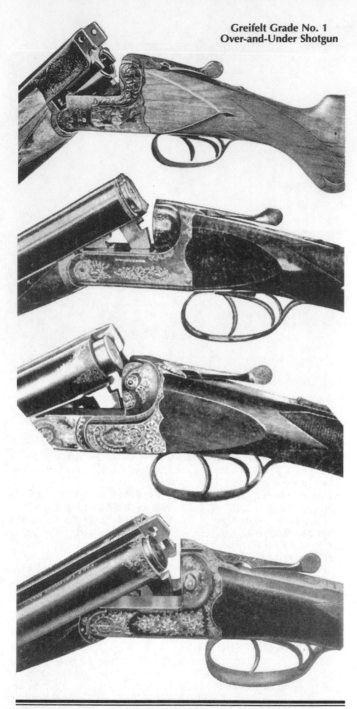

Greifelt Grade No. 1
Over-and-Under Shotgun

GREIFELT & COMPANY — Suhl, Germany

GRADE NO. 1 O/U SHOTGUN
Anson & Deeley boxlock, Kersten fastening. Auto ejectors. Double triggers or single trigger. Elaborately engraved. Gauges: 12, 16, 20, 28, .410. Bbls.: 26- to 32-inch, any combination of chokes, vent or solid matted rib. Weight: 4.25 to 8.25 lbs. depending on ga. and bbl. length. Straight- or pistol-grip stock, Purdey-type forend, both checkered. Manufactured prior to World War II.
W/solid matted-rib bbl.,
except .410 & 28 ga. . . . . **NiB $3653 Ex $3059 Gd $2171**

W/solid matted-rib bbl.,
.410 & 28 ga . . . . **NiB $3691 Ex $2761 Gd $1679**
W/ventilated rib, add. 5%
W/single trigger, add $500

GRADE NO. 3 O/U SHOTGUN
Same general specifications as Grade No. 1 except less fancy engraving. Manufactured prior to World War II.
W/solid matted-rib bbl.,
except .410 & 28 ga. . . . . **NiB $2849 Ex $2294 Gd $1784**
W/solid matted-rib bbl.,
.410 & 28 ga. . . . . **NiB $5000 Ex $3921 Gd $2775**
W/ventilated rib, add 5%
W/single trigger, add. $400

MODEL 22
HAMMERLESS DOUBLE . . . . **NiB $2199 Ex $1677 Gd $1196**
Anson & Deeley boxlock. Plain extractors. Double triggers. Gauges: 12 and 16. Bbls.: 28- or 30-inch, M/F choke. Checkered stock and forend, pistol grip and cheekpiece standard, English-style stock also supplied. Manufactured since World War II.

MODEL 22E
HAMMERLESS DOUBLE . . . . . . **NiB $2754 Ex $2305 Gd $1654**
Same as Model 22 except has automatic ejectors.

MODEL 103
HAMMLERLESS DOUBLE . . . . . **NiB $1985 Ex $1632 Gd $1159**
Anson & Deeley boxlock. Plain extractors. Double triggers. Gauges: 12 and 16. Bbls.: 28- or 30-inch, M and F choke. Checkered stock and forend, pistol grip and cheekpiece standard, English-style stock also supplied. Manufactured since World War II.

MODEL 103E
HAMMERLESS DOUBLE . . . . . . **NiB $2200 Ex $1727 Gd $1224**
Same as Model 103 except has automatic ejectors.

MODEL 143E O/U SHOTGUN
General specifications same as pre-war Grade No. 1 Over-and-Under, except this model is not supplied in 28 and .410 ga. or w/32-inch bbls. Model 143E is not as high quality as the Grade No. 1 gun. Mfd. Since World War II.
W/raised matted rib,
double triggers . . . . **NiB $2400 Ex $1956 Gd $1477**
W/ventilated rib,
selective single trigger . . . . **NiB $2628 Ex $2183 Gd $1763**

HAMMERLESS DRILLING (THREE-BARREL
COMBINATION GUN) . . . . **NiB $3500 Ex $3090 Gd $1956**
Boxlock. Plain extractors. Double triggers, front single set for rifle bbl. Gauges: 12, 16, 20; rifle bbl. in any caliber adapted to this type of gun. 26-inch bbls. Weight: About 7.5 lbs. Auto rear sight operated by rifle bbl. selector. Checkered stock and forearm, pistol-grip and cheekpiece standard. Manufactured prior to WW II. Note: Value shown is for guns chambered for cartridges readily obtainable. If rifle bbl. is an odd foreign caliber, value will be considerably less.

O/U COMBINATION GUN
Similar in design to this maker's over-and-under shotguns. Gauges: 12, 16, 20, 28, .410; rifle bbl. in any caliber adapted to this type of gun. Bbls.: 24- or 26-inch, solid matted rib. Weight: From 4.75 to 7.25 lbs. Folding rear sight. Manufactured prior to WWII. Note: Values shown are for gauges other than .410 w/rifle bbl. Chambered for a cartridge readily obtainable; if in an odd foreign caliber, value will be considerably less. .410 ga. increases in value by about 50%.
W/non-automatic ejector . . . . . **NiB $5224 Ex $4421 Gd $3607**
W/automatic ejector . . . . **NiB $5925 Ex $5125 Gd $4210**

HARRINGTON & RICHARDSON ARMS COMPANY — Gardner, Massachusetts, Now H&R 1871, Inc.

Formerly Harrington & Richardson Arms Co. of Worcester, Mass. One of the oldest and most distinguished manufacturers of handguns, rifles and shotguns, H&R suspended operations on January 24, 1986. In 1987, New England Firearms was established as an independent company producing selected H&R models under the NEF logo. In 1991, H&R 1871, Inc. was formed from the residual of the parent company and then took over the New England Firearms facility. H&R 1871 produced firearms under both their logo and the NEF brand name until 1999, when the Marlin Firearms Company acquired the assets of H&R 1871.

NO. 3 HAMMERLESS
SINGLE-SHOT SHOTGUN . . . . NiB $198 Ex $103 Gd $79
Takedown. Automatic ejector. Gauges: 12, 16, 20, .410. Bbls.: plain, 26- to 32-inch, F choke. Weight: 6.5 to 7.25 lbs. depending on ga. and bbl. length. Plain pistol-grip stock and forend. Discontinued 1942.

NO. 5 STANDARD LIGHTWEIGHT
HAMMER SINGLE . . . . NiB $199 Ex $110 Gd $84
Takedown. Auto ejector. Gauges: 24, 28, .410. Bbls.: 26- or 28-inch, F choke. Weight: About 4 to 4.75 lbs. Plain pistol-grip stock/forend. Discontinued 1942.

NO. 6 HEAVY BREECH SINGLE-SHOT
HAMMER SHOTGUN . . . . NiB $199 Ex $110 Gd $84
Takedown. Automatic ejector. Gauges: 10, 12, 16, 20. Bbls.: Plain, 28- to 36-inch, F choke. Weight: About 7 to 7.25 lbs. Plain stock and forend. Discontinued 1942.

NO. 7 OR 9 BAY STATE SINGLE-SHOT
HAMMER SHOTGUN . . . . NiB $198 Ex $110 Gd $84
Takedown. Automatic ejector. Gauges: 12, 16, 20, .410. Bbls.: Plain 26- to 32-inch, F choke. Weight: 5.5 to 6.5 lbs. depending on ga. and bbl. length. Plain pistol-grip stock and forend. Discontinued 1942.

NO. 8 STANDARD SINGLE-SHOT
HAMMER SHOTGUN . . . . NiB $215 Ex $120 Gd $89
Takedown. Automatic ejector. Gauges: 12, 16, 20, 24, 28, .410. Bbl.: plain, 26- to 32-inch, F choke. Weight: 5.5 to 6.5 lbs. depending on ga. and bbl. length. Plain pistol-grip stock and forend. Made from 1908 to 1942.

MODEL 348 GAMESTER
BOLT-ACTION SHOTGUN . . . . NiB $170 Ex $104 Gd $79
Takedown. 12 and 16 ga. Two round tubular magazine, 28-inch bbl, F choke. Plain pistol-grip stock. Weight: About 7.5 lbs. Made from 1949 to 1954.

MODEL 349 GAMESTER DELUXE . . NiB $199 Ex $110 Gd $84
Same as Model 348 except has 26-inch bbl. W/adj. choke device, recoil pad. Made from 1953 to 1955.

MODEL 351 HUNTSMAN
BOLT-ACTION SHOTGUN . . . NiB $199 Ex $155 Gd $115
Takedown. 12 and 16 ga. Two round tubular magazine. Pushbutton safety. 26-inch bbl. w/H&R variable choke. Weight: About 6.75 lbs. Monte Carlo stock w/recoil pad. Made from 1956 to 1958.

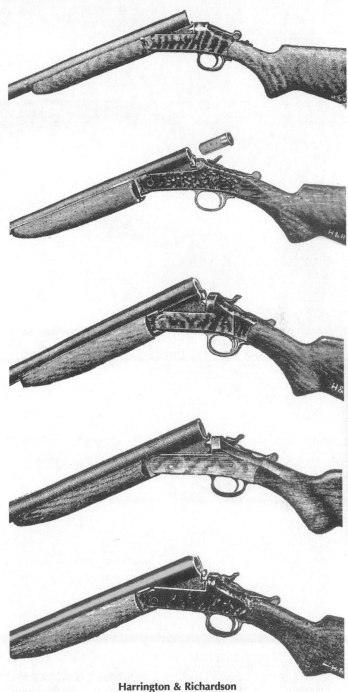

**Harrington & Richardson
No. 3, 5, 6, 7 and 8 Shotguns**

MODEL 400 PUMP . . . . NiB $283 Ex $218 Gd $161
Hammerless. Gauges: 12, 16, 20. Tubular magazine holds 4 shells. 28-inch bbl., F choke. Weight: About 7.25 lbs. Plain pistol-grip stock (recoil pad in 12 and 16 ga.), grooved slide handle. Made from 1955 to 1967.

SHOTGUNS

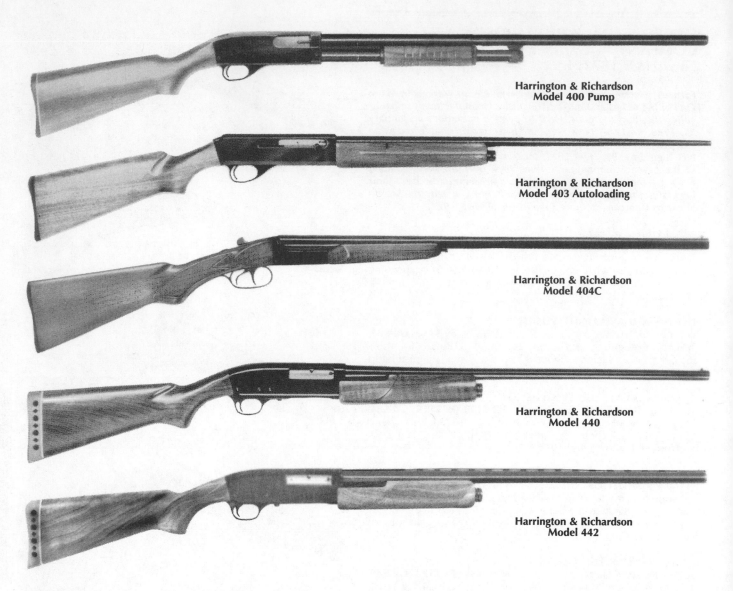

Harrington & Richardson
Model 400 Pump

Harrington & Richardson
Model 403 Autoloading

Harrington & Richardson
Model 404C

Harrington & Richardson
Model 440

Harrington & Richardson
Model 442

MODEL 401 . . . . **NiB $299 Ex $201 Gd $154**
Same as Model 400 on previous page, except has H&R variable choke. Made from 1956-63.

MODEL 402 . . . . **NiB $279 Ex $202 Gd $162**
Similar to Model 400 except .410 ga., weight: About 5.5 lbs. Made from 1959-67.

MODEL 403 AUTOLOADING
SHOTGUN . . . . **NiB $292 Ex $227 Gd $165**
Takedown. .410 ga. Tubular magazine holds four shells. 26-inch bbl., F choke. Weight: About 5.75 lbs. Plain pistol-grip stock and forearm. Made in 1964.

MODEL 404/404C . . . . **NiB $332 Ex $265 Gd $191**
Boxlock. Plain extractors. Double triggers. Gauges: 12, 20, .410. Bbls.: 28-inch in 12 ga. (M/F choke), 26-inch in 20 ga. (IC/M and .410 (F/F). Weight: 5.5 to 7.25 lbs. Plain walnut-finished hardwood stock and forend on Model 404; 404C checkered. Made in Brazil by Amadeo Rossi from 1969-1972.

MODEL 440 PUMP . . . . **NiB $228 Ex $181 Gd $134**
Hammerless. Gauges: 12, 16, 20. 2.75-inch chamber in 16 ga., 3-inch in 12 and 20 ga. Three round magazine. Bbls.: 26-, 28-, 30-inch; IC, M, F choke. Weight: 6.25 lbs. Plain pistol-grip stock and slide handle, recoil pad. Made from 1968-73.

MODEL 442 . . . . **NiB $269 Ex $222 Gd $162**
Same as Model 440 except has vent rib bbl., checkered stock and forearm, weight: 6.75 lbs. Made from 1969-73.

ULTRA SLUG SERIES . . . . **NiB $231 Ex $161 Gd $120**
Singel shot 12 or 20 ga w/3-inch chamber w/heavy-wall 24-inch fully rifled bbl. w/scope . Weight: 9 lbs. Walnut-stained Monte Carlo stock, sling swivels, black nylon sling. Made from 1995 to date.

MODEL 1212 FIELD . . . . **NiB $398 Ex $309 Gd $223**
Boxlock. Plain extractors. Selective single trigger. 12 ga., 2.75-inch chambers. 28-inch bbls., IC/IM, vent rib. Weight: 7 lbs. Checkered walnut pistol-gip stock and fluted forearm. Made 1976-80 by Lanber Arms S. A., Zaldibar (Vizcaya), Spain.

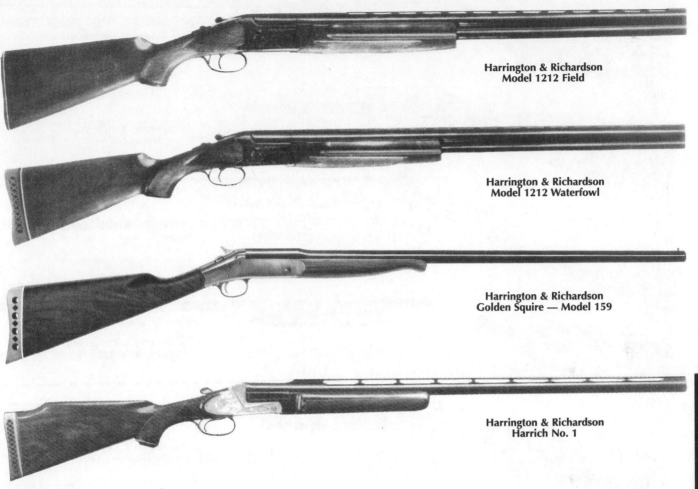

Harrington & Richardson
Model 1212 Field

Harrington & Richardson
Model 1212 Waterfowl

Harrington & Richardson
Golden Squire — Model 159

Harrington & Richardson
Harrich No. 1

MODEL 1212
WATERFOWL GUN . . . . **NiB $457 Ex $343 Gd $247**
Same as Field Gun except chambered for 12-ga, 3-inch mag. shells, has 30-inch bbls., M/F chokes, stock and recoil pad, weight: 7.5 lbs. Made from 1976 to 1980.

MODEL 1908
SINGLE-SHOT SHOTGUN . . . . **NiB $190 Ex $129 Gd $93**
Takedown. Automatic ejector. Gauges: 12, 16, 24 and 28. Bbls.: 26- to 32-inch, F choke. Weight: 5.25 to 6.5 lbs. depending on ga. and bbl. length. Casehardened receiver. Plain pistol-grip stock. Bead front sight. Made from 1908 to 1934.

MODEL 1908 .410 (12MM)
SINGLE-SHOT SHOTGUN . . . . **NiB $199 Ex $146 Gd $110**
Same general specifications as standard Model 1908 except chambered for .410 or 12mm shot cartridge w/bbl. milled down at receiver to give a more pleasing contour.

MODEL 1915 SINGLE-SHOT SHOTGUN
Takedown. Both non-auto and auto-ejectors available. Gauges: 24, 28, .410, 14mm and 12mm. Bbls.: 26- or 28-inch, F choke. Weight: 4 to 4.75 lbs. depending on ga. and bbl. length. Plain black walnut stock w/semi pistol-grip.
24 ga. . . . . **NiB $276 Ex $216 Gd $150**
28, .410 ga. . . . . **NiB $244 Ex $170 Gd $126**

FOLDING GUN . . . . **NiB $254 Ex $170 Gd $126**
Single bbl. hammer shotgun hinged at the front of the frame, the bbl. folds down against the stock. Light Frame model: gauges — 28, 14mm, .410; 22-inch bbl.; weighs about 4.5 lbs. Heavy Frame model: gauges — 12, 16, 20, 28, .410; 26-inch bbl.; weighs from 5.75 to 6.5 lbs. Plain pistol-grip stock and forend. Disc. 1942.

GOLDEN SQUIRE MODEL 159
SINGLE-BARREL
HAMMER SHOTGUN . . . . **NiB $188 Ex $134 Gd $101**
Hammerless. Side lever. Automatic ejection. Gauges: 12, 20. Bbls.: 30-inch in 12 ga., 28-inch in 20 ga., both F choke. Weight: About 6.5 lbs. Straight-grip stock w/recoil pad, forearm w/Schnabel. Made from 1964 to 1966.

GOLDEN SQUIRE JR. MODEL 459 . **NiB $210 Ex $149 Gd $112**
Same as Model 159 except gauges 20 and .410, 26-inch bbl., youth stock. Made in 1964.

HARRICH NO. 1 SINGLE-BARREL
TRAP GUN . . . . **NiB $1650 Ex $1335 Gd $844**
Anson & Deeley-type locking system w/Kersten top locks and double underlocking lugs. Sideplates engraved w/hunting scenes. 12 ga. Bbls.: 32-, 34-inch; F choke; high vent rib. Weight: 8.5 lbs. Checkered Monte Carlo stock w/pistol-grip and recoil pad, beavertail forearm, of select walnut. Made in Austria 1971 to 1975.

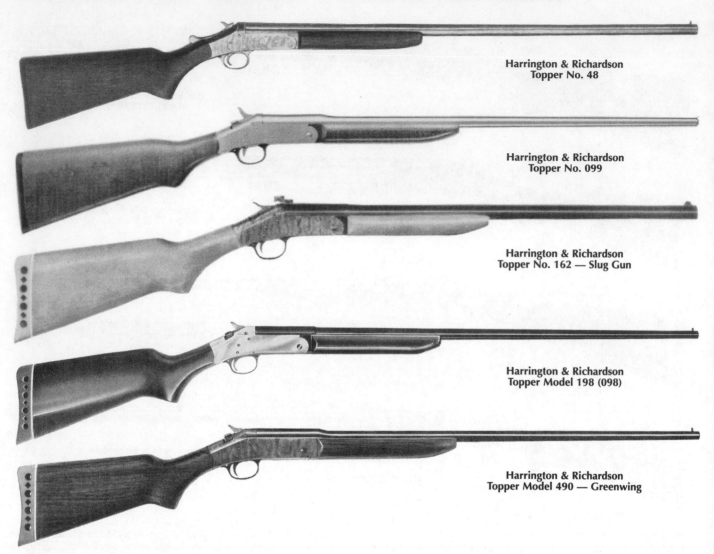

Harrington & Richardson
Topper No. 48

Harrington & Richardson
Topper No. 099

Harrington & Richardson
Topper No. 162 — Slug Gun

Harrington & Richardson
Topper Model 198 (098)

Harrington & Richardson
Topper Model 490 — Greenwing

"TOP RIB"
SINGLE-BARREL SHOTGUN . . . . **NiB $269 Ex $213 Gd $168**
Takedown. Auto ejector. Gauges: 12, 16 and 20. Bbls.: 28- to 30-inch, F choke w/full-length matted top rib. Weight: 6.5 to 7 lbs. depending on ga. and bbl. length. Black walnut pistol-grip stock (capped) and forend; both checkered. Flexible rubber buttplate. Made during 1930s.

TOPPER NO. 48 SINGLE-BARREL
HAMMER SHOTGUN . . . . **NiB $233 Ex $171 Gd $128**
Similar to old Model 8 Standard. Takedown. Top lever. Auto ejector. Gauges: 12, 16, 20, .410. Bbls.: plain; 26- to 30-inch; M or F choke. Weight: 5.5 to 6.5 lbs. depending on ga. and bbl. length. Plain pistol-grip stock and forend. Made from 1946 to 1957.

TOPPER MODEL 099 DELUXE . . . . NiB $200 Ex $135 Gd $100
Same as Model 158 except has matte nickel finish, semipistol grip walnut-finished American hardwood stock; semibeavertail forearm; 12, 16, 20, and .410 ga. Made from 1982 to 1986.

TOPPER MODEL 148 SINGLE-SHOT
HAMMER SHOTGUN . . . . **NiB $169 Ex $140 Gd $104**
Takedown. Side lever. Auto-ejection. Gauges: 12, 16, 20, .410.

Bbls.: 12 ga.,30-, 32- and 36-inch; 16 ga., 28- and 30-inch; 20 and .410 ga., 28-inch; F choke. Weight: 5 to 6.5 lbs. Plain pistol-grip stock and forend, recoil pad. Made from 1958 to 1961.

TOPPER MODEL 158 (058) SINGLE-SHOT
HAMMER SHOTGUN . . . . **NiB $195 Ex $145 Gd $108**
Takedown. Side lever. Automatic ejection. Gauges: 12, 20, .410 (2.75-inch and 3-inch shells); 16 (2.75-inch). bbl. length and choke combinations: 12 ga., 36-inch/F, 32-inch/F, 30-inch/F, 28-inch/F or M; .410, 28-inch/F. Weight: about 5.5 lbs. Plain pistol-grip stock and forend, recoil pad. Made from 1962 to 1981. Note: Designation changed to 058 in 1974.

TOPPER MODEL 162
SLUG GUN . . . . **NiB $251 Ex $182 Gd $133**
Same as Topper Model 158 except has 24-inch bbl., Cyl. bore, w/rifle sights. Made from 1968 to 1986.

TOPPER MODEL 176 10 GA.
MAGNUM . . . . **NiB $243 Ex $176 Gd $129**
Similar to Model 158, but has 36-inch heavy bbl. chambered for 3.5-inch 10- ga. Mag. shells, weight: 10 lbs.; stock w/Monte Carlo comb and recoil pad, longer and fuller forearm. Made from 1977 to 1986.

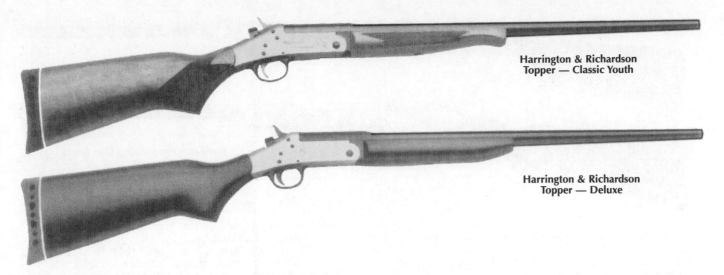

**Harrington & Richardson
Topper — Classic Youth**

**Harrington & Richardson
Topper — Deluxe**

TOPPER MODEL 188 DELUXE . . . . NiB $219 Ex $155 Gd $115
Same as standard Topper Model 148 except has chromed frame, stock and forend in black, red, yellow, blue, green, pink, or purple colored finish. .410 ga. only. Made from 1958 to 1961.

TOPPER MODEL 198 (098) DELUXE . . . . . NiB $214 Ex $161 Gd $118
Same as Model 158 except has chrome-plated frame, black finished stock and forend; 12, 20 and .410 ga. Made 1962 to 1981. Note: Designation changed to 098 in 1974.

TOPPER JR. MODEL 480 . . . . NiB $199 Ex $125 Gd $99
Similar to No. 48 Topper except has youth-size stock, 26-inch bbl, .410 ga. only. Made from 1958-61.

TOPPER NO. 488 DELUXE . . . . NiB $202 Ex $151 Gd $112
Same as standard No. 48 Topper except chrome-plated frame, black lacquered stock and forend, recoil pad. Disc. 1957.

TOPPER MODEL 490 . . . . NiB $195 Ex $145 Gd $108
Same as Model 158 except has youth-size stock (3 inches shorter), 26-inch bbl.; 20 and 28 ga. (M choke), .410 (F). Made 1962 to 1986.

TOPPER MODEL 490 GREENWING . . . . . . NiB $194 Ex $161 Gd $118
Same as the Model 490 except has a special high-polished finish. Made from 1981 to 1986.

TOPPER JR. MODEL 580 . . . . NiB $174 Ex $149 Gd $96
Same as Model 480 except has colored stocks as on Model 188. Made from 1958 to 1961.

TOPPER MODEL 590 . . . . NiB $172 Ex $134 Gd $99
Same as Model 490 except has chrome-plated frame, black finished stock and forend. Made from 1962 to 1963.

The following models are manufactured and distributed by the reorganized company of H&R 1871, Inc.

MODEL 098 TOPPER CLASSIC YOUTH . . . . NiB $158 Ex $124 Gd $93
Same as Topper Junior except also available in 28 ga. and has checkered American black walnut stock/forend w/satin finish and recoil pad. Made from 1991 to date.

MODEL 098 TOPPER DELUXE . . . . . NiB $158 Ex $124 Gd $93
Same as Model 098 Single Shot Hammer except in 12 ga., 3-inch chamber only. 28-inch bbl.; Mod. choke tube. Made from 1992 to date.

**MODEL 098 TOPPER
DELUXE RIFLED SLUG GUN . . . . . NiB $159 Ex $1049 Gd $80**
Same as Topper Deluxe Shotgun except has compensated 24-inch rifled slug bbl. Nickel plated receiver and blued bbl. Black finished hardwood stock. Made from 1996 to date.

**MODEL 098 TOPPER HAMMER
SINGLE-SHOT SHOTGUN . . . . NiB $139 Ex $109 Gd $82**
Side lever. Automatic ejector. Gauges: 12, 20 and .410; 3-inch chamber. Bbls.: 28-inch, (12 ga./M); 26-inch, (20 ga./M); 26-inch (.410/F). Weight: 5 to 6 lbs. Satin nickel receiver, blued bbl. Plain pistol-grip stock and semibeavertail forend w/black finish. Re-Intro. 1992.

MODEL 098 TOPPER JUNIOR . . . . . NiB $165 Ex $114 Gd $86
Same as Model 098 except has youth-size stock and 22-inch bbl. 20 or .410 ga. only. Made 1991 to date.

MODEL .410 TAMER SHOTGUN . . . NiB $150 Ex $124 Gd $93
Takedown. Topper-style single-shot, side lever action w/auto ejector. Gauge: .410; 3-inch chamber. 19.5-inch bbl. 33 inches overall. Weight: 5.75 lbs. Black polymer thumbhole stock designed to hold 4 extra shotshells. Matte nickel finish. Made from 1994 to date.

MODEL N. W. T. F. TURKEY MAG
Same as Model 098 Single-Shot Hammer except has 24-inch bbl. chambered 10 or 12 ga. w/3.5-inch chamber w/screw-in choke tube. Weight: 6 lbs. American hardwood stock, Mossy Oak camo finish. Made from 1991 to 1996.
NWTF 10 ga. Turkey Mag (Made 1996) . . . . NiB $150 Ex $101 Gd $88
NWTF 12 ga. Turkey Mag (Made 1991-95) . . NiB $150 Ex $101 Gd $88

**MODEL N. W. T. F.
YOUTH TURKEY GUN . . . . NiB $140 Ex $109 Gd $803**
Same as Model N.W.T.F. Turkey Mag except has 22-inch bbl. chambered in 20 ga. w/3-inch chamber and fixed full choke. Realtree camo finish. Made from 1994 to 1995.

**MODEL SB1-920
ULTRA SLUG HUNTER . . . . NiB $248 Ex $180 Gd $132**
Special 12 ga. action w/12 ga. bbl. blank underbored to 20 ga. to form a fully rifled slug bbl. Gauge: 20 w/3 inch chamber. 24-inch bbl. Weight: 8.5 lbs. Satin nickel receiver, blued bbl. Walnut finished hardwood Monte Carlo stock. Made from 1996 to 1998.

SHOTGUNS

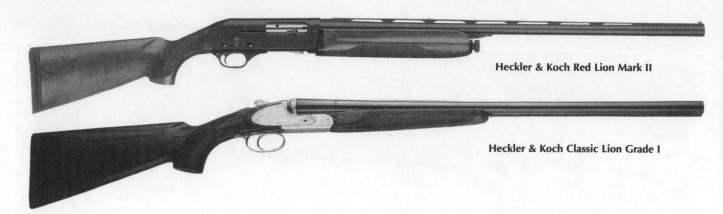

Heckler & Koch Red Lion Mark II

Heckler & Koch Classic Lion Grade I

MODEL ULTRA SLUG HUNTER . . . NiB $245 Ex $205 Gd $165
12 or 20 ga. w/3-inch chamber. 22- or 24-inch rifled bbl. Weight: 9 lbs. Matte black receiver and bbl. Walnut finished hardwood Monte Carlo stock. Made from 1997 to date.

MODEL ULTRA SLUG HUNTER DELUXE . . . . . NiB $315 Ex $195 Gd $134
Similar to Ultra Slug Hunter model except with compensated bbl. Made from 1997 to date.

HECKLER & KOCH FABARM SHOTGUNS — Oberndorf am Neckar, West Germany, and Sterling, Virginia

CLASSIC LION SIDE-BY-SIDE SHOTGUN
12 ga. only. 28- or 30-inch non-ported Tribor bbl. w/3-inch chamber. 46.5 to 48.5-inches overall. Weight: 7 to 7.2 lbs. Five choke tubes; C, IC, M, IM, F. Traditional boxlock design. Oil-finished walnut forearms and stocks w/diamond-cut checkering. Imported from 1999 to date.
Classic Lion Grade I . . . . NiB $1393 Ex $1131 Gd $795
Classic Lion Grade II . . . . NiB $2092 Ex $1675 Gd $1168

CAMO LION SEMI-AUTO SHOTGUN . . . . NiB $917 Ex $789 Gd $509
12 ga. Only. 24 to 28-inches Tribor bbl. 44.25-48.25-inches overall. Weight: 7-7.2 lbs. 3 inch chamber w/5 choke tubes - C, IC, M, IM, F. Two round mag. Camo covered walnut stock w/rear front bar sights. Imp. 1999 to date.

MAX LION O/U SHOTGUN . . . . NiB $1845 Ex $1565 Gd $902
12 or 20 ga. 26- 28- or 30-inch TriBore system bbls. 42.5-47.25-inches overall. Weight: 6.8-7.8 lbs. 3-inch chamber w/5 choke tubes - C, IC, M, IM, F. Single selective adj. trigger and auto ejectors. Side plates w/high-grade stock and rubber recoil pad. Made from 1999 to date.

RED LION MARK II SEMI-AUTO
SHOTGUN . . . . NiB $829 Ex $657 Gd $463
12 ga. Only. 24- 26- or 28-inch TriBore system bbls. 44.25 to 48.25-inches overall. Weight: 7 to 7.2 lbs. 3-inch chamber w/five choke tubes- C, IC, M, IM, F. Two round magazine. Matte finish w/walnut wood stock. Rubber vented recoil pad w/leather cover. Made from 1999 to date.

SILVER LION O/U SHOTGUN . . . . NiB $1243 Ex $991 Gd $699
12 or 20 ga. 26- 28- or 30-inch TriBore system bbls. 43.25-47.25 inchesoverall. 3-inch chamber w/5 choke tubes - C, IC, M, IM, F. Single selective trig. and auto ejectors. Wal. stock w/rubber recoil pad. Made from 1999 to date.

SPORTING CLAY LION
SEMI-AUTO SHOTGUN . . . . NiB $975 Ex $758 Gd $531
12 ga. only. 28- or 30-inch bbl. w/3-inch chamber and ported Tribore system barrel. Matte finish w/gold plated trigger and carrier release button. Made from 1999 to date.

HERCULES SHOTGUNS

See Listings under "W" for Montgomery Ward.

HEYM SHOTGUNS — Münnerstadt, Germany

MODEL 22S
"SAFETY" SHOTGUN/
RIFLE COMBINATION . . . . NiB $3675 Ex $2798 Gd $1953
16 and 20 ga. Cal.: .22 Mag., .22 Hornet, .222 Rem., .222 Rem. Mag., 5.6x50R Mag., 6.5x57R, 7x57R, .243 Win. 24-inch bbls. 40 inches overall. Weight: About 5.5 lbs. Single-set trigger. Left-side bbl. selector. Integral dovetail base for scope mounting. Arabesque engraving. Walnut stock. Disc. 1993.

MODEL 55 BF SHOTGUN/
RIFLE COMBO . . . . NiB $6500 Ex $5026 Gd $4214
12, 16 and 20 ga. Calibers: 5.6x50R Mag., 6.5x57R, 7x57R, 7x65R, .243 Win., .308 Win., .30-06. 25-inch bbls., 42 inches overall. Weight: About 6.75 lbs. Black satin-finished, corrosion-resistant bbls. of Krupp special steel. Hand-checkered walnut stock w/long pistol-grip. Hand-engraved leaf scroll. German cheekpiece. Disc. 1988.

J. C. HIGGINS

See Sears, Roebuck & Company.

HUGLU HUNTING FIREARMS — Huglu, Turkey. Imported by Turkish Firearms Corp.
MODEL 101 B 12 AT-DT
COMBO O/U TRAP . . . . NiB $2299 Ex $1792 Gd $1363
Over/Under boxlock. 12 ga. w/3-inch chambers. Combination 30- or 32-inch top single & O/U bbls. w/fixed chokes or choke tubes. Weight: 8 lbs. Automatic ejectors or extractors. Single selective trigger. Manual safety. Circassian walnut Monte Carlo trap stock w/palm-swell grip and recoil pad. Silvered frame w/engraving. Imported from 1993 to 1997.

Heym Model 22S
"Safety" Shotgun/Rifle Combination Gun

Heym Model 55
BF Shotgun/Rifle

MODEL 101 B 12 ST O/U TRAP.... NiB $1499 Ex $1208 Gd $856
Same as Model 101 AT-DT except in 32-inch O/U configuration only. Imported from 1994 to 1996.

MODEL 103 B 12 ST O/U
Boxlock. Gauges: 12, 16, 20, 28 or .410. 28-inch bbls. w/fixed chokes. Engraved action w/inlaid game scene and dummy sideplates. Double triggers, extractors and manual safety. Weight: 7.5 lbs. Circassian walnut stock. Imported 1995 to 1996.
Model 103B w/extractors .... NiB $1135 Ex $907 Gd $650
28 and .410, add $100

MODEL 103 C 12 ST O/U
Same general specs as Model 103 B 12 S except w/extractors or ejectors. 12 or 20 ga. w/3-inch chambers. Black receiver w/50% engraving coverage. Imported from 1995 to 1097.
Model 103C w/extractors .... NiB $809 Ex $615 Gd $456
Model 103C w/ejectors.......... NiB $899 Ex $715 Gd $556

MODEL 103 D 12 ST O/U
Same gen. specs as Mdl. 103 B 12 ST except stand. boxlock. Ext. or eject. 12 or 20 ga. w/3-inch chambers. 80% engraving coverage. Imp. from 1995 to 1997.
Model 103D w/extractors .... NiB $899 Ex $676 Gd $524
Model 103D w/ejectors .... NiB $999 Ex $776 Gd $624

MODEL 103 F 12 ST O/U
Same as Model 103 B except extractors or ejectors. 12 or 20 ga. only. 100% engraving coverage. Imported from 1996 to 1997.
Model 103F w/extractors .... NiB $949 Ex $775 Gd $598
Model 103F w/ejectors .... NiB $1060 Ex $892 Gd $649

MODEL 104 A 12 ST O/U
Boxlock. Gauges: 12, 20, 28 or .410. 28-inch bbls. w/fixed chokes or choke tubes. Silvered, engraved receiver w/15% engraving coverage. Double triggers, manual safety and extractors or ejectors. Weight: 7.5 lbs. Circassian walnut stock w/field dimensions. Imported 1995 to 1997.
Model 104A w/extractors ....NiB $699 Ex $565 Gd $420

Model 104A w/ejectors.......... NiB $709 Ex $478 Gd $368
28 and .410, add $100
W/Choke Tubes, add $50

MODEL 200 SERIES DOUBLE
Boxlock. Gauges: 12, 20, 28, or .410 w/3-inch chambers. 28-inch bbls. w/fixed chokes. Silvered, engraved receiver. Extractors, manual safety, single selective trigger or double triggers. Weight: 7.5 lbs. Circassian walnut stock. Imported from 1995 to 1997.
Model 200 (w/15%
engraving coverage, SST) .... NiB $910 Ex $796 Gd $544
Model 201 (w/30%
engraving coverage, SST)....... NiB $1187 Ex $1033 Gd $808
Model 202 (w/Greener
cross bolt, DT)................. NiB $799 Ex $559 Gd $390
28 and .410, add $100

HIGH STANDARD SPORTING ARMS — East Hartford, Connecticut, Formerly High Standard Mfg. Corp. of Hamden, Conn.

In 1966, High Standard introduced new series of Flite-King Pumps and Supermatic autoloaders, both readily identifiable by the damascened bolt and restyled checkering. To avoid confusion, these models are designated "Series II" in this text. This is not an official factory designation. Operation of this firm was discontinued in 1984.

FLITE-KING FIELD
PUMP—12 GA.................. NiB $210 Ex $152 Gd $92
Hammerless. Magazine holds five rounds. Bbls.: 26-inch IC, 28-inch M or F, 30-inch F choke. Weight: 7.25 lbs. Plain pistol-grip stock and slide handle. Made from 1960 to 1966.

FLITE-KING BRUSH—12 GA. ...... NiB $237 Ex $207 Gd $166
Same as Flite-King Field 2 except has 18- or 20-inch bbl. (cylinder bore) w/rifle sights. Made from 1962 to 1964.

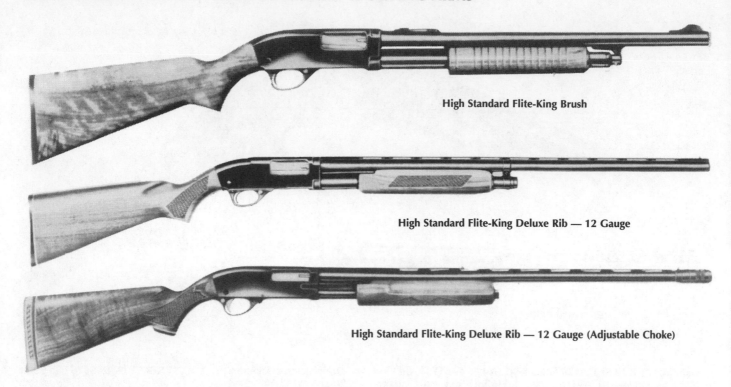

High Standard Flite-King Brush

High Standard Flite-King Deluxe Rib — 12 Gauge

High Standard Flite-King Deluxe Rib — 12 Gauge (Adjustable Choke)

FLITE-KING BRUSH DELUXE . . . . . . NiB $235 Ex $177 Gd $105
Same as Flite-King Brush except has adj. peep rear sight, checkered pistol grip, recoil pad, fluted slide handle, swivels and sling. Not available w/18-inch bbl. Made from 1964 to 1966.

FLITE-KING BRUSH (SERIES II) . . . . NiB $235 Ex $177 Gd $105
Same as Flite-King Deluxe 12 (II) except has 20-inch bbl., cylinder bore, w/rifle sights. Weight: 7 lbs. Made from 1966 to 1975.

FLITE-KING BRUSH DELUXE (II) . . NiB $247 Ex $187 Gd $115
Same as Flite-King Brush (II) except has adj. peep rear sight, swivels and sling. Made from 1966-75.

FLITE-KING DELUXE 12 GA. (SERIES II)
Hammerless. Five round magazine. 27-inch plain bbls.w/adj. choke. 26-inch IC, 28-inch M or F. 30-inch F choke. Weight: About 7.25 lbs. Checkered pistol-grip stock and forearm, recoil pad. Made from 1966 to 1975.
W/adj. choke . . . . NiB $207 Ex $147 Gd $99
W/O adj. choke . . . . NiB $207 Ex $147 Gd $99

FLITE-KING DELUXE
20, 28, .410 GA. (SERIES II) . . . . . . NiB $225 Ex $158 Gd $112
Same as Flite-King Deluxe 12 (II) except chambered for 20 and .410 ga. 3-inch shell, 28 ga. 2.75-inch shell w/20- or 28-inch plain bbl. Weight: About 6 lbs. Made from 1966 to 1975.

FLITE-KING DELUXE RIB 12 GA. . . . . . NiB $245 Ex $191 Gd $125
Same as Flite-King Field 12 except vent rib bbl. (28-inch M or F. 30-inch F). Checkered stock and forearm. Made from 1961-66.

FLITE-KING DELUXE RIB 12 GA. (II)
Same as Flite-King Deluxe 12 (II) except has vent rib bbl., available in 27-inch w/adj. choke, 28-inch M or F, 30-inch F choke. Made from 1966 to 1975.
W/adj. choke . . . . NiB $245 Ex $191 Gd $115
W/O adj. choke. . . . . NiB $245 Ex $191 Gd $115

FLITE-KING DELUXE RIB 20 GA. . . . . . NiB $230 Ex $174 Gd $112
Same as Flite-King Field 20 except vent-rib bbl. (28 inch M or F), checkered stock and slide handle. Made from 1962 to 1966.

FLITE-KING DELUXE RIB 20, 28, .410 GA. (SERIES II)
Same as Flite-King Deluxe 20, 28, .410 (II) except 20 ga. available w/27-inch adj. choke, 28-inch M or F choke. Weight: about 6.25 lbs. Made from 1966 to 1975.
W/adj. choke. . . . . NiB $230 Ex $174 Gd $112
W/O adj. choke. . . . . NiB $230 Ex $174 Gd $112

FLITE-KING DELUXE SKEET GUN
12 GA. (SERIES II) . . . . NiB $293 Ex $198 Gd $94
Same as Flite-King Deluxe Rib 12 (II) except available only w/26-inch vent rib bbl., SK choke, recoil pad optional. Made from 1966 to 1975.

FLITE-KING DELUXE SKEET GUN
20, 28, .410 GA. (SERIES II) . . . . NiB $454 Ex $39 Gd $243
Same as Flite-King Deluxe Rib 20, 28, .410 (II) except available only w/26-inch vent-rib bbl., SK choke. Made 1966 to 1975.

FLITE-KING DELUXE
TRAP GUN (II) . . . . NiB $277 Ex $195 Gd $115
Same as Flite-King Deluxe Rib 12 (II) except available only w/30-inch vent-rib bbl., F choke; trap-style stock. Made 1966 to 1975.

FLITE-KING FIELD PUMP 20 GA. . . . . . NiB $200 Ex $132 Gd $109
Hammerless. Chambered for 3-inch Magnum shells, also handles 2.75-inch. Magazine holds four rounds. Bbls.: 26-inch IC, 28-inch M or F choke. Weight: About 6 lbs. Plain pistol-grip stock and slide handle. Made from 1961 to 1966.

FLITE-KING PUMP SHOTGUNS 16 GA.
Same general specifications as Flite-King 12 except not available in Brush, Skeet and Trap Models or 30-inch bbl. Values same as for 12-ga. guns. Made from 1961 to 1965.

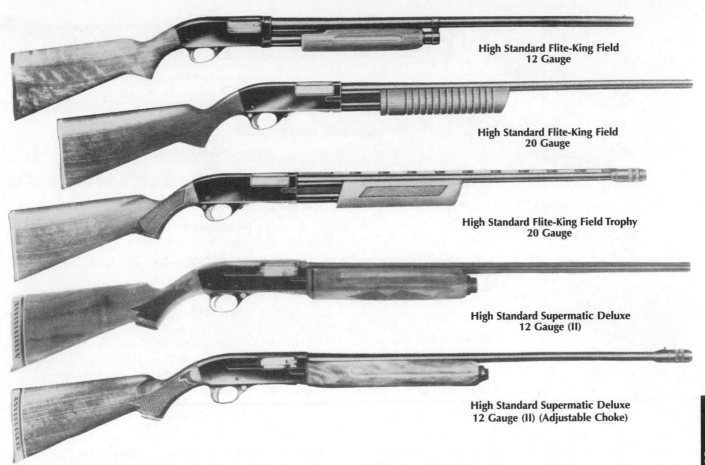

High Standard Flite-King Field
12 Gauge

High Standard Flite-King Field
20 Gauge

High Standard Flite-King Field Trophy
20 Gauge

High Standard Supermatic Deluxe
12 Gauge (II)

High Standard Supermatic Deluxe
12 Gauge (II) (Adjustable Choke)

FLITE-KING PUMP SHOTGUNS (.410 GA.)
Same general specifications as Flite-King 20 except not available in Special and Trophy Models, or w/other than 26-inch choke bbl. Add $100 to 20 gauge price. Made from 1962 to 1966.

FLITE-KING SKEET
12 GA. . . . . **NiB $290 Ex $219 Gd $147**
Same as Flite-King Deluxe Rib except 26-inch vent rib bbl., w/SK choke. Made from 1962 to 1966.

FLITE-KING SPECIAL 12 GA. . . . . . . **NiB $200 Ex $126 Gd $109**
Same as Flite-King Field 12 except has 27-inch bbl. w/adj. choke. Made from 1960 to 1966.

FLITE-KING SPECIAL 20 GA. . . . . . **NiB $200 Ex $126 Gd $109**
Same as Flite-King Field 20 except has 27-inch bbl. w/adj. choke. Made from 1961 to 1966.

FLITE-KING TRAP 12 GA. . . . . **NiB $275 Ex $197 Gd $105**
Same as Flite-King Deluxe Rib 12 except 30-inch vent rib bbl., F choke, special trap stock w/recoil pad. Made from 1962 to 1966.

FLITE-KING TROPHY 12 GA. . . . . . . **NiB $220 Ex $177 Gd $92**
Same as Flite-King Deluxe Rib 12 except has 27-inch vent rib bbl. w/adj. choke. Made from 1960 to 1966.

FLITE-KING TROPHY 20 GA. . . . . . . **NiB $220 Ex $177 Gd $92**
Same as Flite-King Deluxe Rib 20 except has 27-inch vent rib bbl. w/adj. choke. Made from 1962 to 1966.

SUPERMATIC DEER GUN . . . . **NiB $277 Ex $135 Gd $93**
Same as Supermatic Field 12 except has 22-inch bbl. (cylinder bore) w/rifle sights, checkered stock and forearm, recoil pad. Weight: 7.75 lbs. Made in 1965.

SUPERMATIC DELUXE 12 GA. (SERIES II)
Gas-operated autoloader. Four round magazine. Bbls.: Plain; 27-inch w/adj. choke (disc. about 1970); 26-inch IC, 28-inch M or F. 30-inch F choke. Weight: About 7.5 lbs. Checkered pistol-grip stock and forearm, recoil pad. Made from 1966 to 1975.
W/adj. choke . . . . **NiB $277 Ex $135 Gd $93**
Vent rib . . . . **Add $20**

SUPERMATIC DELUXE 20 GA. (SERIES II)
Same as Supermatic Deluxe 12 (II) except chambered for 20 ga. Three inch shell; bbls. available in 27-inch w/adj. choke (disc. about 1970), 26-inch IC, 28-inch M or F choke. Weight: About 7 lbs. Made from 1966 to 1975.
W/adj. choke . . . . **NiB $315 Ex $199 Gd $99**
Vent Rib . . . . **Add $20**

SUPERMATIC DELUXE DEER GUN (II) NiB $270 Ex $195 Gd $110
Same as Supermatic Deluxe 12 (II) except has 22-inch bbl., cylinder bore, w/rifle sights. Weight: 7.75 lbs. Made from 1966 to 1974.

SUPERMATIC DELUXE DUCK
12 GA. MAGNUM (SERIES II) . . . . . **NiB $286 Ex $170 Gd $100**
Same as Supermatic Deluxe 12 (II) except chambered for 3-inch magnum shells, 3-round magazine, 30-inch plain bbl., F choke. Weight: 8 lbs. Made from 1966 to 1974.

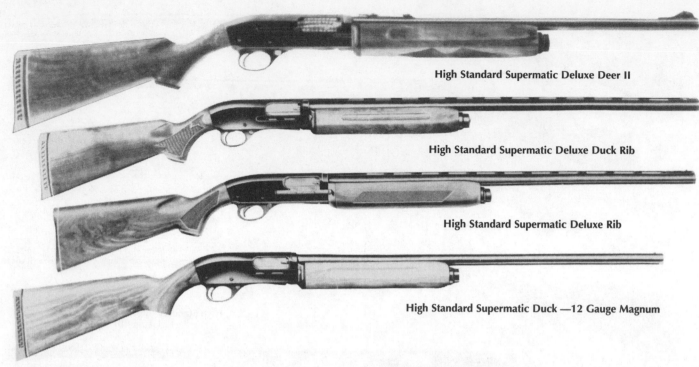

High Standard Supermatic Deluxe Deer II

High Standard Supermatic Deluxe Duck Rib

High Standard Supermatic Deluxe Rib

High Standard Supermatic Duck —12 Gauge Magnum

SUPERMATIC DELUXE RIB
12 GA. . . . . **NiB $270 Ex $190 Gd $100**
Same as Supermatic Field 12 except vent rib bbl. (28-inch M or F, 30-inch F), checkered stock and forearm. Made from 1961 to 1966.

SUPERMATIC DELUXE RIB 12 GA. (II)
Same as Supermatic Deluxe 12 (II) except has vent rib bbl.; available in 27-inch w/adj. choke, 28-inch M or F, 30-inch F choke. Made from 1966 to 1975.
W/adj. choke . . . . **NiB $270 Ex $190 Gd $125**
Vent rib . . . . **Add $25**

SUPERMATIC DELUXE RIB
20 GA. . . . . **NiB $299 Ex $211 Gd $125**
Same as Supermatic Field 20 except vent rib bbl. (28-inch M or F), checkered stock and forearm. Made from 1963 to 1966.

SUPERMATIC DELUXE RIB 20 GA. (II)
Same as Supermatic Deluxe 20 (II) except has vent rib bbl. Made from 1966 to 1975.
W/adj. choke . . . . **NiB $299 Ex $211 Gd $125**
Vent rib . . . . **Add $20**

SUPERMATIC DELUXE
SKEET GUN
12 GA. (SERIES II) . . . . **NiB $290 Ex $188 Gd $108**
Same as Supermatic Deluxe Rib 12 (II) except available only w/26-inch vent rib bbl., SK choke. Made from 1966 to 1975.

SUPERMATIC DELUXE SKEET GUN
20 GA. (SERIES II) . . . . **NiB $320 Ex $227 Gd $125**
Same as Supermatic Deluxe Rib 20 (II) except available only w/26-inch vent rib bbl., SK choke. Made from 1966 to 1975.

SUPERMATIC DELUXE
TRAP GUN (SERIES II)
 . . . . **NiB $275 Ex $207 Gd $122**
Same as Supermatic Deluxe Rib 12 (II) except available only w/30-inch vent rib bbl., full choke; trap-style stock. Made 1966 to 1975.

SUPERMATIC DELUXE DUCK RIB
12 GA. MAG. (SERIES II) . . . . **NiB $305 Ex $219 Gd $139**
Same as Supermatic Deluxe Rib 12 (II) except chambered for 3-inch magnum shells, 3-round magazine; 30-inch vent rib bbl., F choke. Weight: 8 lbs. Made from 1966 to 1975.

SUPERMATIC DUCK 12 GA. MAG. . . . . **NiB $285 Ex $189 Gd $119**
Same as Supermatic Field 12 except chambered for 3-inch Magnum shell, 30-inch F choke bbl., recoil pad. Made from 1961 to 1966.

SUPERMATIC TROPHY 12 GA. . . . . **NiB $225 Ex $149 Gd $102**
Same as Supermatic Deluxe Rib 12 except has 27-inch vent-rib bbl. w/adj. choke. Made from 1961 to 1966.

SUPERMATIC DUCK RIB 12 GA. MAG. . . . . . **NiB $325 Ex $239 Gd $159**
Same as Supermatic Duck 12 Magnum except has vent rib bbl., checkered stock and forearm. Made from 1961 to 1966.

SUPERMATIC FIELD AUTOLOADING
SHOTGUN 12 GA. . . . . **NiB $225 Ex $178 Gd $106**
Gas-operated. Magazine holds four rounds. Bbls.: 26-inch IC, 28-inch M or F choke, 30-inch F choke. Weight: About 7.5 lbs. Plain pistol-grip stock and forearm. Made from 1960 to 1966.

SUPERMATIC FIELD AUTOLOADING
SHOTGUN 20 GA. . . . . **NiB $245 Ex $189 Gd $120**
Gas-operated. Chambered for 3-inch mag. shells, also handles 2.75-inch. Magazine holds three rounds. Bbls.: 26-inch IC, 28-inch M or F choke. Weight: About 7 lbs. Plain pistol-grip stock and forearm. Made from 1963 to 1966.

SUPERMATIC SHADOW AUTOMATIC . . . **NiB $400 Ex $334 Gd $261**
Gas-operated. Ga.: 12, 20, 2.75- or 3-inch chamber in 12 ga., 3-inch in 20 ga. Mag. holds four 2.75-inch shells, three 3-inch. Bbls.: Full-size airflow rib; 26-inch (IC or SK choke), 28-inch (M, IM or F), 30-inch (trap or F choke), 12-ga. 3-inch Mag. available only in 30-inch F choke; 20 ga. not available in 30-inch. Weight: 12 ga., 7 lbs. Checkered walnut stock and forearm. Made 1974 to 1975 by Caspoll Int'l., Inc., Tokyo.

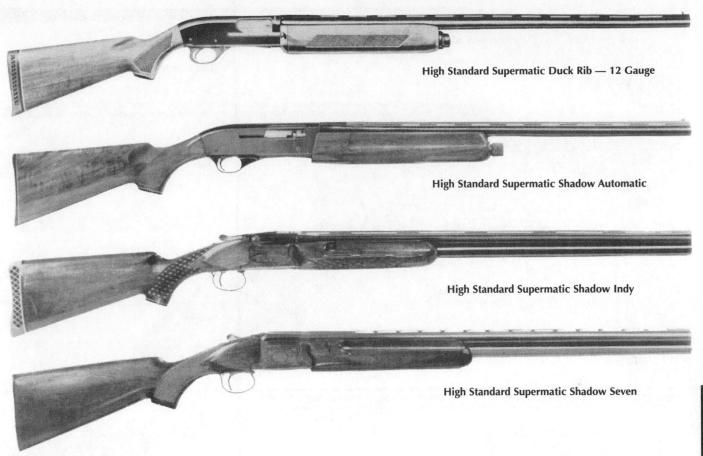

High Standard Supermatic Duck Rib — 12 Gauge

High Standard Supermatic Shadow Automatic

High Standard Supermatic Shadow Indy

High Standard Supermatic Shadow Seven

SUPERMATIC SHADOW

INDY O/U . . . . **NiB 860 Ex $716 Gd $457**
Boxlock. Fully engraved receiver. Selective auto ejectors. Selective single trigger. 12 ga. 2.75-inch chambers. Bbls.: Full-size airflow rib; 27.5 inch both SK choke, 29.75-inch IM/F or F/F. Weight: W/29.75-inch bbls., 8 lbs. 2 oz. Pistol-grip stock w/recoil pad, ventilated forearm, skip checkering. Made 1974 to 1975 by Caspoll Int'l., Inc., Tokyo.

SUPERMATIC SHADOW SEVEN . . . **NiB $695 Ex $467 Gd $346**
Same general specifications as Shadow Indy except has conventional vent rib, less elaborate engraving, standard checkering forearm is not vented, no recoil pad. 27.5-inch bbls.; also available in IC/M, M/F choke. Made from 1974 to 1975.

SUPERMATIC SKEET 12 GA. . . . . . . **NiB $290 Ex $203 Gd $173**
Same as Supermatic Deluxe Rib 12 except 26-inch vent-rib bbl. w/SK choke. Made from 1962 to 1966.

SUPERMATIC SKEET 20 GA. . . . . . . **NiB $338 Ex $239 Gd $193**
Same as Supermatic Deluxe Rib 20 except 26-inch vent-rib bbl. w/SK choke. Made from 1964 to 1966.

SUPERMATIC SPECIAL 12 GA. . . . . . **NiB $230 Ex $178 Gd $116**
Same as Supermatic Field 12 except has 27-inch bbl. w/adj. choke. Made from 1960 to 1966.

SUPERMATIC SPECIAL 20 GA. . . . . . **NiB $260 Ex $197 Gd $128**
Same as Supermatic Field 20 except has 27-inch bbl. w/adj. choke. Made from 1963 to 1966.

SUPERMATIC TRAP 12 GA. . . . . **NiB $275 Ex $173 Gd $103**
Same as Supermatic Deluxe Rib 12 except 30-inch vent rib bbl., F choke, special trap stock w/recoil pad. Made from 1962 to 1966.

SUPERMATIC TROPHY 20 GA. . . . . **NiB $300 Ex $190 Gd $123**
Same as Supermatic Deluxe Rib 20 except has 27-inch vent rib bbl. w/adj. choke. Made from 1963 to 1966.

HOLLAND & HOLLAND, LTD. —
London England

BADMINTON MODEL HAMMERLESS DOUBLE-BARREL SHOTGUN. ORIGINALLY NO. 2 GRADE
General specifications same as Royal Model except without self-opening action. Made as a game gun or pigeon and wildfowl gun. Introduced in 1902. Disc.
W/double triggers . . . . . . **NiB $24,966 Ex $19,794 Gd $16,015**
W/single trigger . . . . **NiB $25,966 Ex $20,800 Gd $17,015**
20 ga., add. 25%
28 ga., add. 40%
.410, add 65%

CENTENARY MODEL HAMMERLESS DOUBLE-BARREL SHOTGUN
Lightweight (5.5 lbs.). 12 ga. game gun designed for 2-inch shell. Made in four grades — Model Deluxe, Royal, Badminton, Dominion. Values: Add 35% to prices shown for standard guns in those grades. Disc. 1962.

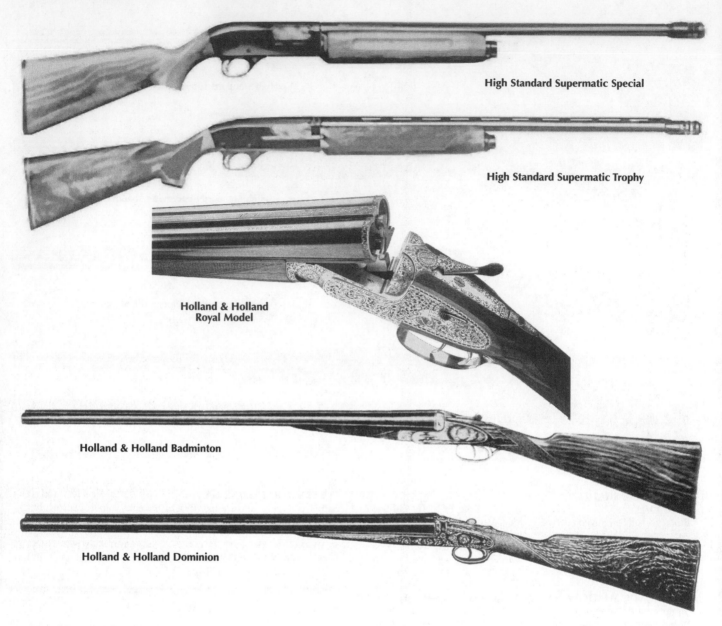

High Standard Supermatic Special

High Standard Supermatic Trophy

Holland & Holland
Royal Model

Holland & Holland Badminton

Holland & Holland Dominion

DOMINION MODEL HAMMERLESS
DOUBLE-BBL. SHOTGUN .... NiB $6750 Ex $5438 Gd $3798
Game Gun. Sidelock. Auto ejectors. Double triggers. Gauges: 12, 16, 20. bbls. 25- to 30-inch, any standard boring. Checkered stock and forend, straight grip standard. Disc. 1967.

MODEL DELUXE HAMMERLESS DOUBLE
Same as Royal Model except has special engraving and exhibition grade stock and forearm. Currently manufactured.
W/double triggers ...... NiB $42,150 Ex $40,320 Gd $32,178
W/single trigger .... NiB $64,675 Ex $51,740 Gd $35,183

NORTHWOOD MODEL HAMMERLESS
DOUBLE-BARREL SHOTGUN .. NiB $5974 Ex $4577 Gd $3815
Anson & Deeley system boxlock. Auto ejectors. Double triggers. Gauges: 12, 16, 20, 28 in Game Model; 28 ga. not offered in Pigeon Model; Wildfowl Model in 12 ga. only (3-inch chambers available). Bbls.: 28-inch standard in Game and Pigeon Models, 30-inch in

Wildfowl Model; other lengths, any standard choke combination available. Weight: From 5 to 7.75 lbs. depending on ga. and bbls. Checkered straight-grip or pistol-grip stock and forearm. Disc. 1990.

RIVIERA MODEL
PIGEON GUN .... NiB $31,174 Ex $22,172 Gd $18,328
Same as Badminton Model but supplied w/two sets of bbls., double triggers. Disc. 1967.

ROYAL MODEL HAMMERLESS DOUBLE
Self-opening. Sidelocks hand-detachable. Auto ejectors. Double triggers or single trigger. Gauges: 12, 16, 20, 28 .410. Built to customer's specifications as to bbl. length, chokes, etc. Made as a Game Gun or Pigeon and Wildfowl Gun, the latter having treble-grip action and side clips. Checkered stock and forend, straight grip standard. Made from 1885, disc. 1951.
W/double triggers ...... NiB $37,826 Ex $30,060 Gd $26,000
W/single trigger .... NiB $43,376 Ex $40,700 Gd $34,476

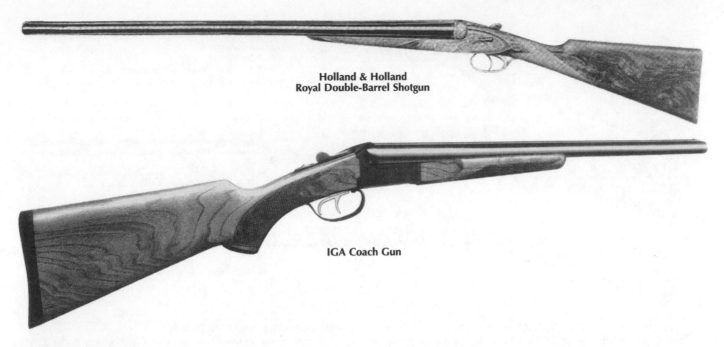

**Holland & Holland
Royal Double-Barrel Shotgun**

IGA Coach Gun

ROYAL MODEL O/U

Sidelocks, hand-detachable. Auto-ejectors. Double triggers or single trigger. 12 ga. Built to customer's specifications as to bbl. length, chokes, etc. Made as a Game Gun or Pigeon and Wildfowl Gun. Checkered stock and forend, straight grip standard. Note: In 1951 Holland & Holland introduced its New Model Under/Over w/an improved, narrower action body. Disc. 1960.

**New model
(double triggers)** . . . . NiB $38,026 Ex $30,420 Gd $20,686
**New model
(single trigger)** . . . . NiB $39,650 Ex $31,720 Gd $21,570
**Old model
(double triggers)** . . . . NiB $32,436 Ex $25,948 Gd $17,645
**Old model
(single trigger)** . . . . NiB $34,450 Ex $27,560 Gd $18,741

SINGLE-SHOT SUPER TRAP GUN

Anson & Deeley system boxlock. Auto-ejector. No safety. 12 ga. Bbls.: Wide vent rib, 30- or 32-inch, w/Extra Full choke. Weight: About 8.75 lbs. Monte Carlo stock w/pistol grip and recoil pad, full beavertail forearm. Models differ in grade of engraving and wood used. Disc.

**Standard
grade.** . . . . NiB $4500 Ex $2797 Gd $1342
**Deluxe
grade** . . . . NiB $7015 Ex $5561 Gd $3123
**Exhibition
grade** . . . . NiB $8,901 Ex $6755 Gd $4009

SPORTING O/U . . . . NiB $27,985 Ex $22,395 Gd $15,240
Blitz action. Auto ejectors; single selective trigger. Gauges: 12 or 20 w/2.75-inch chambers. Barrels: 28- to 32-inch w/screw-in choke tubes. Hand-checkered European walnut straight-grip or pistol grip stock, forearm. Made from 1993 to 2003   .

HOLLAND & HOLLAND SPORTING

O/U DELUXE . . . . NiB $36,736 Ex $29,468 Gd $20,166
Same general specs as Sporting O/U except better engraving and select wood. Made from 1993 to date.

HUNTER ARMS COMPANY —
Fulton, New York

FULTON HAMMERLESS DOUBLE-BARREL SHOTGUN

Boxlock. Plain extractors. Double triggers or non-selective single trigger. Gauges: 12 16, 20. Bbls.: 26- to 32-inch various choke combinations. Weight: about 7 lbs. Checkered pistol-grip stock and forearm. Disc. 1948.
W/double triggers . . . . NiB $700 Ex $417 Gd $316
W/single trigger . . . . NiB $900 Ex $617 Gd $516

SPECIAL HAMMERLESS DOUBLE-BARREL SHOTGUN

Boxlock. Plain extractors. Double triggers or non-selective single trigger. Gauges: 12,16, 20. Bbls.: 26- to 30-inch various choke combinations. Weight: 6.5 to 7.25 lbs. depending on bbl. length and ga. Checkered full pistol-grip stock and forearm. Disc. 1948.
W/double triggers . . . . NiB $830 Ex $576 Gd $422
W/single trigger . . . . NiB $1030 Ex $776 Gd $522

IGA SHOTGUNS — Veranopolis, Brazil
Imported by Stoeger Industries, Inc.
Accokeek, Maryland

COACH GUN

Side-by-side double. Gauges: 12, 20 and .410. 20-inch bbls. w/3-inch chambers. Fixed chokes (standard model) or screw-in tubes (deluxe model). Weight: 6.5 lbs. Double triggers. Ejector and automatic safety. Blued or nickel finish. Hand-rubbed oil-finished pistol grip stock and forend w/hand checkering (hardwood on standard model or Brazilian walnut (deluxe). Imported from 1983 to 2000.
Standard Coach Gun (blued finish) . . . . NiB $350 Ex $258 Gd $159
Standard Coach Gun (nickel finish) . . . NiB $420 Ex $325 Gd $229
**Standard Coach Gun
(engraved stock)** . . . . NiB $385 Ex $292 Gd $190
Deluxe Coach Gun (intro. 1997) . . . NiB $350 Ex $260 Gd $163
Choke tubes, add $50

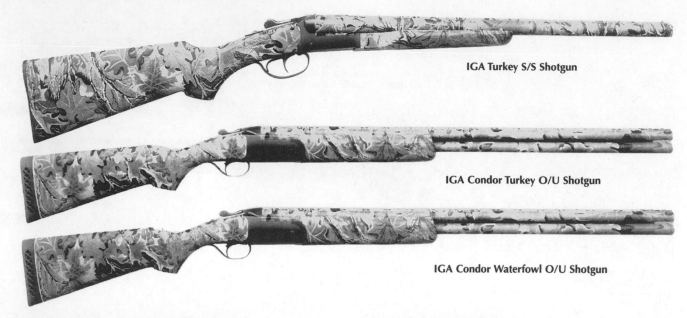

IGA Turkey S/S Shotgun

IGA Condor Turkey O/U Shotgun

IGA Condor Waterfowl O/U Shotgun

CONDOR I O/U SINGLE-TRIGGER SHOTGUN
Gauges: 12 or 20. 26- or 28-inch bbls. of chrome-molybdenum steel. Chokes: Fixed — M/F or IC/M; screw-in choke tubes (12 and 20 ga.). Three inch chambers. Weight: 6.75 to 7 lbs. Sighting rib w/anti-glare surface. Hand-checkered hardwood pistol-grip stock and forend. Imported from 1983 to 1985.
W/fixed chokes . . . . NiB $350 Ex $292 Gd $180
W/screw-in tubes . . . . NiB $450 Ex $390 Gd $276

CONDOR II O/U DOUBLE-TRIGGER
SHOTGUN . . . . NiB $397 Ex $326 Gd $237
Same general specifications as the Condor I O/U except w/double triggers and fixed chokes only; 26-inch bbls., IC/M; 28-inch bbls., M/F.

CONDOR SUPREME . . . . NiB $525 Ex $486 Gd $347
Same general specifications as Condor I except upgraded w/fine-checkered Brazilian walnut buttstock and forend, a matte-laquered finish, and a massive monoblock that joins the bbls. in a solid one-piece assembly at the breech end. Bbls. w/recessed interchangeable choke tubes formulated for use w/steel shot. Automatic ejectors. Imported from 1995 to 2000.

CONDOR TURKEY MODEL
O/U SHOTGUN . . . . NiB $697 Ex $560 Gd $398
12 gauge only. 26-inch vent-rib bbls. w/3-inch chambers fitted w/recessed interchangeable choke tubes. Weight: 8 lbs. Mechanical single trigger. Ejectors and automatic safety. Advantage camouflage on stock and bbls. Made from 1997 to 2000.

CONDOR WATERFOWL MODEL . . . . . NiB $721 Ex $571 Gd $405
Similar to Condor Turkey-Advantage camo model except w/30-inch bbls. Made from 1998 to 2000.

DELUXE HUNTER CLAY SHOTGUN
Same general specifications and values as IGA Condor Supreme. Imported from 1997 to 1999.

MODEL 2000 SHOTGUN. . . . . NiB $415 Ex $324 Gd $254
Gauge: 12 w/3-inch chambers. 26- or 28-inch bbls. of chrome-molybdenum steel w/screw-in choke tubes. Extractors. Manual safety. (Mechanical triggers.) Weight: 7 lbs. Checkered Brazilian hardwood stock w/oil finish. Imported from 1992 to 1995.

REUNA SINGLE-SHOT SHOTGUN
Visible hammer. Under-lever release. Gauges: 12, 20 and .410; 3-inch chambers. 26- or 28-inch bbls. w/fixed chokes or screw-in choke tubes (12 ga. only). Extractors. Weight: 5.25 to 6.5 lbs. Plain Brazilian hardwood stock and semi-beavertail forend. Imported from 1992 to1998.
W/fixed choke . . . . NiB $154 Ex $113 Gd $73
W/choke tubes . . . . NiB $231 Ex $174 Gd $127

UPLANDER SIDE-BY-SIDE SHOTGUN
Gauges: 12, 20, 28 and .410. 26- or 28-inch bbls. of chrome-molybdenum steel. Various fixed-choke combinations; screw-in choke tubes (12 and 20 ga.). Three inch chambers (2.75-inch in 28 ga.). Weight: 6.25 to 7 lbs. Double triggers. Automatic safety. Matte-finished solid sighting rib. Hand checkered pistol-grip or straight stock and forend w/hand-rubbed, oil-finish. Imported from 1997 to 2000.
Upland w/fixed chokes. . . . . .NiB $320 Ex $237 Gd $201
Upland w/screw-in tubes . . . . NiB $350 Ex $289 Gd $226
English model (straight grip) . . . . . . NiB $425 Ex $315 Gd $228
Ladies model . . . . NiB $395 Ex $326 Gd $234
Supreme model . . . . NiB $518 Ex $420 Gd $300
Youth model . . . . NiB $358 Ex $296 Gd $214

UPLANDER TURKEY
MODEL S/S DOUBLE . . . . NiB $513 Ex $419 Gd $299
12 gauge only. 24-inch solid rib bbls. w/3-inch chambers choked F&F. Weight: 6.75 lbs. Double triggers. Automatic safety. Advantage camouflage on stock and bbls. Made from 1997 to 2000.

ITHACA GUN COMPANY — King Ferry (formerly Ithaca), New York. Ithaca Acquisition Corp./Ithaca Gun Co.

MODEL 37 BICENTENNIAL
COMMEMORATIVE. . . . . NiB $595 Ex $497 Gd $359
Limited to issue of 1976. Similar to Model 37 Supreme except has special Bicentennial design etched on receiver, fancy walnut stock and slide handle. Serial numbers U.S.A. 0001 to U.S.A. 1976. Originally issued w/presentation case w/cast-pewter belt buckle. Made in 1976. Best value is for gun in new, unfired condition.

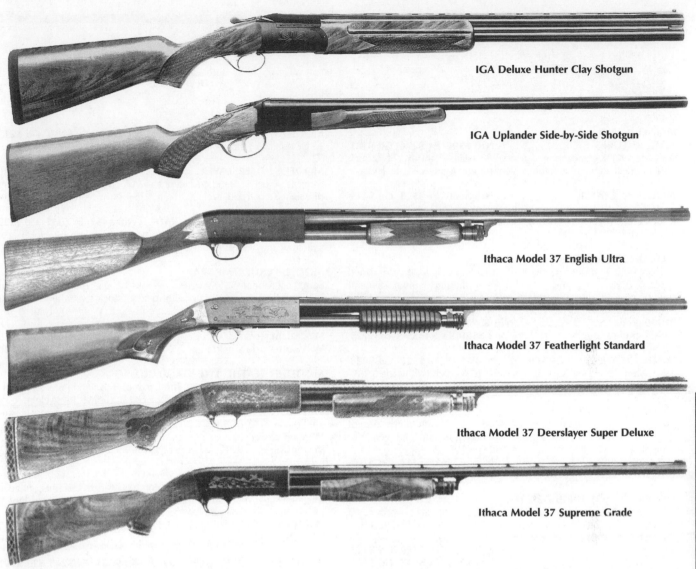

IGA Deluxe Hunter Clay Shotgun

IGA Uplander Side-by-Side Shotgun

Ithaca Model 37 English Ultra

Ithaca Model 37 Featherlight Standard

Ithaca Model 37 Deerslayer Super Deluxe

Ithaca Model 37 Supreme Grade

MODEL 37 DEERSLAYER DELUXE

Formerly "Model 87 Deerslayer Deluxe" reintroduced under the original Model 37 designation w/the same specifications. Available w/smooth bore or rifled bbl. Reintroduced 1996. Disc.

Deluxe model (smoothbore) . . . . . . NiB $498 Ex $428 Gd $294
Deluxe model (rifled bbl.) . . . . NiB $520 Ex $451 Gd $322

MODEL 37 DEERSLAYER II . . . . NiB $520 Ex $478 Gd $342

Gauges: 12 or 20 ga. Five round capacity. 20- or 25-inch rifled bbl. Weight: 7 lbs. Monte Carlo checkered walnut stock and forearm. Receiver drilled and tapped for scope mount. Made 1996 to 2000.

MODEL 37 DEERSLAYER STANDARD . . . . NiB $300 Ex $251 Gd $189

Same as Model 37 Standard except has 20- or 26-inch bbl. bored for rifled slugs, rifle-type open rear sight and ramp front sight. Weight: 5.75 to 6.5 lbs. depending on ga. and bbl. length. Made from 1959-86.

MODEL 37 DEERSLAYER
SUPER DELUXE . . . . NiB $375 Ex $279 Gd $183

Formerly "Deluxe Deerslayer." Same as Model 37 Standard Deerslayer except has stock and slide handle of fancy walnut. Made 1962 to 1986.

MODEL 37 ENGLISH UL. . . . . NiB $525 Ex $429 Gd $308

Same general specifications as Model 37 Ultralite except straight buttstock, 25-inch Hot Forged vent-rib bbl. Made 1984 to 1987.

MODEL 37 FEATHERLIGHT STANDARD GRADE
SLIDE-ACTION REPEATING SHOTGUN

Adaptation of the earlier Remington Model 17, a Browning design patented in 1915. Hammerless. Takedown. Gauges: 12, 16 (disc. 1973), 20. Four round magazine. Bbl. lengths: 26-, 28-, 30-inch (the latter in 12 ga. only); standard chokes. Weight: From 5.75 to 7.5 lbs. depending on ga. and bbl. length. Checkered pistol-grip stock and slide handle. Some guns made in the 1950s and 1960s have grooved slide handle; plain or checkered pistol-grip. Made 1937 to 1984.

Standard w/checkered pistol-grip . . NiB $600 Ex $471 Gd $298
W/plain stock . . . . NiB $295 Ex $206 Gd $181
Mdl 37D Deluxe (1954-77) . . . . NiB $600 Ex $334 Gd $242
Mdl 37DV Deluxe vent rib (1962-84) . . . NiB $600 Ex $334 Gd $242
Mdl 37R Deluxe
solid rib (1955-61) . . . . NiB $600 Ex $334 Gd $242
Mdl 37V Standard
vent rib (1962-84) . . . . NiB $315 Fx $244 Gd $148

**Ithaca Model 51
Deluxe Trap**

**MODEL 37 FIELD GRADE
MAG. W/TUBES** .... NiB $300 Ex $276 Gd $181
Same general specifications as Model 37 Featherlight except 32-inch bbl. and detachable choke tubes. Vent rib bbl. Made 1984 to 1987.

MODEL 37 CLASSIC .... NiB $680 Ex $513 Gd $419
Ggs: 12 or 20 ga. 20- or 28-inch vent rib bbl. w/choke tubes. Knuckle-cut receiver and orig. style "ring-tail" forend. Lim. prod. Made from 1998 to 2005.

MODEL 37 $1000 GRADE
Custom built, elaborately engraved and inlaid w/gold, hand-finished working parts, stock and forend of select figured walnut. General specifications same as standard Model 37. Note: Designated The $1000 Grade prior to World War II. Made 1937 to 1967.
$1000 grade .... NiB $5756 Ex $4590 Gd $3889
$5000 grade................. NiB $520 Ex $4355 Gd $3723

MODEL 37 SUPREME GRADE..... NiB $895 Ex $555 Gd $424
Available in Skeet or Trap Gun, similar to Model 37T. Made 1967-86 and 1997. Subtract $225 for newer models.

MODEL 37 ULTRALITE
Same general specifications as Model 37 Featherlight except streamlined forend, gold trigger, Sid Bell grip cap and vent rib. Weight: 5 to 5.75 lbs. Made from 1984 to 1987.
Standard .... NiB $474 Ex $341 Gd $262
W/choke tubes .... Add $100

MODEL 37R SOLID RIB GRADE
Same general specifications as the Model 37 Featherlight except has a raised solid rib, adding about .25 pounds of weight. Made 1937 to 1967.
W/checkered grip
and slide handle .... NiB $345 Ex $250 Gd $152
W/plain stock .... NiB $245 Ex $147 Gd $101

MODEL 37S SKEET GRADE....... NiB $499 Ex $380 Gd $272
Same general specifications as the Model 37 Featherlight except has vent rib and large extension-type forend; weight: About .5 lb. more. Made from 1937 to 1955.

MODEL 37T TARGET GRADE ..... NiB $475 Ex $349 Gd $219
Same general specifications as Model 37 Featherlight except has vent-rib bbl., checkered stock and slide handle of fancy walnut (choice of skeet- or trap-style stock). Note: This model replaced Model 37S Skeet and Model 37T Trap. Made from 1955- to 191.

MODEL 37T TRAP GRADE .... NiB $475 Ex $382 Gd $244
Same gen. specs. as Mdl. 37S except has straighter trap-style stock of select walnut, recoil pad; weight: About .5 lb. more. Made from 1937-55.

MODEL 37 TURKEYSLAYER
Gauges: 12 ga. (Standard) or 20 ga. (youth). Slide action. 22-inch bbl. Extended choke tube. Weight: 7 lbs. Advantage camouflage or Realtree pattern. Made from 1996 to 2005.
Standard model .... NiB $375 Ex $222 Gd $175
Youth model(intro. 1998)........ NiB $500 Ex $419 Gd $320

MODEL 37 WATERFOWLER ...... NiB $426 Ex $339 Gd $213
12 ga. only w/28-inch bbl. Wetlands camouflage. Made 1998 to 2005.

MODEL 51 DEERSLAYER......... NiB $354 Ex $240 Gd $146
Same as Model 51 Standard except has 24-inch plain bbl. w/slug boring, rifle sights, recoil pad. Weight: About 7.25 lbs. Made from 1972 to 1984.

MODEL 51 SUPREME SKEET GRADE.. NiB $462 Ex $351 Gd $222
Same as Model 51 Standard except 26-inch vent-rib bbl. only, SK choke, skeet-style stock, semi-fancy wood. Weight: About 8 lbs. Made from 1970 to 1987.

MODEL 51 SUPREME TRAP
Same as Model 51 Standard except 12 ga. only, 30-inch bbl. w/broad floating rib, F choke, trap-style stock w/straight or Monte Carlo comb, semifancy wood, recoil pad. Weight: About 8 lbs. Made from 1970 to 1987.
W/straight stock .... NiB $453 Ex $366 Gd $275
W/Monte Carlo stock............................. Add $40

MODEL 51 FEATHERLITE STANDARD
Gas-operated. Gauges: 12, 20. Three round. Bbls.: Plain or vent rib, 30-inch F choke (12 ga. only), 28-inch F or M, 26-inch IC. Weight: 7.25-7.75 lbs. depending on ga. and bbl. Checkered pistol-grip stock, forearm. Made 1970 to 1980. Avail. in 12 and 20 ga., 28-inch M choke only.
W/plain barrel................. NiB $250 Ex $179 Gd $103
W/vent rib .... Add $45

MODEL 51A STANDARD MAGNUM
Same as Model 51 Standard except has 3-inch chamber, handles Magnum shells only; 30-inch bbl. in 12 ga., 28-inch in 20 ga., F or M choke, stock w/recoil pad. Weight: 7.75-8 lbs. Made 1972 to 1982.
W/plain bbl. (disc. 1976) .... NiB $324 Ex $246 Gd $192
W/camo finish .... Add $40

MODEL 51A TURKEY GUN....... NiB $365 Ex $243 Gd $161
Same general specifications as standard Model 51 Magnum except 26-inch bbl. and matte finish. Disc. 1986.

MODEL 66 LONG TOM .... NiB $152 Ex $117 Gd $94
Same as Model 66 Standard except has 36-inch F choke bbl., 12 ga. only, checkered stock and recoil pad standard. Made 1969 to 1974.

MODEL 66 STANDARD SUPER SINGLE LEVER
Single shot. Hand-cocked hammer. Gauges: 12 (disc. 1974), 20, .410, 3-inch chambers. Bbls.: 12 ga., 30-inch F choke, 28-inch F or M; 20 ga., 28-inch F or M; .410, 26-inch F. Weight: About 7 lbs. Plain or checkered straight-grip stock, plain forend. Made from 1963 to 1978.
Standard model .... NiB $150 Ex $103 Gd $82
Vent rib model (20 ga., checkered
stock, recoil pad, 1969-74) ...... NiB $180 Ex $133 Gd $106
Youth model (20 & .410 ga., 26-inch bbl.,
shorter stock, recoil pad, 1965-78).... NiB $204 Ex $152 Gd $112

MODEL 66RS BUCKBUSTER...... NiB $199 Ex $170 Gd $131
Same as Model 66 Standard except has 22-inch bbl. cylinder bore w/rifle sights, later version has recoil pad. Originally offered in 12 and 20 ga.; the former was disc. in 1970. Made from 1967 to 1978.

**Ithaca Model
66RS Buckbuster**

Previously issued as the Ithaca Model 37, the Model 87 guns listed below were made available through the Ithaca Acquisition Corp. From 1986-95. Production of the Model 37 resumed under the original logo in 1996.

MODEL 87 DEERSLAYER SHOTGUN
Gauges: 12 or 20, 3-inch chamber. Bbls.: 18.5-, 20- or 25-inch (w/special or rifled bore). Weight: 6 to 6.75 lbs. Ramp blade front sight, adj. rear. Receiver grooved for scope. Checkered American walnut pistol-grip stock and forearm. Made from 1988 to 1996.

Basic model	NiB $362	Ex $292	Gd $192
Basic Field Combo (w/extra 28-inch bbl.)			
. . . .	NiB $400	Ex $342	Gd $258
Deluxe model	NiB $437	Ex $342	Gd $246
Deluxe Combo (w/extra 28-inch bbl.)			
. . . .	NiB $551	Ex $425	Gd $303
DSPS (8-round model)	NiB $420	Ex $327	Gd $235
Field model	NiB $360	Ex $286	Gd $204
Monte Carlo model	NiB $376	Ex $301	Gd $216
Ultra model (disc. 1991)	NiB $445	Ex $340	Gd $286

MODEL 87 DEERSLAYER II
RIFLED SHOTGUN . . . . NiB $444 Ex $371 Gd $268
Similar to Standard Deerslayer except w/solid frame construction and 25-inch rifled bbl. Monte Carlo stock. Made 1988 to 1996.

MODEL 87 ULTRALITE
FIELD PUMP SHOTGUN . . . . NiB $445 Ex $358 Gd $258
Gauges: 12 and 20; 2.75-inch chambers. 25-inch bbl. w/choke tube. Weight: 5 to 6 lbs. Made from 1988 to 1990.

MODEL 87 FIELD GRADE
Gauge: 12 or 20.; 3-inch chamber. Five round magazine. Fixed chokes or screw-in choke tubes (IC, M, F). Bbls.: 18.5-inch (M&P); 20- and 25-inch (Combo); 26-, 28-, 30-inch vent rib. Weight: 5 to 7 lbs. Made from 1988 to 1996.

Basic field model (disc. 1993) . . .	NiB $360	Ex $239	Gd $143
Camo model	NiB $445	Ex $314	Gd $221
Deluxe model	NiB $435	Ex $390	Gd $279
Deluxe Combo model	NiB $503	Ex $465	Gd $343
English model	NiB $439	Ex $344	Gd $248
Hand grip model			
(w/polymer pistol-grip)	NiB $457	Ex $375	Gd $268
M&P model (disc. 1995)	NiB $400	Ex $329	Gd $237
Supreme model	NiB $639	Ex $504	Gd $357
Turkey model.	NiB $365	Ex $274	Gd $178
Ultra Deluxe model (disc. 1992) .	NiB $359	Ex $295	Gd $216

HAMMERLESS DOUBLE-BARREL SHOTGUNS
Boxlock. Plain extractors, auto ejectors standard on the "E" grades. Double triggers, non-selective or selective single trigger extra. Gauges: Magnum 10, 12; 12, 16, 20, 28, .410. Bbls.: 26- to 32-inch, any standard boring. Weight: 5.75 (.410) to 10.5 lbs. (Magnum 10). Checkered pistol-grip stock and forearm standard.

Higher grades differ from Field Grade in quality of workmanship, grade of wood, checkering, engraving, etc.; general specifications are the same. Ithaca doubles made before 1925 (serial number 425,000) the rotary bolt and a stronger frame were adopted. Values shown are for this latter type; earlier models valued about 50% lower. Smaller gauge guns may command up to 75% higher. Disc. 1948.

Field grade	NiB $995	Ex $760	Gd $537
No. 1 grade.	NiB $1224	Ex $908	Gd $772
No. 2 grade	NiB $2400	Ex $1811	Gd $1054
No. 3 grade	NiB $2293	Ex $1719	Gd $1264
No. 4E grade (ejector)	NiB $5786	Ex $3598	Gd $2886
No. 5E grade (ejector)	NiB $4769	Ex $3669	Gd $4379

Extras:
Magnum 10 or 12 ga.	
(in other than the four highest grades), add	20%
Automatic ejectors (grades No. 1, 2, 3, w/ejectors designated	
No. 1E, 2E, 3E), add	33%
Selective single trigger, add	$200
Non-selective single trigger, add.	$155
Beavertail forend (Field No. 1 or 2), add	$175
Beavertail forend (No. 3 or 4), add.	$175
Beavertail forend (No. 5, 7 or $2000 grade), add	$175
Ventilated rib (No. 4, 5, 7 or $2000 grade), add.	$350
Ventilated rib (lower grades), add.	$200

LSA-55 TURKEY GUN . . . . NiB $836 Ex $693 Gd $531
Over/under shotgun/rifle combination. Boxlock. Exposed hammer. Plain extractor. Single trigger. 12 ga./222 Rem. 24.5-inch ribbed bbls. (rifle bbl. has muzzle brake). Weight: About 7 lbs. Folding leaf rear sight, bead front sight. Checkered Monte Carlo stock and forearm. Made 1970 to 1977 by Oy Tikkakoski AB, Finland.

MAG-10 AUTOMATIC SHOTGUN
Gas-operated. 10 ga. 3.5-inch Magnum. Three round capacity. 32-inch plain (Standard Grade only) or vent-rib bbl. F choke. Weight: 11 lbs., plain bbl.; 11.5 lbs., vent rib. Standard grade has plain stock and forearm. Deluxe and Supreme Grades have checkering, semi-fancy and fancy wood respectively, and stud swivel. All have recoil pad. Deluxe and Supreme grades made 1974 to 191982. Standard Grade intro. in 1977. All grades disc. 1986.

Camo model	NiB $677	Ex $533	Gd $349
Deluxe grade.	NiB $800	Ex $662	Gd $468
Roadblocker	NiB $747	Ex $681	Gd $482
Standard grade, plain barrel	NiB $678	Ex $565	Gd $403
Standard grade,			
ventilated rib	NiB $750	Ex $589	Gd $419
Standard grade, w/tubes	NiB $893	Ex $662	Gd $468
Supreme grade.	NiB $994	Ex $759	Gd $534

SHOTGUNS

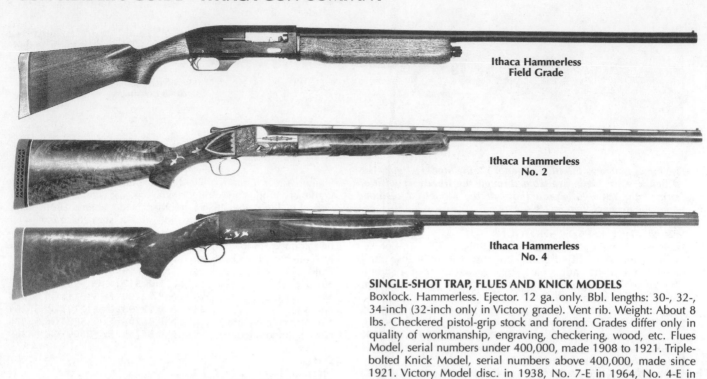

Ithaca Hammerless
Field Grade

Ithaca Hammerless
No. 2

Ithaca Hammerless
No. 4

Ithaca Hammerless
Field Grade

Ithaca Model 5-E

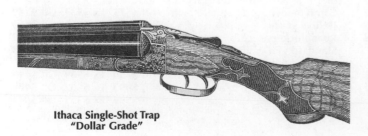

Ithaca Single-Shot Trap
"Dollar Grade"

SINGLE-SHOT TRAP, FLUES AND KNICK MODELS

Boxlock. Hammerless. Ejector. 12 ga. only. Bbl. lengths: 30-, 32-, 34-inch (32-inch only in Victory grade). Vent rib. Weight: About 8 lbs. Checkered pistol-grip stock and forend. Grades differ only in quality of workmanship, engraving, checkering, wood, etc. Flues Model, serial numbers under 400,000, made 1908 to 1921. Triple-bolted Knick Model, serial numbers above 400,000, made since 1921. Victory Model disc. in 1938, No. 7-E in 1964, No. 4-E in 1976, No. 5-E in 1986, Dollar Grade in 1991. Values shown are for Knick Model; Flues models about 50% lower.

Victory grade	NiB $1247	Ex $1044	Gd $746
No. 4-E	NiB $2949	Ex $2399	Gd $1683
No. 5-E	NiB $4000	Ex $2712	Gd $1932
No. 6-E	NiB $15,750	Ex $12,630	Gd $8636
No. 7-E	NiB $6498	Ex $5242	Gd $3646
$5000 grade (prewar $1000 grade)	NiB $9,494	Ex $7394	Gd $5439
Sousa grade (rare)	NiB $13,200+	Ex $10,600+	Gd $7272+

NOTE: *The following Ithaca-Perazzi shotguns were manufactured by Manifattura Armi Perazzi, Brescia, Italy. See also separate Perazzi listings.*

PERAZZI COMPETITION I SKEET . . . NiB $13,655 Ex $12,005 Gd $10,104
Boxlock. Auto ejectors. Single trigger. 12 ga. 26.75-inch vent-rib bbls. SK choke w/integral muzzle brake. Weight: About 7.75 lbs. Checkered skeet-style pistol-grip buttstock and forearm; recoil pad. Made from 1969 to 1974.

PERAZZI COMPETITION TRAP I O/U . . . .
NiB $13,775 Ex $12,045 Gd $10,134
Boxlock. Auto ejectors. Single trigger. 12 ga. 30- or 32-inch vent-rib bbls. IM/F choke. Weight: About 8.5 lbs. Checkered pistol-grip stock, forearm; recoil pad. Made from 1969 to 1974.

PERAZZI COMPETITION I
TRAP SINGLE BARREL . . . . NiB $10,738 Ex $8200 Gd $6551
Boxlock. Auto ejection. 12 ga. 32- or 34-inch bbl., vent rib, F choke. Weight: 8.5 lbs. Checkered Monte Carlo stock and beavertail forearm, recoil pad. Made from 1973 to 1978.

PERAZZI COMPETITION IV
TRAP GUN . . . . NiB $12,299 Ex $10,670 Gd $9,873
Boxlock. Auto ejection. 12 ga. 32- or 34-inch bbl. With high, wide vent rib, four interchangeable choke tubes (Extra Full, F, IM, M). Weight: About 8.75 lbs. Checkered Monte Carlo stock and beavertail forearm, recoil pad. Fitted case. Made from 1977 to 1978.

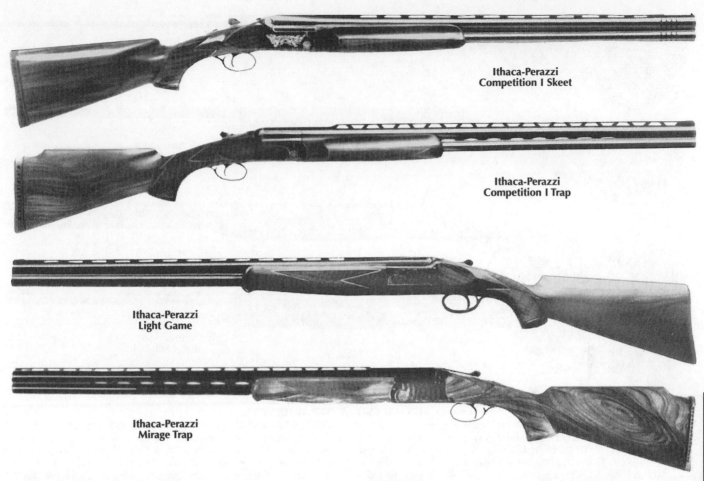

Ithaca-Perazzi Competition I Skeet

Ithaca-Perazzi Competition I Trap

Ithaca-Perazzi Light Game

Ithaca-Perazzi Mirage Trap

PERAZZI LIGHT GAME O/U FIELD
. . . . **NiB $14,122 Ex $13,322 Gd $12,311**
Boxlock. Auto ejectors. Single trigger. 12 ga. 27.5-inch vent rib bbls., M/F or IC/M choke. Weight: 6.75 lbs. Checkered field-style stock and forearm. Made from 1972 to 74.

PERAZZI MIRAGE . . . . **NiB $6000 Ex $4429 Gd $2584**
Same as Mirage Trap except has 28-inch bbls., M and Extra Full choke, special stock and forearm for live bird shooting. Weight: About 8 lbs. Made from 1973 to 1978.

PERAZZI MIRAGE SKEET . . . . . . **NiB $3893 Ex $2962 Gd $2282**
Same as Mirage Trap except has 28-inch bbls. w/integral muzzle brakes, SK choke, skeet-stype stock and forearm. Weight: About 8 lbs. Made from 1973 to 1978.

PERAZZI MIRAGE TRAP . . . . . . **NiB $4076 Ex $3198 Gd $2261**
Same general specifications as MX-8 Trap except has tapered rib. Made from 1973 to 1978.

PERAZZI MT-6 SKEET . . . . **NiB $4056 Ex $3198 Gd $2222**
Same as MT-6 Trap except has 28-inch bbls. w/two skeet choke tubes instead of Extra Full and F, skeet-style stock and forearm. Weight: About 8 lbs. Made from 1976 to 1978.

PERAZZI MT-6 TRAP COMBO . . . . **NiB $5191 Ex $4119 Gd $2854**
MT-6 w/extra single under bbl. w/high-rise aluminum vent rib, 32- or 34-inch; seven interchanageable choke tubes (IC through Extra Full). Fitted case. Made from 1977 to 1978.

PERAZZI MT-6
TRAP O/U . . . . **NiB $3565 Ex $2474 Gd $1992**
Boxlock. Auto selective ejectors. Non-selective single trigger. 12 ga. Barrels separated, wide vent rib, 30-or 32-inch, five interchangeable choke tubes (Extra full, F, IM, M, IC). Weight: About 8.5 lbs. Checkered pistol-grip stock/forearm, recoil pad. Fitted case. Made from 1976 to 1978.

PERAZZI MX
8 TRAP COMBO . . . . **NiB $5585 Ex $4197 Gd $3117**
MX-8 w/extra single bbl., vent rib, 32- or 34-inch, F choke, forearm; two trigger groups included. Made from 1973 to 1978.

PERAZZI MX-8 TRAP
O/U . . . . **NiB $4155 Ex $3334 Gd $2324**
Boxlock. Auto selective ejectors. Non-selective single trigger. 12 ga. Bbls.: High vent rib; 30- or 32-inch, IM/F choke. Weight: 8.25 to 8.5 lbs. Checkered Monte Carlo stock and forearm, recoil pad. Made from 1969 to 1978.

PERAZZI SINGLE-BARREL
TRAP GUN . . . . **NiB $2751 Ex $2015 Gd $1543**
Boxlock. Auto ejection. 12 ga. 34-inch vent rib bbl., F choke. Weight: Abaout 8.5 lbs. Checkered pistol-grip stock, forearm; recoil pad. Made from 1971 to 1972.

The following Ithaca-SKB shotguns, manufactured by SKB Arms Company, Tokyo, Japan, were distributed in the U.S. by Ithaca Gun Company from 1966-1976. See also listings under SKB.

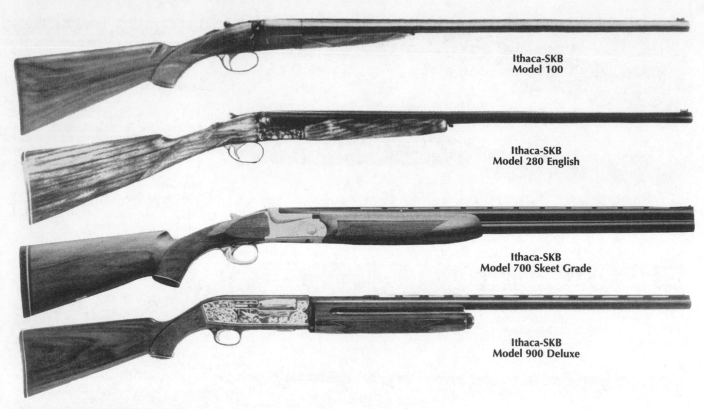

**Ithaca-SKB
Model 100**

**Ithaca-SKB
Model 280 English**

**Ithaca-SKB
Model 700 Skeet Grade**

**Ithaca-SKB
Model 900 Deluxe**

SKB MODEL 100 SIDE-BY-SIDE. . . . NiB $690 Ex $475 Gd $341
Boxlock. Plain extractors. Selective single trigger. Auto safety. Gauges: 12 and 20; 2.75-inch and 3-inch chambers respectively. Bbls.: 30-inch, F/F (12 ga. only); 28-inch, F/M; 26-inch, IC/M (12 ga. only); 25-inch, IC/M (20 ga. only). Weight: 12 ga., about 7 lbs.; 20 ga., about 6 lbs. Checkered stock and forend. Made 1966 to 1976.

SKB MODEL 150 FIELD GRADE . . . NiB $695 Ex $530 Gd $358
Same as Model 100 except has fancier scroll engraving, beavertail forearm. Made from 1972 to 1974.

SKB 200E FIELD GRADE S/S . . . . . . NiB $995 Ex $687 Gd $485
Same as Model 100 except auto selective ejectors, engraved and silver-plated frame, gold-plated nameplate and trigger, beavertail forearm. Made from 1966 to 1976.

SKB MODEL 200E SKEET GUN . . . . NiB $995 Ex $687 Gd $485
Same as Model 200E Field Grade except 26-inch (12 ga.) and 25-inch (20 ga./2.75-inch chambers) bbls., SK choke; nonautomatic safety and recoil pad. Made from 1966 to 1976.

SKB MODEL 200 ENGLISH . . . . . . NiB $1048 Ex $880 Gd $626
Same as Model 200E except has scrolled game scene engraving on frame, English-style straight-grip stock; 30-inch bbls. not available; special quail gun in 20 ga. has 25-inch bbls., both bored IC. Made from 1971 to 1976.

**SKB MODEL 300 STANDARD
AUTOMATIC SHOTGUN**
Recoil-operated. Gauges: 12, 20 (3-inch). Five round capacity. Bbls.: plain or vent rib; 30-inch F choke (12 ga. only), 28-inch F or M, 26-inch IC. Weight: about 7 lbs. Checkered pistol-grip stock and forearm. Made from 1968 to 1972.
W/plain barrel . . . . NiB $997 Ex $685 Gd $407
20 ga. . . . . Add 30%

**SKB MODEL 500
FIELD GRADE O/U . . . . NiB $525 Ex $392 Gd $251**
Boxlock. Auto selective ejectors. Selective single trigger. Non-automatic safety. Gauges: 12 and 20; 2.75-inch and 3-inch chambers respectively. Vent-rib bbls.: 30-inch M/F (12 ga. only); 28-inch M/F; 26-inch IC/M. Weight: 12 ga., about 7.5 lbs; 20 ga., about 6.5 lbs. Checkered stock and forearm. Made from 1966 to 1976.

SKB MODEL 500 MAGNUM . . . . . . NiB $549 Ex $368 Gd $283
Same as Model 500 Field Grade except chambered for 3-inch 12 ga. shells, has 30-inch bbls., IM/F choke. Weight: About 8 lbs. Made 1973 to 1976.

SKB MODEL 600 DOUBLES GUN . . . . NiB $995 Ex $660 Gd $466
Same as Model 600 Trap Grade except specially choked for 21-yard first target, 30-yard second. Made from 1973 to 1975.

SKB MODEL 600 FIELD GRADE . . . NiB $950 Ex $625 Gd $441
Same as Model 500 except has silver-plated frame, higher grade wood. Made from 1969 to 1976.

SKB MODEL 600 MAGNUM . . . . . . NiB $975 Ex $657 Gd $457
Same as Model 600 Field Grade except chambered for 3-inch 12 ga. shells; has 30-inch bbls., IM/F choke. Weight: 8.5 lbs. Made from 1969 to 1972.

SKB MODEL 600 SKEET GRADE
Same as Model 500 except also available in 28 and .410 ga., has silver-plated frame, higher grade wood, recoil pad, 26- or 28-inch bbls. (28-inch only in 28 and .410), SK choke. Weight: 7 to 7.75 lbs. depending on ga. and bbl. length. Made from 1966 to 1976.
12 or 20 ga. NiB $995 Ex $827 Gd $624
28 or .410 ga. . . . . NiB $1426 Ex $1174 Gd $966

SKB MODEL 600 SKEET SET . . . . NiB $2549 Ex $1769 Gd $1233
Model 600 Skeet Grade w/matched set of 20, 28 and .410 ga. bbls., 28-inch, fitted case. Made from 1970-76.

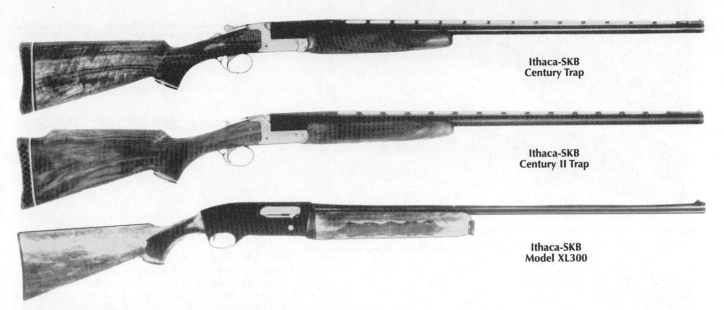

Ithaca-SKB
Century Trap

Ithaca-SKB
Century II Trap

Ithaca-SKB
Model XL300

SKB MODEL 600
TRAP GRADE O/U . . . . NiB $995 Ex $618 Gd $450
Same as Model 500 except 12 ga. only, has silver-plated frame, 30-
or 32-inch bbls. choked F/F or F/IM, choice of Monte Carlo or
straight stock of higher grade wood, recoil pad. Weight: About 8 lbs.
Made from 1966 to 1976.

SKB MODEL 680 ENGLISH . . . . . . NiB $1295 Ex $939 Gd $650
Same as Model 600 Field Grade except has intricate scroll engraving, English-style straight-grip stock and forearm of extra-fine walnut; 30-inch bbls. not available. Made from 1973 to 1976.

SKB MODEL 700
SKEET COMBO SET . . . . NiB $3846 Ex $2786 Gd $1942
Model 700 Skeet Grade w/matched set of 20, 28 and .410 ga. bbls.,
28-inch fitted case. Made from 1970 to 1971.

SKB MODEL 700 SKEET GRADE . . . NiB $841 Ex $711 Gd $500
Same as Model 600 Skeet Grade except not available in 28 and
.410 ga., has more elaborate scroll engraving, extra-wide rib, higher grade wood. Made from 1969 to 1975.

SKB MODEL 700 TRAP GRADE . . . . NiB $824 Ex $601 Gd $466
Same as Model 600 Trap Grade except has more elaborate scroll
engraving, extra-wide rib, higher grade wood. Made 1969 to 1975.

SKB MODEL 700
DOUBLES GUN . . . . NiB $795 Ex $595 Gd $446
Same as Model 700 Trap Grade except choked for 21-yard first tar-
get, 30-yard second target. Made from 1973 to 1975.

SKB MODEL 900
DELUXE AUTOMATIC . . . . NiB $368 Ex $276 Gd $171
Same as Model 30 except has game scene etched and gold-filled on
receiver, vent rib standard. Made 1968 to 1972.

SKB MODEL 900 SLUG GUN . . . . . NiB $350 Ex $264 Gd $190
Same as Model 900 Deluxe except has 24-inch plain bbl. w/slug
boring, rifle sights. Weight: About 6.5 lbs. Made 1970 to 1972.

SKB CENTURY SINGLE-SHOT
TRAP GUN . . . . NiB $555 Ex $312 Gd $242
Boxlock. Auto ejector. 12 ga. Bbls.: 32- or 34-inch, vent rib, F choke.

Weight: About 8 lbs. Checkered walnut stock w/pistol grip, straight or
Monte Carlo comb, recoil pad, beavertail forearm. Made 1973 to 1974.

SKB CENTURY II TRAP . . . . NiB $603 Ex $453 Gd $362
Boxlock. Auto ejector. 12 ga. Bbls.: 32- or 34-inch, vent rib, F choke.
Weight: 8.25 lbs. Improved version of Century. Same general specifications except has higher comb on checkered stock stock, reverse-taper
beavertail forearm w/redesigned locking iron. Made from 1975 to 1976.

SKB MODEL XL300 STANDARD AUTOMATIC
Gas-operated. Gauges: 12, 20 (3-inch). Five round capacity. Bbls.:
Plain or vent rib; 30-inch F choke (12 ga. only), 28-inch F or M, 26-
inch IC. Weight: 6 to 7.5 lbs. depending on ga. and bbl. Checkered
pistol-grip stock, forearm. Made from 1972 to 1976.
W/plain barrel . . . . NiB $329 Ex $263 Gd $190
W/ventilated rib . . . . NiB $365 Ex $283 Gd $205

SKB MODEL XL900
DELUXE AUTOMATIC . . . . NiB $349 Ex $305 Gd $233
Same as Model XL300 except has game scene finished in silver on
receiver, vent rib standard. Made from 1972 to 1976.

SKB MODEL XL
900 SKEET GRADE . . . . NiB $400 Ex $339 Gd $278
Gas-operated. Gauges: 12, 20 (3-inch). Five round tubular magazine. Same as Model XL900 Deluxe except has scrolled
receiver finished in black chrome, 26-inch bbl. only, SK choke,
skeet-style stock. Weight: 7 or 7.5 lbs. depending on ga. Made
from 1972 to 1976.

SKB MODEL XL
900 SLUG GUN . . . . NiB $350 Ex $308 Gd $250
Same as Model XL900 Deluxe except has 24-inch plain bbl. w/slug
boring, rifle sights. Weight: 6.5 or 7 lbs. depending on ga. Made
from 1972 to 1976.

SKB MODEL
XL900 TRAP GRADE . . . . NiB $399 Ex $301 Gd $243
Same as Model XL900 Deluxe except 12 ga. only, has scrolled
receiver finished in black chrome, 30-inch bbl. only, IM or F choke,
trap style w/straight or Monte Carlo comb, recoil pad. Weight:
About 7.75 lbs. Made from 1972 to 1976.

SHOTGUNS

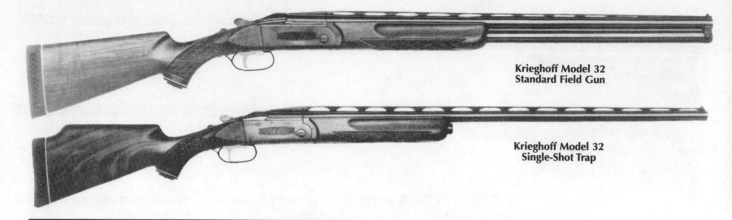

Krieghoff Model 32 Standard Field Gun

Krieghoff Model 32 Single-Shot Trap

IVER JOHNSON ARMS & CYCLE WORKS — Fitchburg, Massachusetts. Currently a division of the American Military Arms Corp., Jacksonville, Arkansas

CHAMPION GRADE TOP SNAP
Auto ejector. Gauges: 12,16, 20, 28 and .410. Bbls.: 26- to 36-inch, F choke. Weight: 5.75 to 7.5 lbs. depending on ga. and bbl.length. Plain pistol-grip stock and forend. Extras include checkered stock and forend, pistol-grip cap and knob forend. Known as Model 36. Also made in a Semi-Octagon Breech, Top Matted and Jacketed Breech (extra heavy) models. Made in Champion Lightweight as Model 39 in gauges 24, 28, 32 and .410, .44 and .45 caliber, 12 and 14mm w/same extras. $200; add $100 in the smaller and obsolete gauges. Made from 1909 to 1973.

Standard model . . . . NiB $301 Ex $19 4 Gd $126
Semi-octagon breech. . . . . NiB $378 Ex $268 Gd $190
Top matted rib (disc. 1948) . . . . NiB $360 Ex $253 Gd $180

HERCULES GRADE HAMMERLESS DOUBLE
Boxlock. (Some made w/false sideplates.) Plain extractors and auto ejectors. Double or Miller single triggers (both selective or non-selective). Gauges: 12, 16, 20 and .410. Bbl. lengths: 26- to 32-inch, all chokes. Weight: 5.75 to 7.75 lbs. depending on ga. and bbl. length. Checkered stock and forend. Straight grip in .410 ga. w/both 2.5- and 3-inch chambers. Extras include Miller single trigger, Jostam Anti-Flinch recoil pad and Lyman ivory sights at extra cost. Disc. 1946.

W/double triggers, extractors . . . . NiB $1091 Ex $840 Gd $659
W/double triggers, auto. ejectors . . . . Add 30%
W/non-selective single trigger, add $25
W/selective single trigger, add. $25
.410 ga., add 100%

MATTED RIB SINGLE-SHOT HAMMER SHOTGUN
IN SMALLER GAUGES. . . . . NiB $315 Ex $255 Gd $233
Same general specifications as Champion Grade except has solid matted top rib, checkered stock and forend. Weight: 6 to 6.75 lbs. Disc. 1948.

SILVER SHADOW
O/U SHOTGUN
Boxlock. Plain extractors. Double triggers or non-selective single trigger. 12 ga., 3-inch chambers. Bbls.: 26-inch IC/M; 28-inch IC/M, 28-inch M/F; 30-inch both F choke; vent rib. Weight: w/28-inch bbls., 7.5 lbs. Checkered pistol-grip stock/forearm. Made by F. Marocchi, Brescia, Italy from 1973 to 1977.

Model 412 w/double triggers . . . . . NiB $500 Ex $403 Gd $308
Model 422 w/single trigger . . . . . . NiB $675 Ex $532 Gd $376

SKEETER MODEL HAMMERLESS DOUBLE
Boxlock. Plain extractors or selective auto ejectors. Double triggers or Miller single trigger (selective or non-selective). Gauges: 12, 16, 20, 28 and .410. 26- or 28-inch bbls., skeet boring standard. Weight: About 7.5 lbs.; less in smaller gauges. Pistol- or straight-grip stock and beavertail forend, both checkered, of select fancy-figured black walnut. Extras include Miller single trigger, selective or non-selective, Jostam Anti-Flinch recoil pad and Lyman ivory rear sight at additional cost. Disc. 1942.

W/double triggers,
plain extractors . . . . NiB $2197 Ex $1808 Gd $950
W/double triggers,
automatic ejectors . . . . Add 20%
W/non-selective
single trigger, add . . . . Add 20%
W/selective single
trigger . . . . Add 50%
20 ga. . . . . Add 30%
28 ga., add 100%
.410 ga., add 90%

SPECIAL TRAP SINGLE-SHOT
HAMMER SHOTGUN . . . . NiB $400 Ex $304 Gd $252
Auto ejector. 12 ga. only. 32-inch bbl. w/vent rib, F choke. Checkered pistol-grip stock and forend. Weight: about 7.5 lbs. Disc. 1942.

SUPER TRAP HAMMERLESS DOUBLE
Boxlock. Plain extractors. Double trigger or Miller single trigger (selective or non-selective), 12 ga. only, F choke 32-inch bbl., vent rib. Weight: 8.5 lbs. Checkered pistol-grip stock and beavertail forend, recoil pad, Disc. 1942.

W/double triggers . . . . NiB $1600 Ex $1044 Gd $880
W/non-selective
single trigger, add $100
W/selective single trigger, add. $100

KBI INC. SHOTGUNS

See listings under Armscor, Baikal, Charles Daly, Fias, & Omega

KESSLER ARMS CORP. — Deggendorf, Germany

LEVER-MATIC REPEATING SHOTGUN   NiB $237 Ex $170 Gd $124
Lever action. Takedown. Gauges: 12, 16, 20; three-round magazine. Bbls.: 26-, 28-, 30-inch; F choke. Plain pistol-grip stock, recoil pad. Weight: 7 to 7.75 lbs. Disc. 1953.

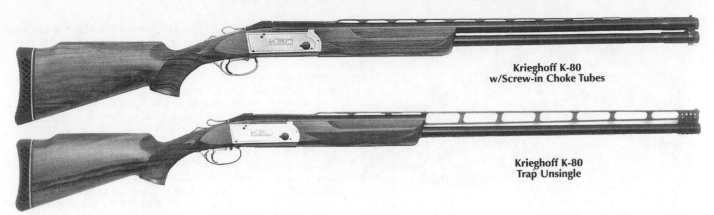

Krieghoff K-80
w/Screw-in Choke Tubes

Krieghoff K-80
Trap Unsingle

THREE SHOT BOLT-ACTION REPEATER NiB $142 Ex $102 Gd $78
Takedown. Gauges: 12, 16, 20. Two-round detachable box magazine. Bbls.: 28-inch in 12 and 16 ga.; 26-inch in 20 ga.; F choke. Weight: 6.25 to 7.25 lbs. depending on ga. and bbl. length. Plain one-piece pistol-grip stock recoil pad. Made from 1951 to 1953.

H. KRIEGHOFF JAGD UND SPORTWAFFEN-FABRIK — Ulm (Donau), West Germany

MODEL 32 FOUR-BARREL SKEET SET
Over/under w/four sets of matched bbls.: 12, 20, 28 and .410 ga., in fitted case. Available in six grades that differ in quality of engraving and wood. Disc. 1979.

Standard grade	NiB $8,454	Ex $6218	Gd $4269
München grade	NiB $9,911	Ex $7,249	Gd $5969
San Remo grade	NiB $12,752	Ex $10,617	Gd $9580
Monte Carlo grade	NiB $18,756	Ex $16,428	Gd $11,171
Crown grade	NiB $25,000	Ex $20,342	Gd $13,833
Super Crown grade	NiB $27,681	Ex $22,145	Gd $15,059
Exhibition grade	NiB $30,000	Ex $27,849	Gd $20,977

MODEL 32 STANDARD GRADE O/U
Similar to prewar Remington Model 23. Boxlock. Auto ejector. Single trigger. Gauges: 12, 20, 28, .410. Bbls.: Vent rib, 26.5- to 32-inch, any chokes. Weight: 12 ga. Field gun w/28-inch bbls., about 7.5 lbs. Checkered pistol-grip stock and forearm of select walnut; available in field, skeet and trap styles. Made from 1958 to 1981.

W/one set of bbls.	NiB $2748	Ex $2383	Gd $1959
Low-rib two-bbl. trap combo	NiB $3946	Ex $3088	Gd $2699
Vandalia (high-rib) two- bbl. trap combo	NiB $5166	Ex $4139	Gd $2878

MODEL 32 STANDARD GRADE
SINGLE-SHOT TRAP GUN .... NiB $3949 Ex $3040 Gd $2750
Same action as over/under. 28 ga.or .410 bore w/low vent rib on bbl.; M, IM, or F choke. Checkered Monte Carlo buttstock w/thick cushioned recoil pad, beavertail forearm. Disc. 1979.

MODEL K-80
Refined and enhanced version of the Mdl. 32. Single selective mech. trig., adj. for position; release trigger optional. Fixed chokes or screw-in choke tubes. Interchangeable front bbl. Hangers to adjust point of impact. Quick-removable stock. Color casehardened or satin grey fin. rec.; alum. alloy rec. on lightweight models. Avail. in stand. plus 5 engraved grades. Made from 1980 to date. Standard grade shown except where noted.

SKEET MODELS
Skeet International	NiB $8477	Ex $5046	Gd $3501
Skeet Special	NiB $9180	Ex $6444	Gd $4081
Skeet standard model	NiB $8400	Ex $4252	Gd $2951
Skeet w/choke tubes	NiB $11,344	Ex $9090	Gd $6526

SKEET SETS - Disc. 1999.
Standard grade 2-bbl. set	NiB $11,846	Ex $7886	Gd $5404
Standard grade 4-bbl. set	NiB $13,279	Ex $10,623	Gd $7224
Bavaria grade 4-bbl. set	NiB $10,926	Ex $8,141	Gd $6,296
Danube grade 4-bbl. set	NiB $22,643	Ex $19,714	Gd $13,405
Gold Target grade 4-bbl. set	NiB $29,675	Ex $23,175	Gd $15,759

SPORTING MODELS
Pigeon	NiB $8896	Ex $5546	Gd $3845
Sporting Clays	NiB $8919	Ex $5580	Gd $3867

TRAP MODELS
Trap Combo Add		30%
Trap Single Add		$550
Trap Standard	NiB $9485 Ex $6972	Gd $4458
Trap Unsingle	NiB $10,800 Ex $7545	Gd $5850
RT models (removable trigger) add		$1300

KRIEGHOFF MODEL KS-5 SINGLE-BARREL TRAP
Boxlock w/no sliding top-latch. Adjustable or optional release trigger. Gauge: 12; 2.75-inch chamber. Bbl.: 32-, 34-inch w/fixed choke or screw-in tubes. Weight: 8.5 lbs. Adjustable or Monte Carlo European walnut stock. Blued or nickel receiver. Made from 1985 to 1999. Redesigned and streamlined in 1993.

Standard model w/fixed chokes	NiB $2475	Ex $1777	Gd $1037
Standard model w/tubes			Add $200
Special model w/adj. rib & stock			Add $200
Special model w/adj. rib & stock, choke tubes			Add $400

TRUMPF DRILLING ...... NiB $13,672 Ex $11,161 Gd $9317
Boxlock. Steel or Dural receiver. Split extractor or ejector for shotgun bbls. Double triggers. Gauges: 12, 16, 20; latter w/either 2.75- or 3-inch chambers. Calibers: .243, 6.5x57r5, 7x57r5, 7x65r5, .30-06; other calibers available. 25-inch bbls. w/solid rib, folding leaf rear sight, post or bead front sight; rifle bbl. soldered or free floating. Weight: 6.6 to 7.5 lbs. depending on type of receiver, ga. and caliber. Checkered pistol-grip stock w/cheekpiece and forearm of figured walnut, sling swivels. Made from 1953 to 2003.

NEPTUN DRILLING ...... NiB $13,556 Ex $10,096 Gd $8299
Same general specifications as Trumpf model except has sidelocks w/hunting scene engraving. Disc. 2003.

NEPTUN-PRIMUS DRILLING NiB $18,400 Ex $15,578 Gd $12,969
Deluxe version of Neptun model; has detachable sidelocks, higher grade engraving and fancier wood. Disc. 2003.

SHOTGUNS

**Krieghoff
Neptun Drilling**

**Krieghoff ULM
Over/Under**

**TECK O/U
RIFLE-SHOTGUN** . . . . **NiB $8774 Ex $5775 Gd $3982**
Boxlock. Kersten dble. crossbolt system. Steel or Dural receiver.
Split extractor or eject. for shotgun bbl. Single or double triggers.
Gauges: 12, 16, 20; latter w/either 2.75- or 3-inch chamber. Cal:
.22 Hornet, .222 Rem., .222 Rem. Mag., 7x57r5, 7x64, 7x65r5, .30-
30, .300 Win. Mag., .30-06, .308, 9.3x74R. 25-inch bbls. With solid
rib, folding leaf rear sight, post or bead front sight; over bbl. is shot-
gun, under bbl. rifle (later fixed or interchangeable; ext. rifle bbl.,
$175). Wt: 7.9-9.5 lbs. depending on type of rec. and caliber.
Checkered pistol-grip stock w/cheekpiece and semi-beavertail forearm of fig. walnut, sling swivels. Made from 1967 to 2004. Note:
This comb. gun is similar in appearance to the same model shotgun.

TECK O/U SHOTGUN . . . . **NiB $6650 Ex $5385 Gd $3735**
Boxlock. Kersten double crossbolt system. Auto ejector. Single or
double triggers. Gauges: 12, 16, 20; latter w/either 2.75- or 3-inch
chambers. 28-inch vent-rib bbl., M/F choke. Weight: About 7 lbs.
Checkered walnut pistol-grip stock and forearm. Made 1967 to 1989.

**ULM O/U
RIFLE-SHOTGUN** . . . . **NiB $14,416 Ex $11,162 Gd $9279**
Same general specifications as Teck model except has sidelocks w/leaf
Arabesque engraving. Made from 1963-2004. Note: This combination
gun is similar in appearance to the same model shotgun.

ULM O/U SHOTGUN . . . . . **NiB $12,325 Ex $10,192 Gd $7590**
Same general specifications as Teck model except has sidelocks
w/leaf Arabesque engraving. Made from 1958 to 2004.

ULM-P LIVE PIGEON GUN
Sidelock. Gauge: 12. 28- and 30-inch bbls. Chokes: F/IM. Weight: 8 lbs.
Oil-finished, fancy English walnut stock w/semi-beavertail forearm.
Light scrollwork engraving. Tapered, vent rib. Made from 1983 to 2004.
Standard . . . . **NiB $17,454 Ex $14,935 Gd $10,815**
Dural . . . . **NiB $12,329 Ex $10,690 Gd $8609**

ULM-PRIMUS O/U . . . . . . **NiB $18,729 Ex $16,406 Gd $12,431**
Deluxe version of Ulm model; detachable sidelocks, higher grade
engraving and fancier wood. Made from 1958 to 2004.

**ULM-PRIMUS O/U
RIFLE-SHOTGUN** . . . . **NiB $19,748 Ex $16,444 Gd $13,381**
Deluxe version of Ulm model; has detachable sidelocks, higher grade
engraving and fancier wood. Made 1963 to 2004. Note: This combination gun is similar in appearance to the same model shotgun.

ULM-S SKEET GUN
Sidelock. Gauge: 12. Bbl.: 28-inch. Chokes: Skeet/skeet. Other
specifications similar to the Model ULM-P. Made from 1983-86.
Bavaria . . . . **NiB $12,164 Ex $10,208 Gd $7905**
Standard . . . . **NiB $1066 Ex $8530 Gd $6554**

ULM-P O/U LIVE TRAP GUN
Over/under sidelock. Gauge: 12. 30-inch bbl. Tapered vent rib.
Chokes: IM/F; optional screw-in choke. Custom grade versions
command a higher price. Disc. 1986.
Bavaria . . . . **NiB $17,032 Ex $14,878 Gd $10,840**
Standard . . . . **NiB $14,299 Ex $11,890 Gd $8809**

ULTRA TS RIFLE-SHOTGUN
Deluxe Over/Under combination w/25-inch vent-rib bbls.
Chambered 12 ga. only and various rifle calibers for lower bbl.
Kickspanner design permits cocking w/thumb safety. Satin receiver.
Weight: 6 lbs. Made from 1985 to 1995 Disc.
Ultra O/U combination . . . . **NiB $4055 Ex $3443 Gd $2788**
Ultra B w/selective front trigger . . . **NiB $5369 Ex $4649 Gd $3727**

LANBER SHOTGUNS — Zaldibar, Spain

MODEL 82 O/U SHOTGUN . . . . . . **NiB $500 Ex $403 Gd $351**
Boxlock. Gauge: 12 or 20; 3-inch chambers. 26- or 28-inch vent-rib
bbls. w/ejectors and fixed chokes. Weight: 7 lbs., 2 oz. Double or
single-selective trigger. Engraved silvered receiver. Checkered
European walnut stock and forearm. Imported 1994.

MODEL 87 DELUXE . . . . **NiB $800 Ex $700 Gd $514**
Over/Under; boxlock. Single selective trigger. 12 or 20 gauge w/3-
inch chambers. Barrels: 26- or 28-inch w/choke tubes. Silvered
engraved receiver. Imported 1994 only.

MODEL 97 SPORTING CLAYS . . . . **NiB $835 Ex $747 Gd $534**
Over/Under; boxlock. Single selective trigger. 12 ga. w/2.75-inch
chambers. Bbls: 28-inch w/choke tubes. European walnut stock,
forend. Engraved receiver. Imported 1994 only.

MODEL 844 MST MAGNUM O/U . . . . **NiB $407 Ex $330 Gd $240**
Field grade. Gauge: 12. 3-inch Mag. chambers. 30-inch flat vent-rib
bbls. Chokes: M/F. Weight: 7 lbs., 7 oz. Single selective trigger.
Blued bbls. and engraved receiver. European walnut stock w/hand-
checkered pistol grip and forend. Imported from 1984 to 1986.

MODEL 2004 LCH O/U . . . . **NiB $575 Ex $449 Gd $323**
Field grade. Gauge: 12. 2.75-inch chambers. 28-inch flat vent-rib
bbls. 5 interchangeable choke tubes: Cyl, IC, M, IM, F. Weight:
About 7 lbs. Single selective trigger. Engraved silver receiver w/fine-
line scroll. Walnut stock w/checkered pistol-grip and forend. Rubber
recoil pad. Imported from 1984 to 1986.

MODEL 2004 LCH O/U SKEET . . . . **NiB $740 Ex $579 Gd $483**
Same as Model 2004 LCH except 28-inch bbls. w/5 interchangeable
choke tubes. Imported from 1984 to 1986.

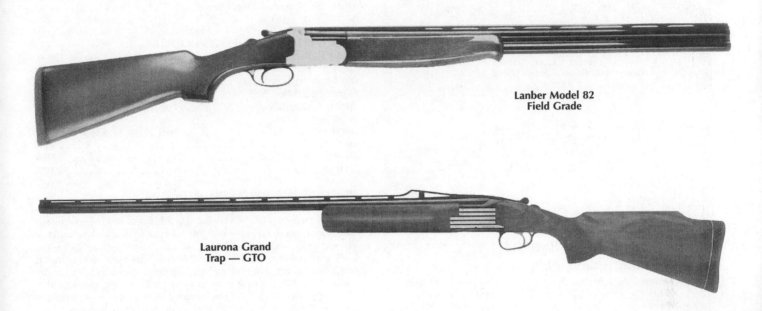

Lanber Model 82
Field Grade

Laurona Grand
Trap — GTO

MODEL 2004
LCH O/U TRAP . . . . **NiB $675 Ex $454 Gd $362**
Gauge: 12. 30-inch vent-rib bbls. Three interchangeable choke tubes: M, IM, F. Manual safety. Other specifications same as Model 2004 LCH O/U. Imported from 1984 to 1986.

CHARLES LANCASTER — London, England

"TWELVE-TWENTY" DOUBLE-BARREL
SHOTGUN . . . . **NiB $15,313 Ex $12,250 Gd $8330**
Sidelock, self-opener. Gauge: 12. Bbls.: 24 to 30 inches standard. Weight: About 5.75 lbs. Elaborate metal engraving. Highest quality English or French walnut buttstock and forearm. Imported by Stoeger in the 1950s.

JOSEPH LANG & SONS — London, England

HIGHEST QUALITY
O/U SHOTGUN . . . . **NiB $29,000 Ex $21,600 Gd $14,688**
Sidelock. Gauges: 12, 16, 20, 28 and .410. Bbls.: 25 to 30 inches standard. Highest grade English or French walnut buttstock and forearm. Selective single trigger. Imported by Stoeger in 1950s.

LAURONA SHOTGUNS — Eibar, Spain

MODEL 300 SERIES
Same general specifications as Model 300 Super Series except supplied w/29-inch over/under bbls. and beavertail forearms. Disc. 1992.
Trap model . . . . **NiB $1252 Ex $1043 Gd $857**
Sporting Clays model . . . . **NiB $1250 Ex $1240 Gd $931**

SILHOUETTE 300 O/U
Boxlock. Single selective trigger. Selective automatic ejectors. Gauge: 12; 2.75-, 3- or 3.5-inch chambers. 28- or 29-inch vent-rib bbls. w/flush or knurled choke tubes. Weight: 7.75 to 8 lbs. Checkered pistol-grip European walnut stock and beavertail forend. Engraved receiver w/silvered finish and black chrome bbls. Made from 1988 to 1992.
Model 300 Sporting Clays . . . . . . **NiB $1317 Ex $1114 Gd $780**
Model 300 Trap, single . . . . **NiB $1417 Ex $1114 Gd $780**
Model 300 Ultra-Magnum . . . . . . **NiB $1469 Ex $1176 Gd $890**

SUPER MODEL O/U SHOTGUNS
Boxlock. Single selective or twin single triggers. Selective automatic ejectors. Gauges: 12 or 20; 2.75- or 3-inch chambers. 26-, 28- or 29-inch vent-rib bbls. w/fixed chokes or screw-in choke tubes. Weight: 7 to 7.25 lbs. Checkered pistol-grip European walnut stock. Engraved receiver w/silvered finish and black chrome bbls. Made from 1985 to 1989.
Model 82 Super Game (disc.) . . . . . **NiB $575 Ex $402 Gd $330**
Model 83 MG Super Game . . . . **NiB $995 Ex $755 Gd $602**
Model 84 S Super Trap . . . . **NiB $1249 Ex $1020 Gd $875**
Model 85 MS Super Game . . . . **NiB $999 Ex $761 Gd $595**
Model 85 MS 2-bbl. set . . . . **NiB $2048 Ex $1647 Gd $1176**
Model 85 MS Special Sporting (disc.) . . . **NiB $1247 Ex $1075 Gd $839**
Model 85 MS Super Trap . . . . **NiB $1250 Ex $1079 Gd $846**
Model 85 MS Pigeon . . . . **NiB $1245 Ex $1086 Gd $930**
Model 85 MS Super Skeet . . . . . . **NiB $1245 Ex $1086 Gd $930**

LEBEAU-COURALLY SHOTGUNS — Belgium

BOXLOCK SIDE
BY-SIDE SHOTGUNS . . . . . . **NiB $17,438 Ex $13,950 Gd $9486**
Gauges: 12, 16, 20 and 28. 26- to 30-inch bbls. Weight: 6.5 lbs. average. Checkered, hand-rubbed, oil-finished, straight-grip stock of French walnut. Classic forend. Made from 1986 to 1988 and 1993.

SHOTGUNS

**Lefever A Grade
Hammerless Double-Barrel Shotgun**

LEFEVER ARMS COMPANY —
Syracuse and Ithaca, N.Y.

Lefever sidelock hammerless double-barrel shotguns were made by Lefever Arms Company of Syracuse, New York from about 1885-1915 (serial numbers 1 to 70,000) when the firm was sold to Ithaca Gun Company of Ithaca, New York. Production of these models was continued at the Ithaca plant until 1919 (serial numbers 70,001 to 72,000). Grades listed are those that appear in the last catalog of the Lefever Gun Company, Syracuse. In 1921, Ithaca introduced the boxlock Lefever Nitro Special double, followed in 1934 by the Lefever Grade A; there also were two single-barrel Lefevers made from 1927-42. Manufacture of Lefever brand shotguns was disc. in 1948. Note: "New Lefever" boxlock shotguns made circa 1904 to 1906 by D. M. Lefever Company, Bowling Green, Ohio, are included in a separate listing.

GRADE A HAMMERLESS DOUBLE-BARREL SHOTGUN
Boxlock. Plain extractors or auto ejector. Single or double triggers. Gauges: 12, 16, 20, .410. Bbls.: 26-32 inches, standard chokes. Weight: About 7 lbs. in 12 ga. Checkered pistol-grip stock and forearm. Made from 1934 to 1942.

W/plain extractors, double triggers. NiB $1100 Ex $888 Gd $650
W/automatic ejector add 33%
W/single trigger add 10%
W/Beavertail Forearm, add $75
16 ga., add 25%
20 ga., add 45%
.410 ga., add 200%

GRADE A SKEET MODEL
Same as A Grade except standard features include auto ejector, single trigger, beavertail forearm; 26-inch bbls., skeet boring. Disc. 1942.

A Grade Skeet model, 12 ga. . . . . NiB $1599 Ex $1059 Gd $760
16 ga., add 40%
20 ga., add 80%
.410 ga., add 200%

HAMMERLESS SINGLE-SHOT
TRAP GUN . . . . NiB $649 Ex $531 Gd $380
Boxlock. Ejector. 12 ga. only. 26- or 32-inch bbl.; Full choke. Weight: About 8 lbs. Checkered pistol-grip stock. Auto ejector; boxlock. Made from 1904 to 1906. Rare.

LONG RANGE HAMMERLESS
SINGLE-BARREL FIELD GUN . . . . . NiB $397 Ex $329 Gd $233
Boxlock. Plain extractor. Gauges: 12, 16, 20, .410. Bbl. lengths: 26-32 inches. Weight: 5.5 to 7 lbs. depending on ga. and bbl. length. Checkered pistol-grip stock and forend. Made from 1927 to 1942.

NITRO SPECIAL HAMMERLESS DOUBLE
Boxlock. Plain extractors. Single or double triggers. Gauges: 12, 16, 20, .410. Bbls.: 26- to 32-inch, standard chokes. Weight: about 7 lbs. in 12 ga. Checkered pistol-grip stock and forend. Made 1921 to 1948.
**Nitro Special W/
double triggers . . . . NiB $728 Ex $459 Gd $294**
**Nitro Special W/
single trigger . . . . NiB $798 Ex $563 Gd $398**
16 ga., add 25%
20 ga., add 50%
.410 ga., add 200%

SIDELOCK HAMMERLESS DOUBLES
Plain extractors or auto ejectors. Boxlock. Double triggers or selective single trigger. Gauges: 10, 12, 16, 20. Bbls.: 26-32 inches; standard choke combinations. Weight: 5.75 to 10.5 lbs. depending on ga. and bbl. length. Checkered walnut straight-grip or pistol-grip stock and forearm. Grades differ chiefly in quality of workmanship, engraving, wood, checkering, etc.; general specifications are the same. DS and DSE Grade guns lack the cocking indicators found on all other models. Suffix "E" means model has auto ejector; also standard on A, AA, Optimus, and Thousand Dollar Grade guns.

H grade	NiB $2179	Ex $1642	Gd $1309
HE grade	NiB $3000	Ex $2148	Gd $1477
G grade	NiB $2175	Ex $1899	Gd $1315
GE grade	NiB $3199	Ex $2521	Gd $1744
F grade.	NiB $2375	Ex $1696	Gd $1191
FE grade.	NiB $3255	Ex $2563	Gd $1791
E grade.	NiB $3605	Ex $2454	Gd $1690
EE grade.	NiB $5400	Ex $3698	Gd $2568
D grade	NiB $4556	Ex $2997	Gd $2070
DE grade	NiB $6600	Ex $4660	Gd $3266
DS grade	NiB $1550	Ex $1353	Gd $950
DSE grade	NiB $1999	Ex $1661	Gd $1174
C grade	NiB $6354	Ex $4092	Gd $2899
CE grade	NiB $8414	Ex $7595	Gd $5297
B grade	NiB $9300	Ex $4885	Gd $3399
BE grade	NiB $9984	Ex $7452	Gd $5869
A grade.	NiB $18,499	Ex $16,054	Gd $14,829
AA grade.	NiB $26,170	Ex $21,736	Gd $14,780
Optimus grade	NiB $45,050	Ex $29,640	Gd $20,155
Thousand Dollar grade . . .	NiB $75,250	Ex $44,200	Gd $30,056

W/single trigger, add 10%
10 ga., add 15%
16 ga., add 45%
20 ga., add 90%

D. M. LEFEVER COMPANY —
Bowling Green, Ohio

In 1901, D. M. "Uncle Dan" Lefever, founder of the Lefever Arms Company, withdrew from that firm to organize D. M. Lefever, Sons & Company (later D. M. Lefever Company) to manufacture the "New Lefever" boxlock double- and single-barrel shotguns. These were produced at Bowling Green, Ohio, from about 1904-1906, when Dan Lefever died and the factory closed permanently. Grades listed are those that appear in the last catalog of D. M. Lefever Co.

HAMMERLESS DOUBLE-BARREL SHOTGUNS

"New Lefever." Boxlock. Auto ejector standard on all grades except O Excelsior, which was regularly supplied w/plain extractors (auto ejector offered as an extra). Double triggers or selective single trigger (latter standard on Uncle Dan Grade, extra on all others). Gauges: 12, 16, 20. Bbls.: Any length and choke combination. Weight: 5.5 to 8 lbs. depending on ga. and bbl. length. Checkered walnut straight-grip or pistol-grip stock and forearm. Grades differ chiefly in quality of workmanship, engraving, wood, checkering, etc. General specifications are the same.

O Excelsior grade
w/plain extractors . . . . NiB $2794 Ex $2070 Gd $1791
O Excelsior grade
w/automatic ejectors. . . . . NiB $3156 Ex $2794 Gd $2072
No. 9, F grade . . . . NiB $3155 Ex $2749 Gd $1974
No. 8, E grade . . . . NiB $4000 Ex $3677 Gd $2273
No. 7, D grade. . . . . NiB $4950 Ex $4395 Gd $3492
No. 6, C grade . . . . NiB $6251 Ex $5490 Gd $3981
No. 5, B grade . . . . NiB $6599 Ex $4499 Gd $3199
No. 4, AA grade. . . . . NiB $9250 Ex $7400 Gd $5372
Uncle Dan grade . . . . Very rare: $150,000+
W/single trigger, add 10%
16 ga., add 45%
20 ga., add 15%

D. M. LEFEVER SINGLE-BARREL TRAP GUN

Boxlock. Auto ejector. 12 ga. only. Bbls.: 26- to 32 inches, F choke. Weight: 6.5 to 8 lbs. depending on bbl. length. Checkered walnut pistol-grip stock and forearm. Made 1904 to 1906. Extremely rare.

MAGTECH SHOTGUNS — San Antonio, Texas
Mfd. by CBC in Brazil

MODEL 586-2 SLIDE-ACTION SHOTGUN

Gauge: 12; 3-inch chamber. 19-, 26- or 28-inch bbl.; fixed chokes or integral tubes. 46.5 inches overall. Weight: 8.5 lbs. Double-action slide bars. Brazilian hardwood stock. Polished blued finish. Imported 1992 to 1995.
Model 586.2F
(28-inch bbl., fixed choke) . . . . NiB $194 Ex $139 Gd $90
Model 586.2P
(19-inch plain bbl., cyl. bore) . . . . . . NiB $184 Ex $129 Gd $92
Model 586.2 S
(24-inch bbl., rifle sights, cyl. bore) . . . NiB $190 Ex $120 Gd $106
Model 586.2 VR
(vent rib w/tubes) . . . . NiB $220 Ex $179 Gd $112

MARLIN FIREARMS CO. — North Haven
(formerly New Haven), Conn.

MODEL 16 VISIBLE HAMMER SLIDE-ACTION REPEATER

Takedown. 16 ga. Five round tubular magazine. Bbls.: 26- or 28-inch, standard chokes. Weight: About 6.25 lbs. Pistol-grip stock, grooved slide handle; checkering on higher grades. Difference among grades is in quality of wood, engraving on Grades C and D. Made from 1904 to 1910.
Grade A . . . . NiB $325 Ex $304 Gd $268
Grade B . . . . NiB $495 Ex $406 Gd $359
Grade C . . . . NiB $635 Ex $420 Gd $340
Grade D. . . . . NiB $1328 Ex $1231 Gd $874

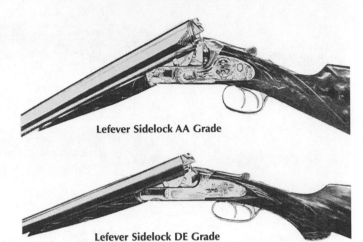

Lefever Sidelock AA Grade

Lefever Sidelock DE Grade

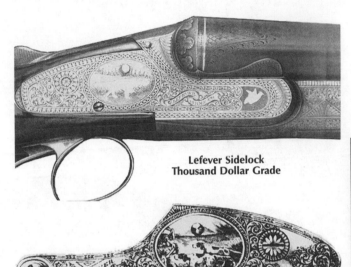

Lefever Sidelock
Thousand Dollar Grade

Lefever Sidelock Sideplate BE Grade

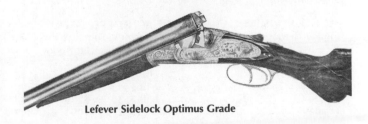

Lefever Sidelock Sideplate CE Grade

Lefever Sidelock Optimus Grade

SHOTGUNS

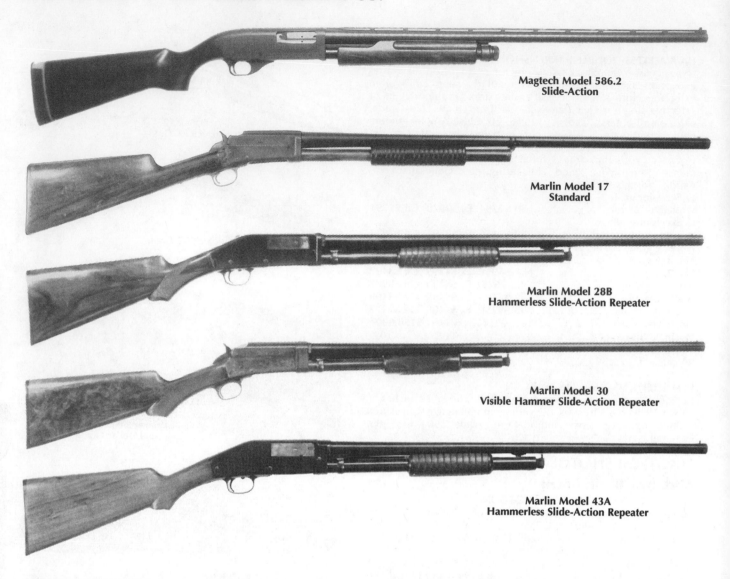

**Magtech Model 586.2
Slide-Action**

**Marlin Model 17
Standard**

**Marlin Model 28B
Hammerless Slide-Action Repeater**

**Marlin Model 30
Visible Hammer Slide-Action Repeater**

**Marlin Model 43A
Hammerless Slide-Action Repeater**

MODEL 17 BRUSH GUN . . . . NiB $323 Ex $252 Gd $140
Same as Model 17 Standard except has 26-inch bbl., cylinder bore.
Weight: About 7 lbs. Made from 1906 to 1908.

MODEL 17 RIOT GUN . . . . NiB $325 Ex $251 Gd $1253
Same as Model 17 Standard except has 20-inch bbl., cylinder bore.
Weight: About 6.88 lbs. Made from 1906 to 1908.

**MODEL 17 STANDARD VISIBLE HAMMER
SLIDE-ACTION REPEATER** . . . . NiB $335 Ex $242 Gd $140
Solid frame.12 ga. Five round tubular magazine. Bbls.: 30- or 32-
inch, F choke. Weight: About 7.5 lbs. Straight-grip stock, grooved
slide handle. Made from 1906 to 1908.

MODEL 19 VISIBLE HAMMER SLIDE-ACTION REPEATER
Similar to Model 1898 but improved, lighter weight, w/two extrac-
tors, matted sighting groove on receiver top. Weight: About 7 lbs.
Made from 1906-07.
Grade A . . . . NiB $325 Ex $237 Gd $144
Grade B . . . . NiB $495 Ex $358 Gd $298
Grade C . . . . NiB $635 Ex $299 Gd $174
Grade D . . . . NiB $1322 Ex $1004 Gd $847

**MODEL 21 TRAP VISIBLE HAMMER
SLIDE-ACTION REPEATER**
Similar to Model 19 w/same general specifications except has
straight-grip stock. Made from 1907 to 1909.
Grade A . . . . NiB $325 Ex $234 Gd $142
Grade B . . . . NiB $494 Ex $269 Gd $135
Grade C . . . . NiB $635 Ex $286 Gd $176
Grade D . . . . NiB $1327 Ex $1059 Gd $818

MODEL 24 VISIBLE HAMMER SLIDE-ACTION REPEATER
Similar to Model 19 but has improved takedown system and auto
recoil safety lock, solid matted rib on frame. Weight: About 7.5 lbs.
Made from 1908 to 1915.
Grade A . . . . NiB $295 Ex $119 Gd $84
Grade B . . . . NiB $326 Ex $196 Gd $94
Grade C . . . . NiB $660 Ex $414 Gd $235
Grade D. NiB $1385 Ex $1256 Gd $865

**MODEL 26
BRUSH GUN** . . . . NiB $275 Ex $180 Gd $92
Same as Model 26 Standard except has 26-inch bbl., cylinder bore.
Weight: About 7 lbs. Made from 1909 to 1915.

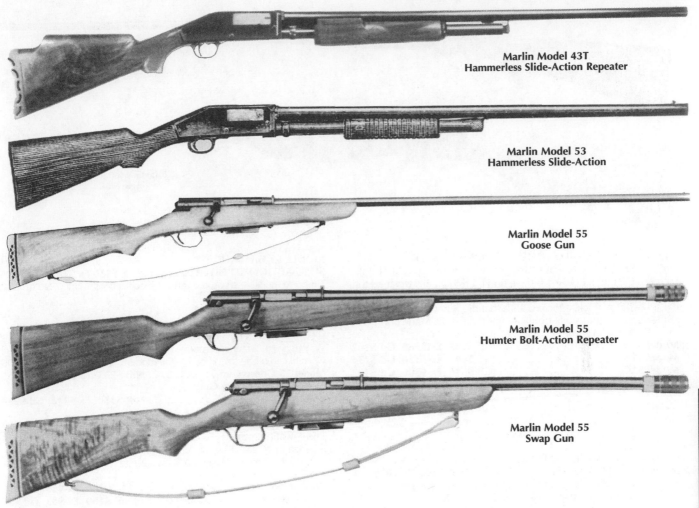

Marlin Model 43T
Hammerless Slide-Action Repeater

Marlin Model 53
Hammerless Slide-Action

Marlin Model 55
Goose Gun

Marlin Model 55
Humter Bolt-Action Repeater

Marlin Model 55
Swap Gun

MODEL 26 RIOT GUN . . . . **NiB $250 Ex $153 Gd $94**
Same as Model 26 Standard except has 20-inch bbl., cylinder bore.
Weight: About 6.88 lbs. Made from 1909 to 1915.

**MODEL 26 STANDARD VISIBLE HAMMER
SLIDE-ACTION REPEATER** . . . . **NiB $275 Ex $203 Gd $171**
Similar to Model 24 Grade A except solid frame and straight-grip
stock. 30- or 32-inch full choke bbl. Weight: About 7.13 lbs. Made
from 1909-15.

MODEL 28 HAMMERLESS SLIDE-ACTION REPEATER
Takedown. 12 ga. Five round tubular magazine. Bbls.: 26-, 28-,
30-, 32-inch, standard chokes; matted-top bbl. except on Model
28D, which has solid matted rib. Weight: About 8 lbs. Pistol-grip
stock, grooved slide handle; checkering on higher grades. Grades
differ in quality of wood, engraving on Models 28C and 28D.
Made 1913 to 1922; all but Model 28A disc. in 1915.
Model 28A . . . . **NiB $295 Ex $209 Gd $120**
Model 28B . . . . **NiB $490 Ex $403 Gd $218**
Model 28C . . . . **NiB $639 Ex $468 Gd $306**
Model 28D . . . . **NiB $1321 Ex $1056 Gd $816**

MODEL 28T TRAP GUN . . . . **NiB $600 Ex $522 Gd $388**
Same as Model 28 except has 30-inch matted-rib bbl., Full choke,
straight-grip stock w/high-fluted comb of fancy walnut, checkered.
Made in 1915.

**MODEL 28TS
TRAP GUN** . . . . **NiB $415 Ex $308 Gd $237**
Same as Model 28T except has matted-top bbl., plainer stock. Made
in 1915.

MODEL 30 FIELD GUN . . . . **NiB $335 Ex $290 Gd $200**
Same as Model 30 Grade B except has 25-inch bbl., Mod. choke,
straight-grip stock. Made from 1913 to 1914.

MODEL 30 VISIBLE HAMMER SLIDE-ACTION REPEATER
Similar to Model 16 but w/Model 24 improvements. Made from
1910-14. See illustration previous page.
Grade A . . . . **NiB $325 Ex $237 Gd $143**
Grade B . . . . **NiB $495 Ex $370 Gd $254**
Grade C . . . . **NiB $635 Ex $438 Gd $252**
Grade D . . . . **NiB $1319 Ex $1047 Gd $947**

MODELS 30A, 30B, 30C, 30D
Same as Model 30; designations were changed in 1915. Also avail-
able in 20 ga. w/25- or 28-inch bbl., matted-top bbl. on all grades.
Suffixes "A," "B," "C" and "D" correspond to former grades. Made
in 1915.
Model 30A . . . . **NiB $325 Ex $237 Gd $143**
Model 30B . . . . **NiB $495 Ex $370 Gd $254**
Model 30C . . . . **NiB $635 Ex $438 Gd $252**
Model 30D . . . . **NiB $1319 Ex $1047 Gd $947**

Marlin Model 59
Bolt-Action Single

Marlin Model 60
Single Shot

MODEL 31 HAMMERLESS SLIDE-ACTION REPEATER
Similar to Model 28 except scaled down for 16 and 20 ga. Bbls.: 25-inch (20 ga. only), 26-inch (16 ga. only), 28-inch, all w/matted top, standard chokes. Weight: 16 ga., about 6.75 lbs.; 20 ga., about 6 lbs. Pistol-grip stock, grooved slide handle; checkering on higher grades; straight-grip stock optional on Model 31D. Made from 1915 to 1917; Model 31A until 1922.

Model 31A . . . . NiB $385 Ex $260 Gd $162
Model 31B . . . . NiB $495 Ex $336 Gd $234
Model 31C . . . . NiB $636 Ex $506 Gd $422
Model 31D . . . . NiB $1320 Ex $1060 Gd $887

MODEL 31F FIELD GUN. . . . . NiB $395 Ex $295 Gd $233
Same as Model 31B except has 25-inch bbl., M choke, straight- or pistol-grip stock. Made from 1915 to 1917.

MODEL 42A VISIBLE HAMMER
SLIDE-ACTION REPEATER . . . . NiB $395 Ex $255 Gd $179
Similar to pre-World War I Model 24 Grade A w/same general specifications but not as high quality. Made from 1922-34.

MODEL 43 HAMMERLESS SLIDE-ACTION REPEATER
Similar to pre-World War I Models 28A, 28T and 28TS, w/same general specifications but not as high quality. Made from 1923 to 1930.
Model 43A . . . . NiB $275 Ex $186 Gd $102
Model 43TS . . . . NiB $525 Ex $334 Gd $180

MODEL 44 HAMMERLESS SLIDE-ACTION REPEATER
Similar to pre-World War I Model 31A w/same general specifications but not as high quality. 20 ga. only. Model 44A is a standard-grade field gun. Model 44S Special Grade has checkered stock and slide handle of fancy walnut. Made from 1923 to 1935.
Model 44A . . . . NiB $360 Ex $251 Gd $155
Model 44S . . . . NiB $470 Ex $360 Gd $280

MODEL 49 VISIBLE HAMMER SLIDE-
ACTION REPEATING SHOTGUN . . NiB $440 Ex $316 Gd $290
Economy version of Model 42A, offered as a bonus on the purchase of four shares of Marlin stock. About 3000 made 1925 to 1928.

MODEL 50DL BOLT
ACTION SHOTGUN . . . . NiB $257 Ex $193 Gd $94
Gauge: 12 w/3-inch chamber. Two round magazine. 28-inch bbl. w/modified choke. 48.75 inches overall. Weight: 7.5 lbs. Checkered black synthetic stocks w/ventilated rubber recoil pad. Made 1997 to 1999.

MODEL 53 HAMMERLESS
SLIDE-ACTION REPEATER . . . . NiB $330 Ex $147 Gd $125
Similar to Model 43A w/same general specifications. Made 1929 to 1930.

MODEL 55 GOOSE GUN
Same as Model 55 Hunter except chambered for 12-ga. 3-inch Magnum shell, has 36-inch bbl., F choke, swivels and sling. Weight: About 8 lbs. Walnut stock (standard model) or checkered black synthetic stock w/ventilated rubber recoil pad (GDL model). Made from 1962 to 1996.
Model 55 Goose Gun . . . . NiB $235 Ex $202 Gd $155
Model 55GDL Goose Gun
(intro. 1997) . . . . NiB $330 Ex $218 Gd $214

MODEL 55 HUNTER BOLT-ACTION REPEATER
Takedown. Gauges: 12, 16, 20. Two round clip magazine. 28-inch bbl. (26-inch in 20 ga.), F or adj. choke. Plain pistol-grip stock; 12 ga. has recoil pad. Weight: About 7.25 lbs.; 20 ga., 6.5 lbs. Made 1954 to 1965.
W/plain bbl. . . . . NiB $90 Ex $59 Gd $38
W/adj. choke . . . . NiB $100 Ex $65 Gd $50

MODEL 55 SWAMP GUN. . . . . NiB $105 Ex $85 Gd $62
Same as Model 55 Hunter except chambered for 12-ga. 3-inch Magnum shell, has shorter 20.5-inch bbl. w/adj. choke, sling swivels and slightly better-quality stock. Weight: About 6.5 lbs. Made from 1963 to 1965.

MODEL 55S SLUG GUN. . . . . NiB $140 Ex $93 Gd $66
Same as Model 55 Goose Gun except has 24-inch bbl., cylinder bore, rifle sights. Weight: About 7.5 lbs. Made from 1974 to 1979.

MODEL 59 AUTO-SAFE
BOLT-ACTION SINGLE . . . . NiB $150 Ex 103 Gd $85
Takedown. Auto thumb safety, .410 ga. 24-inch bbl., F choke. Weight: About 5 lbs. Plain pistol-grip stock. Made 1959 to 1961.

MODEL 60 SINGLE-SHOT
SHOTGUN . . . . NiB $150 Ex $100 Gd $79
Visible hammer. Takedown. Boxlock. Automatic ejector. 12 ga. 30- or 32-inch bbl., F choke. Weight: About 6.5 lbs. Pistol-grip stock, beavertail forearm. Note: Only about 600 were produced in 1923.

MODEL 63 HAMMERLESS SLIDE-ACTION REPEATER
Similar to Models 43A and 43T w/same general specifications. Model 63TS Trap Special is same as Model 63T Trap Gun except stock style and dimensions to order. Made from 1931-35.
Model 63A . . . . NiB $333 Ex $267 Gd $171
Model 63T or 63TS . . . . NiB $388 Ex $282 Gd $193

Marlin Model 90
Standard Over-and-Under

Marlin Model 120
Magnum Slide-Action Repeater

Marlin Model 410
Lever-Action Repeater

Marlin Model 512
Slugmaster

Marlin Model 55-10
Super Goose 10

Marlin Premier Mark I
Slide-Action Repeater

Marlin Premier Mark IV

Marlin-Glenfield
Model 50 Bolt-Action Repeater

SHOTGUNS

**Marocchi Conquista
Sporting Clays**

MODEL 90 STANDARD O/U SHOTGUN
Hammerless. Boxlock. Double triggers; non-selective single trigger was available as an extra on pre-war guns except .410. Gauges: 12, 16, 20, .410. Bbls.: Plain; 26-, 28- or 30-inch; chokes IC/M or M/F; bbl. design changed in 1949, eliminating full-length rib between bbls. Weight: 12 ga., about 7.5 lbs.; 16 and 20 ga., about 6.25 lbs. Checkered pistol-grip stock and forearm, recoil pad standard on prewar guns. Postwar production: Model 90-DT (double trigger), Model 90-ST (single trigger). Made from 1937 to 1958.

W/double triggers	NiB $475	Ex $352	Gd $200
W/single trigger	NiB $625	Ex $519	Gd $366
Combination model	NiB $2750	Ex $1744	Gd 1560
16 ga., deduct			10%
20 ga., add			15%
.410, add			30%

MODEL 120 MAGNUM
SLIDE-ACTION REPEATER . . . . NiB $290 Ex $189 Gd $112
Hammerless. Takedown. 12 ga. (3-inch). Four round tubular magazine. Bbls.: 26-inch vent rib, IC; 28-inch vent rib M choke; 30-inch vent rib, F choke; 38-inch plain, F choke; 40-inch plain, F choke; 26-inch slug bbl. w/rifle sights, IC. Weight: About 7.75 lbs. Checkered pistol-grip stock and forearm, recoil pad. Made from 1971 to 1985.

MODEL 120 SLUG GUN . . . . NiB $290 Ex $189 Gd $112
Same general specifications as Model 120 Magnum except w/20-inch bbl. and about .5 lb. lighter in weight. No vent rib. Adj. rear rifle sights; hooded front sight. Disc. 1990.

MODEL 410 LEVER-ACTION REPEATER
Action similar to that of Marlin Model 93 rifle. Visible hammer. Solid frame. .410 ga. (2.5-inch shell). Five round tubular magazine. 22- or 26-inch bbl., F choke. Weight: About 6 lbs. Plain pistol-grip stock and grooved beavertail forearm. Made from 1929-32.

Model 410 w/22-inch bbl.	NiB $1475	Ex $1374	Gd $1273
Model 410 w/26-inch bbl.	NiB $1363	Ex $1266	Gd $1058
Deluxe model, add			30%

MODEL 512 SLUGMASTER SHOTGUN
Bolt-action repeater. Gauge: 12; 3-inch chamber, 2-round magazine. 21-inch rifled bbl. w/adj. open sight. Weight: 8 lbs. Walnut-finished birch stock (standard model) or checkered black synthetic stock w/ventilated rubber recoil pad (GDL model). Made from 1994 to 1999.

Model 512 Slugmaster	NiB $379	Ex $279	Gd $201
Model 512DL Slugmaster (intro. 1998)	NiB $295	Ex $200	Gd $126
Model 512P Slugmaster w/ported bbl. (intro. 1999)	NiB $388	Ex $305	Gd $220

MODEL 1898 VISIBLE HAMMER SLIDE-ACTION REPEATER
Takedown. 12 ga. Five shell tubular magazine. Bbls.: 26-, 28-, 30-, 32-inch; standard chokes. Weight: About 7.25 lbs. Pistol-grip stock, grooved slide handle; checkering on higher grades. Difference among grades is in quality of wood, engraving on Grades C and D. Made 1898 to 1905. Note: This was the first Marlin shotgun.

Grade A (Field)	NiB $325	Ex $218	Gd $142
Grade B	NiB $495	Ex $348	Gd $249
Grade C	NiB $635	Ex $505	Gd $399
Grade D	NiB $1981	Ex $1681	Gd $852

MODEL 5510 SUPER GOOSE . . . . . NiB $220 Ex $172 Gd $155
Similar to Model 55 Goose Gun except chambered for 10 ga. 3.5-inch Magnum shell, has 34-inch heavy bbl., F choke. Weight: About 10.5 lbs. Made from 1976 to 1985.

PREMIER MARK I
SLIDE-ACTION REPEATER . . . . NiB $200 Ex $154 Gd $80
Hammerless. Takedown. 12 ga. Magazine holds 3 shells. Bbls.: 30-inch F choke, 28-inch M, 26-inch IC or SK choke. Weight: About 6 lbs. Plain pistol-grip stock and forearm. Made in France from 1960-63.

PREMIER MARK II AND IV
Same action and mechanism as Premier Mark except engraved receiver (Mark IV is more elaborate), checkered stock and forearm, fancier wood, vent rib and similar refinements. Made 1960 to 1963.

Premier Mark II	NiB $275	Ex $208	Gd $195
Premier Mark IV (plain barrel)	NiB $306	Ex $274	Gd $182
Premier Mark IV (vent rib barrel)	NiB $330	Ex $280	Gd $244

GLENFIELD MODEL 50
BOLT-ACTION REPEATER . . . . NiB $225 Ex $185 Gd $64
Similar to Model 55 Hunter except chambered for 12-or 20-ga., 3-inch Magnum shell; has 28-inch bbl. in 12 ga., 26-inch in 20 ga., F choke. Made from 1966 to 1974.

GLENFIELD 778 SLIDE-ACTION
REPEATER . . . . NiB $225 Ex $185 Gd $135
Hammerless. 12 ga. 2.75-inch or 3-inch. Four round tubular magazine. Bbls.: 26-inch IC, 28-inch M, 30-inch F, 38-inch MXR, 20-inch slug bbl. Weight: 7.75 lbs. Checkered pistol-grip. Made from 1979 to 1984.

MAROCCHI SHOTGUNS — Brescia, Italy Imported by Precision Sales International of Westfield, MA

CONQUISTA MODEL O/U SHOTGUN
Boxlock. Gauge: 12; 2.75-inch chambers. 28-, 30- or 32-inch vent rib bbl. Fixed choke or internal tubes. 44.38 to 48 inches overall. Weight: 7.5 to 8.25 lbs. Adj. single-selective trigger. Checkered American walnut stock w/recoil pad. Imported 1994 to 2003.

Lady Sport Grade I	NiB $1868	Ex $1655	Gd $1164
Lady Sport Grade II	NiB $1995	Ex $1673	Gd $1386
Lady Sport Grade III	NiB $3234	Ex $2685	Gd $2029
Skeet Model Grade I	NiB $1722	Ex $1439	Gd $1019
Skeet Model Grade II	NiB $1995	Ex $1683	Gd $1261
Skeet Model Grade III	NiB $3225	Ex $2810	Gd $1962
Sporting Clays Grade I	NiB $1729	Ex $1577	Gd $1115
Sporting Clays Grade II	NiB $1995	Ex $1616	Gd $1275
Sporting Clays Grade III	NiB $3225	Ex $2768	Gd $1927
Trap Model Grade I	NiB $1725	Ex $1412	Gd $1124
Trap Model Grade II	NiB $1995	Ex $1731	Gd $1350
Trap Model Grade III	NiB $3227	Ex $2942	Gd $2053
Left-handed model, add			10%

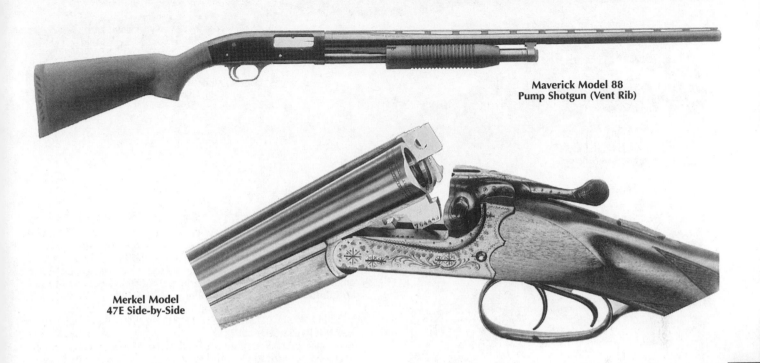

**Maverick Model 88
Pump Shotgun (Vent Rib)**

**Merkel Model
47E Side-by-Side**

MAVERICK ARMS, INC. — Eagle Pass, Texas

MODEL 88 BULLPUP . . . . **NiB $190 Ex $135 Gd $95**
Gauge: 12; 3-inch chamber. Bbl.: 18.5-inch w/fixed choke, blued.
Weight: 9.5 lbs. Dual safeties: Grip style and crossbolt. Fixed sights
in carrying handle. High-impact black synthetic stock; trigger-forward
bullpup configuration w/twin pistol-grip design. Made 1990 to 1995.

MODEL 88 DEER GUN . . . . **NiB $245 Ex $181 Gd $131**
Crossbolt safety and dual slide bars. Cylinder bore choke. Gauge:
12 only w/3-inch chamber. Bbl.: 24-inch. Weight: 7 lbs. Synthetic
stock and forearm. Disc. 1995.

MODEL 88 PUMP SHOTGUN
Gauge: 12; 2.75- or 3-inch chamber. Bbl.: 28 inches/M or 30 inch-
es/F w/fixed choke or screw-in integral tubes; plain or vent rib,
blued. Weight: 7.25 lbs. Bead front sight. Black synthetic or wood
buttstock and forend; forend grooved. Made from 1989 to date.
**Synthetic stock
w/plain bbl.** . . . . **NiB $190 Ex $164 Gd $120**
**Synthetic stock
w/vent-rib bbl.** . . . . **NiB $200 Ex $179 Gd $130**
**Synthetic Combo
w/18.5 inch bbl.** . . . . **NiB $253 Ex $199 Gd $144**
**Wood stock
w/vent-rib bbl./tubes** . . . . **NiB $226 Ex $174 Gd $140**
Wood Combo w/vent-rib bbl./tubes . . . . **NiB $255 Ex $200 Gd $162**

MODEL 88 SECURITY . . . . **NiB $190 Ex $160 Gd $124**
Crossbolt safety and dual slide bars. Optional heat shield.
Cylinder bore choke. Gauge: 12 only w/3-inch chamber. Bbl.:
18.5-inches. Weight: 6 lbs., 8 ozs. Synthetic stock and forearm.
Made 1993 to date.

MODEL 91 PUMP SHOTGUN
Same as Model 88, except w/2.75-, 3- or 3.5-inch chamber, 28-inch
bbl. W/ACCU-F choke, crossbolt safety and synthetic stock only.
Made from 1991 to 1995.
Synthetic stock w/plain bbl. . . . . . . **NiB $229 Ex $133 Gd $153**
Synthetic stock w/vent-rib bbl. . . . . **NiB $231 Ex $200 Gd $161**

MODEL 95 BOLT-ACTION . . . . **NiB $155 Ex $126 Gd $106**
Modified, fixed choke. Built-in two round magazine. Gauge: 12
only. Bbl.: 25-inch. Weight: 6.75 lbs. Bead sight. Synthetic stock
and rubber recoil pad. Made from 1995 to 1997.

GEBRÜDER MERKEL — Suhl, Germany
Mfd. by Suhler Jagd-und Sportwaffen GmbH,
*Imported by GSI, Inc., Trussville, AL,
(Previously by Armes de Chasse)*

MODEL 8 HAMMERLESS DOUBLE NiB $1378 Ex $1067 Gd $758
Anson & Deeley boxlock action w/Greener double-bbl. hook
lock. Double triggers. Extractors. Automatic safety. Gauges: 12,
16, 20; 2.75- or 3-inch chambers. 26-or 28-inch bbls. w/fixed
standard chokes. Checkered European walnut stock, pistol-grip
or English-style w/or w/o cheekpiece. Scroll-engraved receiver
w/tinted marble finish.

SIDE-BY-SIDE MODEL 47E . . . . **NiB $2568 Ex $2448 Gd $1703**
Hammerless boxlock similar to Model 8 except w/automatic
ejectors and cocking indicators. Double hook bolting. Single
selective or double triggers. 12, 16 or 20 ga. w/2.75-inch chambers. Standard bbl lengths, choke combos. Hand-checkered
European walnut stock, forearm; pistol-grip and cheekpiece or
straight English style; sling swivels.

SHOTGUNS

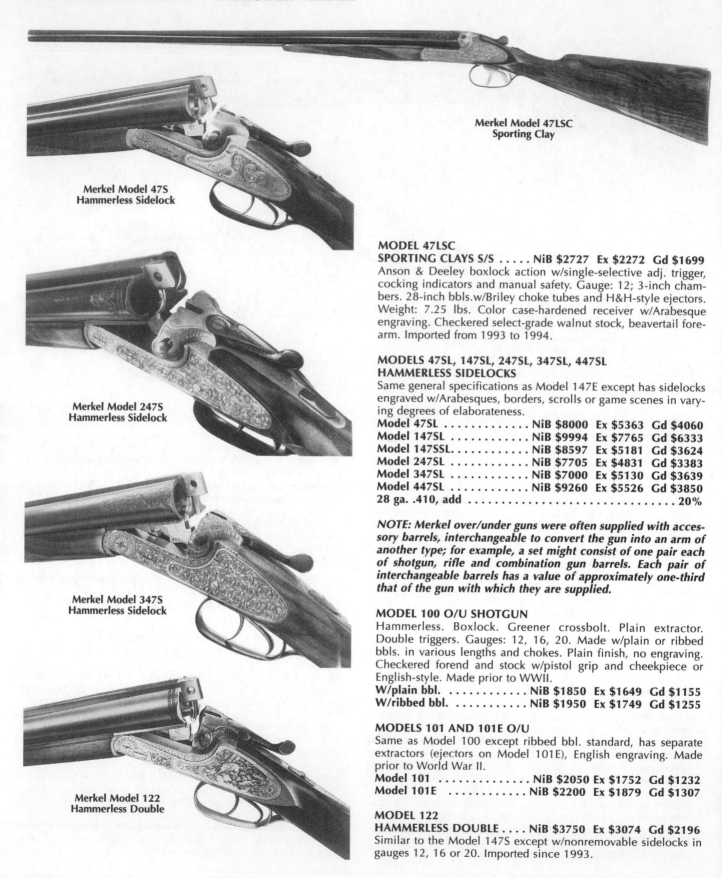

Merkel Model 47LSC
Sporting Clay

Merkel Model 47S
Hammerless Sidelock

Merkel Model 247S
Hammerless Sidelock

Merkel Model 347S
Hammerless Sidelock

Merkel Model 122
Hammerless Double

MODEL 47LSC
SPORTING CLAYS S/S . . . . . NiB $2727 Ex $2272 Gd $1699
Anson & Deeley boxlock action w/single-selective adj. trigger, cocking indicators and manual safety. Gauge: 12; 3-inch chambers. 28-inch bbls.w/Briley choke tubes and H&H-style ejectors. Weight: 7.25 lbs. Color case-hardened receiver w/Arabesque engraving. Checkered select-grade walnut stock, beavertail forearm. Imported from 1993 to 1994.

MODELS 47SL, 147SL, 247SL, 347SL, 447SL
HAMMERLESS SIDELOCKS
Same general specifications as Model 147E except has sidelocks engraved w/Arabesques, borders, scrolls or game scenes in varying degrees of elaborateness.

Model 47SL	NiB $8000	Ex $5363	Gd $4060
Model 147SL	NiB $9994	Ex $7765	Gd $6333
Model 147SSL.	NiB $8597	Ex $5181	Gd $3624
Model 247SL	NiB $7705	Ex $4831	Gd $3383
Model 347SL	NiB $7000	Ex $5130	Gd $3639
Model 447SL	NiB $9260	Ex $5526	Gd $3850
28 ga. .410, add			20%

NOTE: Merkel over/under guns were often supplied with accessory barrels, interchangeable to convert the gun into an arm of another type; for example, a set might consist of one pair each of shotgun, rifle and combination gun barrels. Each pair of interchangeable barrels has a value of approximately one-third that of the gun with which they are supplied.

MODEL 100 O/U SHOTGUN
Hammerless. Boxlock. Greener crossbolt. Plain extractor. Double triggers. Gauges: 12, 16, 20. Made w/plain or ribbed bbls. in various lengths and chokes. Plain finish, no engraving. Checkered forend and stock w/pistol grip and cheekpiece or English-style. Made prior to WWII.
W/plain bbl. . . . . NiB $1850 Ex $1649 Gd $1155
W/ribbed bbl. . . . . NiB $1950 Ex $1749 Gd $1255

MODELS 101 AND 101E O/U
Same as Model 100 except ribbed bbl. standard, has separate extractors (ejectors on Model 101E), English engraving. Made prior to World War II.
Model 101 . . . . NiB $2050 Ex $1752 Gd $1232
Model 101E . . . . NiB $2200 Ex $1879 Gd $1307

MODEL 122
HAMMERLESS DOUBLE . . . . NiB $3750 Ex $3074 Gd $2196
Similar to the Model 147S except w/nonremovable sidelocks in gauges 12, 16 or 20. Imported since 1993.

MODEL 122E

HAMMERLESS SIDELOCK............ **NiB $4099 Ex $3620 Gd $2544**
Similar to the Model 122 except w/removable sidelocks and cocking indicators. Importation disc. 1992.

MODEL 126E

HAMMERLESS SIDELOCK........ **NiB $24,254 Ex $21,460 Gd $16,044**
Holland & Holland system, hand-detachable locks. Auto ejectors. Double triggers. 12, 16 or 20 gauge w/standard bbl. lengths and chokes. Checkered forend and pistol-grip stock; available w/cheekpiece or English-style buttstock. Elaborate game scenes and engraving. Made prior to WW II.

MODEL 127E

HAMMERLESS SIDELOCK........ **NiB $24,849 Ex $21,939 Gd $16,374**
Similar to the Model 126E except w/elaborate scroll engraving on removable sidelocks w/cocking indicators. Made prior to WW II.

MODEL 128E

HAMMERLESS BOXLOCK DOUBLE . **NiB $28,679 Ex $22,167 Gd $16,954**
Scalloped Anson & Deeley action w/hinged floorplate and removable sideplates. Auto-ejectors. Double triggers. Elaborate hunting scene or Arabesque engraving. 12, 16 or 20 gauge w/various bbl. lengths and chokes. Checkered forend and stock w/pistol grip and cheekpiece or English-style. Made prior to WW II.

MODEL 130

HAMMERLESS BOXLOCK DOUBLE . **NiB $19,979 Ex $16,167 Gd $14,954**
Similar to Model 128E except w/fixed sideplates. Auto ejectors. Double triggers. Elaborate hunting scene or Arabesque engraving. Made prior to WW II.

MODESL 147 & 147E HAMMERLESS
BOXLOCK DOUBLE-BARREL SHOTGUN

Anson & Deeley system w/extractors or auto ejectors. Single selective or double triggers. Gauges: 12, 16, 20 or 28 ga. (Three-inch chambers available in 12 and 20 ga.). Bbls.: 26-inch standard, other lengths available w/any standard choke combination. Weight: 6.5 lbs. Checkered straight-grip stock and forearm. Disc. 1998.
Model 147 w/extractors ...... **NiB $2391 Ex $2067 Gd $1590**
Model 147E w/ejectors .... **NiB $5155 Ex $3662 Gd $2638**

Merkel Model 147E
Hammerless Boxlock Double-Barrel Shotgun

MODELS 200, 200E, 201, 201E,
202 AND 202E O/U SHOTGUNS

Hammerless. Boxlock. Kersten double crossbolt. Scalloped frame. Sideplates on Models 202 and 202E. Arabesque or hunting engraving supplied on all except Models 200 and 200E. "E" models have ejectors, others have separate extractors, signal pins, double triggers. Gauges: 12, 16, 20, 24, 28, 32 (last three not available in postwar guns). Ribbed bbls. in various lengths and chokes. Weight: 5.75 to 7.5 lbs. depending on bbl. length and gauge. Checkered forend and stock w/pistol grip and cheekpiece or English-style. The 200, 201, and 202 differ in overall quality, engraving, wood, checkering, etc.; aside from the faux sideplates on Models 202 and 202E, general specifications are the same. Models 200, 201, 202, and 202E, all made before WW II, are disc. Models 201E &202E in production w/revised 2000 series nomenclature.

Model 200	NiB $2748	Ex $2079	Gd $1493
Model 200E	NiB $3584	Ex $2871	Gd $1969
Model 200 ES Skeet...................	NiB $4548	Ex $4096	Gd $2888
Model 200ET Trap	NiB $4400	Ex $3996	Gd $2796
Model 200 SC Sporting Clays	NiB $6751	Ex $4442	Gd $3095
Model 201 (disc.)......................	NiB $3252	Ex $2487	Gd $1799
Model 201E (Pre-WW II)	NiB $7000	Ex $4799	Gd $2976
Model 201E (Post-WW II)...............	NiB $4799	Ex $3894	Gd $2788
Model 201 ES Skeet....................	NiB $7599	Ex $6198	Gd $4294
Model 201 ET Trap.....................	NiB $7491	Ex $6092	Gd $4292
Model 202 (disc.)......................	NiB $8000	Ex $5198	Gd $3281
Model 202E (Pre-WW II)	NiB $7999	Ex $4795	Gd $3691
Model 202 E (Post-WW II & 2002EL).....	NiB $7091	Ex $5897	Gd $3994

Merkel Model 200E
O/U Shotgun

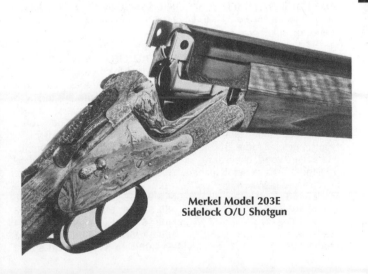

Merkel Model 203E
Sidelock O/U Shotgun

**Merkel Model 303E
O/U Shotgun**

MODEL 203E SIDELOCK O/U SHOTGUNS
Hammerless action w/hand-detachable sidelocks. Kersten double cross bolt, auto ejectors and double triggers. Gauges: 12 or 20 (16, 24, 28 and 32 disc.). 26.75- or 28-inch vent rib bbls. Arabesque engraving standard or hunting engraving optional on coin-finished receiver. Checkered English or pistol-grip stock and forend.
Model 203E sidelock (disc. 1998) .. NiB $9750 Ex $7243 Gd $5682
Model 203ES skeet
(imported 1993-97) . . . . NiB $12,080 Ex $11,380 Gd $9086
Model 203ET trap (disc. 1997) . NiB $12,071 Ex $11,451 Gd $9198

MODEL 204E
O/U SHOTGUN . . . . NiB $8500 Ex $6322 Gd $4427
Similar to Model 203E; has Merkel sidelocks, fine English engraving. Made prior to World War II.

MODEL 210E
SIDE-LOCK O/U SHOTGUN. . . NiB $7000 Ex $5134 Gd $3604
Kersten double cross-bolt, scroll-engraved, casehardened receiver. 12, 16 or 20 ga. Double-triggers; pistol-grip stock w/cheekpiece.

MODEL 211E
SIDE-LOCK O/U SHOTGUN. . . NiB $6654 Ex $5177 Gd $4325
Same specifications as Model 210E except w/engraved hunting scenes on silver-gray receiver.

MODELS 300, 300E, 301, 301E AND 302 O/U
Merkel-Anson system boxlock. Kersten double crossbolt, two underlugs, scalloped frame, sideplates on Model 302. Arabesque or hunting engraving. "E" models and Model 302 have auto ejectors, others have separate extractors. Signal pins. Double triggers. Gauges: 12, 16, 20, 24, 28, 32. Ribbed bbls. in various lengths and chokes. Checkered forend and stock w/pistol grip and cheekpiece or English-style. Grades 300, 301 and 302 differ in overall quality, engraving, wood, checkering, etc.; aside from the dummy sideplates on Model 302, general specifications are the same. Manufactured prior to World War II.
Model 300 . . . . NiB $5155 Ex $3455 Gd $2648
Model 300E . . . . NiB $7956 Ex $6798 Gd $4998
Model 301 . . . . NiB $6750 Ex $4862 Gd $3084
Model 301E . . . . NiB $7950 Ex $6068 Gd $4863
Model 302 . . . . NiB $14,000 Ex $11,992 Gd $9252

MODEL 303EL O/U SHOTGUN   NiB $26,529 Ex $24,059 Gd $19,618
Similar to Model 203E. Has Kersten crossbolt, double underlugs, Holland & Holland-type hand-detachable sidelocks, auto-ejectors. This is a finer gun than Model 203E. Currently manufactured. Special order items.

MODEL 304E O/U
SHOTGUN . . . . NiB $22,556 Ex $18,002 Gd $12,384
Special version of the Model 303E-type, but higher quality throughout. This is the top grade Merkel over/under. Currently manufactured. Special order items.

MODELS 400, 400E, 401, 401E O/U
Similar to Model 101 except have Kersten double crossbolt, Arabesque engraving on Models 400 and 400E, hunting engraving on Models 401 and 401E, finer general quality. "E" models have Merkel ejectors, others have separate extractors. Made prior to World War II.
Model 400 . . . . NiB $2077 Ex $1938 Gd $1376
Model 400E . . . . NiB $2250 Ex $2019 Gd $1703
Model 401 . . . . NiB $2679 Ex $2051 Gd $1453
Model 401E . . . . NiB $4298 Ex $3307 Gd $2319

O/U COMBINATION GUNS ("BOCKBÜCHSFLINTEN")
Shotgun bbl. over, rifle bbl. under. Gauges: 12, 16, 20; calibers: 5.6x35 Vierling, 7x57r5, 8x57JR, 8x60R Mag., 9.3x53r5, 9.3x72r5, 9.3x74R and others including domestic calibers from .22 Hornet to .375 H&H. Various bbl. lengths, chokes and weights. Other specifications and values correspond to those of Merkel over/under shotguns listed below. Currently manufactured. Model 210 & 211 series disc. 1992.
Models 410, 410E, 411E (see shotgun models 400, 400E, 401, 401E)
Models 210, 210E, 211, 211E, 212, 212E
(see shotgun models 200, 200E, 201, 201E, 202, 202E)

MODEL 2000EL O/U SHOTGUNS
Kersten double cross-bolt. Gauges: 12 and 20. 26.75- or 28-inch bbls. Weight: 6.4 to 7.28 lbs. Scroll engraved silver-gray receiver. Automatic ejectors and single selective or double triggers. Checkered forend and stock w/pistol grip and cheekpiece or English-style stock w/luxury grade wood. Imported from 1998 to 2005.
Model 2000EL Standard   . . . . . NiB $5692 Ex $4350 Gd $3003
Model 2000EL Sporter . . . . NiB $5700 Ex $4454 Gd $3115

MODEL 2001EL O/U SHOTGUNS
Gauges: 12, 16, 20 and 28; Kersten double cross-bolt lock receiver. 26.75- or 28-inch IC/mod, mod/full bbls. Weight: 6.4 to 7.28 lbs. Three-piece forearm, automatic ejectors and single selective or double triggers. Imported from 1993 to 2005.
Model 2001EL 12 ga. . . . . NiB $6295 Ex $5090 Gd $3561
Model 2001EL 16 ga.
(disc. 1997) . . . . NiB $6295 Ex $5090 Gd $3561
Model 2001EL 20 ga. . . . . NiB $6295 Ex $5090 Gd $3561
Model 2001EL 28 ga.
(made 1995) . . . . NiB $6989 Ex $5791 Gd $3906

MODEL 2002EL . . . . NiB $10,625 Ex $7692 Gd $5981
Same specifications as Model 2000EL except hunting scenes w/Arabesque engraving.

ANSON DRILLINGS
Three-bbl. combination guns; usually made w/double shotgun bbls., over rifle bbl., although "Doppelbüchsdrillingen" were made w/two rifle bbls. over and shotgun bbl. under. Hammerless.

Miida Model 612
Field Grade O/U

Boxlock. Anson & Deeley system. Side clips. Plain extractors. Double triggers. Gauges: 12, 16, 20; rifle calibers: 7x57r5, 8x57JR and 9.3x74R are most common, but other calibers from 5.6mm to 10.75mm available. Bbls.: standard drilling 25.6 inches; short drilling, 21.6 inches. Checkered pistol-grip stock and forend. The three models listed differ chiefly in overall quality, grade of wood, etc.; general specifications are the same. Made prior to WW II.

Model 142 Engraved . . . . NiB $5599 Ex $4523 Gd $3157
Model 142 Standard . . . . NiB $4286 Ex $3459 Gd $24272
Model 145 Field . . . . NiB $3592 Ex $2928 Gd $2047

MIIDA SHOTGUNS — Manufactured for Marubeni America Corp., New York, N.Y., by Olin-Kodensha Co., Tochigi, Japan

MODEL 612 FIELD GRADE O/U. . . NiB $799 Ex $564 Gd $353
Boxlock. Auto ejectors. Selective single trigger. 12 ga. Bbls.: Vent rib; 26-inch, IC/M; 28-inch, M/F choke. Weight: W/26-inch bbl., 6 lbs., 11 oz. Checkered pistol-grip stock and forearm. Made 1972 to 1974.

MODEL 2100 SKEET GUN . . . . NiB $875 Ex $656 Gd $417
Similar to Model 612 except has more elaborate engraving on frame (50 percent coverage), skeet-style stock and forearm of select grade wood; 27-inch vent-rib bbls., SK choke. Weight: 7 lbs., 11 oz. Made from 1972 to 1974.

MODEL 2200T TRAP GUN,
MODEL 2200S SKEET GUN . . . . . . NiB $925 Ex $691 Gd $541
Similar to Model 612 except more elaborate engraving on frame (60 percent coverage), trap- or skeet-style stock and semi-beavertail forearm of fancy walnut, recoil pad on trap stock. Bbls.: Wide vent rib; 29.75-inch, IM/F choke on Trap Gun; 27-inch, SK choke on Skeet Gun. Weight: Trap, 7 lbs., 14 oz.; Skeet, 7 lbs., 11 oz. Made 1972 to 1974.

MODEL 2300T TRAP GUN,
MODEL 2300S SKEET GUN . . . . . . NiB $975 Ex $753 Gd $585
Same as models 2200T and 2200S except more elaborate engraving on frame (70% coverage). Made from 1972 to 1974.

GRANDEE MODEL GRT/IRS
TRAP/SKEET GUN. . . . . NiB $2500 Ex $2233 Gd $1577
Boxlock w/sideplates. Frame, breech ends of bbls., trigger guard and locking lever fully engraved and gold inlaid. Auto ejectors. Selective single trigger. 12 ga. Bbls.: Wide vent rib; 29-inch, F choke on Trap Gun; 27-inch, SK choke on Skeet Gun. Weight: Trap, 7 lbs., 14 oz.; Skeet, 7 lbs., 11 oz. Trap- or skeet-style stock and semi-beavertail forearm of extra fancy wood, recoil pad on trap stock. Made 1972 to 1974.

MITCHELL ARMS — Santa Ana, California

MODEL 9104/9105 PUMP SHOTGUNS
Slide action in Field/Riot configuration. Gauge: 12; 5-round tubular magazine. 20-inch bbl.; fixed choke or screw-in tubes. Weight: 6.5 lbs. Plain walnut stock. Made from 1994 to 1996.

Model 9104 (w/plain bbl.) . . . . NiB $244 Ex $200 Gd $165
Model 9105 (w/rifle sight). . . . . NiB $244 Ex $200 Gd $165
W/choke tubes, add $20

MODEL 9108/9109 PUMP SHOTGUN
Slide action in Military/Police/Riot configuration. Gauge: 12, 7-round tubular magazine. 20-inch bbl.; fixed choke or screw-in tubes. Weight: 6.5 lbs. Plain walnut stock and grooved slide handle w/brown, green or black finish. Blued metal. Made from 1994 to 1996.

Model 9108 (w/plain bbl.) . . . . NiB $240 Ex $200 Gd $170
Model 9109 (w/rifle sights) . . . . NiB $240 Ex $200 Gd $170
W/choke tubes, add $20

MODEL 9111/9113 PUMP SHOTGUN
Slide action in Military/Police/Riot configuration. Gauge: 12; 6-round tubular magazine. 18.5-inch bbl.; fixed choke or screw-in tubes. Weight: 6.5 lbs. Synthetic or plain walnut stock and grooved slide handle w/brown, green or black finish. Blued metal. Made from 1994 to 1996.

Model 9111 (w/plain bbl.) . . . . NiB $240 Ex $200 Gd $170
Model 9113 (w/rifle sights) . . . . NiB $240 Ex $200 Gd $170
W/choke tubes, add $20

MODEL 9114/9114FS
Slide action in Military/Police/Riot configuration. Gauge: 12; 7-round tubular magazine. 20-inch bbl.; fixed choke or screw-in tubes. Weight: 6.5-7 lbs. Synthetic pistol-grip or folding stock. Blued metal. Made from 1994 to 1996.

Model 9114. . . . . NiB $295 Ex $188 Gd $108
Model 9114FS. . . . . NiB $295 Ex $188 Gd $108

MODEL 9115/9115FS
PUMP SHOTGUN. . . . . NiB $295 Ex $188 Gd $108
Slide action in Military/Police/Riot configuration. Gauge: 12; 6-round tubular magazine. 18.5-inch bbl. w/heat-shield handguard. Weight: 7 lbs. Gray synthetic stock and slide handle. Parkerized metal. Made from 1994 to 1996.

MONTGOMERY WARD

See shotgun listings under "W"

MORRONE SHOTGUN — Manufactured by Rhode Island Arms Company, Hope Valley, RI

STANDARD MODEL 46 O/U . . . . NiB $1100 Ex $774 Gd $525
Boxlock. Plain extractors. Non-selective single trigger. Gauges: 12, 20. Bbls.: Plain, vent rib; 26-inch IC/M; 28-inch M/F choke. Weight: About 7 lbs., 12 ga.; 6 lbs., 20 ga. Checkered straight- or pistol-grip stock and forearm. Made 1949-53. Note: Fewer than 500 of these guns were produced, about 50 in 20 ga.. A few had vent-rib bbls. Value shown is for 12 ga. w/plain bbls.. The rare 20 ga. and vent-rib types should bring considerably more.

SHOTGUNS

Mossberg Model 83D

Mossberg Model 85D
Bolt-Action Repeating Shotgun

Mossberg Model 183K

Mossberg Model 185K

Mossberg Model 200K
Slide-Action Repeater

Mossberg Model 395K
Bolt-Action Repeater

O.F. MOSSBERG & SONS, INC. —
North Haven, Connecticut,
Formerly New Haven, Connecticut

MODEL 83D OR 183D . . . . **NiB $150 Ex $104 Gd $90**
3-round. Takedown. .410 ga. only. Two shell fixed top-loading magazine. 23-inch bbl. w/two interchangeable choke tubes (M/F). Later production had 24-inch bbl. Plain one-piece pistol-grip stock. Weight: about 5.5 lbs. Originally designated Model 83D, changed in 1947 to Model 183D. Made from 1940 to 1971.

MODEL 85D OR 185D BOLT-ACTION
REPEATING SHOTGUN . . . . **NiB $150 Ex $104 Gd $90**
Takedown. Three-round. 20 ga. only. Two-shell detachable box magazine. 25-inch bbl., three interchangeable choke tubes (F, M, IC). Later production had 26-inch bbl. w/F/IC choke tubes.

Weight: About 6.25 lbs. Plain one-piece, pistol-grip stock. Originally designated Model 85D, changed in 1947 to Model 185D. Made from 1940 to 1971.

MODEL 183K . . . . **NiB $175 Ex $128 Gd $96**
Same as Model 183D except has 25-inch bbl. w/variable C-Lect-Choke instead of interchangeable choke tubes. Made 1953 to 1986.

MODEL 185K . . . . **NiB $175 Ex $134 Gd $96**
Same as Model 185D except has variable C-Lect-Choke instead of interchangeable choke tubes. Made from 1950 to 1963.

MODEL 190D . . . . **NiB $175 Ex $128 Gd $96**
Same as Model 185D except in 16 ga. Weight: About 6 lbs. Made from 1955 to 1971.

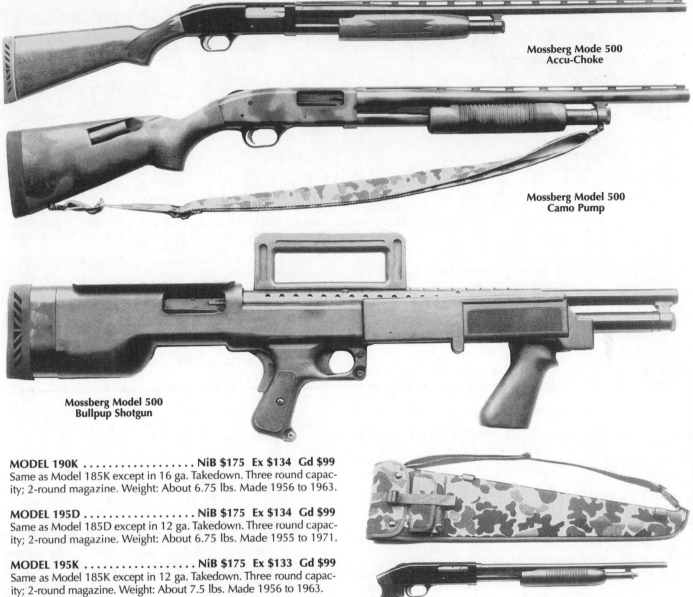

Mossberg Mode 500
Accu-Choke

Mossberg Model 500
Camo Pump

Mossberg Model 500
Bullpup Shotgun

Mossberg Model 500
Camper

MODEL 190K . . . . **NiB $175 Ex $134 Gd $99**
Same as Model 185K except in 16 ga. Takedown. Three round capacity; 2-round magazine. Weight: About 6.75 lbs. Made 1956 to 1963.

MODEL 195D . . . . **NiB $175 Ex $134 Gd $99**
Same as Model 185D except in 12 ga. Takedown. Three round capacity; 2-round magazine. Weight: About 6.75 lbs. Made 1955 to 1971.

MODEL 195K . . . . **NiB $175 Ex $133 Gd $99**
Same as Model 185K except in 12 ga. Takedown. Three round capacity; 2-round magazine. Weight: About 7.5 lbs. Made 1956 to 1963.

MODEL 200D . . . . **NiB $275 Ex $198 Gd $104**
Same as Model 200K except w/two interchangeable choke tubes instead of C-Lect choke. Made from 1955 to 1959.

MODEL 200K
SLIDE-ACTION REPEATER. . . . . **NiB $275 Ex $138 Gd $99**
12 ga. 3-round detachable box magazine. 28-inch bbl. C-Lect choke. Plain pistol-grip stock. Black nylon slide handle. Weight: About 7.5 lbs. Made from 1955 to 1959.

MODEL 395K BOLT-ACTION REPEATER . . . . . **NiB $175 Ex $1389 Gd $99**
Takedown. Three round (detachable-clip magazine holds two rounds).12 ga. (3-inch chamber). 28-inch bbl. w/C-Lect-Choke. Weight: About 7.5 lbs. Monte Carlo stock w/recoil pad. Made 1963 to 1983.

MODEL 385K . . . . **NiB $175 Ex $138 Gd $96**
Same as Model 395K except 20 ga. (3-inch), 26-inch bbl. w/C-Lect-Choke. Weight: About 6.25 lbs.

MODEL 390K . . . . **NiB $175 Ex $138 Gd $99**
Same as Model 395K except 16 ga. (2.75-inch). Made 1963 to 1974.

MODEL 395S SLUGSTER . . . . **NiB $175 Ex $138 Gd $99**
Same as Model 395K except has 24-inch bbl., cylinder bore, rifle sights, swivels and web sling. Weight: About 7 lbs. Made from 1968 to 1981.

MODEL 500 ACCU-CHOKE SHOTGUN . . . . . . **NiB $250 Ex $175 Gd $95**
Pump-action. Gauge: 12. 24- or 28-inch bbl. Weight: 7.25 lbs. Checkered walnut-finished wood stock w/ventilated recoil pad. Available w/synthetic field or Speed-Feed stocks. Drilled and tapped receivers, swivels and camo sling on camo models. Made from 1987 to date.

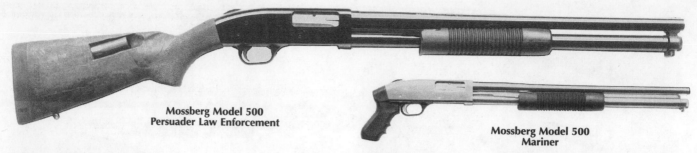

**Mossberg Model 500
Persuader Law Enforcement**

**Mossberg Model 500
Mariner**

MODEL 500 BANTAM SHOTGUN
Same as Model 500 Sporting Pump except 20 or .410 ga. only. 22-inch w/ACCU-Choke tubes or 24-inch w/F choke; vent rib. Scaled-down checkered hardwood or synthetic stock w/standard or Realtree camo finish. Made from 1990 to 1996 and 1998 to 1999.
Bantam Model (hardwood stock) . . . . NiB $200 Ex $184 Gd $124
Bantam Model (synthetic stock) . . . . NiB $292 Ex $204 Gd $146
Bantam Model (Realtree camo), add. $50

MODEL 500 BULLPUP SHOTGUN . . . . . . NiB $651 Ex $424 Gd $301
Pump. Gauge: 12. Six or 8-round capacity. Bbl.: 18.5 to 20 inches. 26.5 and 28.5 inches overall. Weight: About 9.5 lbs. Multiple independent safety systems. Dual pistol grips, rubber recoil pad. Fully enclosed rifle-type sights. Synthetic stock. Ventilated bbl. heat shield. Made from 1987 to 1990.

MODEL 500 CAMO PUMP
Same as Model 500 Sporting Pump except 12 ga. only. Receiver drilled and tapped. QD swivels and camo sling. Special camouflage finish.
Standard model . . . . NiB $345 Ex $216 Gd $157
Combo model (w/ext. Slugster bbl.) . . . NiB $367 Ex $268 Gd $192

MODEL 500 CAMPER . . . . NiB $250 Ex $189 Gd $145
Same general specifications as Model 500 Field Grade except .410 bore, 6-round magazine, 18.5-inch plain cylinder bore bbl. Synthetic pistol grip and camo carrying case. Made 1986 to 1990.

MODEL 500 FIELD GRADE
HAMMERLESS SLIDE-ACTION REPEATER
Pre-1977 type. Takedown. Gauges: 12, 16, 20, .410. Three inch chamber (2.75-inch in 16 ga.). Tubular magazine holds five 2.75-inch rounds or four three-inch. Bbls.: Plain- 30-inch regular or heavy Magnum, F choke (12 ga. only); 28-inch, M or F; 26-inch, IC or adj. C-Lect-Choke; 24-inch Slugster, cylinder bore, w/rifle sights. Weight: 5.75 to lbs. Plain pistol-grip stock w/recoil pad, grooved slide handle. After 1973, these guns have checkered stock and slide handles; Models 500AM and 500AS have receivers etched w/game scenes. The latter has swivels and sling. Made from 1962 to 1976.
Model 500A, 12 ga., ... NiB $250 Ex $186 Gd $132
Model 500AM, 12 ga., hvy. Mag. bbl. . . . . . NiB $250 Ex $180 Gd $126
Model 500AK, 12 ga., C-Lect-Choke . . . . NiB $265 Ex $190 Gd $124
Model 500AS, 12 ga., Slugster . . . . NiB $273 Ex $180 Gd $128
Model 500B 16 ga., ... NiB $285 Ex $180 Gd $122
Model 500BK, 16 ga., C-Lect-Choke . . . . . NiB $267 Ex $180 Gd $121
Model 500BS, 16 ga., Slugster . . . . NiB $275 Ex $180 Gd $124
Model 500C 20 ga., ... NiB $297 Ex $180 Gd $123
Model 500CK, 20 ga., C-Lect-Choke . . . . . NiB $270 Ex $180 Gd $123
Model 500CS, 20 ga., Slugster . . . . NiB $267 Ex $180 Gd $126
Model 500E, .410 ga., ... NiB $273 Ex $180 Gd $120
Model 500EK, .410 ga., C-Lect-Choke . . . . NiB $292 Ex $180 Gd $121

MODEL 500 "L" SERIES
"L" in model designation. Same as pre-1977 Model 500 Field Grade except not available in 16 ga., has receiver etched w/different game scenes; Accu-Choke w/three interchangeable tubes (IC, M, F) standard, restyled stock and slide handle. Bbls.: plain or vent rib; 30- or 32-inch, heavy, F choke (12 ga. Magnum and vent rib only); 28-inch, Accu-Choke (12 and 20 ga.); 26-inch F choke (.410 bore only); 18.5-inch (12 ga. only), 24-inch (12 and 20 ga.) Slugster w/rifle sights, cylinder bore. Weight: 6 to 8.5 lbs. Intro. 1977.
Model 500ALD, 12 ga.,
plain bbl. (disc. 1980) . . . . NiB $237 Ex $180 Gd $91
Model 500ALDR, 12 ga., vent rib . . . . NiB $258 Ex $180 Gd $91
Model 500ALMR, 12 ga.,
Heavy Duck Gun (disc. 1980) . . . . NiB $258 Ex $180 Gd $91
Model 500CLD, 20 ga.,
plain bbl. (disc. 1980) . . . . NiB $297 Ex $180 Gd $91
Model 500CLDR, 20 ga., vent rib . . . . NiB $245 Ex $180 Gd $91
Model 500CLS, 20 ga.,
Slugster (disc. 1980) . . . . NiB $278 Ex $180 Gd $91
Model 500EL, .410 ga.,
plain bbl. (disc. 1980) . . . . NiB $243 Ex $180 Gd $91
Model 500ELR, .410 ga., vent rib . . . . NiB $258 Ex $180 Gd $91

MODEL 500 MARINER SHOTGUN . . . . . . NiB $465 Ex $352 Gd $197
Slide action. Gauge: 12. 18.5 or 20-inch bbl. Six round and 8-round respectively. Weight: 7.25 lbs. High-strength synthetic buttstock and forend. Available in extra round-carrying Speed Feed synthetic buttstock. All metal treated for protection against saltwater corrosion. Intro. 1987.

MODEL 500 MUZZLELOADER COMBO. . NiB $335 Ex $240 Gd $153
Same as Model 500 Sporting Pump except w/extra 24-inch rifled .50-caliber muzzleloading bbl. w/ramrod. Made 1991 to 1996.

MODEL 500 PERSUADER LAW ENFORCEMENT
Similar to pre-1977 Model 500 Field Grade except 12 ga. only, 6- or 8-round capacity, has 18.5- or 20-inch plain bbl., cylinder bore, either shotgun or rifle sights, plain pistol-grip stock and grooved slide handle, sling swivels. Special Model 500ATP8-SP has bayonet lug, Parkerized finish. Intro. 1995.
Model 500ATP6, 6-round, 18.5-inch
bbl., shotgun sights . . . . NiB $350 Ex $236 Gd $172
Model 500ATP6CN, 6-round,
nickle finish "Cruiser" pistol-grip. . . . . . . NiB $365 Ex $246 Gd $189
Model 500ATP6N, 6-round, nickel
finish, 2.75- or 3-inch Mag. shells . . . . . . NiB $350 Ex $241 Gd $175
Model 500ATP6S, 6-round,
18.5-inch bbl., rifle sights . . . . NiB $350 Ex $236 Gd $182
Model 500ATP8, 8-round,
20-inch bbl., shotgun sights . . . . NiB $365 Ex $257 Gd $195
Model 500ATP8S, 8-round,
20-inch bbl., rifle sights . . . . NiB $373 Ex $270 Gd $206
Model 500ATP8-SP Spec. Enforcement . . . NiB $391 Ex $313 Gd $226
Model 500 Bullpup . . . . NiB $650 Ex $471 Gd $335
Model 500 Intimidator w/laser sight, blued . . . NiB $567 Ex $439 Gd $313
Model 500 Intimidator w/laser sight,
parkerized . . . . NiB $350 Ex $250 Gd $120
Model 500 Security combo pack . . . . NiB $274 Ex $203 Gd $151
Model 500 Cruiser w/pistol grip . . . . NiB $400 Ex $273 Gd $151

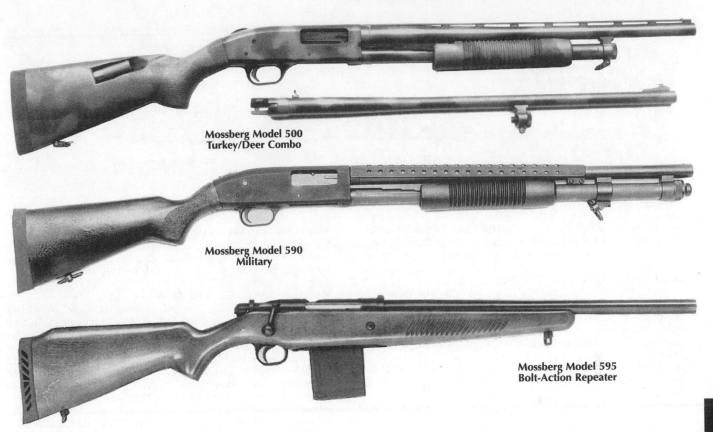

**Mossberg Model 500
Turkey/Deer Combo**

**Mossberg Model 590
Military**

**Mossberg Model 595
Bolt-Action Repeater**

MODEL 500 PIGEON GRADE

Same as Model 500 Super Grade except higher quality w/fancy wood, floating vent rib; field gun hunting dog etching, trap and skeet guns have scroll etching. Bbls.: 30-inch, F choke (12 ga. only); 28-inch, M choke; 26-inch, SK choke or C-Lect-Choke. Made from 1971 to 1975.

Model 500APR, 12 ga., field, trap or skeet . . . NiB $444 Ex $313 Gd $298
Model 500APKR, 12 ga.
field gun, C-Lect-Choke . . . . NiB $385 Ex $224 Gd $105
Model 500 APTR, 12 ga.,
Trap gun, Monte Carlo stock . . . . NiB $375 Ex $253 Gd $153
Model 500CPR, 20 ga., field or skeet gun . . . . NiB $295 Ex $229 Gd $108
Model 500EPR, .410 ga.
field or skeet gun . . . . NiB $295 Ex $229 Gd $108

MODEL 500 CAMO COMBO SHOTGUN. . . . NiB $375 Ex $280 Gd $200

Gauges: 12 and 20. 24- and 28-inch bbl. w/adj. rifle sights. Weight: 7 to 7.25 lbs. Available w/blued or camo finish. Drilled and tapped receiver w/sling swivels and camo web sling. Made from 1987 to 1998.

MODEL 500 PUMP SLUGSTER SHOTGUN

Gauges: 12 or 20 w/3-inch chamber. 24-inch smoothbore or rifled bbl. w/adj. rifle sights or intregral scope mount and optional muzzle break (1997 porting became standard). Weight: 7 to 7.25 lbs. Wood or synthetic stock w/standard or Woodland Camo finish. Blued, matte black or Marinecote metal finish. Drilled and tapped receiver w/camo sling and swivels. Made 1987 to date.

Slugster (w/cyl. bore, rifle sights) . . . . NiB $275 Ex $206 Gd $172
Slugster (w/rifled bore, ported) . . . . NiB $350 Ex $287 Gd $208
Slugster (w/rifled bore, unported). . . . . NiB $275 Ex $206 Gd $172
Slugster (w/rifled bore, ported,
integral scope mount) . . . . NiB $275 Ex $206 Gd $172
Slugster (w/Marinecote and
synthetic stock), add $60
Slugster (w/Truglo fiber optics), add. $30

MODEL 500 REGAL SLIDE-ACTION REPEATER

Similar to regular Model 500 except higher quality workmanship throughout. Gauges: 12 and 20. Bbls.: 26- and 28-inch w/various chokes, or Accu-Choke. Weight: 6.75 to 7.5 lbs. Checkered walnut stock and forearm. Made from 1985 to 1987.

Model 500 w/Accu-Choke . . . . NiB $257 Ex $198 Gd $144
Model 500 w/fixed choke . . . . NiB $237 Ex $178 Gd $124

MODEL 500 SPORTING PUMP

Gauges: 12, 20 or .410, 2.75- or 3-inch chamber. Bbls.: 22 to 28 inches w/fixed choke or screw-in tubes; plain or vent rib. Weight: 6.25 to 7.25 lbs. White bead front sight, brass mid-bead. Checkered hardwood buttstock and forend w/walnut finish.

Standard model . . . . NiB $299 Ex $239 Gd $175
Field combo (w/extra Slugster bbl.) . . . . NiB $375 Ex $293 Gd $212

MODEL 500 SUPER GRADE

Same as pre-1977 Model 500 Field Grade except not made in 16 ga., has vent rib bbl., checkered pistol grip and slide handle. Made from 1965- to 1976.

Model 500AR, 12 ga. . . . . NiB $350 Ex $248 Gd $181
Model 500AMR, 12 ga.,
heavy magnum bbl. . . . . NiB $350 Ex $281 Gd $205
Model 500AKR, 12 ga., C-Lect-Choke . . . . NiB $350 Ex $281 Gd $205
Model 500CR 20 ga. . . . . NiB $350 Ex $281 Gd $205
Model 500CKk, 20 ga., C-Lect-Choke. . . . . NiB $350 Ex $281 Gd $205
Model 500ER, .410 ga. NiB $350 Ex $281 Gd $205
Model 500EKR, .410 ga., C-Lect-Choke . . . . . . NiB $350 Ex $281 Gd $205

MODEL 500 TURKEY/DEER COMBO. . . . . NiB $350 Ex $281 Gd $205

Pump (slide action). Gauge: 12. 20- and 24-inch bbls. Weight: 7.25 lbs. Drilled and tapped receiver, camo sling and swivels. Adj. rifle sights and camo finish. Vent rib. Made from 1987 to 1997.

Mossberg Model 1000
Junior Autoloading

Mossberg Model 5500
Guardian

MODEL 500 TURKEY GUN . . . . . . NiB $345 Ex $287 Gd $206
Same as Model 500 Camo Pump except w/24-inch ACCU-Choke bbl.
w/extra full choke tube and ghost ring sights. Made 1992 to 1997.

MODEL 500 VIKING PUMP SHOTGUN
Gauges: 12 or 20 w/3-inch chamber. 24-, 26- or 28-inch bbls. available
in smoothbore w/Accu-Choke and vent rib or rifled bore w/iron sights
and optional muzzle brake (1997 porting became standard). Optional
optics: Slug Shooting System (SSS). Weight: 6.9 to 7.2 lbs. Moss-green
synthetic stock. Matte black metal finish. Made from 1996 to 1998.
Mdl. 500 Viking
(w/VR & choke tubes, unported) . . . . NiB $230 Ex $191 Gd $103
Mdl. 500 Viking (w/rifled bore, ported) . . . . NiB $338 Ex $299 Gd $211
Mdl. 500 Viking
(w/rifled bore, SSS & ported) . . . . NiB $338 Ex $191 Gd $103
Mdl. 500 Viking
(w/rifled bore, unported) . . . . NiB $230 Ex $191 Gd $102
Mdl. 500 Viking Turkey
(w/VR, tubes, ported) . . . . NiB $230 Ex $173 Gd $106
MODEL 500
WATERFOWL/DEER COMBO . . . . NiB $394 Ex $306 Gd $218
Same general specifications as the Turkey/Deer combo except w/either
28- or 30-inch bbl. along w/the 24-inch bbl. Made from 1987 to date.

MODEL 500 ATR SUPER
GRADE TRAP . . . . NiB $350 Ex $246 Gd $176
Same as pre-1977 Model 500 Field Grade except 12 ga. only
w/vent-rib bbl.; 30-inch F choke, checkered Monte Carlo stock
w/recoil pad, beavertail slide handle. Made from 1968 to 1971.

MODEL 500DSPR DUCK STAMP
COMMEMORATIVE . . . . NiB $525 Ex $408 Gd $232
Limited edition of 1000 to commemorate the Migratory Bird Hunting Stamp
program. Same as Model 500DSPR Pigeon Grade 12-Gauge Magnum Heavy
Duck Gun w/heavy 30-inch vent-rib bbl., F choke; receiver has special wood
duck etching. Gun accompanied by a special wall plaque. Made in 1975.

MODEL 590 BULLPUP . . . . NiB $650 Ex $396 Gd $281
Same general specifications as the Model 500 Bullpup except 20-
inch bbl. and 9-round magazine. Made from 1989 to 1990.

MODEL 590 MARINER PUMP
Same general specifications as the Model 590 Military Security
except has Marinecote metal finish and field configuration synthet-
ic stock w/pistiol-grip conversion included. Made 1989 to 1999.
Model 590 Mariner (w/18.5-inch bbl.) . . . . NiB $565 Ex $389 Gd $267
Model 590 Mariner (w/20-inch bbl.) . . . . . . NiB $565 Ex $389 Gd $267
Model 590 Mariner (w/grip conversion), add $20
Model 590 Mariner (w/ghost ring sight), add $50

MODEL 590 MILITARY SECURITY . . . . . . NiB $457 Ex $359 Gd $259
Same general specifications as the Model 590 Military except there
is no heat shield and gun has short pistol-grip style instead of buttstock. Weight: About 6.75 lbs. Made from 1987 to 1993.

MODEL 590 MILITARY SHOTGUN
Slide-action. Gauge: 12. 9-round capacity. 20-inch bbl. Weight:
About 7 lbs. Synthetic or hardwood buttstock and forend. Ventilated
bbl. heat shields. Equipped w/bayonet lug. Blued or Parkerized fin-
ish. Made from 1987 to date.
Synthetic model, blued . . . . NiB $395 Ex $317 Gd $229
Synthetic model Parkerized . . . . . . NiB $431 Ex $338 Gd $244
Speedfeed model, blued . . . . NiB $424 Ex $332 Gd $240
Speedfeed model, Parkerized . . . . . NiB $424 Ex $332 Gd $240
Intimidator model
w/laser sight, blued . . . . NiB $550 Ex $426 Gd $305
Intimidator model
w/laser sight, Parkerized . . . . NiB $553 Ex $436 Gd $313
For ghost ring sight, add $75

MODEL 595/595K
BOLT-ACTION REPEATER . . . . NiB $356 Ex $199 Gd $123
12 ga. only. Four round detachable magazine. 18.5-inch bbl. Weight: About 7
lbs. Walnut finished stock w/recoil pad and sling swivels. Made 1985 to 1986.

MODEL 695 BOLT-ACTION SLUGSTER
Gauge: 12 w/3-inch chamber. Two round detachable magazine. 22-
inch fully rifled and ported bbl. w/blade front and folding leaf rear
sights. Receiver drilled and tapped for Weaver style scope bases.
Available w/1.5x-4.5x scope or fiber optics installed. Weight: 7.5 lbs.
Black synthetic stock w/swivel studs and recoil pad. Made 1996 to
2002.
Model 695 (w/ACCU-choke bbl.) . . NiB $258 Ex $196 Gd $141
Model 695
(w/open sights) . . . . NiB $335 Ex $246 Gd $176
Model 695
(w/1.5x-4.5x Bushnell scope) . . . . . NiB $345 Ex $344 Gd $244
Model 695 (w/Truglo fiber optics) . . . . NiB $340 Ex $276 Gd $198
Model 695 OFM Camo . . . . NiB $290 Ex $237 Gd $170

MODEL 695 BOLT-ACTION TURKEY GUN NiB $312 Ex $238 Gd $171
Similar to 695 Slugster Model except has smoothbore 22-inch bbl.
w/extra-full turkey Accu-choke tube. Bead front and U-notch rear
sights. Full OFM camo finish. Made from 1996 to 2002.

MODEL 712 AUTOLOADING SHOTGUN
Gas-operated, takedown, hammerless shotgun w/5-round (4-round w/3-inch
chamber) tubular magazine. 12 ga. Bbls.: 28-inch vent rib or 24-inch plain
bbl. Slugster w/rifle sights. Fixed choke or ACCU-choke tube system. Weight:
7.5 lbs. Plain alloy receiver w/top-mounted ambidextrous safety. Checkered.
stained hardwood stock w/recoil pad. Imported from Japan 1986 to 1990.

Mdl. 712 w/fixed chokes . . . . NiB $309 Ex $205 Gd $165
Mdl. 712 w/ACCU-Choke tube system . . . . . NiB $329 Ex $215 Gd $185
Mdl. 712 Regal w/ACCU-Choke tube system . NiB $329 Ex $215 Gd $185
Mdl. 712 Regal w/ACCU-Choke II tube sys. . . NiB $329 Ex $215 Gd $185

MODEL 835 FIELD PUMP SHOTGUN
Similar to the Model 9600 Regal except has walnut-stained hardwood stock and one ACCU-Choke tube only.
Standard model . . . . NiB $270 Ex $159 Gd $108
Turkey model . . . . NiB $270 Ex $159 Gd $108
Combo model (24- & 28-inch bbls.) NiB $310 Ex $199 Gd $148

MODEL 835 "NWTF" ULTI-MA SHOTGUN
National Wild Turkey Federation pump-action. Gauge: 12, 3.5-inch chamber. 24-inch vent-rib bbl. w/four ACCU-MAG chokes. Realtree camo finish. QD swivel and post. Made from 1989 to 1993.
Limited Edition model . . . . NiB $425 Ex $305 Gd $190
Special Edition model . . . . NiB $380 Ex $299 Gd $192

MODEL 835 REGAL ULTI-MAG PUMP
Gauge: 12, 3.5-inch chamber. Bbls.: 24- or 28-inch vent-rib w/ACCU-Choke screw-in tubes. Weight: 7.75 lbs. White bead front, brass mid-bead. Checkered hardwood or synthetic stock w/camo finish. Made 1991 to 1996.
Special model . . . . NiB $342 Ex $275 Gd $201
Standard model . . . . NiB $453 Ex $331 Gd $239
Camo Synthetic model . . . . NiB $442 Ex $355 Gd $256
Combo model . . . . NiB $472 Ex $381 Gd $274

MODEL 835 VIKING PUMP SHOTGUN
Gauge: 12 w/3-inch chamber. 28-inch smoothbore bbl. w/Accu-Choke, vent rib and optional muzzle brake (in 1997 porting became standard). Weight: 7.7 lbs. Green synthetic stock. Matte black metal finish. Made from 1996 to 1998.
Model 835 Viking (w/VR and
choke tubes, ported) . . . . NiB $260 Ex $184 Gd $142
Model 835 Viking (w/VR
and choke tubes, unported) . . . . . . NiB $400 Ex $223 Gd $182

MODEL 1000 AUTOLOADING SHOTGUN
Gas-operated, takedown, hammerless shotgun w/tubular magazine. Gauges: 12, 20; 2.75- or 3-inch chamber. Bbls.: 22- to 30-inch vent rib w/fixed choke or ACCU-Choke tubes; or 22-inch plain bbl, Slugster w/rifle sights. Weight: 6.5 to 7.5 lbs. Scroll-engraved alloy receiver, crossbolt-type safety. Checkered walnut buttstock and forend. Imported from Japan 1986 to 1987.
Junior model, 20 ga., 22-inch bbl. . . NiB $495 Ex $390 Gd $283
Standard model w/fixed choke . . . . NiB $495 Ex $390 Gd $283
Standard model w/choke tubes . . . NiB $495 Ex $390 Gd $283

MODEL 1000 SUPER AUTOLOADING SHOTGUN
Similar to Model 1000, but in 12 ga. only w/3-inch chamber and new gas metering system. Bbls.: 26-, 28- or 30-inch vent rib w/ACCU-Choke tubes.
Standard model w/choke tubes . . . NiB $495 Ex $369 Gd $339
Waterfowler model (Parkerized) . . NiB $510 Ex $442 Gd $260

MODEL 1000S SUPER SKEET . . . . . NiB $575 Ex $450 Gd $396
Similar to Model 1000 in 12 or 20 ga., except w/all-steel receiver and vented jug-type choke for reduced muzzle jump. Bright-point front sight and brass mid-bead. 1 and 2 oz. forend cap weights.

MODEL 5500 AUTOLOADING SHOTGUN
Gas-operated. Takedown. 12 ga. only. Four round magazine (3-round w/3-inch shells). Bbls.: 18.5- to 30-inch; various chokes. Checkered walnut finished hardwood. Made from 1985 to 1986.
Model 5500 w/ACCU-Choke . . . . . NiB $250 Ex $175 Gd $101
Model 5500 modified junior . . . . . . NiB $250 Ex $175 Gd $101

Model 5500 Slugster . . . . NiB $260 Ex $188 Gd $110
Model 5500 12 ga. Mag . . . . NiB $275 Ex $201 Gd $184
Model 5500 Guardian . . . . NiB $260 Ex $188 Gd $110

MODEL 5500 MKII AUTOLOADING SHOTGUN
Same as Model 5500 except equipped w/two Accu-Choke bbls.: 26-inch ported for non-Magnum 2.75-inch shells; 28-inch for magnum loads. Made from 1988 to 1993.
Standard model . . . . NiB $260 Ex $188 Gd $110
Camo model . . . . NiB $303 Ex $237 Gd $163
NWTF Mossy Oak model . . . . NiB $365 Ex $282 Gd $195
USST model (Made 1991-92) . . . . . NiB $325 Ex $243 Gd $190

MODEL 6000 AUTO SHOTGUN. . . NiB $280 Ex $203 Gd $170
Similar to the Model 9200 Regal except has 28-inch vent-rib bbl. w/mod. ACCU-Choke tube only. Made 1993 only.

MODEL 9200 CAMO SHOTGUN
Similar to the Model 9200 Regal except has synthetic stock and forend and is completely finished in camouflage pattern (incl. bbl.). Made from 1993 to date.
Standard model (OFM camo) . . . . . NiB $460 Ex $372 Gd $269
Turkey model (Mossy Oak camo) . . . . . . NiB $415 Ex $376 Gd $272
Turkey model (Shadow Branch camo) . . . NiB $555 Ex $435 Gd $328
Comb. model (24 & 28-inch bbls.
w/OFM camo) . . . . NiB $563 Ex $470 Gd $369

MODEL 9200 CROWN (REGAL) AUTOLOADER
Gauge: 12; 3-inch chamber. Bbls.: 18.5- to 28-inch w/ACCU-Choke tubes; plain or vent rib. Weight: 7.25 to 7.5 lbs. Checkered hardwood buttstock and forend w/walnut finish. Made from 1992 to 2001.
Model 9200 Bantam (w/1-inch shorter stock) . . . . NiB $445 Ex $359 Gd $259
Model 9200 w/ACCU-Choke . . . . NiB $445 Ex $359 Gd $259
Model 9200 w/rifled bbl. . . . . NiB $445 Ex $359 Gd $259
Model 9200 Combo (w/extra Slugster bbl.) . . . . NiB $445 Ex $359 Gd $259
Model 9200 SP (w/matte blue finish,
18.5-inch bbl.) . . . . NiB $445 Ex $359 Gd $259

MODEL 9200 PERSUADER . . . . NiB $445 Ex $359 Gd $259
Similar to the Model 9200 Regal except has 18.5-inch plain bbl. w/fixed mod. choke. Parkerized finish. Black synthetic stock w/sling swivels. Made from 1996 to 2001.

MODEL 9200 A1 JUNGLE GUN . . . NiB $610 Ex $500 Gd $297
Similar to the Model 9200 Persuader except has mil-spec heavy wall 18.5-inch plain bbl. w/cyl. bore designed for 00 Buck shot. 12 ga. w/2.75-inch chamber. Five round magazine. 38.5 inches overall. Weight: 7 lbs. Black synthetic stock. Parkerized finish. Made from 1998 to 2001.

MODEL 9200 SPECIAL HUNTER . . NiB $425 Ex $368 Gd $265
Similar to the Model 9200 Regal except has 28-inch vent-rib bbl. w/ACCU-Choke tubes. Parkerized finish. Black synthetic stock. Made from 1998 to 2001.

MODEL 9200 TROPHY
Similar to the Model 9200 Regal except w/24-inch rifled bbl. or 24- or 28-inch vent-rib bbl. w/ACCU-Choke tubes. Checkered walnut stock w/sling swivels. Made from 1992 to 1998.
Trophy (w/vent rib bbl.) . . . . Add $150
Trophy (w/rifled bbl. & cantilever scope mount) . . . . . . Add $166
Trophy (w/rifled bbl. & rifle sights) . . . . .Add $143

MODEL 9200 USST AUTOLOADER . .NiB $445 Ex $359 Gd $259
Similar to the Model 9200 Regal except has 26-inch vent-rib bbl. w/ACCU-Choke tubes. "United States Shooting Team" engraved on receiver. Made from 1993 to date.

SHOTGUNS

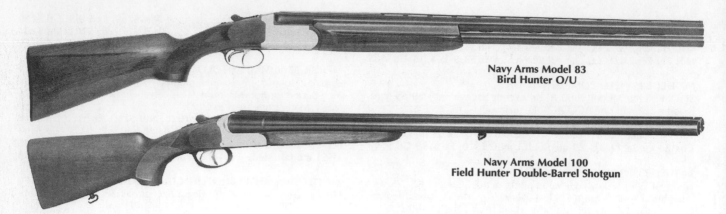

Navy Arms Model 83
Bird Hunter O/U

Navy Arms Model 100
Field Hunter Double-Barrel Shotgun

MODEL 9200
VIKING AUTOLOADER . . . . NiB $365 Ex $29   5 Gd $240
Gauge: 12 w/3-inch chamber. 28-inch smoothbore bbl. W/Accu-Choke and vent rib. Weight: 7.7 lbs. Green synthetic stock. Matte black metal finish. Made from 1996 to 1998.

MODEL HS410
HOME SECURITY PUMP SHOTGUN
Gauge: .410; 3-inch chamber. Bbl.: 18.5-inch w/muzzle brake; blued. Weight: 6.25 lbs. Synthetic stock and pistol-grip slide. Optional laser sight. Made from 1990 to date. A similar version of this gun is marketed by Maverick Arms under the same model designation.
Standard model . . . . NiB $291 Ex $224 Gd $17
Laser model . . . . NiB $481 Ex $368 Gd $261

LINE LAUNCHER. . . . . NiB $949 Ex $765 Gd $543
Gauge: 12 w/blank cartridge. Projectile travels from 250 to 275 feet.

"NEW HAVEN BRAND" SHOTGUNS
Promotional models, similar to their standard guns but plainer in finish, are marketed by Mossberg under the "New Haven" brand name. Values generally are about 20 percent lower than for corresponding standard models.

NAVY ARMS SHOTGUNS —
Ridgefield, New Jersey

MODEL 83/93 BIRD HUNTER O/U
Hammerless. Boxlock, engraved receiver. Gauges: 12 and 20; 3-inch chambers. Bbls.: 28-inch chrome lined w/double vent-rib construction. Checkered European walnut stock and forearm. Gold plated triggers. Imported 1984 to 1990.
Model 83 w/extractors . . . . NiB $280 Ex $205 Gd $161
Model 93 w/ejectors . . . . NiB $325 Ex $286 Gd $208

MODEL 95/96 O/U SHOTGUN
Same as the Model 83/93 except w/five interchangeable choke tubes. Imported 1984 to 1990.
Model 95 w/extractors . . . . NiB $380 Ex $284 Gd $147
Model 96 w/ejectors . . . . NiB $475 Ex $310 Gd $225

MODEL 100/150 FIELD HUNTER
DOUBLE-BARREL SHOTGUN
Boxlock. Gauges: 12 and 20. Bbls.: 28-inch chrome lined. Checkered European walnut stock and forearm. Imported 1984 to 1990.
Model 100 . . . . NiB $380 Ex $305 Gd $243
Model 150 (auto ejectors) . . . . NiB $459 Ex $325 Gd $264

MODEL 100 O/U SHOTGUN . . . . . . NiB $225 Ex $131 Gd $90
Hammerless, takedown shotgun w/engraved chrome receiver. Single trigger. 12, 20, 28, or .410 ga. w/3-inch chambers. Bbls.: 26-inch (F/F or SK/SK); vent rib. Weight: 6.25 lbs. Checkered European walnut buttstock and forend. Imported 1986 to 1990.

NEW ENGLAND FIREARMS —
Gardner, Massachusetts

In 1987, New England Firearms was established as an independent company producing selected H&R models under the NEF logo after Harrington & Richardson suspended operations on January 24, 1986. In 1991, H&R 1871, Inc. was formed from the residual of the parent H&R company and then took over the New England Firearms facility. H&R 1871 produced firearms under both their logo and the NEF brand name until 1999, when the Marlin Firearms Company acquired the assets of H&R 1871.

NEW ENGLAND FIREARMS NWTF TURKEY SPECIAL
Similar to Turkey and Goose models except 10 or 20 gauge w/22- or 24-inch plain bbl. w/screw-in full-choke tube. Mossy Oak camo finish on entire gun. Made from 1992 to 1996.
Turkey Special 10 ga. . . . . NiB $195 Ex $106 Gd $80
Turkey Special 20 ga. . . . . NiB $274 Ex $186 Gd $160

NRA FOUNDATION YOUTH . . . . . . NiB $137 Ex $102 Gd $88
Smaller scale version of Pardner Model chambered for 20, 28 or .410 w/22- inch plain bbl. High luster blue finish. NRA Foundation logo laser etched on stock. Made from 1999 to 2002.

PARDNER SHOTGUN
Takedown. Side lever. Single bbl. Gauges: 12, 20 and .410 w/3-inch chamber; 16 and 28 w/2.75-inch chamber. 26-, 28- or 32-inch, plain bbl. w/fixed choke. Weight: 5-6 lbs. Bead front sight. Pistol grip-style hardwood stock w/walnut finish. Made from 1988 to date.
Standard model . . . . NiB $185 Ex $111 Gd $86
Youth model . . . . NiB $185 Ex $111 Gd $86
Turkey model . . . . NiB $265 Ex $158 Gd $97
W/32-inch bbl., add $15

PARDNER SPECIAL PURPOSE 10 GA. SHOTGUN
Similar to the standard Pardner model except chambered 10 ga. only w/3.5-inch chamber. 24- or 28-inch, plain bbl. w/full choke tube or fixed choke. Weight: 9.5 lbs. Bead front sight. Pistol-grip-style hardwood stock w/camo or matte black finish. Made from 1989 to date.
Special Purpose model w/fixed choke NiB $250 Ex $173 Gd $101
W/camo finish, add $15
W/choke tube, add $20
W/24-inch bbl. turkey option, add $30

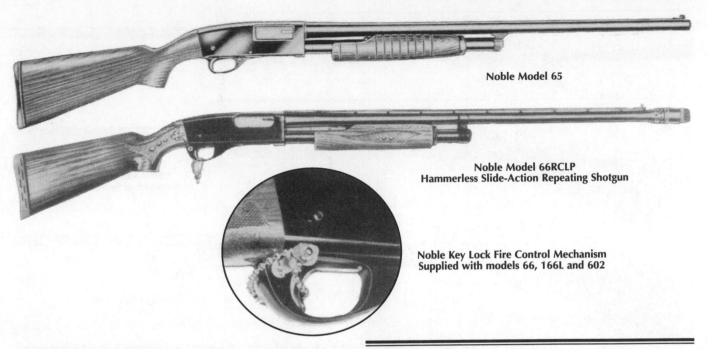

Noble Model 65

Noble Model 66RCLP
Hammerless Slide-Action Repeating Shotgun

Noble Key Lock Fire Control Mechanism
Supplied with models 66, 166L and 602

PARDNER SPECIAL PURPOSE
WATERFOWL SINGLE-SHOT . . . . . **NiB $188 Ex $156 Gd $115**
Similar to Special Purpose 10 Ga. model except w/32-inch bbl.
Mossy Oak camo stock w/swivel and sling. Made from 1988 to date.

PARDNER TURKEY GUN
Similar to Pardner model except chambered in 12 ga. w/3.0- or 3.5-
inch chamber. 24-inch plain bbl. W/turkey full-choke tube or fixed
choke. Weight: 9.5 lbs. American hardwood stock w/camo or matte
black finish. Made from 1999 to date.
Standard Turkey model . . . . **NiB $135 Ex $98 Gd $74**
Camo Turkey model . . . . **NiB $135 Ex $98 Gd $74**

SURVIVOR SERIES
Takedown single bbl. shotgun w/side lever release, Automatic ejector and patented transfer-bar safety. Gauges: 12, 20, and .410/.45
ACP w/3-inch chamber. 22-inch bbl. w/modified choke and bead
sight. Weight: 6 lbs. Polymer stock and forend w/hollow cavity for
storage. Made 1992 to 1993 and 1995 to date.
12 or 20 ga.
w/blued finish . . . . **NiB $155 Ex $103 Gd $88**
12 or 20 ga.
w/nickel finish . . . . **NiB $189 Ex $149 Gd $110**
.410/.45 LC add **$50**

TRACKER SLUG GUN
Similar to Pardner model except in 10, 12 or 20 ga. w/24-inch
w/cylinder choke or rifled slug bbl. (Tracker II). Weight: 6 lbs.
American hardwood stock w/walnut or camo finish, Schnabel
forend, sling swivel studs. Made from 1992 to 2001.
Tracker Slug
(10 ga.) . . . . **NiB $120 Ex $82 Gd $71**
Tracker Slug
(12 or 20 ga.) . . . . **NiB $159 Ex $99 Gd $76**
Tracker II (rifled bore) . . . . **NiB $159 Ex $99 Gd $76**

NIKKO FIREARMS LTD. — Tochigi, Japan

See listings under Golden Eagle Firearms, Inc.

NOBLE MANUFACTURING COMPANY — Haydenville, Massachusetts

Series 602 and 70 are similar in appearance to the corresponding Model 66 guns.

MODEL 40 HAMMERLESS SLIDE-ACTION
REPEATING SHOTGUN . . . . **NiB $199 Ex $141 Gd $103**
Solid frame. 12 ga. only. Five round tubular magazine. 28-inch bbl.
w/ventilated Multi-Choke. Weight: About 7.5 lbs. Plain pistol-grip
stock, grooved slide handle. Made from 1950 to 1955.

MODEL 50
SLIDE-ACTION . . . . **NiB $198 Ex $141 Gd $103**
Same as Model 40 except w/o Multi-Choke. M or F choke bbl.
Made from 1953 to 1955.

MODEL 60 HAMMERLESS SLIDE-ACTION
REPEATING SHOTGUN . . . . **NiB $254 Ex $192 Gd $138**
Solid frame. 12 and 16 ga. Five round tubular magazine. 28-inch
bbl. w/adj. choke. Plain pistol-grip stock w/recoil pad, grooved slide
handle. Weight: About 7.5 lbs. Made from 1955 to 1966.

MODEL 65 . . . . **NiB $267 Ex $165 Gd $121**
Same as Model 60 except without adj. choke and recoil pad. M or
F choke bbl. Made from 1955 to 1966.

MODEL 66CLP . . . . **NiB $199 Ex $155 Gd $111**
Same as Model 66RCLP except has plain bbl. Introduced in 1967. Disc.

MODEL 66RCLP HAMMERLESS SLIDE-ACTION
REPEATING SHOTGUN . . . . **NiB $271 Ex $186 Gd $128**
Solid frame. Key lock fire control mechanism. Gauges: 12, 16. 3-
inch chamber in 12 ga. Five round tubular magazine. 28-inch bbl.,
vent rib, adj. choke. Weight: About 7.5 lbs. Checkered pistol-grip
stock and slide handle, recoil pad. Made from 1967 to 1970.

MODEL 66RLP . . . . **NiB $259 Ex $175 Gd $125**
Same as Model 66RCLP except w/F or M choke. Made 1967 to 1970.

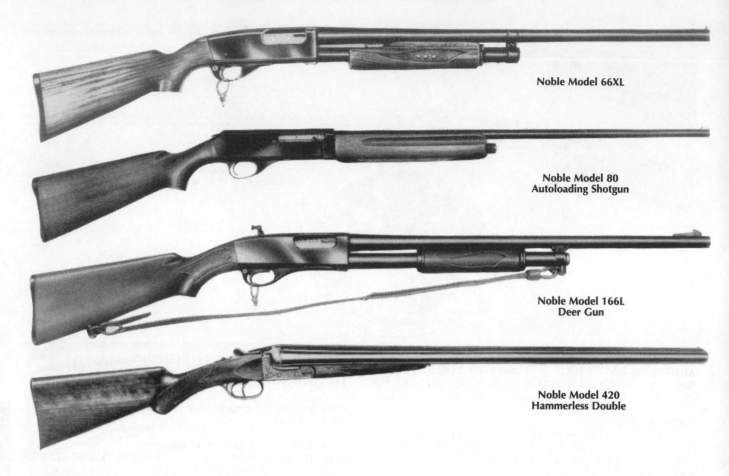

Noble Model 66XL

Noble Model 80
Autoloading Shotgun

Noble Model 166L
Deer Gun

Noble Model 420
Hammerless Double

MODEL 66XL . . . . **NiB $195 Ex $152 Gd $111**
Same as Model 66RCL except has plain bbl., F or M choke, slide handle only checkered, no recoil pad. Made from 1967 to 1970.

MODEL 70CLP HAMMERLESS SLIDE-ACTION
REPEATING SHOTGUN . . . . **NiB $229 Ex $172 Gd $125**
Solid frame. .410 gauge. Magazine holds 5 rounds. 26-inch bbl. w/adj. choke. Weight: About 6 lbs. Checkered buttstock and forearm, recoil pad. Made from 1958 to 1970.

MODEL 70RCLP . . . . **NiB $237 Ex $177 Gd $128**
Same as Model 70CLP except has vent rib. Made 1967 to 1970.

MODEL 70RLP . . . . **NiB $233 Ex $167 Gd $121**
Same as Model 70CLP except has vent rib and no adj. choke. Made from 1967 to 1970.

MODEL 70XL . . . . **NiB $160 Ex $131 Gd $96**
Same as Model 70CLP except without adj. choke and checkering on buttstock. Made from 1958 to 1970.

MODEL 80
AUTOLOADING SHOTGUN . . . . . . **NiB $274 Ex $216 Gd $156**
Recoil-operated. .410 ga. Magazine holds three 3-inch shells, four 2.5-inch shells. 26-inch bbl., full choke. Weight: About 6 lbs. Plain pistol-grip stock and fluted forearm. Made from 1964 to 1966.

MODEL 166L DEER GUN . . . . **NiB $291 Ex $238 Gd $171**
Solid frame. Key lock fire control mechanism. 12 ga. 2.75-inch chamber. Five round tubular magazine. 24-inch plain bbl., specially bored for rifled slug. Lyman peep rear sight, post ramp front sight.

Receiver dovetailed for scope mounting. Weight: About 7.25 lbs. Checkered pistol-grip stock and slide handle, swivels and carrying strap. Made from 1967 to 1970.

MODEL 420
HAMMERLESS DOUBLE . . . . **NiB $392 Ex $313 Gd $225**
Boxlock. Plain extractors. Double triggers. Gauges: 12 ga. 3-inch mag.; 16 ga.; 20 ga. 3-inch mag.; .410 ga. Bbls.: 28-inch, except .410 in 26-inch, M/F choke. Weight: About 6.75 lbs. Engraved frame. Checkered walnut stock and forearm. Made from 1958 to 1970.

MODEL 450E
HAMMERLESS DOUBLE . . . . **NiB $433 Ex $346 Gd $248**
Boxlock. Engraved frame. Selective auto ejectors. Double triggers. Gauges: 12, 16, 20. 3-inch chambers in 12 and 20 ga. 28-inch bbls., M/F choke. Weight: About 6 lbs., 14 oz., 12 ga. Checkered pistol-grip stock and beavertail forearm, recoil pad. Made from 1967 to 1970.

MODEL 602CLP . . . . **NiB $250 Ex $190 Gd $190**
Same as Model 602RCLP except has plain barrel. Made from 1958 to 1970.

MODEL 602RCLP
HAMMERLESS SLIDE-ACTION
REPEATING SHOTGUN . . . . **NiB $252 Ex $200 Gd $145**
Solid frame. Key lock fire control mechanism. 20 ga. 3-inch chamber. Five round tubular magazine. 28-inch bbl., vent rib, adj. choke. Weight: About 6.5 lbs. Checkered pistol-grip stock/slide handle, recoil pad. Made from 1967 to 1970.

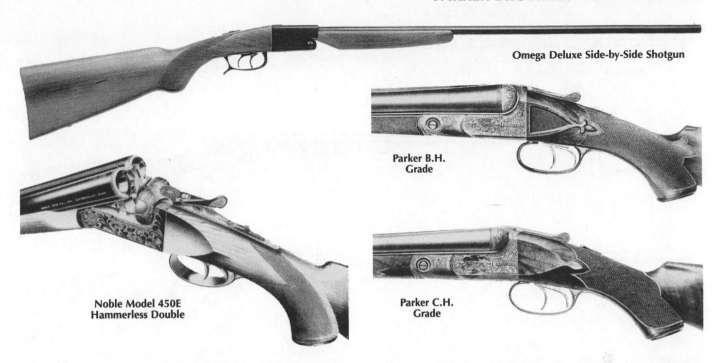

Omega Deluxe Side-by-Side Shotgun

Parker B.H. Grade

Noble Model 450E Hammerless Double

Parker C.H. Grade

MODEL 602RLP . . . . **NiB $240 Ex $187 Gd $131**
Same as Model 602RCLP except without adj. choke, bored F or M choke. Made from 1967 to 1970.

MODEL 602XL . . . . **NiB $199 Ex $155 Gd $114**
Same as Model 602RCL except has plain bbl., F or M choke, slide handle only checkered, no recoil pad. Made from 1958 to 1970.

MODEL 662 . . . . **NiB $231 Ex $186 Gd $134**
Same as Model 602CLP except has aluminum receiver and bbl. Weight: About 4.5 lbs. Made from 1966 to 1970.

OMEGA SHOTGUNS — Brescia, Italy, and Korea

FOLDING OVER/UNDER SHOTGUN, STANDARD
Hammerless Boxlock. Gauges: 12, 20, 28 w/2.75-inch chambers or .410 w/3-inch chambers. Bbls.: 26- or 28-inch vent-rib w/fixed chokes (IC/M, M/F or F/F (.410). Automatic safety. Single trigger. 40.5 inches overall (42.5 inches, 20 ga., 28-inch bbl.). Weight: 6 to 7.5 lbs. Checkered European walnut stock and forearm. Imported from 1984 to 1994.
Standard model (12 ga.) . . . . **NiB $425 Ex $307 Gd $243**
Standard model (20 ga.) . . . . **NiB $425 Ex $307 Gd $243**
Standard model (28 ga. & .410) . . . . **NiB $425 Ex $307 Gd $243**

O/U SHOTGUN, DELUXE . . . . **NiB $335 Ex $209 Gd $180**
Gauges: 20, 28 and .410. 26- or 28-inch vent-rib bbls. 40.5 inches overall (42.5 inches, 20 ga., 28-inch bbl.). Chokes: IC/M, M/F or F/F (.410). Weight: About 5.5-6 lbs. Single trigger. Automatic safety. European walnut stock w/checkered pistol grip and tulip forend. Imported from Italy 1984 to 1990.

OMEGA DELUXE SIDE-BY-SIDE SHOTGUN
. . . . **NiB $220 Ex $179 Gd $114**
Same general specifications as the Standard Side-by-Side except has checkered European walnut stock and low bbl. rib. Made in Italy from 1984 to 1989.

STANDARD SIDE-BY-SIDE SHOTGUN, ... **NiB $195 Ex $118 Gd $75**
Gauge: .410. 26-inch bbl. 40.5 inches overall. Choked F/F. Weight: 5.5 lbs. Double trigger. Manual safety. Checkered beechwood stock and semi-pistol grip. Imported from Italy 1984 to 1989.

DELUXE SINGLE-SHOT SHOTGUN . . . . . . **NiB $179 Ex $122 Gd $86**
Same general specifications as the Standard single bbl. except has checkered walnut stock, top lever break, fully-blued receiver, vent rib. Imported from Korea 1984 to 1987.

STANDARD SINGLE-SHOT SHOTGUN
Gauges: 12, 16, 20, 28 and .410. Bbl. lengths: 26-, 28- or 30-inches. Weight: 5 lbs., 4 oz. to 5 lbs., 11 oz. Indonesian walnut stock. Matte-chromed receiver and top lever break. Imported from 1984 to 1987.
Standard fixed . . . . **NiB $95 Ex $53 Gd $31**
Standard folding . . . . **NiB $167 Ex $105 Gd $74**
Deluxe folding . . . . **NiB $195 Ex $108 Gd $76**

PARKER BROTHERS — Meriden, Connecticut

This firm was taken over by Remington Arms Company in 1934 and its production facilities moved to Remington's Ilion, New York, plant. In 1984, Winchester took over production until 1999.

HAMMERLESS DOUBLE-BARREL SHOTGUNS
Grades V.H. through A-1 Special. Boxlock. Auto ejectors. Double triggers or selective single trigger. Gauges: 10, 12, 16, 20, 28, .410. Bbls.: 26- to 32-inch, any standard boring. Weight: 6.88-8.5 lbs., 12 ga. Stock and forearm of select walnut, checkered; straight, half-or full-pistol grip. Grades differ only in quality of workmanship, grade of wood, engraving, checkering, etc. General specifications are the same for all. Disc. about 1940.
V.H. grade, 12 or 16 ga. . . . . **NiB $5492 Ex $3849 Gd $2013**
V.H. grade, 20 ga. . . . . **NiB $8995 Ex $5064 Gd $2841**
V.H. grade, 28 ga. . . . . **NiB $27998 Ex $26,458 Gd $24,497**
V.H. grade, .410 ga. . . . . **NiB $32,249 Ex $23,398 Gd $19,471**
G.H. grade, 12 ga. . . . . **NiB $7491 Ex $3787 Gd $2668**
G.H. grade, 16 ga. . . . . **NiB $7961 Ex $3986 Gd $2796**

SHOTGUNS

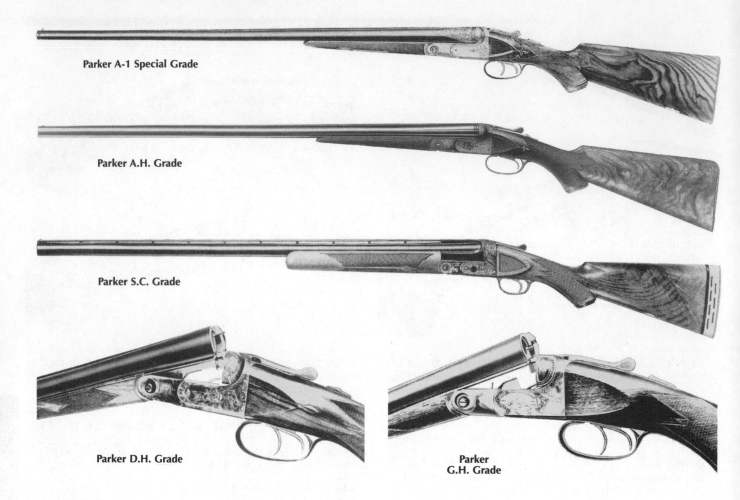

Parker A-1 Special Grade

Parker A.H. Grade

Parker S.C. Grade

Parker D.H. Grade

Parker G.H. Grade

G.H. grade, 20 ga.	NiB $12,000	Ex $9158	Gd $7570
G.H. grade, 28 ga.	NiB $32,990	Ex $27,985	Gd $25,495
G.H. grade, .410 ga.	NiB $42,558	Ex $37,809	Gd $24,595
D.H. grade, 12 or 16 ga.	NiB $9080	Ex $5774	Gd $3973
D.H. grade, 20 ga.	NiB $15,203	Ex $12,395	Gd $10,081
D.H. grade, 28 ga.	NiB $41,888	Ex $37,171	Gd $30692
D.H. grade, .410 ga.	NiB $70,000	Ex $46,462	Gd $34,794
C.H. grade, 12 or 16 ga.	NiB $15,957	Ex $12,397	Gd $10,395
C.H. grade, 20 ga.	NiB $24,404	Ex $18,376	Gd $15,768
C.H. grade, 28 ga.	NiB $70,000	Ex $58,025	Gd $50,825
B.H. grade, 12 or 16 ga.	NiB $19,900	Ex $17,567	Gd $16,580
B.H. grade, 20 ga.	NiB $30,681	Ex $19,587	Gd $15,346
B.H. grade, 28 ga.	NiB $38,639	Ex $30,991	Gd $21,202
A.H. grade, 12 or 16 ga.	NiB $90,000	Ex $71,955	Gd $55,033
A.H. grade, 20 ga.	NiB $55,954	Ex $37,223	Gd $28,630
A.H. grade, 28 ga.	NiB $100,000	Ex $78,186	Gd $62,680
A.A.H. grade, 12 or 16 ga.	NiB $55,323	Ex $49,978	Gd $34,177
A.A.H. grade, 20 ga.	NiB $79,582	Ex $60,646	Gd $41,513
A.A.H. grade, 28 ga.	NiB $200,000	Ex $175,301	Gd $155,724
A-1 Special grade, 12 or 16 ga.	NiB $99,562	Ex $77,250	Gd $52,530
A-1 Special grade, 20 ga.	NiB $150,000	Ex $113,712	Gd $77,324
A-1 Special grade, 28 ga.	NiB $190,035	Ex $152,028	Gd $103,379
W/selective-single trigger, add			20%
W/ventilated rib, add			35%
For non-ejector guns, deduct			30%

SINGLE-SHOT TRAP GUNS

Hammerless. Boxlock. Ejector. 12 ga. only. Bbl. lengths: 30-, 32-, 34-inch, any boring, vent rib. Weight: 7.5-8.5 lbs. Stock and forearm of select walnut, checkered; straight, half-or full-pistol grip. The five grades differ only in quality of workmanship, grade of wood, checkering, engraving, etc. General specifications same for all. Disc. about 1940.

S.C. grade	NiB $9000	Ex $6782	Gd $4927
S.B. grade	NiB $11,000	Ex $7108	Gd $5534
S.A. grade	NiB $15,185	Ex $12,710	Gd $10,950
S.A.1 Special (rare)	NiB $40,000	Ex $29,630	Gd $24,708

SKEET GUN

Same as other Parker doubles from Grade V.H.E. up except selective single trigger and beavertail forearm are standard on this model, as are 26-inch bbls., SK choke. Discontinued about 1940. Values are 35 percent higher.

TROJAN HAMMERLESS DOUBLE-BARREL SHOTGUN

Boxlock. Plain extractors. Double trigger or single trigger. Gauges: 12, 16, 20. Bbls.: 30-inch both F choke (12 ga. only), 26- or 28-inch M and F choke. Weight: 6.25-7.75 lbs. Checkered pistol-grip stock and forearm. Disc. 1939.

12 ga.	NiB $5000	Ex $3990	Gd $2392
16 ga.	NiB $5500	Ex $4211	Gd $2876
20 ga.	NiB $6500	Ex $4362	Gd $3338

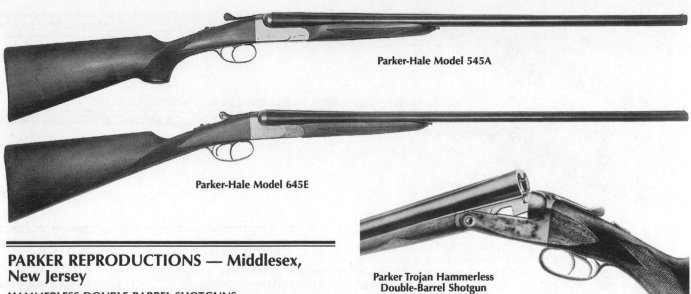

Parker-Hale Model 545A

Parker-Hale Model 645E

Parker Trojan Hammerless
Double-Barrel Shotgun

PARKER REPRODUCTIONS — Middlesex, New Jersey

HAMMERLESS DOUBLE-BARREL SHOTGUNS

Reproduction of the original Parker boxlock. Single selective trigger or double triggers. Selective automatic ejectors. Automatic safety. Gauges: 12, 16, 20, 28 or .410 w/2.75- or 3-inch chambers. Bbls.: 26- or 28-inch w/fixed or internal screw choke tubes SK/SK, IC/M, M/F. Weight: 5.5-7 lbs. Checkered English-style or pistol-grip American walnut stock w/beavertail or splinter forend and checkered skeleton buttplate. Color casehardened receiver with game scenes and scroll engraving. Produced in Japan by Olin Kodensha from 1984-88.

DHE grade, 12 ga.	NiB $3495 Ex $2944 Gd $1243
DHE grade, 12 ga Sporting Clays.	NiB $4041 Ex $3645 Gd $2549
DHE grade, 20 ga.	NiB $4049 Ex $2464 Gd $1731
DHE grade, 28 ga.	NiB $5068 Ex $2716 Gd $1909
DHE grade 2-barrel set (16 & 20 ga.)	NiB $6242 Ex $4647 Gd $3247
DHE grade 2-barrel set (28 & .410)	NiB $7000 Ex $5167 Gd $3602
DHE grade 3-barrel set	NiB $9000 Ex $6392 Gd $4449
B grade Bank Note Lim. Ed., 12 ga.	NiB $5671 Ex $4591 Gd $3209
B grade Bank Note Lim. Ed., 20 ga.	NiB $7050 Ex $5697 Gd $3967
B grade Bank Note Lim. Ed., 28 ga.	NiB $10,816 Ex $8706 Gd $6005
B grade Bank Note Lim. Ed., .410 ga.	NiB $10,194 Ex $8815 Gd $5997
A-1 Special grade, 12 ga.	NiB $9969 Ex $8023 Gd $5441
A-1 Special grade, 16 ga.	NiB $11,799 Ex $9493 Gd $6544
A-1 Special grade, 20 ga.	NiB $9583 Ex $7704 Gd $5299
A-1 Special grade, 28 ga.	NiB $14,259 Ex $12,888 Gd $7929
A-1 Special gr. 2-barrel set	NiB $11,234 Ex $9031 Gd $6223
A-1 Special gr. 3-barrel set	NiB $26,504 Ex $21,225 Gd $14,468
A-1 Special gr. custom engraved	NiB $16,254 Ex $13,035 Gd $9115
A-1 Special gr. custom 2-barrel set	NiB $12,551 Ex $9961 Gd $6804
Extra barrel set, add	$250

PARKER-HALE SHOTGUNS — Mfd. by Ignacio Ugartechea, Spain

MODEL 645A (AMERICAN)

SIDE-BY-SIDE SHOTGUN . . . . NiB $1243 Ex $1081 Gd $729
Gauges: 12, 16 and 20. Boxlock action. 26- and 28-inch bbls. Chokes: IC/M, M/F. Weight: 6 lbs. average. Single non-selective trigger. Automatic safety. Hand-checkered pistol grip walnut stock w/beavertail forend. Raised matted rib. English scroll-design engraved receiver. Discontinued 1990.

MODEL 645E (ENGLISH) SIDE-BY-SIDE SHOTGUN

Same general specifications as the Model 645A except double trig

gers, straight grip, splinter forend, checkered butt and concave rib. Disc. 1990.

12, 16, 20 ga. with 26- or 28-inch bbl.	NiB $1275 Ex $1099 Gd $742
28, .410 ga. with 27-inch bbl.	NiB $1671 Ex $1364 Gd $972

MODEL 645E-XXV
12, 16, 20 ga. with 25-inch bbl.	NiB $1190 Ex $1092 Gd $706
28, .410 ga. with 25-inch bbl.	NiB $1588 Ex $1280 Gd $962

PEDERSEN CUSTOM GUNS — North Haven, Connecticut, Div. of O. F. Mossberg & Sons, Inc.

MODEL 1000 O/U HUNTING SHOTGUN

Boxlock. Auto ejectors. Selective single trigger. Gauges: 12, 20. 2.75-inch chambers in 12 ga., 3-inch in 20 ga. Bbls.: Vent rib; 30-inch M/F (12 ga. only); 28-inch IC/M (12 ga. only), M/F; 26-inch IC/M. Checkered pistol-grip stock and forearm. Grade I is the higher quality gun with custom stock dimensions, fancier wood, more elaborate engraving, silver inlays. Made from 1973 to 1975.
Grade I . . . . NiB $2210 Ex $1881 Gd $1388
Grade II . . . . NiB $1989 Ex $1606 Gd $1130

MODEL 1000 MAGNUM

Same as Model 1000 Hunting Gun except chambered for 12-ga. Magnum 3-inch shells, 30-inch bbls., IM/F choke. Made 1973 to 1975.
Grade I . . . . NiB $2679 Ex $2196 Gd $1504
Grade II . . . . NiB $2187 Ex $1776 Gd $1251

MODEL 1000 SKEET GUN

Same as Model 1000 Hunting Gun except has skeet-style stock; 26- and 28-inch bbls. (12 ga. only), SK choke. Made 1973 to 1975.
Grade I . . . . NiB $2230 Ex $1858 Gd $1496
Grade II . . . . NiB $1998 Ex $1569 Gd $1062

MODEL 1000 TRAP GUN

Same as Model 1000 Hunting Gun except 12 ga. only, has Monte Carlo trap-style stock, 30- or 32-inch bbls., M/F or IM/F choke. Made from 1973 to 1975.
Grade I . . . . NiB $2100 Ex $1697 Gd $1160
Grade II . . . . NiB $1653 Ex $1355 Gd $949

SHOTGUNS

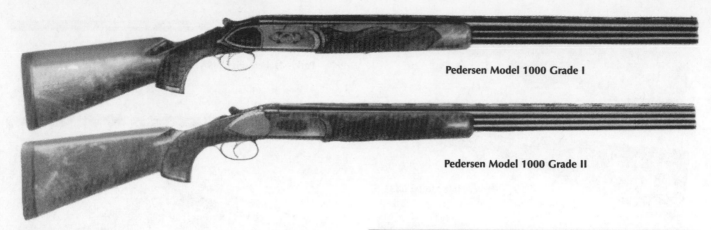

Pedersen Model 1000 Grade I

Pedersen Model 1000 Grade II

MODEL 1500 O/U
HUNTING SHOTGUN . . . . **NiB $700 Ex $585 Gd $385**
Boxlock. Auto ejectors. Selective single trigger. 12 ga. 2.75- or 3-inch chambers. Bbls.: vent rib; 26-inch IC/M; 28- and 30-inch M/F; Magnum has 30-inch, IM/F choke. Weight: 7-7.5 lbs., depending on bbl. length. Checkered pistol-grip stock and forearm. Made from 1973 to 1975.

MODEL 1500 SKEET GUN . . . . NiB $725 Ex $605 Gd $500
Same as Model 1500 Hunting Gun except has skeet-style stock, 27-inch bbls., SK choke. Made from 1973 to 1975.

MODEL 1500 TRAP GUN . . . . NiB $650 Ex $594 Gd $424
Same as Model 1500 Hunting Gun except has Monte Carlo trap-style stock, 30- or 32-inch bbls., M/F or IM/F chokes. Made 1973 to 1975.

MODEL 2000 HAMMERLESS DOUBLE
Boxlock. Auto ejectors. Selective single trigger. Gauges: 12, 20. 2.75-inch chambers in 12 ga., 3-inch in 20 ga. Bbls.: Vent rib; 30-inch M/F (12 ga. only); 28-inch M/F, 26-inch IC/M choke. Checkered pistol-grip stock and forearm. Grade I is the higher quality gun w/custom dimensions, fancier wood, more elaborate engraving, silver inlays. Made from 1973 to 1974.
Grade I . . . . NiB $2678 Ex $2165 Gd $1523
Grade II . . . . NiB $2291 Ex $1999 Gd $1408

MODEL 2500
HAMMERLESS DOUBLE . . . . NiB $573 Ex $419 Gd $298
Boxlock. Auto ejectors. Selective single trigger. Gauges: 12, 20. 2.75-inch chambers in 12 ga., 3-inch in 20 ga. Bbls.: Vent rib; 28-inch M/F; 26-inch IC/M choke. Checkered pistol-grip stock and forearm. Made 1973 to 1974.

MODEL 4000 HAMMERLESS SLIDE-ACTION
REPEATING SHOTGUN . . . . NiB $456 Ex $402 Gd $331
Custom version of Mossberg Model 500. Full-coverage floral engraving on receiver. Gauges: 12, 20, .410. Three-inch chamber. Bbls.: Vent rib; 26-inch IC or SK choke; 28-inch F or M; 30-inch F. Weight: 6-8 lbs. depending on ga. and bbl. Checkered stock and slide handle of select wood. Made in 1975.

MODEL 4000 TRAP GUN . . . . NiB $485 Ex $339 Gd $213
Same as standard Model 4000 except 12 ga. only, has 30-inch F choke bbl., Monte Carlo trap-style stock w/recoil pad. Made in 1975.

MODEL 4500 . . . . NiB $422 Ex $364 Gd $282
Same as Model 4000 except has simpler scroll engraving. Made in 1975.

MODEL 4500 TRAP GUN . . . . NiB $445 Ex $363 Gd $288
Same as Model 4000 Trap Gun except has simpler scroll engraving. Made in 1975.

J. C. PENNEY CO., INC. — Dallas, Texas

MODEL 4011
AUTOLOADING SHOTGUN. . . . . . . NiB $292 Ex $207 Gd $150
Hammerless. Five round magazine. Bbls.: 26-inch IC; 28-inch M or F; 30-inch F choke. Weight: 7.25 lbs. Plain pistol-grip stock and slide handle.

MODEL 6610
SINGLE-SHOT SHOTGUN . . . . NiB $177 Ex $107 Gd $80
Hammerless. Takedown. Auto ejector. Gauges: 12, 16, 20 and .410. Bbl. length: 28-36 inches. Weight: About 6 lbs. Plain pistol-grip stock and forearm.

MODEL 6630
BOLT-ACTION SHOTGUN . . . . NiB $185 Ex $137 Gd $101
Takedown. Gauges: 12, 16, 20. Two round clip magazine. 26- and 28-inch bbl. lengths; with or without adj. choke. Plain pistol-grip stock. Weight: About 7.25 lbs.

MODEL 6670
SLIDE-ACTION SHOTGUN . . . . . . NiB $199 Ex $158 Gd $121
Hammerless. Gauges: 12, 16, 20, and .410. Three round tubular magazine. Bbls.: 26- to 30-inch; various chokes. Weight: 6.25-7.25 lbs. Walnut finished hardwood stock.

MODEL 6870 SLIDE-ACTION
SHOTGUN . . . . NiB $278 Ex $219 Gd $162
Hammerless. Gauges: 12, 16, 20, .410. Four round magazine. Bbls.: Vent rib; 26- to 30-inch, various chokes. Weight: Average 6.5 lbs. Plain pistol-grip stock.

PERAZZI SHOTGUNS — Manufactured by Manifattura Armi Perazzi, Brescia, Italy

See also listings under Ithaca-Perazzi.

DB81 O/U TRAP . . . . NiB $5179 Ex $4190 Gd $2929
Gauge: 12; 2.75-inch chambers. 29.5- or 31.5-inch bbls. w/wide vent rib; M/F chokes. Weight: 8 lbs., 6 oz. Detachable and interchangeable trigger with flat V-springs. Bead front sight. Interchangeable and custom-made checkered stock; beavertail forend. Imported 1988 to 1994.

DB81 SINGLE-SHOT TRAP . . . . NiB $5184 Ex $4190 Gd $2929
Same general specifications as the DB81 over/under except in single bbl. version w/32- or 34-inch wide vent-rib bbl., F choke. Imported 1988 to 1994.

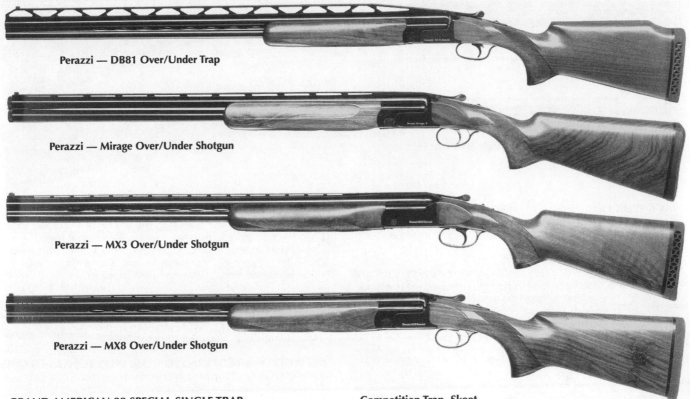

Perazzi — DB81 Over/Under Trap

Perazzi — Mirage Over/Under Shotgun

Perazzi — MX3 Over/Under Shotgun

Perazzi — MX8 Over/Under Shotgun

GRAND AMERICAN 88 SPECIAL SINGLE TRAP
Same general specifications as MX8 Special Single Trap except w/high ramped rib. Fixed choke or screw-in choke tubes.
Model 88 standard . . . . NiB $4595 Ex $3675 Gd $2563
**Model 88 w/interchangeable
choke tubes** . . . . NiB $4878 Ex $3902 Gd $2717

MIRAGE O/U SHOTGUN
Gauge: 12; 2.75-inch chambers. Bbls.: 27.63-, 29.5- or 31.5-inch vent-rib w/fixed chokes or screw-in choke tubes. Single selective trigger. Weight: 7 to 7.75 lbs. Interchangeable and custom-made checkered buttstock and forend.
**Competition Trap,
Skeet, Pigeon, Sporting** . . . . NiB $6000 Ex $5163 Gd $3538
Skeet 4-barrel sets . . . . NiB $13,332 Ex $10,692 Gd $7314
Competition Special (w/adj. 4-position trigger) add $350

MX-1 O/U SHOTGUN
Similar to Model MX8 except w/ramp-style, tapered rib and modified stock configuration.
**Competition Trap, Skeet,
Pigeon & Sporting** . . . . NiB $6399 Ex $4769 Gd $2947
MXIC (w/choke tubes) . . . . NiB $3596 Ex $2913 Gd $2035
MXIB (w/flat low rib) . . . . NiB $3298 Ex $2666 Gd $1867

MX-2 O/U SHOTGUN
Similar to Model MX8 except w/broad high-ramped competition rib.
**Competition-Trap, Skeet,
Pigeon & Sporting** . . . . NiB $6445 Ex $3369 Gd $2324
MX2C (w/choke tubes) . . . . NiB $4699 Ex $3774 Gd $2649

MX-3 O/U SHOTGUN
Similar to Model MX8 except w/ramp-style, tapered rib and modified stock configuration.

**Competition Trap, Skeet,
Pigeon & Sporting** . . . . . . NiB $46,774 Ex $37,517 Gd $25,666
Competition Special (w/adj. 4-position trigger) add $300
Game models . . . . NiB $4292 Ex $3469 Gd $2416
Combo O/U plus SB . . . . NiB $5371 Ex $4273 Gd $2972
SB Trap 32- or 34-inch . . . . NiB $3677 Ex $2933 Gd $2065
Skeet 4-bbl. sets . . . . NiB $11,119 Ex $8916 Gd $6098
Skeet Special 4-bbl. sets . . . . NiB $11,343 Ex $9097 Gd $6221

MX-3 SPECIAL PIGEON SHOTGUN . . NiB $5197 Ex $4142 Gd $2883
Gauge: 12; 2.75-inch chambers. 29.5- or 31.5-inch vent rib bbl.; IC/M and extra full chokes. Weight: 8 lbs., 6 oz. Detachable and interchangeable trigger group w/flat V-springs. Bead front sight. Interchangeable and custom-made checkered stock for live pigeon shoots; splinter forend. Imported 1991 to 1992.

MX-4 O/U SHOTGUN
Similar to Model MX3 in appearance and shares the MX8 locking system. Detachable, adj. 4-position trigger standard. Interchangeable choke tubes optional.
**Competition Trap,
Skeet, Pigeon & Sporting** . . . . . NiB $4398 Ex $3957 Gd $2754
MX4C (w/choke tubes) . . . . NiB $5261 Ex $4218 Gd $3366

MX-5 O/U GAME GUN
Similar to Model MX8 except in hunting configuration, chambered in 12 or 20 ga. Non-detachable single selective trigger.
MX5 Standard . . . . NiB $3894 Ex $2710 Gd $1888
MX5C (w/choke tubes) . . . . NiB $4158 Ex $2983 Gd $2067

MX-6 AMER. TRAP SINGLE-BARREL . . NiB $4199 Ex $2592 Gd $1734
Single shot. Removable trigger group. 12 ga. Barrels: 32- or 34-inch with fixed or choke tubes. Raised vent rib. Checkered European walnut Monte Carlo stock, beavertail forend. Imported 1995 to 1998.

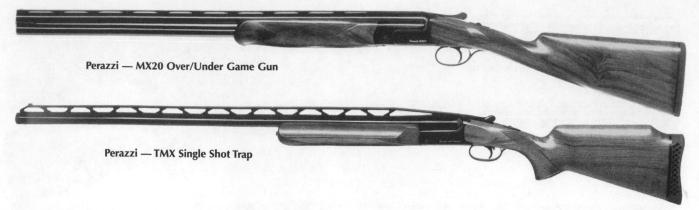

Perazzi — MX20 Over/Under Game Gun

Perazzi — TMX Single Shot Trap

MX-6 SKEET O/U. . . . . **NiB $4195 Ex $2865 Gd $1968**
Same general specs as MX6 American Trap single barrel except over/under; boxlock. Barrels: 26.75- or 27.50-inch. Imported 1995 to 1998.

MX-6 SPORTING O/U . . . . **NiB $4195 Ex $2959 Gd $2059**
Same specs as MX6 American Trap single barrel except over/under; boxlock. Single selective trigger; external selector. Barrels: 28.38-, 29.50-, or 31.50-inch. Imported 1995 to 1998.

MX-6 TRAP O/U . . . . **NiB $4194 Ex $2784 Gd $1728**
Same general specs as MX6 American Trap single barrel except over/under; boxlock. Barrels: 29.50-, 30.75-, or 31.50-inch. Imported 1995 to 1998.

MX-7 O/U SHOTGUN . . . . **NiB $4092 Ex $3534 Gd $2453**
Similar to Model MX12 except w/MX3-style receiver and top-mounted trigger selector. Bbls.: 28.73-, 2.5-, 31.5-inch w/vent rib; screw-in choke tubes. Imported 1992 to 1998.

MX-8 O/U SHOTGUN
Gauge: 12, 2.75-inch chambers. Bbls.: 27.63-, 29.5- or 31.5-inch vent-rib w/fixed chokes or screw-in choke tubes. Weight: 7 to 8.5 lbs. Interchangeable and custom-made checkered stock; beavertail forend. Special models have detachable and interchangeable 4-position trigger group w/flat V-springs. Imported 1968 to date.
MX-8 Standard . . . . **NiB $7900 Ex $3998 Gd $2223**
MX-8 Special (adj. 4-pos. trigger) . . . . . **NiB $4072 Ex $3280 Gd $2280**
MX-8 Special single
(32-or 34-inch bbl.) . . . . **NiB $8210 Ex $6515 Gd $4175**
MX-8 Special combo . . . . **NiB $7895 Ex $6272 Gd $4422**

MX-8/20 O/U SHOTGUN . . . . **NiB $4072 Ex $3240 Gd $2251**
Similar to the Model MX8 except w/smaller frame and custom stock. Available in sporting or game configurations with fixed chokes or screw-in tubes. Imported 1993 to date.

MX-9 O/U SHOTGUN . . . . **NiB $6706 Ex $5537 Gd $4059**
Gauge: 12; 2.75-inch chambers. Bbls.: 29.5- or 30.5-inch w/choke tubes and vent side rib. Selective trigger. Checkered walnut stock w/adj. cheekpiece. Available in single bbl., combo, O/U trap, skeet, pigeon and sporting models. Imported 1993 to 1994.

MX-10 O/U SHOTGUN . . . . . . **NiB $8199 Ex $5700 Gd $3962**
Similar to the Model MX9 except w/fixed chokes and different rib configuration. Imported 1993.

MX-10 PIGEON-ELECTROCIBLES O/U . . . **NiB $8895 Ex $5961 Gd $4368**
Over/Under; boxlock. Removable trigger group; external selector. 12 gauge. Barrels: 27.50- or 29.50-inch. Checkered European walnut adjustable stock, beavertail forend. Imported 1995 to date.

MX–11 AMERICAN TRAP COMBO . **NiB $5220 Ex $4524 Gd $3149**
Over/Under; boxlock. External selector. Removable trigger group; single selective trigger. 12 ga. Bbls: 29-1/2- to 34-inch with fixed or choke tubes; vent rib. European walnut Monte Carlo adjustable stock, beavertail forend. Imported 1995 to date.

MX-11 AMERICAN TRAP
SINGLE BARREL . . . . **NiB $4992 Ex $4100 Gd $2792**
Same general specs as MX11 American Trap combo except 32- or 34-inch single bbl. Imported 1995 to 1996.

MX-11 PIGEON-ELECTROCIBLES O/U. **NiB $5192 Ex $4180 Gd $2912**
Same specs as MX11 American Trap combo except 27.50 O/U bbls. Checkered European walnut pistol grip adjustable stock, beavertail forend. Imported 1995 to 1996.

MX-11 SKEET O/U. . . . . **NiB $5280 Ex $4227 Gd $2943**
Same general specs as MX11 American Trap combo except 26.75 or 27.50-inch O/U bbls. Checkered European walnut pistol-grip adjustable stock, beavertail forend. Imported 1995 to 1996.

MX-11 SPORTING O/U . . . . . . **NiB $5194 Ex $4629 Gd $3209**
Same general specs as MX11 American Trap combo except 28.38, 29.50-, or 31.50-inch O/U bbls. Checkered European walnut pistol-grip adjustable stock, beavertail forend. Imported 1995 to 1996.

MX-11 TRAP O/U . . . . **NiB $5192 Ex $4180 Gd $2912**
Same general specs as MX11 American Trap combo except 29.50,- 30.75, or 31.50-inch O/U bbls. Checkered European walnut pistol-grip adjustable stock, beavertail forend. Imported 1995 to 1996.

MX-12 O/U GAME GUN
Gauge: 12, 2.75-inch chambers. Bbls.: 26-, 27.63-, 28.38- or 29.5-inch, vent rib, fixed chokes or screw-in choke tubes. Non-detachable single selective trigger group w/coil springs. Weight: 7.25 lbs. Interchangeable and custom-made checkered stock; Schnabel forend.
MX12 Standard . . . . **NiB $7892 Ex $4180 Gd $2912**
MX12C (w/choke tubes) . . . . **Add $400**

MX-14 AMERICAN TRAP
SINGLE-BARREL . . . . **NiB $6797 Ex $3524 Gd $2458**
Single shot. Removable trigger group; unsingle configuration. 12 ga. Bbl: 34-inch with fixed or choke tubes; vent rib. Checkered European walnut Monte Carlo adjustable stock, beavertail forend. Imported 1995 to 1996.

MX-15 AMERICAN TRAP
SINGLE-BARREL . . . . **NiB $6500 Ex $3913 Gd $2725**
Full choke. Detachable trigger group. Gauge: 12 only with 2.75-inch chamber. Bbls: 32 and 34-inch. Weight: 8 lbs., 6 oz.

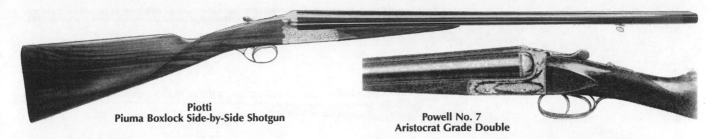

Piotti
Piuma Boxlock Side-by-Side Shotgun

Powell No. 7
Aristocrat Grade Double

MX-20 O/U GAME GUN

Gauges: 20, 28 and .410; 2.75- or 3-inch chambers. 26-inch vent-rib bbls., M/F chokes or screw-in chokes. Auto selective ejectors. Selective single trigger. Weight: 6 lbs., 6 oz. Non-detachable coil-spring trigger. Bead front sight. Interchangeable and custom-made checkered stock w/Schnabel forend. Imported from 1988 to date.
Standard grade . . . . NiB $5190 Ex $4093 Gd $2842
Standard grade
w/gold outline . . . . NiB $8796 Ex $7055 Gd $4979
MX20C w/choke tubes . . . . NiB $5473 Ex $4392 Gd $3047
SC3 grade . . . . NiB $94977 Ex $7643 Gd $5294
SCO grade . . . . NiB $12,950 Ex $10,377 Gd $7127

MX-28 O/U GAME GUN . . NiB $14,263 Ex $11,423 Gd $7814
Similar to the Model MX12 except chambered in 28 ga. w/26-inch bbls. fitted to smaller frame. Imported from 1993 to date.

MX-410 O/U GAME GUN . . . . NiB $14,273 Ex $11,423 Gd $7814
Similar to the Model MX12 except in .410 bore w/3-inch chambers, 26-inch bbls. fitted to smaller frame. Imported from 1993 to date.

TM1 SPECIAL
SINGLE-SHOT TRAP . . . . NiB $2881 Ex $1605 Gd $1123
Gauge: 12- 2.75-inch chambers. 32- or 34-inch bbl. w/wide vent rib; full choke. Weight: 8 lbs., 6 oz. Detachable and interchangeable trigger group with coil springs. Bead front sight. Interchangeable and custom-made stock w/checkered pistol grip and beavertail forend. Imported from 1988 to 1995.

TMX SPECIAL
SINGLE-SHOT TRAP . . . . NiB $3691 Ex $2442 Gd $1618
Same general specifications as Model TM1 Special except w/ultra-high rib. Interchangeable choke tubes optional.

PIOTTI SHOTGUNS — Italy

BOSS O/U . . . . NiB $56,350 Ex $48,350 Gd $33,350
Over/Under; sidelock. Gauges: 12 or 20. Barrels: 26- to 32-inch. Standard chokes. Best quality walnut. Custom-made to customer's specifications. Imported from 1993 to date.

KING NO. 1 SIDELOCK . . NiB $34,110 Ex $27,210 Gd $17,210
Gauges: 10, 12, 16, 20, 28 and .410. 25- to 30-inch bbls. (12 ga.), 25- to 28-inch (other ga.). Weight: About 5 lbs. (.410) to 8 lbs. (12 ga.) Holland & Holland pattern sidelock. Double triggers standard. Coin finish or color casehardened. Level file-cut rib. Full-coverage scroll engraving, gold inlays. Hand-rubbed, oil-finished, straight-grip stock with checkered butt, splinter forend.

KING EXTRA SIDE-BY-SIDE
SHOTGUN . . . . NiB $75,000 Ex $50,000 Gd $40,000
Same general specifications as the Piotti King No. 1 except has choice of engraving, gold inlays, plus stock is of exhibition-grade wood.

LUNIK SIDE-LOCK
SHOTGUN . . . . NiB $33,653 Ex $28,165 Gd $23,701
Same general specifications as the Monte Carlo model except has level, file-cut rib. Renaissance-style, large scroll engraving in relief, gold crown in top lever, gold name, and gold crest in forearm, finely figured wood.

MONTE CARLO
SIDE-LOCK SHOTGUN . . . . . NiB $10,555 Ex $8860 Gd $6060
Gauges: 10, 12, 16, 20, 28 or .410. Bbls.: 25- to 30-inch. Holland & Holland pattern sidelock. Weight: 5-8 lbs. Automatic ejectors. Double triggers. Hand-rubbed oil-finished straight-grip stock with checkered butt. Choice of Purdey-style scroll and rosette or Holland & Holland-style large scroll engraving.

PIUMA BOXLOCK
SIDE-BY-SIDE SHOTGUN. . . NiB $16,794 Ex $11495 Gd $9809
Same general specifications as the Monte Carlo model except has Anson & Deeley boxlock action w/demi-bloc bbls., scalloped frame. Standard scroll and rosette engraving. Hand-rubbed, oil-finished straight-grip stock.

WILLIAM POWELL & SON, LTD. — Birmingham, England

NO. 1 BEST GRADE
DOUBLE-BARREL
SHOTGUN . . . . NiB $40,627 Ex $35,515 Gd $28,515
Sidelock. Gauges: Made to order with 12, 16 and 20 the most common. Bbls.: Made to order in any length but 28 inches was recommended. Highest grade French walnut buttstock and forearm with fine checkering. Metal elaborately engraved. Imported by Stoeger from about 1938 to 1951.

NO. 2 BEST GRADE
DOUBLE-BARREL . . . . . . NiB $27,800 Ex $22,300 Gd $15,260
Same general specifications as the Powell No. 1 except plain finish without engraving. Imported by Stoeger from about 1938 to 1951.

NO. 6 CROWN GRADE
DOUBLE-BARREL . . . . NiB $14,095 Ex $11,345 Gd $7825
Boxlock. Gauges: Made to order with 12, 16 and 20 the most common. Bbls.: Made to order, but 28 inches was recommended. Highest grade French walnut buttstock and forearm with fine checkering. Metal elaborately engraved. Uses Anson & Deeley locks. Imported by Stoeger from about 1938 to 1951.

NO. 7 ARISTOCRAT GRADE
DOUBLE-BARREL
SHOTGUN . . . . NiB $7285 Ex $5880 Gd $4190
Same general specifications as the Powell No. 6 Crown Grade Double-Barrel above, except with lower quality wood and metal engraving.

Premier Ambassador Field Grade

Premier Continental Field Grade

PRECISION SPORTS SHOTGUNS — Cortland, New York; Manufactured by Ignacio Ugartechea, Spain

600 SERIES AMERICAN HAMMERLESS DOUBLES
Boxlock. Single selective trigger. Selective automatic ejectors. Automatic safety. Gauges: 12, 16, 20, 28, .410; 2.75- or 3-inch chambers. Bbls.: 26-,27- or 28-inch w/raised matte rib; choked IC/M or M/F. Weight: 5.75-7 lbs. Checkered pistol-grip walnut buttstock with beavertail forend. Engraved silvered receiver with blued bbls. Imported from 1986 to 1994.

640A (12, 16, 20 ga. w/extractors)	NiB $1091	Ex $837	Gd $614
640A (28, .410 ga. w/extractors)	NiB $1192	Ex $959	Gd $699
640 Slug Gun (12 ga. w/extractors)	NiB $1191	Ex $942	Gd $689
645A (12, 16, 20 ga. w/ejectors)	NiB $1097	Ex $899	Gd $659
645A (28, .410 ga. w/ejectors)	NiB $1364	Ex $1094	Gd $799
645A (20/28 ga. two-bbl. set)	NiB $1563	Ex $1253	Gd $919
650A (12 ga. w/extractors, choke tubes) . .	NiB $1075	Ex $848	Gd $621
655A (12 ga. w/ejectors, choke tubes) . .	NiB $1170	Ex $924	Gd $683

600 SERIES ENGLISH HAMMERLESS DOUBLES
Boxlock. Same general specifications as American 600 series except w/double triggers and concave rib. Checkered English-style walnut stock w/splinter forend, straight grip and oil finish.

640E (12, 16, 20 ga. w/extractors)	NiB $895	Ex $714	Gd $522
640E (28, .410 ga. w/extractors)	NiB $990	Ex $791	Gd $574
640 Slug Gun (12 ga. w/extractors)	NiB $1190	Ex $931	Gd $678
645E (12, 16, 20 ga. w/ejectors)	NiB $1199	Ex $956	Gd $696
645E (28, .410 ga. w/ejectors)	NiB $1189	Ex $915	Gd $668
645E (20/28 ga. two-bbl. set)	NiB $1435	Ex $1188	Gd $883
650E (12 ga. w/extractors, choke tubes) . . .	NiB $1084	Ex $827	Gd $603
655E (12 ga. w/ejectors, choke tubes) . . .	NiB $1084	Ex $876	Gd $636

MODEL 640M MAGNUM 10 HAMMERLESS DOUBLE
Similar to Model 640E except in 10 ga. w/3.5-inch Mag. chambers. Bbls.: 26-, 30-, 32-inch choked F/F.

Model 640M Big Ten, Turkey	NiB $994	Ex $820	Gd $598
Model 640M Goose Gun.	NiB $1020	Ex $841	Gd $613

MODEL 645E-XXV HAMMERLESS DOUBLE
Similar to Model 645E except w/25-inch bbl. and Churchill-style rib.

645E-XXV (12, 16, 20 ga. w/ejectors)	NiB $1094	Ex $876	Gd $636
645E-XXV (28, .410 ga. w/ejectors)	NiB $1294	Ex $989	Gd $715

PREMIER SHOTGUNS

Premier shotguns have been produced by various gunmakers in Europe.

AMBASSADOR MODEL
FIELD GRADE HAMMERLESS
DOUBLE-BARREL SHOTGUN. . . . . NiB $445 Ex $390 Gd $282
Sidelock. Plain extractors. Double triggers. Gauges: 12, 16, 20, .410. 3-inch chambers in 20 and .410 ga., 2.75- inch in 12 and 16 ga. Bbls.: 26-inch in .410 ga., 28 inch in other ga.; choked M/F. Weight: 6 lbs., 3 oz.-7 lbs., 3 oz. depending on gauge. Checkered pistol-grip stock and beavertail forearm. Intro. in 1957; disc.

BRUSH KING . . . . NiB $332 Ex $263 Gd $215
Same as standard Regent model except chambered for 12 (2.75-inch) and 20 ga. (3-inch) only; has 22-inch bbls., IC/M choke, straight-grip stock. Weight: 6 lbs., 3 oz. in 12 ga.; 5 lbs., 12 oz. in 20 ga. Introduced in 1959; disc.

CONTINENTAL MODEL
FIELD GRADE HAMMER
DOUBLE-BARREL SHOTGUN. . . . . NiB $485 Ex $390 Gd $282
Sidelock. Exposed hammers. Plain extractors. Double triggers. Gauges: 12, 16, 20, .410. Three inch chambers in 20 and .410 ga., 2.75-inch in 12 and 16 ga. Bbls.: 26-inch in .410 ga.; 28-inch in other ga.; choked M/F. Weight: 6 lbs., 3 oz.-7 lbs., 3 oz. depending on gauge. Checkered pistol-grip stock and English-style forearm. Introduced in 1957; disc.

MONARCH SUPREME GRADE HAMMERLESS
DOUBLE-BARREL SHOTGUN. . . . . NiB $575 Ex $414 Gd $300
Boxlock. Auto ejectors. Double triggers. Gauges: 12, 20. 2.75-inch chambers in 12 ga., 3-inch in 20 ga. Bbls.: 28-inch M/F; 26-inch IC/M choke. Weight: 6 lbs., 6 oz., 7 lbs., 2 oz. depending on gauge and bbl. Checkered pistol-grip stock and beavertail forearm of fancy walnut. Introduced in 1959; disc.

PRESENTATION
CUSTOM GRADE . . . . NiB $1350 Ex $1039 Gd $744
Similar to Monarch model but made to order of higher quality with hunting scene engraving, gold and silver inlay, fancier wood. Introduced in 1959; disc.

REGENT 10 GA.
MAGNUM EXPRESS . . . . NiB $550 Ex $330 Gd $238
Same as standard Regent model except chambered for 10-ga. Magnum 3.5-inch shells, has heavier construction, 32-inch bbls. choked F/F, stock with recoil pad. Weight: 11.25 lbs. Introduced in 1957; disc.

REGENT 12 GA.
MAGNUM EXPRESS . . . . NiB $374 Ex $300 Gd $218
Same as standard Regent model except chambered for 12-ga. Magnum 3-inch shells, has 30-inch bbls. choked F and F, stock with recoil pad. Weight: 7.25 lbs. Introduced in 1957; disc.

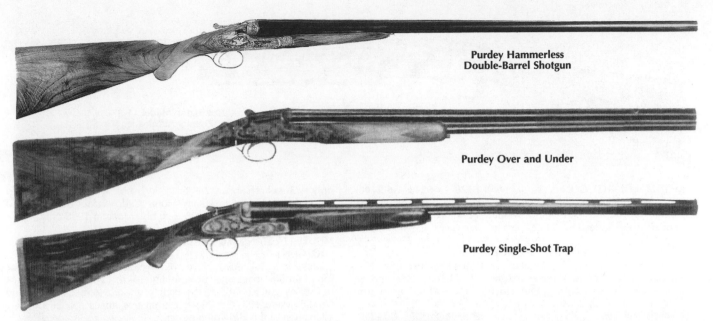

Purdey Hammerless Double-Barrel Shotgun

Purdey Over and Under

Purdey Single-Shot Trap

REGENT FIELD GRADE HAMMERLESS

DOUBLE-BARREL SHOTGUN.....NiB $346 Ex $269 Gd $190
Boxlock. Plain extractors. Double triggers. Gauges: 12,16, 20, 28, .410. Three inch chambers in 20 and .410 ga., 2.75-inch in other gauges. Bbls.: 26-inch IC/M, M/F (28 and .410 ga. only); 28-inch M/F; 30-inch M/F (12 ga. only). Weight: 6 lbs., 2 oz.-7 lbs., 4 oz. depending on gauge and bbl. Checkered pistol-grip stock and beavertail forearm. Introduced in 1955; disc.

JAMES PURDEY & SONS, LTD. — London, England

HAMMERLESS DOUBLE-BARREL SHOTGUN
Sidelock. Auto ejectors. Single or double triggers. Gauges: 12, 16, 20. Bbls.: 26-, 27-, 28-, 30-inch (latter in 12 ga. only);any boring, any shape or style of rib. Weight: 5.25-5.5 lbs. depending on model, gauge and bbl length. Checkered stock and forearm, straight grip standard, pistol-grip also available. Purdey guns of this type have been made from about 1880 to date. Models include: Game Gun, Featherweight Game Gun, Two-Inch Gun (chambered for 12 ga. 2-inch shells), Pigeon Gun (w/3rd fastening and side clips), values of all models are the same.
With double triggers.....NiB $60,025 Ex $52,900 Gd $42,500
With single trigger . . . . Add $1000

OVER/UNDER SHOTGUN
Sidelock. Auto ejectors. Single or double triggers. Gauges: 12 16, 20. Bbls.: 26-, 27-, 28-, 30-inch (latter in 12 ga. only); any boring, any style rib. Weight: 6-7.5 pounds depending on gauge and bbl. length. Checkered stock and forend, straight or pistol grip. Prior to WW II, the Purdey Over/Under Gun was made with a Purdey action; since the war James Purdey & Sons have acquired the business of James Woodward & Sons and all Purdey over/under guns are now built on the Woodward principle. General specifications of both types are the same.
With Purdey action,
double triggers . . . . NiB $75,900 Ex $50,900 Gd $22,900
With Woodward action,
double triggers . . . . Add $3000
W/single trigger, add 10%

SINGLE-BARREL

TRAP GUN. . . . . NiB $11,320 Ex $9595 Gd $6619
Sidelock. Mechanical features similar to those of the over/under model with Purdey action. 12 ga. only. Built to customer's specifications. Made prior to World War II.

REMINGTON ARMS CO. — Ilion, New York

Eliphalet Remington Jr. began making long arms with his father in 1816. In 1828 they moved their facility to Ilion, N.Y., where it remained a family-run business for decades. As the family began to diminish, other people bought controlling interests and today, still a successful gunmaking company, it is a subsidiary of the DuPont Corporation.

MODEL 10A STANDARD GRADE
SLIDE-ACTION REPEATING SHOTGUN . . . . NiB $315 Ex $249 Gd $170
Hammerless. Takedown. Six-round capacity. 12 ga. only. Five shell tubular magazine. Bbls.: Plain; 26- to 32-inch; choked F, M or Cyl. Weight: About 7.5 lbs. Plain pistol-grip stock, grooved slide handle. Made from 1907 to 1929.

MODEL 11 SPECIAL, TOURNAMENT, EXPERT AND PREMIER GRADE GUNS
These higher grade models differ from the Model 11A in general quality, grade of wood, checkering, engraving, etc. General specifications are the same.
Model 11B Special grade . . . . .NiB $682 Ex $517 Gd $370
Model 11D Tournament grade . . NiB $1257 Ex $1007 Gd $712
Model 11E Expert grade . . . . . . .NiB $1751 Ex $1388 Gd $975
Model 11F Premier grade . . . . .NiB $2799 Ex $2209 Gd $1542

MODEL 11A STANDARD GRADE AUTOLOADER
Hammerless Browning type. Five round capacity. Takedown. Gauges: 12, 16, 20. Tubular magazine holds four rounds. Bbls.: Plain, solid or vent rib, lengths from 26-32 inches, F, M, IC, Cyl., SK chokes. Weight: About 8 lbs., 12 ga.; 7.5 lbs., 16 ga.; 7.25 lbs., 20 ga. Checkered pistol grip and forend. Made from 1905 to 1949.
With plain barrel . . . . NiB $299 Ex $216 Gd $193
With solid-rib barrel . . . . .NiB $396 Ex $301 Gd $246
With ventilated-rib barrel . . . . . . .NiB $448 Ex $324 Gd $283

**Remington Model 11-87
Premier Autoloader**

MODEL 11R RIOT GUN . . . . **NiB $328 Ex $243 Gd $148**
Same as Model 11A Standard grade except has 20-inch plain barrel, 12 ga. only. Remington Model 11-48. (See Remington Sportsman-48 Series.)

MODEL 11-87 PREMIER AUTOLOADER
Gas-operated. Hammerless. Gauge: 12; 3-inch chamber. Bbl.: 26-, 28- or 30-inch with REMChoke. Weight: 8.13- 8.38 lbs., depending on bbl. length. Checkered walnut stock and forend in satin finish. Made from 1987 to date.
Premier Deer Gun . . . . NiB $690 Ex $501 Gd $362
Premier Deer Gun w/cant-
ileur scope mount . . . . NiB $768 Ex $572 Gd $379
Premier Skeet . . . . NiB $679 Ex $517 Gd $374
Premier Sporting Clays . . . . NiB $776 Ex $622 Gd $451
Premier Sporting Clays SCNP (nickel plated) . . . NiB $795 Ex $652 Gd $471
Premier Standard Autoloader . . . . NiB $685 Ex $517 Gd $374
Premier Trap . . . . NiB $761 Ex $609 Gd $440
Left-hand models, add. $70

MODEL 11-87 SPECIAL PURPOSE MAGNUM
Same general specifications as Model 11-87 Premier except with non-reflective wood finish and Parkerized metal. 21-, 26- or 28-inch vent-rib bbl. with REMChoke tubes. Made from 1987 to 1993.
Model 11-87 SP Field Magnum . . . . NiB $751 Ex $630 Gd $431
Model 11-87 SP Deer Gun (w/21-inch bbl.) NiB $669 Ex $551 Gd $398
Model 11-87 SP Deer Gun
w/cantilever scope mount. . . . . NiB $739 Ex $590 Gd $455

MODEL 11-87 SPS MAGNUM
Same general specifications as Model 11-87 Special Purpose Magnum except with synthetic buttstock and forend. 21-, 26- or 28-inch vent-rib bbl. with REMChoke tubes. Matte black or Mossy Oak camo finish (except NWTF turkey gun). Made from 1990 to date.
Model 11-87 SPS Magnum (matte black)   NiB $612 Ex $545 Gd $394
Model 11-87 SPS Camo (Mossy Oak camo) NiB $675 Ex $567 Gd $410
Model 11-87 SPS Deer Gun (w/21 inch bbl.)NiB $696 Ex $494 Gd $358
Model 11-87 SPS Deer Gun w/cant. scope mt. NiB $777 Ex $556 Gd $402
Model 11-87 NWTF Turkey Gun
(Brown Trebark) disc. 1993 . . . . NiB $700 Ex $640 Gd $461
Model 11-87 NWTF Turkey Gun
(Greenleaf) disc. 1996 . . . . NiB $673 Ex $518 Gd $446
Model 11-87 NWTF Turkey
Gun (Mossy Oak) disc. 1996 . . . . NiB $676 Ex $529 Gd $454
Model 11-87 NWTF Turkey Gun
(Mossy Oak Breakup) introduced 1999 . . . NiB $676 Ex $529 Gd $454
Model 11-87 NWTF 20 ga. Turkey Gun
(Mossy Oak Breakup)1998 only . . . . NiB $676 Ex $529 Gd $454
Model 11-87 SPST Turkey Gun (matte bl.)   NiB $676 Ex $526 Gd $401

MODEL 11-96 EURO LIGHTWEIGHT
AUTOLOADING SHOTGUN . . . . NiB $719 Ex $588 Gd $420
Lightweight version of Model 11-87 w/reprofiled receiver. 12 ga.

only w/3-inch chamber. 26- or 28-inch bbl. w/6mm vent rib and REM Choke tubes. Semi-fancy Monte Carlo walnut buttstock and forearm. Weight: 6.8 lbs. w/26-inch bbl. Made in 1996 only.

**MODEL 17A STANDARD GRADE SLIDE-ACTION REPEATING
SHOTGUN**
Hammerless. Takedown. Five round capacity. 20 ga. only. Four round tubular magazine. Bbls.: plain; 26- to 32-inch; choked F, M or Cyl. Weight: About 5.75 lbs. Plain pistol-grip stock, grooved slide handle. Made 1921-33. Note: The present Ithaca Model 37 is an adaptation of this Browning design.
Plain barrel . . . . NiB $354 Ex $243 Gd $142
Solid rib. . . . . NiB $455 Ex $357 Gd $221

MODEL 29A STANDARD GRADE
SLIDE-ACTION REPEATING SHOTGUN. . . NiB $324 Ex $267 Gd $188
Hammerless. Takedown. Six round capacity. 12 ga. only. Five round tubular magazine. Bbls.: plain- 26- to 32-inch, choked F, M or Cyl. Weight: About 7.5 lbs. Checkered pistol-grip stock and slide handle. Made from 1929 to 1933.

MODEL 29T TARGET GRADE . . . . . NiB $525 Ex $449 Gd $323
Same general specifications as Model 29A except has trap-style stock with straight grip, extension slide handle, vent rib bbl. Disc. 1933.

MODEL 31 AND 31L SKEET GRADE
Same general specifications as Model 31A except has 26-inch bbl. with raised solid or vent rib, SK choke, checkered pistol-grip stock and beavertail forend. Weight: About 8 lbs., 12 ga. Made from 1932 to 1939.
Model 31 Standard w/raised solid rib . . NiB $395 Ex $193 Gd $97
Model 31 Standard w/ventilated rib . . NiB $474 Ex $320 Gd $262
Model 31L Lightweight w/raised solid rib . NiB $350 Ex $234 Gd $156
Model 31L Lightweight w/ventilated rib NiB $420 Ex $295 Gd $200

**MODEL 31D SPECIAL, TOURNAMENT,
EXPERT AND PREMIER GRADE GUNS**
These higher grade models differ from the Model 31A in general quality, grade of wood, checkering, engraving, etc. General specifications are the same.
Model 31B Special grade . . . . NiB $650 Ex $505 Gd $333
Model 31D Tournament grade . . . NiB $1578 Ex $954 Gd $604
Model 31E Expert grade . . . . NiB $1754 Ex $1186 Gd $843
Model 31F Premier grade . . . . . NiB $2952 Ex $1895 Gd $1337

MODEL 31S TRAP SPECIAL/31TC TRAP GRADE
Same general specifications as Model 31A except 12 ga. only, has 30- or 32-inch vent-rib bbl., F choke, checkered trap stock with full pistol grip and recoil pad, checkered extension beavertail forend. Weight: About 8 lbs. (Trap Special has solid-rib bbl., half pistol-grip stock with standard walnut forend).
Model 31S Trap Special . . . . NiB $550 Ex $405 Gd $342
Model 31TC Trap grade . . . . NiB $875 Ex $611 Gd $435

Remington Model 11-87 SPS

Remington Model 11-87 SPS Camo

Remington Model 11-87 SP Walnut Stock

Remington Model SP-10 Magnum Camo

MODEL 31A SLIDE-ACTION REPEATER
Hammerless. Takedown. 3- or 5-round capacity. Gauges: 12, 16, 20. Tubular magazine. Bbls.: Plain, solid or vent rib; lengths from 26 -32 inches; F, M, IC, C or SK choke. Weight: About 7.5 lbs., 12 ga.; 6.75 lbs., 16 ga.; 6.5 lbs., 20 ga. Earlier models have checkered pistol-grip stock and slide handle; later models have plain stock and grooved slide handle. Made from 1931 to 1949.

Model 31A with plain barrel ..... NiB $405 Ex $272 Gd $170
Model 31A with solid rib barrel ... NiB $468 Ex $499 Gd $318
Model 31A with vent rib barrel ... NiB $474 Ex $320 Gd $237
Model 31H Hunter
w/sporting-style stock .... NiB $395 Ex $241 Gd $188
Model 31R Riot Gun w/20-
inch plain bbl., 12 ga. .... NiB $425 Ex $323 Gd $236

MODEL 32A STANDARD GRADE O/U
Hammerless. Takedown. Auto ejectors. Early model had double triggers, later built with selective single trigger only. 12 ga. only. Bbls.: Plain, raised matted solid or vent rib; 26-, 28-, 30-, 32-inch; F/M choke standard, option of any combination of F, M, IC, C, SK choke. Weight: About 7.75 lbs. Checkered pistol-grip stock and forend. Made from 1932 to 1942.

With double triggers .... NiB $2000 Ex $1695 Gd $1185
With selective single trigger ... NiB $2399 Ex $1997 Gd $1331
With raised solid rib............................. Add 10%
With ventilated rib .... Add 20 %

MODEL 32 TOURNAMENT, EXPERT AND PREMIER GRADE GUNS
These higher-grade models differ from the Model 32A in general quality, grade of wood, checkering, engraving, etc. General specifications are the same. Made from 1932 to 1942.

Model 32D Tournament grade .... NiB $3798 Ex $3067 Gd $2280
Model 32E Expert grade ...... NiB $4492 Ex $3975 Gd $2838
Model 32F Premier grade .... NiB $6488 Ex $5515 Gd $3817

MODEL 32 SKEET GRADE .....NiB $2000 Ex $1675 Gd $1325
Same general specifications as Model 32A except 26- or 28-inch bbl., SK choke, beavertail forend, selective single trigger only. Weight: About 7.5 lbs. Made from 1932 to 1942.

MODEL 32TC
TARGET (TRAP) GRADE ...... NiB $3000 Ex $2655 Gd $1855
Same general specifications as Model 32A except 30- or 32-inch vent-rib bbl., F choke, trap-style stock with checkered pistol-grip and beavertail forend. Weight: About 8 lbs. Made from 1932 to 1942.

MODEL 89 (1889)........... NiB $1998 Ex $1692 Gd $1039
Hammers. Circular action. Gauges: 10, 12, 16, 28- to 32-inch bls.; steel or Damascus twist. Weight 7-10 lbs. Made from 1889 to 1908.

MODEL 90-T SINGLE-SHOT TRAP ..... NiB $1855 Ex $1672 Gd $1246
Gauge: 12; 2.75-inch chambers. 30-, 32- or 34-inch vent-rib bbl. with fixed chokes or screw-in REMChokes; ported or non-ported. Weight: 8.25 lbs. Checkered American walnut standard or Monte Carlo stock with low-luster finish. Engraved sideplates and drop-out trigger group optional. Made from 1990 to 1997.

MODEL 396 O/U
Boxlock. 12 ga. only w/2.75-inch chamber. 28- and 30-inch blued bbls. w/Rem chokes. Weight: 7.50 lbs. Nitride-grayed, engraved receiver, trigger guard, tang, hinge pins and forend metal. Engraved sideplates. Checkered satin-finished American walnut stock w/target style forend. Made from 1996 to 1998.

Sporting Clays .... NiB $1879 Ex $1563 Gd $1169
396 Skeet.................. NiB $1755 Ex $1422 Gd $1011

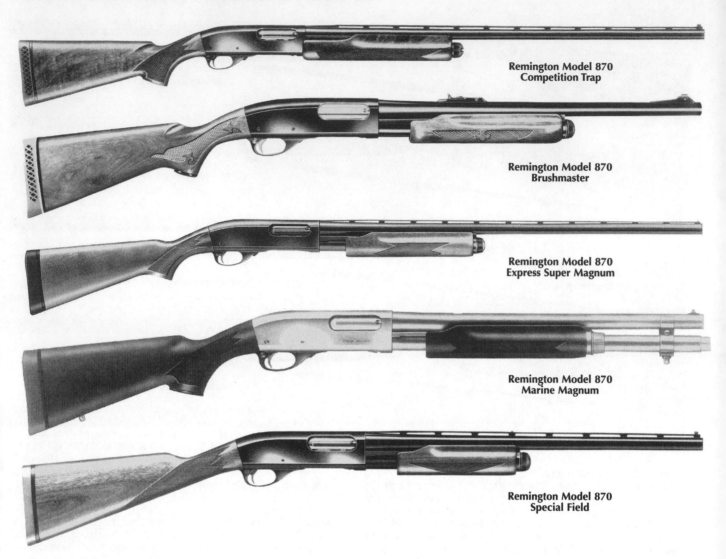

Remington Model 870
Competition Trap

Remington Model 870
Brushmaster

Remington Model 870
Express Super Magnum

Remington Model 870
Marine Magnum

Remington Model 870
Special Field

MODEL 870

"ALL AMERICAN" TRAP GUN . . . NiB $1189 Ex $924 Gd $661
Same as Model 870TB except custom grade with engraved receiver, trigger guard and bbl.; Monte Carlo or straight-comb stock and forend of fancy walnut; available only with 30-inch F choke bbl. Made from 1972 to 1977.

MODEL 870 COMPETITION TRAP   NiB $693 Ex $526 Gd $378
Based on standard Model 870 receiver except is single-shot with gas-assisted recoil-reducing system, new choke design, a high step-up vent rib and redesigned stock, forend with cut checkering and satin finish. Weight: 8.5 lbs. Made from 1981 to 1987.

MODEL 870 STANDARD. . . . . NiB $496 Ex $360 Gd $263
Same as Model 870 Wingmaster Riot Gun, on page 524, except has rifle-type sights.

MODEL 870 BRUSHMASTER DELUXE
Same as Model 870 Standard except available in 20 ga. as well as 12, has cut-checkered, satin-finished American walnut stock and forend, recoil pad.
Right-hand model . . . . NiB $493 Ex $390 Gd $284
Left-hand model . . . . NiB $574 Ex $446 Gd $322
MODEL 870 EXPRESS

Same general specifications Model 870 Wingmaster except has low-luster walnut-finished hardwood stock with pressed checkering and black recoil pad. Gauges: 12, 20 or .410, 3-inch chambers. Bbls.: 26- or 28-inch vent-rib with REMChoke; 25-inch vent-rib with fixed choke (.410 only). Black oxide metal finish. Made from 1987 to date.
Model 870 Express
(12 or20 ga., REMChoke) . . . . NiB $290 Ex $240 Gd $176
Model 870 Express
(.410 w/fixed choke) . . . . NiB $393 Ex $266 Gd $194
Express Combo (w/extra
20-inch deer bbl.) . . . . NiB $390 Ex $312 Gd $224

MODEL 870
EXPRESS DEER GUN
Same general specifications as Model 870 Express except in 12 ga. only, 20-inch bbl. with fixed IC choke, adj. rifle sights and Monte Carlo stock. Made from 1991 to date.
Express Deer Gun
w/standard barrel . . . . NiB $385 Ex $260 Gd $188
Express Deer Gun
w/rifled barrel . . . . NiB $380 Ex $287 Gd $207

**Remington Model 870
Special Purpose Deer Gun**

**Remington Model 870
Wingmaster Field Gun**

MODEL 870 EXPRESS SUPER MAGNUM
Similar to Model 870 Express except chambered for 12 ga. mag. w/3.5-inch chamber. Bbls.: 23-, 26- or 28-inch vent rib w/REM Choke. Checkered low-luster walnut-finished hardwood, black synthetic or camo buttstock and forearm. Matte black oxide metal finish or full camo finish. Made from 1998 to date.
**Model 870 ESM
(w/hardwood stock)** . . . . NiB $325 Ex $248 Gd $181
**Model 870 ESM
(w/black synthetic stock)** . . . . NiB $325 Ex $248 Gd $181
**Model 870 ESM
(w/camo synthetic stock)** . . . . NiB $390 Ex $300 Gd $254
**Model 870 ESM Synthetic
Turkey (w/synthetic stock)** . . . . NiB $390 Ex $300 Gd $254
**Model 870 ESM camo
Turkey (w/full camo)** . . . . NiB $390 Ex $300 Gd $254
**Model 870 ESM combo
(w/full camo, extra bbl.)** . . . . NiB $460 Ex $335 Gd $278

MODEL 870 EXPRESS
SYNTHETIC HOME DEFENSE . . . . . NiB $320 Ex $239 Gd $175
Slide action, hammerless, takedown. 12 ga. only. 18-inch bbl. w/cylinder choke and bead front sight. Positive checkered synthetic stock and forend with non-reflective black finish. Made from 1995 to date.

MODEL 870 EXPRESS TURKEY GUN . . NiB $395 Ex $249 Gd $259
Same general specifications as Model 870 Express except has 21-inch vent-rib bbl. and Turkey Extra-Full REMChoke. Made from 1991 to date.

MODEL 870 EXPRESS YOUTH GUN . . NiB $391 Ex $248 Gd $181
Same general specifications as Model 870 Express except has scaled-down stock with 12.5-inch pull and 21-inch vent rib bbl. with REMChoke. Made from 1991 to date.

MODEL 870 LIGHTWEIGHT
Same as standard Model 870 but with scaled-down receiver and lightweight mahogany stock; 20 ga. only. 2.75-inch chamber. Bbls.: plain or vent rib; 26-inch, IC; 28-inch, M or F choke. REMChoke available from 1987. Weight 5.75 lbs. w/26-inch plain bbl. American walnut stock and forend with satin or Hi-gloss finish. Made from 1972 to 1994.
With plain barrel . . . . NiB $390 Ex $283 Gd $220
With ventilated rib barrel . . . . NiB $410 Ex $297 Gd $216
With REMChoke barrel . . . . NiB $493 Ex $331 Gd $239

MODEL 870 LIGHTWEIGHT MAGNUM
Same as Model 870 Lightweight but chambered for 20 ga. Magnum 3-inch shell; 28-inch bbl., plain or vent rib, F choke. Weight: 6 lbs. with plain bbl. Made from 1972 to 1994.

With plain barrel . . . . NiB $390 Ex $298 Gd $240
With ventilated rib barrel . . . . NiB $490 Ex $398 Gd $340

MODEL 870 MAGNUM DUCK GUN
Same as Model 870 Field Gun except has 3-inch chamber 12 and 20 gauge Magnum only. 28- or 30-inch bbl., plain or vent rib, M or F choke, recoil pad. Weight: About 7 or 6.75 lbs. Made from 1964 to date.
With plain barrel . . . . NiB $250 Ex $184 Gd $108
With ventilated rib barrel . . . . NiB $600 Ex $385 Gd $275

MODEL 870
MARINE MAGNUM . . . . NiB $650 Ex $404 Gd $314
Same general specifications as Model 870 Wingmaster except with 7-round magazine, 18-inch plain bbl. with fixed IC choke, bead front sight and nickel finish. Made from 1992 to date.

MODEL 870
SA SKEET GUN, SMALL GAUGE . . . . NiB $715 Ex $590 Gd $483
Similar to Wingmaster Model 870SA except chambered for 28 and .410 ga. (2.5-inch chamber for latter); 25-inch vent rib bbl., SK choke. Weight: 6 lbs., 28 ga.; 6.5 lbs., .410. Made from 1969 to 1982.

MODEL 870 MISSISSIPPI
MAGNUM DUCK GUN . . . . NiB $710 Ex $497 Gd $388
Same as Remington Model 870 Magnum duck gun except has 32-inch bbl. "Ducks Unlimited" engraved receiver, Made in 1983.

MODEL 870
SPECIAL FIELD SHOTGUN . . . . NiB $383 Ex $269 Gd $183
Pump action. Hammerless. Gauge: 12 or 20. 21-inch vent-rib bbl. with REMChoke. 41.5 inches overall. Weight: 6-7 lbs. Straight-grip checkered walnut stock and forend. Made from 1987 to 1995.

MODEL 870 SPECIAL PURPOSE DEER GUN
Similar to Special Purpose Magnum except with 20-inch IC choke, rifle sights. Matte black oxide and Parkerized finish. Oil-finished, checkered buttstock and forend with recoil pad. Made from 1986 to date.
Model 870 SP Deer Gun . . . . NiB $650 Ex $433 Gd $243
**Model 870 SP Deer Gun,
cant. scope mt.** . . . . NiB $715 Ex $498 Gd $308

MODEL 870 SPECIAL
PURPOSE MAGNUM . . . . NiB $650 Ex $484 Gd $378
Similar to the 870 Magnum duck gun except with 26-, 28- or 30-inch vent rib REMChoke bbl.12 ga. only; 3-inch chamber. Oil-finished field-grade stock with recoil pad, QD swivels and Cordura sling. Made from 1985 to date.

SHOTGUNS

**Remington Model 870TC
Wingmaster Trap**

MODEL 870SPS MAGNUM
Same general specifications Model 870 Special Purpose Magnum except with synthetic stock and forend. 26- or 28-inch vent-rib bbl. with REMChoke tubes. Matte black or Mossy Oak camo finish. Made from 1991 to date.
70 SPS Mag. (black syn. stock) .... NiB $565 Ex $374 Gd $272
870 SPS-T Camo (Mossy Oak camo)...... NiB $759 Ex $427 Gd $325

MODEL 870 WINGMASTER FIELD GUN
Same general specifications as Model 870AP except checkered stock and forend. Later models have REMChoke systems in 12 ga. Made from 1964 to date.
With plain barrel .... NiB $255 Ex $164 Gd $104
With ventilated rib barrel .... NiB $600 Ex $385 Gd $215

MODEL 870 WINGMASTER FIELD GUN, SMALL GAUGE
Same as standard Model 870 except w/scaled-down lightweight receivers. Gauges: 28 and .410. Plain or vent rib 25-inch bbl. choked IC, M or F. Weight: 5.5-6.25 lbs. depending on gauge and bbl. Made 1969 to 1994.
With plain barrel .... NiB $656 Ex $528 Gd $378
With ventilated-rib barrel .... NiB $715 Ex $598 Gd $418

MODEL 870 WINGMASTER
MAGNUM DELUXE GRADE ...... NiB $599 Ex $478 Gd $344
Same as Model 870 Magnum standard grade except has checkered stock and extension beavertail forearm, bbl. with matted top surface. Disc. in 1963.

MODEL 870 WINGMASTER
MAGNUM STANDARD GRADE ... NiB $578 Ex $427 Gd $309
Same as Model 870AP except chambered for 12 ga. 3-inch Magnum, 30-inch F choke bbl., recoil pad. Weight: About 8.25 lbs. Made 1955 to 1963.

MODEL 870 WINGMASTER REMCHOKE SERIES
Slide action, hammerless, takedown with blued all-steel receiver. Gauges: 12, 20; 3-inch chamber. Tubular magazine. Bbls.: 21-, 26-, 28-inch vent-rib with REM Choke. Weight: 7.5 lbs. (12 ga.). Satin-finished, checkered walnut buttstock and forend with recoil pad. Right- or left-hand models. Made from 1986 to date.
Standard model, 12 ga. .... NiB $410 Ex $321 Gd $233
Standard model, 20 ga. .... NiB $433 Ex $339 Gd $246
Youth model, 21-inch barrel ...... NiB $457 Ex $335 Gd $243

MODEL 870ADL WINGMASTER DELUXE GRADE
Same general specifications as Wingmaster Model 870AP except has pistol-grip stock and extension beavertail forend, both finely checkered; matted top surface or vent-rib bbl. Made 1950 to 1963.
With matted top-surface barrel .... NiB $396 Ex $326 Gd $238
With ventilated-rib barrel .... NiB $459 Ex $361 Gd $261

MODEL 870AP WINGMASTER STANDARD GRADE
Hammerless. Takedown. Gauges: 12, 16, 20. Tubular magazine holds four rounds. Bbls.: Plain, matted top surface or vent rib; 26-inch IC, 28-inch M or F choke, 30-inch F choke (12 ga. only). Weight: About 7 lbs., 12 ga.; 6.75 lbs., 16 ga.; 6.5 lbs., 20 ga. Plain pistol-grip stock, grooved forend. Made 1950 to 1963.
With plain barrel .... NiB $293 Ex $242 Gd $176
With matted surface barrel .... NiB $367 Ex $252 Gd $183
With ventilated rib barrel .... NiB $378 Ex $278 Gd $202
Left-hand model .... NiB $395 Ex $288 Gd $209

MODEL 870BDL WINGMASTER DELUXE SPECIAL
Same as Model 870ADL except select American walnut stock and forend. Made from 1950 to 1963.
With matted surface barrel .... NiB $575 Ex $350 Gd $255
With ventilated-rib barrel .... NiB $665 Ex $383 Gd $276

REMINGTON MODEL 870D, 870F WINGMASTER TOURNAMENT AND PREMIER GRADE GUNS
These higher-grade models differ from the Model 870AP in general quality, grade of wood, checkering, engraving, etc. General operating specifications are essentially the same. Made from 1950 to date.
Model 870D Tournament grade ...... NiB $2990 Ex $2191 Gd $1541
Model 870F Premier grade .... NiB $5994 Ex $4695 Gd $3263
Model 870F Premier gr. w/gold inlay ..... NiB $9212 Ex $7436 Gd $5164

REMINGTON MODEL 870R
WINGMASTER RIOT GUN .... NiB $299 Ex $227 Gd $185
Same as Model 870AP except 20-inch bbl., IC choke, 12 ga. only.

REMINGTON MODEL 870SA WINGMASTER SKEET GUN
Same general specifications as Model 870AP except has 26-inch vent-rib bbl., SK choke, ivory bead front sight, metal bead rear sight, pistol-grip stock and extension beavertail forend. Weight: 6.75 to 7.5 lbs. depending on gauge. Made 1950 to 1982.
Model 870SA Skeet grade (disc. 1982) ...... NiB $600 Ex $336 Gd $241
**Model 870SC Skeet Target
grade (disc. 1980)** .... NiB $625 Ex $474 Gd $338

REMINGTON MODEL 870TB
WINGMASTER TRAP SPECIAL .... NiB $550 Ex $408 Gd $293
Same general specifications as Model 870AP Wingmaster except has 28- or 30-inch vent rib bbl., F choke, metal bead front sight, no rear sight. "Special" grade trap-style stock and forend, both checkered, recoil pad. Weight: About 8 lbs. Made from 1950 to 1981.

REMINGTON MODEL
870TC TRAP GRADE .... NiB $795 Ex $554 Gd $400
Same as Model 870 Wingmaster TC except has tournament-grade walnut in stock and forend w/satin finish. Over-bored 30-inch vent rib bbl. w/ 2.75-inch chamber and RemChoke tubes. Reissued in 1996. See separate listing for earlier model.

REMINGTON MODEL 870TC WINGMASTER TRAP GRADE
Same as Model 870TB except higher-grade walnut in stock and forend, has both front and rear sights. Made 1950-79. Model 870 TC reissued in 1996. See separate listing for later model.
Model 870 TC Trap (Standard) .... NiB $425 Ex $359 Gd $203
Model 870 TC Trap (Monte Carlo) ... NiB $450 Ex $370 Gd $215

REMINGTON MODEL
878A AUTOMASTER .... NiB $265 Ex $205 Gd $182
Gas-operated Autoloader. 12 ga., 3-round magazine. Bbls.: 26-inch IC, 28-inch M choke, 30-inch F choke. Weight: About 7 lbs. Plain pistol-grip stock and forearm. Made from 1959-62.

NOTE: *New stock checkering patterns and receiver scroll markings were incorporated on all standard Model 1100 field, magnum, skeet and trap models in 1979.*

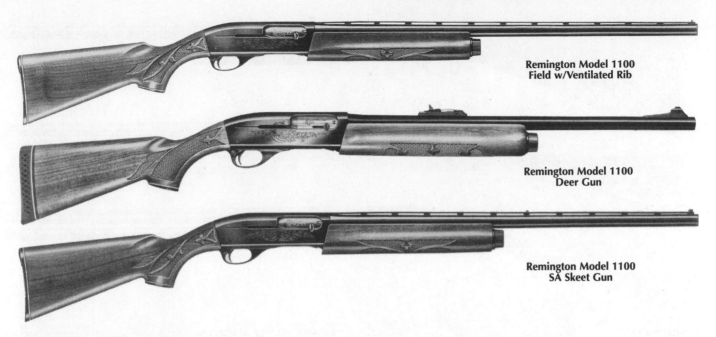

Remington Model 1100
Field w/Ventilated Rib

Remington Model 1100
Deer Gun

Remington Model 1100
SA Skeet Gun

MODEL 1100 AUTO FIELD GUN

Gas-operated. Hammerless. Takedown. Gauges: 12, 16, 20. Bbls.: plain or vent. rib; 30-inch F, 28-inch M or F, 26-inch IC; or REMChoke tubes. Weight: Average 7.25-7.5 lbs. depending on ga. and bbl. length. Checkered walnut pistol-grip stock and forearm in high-gloss finish. Made 1963 to 1988. 16 ga. discontinued 1980.

With plain barrel . . . . NiB $332 Ex $234 Gd $156
With ventilated-rib barrel . . . . NiB $353 Ex $285 Gd $204
REMChoke model . . . . NiB $413 Ex $346 Gd $256
REMChoke, Left-hand action . . . . . NiB $630 Ex $465 Gd $315

MODEL 1100 DEER GUN . . . . NiB $440 Ex $273 Gd $190

Same as Model 1100 Field Gun except has 22-inch barrel, IC, with rifle-type sights; 12 and 20 ga. only; recoil pad. Weight: About 7.25 lbs. Made from 1963 to 1998.

MODEL 1100 DUCKS UNLIMITED
ATLANTIC COMMEMORATIVE. . . NiB $1084 Ex $888 Gd $632
Limited production for one year. Similar specifications to Model 1100 Field except with 32-inch F choke, vent rib bbl. 12-ga. Magnum only. Made in 1982.

MODEL 1100 DUCKS UNLIMITED "THE CHESAPEAKE"
COMMEMORATIVE. . . . . NiB $789 Ex $648 Gd $476
Limited edition 1 to 2400. Same general specifications as Model 1100 Field except sequentially numbered with markings "The Chesapeake." 12 ga. Magnum with 30-inch F choke, vent rib bbl. Made in 1981.

REMINGTON MODEL 1100 FIELD GRADE, SMALL BORE

Same as standard Model 1100 but scaled down. Gauges: 28, .410. 25-inch bbl., plain or vent rib; IC, M or F choke. Weight: 6.25-7 lbs. depending on gauge and bbl. Made from 1969 to 1994.

With plain barrel . . . . NiB $593 Ex $464 Gd $370
With ventilated rib . . . . NiB $789 Ex $590 Gd $424

MODEL 1100 LIGHTWEIGHT

Same as standard Model 1100 but scaled-down receiver and lightweight mahogany stock; 20 ga. only, 2.75-inch chamber. Bbls.: Plain or vent rib; 26-inch IC; 28-inch M and F choke. Weight: 6.25 lbs. Made from 1970 to 1976.

With plain barrel . . . . NiB $589 Ex $444 Gd $322
With ventilated rib . . . . NiB $640 Ex $492 Gd $356

MODEL 1100 LIGHTWEIGHT MAGNUM

Same as Model 1100 Lightweight but chambered for 20 gauge Magnum 3-inch shell; 28-inch bbl., plain or vent rib, F choke. Weight: 6.5 lbs. Made from 1977 to 1998.

With plain barrel . . . . NiB $587 Ex $465 Gd $335
With ventilated rib . . . . NiB $669 Ex $514 Gd $369
With choke tubes . . . . NiB $775 Ex $546 Gd $391

MODEL 1100 LT-20
DUCKS UNLIMITED
SPECIAL COMMEMORATIVE . . . . NiB $1300 Ex $975 Gd $612
Limited edition 1 to 2400. Same general specifications as Model 1100 Field except sequentially numbered with markings, "The Chesapeake." 20 ga. only. 26-inch IC, vent-rib bbl. Made in 1981.

MODEL 1100 LT-20 SERIES

Same as Model 1100 Field Gun except in 20 ga. with shorter 23-inch vent rib bbl., straight-grip stock. REMChoke series has 21-inch vent rib bbl., choke tubes. Weight: 6.25 lbs. Checkered grip and forearm. Made from 1977 to 1995.

Model 1100
LT-20 Special . . . . NiB $512 Ex $404 Gd $341
Model 1100
LT-20 Deer Gun . . . . NiB $435 Ex $362 Gd $226
Model 1100
LT-20 Youth . . . . NiB $513 Ex $364 Gd $233

REMINGTON MODEL
1100 MAGNUM . . . . NiB $509 Ex $418 Gd $303
Limited production. Similar to the Model 1100 Field except with 26-inch F choke, vent rib bbl. and 3-inch chamber. Made in 1981.

MODEL 1100
MAGNUM DUCK GUN

Same as Model 1100 Field Gun except has 3-inch chamber, 12 and 20 ga. Mag. only. 30-inch plain or vent rib bbl. in 12 ga., 28-inch in 20 ga.; M or F choke. Recoil pad. Weight: About 7.75 lbs. Made from 1963 to 1988.

With plain barrel . . . . NiB $420 Ex $316 Gd $275
With ventilated
rib barrel . . . . NiB $450 Ex $350 Gd $314

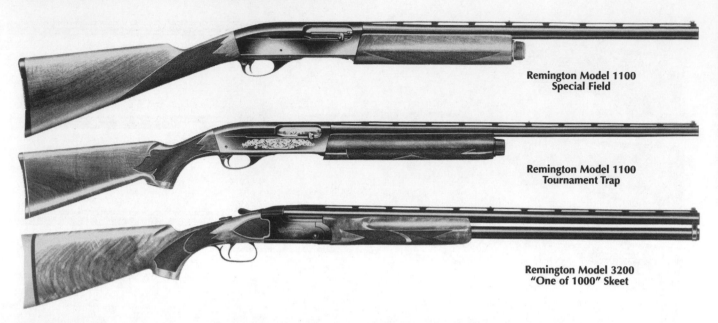

Remington Model 1100 Special Field

Remington Model 1100 Tournament Trap

Remington Model 3200 "One of 1000" Skeet

MODEL 1100
ONE OF 3000 FIELD . . . . NiB $1104 Ex $881 Gd $670
Limited edition, numbered 1 to 3000. Similar to Model 1100 Field except with fancy wood and gold-trimmed etched hunting scenes on receiver. 12 gauge with 28-inch Mod., vent rib bbl. Made in 1980.

MODEL 1100 SA SKEET GUN
Same as Model 1100 Field Gun, 12 and 20 ga. except has 26-inch vent-rib bbl., SK choke or with Cutts Compensator. Weight: 7.25-7.5 lbs. Made from 1963 to 1994.
**With skeet-
choked barrel** . . . . NiB $895 Ex $566 Gd $336
With Cutts Comp . . . . Add $100
Left-hand action . . . . NiB $916 Ex $597 Gd $377

MODEL 1100 SA
LIGHTWEIGHT SKEET . . . . NiB $550 Ex $441 Gd $318
Same as Model 1100 Lightweight except has skeet-style stock and forearm, 26-inch vent-rib bbl., SK choke. Made from 1971 to 1997.

MODEL 1100 SA
SKEET SMALL BORE . . . . NiB $550 Ex $358 Gd $260
Similar to standard Model 1100SA except chambered for 28 and .410 ga. (2.5-inch chamber for latter); 25-inch vent-rib bbl., SK choke. Weight: 6.75 lbs., 28 ga.; 7.25 lbs., .410. Made from 1969 to 1994.

MODEL 1100 SB
LIGHTWEIGHT SKEET . . . . NiB $550 Ex $358 Gd $260
Same as Model 1100SA Lightweight except has select wood. Introduced in 1977.

MODEL 1100
SB SKEET GUN . . . . NiB $550 Ex $358 Gd $260
Same specifications as Model 1100SA except has select wood. Made from 1963 to 1997.

MODEL 1100
SPECIAL FIELD SHOTGUN . . . . NiB $510 Ex $406 Gd $350
Gas-operated. Five round capacity. Hammerless. Gauges: 12 and 20. 21-inch vent-rib bbl. with REMChoke. Weight: 6.5-7.25 lbs. Straight-grip checkered walnut stock and forend. Made from 1983 to 1999.

MODEL 1100 SP MAGNUM
Same as Model 1100 Field except 12 ga. only with 3-inch chambers. Bbls.: 26- or 30-inch F choke; or 26-inch with REM Choke tubes; vent rib. Non-reflective matte black, Parkerized bbl. and receiver. Satin-finished stock and forend. Made 1986.
With fixed choke . . . . NiB $400 Ex $308 Gd $281
With REMChoke . . . . NiB $425 Ex $333 Gd $306

MODEL 1100 TOURNAMENT
AND PREMIER
These higher grade guns differ from standard models in overall quality, grade of wood, checkering, engraving, gold inlays, etc. General specs are the same. Made 1963 to 1994; 1997 to 1999; 2003.
**Model 1100D
Tournament** . . . . NiB $899 Ex $556 Gd $490
**Model 1100F
Premier** . . . . NiB $1191 Ex $936 Gd $750
**Model 1100F Premier
with gold inlay** . . . . NiB $9256 Ex $5393 Gd $3720

MODEL 1100
TOURNAMENT SKEET . . . . NiB $899 Ex $643 Gd $419
Similar to Model 1100 Field except with 26-inch bbl. SK choke. Gauges: 12, LT-20, 28, and .410. Features select walnut stocks and new cut-checkering patterns. Made from 1979- to 1999.

MODEL 1100TA TRAP GUN . . . . . . NiB $420 Ex $344 Gd $282
Similar to Model 1100TB Trap Gun except with regular-grade stocks. Available in both left- and right-hand versions. Made 1979 to 1986.

MODEL 1100TB TRAP GUN
Same as Model 1100 Field Gun except has special trap stock, straight or Monte Carlo comb, recoil pad; 30-inch vent-rib bbl., F or M trap choke; 12 ga. only. Weight: 8.25 lbs. Made 1963 to 1979.
With straight stock . . . . NiB $475 Ex $349 Gd $295
With Monte Carlo stock . . . . NiB $495 Ex $369 Gd $315

MODEL 1900
HAMMERLESS DOUBLE . . . . . . NiB $1790 Ex $1271 Gd $1090
Improved version of Model 1894. Boxlock. Auto ejector. Double triggers. Gauges: 10, 12, 16. Bbls.: 28 to 32 inches. Value shown is for standard grade with ordnance steel bbls. Made 1900 to 1910.

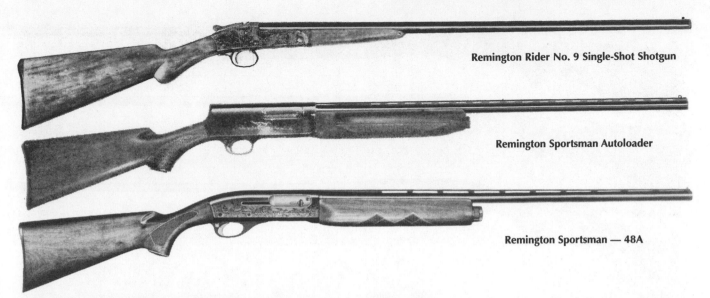

Remington Rider No. 9 Single-Shot Shotgun

Remington Sportsman Autoloader

Remington Sportsman — 48A

MODEL 3200 FIELD GRADE O/U . . NiB $1258 Ex $1048 Gd $742
Boxlock. Auto ejectors. Selective single trigger. 12 ga. 2.75-inch chambers. Bbls.: Vent rib, 26- and 28-inch M/F; 30-inch IC/M. Weight: About 7.75 lbs. with 26-inch bbls. Checkered pistol-grip stock/forearm. Made from 1973 to 1978.

MODEL 3200
COMPETITION SKEET GUN . . . NiB $1710 Ex $1477 Gd $1047
Same as Model 3200 Skeet Gun except has gilded scrollwork on frame, engraved forend, latch plate and trigger guard, select fancy wood. Made from 1973 to 1984.

MODEL 3200
COMPETITION SKEET SET . . . . NiB $5505 Ex $4516 Gd $3146
Similar specifications to Model 3200 Field. 12-ga. O/U with additional, interchangeable bbls. in 20, 28, and .410 ga. Cased. Made from 1980 to 1984.

MODEL 3200
COMPETITION TRAP GUN. . . . NiB $1454 Ex $1121 Gd $1093
Same as Model 3200 Trap Gun except has gilded scrollwork on frame, engraved forend, latch plate and trigger guard, select fancy wood. Made from 1973 to 1984.

MODEL 3200
FIELD GRADE MAGNUM . . . . . NiB $1695 Ex $1426 Gd $1080
Same as Model 3200 Field except chambered for 12 ga. mag. 3-inch shells 30-inch bbls., M and F or both F choke. Made 1975 to 1984.

MODEL 3200
"ONE OF 1000" SKEET . . . . NiB $1930 Ex $1462 Gd $1171
Same as Model 3200 "One of 1000" Trap except has 26- or 28-inch bbls., SK choke, skeet-style stock and forearm. Made in 1974.

MODEL 3200
"ONE OF 1000" TRAP. . . . . NiB $2150 Ex $1660 Gd $1375
Limited edition numbered 1 to 1000. Same general specifications as Model 3200 Trap Gun but has frame, trigger guard and forend latch elaborately engraved (designation "One of 1,000" on frame side), stock and forearm of high grade walnut. Supplied in carrying case. Made in 1973.

MODEL 3200 SKEET GUN . . . . . NiB $1696 Ex $1322 Gd $934
Same as Model 3200 Field Grade except skeet-style stock and full beavertail forearm, 26- or 28-inch bbls., SK choke. Made from 1973-80.

MODEL 3200
SPECIAL TRAP GUN . . . . NiB $1467 Ex $1223 Gd $873
Same as Model 3200 Trap Gun except has select fancy-grade wood and other minor refinements. Made from 1973 to 1984.

MODEL 3200 TRAP GUN . . . . . . NiB $1378 Ex $1135 Gd $813
Same as Model 3200 Field Grade except trap-style stock w/Monte Carlo or straight comb, select wood, beavertail forearm, 30- or 32-inch bbls. w/ventilated rib, IM/F or F/F chokes. Made 1973 to 1977.

RIDER NO. 9
SINGLE-SHOT SHOTGUN . . . . NiB $458 Ex $380 Gd $293
Improved version of No. 3 Single Barrel Shotgun made in the late 1800s. Semi-hammerless. Gauges 10, 12, 16, 20, 24, 28. 30- to 32-inch plain bbl. Weight: About 6 lbs. Plain pistol-grip stock and forearm. Auto ejector. Made from 1902 to 1910.

SP-10
MAGNUM AUTOLOADER . . . . NiB 995 Ex $715 Gd $549
Takedown. Gas-operated with stainless steel piston. 10 ga., 3.5-inch chamber. Bbls.: 26- or 30-inch vent-rib with REMChoke screw-in tubes. Weight: 11 to 11.25 lbs. Metal bead front. Checkered walnut stock with satin finish. Made from 1989 to date.

SP-10
MAGNUM TURKEY COMBO . . . . NiB $1291 Ex $983 Gd $658
Same general specifications as Model SP-10 Magnum except has extra 22-inch REMChoke bbl. with M, F and Turkey extra-full tubes. Rifle sights. QD swivels and camo sling. Made from 1991 to 1994.

PEERLESS O/U. . . . . NiB $1000 Ex $881 Gd $677
Boxlock action and removable, engraved sideplates. Gauge: 12 only with 3-inch chambers. Barrels: 26-, 28-, or 30-inch with vent rib and REMChoke system. Automatic safety and single selective trigger. Weight: 7.25 lbs. to 7.5 lbs. Blued receiver and bbls. Checkered American walnut stock. Made from 1993 to 1998.

SPORTSMAN A STANDARD GRADE
AUTOLOADER
Same general specifications as Model 11A except magazine holds two shells. Also available in "B" Special Grade, "D" Tournament Grade, "E" Expert Grade, "F" Premier Grade. Made from 1931 to 1948. Same values as for Model 11A.
48D . . . . NiB $320 Ex $246 Gd $159

SHOTGUNS

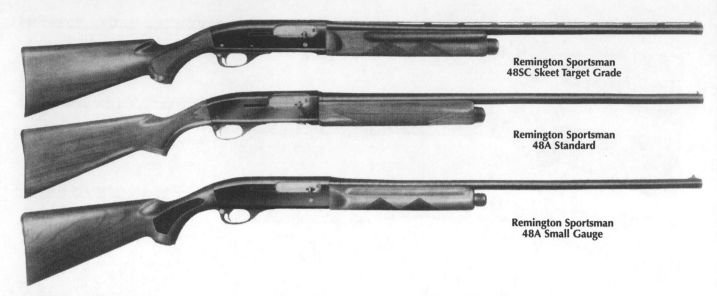

Remington Sportsman
48SC Skeet Target Grade

Remington Sportsman
48A Standard

Remington Sportsman
48A Small Gauge

SPORTSMAN SKEET GUN

Same general specifications as the Sportsman A except has 26-inch bbl. (plain, solid or vent rib), SK choke, beavertail forend. Disc. in 1949.

With plain barrel	NiB $325	Ex $275	Gd $276
With solid-rib barrel	NiB $325	Ex $275	Gd $276
With ventilated rib barrel	NiB $425	Ex $375	Gd $375

SPORTSMAN-48 MOHAWK SPORTSMAN AUTO

Streamlined receiver. Hammerless. Takedown. Gauges: 12, 16, 20. Tubular magazine holds two rounds. Bbls.: Plain, matted top surface or vent rib; 26-inch IC, 28-inch M or F choke, 30-inch F choke (12 ga. only). Weight: About 7.5 lbs., 12 ga.; 6.25 lbs., 16 ga.; 6.5 lbs., 20 ga. Pistol-grip stock, grooved forend, both checkered. Made from 1949 to 1959.

With plain bbl.	NiB $300	Ex $225	Gd $147
With matted top-surface bbl.	NiB $400	Ex $325	Gd $250
With ventilated rib bbl.	NiB $470	Ex $348	Gd $291

SPORTSMAN-48 B, D, F SELECT, TOURNAMENT AND PREMIER GRADE GUNS

These higher grade models differ from the Sportsman-48A in general quality, grade of wood, checkering, engraving, etc. General specifications are the same. Made from 1949 to 1959.

Sportsman-48B Select grade	NiB $420	Ex $288	Gd $196
Sportsman-48D Tournament grade	NiB $1500	Ex $924	Gd $681
Sportsman-48F Premier grade	NiB $5750	Ex $3810	Gd $2280

SPORTSMAN-48SA SKEET GUN

Same general specifications as Sportsman-48A except has 26-inch bbl. with matted top surface or vent rib, SK choke, ivory bead front sight, metal bead rear sight. Made from 1949 to 1960.

With plainbarrel	NiB $305	Ex $241	Gd $151
With ventilated rib barrel	NiB $395	Ex $293	Gd $186
Sportsman-48SC Skeet	NiB $499	Ex $377	Gd $245
Tournament grade	NiB $1500	Ex $1118	Gd $981
Sportsman-48SF Skeet Premier grade	NiB $5755	Ex $3800	Gd $2342

MODEL 11-48A RIOT GUN	NiB $300	Ex $291	Gd $211

Same as Model 11-48A except 20-inch plain barrel and 12 ga. only. Disc. in 1969.

MODEL 11-48A STANDARD
GRADE 4-ROUND AUTOLOADER .410 & 28 GAUGE

Same general specifications as Sportsman-48A except gauge, 3-round magazine, 25-inch bbl. Weight: About 6.25 lbs. 28 ga. introduced 1952, .410 in 1954. Disc. in 1969. Values same as shown for Sportsman-48A.

MODEL 11-48A STANDARD
GRADE AUTOLOADER

Same general specifications as Sportsman-48A except magazine holds four rounds, forend not grooved. Also available in Special Grade (11-48B), Tournament Grade (11-48D) and Premier Grade (11-48F). Made 1949 to 1969. Values same as for Sportsman-48A.

MODEL 11-48SA

.410 AND 28 GA. SKEET	NiB $300	Ex $260	Gd $158

Same general specifications as Model 11-48A 28 gauge except has 25-inch vent rib bbl., SK choke. 28 ga. introduced 1952, .410 in 1954.

SPORTSMAN-58 SKEET, TARGET, TOURNAMENT AND PREMIER GRADES

These higher grade models differ from the Sportsman-58SA in general quality, grade of wood, checkering, engraving, and other refinements. General operating and physical specifications are the same.

Sportsman-58C Skeet Gun.	NiB $450	Ex $331	Gd $273
Sportsman-58D Tournament	NiB $1500	Ex $1162	Gd $954
Sportsman-58SF Premier	NiB $5755	Ex $3451	Gd $2124

SPORTSMAN-58 TOURNAMENT AND PREMIER

These higher grade models differ from the Sportsman-58ADL with vent-rib bbl. in general quality, grade of wood, checkering, engraving, etc. General specifications are the same.

Sportsman-58D Tournament	NiB $1099	Ex $824	Gd $590
Sportsman-58F Premier	NiB $1889	Ex $1488	Gd $1051

SPORTSMAN-58ADL AUTOLOADER

Deluxe grade. Gas-operated. 12 ga. Three round magazine. Bbls.: plain or vent rib, 26-, 28- or 30-inch; IC, M or F choke, or Remington Special Skeet choke. Weight: About 7 lbs. Checkered pistol-grip stock and forearm. Made from 1956 to 1964.

With plain barrel	NiB $275	Ex $217	Gd $159
With ventilated rib barrel	NiB $360	Ex $261	Gd $159

Richland Model 200

Richland Model 202

Richland Model 707 Deluxe

Richland Model 711
Long Range Waterfowl Magnum

SPORTSMAN-58BDL DELUXE SPECIAL GRADE
Same as Model 58ADL except select grade wood.
With plain barrel . . . . **NiB $452 Ex $340 Gd $248**
With ventilated rib barrel . . . . **NiB $484 Ex $389 Gd $282**

SPORTSMAN-58SADL
SKEET GRADE . . . . **NiB $492 Ex $380 Gd $274**
Same general specifications as Model 58ADL with vent-rib bbl.
except special skeet stock and forearm.

REVELATION SHOTGUNS

See Western Auto listings.

RICHLAND ARMS COMPANY — Blissfield, Michigan; Manufactured in Italy and Spain

MODEL 200
FIELD GRADE DOUBLE . . . . **NiB $335 Ex $240 Gd $127**
Hammerless, boxlock, Anson & Deeley-type. Plain extractors.
Double triggers. Gauges: 12, 16, 20, 28, .410 (3-inch chambers in
20 and .410; others have 2.75-inch). Bbls.: 28-inch M/F choke, 26-
inch IC/M; .410 with 26-inch M/F only; 22-inch IC/M in 20 ga. only.
Weight: 6 lbs., 2 oz. to 7 lbs., 4 oz. Checkered walnut stock with
cheekpiece, pistol grip, recoil pad; beavertail forend. Made in Spain
from 1963 to 1985.

MODEL 202
ALL PURPOSE FIELD GUN . . . . **NiB $450 Ex $299 Gd $219**
Hammerless, boxlock, Anson & Deeley-type. Same as Model 200

except has two sets of barrels same gauge. 12 ga.: 30-inch bbls. F/F,
3-inch chambers; 26-inch bbls. IC/M, 2.75-inch chambers. 20
gauge: 28-inch bbls. M/F; 22-inch bbls. IC/M, 3-inch chambers.
Made from 1963. Disc.

MODEL 707
DELUXE FIELD GUN . . . . **NiB $350 Ex $224 Gd $136**
Hammerless, boxlock, triple bolting system. Plain extractors.
Double triggers. Gauges: 12, 2.75-inch chambers; 20, 3-inch
chambers. Bbls.: 12 ga., 28-inch M/F, 26-inch IC/M; 20 ga., 30-
inch F/F, 28-inch M/F, 26-inch IC/M. Weight: 6 lbs., 4 oz. to 6
lbs., 15 oz. Checkered walnut stock and forend, recoil pad.
Made from 1963 to 1972.

MODEL 711 LONG-RANGE
WATERFOWL MAGNUM
DOUBLE-BARREL SHOTGUN
Hammerless, boxlock, Anson & Deeley-type, Purdey triple lock.
Plain extractors. Double triggers. Auto safety. Gauges: 10, 3.5-inch
chambers; 12, 3-inch chambers. Bbls.: 10 ga., 32-inch; 12 ga., 30-
inch; F/F. Weight: 10 ga., 11 pounds; 12 ga., 7.75 lbs. Checkered
walnut stock and beavertail forend; recoil pad. Made in Spain
from 1963 to 1985.
10 ga. magnum . . . . **NiB $410 Ex $302 Gd $226**
12 ga. magnum . . . . **NiB $417 Ex $301 Gd $212**

MODEL 808
O/U SHOTGUN . . . . **NiB $435 Ex $290 Gd $183**
Boxlock. Plain extractors. Non-selective single trigger. 12 ga. only.
Bbls. (Vickers steel): 30-inch F/F; 28-inch M/F; 26-inch IC/M. Weight:
6 lbs., 12 oz. to 7 lbs., 3 oz. Checkered walnut stock/forend. Made in
Italy from 1963 to 1968.

Rigby Regal
Side Lock

JOHN RIGBY & CO. — London, England

HAMMERLESS BOX LOCK DOUBLE-BARREL SHOTGUNS
Auto ejectors. Double triggers. Made in all gauges, barrel lengths
and chokes. Checkered stock and forend, straight grip standard.
Made in two grades: Sackville and Chatsworth. These guns differ
in general quality, engraving, etc.; specifications are the same.
Sackville grade . . . . NiB $5900 Ex $4045 Gd $3525
Chatsworth grade . . . . NiB $4550 Ex $3809 Gd $2669

HAMMERLESS SIDE LOCK DOUBLE-BARREL SHOTGUNS
Auto ejectors. Double triggers. Made in all gauges, barrel
lengths and chokes. Checkered stock and forend, straight grip
standard. Made in two grades: Regal (best quality) and
Sandringham; these guns differ in general quality, engraving,
etc., specifications are the same.
Regal grade . . . . NiB $12,525 Ex $10,125 Gd $6125
Sandringham grade . . . . NiB $9550 Ex $7750 Gd $4025

RIZZINI, BATTISTA — Marcheno, Italy

*Rizzini was purchased by San Swiss AG IN 2002. Imported in
the U. S. by SIB Arms, Exeter, New Hampshire; William Larkin
Moore & Co., Scottsdale, Arizona; and New England Arms Co.,
Kittery, Maine*

AURUM O/U . . . . NiB $2600 Ex $2140 Gd $1935
Gauge: 12, 16 and 20. Boxlock action, light engraving. Case
included. Introduced 1996.

AURUM LIGHT . . . . NiB $3790 Ex $2695 Gd $2245
Similaar to Aurum but 16 gauge only. Imported beginning in
2000.

ARTEMIS . . . . NiB $2600 Ex $2115 Gd $1815
Similarf to Aurum but with improved engraving and gold inlays.

ARTEMIS DELUXE . . . . NiB $5995 Ex $3720 Gd $2995
Similar to Artemis but with detailed game scene engraving.
Available in all gauges

ARTEMIS EL . . . . NiB $16,140 Ex $13,140 Gd $11,640
Same as Artemis Deluxe. Custom gun with superior quality wood
and detailed hand engraving. Disc. 2000.

MODEL 780 FIELD . . . . NiB $1985 Ex $940 Gd $810
Gauge: 10, 12 or 16. Boxlock action, double triggers, extractors,
walnut stock and forearm. Disc. 2000.
10 gauge, add $550
Ejector model (S780EL), add $150
Single selective trigger with ejectors, add $200
SST, ejectors and upgraded stock, add $350

MODEL S780 EMEL . . . . NiB $13,000 Ex $12,044 Gd $9965
Same as Model 780 Field but with special engraving and hand finished.

MODEL 780 COMPETITION . . . . NiB $1375 Ex $1125 Gd $940
Same as Model 780 Field but with skeet, trap or sporting clays features. Disc.1998.

**MODEL 780
SMALL GAUGE SERIES** . . . . NiB $1280 Ex $1010 Gd $790
Same as Model 780 Field but in 20, 28, or 36 gauge. Double trig-
gers, ejectors. Disc. 1998.

MODEL 782 EM FIELD . . . . NiB $1443 Ex $1143 Gd $913
Gauge: 12 or 16. Boxlock action with sideplates, single selective trig-
ger, ejectors and extractors, walnut stock and forearm. Disc. 1998.
MODEL 782 EM SLUG, add $455
MODEL 782 EML, add $350

MODEL S7820 EMEL . . . . NiB $13,130 Ex $10,985 Gd $9660
Same as Model 782 EM Field but specially engraved and hand finished.

MODEL S782 EMEL DELUXE . . . . NiB $12,225 Ex $10,825 Gd $9095
Gauge: 10, 12, 16, 20, 28, 36 and .410. Barrel:28-inch ventilated rib
with choke tubes (except .410); coin-finish engraving; gold inlaids;
fine scroll borders; Deluxe English walnut stock. Imported 1994.

MODEL 790 COMPETITION . . . . NiB $1725 Ex $1517 Gd $1147
Gauge: 12 or 20. Available in trap, skeet or sporting clays models.
Black frame outlined with gold line engraving. Disc. 1999.
20 ga. Sporting (sideplates and QD stock), add $1050
Trap model, 20 gauge, subtract $150

MODEL 790 SMALL GAUGE . . . . NiB $1375 Ex $1068 Gd $913
Similar to Model 790 Competition but in 20, 29, or 36 guages.
Single selective trigger, ejectors. Disc. 2000.

MODEL 790 EL . . . . NiB $6950 Ex $4850 Gd $3525
Same as Model 790 but hand finished with 18k gold inlays, hand
engraving.

MODEL 790 EL . . . . NiB $6950 Ex $4220 Gd $3345
Same as Model 790 but with multiple chokes, fitted case. Disc. 2000.

MODEL S790 EMEL DELUXE . . . . NiB $11,370 Ex $9635 Gd $6280
Guages: All. Custom gun with 27.5-inch ventilated-rib bbls. choke
tubes (except .410); color case-hardened or coin-finished receiver;
ornate engraving with Rizzini crest. Stock is deluxe English walnut;
leather case included.

MODEL 792 SMALL GAUGE MAGNUM NiB $1695 Ex $1347 Gd $1017
Gauge: 20, 28, or 36. Magnum chambers. Single selective trigger;
ejectors; engraved sideplates. Disc. 1998.

MODEL 792 EMEL DELUXE . . . . NiB $8085 Ex $7035 Gd $5080
Same as Model 793 but hand finished with 18k gold inlays and
hand engraving.

MODEL S792 EMEL . . . . NiB $12,255 Ex $10,835 Gd $9180
Guages: All. Custom gun with 27.5-inch ventilated-rib bbls. choke
tubes (except .410); coin-finished receiver; sideplates with fine
game scene engraving and scroll borders; deluxe English walnut
stock; leather case included. Imported 1994.

MODEL 2000 TRAP . . . . NiB $1675 Ex $1372 Gd $1017
Guage: 12 only. Nickel-finished receiver; sideplates; gold trigger; ventilated-
rib bbls.. Disc 1998.

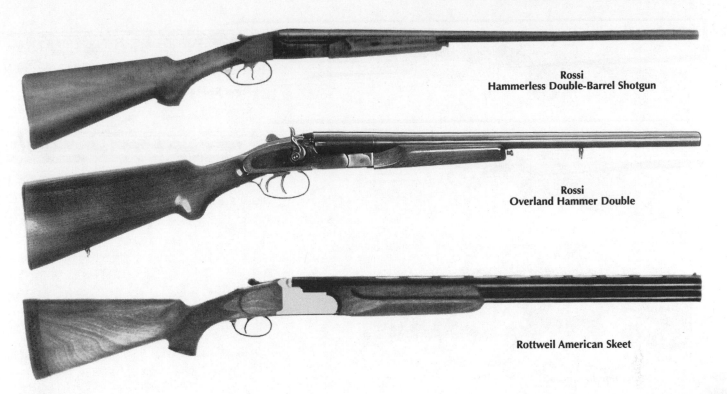

Rossi
Hammerless Double-Barrel Shotgun

Rossi
Overland Hammer Double

Rottweil American Skeet

MODEL 2000

TRAP EL . . . . **NiB $5290 Ex $3950 Gd $3055**
Same as Model 2000 Trap but hand finished with 18k gold inlays and ornate hand engraving.

MODEL 2000-SP . . . . **NiB $3000 Ex $2765 Gd $2040**
Guage: 12 only. Bbls.: 26, 29.5, or 32 inches. Over-bored barrels with choke tubes. Engraved sideplates, semi-fancy select QD stock. Case included. Imported 1994 to 1998.

PREMIER SPORTING . . . . **NiB $2590 Ex $2155 Gd $1625**
Guages: 12 or 20. Bbls.: 28, 29.5 or 32 inches five chokes per bbl.. Custom built on request. Imported 1994

SPORTING EL . . . . **NiB $2975 Ex $2250 Gd $1955**
Same as Premier model but includes multiple chokes and fitted case. Disc. 2000.

UPLAND EL . . . . **NiB $2625 Ex $2150 Gd $1855**
Guages: All. Custom gun with 27.5-inch ventilated-rib bbls. choke tubes (except .410); case-hardened receiver; deluxe walnut stock. Hard case included. Imported 1994.

AMADEO ROSSI, S.A. — Sao Leopoldo, Brazil

SQUIRE HAMMERLESS DOUBLE-
BARREL SHOTGUN . . . . **NiB $320 Ex $312 Gd $226**
Boxlock. Plain extractors. Double triggers. 12 and 20 ga., .410. Three-inch chambers. Bbls.: 20-, 26-inch IC/M; 28-inch M/F choke. Weight: 7 to 7.5 lbs. Pistol-grip hardwood stock and beavertail forearm, uncheckered. Made 1985 to 1990.

OVERLUND
HAMMER DOUBLE. . . . . **NiB $290 Ex $156 Gd $107**
Sidelock. Plain extractors. Double triggers. Gauges: 12, .410; 3-inch chambers. Bbls.: 20-inch, IC/M in 12 g.; 26-inch, F/F choke in .410. Weight: 7 lbs. (12 ga.); 6 lbs. (.410). Pistol-grip stock and beavertail forearm, uncheckered. Note: Because of its resemblance to the short-barreled doubles carried by guards riding shotgun on 19th-century stagecoaches, the 12 ga. version originally was called the "Coach Gun." Made 1968 to 1989.

ROTTWEIL SHOTGUNS — West Germany

MODEL 72 O/U
SHOTGUN. . . . . **NiB $1850 Ex $1585 Gd $1186**
Hammerless, takedown with engraved receiver. 12 ga.; 2.75-inch chambers. 26.75-inch bbls. with SK/SK chokes. Weight: 7.5 lbs. Interchangeable trigger groups and buttstocks. Checkered French walnut buttstock and forend. Imported from Germany.

MODEL 650 FIELD
O/U SHOTGUN . . . . **NiB $750 Ex $610 Gd $504**
Breech action. Gauge: 12. 28-inch bbls. Six screw-in choke tubes. Automatic ejectors. Engraved receiver. Checkered pistol grip stock. Made from 1984 to 1986.

AMERICAN SKEET . . . . **NiB $1850 Ex $1636 Gd $1151**
Boxlock action. Gauge: 12. 27-inch vent-rib bbls. 44.5 inches overall. SK chokes. Weight: 7.5 lbs. Designed for tube sets. Hand-checkered European walnut stock with modified forend. Made from 1984 to 1987.

INTERNATIONAL
TRAP SHOTGUN . . . . **NiB $1850 Ex $1680 Gd $1181**
Box lock action. Gauge: 12. 30-inch bbls. 48.5 inches overall. Weight: 8 lbs. Choked IM/F. Selective single trigger. Metal bead front sight. Checkered European walnut stock w/pistol grip. Engraved action. Made from 1984 to 1987.

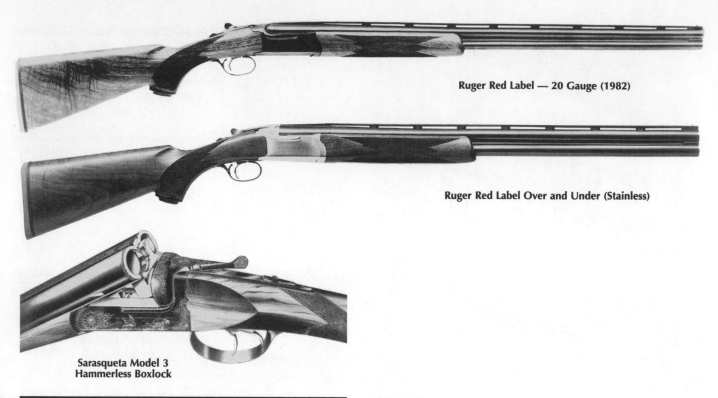

Ruger Red Label — 20 Gauge (1982)

Ruger Red Label Over and Under (Stainless)

Sarasqueta Model 3
Hammerless Boxlock

STURM, RUGER & COMPANY, INC. — Southport, Connecticut

RED LABEL O/U
STANDARD GRADE
Boxlock. Auto ejectors. Selective single trigger. 12, 20 or 28 ga. w/2.75- or 3-inch chambers. 26-inch vent-rib bbl., IC/M or SK choke. Single selective trigger. Selective automatic ejectors. Automatic top safety. Standard gold bead front sight. Pistol-grip or English-style American walnut stock and forearm w/hand-cut checkering. The 20 ga. Model was introduced in 1977; 12 ga. version in 1982 and the stainless receiver became standard in 1985. Choke tubes were optional in 1988 and standard in 1990. Weight: 7.0 to 7.5 lbs.
Red Label w/fixed chokes . . . . . . NiB $1507 Ex $1229 Gd $905
Red Label w/screw-in tubes . . . . . NiB $1547 Ex $1259 Gd $925
Red Label w/grade 1 engraving. . . . NiB $1755 Ex $1388 Gd $1030
Red Label w/grade 2 engraving . . . NiB $2198 Ex $1974 Gd $1527
Red Label w/grade 3 engraving . . . NiB $2539 Ex $2163 Gd $1926

RED LABEL O/U
ALL-WEATHER STAINLESS
Gauges: 12 ga. Only. Bbls.: 26- 28- or 30-inch w/various chokes, fixed or screw-in tubes. Stainless receiver and barrel. Checkered black synthetic stock and forearm. Weight: 7.5 lbs. Made 1999 to 2006.
All-weather stainless model . . . . NiB $1275 Ex $1020 Gd $733
W/30-inch bbl., add $100

RED LABEL
"WOODSIDE" O/U
Similar to the Red Label O/U Stainless except in 12 ga. only with wood sideplate extensions. Made from 1995 to 2002. Disc.
Standard Woodside . . . . NiB $1530 Ex $1306 Gd $928
Engraved Woodside . . . . NiB $2200 Ex $1853 Gd $1303

RED LABEL
SPORTING CLAYS O/U
Similar to the standard Red Label model except chambered 12 or 20 ga. only w/30-inch vent-rib bbls., no side ribs; backbored w/screw-in choke tubes (not interchangeable w/other Red Label O/U models). Brass front and mid-rib beads. Made from 1992 to date.
Standard Sporting Clays. . . . . NiB $1555 Ex $1160 Gd $820
Engraved Sporting Clays . . . . . . NiB $2500 Ex $2031 Gd $1429

RED LABEL SPECIAL EDITION - WILDLIFE FOREVER
Limited edition commemorating the 50th Wildlife Forever anniversary. Similar to the standard Red Label model except chambered 12 ga. only w/engraved receiver enhanced w/gold mallard and pheasant inlays. 300 produced in 1993.
Special edition. . . . . NiB $1594 Ex $1385 Gd $1049
Special edition w/hard case . . . . Add $125

VICTOR SARASQUETA, S. A. — Eibar, Spain
SARASQUETA MODEL 3 HAMMERLESS
BOXLOCK DOUBLE-BARREL SHOTGUN
Plain extractors or auto ejectors. Double triggers. Gauges: 12, 16, 20. Made in various bbl. lengths, chokes and weights. Checkered stock and forend, straight grip standard. Imported from 1985-87.
Model 3, plain extractors . . . . NiB $445 Ex $326 Gd $279
Model 3E, automatic ejectors . . . . . NiB $575 Ex $450 Gd $372

HAMMERLESS SIDELOCK DOUBLES
Automatic ejectors (except on Models 4 and 203 which have plain extractors). Double triggers. Gauges: 12, 16, 20. Barrel lengths, chokes and weights made to order. Checkered stock and forend, straight grip standard. Models differ chiefly in overall quality, engraving, grade of wood, checkering, etc.; general specifications are the same. Imported from 1985 to 1987.

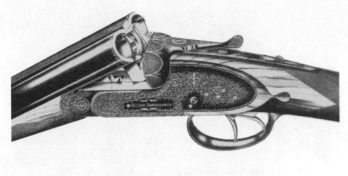

Sarasqueta Models 6E, 11E and 12E

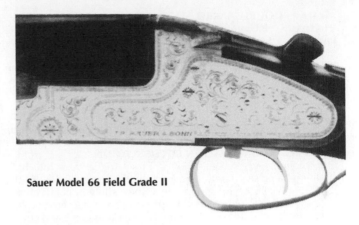

Sauer Model 66 Field Grade II

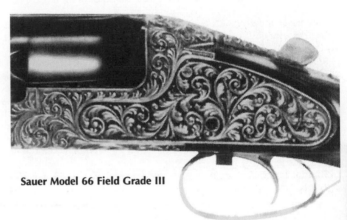

Sauer Model 66 Field Grade III

Model 4	NiB $628	Ex $560	Gd $376
Model 4E	NiB $700	Ex $591	Gd $405
Model 203	NiB $650	Ex $563	Gd $392
Model 203E	NiB $715	Ex $609	Gd $423
Model 6E	NiB $1220	Ex $915	Gd $699
Model 7E	NiB $1309	Ex $1065	Gd $835
Model 10E	NiB $2446	Ex $2027	Gd $1707
Model 11E	NiB $2652	Ex $2373	Gd $2037
Model 12E	NiB $2950	Ex $2688	Gd $2291

J. P. SAUER & SOHN — Eckernförde, Germany, formerly Suhl, Germany

MODEL 66 O/U
FIELD GUN
Purdey-system action with Holland & Holland-type sidelocks. Selective single trigger. Selective auto ejectors. Automatic safety. Available in three grades of engraving. 12 ga. only. Krupp special steel bbls. w/vent rib 28-inch, M/F choke. Weight: About 7.25 lbs. Checkered walnut stock and forend; recoil pad. Made from 1966 to 1975.

Grade I	NiB $2200	Ex $2086	Gd $1472
Grade II	NiB $3090	Ex $2734	Gd $1919
Grade III	NiB $3865	Ex $3523	Gd $2537

MODEL 66
O/U SKEET GUN
Same as Model 66 Field Gun except 26-inch bbls. with wide vent rib, SK choked- skeet-style stock and ventilated beavertail forearm; non-automatic safety. Made from 1966 to 1975.

Grade I	NiB $2200	Ex $2025	Gd $1428
Grade II	NiB $3080	Ex $2737	Gd $1921
Grade III	NiB $3850	Ex $3459	Gd $2702

MODEL 66
O/U TRAP GUN
Same as Model 66 Skeet Gun except has 30-inch bbls. choked F/F or M/F; trap-style stock. Values same as for Skeet model. Made from 1966 to 1975.

MODEL 3000E DRILLING
Combination rifle and double barrel shotgun. Blitz action with Greener crossbolt, double underlugs, separate rifle cartridge extractor, front set trigger, firing pin indicators, Greener side safety, sear slide selector locks right shotgun bbl. for firing rifle bbl. Gauge/calibers 12 ga. (2.75-inch chambers); .222, .243, .30-06, 7x65R. 25-inch Krupp-Special steel bbls.; M/F choke automatic folding leaf rear rifle sight. Weight: 6.5 to 7.25 lbs. depending on rifle caliber. Checkered walnut stock and forend; pistol grip, Monte Carlo comb and cheekpiece, sling swivels. Standard model with Arabesque engraving; Deluxe model with hunting scenes engraved on action. Currently manufactured. Note: Also see listing under Colt.

Standard model	NiB $4299	Ex $3749	Gd $2625
Deluxe model	NiB $5550	Ex $4539	Gd $3256

ARTEMIS DOUBLE-BARREL SHOTGUN

Holland & Holland-type sidelock with Greener crossbolt double underlugs, double sear safeties, selective single trigger, selective auto ejectors. Grade I with fine-line engraving, Grade II with full English Arabesque engraving. 12 ga. (2.75-inch chambers). Krupp special steel bbls., 28-inch, M/F choke. Weight: About 6.5 lbs. Checkered walnut pistol-grip stock and beavertail forend; recoil pad. Made from 1966 to 1977.

Grade I . . . . NiB $5500 Ex $4586 Gd $3338
Grade II . . . . NiB $6600 Ex $5520 Gd $4126

BBF 54 O/U COMBINATION RIFLE/SHOTGUN

Blitz action with Kersten lock, front set trigger fires rifle bbl., slide-operated sear safety. Gauge/calibers: 16 ga.; .30-30, .30-06, 7x65R, 25-inch Krupp special steel bbls.; shotgun bbl. F choke, folding-leaf rear sight. Weight: About 6 lbs. Checkered walnut stock and forend; pistol grip, mod. Monte Carlo comb and cheekpiece, sling swivels. Standard model with Arabesque engraving; Deluxe model with hunting scenes engraved on action. Currently manufactured.

Standard model . . . . NiB $2878 Ex $2332 Gd $1645
Deluxe model . . . . NiB $3318 Ex $2676 Gd $1881

ROYAL DOUBLE-BARREL SHOTGUNS

Anson & Deeley action (boxlock) with Greener crossbolt, double underlugs, signal pins, selective single trigger, selective auto ejectors, auto safety. Scalloped frame with Arabesque engraving. Krupp special steel bbls. Gauges: 12, 2.75-inch chambers, 20, 3-inch chambers. Bbls.: 30-inch (12 ga. only) and 28-inch, M/F- 26-inch (20 ga. only), IC/M. Weight: 12 ga., about 6.5 lbs.; 20 ga., 6 lbs. Checkered walnut pistol-grip stock and beavertail forend; recoil pad. Made from 1955 to 1977.

Standard model . . . . NiB $1650 Ex $1383 Gd $987
20 ga. Add 20%

SAVAGE ARMS — Westfield, Massachusetts
Formerly located in Utica, New York

MODEL 24 22-.410

O/U COMBINATION . . . . NiB $475 Ex $361 Gd $218
Same as Stevens No. 22-.410 with walnut stock and forearm. Made from 1950 to 1965.

MODEL 24C

CAMPER'S COMPANION . . . . NiB $575 Ex $394 Gd $221
Same as Model 24FG except made in .22 Magnum/20 ga. only; has 20-inch bbls., shotgun tube Cyl. bore. Weight: 5.75 lbs. Trap in butt provides ammunition storage; comes with carrying case. Made 1972 to 1989.

MODEL 24 FIELD . . . . NiB $395 Ex $219 Gd $159

Same as Models 24DL and 24MDL except frame has black or casehardened finish. Game scene decoration of frame eliminated in 1974; forearm uncheckered after 1976. Made from 1970 to 1989.

MODEL 24DL . . . . NiB $395 Ex $268 Gd $194

Same general specifications as Model 24S except top-lever opening; satin-chrome-finished frame decorated with game scenes, checkered Monte Carlo stock and forearm. Made from 1962 to 1965.

MODEL 24F-12T TURKEY GUN . . . NiB $600 Ex $421 Gd $286

12- or 20-ga. shotgun bbl./.22 Hornet, .223 or .30-30 caliber rifle. 24-inch blued bbls., 3-inch chambers, extra removable F choke tube. Hammer block safety. Color casehardened frame. DuPont Rynite camo stock. Swivel studs. Made from 1989 to 2007.

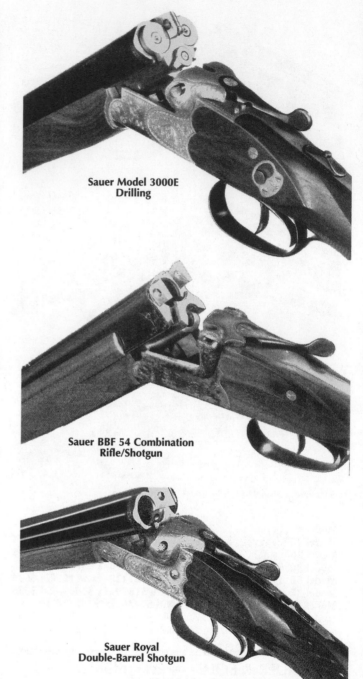

Sauer Model 3000E Drilling

Sauer BBF 54 Combination Rifle/Shotgun

Sauer Royal Double-Barrel Shotgun

MODEL 24FG FIELD GRADE . . . . . NiB $450 Ex $370 Gd $227

Same general specifications as Model 24S except top lever opening. Made 1972. Disc.

MODEL 24MDL. . . . . NiB $496 Ex $279 Gd $193

Same as Model 24DL except rifle bbl. chambered for 22 WMR. Made 1962 to 1969.

MODEL 24MS. . . . . NiB $600 Ex $470 Gd $327

Same as Model 24S except rifle bbl. chambered for 22 WMR. Made 1964 to 1971.

Savage Model 24
.22-/.410 O/U Combination

Savage Model 24-VS
Camper/Survival/Centerfire Rifle/Shotgun

MODEL 24S O/U COMBINATION . NiB $395 Ex $279 Gd $162
Boxlock. Visible hammer. Side lever opening. Plain extractors. Single trigger. 20 ga. or .410 bore shotgun bbl. under 22 LR bbl., 24-inch. Open rear sight, ramp front, dovetail for scope mounting. Weight: About 6.75 lbs. Plain pistol-grip stock and forearm. Made from 1964 to 1971.

MODEL 24V . . . . **NiB $495 Ex $321 Gd $261**
Similar to Model 24D except 20 ga. under .222 Rem., .22 Rem., .357 Mag., .22 Hornet or .30-30 rifle bbl. Made 1967 to 1989.

MODEL 24-CS CAMPER'S COMPANION
CENTERFIRE RIFLE/SHOTGUN. . . . NiB $575 Ex $339 Gd $273
Caliber: .22 LR over 20 ga. Nickel finish full-length stock and accessory pistol-grip stock. Overall length: 36 inches with full stock; 26 inches w/pistol grip. Weight: About 5.75 lbs. Made 1972 to 1988.
Model 24VS (.357 Mag./20 ga.). . . . .**NiB $595 Ex $339 Gd $273**

MODEL 28A STANDARD GRADE
SLIDE-ACTION REPEATING SHOTGUN . . . . . **NiB $370 Ex $296 Gd $214**
Hammerless. Takedown. 12 ga. Five round tubular magazine. Plain bbl., lengths: 26-,28-, 30-, 32-inches, choked C/M/F. Weight: About 7.5 lbs. with 30-inch bbl. Plain pistol-grip stock, grooved slide handle. Made from 1928 to 1931.

MODEL 28B . . . . **NiB $310 Ex $241 Gd $205**
Raised matted rib; otherwise the same as Model 28A.

MODEL 28D TRAP GRADE . . . . **NiB $310 Ex $241 Gd $205**
Same general specifications as Model 28A except has 30-inch F choke bbl. w/matted rib, trap-style stock w/checkered pistol grip, checkered slide handle of select walnut.

MODEL 30 SOLID FRAME HAMMERLESS
SLIDE-ACTION SHOTGUN. . . . . . . **NiB $235 Ex $200 Gd $160**
Gauges: 12, 16, 20, .410. 2.75-inch chamber in 16 ga., 3- inch in other ga. Magazine holds four 2.75-inch shells or three 3-inch shells. Bbls.: Vent rib; 26-, 28-, 30-inch; IC, M, F choke. Weight: Average 6.25 to 6.75 lbs. depending on ga. Plain pistol-grip stock (checkered on later production), grooved slide handle. Made from 1958 to 1970.

MODEL 30 TAKEDOWN SLUG GUN . . **NiB $205 Ex $140 Gd $101**
Same as Model 30FG except 21-inch cyl. bore bbl. with rifle sights. Made from 1971 to 1979.

MODEL 30AC SOLID FRAME . . . . . **NiB $240 Ex $205 Gd $164**
Same as Model 30 Solid Frame except has 26-inch bbl. with adj. choke; 12 ga. only. Made from 1959 to 1970.

MODEL 30AC TAKEDOWN. . . . . . . **NiB $220 Ex $183 Gd $162**

Same as Model 30FG except has 26-inch bbl. with adj. choke; 12 and 20 ga. only. Made from 1971 to 1972.

MODEL 30D TAKEDOWN . . . . **NiB $220 Ex $175 Gd $151**
Deluxe Grade. Same as Model 30FG except has receiver engraved with game scene, vent rib bbl., recoil pad. Made from 1971. Disc.

MODEL 30FG TAKEDOWN HAMMERLESS
SLIDE-ACTION SHOTGUN. . . . . **NiB $195 Ex $107 Gd $88**
Field Grade. Gauges: 12, 20, .410. Three-inch chamber. Magazine holds four 2.75-inch shells or three 3-inch shells. Bbls.: plain; 26-inch F choke (.410 ga. only); 28-inch M/F choke; 30-inch F choke (12 ga. only). Weight: Average 7 to 7.75 lbs. depending on gauge. Checkered pistol-grip stock, fluted slide handle. Made 1970 to 1979.

MODEL 30L SOLID FRAME . . . . . . **NiB $248 Ex $196 Gd $144**
Same as Model 30 Solid Frame except left-handed model with ejection port and safety on left side; 12 ga. only. Made 1959 to 1970.

MODEL 30T SOLID FRAME
TRAP AND DUCK . . . . **NiB $268 Ex $221 Gd $161**
Same as Model 30 Solid Frame except only in 12 ga. w/30-inch F choke bbl.; has Monte Carlo stock with recoil pad, weight: About 8 lbs. Made from 1963 to 1970.

MODEL 30T TAKE DOWN
TRAP GUN . . . . **NiB $256 Ex $211 Gd $147**
Same as Model 30D except only in 12 ga. w/30-inch F choke bbl. Monte Carlo stock with recoil pad. Made from 1970 to 1973.

MODEL 69-RXL SLIDE-ACTION
SHOTGUN . . . . **NiB $271 Ex $191 Gd $140**
Similar to Model 67 (law enforcement configuration). Hammerless, side ejection top tang safe for left- or right-hand use. 12 ga. chambered for 2.75- and 3-inch magnum shells. 18.25-inch bbl. Tubular magazine holds 6 rounds (one less for 3-inch mag). Walnut finish hardwood stock with recoil pad and grooved operating handle. Weight: About 6.5 lbs. Made from 1982 to 1989.

MODEL 210F BOLT-ACTION
SLUG GUN . . . . **NiB $422 Ex $322 Gd $232**
Built on Savage 110 action. Gauge: 12 w/3-inch chamber. Two round detachable magazine. 24-inch fully rifled bbl. Receiver drilled and tapped for scope mounts w/no sights. Weight: 7.5 lbs. Checkered black synthetic stock w/swivel studs and recoil pad. Made from 1997 to 2000.

MODEL 210FT BOLT-ACTION SHOTGUN . . . **NiB $492 Ex $388 Gd $269**
Similar to Model 210F except has smoothbore 24-inch bbl. w/choke tubes. Bead front and U-notch rear sights. Advantage Camo finish. Made from 1997 to 2000.

SHOTGUNS

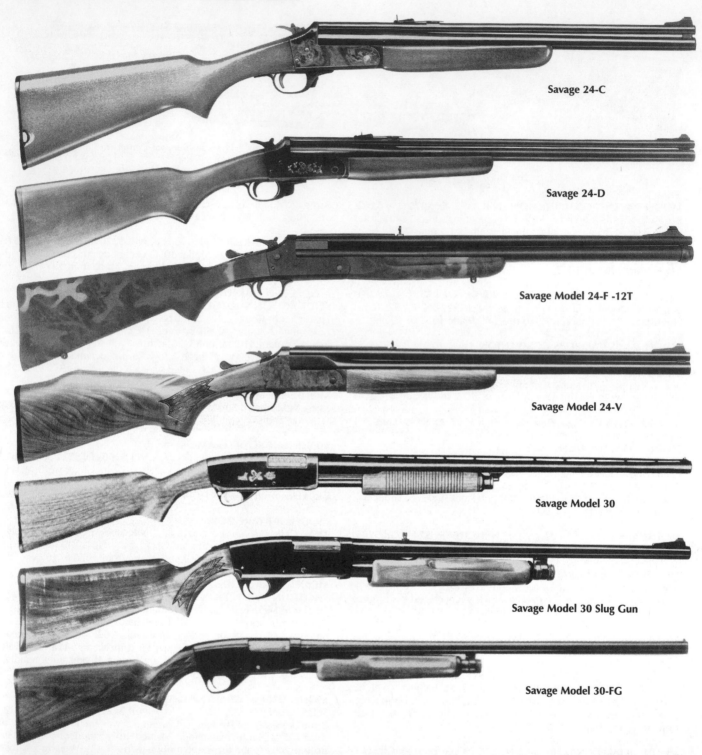

Savage 24-C

Savage 24-D

Savage Model 24-F -12T

Savage Model 24-V

Savage Model 30

Savage Model 30 Slug Gun

Savage Model 30-FG

MODEL 220 SINGLE-BARREL SHOTGUN NiB $414 Ex $309 Gd $197
Hammerless. Takedown. Auto ejector. Gauges: 12,16, 20 .410. Single shot. Bbl. lengths: 12 ga., 28- to 36-inch, 16 ga., 28- to 32-inch; 20 ga., 26- to 32-inch; .410 bore, 26-and 28-inch. F choke. Weight: about 6 lbs. Plain pistol-grip stock and wide forearm. Made 1938 to 1965.

MODEL 220AC . . . . NiB $399 Ex $215 Gd $160
Same as Model 220 except has Savage adj. choke.

MODEL 220L . . . . NiB $399 Ex $215 Gd $160
Same general specifications as Model 220 except has side lever opening instead of top lever. Made from 1965 to 1972.

MODEL 220P . . . . NiB $399 Ex $215 Gd $160
Same as Model 220 except has PolyChoke bbl., made in 12 ga. with 30-inch bbl., 16 and 20 ga. with 28-inch bbl., no .410 bore; recoil pad.

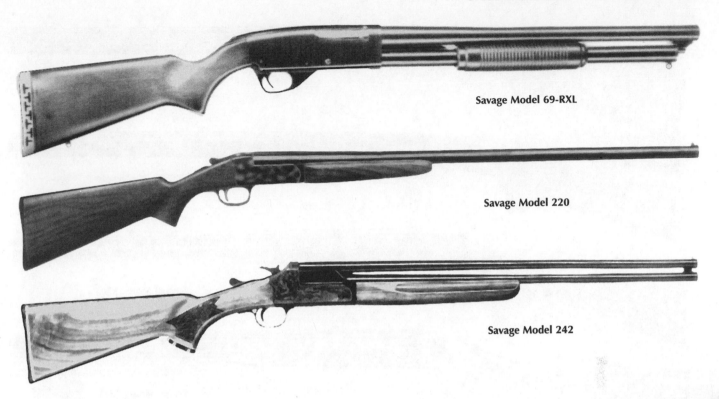

Savage Model 69-RXL

Savage Model 220

Savage Model 242

MODEL 242 O/U SHOTGUN . . . . . NiB $359 Ex $300 Gd $236
Similar to Model 24D except both bbls. .410 bore, F choke. Weight: About 7 lbs. Made from 1977 to 1980.

MODEL 312 FIELD GRADE O/U . . . NiB $590 Ex $471 Gd $335
Gauge: 12; 2.75- or 3-inch chambers. 26- or 28-inch bbls. w/vent rib; F/M/IC chokes. 43 or 45 inches overall. Weight: 7 lbs. Internal hammers. Top tang safety. American walnut stock with checkered pistol grip and recoil pad. Made from 1990 to 1993.

MODEL 312 SPORTING CLAYS O/U . . . . . NiB $595 Ex $495 Gd $359
Same as Model 312 Field Grade except furnished with number 1 and number 2 Skeet tubes and 28-inch bbls. only. Made 1990 to 1993.

MODEL 312 TRAP O/U . . . . NiB $615 Ex $537 Gd $380
Same as Model 312 Field Grade except with 30-inch bbls. only, Monte Carlo buttstock, weight: 7.5 lbs. Made from 1990 to 1993.

MODEL 330 O/U SHOTGUN . . . . . NiB $495 Ex $405 Gd $359
Boxlock. Plain extractors. Selective single trigger. Gauges: 12, 20. 2.75-inch chambers in 12 ga., 3-inch in 20 gauge. Bbls.: 26-inch IC/M; 28-inch M/F; 30-inch M/F choke (12 ga. only). Weight: 6.25 to 7.25 lbs., depending on gauge. Checkered pistol-grip stock and forearm. Made from 1969 to 1978.

MODEL 333 O/U SHOTGUN
Boxlock. Auto ejectors. Selective single trigger. Gauges: 12, 20. 2.75-inch chambers in 12 ga., 3-inch in 20 ga. Bbls.: vent rib; 26-inch SK choke, IC/M; 28-inch M/F; 30-inch M/F choke (12 ga. only). Weight: Average 6.25 to 7.25 lbs. Checkered pistol-grip stock and forearm. Made from 1973 to 1979.
Model 333 12 ga. . . . . NiB $495 Ex $371 Gd $295
Model 333 20 ga. . . . . Add 30%

MODEL 333T TRAP GUN . . . . NiB $550 Ex $432 Gd $365
Similar to Model 330 except only in 12 ga. with 30-inch vent-rib bbls., IM/F choke; Monte Carlo stock w/recoil pad. Weight: 7.75 lbs. Made from 1972 to 1979.

MODEL 420 O/U SHOTGUN
Boxlock. Hammerless. Takedown. Automatic safety. Double triggers or non-selective single trigger. Gauges: 12, 16, 20. Bbls.: Plain, 26-to 30-inch (the latter in 12 ga. only); choked M/F, C/IC. Weight with 28-inch bbls.: 12 ga., 7.75 lbs.; 16 ga., 7.5 lbs.; 20 ga., 6.75 lbs. Plain pistol-grip stock and forearm. Made from 1938 to 1942.
With double triggers . . . . NiB $482 Ex $387 Gd $278
With single trigger . . . . NiB $552 Ex $435 Gd $310

MODEL 430
Same as Model 420 except has matted top bbl., checkered stock of select walnut with recoil pad, checkered forearm. Made from 1938 to 1942.
With double triggers . . . . NiB $543 Ex $430 Gd $310
With single trigger . . . . NiB $582 Ex $473 Gd $337

MODEL 440 O/U SHOTGUN . . . . . NiB $509 Ex $456 Gd $357
Boxlock. Plain extractors. Selective single trigger. Gauges: 12, 20. 2.75-inch chambers in 12 ga., 3-inch in 20 ga. Bbls.: Vent rib; 26-inch SK choke, IC/M; 28-inch M/F; 30-inch M/F choke (12 ga. only). Weight: Average 6 to 6.5 lbs. depending on ga. Made from 1968 to 1972.

MODEL 440T TRAP GUN . . . . NiB $495 Ex $401 Gd $335
Similar to Model 440 except only in 12 ga. with 30-inch bbls., extra-wide vent rib, IM/F choke. Trap-style Monte Carlo stock and semibeavertail forearm of select walnut, recoil pad. Weight: 7.5 lbs. Made from 1969 to 1972.

MODEL 444 DELUXE
O/U SHOTGUN . . . . NiB $560 Ex $403 Gd $337
Similar to Model 440 except has auto ejectors, select walnut stock and semi-beavertail forearm. Made from 1969 to 1972.

SHOTGUNS

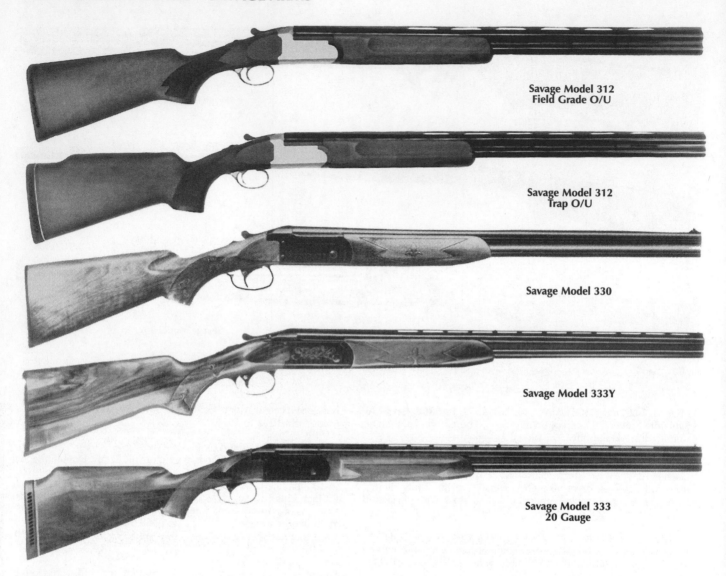

Savage Model 312
Field Grade O/U

Savage Model 312
Trap O/U

Savage Model 330

Savage Model 333Y

Savage Model 333
20 Gauge

MODEL 550
HAMMERLESS DOUBLE . . . . NiB $277 Ex $243 Gd $185
Boxlock. Auto ejectors. Non-selective single trigger. Gauges: 12, 20. 2.75-inch chamber in 12 ga., 3-inch in 20 ga. Bbls.: Vent rib; 26-inch IC/M; 28-inch M/F; 30-inch M/F choke (12 ga. only). Weight: 7 to 8 lbs. Checkered pistol-grip stock and semi-beavertail forearm. Made 1971 to 1973.

MODEL 720 STANDARD GRADE
5 SHOT AUTOLOADING
SHOTGUN . . . . NiB $229 Ex $212 Gd $186
Browning type. Takedown. 12 and 16 ga. Four round tubular magazine. Bbl.: plain; 26- to 32-inch (the latter in 12 ga. only); choked IC, M, F. Weight: About 8.25 lbs., 12 ga. with 30-inch bbl.; 16 ga., about .5 lb. lighter. Checkered pistol-grip stock and forearm. Made from 1930 to 1949.

MODEL 726 UPLAND SPORTER AUTO
SHOTGUN . . . . NiB $275 Ex $208 Gd $187
Same as Model 720 except has 2-round magazine capacity. Made from 1931 to 1949.

MODEL 740C
SKEET GUN . . . . NiB $308 Ex $239 Gd $171
Same as Model 726 except has special skeet stock and full beavertail forearm, equipped with Cutts Compensator. Bbl. length overall with spreader tube is about 24.5 inches. Made from 1936 to 1949.

MODEL 745 LIGHT-WEIGHT
AUTOLOADER . . . . NiB $275 Ex $225 Gd $186
Three- or five-round models. Same general specifications as Model 720 except has lightweight alloy receiver, 12 ga.only, 28-inch plain bbl. Weight: About 6.75 lbs. Made from 1940 to 1949.

MODEL 750
AUTO SHOTGUN . . . . NiB $275 Ex $202 Gd $191
Browning-type autoloader. Takedown. 12 ga. Four round tubular magazine. Bbls.: 28-inch F or M choke; 26-inch IC. Weight: About 7.25 lbs. Checkered walnut pistol-grip stock and grooved forearm. Made from 1960 to 1967.

MODEL 750-AC . . . . NiB $283 Ex $230 Gd $189
Same as Model 750 except has 26-inch bbl. with adj. choke. Made from 1964 to 1967.

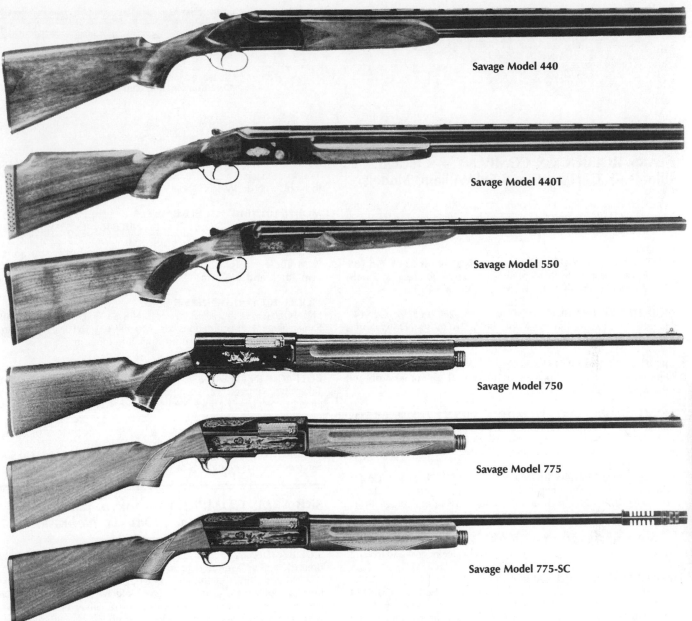

Savage Model 440

Savage Model 440T

Savage Model 550

Savage Model 750

Savage Model 775

Savage Model 775-SC

MODEL 750-SC . . . . **NiB $295 Ex $208 Gd $185**
Same as Model 750 except has 26-inch bbl. with Savage Super Choke. Made from 1962 to 1963.

**MODEL 755 STANDARD
GRADE AUTOLOADER.** . . . . **NiB $275 Ex $206 Gd $187**
Streamlined receiver. Takedown.12 and 16 ga. Four round tubular magazine (a three-round model with magazine capacity of two rounds was also produced until 1951). Bbl.: Plain, 30-inch F choke (12 ga. only), 28-inch F or M, 26-inch IC. Weight: About 8.25 lbs., 12 ga. Checkered pistol-grip stock and forearm. Made from 1949 to 1958.

MODEL 755-SC . . . . **NiB $275 Ex $203 Gd $184**
Same as Model 755 except has 26-inch bbl. w/recoil-reducing, adj. Savage Super Choke.

MODEL 775 LIGHTWEIGHT. . . . . . . **NiB $275 Ex $208 Gd $188**
Same general specifications as Model 755 except has lightweight alloy receiver, weight: About 6.73 lbs. Made from 1950 to 1965.

MODEL 775-SC . . . . **NiB $295 Ex $208 Gd $195**
Same as Model 775 except has 26-inch bbl. with Savage Super Choke.

**MODEL 2400 O/U
COMBINATION** . . . . **NiB $695 Ex $434 Gd $377**
Boxlock action similar to that of Model 330. Plain extractors. Selective single trigger. 12-ga. (2.75-inch chamber) shotgun bbl., F choke over .308 Win. or .222 Rem. rifle bbl.; 23.5-inch; solid matted rib with blade front sight and folding leaf rear, dovetail for scope mounting. Weight: About 7.5 lbs. Monte Carlo stock w/pistol grip and recoil pad, semibeavertail forearm, checkered. Made 1975 to 1979 by Valmet.

Savage Model 2400
O/U Combination Gun

SEARS, ROEBUCK & COMPANY — Chicago, Illinois. (J. C. Higgins and Ted Williams Models)

Although they do not correspond to specific models below, the names Ted Williams and J. C. Higgins have been used to designate various Sears shotguns at various times.

MODEL 18
BOLT-ACTION REPEATER . . . . **NiB $154 Ex $113 Gd $85**
Takedown. Three round top-loading magazine. Gauge: .410 only. Bbl.: 25-inch w/variable choke. Weight: About 5.75 lbs.

MODEL 20 SLIDE-ACTION REPEATER . . **NiB $260 Ex $197 Gd $142**
Hammerless. Five round magazine. Bbls.: 26- to 30-inch w/various chokes. Weight: 7.25 lbs. Plain pistol-grip stock and slide handle.

MODEL 21 SLIDE-ACTION REPEATER . . . . . **NiB $282 Ex $217 Gd $157**
Same general specifications as the Model 20 except vent rib and adustable choke.

MODEL 30 SLIDE-ACTION REPEATER . . . **NiB $271 Ex $206 Gd $149**
Hammerless. Gauges: 12, 16, 20 and .410. Four round magazine. Bbls.: 26- to 30-inch, various chokes. Weight: 6.5 lbs. Plain pistol-grip stock, grooved slide handle.

MODEL 97 SINGLE-SHOT SHOTGUN . . . . . . **NiB $138 Ex $92 Gd $71**
Takedown. Visible hammer. Automatic ejector. Gauges: 12, 16, 20 and .410. Bbls.: 26- to 36-inch, F choke. Weight: Average 6 lbs. Plain pistol-grip stock and forearm.

MODEL 97-AC SINGLE-SHOT SHOTGUN . . . . **NiB $158 Ex $108 Gd $81**
Same general specifications as Model 97 except fancier stock and forearm.

MODEL 101.7 DOUBLE-BARREL
SHOTGUN . . . . **NiB $272 Ex $199 Gd $144**
Boxlock. Double triggers. Gauges: 12, 16, 20, .410. Bbls.: 26- to 32-inch, choked M and F. Weight: From 6 to 7.5 lbs. Plain stock and forend.

MODEL 101.7C DOUBLE-BARREL
SHOTGUN . . . . **NiB $2877 Ex $201 Gd $120**
Same general specifications as Model 101.7 except checkered stock and forearm.

MODEL 101.25 BOLT-ACTION SHOTGUN . . . **NiB $169 Ex $110 Gd $82**
Takedown. .410 gauge. Five round tubular magazine. 24-inch bbl., F choke. Weight: About 6 lbs. Plain, one-piece pistol-grip stock.

MODEL 101.40 SINGLE-SHOT SHOTGUN . **NiB $143 Ex $95 Gd $72**
Takedown. Visible hammer. Automatic ejector. Gauges: 12, 16, 20 and .410. Bbls.: 26- to 36-inch, F choke. Weight: Average 6 lbs. Plain pistol-grip stock and forearm.

MODEL 101.1120 BOLT-ACTION REPEATER . . . . **NiB $148 Ex $108 Gd $81**
Takedown. .410 ga. 24-inch bbl., F choke. Weight: About 5 lbs. Plain one-piece pistol-grip stock.

MODEL 101.1380
BOLT-ACTION REPEATER . . . . **NiB $161 Ex $118 Gd $88**
Takedown. Gauges: 12, 16, 20. Two round detachable box magazine. 26-inch bbl., F choke. Weight: About 7 lbs. Plain one-piece pistol-grip stock.

MODEL 101.1610 DOUBLE-BARREL
SHOTGUN . . . . **NiB $464 Ex $286 Gd $206**
Boxlock. Double triggers. Plain extractors. Gauges: 12, 16, 20 and .410. Bbls.: 24- to 30-inch. Various chokes, but mostly M and F. Weight: About 7.5 lbs, 12 ga. Checkered pistol-grip stock and forearm.

MODEL 101.1701 DOUBLE-BARREL
SHOTGUN . . . . **NiB $377 Ex $285 Gd $205**
Same general specifications as Model 101.1610 except satin chrome frame and select walnut stock and forearm.

MODEL 101.5350-D
BOLT-ACTION REPEATER . . . . **NiB $167 Ex $104 Gd $78**
Takedown. Gauges: 12, 16, 20. Two round detachable box magazine. 26-inch bbl., F choke. Weight: About 7.25 lbs. Plain one piece pistol-grip stock.

MODEL 101.5410
BOLT-ACTION REPEATER . . . . **NiB $158 Ex $106 Gd $80**
Same general specifications as Model 101.5350-D.

SKB ARMS COMPANY — Tokyo, Japan
Imported by G.U. Inc., Omaha, Nebraska

MODEL 385
SIDE-BY-SIDE. . . . . **NiB $1813 Ex $1459 Gd $1032**
Boxlock action w/double locking lugs. Gauges: 12, 20 and 28 w/2.75- and 3-inch chambers. 26- or 28-inch bbls. w/Inter-Choke tube system. Single selective trigger. Selective automatic ejectors and automatic safety. Weight: 6 lbs., 10 oz. Silver nitride receiver w/engraved scroll and game scene. Solid rib w/flat matte finish and metal front bead sight. Checkered American walnut English or pistol-grip stock. Imported from 1992.

MODELS 300 AND 400
SIDE-BY-SIDE DOUBLES
Similar to Model 200E except higher grade. Models 300 and 400 differ in that the latter has more elaborate engraving and fancier wood.
Model 300 . . . . **NiB $995 Ex $827 Gd $590**
Model 400 . . . . **NiB $1395 Ex $1193 Gd $1006**

MODEL 400 SKEET . . . . **NiB $1395 Ex $1193 Gd $1006**
Similar to Model 200E Skeet except higher grade with more elaborate engraving and full fancy wood.

MODEL 480 ENGLISH . . . . **NiB $1675 Ex $1404 Gd $1250**
Similar to Model 280 English except higher grade with more elaborate engraving and full fancy wood.

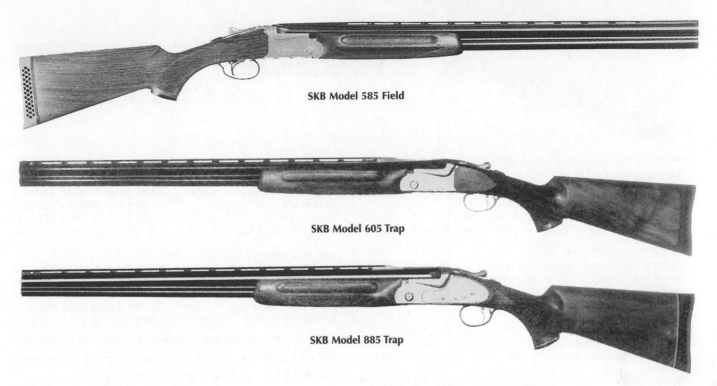

SKB Model 585 Field

SKB Model 605 Trap

SKB Model 885 Trap

MODEL 500 SERIES O/U SHOTGUN
Boxlock. Gauges: 12 and 20 w/2.75-or 3-inch chambers. Bbls.: 26-, 28- or 30-inch with vent rib; fixed chokes. Weight: 7.5 to 8.5 lbs. Single selective trigger. Selective automatic ejectors. Manual safety. Checkered walnut stock. Blue finish with scroll engraving. Imported 1967 to 1980.
500 Field, 12 ga. . . . . **NiB $534 Ex $461 Gd $342**
500 Field, 20 ga. . . . . **Add 20%**
500 Magnum, 12 ga. . . . . **Add 25$**

MODEL 500 SMALL
GAUGE O/U SHOTGUN . . . . **NiB $737 Ex $588 Gd $416**
Similar to Model 500 except gauges 28 and .410; has 28-inch vent-rib bbls., M/F chokes. Weight: About 6.5 lbs.

MODEL 505 O/U SHOTGUN
Blued boxlock action. Gauge: 12, 20, 28 and .410. Bbls.: 26-, 28, 30-inch; IC/M, M/F or inner choke tubes. 45.19 inches overall. Weight: 6.6 to 7.4 lbs. Hand checkered walnut stock. Metal bead front sight, ejectors, single selective trigger and ejectors. Introduced 1988.
Standard Field, Skeet or Trap grade . . . . **NiB $1225 Ex $1079 Gd $9569**
Standard Two-bbl. Field set . . . . . **NiB $1464 Ex $1180 Gd $830**
Skeet grade, three-bbl. set . . . . **NiB $1750 Ex $1662 Gd $1163**
Sporting Clays . . . . **NiB $1100 Ex $838 Gd $593**
Trap grade two-bbl. set . . . . **NiB $875 Ex $716 Gd $594**

MODEL 585 O/U SHOTGUN
Boxlock. Gauges: 12, 20, 28 and .410; 2.75-or 3-inch chambers. Bbls.: 26-, 28-, 30-, 32- or 34-inch with vent rib; fixed chokes or Inter-choke tubes. Weight: 6.5 to 8.5 lbs. Single selective trigger. Selective automatic ejectors. Manual safety. Checkered walnut stock in standard or Monte Carlo style. Silver nitride finish with engraved game scenes. Made from 1992 to 2008.
Field, Skeet, Trap grades . . . . **NiB $1320 Ex $1055 Gd $742**
Field grade, two-bbl. set . . . . . . **NiB $2284 Ex $1843 Gd $1291**
Skeet set (20, 28, .410 ga.) . . . . **NiB $2766 Ex $2223 Gd $1552**
Sporting Clays . . . . **NiB $1575 Ex $1269 Gd $888**
Trap Combo (two-bbl.) . . . . **NiB $2287 Ex $1836 Gd $1284**

MODEL 600 SERIES O/U SHOTGUN
Similar to 500 Series except w/silver nitride receiver. Checkered deluxe walnut stock in both Field and Target Grade configurations . Imported from 1969 to 1980.
600 Field, 12 ga. . . . . **NiB $965 Ex $615 Gd $433**
600 Field, 20 ga. . . . . **NiB $995 Ex $740 Gd $586**
600 Magnum, 12 ga.
3-inch chambers . . . . **NiB $975 Ex $686 Gd $406**
600 Skeet or Trap grade . . . . **NiB $995 Ex $633 Gd $483**
600 Trap Doubles Gun. . . . . **NiB $995 Ex $633 Gd $483**

MODEL 600 SMALL GA. . . . . **NiB $1115 Ex $848 Gd $544**
Same as Model 500 Small Gauge except higher grade with more elaborate engraving and fancier wood.

MODEL 605 SERIES O/U SHOTGUN
Similar to the Model 505 except w/engraved silver nitride receiver and deluxe wood. Introduced 1988.
Field, Skeet, Trap grade . . . . **NiB $1105 Ex $917 Gd $671**
Skeet three-bbl. set . . . . **NiB $2174 Ex $1925 Gd $1413**
Sporting Clays . . . . **NiB $1113 Ex $817 Gd $578**

MODEL 680 ENGLISH O/U SHOTGUN
Similar to 600 Series except w/English style select walnut stock and fine scroll engraving. Imported from 1973 to 1977.
680 English, 12 ga. . . . . **NiB $1325 Ex $1092 Gd $893**
680 English, 20 ga. . . . . **NiB $1610 Ex $1058 Gd $990**

MODEL 685 DELUXE O/U
Similar to the 585 Deluxe except with semi-fancy American walnut stock. Gold trigger and jeweled barrel block. Silvered receiver with fine engraving.
Field, Skeet, Trap grade . . . . **NiB $1365 Ex $1104 Gd $898**
Field grade, two-bbl. set . . . . **NiB $1365 Ex $1104 Gd $898**
Skeet set . . . . **NiB $1365 Ex $1104 Gd $898**
Sporting Clays . . . . **NiB $1365 Ex $1161 Gd $825**
Trap Combo. two bbl. . . . . **NiB $1983 Ex $1692 Gd $1193**

Sile Field Master II

MODEL 800 SKEET/TRAP O/U
Similar to Model 700 Skeet and Trap except higher grade with more elaborate engraving and fancier wood.
Model 800 Skeet . . . . NiB $1200 Ex $1005 Gd $868
Model 800 Trap . . . . NiB $1150 Ex $955 Gd $815

MODEL 880 SKEET/TRAP
Similar to Model 800 Skeet except has sideplates.
Model 880 Skeet . . . . NiB $1533 Ex $1305 Gd $927
Model 880 Trap . . . . NiB $1670 Ex $1375 Gd $1001

MODEL 885 DELUXE O/U
Similar to the 685 Deluxe except with engraved sideplates.
Field, Skeet, Trap grade . . . . NiB $1600 Ex $1388 Gd $1068
Field grade, two-bbl. set . . . . . . NiB $2455 Ex $1999 Gd $1683
Skeet Set . . . . NiB $1650 Ex $1422 Gd $1209
Sporting Clays . . . . NiB $1655 Ex $1381 Gd $968
Trap Combo . . . . NiB $2393 Ex $2160 Gd $1889

The following SKB shotguns were distributed by Ithaca Gun Co. from 1966-76. For specific data, see corresponding listings under Ithaca.

CENTURY SINGLE-BARREL TRAP GUN
The SKB catalog does not differentiate between Century and Century II; however, specifications of current Century are those of Ithaca-SKB Century II.
Century (505) . . . . NiB $875 Ex $752 Gd $595
Century II (605) . . . . NiB $1075 Ex $958 Gd $683

GAS-OPERATED AUTOMATIC SHOTGUNS
Model XL300 with plain barrel . . . . NiB $295 Ex $203 Gd $145
Model XL300 with vent rib . . . . NiB $325 Ex $335 Gd $183
Model XL900 . . . . NiB $366 Ex $269 Gd $152
Model XL900 Trap . . . . NiB $395 Ex $281 Gd $189
Model XL900 Skeet . . . . NiB $400 Ex $260 Gd $194
Model XL900 Slug . . . . NiB $352 Ex $260 Gd $171
Model 1300 Upland, Slug . . . . NiB $450 Ex $339 Gd $221
Model 1900 Field, Trap, Slug . . . . . . NiB $487 Ex $384 Gd $252

SKB OVER/UNDER SHOTGUNS
Model 500 Field . . . . NiB $525 Ex $413 Gd $331
Model 500 Magnum . . . . NiB $550 Ex $441 Gd $359
Model 600 Field . . . . NiB $950 Ex $684 Gd $494
Model 600 Magnum . . . . NiB $975 Ex $707 Gd $510
Model 600 Trap . . . . NiB $995 Ex $647 Gd $470
Model 600 Doubles . . . . NiB $995 Ex $647 Gd $470
Model 600 Skeet—12 or 20 ga. . . . . NiB $995 Ex $647 Gd $470
Model 600 Skeet—28 or .410. . . . . NiB $1424 Ex $1175 Gd $958
Model 600 Skeet Combo. . . . . NiB $2651 Ex $2210 Gd $2085
Model 600 English . . . . NiB $995 Ex $647 Gd $470
Model 700 Trap. . . . . NiB $820 Ex $726 Gd $593
Model 700 Doubles . . . . NiB $795 Ex $538 Gd $433
Model 700 Skeet. . . . . NiB $845 Ex $694 Gd $572
Model 700 Skeet Combo. . . . . NiB $2415 Ex $1963 Gd $1384

SKB RECOIL-OPERATED AUTOMATIC SHOTGUNS
Model 300—with plain barrel . . . . NiB $398 Ex $307 Gd $230
Model 300—with vent rib . . . . NiB $436 Ex $338 Gd $250
Model 900 . . . . NiB $470 Ex $373 Gd $274
Model 900 Slug . . . . NiB $452 Ex $359 Gd $265

SKB SIDE-BY-SIDE DOUBLE-BARREL SHOTGUNS
Model 100 . . . . NiB $695 Ex $565 Gd $335
Model 150 . . . . NiB $695 Ex $565 Gd $335
Model 200E . . . . NiB $1050 Ex $835 Gd $727
Model 200E Skeet . . . . NiB $1050 Ex $835 Gd $727
Model 280 English . . . . NiB $1095 Ex $910 Gd $725

SIG SAUER — (SIG) Schweizerische Industrie-Gesellschaft, Neuhausen, Switzerland

MODEL SA3 O/U SHOTGUN
Monobloc boxlock action. Single selective trigger. Automatic ejectors. Gauges: 12 or 20 w/3- inch chambers. 26-, 28- or 30-inch vent rib bbls. w/choke tubes. Weight: 6.8 to 7.1 lbs. Checkered select walnut stock and forearm. Satin nickel-finished receiver w/game scene and blued bbls. Imported from 1997-98.
Field model . . . . NiB $1175 Ex $1086 Gd $874
Sporting Clays model . . . . NiB $1375 Ex $1212 Gd $1000

MODEL SA5 O/U SHOTGUN
Similar to SA3 Model except w/detachable sideplates. Gauges: 12 or 20 w/3- inch chambers. 26.5-, 28- or 30-inch vent rib bbls. w/choke tubes. Imported from 1997 to 1999.
Field model . . . . NiB $2175 Ex $1973 Gd $1395
Sporting Clays model . . . . NiB $2310 Ex $2200 Gd $1510

SILE SHOTGUNS — Sile Distributors, New York, NY

FIELD MASTER II O/U SHOTGUN. . . . . NiB $647 Ex $520 Gd $372
Gauge: 12, 3-inch chambers. 28-inch bbl., IC, M, IM, F choke tubes. 45.25 inches overall. Weight: 7.25 lbs. Satin-finished walnut, checkered stock and forend. Introduced 1989.

L. C. SMITH SHOTGUNS — Made 1890-1945 by Hunter Arms Company, Fulton, N.Y.; 1946-51 and 1968-73 and 2004 by Marlin Firearms Company, New Haven, Conn.

L. C. SMITH DOUBLE-BARREL SHOTGUNS
Values shown are for L. C. Smith doubles made by Hunter. Those of 1946-51 Marlin manufacture generally bring prices about 1/3 lower. Smaller gauge models, especially in the higher grades, command premium prices: Up to 50 percent more for 20 gauge, up to 400 percent for .410 gauge.

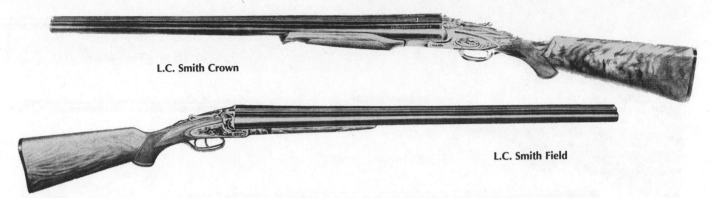

L.C. Smith Crown

L.C. Smith Field

Crown grade, double triggers,
automatic ejectors . . . . NiB $10,000 Ex $8317 Gd $6693
Crown grade, selective single trigger,
automatic ejectors . . . . NiB $10,500 Ex $8815 Gd $7186
Deluxe grade, selective single trigger,
automatic ejectors . . . . . . NiB $78,791 Ex $58,275 Gd $32,507
Eagle grade, double triggers,
automatic ejectors . . . . NiB $7198 Ex $5355 Gd $3032
Eagle grade, selective
single trigger . . . . NiB $7696 Ex $5855 Gd $3330
Field grade, double trigger
plain extractors . . . . NiB $1779 Ex $1584 Gd $978
Field grade, double triggers
auto. ej. . . . . NiB $2280 Ex $2015 Gd $1402
Field grade, non-selective single trigger,
plain extractors . . . . NiB $1653 Ex $1339 Gd $930
Field grade, selective single trigger,
automatic ejectors . . . . NiB $2182 Ex $1815 Gd $1402
Ideal grade, double triggers,
plain extractors . . . . NiB $2500 Ex $1474 Gd $1042
Ideal grade, double triggers,
auto. ej. . . . . NiB $3000 Ex $1972 Gd $1546
Ideal grade, selective single trigger,
automatic ejectors . . . . NiB $2866 Ex $2288 Gd $1614
Monogram grade, selective single trigger,
automatic ejectors . . . . . . NiB $15,596 Ex $11,501 Gd $9782
Olympic grade, selective single trigger,
automatic ejectors . . . . NiB $6000 Ex $4105 Gd $2485
Premier grade, selective single trigger
automatic ejectors . . . . . NiB $39,878 Ex $30,337 Gd $22,805
Skeet Special, non-selective single trigger,
automatic ejectors . . . . NiB $3805 Ex $2735 Gd $1938
Skeet Special, selective single trigger,
auto ejectors . . . . NiB $3815 Ex $2858 Gd $2409
.410 ga. . . . . NiB $12,699 Ex $10,955 Gd $7494
Specialty grade, double triggers,
auto ejectors . . . . NiB $3838 Ex $3455 Gd $2954
Specialty grade, selective single trigger,
automatic ejectors . . . . NiB $3784 Ex $3076 Gd $2459
Trap grade, sel. single trigger,
auto ej. . . . . NiB $3498 Ex $3008 Gd $2461

L C. SMITH HAMMERLESS DOUBLE-BARREL SHOTGUNS

Sidelock. Auto ejectors standard on higher grades, extra on Field and Ideal Grades. Double triggers or Hunter single trigger (non-selective or selective). Gauges: 12, 16, 20, .410. Bbls.: 26- to 32-inch, any standard boring. Weight: 6.5 to 8.25 lbs., 12 ga. Checkered stock and forend; choice of straight, half or full pistol grip, beavertail or standard-type forend. Grades differ only in quality of workmanship, wood, checkering, engraving, etc. Same general specifications apply to all. Manufacture of these L. C. Smith guns was discontinued in 1951. Production of Field Grade 12 ga. was resumed 1968-73. Note: L. C. Smith Shotguns manufactured by the Hunter Arms Co. 1890-13 were designated by numerals to indicate grade with the exception of Pigeon and Monogram.

00 grade . . . . NiB $1452 Ex $1208 Gd $920
0 grade . . . . NiB $1600 Ex $1480 Gd $1106
1 grade . . . . NiB $2000 Ex $1774 Gd $1281
2 grade . . . . NiB $2300 Ex $1944 Gd $1365
3 grade . . . . NiB $3699 Ex $2735 Gd $1911
Pigeon . . . . NiB $5010 Ex $3409 Gd $2375
4 grade . . . . NiB $6000 Ex $5028 Gd $4889
5 grade . . . . NiB $9500 Ex $7697 Gd $5344
Monogram . . . . NiB $12,528 Ex $10,314 Gd $8542
A1 . . . . NiB $6084 Ex $4110 Gd $2899
A2. . . . . NiB $13,821 Ex $10,523 Gd $9581
A3 . . . . NiB $40,000 Ex $35,875 Gd $30,283

L. C. SMITH HAMMERLESS DOUBLE
MODEL 1968 FIELD GRADE . . . . . NiB $1010 Ex $772 Gd $586
Re-creation of the original L. C. Smith double. Sidelock. Plain extractors. Double triggers. 12 ga. 28-inch vent-rib bbls., M/F choke. Weight: About 6.75 lbs. Checkered pistol-grip stock and forearm. Made from 1968 to 1973.

L. C. SMITH HAMMERLESS DOUBLE
MODEL 1968 DELUXE . . . . NiB $1515 Ex $980 Gd $712
Same as 1968 Field Grade except has Simmons floating vent rib, beavertail forearm. Made from 1971 to 1973.

L. C. SMITH SINGLE-SHOT TRAP GUNS

Boxlock. Hammerless. Auto ejector.12 gauge only. Bbl. lengths: 32- or 34-inch. Vent rib. Weight: 8 to 8.25 lbs. Checkered pistol-grip stock and forend, recoil pad. Grades vary in quality of workmanship, wood, engraving, etc.; general specifications are the same. Disc. 1951. Note: Values shown are for L. C. Smith single-barrel trap guns made by Hunter. Those of Marlin manufacture generally bring prices about one-third lower.

Olympic grade. . . . . NiB $2760 Ex $2475 Gd $1907
Specialty grade . . . . NiB $3300 Ex $2976 Gd $2390
Crown grade . . . . NiB $4212 Ex $3380 Gd $2359
Monogram grade . . . . NiB $7800 Ex $5317 Gd $4497
Premier grade . . . . Very rare (fewer than three manufactured)
Deluxe grade . . . . Very rare (fewer than four manufacturered)

SMITH & WESSON SHOTGUNS —
Springfield, Massachusetts

Sold several times, currently Saf-T-Hammer.

SHOTGUNS

L.C. Smith 1968 Field Grade

L.C. Smith 1968 Deluxe

L.C. Smith Single-Shot Trap Gun

Smith & Wesson Model 1000 Magnum

Smith & Wesson Model 3000 Slide Action

MODEL 916 SLIDE-ACTION REPEATER
Hammerless. Solid frame. Gauges: 12, 16, 20. Three inch chamber in 12 and 20 ga. Five round tubular magazine. Bbls.: plain or vent rib; 20-inch C (12 ga., plain only); 26-inch IC- 28-inch M or F; 30-inch F choke (12 ga. only). Weight: With 28-inch plain bbl., 7.25 lbs. Plain pistol-grip stock, fluted slide handle. Made 1972 to 1981.
With plain bbl. . . . . **NiB $179 Ex $105 Gd $81**
With ventilated rib bbl. . . . . **NiB $200 Ex $173 Gd $146**

MODEL 916T
Same as Model 916 except takedown, 12 ga. only. Not available with 20-inch bbl. Made from 1976 to 1981.
With plain bbl. . . . . **NiB $195 Ex $141 Gd $99**
With ventilated rib bbl. . . . . **NiB $225 Ex $188 Gd $141**

MODEL 1000 AUTOLOADER . . . . . **NiB $348 Ex $283 Gd $208**
Gas-operated. Takedown. Gauges: 12, 20. 2.75-inch chamber in 12 ga., 3-inch in 20 ga. Four round magazine. Bbls.: Vent rib, 26-inch SK choke, IC; 28-inch M or F; 30-inch F choke (12 ga. only). Weight: With 28-inch bbl., 6.5 lbs. in 20 ga.,7.5 lbs. in 12 ga. Checkered pistol-grip stock and forearm. Made from 1972. Disc.

MODEL 3000
SLIDE ACTION . . . . **NiB $350 Ex $251 Gd $149**
Hammerless. 20-ga. Bbls.: 26-inch IC; 28-inch M or F. Chambered for 3-inch magnum and 2.75-inch loads. American walnut stock and forearm. Checkered pistol grip and forearm. Introduced 1982.

MODEL 1000 . . . . **NiB $350 Ex $287 Gd $206**
Same as Model 3000 but an earlier version.

MODEL 1000 MAGNUM . . . . **NiB $500 Ex $372 Gd $268**
Same as standard Model 1000 except chambered for 12 ga. magnum, 3-inch shells; 30-inch bbl. only, M or F choke; stock with recoil pad. Weight: About 8 lbs. Introduced in 1977.

SPRINGFIELD ARMS — Built by Savage Arms Company, Utica, New York

SPRINGFIELD DOUBLE-BARREL
HAMMER SHOTGUN . . . . **NiB $489 Ex $376 Gd $270**
Gauges: 12 and 16. Bbls.: 28 to 32 inches. In 12 ga., 32-inch model, both bbls. have F choke. All other gauges and barrel lengths are left barrel, Full; right barrel, Mod. Weight: 7.25 to 8.25 lbs., depending on gauge and barrel length. Black walnut checkered buttstock and forend. Disc. 1934.

SQUIRES BINGHAM CO., INC. — Makati, Rizal, Philippines

MODEL 30
PUMP SHOTGUN . . . . **NiB $265 Ex $189 Gd $137**
Hammerless. 12 ga. Five round magazine. Bbl.: 20-inch Cyl.; 28-inch M; 30-inch F choke. Weight: About 7 lbs. Pulong Dalaga stock and slide handle. Currently manufactured.

Squires Bingham Model 30 Pump Shotgun

J. STEVENS ARMS COMPANY — Chicopee Falls, Massachusetts, Division of Savage Arms Corporation

NO. 20 "FAVORITE" SHOTGUN . . NiB $260 Ex $185 Gd $120
Calibers: .22 and .32 shot. Smoothbore bbl. Blade front sight; no rear. Made from 1893 to 1939.

**NO. 39 NEW MODEL
POCKET SHOTGUN** . . . . NiB $731 Ex $571 Gd $407
Gauge: .410. Calibers: .38-40 shot, .44-40 shot. Bbls.: 10, 12, 15 or 18 inches, half-octagonal smoothbore. Shotgun sights. Made 1895 to 1906.

NO. 22-.410 O/U COMBINATION GUN
.22 caliber rifle barrel over .410 ga. shotgun barrel. Visible hammer. Takedown. Single trigger. 24-inch bbls., shotgun bbl. F choke. Weight: About 6 lbs. Open rear sight and ramp front sight of sporting rifle type. Plain pistol-grip stock and forearm; originally supplied with walnut stock and forearm. "Tenite" (plastic) was used in later production. Made 1939 to 1950. Note: This gun is now manufactured as the Savage Model 24.
With wood stock and forearm . . . . NiB $429 Ex $315 Gd $255
With Tenite stock and forearm . . . . NiB $450 Ex $340 Gd $280

**MODEL 51 BOLT-ACTION
SHOTGUN** . . . . NiB $186 Ex $115 Gd $87
Single shot. Takedown. .410 ga. 24-inch bbl., F choke. Weight: About 4.75 lbs. Plain one-piece pistol-grip stock. checkered on later models. Made from 1962 to 1971.

**MODEL 58 BOLT-ACTION
REPEATER** . . . . NiB $191 Ex $135 Gd $100
Takedown. Gauges: 12, 16, 20. Two round detachable box magazine. 26-inch bbl., F choke. Weight: About 7.25 lbs. Plain one piece pistol-grip stock on early models w/takedown screw on bottom of forend. Made 1933-81. Note: Later production models have 3-inch chamber in 20 ga., checkered stock with recoil pad.

**MODEL 58-.410 BOLT-ACTION
REPEATER** . . . . NiB $154 Ex $129 Gd $97
Takedown. .410 ga. Three round detachable box magazine. 24-inch bbl., F choke. Weight: About 5.5 lbs. Plain one piece pistol-grip stock, checkered on later production. Made from 1937 to 1981.

**MODEL 59 BOLT-ACTION
REPEATER** . . . . NiB $200 Ex $166 Gd $122
Takedown. .410 ga. Five round tubular magazine. 24-inch bbl., F choke. Weight: About 6 lbs. Plain, one piece pistol-grip stock, checkered on later production. Made from 1934 to 1973.

MODEL 67 PUMP SHOTGUN
Hammerless, side-ejection solid-steel receiver. Gauges: 12, 20 and .410, 2.75- or 3-inch shells. Bbls.: 21-, 26-, 28- 30-inch with fixed chokes or interchangeable choke tubes, plain or vent rib. Weight: 6.25 to 7.5 lbs. Optional rifle sights. Walnut-finished hardwood stock with corncob-style forend.

Standard model, plain bbl. . . . . NiB $200 Ex $176 Gd $109
Standard model, vent rib . . . . NiB $210 Ex $186 Gd $120
Standard model, w/choke tubes . . . NiB $230 Ex $206 Gd $134
Slug model w/rifle sights . . . . NiB $200 Ex $176 Gd $142
Lobo model, matte finish . . . . NiB $200 Ex $176 Gd $142
Youth model, 20 ga. . . . . NiB $205 Ex $181 Gd $119
Camo model. w/choke tubes . . . . . NiB $245 Ex $167 Gd $104

MODEL 67 WATERFOWL SHOTGUN . . . . NiB $265 Ex $166 Gd $110
Hammerless. Gauge: 12. Three round tubular magazine. Walnut-finished hardwood stock. Weight: About 7.5 lbs. Made 1972 to 1989.

MODEL 77 SLIDE-ACTION REPEATER . . . . . NiB $185 Ex $108 Gd $87
Solid frame. Gauges: 12, 16, 20. Five round tubular magazine. Bbls.: 26-inch IC, 28-inch M or F choke. Weight: About 7.5 lbs. Plain pistol-grip stock with recoil pad, grooved slide handle. Made from 1954 to 1971.

MODEL 77-AC . . . . NiB $179 Ex $108 Gd $87
Same as Model 77 except has Savage Super Choke.

MODEL 79-VR SUPER VALUE . . . . . NiB $279 Ex $216 Gd $158
Hammerless, side ejection. Bbl.: Chambered for 2.75-inch and 3-inch mag. shells. 12, 20, and .410 ga. vent rib. Walnut finished hardwood stock with checkering on grip. Weight: 6.75-7 lbs. Made 1979 to 1990.

MODEL 94 SINGLE-SHOT SHOTGUN . . . NiB $110 Ex $72 Gd $62
Takedown. Visible hammer. Auto ejector. Gauges: 12, 16, 20, 28, .410. Bbls.: 26-, 28-, 30-, 32-, 36-inch, F choke. Weight: About 6 lbs. depending on gauge and barrel. Plain pistol-grip stock and forearm. Made from 1939 to 1961.

MODEL 94C . . . . NiB $110 Ex $72 Gd $47
Same as Model 94 except has checkered stock, fluted forearm on late production. Made from 1965 to 1990.

MODEL 94Y YOUTH GUN . . . . NiB $110 Ex $75 Gd $55
Same as Model 94 except made in 20 and .410 ga. only; has 26-inch F choke bbl., 12.5-inch buttstock with recoil pad; checkered pistol grip and fluted forend on late production. Made from 1959 to 1990.

MODEL 95 SINGLE-SHOT SHOTGUN . . NiB $165 Ex $122 Gd $92
Solid frame. Visible hammer. Plain extractor. 12 ga. Three-inch chamber. Bbls.: 28-inch M- 30-inch F choke. Weight: About 7.25 lbs. Plain pistol-grip stock, grooved forearm. Made 1965 to 1969.

**MODEL 107 SINGLE-SHOT
HAMMER SHOTGUN** . . . . NiB $158 Ex $117 Gd $89
Takedown. Auto ejector. Gauges: 12, 16, 20, .410. Bbl. lengths: 28- and 30-inch (12 and 16 ga.), 28-inch (20 ga.), 26-inch (.410); F choke only. Weight: About 6 lbs., 12 bore ga. Plain pistol-grip stock and forearm. Made from about 1937 to 1953.

**MODEL 124
BOLT-ACTION REPEATER** . . . . NiB $225 Ex $166 Gd $122
Hammerless. Solid frame. 12 ga. only. Two round tubular magazine. 28-inch bbl.; IC, M or F choke. Weight: About 7 lbs. Tenite stock and forearm. Made from 1947 to 1952.

SHOTGUNS

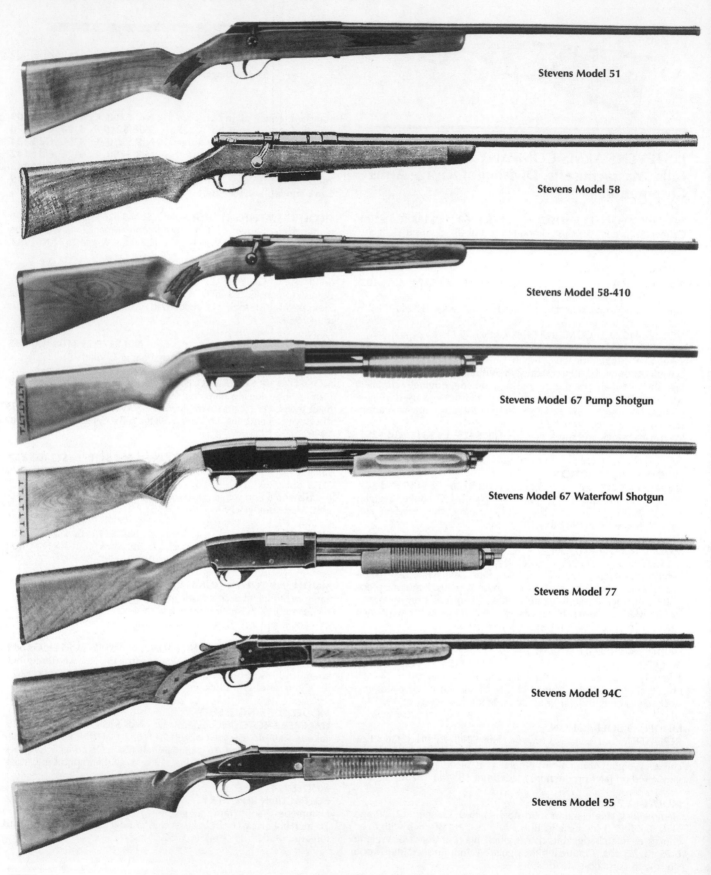

Stevens Model 51

Stevens Model 58

Stevens Model 58-410

Stevens Model 67 Pump Shotgun

Stevens Model 67 Waterfowl Shotgun

Stevens Model 77

Stevens Model 94C

Stevens Model 95

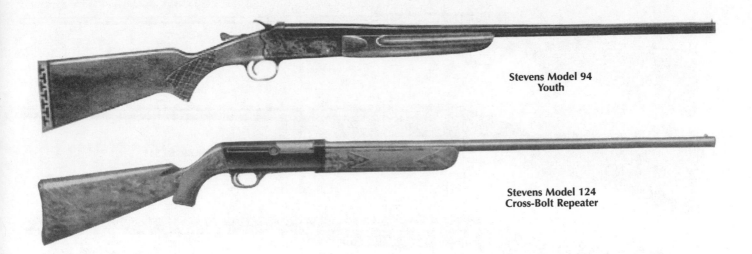

Stevens Model 94 Youth

Stevens Model 124 Cross-Bolt Repeater

MODEL 240 O/U SHOTGUN . . . . . **NiB $353 Ex $290 Gd $209**
Visible hammer. Takedown. Double triggers. .410 ga. 26-inch bbls.,
F choke. Weight: 6 lbs. Tenite (plastic) pistol-grip stock and forearm.
Made from 1940 to 1949.

**MODEL 258 BOLT-ACTION
REPEATER** . . . . **NiB $210 Ex $125 Gd $94**
Takedown. 20-gauge. Two round detachable box magazine. 26-inch
barrel, Full choke. Weight: About 6.25 lbs. Plain, one piece pistol-
grip stock. Made from 1937 to 1965.

**MODEL 311 SPRINGFIELD
HAMMERLESS DOUBLE**
Same general specifications as Stevens Model 530 except earlier
production has plain stock and forearm; checkered on current guns.
Originally produced as a "Springfield" gun, this model became a
part of the Stevens line in 1948 when the Springfield brand name
was discontinued. Made from 1931 to 1989.
Pre-WWII . . . . **NiB $550 Ex $300 Gd $200**
Post-WWII . . . . **NiB $275 Ex $147 Gd $99**

**MODEL 311-R
HAMMERLESS DOUBLE** . . . . **NiB $245 Ex $188 Gd $138**
Same general specifications as Stevens Model 311 except compact
design for law enforcement use. Bbls.: 18.25-inch 12 gauge with
solid rib, chambered for 2.75 and 3-inch Mag. shells. Double triggers and auto top tang safety. Walnut finished hardwood stock with
recoil pad and semi-beavertail forend. Weight: About 6.75 lbs.
Made from 1982 to 1989.

**MODEL 530
HAMMERLESS DOUBLE** . . . . **NiB $275 Ex $208 Gd $172**
Boxlock. Double triggers. Gauges: 12, 16, 20, .410. Bbl. lengths:
26- to 32-inch; choked M/F, C/M, F/F. Weight: 6 to 7.5 pounds
depending on gauge and barrel length. Checkered pistol-grip
stock and forearm; some early models with recoil pad. Made
from 1936 to 1954.

MODEL 530M . . . . **NiB $275 Ex $208 Gd $172**
Same as Model 530 except has Tenite (plastic) stock and forearm.
Disc. about 1947.

MODEL 530ST DOUBLE GUN . . . . . **NiB $275 Ex $208 Gd $172**
Same as Model 530 except has non-selective single trigger. Disc.

**MODEL 620 HAMMERLESS
SLIDE-ACTION
REPEATING SHOTGUN** . . . . **NiB $295 Ex $190 Gd $139**
Takedown. Gauges: 12, 16, 20. Five round tubular magazine. Bbl.
lengths: 26-, 28-, 30-, 32-inch; choked F, M IC, C. Weight: About
7.75 lbs., 12 ga.; 7.25 lbs., 16 ga.- 6 lbs., 20 ga. Checkered pistol-
grip stock and slide handle. Made from 1927 to 1953.

MODEL 620-C . . . . **NiB $285 Ex $190 Gd $139**
Same specifications as Model 620 except equipped with Cutts
Compensator and two choke tubes.

MODEL 620-P . . . . **NiB $195 Ex $190 Gd $139**
Same specifications as Model 620 equipped with Aero-Dyne
PolyChoke and 27-inch bbl.

MODEL 620-PV . . . . **NiB $195 Ex $190 Gd $139**
Same specifications as Model 620 except equipped with ventilated
PolyChoke and 27-inch bbl.

MODEL 621 . . . . **NiB $285 Ex $190 Gd $139**
Same as Model 620 except has raised solid matted-rib barrel.
Disc.

**MODEL 820 HAMMERLESS
REPEATING SHOTGUN** . . . . **NiB $297 Ex $237 Gd $174**
Solid frame. 12 gauge only. Five round tubular magazine. 28-inch
barrel; IC, M or F choke. Weight: About 7.5 lbs. Plain pistol-grip
stock, grooved slide handle. Early models furnished w/Tenite buttstock and forend. Made from 1949 to 1954.

**MODEL
820-SC.** . . . . **NiB $352 Ex $257 Gd $187**
Same as Model 820 except has Savage Super Choke.

**MODEL 940 SINGLE-
SHOT SHOTGUN** . . . . **NiB $210 Ex $119 Gd $91**
Same general specifications as Model 94 except has side lever
opening instead of top lever. Made from 1961 to 1970.

**MODEL 940Y
YOUTH GUN** . . . . **NiB $199 Ex $137 Gd $104**
Same general specifications as Model 94Y except has side lever
opening instead of top lever. Made from 1961 to 1970.

SHOTGUNS

Stevens Model 258

Stevens Model 311

Stevens Model 530

Stevens Model 620

Stevens Model 620-P

Stevens Model 820

MODEL 9478 . . . . **NiB $95 Ex $63 Gd $45**
Takedown. Visible hammer. Automatic ejector. Gauges: 12, 20, .410. Bbls.: 26-, 28-, 30-, 36-inch; Full choke. Weight: Average 6 pounds depending on gauge and barrel. Plain pistol-grip stock and forearm. Made from 1978 to 1985.

MODEL 5151 SPRINGFIELD . . . . . . **NiB $453 Ex $354 Gd $253**
Same specifications as the Stevens Model 311 except with checkered grip and forend; equipped with recoil pad and two ivory sights.

STOEGER SHOTGUNS

See IGA and Tikka Shotguns

TAR-HUNT CUSTOM RIFLES, INC. — Bloomsburg, PA

MODEL RSG-12 MATCHLESS
BOLT-ACTION SLUG GUN . . . . **NiB $2177 Ex $1817 Gd $1470**
Similar to Professional model except has McMillan Fibergrain stock and deluxe blue finish. Made from 1995 to 2004.

MODEL RSG-12 PEERLESS
BOLT-ACTION SLUG GUN . . . . **NiB $2775 Ex $2480 Gd $2112**
Similar to Professional model except has McMillan Fibergrain stock and deluxe NP-3 (Nickel/Teflon) metal finish. Made from 1995 to 2004.

MODEL RSG-12 PROFESSIONAL
BOLT-ACTION SLUG GUN
Bolt action 12 ga. w/2.75-inch chamber, 2-round detachable magazine, 21.5-inch fully rifled bbl. w/ or w/o muzzle brake. Receiver drilled and tapped for scope mounts w/no sights. Weight: 7.75 lbs. 41.5 inches overall. Checkered black McMillan fiberglass stock w/swivel studs and Pachmayr Deacelerator pad. Made from 1991 to 2004.

RSG-12 model
W/O muzzle brake (disc. 1993) . . . NiB $2575 Ex $2250 Gd $1889
RSG-12 model
W/muzzle brake . . . . NiB $2575 Ex $2250 Gd $1889

MODEL RSG-20 MOUNTAINEER
BOLT ACTION SLUG GUN. . . . NiB $2150 Ex $1837 Gd $1312
Similar to Professional model except 20 ga. w/2.75 inch chamber. Black McMillan synthetic stock w/blind magazine. Weight: 6.5 lbs. Made from 1997 to 2004.

TECNI-MEC SHOTGUNS — Italy, Imported by RAHN Gun Work, Inc., Hastings, MI

MODEL SPL 640
FOLDING SHOTGUN
Gauges: 12, 16, 20, 24, 28, 32 and .410 bore. 26-inch bbl. Chokes: IC/IM. Weight: 6.5 lbs. Checkered walnut pistol-grip stock and forend. Engraved receiver. Available with single or double triggers. Imported from 1988 to 1994.
640 w/single trigger . . . . NiB $551 Ex $421 Gd $305
640 w/double trigger. . . . . NiB $579 Ex $467 Gd $337

THOMPSON/CENTER ARMS — Rochester, NH and Springfield, MA.

Purchased by Smith & Wesson in 2006.

CONTENDER
.410 GA. CARBINE . . . . NiB $445 Ex $343 Gd $251
Gauge: .410 smoothbore. 21-inch vent rib bbl. 34.75 inches overall. Weight: About 5.25 lbs. Bead front sight. Rynite stock and forend. Made 1991 to date.

ENCORE
20 GA. SHOTGUN
Gauge: 20 smoothbore w/rifled slug bbl. or 26-inch vent-rib bbl. w/three internal screw choke tubes, 38 to 40.5 inches overall. Weight: About 5.25 to 6 lbs. Bead or fiber optic sights. Walnut stock and forend. Made from 1998 to date.
Encore 20 ga.
W/vent rib. . . . . NiB $415 Ex $361 Gd $245
Encore 20 ga.
w/rifled slug bbl.. . . . . NiB $440 Ex $369 Gd $293
W/extra
bbl., add $260

HUNTER SHOTGUN MODEL . . . . . NiB $520 Ex $431 Gd $310
Single shot. Gauge: 10 or 12, 3.5-inch chamber, 25-inch field bbl. with F choke. Weight: 8 lbs. Bead front sight. American black walnut stock with recoil pad. Made from 1987 to 1992.

HUNTER SLUG MODEL . . . . NiB $520 Ex $431 Gd $310
Gauge: 10 (3.5-inch chamber) or 12 (3-inch chamber). Same general specifications as Model '87 Hunter Shotgun except with 22-inch slug (rifled) bbl. and rifle sights. Made from 1987 to 1992.

TIKKA SHOTGUNS — Manufactured by Sako, Ltd. in Armi Marocchi, Italy

M 07 SHOTGUN/
RIFLE COMBINATION . . . . NiB $1145 Ex $940 Gd $678
Gauge/caliber: 12/.222 Rem. Shotgun bbl.: About 25 inches; rifled bbl.: About 22.75 inches. 40.66 inches overall. Weight: About 7 lbs. Dovetailed for telescopic sight mounts Single trigger with selector between the bbls. Vent rib. Monte Carlo-style walnut stock with checkered pistol grip and forend. Made from 1965 to 1987.

M 77 O/U SHOTGUN. . . . . NiB $1244 Ex $1200 Gd $796
Gauge: 12. 27-inch vent-rib bbls., approx. 44 inches overall, weight: About 7.25 lbs. Bbl. selector. Ejectors. Monte Carlo-style walnut stock with checkered pistol grip and forend; rollover cheekpiece. Made from 1977 to 1987.

M 77K SHOTGUN/ RIFLE
COMBINATION . . . . NiB $1587 Ex $1216 Gd $870
Gauge: 12/70. Calibers: .222 Rem., 5.6x52r5, 6.5x55, 7x57r5, 7x65r5, .308 Win. Vent-rib bbls.: About 25 inches (shotgun); 23 inches (rifle), 42.3 inches overall. Weight: About 7.5 lbs. Double triggers. Monte Carlo-style walnut stock with checkered pistol grip and forend; rollover cheekpiece. Made from 1977 to 1986.

412S/512S SHOOTING SYSTEM
Boxlock action with both under lug and sliding top latch locking mechanism designed to accept interchangeable monobloc barrels, including O/U shotgun, combination and double rifle configurations. Blued or satin nickel receiver w/cocking indicators. Selective single trigger design w/barrel selector incorporated into the trigger (double triggers available). Blued barrels assemblies w/extractors or auto ejectors as required. Select American walnut stock with checkered pistol grip and forend. Previously produced in Finland (same as the former Valmet Model 412) but currently manufactured in Italy by joint venture arrangement with Armi Marocchi. From 1990-93, Stoeger Industries imported this model as the 412/S. In 1993 the nomenclature of this shooting system was changed to 512/S. Disc. 1997. Note: For double rifle values, see Tikka Rifles.

MODEL 412S/512S O/U SHOTGUN
Gauge: 12 w/3-inch chambers. 24-, 26-, 28- or 30-inch chrome-lined bbls. w/blued finish and integral stainless steel choke tubes. Weight: 7.25 to 7.5 lbs. Blue or matte nickel receiver. Select American walnut from stock with checkered pistol grip and forend. Imported 1990 to 1997.
Standard Field model . . . . NiB $1050 Ex $809 Gd $693
Standard Trap model . . . . NiB $1125 Ex $837 Gd $592
Premium Field model . . . . NiB $1425 Ex $1160 Gd $938
Premium Trap model . . . . NiB $1425 Ex $1202 Gd $1007
Sporting Clays model . . . . NiB $1167 Ex $953 Gd $703
W/Extra O/U shotgun bbl., add $575
W/Extra O/U combination bbl., add $695
W/Extra O/U rifle bbl., add $995

MODEL 412S/512S OVER/UNDER COMBINATION
Gauge: 12 w/3-inch chamber. Calibers: .222 Rem., .30-06 or .308 Win. Blue or matte nickel receiver, 24-inch chrome-lined bbls. w/extractors and blued finish. Weight: 7.25 to 7.5 lbs. Select American walnut stock with checkered pistol grip and forend. Imported from 1990 to 1997.
Standard Combination model . . . . NiB $1425 Ex $1209 Gd $1062
Premium Combination model . . . . NiB $1452 Ex $1209 Gd $1062
Extra barrel options. . . . . Add $750

SHOTGUNS

TRADITIONS PERFORMANCE FIREARMS — Importers of shotguns produced by Fausti Stefano of Brescia, Italy and ATA Firearms, Turkey.

CLASSIC SERIES, FIELD I O/U . . . . . . NiB $795 Ex $605 Gd $505
Available in 12, 20, 28 (2 3/4-inch chamber) and .410 gauge, 26- or 28-inch vent rib bbls. W/fixed chokes and extractors. Weight: 6 3/4 to 7 1/4 lbs. Blued finish, silver receiver engraved with game birds. Single, selective trigger. Brass bead front sight. European walnut stock. Overall length 43 to 45 inches. Intro. 2000.

FIELD HUNTER MODEL. . . . . NiB $795 Ex $605 Gd $505
Same as Field I except 12 and 20 gauge, 3-inch chambers, screw-in chokes and extractors.

FIELD II MODEL . . . . NiB $895 Ex $605 Gd $505
Same as Field I except with screw-in chokes and automatic ejectors.

FIELD III GOLD MODEL . . . . NiB $1125 Ex $1005 Gd $905
Same as Field I model except 12 gauge only, high-grade, oil-finish walnut, coin-finish receiver with engraved pheasants and woodcock, deep blue finish on barrels, automatic ejectors and non-slip recoil pad.

CLASSIC SERIES O/U
SPORTING CLAY III . . . . NiB $1115 Ex $905 Gd $705
Available in 12 and 20 gauge, 3-inch chambers, high grade walnut stock, oil-satin finish, palm swell Schnabel forend. 28- and 30-inch bbls. with 3/8-inch top and middle vent rib, red target front bead sight. Automatic ejectors, extended choke tubes. Weight: 8 1/4 lbs. Intro. 2000.

SPORTING CLAY II MODEL. . . . . . . NiB $1075 Ex $705 Gd $505
Same as Sporting Clay III model but with European walnut stocks, cut checkering and extended choke tubes. Overall length: 47 inches. Weight: 7 3/4 lbs.

UPLAND III MODEL. . . . . NiB $1115 Ex $905 Gd $705
Same as Sporting Clay III model but round pistol grip and Schnabel forend, blued receiver with engraved upland scene, weight: 7 1/2 lbs.

UPLAND II MODEL . . . . NiB $995 Ex $605 Gd $505
Same as Upland III model except with English walnut straight-grip stock and Schnabel forend, 24- and 26-inch vent rib bbls., floral engraving on blued receiver, automatic ejectors.

MAG 350 SERIES TURKEY II O/U . . NiB $1050 Ex $805 Gd $605

Magnum 3 1/2-inch chambers in 12 gauge only, 24- and 26-inch bbls., screw-in flush fitting chokes: F and XF. Matte finish, engraved receiver, Mossy Oak or Realtree camo. Intro. 2000.

WATERFOWL II MODEL. . . . . NiB $1050 Ex $805 Gd $605
Same as Turkey II model except with Advantage Wetlands camo stock and barrels, weight: 8 lbs., overall length 45 inches. Waterfowl model has 28-inch bbls.

MAG HUNTER II. . . . . NiB $1050 Ex $805 Gd $605
Same as Turkey II model except blued engraved receiver and matte finish walnut stocks, 3 1/2-inch chambers, 28-inch bbls. with screw-in chokes.

ELITE FIELD III ST . . . . NiB $1825 Ex $1605 Gd $1205
Checkered English walnut straight stock, splinter forend, fixed chokes. Available in 28 and .410 gauge, 26-inch chrome-lined bbls., Cylinder and Modified chokes. Silver trigger guard and receiver with hand-finished engraving of upland game scenes with gold inlays. Automatic ejectors. Brass front sight bead. Weight: About 6 1/2 lbs. Intro. 2000.

ELITE HUNTER . . . . NiB $1185 Ex $905 Gd $625
Same as Elite Field model except 12 and 20 gauge, European walnut stock, beavertail forend, screw-in choke tubes, extractors, three-inch chambers. Blued finish. Vent-rib, tang safety. Weight: 6 1/2 pounds.

ELITE FIELD I ST . . . . NiB $1009 Ex $905 Gd $705
Same as Elite Field III except single trigger, fixed chokes, extractors; European walnut stock. Available in 12, 20, 28 (2 3/4-inch chambers) and .410 gauge; fixed IC/M chokes. Weight: 5 3/4 to 6 1/2 lbs.

ELITE FIELD I DT . . . . NiB $950 Ex $705 Gd $505
Same as Elite Field I except with double triggers, fixed chokes, extractors. Available in 12, 20, 28 (2 3/4-inch chambers) and .410. Bbls: 26 inches, fixed IC/M chokes. Weight: 5 1/2 to 6 1/4 lbs

AL 2100 SEMI-AUTO SHOTGUNS
FIELD SERIES, WALNUT MODEL. . . . NiB $295 Ex $215 Gd $175
Gas-operated, 12 and 20 gauge, 3-inch chambers, cut-checkered Turkish walnut stock and forend, blued 26- and 28-inch vent rib bbls., multi-choke system, chrome bore lining. Weight: About 6 lbs. Rifled barrel with cantilever mount available Intro. 2001.

SYNTHETIC STOCK MODEL . . . . NiB $300 Ex $245 Gd $185
Same as the ALS 2100 Walnut model except with synthetic stock, matted finish on receiver and bbl., weight: About 6 lbs.

YOUTH MODEL . . . . NiB $295 Ex $205 Gd $145
Same as ALS 2100 Walnut model except with a shorter walnut stock (length of pull: 13 1/2 inches). Available in 12 or 20 gauge with 24-inch vent rib barrel, weight: 5 1/2 to 6 lbs.

HUNTER COMBO MODEL
Same as ALS 2100 Walnut model except comes with two bbls. (28-inch vent rib and 24-inch slug), TruGlo adjustable sights and cantilever mount. Available with Turkish walnut or synthetic stock with matte barrel finish. Weight: 6 1/2 lbs.
(Walnut). . . . . NiB $465 Ex $320 Gd $155
(Synthetic) . . . . NiB $435 Ex $290 Gd $125

SLUG HUNTER MODEL. . . . . NiB $300 Ex $205 Gd $115
Same as ALS 2100 Walnut except with fully-rifled barrel, choice of walnut or synthetic stocks, matte or blue finish; rifle or TruGlo adjustable sights. Weight: About 6 1/4 lbs.

TURKEY HUNTER/
WATERFOWL MODEL . . . . NiB $315 Ex $245 Gd $155
Same as ALS 2100 Walnut except with synthetic stock, 3-inch chambers, 26-inch vent rib bbl., screw-in chokes, Mossy Oak or Realtree camo stocks.

HOME SECURITY MODEL. . . . . NiB $275 Ex $205 Gd $165
Same as ALS 2100 Walnut but with 20-inch cylinder-bore bbl., synthetic stock, 3-inch chambers, six-round capacity with 2 3/4-inch shells. Weight: About 6 lbs.

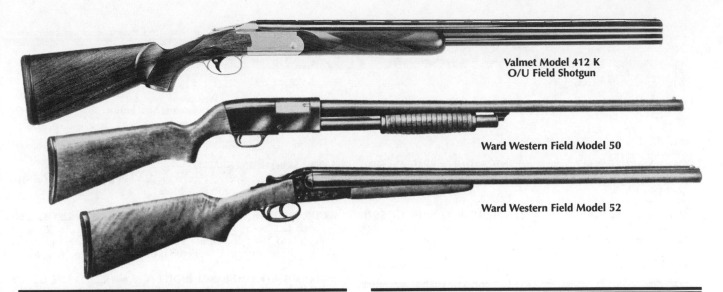

Valmet Model 412 K
O/U Field Shotgun

Ward Western Field Model 50

Ward Western Field Model 52

TRISTAR SPORTING ARMS — North Kansas City, MO

MODEL 1887 LEVER-ACTION REPEATER .... NiB $650 Ex $524 Gd $375
Copy of John Browning's Winchester Model 1887 lever-action shotgun. 12 ga. only. 30-inch bbl. which may be cut down to any desired length of 18 inches or more. Version shown has 20-inch bbl. Imported from 1997 to 1999.

MODEL 300 O/U SHOTGUN..... NiB $395 Ex $290 Gd $183
Similar to the Model 333 except 12 ga. only w/3-inch chambers, 26- or 28-inch vent rib bbls. w/extractors and fixed chokes. Etched receiver w/double triggers and standard walnut stock. Imported 1994 to 1998.

MODEL 311 SIDE-BY-SIDE SHOTGUN
Boxlock action w/underlug and Greener cross bolt. 12 or 20 ga. w/3-inch chambers, 20, 28- or 30-inch bbls. w/choke tubes or fixed chokes (311R). Double triggers. Extractors. Black chrome finish. Checkered Turkish walnut buttstock and forend. Weight: 6.9 to 7.2 lbs. Imported from 1994 to 1997.
311 Model (w/extractors and choke tubes) ... NiB $535 Ex $423 Gd $365
311R Model
(w/20-inch bbls. and fixed chokes) .... NiB $375 Ex $295 Gd $188

MODEL 330 O/U SHOTGUN
Similar to the Model 333 except 12 ga. only w/3-inch chambers. 26-, 28- or 30-inch vent rib bbls w/extractors or ejectors and fixed chokes or choke tubes. Etched receiver and standard walnut stock. Imported from 1994 to 1999.
330 model (w/ extractor and fixed chokes) ... NiB $475 Ex $372 Gd $242
330 D model (w/ejectors and choke tubes) ... NiB $635 Ex $511 Gd $438

MODEL 333 O/U SHOTGUN
Boxlock action. 12 or 20 ga. w/3-inch chambers. 26-, 28- or 30-inch vent rib bbls. w/choke tubes. Single selective trigger. Selective automatic ejectors. Engraved receiver w/satin nickel finish. Checkered Turkish fancy walnut buttstock and forend. Weight: 7.5 to 7.75 lbs. Imported from 1994 to 1998.
333 Field model .... NiB $735 Ex $605 Gd $505
333 Sporting Clays model (1994-97)..... NiB $824 Ex $687 Gd $563
333 TRL Ladies Field model .... NiB $735 Ex $605 Gd $505
333 SCL Ladies Sporting Clays model
(1994-97)...................... NiB $825 Ex $640 Gd $573

SHOTGUNS OF ULM — Ulm, West Germany

See listings under Krieghoff.

U.S. REPEATING ARMS CO. — New Haven, Connecticut

See also Winchester Shotgun listings.

VALMET OY — Jyväskylä, Finland

NOTE: In 1987, Valmet and Sako merged and the Valmet production facilities were moved to Riihimaki, Finland. In 1989 a joint venture agreement was made with Armi Marocchi, and when production began in Italy, the Valmet name was changed to Tikka (Oy Tikkakoski Ab).

See also Savage Models 330, 333T, 333 and 2400, which were produced by Valmet.

VALMET LION O/U SHOTGUN ... NiB $425 Ex $347 Gd $261
Boxlock. Selective single trigger. Plain extractors. 12 ga. only. Bbls.: 26-inch IC/M; 28-inch M/F, 30-inch M/F, F/F. Weight: About 7 lbs. Checkered pistol-grip stock and forearm. Imported 1947 to 1968.

MODEL 412 S O/U FIELD SHOTGUN.... NiB $855 Ex $638 Gd $526
Hammerless. 12-ga., 3-inch chamber, 36-inch bbl., F/F chokes. American walnut Monte Carlo stock. Disc 1989.

MODEL 412 S SHOTGUN RIFLE
COMBINATION .... NiB $1025 Ex $896 Gd $641
Similar to model 412 K except bottom bbl. chambered for .222 Rem., .223 Rem., .243 Win., .308 Win. or .30-06. 12-ga. shotgun bbl. with IM choke. Monte Carlo American walnut stock, recoil pad.

MODEL 412 O/U
FIELD SHOTGUN .... NiB $775 Ex $618 Gd $532
12-ga. chambered for 2.75-inch shells. 26-inch bbl., IC/M chokes; 28-inch bbl., M/F chokes; 12-ga. chambered for 3-inch shells, 30-inch bbl., M/F chokes. 20-ga. (3-inch shells); 26-inch bbl., IC/M chokes; 28-inch bbl., M/ F chokes. American walnut Monte Carlo stock.

**Weatherby Model 82
Autoloading Shotgun**

MODEL 412 ST SKEET . . . . NiB $1040 Ex $816 Gd $676
Similar to Model 412 K except skeet stock and chokes. 12 and 20 ga. Disc. 1989.

MODEL 412 SE TRAP . . . . NiB $1040 Ex $816 Gd $676
Similar to Model 412 K Field except trap stock, recoil pad. 30-inch bbls., IM/F chokes. Disc.1989.

MODEL 412 EXTRA BARREL . . . . .Add $500

MONTGOMERY WARD — Chicago, Illinois
Western Field and Hercules Models

Although they do not correspond to specific models below, the names Western Field and Hercules have been used to designate various Montgomery Ward shotguns at various times.

MODEL 25 SLIDE-ACTION REPEATER . . . . . . NiB $250 Ex $199 Gd $147
Solid frame. 12 ga. only. Two- or 5-round tubular magazine. 28-inch bbl., various chokes. Weight: About 7.5 lbs. Plain pistol-grip stock, grooved slide handle.

MODEL 40 O/U SHOTGUN . . . . . . NiB $778 Ex $628 Gd $447
Hammerless. Boxlock. Double triggers. Gauges: 12, l6, 20, .410. Bbls.: Plain; 26- to 30-inch, various chokes. Checkered pistol-grip stock and forearm.

**MODEL 40N
SLIDE-ACTION REPEATER** . . . . NiB $266 Ex $204 Gd $150
Same general specifications as Model 25.

(WESTERN FIELD) MODEL 50 PUMPGUN . . . NiB $255 Ex $211 Gd $156
Solid frame. Gauges: 12 and 16. Two- and 5-round magazine. 26-, 28- or 30-inch bbl., 48 inches overall w/28-inch bbl. Weight: 7.25 - 7.75 lbs. Metal bead front sight. Walnut stock and grooved forend.

**(WESTERN FIELD) MODEL 52
DOUBLE-BARREL SHOTGUN** . . . . . NiB $295 Ex $236 Gd $173
Hammerless coil-spring action. Gauges: 12, 16, 20 and .410. 26-, 28-, or 30-inch bbls., 42 to 46 inches overall, depending upon bbl. length. Weight: 6 (.410 ga. w/26-inch bbl.) to 7.25 lbs. (12 ga. w/30-inch bbls.), depending upon gauge and bbl. length. Casehardened receiver; blued bbls. Plain buttstock and forend. Made circa 1954.

MODEL 172 BOLT-ACTION SHOTGUN . . . . . . NiB $164 Ex $113 Gd $88
Takedown. Two-round detachable clip magazine.12 ga. 28-inch bbl. with variable choke. Weight: About 7.5 lbs. Monte Carlo stock with recoil pad.

MODEL 550A SLIDE-ACTION REPEATER . . . . NiB $293 Ex $233 Gd $170
Takedown. Gauges: 12, 16, 20, .410. Five-round tubular magazine. Bbls.: Plain, 26- to 30-inch, various chokes. Weight: 6 (.410 ga. w/26-inch bbl.) to 8 lbs. (12 ga. w/30-inch bbls.). Plain pistol-grip stock and grooved slide handle.

**MODEL SB300 DOUBLE-BARREL
SHOTGUN** . . . . NiB $323 Ex $250 Gd $180
Same general specifications as Model SD52A.

MODEL SB312 DOUBLE-BARREL SHOTGUN . . . NiB $361 Ex $281 Gd $203
Boxlock. Double triggers. Plain extractors. Gauges: 12, 16, 20, .410. Bbls.: 24- to 30-inch. Various chokes. Weight: About 7.5 lbs. in 12 ga.; 6.5 lbs in .410 ga. Checkered pistol-grip stock and forearm.

MODEL SD52A DOUBLE-BARREL SHOTGUN . . . . NiB $271 Ex $216 Gd $159
Boxlock. Double triggers. Plain extractors. Gauges: 12, 16, 20, .410. Bbls.: 26- to 32-inch, various chokes. Plain forend and pistol-grip buttstock. Weight: 6 (.410 ga., 26-inch bbls.) to 7.5 lbs. (12 ga., 32-inch bbls.).

WEATHERBY, INC. (Pasa Robles, CA) —

MODEL 82 AUTOLOADING SHOTGUN Hammerless, gas-operated. 12 ga. only. Bbls.: 22- to 30-inch, various integral or fixed chokes. Weight: 7.5 lbs. Checkered walnut stock and forearm. Imported from 1982 to 1989.
Standard Autoloading Shotgun . . . . NiB $497 Ex $394 Gd $287
BuckMaster Auto Slug
w/rifle sights (1986-90) . . . . NiB $494 Ex $399 Gd $291
W/fixed chokes, deduct. $40

MODEL 92 SLIDE-ACTION SHOTGUN
Hammerless, short-stroke action. 12 ga.; 3-inch chamber. Tubular magazine. Bbls.: 22-, 26-, 28-, 30-inch with fixed choke or IMC choke tubes; plain or vent rib with rifle sights. Weight: 7.5 lbs. Engraved, matte black receiver and blued barrel. Checkered high-gloss buttstock and forend. Imported from Japan since 1982.
Standard Model 92 . . . . NiB $330 Ex $261 Gd $195
BuckMaster Pump Slug
w/rifle sights (intro. 1986) . . . . NiB $345 Ex $260 Gd $199
W/fixed chokes, deduct. $30

ATHENA O/U SHOTGUN
Engraved boxlock action with Greener crossbolt and sideplates. Gauges: 12, 20, 28 and .410; 2.75- or 3.5-inch chambers. Bbls.: 26-, 28-, 30- or 32-inch with fixed or IMC Multi-choke tubes. Weight: 6.75 to 7.38 lbs. Single selective trigger. Selective auto ejectors. Top tang safety. Checkered Claro walnut stock and forearm with high-luster finish. Imported from 1982 to 2002.
Field Model w/IMC multi-choke
(12 or 20 ga.) . . . . NiB $2085 Ex $1804 Gd $1552
Field Model w/fixed chokes (28 or .410 ga.) . . . NiB $1865 Ex $1504 Gd $1260
Skeet Model w/fixed chokes (12 or 20 ga.) . . . . NiB $1675 Ex $1309 Gd $1147
Skeet Model w/fixed chokes
(28 or .410 ga.) . . . . NiB $3110 Ex $2794 Gd $2277
Master skeet tube set . . . . NiB $3089 Ex $2683 Gd $2192
Trap Model w/IC tubes . . . . NiB $2271 Ex $1842 Gd $1569
Grade V (1993 to date) . . . . NiB $3339 Ex $2987 Gd $2409

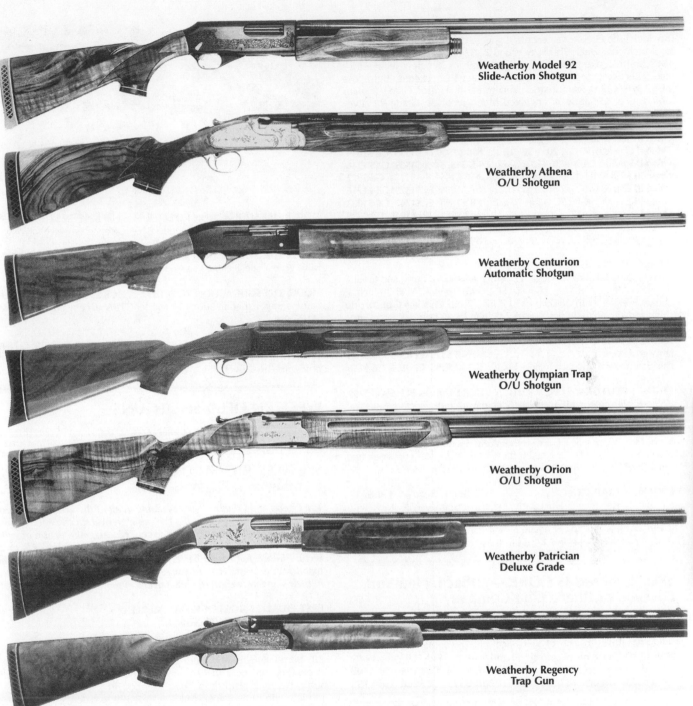

Weatherby Model 92
Slide-Action Shotgun

Weatherby Athena
O/U Shotgun

Weatherby Centurion
Automatic Shotgun

Weatherby Olympian Trap
O/U Shotgun

Weatherby Orion
O/U Shotgun

Weatherby Patrician
Deluxe Grade

Weatherby Regency
Trap Gun

CENTURION AUTOMATIC SHOTGUN

Gas-operated. Takedown. 12 ga. 2.75-inch chamber. Three round magazine. Bbls.: Vent ribs; 26-inch SK, IC or M 28-inch M or F; 30-inch Full choke. Weight: With 28-inch bbl., 7 lbs. 10.5 oz. Checkered pistol-grip stock and forearm, recoil pad. Made in Japan from 1972 to 1981.

Centurion Field grade . . . . NiB $320 Ex $263 Gd $195
Centurion Trap Gun
(30-inch full choke bbl.) . . . . NiB $355 Ex $267 Gd $195
Centurion Deluxe (etched
receiver, fancy wood) . . . . NiB $395 Ex $269 Gd $186

OLYMPIAN O/U SHOTGUN

Gauges: 12 and 20. 2.75- (12 ga.) and 3-inch (20 ga.) chambers. Bbls.: 26-, 28-, 30, and 32-inch. Weight: 6.75 - 8.75 lbs. American walnut stock and forend.

Field
Model . . . . NiB $859 Ex $633 Gd $500
Skeet
Model . . . . NiB $885 Ex $653 Gd $524
Trap
Model . . . . NiB $859 Ex $638 Gd $504

ORION O/U SHOTGUN

Boxlock with Greener crossbolt. Gauges: 12, 20, 28 and .410; 2.75- or 3-inch chambers. Bbls.: 26-, 28, 30-, 32- or 34-inch with fixed or IMC Multi-Choke tubes. Weight: 6.5 to 9 lbs. Single selective trigger. Selective auto ejectors. Top tang safety. Checkered, high-gloss pistol-grip Claro walnut stock and forearm. Finish: Grade I, plain blued receive; Grade II, engraved blued receiver; Grade III, silver gray receiver. Imported from 1982 and 2002.

Orion I Field w/IC (12 or 20 ga.) .... NiB $1243 Ex $1004 Gd $722
Orion II Field w/IC (12 or 20 ga.) .... NiB $1077 Ex $840 Gd $647
Orion II Classic w/IC (12, 20 or 28 ga.) ... NiB $1500 Ex $1223 Gd $1039
Orion II Sporting Clays w/IC (12 ga.)..... NiB $1875 Ex $1583 Gd $1246
Orion III Field w/IC (12 or 20 ga.) .... NiB $1551 Ex $1274 Gd $972
Orion III Classic w/IC (12 or 20 ga.) ..... NiB $1800 Ex $1579 Gd $1216
Orion III English Field w/IC (12 or 20 ga.). NiB $1593 Ex $1247 Gd $1083
Orion Upland w/IC (12 or 20 ga.) .... NiB $1225 Ex $1048 Gd $832
Skeet II w/fixed chokes .... NiB $1220 Ex $1035 Gd $881
Super Sporting Clays .... NiB $1874 Ex $1506 Gd $1074

PATRICIAN SLIDE-ACTION SHOTGUN

Hammerless. Takedown. 12 ga. 2.75-inch chamber. Four round tubular magazine. Bbls.: Vent rib; 26-inch, SK, IC M; 28-inch, M F; 30-inch, F choke. Weight: With 28-inch bbl., 7 lbs., 7 oz. Checkered pistol-grip stock and slide handle, recoil pad. Made in Japan from 1972 to 1982.

Patrician Field grade .... NiB $277 Ex $169 Gd $97
Patrician Deluxe (etched receiver,
fancy grade wood) .... NiB $325 Ex $288 Gd $133
Patrician Trap Gun (30-inch F choke bbl.) .... NiB $295 Ex $184 Gd $136

REGENCY FIELD GRADE O/U SHOTGUN .. NiB $1248 Ex $1118 Gd $799
Boxlock with sideplates, elaborately engraved. Auto ejectors. Selective single trigger. Gauges: 12, 20. 2.75-inch chamber in 12 ga., 3-inch in 20 ga. Bbls.: Vent rib; 26-inch SK, IC/M, M/F (20 ga. only); 28-inch SK, IC/M, M/F; 30-inch M/F (12 ga only). Weight with 28-inch bbls.: 7 lbs., 6 oz., 12 ga.; 6 lbs., 14 oz., 20 ga. Checkered pistol-grip stock and forearm of fancy walnut. Made in Italy from 1965 to 1982.

REGENCY TRAP GUN .... NiB $900 Ex $744 Gd $617
Similar to Regency Field Grade except has trap-style stock with straight or Monte Carlo comb. Bbls. have vent side ribs and high, wide vent top rib; 30- or 32-inch, M/F, IM/F or F/F chokes. Weight: With 32-inch bbls., 8 lbs. Made in Italy from 1965 to 1982.

WESTERN ARMS CORP. — Ithaca, New York
Division of Ithaca Gun Company

LONG RANGE HAMMERLESS DOUBLE

Boxlock. Plain extractors. Single or double triggers. Gauges: 12, 16, 20, .410. Bbls.: 26- to 32-inch, M/F choke standard. Weight: 7.5 lbs., 12 ga. Plain pistol-grip stock and forend. Made 1929 to 1946.
With double triggers .... NiB $278 Ex $195 Gd $100
With single trigger .... NiB $325 Ex $266 Gd $153

WESTERN AUTO SHOTGUNS —
Kansas City, Missouri

MODEL 300H SLIDE-ACTION REPEATER .... NiB $315 Ex $242 Gd $179
Gauges: 12,16, 20, .410. Four round tubular magazine. Bbls.: 26- to 30-inch, various chokes. Weight: About 7 lbs. Plain pistol-grip stock, grooved slide handle.

MODEL 310A SLIDE-ACTION REPEATER .... NiB $299 Ex $232 Gd $173
Takedown. 12 ga. Five round tubular magazine. Bbls.: 28- and 30-inch. Weight: About 7.5 lbs. Plain pistol-grip stock.

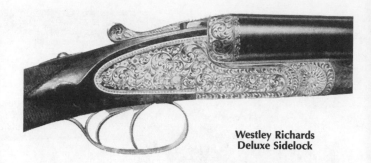

Westley Richards Deluxe Sidelock

MODEL 310B SLIDE-ACTION REPEATER..... NiB $291 Ex $216 Gd $159
Same general specifications as Model 310A except chambered for 16 ga.

MODEL 310C SLIDE-ACTION REPEATER .... NiB $297 Ex $237 Gd $175
Same general specifications as Model 310A except chambered for 20 ga.

MODEL 310E SLIDE-ACTION REPEATER..... NiB $355 Ex $267 Gd $194
Same general specifications as Model 310A except chambered for .410 bore.

MODEL 325BK BOLT-ACTION REPEATER ..... NiB $191 Ex $129 Gd $99
Takedown. Two round detachable clip magazine. 20 ga. 26-inch bbl. with variable choke. Weight: 6.25 lbs.

WESTERN FIELD SHOTGUNS

See "W" for listings under Montgomery Ward.

WESTLEY RICHARDS & CO., LTD. —
Birmingham, England

The Pigeon and Wildfowl gun, available in all of the Westley Richards models except the Ovundo, has the same general specifications as the corresponding standard field gun except has magnum action of extra strength and treble bolting, chambered for 12 gauge only (2.75- or 3-inch); 30-inch full choke barrels standard. Weight: About 8 lbs. The manufacturer warns that 12-gauge magnum shells should not be used in their standard weight double-barrel shotguns.

BEST QUALITY BOXLOCK HAMMERLESS
DOUBLE-BARREL SHOTGUN

Boxlock. Hand-detachable locks and hinged cover plate. Selective ejectors. Double triggers or selective single trigger. Gauges: 12, 16, 20. Barrel lengths and boring to order. Weight: 5.5 to 6.25 lbs. depending on ga. and bbl. length. Checkered stock and forend, straight or half-pistol grip. Also supplied in Pigeon and Wildfowl models with same values. Made from 1899 to date.
With double triggers .... NiB $21,522 Ex $17,260 Gd $11,804
With selective single trigger........ NiB $24,312 Ex $19,500 Gd $13,340

BEST QUALITY SIDELOCK HAMMERLESS
DOUBLE-BARREL SHOTGUN

Hand-detachable sidelocks. Selective ejectors. Double triggers or selective single trigger. Gauges: 12, 16, 20, 28, .410. Bbl. lengths and boring to order. Weight: 4.75 to 6.75 lbs., depending on ga. and bbl. length. Checkered stock and forend, straight or half-pistol grip. Also supplied in Pigeon and Wildfowl models with same values. Currently manufactured.
With double triggers............... NiB $27,581 Ex $24,475 Gd $21,323
With selective single trigger........ NiB $28,525 Ex $25,275 Gd $22,555

Westley Richards
Best Quality Sidelock

Westley Richards
Deluxe Boxlock

Westley Richards
Model E

Winchester Model 12 Classic
Limited Edition Grade I

Winchester Model 12
Field Gun — 1972 Type

SHOTGUNS

MODEL DELUXE BOX LOCK
HAMMERLESS DOUBLE-BARREL SHOTGUN
Same general specifications as standard Best Quality gun except higher quality throughout. Has Westley Richards top-projection and treble-bite lever-work, hand-detachable locks. Also supplied in Pigeon and Wildfowl models with same values. Currently manufactured.
With double triggers .... NiB $11,503 Ex $9265 Gd $6401
**With selective
single trigger** .... NiB $30,325 Ex $28,325 Gd $12,325

MODEL DELUXE SIDELOCK
Same as Best Quality Sidelock except higher grade engraving and wood. Currently manufactured.
With double triggers .... NiB $25,275 Ex $20,275 Gd $13,875
With single trigger ...... NiB $30,300 Ex $24,300 Gd $16,620

MODEL E HAMMERLESS DOUBLE
Anson & Deeley-type boxlock action. Selective ejector or non-ejector. Double triggers. Gauges: 12, 16, 20. Barrel lengths and boring to order. Weight: 5.5 to 7.25 lbs. depending on type, ga. and bbl. length. Checkered stock and forend, straight or half-pistol grip. Also supplied in Pigeon and Wildfowl models with same values. Currently manufactured.
Ejector model .... NiB $5079 Ex $4090 Gd $2866
Non-ejector model .... NiB $4460 Ex $3595 Gd $3039

OVUNDO (O/U) .... NiB $18,000 Ex $15,190 Gd $10,392
Hammerless. Boxlock. Hand-detachable locks. Dummy sideplates. Selective ejectors. Selective single trigger. 12 ga. Barrel lengths and boring to order. Checkered stock/forend, straight or half-pistol grip. Mfd. before WW II.

TED WILLIAMS SHOTGUNS

See Sears shotguns.

WINCHESTER SHOTGUNS —
New Haven, Connecticut

Formerly Winchester Repeating Arms Co., and then mfd. by Winchester-Western Div., Olin Corp., later by U.S. Repeating Arms Company. In 1999, production rights were acquired by Browning Arms Company.

MODEL 12 CLASSIC LIMITED EDITION
Gauge: 20; 2.75-inch chamber. Bbl.: 26-inch vent rib; IC. Weight: 7 lbs. Checkered walnut buttstock and forend. Polished blue finish (Grade I) or engraved with gold inlays (Grade IV). Made from 1993 to 1995.
Grade I (4000) .... NiB $995 Ex $781 Gd $552
Grade IV (1000) .... NiB $1500 Ex $1198 Gd $837

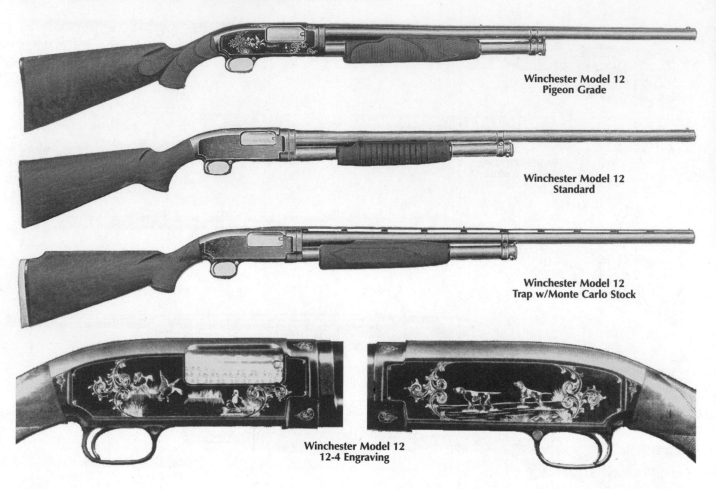

**Winchester Model 12
Pigeon Grade**

**Winchester Model 12
Standard**

**Winchester Model 12
Trap w/Monte Carlo Stock**

**Winchester Model 12
12-4 Engraving**

MODEL 12

FEATHERWEIGHT . . . . **NiB $550 Ex $455 Gd $341**
Same as Model 12 Standard w/plain barrel except has alloy trigger guard. Modified takedown w/redesigned magazine tube, cap and slide handle. 12 ga. only. Bbls.: 26-inch IC; 28-inch M or F; 30-inch F choke. Serial numbers with "F" prefix. Weight: About 6.75 lbs. Made from 1959 to 1962.

MODEL 12 FIELD GUN, 1972 TYPE . . . . . . **NiB $700 Ex $568 Gd $404**
Same general specifications as Standard Model 12 but 12 ga. only, 26- 28- or 30-inch vent rib bbl., standard chokes. Engine-turned bolt and carrier. Hand-checkered stock/slide handle of semifancy walnut. Made from 1972 to 1975.

MODEL 12 HEAVY DUCK GUN
Same general specifications as Standard Grade except 12 ga. only chambered for 3-inch shells. 30- or 32-inch plain, solid or vent rib bbl. w/full choke only. Three round magazine. Checkered slide handle and pistol-grip walnut buttstock w/recoil pad. Weight: 8.5 to 8.75 lbs. Made from 1935 to 1963.

Heavy Duck Gun, plain bbl. . . . . **NiB $1200 Ex $755 Gd $537**
**Heavy Duck Gun, solid
rib (disc. 1959)** . . . . **NiB $1848 Ex $1192 Gd $754**
**Heavy Duck Gun, vent rib
(Special order only)** . . . . **NiB $3000 Ex $2692 Gd $2342**

MODEL 12 PIGEON GRADE
Deluxe versions of the regular Model 12 Standard or Field Gun, Duck Gun, Skeet Gun and Trap Gun made on special order. This grade has finer finish throughout, hand-smoothed action, engine-turned breech bolt and carrier, stock and extension slide handle of high grade walnut, fancy checkering, stock dimensions to individual specifications. Engraving and carving available at extra cost ranging from about $135 to over $1000. Disc. 1965.

Field Gun, plain bbl. . . . . **NiB $4000 Ex $3556 Gd $2903**
Field Gun, vent rib . . . . **NiB $2000 Ex $1892 Gd $1339**
Skeet Gun, matted rib . . . . **NiB $2000 Ex $1892 Gd $1339**
Skeet Gun, vent rib . . . . **NiB $3560 Ex $3145 Gd $2910**
Skeet Gun, Cutts Compensator . . . . **NiB $1500 Ex $1281 Gd $909**
Trap Gun, matted rib . . . . **NiB $2000 Ex $1830 Gd $1292**
Trap Gun, vent rib . . . . **NiB $2120 Ex $1970 Gd $1950**
16 ga. (Field), add 100%
16 ga. (Skeet), add 100%
20 ga. (Field), add 175%
20 ga. (Skeet), add 175%
28 ga. (Skeet), add 550%

MODEL 12 RIOT GUN . . . . **NiB $894 Ex $724 Gd $518**
Same general specifications as plain barrel Model 12 Standard except has 20-inch cylinder bore bbl.,12 gauge only. Made from 1918 to 1963.

MODEL 12 SKEET GUN . . . . . . **NiB $2000 Ex $1892 Gd $1339**
Gauges: 12, 16, 20, 28. Five round tubular magazine. 26-inch matted rib bbl., SK choke. Weight: About 7.75 lbs., 12 ga.; 6.75 lbs., other gauges. Bradley red or ivory bead front sight. Winchester 94B middle sight. Checkered pistol-grip stock and extension slide handle. Disc. after WWII.

**Winchester Model 21
Custom Grade**

**Winchester Model 21
Pigeon Grade**

MODEL 12 SKEET GUN, CUTTS COMPENSATOR . . . . NiB $1000 Ex $831 Gd $596
Same general specifications as standard Model 12 Skeet Gun except has plain bbl. fitted with Cutts Compensator, 26 inches overall. Disc. 1954.

MODEL 12 SKEET GUN, PLAIN-BARREL . . NiB $2000 Ex $1778 Gd $1560
Same general specifications as standard Model 12 Skeet except w/no rib.

MODEL 12 SKEET GUN, VENT RIB . . . . . . NiB $4000 Ex $3514 Gd $3025
Same general specifications as standard Model 12 Skeet Gun except has 26-inch bbl. with vent rib, 12 and 20 ga. Disc. in 1965.

MODEL 12 SKEET GUN, 1972 TYPE . . . . NiB $1195 Ex $845 Gd $606
Same gen. specifications as Standard Model 12 but 12 ga. only. 26-inch vent rib bbl., SK choke. Engine-turned bolt and carrier. Hand-checkered skeet-style stock and slide handle of choice walnut, recoil pad. Made from 1972 to 1975.

MODEL 12 STANDARD GR., MATTED RIB . . . . NiB $750 Ex $542 Gd $359
Same general specifications as plain bbl. Model 12 Standard except has solid raised matted rib. Disc. after World War II.

MODEL 12 STANDARD GR., VENT RIB . . . . . . NiB $750 Ex $542 Gd $359
Same general specifications as plain barrel Model 12 Standard except has vent rib. 26.75- or 30-inch bbl.,12 ga. only. Disc. after World War II.

MODEL 12 STANDARD SLIDE-ACTION REPEATER
Hammerless. Takedown. Gauges: 12, 16, 20, 28. Six round tubular magazine. Plain bbl. Lengths: 26- to 32-inches; choked F to Cyl. Weight: About 7.5 lbs., 12 ga. 30-inch, 6.5 lbs. in other ga. with 28-inch bbl. Plain pistol-grip stock, grooved slide handle. Made from 1912 to 1964.

12 ga., 28-inch bbl. (full choke) . . . . NiB $700	Ex $603	Gd $497
16 ga. . . . . NiB $800	Ex $700	Gd $448
20 ga. . . . . NiB $1100	Ex $796	Gd $567
28 ga. . . . . NiB $5500	Ex $3343	Gd $2366

MODEL 12 SUPER PIGEON GRADE . NiB $4000 Ex $3692 Gd $2903
Custom version of Model 12 with same general specifications as standard models. 12 ga. only. 26-, 28- or 30-inch vent-rib bbl., any standard choke. Engraved receiver. Hand-smoothed and fitted action. Full fancy walnut stock and forearm made to individual order. Made from 1965 to 1972.

MODEL 12 TRAP GUN
Same general specifications as Standard Model 12 except has straighter stock, checkered pistol grip and extension slide handle, recoil pad, 30-inch matted-rib bbl., F choke, 12 ga. only. Disc. after World War II; vent rib model disc. 1965.

Matted rib bbl. . . . . NiB $2000	Ex $1808	Gd $1476
With straight stock, vent rib . . . NiB $2200	Ex $2000	Gd $1875
With Monte Carlo stock, vent rib . . . NiB $2000	Ex $1808	Gd $1476

MODEL 12 TRAP GUN, 1972 TYPE . . . . NiB $1110 Ex $876 Gd $599
Same general specifications as Standard Model 12 but 12 gauge only. 30-inch vent-rib bbl., F choke. Engine-turned bolt and carrier. Hand-checkered trap-style stock (straight or Monte Carlo comb) and slide handle of select walnut, recoil pad. Intro. in 1972. Disc.

MODEL 20 SINGLE-SHOT HAMMER GUN . . NiB $1220 Ex $1049 Gd $863
Takedown. .410 bore. 2.5-inch chamber. 26-inch bbl., F choke. Checkered pistol-grip stock and forearm. Weight: About 6 lbs. Made from 1919 to 1924.

ORIGINAL MODEL 21 DOUBLE-BARREL SHOTGUNS (ORIGINAL PRODUCTION SERIES - 1930 to 1959)
Hammerless. Boxlock. Automatic safety. Double triggers or selective single trigger, selective or non-selective ejection (all postwar Model 21 shotguns have selective single trigger and selective ejection). Gauges: 12, 16, 20, 28 and .410 bore. Bbls.: Raised matted rib or vent rib; 26-, 28-, 30-, 32-inch, the latter in 12 ga. only; F, IM, M, IC, SK chokes. Weight: 7.5 lbs., 12 ga. w/30-inch bbl.; about 6.5 lbs. 16 or 20 ga. w/28-inch bbl. Checkered pistol- or straight-grip stock, regular or beavertail forend. Made from 1930 to 1959.

Standard grade, 12 ga.	NiB $6996	Ex $4259	Gd $3008
Standard grade, 16 ga.	NiB $8551	Ex $5270	Gd $3695
Standard grade, 20 ga.	NiB $9547	Ex $5443	Gd $3814
Tournament grade, 12 ga. (1933-34)	NiB $5494	Ex $4465	Gd $3149
Tournament grade, 16 ga. (1933-34)	NiB $6749	Ex $5443	Gd $3822
Tournament grade, 20 ga. (1933-34)	NiB $8070	Ex $6582	Gd $4439
Trap grade, 12 ga. (1940-59)	NiB $5377	Ex $4335	Gd $3037
Trap grade, 16 ga. (1940-59)	NiB $5896	Ex $4784	Gd $3362
Trap grade, 20 ga. (1940-59)	NiB $7360	Ex $5952	Gd $4175
Skeet grade, 12 ga. (1936-59)	NiB $5241	Ex $4264	Gd $2993
Skeet grade, 16 ga. (1936-59)	NiB $5975	Ex $4861	Gd $3392
Skeet grade, 20 ga. (1936-59)	NiB $6972	Ex $5663	Gd $4056
Duck Gun, 12 ga. 3-inch (1940-52) . . .	NiB $5766	Ex $4666	Gd $3284
Magnum, 12 ga. 3-inch (1953-59) . . .	NiB $5540	Ex $4546	Gd $3172
Magnum, 20 ga. 3-inch (1953-59) . . .	NiB $6794	Ex $5568	Gd $3887
Cust. built/deluxe gr., 12 ga.(1933-59)	NiB $8339	Ex $6775	Gd $4799
Cust. built/deluxe gr., 16 ga. (1933-59)	NiB $9539	Ex $7738	Gd $5448
Cust. built/deluxe gr., 20 ga. (1933-59)	NiB $10,290	Ex $8319	Gd $5798
Custom built/deluxe grade, 28 ga.(1933-59)			Very Rare*
Custom built/deluxe grade, .410 (1933-59)			Very Rare*

*Fewer than 100 sm. bore models (28 ga. and .410) were built, which precludes accurate pricing, but projected values could exceed $30,000. Such rare specimens should be authenticated by factory letter and/or independent appraisals.

SHOTGUNS

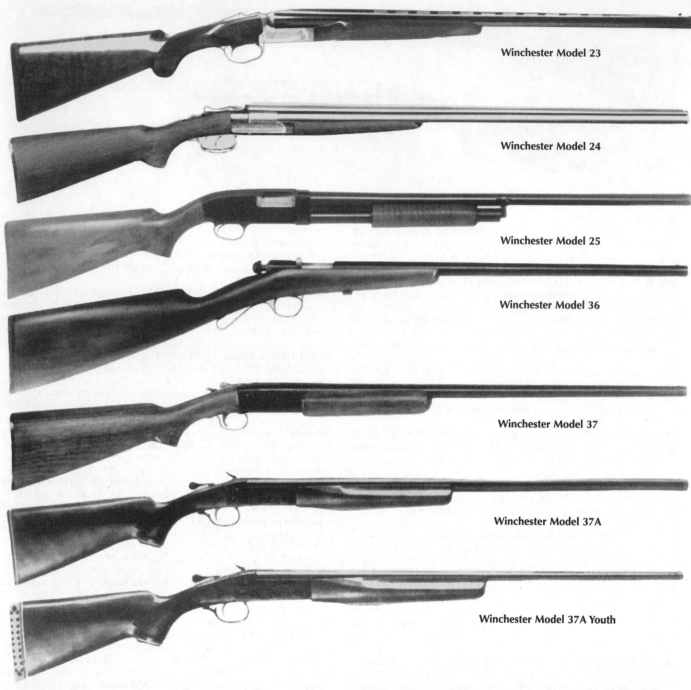

Winchester Model 23

Winchester Model 24

Winchester Model 25

Winchester Model 36

Winchester Model 37

Winchester Model 37A

Winchester Model 37A Youth

W/vent rib on 12 ga. models, add $750
W/vent rib on 16 ga. models, add $1650
W/vent rib on 20 ga. models, add $1145
W/double triggers ans extractors, deduct 30%
W/double trigger, selective ejection, deduct 20%
For Custom Engraving from this period:
No. 1 Pattern, add 25%
No. 2 Pattern, add 35%
No. 3 Pattern, add 50%
No. 4 Pattern, add 35%
No. 5 Pattern, add 65%
No. 6 Pattern, add 75%

MODEL 21 CUSTOM, PIGEON, GRAND AMERICAN (CUSTOM SHOP SERIES - PRODUCTION 1959 TO 1981)

Since 1959 the Model 21 has been offered through the Custom Shop in deluxe models. (Custom, Pigeon, Grand American) on special order. General specifications same as for Model 21 standard models except these custom guns have full fancy American walnut stock and forearm with fancy checkering, finely polished and hand-smoothed working parts, etc.; engraving inlays, carved stocks and other extras are available at additional cost. Made 1959 to 1981.
Custom grade, 12 ga. . . . . NiB $10,071 Ex $8126 Gd $5638
Custom grade, 16 ga. . . . . NiB $15,161 Ex $12,200 Gd $8410
Custom grade, 20 ga. . . . . NiB $13,533 Ex $10,892 Gd $7514

Winchester
Model 40 Skeet

Winchester
Model 41 Deluxe

Pigeon grade, 12 ga. . . . . NiB $15,479 Ex $12,452 Gd $8580
Pigeon grade, 16 ga. . . . . NiB $21,444 Ex $17,195 Gd $11,757
Pigeon grade, 20 ga. . . . . NiB $19,835 Ex $15,907 Gd $10,881
Grand American, 12 ga. . . . . NiB $23,361 Ex $18,738 Gd $12,822
Grand American, 16 ga. . . . . NiB $37,094 Ex $29,755 Gd $20,361
Grand American, 20 ga. . . . . NiB $27,660 Ex $29,655 Gd $15,183
Grand American 3-barrel Set . . . . $23,175 to $39,140
Small Bore Models
(28 ga. And .410) . . . . Very Rare*
*Fewer than 20 Small Bore models (28 ga. and .410) were built dur-
ing this period, which precludes accurate pricing, but projected val-
ues could exceed $35,000. Such rare specimens should be authen-
ticated by factory letter and/or independent appraisals.
For Custom Shop Engraving from this period:
#1 Pattern, add 10%
#2 Pattern, add 15%
#3 Pattern, add 25%
#4 Pattern, add 35%
#5 Pattern, add 45%
#6 Pattern, add 50%

MODEL 21 - U.S.R.A. CUSTOM-BUILT SERIES (CUSTOM SHOP PRODUCTION 1982 TO DATE)

Individual model designations for the Model 21 (made from 1931 to
1982) were changed when U. S. Repeating Arms Company assumed
production. The new model nomenclature for the Custom/Built
catagory, includes: Standard Custom, Special Custom and Grand
American — all of which are available on special order through the
Custom Shop. General specifications remained the same on these
consolidated model variations and included the addition of a Small
Bore 2-Barrel Set (28/.410) and a 3-Barrel Set (20/28/.410). Made
1982 to date.
Custom Built -
Standard Custom.. . . . . NiB $6630 Ex $5390 Gd $3792
Custom Built -
Special Custom . . . . NiB $7889 Ex $6407 Gd $4492
Custom Built - Grand American . . . . . . NiB $13,849 Ex $11,125 Gd $7664
Custom Built - Grand
American 2-barrel set. . . . . NiB $45,499 Ex $36,498 Gd $24,979
Custom Built - Grand
American 3-barrel set. . . . . NiB $68,294 Ex $54,775 Gd $37,471
The values shown above represent the basic model in each catago-
ry. Since many customers took advantage of the custom built
options, individual gun appointments vary and values will need to
be adjusted accordingly. For this reason, individual appraisals
should be obtained on all subject firearms.
MODEL 23 SIDE-BY-SIDE SHOTGUN
Boxlock. Single trigger. Automatic safety. Gauges: 12, 20, 28, .410.
Bbls.: 25.5-, 26-, 28-inch with fixed chokes or Winchoke tubes.

Weight: 5.88 to 7 lbs. Checkered American walnut buttstock and
forend. Made in 1979 for Olin at its Olin-Kodensha facility, Japan.
Classic 23 — Gold inlay, engraved . . . . NiB $2650 Ex $2395 Gd $2210
Custom 23 — Plain receiver,
Winchoke system . . . . NiB $1321 Ex $1090 Gd $795
Heavy Duck 23 — Standard . . . . NiB $2600 Ex $2224 Gd $1902
Lightweight 23 — Classic . . . . NiB $1940 Ex $1665 Gd $1183
Light Duck 23 — Standard . . . . NiB $2890 Ex $2581 Gd $2129
Light Duck 23 — 12 ga. Golden Quail . . NiB $2779 Ex $2472 Gd $21337
Light Duck 23 — .410 Golden Quail . . . . . NiB $4351 Ex $4145 Gd $3815
Custom Set 23 — 20 & 28 ga.. . . . . NiB $6000 Ex $4877 Gd $3415

MODEL 24 HAMMERLESS DOUBLE
Boxlock. Double triggers. Plain extractors. Auto safety. Gauges: 12, 16, 20.
Bbls.: 26-inch IC/M; 28-inch M/F (also IC/M in 12 ga. only); 30-inch M
and F in 12 ga. only. Weight: About 7.5 lbs., 12 ga. Metal bead front sight.
Plain pistol-grip stock, semi-beavertail forearm. Made from 1939 to 1957.
Model 24, 12 ga. . . . . NiB $825 Ex $650 Gd $479
Model 24, 16 ga. . . . . NiB $989 Ex $709 Gd $519
Model 24, 20 ga. . . . . NiB $1111 Ex $874 Gd $668

MODEL 25 RIOT GUN . . . . NiB $550 Ex $404 Gd $358
Same as Model 25 Standard except has 20-inch cylinder bore bbl.,
12 ga. only. Made from 1949 to 1955.

MODEL 25 7550 . . . . Ex $404 Gd $358
Hammerless. Solid frame. 12 ga. only. Four round tubular maga-
zine. 28-in. Plain bbl.; IC, M or F choke. Weight: About 7.5 lbs.
Metal bead front sight. Plain pistol-grip stock, grooved slide handle. Made from 1949 to 1955.

MODEL 36 SINGLE-SHOT BOLT ACTION NiB $1720 Ex $1573 Gd $1395
Takedown. Uses 9mm Short or Long shot or ball cartridges interchangeably.
18-inch bbl. Plain stock. Weight: About 3 lbs. Made from 1920 to 1927.

MODEL 37 SINGLE-SHOT SHOTGUN
Semi-hammerless. Auto ejection. Takedown. Gauges: 12, 16, 20,
28, .410. Bbl. lengths: 28-, 30-, 32-inch in all gauges except .410;
26- or 28-inch in .410; all barrels plain with F choke. Weight: About
6.5 pounds, 12 ga. Made from 1937 to 1963.
12 ga. . . . . NiB $459 Ex $300 Gd $220
16 ga. . . . . NiB $459 Ex $300 Gd $220
20 ga. . . . . NiB $495 Ex $345 Gd $266
20 ga. (Youth w/red dot indicator) . . . . NiB $495 Ex $427 Gd $309
28 ga. (red letter only) . . . . NiB $2500 Ex $2353 Gd $1940
410 ga. . . . . NiB $650 Ex $507 Gd $398
Other "Red Letter" models, add 20%
W/32-inch bbl., add 15%

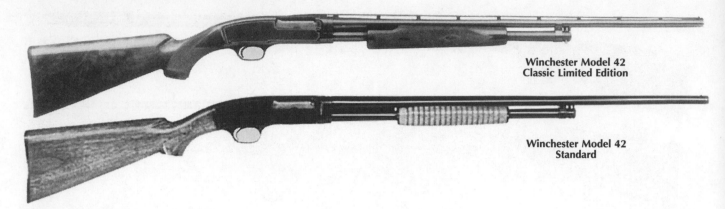

Winchester Model 42
Classic Limited Edition

Winchester Model 42
Standard

MODEL 37A SINGLE SHOT SHOTGUN
Similar to Model 370 except has engraved receiver and gold trigger, checkered pistol-grip stock, fluted forearm; 16 ga. available with 30-inch bbl. only. Made from 1973 to 1980.
Model 37A, 12, 16, or 20 ga. . . . . . NiB $450 Ex $261 Gd $190
Model 37A, 28 ga. . . . . NiB $2488 Ex $2231 Gd $2170
Model 37A, .410 . . . . NiB $650 Ex $472 Gd $298
W/32-inch bbl., add $20

MODEL 37A YOUTH. . . . . NiB $500 Ex $325 Gd $195
Similar to Model 370 Youth except has engraved receiver and gold trigger, checkered pistol-grip stock, fluted forearm. Made 1973 to 1980.

MODEL 40 STANDARD AUTOLOADER. . NiB $825 Ex $649 Gd $459
Streamlined receiver. Hammerless. Takedown. 12 ga. only. Four round tubular magazine. 28- or 30-inch bbl.; M or F choke. Weight: About 8 lbs. Bead sight on ramp. Plain pistol-grip stock, semi-beavertail forearm. Made from 1940 to 1941.

MODEL 40 SKEET GUN . . . . NiB $1096 Ex $892 Gd $645
Same general specifications as Model 40 Standard except has 24-inch plain bbl. w/Cutts Compensator and screw-in choke tube, checkered forearm and pistol grip, grip cap. Made 1940 to 1941.

MODEL 41 SINGLE-SHOT BOLT ACTION
Takedown. .410 bore. 2.5-inch chamber (chambered for 3-inch shells after 1932). 24-inch bbl., F choke. Plain straight stock standard. Also made in deluxe version. Made from 1920 to 1934.
Standard model . . . . NiB $722 Ex $593 Gd $429
Deluxe model . . . . NiB $872 Ex $698 Gd $500

MODEL 42 STANDARD GRADE
Hammerless. Takedown. .410 bore (3- or 2.5-inch shell). Tubular magazine holds five 3-inch or six 2.5-inch shells. 26- or 28-inch plain or solid-rib bbl.; cylinder bore, M or F choke. Weight: 5.8 to 6.5 lbs. Plain pistol-grip stock; grooved slide handle. Made from 1933 to 1963.
Model 42 Standard w/plain bbl NiB $2500 Ex $1935 Gd $1497
Model 42 Standard w/solid rib . . . . NiB $3750 Ex $3396 Gd $3184

MODEL 42 CLASSIC LTD. EDITION NiB $1725 Ex $1402 Gd $990
Gauge: .410 with 2.75-inch chamber. Bbl.: 26-inch vent rib; F choke. Weight: 7 lbs. Checkered walnut buttstock and forend. Engraved blue with gold inlays. Limited production of 850. Made from 1993.

MODEL 42 DELUXE. . . . . NiB $21,000 Ex $18,878 Gd $16,402
Same general specifications as the Model 42 Trap Grade except available w/vent rib after 1955. Finer finish throughout w/hand-smoothed action, engine-turned breech bolt and carrier, stock and extension slide handle of high grade walnut, fancy checkering, stock dimensions to individual specifications. Engraving and carving were

offered at extra cost. Made 1940-63. Note: Exercise caution on VR models not marked "DELUXE" on the bottom of the receiver. A factory letter will insure that the rib was installed during the initial manufacturing process. Unfortunately, factory authentication is not always possible due to missing or destroyed records. To further complicate this matter, not all VR ribs were installed by Winchester. From 1955-63, both Deluxe and Skeet Grade models were available with Simmons style ribs. After-market rib installations are common.

MODEL 42 PIGEON GRADE
This higher-grade designation is similar to the Deluxe grade and is available in all configurations. May be identified by engraved Pigeon located at the base of the magazine tube. Most production occurred in the late 1940's. *NOTE: To determine the value of any Model 42 Pigeon Grade, add 50 % to value listed under the specified Model 42 configuration.*

MODEL 42 SKEET GUN
Same general specifications as Model 42 Standard except has checkered straight or pistol-grip stock and extension slide handle, 26- or 28-inch plain, solid-rib or vent-rib bbl. May be choked F., Mod., Imp. Cyl. or Skeet. Note: Some Model 42 Skeet Guns are chambered for 2.5-inch shells only. Made from 1933 to 1963.
Model 42 Skeet
w/plain bbl. . . . . NiB $6000 Ex $4277 Gd $3552
Model 42 Skeet
w/solid rib . . . . NiB $6000 Ex $4277 Gd $3552
Model 42 Skeet
w/vent rib . . . . NiB $6673 Ex $5760 Gd $4656
W/2.5-inch
chamber, add 35%

MODEL 42 TRAP GRADE
This higher grade designation was available in both field and skeet configurations and is fitted w/deluxe wood w/trap grade checkering pattern and marked "TRAP" on bottom of receiver. Made 1934 to 1939. Superseded by the Deluxe model in 1940.
Model 42 Trap grade
w/plain bbl. . . . . NiB $25,000 Ex $22,840 Gd $20,035
Model 42 Trap grade
w/solid rib . . . . NiB $25,000 Ex $22,840 Gd $20,035
Model 42 Trap grain
w/vent rib. . . . . NiB $25,645 Ex $23,470 Gd $21,637

MODEL 50 FIELD GUN, VENT RIB . . . NiB $650 Ex $465 Gd $335
Same as Model 50 Standard except has vent rib.

MODEL 50 SKEET GUN . . . . NiB $1300 Ex $1123 Gd $973
Same as Model 50 Standard except has 26-inch vent-rib bbl. with SK choke, skeet-style stock of select walnut.

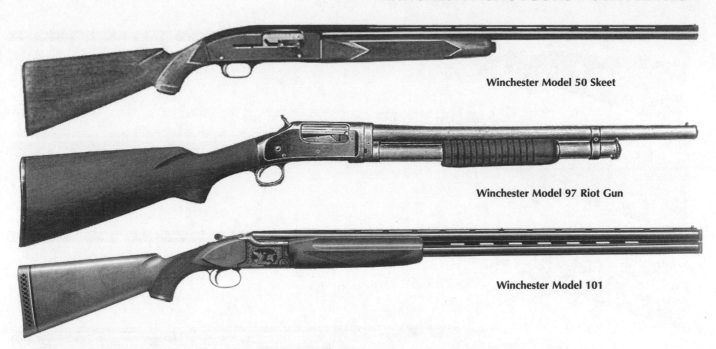

Winchester Model 50 Skeet

Winchester Model 97 Riot Gun

Winchester Model 101

MODEL 50 STANDARD GRADE . . . NiB $650 Ex $412 Gd $296
Non-recoiling bbl. and independent chamber. Gauges: 12 and 20. Two round tubular magazine. Bbl.: 12 ga. — 26-, 28-, 30-inch; 20 ga. — 26-, 28-inch; IC, SK, M, F choke. Checkered pistol-grip stock and forearm. Weight: About 7.75 lbs. Made from 1954 to 1961.

MODEL 50 TRAP GUN . . . . NiB $1300 Ex $1187 Gd $955
Same as Model 50 Standard except 12 ga. only, has 30-inch vent-rib bbl. with F choke, Monte Carlo stock of select walnut.

MODEL 59 AUTO-LOADING SHOTGUN . . . NiB $759 Ex $581 Gd $426
Gauge: 12. Magazine holds two rounds. Alloy receiver. Win-Lite steel and fiberglass bbl.: 26-inch IC, 28-inch M or F choke, 30-inch F choke; also furnished with 26-inch bbl. with Versalite choke (interchangeable F, M, IC tubes; one supplied with gun). Weight: About 6.5 lbs. Checkered pistol-grip stock and forearm. Made 1959 to 1965.

MODEL 1897 BUSH GUN
Takedown or solid frame. Same general specifications as standard Model 97 except w/26-inch cylinder bore bbl. Made 1897 to 1931.
Model 97 Bush Gun w/solid frame   NiB $882 Ex $602 Gd $477
Model 97 Bush Gun takedown . . . . NiB $1144 Ex $912 Gd $640

MODEL1897 RIOT GUN
Takedown or solid frame. Same general specifications as standard Model 97 except 12 ga. only, 20-inch cylinder bore bbl. Made from 1898 to 1935.
Model 97 Riot Gun w/solid frame . . NiB $1349 Ex $1073 Gd $760
Model 97 Riot Gun takedown . . . . NiB $1157 Ex $945 Gd $673

MODEL 1897 TRAP, TOURNAMENT AND PIGEON
These higher grade models offer higher overall quality than the standard grade. Made from 1897 to 1939.
Standard Trap grade . . . . NiB $1589 Ex $1259 Gd $888
Special Trap grade . . . . NiB $1664 Ex $1413 Gd $993
Tournament grade (Black Diamond) . . . . NiB $2739 Ex $2207 Gd $1550
Pigeon grade . . . . NiB $5192 Ex $4200 Gd $2931

MODEL 97 TRENCH GUN . . . . NiB $2158 Ex $1757 Gd $1222
Solid frame. Same as Model 97 Riot Gun except has handguard and is equipped with a bayonet. World War I government issue,

from 1917 to 1918.
Model 97 Trench Gun
w/solid frame . . . . NiB $3143 Ex $2540 Gd $1769
Model 97 Trench Gun takedown. . . . NiB $1338 Ex $1100 Gd $773

MODEL 1897
SLIDE-ACTION REPEATER
Standard Grade. Takedown or solid frame. Gauges: 12 and 16. Five-round tubular magazine. Bbl.: Plain; 26 to 32 inches, the latter in 12 ga. only; choked F to Cyl. Weight: About 7.75 lbs. (12 ga. w/28-inch barrel). Plain pistol-grip stock, grooved slide handle. Made from 1897 to 1957.
Model 97, 12 ga. w/solid frame . . NiB $1000 Ex $766 Gd $547
Model 97, 16 ga. w/solid frame . . NiB $1000 Ex $766 Gd $547
Model 97, 12 ga. takedown. . . . . . NiB $1250 Ex $990 Gd $764
Model 97, 16 ga. takedown. . . . . . NiB $1250 Ex $990 Gd $764

NOTE: All Winchester Model 101s are mfd. for Olin Corp. at its Olin-Kodensha facility in Tochigi, Japan. Production for Olin Corp. stopped in Nov. 1987. Importation of Model 101s was continued by Classic Doubles under that logo until 1990. See separate heading for additional data.

MODEL 101 DIAMOND
GRADE TARGET . . . . NiB $1879 Ex $1498 Gd $1071
Similar to Model 101 Standard except silvered frame and Winchoke interchangeable choke tubes. Made from 1981 to 1990.

MODEL 101 FIELD GUN O/U
Boxlock. Engraved receiver. Auto ejectors. Single selective trigger. Combination bbl. selector and safety. Gauges: 12 and 28, 2.75-inch chambers; 20 and .410, 3-inch chambers. Vent rib bbls.: 30- (12 ga. only) and 26.5-inch, IC/M. Weight: 6.25 to 7.75 lbs. depending on gauge and bbl. length. Hand-checkered French walnut and forearm. Made from 1963 to 1981. Gauges other than 12 introduced 1966.
12 and 20 ga. . . . . NiB $995 Ex $757 Gd $610
28 and .410 ga. . . . . NiB $1491 Ex $1042 Gd $838
12 and 20 ga. mag. . . . . NiB $1119 Ex $914 Gd $652

SHOTGUNS

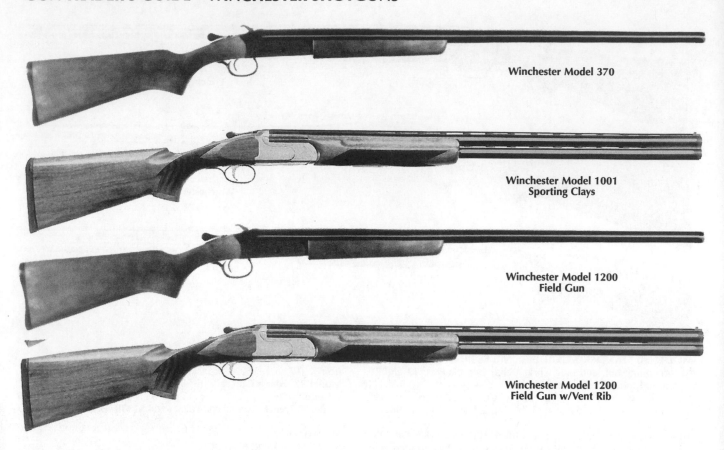

Winchester Model 370

Winchester Model 1001
Sporting Clays

Winchester Model 1200
Field Gun

Winchester Model 1200
Field Gun w/Vent Rib

MODEL 101 QUAIL SPECIAL O/U
Same specifications as small-frame Model 101 except in 28 and .410 ga. with 3-inch chambers. 25.5-inch bbls. with choke tubes (28 ga.) or M/F chokes (.410). Imported from Japan in 1984 to 1987.
12 ga. . . . . NiB $2921 Ex $2679 Gd $2328
20 ga. . . . . NiB $3538 Ex $3204 Gd $3049
28 ga. . . . . NiB $5250 Ex $4731 Gd $3968
.410 ga. NiB $4500 Ex $3939 Gd $3568

MODEL 101 SHOTGUN/RIFLE
COMBINATION GUN . . . . NiB $2790 Ex $2592 Gd $2206
12-ga. Winchoke bbl. on top and rifle bbl. chambered for .30-06 on bottom (over/under). 25-inch bbls. Engraved receiver. Hand checkered walnut stock and forend. Weight: 8.5 lbs. Mfd. for Olin Corp. in Japan.

MODEL 370
SINGLE-SHOT SHOTGUN . . . . NiB $203 Ex $129 Gd $98
Visible hammer. Auto ejector. Takedown. Gauges: 12, 16, 20, 28, .410. 2.75-inch chambers in 16 and 28 ga., 3-inch in other ga. Bbls.: 12 ga., 30-, 32- or 36-inch,16 ga; 30- or 32-inch; 20 and 28 ga., 28-inch; .410 bore, 26-inch, all F choke. Weight: 5.5-6.25 lbs. Plain pistol-grip stock and forearm. Made from 1968 to 1973.

MODEL 370 YOUTH
Same as standard Model 370 except has 26-inch bbl. and 12.5-inch stock with recoil pad; 20 gauge with IM choke, .410 bore with F choke. Made from 1968 to 1973.
Model 370, 12,
16, or 20 ga. . . . . NiB $152 Ex $144 Gd $107
Model 37A, 28 ga. . . . . NiB $223 Ex $192 Gd $141
Model 37A, .410 ga. . . . . NiB $252 Ex $200 Gd $165

MODEL 1001 O/U SHOTGUN
Boxlock. 12 ga., 2.75- or 3-inch chambers. Bbls.: 28- or 30-inch vent rib; WinPlus choke tubes. Weight: 7-7.75 lbs. Checkered walnut buttstock and forend. Blued finish with scroll engraved receiver. Made from 1993 to 1998.
Field model
(28-inch bbl., 3-inch) . . . . NiB $977 Ex $883 Gd $633
Sporting
Clays . . . . NiB $1080 Ex $980 Gd $700
Sporting
Clays Lite . . . . NiB $1003 Ex $911 Gd $653

MODEL 1200
DEER GUN . . . . NiB $257 Ex $207 Gd $136
Same as standard Model 1200, except has special 22-inch bbl. with rifle-type sights, for rifled slug or buckshot; 12 ga. only. Weight: 6.5 lbs. Made from 1965 to 1974.

MODEL 1200 DEFENDER SERIES
SLIDE-ACTION SECURITY SHOTGUNS
Hammerless. 12 ga. w/3-inch chamber. 18-inch bbl. w/cylinder bore and metal front bead or rifle sights. Four- or 7-round magazine. Weight: 5.5 to 6.75 lbs. 25.6 inches (PG Model) or 38.6 inches overall. Matte blue finish. Synthetic pistol grip or walnut finished hardwood buttstock w/grooved synthetic or hardwood slide handle. NOTE: Even though the 1200 series was introduced in 1964 and was supplanted by the Model 1300 in 1978, the Security series (including the Defender model) was marketed under 1200 series alpha-numeric product codes (G1200DM2R) until 1989. In 1990, the same Defender model was marketed under a 4-digit code (7715) and was then advertised in the 1300 series.

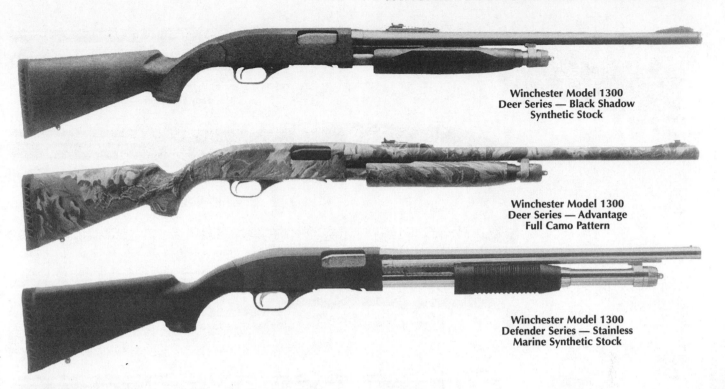

**Winchester Model 1300
Deer Series — Black Shadow
Synthetic Stock**

**Winchester Model 1300
Deer Series — Advantage
Full Camo Pattern**

**Winchester Model 1300
Defender Series — Stainless
Marine Synthetic Stock**

Defender
w/hardwood stock,bead sight . . . . . NiB $246 Ex $204 Gd $150
Defender
W/hardwood stock, rifle sights . . . . NiB $246 Ex $204 Gd $150
Defender model w/pistol-grip stock . . . NiB $246 Ex $204 Gd $150
Defender Combo model
W/extra 28-inch plain bbl. . . . . NiB $297 Ex $245 Gd $178
Defender Combo model
W/extra 28-inch vent rib bbl. . . . . . NiB $337 Ex $260 Gd $189

MODEL 1200 FIELD GUN — MAGNUM
Same as standard Model 1200 except chambered for 3-inch 12 and 20 ga. magnum shells; plain or vent-rib bbl., 28- or 30-inch, F choke. Weight: 7.38 to 7.88 lbs. Made from 1964 to 1983.
With plain bbl. . . . . NiB $220 Ex $170 Gd $140
With vent rib bbl. . . . . NiB $250 Ex $190 Gd $160
Add for Winchester recoil reduction system $65

MODEL 1200 RANGER
SLIDE-ACTION SHOTGUN . . . . NiB $220 Ex $170 Gd $140
Hammerless. 12 and 20 ga.; 3-inch chambers. Walnut finished hardwood stock, ribbed forearm. 28-inch vent-rib bbl.; Winchoke system. Weight: 7.25 lbs. Made from 1982 to 1990 by U. S. Repeating Arms.

MODEL 1200 RANGER YOUTH
SLIDE-ACTION SHOTGUN . . . . NiB $220 Ex $170 Gd $140
Same general specifications as standard Ranger Slide-Action except chambered for 20 ga. only, has Four round magazine, recoil pad on buttstock, weight: 6.5 lbs. Mfd. by U. S. Repeating Arms.

MODEL 1200 SLIDE-ACTION FIELD GUN
Front-locking rotary bolt. Takedown. Four round magazine. Gauges: 12, 16, 20 (2.75-inch chamber). Bbl.: Plain or vent rib; 26-, 28-, 30-inch; IC, M, F choke or with Winchoke (interchangeable tubes IC-M-F). Weight: 6.5 to 7.25 lbs. Checkered pistol-grip stock and fore arm (slide handle), recoil pad; also avail. 1966 to 1970 w/Winchester recoil reduction system (Cycolac stock), Made from

1964 to 1983.
With plain bbl. . . . . NiB $200 Ex $157 Gd $109
With vent rib bbl. . . . . NiB $220 Ex $177 Gd $129
Add for Winchester recoil reduction system $65
Add for Winchoke $25

MODEL 1200 STAINLESS
MARINE SERIES SLIDE-ACTION
SECURITY SHOTGUN
Similar to Model 1200 Defender except w/6-round magazine. 18-inch bbl. of ordnance stainless steel w/cylinder bore and rifle sights. Weight: 7 lbs. Bright chrome finish. Synthetic pistol grip or walnut finished hardwood buttstock w/grooved synthetic or hardwood slide handle.Made from 1984 to 1990.
Marine model w/hardwood stock . . NiB $255 Ex $202 Gd $125
Marine model w/pistol-grip stock . NiB $255 Ex $202 Gd $125

MODEL 1200 STAINLESS
POLICE SERIES SLIDE-ACTION
SECURITY SHOTGUN
Similar to Model 1200 Defender except w/6-round magazine. 18-inch bbl. of ordnance stainless steel w/cylinder bore and rifle sights. Weight: 7 lbs. Matte chrome finish. Synthetic pistol grip or walnut-finished hardwood buttstock w/grooved synthetic or hardwood slide handle.Made from 1984-90.
Police model w/hardwood stock . . . NiB $255 Ex $202 Gd $125
Police model w/pistol grip stock . . . NiB $255 Ex $202 Gd $125

MODEL 1200 TRAP GUN
Same as standard Model 1200 except 12 gauge only. Has 2-round magazine, 30-inch vent-rib bbl., Full choke or 28-inch with Winchoke. Semi-fancy walnut stock, straight Made from 1965-73. Also available 1966 to 1970 w/Winchester recoil reduction system.
With straight-trap stock. . . . . NiB $305 Ex $215 Gd $155
With Monte Carlo stock . . . . NiB $305 Ex $215 Gd $155
Add for Winchester recoil reduction system $75
Add for Winchoke $30

Winchester Model 1300
Lady Defender — Synthetic Full Stock

Winchester Model 1300
Lady Defender — Synthetic Pistol Grip Stock

Winchester Model 1300
Defender 5-Shot Combo

Winchester Model 1300
Turkey Gun

Winchester Model 1300
XTR w/Winchoke

Winchester Model 1300
Magnum Waterfowl

MODEL 1200 RANGER
COMBINATION SHOTGUN . . . . . . **NiB $354 Ex $260 Gd $191**
Same as Ranger Deer combination except has one 28-inch vent-rib bbl. with M choke and one 18-inch Police Cyl. bore bbl. Made 1987 to 1990.

MODEL 1200 SKEET GUN . . . . **NiB $364 Ex $305 Gd $228**
Same as standard Model 1200 except 12 and 20 ga. only; has 2-round magazine, specially tuned trigger, 26-inch vent-rib bbl. SK choke, semi-fancy walnut stock and forearm. Weight: 7.25 to 7.5 lbs. Made 1965 to 1973. Also avail. 1966 to 1970 with Winchester recoil reduction system (add $50 to value).

MODEL 1300 CAMOPACK . . . . **NiB $396 Ex $350 Gd $252**
Gauge: 12.3-inch Magnum. Four round magazine. Bbls.: 30-and 22-inch with Winchoke system. Weight: 7 lbs. Laminated stock with Win-Cam camouflage green, cut checkering, recoil pad, swivels and sling. Made from 1987-88.

MODEL 1300 DEER SERIES
Similar to standard Model 1300 except 12 or 20 ga. only w/special 22-inch cyl. bore or rifled bbl. and rifle-type sights. Weight: 6.5 lbs. Checkered walnut or synthetic stock w/satin walnut, black or Advantage Full Camo Pattern finish. Matte blue or full-camo metal finish. Made from 1994 to 2006.
Deer model
w/walnut stock (intro. 1994) . . . . . . **NiB $359 Ex $309 Gd $238**
Black Shadow Deer
w/synthetic stock (intro. 1994) . . . . **NiB $300 Ex $238 Gd $176**
Advantage Full Camo
Pattern (1995-98) . . . . **NiB $356 Ex $317 Gd $230**
Deer Combo
w/22- and 28-inch bbls. (1994-98) . . . . **NiB $446 Ex $389 Gd $275**
W/rifled bbl. (intro. 1996), add $25

MODEL 1300 DEFENDER SERIES
Gauges: 12 or 20 ga. 18- 24- 28-inch vent rib bbl. w/3-inch chamber. Four-, 7- or 8- round magazine. Weight: 5.6 to 7.4 lbs. Blued, chrome or matte stainless finish. Wood or synthetic stock. Made from 1985 to 2006.
Combo model . . . . **NiB $370 Ex $283 Gd $203**
Hardwood stock model . . . . **NiB $270 Ex $241 Gd $178**
Synthetic pistol-grip model . . . . **NiB $270 Ex $283 Gd $203**
Synthetic stock . . . . **NiB $255 Ex $201 Gd $185**
Lady Defender synthetic
stock (made 1996) . . . . **NiB $235 Ex $207 Gd $195**
Lady Defender synthetic
Pistol-grip (made 1996) . . . . **NiB $235 Ex $207 Gd $179**
Stainless marine synthetic stock . . **NiB $480 Ex $377 Gd $270**

MODEL 1300 DELUXE SLIDE-ACTION
Gauges: 12 and 20 w/3-inch chamber. Four round magazine. Bbl.:22, 26 or 28 inch vent rib bbl. w/Winchoke tubes. Weight: 6.5 lbs. Checkered walnut buttstock and forend w/high luster finish. Polished blue metal finish with roll-engraved receiver. Made from 1984 to 2006.
Model 1300 Deluxe
w/high gloss finish . . . . **NiB $427 Ex $329 Gd $237**
Model 1300 Ladies/Youth
w/22-inch bbl.(disc. 1992) . . . . **NiB $376 Ex $294 Gd $214**

MODEL 1300 FEATHERWEIGHT SLIDE-ACTION SHOTGUN
Hammerless. Takedown. Four round magazine. Gauges: 12 and 20 (3-inch chambers). Bbls.: 22, 26 or 28 inches w/plain or vent rib w/Winchoke tubes. Weight: 6.38 to 7 lbs. Checkered walnut butt-stock, grooved slide handle. Made from 1978 to 1994.
Model 1300 FW (plain bbl.) . . . . . . **NiB $300 Ex $267 Gd $195**
Model 1300 FW (vent rib) . . . . **NiB $300 Ex $267 Gd $195**
Model 1300 FW XTR . . . . **NiB $300 Ex $277 Gd $230**

MODEL 1300 RANGER SERIES
Gauges: 12 or 20 ga. w/3-inch chamber. Five round magazine. 22-(Rifled), 26- or 28-inch vent-rib bbl. w/Winchoke tubes. Weight: 7.25 lbs. Blued finish. Walnut-finished hardwood buttstock and forend. Made from 1984 to 2006.
Standard model . . . . **NiB $285 Ex $258 Gd $199**
Combo model . . . . **NiB $394 Ex $324 Gd $234**
Ranger Deer combo
(D&T w/rings & bases) . . . . **NiB $350 Ex $289 Gd $244**
Ranger Ladies/Youth . . . . **NiB $285 Ex $208 Gd $173**

MODEL 1300 SLIDE-ACTION FIELD GUN
Takedown w/front-locking rotary bolt. Gauges: 12, 20 w/3-inch chamber. Four round magazine. Bbl.: Vent rib; 26-, 28-, 30-inch w/ Win-choke tubes IC-M-F). Weight: 7.25 lbs. Checkered walnut or synthetic stock w/standard, black or Advantage Full Camo Pattern finish. Matte blue or full-camo metal finish. Made from 1994 to 2006.
Model 1300 Standard Field
(w/walnut stock) . . . . **NiB $353 Ex $250 Gd $184**
Model 1300 Black Shadow
(w/black synthetic stock) . . . . **NiB $275 Ex $220 Gd $162**
Model 1300 Advantage Camo . . . . . **NiB $340 Ex $301 Gd $217**

MODEL 1300 SLUG HUNTER SERIES
Similar to standard Model 1300 except chambered 12 ga. only w/special 22-inch smoothbore w/sabot-rifled choke tube or fully rifled bbl. w/rifle-type sights. Weight: 6.5 lbs. Checkered walnut, hardwood or laminated stock w/satin walnut or WinTuff finish. Matte blue metal finish. Made from 1988 to 1994.
Slug Hunter w/hardwood stock . . . **NiB $364 Ex $284 Gd $206**
Slug Hunter w/laminated stock . . . . **NiB $397 Ex $326 Gd $236**
Slug Hunter w/walnut stock . . . . . . **NiB $380 Ex $305 Gd $222**
Whitetails Unlimited
w/beavertail forend . . . . **NiB $399 Ex $310 Gd $245**
W/sabot-rifled choke tubes, add $15

MODEL 1300 TURKEY SERIES
Gauges: 12 or 20 ga. 22-inch bbl. w/3-inch chamber. Four round magazine. 43 inches overall. Weight: 6.4 to 6.75 lbs. Buttstock and magazine cap, sling studs w/Cordura sling. Drilled and tapped to accept scope base. Checkered walnut, synthetic or laminated wood stock w/low luster finish. Matte blue or full camo finish. Made from 1985 to 2006.
Turkey Advantage Full Camo . . . . **NiB $295 Ex $205 Gd $173**
Turkey Realtree All-Purpose Full Camo . . . . **NiB $399 Ex $318 Gd $231**
Turkey Realtree Gray
All-Purpose Full Camo . . . . **NiB $430 Ex $329 Gd $237**
Turkey Realtree All-Purpose
Camo (matte metal) . . . . **NiB $35 Ex $284 Gd $206**
Turkey Black Shadow
(black synthetic stock) . . . . **NiB $259 Ex $208 Gd $155**
Turkey Win-Cam (green laminated wood) . . . **NiB $353 Ex $299 Gd $217**
Turkey Win-Cam Combo
(22- and 30-inch bbls.) . . . . **NiB $365 Ex $310 Gd $237**
Turkey Win-Cam NWTF
(22- and 30-inch bbls.) . . . . **NiB $425 Ex $320 Gd $247**
Turkey Win-Cam Youth/
Ladies model (20 ga.) . . . . **NiB $472 Ex $362 Gd $580**
Turkey Win-Tuf (br. laminated wood) . . **NiB $379 Ex $307 Gd $224**

MODEL 1300 WATERFOWL SLIDE-ACTION SHOTGUN
Similar to 1300 Standard model except has 28- or 30-inch vent rib bbl. w/Winchoke tubes. Weight: 7 lbs. Matte blue metal finish. Checkered walnut finished hardwood or brown laminated Win-Tuffwood stock w/camo sling, swivels and recoil pad. Made from 1984 to 1992.
Model 1300 Waterfowl w/hardwood stock . . . **NiB $295 Ex $204 Gd $176**
Model 1300 Waterfowl w/laminated stock . . . . **NiB $295 Ex $204 Gd $176**

SHOTGUNS

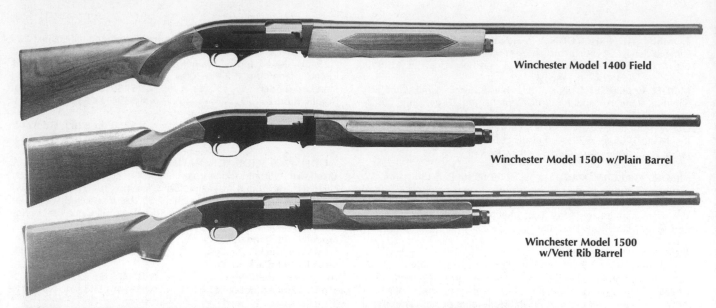

Winchester Model 1400 Field

Winchester Model 1500 w/Plain Barrel

Winchester Model 1500
w/Vent Rib Barrel

MODEL 1300 XTR SLIDE-ACTION . NiB $460 Ex $360 Gd $260
Hammerless. Takedown. Four shot magazine. Gauges: 12 and 20 (3-inch chambers). Bbl.: Plain or vent rib; 28-inch bbls.; Winchoke (interchangeable tubes IC-M-F). Weight: About 7 lbs. Disc. 2006.

MODEL 1400 AUTOMATIC FIELD GUN
Gas-operated. Front-locking rotary bolt. Takedown. Two round magazine. Gauges: 12, 16, 20 (2.75-inch chamber). Bbl.: Plain or vent rib; 26-, 28-, 30-inch; IC, M, F choke, or with Winchoke (interchangeable tubes IC-M-F). Weight: 6.5 to 7.25 lbs. Checkered pistol-grip stock and forearm, recoil pad, also available with Winchester recoil reduction system (Cycolac stock). Made from 1964 to 1968.
With plain bbl. . . . . NiB $276 Ex $185 Gd $157
With vent rib bbl. . . . . NiB $316 Ex $190 Gd $157
Add for Winchester recoil reduction system $100
Add for Winchoke $25

MODEL 1400 DEER GUN . . . . NiB $264 Ex $204 Gd $156
Same as standard Model 1400 except has special 22-inch bbl. with rifle-type sights, for rifle slug or buckshot; 12 ga. only. Weight: 6.25 lbs. Made from 1965 to 1968.

MODEL 1400 MARK II DEER GUN. NiB $394 Ex $324 Gd $234
Same general specifications as Model 1400 Deer Gun. Made from 1968-73.

MODEL 1400 MARK II FIELD GUN
Same general specifications as Model 1400 Field Gun, except not chambered for 16 gauge; Winchester Recoil Reduction System not available after 1970. Only 28-inch barrels w/Winchoke offered after 1973. Made from 1968 to 1978.
With plain bbl. . . . . NiB $354 Ex $300 Gd $217
With plain bbl. and Winchoke. . . . . NiB $391 Ex $321 Gd $235
With vent-rib bbl. . . . . NiB $461 Ex $337 Gd $243
With vent-rib bbl. and Winchoke . . NiB $440 Ex $360 Gd $260
Add for Winchester recoil reduction system $100

MODEL 1400 MARK II
SKEET GUN. . . . . NiB $459 Ex $360 Gd $270
Same general specifications as Model 1400 Skeet Gun. Made from 1968 to 1973.

MODEL 1400 MARK II TRAP GUN
Same general specifications as Model 1400 Trap Gun except also furnished with 28-inch bbl. and Winchoke. Winchester recoil reduction system not available after 1970. Made from 1968 to 1973.
With straight stock . . . . NiB $544 Ex $414 Gd $299
With Monte Carlo stock . . . . NiB $571 Ex $452 Gd $326
With Winchester recoil reduction system, add $100
With Winchoke, add $25

MODEL 1400 MARK II UTILITY SKEET NiB $446 Ex $324 Gd $238
Same general specifications as Model 1400 Mark II Skeet Gun except has stock and forearm of field grade walnut. Made 1970 to 1973.

MODEL 1400 MARK II UTILITY TRAP . NiB $446 Ex $352 Gd $257
Same as Model 1400 Mark II Trap Gun except has Monte Carlo stock/forearm of field grade walnut. Made from 1970 to 1973.

MODEL 1400 RANGER
SEMIAUTOMATIC SHOTGUN . . . . NiB $284 Ex $251 Gd $185
Gauges: 12, 20. Two round magazine. 28-inch vent rib bbl. with F choke. Overall length: 48.63 inches. Weight: 7 to 7.25 lbs. Walnut finish, hardwood stock and forearm with cut checkering. Made from 1984 to 1990 by U. S. Repeating Arms.

MODEL 1400 RANGER SEMIAUTOMATIC
DEER SHOTGUN. . . . . NiB $427 Ex $262 Gd $192
Same general specifications as Ranger Semiautomatic except 24.13-inch plain bbl. with rifle sights. Mfd. by U.S. Repeating Arms.

MODEL 1400 SKEET GUN . . . . NiB $425 Ex $353 Gd $254
Same as standard Model 1400 except 12 and 20 ga. only, 26-inch vent-rib bbl., SK choke, semi-fancy walnut stock and forearm. Weight: 7.25 to 7.5 lbs. Made from 1965 to 1968. Also available with Winchester recoil reduction system (add $50 to value).

MODEL 1400 TRAP GUN
Same as standard Model 1400 except 12 ga. only with 30-inch vent-rib bbl., F choke. Semi-fancy walnut stock, straight or Monte Carlo trap style. Also available with Winchester recoil reduction system. Weight: About 8.25 lbs. Made from 1965 to 1968.
With straight stock . . . . NiB $360 Ex $288 Gd $197
With Monte Carlo stock . . . . NiB $375 Ex $300 Gd $214
Add for Winchester recoil red. system. $100

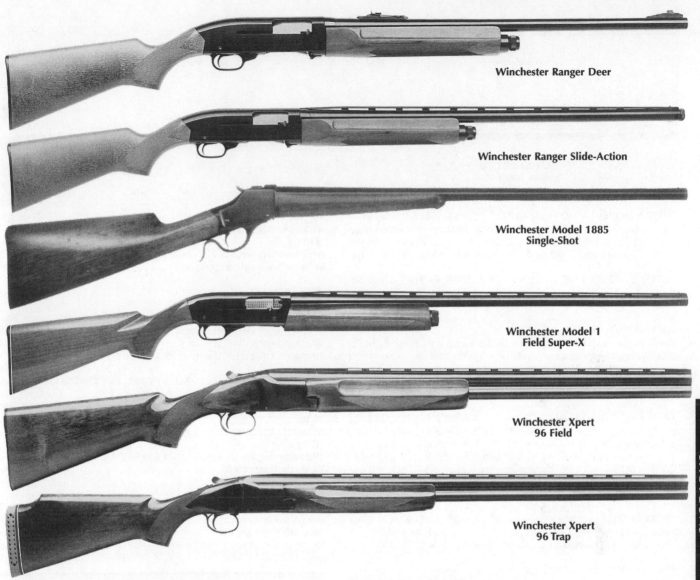

Winchester Ranger Deer

Winchester Ranger Slide-Action

Winchester Model 1885
Single-Shot

Winchester Model 1
Field Super-X

Winchester Xpert
96 Field

Winchester Xpert
96 Trap

SHOTGUNS

MODEL 1500 XTR SEMIAUTOMATIC . . NiB $330 Ex $271 Gd $219
Gas-operated. Gauges: 12 and 20 (2.75-inch chambers). Bbl.: Plain or vent rib; 28-inch; WinChoke (interchangeable tubes IC-M-F). American walnut stock and forend; checkered grip and forend. Weight: 7.25 lbs. Made from 1978 to 1982.

MODEL 1885
SINGLE-SHOT SHOTGUN . . . . NiB $4034 Ex $3280 Gd $2293
Falling-block action, same as Model 1885 Rifle. Highwall receiver. Solid frame or takedown. 20 ga. 3-inch chamber. 26-inch bbl.; plain, matted or matted rib; Cyl. bore, M or F choke. Weight: About 5.5 lbs. Straight-grip stock and forearm. Made from 1914 to 1916.

MODEL 1887 LEVER-ACTION SHOTGUN
First of John Browning's patent shotgun designs produced by Winchester. 10 or 12 ga. on casehardened frame fitted w/20-inch blued, cylinder bore or full choke 30- or 32-inch bbl. Plain or checkered walnut stock and forend. Made from 1887 to 1901.
Model 1887 10 or 12 ga. standard . . . . NiB $3854 Ex $3595 Gd $3081
Model 1887 10 or 12 ga. deluxe. . . NiB $8166 Ex $7342 Gd $6057
Model 1887 10 or 12 ga. riot gun . . . . NiB $2480 Ex $2003 Gd $1418

W/.70-150 Ratchet rifled bbl.
.70 cal. rifle/87 produced) . . . . NiB $3529 Ex $2840 Gd $2011
W/3 or 4 blade Del. Damascus bbl., add. 20%

MODEL 1901 LEVER-ACTION SHOTGUN
Same general specifications as Model 1887, of which this is a redesigned version. 10 ga. only. Made from 1901 to 1920.
Model 1901 Standard. . . . . NiB $3850 Ex $3678 Gd $3271
Model 1901 Deluxe . . . . NiB $5369 Ex $4629 Gd $3076

MODEL 1911 AUTO-
LOADING SHOTGUN. . . . . NiB $610 Ex $549 Gd $423
Hammerless. Takedown. 12 gauge only. Four round tubular magazine. Bbl.: plain, 26- to 32-inch, standard borings. Weight: About 8.5 lbs. Plain or checkered pistol-grip stock and forearm. Made from 1911 to 1925.

RANGER DEER COMBINATION . . . NiB $357 Ex $268 Gd $193
Gauge: 12, 3-inch Magnum. Three round magazine. Bbl.: 24-inch Cyl. bore deer bbl. and 28-inch vent rib bbl. with WinChoke system. Weight: 7.25 lbs. Made from 1987 to 1990.

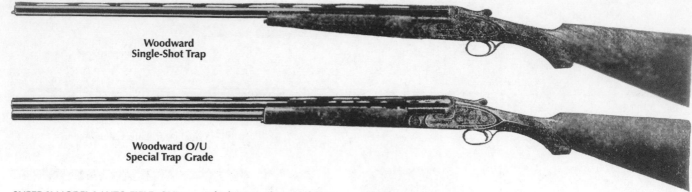

Woodward
Single-Shot Trap

Woodward O/U
Special Trap Grade

SUPER-X MODEL I AUTO FIELD GUN. . . . NiB $315 Ex $231 Gd $137
Gas-operated. Takedown.12 ga. 2.75-inch chamber Four round magazine. Bbl.: Vent rib 26-inch IC; 28-inch M or F; 30-inch F choke. Weight: About 7 lbs. Checkered pistol-grip stock. Made 1974 to 1984.

SUPER-X MODEL I SKEET GUN . . . NiB $840 Ex $645 Gd $459
Same as Super-X Field Gun except has 26-inch bbl., SK choke, skeet-style stock and forearm of select walnut. Made 1974 to 1984.

SUPER-X MODEL I TRAP GUN
Same as Super-X Field Gun except has 30-inch bbl., IM or F choke, trap-style stock (straight or Monte Carlo comb) and forearm of select walnut, recoil pad. Made from 1974 to 1984.
With straight stock . . . . NiB $659 Ex $514 Gd $367
With Monte Carlo stock   . . . . NiB $723 Ex $590 Gd $419

XPERT MODEL 96 O/U FIELD GUN . . . . . NiB $875 Ex $729 Gd $595
Boxlock action similar to Model 101. Plain receiver. Auto ejectors. Selective single trigger. Gauges: 12, 20. 3-inch chambers. Bbl.: Vent rib; 26-inch IC/M; 28-inch M/F, 30-inch F/F choke (12 ga. only). Weight: 6.25 to 8.25 lbs. depending on ga. and bbls. Checkered pistol-grip stock and forearm. Made from 1976-81 for Olin Corp. at its Olin-Kodensha facility in Japan.

XPERT MODEL 96 SKEET GUN. . . . NiB $875 Ex $697 Gd $530
Same as Xpert Field Gun except has 2.75-inch chambers, 27-inch bbls., SK choke, skeet-style stock and forearm. Made 1976 to 1981.

XPERT MODEL 96 TRAP GUN
Same as Xpert Field Gun except 12 ga. only, 2.75-inch chambers, has 30-inch bbls., IM/F or F/F choke, trap-style stock (straight or Monte Carlo comb) with recoil pad. Made from 1976 to 1981.
With straight stock . . . . NiB $875 Ex $809 Gd $582
With Monte Carlo stock   . . . . . . NiB $10410 Ex $828 Gd $595

JAMES WOODWARD & SONS —
London, England

James Woodward & Sons was acquired by James Purdey & Sons after World War II.

BEST QUALITY HAMMERLESS DOUBLE
Sidelock. Automatic ejectors. Double triggers or single trigger. Built to order in all standard gauges, bbl. lengths, boring and other specifications. Made as a field gun, pigeon and wildfowl gun, skeet gun or trap gun. Manufactured prior to World War II.
12 ga.
w/double triggers . . . . . . NiB $27,176 Ex $21,775 Gd $14,907
20 ga.
w/double triggers . . . . . . NiB $30,831 Ex $24,727 Gd $16,915

28 ga.
w/double triggers . . . . . . NiB $38,131 Ex $30,587 Gd $20,927
.410 ga.
w/double triggers . . . . . . NiB $43,156 Ex $34,575 Gd $23,655
W/selective single trigger, add 5%

**BEST QUALITY
O/U SHOTGUN**
Sidelock. Automatic ejectors. Double triggers or single trigger. Built to order in all standard gauges, bbl. lengths, boring and other specifications, including Special Trap Grade with vent rib. Woodward introduced this type of gun in 1908. Made until World War II.
12 ga.
w/double triggers . . . . . . NiB $29,831 Ex $23,725 Gd $16,365
20 ga.
w/double triggers . . . . . . NiB $40,103 Ex $32,162 Gd $21,998
28 ga.
w/double triggers . . . . . . NiB $52,722 Ex $42,287 Gd $28,931
.410 ga.
w/double triggers . . . . NiB $59,662 Ex $47,850 Gd $32,730
W/single trigger, add 5%

**BEST QUALITY
SINGLE-SHOT TRAP . . . . . . NiB $12,711 Ex $10,130 Gd $7054**
Sidelock. Mechanical features of the O/U gun. Vent rib bbl. 12 ga. only. Built to customer's specifications and measurements, including type and amount of checkering, carving and engraving. Made prior to World War II.

ZEPHYR SHOTGUNS — Manufactured by
Victor Sarasqueta Company, Eibar, Spain

MODEL 1
O/U SHOTGUN . . . . NiB $1341 Ex $1083 Gd $778
Same general specifications as Field Model O/U except with more elaborate engraving, finer wood and checkering. Imported by Stoeger 1930s- to 1951.

MODEL 2
O/U SHOTGUN . . . . NiB $1746 Ex $1393 Gd $994
Sidelock. Auto ejectors. Gauges: 12, 16, 20, 28 and .410. Bbls.: 25 to 30 inches most common. Modest scroll engraving on receiver and sideplates. Checkered, straight-grain select walnut buttstock and forend. Imported by Stoeger 1930s to 1951.

MODEL 3
O/U SHOTGUN . . . . NiB $2369 Ex $1888 Gd $1337
Same general specifications as Zephyr Model 2 O/U except with more elaborate engraving, finer wood and checkering. Imported by Stoeger 1930s to 1951.

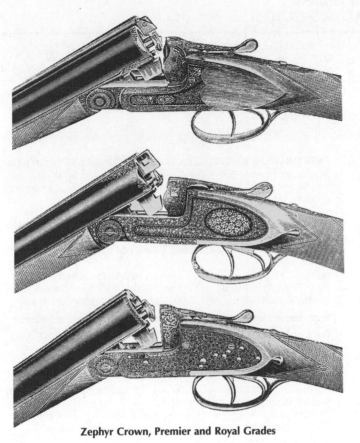

Zephyr Crown, Premier and Royal Grades

MODEL 400E FIELD GRADE DOUBLE-BARREL SHOTGUN

Anson & Deeley boxlock system. Gauges: 12 16, 20, 28 and .410. Bbls.: 25 to 30 inches. Weight: 4.5 lbs. (.410) to 6.25 lbs. (12 ga.). Checkered French walnut buttstock and forearm. Modest scroll engraving on bbls., receiver and trigger guard. Imported by Stoeger 1930s to 1950s.

12, 16 or 20 ga.	NiB $2077	Ex $1275	Gd $894
28 or .410 ga.	NiB $1712	Ex $1395	Gd $889
W/selective single trigger, add			$200

MODEL 401 E SKEET GRADE DOUBLE-BARREL SHOTGUN

Same general specifications as Field Grade except with beavertail forearm. Bbls.: 25 to 28 inches. Imported by Stoeger 1930s to 1950s.

12, 16 or 20 ga.	NiB $1848	Ex $1472	Gd $1042
28 or .410 ga.	NiB $1983	Ex $1583	Gd $1140
W/selective single trigger, add			$350
W/nonselective single trigger, add			$250

MODEL 402E DELUXE

DOUBLE-BARREL SHOTGUN . . NiB $2298 Ex $1860 Gd $1312
Same general specifications as Model 400E Field Grade except for custom refinements. The action was carefully hand-honed for smoother operation; finer, elaborate engraving throughout, plus higher quality wood in stock and forearm. Imported by Stoeger 1930s to 1950s.

CROWN GRADE . . . . NiB $1682 Ex $1350 Gd $954
Boxlock. Gauges: 12, 16, 20, 28 and .410. Bbls.: 25 to 30 inches standard but any lengths could be ordered. Weight: 6 lbs., 4 oz. (.410) to 7 lbs., 4 oz. (12 ga.). Checkered Spanish walnut stock and beavertail forearm. Receiver engraved with scroll patterns. Imported

by Stoeger 1938 to 1951.

FIELD MODEL

O/U SHOTGUN . . . . NiB $828 Ex $678 Gd $490
Anson & Deeley boxlock. Auto ejectors. Gauges: 12, 16 and 20. Bbls.: 25 to 30 inches standard- full-length matt rib. Double triggers. Checkered buttstock and forend. Light scroll engraving on receiver. Imported by Stoeger 1930s to 1951.

HONKER SINGLE-SHOT SHOTGUN . . . . . NiB $576 Ex $474 Gd $343
Sidelock. Gauge: 10; 3.5-inch magnum. 36-inch vent rib barrel w/F choke. Weight: 10.5 lbs. Checkered select Spanish walnut buttstock and beavertail forend; recoil pad. Imported by Stoeger 1950s to 1972.

PINEHURST

DOUBLE-BARREL SHOTGUN . . . . NiB $1174 Ex $955 Gd $674
Boxlock. Gauges: 12, 16, 20, 28 and .410. Bbls.: 25 to 28 inches most common. Checkered, select walnut buttstock and forend. Selective single trigger and auto ejectors. Imported by Stoeger 1950s to 1972.

PREMIER GRADE

DOUBLE-BARREL SHOTGUN . . . . NiB $2517 Ex $2042 Gd $1434
Sidelock. Gauges: 12, 16, 20, 28 and .410. Bbls.: Any length, but 25 to 30 inches most popular. Weight: 4.5 lbs. (.410) to 7 lbs. (12 ga.). Checkered high-grade French walnut buttstock and forend. Imported by Stoeger 1930s to 1951.

ROYAL GRADE

DOUBLE-BARREL SHOTGUN . . . . NiB $3871 Ex $1118 Gd $2181
Same general specifications as the Premier Grade except with more elaborate engraving, finer checkering and wood. Imported by Stoeger 1930s to 1951.

STERLINGWORTH II

DOUBLE-BARREL SHOTGUN . . . . . NiB $811 Ex $736 Gd $601
Genuine sidelocks with color-casehardened sideplates. Gauges: 12, 16, 20 and .410. Bbls.: 25 to 30 inches. Weight: 6 lbs., 4 oz. (.410) to 7 lbs., 4 oz. (12 ga.). Select Spanish walnut buttstock and beavertail forearm. Light scroll engraving on receiver and sideplates. Automatic, sliding-tang safety. Imported by Stoeger 1950s to 1972.

THUNDERBIRD

DOUBLE-BARREL SHOTGUN . . . NiB $1062 Ex $847 Gd $602
Sidelock. Gauges: 12 and 10 Magnum. Bbls.: 32-inch, both F choke. Weight: 8 lbs., 8 oz. (12 ga.), 12 lbs. (10 ga.). Receiver elaborately engraved with waterfowl scenes. Checkered select Spanish walnut buttstock and beavertail forend. Plain extractors, double triggers. Imported by Stoeger 1950 to 1972.

UPLAND KING

DOUBLE-BARREL SHOTGUN . . . NiB $1198 Ex $974 Gd $710
Sidelock. Gauges: 12, 16, 20, 28 and .410. Bbls.: 25 to 28 inches most popular. Checkered buttstock and forend of select walnut. Selective single trigger and auto ejectors. Imported by Stoeger 1950 to 1972.

UPLANDER 4E

DOUBLE-BARREL SHOTGUN . . . . NiB $779 Ex $595 Gd $473
Same general specifications as the Zephyr Sterlingworth II except with selective auto ejectors and highly polished sideplates. Imported by Stoeger 1951 to 1972.

WOODLANDER II

DOUBLE-BARREL SHOTGUN . . . . NiB $517 Ex $374 Gd $229
Boxlock. Gauges: 12, 20 and .410. Bbls.: 25 to 30 inches. Weight: 6 lbs., 4 oz. (.410) to 7 lbs., 4 oz. (12 ga.). Checkered Spanish walnut stock and beavertail forearm. Engraved receiver. Imported by Stoeger 1950 to 1972.

SHOTGUNS

New Listings

HANDGUNS

BENELLI PISTOLS — Urbino, Italy

Imported by Benelli USA

MODEL B-76. . . . . NiB $420 Ex $310 Gd $245
Semi-auto, SA/DA. Cal.: 9 mm Para. Bbl.: 4.25 inches. 8-round mag. Weight: 34 oz. Disc. 1990.

MODEL B-765 TARGET . . . . NiB $576 Ex $450 Gd $325
Cal.: 9 mm Para. Similar to B-76 model but w/5.5-inch bbl., target grips, adj. rear sight. Disc. 1990.

MODEL B-77 . . . . NiB $400 Ex $295 Gd $210
Semi-auto, SA/DA. Cal.: 32 ACP. Bbl.: Steel, 4.25 inches. 8-round mag. Disc. 1995.

MODEL B-80 . . . . NiB $405 Ex $300 Gd $235
Semi-auto, SA/DA. Cal.: .30 Luger. Bbl.: Steel, 4.25 inches. 8-round mag. Weight: 34 oz. Disc. 1995.
B-80s Target, add $120

MODEL B-82 . . . . NiB $775 Ex $525 Gd $395
Limited production Italian police model; serial no. with "D" suffix. Cal.: .30 Luger, .32 ACP, 9 mm Ultra.

MODEL MP3S . . . . NiB $575 Ex $445 Gd $320
Semi-auto, target model. Cal.: .32 S&W Long Wadcutter. Bbl.: 5.5 inches. High gloss blued finish, target grips. Adj. rear sight. Disc. 1995.

GLISENTI PISTOL — Carcina (Brescia), Italy

Mfd. By Societa Siderurgica Glisenti

BRIXIA MODEL . . . . NiB $1595 Ex $1100 Gd $925
Similar to Glisenti Model 1910 except mass produced using simplified mfg. techniques for the civilian market.

SOSSO MODEL . . . . .EXTREMELY RARE
Experimental semi-auto. Cal.: 9 mm Para. Double action (marked "Sosso"), later single action. Mag.: 19 or 21 rounds. Made by FNA. Fewer than 10 made.

GREAT WESTERN ARMS CO. — North Hollywood, California

SHERIFF'S MODEL . . . . NiB $775 Ex $625 Gd $500
Reportedly made from old Colt parts inventory. Cal.: .45 Long Colt. Blue, nickel, or case-colored finish. Plastic staghorn grips.

FAST DRAW MODEL. . . . . NiB $700 Ex $595 Gd $430
Similar to Frontier Six Shooter. Bbl.: 4.75 inches. Brass backstrap and trigger guard; blue finish; plastic staghorn grips. Longer, turned-up hammer spur.

TARGET MODEL . . . . NiB $725 Ex $610 Gd $465
Similar to Frontier Six Shooter. Cal.: .22 LR. Adj. rear sights, Micro front blade. Blue or case colored frame. Bbl.: Various lengths.

DEPUTY MODEL . . . . NiB $815 Ex $695 Gd $500
Cal.: .22 LR, .38 Spl., .357 Mag. Bbl.: 4 inches. Deluxe blue finish, walnut grips. Adj. rear sight. Fewer than 100 made.

KEL-TECH CNC INDUSTRIES, INC. — Cocoa, Florida

P-32 . . . . NiB $285 Ex $170 Gd $90
Semi-auto, double-action. Cal.: .32 ACP. Internal block safety. 7-round mag. Bbl.: 2.68 inches; Parkerized, blue, or chrome finish. Choice of ivory or colored grips. Weight: 6.6 oz.

P-3AT . . . . NiB $295 Ex $180 Gd $95
Similar to P-32. Cal.: .380 ACP. Bbl.: 2.76 inches. 6-round mag. Black composite frame with Parkerized steel slide. Weight: 8.3 oz.

P-40 . . . . NiB $290 Ex $175 Gd $85
Semi-auto, double-action. 9- or 10-round mag. Composite frame with steel slide. Bbl.: 3.3 inches. Parkerized, blue, or chrome finish. Made from 1999 to 2001.
Parkerized finish, add $50
Hard chrome finish, add $70

PLR-16 . . . . NiB $625 Ex $495 Gd $275
M-16-type gas operated. Cal.: .223 Rem., 10-round mag. Bbl.: 9.2 inches. Upper w/Picatinny accessory rail. Black composite frame. Weight: 3.2 lbs.

PLR-22 . . . . NiB $350 Ex $255 Gd $170
Similar to PLR-16 except in .22 LR; 26-round mag. Weight: 2.8 lbs.

PF-9. . . . . NiB $300 Ex $195 Gd $140
Similar to P-11, cal.: 9 mm Para. Bbl.: 3.1 inches. 7-round mag., lower accessory rail. Black finish. Weight: 12.7 oz. Limited production in 2006, reintro. 2008.
Parkerized finish, add $50
Hard chrome finish, add $65

PMR-30 . . . . NiB $400 Ex $295 Gd $185
Cal.: .22 Mag. Bbl.: 4.3 inches. 30-round mag, blowback action, manual safety. Black finished aluminum frame. Lower Picatinny accessory rail. Steel slide and bbl., fiber optic sights. Weight: 19.5 oz.

Century International Arms GP WASR-10

Century International Arms GP 1975

Century International Arms Tantal Sporter

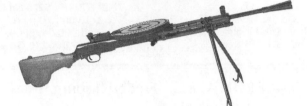

Century International Arms Degtyarev DP28

Century International Arms VZ 2008 Sporter

Century International Arms Sterling SA

RIFLES

CENTURY INTERNATIONAL ARMS, INC — Delray Beach, Florida

Imported by Benelli USA

GAMESTALKER . . . . **NiB $1310 Ex $1025 Gd $895**
Cal.: .243 WSSM, .25 WSSM, .300 WSSM. Bbl.: 22 inches, stainless steel, flattop upper, free-floating aluminum hand guard. ACE skeleton stock with ERGO Sure Grip. 100% camo. Weight: 7 lbs.

G-3 SPORTER . . . . **NiB $815 Ex $575 Gd $375**
Semi-auto. Cal.: .308 Win. Made from G3 parts, American-made receiver with integrated scope rail. Bbl.: 19 inches. 20-round mag. Pistol grip stock, matte black finish. Weight: 9.3 pounds. Imported 1999 to 2006.

CETME SPORTER . . . . **NiB $650 Ex $485 Gd $325**
Cal.: .308 Win. Bbl.: 19.5 inches. 20-round mag. Blue or Mossy Oak Break-Up camo finish, wood or synthetic stock w/pistol grip. Vented forearm. Weight: 9.7 lbs.

S.A.R. 1 . . . . **NiB $775 Ex $550 Gd $325**
AK-47-type by Romarm. Cal.: 7.62x39mm. Bbl.: 16 inches. Wood stock and forearm. Includes one 10 and one 30-round double-stack magazine. Disc. 2003
S.A.R. 2 (5.45x39mm) . . . . **NiB $775 Ex $550 Gd $325**
S.A.R. 3 (.223 Rem.) . . . . **NiB $775 Ex $550 Gd $325**

MODEL B-82 . . . . **NiB $775 Ex $525 Gd $395**
Limited production Italian police model; serial no. with "D" suffix. Cal.: .30 Luger, .32 ACP, 9 mm Ultra.

GP WASR-10 . . . . **NiB $475 Ex $295 Gd $185**
AK-47 type by Romarm. Cal.: 7.62x39mm. Bbl.: 16.25 inches. Wood stock and forearm, includes one 5- and one 10-round mag. Weight: 7.5 lbs.
High-Cap series . . . . **NiB $475 Ex $295 Gd $185**

L1A1/R1A1 SPORTER . . . . **NiB $995 Ex $750 Gd $585**
Modeled after British L1A1. Cal.: .308 Win. Bbl.: 22.5 inches. Carrying handle, synthetic furn. 20-round mag. Folding rear sight. Weight: 9.5 lbs.

GOLANI SPORTER . . . . **NiB $795 Ex $550 Gd $355**
Made in Israel. Cal.: .223 Rem. Bbl.: 21 inches. Folding stock, opt. bayonet lug., 35-round mag. Weight: 8 lbs.

TANTAL SPORTER . . . . **NiB $675 Ex $500 Gd $395**
Cal.: 5.45x39mm. Bbl.: 18 inches, flash hider. Folding wire stock. Parkerized finish. Includes extra mag. Weight. 8 lbs.

VZ 2008 SPORTER . . . . **NiB $725 Ex $550 Gd $380**
Copy of the Czech V258. Cal.: 7.62x39mm. Bbl.: 16.25 inches; steel receiver w/matte finish; wood or plastic stock. Weight: 7 lbs.

M-76 SNIPER . . . . **NiB $1875 Ex $1450 Gd $900**
Semi-auto version of Yugoslav M76. Cal.: 8mm Mauser. Bbl.: 21.5 inches. U.S.-made receiver. Includes scope, mount and 10-round mag. Weight: 11.3 lbs.

GP 1975 . . . . **NiB $550 Ex $395 Gd $255**
Cal.: 7.62x39mm. Bbl.: 16.25 inches. Black synthetic furniture, U.S.-made receiver and bbl. Weight: 7.4 lbs.

DEGTYAREV DP28 . . . . **NiB $3750 Ex $2955 Gd $2250**
Semi-auto, top-mounted magazine. Cal.: 7.62x54R. Gas oper-

---

ated. Full stock. 47- to 50-round mag. Weight: 10 lbs.
DPM 28 (pistol grip) . . . . . . NiB $3750 Ex $2955 Gd $2250
DPX Tank Model . . . . NiB $3750 Ex $2955 Gd $2250

STERLING SA. . . . . NiB $700 Ex $525 Gd $320
Semi-auto version of Sterling sub-machine gun. Cal.: 9mm Para.,
34-round mag. Bbl.: 16 inches. U.S.-made receiver and bbl., crin-
kle finish; folding stock.

PAR 1 . . . . NiB $395 Ex $270 Gd $190
AK-47 receiver, made by PAR. Cal.: 7.62x39mm; 10-round mag.
Bbl.: 20.9 inches. Weight: 7.6 lbs. Imported 2002 to 2009.
PAR 3 (.223 Rem.) . . . . NiB $395 Ex $270 Gd $190

CIMARRON ARMS—Fredericksburg, Texas

1883 BURGESS RIFLE . . . . NiB $1400 Ex $975 Gd $675
Caliber: .45 Long Colt. Bbl.: 20 or 25 ½ inches. Reproduction.
Importation began in 2010.

LIGHTNING MAGAZINE RIFLE NiB $1390 Ex $1000 GD $650
Reproduction of Colt Lightning Rifle. Cal.: .357 Mag., .44-40
WCF or .45 Long Colt. Bbl.: round; 20 or 24 inches; octagon: 20,
24, or 26 inches. Blue or case-colored frame.
Octagon bbl, add $100
Case colored frame, add $250

**MODEL 1871 ROLLING BLOCK
BABY CARBINE** . . . . NiB $325 Ex $250 Gd $175
Remington repro. Caliber: .22 LR, .22 Hornet, .22 Mag. Or .357 Mag.
Bbl: 22 inches. Walnut stock and forearm. Brass trigger guard and
buttplate. Disc. 1990.
Deluxe model . . . . NiB $725 Ex $550 Gd $275

LONG RANGE CREEDMOOR. . . . . NiB $1250 Ex $875 Gd $600
Cal.: .45-70 Gov't. Barrel: 30-inch octagon. Deluxe checkered walnut stock.

**ADOBE WALLS FALLING
BLOCK RIFLE.** . . . . NiB $1650 Ex $1200 Gd $845
Cal.: .45-70 Gov't. Bbl.: 30 inches, octagon. Case hardened receiv-
er, hand checkered walnut stock, German silver nose cap. Optional
Creedmoor sights.

SHARPS NO. 1 RIFLE . . . . NiB $1000 Ex $695 Gd $475
Sharps reproduction. Cal.: .40-65 Win. or .45-70 Gov't. Bbl.: 32
inches, octagon; pistol grip stock. Imported 2000 to 2002.
No. 1 Silhouette . . . . NiB $1500 Ex $975 Gd $625

MODEL 1874 SPORTING RIFLE . . . NiB $1225 Ex $800 Gd $550
Armi-Sport Billy Dixon model. Cal.: .38-55 WCF, .45-70 Gov't., .45-
90 Win., .45-110, .50-90. Bbl.: 32 inches. Checkered deluxe wal-
nut stock. Double set triggers.
Pedersoli model . . . . NiB $1725 Ex $1290 Gd $995
Quigley II model . . . . NiB $1320 Ex $950 Gd $775
Pedersoli Quigley. . . . . NiB $2000 Ex $1395 Gd $900
Big 50 model . . . . NiB $2550 Ex $1895 Gd $1300
Sharps Pride model . . . . NiB $1900 Ex $1400 Gd $1125
Pride II model . . . . NiB $1300 Ex $975 Gd $700
Professional Hunter . . . . NiB $1300 Ex $975 Gd $700
Texas Ranger . . . . NiB $1175 Ex $825 Gd $600

**SHARPS ROCKY MOUNTAIN II
MODEL 74.** . . . . NiB $1375 Ex $965 Gd $595

Cimarron 1883 Burgess Rifle

Cimarron Adobe Walls Falling Block Rifle

Cimarron Sharps Rocky Mountain II Model 74

Cimarron Civil War Henry Rifle

Cimarron 1876 Centennial Sporting Rifle

Cimarron 1892 Carbine

Repro. Cal.: .45-70 Gov't. Bbl.: 30 inches, octagon. Silver receiver,
checkered walnut stock. Optional 6x Malcolm rifle scope.
Scoped model, add $600

MODEL 1860 SPENCER RIFLE. . . . NiB $1500 Ex $1095 Gd $800
By Armi Sport. Cal.: 56-50. Bbl.: 30 inches. Plain walnut stock and
forearm. Case hardened receiver, trigger guard and hammer. Three
barrel bands.

**MODEL 1865 SPENCER
REPEATING RIFLE** . . . . NiB $1325 Ex $995 Gd $700
By Armi Sport. Cal.: .44-40 WCF, .45 Schofield, .45 Long Colt, .56-
50. Bbl.: 20 or 30 inches (in 56-50 only, disc. 2009). Blue finish,
color case hardened frame. Straight grip walnut stock.
30-inch bbl., add $200

CIVIL WAR HENRY RIFLE . . . . NiB $1450 Ex $1195 Gd $895
By Uberti. Cal.: .44-40 WCF or .45 Long Colt. Bbl.: 24 inches.
Includes military inspector's marks and cartouche; military-type
sling swivels.

1866 YELLOWBOY CARBINE . . . . . NiB $1125 Ex $995 Gd $550
By Uberti. Cal.: .32-20 WCF, .38 SP, .38-55 WCF, .44 SP, .44-40
WCF, .45 Long Colt. Similar to Model 1866 Sporting Rifle except
w/19-inch round bbl., two barrel bands, saddle ring, smooth walnut
stock, and forearm.

Trapper . . . . **NiB $1025 Ex $795 Gd $495**
Indian Carbine. . . . . **NiB $915 Ex $600 Gd $435**
Red Cloud . . . . **NiB $915 Ex $600 Gd $435**

1873 SADDLE RING CARBINE . . . . **NiB $1250 Ex $975 Gd $665**
Cal.: .22 LR, .22 Mag., .32-20 WCF, .357 Mag./.38 SP, .38-40 WCF, .44 SP., .44-40 WCF, .45 Long Colt. Bbl.: 19 inches, round. Blued receiver, saddle ring.
Trapper Carbine. . . . . **NiB $1350 Ex $1050 Gd $900**

1876 CENTENNIAL
SPORTING RIFLE. . . . . **NiB $1525 Ex $1250 Gd $995**
Cal.: .40-60 WCF, .45-60 WCF, .45-70 WCF,.50-95 WCF; bbl.: 22 or 28 inches, octagon. Blue finish, case hardened frame. Full-length magazine, iron sights, walnut stock, and forearm.

1876 CARBINE . . . . **NiB $1645 Ex $1290 Gd $1055**
By Uberti. Cal.: .45-60 WCF, .45-75. Bbl.: 22 inches, round. Full length fore end and barrel band. Canadian NWMP model has blued frame and saddle ring.

1885 HI-WALL RIFLE. . . . . **NiB $1055 Ex $850 Gd $675**
Cal.: .30-40 Krag, .348 Win., .38-55 Win., .405 Win., .40-65 WCF, .45-70 Gov't., .45-90 WCF, .45-120 WCF. Bbl.: 28 or 30 inches, octagon. Case hardened finish frame. Iron sights standard or optional aperture rear and globe front offered.
Pedersoli mode . . . . **NiB $2250 Ex $1875 Gd $1095**

1885 LOW-WALL RIFLE. . . . . **NiB $975 Ex $700 Gd $545**
Cal.: .22 LR, .22 Hornet, .22 Mag., .30-30 Win., .32-20 WCF, .357 Mag., .38-40 WCF, .44 Mag., .38-55, .44-40 WCF, .45-70 Gov't., .45 Long Colt. Bbl.: 30 inches. Hand checkered walnut stock, single- or double-set trigger.
Deluxe model, add $150
Standard custom engraving, add $1500
Double set triggers, add $300

1892 RIFLE . . . . **NiB $1150 Ex $750 Gd $575**
Cal.: .357 Mag., .44 Mag., .44-40 WCF, .45 Long Colt. Bbl.: 20 or 24 inches. Solid or take-down frame, smooth walnut stock and forearm, case colored receiver.
Take-down frame, add $175
.44-40 WCF, .44 Mag., add $40

1892 CARBINE . . . . **NiB $1100 Ex $735 Gd $525**
Cal.: .357 Mag., .44 Mag., .44-40 WCF, .45 Long Colt. Bbl.: 16 (Trapper model) or 20 inches. Solid frame, choice of big loop lever (El Dorado) or standard with 20-inch bbl. Saddle ring with 20-inch bbl. only.

NEW ENGLAND FIREARMS—Gardner, Massachusetts

In 1987, New England Firearms was established as an independent company producing selected H&R models under the NEF logo. In 1991, H&R 1871, Inc., was formed from the residual of the parent company that took over the New England Firearms facility. H&R 1871, Inc., produced firearms under both its logo and the NEF brand until 1999, when the Marlin Firearms Company acquired the assets of H&R 1871, Inc. Since 2007, all guns manufactured in the U.S. carry the H&R 1871, Inc. All imported guns are sold under the NEF brand. The Handi-Rifle, Super Light Handi-Rifle, Sportster and Survivor are now sold under the H&R 1871, Inc., brand.

HANDI-RIFLE . . . . **NiB $240 Ex $175 Gd $90**
Single-shot, break-open action w/side lever release. Cal.: .22 Hornet, .22-250 Rem., .223 Rem., .243 Win., .270 Win., .30-30 Win., .30-06, .45-70 Gov't., .204 Ruger, .25-06 Rem., .280 Rem., .308 Win., .35 Whelen, .357 Mag., 7mm-08 Rem., .444 Marlin, .500 S&W, 7x57 Mauser, 7.62x39mm, 7x64mm Brenneke. Bbl.: 22 or 26 inches, regular or bull. Blued receiver. Stock: Walnut finished hardwood, regular or Monte Carlo. Scope mount or ramp front, adj. rear sights. Sling swivels. Weight: 7 lbs. Mfg. 1989 to 2008.
Handi-Rifle Synthetic. . . . . **NiB $240 Ex $175 Gd $90**
Synthetic/Stainless. . . . . **NiB $275 Ex $200 Gd $110**
Youth model . . . . **NiB $260 Ex $185 Gd $100**
10th Anniversary. . . . . **NiB $715 Ex $395 Gd $250**
Trapper's Edition . . . . **NiB $255 Ex $190 Gd $125**

SUPER LIGHT HANDI-RIFLE. . . . . **NiB $240 Ex $175 Gd $90**
Cal.: .22 Hornet, .223 Rem., .243 Win. Same as Handi Rifle but with black synthetic stock and forearm, recoil pad. Bbl.: 20-inch special contour w/rebated muzzle. .223 Rem. model includes scope base and hammer extension. Weight: 5.5 lbs. Made 1997 to 2008.

SPORTSTER . . . . **NiB $145 Ex $90 Gd $75**
Cal.: .17 HMR, .17 Mach 2, .22 LR, .22 Mag. Bbl.: 20 or 22 inches, Weaver-style rail, no sights. Adult or youth (.22 LR only) dimensions. Stock and forearm: Black polymer. Made 1999 to 2008.

SURVIVOR. . . . . **NiB $255 Ex 180 Gd $100**
Cal.: .223 Rem., .308 Win., .357 Mag., .410/.45 Long Colt. Similar to Survivor series shotgun but with removable forearm and thumbhole stock (both with ammo compartments). Bbl.: 20 or 22 inches, blue or nickel finish. Weight: 6 lbs. Made 1996 to 2008.

OLYMPIC ARMS—Olympia, Washington

BOLT-ACTION SAKO. . . . . **NiB $675 Ex $525 Gd $395**
Cal.: Various from .17 Rem. to .416 Rem. Mag. Bbl.: Fluted; various stock options. Value is for base model without custom options.

ULTRA CSR TACTICAL . . . . **NiB $1525 Ex $1150 Gd $895**
Cal.: .308 Win. Sako action. Bbl.: Heavy, 26 inches, broach cut. Stock: Bell & Carlson black or synthetic with aluminum bedding. Harris bipod included. Made from 1996 to 2000.

COUNTER SNIPER RIFLE. . . . . **NiB $1425 Ex $1175 Gd $950**
Bolt action. Cal.: .308 Win. Bbl.: Heavy, 26-inches. Stock: Camo fiberglass. Weight: 10.5 lbs. Disc. 1987.

SURVIVOR 1 . . . . **NiB $325 Ex $200 Gd $155**
Converts M1911 into bolt-action carbine. Cal.: .223 Rem., .45 ACP. Bbl.: 16.25 inches. Collapsible stock. Available for S&W and Browning Hi-Power. Weight: 5 lbs.

CAR 97 . . . . **NiB $825 Ex $620 Gd $550**
Cal.: .223 Rem., 9mm Para., 10mm, .40 S&W, .45 ACP. Similar to PCR-5 but w/ 16-inch button-rifled barrel. A2 sights, fixed CAR stock, post-ban muzzle brake. Weight: 7 lbs. Made from 1997 to 2004.
M-4 version (Disc. 2004), add. $50

FAR-15. . . . . **NiB $825 Ex $620 Gd $550**
Featherweight model. Cal.: .223 Rem. Bbl.: 16 inches, lightweight, button-rifled, collapsible stock. Made from 2001 to 2004.

NEW LISTINGS

Olympic Arms OA-93 Carbine

Olympic Arms LTF Tactical Rifle

Olympic Arms K4B

Olympic Arms K7 Eliminator

GI-16 . . . . **NiB $825 Ex $620 Gd $550**
Cal.: .223 Rem. Forged aluminum receiver, matte finish. Bbl.: Match grade, 16 inches, button rifled. Collapsible stock. Weight: 7 lbs. Made 2004 and 2006.

GI-20 . . . . **NiB $750 Ex $590 Gd 505**
Cal. .223 Rem. Similar to GI-16 except w/20-inch heavy bbl., A-2 lower. Weight: 8.4 lbs. Made 2004.

OA-93 Carbine . . . . **NiB $1300 Ex $1090 Gd $895**
Based on OA-93 pistol. Cal.: .223 Rem. Bbl.: 16 inches. Flattop receiver. Aluminum side folding stock, round aluminum handguard, Vortex flash supp. Weight: 7.5 lbs. Made 1998 and from 2004 to 2007.

OA-93PT . . . . **NiB $1000 Ex $850 Gd $595**
Similar to OA-93 carbine but with aluminum receiver, black matte anodized finish. Bbl.: 16 inches, match grade chromemoly steel with removable muzzle brake, push-button removable stock. Weight: 7 lbs. Made from 2006 to 2007.

LTF TACTICAL RIFLE . . . . **NiB $1200 Ex $995 Gd $625**
Cal. .223 Rem. Bbl.: 16 inches, fluted or non-fluted w/flash supp. Black matte anodized receiver. Firsh-type forearm, Picatinny rails, Parkerized steel parts. Tube-style stock. Weight: 6.4 lbs.
Fluted bbl., add **10%**

K3B CARBINE . . . . . . **NiB $900 Ex $775 Gd $550**
Cal. .223 Rem. Bbl.: 16 inches, match grade chromemoly steel w/flash supp. A2 rear sight and buttstock; adj. front post sight.

A3 Flattop receiver, add **$40**
FAR carbine, add **$50**
M4 carbine, add **$50**
A3-TC carbine, add **$220**

K4B/K4B68 . . . . **NiB $920 Ex $675 Gd $495**
Cal.: .223 Rem., 6.8 SPC. Bbl.: 20 inches, match grade, chromemoly steel, button rifled; flash supp. Adj. A2 rear sight and front post; A2 buttstock, upper receiver and hand guard. Weight: 8.5 lbs.
Flattop receiver, add **$100**

K4B-A4 . . . . **NiB $895 Ex $650 Gd $510**
Cal.: .223 Rem. Bbl.: 20 inches w/A2 flash supp.; bayonet lug. Flattop receiver. Adj. post front sight. Firsh handguard, Picatinny rails. Made from 2006 to 2008.

K7 ELIMINATOR . . . . **NiB $925 Ex $680 Gd $525**
Cal.: .223 Rem. Bbl.: 16 inches, stainless steel w/flash supp.; adj. A2 rear sight and front post; A2 buttstock. Weight: 7.8 lbs.

K8 TARGET MATCH . . . . **NiB $895 Ex $600 Gd $475**
Cal.: .223 Rem. Bbl.: 20-inch bull bbl., stainless, button rifling; Picatinny flattop upper, A2 buttstock. Weight: 8.5 lbs.

K8-MAG . . . . **NiB $1300 Ex $1095 Gd $875**
Similar to Target Match model. Cal.: .223 WSSM, .243 WSSM, .25 WSSM, .300 WSM. 24-inch bbl. Weight: 9.4 lbs.

K9/K10/K40/K45 . . . . **NiB $960 Ex $785 Gd $610**
Cal.: 9mm Para., 10mm Norma, .40 S&W, .45 ACP. Blow-back action. Bbl.: 16 inches w/flash suppressor and bayonet lug. Adj. A2 rear sight. Collapsible stock. Weight: 6.7 lbs.

K9GL/K40GL . . . . **NiB $1050 Ex $895 Gd $600**
Similar to K9 series. Cal.: 9mm Para., .40 S&W. Lower designed to accept Glock magazines. Bbl.: 16 inches; flash suppressor. Collapsible stock. No magazine furnished.
A3 upper, add **$100**

K16 . . . . **NiB $810 Ex $650 Gd $495**
Cal.: .223 Rem. Bbl.: 16 inches, free-floating, button rifled. Picatinny flattop upper; A2 buttstock. Weight: 7.5 lbs.
K-30 (.30 carbine) . . . . **NiB $850 Ex $600 Gd $450**

K30R . . . . **NiB $925 Ex $725 Gd$550**
Cal.: 7.62x39mm. Bbl.: 16-inch stainless steel, adj. rear sight. Parkerized steel parts. Six-point collapsible stock.
A3 upper, add **$100**

K68 . . . . **NiB $1025 Ex $850 Gd $595**
Cal.: 6.8 Rem. SPC. Bbl.: 16-inch stainless steel, A2 upper with adj. rear sight and flash suppressor. Matte black anodized receiver, Parkerized steel parts. Six-position collapsible A2 stock w/pistol grip.
A3 receiver, add **$100**

K74 . . . . **NiB $910 Ex $775 Gd $550**
Cal.: 5.45x39mm. Bbl.: 16-inches, button rifling; flash suppressor and adj. front sight. Six-position collapsible stock. Weight 6.75 lbs.

THOMPSON/CENTER ARMS—(Div. of Smith & Wesson, Springfield, MA; formerly Rochester, NH)

ICON . . . . **NiB $1020 Ex $775 Gd $525**
Bolt action. Cal.: .22-250 Rem., .270 Win., .30-06, .300 Win. Mag., .308 Win., .30 TC, 6.5 Creedmoor, 7mm Mag. Bbl.: 24 inches.

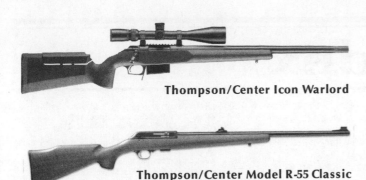

Thompson/Center Icon Warlord

Thompson/Center Model R-55 Classic

Thompson/Center Encore Katahdin

Medium or long action, hinged floor plate (on long action). Stock: Black synthetic or RealTree camo, checkered American walnut, classic walnut or Ultra Wood; pistol grip and forearm. Adj. trigger, cocking indicator, three-shot magazine (on medium action). Jeweled bolt handle. Weaver-style bases. Weight: 7.5 pounds. Guaranteed to shoot 1-inch or less at 100 yards.
Walnut stock models, add **$25**

ICON PRECISION HUNTER . . . . . . NiB $1200 Ex $895 Gd $650
Bolt action. Cal.: .204 Ruger, .223 Rem., .22-250 Rem., .243 Win., 6.5 Creedmoor, .308 Win. Bbl.: 22 inches, fluted; 5R button rifling. Tactical-style bolt handle. Stock: Brown synthetic with cheekpiece and beavertail fore end. Detachable 3-round magazine with single-shot adapter. Picatinny rail, adj. trigger, sling studs.

ICON WARLORD . . . . NiB $1295 Ex $950 Gd $775
Bolt action. Cal.: .308 Win. or .338 Lapua; 5- or 10-round magazine. Bbl.: Fluted, stainless steel, hand lapped. Stock: Carbon fiber tactical style with adj. cheek piece available in OD, flat black or desert sand. Adj. trigger, Picatinny rail. Weight: 12.75 to 13.75 lbs.

VENTURE . . . . NiB $495 Ex $350 Gd$290
Bolt action. Cal.: 270 Win., .30-06, 7 mm Rem. Mag., .300 Win. Mag. Bbl.: 24 inches, tapered match grade with 5R button rifling. Stock: Black synthetic, sporter design, textured grip. Adj. trigger, two-position safety.

VENTURE PREDATOR . . . . NiB $595 Ex$425 Gd $325
Bolt action. Cal.: .204 Ruger, .223 Rem., .22-250 Rem. or .308 Win. Bbl.: 22 inches, fluted, 3-round magazine. Stock: Composite with 100% Realtree Max-1 camo coating; Hogue panels, Weather Shield bolt handle. Weight: 6.75 lbs.

SILVER LYNX . . . . NiB $365 Ex $400 Gd $310
Semi-auto. Cal.: .22 LR. Bbl.: 20 inches, match grade; 5-round magazine, stainless steel action and bbl. Stock: Black composite with Monte Carlo cheek piece. Weight: 5.5 lbs.

MODEL R-55 CLASSIC . . . . NiB $510 Ex 355 Gd $285
Semi-auto. Cal.: .17 Mach 2, .22 LR. Bbl.: 22 inches, match grade; adj. rear sight; blue finish. Blow-back action. Smooth Monte Carlo walnut stock. Weight: 5.5 lbs.
R-55 Target . . . . NiB $545 Ex $415 Gd $300
R-55 Sporter . . . . NiB $500 Ex $395 Gd $240

ENCORE RIFLE. . . . . Nib $695 Ex $450 Gd $325
Single-shot, break-action. Cal.: Rimfire and centerfire from .17 Mach 2 to .45-70 Gov't. Bbl.: 24 to 16 inches, interchangeable. Hammer block safety, trigger guard opening lever. Stock: Synthetic black, Realtree camo or American walnut; smooth forearm, Monte Carlo stock w/pistol grip.; adj. rear sight.
Extra bbls (blued), add. **$295**
Camo models, add. **$125**
Thumbhole stock, add **$195**
.17 Mach 2, add **$50**
Stainless bbl., add **$350**
Hunter Pkg. (scope, bases, case), add **$250**

ENCORE KATAHDIN . . . . NiB $525 Ex $400 Gd $295
Same as Encore but with 18-inch blued bbl. Cal.: .444 Marlin, .450 Marlin or .45-70 Gov't. Stock: Black composite. Fiber optic sights, drilled and tapped for scope. Weight: 6.6 lbs. Made from 2002 to 2005.

PRO HUNTER RIFLE. . . . . NiB $800 Ex $545 Gd $315
Cal.: Various. Bbl.: 28 inches, stainless steel. Recoil reducing Flex-Tech stock (thumbhole option) in black or camo.
Camo stock, add **$75**
Extra bbl., add **$355**

HOTSHOT (Pink) . . . . NiB $325 Ex $280 Gd $195
Youth model. Cal.: 22 LR. Bbl.: 19 inches. Stock: Black synthetic, Realtree AP camo or AP pink camo. Auto safety; drilled and tapped for scope. Weight: 3 lbs.

SHOTGUNS

CENTURY INTERNATIONAL ARMS INC.— St. Albans, VT, and Boca Raton, FL

ARTHEMIS O/U. . . . . NiB $475 Ex $310 Gd $245
Gauge: 12, 20, 28, .410. Bbl.: 28 inches, vent. rib, 3-inch chamber. Single selective trigger, extractors. Stock: Checkered walnut. Weight: 5.3 to 7.4 lbs. Mfg. by PAR. Imported from 2002 to 2009.

PHANTOM . . . . NiB $295 Ex $240 Gd $190
Semi-auto. Gauge: 12. 3-inch chamber. Bbl.: 24, 26 or 28 inches; vent. rib. Three choke tubes. Stock: Black synthetic. Mfg. in Turkey. Disc.

SAS-12 . . . . NiB $250 Ex $185 Gd $100
Semi-auto. Gauge: 12. 2.75-inch chamber. Bbl.: 22 or 23.5 inches. Detachable 3- or 5-round mag.
Ghost ring rear sight, add **$25**

COACH MODEL . . . . NiB $325 Ex $200 Gd $140
Side-by-side. Gauge: 12, 20, .410. Bbl.: 20 inches, exposed hammers, double trigger. Stock: Checkered walnut. Sling swivels. Mfg. in China.

MODEL IJ2 . . . . NiB $220 Ex $155 Gd $100
Slide-action. Gauge: 12; 2.75-inch or 3-inch chamber. Bbl.: 19 inches, fixed choke. Ghost ring rear or fiber optic sights. Weight: 7 lbs. Mfg. in China.

ULTRA 87 . . . . NiB $255 Ex $180 Gd $110
Slide-action. Gauge: 12. Bbl.: 19 inches. Optional heat shield and pistol grip. Side folding stock. Includes extra 28-inch bbl. Weight: 8.2 lbs.

NEW LISTINGS

Index

INDEX

INDEX

INDEX

Model 80G, 287
Model 81G, 288
Model 99G, 288
Model 101G, 287
Model 989G Autoloading Rifle, 288

SHOTGUNS
Model 16 Visible Hammer Slide-Action, 491
Model 17 Brush Gun, 492
Model 17 Riot Gun, 492
Model 17 Standard Visible Hammer Slide-Action, 492
Model 19 Visible Hammer Slide-Action Repeater, 492
Model 21 Trap Visible Hammer Slide-Action Repeater, 492
Model 24 Visible Hammer Slide-Action Repeater, 492
Model 26 Brush Gun, 492
Model 26 Riot Gun, 493
Model 26 Standard Visible Hammer Slide-Action Repeater, 493
Model 28 Hammerless Slide-Action Repeater, 493
Model 28T Trap Gun, 493
Model 28TS Trap Gun, 493
Model 30 Field Gun, 493
Model 30 Visible Hammer Slide-Action Repeater, 493
Models 30A, 30B, 30C, 30D, 493
Model 31 Hammerless Slide-Action Repeater, 494
Model 31F Field Gun, 494
Model 42A Visible Hammer Slide-Action Repeater, 494
Model 43 Hammerless Slide-Action Repeater, 494
Model 44 Hammerless Slide-Action Repeater, 494
Model 49 Visible Hammer Slide-Action Repeating, 494
Model 50DL Bolt Action Shotgun, 494
Model 53 Hammerless Slide-Action Repeater, 494
Model 55 Goose Gun, 494
Model 55 Hunter Bolt-Action Repeater, 494
Model 55 Swamp Gun, 494
Model 55S Slug Gun, 494
Model 59 Auto-Safe Bolt-Action Single, 494
Model 60 Single-Shot Shotgun, 494
Model 63 Hammerless Slide-Action Repeater, 494
Model 90 Standard Over/Under Shotgun, 496
Model 120 Magnum Slide-Action, 496
Model 120 Slug Gun, 496
Model 410 Lever-Action Repeater, 496
Model 512 Slugmaster Shotgun, 496
Model 1898 Visible Hammer Slide-Action Repeater, 496
Model 55-10 Super Goose 10, 496
Premier Mark I Slide-Action Repeater, 496
Premier Mark II and IV, 496
Model 50 Bolt-Action, 496
Model 778 Slide-Action Repeater, 496

MAROCCHI SHOTGUNS
Conquista Model Over/Under Shotguns:
Lady Sport Garde I, 496
Lady Sport Grade II, 496
Lady Sport Grade III, 496
Skeet Model Grade I, 496
Skeet Model Grade II, 496
Skeet Model Grade III, 496
Sporting Clays Grade I, 496
Sporting Clays Grade II, 496
Sporting Clays Grade III, 496
Trap Model Grade I, 496
Trap Model Grade II, 496
Trap Model Grade III, 496
Left-Handed Model, 496

MAUSER
PISTOLS
Model 80-SA, 126
Model 90 DA, 126
Model 90 DAC Compact, 126
Model 1898 (1896) Military, 126 - 127
Model HSC DA, 126
Luger Lange Pistole 08, 126-127
Parabellum Luger, 127
Pocket Model 1910, 127
Pocket Model 1914, 127
Pocket Model 1934, 127
WTP Model I, 127
WTP Model II, 127

RIFLES
PRE-WORLD WAR I MODELS
Bolt-Action Sporting Carbine, 289
Bolt-Action Sporting Rifle, 289
Bolt-Action Sporting Rifle, Military "Type C", 289
Bolt-Action Sporting Rifle, Short "Type K", 289

PRE-WORLD WAR II MODELS
Model DSM34 Bolt-Action Single-Shot Sporting, 289
Model EL320 BA - SS Sporting Rifle, 289
Model EN310 BA - SS Sporting Rifle, 289
Model ES340 BA - SS Target Rifle, 289
Model ES340B BA - SS Target Rifle, 289
Model ES350 BA - SS Target Rifle, 289
Model ES350B BA - SS Target Rifle, 289
Model KKW BA - SS Target Rifle, 289
Model M410 Bolt-Action Repeating Sporting Rifle, 289
Model MM410B Bolt-Action Repeating Sporting Rifle, 290
Model MS350B Target Rifle, 290
Model MS420 Sporting Rifle, 290
Model MS420B Target Rifle, 290
Standard Model Rifle, 290
Type "A" Bolt-Action Sporting Rifle , 290
Type "A" BA Sporting Rifle, Magnum, 290
Type "A" BA Sporting Rifle, Short, 290
Type "B" Bolt-Action Sporting Rifle, 290
Type "K" BA Sporting Rifle, 290
Type "M" BA Sporting Carbine, 290
Type "S" BA Sporting Carbine, 291

POST-WORLD WAR II MODELS
Model 66S Standard Sporting Rifle, 291
Model 66S Deluxe Sporter, 291
Model 66S Ultra, 291
Model 66SG Big Game, 291
Model 66SH High Performance, 292
Model 66SP Super Match Target, 292
Model 66ST Carbine, 292
Model 83 Bolt-Action Rifle, 292
Model 96, 292
Model 99 Classic Bolt-Action Rifle, 292
Model 107 Bolt-Action Rifle, 292
Model 201/201 Luxus BA Rifle, 292
Model 2000 Bolt-Action Sporting Rifle, 293
Model 2000 Classic DA Sporting Rifle, 293
Model 3000 Bolt-Action Sporting Rifle, 293
Model 3000 Magnum, 293
Model 4000 Varmint Rifle, 293

MAVERICK ARMS SHOTGUNS
Model 60 Autoloading Shotgun, 497
Model 88 Bullpup, 497
Model 88 Deer Gun, 497
Model 88 Pump Shotgun, 497
Model 88 Security, 497
Model 91 Pump Shotgun, 497
Model 95 Bolt Action, 497

McMILLAN — *See listing under Harris Gunworks*
MERKEL
RIFLES
Over/Under Rifles ("Bock- Doppelbüchsen"), 293
Model 220, 293
Model 220E, 293
Model 221, 293
Model 221E, 293
Model 320, 293
Model 320E, 293
Model 321, 293
Model 321E, 293
Model 322, 293
Model 323E, 293
Model 324, 293

SHOTGUNS
Model 8 Hammerless Double , 497
Model 47E Side-by-Side, 497
Model 47LSC Sporting Clays S/S, 498
Models 47SL, 147SL, 247SL, 347S, 447S Hammerless Sidelocks, 498
Models 100 Over/Under, 498
Models 101 and 101E Over/Unders, 498
Model 122 Hammerless Double, 498
Model 122E Hammerless Sidelock, 499
Model 126E Hammerless Sidelock, 499
Model 127E Hammerless Sidelock, 499
Model 128E Hammerless Sidelock Double, 499
Model 130 Hammerless Boxlock Double, 499
Model 147, 147E Hammerless Boxlock Double-Barrel, 499
Models 200, 200E, 201, 201E, 202 and 202E, 499
Model 203E Sidelock Over/Under Shotguns, 500
Model 204E Over/Under Shotgun, 500
Model 210E Sidelock Over/Under Shotgun, 500
Model 211E Sidelock Over/Under Shotgun, 500
Models 300, 300E, 301, 301E and 302 Over/Under, 500
Model 303EL Over/Under Shotgun, 500
Model 304E Over/Under Shotgun , 500
Models 400, 400E, 401, 401E, 500

Over/Under Combination ("Bock-Büchsflinten"), 500
Model 2000EL Over/Under Shotguns, 500
Model 2001EL Over/Under Shotguns, 500
Model 2002EL, 500
Anson Drillings, 500-501

MERWIN
First Model Frontier Army, 127
Second Model Frontier Army, 127
Second Model Pocket Army, 127
Third Model Frontier Army, 127
Third Model Frontier Army DA, 127
Third Model Pocket Army, 127
Third Model Pocket Army DA, 127
Third Model Pocket Army DA, 127
Fourth Model Pocket Army, 127
Fourth Model Pocket Army DA, 127
First Pocket Model, 127
Second Pocket Model, 127
Third Pocket Model, 127
Third Pocket Model w/Trigger Guard, 127
Medium Frame Pocket Model, 128
Medium Frame Pocket Model 32, 128
Tip-Up Model 32, 128

MEXICAN MILITARY RIFLE
Model 1936, 293

MIIDA SHOTGUNS
Model 612 Field Grade Over/Under, 501
Model 2100 Skeet Gun, 501
Model 2200T Trap Gun, Model 2200S Skeet Gun, 501
Model 2300T Trap Gun,Model 2300S Skeet Gun, 501
Grandee Model GRT/IRS Trap/Skeet Gun, 501

MIDLAND RIFLES
Model 2100, 294
Model 2600, 294
Model 2700, 294
Model 2800, 294

MITCHELL ARMS
HANDGUNS
Model 1911 Gold Signature, 128
Alpha Model, 128
American Eagle, 128
Citation II, 128
Olympic I.S.U., 128
Sharpshooter II, 128
SA Sport King II, 128
SA Army Revolver, 128
Trophy II, 128
Victor II, 129
Model Guardian Angel Derringer, 129
Model Guardian II, 129
Model Guardian III, 129
Model Titan II DA, 129
Model Titan III DA, 129

RIFLES
Model 15/22 Semiautomatic, 294
Model 9300 Series, 294
Model 9302, 294
Model 9303, 294
Model 9304, 294
Model 9305, 294
AK-22, 294
CAR-15 22 Semiautomatic Rifle, 294
Galil 22 Semiautomatic Rifle, 294
M-16A 22 Semiautomatic Rifle, 243
MAS 22 Semiautomatic Rifle, 294
PPS Semiautomatic Rifle, 294

SHOTGUNS
Model 9104/9105 Pump Shotguns, 501
Model 9108/9109 Pump Shotgun, 501
Model 9111/9113 Pump Shotgun, 501
Model 9114/9114FS, 501
Model 9115/9115FS Pump Shotgun, 501

MKE PISTOL
Kirikkale DA, 129

MOA CORPORATION
Maximum Carbine Pistol, 129
Maximum Single-Shot, 129

MONTGOMERY WARD — *See shotgun listings under "W"*

MORRONE SHOTGUN
Standard Model 46 Over-and-Under, 501

MOSSBERG & SONS
PISTOLS
Brownie "Pepperbox" Pistol, 130
RIFLES
Model 10, 294
Model 14, 294
Model 20, 294
Model 25/25A, 294

INDEX

INDEX

INDEX